BEST 290
BUSINESS SCHOOLS

PrincetonReview.com

BEST 290 BUSINESS SCHOOLS

2008 EDITION

**Nedda Gilbert
and the Staff
of The Princeton Review**

*Random House, Inc.
New York*

The Princeton Review, Inc.
2315 Broadway
New York, NY   10024
E-mail: bookeditor@review.com

© 2008 by The Princeton Review, Inc.

ISBN: 978-0-375-76627-5

Editorial Director: Robert Franek
Editor: Laura Braswell
Director, Production Editorial: Christine LaRubio
Director, Print Production: Scott Harris
Account Manager: David Soto

Printed in the United States of America.

9 8 7 6 5 4 3 2 1

2008 Edition

ACKNOWLEDGMENTS

This book absolutely would not have been possible without the help of my husband, Paul. With each edition of this guide, his insights and support have been invaluable—this book continues to be as much his as it is mine. That said, I also need to thank my twelve-year-old daughter, Kaela, and her eight-year-old sister, Lexi, for enduring all the time I have spent immersed in this project.

A big thanks goes to Tom Meltzer and Anna Weinberg for their smart and savvy profile writing. The following people were also instrumental in the completion of this book: Scott Harris, Christine LaRubio, Laura Braswell, Adrinda Kelly, David Soto, Ben Zelevansky, Steven Aglione, Sarah Kruchko, and Jeff Adams for putting all the pieces together; the sales staff at The Princeton Review, Josh Escott; Robert Franek and Young Shin, as well as Alicia Ernst and John Katzman, for giving me the chance to write this book; and to the folks at Random House, who helped this project reach fruition.

Thanks go to Kristin Hansen (Tuck '01) and Matt Camp (Tuck '02), and to Ramona Payne and all the folks at The Diversity Pipeline Alliance. I am also grateful for the unique insights provided by Cathy Crane-Moley, Stanford Graduate School of Business, Class of '92; Patricia Melnikoff and Chiara Perry, Harvard Business School, Class of '92; Caroline Grossman, University of Chicago Graduate School of Business, Class of '03; Sara Weiss, MIT Sloan School of Management, Class of '04; and Stephen Hazelton, MIT Sloan School of Management, Class of '05. Thanks are also due to the business school folks who went far out of their way to provide essential information. They continue to make this book relevant and vital.

Linda Baldwin, Director of Admissions, The Anderson School, UCLA

Derek Bolton, Assistant Dean and Director of Admissions, Stanford University School of Business

Eileen Chang, former Associate Director of Admissions, Harvard Business School

Allan Friedman, Director of Communications and Public Relations, University of Chicago

Wendy Hansen, Associate Director of Admissions, Stanford Business School

Stacey Kole, Deputy Dean for the full-time MBA Program and clinical professor of Economics, University of Chicago Graduate School of Business

Steven Lubrano, Assistant Dean and Director of the MBA Program, Tuck School of Business

Rose Martinelli, former Director of Admissions and Financial Aid, The Wharton School MBA Program

Jon McLaughlin, Assistant MBA Admissions Director, Sloan School of Management, MIT

Julia Min, Executive Director of MBA Admissions, UC—Berkeley, Haas School of Business

Jeanne Wilt, Assistant Dean of Admissions and Career Development, Michigan

Linda Meehan, Assistant Dean for Admissions, Columbia University

CONTENTS

INTRODUCTION

A RETURN TO OUR ROOTS

Over the past 14 years, The Princeton Review has annually published a guide to business schools. For the early editions of the guide, we collected opinion surveys from thousands of students at a select group of graduate business schools as well as school statistics from school administrators that include enrollment and demographic figures, tuition, and the average GMAT scores of entering students. We used the students' opinions to craft descriptive narratives of the schools they attended and reported the statistics in the sidebars of those narrative profiles.

For the 2001–2004 editions of this guide, we discontinued collecting opinion surveys from students and writing narrative descriptions of the schools; instead we focused solely on collecting and reporting school statistics. While we were able to report statistics for many more business schools in the new format (the last [2000] edition of the guide with narrative descriptions profiled only 80 schools, and the first edition of the statistics-only guide profiled 372 schools), we learned over the next few years that readers are interested in more than just school-reported statistics. They want to read what the experts—current graduate business school students—have to say about the experiences of today's graduate business student. They want from-the-horse's-mouth accounts of what's great (*and* what's not) at each school.

So in 2005 we decided to reintroduce the student survey-driven descriptive narrative, offering students a more intimate look at the inner workings of each school, and we've continued with this approach ever since.

We also brought back several top 10 lists that rank the profiled schools according to various metrics (more on the rankings later). You'll find those rankings on page 67.

Taken together, we believe that these candid student opinions, school statistics, and rankings provide a unique and helpful resource to help you decide what business schools to apply to. But let us stress that we hope that this book will not be the *only* resource you turn to when making this expensive (both in terms of time and treasure) decision to enter a graduate business program. Do additional research on the Internet and in newspapers, magazines, and other periodicals. Talk to Admissions Officers and current students at the programs that interest you. If at all possible, visit the campuses you are seriously considering. But treat the advice of all these resources (including ours) as you would treat advice from anyone regarding any situation: as input that reflects the values and opinions of others as you *form your own opinion*.

TWO TYPES OF ENTRIES

For each of the 445 business programs in this book, you will find one of two possible types of entries: a two-page profile with lots of descriptive text and statistics, or a straight statistical listing. Our descriptive profiles are driven primarily by 1) comments business students provide in response to open-ended questions on our student survey, and 2) our own statistical analysis of student responses to the many multiple-choice questions on the survey. While many business students complete a survey unsolicited by us at http://survey.review.com, in the vast majority of cases we rely on business school administrators to get the word out about our survey to their students. In the ideal scenario, the business school administration sends a Princeton Review-authored e-mail to all business students with an embedded link to our survey website (again, http://survey.review.com). If for some reason there are restrictions that prevent the administration from contacting the entire graduate business school student body on behalf of an outside party, they often help us find other ways to notify students of the fact that we are seeking their opinions, such as advertising in business student publications or posting on business student community websites. In almost all cases, when the administration is cooperative, we are able to collect opinions from a sufficient number of students to produce an accurate descriptive profile and ratings of its business school.

There is a group of business school administrators, however, that doesn't agree with us that current business school student opinions presented in descriptive profile and rankings formats are useful to prospective business school students. Administrators at the many AACSB-accredited business schools not appearing with two-page descriptive profiles are a part of this group. They either ignored our multiple attempts to contact them in order to request their assistance in notifying their students about our survey, or they simply refused to work with us at all. While we would like to be able to write a descriptive profile each of these many schools anyway, we won't do so with minimal business student opinion.

So if you are a prospective business school student and would like to read current business student opinion about schools that do not appear with a two-page descriptive profile, contact the schools and communicate this desire to them. (We include contact information in each of the business school data listings.) If you are a current business student at one of the many AACSB-accredited business schools without a two-page descriptive profile, please don't send us angry letters; instead, go to http://survey.review.com, complete a survey about your school, and tell all of your fellow students to do the same.

You will find statistics for business schools whose administrators were willing to report their school statistics to us but unwilling to allow us to survey their students under the school's name in the section of the book entitled "Business School Data Listings."

One more thing to note about the different entries: The majority of our various rankings lists are based wholly or partly on student feedback to our survey. Only one top 10 ranking, The Toughest to Get Into, is based on school-reported statistics alone. So while *any* of the 444 programs listed in the book may appear on that list, *only those schools with two-page descriptive profiles will appear on all other rankings lists.*

BUT SOME THINGS NEVER CHANGE

Admission to the business school of your choice, especially if your choice is among the most selective programs, will require your absolute best shot. One way to improve your chances is to make sure you apply to schools that are a good fit—and the comments provided by students in our descriptive profiles will provide more insight into the personality of each school than does its glossy view book.

In addition, you'll find plenty of useful information in Part I of this book on how to get in to business school and what to expect once you arrive. You'll find out what criteria are used to evaluate applicants and who decides your fate. You will also hear directly from admissions officers on what dooms an application and how to ace the interview. We've even interviewed deans at several of the top schools to share with you their take on recent events, including trends in business, b-school applications, recruitment, and placement.

Again, it is our hope that you will consult our profiles as a resource when choosing a list of schools that suit your academic and social needs, and that our advice is helpful to you during the application process. Good luck!

HOW WE PRODUCE THIS BOOK

In August 1999, we published *The Best 80 Business Schools, 2000 Edition*. By the time the 2001 edition of the guide was published, we had shifted our focus from student opinion-driven profiles of a select number of schools to more data-driven profiles of every graduate business school accredited by the AACSB. Although we continue to present readers with data from 444 accredited graduate b-school programs, we have reintroduced the student survey-based descriptive profile. In order to clarify our position, intent, and methodology, we've created a series of questions and answers regarding the collection of data and the production of our descriptive profiles.

How do we choose which b-schools to survey and profile? And why do some competitive schools have only a data listing?

Any business school that is AACSB-accredited and offers a Master of Business Administration degree may have a data listing included in the book, as long as that school provides us with a sufficient amount of school-specific data. In addition, this year we offered each of those accredited schools in which the primary language of instruction is English an opportunity to assist us in collecting online business student surveys.

Some schools were unable to solicit surveys from their students via e-mail due to restrictive privacy policies; others simply chose not to participate. Schools that declined to work with us to survey their students remain in the book, although they do not have a descriptive profile. A school with only a data listing does not suggest that the school is less competitive or compelling; we only separated these profile types into two sections for easier reference. If you're not sure where to find information on a school in which you're interested, you can refer to our alphabetical b-school listing in the back of the book.

There is no fee to be included in this book. If you're an administrator at an accredited business school and would like to have your school included, please send an e-mail to surveysupport@review.com.

What's the AACSB, and by what standards are schools accredited?

The AACSB stands for the Association to Advance Collegiate Schools of Business. In April 2003, the AACSB made some significant changes to its standards for accreditation. In fact, the actual number of standards went from 41 to 21. Some of the changes in accreditation included a shift from requiring a certain number of full-time faculty members with doctorates to a focus on teacher participation. Schools may employ more part-time faculty members if they are actively involved in the students' business education. The onus of both the development of a unique curriculum and the evaluation of the success of that curriculum will fall on each b-school, and schools will be reviewed by the association every five years instead of every ten. As a result of the changes in accreditation standards, a number of schools have been newly accredited or reaccredited.

How were the student surveys collected?

Back in Fall 2005, we contacted Admissions Officers at all accredited graduate b-schools and requested that they help us survey their students by distributing our Princeton Review–authored survey message to the student body via e-mail. The survey message explained the purpose of the survey and contained a link to our online business student survey. We had a phenomenal response from students—at least ten percent of full-time students responded at almost all institutions we surveyed; at many schools, we scored responses from as many as one-third or one-half of the student body—and nearly all students in a few cases.

The surveys are made up of 78 multiple-choice questions and 7 free-response questions, covering 5 sections: About Yourself, Students, Academics, Careers, and Quality of Life. Students may complete the secure online survey at any time and may save their survey responses, returning later, until the survey is complete and ready for submission. Students sign in to the online survey using their school-issued .edu e-mail address to ensure that their response is attributed to the correct school, and the respondent certifies before submission that he or she is indeed a current student enrolled in said program. In addition, an automated message is sent to this address once the student has submitted the survey, and they must click on a link in the e-mail message in order to validate their survey. We also offered a paper version of the survey to a few schools that were unable to e-mail their students regarding our online survey.

We use the resulting responses to craft descriptive profiles that are representative of the respondents' feelings toward the b-school they attend. Although well-written and/or humorous comments are especially appreciated, they would never be used unless they best stated what numerous students have told us.

What about the ranking lists and ratings?

When we decided to bring the student opinion-driven resources back into the fold, we updated our online survey and reconsidered all ranking lists. You will find that only a few of the rankings in this year's book resemble our b-school rankings of yesteryear. We've done our best to include only those topics most vital to success in business school, and we have added a few brand new lists that you will find timely and relevant.

We offer several ranking lists on a variety of considerations, from academic experience to career expectations, to the atmosphere for women and minority students. It must be noted, however, that none of these lists purport to rank the business schools by their overall quality. Nor should any combination of the categories we've chosen be construed as representing the raw ingredients for such a ranking. We have made no attempt to gauge the "prestige" of these schools, and we wonder whether we could accurately do so even if we tried. What we have done, however, is presented a number of lists using information from two very large databases—one of statistical information collected from business schools and another of subjective data gathered via our survey of 11,000 business students at 290 AACSB-accredited business schools. We do believe that there is a right business school for you, and that our rankings, when used in conjunction with our profile of each school, will help you select the best schools to apply to.

New to our rankings this year is our "Best Classroom Experience" list, based on students' answers to survey questions concerning their professors' teaching ability and recognition in the field, the integration of new business trends and practices into course offerings, and the level of student engagement in the classroom.

What do the schools have to say about all this?

Our contact at each school is kept abreast of the profile's status throughout the production process. After establishing a contact through whom we are able to reach online student respondents, we get to work writing our profiles and crunching the data. Once this information has been poured into profile pages, we send a copy of the school's profile to our contact via e-mail and snail mail. We request that the administrator review the data and comments included in the profile, and we invite their corrections to any inaccurate data, or text that may be misrepresentative of overall student opinion. With their suggestions in hand, we revisit survey responses and investigate any such claims of inaccuracy.

We are aware that a general distaste for rankings permeates the business school community, and that top schools have recently backed down from providing the data necessary for such calculations. We agree that overall rankings that purport to decide the "best" overall school are not so helpful to students, and that they may be tainted by the agendas of school administrators hoping to advance their schools' reputations, without taking the necessary measures to actually improve the quality of the school. This is why the meat of our book is the schools' descriptive profiles, which are meant to showcase each school's unique personality. The ranking lists are simply used as reference tools for students looking for a particular attribute in a prospective b-school. We don't claim to be the final word on what school has the best MBA program in the country—that's nearly impossible to determine. We simply relay the messages that the students at each school are sending us, and we are clear about how our rankings are determined.

HOW THIS BOOK IS ORGANIZED

This book is packed with information about business schools, and we want to make sure you know how to find what you're looking for. So here's a breakdown of how this book is organized.

Part I is comprised of several chapters that give you an idea of what to expect at business school and tell you how to put together a winning application.

Part II has our b-school ranking lists. Of the 11 lists, 7 are based entirely on student survey responses; 1 is based solely on institutionally reported data; and 4 are based on a combination of survey responses and statistical information. Along with each list, you will find information about which survey questions or statistical factors were used to calculate the rankings.

Part III contains profiles of all AACSB-accredited graduate schools with MBA programs divided into two sections: those with descriptive profiles based on student surveys, and those with only a statistical listing.

PART III-A: BUSINESS SCHOOL DESCRIPTIVE PROFILES

Please see the sample descriptive profile below.

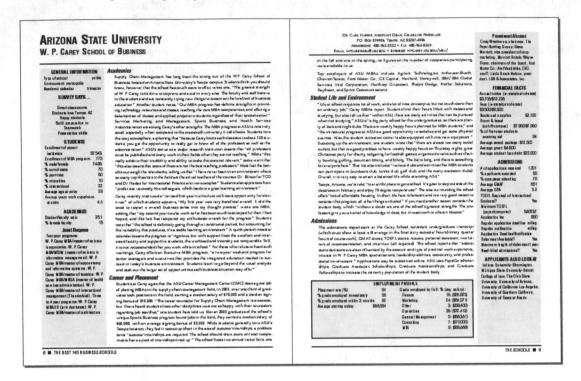

Each two-page spread is made up of eight major components. At the top of each page, you'll find the name of the business school, along with the name of an admissions contact and his or her address, phone number, fax number, if applicable, and e-mail address. This section also includes the b-school's website address. There are two sidebars (the narrow columns on the outer edge of each page) that contain information reported by the schools through the Business Data Set (BDS) and some student survey data as well. The Survey Says information reflects aspects of the school about which students feel the strongest; there are nine different possible results. We also offer an Employment Profile for each school, which is made up of statistical information from the BDS. The main body of the profile contains descriptive text discussing Academics, Placement and Recruiting, Student/Campus Life, and Admissions. Each description is based on student survey responses and may call upon statistical data where necessary.

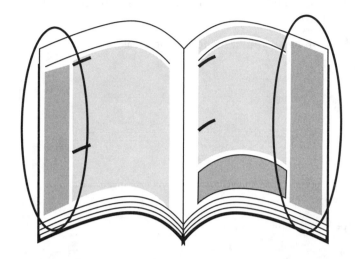

All information in the sidebars falls under the following categories: General Information, Academics, Financial Facts, and Admissions. Please note that not every category will appear for every school; in some cases the information is not reported or not applicable. These are the same data fields that are reported for those schools listed in Part III-B: Business School Data Listings, save for 4 of the 5 ratings, which appear only in the descriptive profiles.

Here is what each sidebar heading tells you.

General Information

Type of school

Public or private school

Affiliation

Any religious order with which the school is affiliated

Environment

Whether the campus is located in a metropolis, city, town, village, or rural setting

Academic Calendar

Whether the school schedule runs according to trimesters, semesters, quarters, or another calendar type like a 4-1-4 (4-month semester, 1-month interim term, 4-month semester)

Survey Says

Survey Says gives you an at-a-glance look at what students are most in agreement about at their school. You'll find up to six results per school. Three will reflect the top three subject areas as indicated by responses to the following question:

How well has your school prepared you in the following areas:

Marketing

Finance

Accounting

General management

Operations

Teamwork

Communication/Interpersonal skills

Presentation skills

Quantitative skills

Computer skills

Doing business in a global economy

Entrepreneurial studies

In addition, Survey Says may include (up to) three things from the following list that students were most in agreement about:

- Students like Hometown, State. Based on level of agreement with the statement, "I like the town where my school is located."

- Friendly students. Based on level of agreement with the statement, "Your business school classmates are friendly."

- Good social scene. Based on level of agreement with the statement, "Your business school classmates have active social lives."

- Good peer network. Based on level of agreement with the statement, "Your business school classmates are the type of people you want to network with after graduation."

- Cutting-edge classes. Based on responses to the question, "How well has your school integrated new business trends and practices into course offerings?"

- Helpful alumni. Based on responses to the question, "How helpful have alumni been in assisting you in your job search?"

- Happy students. Based on level of agreement with the statement, "Overall, I am happy here."

- Smart classrooms. Based on level of agreement with the statement, "Classroom facilities are equipped with computer/multimedia resources."

Students

Enrollment of parent institution

Total number of undergraduate and graduate students enrolled in parent institution program

Enrollment of MBA program

Total number of students enrolled in MBA programs at the business school, including both full- and part-time programs

"% male/female" through "% international"

Items based on demographic information about full-time b-school students as reported by the schools

Average age at entry

The average age of incoming first-year MBA students

Average years work experience at entry

The average years of work experience for incoming first-year MBA students

Academics

Academic Experience Rating

This rating measures the quality of the learning environment. Each school is given a score between 60 and 99 Factors taken into consideration include GMAT scores and undergraduate grades of enrolled students; percent accepted; percent enrolled; student/faculty ratio; and student survey questions pertaining to faculty, fellow students, and realization of academic expectations. This rating is intended to be used only to compare those schools within this edition of the book whose students completed our business student survey.

Please note that if a 60* Academic Experience Rating appears for any school, it means that the school didn't report all the rating's underlying data points by our deadline, so we were unable to calculate an accurate rating. In such cases, the reader is advised to follow up with the school about specific measures this rating takes into account.

Please also note that many foreign institutions use a grading system that is different from the standard U.S. GPA; as a result, we approximated their Admissions Selectivity and Academic Ratings, indicating this with a † following the rating.

Student/Faculty Ratio

The ratio of full-time graduate instructional faculty members to all enrolled MBA students

Professors Interesting Rating

Based on the answers given by students to the survey question, "Overall, how good are your professors as teachers?" Ratings fall between 60 and 99. This rating is intended to be used to compare those schools within this edition of the book whose students completed our business student survey.

Professors Accessible Rating

Based on the answers given by students to the survey question, "How accessible are your professors outside of the classroom?" Ratings fall between 60 and 99. This rating is intended to be used to compare those schools within this edition of the book whose students completed our business student survey.

% female faculty

Percent of graduate business faculty in the 2006–2007 academic year who were women

% minority faculty

Percent of graduate business faculty in the 2006–2007 academic year who were members of minority groups

Joint Degrees

A list of joint degrees offered by the business school. See Decoding Degrees on page 519 for the full name of each degree.

Prominent Alumni

School administrators may submit the name, title, and company of up to five prominent alumni.

Financial Facts

Please note that we rely on foreign institutions to convert financial figures into U.S. dollars. Please check with any foreign schools you are considering for up-to-date figures and conversion rates.

"Tuition (in-state/out-of-state)" and "Fees (in-state/out-of-state)"

In-state and out-of-state tuition and fees per academic year. At state-supported public schools, in-state tuition and fees are likely to be significantly lower than out-of-state expenses.

Books and supplies

Estimated cost of books and supplies for one academic year

Room and board

Cost of room and board on campus per academic year, and estimate of off-campus living expenses for this time period

"% of students receiving aid" through "% of students receiving grants"

Percent of students receiving aid, then specifically those receiving grants and loans. These numbers reflect the percentage of all enrolled MBA students that receive financial aid, regardless of whether or not they applied for financial aid or for specific aid types. Likewise, the second figure, "% of first year students receiving aid" takes into account all first-year MBA students, regardless of whether they applied for financial aid or specific aid types.

Average award package

For students who received financial aid, this is the average award amount.

Average grant

For students who received grants, this is the average amount of grant money awarded.

Average student loan debt

The average dollar amount of outstanding educational MBA loans per graduate (class of 2006) at the time of graduation

Admissions

Admissions Selectivity Rating

This rating measures the competitiveness of the school's admissions. Factors taken into consideration include the average GMAT score and undergraduate GPA of the first-year class, the percent of students accepted, and the percent of applicants who are accepted and ultimately enroll. No student survey data is used in this calculation. Ratings fall between 60 and 99. This rating is intended to be used to compare all schools within this edition of the book, regardless of whether their students completed our business student survey.

Please note that if a 60* Admissions Selectivity Rating appears for any school, it means that the school did not report all of the rating's underlying data points by our deadline, so we were unable to calculate an accurate rating. In such cases, the reader is advised to follow up with the school about specific measures this rating takes into account.

Please also note that many foreign institutions use a grading system that is different from the standard U.S. GPA; as a result, we approximated their Admissions Selectivity and Academic Ratings, indicating this with a † next to the rating.

of applications received

The total number of applications received for any and all MBA programs at the school

% applicants accepted

The percentage of applicants to which the school offered admission

% acceptees attending

Of those accepted students, the percentage of those who enrolled

Average GMAT

The average GMAT score for the first-year class

Average GPA

The average undergraduate GPA of the first year class, reported on a 4-point scale

TOEFL required of international applicants?

For those international students interested in applying, the b-school reports whether the Test of English as a Foreign Language (TOEFL) is required.

Minimum TOEFL (paper/computer)

The minimum TOEFL score necessary for consideration. We list acceptable scores for both the paper and computer versions of the test.

Application fee

The amount it costs to file an application with the school

"Application deadline" and "Regular notification"

This regular application deadline reflects the date by which all materials must be postmarked; the notification date tells you when you can expect to hear back.

International Application Fee

The amount it costs an international student to file an application with the school if it is different from the cost of the regular application.

"Early decision program" and "ED deadline/notification"

If a school offers an early decision option, we'll tell you when early decision apps are due to be postmarked, and when you'll be notified of the school's decision.

"Deferment available?" and "Maximum length of deferment"

Some schools allow accepted students to defer enrollment for a year or more, while others require students who postpone attendance to reapply.

Transfer students accepted?

Whether or not students are accepted from other MBA programs

Transfer Application Policy

Lets you know how transfer applications are reviewed and how many credits will be allowed to transfer from another program.

Non-fall admissions?

Some business schools may allow students to matriculate at the beginning of each semester, while for others, the invitation to attend stipulates that fall attendance is mandatory.

Need-blind admissions?

Whether or not the school considers applications without regard to the candidate's financial need

Applicants also look at

The school reports that students applying to their school are also known to apply to a short list of other schools.

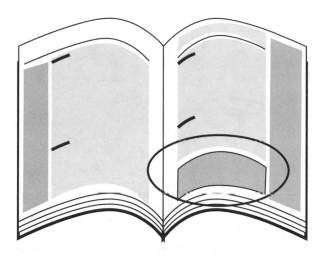

Career Rating

Taking into account both student survey responses and statistical data, this rating measures the confidence students have in their school's ability to lead them to fruitful employment opportunities, as well as the school's own record of having done so. Factors taken into consideration include statistics on the average starting salary and percent of students employed at graduation from the Business Data Set and comments from the student survey, assessing the efforts of the placement office, the quality of recruiting companies, level of preparation, and opportunities for off-campus projects, internships, and mentorships. Ratings fall between 60 and 99. This rating is intended to be used to compare only those schools within this edition of the book whose students completed our business student survey.

* Please note that if a 60* Career Rating appears for any school, it means that the school did not report all of the rating's underlying data points by our deadline, so we were unable to calculate an accurate rating. In such cases, the reader is advised to follow up with the school about the specific attributes this rating takes into account.

% grads employed within three months of graduation

This reflects the percentage of MBA grads who earned a job within three months of graduation.

Average starting salary

Average starting salary of all 2006 graduates

Grads employed by field %: avg. salary

Reflects the distribution of 2006 graduates across many different industries and the average starting salary for each field.

Top 5 employers hiring grads

Reflects the top five employers who hired 2006 job seeking full-time MBA graduates, and the number of students they hired.

Each school's descriptive profile is made up of four sections which highlight those qualities that characterize the school as a unique institution. *Academics* covers students' opinions on the quality of professors, curriculum, special or noteworthy programs, the administration, and anything else academic in nature. *Career and Placement* deals with the school's efforts to secure internships and jobs for its current students and graduates; information about alumni assistance and popular recruiters of MBAs at the school may also be included. In *Student Life and Environment*, you'll find out how students balance work and play and whether they find it manageable to do so; often, you'll also find reviews of the school's facilities as well. Finally, the *Admissions* section describes what the Admissions Committee is looking for in potential students.

All quotes in these sections are taken from students' responses to our survey. We choose quotes that were consistent with the overall survey results.

PART III-B: BUSINESS SCHOOL DATA LISTINGS

This section contains all of the statistical info that is presented in the sidebars of the descriptive profile. Each school in this section will include an Admissions Selectivity rating but will not include the other 3 ratings, the Survey Says section, or a descriptive profile.

PART IV: SCHOOL SAYS

Part IV offers more detailed information about particular business schools authored by the schools themselves. The business schools included in this section pay a small fee for this space. These schools also have descriptive profiles or data listings in Part III.

EVERYTHING ELSE

Following Part IV, we offer a small section of profiles of b-schools who may pay a small fee for inclusion. Next is a section entitled *Decoding Degrees* that will help you make sense of the myriad degree abbreviations you'll see listed in the book. You'll then find the indexes—alphabetical by school name, and then by location. Finally, you'll have an opportunity to learn more about our author, Nedda Gilbert.

Enjoy and good luck!

PART I
ALL ABOUT BUSINESS SCHOOL

CHAPTER 1

THIS ISN'T YOUR FATHER'S (OR MOTHER'S) B-SCHOOL ANYMORE

THE NEW MBA CLASS: FEWER, YOUNGER, AND WORKING WHILE THEY LEARN

The MBA has always been seen as a golden passport, the trip ticket to romance and riches. The destination: career acceleration, power networks and recruiters, elite employers, and of course, generous paychecks.

But not everyone wants to make the trip. Several factors will always impact on the popularity of the MBA: 1) the state of the economy—interest in getting the MBA has generally waxed and waned with economic times; 2) trends and favorable or unfavorable press—in the 1980s, a rash of insider trading scandals in which MBAs were ensnared made the degree look smarmy and other graduate programs, notably law and medicine, look more appealing; 3) the immediacy of good professional opportunities—the collapse of the dot-com boom, followed by the severe retrenchment of traditional MBA destinations (such as investment banks and consulting firms) in a depressed economy, has left many current MBAs stranded; and 4) recruiter demand for newly minted MBAs—do employers see the skill sets of today's MBAs bringing measurable value to their companies?

B-SCHOOL: INTEREST AND APPLICATIONS ON UPSWING

After three straight years of declining applications, the numbers increased in 2006. Two-thirds of full-time MBA programs participating in the 2006 GMAC Application Trends Survey saw application levels rise in 2006, up from only 21 percent from last year. Part-time programs reported a similar increase in volume: 62 percent in 2006, compared with 46 percent last year. Among executive MBA programs, 69 percent saw applications increase, up from 38 percent in 2005.

A STRONGER ECONOMY + A HEFTY PRICE TAG = SCARING STUDENTS AWAY

The weak economy of the past few years has been behind the wheel in driving MBA unpopularity. Concerns about the lingering effects of the recession have made the once-golden MBA an unsure investment. In an already tight job market, fewer students wanted to take on the opportunity costs of leaving their current jobs, paying a hefty sum for tuition, and still having to scramble for a job after they graduate. The numbers do tell: B-school has lost its appeal as a safe haven from turbulent times, much less a straight-shot pathway to guaranteed riches.

Fortunately, the economy does appear to be recovering. But application numbers are still less than stellar and the hiring of new MBAs has not fully rebounded. One note of difference: at top-brand schools, the picture is much rosier. Placement rates are fast returning to pre-September 11 levels.

YOUNGER MINDS

Although growing applicant pools may make admission seem more competitive, there are now some unrecognized opportunities for candidates with less than the traditional two to four years of work experience to make a strong case for admittance.

Admissions officers at large benchmark schools such as Stanford say that this trend pre-dates the economic downturn. Derek Bolton, director of admissions at Stanford notes, "The pendulum has gone too far in one direction in terms of the number of younger candidates applying to b-school. It has not kept pace with the overall pace of applicants. We want more young applicants applying. The goal is to bring the average age down in the next couple of years."

"What's driving this is the willingness on the part of the b-schools to not be rigidly fixed on what's right for someone. We may not always be the best judge of when the best time is for a candidate to go to b-school," continues Bolton.

Wharton's former Director of Admissions Rose Martinelli observed "a shift in that we became more tuned in to when students are ready in their leadership, professional, and personal development. We see so many nontraditional students that we don't want to have rules on when they can apply. We don't want to miss out on fabulous applicants because they don't think they can get in."

"When the applicant pool continues to get older and older, then we're closing out younger applicants who are on a fast track." Martinelli continues, "Why should we wait? Why should they wait? We want to catch the human element in the application process."

This perspective continues to hold true. As University of Chicago's Stacey Kole sums up, "The pendulum had swung too far in terms of the type of student who should be admitted and when. Now schools are correcting that and experimenting, taking less experienced candidates. We believe that this experimentation is a good thing."

THE DRAW OF THE PART-TIME PROGRAM

Ironically, even as the economy appears to be in a slight upswing, many young adults are choosing to brave a newly robust job market over immersing themselves in the uncertainty—not to mention the high costs—of a graduate program in business or even law. Because part-time and executive education programs have not suffered the decline that full-time programs have, pundits say that the future of b-school may lie in programs that offer more flexible part-time opportunities, allowing students to get the degree without making a full-time commitment. In fact, Stacey Kole, Deputy Dean for the full-time MBA Program and Clinical Professor of Economics, University of Chicago Graduate School of Business states, "There is this tendency to think of the MBA as a full-time-only product. But schools like Chicago offer MBA programs in the evening, on weekends, and in executive program formats. For us, whether the student matriculates in our part-time or full-time program, the process is exactly the same. Ours is the same degree, only delivered in full-time, part-time, and weekend formats with different scheduling options. Chicago GSB offers individuals interested in an MBA considerable flexibility in how they pursue their education."

Kole continues, "Part-time and executive programs are now providing more of the outside-the-classroom, extracurricular experience that did not exist 10 years ago. For example, they are offering student-led clubs, speakers, and recruiter events that historically were the exclusive domain of full-time programs. This is one explanation for why part-time programs are looking like better substitutes for a full-time program."

There may be more to the story, too. Because they may be less likely to be in committed relationships or have families, younger students are more active, generous alumni, and b-schools can't afford to ignore the market that these younger students represent. Despite the heightened competition, candidates with less experience are increasingly being deemed worthy of a coveted b-school acceptance.

PAYBACK TIME

The MBA, particularly at the top schools, continues to pay out high dividends to grads. The salaries of 2006 alumni have risen against MBA 2005 salaries within every sector—from investment banking to the retail sector. Although salaries for U.S. alumni are still higher than those paid to their European counterparts, the gap is closing rapidly. That's a hefty return on investment. But the degree doesn't come with any promises. The world of business requires some risk, as many MBA wannabes found out several years go: You can enter a business school program at the height of the economy only to graduate when things are dismal. But you can also enter b-school at low tide then watch as the job market swells and employers are fighting over the newest and brightest MBA grads, including you.

FOREIGN MBA STUDENTS: THE NEW REALITY

Opportunities to study or work abroad during an MBA program are considered highly relevant. Likewise, international enrollment at U.S. business schools has always been a priority. At some schools, the percentage of foreign students has been sky-high, anywhere from 30 to 40 percent. Of course, that was before the new screening and tracking processes for international applicants went into effect.

Previously, our position was clear: International students represent a win-win proposition for both U.S. business schools and the foreign industries that send them here. American business schools prize the global perspective and diversity international students bring into the classroom and community; foreign businesses operating in a global economy desire expertise in U.S. business practices which are becoming the international standard.

Unfortunately, due to international security issues, this informal but critical partnership faces greater challenges. These have come primarily in the form of increased scrutiny. Foreign students must slog through tougher rules and procedures for obtaining and maintaining a visa under the United States Citizenship and Immigration Services (USCIS). And many foreign students feel that even if they are successful in obtaining a student visa, they will face an even tougher battle after they graduate: trying to get a work visa. That puts them back at square one. Though armed with an American MBA, they often find themselves looking for work in their home country—a scenario from which they may originally have wanted a professional out.

Foreign Students: Getting In

As of January 2003, U.S. institutions must comply with the Student and Exchange Visitor Information System, or SEVIS, which tracks foreign students and exchange visitors, as well as some foreign professors. While there is hope that SEVIS will prevent potential terrorists from slipping through the cracks, critics fear that the intensified scrutiny drives away many foreign applicants. The system causes major delays in obtaining a student visa and leaving or reentering the country. In addition, compliance with SEVIS requires the staff of international student offices to perform a great deal of data entry, detracting from the face-time advisors can spend with foreign students.

For the foreseeable future, students wishing to obtain a visa will not be able to escape the shadow of world events, but they should not be deterred. Most business schools stand firm on their commitment to foreign applicants throughout the entire process.

In fact, Don Martin, Director of Admissions at the University of Chicago notes that the number of international students enrolled at UChicago has remained constant. Martin says, "We have made no change in terms of our desire and commitment to enroll foreign students. This world will never go back to what it was before it became a global village. For the sake of diversity and the perspective international students bring to the table, or for understanding foreign business culture, we need to have people who represent that world in every sense."

Martin does agree that for foreign MBA students intending to study on American soil, "The journey of enrolling them is going to be more challenging. A part of that is tied into the changes the U.S. government has imposed on getting visas. Some applicants will need to take another year for the paperwork." But most notably, he sees different forces at play in the shrinking foreign MBA market, namely, the competition U.S. schools are feeling from business schools abroad. Martin continues, "The issue influencing more international business students away from U.S. business schools is the large amount of European, Australian, and Latin American business schools that heretofore I would not have thought would have had as much pull as they did. These business schools have become more visible and prominent. They are being ranked by the large news organizations and magazines. So I would say American business schools still want international students, but the ability to recruit and draw them here to us will be difficult against this new competition."

To those applying for a visa, Wharton's former Director of Admissions Rose Martinelli offers this advice: "Emphasize plans to return home, [not] plans to immigrate to the United States." If a visa is denied, many schools will defer admission and hold that student's spot until the visa is obtained. "It may take a little longer for students from some countries to get their visas. But decisions here are not made based on whether they got a visa or not. Decisions are made based on what they'll do at our school and on the contributions they'll make," sums up Martinelli.

Of course, all this is subject to change, perhaps even by the time of this book's publication. Non-U.S. citizens should visit the USCIS website (www.uscis.gov) for the latest information on student visas.

Foreign Students: Getting a Job

Just when a foreign student is ready to reap the rewards of his or her hard-won business degree, he or she hits another roadblock. And this one's a brick wall: an unforgiving and limited job market fueled not just by a new wartime security, but also a new nationalism.

Historically, foreign students have always had a tougher time than their American counterparts in trying to get that first job out of b-school. That's because of the hassle of sponsoring a foreigner on a visa, rigid immigration rules, and other cultural and relocation issues. Nonetheless, for grads of the top schools, there has always been a pot of gold waiting at the end of that long journey. That pot of gold has meant the opportunity to embark on an entirely new career and life—to be sponsored by a U.S. company, on U.S. soil, with post-MBA pay scales that supersede those of their home countries and launch them on a high-earnings career path.

Since September 11, the environment in the United States has changed, and the home-field advantage of American MBAs is even greater. Simply put, U.S. companies have been reluctant to offer a foreign MBA a plush job over an American MBA who is equally talented and qualified. The result is that foreign hires have been more limited to hard-to-fill positions, to employment in their locations abroad, or to positions in the student's home country. Many MBA recruiters won't even offer an international student an interview.

As for companies shrinking their foreign MBA hires down to bare bones, as we've said many times before, and Don Martin concurs, where you go to school matters. He explains, "Some companies have changed their hiring strategies. Fewer overall international students are being hired, but not at our school. Companies typically will drop down from their list of 10 schools they go to, to a much smaller number of programs. In a high percentage, we've remained on their lists. We are seeing 90 percent of our international students placed in internships and going on to full-time hires."

The result of the shrinking job market for most foreign students is that business schools have begun to cut back on the number of applicants admitted, and this has made it even tougher to get accepted. Many schools have begun to be upfront about the limited career opportunities on U.S. soil for foreigners. Indeed, this will soon be compounded by a reduction of more than 50 percent in the number of work visas the government issues annually to employees sponsored by their company.

But as the economy heats up and MBA hiring begins to rebound, it is possible that recruiters, particularly Wall Street and the top-flight consulting firms, will once again open their doors to whomever is most qualified, foreign or not. History, it should be remembered, shows us that the top jobs always go to the most capable applicants. This next cycle should be no different than the preceding cycles. Talent still rules.

In the meantime, buyers beware: An MBA is not the passport to riches it once was for foreign applicants. International students should think twice about the costs of pursuing a degree that may only deliver them back into the hands of their home countries saddled with the expense, but not the benefit, of an MBA education.

THE CONTINUING RELEVANCE OF BUSINESS SCHOOL

The MBA is such an attractive option because it *does* confer huge value on the recipient. Business schools know how to keep pace with the rapidly changing face of business. After all, that's *their* business, so you're never really out of the game. In fact, if you look at the nation's top business programs, you'll find exciting innovations in curriculum that reflect all that's new and relevant. This includes unique opportunities for teamwork, internships, and laboratory simulations that replicate real-world, real-time business scenarios.

The integration of these real-world experiences into the basics produces better-trained, more well-rounded managers, as graduates are more adept at discerning the correlation between principle and reality. Even so, programs and students in search of business knowledge that is more widely applicable and more relevant long-term has caused a strong return to fundamentals.

BACKPEDALING TO THE BASICS

Many top schools are reviving the old classics: It's back to basics. Both schools and students now have enough of a perspective to look back at the frenzy of the last business cycle and understand that enduring values are rooted in a solid foundation. Gone is the frothy demand for trendy courses on e-commerce and other hype-driven topics. Just four years ago, a class at Stanford on the principles of Internet marketing was oversub-scribed. Last year, only a few people signed up for it.

So here's a sampler of the back-to-basics you'll get at b-school: An in-depth immersion in all of the key functional areas of an organization: marketing, management, sales, finance, operations, logistics, and so on. You'll look at these areas across dozens of industries and organizational types, from start-ups to Fortune 500 companies.

The renewed focus on basics doesn't mean that you'll find yourself shorted on current trends and events. Expect plenty of case study debate on corporate governance and the Enron debacle, and expect the themes of global perspective and technological competence to permeate many programs. You'll also find classes and seminars on leadership gaining popularity. "We're seeing a resurgence of leadership courses as students seek out professions and business models that are other-oriented," notes Stanford's Bolton. "This may be a new generation. But these are students who look at business as a positive force in the world, a more noble calling."

SURVIVOR POWER

Once you have your MBA, you can expect to hit the ground running. You'll start off your post b-school career with a load of contacts that you will periodically leverage over your career. Many graduates use the degree to embark on entirely new career paths than those that brought them to the school; consultants become bankers, entrepreneurs become consultants, marketers become financiers, and so on. The MBA has and will continue to be a terrific opportunity to reinvent oneself.

"An MBA is unlike any other professional degree because the breadth of knowledge poises you for a multitude of career choices," says Julia Min, Director of MBA Admissions for NYU Stern School of Business. "You can be an investment banker, yet two years from that point, segue into nonprofit work. You can move from banking to corporate finance, to a venture-capital proposition, to ultimately having an entrepreneurial experience. So it's a credential that allows you the flexibility to explore different industries; it's a long-term investment that will give you the tools to transition if you want to."

"What's wonderful about the MBA is that it provides fundamental skills that you can use whenever and wherever you need them," champions Martinelli. "I'm a cheerleader for the nontraditional because I feel the MBA is such a fundamental tool. It offers an ability to enter the business world and link passion with functionality."

"For example, for folks who want to go into public service or nonprofit, even the arts industry, they're very narrow fields. You need the passion and vision to be successful in them. But often credibility is undermined when you don't understand the business world's perspective," states Martinelli.

"You've got to know that industry if you're going to make it viable for the future. But you have to be able to know how to talk to the business world in order to get those investments to make it happen. And that's one of the reasons why an MBA is so valuable. It bestows credibility in the marketplace and helps us maintain these organizations in a world that doesn't often respect passion over the bottom line," she continues.

After a tough slog in 2002 and 2003, job prospects for recent MBA graduates are looking up. Hundreds of companies continue to visit and recruit from business school campuses, with today's MBA candidates receiving two job offers on average. Recruiters exist in a symbiotic relationship with business schools. Employers like to maintain a strong presence on campus—even during an economic downturn—so that they'll have their top picks of MBA talent when the good times return. Thus, MBA programs remain one of the most effective means to get oneself in front of recruiters and senior managers from the most desirable companies. And while that may not grant you "immunity" from an economy characterized by up and downs, it will absolutely improve your survivor power.

COMPETITION HAS EASED UP

With an economic recovery seemingly underway, the chance to dive into any number of secure, well-paying jobs will lure a percentage of professionals away from the MBA. After years of struggling through economic hardship, a decent paycheck from the pocket of a much improved labor market may seem the best bet. There's no doubt that risk-averse individuals would prefer the stability of a secure job to what might-be, could-be, or should-be two years down the road—even with an MBA in hand. This may keep the applicant pool smaller.

Additionally, the continued decrease in the number of foreign applicants, who at many schools comprised well over 20 percent of students, will keep applications down, too. Other factors include the fact that there are currently smaller percentages of people in the country who are in the typical age bracket of business school applicants. Lastly, the increased interest in part-time MBA programs may continue to drive the decline in full-time business school applications.

What does all of this mean? Basically this: If you have a handsome application and you plan on applying to the most competitive programs this year, you may find yourself met with welcoming arms.

As the Song Goes...Money, Money, Money, Money...

But don't go buying the flashy car to go with that flashy degree quite yet. It needs to be said that, after several years of a slump, there could actually be a surge in this upcoming applicant pool that would correspond with improvements in the economy. Recruiters are once again storming the top business schools as hiring slowly returns to healthy levels. At programs like Chicago, Harvard, and Stanford, six-figure salaries and signing bonuses of $15,000-plus are still the norm. That's why it's important to remember that the MBA from the right school can deliver an immediate and hefty return on investment. According to the Graduate Management Admission Council Global MBA Graduate Survey of 2006, respondents reported an annual (mean) salary of $59,635 before entering business school and a (mean) salary of $92,000 in their first job out. This number is expected to continue to rise for the class of 2007. Amid a healthy recruiting environment built on strong employer confidence in the economy, the average new MBA with a job offer in hand will earn $92,360 during the first year of employment, up 4.2 percent from the $88,626 graduates in 2005 received. Moreover, two-thirds of job offers to MBAs in 2006 come with signing bonuses that average $17,603, up slightly from last year.

Another trend worth noting: Although applications are down overall at b-schools, that doesn't mean the quality of applicants has suffered. Notes Chicago's Kole, "Our applications are of high quality, and applicants appear to be quite focused with regard to why they seek an advanced degree. Whether they are career switchers or planning to resume their career path, those applicants who present a compelling story for why they want to be here leave a stronger impression with the admissions committee."

Top schools are always going to have people knocking at their doors. The possibility that business school applications in general could once again rise means you'll still want to be competitive. The long application process starts with developing a solid application strategy and applying to a diverse portfolio of schools.

Let Us Help You Decide

There are many factors to consider when deciding whether or not to pursue an MBA, and we'll help you make that decision in the following chapters. We'll also tell you a bit about each school in our profiles and prepare you to do further research on the schools on your list. We've worked hard to provide you with thorough information on every aspect of the MBA, but you don't have to take our word for it—see for yourself. Stanford's Bolton advises future applicants, "Start early. Visit as many schools as you can, because it's very hard to differentiate among programs from websites, books, and marketing materials. You need to get a feeling from walking down the halls."

After you decide to go, finding the right program can be extremely difficult. Bolton explains, "Applicants really have to dig beneath the programs they're looking at to determine what's going to make them happy. A lot of people wind up going to the wrong school. A lot of external factors contribute to that. People shouldn't worry about justifying the decision to others, but to themselves."

Making the Decision to Go

The next step for you may be b-school. Indeed, armed with an MBA you may journey far. But the success of your trip and the direction you take will depend on knowing exactly why you're going to b-school and just what you'll be getting out of it.

The most critical questions you need to ask yourself are the following: Do you really want a career in business? What do you want the MBA to do for you? Are you looking to gain credibility, accelerate your development, or move into a new job or industry? Perhaps you're looking to start your own business, in which case entrepreneurial study will be important.

Knowing what you want doesn't just affect your decision to go, it also affects your candidacy; admissions committees favor applicants who have clear goals and objectives. Moreover, once at school, students who know what they want make the most of their two years. If you're uncertain about your goals, opportunities for career development—such as networking, mentoring, student clubs, and recruiter events—are squandered.

You also need to find a school that fits your individual needs. Consider the personal and financial costs. This may be the single biggest investment of your life. How much salary will you forego by leaving the workforce? What will the tuition be? How will you pay for it? If you have a family, spouse, or significant other, how will getting your MBA affect them?

If you do have a spouse, you may choose a program that involves partners in campus life. If status is your top priority, you should simply choose the most prestigious school you can get into.

The MBA presents many opportunities but no guarantees. As with any opportunity, you must make the most of it. Whether you go to a first-tier school or to a part-time program close to home, you'll acquire the skills that can jump-start your career. But your success will have more to do with you than with the piece of paper your MBA is printed on.

Chapter 2

Blackberrys and Power Lunches: What Does an MBA Offer?

NUTS-AND-BOLTS BUSINESS SKILLS

Graduate business schools teach the applied science of business. The best business schools combine the latest academic theories with pragmatic concepts, hands-on experience, and real-world solutions.

B-schools also teach the analytical skills used to make complicated business decisions. You learn how to define the critical issues, apply analytical techniques, develop the criteria for decisions, and make decisions after evaluating their impact on other variables.

After two years, you're ready to market a box of cereal. Or prepare a valuation of the cereal company's worth. You'll speak the language of business. You'll know the tools of the trade. Your expertise will extend to many areas and industries. In short, you will have acquired the skills that open doors.

ACCESS TO RECRUITERS, ENTRÉE TO NEW FIELDS

Applicants tend to place great emphasis on "incoming" and "outgoing" statistics. First they ask, "Will I get in?" Then they ask, "Will I get a job?"

Obviously, the first is largely dependent on how selective the school is and the quality of your credentials. The latter question can almost assuredly be answered in the positive, "Yes, you will."

But the real question is: How many—and what kind—of offers will you receive? Again, that is dependent on the appeal of the school to recruiters (which is a readily available statistic you can get from each school) and the particular industry you elect to pursue. For example, investment banks and consulting firms are always going to come to the schools for formal recruiting periods, whereas more off-the-beaten-path choices will possibly require you to go off campus in search of opportunity.

It's Good to Be Wanted, It's Great to Be Paid

According to many top schools, recruiter appetite for new grads is up. The latest figures suggest a strong market for newly minted MBAs. This comes after several years of depressed interest in which the immediate economic value of the MBA was in question.

As we reported in Chapter 1, the average return on investment for business school grads in 2006 was an impressive 30 percent increase in annual salary. According to the Graduate Management Council, the before and after picture looks something like this: Average entering salary: roughly $59,635. Average first job out of school salary: $92,360. Presumably, starting salaries will continue to increase as the economy improves.

The majority of top grads receive a generous relocation package too. Indeed, if you were fortunate enough to have spent the summer between your first and second year at a consulting company, then you will, in all likelihood, also receive a "rebate" on your tuition. These companies often pick up a student's second-year tuition bill. The best package, however, goes to those MBA students who worked at the firm before b-school. These lucky capitalists often get their whole tuition paid for.

Getting the MBA for the Long Run

Although MBA hiring appears to be on an upswing, going to business school still requires you to take a bit of a gamble. Leaner years make business school a riskier proposition. The nation appears to be heading out of what has been a lingering recession, but economic factors are always unpredictable. Furthermore, the world has witnessed great political turmoil. All of these factors can quickly and negatively impact the job market for newly minted MBAs.

So as you make plans to go to b-school, you need to accept that there is some risk that the labor market won't greet you with open arms at graduation. Consider the plight of MBAs from just three years ago: when they entered b-school, the economy was roaring ahead. The immediate future looked exceptionally bright. Most MBAs probably thought that once they got in, they had it made, and they looked forward to generous starting salaries and bonuses. Few probably anticipated that tough times could hit so dramatically.

But that's just the point. Good times and bad times cycle in and out. Fortunately, it looks as though we are cycling into a good time. Many economic experts agree that the economy is looking up and the markets will continue to improve. This means traditional hirers of MBAs, such as the investment banks and consulting firms, may once again be wooing many a b-school grad. Still, it's hard to know when all of the recruiters who typically hire MBAs will feel comfortable again about bringing their hiring levels back up to what they were before the downturn.

The best way to consider the value of the degree is by focusing on its long-lasting benefits. "When people come here for their MBA, they talk about retooling for their life. They think about the long term and recognize that there are some short term hurdles," says Rose Martinelli, former director of admissions at the Wharton School. "Just out of business school, this is the very first job in a long career. This is really about building blocks and going for the long run. You may have to work harder to find a job now, but building your career is a lifelong process." The MBA gives you the tools, networking, and polish to meaningfully enhance your long-term prospects and earning potential.

"There is real opportunity here. The opportunity right now is to pursue your passion and perhaps not your wallet," continues Martinelli. "We're seeing more of an equalization in salary. Those high-paying jobs in finance, investment banking, and consulting are fewer and harder to find. So here you have an opportunity for a job with a true learning experience rather than one that just pays a lot. More people are going into nonprofit and government and making contributions back to the community."

Brand Power Counts

Of course, there is great variability with placement rates and starting salaries among schools. The MBA does not swap your tuition bill for a guarantee that you'll get rich quick. As we've noted, it is at the best schools—those that have the greatest prestige and global recognition—where the strongest recovery is taking place. It's brand power at work. Even in an uncertain economy, top schools will continue to produce in-demand MBAs for the marketplace.

Branded schools tend to have an extensive history with big recruiting companies because the schools are a steady source of exceptional talent. As the economy stabilizes and hiring creeps up again, recruiters are naturally going to orient themselves at the top-brand schools.

At the University of Chicago, Deputy Dean Stacey Kole notes: "Recruiting activity is up, in the order of 20 percent. Hiring activity has really skyrocketed. I think that companies are feeling more comfortable that the economy is in good shape and are resuming their pre-September 11 hiring patterns. We had thousands of interviews available for our grads."

At less prominent schools, the picture may not be quite as optimistic. It is important to consider placement rates and the list of companies that typically recruit on campus at any school you are considering.

GETTING A JOB

For most would-be MBAs, b-school represents a fresh beginning—either in their current profession or in an entirely different industry. Whatever promise the degree holds for you, it's wise to question what the return on your investment will be.

Several factors affect job placement and starting salary. School reputation and ties to industries and employers are important. At the top programs, the lists of recruiters read like a "Who's Who" of American companies. These schools not only attract the greatest volume of recruiters, but consistently get the attention of those companies considered to be "blue chip."

Not to be overlooked are lesser-known, regional schools that often have the strongest relationships with local employers and industries. Some b-schools (many of them state universities) are regarded by both academicians and employers as number one in their respective regions. In other words, as far as the local business community is concerned, these programs offer as much prestige and pull as a nationally ranked program.

Student clubs also play a big part in getting a job because they extend the recruiting efforts at many schools. They host a variety of events that allow you to meet leading business people, so that you can learn about their industries and their specific companies. Most important, these clubs are very effective at bringing in recruiters and other interested parties that do not recruit through traditional mainstream channels. For example, the high-tech, international, and entertainment student clubs provide career opportunities not available through the front door.

Your background and experiences also affect your success in securing a position. Important factors are academic specialization, academic standing, prior work experience, and intangibles such as your personal fit with the company. These days, what you did before b-school is particularly important; it helps establish credibility and gives you an edge in competing for a position in a specific field. For those using b-school to switch careers to a new industry, it's helpful if something on your resume ties your interest to the new profession. It's also smart to secure a summer job in the new area.

Finally, persistence and initiative are critical factors in the job search. Many fast tracks have been narrowed since the beginning of the decade. Increasingly, even at the best schools, finding a job requires off-campus recruiting efforts and ferreting out the hidden jobs.

A RETURN ON YOUR INVESTMENT

Not everyone measures their return on investment from business school with a dollar amount. (See the interview at the end of this chapter as one example.) We've heard many b-school grads explain that the fundamental skills, the network of people, and the proper environment in which to formulate their long-term career path were the most valuable things they wanted to get back from their MBA programs—in doing so, they considered the experience a success, regardless of their starting salary at graduation.

But for those who are anxious to start paying back those school loans, it's important to note that the industry in which you are hired can strongly affect your job prospects. Traditionally heavy hirers such as investment banking and consulting companies continue to lead the salary pack. Historically these sectors have offered the highest starting salaries and sign-on bonuses, with recruiters gravitating to the name-brand schools. At Chicago, Kole notes, "We saw tremendous activity in consulting, investment banking, investment management, and in leadership development programs. We are up in all of these areas, but most significantly in management consulting."

Also impacting your placement outlook is the geographic location of the school. Regional powerhouses such as Rutgers University in New Jersey may hold great sway at nearby, national employers such as Johnson & Johnson and Warner Lambert/Pfizer, providing graduates of those programs a unique competitive advantage. Although these companies reach out far and wide to recruit everywhere, a homegrown MBA may catch their attention and hold greater appeal.

As always, prioritize your criteria for school selection. Research who the top hirers are at any school you are considering. If you know what field you are interested in, look at how strong a particular business school's track record is in finding jobs for their graduates in that industry. To cement the relationships between school and recruiter, companies often foster a partnership with the school that includes sponsoring academic projects and internships, and hosting school club functions and informational cocktail hour events.

You may indeed be accepted at one of the nation's most prestigious schools, but if they lack real access to the type of industry you desire to work in, you are better off elsewhere.

FRIENDS WHO ARE GOING PLACES, ALUMNI WHO ARE ALREADY THERE

Most students say that the best part about b-school is meeting classmates with whom they share common goals and interests. Many students claim that the "single greatest resource is each other." Not surprisingly, with so many bright and ambitious people cocooned in one place, b-school can be the time of your life. It presents numerous professional and social opportunities. It can be where you find future customers, business partners, and mentors. It can also be where you establish lifelong friendships. After graduation, these classmates form an enduring network of contacts and professional resources.

Alumni are also an important part of the b-school experience. While professors teach business theory and practice, alumni provide insight into the real business world. When you're ready to interview, they can provide advice on how to get hired by the companies recruiting at your school. In some cases, they help you secure the interview and shepherd you through the hiring process.

B-schools love to boast about the influence of their alumni network. To be sure, some are very powerful, but this varies from institution to institution. At the very least, alumni will help you get your foot in the door. A resume sent to an alum at a given company, instead of to "Sir or Madam" in the personnel department, has a much better chance of being noticed and acted on.

After you graduate, the network continues to grow. Regional alumni clubs and alumni publications keep you plugged in to the network with class notes detailing who's doing what, where, and with whom.

Throughout your career, an active alumni relations department can give you continued support. Post-MBA executive education series, fund-raising events, and continued job placement efforts are all resources you can draw on for years to come.

In the interview below, you will see how a recent grad's professor is the source of the connections that will help this student him start his own business overseas.

STEPHEN HAZELTON, MIT SLOAN SCHOOL OF MANAGEMENT, CLASS OF 2005

Q: What made you decide to get the MBA and go to the MIT Sloan School of Business?

A: There are probably three different reasons why I went to school. First, there were skills I needed to learn. Examples of key courses I took include Entrepreneurial Finance, which will be very relevant for me in the coming months when I begin to negotiate with investors; Law for the Entrepreneur which was practical and relevant; Negotiations was another—whether it is for life in general or business—and Accounting—that's a very standard course, but it was an area in which I did not have much experience. So, the curriculum was a big draw for me.

The second draw was MIT Sloan's strong focus on entrepreneurship. If you look at the world of entrepreneurship on a map, the two hotspots are Silicon Valley and Route 128 (a highway in the Boston area where most start-ups and venture capital firms are located). I wanted to be in that community and understand and have access to it. Finally, I wanted to meet and learn from my classmates, given their diverse backgrounds.

Q: Now as you approach graduation, has the MBA performed for you in the way you thought it would?

A: I wanted to pursue entrepreneurship internationally. I have a background in Latin American markets, and for me the MBA has been highly relevant. The way I gauge that is how the MBA helped me with what I'm going to be doing after school, which is starting a business focused on financial services in Vietnam. A professor of mine went out of her way to put me in touch with a venture capitalist in Hanoi and things went on from there. This investor has a network in Vietnam and is going to support me both financially and otherwise; without this it would be a bit daunting to take a shot on my own.

Had I not gone to MIT Sloan and gotten to know this professor I'm not sure all this would have happened. So the MBA has been highly relevant because what I'm going to be doing is a direct result of my attending MIT Sloan.

Q: Specifically, how else did MIT Sloan provide you with real exposure and access?

A: Because of MIT's rich tradition in entrepreneurship, we get a lot of interest from that community. We have numerous opportunities to build business plans, receive feedback, pitch to investors, and learn from successful entrepreneurs that come to campus. It's a really special environment.

Another unique way is the popular course, Global Entrepreneurship Lab. Students in the course spend the month of January working with a start-up in emerging markets around the world. Companies host students and provide a view into how entrepreneurship is done in, for instance, Brazil or China.

Q: What were you doing before business school?

A: I was working for a nonprofit called Endeavor. Its mission is to promote entrepreneurship in emerging markets. They're in Africa and South America. My focus was on South America; I lived in Chile for a while and helped restart the local office there.

Q: Does it matter where you go to school?

A: In my case it definitely did.

Q: What advice would you give to today's applicant?

A: Make sure you understand why you want to go business school and what you want to get out of it. I would advise someone attending a program to use that two-year window to assess what they really are passionate about rather than pursue some of the fast-track careers by default.

Q: What do you mean by "fast-track career by default?"

A: Just because a company comes to campus to recruit doesn't mean it's necessarily right for you. I would consider those opportunities, but I think some people go into that track without considering other options. Consider other options based on your interests as well.

Q: If you had to do it all over again would you do anything differently?

A: I would apply to fewer schools. I applied to four. I would have applied to two b-schools because what I was looking for was at MIT Sloan and Stanford.

Q: How do you measure return on investment?

A: First off, I should say that I have a fellowship from Sloan that covers almost all of my tuition. I think that gives me a little bit of a different perspective. The flip side is I have the average debt that others do in my living expenses. So I invested a fair amount of my own money, although I will not have those huge tuition bills to pay off.

I think some people look at the MBA payoff based on what kind of job they will get that's well regarded or pays them better than what they were making before business school. I don't. I don't look at education as a financial thing. It's a lifelong thing. I feel very closely connected to MIT and will come back here for support for the rest of my career.

As for money, I will be making very little money starting my own business.

It's true, a business education costs a lot of money, but it should not be a financial decision.

I want to add that I'm an immigrant to this country. The MBA is a wonderful way for an immigrant to assimilate into the business world.

Q: How would you describe your experience with your peers at Sloan?

A: In going into any situation where there are relationships to be made, I'm a quality versus quantity type of person. So I've made some really great friends here—people I will keep in touch with for the rest of my life. It's what I expected and hoped for.

Chapter 3

Admissions

PREPARING TO BE A SUCCESSFUL APPLICANT

Get Good Grades

If you're still in school, concentrate on getting good grades. A high GPA says you've got not only brains but also discipline. It shows the Admissions Committee you have what you need to make it through the program. If you're applying directly from college or have limited job experience, your grades will matter even more. The Admissions Committee will have little else on which to evaluate you.

It's especially important that you do well in courses such as economics, statistics, and calculus. Success in these courses is more meaningful than success in classes like "Monday Night at the Movies" film appreciation. Of course, English is also important; b-schools want students who communicate well.

Strengthen Math Skills

Number-crunching is an inescapable part of b-school. If your work experience has failed to develop your quantitative skills, take an accounting or statistics course for credit at a local college or b-school. If you have a liberal arts background and did poorly in math, or got a low GMAT Math score, this is especially important. Getting a decent grade will go a long way toward convincing the Admissions Committee you can manage the quantitative challenges of the program.

Work for a Few Years—But Not Too Many

Business schools have traditionally favored applicants who have worked full-time for several years. There are three primary reasons for this:

1. With experience comes maturity.

2. You're more likely to know what you want out of the program.

3. Your experience enables you to bring real-work perspectives to the classroom. Because business school is designed for you to learn from your classmates, each student's contribution is important.

Until recently, b-schools preferred to admit only those students with two to five years of work experience. The rationale was that at two years you have worked enough to be able to make a solid contribution, while beyond four or five, you might be too advanced in your career to appreciate the program fully. However, as we noted earlier in this book, there is a new trend among top schools toward admitting "younger" applicants—that is, candidates with limited work experience as well as those straight from college.

Depending on the schools to which you're applying and the strength of your resume of accomplishments, you may not need full-time, professional work experience. Of course, there's a catch: The younger you are, the harder you'll have to work to supply supporting evidence for your case as a qualified applicant. Be prepared to convince Admissions Committees that you've already done some incredible things, especially if you're hailing straight from college.

If you've targeted top-flight schools like Wharton, Columbia, or Stanford, applying fresh out of college is still a long shot. While your chances of gaining admission with little work experience have improved, your best shot is still to err on the conservative side and get a year or two of some professional experience under your belt.

If you're not interested in the big league or you plan on attending a local program, the number of years you should work before applying may vary. Research the admissions requirements at your target school. There's no doubt the MBA will jumpstart your career and have long-lasting effects on your business (and perhaps personal) outlook. If you're not ready to face the real world after college, plenty of solid b-schools will welcome you to another two years of academia.

There is one caveat to this advice, however. If your grades are weak, consider working at least three years before applying. The more professional success you have, the greater the likelihood that Admissions Committees will overlook your GPA.

Let Your Job Work for You

Many companies encourage employees to go to b-school. Some of these companies have close ties to a favored b-school and produce well-qualified applicants. If their employees are going to the kinds of schools you want to get into, these may be smart places to work.

Other companies, such as investment banks, feature training programs, at the end of which trainees go to b-school or leave the company. These programs hire undergraduates right out of school. They're known for producing solid, highly skilled applicants. Moreover, they're full of well-connected alumni who may write influential letters of recommendation.

Happily, the opposite tactic—working in an industry that generates few applicants—can be equally effective. Admissions Officers look for students from underrepresented professions. Applicants from biotechnology, health care, not-for-profit, and even the Peace Corps are viewed favorably.

One way to set yourself apart is to have had two entirely different professional experiences before business school. For example, if you worked in finance, your next job might be in a different field, like marketing. Supplementing quantitative work with qualitative experiences demonstrates versatility.

Finally, what you do in your job is important. Seek out opportunities to distinguish yourself. Even if your responsibilities are limited, exceed the expectations of the position. B-schools are looking for leaders.

March from the Military

A surprising number of b-school students hail from the military (although the armed forces probably had commanders in mind, not CEOs, when they designed their regimen). Military officers know how to be managers because they've held command positions. And they know how to lead a team under the most difficult of circumstances.

Because most have traveled all over the world, they also know how to work with people from different cultures. As a result, they're ideally suited to learn alongside students with diverse backgrounds and perspectives. B-schools with a global focus are particularly attracted to such experience.

The decision to enlist in the military is a very personal one. However, if you've thought of joining those few good men and women, this may be as effective a means of preparing for b-school as more traditional avenues.

CHECK OUT THOSE ESSAY QUESTIONS NOW

You're worried you don't have interesting stories to tell. Or you just don't know what to write. What do you do?

Ideally, several months before your application is due, you should read the essay questions and begin to think about your answers. Could you describe an ethical dilemma at work? Are you involved in anything outside the office (or classroom)? If not, now is the time to do something about it. While this may seem contrived, it's preferable to sitting down to write the application and finding you have to scrape for or, even worse, manufacture situations.

Use the essay questions as a framework for your personal and professional activities. Look back over your business calendar, and see if you can find some meaty experiences for the essays in your work life. Keep your eyes open for a situation that involves questionable ethics. If all you do is work, work, work, get involved in activities that round out your background. In other words, get a life.

Get involved in community-based activities. Some possibilities are being a big brother/big sister, tutoring in a literacy program, or initiating a recycling project. Demonstrating a concern for others looks good to Admissions Committees, and hey, it's good for your soul, too.

It's also important to seek out leadership experiences. B-schools are looking for individuals who can manage groups. Volunteer to chair a professional committee or run for an office in a club. It's a wide-open world; you can pick from any number of activities. The bottom line is this: The extracurriculars you select can show that you are mature, multifaceted, and appealing.

We don't mean to sound cynical. Obviously, the best applications do nothing more than describe your true, heartfelt interests and show off your sparkling personality. We're not suggesting you try to guess which activity will win the hearts of admissions directors and then mold yourself accordingly. Instead, think of projects and activities you care about, that maybe you haven't gotten around to acting on, and act on them now!

PICK YOUR RECOMMENDERS CAREFULLY

By the time you apply to business school, you shouldn't have to scramble for recommendations. Like the material for your essays, sources for recommendations should be considered long before the application is due.

How do you get great recommendations? Obviously, good work is a prerequisite. Whom you ask is equally important. Bosses who know you well will recommend you on both a personal and professional level. They can provide specific examples of your accomplishments, skills, and character. Additionally, they can convey a high level of interest in your candidacy.

There's also the issue of trust. B-school recommendations are made in confidence; you probably won't see exactly what's been written about you. Choose someone you can trust to deliver the kind of recommendation that will push you over the top. A casual acquaintance may fail you by writing an adequate, yet mostly humdrum letter.

Cultivate relationships that yield glowing recommendations. Former and current professors, employers, clients, and managers are all good choices. An equally impressive recommendation can come from someone who has observed you in a worthwhile extracurricular activity.

We said before you won't see *exactly* what's being written about you, but that doesn't mean you should just hand a blank piece of paper to your recommender. Left to their own devices, recommenders may create a portrait that leaves out your best features. You need to prep them on what to write. Remind them of those projects or activities in which you achieved some success. You might also discuss the total picture of yourself that you are trying to create. The recommendation should reinforce what you're saying about yourself in your essays.

About "big shot" recommendations: Don't bother. Getting some professional athlete who's a friend of your parent's to write you a recommendation will do you no good if he or she doesn't know you very well. Don't try to fudge your application; let people who really know you and your work tell the honest, believable, and impressive truth.

Prepare for the Graduate Management Admission Test (GMAT)

Most b-schools require you to take the GMAT. The GMAT is now a three-and-a-half-hour computer adaptive test (CAT) with multiple-choice Math and Verbal sections as well as an essay section. It's the kind of test you hate to take and schools love to require.

Why is the GMAT required? B-schools believe it measures your verbal and quantitative skills and predicts success in the MBA program. Some think this is a bunch of hooey, but most schools weigh your GMAT scores heavily in the admissions decision. If nothing else, it gives the school a quantitative tool to use to compare you with other applicants.

The test begins with the Analytical Writing Assessment (AWA) containing two essays questions. In the past, all questions that have appeared on the official GMAT have been drawn from a list of about 150 topics that appear in *The Official Guide to the GMAT* (published by the Educational Testing Service). Review that list and you'll have a pretty good idea of what to expect from the AWA. You will have 30 minutes to write each essay. By the way, you will be required to type your essay at the computer. Depending on how rusty your typing skills are, you may want to consider a bit of practice.

Next comes the multiple-choice section which has two parts: a seventy-five-minute Math section and a seventy-five-minute Verbal section. The Math section includes problem-solving questions (e.g., "Train A leaves Baltimore at 6:32 A.M. . . .") and data-sufficiency questions. Data-sufficiency questions require you to determine whether you have been given enough information to solve a particular math problem. The good news about these types of questions is that you don't actually have to solve the problem; the bad news is that these questions can be very tricky. The Verbal section tests reading skills (reading comprehension), grammar (sentence correction), and logic (critical reasoning).

For those unfamiliar with CAT exams, here's a brief overview of how they work: On multiple-choice sections, the computer starts by asking a question of medium difficulty. If you answer it correctly, the computer asks you a question that is slightly more difficult than the previous question. If you answer incorrectly, the computer asks a slightly easier question next. The test continues this way until you have answered enough questions that it can make an accurate (or so they say) assessment of your performance and assign you a score.

Most people feel they have no control over the GMAT. They dread it as the potential bomb in their application. Relax; you have more control than you think. You can take a test-preparation course to review the Math and Verbal material, learn test-taking strategies, and build your confidence. Test-prep courses can be highly effective. The Princeton Review offers what we think is the best GMAT course available. Even better, it offers two options for online preparation in addition to the traditional classroom course and one-on-one tutoring. Another option is to take a look at our book *Cracking the GMAT CAT*, which reviews all the subjects and covers all the tips you would learn in one of our courses.

How many times should you take the GMAT? More than once if you didn't ace it on the first try. But watch out: Multiple scores that fall in the same range make you look unprepared. Don't take the test more than once if you don't expect a decent increase, and don't even think of taking it the first time without serious preparation. Limiting your GMAT attempts to two is best. Three tries are okay if there were unusual circumstances. If you take it more than three times, the Admissions committee will think you have an unhealthy obsession. A final note: If you submit more than one score, most schools will take the highest.

If you don't have math courses on your college transcript or numbers-oriented work experience, it's especially important to get a solid score on the quantitative section. There's a lot of math between you and the MBA.

HOW THE ADMISSIONS CRITERIA ARE WEIGHTED

Although admissions requirements vary among business schools, most rely on the following criteria: GMAT score, college GPA, work experience, your essays, letters of recommendation (academic and/or professional), an interview with an admissions representative, and your extracurriculars. The first four are generally the most heavily weighted. The more competitive the school, the less room there is for weakness in any area. Any component out of sync, such as a weak GMAT score, is potentially harmful.

Happily, the admissions process at business school is one where great emphasis is placed on getting to know you as a person. The essay component is the element that allows the schools to do just that. Your essays can refute weaknesses, fill in gaps, and in general, charmingly persuade an admissions board you've got the right stuff. They are the single most important criteria in business school admissions.

But as we've just said, they're not the only criteria. All pieces of your application must come together to form a cohesive whole. It is the *entire application* that determines whether you win admission.

ANTICIPATE AND COORDINATE

The application process is very time-consuming, so anticipating what you need to accomplish within the admissions time frame is critical. To make the best use of our advice, you should first contact each of the programs on your personal list of schools. Their standards and criteria for admission may vary, and you'll need to follow their specific guidelines. Please note that the less competitive a school is, the more easily you may be able to breeze through (or completely omit) the rigorous requirements we identify as crucial in the application process for the top programs.

In addition, business school applicants are often overwhelmed by how much they have to do to complete not only one, but several applications. Proper management of the process is essential, since there are so many factors to coordinate in each application.

You'll have to prep for the GMAT, then actually take the test, round up some writers for your recommendations, follow up with those chosen to write recommendations, make sure the recommendations are mailed in on time, have your college transcript sent, and finally, write the essays. Of course, some schools require an interview as well. What makes all of this particularly challenging is that many applicants have to do all of this while balancing the demands of a full-time job.

We know that it takes a supreme force of will to complete even one application. As grad school applications go, a top business school's is pretty daunting. So if you don't stay focused on the details and deadlines, you may drop the ball.

There are many common and incredibly embarrassing mistakes you can avoid with prudent early planning. These include allowing your recommenders to miss the deadline, submitting an application full of typos and grammatical errors, sending one school an essay intended for another, or forgetting to change the school name when using the same essay for several applications. Applicants who wind up cramming for the GMAT or squeezing their essay writing into several all-nighters end up seriously shortchanging themselves.

APPLY EARLY

The best advice is to plan early and apply early. The former diminishes the likelihood of an accidental omission or a missed deadline. The latter increases your chances of acceptance.

The filing period ranges anywhere from six to eight months. The earlier you apply, the better your chances. There are a number of reasons for this:

First, there's plenty of space available early on. As the application deadline nears, spaces fill up. The majority of applicants don't apply until the later months because of procrastination or unavoidable delays. As the deadline draws close, the greatest number of applicants compete for the fewest number of spaces.

Second, in the beginning, Admissions Officers have little clue about how selective they can be. They haven't reviewed enough applications to determine the competitiveness of the pool. An early application may be judged more on its own merit than on how it stacks up against others. This is in your favor if the pool turns out to be unusually competitive. Above all, Admissions Officers like to lock their classes in early; they can't be certain they'll get their normal supply of applicants. Admissions decisions may be more generous at this time.

Third, by getting your application in early you're showing a strong interest. The Admissions Committee is likely to view you as someone keen on going to their school.

To be sure, some Admissions Officers report that the first batch of applications tend to be from candidates with strong qualifications, confident of acceptance. In this case, you might not be the very first one on line; but being closer to the front is still better than getting lost in the heap of last-minute hopefuls.

Of course, if applications are down that year at all b-schools or—thanks to a drop in its ranking—at the one to which you are applying, then filing later means you can benefit from admissions officers' desperate scramble to fill spaces. But this is risky business, especially since the rankings don't come out until the spring.

Conversely, if the school to which you are applying was recently ranked number one or two, applying early may make only a marginal difference. Swings in the rankings from year to year send school applications soaring and sagging. A newly crowned number-one or two school will be flooded with applications of a potential edge to be gained by filing earlier or later. Regardless from the beginning to the end of its filing period, do not put in your application until you are satisfied that it is the best you can make it. Once a school has passed on your application, it will not reconsider you until the following year.

ROUNDS VS. ROLLING ADMISSIONS

Applications are processed in one of two ways: rounds or rolling admissions. Schools that use rounds divide the filing period into three or so timed cycles. Applications are batched into the round in which they are received and reviewed in competition with others in that round. A list of a b-school's round dates can be obtained by contacting its Admissions Office if it employs this method. Applications to schools with rolling admissions are reviewed on an ongoing basis as they are received.

GMAT AND GPA

The GMAT and GPA are used in two ways. First, they're "success indicators" for the academic work you'll have to slog through if admitted—will you have the brainpower to succeed in the program? Second, they're used as benchmarks to compare each applicant to other applicants within the pool. At the more selective schools, you'll need a higher score and average to stay in the game.

Pearson VUE and the American College Testing Program (ACT) administer the GMAT. You'll need to register to take the exam by registering online at www.mba.com. Many applicants take the exam more than once to improve their scores. Test preparation is also an option for boosting your numbers—visit PrincetonReview.com for more information about The Princeton Review's GMAT courses.

Your college transcript is a major factor in the strength of your candidacy. Some schools focus more closely on the junior- and senior-year grades than the overall GPA, and most consider the reputation of your college and the difficulty of your course selections. A transcript loaded with offerings like "Environmental Appreciation" and "The Child in You" won't be valued as highly as one packed with calculus and history classes.

The Essays

Admissions committees consider the essays the clincher, the swing vote on the admit/deny issue. Essays offer the most substantive information about who you really are. The GMAT and GPA reveal little about you, only that you won't crash and burn. Your work history provides a record of performance and justifies your stated desire to study business. But the essays tie all the pieces of the application together and create a summary of your experiences, skills, background, and beliefs.

The essays do more than give answers to questions. They create thumbnail psychological profiles. Depending on how you answer a question or what you present, you reveal yourself in any number of ways—creative, witty, open-minded, articulate, mature, to name a few. On the other hand, your essay can also reveal a negative side, such as arrogance, sloppiness, or an inability to think and write clearly.

CHECK IT OUT: Most top schools require multiple essays, and our popular book *Business School Essays that Made a Difference* lets you know how to ace them all. Including sample essays from successful applicants with comments from admissions officers on what worked and what didn't, *Business School Essays that Made a Difference* lets you know how to write the essays that will get you admitted. Pick it up at princetonreview.com/bookstore.

Letters of Recommendation

Letters of recommendation function as a reality check. Admissions committees expect them to support and reinforce what they're seeing in the rest of your application. When the information doesn't match up with the picture you've painted, it makes you look bad. Because you won't see the recommendation (it's sent in "blind"), you won't even know there's a problem. This can mean the end of your candidacy.

That's why you need to take extreme care in selecting your references.

Scan each application for guidelines on choosing your references—business schools typically request an academic and a professional reference. The academic reference should be someone who can evaluate your performance in an academic environment. It's better to ask an instructor, teacher's aide, or mentor who knew you well than a famous professor who barely knew your name.

The same holds true for your professional reference. Seek out individuals who can evaluate your performance on many levels. The reference will be far more credible. Finding the right person to write your professional reference, however, can be trickier. You may not wish to reveal to your boss early on that you plan on leaving, and if the dynamics of your relationship are not ideal (hey, it happens once in a while), he or she might not make an appropriate reference. If this is the case, seek out a boss at a former job or someone who was your supervisor at your current job but has since moved to another organization. Avoid friends, colleagues, and clients as references unless the school explicitly says it's okay.

Advise your writers on themes and qualities you highlighted in your application. Suggest that they include real-life examples of your performance to illustrate their points. In other words, script the recommendation as best you can. Your boss, even if he or she is your biggest fan, may not know what your recommendation should include.

A great recommendation is rarely enough to save a weak application from doom. But it might push a borderline case over to the "admit" pile. Mediocre recommendations can be damaging; an application that is strong in all other areas now has a weakness, an inconsistency.

A final warning on this topic: Procrastination is common here. Micromanage your references so that each recommendation arrives on time! If need be, provide packaging for an overnight letter, have your reference seal it up, and then ship it out yourself.

THE INTERVIEW

Not all business schools attach equal value to the interview. For some, it's an essential screening tool. For others, it's used to make a final decision on those caught somewhere between "admit" and "reject." Some schools may encourage, but not require, the interview. Others make it informative, with little connection to the admissions decision.

Like the letters of recommendation, an interview may serve as a reality check to reinforce the total picture. It may also be used to fill in the blanks, particularly in borderline cases.

If an interview is offered, take it. In person, you may be a more compelling candidate. You can use the interview to further address weaknesses or bring dull essays to life. Most importantly, you can display the kinds of qualities—enthusiasm, sense of humor, maturity—that can positively sway an admissions decision.

Act quickly to schedule your interview. Admissions Departments often lack the time and staff to interview every candidate who walks through their doors. You don't want your application decision delayed by several months (and placed in a more competitive round or pool) because your interview was scheduled late in the filing period.

A great interview can tip the scale in the "admit" direction. How do you know if it was great? You were calm and focused. You expressed yourself and your ideas clearly. Your interviewer invited you to go rock climbing with him or her the following weekend. (Okay, let's just say you developed a solid personal rapport with the interviewer.)

A mediocre interview may not have much impact, unless your application is hanging on by a thread. In such a case, the person you're talking to (harsh as it may seem) is probably looking for a reason not to admit you, rather than a reason to let you in. If you feel your application may be in that hazy, marginal area, try to be extra-inspired in your interview.

Approach this meeting as you would a job interview. Remember, you're being sized up as a person in all of your dimensions. Here are a few tips to use during the interview.

- Dress and act the part of a professional but avoid being stiff or acting like a stuffed shirt.

- Limit your use of business jargon. Interviewers often hear a lot of the same generic answers. They are more interested in you being your witty, charming, natural self.

- Be personable and talk about your passions, such as hobbies or a recent trip you've taken. The idea is to get the interviewer thinking of you as someone who will contribute greatly to the quality of campus life.

Highlight your achievements and excellence, even in something like gourmet cooking, but avoid stunts, such as pulling out a platter of peppercorn pate sautéed in anchovy sauce.

Chapter 4

Quotas, Recruitment, and Diversity

B-schools don't have to operate under quotas—governmental or otherwise. However, they probably try harder than most corporations to recruit diverse groups of people. Just as the modern business world has become global and multicultural, so too have b-schools. They must not only teach diversity in the classroom but also make it a reality in their campus population and, if possible, faculty.

Schools that have a diverse student body tend to be proud of it. They tout their success in profiles that demographically slice and dice the previous year's class by gender, race, and geographic and international residency. Prospective students can review this data and compare the diversity of the schools they've applied to.

However, such diversity doesn't come naturally from the demographics of the applicant pool. Admissions Committees have to work hard at it. In some cases, enrollment is encouraged with generous financial aid packages and scholarships.

While they don't have quotas per se, they do target groups for admission, seeking a demographic balance in many areas. Have they admitted enough women, minorities, foreign students, marketing strategists, and liberal arts majors? Are different parts of the country represented?

As we've said before, the best b-schools tend to attract top talent, students, and recruiters to their campus. Women and minorities are the most sought-after groups targeted for admission. So it's no surprise that programs that report higher-than-average female and minority enrollments tend to be among the very best.

AN INITIATIVE FOR MINORITIES

Some schools report higher minority enrollments than others, so our advice is consistent: You need to thoroughly research the program you've set your sights on. Consider your goals. Do you simply want to attend the most prestigious program? How will social factors impact your goals and experiences on campus?

Most business schools aspire to diversify their programs. It's the number of minorities applying to business school that has remained consistently low. An initiative of the Graduate Management Admissions Council called The Diversity Pipeline Alliance (DiversityPipeline.org) was formed to reverse this trend and increase the number of underrepresented minorities pursuing a business career. Much like the initiative for women, this organization plans a powerful marketing campaign with a pro-business career message for minority students from middle school to graduate school. It offers information on current opportunities for mentorships, internships, and financial assistance and provides an impressive roster of member organizations, services, and educational opportunities.

Minority enrollment at business schools is still quite low, so in all likelihood, you will not experience the dramatic upward shift in b-school demographics in the near future that initiatives like the Diversity Pipeline Alliance hope to influence. However, by recognizing the disparity between the minority presence in the U.S. and minority involvement in business education and practice, we are working toward a solution.

As you make up your mind about where you want to go for b-school, know that the scenario is positive and that new infrastructures exist to support your business career.

FEMALE APPEAL: BUSINESS SCHOOLS GET UP TO SPEED

If you've toured the campus and classrooms of a business school, you may have noticed something: On average, roughly 70 percent of any given MBA program's students are male. While this may make a nice pool of dating prospects for the women who are enrolled, it's not something business schools are happy with—far from it! In fact, it's something they are working to change as quickly as they can.

Beyond showing significantly higher application volume, MBA programs of all types are seeing female applications increase. About 64 percent of full-time MBA programs saw applications from women rise in 2006; the figure is 47 percent for part-time-programs and 50 percent for executive programs. While these numbers may not match the 50 percent male-to-female ratio of other graduate programs, closing the MBA gap is only a matter of time.

SCHOOL INITIATIVES

How can we be sure that female enrollment will continue to increase? One reason is that getting women enthused about a career in business is a sky-high priority at business schools across the country these days. To wit, many business schools have launched their own women-only outreach and recruiting events. Columbia University hosts an annual "Women in Business" conference that brings together more than 700 alumnae, business leaders, students and prospective students to network and share ideas on achieving success in the marketplace. Linda Meehan, Assistant Dean for Admissions at Columbia Business School, knows that this outreach is working because "applicants walk away wowed by the extraordinary experience of being surrounded by so many intelligent, passionate and successful women." Events like these aim to dispel myths, discuss the perceived lack of role models, and help women make informed decisions.

Stanford's events, says Wendy Hansen, Associate Director of Admissions at the Stanford Business School, "focus on the educational experience, but also on the unique types of issues women have, such as: how does getting the MBA fit in with having a family or having a spouse? How do I make this experience fit in with my life?" Julia Min, Executive Director of Admissions at UC Berkeley's Haas School of Business, says attendees often find comfort in numbers. "Seeing such a large presence of women is empowering. They realize they're not in this alone, that there are other women around like them."

If all this sounds like good public relations, it is. Schools want to get the word out: MBAs offer women viable opportunities. But if the business schools are talking the talk, they're also walking the walk. There's nothing superficial about this campaign. Bit by bit, the MBA landscape for women is changing.

Opportunities begin even before the first day of class. At Stanford, admitted women are treated to one-on-one admit-lunches with female alumni. Once an admit gets to campus, they find MBA life is chock-full of student-run women and management programs, support groups, retreats, executive conferences, mentoring programs, and other dedicated resources for women only.

For many years now, most business programs have had an on-campus Partners Club for spouses and significant others—a benefit to both female and male students. Newcomers to the business-school scene include groups like The Parents Club and Biz Kids where students can find family-oriented classmates and activities. Columbia University's Mother's Network is an initiative that provides a formal support network for new, current and future b-school moms. Perhaps the most symbolic gesture of the increasing influence of women in business school is Stanford's provision of a private nursing room for MBA moms and their babies in its main classroom facility.

More Flexibility and Making it Work

Of course, there's still room for improvement. A continuing problem at business schools is a lack of course work and case study material featuring women leaders. Likewise, there is an absence of female professors on the academic front.

Apart from these lingering issues, business schools continue to tackle the particular challenges female students face. For many women, the late starting age can be a turn-off. But even here, there are new options and opportunities to consider.

If you are stressed out from trying to have it all and have written off getting an MBA, new early-initiative programs might make you pause and reconsider your decision. Harvard and Stanford have developed an early career track that aims to minimize the impact of the biological clock on a prospective applicant's decision to pursue an MBA. Other schools are likely to follow suit.

The early career track offers a solution that is as simple as it is practical: Admit women (and men) to the MBA program either straight out of college or with just a few years of work experience. Business schools hope that the option to attain their MBA early on in their careers will prompt more women to apply to their programs. With a bigger window to accomplish their professional goals, more women will turn to the MBA as a viable option that won't require them to sacrifice their personal lives.

Beginning a business career earlier eliminates the immediate problem of timing. But what happens down the road? While it helps to remove one timing issue, it can't indefinitely postpone the balancing act that shadows many women's careers. It's hard to rationalize the opportunity costs of the MBA knowing that the investment might be forsaken when tough choices have to be made.

Business schools blame misconceptions about the utility of the MBA for women's reticence on this front. They feel that many women underestimate the broad reach of the degree. The MBA is not just for hard-core careers like banking and finance, but is also useful in not-for-profit work, less high-stress industries such as consumer goods, and leadership positions in a wide range of fields.

Further, says Hansen, "There is a tremendous amount of flexibility in a general management degree. The MBA positions you much more effectively to make an impact wherever you fall at different points in your life. It gives you the tools and framework to apply those skills at different levels and in different intensities. For example, women can rise to a partner level or a senior leadership position and then scale back to a different role within the organization. They can also scale back to part-time work." In other words, the investment doesn't have to be forsaken; it might instead be redirected.

There's no doubt the return on investment (that's ROI in business speak) for the MBA is high. Six-figure salaries and sign-on bonuses that pay you back for the cost of your MBA tuition are hard to beat (and unlike medical, veterinary, and law school grads, you won't have malpractice premiums eating into your take-home pay). If you've thought business school might be right for you, keep investigating—you might be right.

WHERE ARE THE WOMEN IN MBA PROGRAMS?

Are you a professional woman in her mid-to-late twenties? Do you see graduate school in your future? During these tough times, you might envision yourself back on campus sooner rather than later. Downturns do tend to fuel grad school applications. After all, what better place to wait out the economy and avoid the gaping pit of joblessness?

Grad school can be a cure-all for many ills: It can jump-start or redirect a stubbornly off-track career; it can give you a place to hang out while you figure out what you want to be when you grow up (law school, a three-year degree, offers an even longer alternative); and it can transform your personal life as you vault into a new career. Even in uncertain times there is certainty in knowing that after two years in school you can emerge reborn as a professional with a spanking new identity, prescribed career track, and a solid alumni network.

Despite the huge appeal of graduate school, be it as an escape from bad times or as your true, chosen path, MBA programs have remained a problematic choice for many women. Female enrollment at law, medical, and veterinary schools now hovers at, or near, the 50 percent mark. So what's up with business schools? Why has female enrollment at business schools stagnated at about 30 percent?

Even during the best of times, business schools have struggled to attract women. Is this due to the unique challenges women face in building and sustaining their careers over a lifetime of choices, both professional and personal, or is there another reason? Clearly an MBA presents many opportunities, but, for women, will these opportunities upset their already delicate balancing acts?

THINKING OF FAMILY

Let's start with biology—as in biological clocks. Since a prerequisite for admission to many business programs is prior work experience, first-year business school students are typically a bit older than their law or med school counterparts. In fact, the average age for entering full-time MBA students is 28. This means that by the time graduation rolls around, MBA students are heading into their thirties—a prime time for marriage and children. For some women, that timing couldn't be worse.

Newly minted MBAs in their early thirties are just starting to reap the rewards of their business school investments by scoring brand new, mid to senior level jobs. With these jobs come ever-greater demands and time pressures. But, for many, the pressure to have a personal life is just as great. Those kinds of competing priorities are the very headaches women hope to avoid. Making matters worse, MBA jobs at the senior level can vault women into a culture that may still be dominated by old-school thinking (translation: men) and a culture that may be less tolerant of efforts to balance work commitments with family.

These dilemmas begin long before business school graduation. Again, because MBA students tend to be older, many women have to factor a partner or child into their graduate school decision, especially if it involves relinquishing a paycheck and/or relocation. Many of these women encounter a potential double standard: Husbands and boyfriends, especially those with careers, are often less willing to relocate on their female partner's behalf than vice versa.

NO URGENT MATTER

Another reason business school enrollment for women may be low is that an MBA is not a barrier to entry nor is it a requirement for success in business. In addition, it isn't a rite of passage in many fields that appeal to high numbers of women: marketing, publishing, fashion, and teaching. By contrast, notes Eileen Chang, former Associate Director of Admissions at the Harvard Business School, "If your objective is to be a lawyer or doctor, you simply can't practice without the requisite degree. Business school is fundamentally different because the career path is one where the MBA can put you on any number of tracks—be it banking, accounting, or management—but doesn't require a credential." Between the lack of a required degree for entering business and the late starting age to enter a program, some women perceive a high opportunity cost for the MBA.

FEAR OF MATH?

Why more women aren't pursuing an MBA is a question that business schools have been asking themselves for years. Some hard answers came in the form of a recent study by the University of Michigan's Business School Center for the Education of Women and the Catalyst Foundation. The following issues were identified as key deterrents to business school for women: the MBA is still seen as a male domain; there is a lack of support from employers; a lack of career opportunity and flexibility; a lack of access to powerful business networks and role models; and a perception that b-school is overloaded with math.

According to many schools, math fears are just that—fears. Harvard's Chang observes, "Maybe historically, math was considered a hurdle. But we see so many women who have strong skills coming from fields that are quantitative, such as banking and engineering, that I think the math fears are almost a myth. But this is a myth we want to work against. We want applicants to know they can handle the math."

Julia Min, Executive Director of Admissions at UC Berkeley's Haas School of Business, concurs, "The math phobia may be unfounded to a certain degree, and still it's a perception that has been long-lasting. Women [enter business school] and perform extremely well."

If you're frightened by math, you need to know that a business school education does require a basic command of the subject. "You do need to be comfortable with numbers," advises Wendy Hansen, Associate Director of Admissions at the Stanford Business School. "The strongest MBA programs are going to be rigorous in math. Knowing how to influence and lead an organization requires understanding the language of business, which includes accounting and finance."

Still, prospective MBAs with a math phobia need not panic; most programs will work with students who lack the necessary math background. "At Stanford, we have a pre-term program of courses before classes begin to get students up to speed," says Hansen, "We also encourage people to take quantitative courses before they come to our school to develop their skills."

If your math fears are not so easily assuaged, concerns about a persistent Old Boys Network might be. As Hansen notes, "Women may say, I don't see the masses of female role models doing what I want to do. That is going to change slowly. But it is going to change. We have to reach a point where those in school reach a place where they are out in the world having an impact."

OUR ADVICE

Look at the number of female MBA students attending your targeted school and evaluate whether you would feel comfortable there. Research the number and range of student organizations for women and speak with female MBAs about school life.

WHERE ARE THEY NOW?

It takes a monumental leap of faith to go to business school—to take two years out of your professional life, go to zero income, and drop $60,000 or more on tuition. By contrast, making the decision to go to medical or law school is more straightforward. Of the three so-called primary professions—business, medicine, and law—business is the only one you can pursue without a degree. In fact, you can become highly successful (and may already be) without an MBA. So how do you decide if going to business school is the best option for you?

Perhaps the best way to assess the value of the MBA is to talk to the people who have already gone through the program and can reflect on the experience and the credential. Over the next several pages, you'll find a series of interviews with women who have graduated with an MBA. Their graduation dates range from 1992 to 2004, but their common thread lies in how valuable each of them found their advanced degree to be. Each of the women came from different backgrounds, went to different schools, were hoping for different things from their b-school experiences, and took different approaches to their career paths. Here, they share their choices, advice, and what they might change if they were to do it all again.

We begin with Cathy Crane-Moley, an outstanding MBA with the talent, passion, and drive that have made her one of America's most successful businesswomen. In fact, Entelos, Inc., which Cathy co-founded in 1996, was named one of the 13 coolest companies in the nation by *Fortune* magazine.

Ten years out, Crane-Moley is the co-founder and senior vice-president of strategy for Entelos, Inc., and former chief financial officer and head of corporate development.

CATHY CRANE-MOLEY, STANFORD GRADUATE SCHOOL OF BUSINESS, CLASS OF '92

Q: Cathy, as a newly minted MBA, what were your thoughts on what the degree could do for you?

A: At that point in time, I didn't have a 10-plus-year horizon in my view. My thoughts were more about the immediate future of my career. I was a molecular biology major as an undergrad. I had worked in sales and in the field and had a big passion for health care. So that's really why I went to get an MBA, to follow through on my passion and vision for a business career in the health care sector.

Q: How did you target Stanford as the school that would deliver on that vision?

A: That's an interesting question. I lived in Virginia at the time and I did a lot of research on schools. I had a number of goals, some of which changed once I got to business school, but one of the goals was to go to a top school—which Stanford is. And I was really interested in somehow combining international business and entrepreneurship, so another goal was to find an environment that would support my exposure to that. So I applied to Stanford and Harvard and Wharton and all the types of schools that would have recruiters coming on campus from an international background. I chose Stanford as the best environment for my combined vision.

Q: What was it about Stanford that fit with your career aspirations in particular?

A: What I really wanted from the MBA was to have the credibility to go build a company in health care. I had an expectation that business school would help me be a better businessperson in science. My goal was to be able to tie together the business and science and pursue a business career in biotechnology health care.

When I went to Stanford I was pretty nervous because all these investment bankers and consultants were using intimidating terms like "run the numbers." When I got to business school I learned that it just meant 2 + 2. So for me it was really about learning a whole new language. Every domain has its own jargon and half the battle is learning the language. Business isn't rocket science. It has some very pragmatic, practical, and even intuitive components to it. So putting a language to it was a critical step for me.

Q: Did you use Stanford's formal on-campus recruiting to get your first job or did you have to do a one-of-a-kind type of job search?

A: I did a little bit of both. The [formalized] on-campus recruiting I did was more for the sake of exposure. Mostly, I created my own job search, which touches on the MBA and [the] important[ance] [of] the school's networks. The Stanford community was pivotal to my getting the job. There is no question that if I hadn't come out of Stanford, I would not have had the job I had.

Q: Why?

A: A couple of things. Right out of school, I became an entrepreneur-in-residence at the Mayfield Fund, a venture firm on Sand Hill Road [one of the most nationally prominent addresses for ventures funding]. The combination of my background and MBA was a big plus, but mostly getting my foot in the door was the result of befriending a wonderful woman who was from Stanford's Class of '87. She became a really strong mentor and made endless introductions in the venture community for me. She is now a dear friend of mine and was instrumental in my soul-searching.

Until 1995, when we merged with a public company. Then I started my current company with my four co-founders in 1996, which is also in the biotechnology sector.

Q: It sounds as though the Stanford networks were invaluable to this first experience out. What about this next stage?

A: Absolutely invaluable. Not just because of the connections—that's one component—but in your own brainstorming about what you want to be in your life.

At business school, you are surrounded by people who have done everything. There were people in my environment who had been entrepreneurs, venture capitalists, investment bankers, and international marketers at pharmaceutical companies. There were incredibly helpful connected professors and alumni. It was all at your fingertips as you were solidifying your own vision.

Q: I'm guessing that you would advise students beginning their MBA studies to think hard about why they're there and to take advantage of all the opportunities?

A: Absolutely. What can happen is that it's easy to do it [pursue the opportunities], but it's also easy not to do it.

Stanford is a classic example. It's in such a beautiful location, and people want to experience California; you can easily be distracted. But this is two years when anyone will return your call. You have heads of state, heads of corporations visiting, people in the nonprofit area showing up. And all you have to do is get on your bike and ride over there.

The other thing is, there are people who have come from a particular background, like investment banking and consulting, who know they intend to return to those careers after business school. But even if that is your goal, you still should use the two years to check everything out. You should use the two years to get more exposure and think about [your] long-term [goals].

Q: It's clear the networking opportunities were critical to your future career developments, but how important would you say actual content learning at school was?

A: It actually was. But you'll see differences depending on people's backgrounds. For my husband, who was an undergrad at Wharton (I met him at Stanford), he could do corporate finance with his eyes closed. But for me, a molecular biology major as an undergrad, I had never taken business classes, so the academic training was critical. Take corporate finance, for example. I cannot imagine anyone being in the business world without formal corporate finance. Our strategy classes, entrepreneurial classes, small business classes were all great for me. Anything like cost accounting or some of the options theory, I could have done without. But the pragmatic fundamentals gave me the tools to build two businesses from nothing.

Q: How was being a woman at Stanford?

A: It was wonderful. The quality of people, male and female, was superb. I believe we have a ratio of 33 percent female. We had strong women and we did great. I never noticed any sort of difference in abilities based on gender.

Q: **Was the business school environment intimidating?**

A: I didn't think so. I felt very inspired by the people around me.

Q: **What advice do you have for someone thinking about going to business school now?**

A: I think it comes back to the theme we've already touched on: make the most of the community that you can, way over and above what the classes offer. Business school is a very unique opportunity—live it while you are there.

CHIARA PERRY, HARVARD BUSINESS SCHOOL, CLASS OF '92
SENIOR PRICING ANALYST, A DIVISION OF UNITED TECHNOLOGIES

Q: **In 1992 the nation was in a recession. Jobs, even for Harvard b-school grads, were scarce. What was your mindset coming out of the program?**

A: Well, I was fortunate in that I had a job in place before graduating. And I was thinking about the opportunities and challenges I'd face in that position. The company that made me the offer was part of United Technologies, and they had come on campus looking for MBAs. I was really happy to already have the offer by graduation so I didn't have to worry about looking for some great job over the summer.

It's true that in 1992 the economy wasn't in great shape, so many people were heading into graduation without an offer yet. I had a lot of things going on in my life at that time: I got married and moved a thousand miles away from the East Coast to the middle of the Midwest [Indiana].

In terms of my expectations about the degree, I think [I expected] that it [would] put me into an elevated position and salary compared to the people I would be working with at my new job.

Q: **Given your job offer, were you happy with what the MBA did for you?**

A: Oh, absolutely. The company was excited to have hired me, and I was excited to work for them. I still work for the same company in the same location.

Q: **To what do you attribute having stayed with the same company for so long?**

A: I think it's several things. It's a great place to work. They treat their employees really well. And I don't like to play the sexist card, but it's a wonderful company to work for if you're a woman. My husband and I also really love Bloomington, Indiana. We have two children, and this is a great place to raise a family. So it's been several factors, including having children come into the equation. I only work three days a week now, but I have a professional position.

Q: **Switching subjects, what kind of person is ideally suited for an MBA?**

A: I think the type of person that benefits from the MBA is someone who wants to learn a lot, but also realizes that this isn't rocket science. Yes, there are challenging courses, and I learned a tremendous amount when I was at school. But I thought it was hard because of the overwhelming amount of work, the perceived competitiveness within the class, at least the first year. It wasn't necessarily hard academically. There was only one class I felt a bit overwhelmed by. Mostly, I pretty much felt, "Oh, I can do this."

So, back to your question. Someone who can go into a business school program with the attitude that this is a good thing to have, that you're going to challenge yourself and expand your expertise is going to benefit the most. It's great if you can do it full-time because you can really devote yourself to the program and figure out what you want to do with your life.

Q: So how important is it to go to a really good school?

A: I think it is important because people look at the school you've gone to and are impressed with you. And I have to be honest, that will make you feel good. People will say, "Oh my gosh, you went to Harvard!" In a social setting, when people ask me where I went to school, I almost hesitate, because I know there will be this big reaction, especially out here in the Midwest. Not very many people out here went to Harvard.

Right out of business school, I felt, you know, if this job doesn't work, I can go almost anywhere I want with this degree. I know that sounds kind of arrogant but I knew that with my business experience before I went to Harvard, and now with my MBA, I could take a risk. I could come out to this small town in the Midwest and if I needed to, I could leave and be okay.

Even 10 years later, I think that's still true. A Harvard MBA certainly is helpful when you're trying to move to the next place or job. I don't think I can go anywhere I want now, because I've taken a little curve in my career track to be with my children. I've been working part-time for three years now, three days a week. But the MBA from Harvard is going to be very helpful if we decide to leave.

Q: Do you ever anticipate reentering the workforce as a full-time person or leaving your job? And if so, how do you think the opportunities will be enhanced with the MBA?

A: It's actually good you ask that question, because right now I'm grappling with that. Our factory is moving all of its manufacturing to Mexico. And so the question is, what will happen to the office staff? Will we go, have some role, or be laid off? That's an unanswered question right now.

Because we'd like to stay in the area, my husband and I have been thinking about different things I can do. So the MBA will be very beneficial as I face these issues.

Q: What else did you get out of the two years you were at school?

A: I met a lot of wonderfully diverse and interesting people. Many people were like Wall Street–Harvard–back to Wall Street, or consulting–Harvard–back to consulting. Or people were switching careers. There were people who had been in the Peace Corps, done public not-for-profit work, or come from the military. So from that perspective, it was just wonderful to meet all those incredible people.

And how many smart people can you put in a room? I mean students were just incredibly bright. It was impressive and added tremendously to the classes.

Q: As you have passed the 10-year mark, how do you feel about the value of your business school training?

A: I absolutely still utilize it. I still think back on cases and situations and examples that I use to resolve issues going on in work. For example, we are moving some aspect of the business to Mexico, and I can remember that I did a case on that. Plus, with this colleague of mine who is currently getting his MBA, we'll chat even more about some of those issues from class.

But looking back, I can still remember comments I made in class, and my teachers and the classes themselves. It was a very valuable, memorable time in my life. But it wasn't always pleasant . . . .

Q: **Why wasn't it pleasant?**

A: The first year class set-up and the overwhelming desire to make value-added comments was an immense amount of pressure on me. I mean, I'm probably obsessive, but I even think of comments now!

Q: **Someone reading this book might not understand what this comment thing is all about.**

A: Comments you made to contribute to classroom discussion which, depending on the class, counted toward your grade. Comments could almost define the class—coming up with comments to be brilliant or prove yourself to the others. I remember I was always second-guessing what I said in class. I could have said it better, or I could have said it a different way, that kind of thing.

Q: **Looking back, if you could do anything differently, what would it be?**

A: Well, probably I would do a little better at networking and then keeping in touch with section mates, because I may need to call them at some point. I think if you have those networks in place, it's not really calling to ask for a job, it's talking about your situation, and then those people know what's going on and may be able to let you know about an opportunity.

Having been at the same job for more than 10 years, and being out in the Midwest, I'm a little less connected to the pipeline of, "Hey, do you need someone like me at your company?" And that goes both ways. You know, time is a problem, and when kids come along, things change greatly. It's just hard to fit everything in.

Q: **Summing up, what advice do you have for someone reading this book?**

A: The MBA gives you an extra couple of years to go and figure out what you want to do. I liken it to what college does for you, but this is your second breath. And it's a very valuable one. I recommend you go full-time, so you can really focus.

PATRICIA MELNIKOFF, HARVARD BUSINESS SCHOOL, CLASS OF '92
VICE PRESIDENT, MARKETING AND BUSINESS DEVELOPMENT, ARIAT INTERNATIONAL, A MANUFACTURER OF EQUESTRIAN FOOTWEAR AND APPAREL

Q: **Patty, what kind of opportunities were you looking for post-MBA?**

A: I was looking for an opportunity with a consumer-oriented company that sold goods and services. I was seeking product management, marketing, or strategic planning opportunities.

I was interested in working for a large multinational company, so I interviewed with companies like Disney and Sara Lee Corporation.

Q: Did they come on campus?

A: Yes they did.

Q: So you relied heavily on on-campus recruiters?

A: Very heavily. My second year I attended quite a few corporate presentations from different sectors: technology, packaged goods, and so forth.

At that time, we had the opportunity to attend recruiting presentations and weekly Q&A sessions with well-known business leaders that are part of the second-year general management course. So by going to the more general presentations and learning about the companies or going to specific recruiting presentations, I actually came across quite a varied group of organizations.

Q: What was your summer position between your first and second year?

A: I participated in a fellowship in Eastern Europe. I worked with a group that was consulting with factories in Poland that were at risk of going out of business. It was 1991, so it was right after the fall of the communist system in Poland and there were a number of state-run factories and businesses that were in a state of collapse.

Q: How did you find your way to Poland?

A: I had worked previously with two of the founders of a consulting practice in Poland.

Q: You learned of this opportunity for a fellowship in Poland at Harvard? How did you unearth that?

A: Actually, it was a formalized program of doing nonprofit work. There were a number of HBS students who participated in the program.

I had to complete an application that explained the nature of the nonprofit work, and upon my return, I was required to write a summary report.

Q: Why did you seek out this particular opportunity in Europe for your summer job? A lot of MBAs expect that summer job to be the one that leads to a final job offer.

A: I'm always looking for interesting experiences in my life. I wanted to work overseas. I figured I probably wouldn't end up living my life in Eastern Europe, and so it was a unique opportunity at the time.

Q: How relevant were the things you learned at business school for your first job out?

A: I probably learned more basic analytical, communication, and process management skills from my experience at Bain & Co. My HBS education helped me to understand many of the big-picture issues facing the corporation.

Q: What did you learn at business school?

A: (Long pause) I can tell you more about how business school helps me today than how it helped me then. [Several people told me] that I would understand the true value of my MBA after 10 years. I would say that is mostly true.

In the short term, however, I did find that the finance courses I took helped me in my first job. I chose to take several finance courses at HBS because I wanted to develop a more in-depth understanding of that area. I did not plan on working in finance post-HBS, and I didn't think I would ever have another opportunity to learn about it.

Ten years out, it's all about the leadership and people issues. For example, my company was facing a potential product recall recently. I found myself drawing upon the case we studied on the Tylenol recall at J&J. I asked myself, what were the big-picture decisions they had to make? How fast? How serious? What is the potential damage? What is the action plan and how will we communicate it? Being able to draw from that exposure to a crisis management situation was very helpful. Over a decade ago, I sat in a classroom and discussed for 90 minutes how to approach a crisis. Somehow that exercise of analyzing and debating potential scenarios left an impression on me that helped me years later.

Q: **If there were anything you could go back and do differently at business school what would it be?**

A: I would take more of those organizational behavior classes that I laughed at.

Q: **Because?**

A: Oh you know, power, "group norms," and other people issues. None of those issues seemed that important to me at the time. I was still focused on mastering my knowledge in academic disciplines.

Q: **Did you all laugh at them?**

A: I don't think we valued those courses as much as other courses in the curriculum. But now I see the value, having managed so many people. In the second year, I might have taken more leadership courses and those organizational behavior courses.

Q: **Do you think it was more intimidating for you to go to business school as a woman?**

A: No. But I think I had to work harder in certain ways earlier on to establish myself as a credible voice in the class. Somehow I felt that if a woman was perceived to be too harsh or too focused, there was a natural tendency not to like her. And so I do think that women have to work harder at finding their place and fitting in.

Q: **Overall would you say business school is an intimidating place?**

A: No. I enjoyed it. I made great friends at HBS. I think the first week is terrifying for everyone, but overall, no.

Q: **What would you say to someone who said, should I get my MBA today?**

A: I think it depends on their circumstances. If they're very successful in business already and they are financially secure, I'm not sure business school is necessary. I meet incredible business people all the time who don't have MBAs.

But I think if you're younger in your career, or you're trying to make a career change, or you've found yourself limited, then I think it's a wonderful opportunity to go for two years and get the MBA.

Q: **Do you think you went at the right time for the right reasons?**

A: Absolutely. I was 25. It was perfect for a young woman with three years of business experience post-college, with my objectives, to go and get the MBA from the very best school I could.

CAROLINE GROSSMAN, UNIVERSITY OF CHICAGO GRADUATE SCHOOL OF BUSINESS, CLASS OF 2003
SENIOR ASSOCIATE BRAND MANAGER, KRAFT

Q: Did you have a specific career path in mind, or an industry you wanted to gain entry to in deciding to get your MBA?

A: My interests were fairly broad. I wanted to gain general management experience. So I was thinking about using the MBA to pursue either general management or consulting.

Q: What did you do before business school?

A: I worked as a teacher for three years, both abroad and in inner-city schools, and then worked in program management at an educational nonprofit. I had a liberal arts background.

Q: So this was a big career change for you. What made you decide to switch gears?

A: Although I liked the social service mission of the jobs I was doing, I wasn't fulfilled by the specific job functions in those positions. I wanted to go to business school to get to a place where I could be satisfied by and challenged by the actual work. When I thought about the kinds of work I liked most, I realized it was strategic thinking and project leadership. That pointed me toward business and the MBA.

Q: So, how did you wind up at Kraft?

A: I had an internship there in the summer between my first and second years. Now I'm working in a brand management position, and at Kraft, this offers me a perfect mix of marketing and general business management experiences. Brand Managers at Kraft have profit and loss responsibility in addition to setting the strategic vision for the business. Ultimately, they are responsible for achieving the business results on their brand. As my first job out of business school, it has very much met my needs.

Q: What was your sense of the value of the degree around graduation, and now, one and a half years later?

A: My MBA facilitated a major job transition. I had access to this specific opportunity through on-campus recruiting, and my course work and extracurricular activities helped prepare me to do the job. I feel very pleased to have landed where I have, and I certainly needed the MBA to get started in this direction. I felt pretty confident that coming out of Chicago I would have the tool kit I needed for the job I was going to be doing.

Q: In what ways is the MBA relevant and not relevant in today's world?

A: The MBA opens a lot of doors. It allows a candidate access to companies to which one otherwise might not have access. The MBA is a ticket to a conversation with those organizations. Mind you, the ticket is only to a conversation—the job you have to get yourself. There are some companies who simply won't look at someone who does not have the MBA; it's a prerequisite.

I have to add that most of one's career is built in the workplace, not in the classroom. But school sets you up for success. You're creating a foundation of knowledge, as well as the strategic frameworks that you'll need to process all of the learning once you're in the workplace. For a very short time after business school, perhaps you could perform in my kind of job without the MBA. But over time, for strategy, decision-making, and being able to truly lead, the MBA will be highly relevant.

Q: What advice would you give those considering leaving the workforce for an MBA?

A: Be ready to hit the ground running because the job search process begins day one. Do some thinking about what you want to do with your career before you get to campus so you can focus your career exploration at school once you arrive.

Q: How do you measure return on investment for the MBA?

A: I was looking to make a major career switch, so my reasons for going to business school were very straightforward. Because I came from the teaching field, and am now in a position at a leading consumer goods company, I would have to say I am completely satisfied with the return on my investment.

But I think this will vary depending on the type of job you left behind. It will also depend on where you land after the MBA and the extent to which that new position meets your goal. The more introspection you have about what you are looking for, the greater your return on investment.

I also measure ROI (return on investment) in terms of long- and short-term returns. At Chicago, I learned a lot of frameworks for making business decisions, which will help me in the long run. And in the short run, I acquired the skills and knowledge I needed to hit the ground running at work.

Q: How important is it where you go to school?

A: I think it's very important. You should ask yourself what it is that you want to get out of the experience and then consider what the school offers and if it's a good fit.

In my case, I wanted a lens for looking at business challenges and problems. Because I had a liberal arts background, I was looking for quantitative rigor to balance that out, and wanted to be sure that I'd be somewhere I could master business fundamentals. Chicago gave me that. The economics courses, in particular, really helped frame my thinking, and it was in the Marketing course that I learned the basis of what I do every day at work.

You might also consider the regional location of the schools you're looking at. In certain industries, such as consulting and investment banking, firms interview at many business schools, then place hires in different offices nationally. But other companies tend to recruit in the geographic region in which they are based.

Q: If you could go back in time, is there anything you would do differently with your time at Chicago?

A: I'm not one for regrets. I had a balanced experience at Chicago. I had a leadership position in a student organization, and was a member of a couple of others, which helped me. I built a strong network, which facilitated the career transition I was looking for. I learned a lot, and I had a good time. What more could I ask for?

I think the key to achieving this level of satisfaction with business school is picking your mandatories (for me, a career transition) and balance. There is so much to do that you can't do everything to the fullest, so you have to either focus or do a little of everything. The latter approach was a good fit for me.

Sara Weiss, MIT Sloan School of Management, Class of 2004

Q: What were your reasons for going to b-school?

A: I was looking for a career change. At the time, I wanted to become an energy trader. In fact, in my b-school essays I wrote about how I wanted to work for Enron. And then within three days of submitting my last application, Enron just imploded.

Q: Isn't that a little unusual, having a specific company to work for in mind?

A: Yes, it is. But Enron was unique in the role that they played in this field. That is why I had so specifically targeted the company. In the end, I wound up working in the financial market, which naturally is very different from the energy markets. But a lot of the attributes and experiences I was looking for in a job, I found in the financial markets.

Q: What were you doing before business school?

A: I was doing management consulting. I did process design and systems implementation for electric utilities. This is why I first got interested in energy-related fields.

Q: So how was the MBA going to advance your career? It sounds like you already had a strong career path and future.

A: I had a strong career path in consulting, but I didn't find myself fulfilled by that job. By the time I arrived at Sloan, I knew what I was looking for. It was something more dynamic and fast-paced. I wanted something where I had more control over my career path. I was looking for a job where I had immediately measurable results versus consulting, where you do these projects and you never really know if the project was successful until many years later.

It was really my Sloan classmates who helped me find my new focus. The community at Sloan is extremely supportive, and people are very willing to share their experiences and offer insight to each other. When I got to Sloan, I immediately knew that I had joined an incredible network. The students back each other up and help each other out. Without my peers, I would not have been able to find my focus so quickly or make such a successful transition.

Q: How did you feel about the value of the MBA as graduation approached?

A: I was able to look back and pinpoint several things I had gotten out of the MBA. First, I learned about finance, accounting, and other disciplines, which was the content I needed to start my new job. More importantly, I developed tremendously as a person. In a lot of ways, I became more level-headed in my decision-making, and I fine-tuned my skills as a professional. I think I just came out as a better package. I looked back right after I graduated and thought, "Wow, this is a huge transformation I've undergone in these two years."

But probably the most important thing I got out of business school is a network of incredible friends. I really got to know my classmates well, because we spent so much time together doing a wide range of activities inside and outside the classroom. My Sloan friends are closer to me than my college friends. Not only are they valued friends, but they are also people I will turn to for career support for the rest of my life.

Q: How, if at all, has your perception of the value of the degree changed?

A: I definitely feel the value. I absolutely use the finance content I learned directly in my job. Even the classes I thought were useless at the time, such as the organizational behavior classes, the touchy-feely classes, I have found those extraordinarily relevant.

Q: Why is that?

A: In my current job, I have many different layers of colleagues and clients. The dynamics of the teams I work with and am expected to perform with are complicated. So all of that stuff about how people interact with each other, require motivation, ownership, etc.—I'm using all of that.

Q: Does it matter where you get your MBA?

A: Yes, of course. But it matters more what you decide to get out of it. A program is only as good as what you decide to invest in it and in turn what you take away from it.

Q: Do you notice a difference among graduates of different programs?

A: Yes, in their soft skills. For example, anyone can learn textbook accounting. Just about every business program has accounting courses and most schools will require you to take at least one. But not every school has a community that is team-oriented or is involved in projects with the local business community. Not every school provides students with presentation experience. Students in programs that support class participation learn to express themselves eloquently on the fly.

Q: In what ways is the MBA relevant and not relevant in today's world?

A: I think that everything you learn in business school can also be learned in the real world. I don't think there is anything new. You just learn it faster, better, and have more fun doing it in a full-time MBA program. That makes it ultimately relevant and yet completely unnecessary. Nobody ever needs an MBA, but it's a huge leg up. The MBA gives you a much more focused and concentrated experience. The magic of it is in the environment and the people.

Q: How do you measure return on investment?

A: Personally, I actually don't measure my experience in terms of return on investment. I believe very strongly that education is worth its cost, as long as you give it your all, so you don't just spend all this money and cut class. Some people I know look at it differently. They measure the opportunity cost in dollars and ensure for themselves that they will make back those dollars. I think those people are missing a big piece of what is most important about business school. The real value isn't measurable.

Q: What advice would you give to today's applicants?

A: Try to do as much thinking as you can (even if it's in abstract terms), before you do your applications. Think about what is important to you, what you're looking for, what's missing from your life today, and who you want to be in the future. You don't need to know specifically what your next steps are. But the more focused you are, the more you are prepared to take advantage of what business school has to offer.

Q: If you had to do b-school all over again, what would you do differently?

A: I would study less. I would stress less. I would join more extracurricular clubs unrelated to my chosen career path. I would definitely throw that cocktail party on my roof deck in Beacon Hill, something that I never got around to doing. And I would take a class at Harvard's Kennedy School. There. That's my list.

Chapter 5

Money Matters

HOW MUCH WILL IT COST?

The Truth

To say that business school is an expensive endeavor is an understatement. In fact, to really gauge how expensive business school is, you need to look not only at your tuition costs and living expenses, but also at the opportunity cost of foregoing a salary for the length of your program. Think about it: You'll have a net outflow of money.

But keep in mind that, unlike law school or medical school, business school is just a two-year program. Once those two years are over, you can expect to reap the rewards of your increased market value. Unfortunately, business school differs from law school and medical school in a much less desirable way as well—there are serious limitations on the amount of money available through scholarships and grants. Most business school students will be limited to loans, and lots of them.

Try not to get too upset about borrowing the money for business school; think of it as an investment in yourself. But, like all investments, it should be carefully thought out and discussed with everyone (spouse, partner, etc.) concerned. This is especially important for those of you considering business school. You need a law degree to practice law, and a medical degree to practice medicine, but a business degree is not required to work in business. That said, certain professional opportunities may be tougher to pursue without an MBA on your resume.

The Cost of B-School

So get out some paper, a pencil, and a calculator, and figure out how much it will cost you to attend school. What should you include? Your opportunity cost (lost income) and your cost of attending b-school (tuition and fees). One more thing: For a more accurate assessment of your investment, you should figure taxes into the equation by dividing tuition cost by 0.65 (this assumes taxes of about 35 percent). Why? Because in order to pay tuition of $25,000, you would have to make a pre-tax income of about $38,500. If you are lucky enough to have a source of aid that does not require repayment, such as a grant, scholarship, or wealthy benefactor, subtract that amount from the cost of attending b-school.

For example, if you currently make $50,000 and plan to attend a business school that costs $25,000 per year, your investment would be approximately $177,000.

$(50,000 \times 2) + [(25,000 \times 2)/.65] = 177,000$

Now say you receive an annual grant of $5,000. Your investment would now be approximately $161,500.

$(50,000 \times 2) + [(20,000 \times 2)/.65] = 161,500$

How Long Will It Take You to Recoup Your Investment?

To estimate this figure, you first need to estimate your expected salary increase post-MBA. Check out the average starting salaries for graduates of the programs you are looking at and adjust upward/downward based on the industry you plan to enter. Subtract your current salary from your expected salary and you'll get your expected salary increase.

Once you complete the step above, divide your investment (tuition and fees plus lost income) by your expected salary increase, and then add 2 (the length of a full-time MBA program). If you are contemplating a one-year MBA program, just add 1.

Going back to the example above, if your pre-MBA salary is $50,000 and you expect to make $75,000 when you graduate, your expected salary increase is $25,000 (a 50 percent increase). Let's assume you did not receive a grant and that your investment will be about $177,000.

$(177,000/25,000) + 2 = 9.08$

It will take you approximately nine years to earn back your investment.

Keep in mind, these are approximations and don't take into account annual raises, inflation, and so on. But it is interesting, isn't it?

While business school is an expensive proposition, the financial rewards of having your MBA can be immensely lucrative as we discussed before. You won't be forced into bankruptcy if you finance it correctly. There are tried-and-true ways to reduce your initial costs, finance the costs on the horizon, and manage the debt you'll leave school with—all without selling your soul to the highest bidder.

Comparison Shopping

While cost shouldn't be the first thing on your mind when you are choosing a school, depending on your goals in getting an MBA, it might be fairly high on your list. Private schools aren't the only business schools. Many state schools have fantastic reputations. Regional schools may be more generous with financial aid. Tuition costs will vary widely between public and private schools, especially if you qualify as an in-state student. Keep in mind, however, that salary gains tend to be less dramatic at more regional schools.

HOW DO I FUND MY MBA?

The short answer: loans. Unless your company is underwriting your MBA, or you're able to pay your way in cash, you'll be financing your two years of business school through a portfolio of loans. Loans typically come in one of two forms: federal and private. Only a few of you will be lucky enough to qualify for, and get, grants and scholarships.

Anyone with reasonably good credit, regardless of financial need, can borrow money for business school. If you have financial need, you will probably be eligible for some type of financial aid if you meet the following basic qualifications:

- You are a United States citizen or a permanent U.S. resident.

- You are registered for Selective Service if you are a male, or you have documentation to prove that you are exempt.

- You are not in default on student loans already.

- You don't have a horrendous credit history.

International applicants to business school should take note: Most U.S. business schools will require all international students to pay in full or show proof that they will be able to pay the entire cost of the MBA prior to beginning the MBA program.

FEDERAL LOANS

The federal government funds federal loan programs. Federal loans are usually the "first resort" for borrowers because many are subsidized by the federal government and offer generous interest rates. Some do not begin charging you interest until after you complete your degree. Most federal loans are need-based, but some higher interest federal loans are available regardless of financial circumstances. Your business school's Financial Aid Office will determine what your need is, if any.

PRIVATE LOANS

Private loans are funded by banks, foundations, corporations, and other associations. A number of private loans are targeted to aid particular segments of the population. You may have to do some investigating to identify private loans for which you might qualify. As always, contact your law school's Financial Aid Office to learn more.

ALTERNATIVE SOURCES OF FUNDING

We've already mentioned these in one form or other, but they are worthy of a bit more attention.

The first alternative is sponsorship of your employer or educational reimbursement. Not all companies treat this the same way, but if you are able to get your employer to kick in a portion of the cost, you are better off than before. But beware, this benefit also comes with strings attached. Most companies that pay for your MBA will require a commitment of several years upon graduation. If you renege, you could be liable for the full cost of your education. Others will require that you attend business school part-time, which you may or may not want to do. Often, part-time students are ineligible to participate in on-campus recruiting efforts to the same extent as full-time students.

Educational reimbursement can come in another form as well. Some companies will provide sign-on bonuses to new MBAs that will cover the cost of a year's tuition. This is a fantastic development from the years of a robust economy, but it is by no means a guarantee during tougher times. Don't assume that you will have this option open to you just because it has been a common occurrence in past years.

The other "alternative" source of funding is a financial gift from family or another source. Either you have a resource that is willing and able to fund all or part of your MBA, or you don't. If you do, be thankful.

APPLYING FOR FINANCIAL AID

In order to become eligible for financial aid of any kind, you will need to complete the Free Application for Federal Student Aid, also known as the FAFSA. You complete and submit this form after January 1 of the year in which you plan to enter business school. You should aim to complete and submit this form as soon as possible after the first of the year to avoid any potential delays. The FAFSA is available from a school's Financial Aid Office. You can also download the form directly from the website of the U.S. Department of Education at FAFSA.ed.gov. A third option is to use the FAFSA Express software (also downloadable from the website) and transmit the application electronically.

It is important to note that the form requires information from your federal income tax returns. Plan to file your taxes early that year.

In addition to the FAFSA form, most schools will have their own financial aid form that you will be required to complete and submit. These often have their own deadlines, so it is wise to keep careful track of all the forms you must complete and all their respective deadlines. Yes, it's a lot of paperwork, but get over it. You'll be much happier when the tuition bill arrives.

LOAN SPECIFICS

GUIDE TO FEDERAL LOANS

Stafford Loans

Stafford loans require you to complete the FAFSA form in order to qualify. These are very desirable loans because they offer low-interest rates capped at 8.25 percent and are federally guaranteed. There is a limit to how much you can borrow in this program. The maximum amount per year you may borrow as a graduate student is $18,500; $10,000 of which must be unsubsidized loans. The maximum amount you may borrow in total is $138,500 (only $65,500 of this may be in subsidized loans). The aggregate amount includes any Stafford loans you may have from your undergraduate or other graduate studies.

Stafford loans come in two types: subsidized and unsubsidized. Subsidized loans are need-based as determined by your business school. They do not accrue interest while you are in school or in an authorized deferment period (such as the first six months after graduation). This cost is picked up by the government (hence the name "subsidized"). Repayment begins at that time. Unsubsidized loans are not need-based and do charge interest from the time of disbursement to the time of full repayment. You can pay the interest while you are in school or opt for capitalization, in which case the interest is added to the principal. You will pay more in the long run if you choose capitalization. Interest payments may be tax deductible, so be sure to check. The standard repayment period for both is 10 years.

You will pay a small origination and guarantee fee for each loan, but this is not an out-of-pocket expense. It is simply deducted from the loan amount. Some schools will allow you to borrow the money under the Stafford program directly from them, while others will require you to borrow from a bank. For more information on federal loans, call the Federal Student Aid Information Center at 800-433-3243.

Perkins Loans

Perkins loans are available to graduate students who demonstrate exceptional financial need. The financial aid office will determine your eligibility for a Perkins Loan. If you qualify for a Perkins Loan as part of your financial aid package, take it. The loans are made by the schools and are repaid to the schools, although the federal government provides a large portion of the funds. You can borrow up to $6,000 for each year of graduate study up to a total of $40,000 (this includes any money borrowed under this program during undergraduate study). The interest rates on this loan are low, usually 5 percent. There are no fees attached. The grace period is nine months upon graduation.

PRIVATE/COMMERCIAL LOANS

This is expensive territory. Not only are interest rates high, but terms are also quite different from those found with federal loans. You may not be able to defer payment of interest or principal until after graduation. Origination and guarantee fees are also much higher since these loans are unsecured. After all, banks and other specialized lenders exist to loan money to folks like you, and unlike the federal government, want to make money doing it. If you go this route, shop around diligently. Think of it as good practice for your post-MBA executive career.

Scholarships and Grants

The usual sources for this type of funding are alumni groups and civic organizations. This funding is limited, and actual awards tend to be small. Even if you benefited from generous scholarship funding as an undergraduate, it would be unwise to assume you'll have the same experience as a graduate student. But do investigate. You never know what's out there. Schools will frequently list any scholarships and grants that are available at the back of their financial aid catalog.

For more information

Find out more about your financing options for business school education at PrincetonReview.com.

Chapter 6

What B-School is Really Like

AN ACADEMIC PERSPECTIVE

The objective of all MBA programs is to prepare students for a professional career in business. One business school puts it this way:

Graduates should be all of the following:

1. Able to think and reason independently, creatively, and analytically.

2. Skilled in the use of quantitative techniques.

3. Literate in the use of software applications as management tools.

4. Knowledgeable about the world's management issues and problems.

5. Willing to work in and successfully cope with conditions of uncertainty, risk, and change.

6. Astute decision makers.

7. Ethically and socially responsible.

8. Able to manage in an increasingly global environment.

9. Proficient in utilizing technology as a mode of doing business.

Sound like a tall order? Possibly. But this level of expectation is what business school is all about.

Nearly all MBA programs feature a core curriculum that focuses on the major disciplines of business: finance, management, accounting, marketing, manufacturing, decision sciences, economics, and organizational behavior. Unless your school allows you to place out of them, these courses are mandatory. Core courses provide broad functional knowledge in one discipline. To illustrate, a core marketing course covers pricing, segmentation, communications, product-line planning, and implementation. Electives provide a narrow focus that deepen the area of study. For example, a marketing elective might be entirely devoted to pricing.

Students sometimes question the need for such a comprehensive core program, but the functional areas of a real business are not parallel lines. All departments of a business affect each other every day. For example, an MBA in a manufacturing job might be asked by a financial controller why the company's product has become unprofitable to produce. Without an understanding of how product costs are accounted for, this MBA wouldn't know how to respond to a critical and legitimate request.

At most schools, the first term or year is devoted to a rigid core curriculum. Some schools allow first-years to take core courses side by side with electives. Still others have come up with an entirely new way of covering the basics, integrating the core courses into one cross-functional learning experience, which may also include sessions on topics such as globalization, ethics, and managing diversity. Half-year to year-long courses are team-taught by professors who will see you through all disciplines.

TEACHING METHODOLOGY

Business schools employ two basic teaching methods: case study and lecture. Usually, they employ some combination of the two. The most popular is the case study approach. Students are presented with either real or hypothetical business scenarios and are asked to analyze them. This method provides concrete situations (rather than abstractions) that require mastery of a wide range of skills. Students often find case studies exciting because they can engage in spirited discussions about possible solutions to given business problems and because they get an opportunity to apply newly acquired business knowledge.

On the other hand, lecturing is a teaching method in which—you guessed it—the professor speaks to the class and the class listens. The efficacy of the lecture method depends entirely on the professor. If the professor is compelling, you'll probably get a lot out of the class. If the professor is boring, you probably won't listen, which isn't necessarily a big deal since many professors make their class notes available on computer disc or in the library.

THE CLASSROOM EXPERIENCE

Professors teaching case methodology often begin class with a "cold call." A randomly selected student opens the class with an analysis of the case and makes recommendations for solutions. The cold call forces you to be prepared and to think on your feet.

No doubt, a cold call can be intimidating. But unlike law school, b-school professors don't use the Socratic Method to torture you, testing your thinking with a pounding cross-examination. They're training managers, not trial lawyers. At worst, particularly if you're unprepared, a professor will abruptly dismiss your contribution.

Alternatively, professors ask for a volunteer to open a case, particularly someone who has had real industry experience with the issues. After the opening, the discussion is broadened to include the whole class. Everyone tries to get in a good comment, particularly if class participation counts heavily toward the grade. "Chip shots"—unenlightened, just-say-anything-to-get-credit comments—are common. So are "air hogs," students who go on and on because they like nothing more than to hear themselves pontificate.

Depending on the school, class discussions can degenerate into wars of ego rather than ideas. But for the most part, debates are kept constructive and civilized. Students are competitive, but not offensively so, and learn to make their points succinctly and persuasively.

A Glossary of Insider Lingo

B-school students, graduates, and professors—like most close-knit, somewhat solipsistic groups—seem to speak their own weird language. Here's a sampler of MBA jargon (with English translations):

Admissions Mistake: How each student perceives him or herself until getting first-year grades back from midterms.

Air Hogs: Students who monopolize classroom discussion and love to hear themselves speak.

B2B: "Business to Business"—a company that sells not to retail consumers, but to other enterprises. With the renewed focus on more traditional industries, this now stands for "Back to Basics."

B2C: "Business to Consumer"—a company that sells primarily to individual retail consumers. As with the above joke about B2B, business students occasionally say this really means "Back to Consulting."

Back of the Envelope: A quick analysis of numbers, as if scribbled on the back of an envelope.

Benchmarking: Comparing a company to others in the industry.

Burn Rate: Amount of cash a money-losing company consumes during a period of time.

Case Study Method: Popular teaching method that uses real-life business cases for analysis.

Cold Call: Unexpected, often dreaded request by the professor to open a case discussion.

Chip Shot: Vacant and often cheesy comments used not to truly benefit class discussion, but rather to get credit for participation.

Cycle Time: How fast you can turn something around.

Deliverable: Your end product.

Four Ps: Elements of a marketing strategy: Price, Promotion, Place, Product.

Fume Date: Date the company will run out of cash reserves.

Functional Areas: The basic disciplines of business (e.g., finance, marketing, R&D).

HP12-C: A calculator that works nothing like a regular one, used by finance types when they don't have Excel handy.

Lingo Bingo: A furtive game of Bingo whereby he who "wins" must work a decided upon, often trite phrase (see "chip shot") into the class discussion. For example: "I didn't actually read the case last night, but the protagonist is *two beers short of a six-pack*." The winner also earns a prize and the admiration of classmates.

Low Hanging Fruit: Tasks or goals that are easiest to achieve (consultant jargon).

Monitize: To turn an idea into a moneymaking scheme.

Net Net: End result.

Power Nap: Quick, intense, in-class recharge for the continually sleep-deprived.

Power Tool: Someone who does all the work and sits in the front row of the class with his or her hand up.

Pre-enrollment Courses: Commonly known as MBA summer camp—quantitative courses to get the numerically challenged up to speed.

Pro Forma: Financial presentation of hypothetical events, such as projected earnings.

Quant Jock: A numerical athlete who is happiest crunching numbers.

Rule of Three: You should not talk more than three times in any given class, but you should participate at least once over the course of three classes.

Run the Numbers: Analyze quantitatively.

Shrimp Boy: A student who comes to a corporate event just to scarf down the food.

Skydeck: Refers to the back row of the classroom, usually when it's amphitheater style.

Slice and Dice: Running all kinds of quantitative analysis on a set of numbers.

Soft Skills: Conflict resolution, teamwork, negotiation, oral and written communication.

Take-aways: The key points of a lecture or meeting that participants should remember.

The Five Forces: Michael Porter's model for analyzing the strategic attractiveness of an industry.

Three Cs: The primary forces considered in marketing: Customer, Competition, Company.

Value-Based Decision Making: Values and ethics as part of the practice of business.

YOUR FIRST YEAR

The first six months of b-school can be daunting. You're unfamiliar with the subjects. There's a tremendous amount of work to do. And when you least have the skills to do so, there's pressure to stay with the pack. All of this produces anxiety and a tendency to overprepare. Eventually, students learn shortcuts and settle into a routine, but until then, much of the first year is just plain tough. The programs usually pack more learning into the first term than they do into each of the remaining terms. For the schools to teach the core curriculum (which accounts for as much as 70 percent of learning) in a limited time, an intensive pace is considered necessary. Much of the second year will be spent on gaining proficiency in your area of expertise and on searching for a job.

The good news is that the schools recognize how tough the first year can be. During the early part of the program, they anchor students socially by placing them in small sections, sometimes called "cohorts." You take many or all of your classes with your section-mates. Sectioning encourages the formation of personal and working relationships and can help make a large program feel like a school within a school.

Because so much has to be accomplished in so little time, getting an MBA is like living in fast-forward. This is especially true of the job search. No sooner are you in the program than recruiters for summer jobs show up, which tends to divert students from their studies. First-years aggressively pursue summer positions, which are linked with the promise of a permanent job offer if the summer goes well. At some schools, the recruiting period begins as early as October, at others in January or February.

A DAY IN THE LIFE

MATT CAMP, FIRST YEAR
Tuck School of Business, Dartmouth College

7:00 A.M.: Get dressed. Out of the door by 7:45 A.M. to head to the campus dining hall for breakfast. If I have time, I'll grab the *Financial Times* and *The Wall Street Journal* and gloss over the front page. Today, I have an informal get-to-know-you-better meeting with a marketing professor over breakfast.

8:30 A.M.: Core class in Corporate Finance. Grab any seat in a tiered classroom set-up. I'm usually in the middle toward the side. If possible, the front row stays empty.

10:00 A.M.: Go to e-mail kiosk on campus and check messages. Hang out or do a quick run to the library to read more of the *Times*.

10:30 A.M.: Macroeconomics lecture/case study class. Again, no assigned seating. Expect cold calls on case. Cold calls are not terrifying. Professors are supportive, not out to embarrass you. Class discussion is lively, with a mix of people offering their views.

Noon: Back to the cafeteria. Tuck may be one of the few schools where everyone eats together at the same place. There isn't much in town, and you're tight on time, so it doesn't make sense to go back home or elsewhere. It's crowded, so I look for friends, but basically grab a seat anywhere at one of the large tables that seat six to seven. Professors, administrators, and students all eat at the same place. Food is above-average.

1:15 P.M.: Classes are over for the day. From this point, I begin to start homework; there's a lot of work to do. I can go to a study room on campus, but they get booked up pretty quickly for groups, so I head to the library. The majority of the people are doing work for tomorrow. It's rare to have someone working on a project that's due the following week. It's pretty much day-to-day.

4:00 P.M.: I head off to one of the scheduled sports I've signed up for. Today it's soccer, played about one mile from campus. I drive; friends hitch a ride with me. This is a big international scene, mostly men, but there's a small group of women too. It's definitely a game we play hard, but in a very congenial way.

6:00 P.M.: Head back to campus. I'm hungry. It's off to the dining hall again. Most first-years live in dorms, so home cooking is not an option. Almost all second-years live off-campus, so they head back for a home-cooked meal. Cafeteria is not crowded; I may eat alone.

7:00 P.M.: Head home for a quick shower and change. The night is just beginning.

7:30 P.M.: Meet with study group at school to flesh out rest of work that needs to be done in preparation for tomorrow's classes.

11:00 P.M.: Students and their wives/husbands or partners head out to play ice hockey at one of the two rinks here. Wives/husbands and partners play. There are different games going on for different skill levels. It's a lot of fun.

Midnight: Time to go and celebrate either a hard game or a sore butt, but everyone goes to get some wings and a beer. There are only two bars on campus, and they close at 1:00 A.M. so we head to one of them.

1:00 A.M.: After the bar closes, people head home.

1:15 A.M.: Exhausted, I go to bed. No TV. I've forgotten what that is.

YOUR SECOND YEAR

Relax, the second year is easier. By now, students know what's important and what's not. Second-years work more efficiently than first-years. Academic anxiety is no longer a factor. Having mastered the broad-based core curriculum, students now enjoy taking electives and developing an area of specialization.

Anxiety in the second year has more to do with the arduous task of finding a job. For some lucky students, a summer position has yielded a full-time offer. But even those students often go through the whole recruiting grind anyway because they don't want to cut off any opportunities prematurely.

Most MBAs leave school with a full-time offer. Sometimes it's their only offer. Sometimes it's not their dream job, which may be why most grads change jobs after just two years. One student summed up the whole two-year academic/recruiting process like this: "The first-year students collapse in the winter quarter because of on-campus recruiting. The second-years collapse academically in the first quarter of their second year because it's so competitive to get a good job. And when a second-year does get a job, he or she forgets about class entirely. That's why pass/fail was invented."

A DAY IN THE LIFE

KRISTIN HANSEN, SECOND-YEAR
Tuck School of Business, Dartmouth College

9:00 A.M.: Wake-up (my first class is at 10:30 A.M.) and finish work for Monday classes.

10:15 A.M.: Ride my bike to campus for 10:30 A.M. class.

10:30 A.M.: Head to International Economics class, an elective. I have only three classes this semester, my last. Prior to this I had four and a half classes each term. I front-loaded so I would have a light last semester. Grab a yogurt and juice on way in. Eat in class. We discuss a currency crisis case.

Noon: Head to study room to plug my personal computer into one of the many networked connections on campus to check e-mail. Finish work for next class.

1:00 P.M.: Grab a quick lunch in the dining hall. Will bring it to eat during class.

1:15 P.M.: Managerial Decision Making class, another elective. Today is the very last class that second-years will have at Tuck; we're off to graduation! Our professor brings in strawberries and champagne to celebrate. We all hang out and toast each other. This obviously doesn't happen everyday, but this is just the kind of thing a Tuck professor would do.

2:45 P.M.: I'm one of four Tuck social chairpersons, so I use this time to send e-mails to my co-chairs about the upcoming chili cook-off and farm party. Then I send a message to the school regarding other social events for the weekend. I get an e-mail from the New York office of CS First Boston, with whom I've accepted a job offer, with a calendar of the dates for my private client-services training.

3:00 P.M.: Go for a run, swim, or bike ride.

5:00 P.M.: Head home to shower and change. Usually I'd make dinner at home and eat, but tonight, I'm heading out to a social event. So I relax a bit and do an hour of preparation for the next day. On Monday, Tuesday, and Wednesday nights, the workload is heavier.

7:00 P.M.: Off to a Turkey Fry Dinner. This is a meal that will be prepared by my two economics professors. They donated this "dinner" for the charity student auction. Friends of mine bid on it and won. Each of eight bidders gets to bring a guest, and I'm one of the guests. The professors are hosting this at one of their homes. Basically, they're taking three large turkeys and fry-o-lating them.

8:30 P.M.: We all head out to an open mic night, led by the same two economics professors that hosted the Turkey Fry. It's held at a local bar. Anyone in the audience can get onstage and perform. I'm a member of the Tuck band, so I get up on stage with my acoustic guitar and play various folk and bluegrass songs. This is a great warm-up for the open mic night at Tuck.

10:45 P.M.: We head out for Pub Night in downtown Hanover.

1:00 A.M.: The bar closes, so we head to "The End Zone," one of the second-year houses close to campus. All the second-year houses are named; these are names that have been passed down from generation to generation. On a typical Thursday night at Tuck, a small number of students will stay out until 3:00 A.M. I'm usually one of them.

3:00 A.M.: I walk home. My house, called "Girls in the Hood," is just a ten-minute stroll away. I may grab a 3:00 A.M. snack. Then, I quickly fall asleep, exhausted.

Life Outside of Class

Business school is more than academics and a big-bucks job. A spirited community provides ample opportunity for social interaction, extracurricular activity, and career development.

Much of campus life revolves around student-run clubs. There are groups for just about every career interest and social need—from MBAs for a Greener America to the Small Business Club. There's even a group for significant others on most campuses. The clubs are a great way to meet classmates with similar interests and to get in on the social scene. They might have a reputation for throwing the best black-tie balls, pizza-and-keg events, and professional mixers. During orientation week, these clubs aggressively market themselves to first-years.

Various socially responsible projects are also popular on campus. An emphasis on volunteer work is part of the overall trend toward good citizenship. Perhaps to counter the greed of the 1980s, "giving back" is the b-school style of the moment. There is usually a wide range of options—from tutoring in an inner-city school to working in a soup kitchen to renovating public buildings.

Still another way to get involved is to work on a school committee. Here you might serve on a task force designed to improve student quality of life, 0r you might work in the admissions office and interview prospective students.

For those with more creative urges there are always the old standbys: extracurriculars such as the school paper, yearbook, or school play. At some schools, the latter is a dramatization of "b-school follies" and is a highlight of the year. Like the student clubs, these are a great way to get to know your fellow students.

Finally, you can play on intramural sports teams or attend the numerous informal get-togethers, dinner parties, and group trips. There are also plenty of regularly scheduled pub nights, just in case you thought your beer-guzzling days were over.

Most former MBA students say that going to b-school was the best decision they ever made. That's primarily because of nonacademic experiences. Make the most of your classes, but take the time to get involved and enjoy yourself.

PART II
SCHOOLS RANKED BY CATEGORY

On the following pages you will find eleven top 10 lists of business schools ranked according to various metrics. As we noted earlier, none of these lists purports to rank the business schools by their overall quality. Nor should any combination of the categories we've chosen be construed as representing the raw ingredients for such a ranking. We have made no attempt to gauge the "prestige" of these schools, and we wonder whether we could accurately do so even if we tried. What we have done, however, is presented a number of lists using information from two very large databases—one of statistical information collected from business schools, and another of subjective data gathered via our survey of 19,000 business students at 290 business schools.

Ten of the ranking lists are based partly or wholly on opinions collected through our business student survey. The only schools that may appear in these lists are the 290 business schools from which we were able to collect a sufficient number of student surveys to accurately represent the student experience in our various ratings and descriptive profiles.

One of the rankings, Toughest to Get Into, incorporates *only* admissions statistics reported to us by the business schools. Therefore, any business school appearing in this edition of the guide, whether we collected student surveys from it or not, may appear on this list.

Under the title of each list is an explanation of what criteria the ranking is based on. For explanations of many of the individual rankings components, turn to the "How This Book is Organized" section, on page 5.

It's worth repeating: There is no one best business school in America. There is a best business school for you. By using these rankings in conjunction with the descriptive profiles and data listings in subsequent sections of this book, we hope that you will begin to identify the attributes of a business school that are important to you, as well as those schools that can best help you to achieve your personal and professional goals.

Please note that in an effort to avoid comparing apples to oranges, we have not placed any international business schools on any of our rankings lists.

The top schools in each category appear in descending order.

TOUGHEST TO GET INTO
BASED ON THE ADMISSIONS SELECTIVITY RATING (SEE PAGE 11 FOR EXPLANATION)

1. Stanford University
2. Harvard University
3. Columbia University
4. University of Pennsylvania
5. Massachusetts Institute of Technology
6. University of California—Berkeley
7. Dartmouth College
8. New York University
9. Northwestern University
10. Yale University

BEST CAREER PROSPECTS
BASED ON THE CAREER RATING (SEE PAGE 13 FOR EXPLANATION)

1. Stanford University
2. The University of Chicago
3. Harvard University
4. Dartmouth College
5. University of California—Berkeley
6. University of Michigan—Ann Arbor
7. University of Pennsylvania
8. New York University
9. University of Virginia
10. Massachusetts Institute of Technology

BEST CLASSROOM EXPERIENCE
BASED ON STUDENT ASSESSMENT OF PROFESSORS' TEACHING ABILITIES AND RECOGNITION IN THEIR FIELDS, THE INTEGRATION OF NEW BUSINESS TRENDS AND PRACTICES IN THE CURRICULA, AND THE INTELLECTUAL LEVEL OF CLASSMATES' CONTRIBUTIONS IN COURSE DISCUSSIONS

1. Indiana University—Bloomington
2. Harvard University
3. Millsaps College
4. The University of Chicago
5. University of Virginia
6. Acton MBA in Entrepreneurship
7. East Tennessee State University
8. Miami University Ohio
9. The University of Alabama at Tuscaloosa
10. Claremont Graduate University

BEST PROFESSORS
BASED ON THE PROFESSORS INTERESTING AND PROFESSORS ACCESSIBLE RATINGS (SEE PAGES 9 AND 10 FOR EXPLANATIONS)

1. University of Virginia
2. Indiana University—Bloomington
3. The College of William & Mary
4. Northern Arizona University
5. Acton MBA in Entrepreneurship
6. Claremont Graduate University
7. Washington University in St. Louis
8. Penn State University
9. Harvard University
10. The University of North Carolina at Chapel Hill

MOST COMPETITIVE STUDENTS

BASED ON STUDENT ASSESSMENT OF HOW COMPETITIVE CLASSMATES ARE, HOW HEAVY THE WORKLOAD IS, AND THE PERCEIVED ACADEMIC PRESSURE

1. Brigham Young University
2. Vanderbilt University
3. University of Pennsylvania
4. University of Rochester
5. University of Mississippi
6. The University of Iowa
7. Purdue University
8. Georgia State University
9. Texas A&M University—College Station
10. Rutgers, The State University of New Jersey

BEST CAMPUS ENVIRONMENT

BASED ON STUDENT ASSESSMENT OF THE SAFETY, ATTRACTIVENESS AND LOCATION OF THE SCHOOL

1. University of California—Los Angeles
2. American University
3. Rice University
4. University of Virginia
5. University of Portland
6. University of Washington
7. Stanford University
8. Loyola Marymount University
9. Emory University
10. Appalachian State University

MOST FAMILY FRIENDLY

BASED ON STUDENT ASSESSMENT OF: HOW HAPPY MARRIED STUDENTS ARE, HOW MANY STUDENTS HAVE CHILDREN, HOW HELPFUL THE BUSINESS SCHOOL IS TO STUDENTS WITH CHILDREN, AND HOW MUCH THE SCHOOL DOES FOR THE SPOUSES OF STUDENTS

1. Dartmouth College
2. Brigham Young University
3. Stanford University
4. Indiana University—Bloomington
5. Harvard University
6. East Tennessee State University
7. University of Utah
8. University of Virginia
9. Northwestern University
10. The University of North Carolina at Chapel Hill

BEST CAMPUS FACILITIES

BASED ON STUDENT ASSESSMENT OF THE QUALITY OF CLASSROOM, LIBRARY AND GYM FACILITIES

1. Penn State University
2. Indiana University—Bloomington
3. University of Virginia
4. The University of Alabama at Tuscaloosa
5. Harvard University
6. University of Oregon
7. Bentley College
8. Baylor University
9. Northern Arizona University
10. University of Georgia

BEST ADMINISTERED

BASED ON STUDENT ASSESSMENT OF HOW SMOOTHLY THE SCHOOL IS RUN, AND THE EASE WITH WHICH STUDENTS CAN GET INTO REQUIRED AND POPULAR COURSES

1. New York University
2. The George Washington University
3. Brigham Young University
4. West Virginia University
5. Washington University in St. Louis
6. Stanford University
7. The University of Iowa
8. University of Alabama—Tuscaloosa
9. Colorado State University
10. University of California—Berkeley

GREATEST OPPORTUNITY FOR MINORITY STUDENTS

BASED ON THE PERCENT OF STUDENTS FROM MINORITIES, THE PERCENT OF FACULTY FROM MINORITIES, AND STUDENT ASSESSMENT OF RESOURCES FOR MINORITY STUDENTS, HOW SUPPORTIVE THE CULTURE IS OF MINORITY STUDENTS, AND WHETHER FELLOW STUDENTS ARE ETHNICALLY AND RACIALLY DIVERSE

1. Howard University
2. University of Houston—Victoria
3. Barry University
4. Florida International University
5. Bowling Green State University
6. University of West Georgia
7. Texas A&M International University
8. San Francisco State University
9. The University of Texas at San Antonio
10. Northern Arizona University

GREATEST OPPORTUNITY FOR WOMEN

BASED ON THE PERCENT OF STUDENTS WHO ARE FEMALE, THE PERCENT OF FACULTY WHO ARE FEMALE, AND STUDENT ASSESSMENT OF: RESOURCES FOR FEMALE STUDENTS, HOW SUPPORTIVE THE CULTURE IS OF FEMALE STUDENTS, WHETHER THE BUSINESS SCHOOL OFFERS COURSEWORK FOR WOMEN ENTREPRENEURS, AND WHETHER CASE STUDY MATERIALS FOR CLASSES PROPORTIONATELY REFLECT WOMEN IN BUSINESS

1. Mercer University—Atlanta
2. Jacksonville State University
3. University of Massachusetts Amherst
4. The University of Tennessee at Chattanooga
5. St. Mary's University
6. The University of Vermont
7. California State University—Chico
8. University of California—Davis
9. Seattle University
10. Babson College

PART III-A
BUSINESS SCHOOL
DESCRIPTIVE PROFILES

ACTON SCHOOL OF BUSINESS
THE ACTON MBA IN ENTREPRENEURSHIP

GENERAL INFORMATION

Type of school	Private
Academic calendar	Aug.–Apr.

SURVEY SAYS . . .

Cutting-edge classes
Solid preparation in:
Finance
Accounting
General management
Operations
Entrepreneurial studies

STUDENTS

Enrollment of parent institution	2,200
Enrollment of business school	21
% male/female	90/10
% out-of-state	19
% minorities	5
% international	10
Average age at entry	31
Average years work experience at entry	7

ACADEMICS

Academic Experience Rating	**99**
Student/faculty ratio	2:1
Profs interesting rating	99
Profs accessible rating	87

FINANCIAL FACTS

Annual tuition	$35,000
% of students receiving aid	100
% of first-year students receiving aid	100
% of students receiving loans	43

Academics

The Acton MBA in Entrepreneurship is a rigorous, progressive, and unique business program offered through Hardin-Simmons University in Austin, Texas. Cramming 2 years worth of material into just 12 months, Acton students are ambitious and focused, willing "to work 100-hour weeks to accomplish what 'traditional' schools accomplish in 2" weeks. All classes are taught in the case-based or Socratic Method and, in a single year, students analyze over 300 cases. Preparation is crucial, as class participation accounts for 50 percent of your grade, and professors "place a high emphasis on quality listening and on conversational continuity (i.e., building on previous comments) versus merely making a brilliant point that is unconnected to the dialogue." Plus, there's no wiggle room for slackers: The curriculum is tightly integrated, with each class building on the next.

The Acton program is built upon three pillars: learning to learn, learning how to make money, and learning how to live a life of meaning. Students say the program delivers on all three points and distinguishes itself by focusing on the personal side of career development. "Acton helps us learn about ourselves by aiding us in our search for our true calling in life—the one thing that we are the best at that intertwines with what the world needs," explains one student. "This help in our personal lives as well as our business lives is unparalleled by any other MBA program."

At the same time, Acton emphasizes a "concrete, nuts-and-bolts approach to business and entrepreneurship," including many hands-on projects such as operations simulation and plant tours. Promoting an entrepreneurial spirit, Acton is "the only program in which 100 percent of the professors are actively running businesses." While they put their students through the wringer in the classroom, these "entrepreneur-teachers" are "all leaders in their fields with a real heart for teaching." There is no traditional tenure track at Acton, and teachers (like students) are expected to perform. To ensure their success, students fill out a weekly survey that "brings about change almost immediately. The administration is very focused on making the Acton program the best entrepreneurial program in the world, and so they take the input of their customer (the student) very seriously." One student goes so far as to say the administrative staff treats students "like we are at a Ritz-Carlton; customer service is outstanding."

Fellow students also form an important part of the academic environment at Acton with, "a highly varied set of backgrounds, ranging from home building, to e-commerce, to manufacturing, to the military, to public radio. Everyone is passionate about learning, and we hold each other to the highest of standards." In fact, students tell us that "competition and debate is held to a standard of high conflict, in which ideas are challenged and efforts are tested but the individuals are held in high regard and treated with respect."

Career and Placement

It is Acton's philosophy that sending out hundreds of resumes is a waste of time for both employers and applicants. Therefore, Acton takes a very unique approach to career planning. First, students complete the Life of Meaning course—a required part of the Acton curriculum—during which they profoundly consider both their skill set and career goals. As a part of the course, students identify a specific job at a specific company which represents the next step in their career development. Once entrepreneur-teachers believe that a student has made an appropriate and well-considered choice, the teacher will call the potential employer and personally introduce you to the company.

JESSICA BLANCHARD, DIRECTOR OF ENROLLMENT
515 CONGRESS AVENUE, SUITE 1875 AUSTIN, TX 78701 UNITED STATES
PHONE: 512-703-1231 • FAX: 512-495-9480
E-MAIL: JBLANCHARD@ACTONMBA.ORG • WEBSITE: WWW.ACTONMBA.ORG

In addition to the support they receive from teachers, Acton students are confident that their top-notch program will continue to open doors for them as the school's reputation grows. A current student insists, "The name recognition of Acton literally grows every day, and for a school that has only been around for 4 years, we have an incredible presence in the business world."

Student Life and Environment

A day in the life of an Acton MBA is nothing short of a marathon. Set that alarm clock: "Mandatory study group begins at 6:30 A.M. every morning and last until classes start at 8:00 A.M." After that, it's off to lively, discussion-based classes and then hours of prep time for the next day (according to most, roughly 6 to 8 prep hours per class.) Shares a current student, "It is brutally intense, and there are weeks where I get 5 hours of sleep per night. . . . The competition in class is fierce, and if you are not prepared you will be called on it. That said, there is nothing in this world I would rather be doing right now, and there is nowhere that will better prepare me to start a company. This program will push you well beyond what you thought you could achieve."

The required dedication makes for a close-knit college community comprised of "some of the brightest and most insightful people I have ever met. They manage to compete fiercely while still caring for each other in amazing ways." However, students explain that while "The class is tight and does have activities, both planned and informal," they are not socializing "to the degree that a traditional MBA program does. It is not about happy hours or networking events."

Although the pace rarely lets up, students mention that "the breaks we have in the school year are wonderful times where we can recharge our batteries before heading back into the fray." In those rare moments of relaxation, "Acton is located in the great city of Austin, Texas which provides for a fun, relaxed atmosphere when we are not in school."

Admissions

Acton looks for students who display perseverance, a curious intellect, and integrity. You must also demonstrate a high level of achievement in your undergraduate academic record, an aptitude for graduate study as evidenced by your GMAT score, and a history of leadership and involvement in extracurricular activities. With such a low enrollment (around 20 students currently), Acton takes a personal interest in getting to know their applicants. In addition to essay questions and letters of recommendation, every student is personally interviewed before being admitted to the program.

ADMISSIONS

Admissions Selectivity Rating	**90**
# of applications received	50
% applicants accepted	50
% acceptees attending	84
Average GMAT	640
Range of GMAT	540–760
Average GPA	3.2
TOEFL required	
of international students	Yes
Minimum TOEFL	
(paper/computer)	620/260
Application fee	$50
Regular notification	
Application Deadline/Notification	
Round 1:	11/15 / 12/15
Round 2:	3/1 / 4/1
Round 3:	5/1 / 6/1

Applicants Also Look At

Babson College, Duke University, University of Virginia.

EMPLOYMENT PROFILE

Career Rating	81	Grads Employed by Function	%	Avg. Salary
Primary Source of Full-time Job Acceptances		Finance/Accounting	20	$70,000
School-facilitated activities	2 (16%)	Marketing/Sales	10	$60,000
Graduate-facilitated activities	8 (62%)	Consulting	10	$50,000
Unknown	3 (22%)	Entrepreneurship	10	$80,000
Average base starting salary	$80,000	General Management	20	$80,000
Percent employed	69	Other	30	$70,000

ALFRED UNIVERSITY
COLLEGE OF BUSINESS

Academics

If you're looking for an "intimate environment" for your MBA experience, Alfred University is well worth a look. This program serves a population of 60 graduate students, only 15 of whom attend full-time. The result is a program with a "family atmosphere" where everyone is "really friendly and willing to help." As one student told us, "The greatest strength of Alfred University is its size. The classes are between 10 and 20 people, and the interaction is incredible. One really feels a part of the class discussions." The school is especially strong in entrepreneurial studies, an area abetted by the university's Center for Family Business and Entrepreneurial Leadership, a research center.

Professors at Alfred have the time to go the extra mile for students, and they "work hard to make sure you understand what they are teaching, but they also expect you to do your share of the work." Students also appreciate that "professors here are very diverse and have experiences [in other countries] ranging from Japan to Tunisia." With no crowd to fight, Alfred students have a better chance to shine (though keep in mind this also means there's no anonymity for anyone—"Show up to class prepared and hand your work in on time," advises one student). Another writes, "One professor liked a paper I wrote for his class. He offered to coauthor another paper with me and pursue getting it published. These opportunities are so valuable to me and something I would never have expected." And this sense of support and enterprise doesn't end in the classroom. As one student explains, "MBA students at Alfred receive great amounts of attention not only from faculty but also from business school staff. The Assistant Dean keeps a close eye on all of us to make sure we're getting everything we need: from bindings for term papers to a listening ear [for our] concerns."

Of course, a small school can only offer students so much. Some students find that there are "few academic options within the program," "too few courses," and "limited electives." Even so, they regard their MBA experience as extremely "positive." They approve of the school's "active learning" strategies, which emphasize teamwork, case studies, simulations, and field experience (usually gained through an internship). "As a result, I have found the program challenging, rewarding, and enriching," explains one student.

Career and Placement

All Alfred students receive career services through the Robert R. McComsey Career Development Center. The office provides one-on-one counseling sessions; workshops in interviewing, resume writing, and networking; a career library with online and conventional print resources; and annual job fairs. The school also boasts a 100 percent placement rate for its MBAs. Students point out, however, that Alfred's remote location complicates their search for jobs and internships. Many agree that "Alfred is a small community" and that "outside internships and projects are more difficult to obtain due to the university's rural location." However, over the past few years the administration had worked "to expand local, as well as international, opportunities with particular focus on MBA students," and as such, many find that the school currently "does very well in providing big city opportunities."

Prominent employers of Alfred MBAs include Alstom, AOL Communications, Avantt Consulting, Met Life/New England Financial, General Electric Company, Eli Lilly and Company, Citynet, Corning, Dresser Rand, Nestlé, NYSEG, Toro Energy, and Wal-Mart.

VALERIE STEPHENS, ASSISTANT DIRECTOR/TECHNICAL COORDINATOR
OFFICE OF GRADUATE ADMISSIONS, ALUMNI HALL, SAXON DRIVE ALFRED, NY 14802 U.S.
PHONE: 800-541-9229 • FAX: 607-871-2198
E-MAIL: GRADINQUIRY@ALFRED.EDU • WEBSITE: BUSINESS.ALFRED.EDU/MBA.HTML

Student Life and Environment

Alfred, New York, is a quiet, rural town with few distractions, and accordingly, student life centers on campus. The university is a community of about 2,500 students, including 250 business undergrads and 60 MBAs, making it large enough to support all manner of activity. The "wide variety of clubs and organizations offer great opportunity for individual growth" and if you want a club "All you have to do is ask." One student explains, "Alfred's clubs and activities are astounding. Diverse clubs and organizations regularly attend student senate to discuss concerns that are circulating the student population."

Alfred's infrastructure includes "plenty of computers and good Internet bandwidth"; however, "The recreational facilities aren't the best, and the library needs help." Fortunately, a "large renovation and expansion project" is underway, which could be "the largest project for the university within the last few decades." The renovations are expected to "address shortcomings of the university, greatly enhance the campus, and benefit students." Also, while the "huge" dorms get glowing reviews, "Housing is really poor off campus."

Alfred's 16 Division III intercollegiate teams provide entertainment, as does the popular intramural sports program. The school's divisions of music, theater, and dance frequently hold performances. Alfred also has an active visual-arts community; it houses one of the best ceramic arts programs in the country. The "peaceful and safe" village of Alfred has a year-round population of 1,000 and surrounding towns are not much larger. These "secluded" surroundings lessen "the chances of distractions from studies," though when students need a break from the books, Rochester is only 80 miles away, with Buffalo only a little farther down the road—provided you have four-wheel drive in the winter.

Admissions

Applicants must provide the school with official copies of undergraduate transcripts, GMAT scores, TOEFL scores (for international students whose first language is not English), a personal statement, and letters of recommendation (preferably from former employers or professors). Previous work experience is not required, and an interview, while always recommended, is optional.

ADMISSIONS	
Admissions Selectivity Rating	**78**
# of applications received	46
% applicants accepted	43
% acceptees attending	50
Average GMAT	448
Average GPA	3.08
TOEFL required of international students	Yes
Minimum TOEFL (paper/computer)	590/243
Application fee	$50
Deferment available	Yes
Maximum length of deferment	2 years
Transfer students accepted	Yes
Transfer application policy Transfer a maximum of 6 credit hours from an AACSB-accredited institution.	
Non-fall admissions	Yes
Need-blind admissions	Yes

AMERICAN UNIVERSITY
KOGOD SCHOOL OF BUSINESS

Academics

The "small and friendly" MBA program at American University's Kogod School of Business offers a "solid academic program" that, like its namesake (Robert P. Kogod, Charles E. Smith Co.), excels in the area of real estate. American's Washington, DC location situates it ideally to focus on international matters, and the school exploits that opportunity well, interjecting "an international perspective in class discussions that is second to none. Almost all classes integrate an international component."

Kogod's strengths extend far beyond real estate and international business, however. The school boasts a finance faculty that is "internationally recognized for their research. They are great instructors too." Students praise the commercial banking career track offered here and love the fact that the program "allows you to concentrate in two areas of expertise," which "lets you design your own MBA" and "is a great advantage in the job market." Kogod recently "created the first LLM/MBA in the country, which is an excellent way to combine international law studies and business."

Kogod's pedagogical approach embraces a mixture of case studies and theory, combined with plenty of group work that acts as good practice for the real world. Professors "have a great reputation and have done interesting research." They are also easy to contact because of an "open-door policy." Faculty members "bring a lot of academic and professional experience" to the program—another plus. "We have former investment bankers, former consultants, former CFOs, and lifelong academics," brags one student. Small class sizes "give Kogod an advantage over the other DC schools like Georgetown and GW. I know everyone by name, and that's a nice feeling." As a result, the program "feels like being in a big family. Everyone knows you and does their best to help you."

Kogod's DC address "creates many opportunities for networking, internships, etc." As one student puts it, "The DC location gives Kogod a huge advantage. There are so many more opportunities to pursue when you are in a big city. It also helps Kogod draw "international students from very diverse countries," enhancing in-class and networking experiences. Perhaps best of all, this is a school that "is in the middle of overhauling its curriculum" and is in construction on a new building that "will allow for more space to gather in study groups, do group projects, etc." One MBA professes, "I think there will be some great changes" in the school's near future.

Career and Placement

Career Services at Kogod "does a great job in involving alumni in school life. There are lots of networking opportunities . . . [and] lots of on-site visits with direct interactions with alumni, both young and more experienced." A Wall Street trip includes visits to "all the major financial institutions with alumni as tour guides and a session for Q & As and recruiting procedures and tips, concluded by an alumni networking dinner." Career Services Counselors also provide "constant information about new jobs/internship opportunities in the DC area and beyond."

Companies that have recently hired Kogod MBAs include: America Online, BearingPoint, Booz Allen Hamilton, Citigroup, Deloitte Touche Tohmatsu, Discovery Communications, Ernst & Young, ExxonMobil, Fannie Mae, Freddie Mac, The Gallup Organization, Goldman Sachs, IBM, Johnson & Johnson, JPMorgan, Lehman Brothers, Marriott International, MetLife, MSN, PricewaterhouseCoopers, Raytheon, U.S. Bank, the U.S. Government Accountability Office, the U.S. Securities and Exchange Commission, the U.S. Senate, and Unisys.

SONDRA SMITH, SENIOR DIRECTOR FOR ENROLLMENT MANAGEMENT
4400 MASSACHUSETTS AVENUE NW WASHINGTON, DC 20016-8044 UNITED STATES
PHONE: 202-885-1913 • FAX: 202-885-1078
E-MAIL: KOGODMBA@AMERICAN.EDU • WEBSITE: WWW.KOGOD.AMERICAN.EDU

Student Life and Environment

The atmosphere in the Kogod MBA program "is low key, friendly, and accessible," with "a great learning environment. The students are all very friendly and socialize together regularly. The professors are very approachable and friendly, and have some impressive resumes. The academics are tough and the program is effective but not cutthroat." Kogod offers "many clubs and organizations in different fields," and students report that "involvement is highly encouraged."

Some here feel that "the program is not as social as others, and this is due in large part to the fact that the school is located in a relatively upscale neighborhood, and there are few restaurants or bars in the immediate area. Also, students tend to live all over Washington, DC," so "Getting large groups together can be difficult." Most agree that's a small trade-off for living "in one of the most exciting and fun cities in the country." As an added bonus, "There is so much work in DC that making $100K a year is almost automatic if you connect with the right government-related job."

Students here represent a variety of backgrounds. "I come from a military background," says one MBA, "and I really enjoy mingling and working with people from nonprofits, other government agencies, small companies, and large companies." The population includes a substantial international contingent.

Admissions

The Kogod Admissions Office requires the following from all applicants: a completed online application form; a personal statement of purpose in pursuing the MBA; a current resume; two letters of recommendation; an official transcript from all attended undergraduate and graduate institutions; and an official GMAT score report. International applicants whose first language is not English must also submit an official score report for other the TOEFL or the IELTS. An interview is required of all applicants.

FINANCIAL FACTS

Annual tuition	$27,404
Fees	$380
Room & board	$20,000
% of students receiving grants	25
Average award package	$17,210
Average student loan debt	$43,488

ADMISSIONS

Admissions Selectivity Rating	**80**
# of applications received	410
% applicants accepted	55
% acceptees attending	39
Average GMAT	580
Range of GMAT	500–680
Average GPA	3.01
TOEFL required of international students	Yes
Minimum TOEFL (paper/computer)	600/100
Application fee	$75
Regular application deadline	Rolling
Regular notification	Rolling
Deferment available	Yes
Maximum length of deferment	1 year
Transfer students accepted	Yes
Transfer application policy	

They must meet the same requirements as a non-transfer student. Nine credits may be transferred into the program from an AACSB-accredited MBA program.

Non-fall admissions	Yes
Need-blind admissions	Yes

Applicants Also Look At

The George Washington University, Georgetown University, University of Maryland.

EMPLOYMENT PROFILE				
Career Rating	**75**	**Grads Employed by Function**	**%**	**Avg. Salary**
Primary Source of Full-time Job Acceptances		Finance/Accounting	27	$72,409
School-facilitated activities	40%	Human Resources	2	NR
Graduate-facilitated activities	60%	Marketing/Sales	5	NR
Average base starting salary	$71,487	Consulting	37	$74,615
Percent employed	81.8	General Management	10	$70,750
		Other	17	$67,000
		Top 5 Employers Hiring Grads		
		Deloitte Touche Tohmatsu; Bearing Point; Ernst & Young; IBM; KPMG International.		

APPALACHIAN STATE UNIVERSITY
WALKER COLLEGE OF BUSINESS

GENERAL INFORMATION

Type of school	Public
Environment	Village
Academic calendar	Semester

SURVEY SAYS...

Students love Boone, NC
Smart classrooms
Solid preparation in:
Finance
Accounting
Quantitative skills

STUDENTS

Enrollment of parent institution	14,653
Enrollment of business school	27
% male/female	75/25
% out-of-state	7
% minorities	3
% international	3
Average age at entry	26
Average years work experience at entry	4

ACADEMICS

Academic Experience Rating	**70**
Student/faculty ratio	20:1
Profs interesting rating	67
Profs accessible rating	81
% female faculty	18

FINANCIAL FACTS

Annual tuition (in-state/ out-of-state)	$2,096/$6,888
Fees	$915
Cost of books	$1,200
Room & board (on/off-campus)	$4,082/$7,200
Average grant	$1,000

Academics

The nascent graduate business program at Appalachian State University's Walker College of Business offers a select few students "what is probably the most reasonably priced graduate program in the state—incredible bargain." At present, fewer than 20 students are enrolled in the program, which offers a conventional MBA, an MS in accounting, and graduate certificate programs in finance, human-resource management, and information systems. Housed in the same hall as the university's mainframe computer, the MBA program puts computers to good use, employing computer simulations and computer analysis as well as computer-aided instruction in the classroom.

First-year studies at Walker commence with MBA Enrichment, a required program that includes "orientation sessions, workshops, a team-building outdoor experience, and social time for students to get acquainted." The freshman curriculum is entirely prescribed and is designed to "provide students with a broad foundation of knowledge." Students must complete an internship or international experience between their first and second years. Second-year studies consist of five required courses and five electives. Instruction at Walker incorporates case study, group discussion, role playing, guest-led seminars, field projects, team projects, and individual presentations. Students tell us that the Walker approach consists of "lots of work: You have to read and study a lot, [and] you get to learn! With so many assignments and reading, we are turning ourselves into sources of knowledge."

MBAs tell us that faculty members "are very well prepared; they have both the academic and professional experience that makes their teaching valuable. Academic quality is one of the greatest strengths of the school." They warn, however, that the program has a few kinks to iron out. One student warns, "Organization and overall program direction are currently being reassessed and will be better defined and articulated by next year. Once the restructuring has had time to develop, the MBA program will be one of the best buys in the state for the money."

Career and Placement

ASU's MBA program is much too small to support its own Career Services Office; students must use the school's Career Development Center, which serves all ASU enrollees. The office offers a variety of career-prep classes in interviewing, resume writing, networking, cover letters, and job hunting. It also sponsors career fairs and provides online support including links to job boards and major-related resources.

Students recognize the limitations of their situation. They approvingly report, "The school has a good relationship with alumni and companies in nearby Charlotte, the second-largest financial mecca in the U.S.," but concede that that's not always enough. One student writes, "They need to do more to help students get internships and job positions. They do have departments and people that guide us and show us what steps we should take, but they should also have more agreements with some companies for sending students every year for internships." Companies most likely to hire Walker grads include Bank of America, BB&T, Duke Energy, IBM, Lowe's Companies, MDI, Murray Supply, North Carolina State University, Regeneron Pharmaceuticals, Rubbermaid Newell, Wachovia, and Wake Tech.

ADMISSIONS CONTACT: ANNA BASNIGHT, ADMISSIONS CONTACT
ADDRESS: ASU BOX 32068, BOONE, NC 28608-2068 UNITED STATES
PHONE: 828-262-2130 • FAX: 828-262-2709
E-MAIL: BASNIGHTAL@APPSTATE.EDU • WEBSITE: WWW.MBA.APPSTATE.EDU

Student Life and Environment

Unlike most MBA programs, Walker does not support much of an extracurricular scene; with its tiny student body, it can barely populate one club, let alone several. Accordingly, "most people pursue their own personal hobbies during their spare time. Being near the Blue Ridge Parkway and several ski slopes, a lot of people are involved in outdoor activities." As one student puts it, "If you like nature, long winters, and small, close-knit groups of friends, then you should look into ASU. And if you like skiing, you're golden."

On the other hand, "when you want to have some nightlife, there is almost none." That's because "[hometown] Boone is a very small town. It has several movie theaters, including one that is $1.50," but not much else to offer. As one student explains it, "This is a beautiful place, meant for studying." Fortunately, the university community at large (which numbers over 15,000 students) offers up many forms of diversion, including ASU's 18 intercollegiate athletic teams. The university houses several museums and is host to numerous performing-arts series.

When students crave a more urban environment, they road-trip to either Asheville or Winston-Salem; each is just under a two-hour drive from campus. Lexington, NC, is also only two hours away. It's not a huge city, but it is home to arguably the best barbecue in the state (and thus, from a Tar Heel perspective, the best barbecue in the world).

Admissions

Applications to the Walker MBA program are processed by the Admissions Office at the Cratis D. Williams Graduate School. Prospective students must submit GMAT scores, an undergraduate transcript, letters of recommendation, a resume (at least one year of work experience is required), and two essays. An interview is strongly recommended but not required. Applicants must have completed at least one undergraduate class in each of the following areas: calculus, microeconomics, and statistics (summer courses in these subjects are offered for applicants who do not meet this requirement). Students should arrive with a working knowledge of Microsoft Excel®, Word®, and PowerPoint®.

The school uses a formula to set minimum admissions requirements. The formula is (GPA x 200) + GMAT = admissions score; GPA is tallied based only on the final 60 hours of undergraduate course work. An admissions score of at least 1050 is required but does not guarantee admission. Application materials must arrive no later than 3/1; admission is for the fall term only.

ADMISSIONS

Admissions Selectivity Rating	**79**
# of applications received	30
% applicants accepted	67
% acceptees attending	95
Average GMAT	540
Range of GMAT	470–700
Average GPA	3.4
TOEFL required of international students	Yes
Minimum TOEFL (paper/computer) 550/233	
Application fee	$45
Regular application deadline	3/1
Regular notification	3/31
Deferment available	Yes
Maximum length of deferment	1 year
Transfer students accepted	Yes
Transfer application policy	Up to 6 hours of graduate credit may be transferred for equivalent courses completed with at least grade of B.
Non-fall admissions	Yes
Need-blind admissions	Yes

Applicants Also Look At

North Carolina State University, The University of North Carolina at Chapel Hill, The University of North Carolina at Greensboro, Western Carolina University.

ARIZONA STATE UNIVERSITY
W.P. CAREY SCHOOL OF BUSINESS

Academics

Students at Arizona State University's W.P. Carey School of Business say their school is "by far, the best b-school in the Southwest," boasting a range of progressive MBA programs, a strong foothold in the Phoenix business community, and a practical but fun approach to business education. A rising star in the business world, "The school is constantly striving to be recognized as one of the top business schools in the country by recruiting top faculty and remaining selective with student admission." As one student observes, "Each year we are getting more and more professors from distinguished b-schools. For the most part, the faculty is outstanding, and as you get into your specialization courses, they become recognized leaders in their fields." Academically, the school emphasizes case-based and team-oriented learning, maintaining a "good mix of lecture, cases, and project work in classes." ASU professors bring "current practical research, knowledge, and excellent teaching skills into the classroom." A current student attests, "I have taken away a tremendous amount of applicable information (both theoretical and practical) which I am able to apply to my job."

ASU offers a number of MBA options, including full-time and part-time programs, an online program, an executive MBA program, and the "Technology, Science, and Engineering MBA program, which has extremely challenging electives and several attractive certifications available." While the school is traditionally recognized for its excellence in Supply Chain Management and Sports Business, students reassure us that there is a "good variety of courses from all disciplines" at ASU, including many "creative offerings to meet emerging market trends." With a lockstep core program in the first year, ASU is characterized by "challenging course work with very high expectations from students." This intensity is balanced by a lively and fun academic environment, thanks to professors who are "professional and intelligent, but still know how to relate to students and bring humor into classes."

You won't have to worry about red tape and registration headaches at ASU. Unlike many public schools, "ASU's administration team takes many tasks off of the student's plate. They register students for classes, pick up their books and parking passes, and are easily accessible." The popular Dean Keim also draws his share of praises. A student relates, "We have brought in a relatively new dean who has created a culture of excellence and, to be honest, an environment of academic rigor beyond what I expected." An ideal learning environment, the "program is hosted in a high-tech facility, so it gives it a nice progressive feel. We're surrounded by clean rooms and technology labs."

Career and Placement

Students say "the Career Management Center is phenomenal, helping all students with every aspect of finding both an internship and a full-time position upon graduation." Working with the school's extensive alumni network and strong connections in the local business community, "The people in the Career Management Center sincerely want you to succeed, and they will do anything to get you the job/internship that you want."

Thanks to the "economic growth being experienced in Phoenix and the Southwest in general," as well as the school's great regional reputation, it's easy for students to land a plum position in Phoenix. "For supply-chain management students [in particular], the Career Management Center is superb. Recruiters are here nonstop throughout the year looking for both interns and full-time hires. From day one, it is made clear that it is the school's goal to get you a quality job." While Supply Chain students may receive the undivided attention of many recruiters, ASU students do well on the whole. "The class of 2007 had 100 percent

Dr. Gerry Keim, Associate Dean, W. P. Carey MBA
PO Box 874906 Tempe, AZ 85287-4906 United States
Phone: 480-965-3332 • Fax: 480-965-8569
E-mail: wpcareymba@asu.edu • Website: wpcarey.asu.edu/mba

summer internship placement in 2006," and over 95 percent of last year's graduating class was employed within 3 months of graduation.

Student Life and Environment

Students at ASU are as warm and sunny as the desert itself. As one student explains, "Whether it be helping with homework, assisting with interview preparation, or just going out on a Thursday night, you know that somebody will be there for you." While the class size is growing annually, the ASU business program is still fairly community oriented. "On any given night off you will find many of us hanging out together socializing; we are an extremely close-knit community," says a current student. Part-timers admit that "being enrolled in a part-time program leads to little time for an active social life"; even so, these students "still make time for one another."

On campus, there are plenty of opportunities to get involved in the school community. When students need to burn off some stress they head to the intramural fields which are "filled every evening with soccer games, softball games—you name it." On top of that, "There is always something new and interesting happening, including study groups for classes, social events like skydiving and happy hours, networking events with alumni," and "opportunities to hear outstanding speakers (such as the Dutch ambassador to the U.S.)." Aside from school events, hometown Phoenix provides plenty of social and recreational opportunities, and "The weather and beautiful campus make getting up in the morning a lot easier."

Admissions

Admissions vary for the full-time; executive; and technology, science, and engineering programs. Applicants to all programs must submit a completed application form, undergraduate transcripts, and official GMAT scores. In the fall of 2006, full-time entering students had an average GMAT score of 655 and an average undergraduate GPA of 3.46. Students entering the evening program had an average GPA of 3.28 and an average GMAT score of 561. The school admits students who demonstrate a combination of strong academic credentials, leadership potential, work experience, and strong communication skills.

EMPLOYMENT PROFILE

Career Rating	83	Grads Employed by Function	%	Avg. Salary
		Finance/Accounting	25	$76,529
		Marketing/Sales	17	$69,417
		MIS	7	$74,166
		Operations/Production	26	$71,522
		Consulting	11	$63,556
		General Management	9	$58,820
		Other	5	$74,000

Prominent Alumni

Craig Weatherup, chairman, The Pepsi Bottling Group; Steve Marriott, vice president of corporate marketing, Marriott Hotels; Wayne Doran, chairman of the board, Ford Motor Co.; George Schreiber, CEO, SEMCO ENERGY, Inc.; Jack Furst, partner, Hicks, Muse, Tate and Furst, Inc.

FINANCIAL FACTS

Annual tuition (in-state/ out-of-state)	$5,561/$15,825
Fees	$9,500
Cost of books	$2,100
Room & board	$7,960
% of students receiving aid	86
% of first-year students receiving aid	86
% of students receiving loans	83
% of students receiving grants	13
Average award package	$15,622
Average grant	$8,052
Average student loan debt	$31,245

ADMISSIONS

Admissions Selectivity Rating	82
# of applications received	1,108
% applicants accepted	64
% acceptees attending	72
Average GMAT	588
Range of GMAT	540–640
Average GPA	3.08
TOEFL required of international students	Yes
Minimum TOEFL (paper/computer)	600/250
Application fee	$50
Application Deadline/Notification	
Round 1:	11/15 / 1/10
Round 2:	1/13 / 3/10
Round 3:	3/15 / 5/10
Round 4:	5/15 / 6/30
Deferment available	Yes
Maximum length of deferment	1 year
Non-fall admissions	Yes
Need-blind admissions	Yes

Applicants Also Look At

Indiana University—Bloomington, Michigan State University—College of Law, University of Arizona, University of California, Los Angeles (UCLA), University of Maryland, University of Southern California, The University of Texas at Austin.

AUBURN UNIVERSITY
COLLEGE OF BUSINESS

GENERAL INFORMATION
Type of school	Public
Environment	Town
Academic calendar	Semester

SURVEY SAYS . . .
Happy students
Smart classrooms
Solid preparation in:
Teamwork

STUDENTS
Enrollment of parent institution	23,547
Enrollment of business school	375
% male/female	65/35
% out-of-state	63
% part-time	80
% minorities	7
% international	32
Average age at entry	26
Average years work experience at entry	4

ACADEMICS
Academic Experience Rating	**88**
Student/faculty ratio	29:1
Profs interesting rating	94
Profs accessible rating	79
% female faculty	20
% minority faculty	5

Joint Degrees
Dual degree program with industrial and systems engineering 2.5 years. Other dual-degree options available on case-by-case basis with approval of AU Graduate School.

Prominent Alumni
Mohamed Mansour, CEO, Mansour Group; Joanne P. McCallie, head coach, Michigan State University women's basketball; Wendell Starke, past president, INVESCO.

Academics

Students seeking an MBA from Auburn University can follow one of three curriculum models: the traditional on-campus model; the new, increasingly popular distance model, called the Outreach Program, which allows students to fulfill most of the obligations toward their degrees from the comfort of their own homes (students must attend one five-day case analysis during their final fall semester, but otherwise never need to visit campus); and the Executive MBA program (EMBA), which requires five one-week residencies over a two-year period, with the larger portion of instruction coming via Internet and DVD technologies. The distance program offers concentrations in finance, health care administration, human resource development, management information systems, technology management, marketing, and production/operations management. The full-time program offers all of these, plus concentrations in agribusiness, economic development, and sports management. The EMBA offers specializations in technology management and health care administration.

Full-time students warn that "it can be too much of a course load in the first semester, an absolute killer!" However, they appreciate how "everything is organized" so that "students take the same classes, [meaning that] getting the right courses is not a problem," and also recognize other benefits of this curricular approach; one student explains, "This degree has taught me as much about life as it did business. You get to see the synergistic effect of these lessons when you reach the end of the curriculum." The workload and the design of the program "encourage us to work as a team, and participate in class. This provides us an opportunity to realize what we are strong at, and what we are not so strong at." One shortcoming of the program is that "the different course offerings at Auburn are limited. Currently, Auburn is working toward expanding the concentrations in which MBA students can focus."

Students tell us that "the atmosphere is the best aspect of Auburn. The academics are great and the faculty and administration are excellent, but that's just a part of . . . the MBA program at Auburn University. Auburn will prepare you inside and outside of the classroom to be successful. [It's] a choice that you'll never regret." Another student agrees, "The courses have been great, but the . . . extra training and development in things such as leadership and impression management have really made the program stand out." The program is challenging, but an administration that "is extremely helpful and always available to help with questions and problems" and professors who "treat us with respect and . . . as professionals" help students shoulder the load.

Career and Placement

Auburn's Careers Services Office handles career counseling and recruitment services for MBAs. The office provides one-on-one counseling, seminars, workshops, and a career library; it also organizes career expos and on-campus recruiting events. Students approve, telling us that "over a hundred companies recruit on campus every semester" and touting "a huge alumni base with which to network. The alumni are a great strength of this school." Employers who often hire Auburn MBAs include AmSouth Bank, Colonial Bank, Home Depot, Total Systems, and Wal-Mart.

Mr. J. Don Flowers, Director MBA Admissions and Operations
415 West Magnolia Ave., Suite 503, Lowder Business Building Auburn U., AL 36849 U.S.
Phone: 334-844-4060 • Fax: 334-844-2964
E-mail: mbadmis@auburn.edu • Website: www.mba.business.auburn.edu

Student Life and Environment

"There is more to Auburn than an MBA program," students at this large, southern university remind us. "The school has quality sports teams and multitudes of other activities that allow you to really enjoy your time here." The town of Auburn itself is a source of pride and comfort for many MBAs; "There isn't a better college town in the country," writes a typical student, pointing out that "football season is always exciting and game days present a great tailgating atmosphere. The nightlife is good as well, with a good number of bars close to campus." With its "smaller-town atmosphere with plenty of things to do and people to meet," Auburn "can provide something to appeal to everybody," but especially to those who "like sweet tea, chicken fingers, and football."

Auburn's full-time MBA program "offers numerous opportunities for students to meet people and network. In addition to social events, the MBA program has an established mentor program that pairs first-year students with second-year students." Students note that "the way the program is structured, you can't help but know everyone in the on-campus MBA program, which creates a cohesive group that can be drawn on for help." Accordingly, MBA students note that they "all stick together and are willing to help each other out with studying and doing projects. Nobody is going to stab you in the back to get a better grade. We try to lift each other up."

Auburn MBAs evince "Southern hospitality in full force" by not only "tailgating, playing intramurals, and barhopping together" but also by "getting very involved in the community through volunteer organizations." It's "a very diverse group with different backgrounds. Some are married with children; some are international; some are businesspeople; some are engineering; some have years of work experience; some came straight from undergrad. Anyone of any age could fit in at Auburn because the students are so diverse."

Admissions

All applicants to the Auburn MBA program must submit official transcripts for all post-secondary academic work, an official GMAT score report, three letters of recommendation, a completed application to the graduate school, and a completed application to the MBA program, including a signed copy of the MBA Code of Ethics and Responsibilities. Work experience is encouraged, but a personal interview is required. International students whose first language is not English must also submit TOEFL scores. Undergraduate-level competency in accounting, calculus, economics, finance, management, marketing, and statistics are all prerequisites to starting the Auburn MBA program. Students lacking appropriate undergraduate credentials may purchase the corresponding courses on CD, and must subsequently pass a competency exam in each course prior to commencing work on the MBA. In an effort to boost the population of underrepresented students, Auburn makes recruiting trips to minority campuses.

FINANCIAL FACTS

Annual tuition (in-state/ out-of-state)	$5,250/$15,750
Fees	$430
Cost of books	$1,200
Room & board (off-campus)	$10,746
% of students receiving aid	95
% of first-year students receiving aid	81
% of students receiving grants	30
Average award package	$6,115
Average grant	$1,200
Average student loan debt	$14,665

ADMISSIONS

Admissions Selectivity Rating	89
# of applications received	131
% applicants accepted	45
% acceptees attending	61
Average GMAT	619
Range of GMAT	580–640
Average GPA	3.34
TOEFL required of international students	Yes
Minimum TOEFL (paper/computer)	550/213
Application fee	$25
International application fee	$50
Regular application deadline	3/1
Deferment available	Yes
Maximum length of deferment	1 year
Transfer students accepted	Yes
Transfer application policy	
AACSB schools only. Case-by-case basis and accepted in lieu of elective courses only. Limit of 12 credit hours.	
Need-blind admissions	Yes

EMPLOYMENT PROFILE

Career Rating	67	Grads Employed by Function	%	Avg. Salary
Primary Source of Full-time Job Acceptances		Finance/Accounting	21	$49,840
School-facilitated activities	15 (63%)	Marketing/Sales	12	$52,000
Graduate-facilitated activities	9 (38%)	MIS	17	$57,000
Average base starting salary	$56,488	Operations/Production	17	$57,750
Percent employed	33	Consulting	17	$54,500
		General Management	12	$77,167
		Other	4	$42,000

AUBURN UNIVERSITY—MONTGOMERY
SCHOOL OF BUSINESS

GENERAL INFORMATION
Type of school	Public
Environment	City

SURVEY SAYS . . .
Cutting-edge classes
Happy students
Solid preparation in:
General management
Teamwork
Communication/interpersonal skills
Presentation skills

STUDENTS
Enrollment of parent institution	5,079
Enrollment of business school	220
Average age at entry	28

ACADEMICS
Academic Experience Rating	**67**
Student/faculty ratio	20:1
Profs interesting rating	74
Profs accessible rating	66
% female faculty	25
% minority faculty	10

FINANCIAL FACTS
Annual tuition (in-state)	$180 per credit hour
Annual tuition (out-of-state)	$540 per credit hour
Cost of books	$1,500
% of students receiving aid	60
% of first-year students receiving aid	65
% of students receiving loans	45
% of students receiving grants	15
Average award package	$14,750
Average grant	$3,000

Academics

The AACSB-accredited MBA program at Auburn University—Montgomery is designed for part-time students; in fact, any student wishing to exceed a course load of nine hours per semester must first receive approval from the dean of the School of Business. Students in this program appreciate how "course offerings cater to students' work schedules" by meeting during convenient evening hours.

The MBA program at AUM is divided into three parts. The first is called the Basic Program, consisting of 11 half-term courses covering business concepts typically taught at the undergraduate level (accounting, management, marketing, business law, microeconomics, macroeconomics, operations management, statistics, MIS, and finance). Students who can demonstrate sufficient background in these areas may petition to be exempted from some or all of these requirements. The second part of the program is the Business Core, a 7-course set of classes covering such integrative concepts as managerial applications of accounting information and synergistic organizational strategy (the latter is a capstone course), as well as such essential functions as marketing, data analysis, and managing personnel. The program concludes with either three or four electives, depending on whether the student chooses a general MBA or a specialization. Specializations are offered in contract management, economics, finance, global business management, information systems, management of information technology, management, and marketing.

AUM MBAs brag that "the teachers are great and enjoy what they do," although some feel that some classes rely too heavily on lectures and that "professors could try to involve students more in the classroom and encourage more interaction." Many also agree that the program "would benefit from more offerings in high-tech and computer-related fields." Comprehensive exit exams are required of all students who complete the program with a GPA below 3.25. Comprehensive exams may be taken no more than three times.

Career and Placement

The Career Development Center (CDC) at AUM serves all university students and alumni. The office maintains a library of career-related material, including documents tracking salary and hiring trends around the region, state, country, and world. Career counseling services are available, as are job fairs, seminars, and workshops in interviewing, job hunting, and resume and cover-letter writing. Students agree that the CDC's services are adequate, though on many students' wish lists are "better career advice and job placement" options. The office arranges internships and recruiting events for qualifying MBA students.

Student Life and Environment

AUM MBAs are typically "commuters who attend mostly for education and do not contribute much to the university outside of classes." There are "lots of military" here as well as a large number of international students. Most students "are in their 20s or 30s and hold full-time jobs. Many have spouses and children" who take up what little free time they have. As a result, "social life isn't huge here, but that's great; there are no distractions!" notes one student. International students occasionally recreate through "a club called ISA (International Students Association), which helps new foreign students get together and socialize as well as share their culture with others, through banquets."

SHARON JONES, ADMISSION SPECIALIST
PO BOX 244023 MONTGOMERY, AL 36124 UNITED STATES
PHONE: 334-244-3623 • FAX: 334-244-3927
E-MAIL: VJONES1@MAIL.AUM.EDU • WEBSITE: WWW.AUM.EDU

ADMISSIONS	
Admissions Selectivity Rating	**66**
# of applications received	82
% applicants accepted	87
% acceptees attending	100
Average GMAT	500
Average GPA	2.92
TOEFL required of international students	Yes
Minimum TOEFL (paper)	500
Application fee	$25
Regular application deadline	Rolling
Regular notification	Rolling
Non-fall admissions	Yes
Need-blind admissions	Yes

Montgomery is a midsize southern city well known for its integral part in the civil rights movement. The population of the city is about evenly split between whites and blacks, with small Hispanic, Native American, and Asian populations accounting for a small minority. The city is home to the Alabama Shakespeare Festival, a year-round enterprise that mounts a dozen or more productions and draws over 300,000 visitors annually. Another major attraction is the minor-league baseball team, Montgomery Biscuits, the AA affiliate of the Tampa Bay Devil Rays. And no Montgomery summer is complete without City Stages, a three-day outdoor music festival that in recent years has attracted such headliners as Ralph Stanley, P-Funk, Al Green, Kid Rock, Jurassic 5, and Shelby Lynne. The all-day event closes a good portion of the downtown area to traffic.

Admissions

Applicants to the AUM MBA program must submit official transcripts for all previous postsecondary academic work, official GMAT score reports, and a completed application form. The screening committee may request an interview, typically in the case of borderline candidates; otherwise, interviews are not required. The admissions committee applies an undisclosed mathematical formula to applicants' GPA and GMAT, using the formula results and other considerations in reaching its decision. International applicants must meet all of the above requirements and must also provide certified English translations of any academic transcripts not in English and a course-by-course evaluation of undergraduate work "by a recognized, expert service in the field of foreign credential evaluations and international admissions." Applicants whose first language is not English must submit TOEFL scores. Candidates may be admitted conditionally pending completion of prerequisite undergraduate-level classes in business.

EMPLOYMENT PROFILE	
Career Rating	**61**

AUGUSTA STATE UNIVERSITY
COLLEGE OF BUSINESS ADMINISTRATION

Academics

Convenience and cost are the two main reasons students cite for choosing the MBA program at Augusta State University. Many students here tell us that they attended the school as undergraduates and saw no reason to leave.

At ASU's MBA program, "Personal attention and career development are a given. Students have to actively work at not being known by the administration and faculty of the Business School." Service is key; despite its relatively small MBA enrollment, "ASU has a dedicated educational professional to usher graduate students through the program." One student notes, "The school is the perfect size. It is small enough to allow for more personal relations between the student and the teacher but is big enough to enjoy all the aspects of attending a college." A "low teacher/student ratio" and "professors who are approachable and willing to help students" are among the other perks of attending. ASU works hard to accommodate its students' schedules by offering "almost every needed subject in the program" during the fall and spring semesters.

MBAs at ASU must complete a 12-course sequence that includes 2 electives and 10 required courses in human resources management, marketing, finance, accounting, economics, production management, ethics, communications, management information systems, business research methods, and an integrating course in strategic management. Students tell us that the school has traditionally been recognized for strengths for economics, finance, and accounting, as well as in "certain quantitative-based courses like market research." In addition, ASU has taken steps in order to better prepare the students for information-based knowledge. Those steps include "recently naming an information technology professor to chair the program."

Career and Placement

The ASU Career Center serves all undergraduates and graduate students at the university. Services are geared primarily toward undergraduates, in part because the school's graduate divisions are so small and in part because many graduate students—including many MBAs—attend while continuing in jobs they intend to keep post-graduation. The office sponsors an annual Career Fair and offers the standard battery of career services: job posting, counseling, mock interviews, on-campus recruiting, and more.

Student Life and Environment

Most ASU MBAs "work full-time during the day and attend classes at night," which means they have limited time to devote to extracurricular activities. Students tell us that "many professors acknowledge the average students' work/demand schedule and design their courses to allow students to catch up on the weekends." MBAs also appreciate how the small-school environment creates "the opportunity to get to know the students and faculty on a greater than superficial level," an opportunity students take advantage of by "congregating in a small centralized area of the building before classes." With so many chances to bond with peers and professors, it's no wonder students tell us that "the school feels like a family."

Full-time students—consisting primarily of international students and undergraduates proceeding directly from their BA program to the MBA—tell us that "there is an active campus life at ASU even though few students actually live on campus. There are so many groups to be involved with and [there are] always activities going on. The school spirit at ASU is so alive, and the students there really love their campus. Most of the MBA students are graduates of ASU, so I believe they feel the same as well." Clubs "are very active on campus." Phi Beta Lambda is one of the major ones for business students.

MIYOKO JACKSON, DEGREE PROGRAM SPECIALIST, COLLEGE OF BUSINESS ADMINISTRATION
MBA OFFICE, 2500 WALTON WAY AUGUSTA, GA 30904-2200 U.S.
PHONE: 706-737-1565 • FAX: 706-667-4064
E-MAIL: MBAINFO@AUG.EDU • WEBSITE: WWW.AUG.EDU/COBA

MBAs tell us that the school has worked hard to beautify and improve this campus, which, they note, "was an arsenal during the Civil War. The school has done a great job of keeping that heritage intact" while simultaneously adding such assets as a " beautiful new student center" that "provides study areas, gym equipment, billiards, and a host of other activities for students that help to release school stress." Commuters warn that "parking is limited during morning hours, but afternoon and evening parking is very good."

The ASU student body is "broadly diverse in age, occupation, race, and educational background, but [they are] uniformly goal oriented, serious, and competitive, [while also] capable or working in a team environment." Students seem to appreciate this diversity. One student says, "I have come in contact with people from many different cultures, and it gives me a different outlook on business." Even though there are "so many international students," most "seem to be regular people with careers who have felt a need to improve themselves."

Admissions

Applicants to the Hull School of Business MBA program must submit all of the following: official transcripts for all undergraduate and graduate work; an official score report for the GMAT (test score can be no more than 5 years old); and a completed application form. In addition, international students whose first language is not English must submit an official score for the TOEFL and a financial responsibility statement. International transcripts must be submitted via Educational Credential Evaluators, Inc., a company that matches international course work to its American equivalent. The Admissions Committee looks for students with significant and diverse work experience, varied educational backgrounds, and sound academic achievement. Incoming students must be able to run word processing, spreadsheet, and database programs.

ADMISSIONS	
Admissions Selectivity Rating	**77**
# of applications received	33
% applicants accepted	58
% acceptees attending	79
Average GMAT	520
Range of GMAT	450–590
Average GPA	3.12
TOEFL required of international students	Yes
Minimum TOEFL (paper/computer)	550/213
Application fee	$20
Regular application deadline	Rolling
Regular notification	Rolling
Deferment available	Yes
Maximum length of deferment	1 year
Transfer students accepted	Yes
Transfer application policy Must meet regular MBA admission standards. Up to 9 semester credit hours may be accepted for transfer.	
Non-fall admissions	Yes

BABSON COLLEGE
F. W. OLIN GRADUATE SCHOOL OF BUSINESS

Academics

Students tell us that Babson College's F.W. Olin Graduate School of Business has "an excellent reputation for entrepreneurship," meaning that it "is 100 percent focused on the number-one trend in business today." Some, in fact, are convinced that this is "the best entrepreneurship program in the United States," and can point to top rankings in entrepreneurial business management and opportunity identification and assessment to back their opinions.

Babson's highly integrated curriculum "is incredibly rigorous. . . . None of the academic cases focuses on any one discipline. Instead, we look at a business case from many perspectives, just as a businessperson must in the 'real world.' A strategy problem is not simply a strategy problem. It has marketing, operational, organizational, and financial implications (among others) as well." One student adds, "Babson is known for developing the full thinker. The teaching methods and courses encourage creative thinking and idea generation. The professors and students, the clubs and the environment all weave together to support a balanced education focused on integrated business management from finances to leadership, both inside and outside of the classroom." This approach makes Babson "a good program for general management" as well as for entrepreneurship. Students also praise Babson's curriculum in technology management and tell us that "the school is making significant ground in areas that support entrepreneurship, such as the private equity and venture capital arenas."

Babson offers students a variety of program options. Full-time students may choose from a traditional 2-year program or an intensive 1-year program. Part-timers may choose from a traditional evening program and a fast-track, blended, partially online program. Students in all programs benefit from a faculty "as good as any business school in the world. Their rankings reflect this, and in my experience, their reputation is well deserved. The Babson faculty is comprised of many professors who left top-10 business schools to teach in a more innovative, leading-edge curriculum. They also tend to be leading practitioners within their fields."

Career and Placement

Babson's Center for Career Development "has made great progress in the last 2 years" and "has improved tremendously. It has taken a 'product management' approach, where the students are the product." One student notes, "The CCD has also gone way out of its way to get to know us. At the end of our first semester, the CCD had champagne and hors d'oeuvres for each BCAP group as we completed our final presentation. CCD has also undergone massive quantitative analysis of the market as it applies to Babson students. The results from this analysis and the new system have dramatically improved the internship/employment stats." Another adds, "While there are challenges in bringing in diverse employers, the companies visiting the school are of exceptional quality and provide real opportunities after graduation for those not starting their own businesses."

Employers who most frequently hire Babson MBAs include: Fidelity Investments, EMC Corporation, Adventis, Bose, Boston Scientific Corporation, IBM, Liberty Mutual Group, Merrill Lynch, Our Group, PricewaterhouseCoopers, Staples, Estee Lauder, General Electric Company, Deloitte Touche Tohmatsu, Proctor & Gamble, Morgan Stanley, and Dunkin' Brands.

Student Life and Environment

Babson offers graduate business students a modern campus at which "facilities are generally exceptionally well maintained." Students attend class in "modern classrooms" and

DENNIS NATIONS, DIRECTOR OF GRADUATE ADMISSIONS
OLIN HALL BABSON PARK (WELLESLEY), MA 02457-0310 UNITED STATES
PHONE: 781-239-5591 • FAX: 781-239-4194
E-MAIL: MBAADMISSION@BABSON.EDU • WEBSITE: WWW.BABSON.EDU/MBA

"a clean and tidy environment, with wireless network access on most of the campus." The library "seems to have everything you need to do research and also offers free tutorials on important skills, such as b-plan writing, etc." As one student sums up, "Everything I need is at my fingertips, and all staff are very responsive. Computers, IT support, librarians, on-site cafes, on and on. It really is a privilege to attend here!" All that support is especially welcome given that "the course load is tough. We need to study long hours before class. It is overwhelming, and the idea of the school is to overwhelm students and make them learn things the hard way."

The Babson campus "is usually full of activity ranging from panel events, social gatherings, recruiting, to general student interaction." The "centralized structure of graduate activities lends itself to a high degree of interaction among MBA students," especially among full-time students, who also take advantage of "two campus bars—one graduate, one for undergrads—provide a nice outlet to unwind after class." One student in the 2-year full-time program describes the experience as "very social. In fact, I'm headed out in a few to see a fellow student's band play in Boston. There will be at least 20 other MBAs attending. Should be a blast! I love it here. Wish it was 3 years . . . ha!" The school works hard to acknowledge that students have lives beyond the classroom. One MBA reports, "Babson hosts a friends and family day with food and different activities. Babson also offers classes in which spouses can participate with very little cost. Movies are shown, and students and student's family are welcome."

Admissions

Applicants to Babson MBA programs must submit the following materials: official transcripts covering undergraduate work; an official GMAT score report; a resume or curriculum vitae (2 years of full-time post-undergraduate work experience is required); a completed application form; and personal essays. Candidates whose native language is other than English and who have not earned a degree in the United States, United Kingdom, Canada, Australia, or New Zealand must also submit: an official TOEFL iBT score report; and, official English translation and interpretation of all transcripts. Babson contacts all candidates to schedule an admissions interview.

FINANCIAL FACTS

Annual tuition	$35,110
Cost of books	$2,270
Room & board (on-campus)	$18,580
% of students receiving aid	66
% of first-year students receiving aid	58
% of students receiving loans	51
% of students receiving grants	46
Average award package	$19,890
Average grant	$16,254
Average student loan debt	$58,903

ADMISSIONS

Admissions Selectivity Rating	**86**
# of applications received	580
% applicants accepted	58
% acceptees attending	50
Average GMAT	630
Range of GMAT	600–680
Average GPA	3.06
TOEFL required of international students	Yes
Minimum TOEFL (paper/computer)	600/250
Application fee	$100
Application Deadline/Notification	
Round 1:	11/15 / 1/15
Round 2:	1/15 / 3/30
Round 3:	3/15 / 4/30
Round 4:	4/15 / 5/15
Deferment available	Yes
Maximum length of deferment	1 year
Transfer students accepted	Yes
Transfer application policy	
We accept transfer credit from an AACSB-accredited programs into our evening MBA program.	
Non-fall admissions	Yes
Need-blind admissions	Yes

Applicants Also Look At

Boston College, Boston University, Dartmouth College, Harvard University, Massachusetts Institute of Technology, New York University, Northwestern University.

EMPLOYMENT PROFILE				
Career Rating	**93**	**Grads Employed by Function**	**%**	**Avg. Salary**
Primary Source of Full-time Job Acceptances		Finance/Accounting	16	$90,375
School-facilitated activities	45%	Human Resources	2	$65,000
Graduate-facilitated activities	55%	Marketing/Sales	20	$77,938
Percent employed	94	MIS	2	$84,000
		Operations/Production	4	$67,400
		Consulting	11	$96,500
		Entrepreneurship	23	$66,670
		General Management	17	$88,636
		Other	1	$80,000
		Nonprofit	4	$65,800

BARRY UNIVERSITY
ANDREAS SCHOOL OF BUSINESS

GENERAL INFORMATION
Type of school	Private
Affiliation	Roman Catholic
Academic calendar	All year

SURVEY SAYS . . .
Friendly students
Good peer network
Happy students
Solid preparation in:
Teamwork
Communication/interpersonal skills
Presentation skills
Doing business in a global economy

STUDENTS
Enrollment of parent institution	9,324
Enrollment of business school	114
% male/female	46/54
% part-time	72
% minorities	78
% international	51

ACADEMICS
Academic Experience Rating	**87**
Student/faculty ratio	9:1
Profs interesting rating	91
Profs accessible rating	77
% female faculty	30
% minority faculty	48

Joint Degrees
MBA/Master of Science (human resources development) 60 credits, MBA/Master of Science (sports management) 57 credits, MBA/Master of Science (nursing)69 credits, MBA/Doctor of Podiatric Medicine 205 credits.

Prominent Alumni
Gary Spulak, president, Embraer Aircraft of North America; Gregory Greene, senior vice president, strategy, Ryder Systems; John Primeau, president, Valley Bank; Arthur Snyder, president, Indiana Institute of Technology; Craig Lemasters, president and CEO, Assurant Solutions.

Academics

Besides offering all of the advantages of a small, private school, the Andreas School of Business at Barry University manages to offer a surprising number of custom-tailored options to meet the needs and goals of its student body. Part-timers, who make up about two-thirds of the student body here, can choose between evening classes (on both the main campus and the West Broward campus) or the Saturday MBA program. Full-time students can complete their program of study at the main campus. All students can opt for dual degrees in Human Resource Development, Nursing, Podiatry, and Sports Management: The last is an especially popular option, cited by a number of MBAs as their primary reason for choosing Barry. Besides a general MBA, Andreas also offers a full complement of areas of specialization, with options including accounting, e-commerce, finance, health services administration, international business, management, MIS, and marketing. Besides the MBA, the School of Business also offers a Master of Science in Accounting (MSA) and a Master of Science in Management (MSM).

All told, Barry provides choices that are typically available only at larger universities. Yet this program is relatively pint-size, to the great advantage of its MBAs. One such MBA explains, "Because the business school is small, you get the benefit of personalized attention. The administrators and class coordinators know your name, and professors can always make time for you to visit them." Another agrees, "No other school would give you such personal attention. Several of my classes have had fewer than 10 students, and the professor tailors the material to fit our schedules and individual ambitions. And because there's such close contact, it's easy to build relationships with professors. I even was able to collaborate with one professor on writing a business case that will appear in a textbook supplement."

Andreas classes "are designed to challenge students in several ways. One is the explanation of theories; others include the implementation of practical assignments or case studies." In keeping with the school's Catholic worldview, many courses "promote social responsibility." The school's religious affiliation also helps it attract international students, whose presence "truly prepares students for working with many different types of people in many different contexts."

Career and Placement

The School of Business Career Resource & Alumni Relations Center maintains a close working relationship with local, state, and national companies. One student in the past indicated, "While job placement efforts could certainly be improved, I, like most Barry MBAs, have a job already, so I'm not really worried about the post-graduation job hunt, and that might be why Barry doesn't bring more companies to campus and be more aggressive in job placement. But for those students who do need to find work after school, Barry isn't equipped to be the kind of resource they really need." Additionally, international students are among those who feel most strongly that these services must be improved. However, since then, the school has reported that during the 2005 school year the center increased its placement by 27.6 percent along with an accompanying wage increase. The Career Resource Center has also partnered with the following firms and companies: Burger King Corporation, Microsoft Latin America, Franklin Templeton, KPMG International, FBI, JM Family Enterprises, Robert Half International, Northwestern Mutual, Morgan Stanley, and MTV Networks Latin America.

Jose J. Poza Jr., Assistant Dean for Marketing
11300 Northeast Second Avenue Miami Shores, FL 33161 United States
Phone: 305-899-3535 • Fax: 305-892-6412
E-mail: jpoza@mail.barry.edu • Website: www.barry.edu/business

Student Life and Environment

For MBA students, Barry is "mostly a commuter school, so most MBA students are on campus in the evenings or weekends. As a result, there is not much extracurricular life. Not that that's necessarily a bad thing; as one student observes, "Barry is tranquil and laid-back, the ideal place for a person who would get overwhelmed by a high-stress, backstabbing MBA program. The MBA school is also made for people already working full-time." The school offers "limited clubs" and didn't even have a graduate business association until students took the initiative to form one. Those who truly desire a higher level of involvement can find it here, though. One student explains, "I have made myself get involved. I am a former student-athlete, currently a residence assistant as well as a graduate assistant. So my life has been great here. There is potential for everyone if you look for it."

"There is a vast cultural diversity within the university" and the MBA program at Barry. "It is delightful to see the peace that exists among classmates." Students "are very willing to help one another. There are always study groups, and in every class all students have each others' phone numbers, e-mails, etc. so that we can discuss the class when we need to." One MBA notes, "Learning in a cohort group has been the number one reason my MBA experience at Barry has been so successful. We've bonded as classmates, collaborated on projects, and built friendships that will extend beyond our MBA studies. In general, Barry MBA students are culturally diverse, unfailingly nice, and, since most work full-time while going to school, eager to use their degree to move up the career ladder."

Barry is located in Miami Shores, a central location offering easy access to the entire Miami metropolitan area. The area surrounding the campus offers access to the beach, and plenty of shopping, dining, and housing.

Admissions

The Admissions Committee at Barry University School of Business looks closely at the following components of the application: undergraduate GPA; GMAT scores (in lieu of the GMAT, we also accept the GRE, LSAT, or the MCAT); quality of undergraduate curriculum; personal essay; resume; two letters of reference supporting the resume; and TOEFL scores (for non-native English speakers). The GMAT requirement may be waived for applicants with substantial managerial experience. All of the following are prerequisites to MBA study: 6 credit hours of introductory accounting; 6 credit hours of macro and microeconomics; 3 credit hours of algebra or precalculus; 3 credit hours of statistics; 3 credit hours of introductory computer skills; 3 credit hours of operations management; and 3 credit hours of marketing. Students may demonstrate competency in any of these areas through undergraduate work or, in some cases, CLEP testing.

FINANCIAL FACTS

Annual tuition	$26,100
Cost of books	$1,500
Room & board (on-campus)	$13,000
% of students receiving aid	100
% of first-year students receiving aid	52
% of students receiving loans	41
% of students receiving grants	48
Average award package	$15,731
Average grant	$6,225

ADMISSIONS

Admissions Selectivity Rating	79
# of applications received	154
% applicants accepted	36
% acceptees attending	85
Average GMAT	469
Range of GMAT	400–640
Average GPA	3.08
TOEFL required of international students	Yes
Minimum TOEFL (paper/computer)	550/213
Application fee	$30
Regular application deadline	Rolling
Regular notification	Rolling
Deferment available	Yes
Maximum length of deferment	1 year
Transfer students accepted	Yes
Transfer application policy Up to 6 transfer credits.	
Non-fall admissions	Yes

Applicants Also Look At
Florida Atlantic University, Florida International University, Nova Southeastern University, University of Miami.

EMPLOYMENT PROFILE

Career Rating	61	Grads Employed by Function	%	Avg. Salary
Primary Source of Full-time Job Acceptances		Finance/Accounting	32	NR
School-facilitated activities	22 (42%)	Human Resources	9	NR
Graduate-facilitated activities	3 (14%)	Marketing/Sales	9	NR
Unknown	32 (62%)	MIS	5	NR
Percent employed	9	Operations/Production	9	NR
		General Management	18	NR
		Other	18	NR

BAYLOR UNIVERSITY
HANKAMER SCHOOL OF BUSINESS

GENERAL INFORMATION
Type of school	Private
Affiliation	Baptist
Environment	City
Academic calendar	Semester

SURVEY SAYS . . .
Friendly students
Good peer network
Smart classrooms
Solid preparation in:
Teamwork
Communication/interpersonal skills
Presentation skills

STUDENTS
Enrollment of parent institution	14,040
Enrollment of business school	88
% male/female	70/30
% minorities	9
% international	36
Average age at entry	26
Average years work experience at entry	3

ACADEMICS
Academic Experience Rating	**85**
Student/faculty ratio	14:1
Profs interesting rating	86
Profs accessible rating	88
% female faculty	20
% minority faculty	2

Joint Degrees
MBA/MSIS 2 years, MBA/Master of Engineering 3 years, MBA/MS (computer science) 3 years, JD/MBA 4 years, JD/MTax 4 years.

FINANCIAL FACTS
Annual tuition	$22,220
Fees	$2,857
Cost of books	$8,000
Room & board	$10,000
% of students receiving aid	80
% of first-year students receiving aid	80

Academics

A "Christian school with a strong emphasis on ethics," the Hankamer School of Business at Baylor University offers "high standards, a great reputation, and an intimate learning environment" to its small, full-time student population. Students tell us the program "strikes a perfect balance between holding students accountable for work and providing resources and mentoring for those who need a little extra assistance."

The Baylor MBA can be completed in 16 to 21 months, a plus for managers on the go. The curriculum is fully integrated "to tie everything together nicely" with a focus on "strong communication skills and management preparation." Study includes a series of 5-week, cross-disciplinary courses covering accounting, finance, statistics, marketing, information systems, and strategy; these classes are spread out over three semesters. The program also includes four semester-long core courses covering operations management, microeconomics, communications management, and organizational behavior. Students supplement the core with one elective during each of the three lockstep semesters. All students complete either a summer internship or a summer abroad as part of the program. The program also includes the Focus Firm practicum, a project in which students assess a real-life business problem and propose solutions. One MBA enjoyed the fact that "in the fall of 2006, students worked with executives at Hewlett-Packard to address core problems within the company."

The size of the program and the lockstep curriculum combine to create an "intimate environment where everyone knows everyone and we can build great relationships and friendships that I hope last a lifetime," says one MBA. Professors contribute to this environment; they "are readily available for one-on-one sessions during office hours and by appointment. . . . I am thoroughly impressed by the level of attention to detail that the staff and professors exert to provide us with a superb education," says a first-year student. The program also boasts "amazing facilities" and "an administration that works hard at making sure we have a great business school." Still another benefit of a Baylor MBA: "Great alumni networking in Texas to use for future jobs."

Career and Placement

Baylor employs two full-time career placement professionals to work exclusively with the school's approximately 90 MBA students as well as with alumni. Students tell us that "Career Services has picked up the pace a lot this year. You almost have to try to avoid them." Some still grumble that "placement rates for graduates are low" as are the "campus recruiting opportunities."

Employers who most frequently hire Baylor MBAs include: Accenture, Allergan, American Express, Annuity Board of the Southern Baptist Convention, Anadarko Petroleum, Bank One, Bearing Point, Capgemini, Comerica, Community Bank and Trust, ConocoPhillips Company, Countrywide, Deloitte Touche Tohmatsu, Echostar Communications, Ernst & Young, ExxonMobil, The Gallup Organization, Goldman Sachs, IBM, Intecap, the IRS, Johnson & Johnson, JPMorgan Chase, KPMG International, Kraft Foods, Merck, Perot Systems, PricewaterhouseCoopers, Protiviti, Q Investments, RSM McGladrey, Shell Oil, Southwest Airlines, Sprint, Steak 'n Shake Operations, UBS Financial Services, Verizon Wireless, Wal-Mart, and Zale Corporation.

Student Life and Environment

"The MBA class is very social" at Hankamer, where students "work hard together and play in our spare time." "Everyone in the MBA program is very close" "due to the small number of students in classes. Everyone knows everyone else" and "is willing and able

LAURIE WILSON, DIRECTOR, GRADUATE BUSINESS DEGREE PROGRAMS
ONE BEAR PLACE #98013, 1311 SOUTH FIFTH STREET WACO, TX 76798-8013 UNITED STATES
PHONE: 254-710-3718 • FAX: 254-710-1066
E-MAIL: MBA_INFO@BAYLOR.EDU • WEBSITE: WWW.BAYLOR.EDU/MBA

to help one another and work together." "Almost all students work out in the student center after class, and there are always study groups and tutoring if you want to join them." Unsurprisingly, at this Christian university, "Religious resources are outstanding." Perhaps more surprising is the fact that "if a student wants a nightlife, that is also available." One student sums up, "School life is study hard and play hard. . . . We have an excellent wireless network through the entire campus. The health care facilities are top notch. Eateries are nice. Quality of life is good. Isn't life what we make of it anyway? We make it enjoyable here!"

Baylor's "easygoing" but "ambitious" MBAs "come from diverse backgrounds with different levels and backgrounds of experiences. Each of us has something excellent to contribute to our program. During team projects, we diligently engage in the activities to produce results. We respect one another," and "Each of us listens to our individual perspectives. We have learned and continue to learn to collaborate and build good relationships." Students tend to be "mostly recent undergraduates." The student body is ethnically diverse "in regards to international students."

Admissions

Those seeking admission to the Hankamer School must submit the following materials: a completed application (online application preferred); two letters of recommendation from individuals who know you professionally and can assess your skills and potential; official undergraduate transcripts (international students who attended a non-English-speaking school must provide professionally translated and interpreted academic records); a GMAT score report; a current resume; and personal essays detailing qualifications, experiences, and objectives in pursuing a Hankamer MBA. International students whose first language is not English must also submit a score report for the TOEFL (minimum score: 600, paper-based test; 250, computer-based test; or 100, Internet-based test). Hankamer processes applications on a rolling basis; candidates are notified of their admission status as soon as a decision is made.

ADMISSIONS

Admissions Selectivity Rating	**83**
# of applications received	118
% applicants accepted	66
% acceptees attending	69
Average GMAT	604
Range of GMAT	530–690
Average GPA	3.37
TOEFL required of international students	Yes
Minimum TOEFL (paper/computer)	600/250
Application fee	$50
Regular application deadline	6/15
Regular notification	Rolling
Deferment available	Yes
Maximum length of deferment	1 year
Transfer students accepted	Yes

Transfer application policy
A student who has been admitted to a graduate program at another university, and who desires admission to Baylor, must present a transcript that presents the student's active, satisfactory work toward the same degree. Only 6 hours may be transferred into the MBA program.

Non-fall admissions	Yes
Need-blind admissions	Yes

Applicants Also Look At
Babson College, Rice University, Southern Methodist University, Texas A&M University System Health Science Center, Texas Christian University (TCU), The University of Texas at Arlington, The University of Texas at Dallas.

EMPLOYMENT PROFILE

		Grads Employed by Function	%	Avg. Salary
Career Rating	**78**	Finance/Accounting	39	$61,000
Primary Source of Full-time Job Acceptances		Marketing/Sales	5	$48,000
Percent employed	89	MIS	5	$63,000
		Operations/Production	28	$55,600
		General Management	11	$66,000
		Other	11	$66,000

BELMONT UNIVERSITY
THE JACK C. MASSEY GRADUATE SCHOOL OF BUSINESS

Academics

The Jack C. Massey School of Business at Belmont University offers an academically rigorous program that is designed to meet the needs of nontraditional students. As one such student explains, "Belmont offers a flexible approach to taking classes—I could take classes [if] I needed that experience in my work." Most classes are offered in the evening, and students may elect to enroll in a full- or part-time program. Undergraduate courses in business areas such as accounting and economic analysis, along with competency in language and quantitative skills, are required to begin the graduate program. Belmont offers guidance on meeting or waiving these requirements where appropriate, including "the opportunity to take a year of prerequisite classes as part of the program," which helps students to prepare for the core.

The MBA program itself consists of 34 credit hours, 24 of which are taken up by required courses. These classes focus on the management aspects of technology, human resources, finance, and international business, and well as advanced skills in leadership, cost analysis, and entrepreneurship. With the 10 remaining credits, students may continue with a general business degree or pursue concentrations in accounting, finance, health care management, management of business processes and operations, or music business. Located in Nashville's West End, just blocks from Music Row and down the street from the classically oriented programs at Vanderbilt University's Blair School of Music, Belmont owns and operates the historic Studio B recording complex in conjunction with the Country Music Hall of Fame. "I chose Belmont because of its excellent music business program elective and because of its proximity to the music industry in Nashville," one student said. Opportunities for international study abound, with programs in Ireland, the Czech Republic, China, Chile, France, Germany, and Brazil.

All of the professors at Belmont "were top executives at one point in their careers." "The professors have business experience that I feel will create a richer learning experience," says one satisfied student. Described by students as "good, knowledgeable people who have a desire to teach," the professors at Belmont "are well educated and have impressive backgrounds in their fields." "I feel completely comfortable approaching the professors and am confident they are willing and eager to help me succeed," says one student. Students say the "administration is seamless," although they wish it were "more racially diverse." "Overall though, I think the school has a strong program," says one student, echoing the sentiments of his peers.

Career and Placement

Belmont employs a staff of advisors dedicated to meeting the needs of business students. At the university's Career Center, MBA students have access to a wide array of services including career planning, resume review, and alumni mentorship programs, as well as workshops on topics such as networking and salary negotiation. With many of Belmont's MBA graduates still living in middle Tennessee, both the school and currently-enrolled students find these alums to be the most useful resources in their job search. Students appreciate the "amount of contacts to the business world" that Belmont offers, but feel that "the school needs to improve its career services." Bridgestone/Firestone, Caterpillar, Hospital Corporation of America, Deloitte Touche Tohmatsu, and Ernst &Young are among the top firms that recruit at Belmont.

TONYA HOLLIN, ADMISSIONS ASSISTANT
1900 BELMONT BOULEVARD NASHVILLE, TN 37212 UNITED STATES
PHONE: 615-460-6480 • FAX: 615-460-6353
E-MAIL: MASSEYADMISSIONS@MAIL.BELMONT.EDU • WEBSITE: MASSEY.BELMONT.EDU

Student Life and Environment

Although the classes at Belmont take place in the evening, there is still a strong sense of community among students. As one student explains, "The main reason I went here is for the people." Students here are "very supportive and diverse. I have met a lot of great friends and contacts in the graduate school at Belmont." Many students are "young and recent graduates" and "don't have the level of contacts or job that would make them a good networking contact." While these students may not be "as mature or as settled" as some of the older students on campus, "Most are friendly and helpful." "Other [students] are older and have families" and can "provide knowledge from their career." Some students say their family situation could use some recognition from the university. "Because such a large population of students have children," students say it would be "extremely helpful if [the school] offered child care." Students have nothing but praise for their fellow students: "They are tomorrow's leaders. I look forward to working with each of them." "They are the type of people I would have chosen could I have hand-picked people to go to school with."

Admissions

To apply to the Jack C. Massey School of Business at Belmont, you'll need to submit your undergraduate transcript, GMAT scores, two references, a resume, and a one page statement of your career goals. At least 2 years of work experience is required, along with prior course work or competency in basic business subjects, quantitative skills, and communication skills. In 2006, the average GMAT score of the entering class was 503 and the average undergraduate GPA was 3.22. Students averaged about 6 and a half years of work experience.

ADMISSIONS

Admissions Selectivity Rating	**67**
# of applications received	53
% applicants accepted	83
% acceptees attending	77
Average GMAT	503
Range of GMAT	450–560
Average GPA	3.22
TOEFL required of international students	Yes
Minimum TOEFL (paper/computer)	550/213
Application fee	$50
Regular application deadline	7/1
Regular notification	7/1
Deferment available	Yes
Maximum length of deferment	1 year
Transfer students accepted	Yes
Transfer application policy Application process is the same for all students. May transfer up to 6 hours from an-accredited university.	
Non-fall admissions	Yes
Need-blind admissions	Yes

Applicants Also Look At

Middle Tennessee State University, University of Tennessee, Vanderbilt University.

EMPLOYMENT PROFILE			
Career Rating	**77**	**Grads Employed by Function%**	**Avg. Salary**
		Finance/Accounting 11	NR
		Human Resources 2	NR
		Marketing/Sales 5	NR
		MIS 2	NR
		Operations/Production 9	NR
		Consulting 3	NR
		General Management 5	NR
		Other 17	NR

BENTLEY COLLEGE
THE ELKIN B. MCCALLUM GRADUATE SCHOOL OF BUSINESS

GENERAL INFORMATION

Type of school	Private
Environment	Town
Academic calendar	Semester

SURVEY SAYS . . .
Cutting-edge classes
Smart classrooms
Solid preparation in:
Computer skills

STUDENTS

Enrollment of parent institution	5,497
Enrollment of business school	548
% male/female	64/36
% out-of-state	12
% part-time	91
% international	36
Average age at entry	26
Average years work experience at entry	3

ACADEMICS

Academic Experience Rating	**84**
Student/faculty ratio	10:1
Profs interesting rating	82
Profs accessible rating	81
% female faculty	30
% minority faculty	12

Joint Degrees
Dual degrees are available.

Prominent Alumni
Joseph Antonellis, CIO and ex vice president, State Street Corporation; Ullas Naik, managing director, JAFCO Ventures; Thomas Venables, founder and CEO, Lighthousebank.com; Amy Hunter, executive vice president, Boston Private Bank and Trust; Anthony P. DiBona, vice president PTC.

Academics

With both "one of the most technologically advanced schools" in the country and "the ability to combine technology and people to create a phenomenal learning environment," The McCallum MBA program at Bentley College "has done a good job of creating a niche for itself in the Boston-area business-school environment." This predominantly part-time program boasts "amazing facilities" and strength in a number of technology-related and technology-assisted disciplines.

High-tech perks are what first catch prospective MBAs' attention here and for good reason. Bentley's resources include "an awesome trading center," a 3,500-square-foot facility complete with a trading floor with two Trans-Lux data walls, 60 work stations, an adjacent business suite, and a marketing center that features numerous state-of-the-art research and analysis labs. Bentley "blows other schools' facilities away," one student assures us. Also available are "top-notch centers to serve students in accounting, information technology, and cyberlaw; and a library that recently received a $16 million makeover. The library is "ideal for group projects, with its dozens of collaboration rooms, which can be reserved electronically and are equipped with LCD monitors, white boards, conference tables etc."

Bentley puts those facilities to excellent use in such diverse fields as marketing technology, finance, accounting, and information technology. In these areas especially, Bentley has an "excellent reputation that provides the best in career opportunities." The school also offers both an MS and a concentration in real estate management ("It offers Argus training for real estate"), and is "a leader in the field of human-computer interaction." Professors here "are presently involved in the Boston business community" and so transport "actual experience in the business world" to the classroom. "They bring creative approaches to challenge students in the classroom," although incoming students should also note that "most are hard-asses, but [the workload] really prepares you for the real world." Bentley "keeps the classes small, allowing for individual attention when needed." One student says, "I really didn't want any auditorium-style classes." Students also love the "flexibility in terms of scheduling, which makes it possible to take two courses a night after work if you need to." Ultimately, though, it's "Bentley's eagerness to set the bar for education in business/IT integration" that sets the school apart from the crowd.

Career and Placement

Bentley's Nathan R. Miller Center for Career Services (CCS) "is excellent" at serving the school's MBA students, who tell us that "everyone . . . is personally involved in helping you out." Counselors receive a strong assist from Bentley's solid "reputation among Boston-area employers." Students here benefit from the Career Management Series (CMS), a program designed to help them better position themselves in the battle for top jobs. CMS programs vary by area of concentration, meaning students receive plenty of field-specific assistance. The CSS provides lifetime service to alumni, another huge plus.

Top employers of Bentley MBAs include: Deloitte Touche Tohmatsu, Raytheon, Staples, State Street, Liberty Mutual, PepsiCo, PricewaterhouseCoopers, GE, Yankee Group, BearingPoint, Thermo Electron, Yahoo!, EMC, Fidelity, and Tyco.

SHARON HILL, DIRECTOR OF GRADUATE ADMISSIONS
175 FOREST STREET WALTHAM, MA 02452 UNITED STATES
PHONE: 781-891-2108 • FAX: 781-891-2464
E-MAIL: GRADADM@BENTLEY.EDU • WEBSITE: WWW.BENTLEY.EDU

Student Life and Environment

Full-time MBA students describe a full grad school experience, one buttressed by lots of group work, meetings, and events held by graduate student associations, and such on campus amenities as numerous food options and "an excellent gym with flat-screen LCDs to watch while [working out] on the cardio machines." Students tell us that "there are tons of activities" in the Bentley community, but note that "it is also true that those activities and clubs are targeted to full-time students. For those who work 9 to 5, it is impossible to get involved in events." Full-timers and part-timers alike agree that "the campus is absolutely gorgeous, and it's great that it's completely wireless."

Full-time students also enjoy being a part of "a tight-knit group," which, in part, begins because they participate in a cohort program. "We spend a lot of time together, for better or worse. It's great for building tight bonds, but it's a little harder to meet people outside of that group." MBAs report that "students appear happy here. There is lots of mingling in between classes, and it appears people genuinely like meeting new people." One student adds, "The different backgrounds and experiences of my classmates really add a lot of value to class time."

Admissions

Applicants to the Bentley MBA program must submit all of the following materials to the Admissions Committee: a completed application form; official copies of all transcripts for all postsecondary academic work; an official GMAT score report; two letters of recommendation; three essays (topics detailed in application); and a resume. Applicants to the full-time, daytime MBA program or the MS plus MBA program must sit for an interview; interviews are optional for all other applicants. In addition to all of the above, international applicants must also submit an official score report for the TOEFL, IBT, or IELTS; an international student data form; a bank statement; and a letter detailing how the student intends to support him/herself while attending school. Bentley Admissions Officers pride themselves on personalizing the admissions process by looking at the whole person when making admissions decisions. Work experience is strongly preferred but not required.

FINANCIAL FACTS

Annual tuition	$22,752
Fees	$204
Cost of books	$1,080
Room & board	$12,390
% of students receiving aid	29
% of first-year students receiving aid	44
% of students receiving loans	20
% of students receiving grants	14
Average award package	$17,410
Average grant	$13,939
Average student loan debt	$24,523

ADMISSIONS

Admissions Selectivity Rating	**80**
# of applications received	420
% applicants accepted	60
% acceptees attending	55
Average GMAT	562
Range of GMAT	510–610
Average GPA	3.54
TOEFL required of international students	Yes
Minimum TOEFL (paper/computer)	600/250
Application fee	$50
Regular application deadline	3/1
Regular notification	Rolling
Early decision program?	Yes
ED Deadline/Notification	12/1, 1/15
Deferment available	Yes
Maximum length of deferment	1 year
Non-fall admissions	Yes
Need-blind admissions	Yes

Applicants Also Look At

Babson College, Boston College, Boston University, Northeastern University.

EMPLOYMENT PROFILE

Career Rating	86	Grads Employed by Function	%	Avg. Salary
Primary Source of Full-time Job Acceptances		Finance/Accounting	18	$60,000
School-facilitated activities	10 (45%)	Marketing/Sales	5	$57,500
Graduate-facilitated activities	7 (32%)	MIS	27	$70,000
Unknown	5 (23%)	Operations/Production	14	$62,500
Average base starting salary	$65,278	Communications	4	$82,500
Percent employed	95	Other	32	$62,500

Top 5 Employers Hiring Grads

Deloitte Consulting; Fidelity Investments; EMC; GE; Reebok.

Berry College

Campbell School of Business

GENERAL INFORMATION

Type of school   Private

SURVEY SAYS . . .
Friendly students
Good peer network
Happy students
Smart classrooms
Solid preparation in:
Marketing
General management
Operations

STUDENTS
Enrollment of parent
  institution   1,800
Enrollment of
  business school   29
Average age at entry   24

ACADEMICS
Academic Experience Rating   61
Profs interesting rating   86
Profs accessible rating   91

FINANCIAL FACTS
Annual tuition $343
                        per credit

Academics

The Campbell School of Business at Berry College offers a broad and contemporary business education in the context of a small, private school environment. Taking a whole-picture approach to learning, the program's stated mission is to "educate the head, heart, and hands" of future business leaders—a goal they achieve through a series of core courses in a range subject areas, including: analysis and problem solving, application of theory, technology, oral and written communication, global and political issues, demographic diversity, lifelong learning, and more. After completing the core course work, students must take at least four electives (or an equivalent of 12 semester hours) and may also earn course credit through internship experiences.

Many students chose Berry because it "is small in size, and the teacher-to-student ratio is excellent." Indeed, the "community atmosphere on the campus" is one of the program's greatest strengths, and students say it's easy to receive plenty of "personal attention from the faculty." While they maintain a friendly and relaxed attitude, Campbell faculty promotes a high academic standard on campus. A current student raves, "We have some top-notch professors here who most definitely know their stuff and could rival Stanford professors any day of the week." Students admit, however, that there are a few drawbacks to attending a small school. Specifically, "Course offerings are slim" and do not always meet student needs.

The MBA program at the Campbell School of Business is designed for working professionals and managers in every business field, attracting students who are "goal oriented and are trying to better themselves in their current or future careers." In order to accommodate the special needs of students struggling to balance a career and an education, classes at Campbell meet 1 night a week. Furthermore, Berry professors are sensitive to the difficulties of keeping up with the work and school schedule, and they "take into consideration the outside responsibilities when it comes to assessing their students."

Campbell is an increasingly important presence in the North Georgia economic community, enjoying "great school recognition in the area." Playing an active role in the region and encouraging a sense of social consciousness in the student body, the school's involvement in the community goes beyond churning out talented business graduates. A current student explains, "Berry doesn't just try to trade cash for knowledge. It truly wants to change students for the better. The students here are very caring and go out of their way to make an impact in the community." Another adds, "Berry emphasizes the head, heart, and hands and abides by this with what the professors teach."

Career Placement

Campbell MBA students have access to the Berry College Career Development Center, through which they can work with professional career counselors and receive assistance looking for jobs and internships. The center provides job counseling and resume-preparation services, workshops, and online career search tools, as well as extensive materials on their website. Through the center, students can register for and attend a number of career fairs in the region, which draw major employers from the area. In February, the Career Development Center hosts the Employer Expo, a 2-day career fair held on the Berry campus.

DANA PAUL, DEAN, ADMISSIONS AND FINANCIAL AID
2277 MARTHA BERRY HIGHWAY NW ROME, GA 30165-9987 UNITED STATES
PHONE: 706-236-2215 • FAX: 706-290-2178
E-MAIL: WWW.ADMISSIONS@BERRY.EDU • WEBSITE: CAMPBELL.BERRY.EDU

Student Life and Environment

Berry College's "peaceful and gorgeous" campus is one of the school's chief attractions. At 28,000 acres, these beautiful and green grounds are among the largest college campuses in the world. Graduate students may participate in all student activities at Berry, including movie nights, intramural sports, and cultural activities; however, MBA students admit that "there are no purely graduate focused resources." For graduate students who choose to live on the Berry campus, "Housing is great with fairly large rooms and many dorms have wireless Internet."

Between school and career, Campbell students have plenty of responsibilities to keep them busy. Even so, most are "very outgoing, and many help out in the community with volunteer work." A great place to live, work, and study, Rome, Georgia is a small city that nonetheless offers plenty of entertainment options, such as art museums and parks as well as proximity to other Georgia cities. Students appreciate the town's pleasant culture, as well as its affordability. In fact, "Rent is fairly cheap" for those who wish to live off campus.

Admissions

To apply to Berry College Campbell School of Business, all prospective students must possess an undergraduate degree from an accredited college or university. Candidates must submit the graduate application form, an official transcript from all colleges and universities attended, official GMAT score, two letters of recommendation, an essay explaining their reasons for pursuing an MBA, and, for international applicants, a score of 550 or better on the TOEFL. Usually a GMAT score of at least 400 is required for entry to the program and an undergraduate GPA of at least 3.0. For all candidates, the school looks for students who display a promise of growth, seriousness of purpose, and a sense of responsibility. Undergraduate business majors with a grade point average of 3.0 or better may request permission from the Dean to be admitted to the postbaccalaureate MBA program.

ADMISSIONS

Admissions Selectivity Rating	**63**
% applicants accepted	88
% acceptees attending	100
Average GMAT	525
TOEFL required of international students	Yes
Minimum TOEFL (paper/computer)	550/213
Application fee	$25
International application fee	$30
Deferment available	Yes
Maximum length of deferment	1 semester
Transfer students accepted	Yes
Transfer application policy The curriculum committee may grant transfer credit for appropriate graduate-level work completed at other institutions to a maximum of three 3-semester-hour courses, for a total of 9 semester hours. Transfer credit is not given for BUS 685.	
Non-fall admissions	Yes

BIRMINGHAM-SOUTHERN COLLEGE

Academics

Birmingham-Southern College is a relative rarity in the graduate business world in that it is a tiny liberal arts school. It is so small, in fact, that business is the only area in which it offers any type of graduate instruction. The school is also unique in the degree it awards. Rather than offering a traditional MBA, the school offers a Master's of Arts in Public and Private Management (MPPM), a degree that stresses "a holistic approach to managerial leadership through a liberal arts curriculum." As one student puts it, the focus here is "more on leadership and management than on the numbers." The school also offers a 1-year certificate program in Public and Private Management for international students.

BSC has built a graduate business curriculum based on the themes of leadership, entrepreneurship, teamwork, ethics, critical analysis, business strategy, quantitative analysis, creativity, communication, and global perspectives. The incorporation of the school's strong liberal arts programs means that "Behavioral and political science professors have a place in the MPPM program," too, although some here feel that "the program places too much emphasis on those types of courses." All students must complete 16 three-credit classes, nine of which form the program's foundation requirements. Elective choices are limited, as are concentration options; students may currently concentrate only in public sector management, private sector management, or health care management. The program could improve by "increasing concentrations to include entrepreneurship, transportation/logistics, marketing, strategic management, corporate finance/controller, and IT/technology management," says one student. "I believe that by offering concentrations that are more specific, BSC can increase enrollment and provide a more individualized experience that could better serve the greater Birmingham area."

BSC's size may have some drawbacks, but it also ensures "small classes" and "personal attention" for each student in the program. The school's solid commitment to the program means also that a "dedicated administration" demonstrates a serious "interest in improving the program." Students agree the majority of "Professors are good communicators, experts in their fields, and appear to genuinely care about the students." "My overall academic experience is very good and appropriately challenging."

Career and Placement

BSC is primarily an undergraduate institution, and its Career Counseling Center is designed to provide placement and counseling services to undergraduates. Services here include self-assessments instruments; seminars and workshops in job search skills, resume writing, interviewing, and salary negotiation; mentoring and internship placement; and the administration of networking and recruiting events both on and off campus.

The school does not provide employment data for graduates of its MPPM program. Major employers in the Birmingham area include The University of Alabama at Birmingham, BellSouth, Baptist Health System, AmSouth Bank, American Cast Iron Pipe, Alabama Gas, BE&K, Alabama Power, Blue Cross and Blue Shield Association, Compass Bank, and federal, state, and local government.

Student Life and Environment

"Graduate students, for the most part, come to campus to attend classes at night and have jobs during the day" at Birmingham-Southern, meaning that most students attend part-time, taking two classes per semester to complete the program in 3 to 4 years. While on campus, students "frequently utilize the business school building, the cafeteria, the computer lab," and the library. One commuter students says, "I try to interact with fac-

CAMILLE SPRATLING, ASSOCIATE DIRECTOR OF MPPM ADMISSION
900 ARKADELPHIA ROAD, BOX 549008 BIRMINGHAM, AL 35254 UNITED STATES
PHONE: 205-226-4653 • FAX: 205-226-3074
E-MAIL: GRADUATE@BSC.EDU • WEBSITE: WWW.BSC.EDU/ACADEMICS/BUSINESS/MPPM/INDEX.HTM

ADMISSIONS	
Admissions Selectivity Rating 60*	
TOEFL required of international students	Yes
Application fee	$25
Deferment available	Yes
Maximum length of deferment	1 year
Non-fall admissions	Yes

ulty and staff whenever possible." Classes convene in the Marguerite Jones Harbert Building, built in 1987–1988. The complex includes computer labs, an auditorium, a conference center, and a behavioral science research center, which is utilized for the MPPM program.

The city of Birmingham is one of the major banking centers of the South, and its banks help feed the program's student body. The city is also the state's capital, and the government workforce also contributes to the population here. Birmingham-Southern is located on a wooded, 192-acre campus just three miles west of downtown Birmingham, making it both convenient and comfortable. The acreage means there's plenty of room for a baseball field, a softball field, a soccer field, tennis courts, an intramural field, and EcoScape, an art park that combines the work of local artists with a nature center. Mild winters help relieve the winter doldrums suffered by students' peers farther north. Spring and fall are reasonably mild, while summers can be oppressive.

BSC draws a "very diverse" student body "by race, gender, age, and economic background" to its MPPM program, meaning "Discussions are always interesting." "Classroom interaction is the best part of the MPPM program," offers one student. Most here have "white-collar careers, are married" and are in "their mid- to late 30s." They are typically "dedicated to work, school, and home." Some feel the program needs to tighten admissions requirements in order to push the program to the next level.

Admissions

Applicants to the Birmingham-Southern MPPM program must apply to the college's Office of Graduate Programs. The school requires applicants to submit a completed application, an essay discussing career goals and program objectives, a resume, two letters of recommendation, official transcripts for all postsecondary institutions attended, and any of the following entrance exams: the GMAT, the GRE, or the Miller Analogy Test (MAT). Applicants already holding advanced degrees are exempted from entrance exam requirements. Foreign students whose first language is not English must submit either an official TOEFL score report (minimum required score: 600, paper-based test; or 214, computer-based test) or comparable evidence of proficiency in written and spoken English. After initial review of applications, the school contacts potential candidates to schedule an entrance interview. BSC requires students to enter with at least 3 years of management experience.

BOSTON COLLEGE
CARROLL SCHOOL OF MANAGEMENT

Academics

The Carroll School of Management at Boston College enjoys a "great reputation with industry for producing graduates who can immediately produce" as well as a "strong reputation in finance" and several other disciplines. Add to the mix a "huge resource in our alumni network: BC alums are always eager to help fellow Eagles," and you understand why so many students here describe this as an "amazing program."

BC's marquee discipline is finance, but students are adamant that "BC is as strong a marketing school as it is a finance school" and that the school offers "a good marketing curriculum." Also, according to at least one student, "A hidden gem is Boston College's organizational studies focus. Holding many highly touted organizational behavior and organizational development professors, BC offers the opportunity for MBA students to take PhD-level classes in organization studies during the second year. The high quality of professors is recognized in the academic and business community." Throughout the MBA program, BC implements "an experiential curriculum." One student writes, "Not only does BC offer the MBA consulting project but also a business plan project during the second year and several investment management opportunities. It is extremely valuable to combine these opportunities with a traditional classroom education to provide an overall world-class experience." BC offers specializations in asset management, change leadership, competitive service delivery, corporate finance, entrepreneurial management, financial reporting and controls, global management, marketing informatics, and product and brand management. Students may also design their own fields of specialization.

BC "does a good job at teaching the hard technical skills as well as soft skills like communication and leadership." Prospective students should be aware that "the program has gone through some administrative changes in the past few years" and that "the program is changing," making it "feel a bit like an experiment right now." Students report that "the school has recently taken great effort to expand the curriculum and opportunities available to students, making it increasing more relevant to current business issues," and that the curriculum was completely overhauled for the Class of 2008. Students remain confident that, regardless of the changes, "BC is a school that is climbing in the rankings—small enough to have amazing faculty interaction—and will prepare me well for my intended career."

Career and Placement

BC's Office of Career Strategies "is unique in the time and effort spent working with every single student. We meet regularly with our career counselors. They are constantly working to coordinate events and seek increasingly more job opportunity for graduate management students." Still, some here complain that "on-campus recruiting is disappointing in terms of quality of employer and intern positions available" and that "there is little effort made to place students outside the Boston area." Fortunately, the alumni network is a "huge resource." One MBA explains, "Many of the big consulting or investment banking firms don't recruit on campus, but we have plenty of alumni at those firms. It's really up to the students to make the connections and ask for a lead."

Employers who most frequently hire BC MBAs include: Liberty Mutual, Staples, EMC Corporation, Boston Scientific Corporation, Fidelity Investments, Strategic Pricing Group, Gillette, Merrill Lynch, State Street Global Markets, UBS Warburg, and Wellington Management.

SHELLEY CONLEY, DIRECTOR OF GRADUATE ENROLLMENT
FULTON HALL 315, 140 COMMONWEALTH AVENUE CHESTNUT HILL, MA 02467-3808 UNITED STATES
PHONE: 617-552-3920 • FAX: 617-552-8078
E-MAIL: BCMBA@BC.EDU • WEBSITE: WWW.BC.EDU/MBA

Student Life and Environment

Life in the graduate management program at BC is "the best." One student explains, "BC is a very tight-knit community, and students spend a lot of time together both inside and outside of the classroom. Whether it's working in teams as part of the Diane Weiss Consulting Competition or having drinks at the weekly 'Thirsty Thursday' get-togethers, BC students form relationships that will last forever." Students remind us "not to forget the football games and the tailgate events organized by the GMA (Graduate Management Association)," or that "the strong nationally ranked athletics programs in football, basketball, and hockey create a wonderful bonding experience for students." One student sums up, "If you don't want to know your classmates, mingle with alumni, and study hard, Boston College is not the place for you."

Students also point out that "for such a small school there are a lot of clubs and activities for MBA students to partake in. Almost everyone is involved in some sort of activity, and many people belong to more than one club or organization," especially as students move through the program; first year "is hectic" enough that sometimes "School is the only thing that you seem to have time for," because "The academic workload is substantial. Fortunately, the camaraderie among students and the teamwork that takes place makes the experience worthwhile."

Admissions

Applicants to the MBA program at Boston College must submit the following materials to the school: a completed application; a current resume and a separate employment history; two personal essays (students may submit a third optional essay); two letters of recommendation, an official transcript from each degree-granting undergraduate and graduate program attended; and an official GMAT score report. International applicants who attended a non-English language institution must have their transcripts translated and interpreted by a professional service. International students whose first language is not English must submit an official TOEFL score report unless they received their undergraduate degrees from an institution at which the language of instruction is English. BC strongly encourages applicants to apply online.

Prominent Alumni

John Fisher, president and CEO, Saucony; Norman Chambers, president and COO of NCIS Building Systems, Inc.; Paul LaCamera, president and GM, WCVB-TV, channel 5; Alexis Sarkissian, CEO, Vivid Collection; Ronald Logue, chairman and CEO, State Street

FINANCIAL FACTS

Annual tuition	$33,232
Fees	$150
Cost of books	$1,500
Room & board	$18,390
% of students receiving loans	45
% of students receiving grants	65
Average award package	$47,972
Average grant	$18,874
Average student loan debt	$46,301

ADMISSIONS

Admissions Selectivity Rating	90
# of applications received	463
% applicants accepted	46
% acceptees attending	44
Average GMAT	645
Range of GMAT	593–690
Average GPA	3.39
TOEFL required of international students	Yes
Minimum TOEFL (paper/computer)	600/250
Application fee	$100
Application Deadline/Notification	
Round 1:	11/15 / 1/15
Round 2:	1/15 / 3/15
Round 3:	3/15 / 5/1
Transfer students accepted	Yes
Transfer application policy	
4 courses are accepted (with a grade of B or higher) from other AACSB MBA programs.	
Need-blind admissions	Yes

Applicants Also Look At

Babson College, Boston University, Columbia University, Georgetown University, Harvard University, Massachusetts Institute of Technology, New York University.

EMPLOYMENT PROFILE

Career Rating	89	Grads Employed by Function	%	Avg. Salary
Primary Source of Full-time Job Acceptances		Finance/Accounting	38	$82,271
School-facilitated activities	34 (49%)	Human Resources	1	NR
Graduate-facilitated activities	35 (51%)	Marketing/Sales	23	$85,857
		MIS	1	NR
		Operations/Production	1	NR
		Consulting	10	$96,286
		General Management	16	$88,389
		Other	10	NR

Top 5 Employers Hiring Grads
EMC; Liberty Mutual; State Street; Monitor Group (Formerly Strategic Pricing Group); Talbot's.

BOSTON UNIVERSITY
SCHOOL OF MANAGEMENT

GENERAL INFORMATION

Type of school	Private
Environment	Metropolis
Academic calendar	Semester

SURVEY SAYS . . .
Students love Boston, MA
Smart classrooms
Solid preparation in:
Teamwork
Communication/interpersonal skills

STUDENTS

Enrollment of parent institution	
Enrollment of business school	786
% male/female	63/37
% part-time	62
% minorities	22
% international	36
Average age at entry	26
Average years work experience at entry	5

ACADEMICS

Academic Experience Rating	**88**
Student/faculty ratio	17:1
Profs interesting rating	85
Profs accessible rating	92
% female faculty	25

Joint Degrees
MS/MBA (information systems and traditional MBA) 84 credits in 21 months, MBA/MS (television management), MBA/MA international relations), MBA/MS (manufacturing engineering), MBA/MA (economics), MBA/MA (medical sciences) 80 credits, MBA/JD 116 credits, MBA/MPH 85 credits MBA/MD 114 credits.

Prominent Alumni
Christine Poon, vice chairman, Pharmacy Group, Johnson & Johnson; Millard S. (Mickey) Drexler, chairman and CEO, J. Crew, Inc.; Edward J. Zander, chairman and CEO, Motorola; Walter Skowronski, president, Boeing.

Academics

The Boston University School of Management boasts a number of first-rate programs, including a number of combined MS/MBAs to suit the needs of the especially ambitious. Students praise the school and love the direction in which the program is headed, telling us that "the Dean of the school is a powerhouse of influence for our community and is continuously upgrading the facilities and the resources available to students and alumni."

BU excels in finance, marketing, and strategy departments, "all of which have renowned professors teaching MBA students in them. Many formerly taught at the Harvard Business School." Students also approve of the Health Sector Management program, which "excels in putting students in contact with leading health companies and service providers. Boston is a great place for both world-class hospital systems and a burgeoning biotechnology community. For students interested in the health sector, it's a great program that is continuing to evolve." BU's MBA in public nonprofit management is "extremely strong, teaching not only the management skills necessary for public and nonprofit organizations, but the benefit and skills necessary for the management of for-profit social enterprise companies." An MS/MBA in information systems offers "a great technology program in a city that is a hotbed for innovation."

The SMC's faculty is "passionate about what they teach and are available to answer questions outside of class. In addition, professors collaborate with each other to make sure students develop completely. For example, just recently our marketing professor spoke with our data analysis professor about a common shortcoming that arose in our marketing presentations." BU also offers its MBA Program "a strong and developing alumni network. BU has a large Executive MBA program, as well as part-time MBA students who are all integrated into the business environment of Boston and prove to be extremely useful in career efforts."

Career and Placement

Students report a much-improved Career Center at BU, reporting that "they are doing a great job and have shown great improvement in the past [few] years." Students also tell us that "there is now an extremely strong pharma presence recruiting at BU. Phizer, Eli Lilly, and Bristol Meyers all are recruiting heavily from BU." Some still see room for improvement; one such student writes, "Many of the companies that come to campus to recruit are local. Although some big names that have national or even global presence do recruit here, it is a challenge to find a job if you are looking in a specific area that is not Boston."

Top employers of BU MBAs include: BearingPoint, Medtronic, Citigroup, IBM Corporation, Ernst & Young, Fidelity Investments, IDC, Intel, Raytheon, Colgate Palmolive, EMC Corporation, HSBC, JPMorgan Chase, L'Oréal, and Reebok.

Student Life and Environment

Life at BU "is busy," writes one full-time student. "Although we're only in class for an average of 3 hours per day, I spend an average of 8 hours on campus, working individually or within my groups in between classes, meeting with professors, etc. Weekends (Fridays through Sunday) are days to read, work on individual assignments, and meet with groups." The workload isn't overwhelming, though; "The School of Management does an excellent job of maintaining a rigorous academic environment while still concentrating on creating a career network that will enable you to succeed after school." Beyond the classroom, students enjoy various club activities and school events. "Organized groups constantly make their presence known through on-campus speakers and events, and most do a good job of mixing social and academic pursuits." One student notes, "The school facilities are excellent, and membership to a great fitness center comes with your tuition: weights, cardio, pool, basketball court, and climbing wall."

Only about 40 percent of MBAs here attend full-time, about 30 percent of whom are international students (students from India and China are especially well represented, according to student response). Students also tell us that "classmates include a good mix of younger and older students, ranging in backgrounds from acting to engineering. They are gregarious, nerdy, competitive, and entertaining." There is a sense among some, however, that "there is somewhat too little work experience from members of our class" (even though the average full-time student enters the program with 4-plus years of work experience).

Those who have the time to socialize (part-timers typically include a number of students with full-time jobs, leaving them little spare time) extol the school's "exciting location near nightlife and Fenway Park. Parking is pretty good, with metered spots close to the school." There is also a parking garage located directly under the school itself. Social life "is extensive and highly important. Boston nightlife is omnipresent and enjoyed to the nth degree. This city allows for adventure right outside of the classroom and the students take advantage of it intensely."

Admissions

Applicants to the BU MBA program must submit the following materials: a completed application; a current resume, personal essays, in response to application questions; two letters of recommendation; official copies of transcripts for all undergraduate and graduate work; and an official GMAT score report. Interviews are required for some applicants and are scheduled at the request of the school. In addition to the above materials, international students must also submit an official score report for the TOEFL or IELTS (students whose first language is other than English only; minimum TOEFL score of 250 on paper-based exam, 250 on the old computer-based exam; minimum IELTS score of 7 across each band); a financial declaration; copies of all current visa or I-20 documentation; and a copy of the initial passport page.

FINANCIAL FACTS

Annual tuition	$33,330
Fees	$428
Cost of books	$1,380
Room & board (off-campus)	$11,008
% of students receiving aid	96
% of first-year students receiving aid	89
% of students receiving loans	56
% of students receiving grants	75
Average award package	$25,157
Average grant	$17,581

ADMISSIONS

Admissions Selectivity Rating	92
# of applications received	1,402
% applicants accepted	42
% acceptees attending	48
Average GMAT	663
Range of GMAT	600–730
Average GPA	3.28
TOEFL required of international students	Yes
Minimum TOEFL (paper/computer)	600/250
Application fee	$125
Regular application deadline	3/15
Regular notification	5/1
Application Deadline/Notification	
Round 1:	11/15 / 1/1
Round 2:	1/15 / 3/1
Round 3:	3/15 / 5/1
Deferment available	Yes
Maximum length of deferment	1 year
Transfer students accepted	Yes
Transfer application policy Classes must be AACSB-accredited.	
Need-blind admissions	Yes

Applicants Also Look At

Duke University, Georgetown University, Massachusetts Institute of Technology, New York University, University of Maryland.

EMPLOYMENT PROFILE

Career Rating		85	Top 5 Employers Hiring Grads
Primary Source of Full-time Job Acceptances			EMC Corporation; JPMorgan Chase; PA Consulting; Bristol-Myers Squibb; GE.
Percent employed		86	
Grads Employed by Function	**%**	**Avg. Salary**	
Finance/Accounting	18	$83,556	
Human Resources	1	$72,000	
Marketing/Sales	14	$81,417	
MIS	4	$85,333	
Consulting	19	$78,500	
General Management	8	$84,667	
Other	2	$81,667	

BOWLING GREEN STATE UNIVERSITY
COLLEGE OF BUSINESS ADMINISTRATION

Academics

Looking for a "quality education" with "high standards" that keep "student success as a primary goal"—all while offering an MBA degree that can be completed in 14 months? For those hoping to fast-track their business careers, the MBA program at the College of Business Administration at Bowling Green State University provides an excellent (and speedy) opportunity for students, even if they didn't get their undergraduate degree in business. And for only one additional semester's work, a specialization in accounting, finance, or management information systems can be added.

"The workload is heavy, and the classes are demanding," students tell us. However this is bolstered by the "very supportive" professors. One student explains, "When I started BGSU, I thought it would be a piece of cake for me. But I soon realized that the professors were serious about their work and expectations and settled for nothing but the best." Despite the rigors of the curriculum, most students find the program manageable thanks to the fact that "everyone seems willing to help each other out." Even those without prior business degrees or experience note that this collegial atmosphere and the "professors' accessibility outside the classroom and readiness to assist in learning were of great importance to my success in BGSU MBA program."

Students agree that the majority of professors "are very knowledgeable and willing to help." "Some are outstanding, while some are just okay," explains one student. "Two out of every three classes . . . were great," adds another; however, "It seemed like each semester we had one professor that wasn't the best." The curriculum puts a heavy emphasis on group projects and teamwork, which functions to help students make "a connection between theory and practice and help to develop skills."

The College of Business' full-time program features "a leadership assessment and development component consisting of a series of workshops" that "lead students through an ongoing process of reflection and self-discovery so that each obtains a better understanding of his or herself in relation to a desired management career." Students find the workshops helpful in their career development, especially the "Professional Development Sessions on Fridays," where they meet and interact "with industry leaders . . . in a professional and mentorship atmosphere."

Career and Placement

To assist BGSU students in their job searches, the College of Business offers "a series of co-curricular professional development seminars, covering topics such as oral presentation and report writing, team facilitation, effective negotiations, career planning, and organizational politics." Some report though that "career opportunities for MBAs are not well organized" and that students are "mostly on their own" in the job hunt. In particular, international students find it "very tough to find a job."

Recent employers of BGSU MBAs include American Express, American Greetings, Ernst & Young, Marathon Ashland, National City Corporation, Nationwide Insurance, Owens Corning, Plante & Moran, Progressive Insurance, and State Farm Insurance. The school reports that over half its graduates find their first job outside the United States.

SHEILA K. IRVING, DIRECTOR, GRADUATE STUDIES IN BUSINESS
369 BUSINESS ADMINISTRATION BUILDING BOWLING GREEN, OH 43403 UNITED STATES
PHONE: 419-372-2488 • FAX: 419-372-2875
E-MAIL: MBA-INFO@BGSU.EDU • WEBSITE: WWW.BGSUMBA.COM

Student Life and Environment

Students at BGSU agree that the student body is a "very diverse group from almost every continent" that consists of "very intelligent, committed, and dedicated" individuals. Statistics state that for the school at large, while "90 percent" of students are from Ohio, a whopping 55 countries are represented on campus. Additionally, about one-third of the MBAs are international students. The school also notes that "across all programs, students range in age from 22 to 52, with an average of 29. The average work experience of full-time, part-time, and executive students is 3, 6, and 10 years, respectively, but work experience is not required of full-time or part-time students."

On a campus of over 19,000 students, the College of Business facility is home to "a smaller community of professors, business students, and equipment where it is extremely easy to locate resources. Classrooms and a computer lab are located on the main floor, and professors and more computer labs are located upstairs. At BGSU, time is not wasted locating resources." MBAs also appreciate the "high standards" of "the school's programs" and "extracurricular activities" that "provide a well-rounded educational experience." They also tell us that "there are many diverse clubs and activities," such as The Business Club that "has social activities ranging from guest speakers to having beers at the local bar. Sometimes we even invite our professors."

While no one would mistake Bowling Green for a megalopolis, students find this "quiet" and "friendly" town charming and completely lacking in "distractions." "The university is the city for the most part," says one student. Others extol the "low prices" and "very cheap places to live off campus." But, "More than anything, it's safe." BGSU's location provides "easy access to Chicago, Cleveland, and Detroit." But if you crave "a large city," Toledo is "only 15 to 20 [minutes] away." But be sure to bundle up as "The weather may be a bit harsh during winter."

Admissions

The College of Business Administration at BGSU doesn't require applicants to have business experience for admission as "the full-time program is designed for students who will be new to their chosen fields." That said, prior work experience is a factor when it comes to securing an assistantship. Applicants must submit two official transcripts from each college attended, GMAT scores, a current resume, three letters of recommendation, and a personal statement; interviews are optional and can be conducted in person or by telephone. International students must also provide the school with TOEFL scores if their native language is not English.

ADMISSIONS

Admissions Selectivity Rating	**84**
# of applications received	135
% applicants accepted	49
% acceptees attending	77
Average GMAT	550
Range of GMAT	400–650
Average GPA	3.27
TOEFL required of international students	Yes
Minimum TOEFL (paper/computer)	550/213
Application fee	$30
Regular application deadline	Rolling
Regular notification	Rolling
Deferment available	Yes
Maximum length of deferment	1 year
Transfer students accepted	Yes

Transfer application policy
Students in the MBA programs (full-time, evening, and executive) are limited to a maximum of 6 graduate credit hours of transfer credit from AACSB-accredited institutions. Transfer credit may be applied to the foundation and core courses and to electives. Transfer credit is not permitted for MBA 609.

Non-fall admissions	Yes
Need-blind admissions	Yes

BRIGHAM YOUNG UNIVERSITY
MARRIOTT SCHOOL OF MANAGEMENT

GENERAL INFORMATION
Type of school Private
Affiliation Church of Jesus
Christ of Latter-day Saints
Environment City
Academic calendar Semester

SURVEY SAYS . . .
Friendly students
Good peer network
Happy students
Solid preparation in:
Accounting
Teamwork
Quantitative skills

STUDENTS
Enrollment of parent
institution 34,185
Enrollment of
business school 269
% male/female 84/16
% minorities 9
% international 12
Average age at entry 28
Average years work
experience at entry 3

ACADEMICS
Academic Experience Rating 89
Profs interesting rating 92
Profs accessible rating 89
% female faculty 15
% minority faculty 1

Joint Degrees
MBA/JD 4 years, MBA/MS, IPD
program with engineering department, 3 years, MAcc/JD 4 years,
MPA/JD 4 years.

Prominent Alumni
Andrea Thomas, vice president of
Global Chocolate, Hershey; D.
Fraser Bullock, founder/managing
director, Sorenson Capital; Robert
Parsons, executive vice president
and CFO, Exclusive Resorts; David
W. Checketts, chair, Sports Capital
Partners; Bill P. Benac, Sr., senior
vice president and CFO, American
Rail Car Industries.

Academics

The MBA program at Brigham Young's Marriott School of Management "provides a success-oriented environment that also promotes students' finding an elusive work-life balance," report students at this full-time-only Utah institution. At Marriott, "the course work is intense but manageable, and professors are almost always available for private consultations with students who are experiencing difficulties or who simply want to discuss applications of concepts that go beyond the scope of the course."

Students love the finance and accounting tracks at Marriott, reporting that "many big companies come to recruit good accounting students." Organizational behavior/human resources is also "a well-developed track." Marriott is home to four career training centers: the Rollins Center for eBusiness, the Center for Entrepreneurship, and the GMC (Global Management Center), which offers an International Management Certificate. The school has also recently added the H. Taylor Peery Institute of Financial Services to enhance its already solid finance program as well as the ESR Center (Economic Self-Reliance) and the Dyer Institute.

Across the curriculum, students praise their "extremely impressive professors, nearly all of whom come from a top-five school." Professors here "push you to your edge, but are very willing to lend a hand when you're slipping." While "most of them have extensive real-world and consulting experience, not all professors are recognized experts in their academic fields. This is primarily a teaching university." For the most part, students are glad to receive "a practical education that might not be possible from a pure 'academic' professor," but some wonder whether "the school could benefit from recruiting and retaining more top-talent professors."

With a first year that requires the completion of 33 credits, students quickly learn "how to prioritize," a skill they acquire "by being overwhelmed with work." The second year is not quite as rigorous, as students are given much more freedom to pursue electives and fields of specialization (here termed "tracks"). Students appreciate the "academic rigor balanced by charity for the individual" as well as the "religious and ethical emphasis" of the curriculum. They also boast that "tuition is amazingly low." (Note that rates are slightly higher for non-LDS members.)

Career and Placement

Career services at Marriott are provided by the Steven and Georgia White Business Career Center, which are described in school brochures as "the focal point for the school's placement, internship, and field study efforts." Facilities include a reference library, interview rooms, a large presentation room, and an eRecruiting system. School materials identify nearly 100 companies that recruit at the Marriott School.

Employers most likely to hire Marriott MBAs include American Express, Cigna, Daimler Chrysler, Dell, DOW Chemical, Ernst & Young, Ford Motor Company, Gap, Inc., General Electric Company, General Mills, Hewlett-Packard, Hollywood Entertainment, Honeywell, IBM, Intel, Nutraceutical, Payless Shoes, Partners Group, Procter & Gamble, Union Pacific, U.S. Department of Agriculture, and Yellow Freight.

Student Life and Environment

The typical Marriott MBA student "is married, has at least one child, and has three years of work experience. He or she is very smart, competitive, socially active, team-oriented, and religious." (BYU is affiliated with the Church of Jesus Christ of Latter-day Saints, as are, in one student's estimate, 80 percent of students here.) They are also typically "a bit

YVETTE ANDERSON, MBA PROGRAM ADMISSION DIRECTOR
635 TNRB PROVO, UT 84602 UNITED STATES
PHONE: 801-422-3500 • FAX: 801-422-0513
E-MAIL: MBA@BYU.EDU • WEBSITE: MARRIOTTSCHOOL.BYU.EDU/MBA

older than usual business school students, and they serve in the community more." It is important to note that "the ethical standards at BYU are extremely high." Religious life imposes many restrictions that students outside the faith may find surprising. Indeed, "students have many lifestyle limitations." These include abstaining from consumption of alcohol and coffee.

For those comfortable in "such an undiverse place," students agree that "there is no better program in the world for students with families. The MBA spouses' association is the most active group on campus and provides unparalleled support" for family members of MBA students. In their leisure time, students enjoy "plenty of activities, many of them multicultural, including Asian, Polynesian, Latino-American festivals." There are also lots of opportunities for outdoor activities. Students boast of the school's proximity to "the Wasatch Front," a natural retreat that "offers an excellent opportunity to enjoy life outside the classroom." Fortunately, these concerns are being addressed as the Tanner Building is under construction.

The Marriott MBA program is housed in the Tanner Building, "a great place to eat, socialize, get to know each other, and bond—but not a great place to do work. The study rooms ought to be quiet, well-lit, have an Internet jack (the wireless fails sometimes), and a power outlet. Power outlets come at a premium if you want one, so it's best to bring your own power strip to share." Fortunately, these concerns are being addressed as the Tanner Building is under construction. Students would like to see these problems remedied by the addition of new study areas.

Admissions

A completed application to the Marriott MBA program includes an application form, personal essays, an official GMAT score report, official transcripts for all postsecondary academic work, three letters of recommendation (one academic, two professional), an honor code commitment form, and a personal statement of intent. An interview is required; the school contacts applicants who have cleared initial screening to set up an interview appointment. International students must submit all of the above and must also provide financial disclosure forms and, if appropriate, TOEFL scores. A minimum of two years of full-time, post-undergraduate professional experience is required, but management experience is strongly preferred. Personal attributes are also considered; the school "values applicants who exemplify a sense of directedness and a commitment to the principles of the restored gospel of Jesus Christ," according to the school's brochure.

FINANCIAL FACTS

Annual tuition	$8,200
Cost of books	$1,600
Room & board	$6,080
Average award package	$7,806
Average grant	$4,994
Average student loan debt	$19,317

ADMISSIONS

Admissions Selectivity Rating	**90**
# of applications received	341
% applicants accepted	57
% acceptees attending	70
Average GMAT	648
Average GPA	3.54
TOEFL required of international students	Yes
Minimum TOEFL (paper/computer)	590/240
Application fee	$50
Regular application deadline	3/1
Regular notification	7/1
Application Deadline/Notification	
Round 1:	12/1 / 2/1
Round 2:	1/15 / 3/15
Round 3:	3/1 / 5/1
Round 4:	5/1 / 7/1
Early decision program?	Yes
ED Deadline/Notification	1/15 / 2/28
Deferment available	Yes
Maximum length of deferment	2 years
Transfer students accepted	Yes
Transfer application policy 15 credit hours of approved graduate-level courses, no pass/fail grades, and a minimum grade of B.	
Need-blind admissions	Yes

Applicants Also Look At
Arizona State University, Harvard University, Stanford University, University of Utah, Utah State University, Weber State University.

EMPLOYMENT PROFILE			
Career Rating	**83**	**Grads Employed by Function**	**% Avg. Salary**
Primary Source of Full-time Job Acceptances		Finance/Accounting	25 $79,361
Average base starting salary	$79,717	Human Resources	17 $74,406
Percent employed	17	Marketing/Sales	10 $84,100
		MIS	1 NR
		Operations/Production	14 $77,179
		Consulting	3 $79,667
		General Management	14 $76,864
		Other	11 $76,858
		Top 5 Employers Hiring Grads	
		AMEX, Woodside Group; Intel; Ford Motor Co.; General Mills.	

BROCK UNIVERSITY
FACULTY OF BUSINESS

GENERAL INFORMATION
Type of school   Public
Academic calendar

SURVEY SAYS . . .
Cutting-edge classes
Helpful alumni
Happy students
Smart classrooms

STUDENTS
Enrollment of parent
  institution   17,453
Enrollment of
  business school   82
% male/female   60/40
% part-time   23
% international   10
Average age at entry   27
Average years work
  experience at entry   4

ACADEMICS
Academic Experience Rating   84
Student/faculty ratio   1:1
Profs interesting rating   81
Profs accessible rating   65
% female faculty   23

Prominent Alumni
Doug Wilkinson, partner, Deloitte; Debi Rosati, venture capitalist, RosatiNet, Inc.; Paul Ingram, professor, Columbia University; Debbie Sevenpifer, president and CEO, Niagara Health System.

FINANCIAL FACTS
Annual tuition (in-state/
  out-of-state) $6,160/$14,521
Fees $450
Cost of books $1,500
Room & board
  (on/off-campus) $8,800/$7,050

Academics

Ontario's Brock University enjoys "a good reputation for business and accounting" among students and area businesses. As one student puts it, "Overall, considering the fact that the MBA program is new, the administration has done a great job. They have accomplished AACSB accreditation within a few short years and are making excellent hiring decisions for professors."

Brock's chief asset, students tell us, is its small classes, which "help encourage a lot of discussion with teachers and students. The teachers here are eager to hear your insight on situations while still educating you on how to take your thinking to the next level." Students also love the "great facilities that provide easy wireless Internet access" and the "many computers on campus," and they appreciate the "great opportunities to become involved with the school. This school provides anyone interested in becoming an active and contributing member of university society the chance to get involved." Prospective students should note that the workload here can be quite heavy, as one student explains: "As I've always heard about MBA programs anywhere, it's not rocket science, but the volume [of work] may kill you!"

The Brock MBA includes a sequence of required courses and an option for specialization in one of four "streams": accounting, finance, human resource management, and marketing. Students may also opt for a general MBA. Students may choose to replace up to three of their specialization courses with independent research projects; such projects are subject to the approval of the dean and the MBA Committee.

Career and Placement

The Faculty of Business at Brock University maintains a Business Center Development Office to serve all undergraduates and graduates enrolled at the faculty. The office manages the Graduate Recruitment Program for MBA students; through this program, students have access to employer information sessions and on-campus interviews. A Career Expo in the fall brings employers to campus for recruiting purposes. The office also offers resume review, interviewing and job search workshops, online job search tools, and assistance with international job placement. While Brock's website claims that the school boasts "the highest employment rate of any university in Ontario," students counter that "there are not a lot of companies recruiting from our program due to lack of knowledge about it." But students expect that career and placement issues will sort themselves out as the school sends more MBAs into the business world to "help other Brock students as they enter their careers."

Student Life and Environment

Brock University is located in St. Catharines, a mere 12 miles from Niagara Falls and just 70 miles from Toronto. Students call the location "a great strength," pointing out that St. Catharines is "a great city that is near Toronto and the States. It is very safe and the rent is super cheap. There are tons of bars to party at and everyone in St. Catharines just wants to have a good time. That can really make a difference when you are stressed out from working too much and you need a break." "Great weather" and "a nice campus" that is "not too big so that it is comfortable for newcomers" complete the picture. Students accustomed to more cosmopolitan locales claim, however, that St. Catharines is "a small town with not a lot to offer in terms of extracurriculars."

Most of Brock's MBAs are younger full-time students with little professional experience. They "are interested in school but also enjoy hanging out together. There are lots of great

ANDREA NAVIN, GRADUATE RECRUITMENT OFFICER, FACULTY OF BUSINESS
BROCK UNIVERSITY, 500 GLENRIDGE AVENUE ST. CATHARINES, ON L2S 3A1 CANADA
PHONE: 905-688-5550, EXT. 5362 • FAX: 905-688-4286
E-MAIL: MLSA@BROCKU.CA • WEBSITE: WWW.BUS.BROCKU.CA/GRADSTUDENTS

people to get to know and you become close friends." As one student observes, "Due to the fact that this program has relatively younger students, participation in activities is very high. The students have to participate because if we don't do it, there is not a large student body behind us to carry us." Brock does its part to facilitate extracurricular life: "The school provides opportunities to get involved with athletics and clubs," notes one MBA. One such exciting opportunity is the Corporate Social Responsibility Center, which "will match students to projects in the nonprofit sector. This will help students with connecting to opportunities off campus."

Admissions

Admission to the MBA program at Brock is based on five main criteria. The quality of one's undergraduate education is most important; Brock seeks students with at least a 3.0 undergraduate GPA. A minimum GMAT score of 550 is required, as are three letters of recommendation from professors and/or supervisors at work; a personal statement; and, as the Brock website states, a "resume detailing the applicant's education and career to date." Applications are assessed holistically; strength in one area may be sufficient to compensate for weaknesses elsewhere, according to the school's website. Professional experience, though preferred, is not required. Those whose first language is not English must demonstrate English proficiency through the TOEFL (minimum score 575, or 230 on the TOEFL (CBE), or 4.5 on the TWE).

ADMISSIONS

Admissions Selectivity Rating	**85**
# of applications received	156
% applicants accepted	53
% acceptees attending	43
Average GMAT	600
Range of GMAT	550–700
Average GPA	3.4
TOEFL required of international students	Yes
Minimum TOEFL (paper/computer)	620/260
Application fee	$100
Deferment available	Yes
Maximum length of deferment	1 year
Transfer students accepted	Yes
Transfer application policy Up to 10 courses of advanced standing plus 2 courses of transfer credit.	
Non-fall admissions	Yes
Need-blind admissions	Yes

Applicants Also Look At
McMaster University, Wilfrid Laurier University (Canada).

EMPLOYMENT PROFILE

Career Rating	73	Grads Employed by Function	%	Avg. Salary
Primary Source of Full-time Job Acceptances		Finance/Accounting	61	NR
School-facilitated activities	4 (22%)	Human Resources	5	NR
Unknown	14 (78%)	Marketing/Sales	8	NR
Percent employed	85	Operations/Production	5	NR
		General Management	5	NR
		Other	16	NR

Top 5 Employers Hiring Grads
HydroOne; Canadian Tire Financial Services; Ministry of Transportation; TD Bank Financial; Ministry of Finance.

Bryant University

Graduate School of Business

GENERAL INFORMATION

Type of school	Private
Environment	Town
Academic calendar	Semester

SURVEY SAYS . . .

Cutting-edge classes
Solid preparation in:
Teamwork
Communication/interpersonal skills

STUDENTS

Enrollment of parent institution	3,651
Enrollment of business school	298
% part-time	100
Average age at entry	28
Average years work experience at entry	6

ACADEMICS

Academic Experience Rating	**79**
Student/faculty ratio	20:1
Profs interesting rating	85
Profs accessible rating	80
% female faculty	27
% minority faculty	20

Prominent Alumni

David M. Beirne, general partner, Benchmark Capital Partners; William J. Conaty, senior vice president, GE; Robert P. Mead, president, Tyco Engineered Products and Services; Thomas Taylor, president and CEO, Amica Insurance; Kristian P. Moor, executive vice president, Domestic General Insurance.

FINANCIAL FACTS

Annual tuition	$666 per credit
Room & board (off-campus)	$10,000
Average award package	$13,640
Average grant	$16,235
Average student loan debt	$21,683

Academics

Students choose Bryant University's MBA program for the school's "reputation of being a top business school in the area" and for its "amazing facilities." In January 2006, the school gave students another reason to select Bryant: a revamped program that allows part-time students to enjoy the same benefits of cohort learning that full-time students enjoy. Under this new system, part-time students are grouped in cohorts of 30 to 35 with whom they move through the program (which they typically complete in 2 years). Each student is also assigned to a study team for the length of the program. Teams are constructed by administrators to provide the widest possible range of life and career experiences to the study group.

The MBA at Bryant consists of two preparatory courses in economics and statistics; eight core in accounting, computer information systems, finance, management, marketing, and operations; and four electives offered in a wide range of disciplines. "The academics are far from stressful but keep a steady pace." Students praise the program's "very educational methods of teaching: case study, group learning, and projects" and tell us that they do "plenty of presentations to prepare us for the business world." Even more importantly, the program focuses on "practical applications of theories and concepts." Students also enjoy the extent of the curriculum, describing it as "very oriented toward the overall business world. I have friends attending other business schools, and they are not getting the breadth of information that we are getting."

Bryant faculty typically "have been in the actual workforce and have an understanding of how the ideas that they are teaching apply to the real world," yet don't lack for academic credentials. "Many of the relevant writings were written by our professors," points out one student. Students find the faculty "dedicated and passionate as a whole."

Career and Placement

The Amica Center for Career Education serves the undergraduate students, graduate students, and alumni of Bryant University. The office provides counseling services, assessment instruments, and workshops on resume writing, interviewing, and job-search skills. The center maintains a career services library and facilitates contact with alumni through the school's Alumni Career Network. Students wish that the school would "improve in the number and diversity of on-campus recruiting companies, for example, companies based outside of Rhode Island."

Student Life and Environment

Bryant University is a "tight-knit, small school" where "people genuinely care about the community and each other." Explains one part time student in the MBA program, "I wasn't expecting to become as connected to Bryant as I was to my undergraduate university. They have made me feel like part of the community very well here." Students praise the "attractive" campus for both its beauty ("There is a fountain and a bridge in the middle of campus.") and its convenience. One student reports, "Parking is convenient and close to the classrooms. All of the classes are in one building, which reduces walking from building to building in inclement weather. The library is huge and offers unparalleled resources."

While "The Graduate Student Council is very active in getting graduate participation at all school sporting events," this is still largely a program of overcommitted part-time students, people managing not only an academic career but also full-time jobs and, often, family obligations. While students enjoy a strong esprit de corps—one reinforced by the school's recent switchover to cohort-based learning—they do not have much time to bond outside their classrooms and study groups.

KRISTOPHER SULLIVAN, ASSISTANT DEAN OF THE GRADUATE SCHOOL
1150 DOUGLAS PIKE SMITHFIELD, RI 02917-1284 UNITED STATES
PHONE: 401-232-6230 • FAX: 401-232-6494
E-MAIL: GRADPROG@BRYANT.EDU • WEBSITE: WWW.BRYANT.EDU

Bryant is located just outside the city of Providence. The location provides access not only to Rhode Island's biggest city but also to Boston, just an hour's drive to the north. The city of Providence offers a wide selection of great dining and entertainment options; it is also one of the nation's leaders in jewelry design and manufacturing. Major employers include the Bank of America, Verizon, and Blue Cross and Blue Shield Association.

Bryant MBAs "have diverse backgrounds. There is a wide dispersion of ages and social status. There are students who are married with children, newlyweds, single, and just out of undergrad. The wide diversity of experience and lifestyles has made the program interesting." The cohort system means that "moving through the program with the same group enables you to make lasting friendships with your colleagues."

Admissions

Applicants to graduate programs at Bryant University must provide the Admissions Department with the following materials: a completed application form; a personal statement of objectives (no less than 500 words long); a current resume; one letter of recommendation from a professional who can evaluate your skills and potential; official transcripts for all previous undergraduate and graduate work (regardless of whether it resulted in a degree); and an official GMAT score report. In addition to the above, international students must also provide a statement of finances, professional translation and interpretation of any foreign language transcripts, and, for those whose first language is not English and who did not earn an undergraduate degree from an English-speaking institution, an official TOEFL score report.

ADMISSIONS

Admissions Selectivity Rating	**81**
# of applications received	106
% applicants accepted	64
% acceptees attending	69
Average GMAT	579
Range of GMAT	530–630
Average GPA	3.2
TOEFL required of international students	Yes
Minimum TOEFL (paper/computer)	580/237
Application fee	$80
Regular application deadline	7/1
Regular notification	Rolling
Deferment available	Yes
Maximum length of deferment	1 year
Transfer students accepted	Yes
Transfer application policy Transfer credits are limited to 2 courses taken within the last 3 years with a grade of B (3.0) or better from an AACSB-international-al-accredited master's program.	
Non-fall admissions	Yes
Need-blind admissions	Yes

Applicants Also Look At

Babson College, Bentley College, Suffolk University, University of Rhode Island.

BUTLER UNIVERSITY
COLLEGE OF BUSINESS ADMINISTRATION

GENERAL INFORMATION

Type of school	Private
Environment	Metropolis
Academic calendar	Semester

SURVEY SAYS . . .
Cutting-edge classes
Solid preparation in:
Marketing

STUDENTS

Enrollment of parent institution	4,437
Enrollment of business school	220
% male/female	70/30
% out-of-state	17
% part-time	93
% international	6
Average age at entry	28
Average years work experience at entry	5

ACADEMICS

Academic Experience Rating	**75**
Student/faculty ratio	20:1
Profs interesting rating	88
Profs accessible rating	91
% female faculty	20
% minority faculty	12

Joint Degrees
PharmD/MBA 6 years.

FINANCIAL FACTS

Annual tuition	$10,000
Cost of books	$800
Room & board (on-campus)	$8,530

Academics

At Butler, an MBA student may major in finance, international business, leadership, or marketing. There is also a combined program leading to both a Doctor of Pharmacy and an MBA. All students must take a core curriculum, which begins with what's known as a Gateway Experience, a day-long immersion in the activities of a local business followed by an evening of analysis by the students. Students "love how this school works with local businesses to enhance experiential learning and to also provide a sort of 'symbiotic' relationship." The students "help the businesses by offering solutions to their current problems, and they also help us learn by providing us with actual business problems." That practical exercise gets students thinking about scenarios that will show up in future courses such as ethics, financial management, managerial finance, and related subjects, which account for about half the credits needed for the degree. The students then move into areas of specialization and finish things off with what's known as a Capstone Experience, which is somewhat of an extended version of the Gateway Experience they encountered at the beginning of the program. It addresses more complex issues and allows the student to make good use of the knowledge gained during the program.

"Flexibility" is a definite key word when in comes to describing the MBA program at Butler. "It is not a lockstep program, meaning that if I missed a class, I would not have to wait an entire year to retake it," one student explains. "The approach that the school takes at understanding that the part-time MBA students have lives outside of the classroom" is a strength of the program, students say, and "I travel frequently for my job, and I have yet to encounter a professor who has not attempted to help ensure I would be caught up when I return," adds another. Classes are offered on evenings and weekends, and though some students would like to see the schedule of classes expanded, they uniformly praise the quality of teaching that goes on in them. "The professors at Butler are excellent. They make themselves available to their students and truly enjoy interaction in the classroom," and "Professors have demonstrated mastery of their subject as well as an ability to relate theory of a subject to real-world situations," students say.

Throughout the program students find that the emphasis is on "high-quality and high-value, in-class lessons, and great real-world learning." Many courses are taught by professors in conjunction with business leaders, and the case studies and problems students work on in class are most often real-world business issues. "Incorporation of practical business cases and scenarios in conjunction with the course work" is a hallmark of the program, as are "up-to-date, relevant [classroom] activities and problems" and "small class size, so that one can really get to know the other students and the professors."

Career and Placement

Most of Butler's MBA students are employed while completing the degree. Some students feel that "since almost all students are already working full-time, there is little emphasis on new career opportunities," remarking that Career Services seem to be geared toward undergraduates. However, being located in Indianapolis, a city ranked in the "Top 10 Best Places for Business and Careers" in a ranking of the 200 largest metropolitan areas in the United States by *Forbes*, helps with prospects. "There are thousands of top companies right in our backyard," students point out. "Many local companies have allowed students to participate in hands-on business simulations, and prominent business leaders have come to campus to speak and network." Butler's "regional reputation with business and community leaders and the number of very successful alumni working in the region" are also strong points for those who are job hunting.

STEPHANIE JUDGE, DIRECTOR OF MARKETING
COLLEGE OF BUSINESS ADMINISTRATION, 4600 SUNSET AVENUE INDIANAPOLIS, IN 46208-3485 U.S.
PHONE: 317-940-9221 • FAX: 317-940-9455
E-MAIL: MBA@BUTLER.EDU • WEBSITE: WWW.BUTLERMBA.COM

Eli Lilly and Company, Roche, First Indiana Bank, Regions Bank, Firestone, and the NCAA are among those who employ Butler's MBA graduates.

Student Life and Environment

MBA students love Butler's small-school atmosphere and personal touch. "Butler is a beautiful campus. Although I live off campus, I am always surprised by how many students are around participating in various on-campus activities," notes one student. "My classes include students from different ethnic, cultural, social, and religious backgrounds. This leads to great discussions on the wide varieties of experiences we have had in our careers." "Everyone on campus is engaging and helpful. Because of the small campus and class size, you get to know a number of peers, professors and administration well," others say. Students find the workload moderate, the administration responsive, and their fellow students friendly and focused. Noting that "the school is small enough to have a personal touch," "You can easily get the help and support that you need." Some would like better child care support and more opportunities to involve spouses in their academic lives, but they like the attention both faculty and staff pay to the needs of working students with families. "Most are busy with careers just like I am, but that gives us common ground to support each other in balancing work, school, and life," one student says.

Admissions

The Admissions Committee for the MBA program at Butler weighs an applicant's undergraduate GPA, GMAT score, letters of recommendation, and work experience most heavily. Though most students are from the Midwest, residency is not a factor that Butler, a private institution, takes into account, and it also does not consider a student's extracurricular activities. In 2006 the average GPA of admitted students was 3.32/4.0, and their GMAT score ranged from 470–690. Most students had 5 or more years of work experience.

ADMISSIONS

Admissions Selectivity Rating	**72**
# of applications received	76
% applicants accepted	84
% acceptees attending	78
Average GMAT	540
Range of GMAT	470–690
Average GPA	3.32
TOEFL required of international students	Yes
Minimum TOEFL (paper/computer)	550/213
Regular application deadline	7/15
Regular notification	8/10
Deferment available	Yes
Maximum length of deferment	1 year
Transfer students accepted	Yes
Transfer application policy Up to 9 credit hours, pending approval.	
Non-fall admissions	Yes

Applicants Also Look At

Indiana University—Bloomington, Indiana University—Purdue University Indianapolis.

CALIFORNIA POLYTECHNIC STATE UNIVERSITY—SAN LUIS OBISPO
ORFALEA COLLEGE OF BUSINESS

GENERAL INFORMATION
Type of school	Public
Environment	Town
Academic calendar	Quarter

SURVEY SAYS . . .
Students love San Luis Obispo, CA
Good social scene
Good peer network
Solid preparation in:
Teamwork
Communication/interpersonal skills
Presentation skills

STUDENTS
Enrollment of parent institution	18,500
Enrollment of business school	84
% male/female	65/35
% out-of-state	20
% part-time	10
% minorities	12
% international	10
Average age at entry	27
Average years work experience at entry	3

ACADEMICS
Academic Experience Rating	**70**
Student/faculty ratio	25:1
Profs interesting rating	71
Profs accessible rating	81
% female faculty	20
% minority faculty	20

Joint Degrees
MBA/MS (engineering management) 2 years, MBA/MS (computer science) 2 years, MBA/MS (electrical engineering) 2 years, MBA/MS (mechanical engineering) 2 years, MBA/MS (industrial and technical studies) 2 years, MBA/MS (industrial engineering) 2 years, MBA/MS (civil and environmental engineering) 2 years, MBA/master of public policy 2 years. Various additional dual degree options are available.

Academics

Students praise "the focus on career preparation" in the MBA program at California Polytechnic State University's Orfalea College of Business, telling us that "Orfalea has a hands-on approach. It's not as theoretical as some programs; here, you take on real-world challenges. Companies that recruit here frequently comment that they prefer Cal Poly grads because they 'hit the ground running' after being hired." Students also greatly appreciate the reasonable tuition; one writes, "This place is a great deal in terms of bang for your buck. If I had gone someplace else, I'd be in debt for decades." The school is an exceptionally good deal for students in the accelerated Track 1 full-time MBA; they complete the program in 1 year, saving the additional tuition, expenses, and fees that some in the Track 2 program (one year full-time plus additional part-time study) incur.

In either program, students pursue "a learn-by-doing policy adhered to throughout the college." One student reports, "In the upcoming quarter, I will be involved in a team competing against teams from other schools in making important business decisions for a simulated company in a simulated market. Not only will this help me learn what types of decisions and information I will encounter in the real world, it also gives me a great add-on for my resume and subject to talk about during interviews." A mentoring program provides another great add-on; it "allows students to 'hook up' with a mentor prominent in the business world (mine is the vice president of a large chain of banks) starting from the second week of classes." Yet another perk of the program is a two-and-a-half week trip to China (mandatory for Track 1, encouraged for Track 2), which some here feel is the "most informative" part of the program.

Orfalea's faculty is "well prepared and knowledgeable" with professors who "emphasize the importance of teamwork." Small class sizes "really allow students to get to know one another and create a friendly atmosphere conducive to creating strong bonds." On the downside, students complain that "the short time period of the program leaves out room for some electives that would be beneficial or exciting to take" and that "most of the teachers focus too heavily on grades. The school will improve when more focus is on learning and less on grades. The design does not encourage risk taking so students select easier classes." Nearly 20 percent of Orfalea MBAs pursue dual-degree programs, taking second degrees in such areas as engineering, architecture, and public policy.

Career and Placement

Orfalea's Career Placement Services "do a great job of preparing students for the recruiting process and following through with companies to ensure that they continue to recruit Cal Poly grads." The school has strong "connections to Bay Area companies." The small size of the program, however, may affect recruitment activities somewhat; one student says, "Since this is a technical school, the majority of employers are seeking engineers or related fields. It's difficult for someone with a non-technical background (like a degree in management) to find a range of employers at the job fair."

Orfalea MBAs most often work for: Northrup Grumman, Raytheon, Rantec, General Dynamics, Sun MicroSystems, Deloitte Touche Tohmatsu, Qualcomm, IBM, Agilent Technology, Amgen, Lawrence Livermore Labs, Pacific Gas & Electric, USDA, Department of Veterans Affairs, KPMG International, Pratt & Whitney, Morgan Stanley, Boston Scientific Corporation, PricewaterhouseCoopers, Sandia National Lab, Lam Research, Columbia Sportswear, and Adelaida Cellars.

CHRIS CARR, ASSOCIATE DEAN OF GRADUATE PROGRAMS
ONE GRAND AVENUE, OCOB SAN LUIS OBISPO, CA 93407 UNITED STATES
PHONE: 805-756-2637 • FAX: 805-756-0110
E-MAIL: MBA@CALPOLY.EDU • WEBSITE: MBA.CALPOLY.EDU

Student Life and Environment

San Luis Obispo is "primarily an undergrad campus," but grad students find ways to get in on the action. They're "very social; everyone wants to be involved with each other and with the events taking place. There are speakers every week, and the attendance is fairly good." The fact that "the program is relatively small" means "Everyone gets to know each other well. This is not like a commuter school."

The town of San Luis Obispo "is a great place loaded with clubs and situated in a great location for all manner of activities. Public transit is free for students. Because the town is so attractive, there is often less activity on campus than you would see at other schools, but the student population is 50 percent of the city, so almost any place becomes a gathering place for students." Students arriving from big cities may find that the leisurely pace of life here requires some adjustment.

Orfalea students "come from a variety of different backgrounds but are all very motivated to further their careers. The attitude at the school is more of camaraderie and cooperation than competition." The population "is very young compared to other grad schools, but most students have at least a few . . . years of experience."

Admissions

The Admissions Office at the Orfalea College of Business consider all of the following components of a student's application: GMAT score (middle 80 percent of student body scores between 540 and 680); TOEFL score (where applicable); two official copies of undergraduate transcript (the middle 80 percent of student body earns between 2.9 and 3.7); two letters of recommendation; a personal statement; and a resume. Prior work experience, while preferred, is not required. Prospective dual-degree candidates must apply to, and be accepted to, each program separately. All international applicants must provide statements of purpose and financial responsibility, a spouse/dependent declaration, and a signed health insurance contract; they must also submit to an educational background check.

Prominent Alumni

Robert Rowell, president, Golden State Warriors; Linda Ozawa Olds, founder, Jamba Juice; Bill Swanson, chairman and CEO, Raytheon Company; Burt Rutan, president, Scaled Composites, designer SpaceShipOne; Gary Bloom, CEO, Veritas.

FINANCIAL FACTS

Annual tuition (in-state/ out-of-state)	$3,102/$13,950
Fees	$1,830
Cost of books	$1,500
Room & board	$8,745
% of students receiving aid	45
% of first-year students receiving aid	25
% of students receiving loans	45
% of students receiving grants	5
Average award package	$11,634
Average grant	$2,176

ADMISSIONS

Admissions Selectivity Rating	**90**
# of applications received	135
% applicants accepted	47
% acceptees attending	90
Average GMAT	610
Range of GMAT	580–640
Average GPA	3.26
TOEFL required of international students	Yes
Minimum TOEFL (paper/computer)	550/213
Application fee	$55
Regular application deadline	7/1
Regular notification	Rolling
Transfer students accepted	Yes
Transfer application policy Maximum of 8 units transfer.	
Need-blind admissions	Yes

Applicants Also Look At

Arizona State University, California State University—Sacramento, San Diego State University, University of California—Berkeley, University of California—Davis, University of California—Irvine, University of California—Los Angeles (UCLA).

EMPLOYMENT PROFILE	
Career Rating	**86**
Primary Source of Full-time Job Acceptances	
Percent employed	100

CALIFORNIA STATE POLYTECHNIC UNIVERSITY—POMONA
COLLEGE OF BUSINESS ADMINISTRATION

GENERAL INFORMATION

Type of school	Public
Environment	City
Academic calendar	Quarter

SURVEY SAYS . . .
Helpful alumni
Happy students
Solid preparation in:
Teamwork
Communication/interpersonal skills
Presentation skills
Quantitative skills

STUDENTS

Enrollment of parent institution	19,800
Enrollment of business school	350
% male/female	55/45
% minorities	20
% international	18
Average age at entry	32
Average years work experience at entry	10

ACADEMICS

Academic Experience Rating	**85**
Student/faculty ratio	15:1
Profs interesting rating	76
Profs accessible rating	69

FINANCIAL FACTS

Annual tuition (in-state/ out-of-state)	$4,420/$6,100
Cost of books	$3,000
Room & board (on/off-campus)	$5,000/$8,000
Average grant	$18,500
Average student loan debt	$12,000

Academics

Cal Poly Pomona offers a number of intriguing MBA options to its predominantly part-time student body. Like nearly all business schools, Cal Poly Pomona offers a general MBA, but unlike many schools, Cal Poly Pomona offers required courses for the degree both on campus and "off campus at a variety of locations throughout Southern California," through its Professional MBA (PMBA) program. For students with precisely defined goals, Cal Poly Pomona offers the Career MBA, through which students may specialize in one of 11 predefined areas or design a custom emphasis of their own. Finally, Cal Poly Pomona offers the only MSBA in Information Systems Auditing in the United States.

Cal Poly Pomona stresses a "learn-by-doing teaching/learning style" that students appreciate. The approach "forces students to work in groups and deal with teamwork while polishing presentation skills. This is very valuable." Students also appreciate the fact that Cal Poly "has decent technology and wireless access. I like the fact the school can keep up with technology." Cal Poly Pomona's MBA program "offers a high-quality, well-structured education with challenging courses, and students definitely learn a lot." The faculty "brings real business experiences and problems to the table. They are still active in the business world—not a bunch of stuffy academics with outdated information and notes." As one student sums up, "The overall experience here has been exceptional, especially considering the fact that it is a state school! The administration bends over backward for the students to fix any problems students or faculty may have. Professors are all top-quality and have a definite interest in seeing the students learn."

PMBA students at remote sites are particularly impressed with the level of service they receive. One PMBA student writes, "I live in a remote area, and the school provides instructors to teach not online but in person. The experience is perfect and quite rewarding." Faculty members "are very helpful and accessible despite the fact that classes are off campus."

Career and Placement

Career services for MBAs here are provided by the Cal Poly Pomona Career Center (CPPCC), a central office serving all undergraduate and graduate students at the university. The CPPCC provides all standard counseling and placement services. Many students do not even use the service; they already have jobs that they hope to advance in by earning a graduate degree. Those who do visit the office wish that it would "focus on providing more internships, part-time jobs, and full-time job opportunities."

Student Life and Environment

Cal Poly Pomona "is a commuter campus" for MBAs, who largely agree that "campus life is for undergrads who don't work. There is little time for working adults to enjoy campus life, but there is no shortage of clubs and organizations to join for those who want to." When students here get together outside of class, it is to complete required group projects, not to pound some brews or organize a lecture series. Cal Poly Pomona's MBAs appreciate the fact that "the campus is also continually improving its facilities and growing to become more modern and state-of-the-art every year."

ADMINISTRATIVE COORDINATOR
3801 WEST TEMPLE AVENUE, POMONA, CA 91768 UNITED STATES
PHONE: 909-869-3210 • FAX: 909-869-4529
E-MAIL: ADMISSIONS@CSUPOMONA.EDU • WEBSITE: WWW.CSUPOMONA.EDU

Those who take classes at one of the school's satellite sites report that "classrooms are rented by the university at our site; thus, there are few student activities or resources here. There is no need for us to travel to the main campus, so we don't. The online services are excellent and that makes dealing with the university easy. And even though I am not at the main campus, I do have access to all main campus services and resources if I ever decide to travel there."

The MBA student body is "extremely diverse in terms of age, ethnicity, undergrad majors, and experience levels. Most are commuters who work full-time, come to class, and can't wait to get home after class is over. Most have very busy lives and do not network too strongly within this campus. It's a good group, but career- and family-minded, not socially minded." A substantial number are "enginerds" who "are broadening their intellect by going to b-school."

Admissions

Cal Poly Pomona operates on a quarterly academic schedule; the school accepts MBA applications for each quarter. All of the following components of the application are carefully considered: complete postsecondary academic record as reflected in official transcripts; GMAT scores (must be no more than five years old); two letters of recommendation from current or former employers; and a resume. Applicants who attended an undergraduate institution at which English is not the primary language of instruction must provide official TOEFL scores. Applicants must meet the following criteria to be considered for admission: an overall undergraduate GPA of at least 3.0; a minimum GMAT score of 450; and, if required, TOEFL scores of at least 580 on the paper and-pencil test or 237 on the computer-based test. Meeting minimum requirements does not guarantee admission to the program.

ADMISSIONS

Admissions Selectivity Rating	**86**
# of applications received	163
% applicants accepted	30
% acceptees attending	59
Average GMAT	540
Range of GMAT	450–720
Average GPA	3.2
TOEFL required of international students	Yes
Minimum TOEFL (paper/computer)	580/237
Application fee	$55
Regular application deadline	Rolling
Regular notification	Rolling
Deferment available	Yes
Maximum length of deferment	1–2 quarters
Transfer students accepted	Yes
Transfer application policy Maximum of 3 transferrable classes (13 units).	
Non-fall admissions	Yes
Need-blind admissions	Yes

EMPLOYMENT PROFILE	
Career Rating	75

CALIFORNIA STATE UNIVERSITY—CHICO
COLLEGE OF BUSINESS

GENERAL INFORMATION
Type of school	Public
Environment	Village
Academic calendar	Semester

SURVEY SAYS . . .
Students love Chico, CA
Friendly students
Solid preparation in:
Finance
Teamwork
Presentation skills
Computer skills

STUDENTS
Enrollment of parent institution	15,000
Enrollment of business school	76
% male/female	53/47
% part-time	30
% international	22
Average age at entry	30
Average years work experience at entry	3

ACADEMICS
Academic Experience Rating	**69**
Student/faculty ratio	25:1
Profs interesting rating	65
Profs accessible rating	62
% female faculty	30
% minority faculty	10

Prominent Alumni
Prabhakar Kalavacharla, managing partner, KPMG International; Ed Byers, managing partner, Deloitte Touche Tohmatsu; Masayuki Ishizaki, managing partner, Accenture; Bill Bales, CFO, Sierra Nevada Brewing Company; Abhijit Joshi, Manager, KPMG International.

Academics

Many students choose California State University—Chico for its "emphasis on cutting-edge information system knowledge and technologies," citing "their focus on IT, the future of business," as a primary reason for choosing to enroll in the program. Chico was the first school to participate in the SAP University Alliance Program, which trains students in software that manages and integrates information in a corporate business setting. College of Business students also publish an annual magazine, *Link*, dedicated to business and technology issues. Students tell us that they also enjoy excellent industry contacts through the teaching staff, internship office, and career services.

Chico stands out for its "outstanding achievement teaching MIS," though students report that the quality of instruction is generally very high. "Small classes mean good opportunity for individual attention from teachers," and applied learning is a foundation of the program. Course work emphasizes "tons of teamwork and presentation" and "most business professors choose the hands-on approach in teaching and are open-minded to suggestions and ideas." However, while students are highly satisfied with the instruction in modern topics such as e-commerce and technology, they warn that more traditional subjects do not always receive the attention they might at more conventional business schools. Students admit that "professors range from excellent to to-be-avoided," and that "instruction in finance is weak."

The College of Business at Chico "is geared toward MBA students who did not have business undergrad," and therefore the curriculum comprises a broad base of courses in accounting, finance, management, international business, technology, and e-commerce. For students with extensive professional experience or who pursued an undergraduate degree in business, the curriculum provides a worthy examination of these concepts, but such students tells us that "the workload is moderate" and easy to balance alongside full-time employment. In the words of a second-year student, "Coming from industry, the workload is not that difficult to manage." Those entering the program with a less intensive business background, however—particularly for those with less technology know-how—find the program rather challenging; writes one such student, "I was not prepared in computers for my accounting BS, so it's been a little overwhelming." As the curriculum is broad-based, with the exception of the technology focus, students at Chico may design a moderately focused business education. Chico does not offer concentrations in special areas of study, nor highly focused electives in certain industries or topics.

As part of the California State school system, Chico has been affected by the state's widely publicized budget cuts. As a result, the school is "sometimes a bit of a logistical nightmare." In addition, facilities and resources do not always meet student needs. For example, "the library is hardly ever open and closes early" and "the cash-strapped school needs updated computers for some labs."

Career and Placement

Chico graduates tend to find work in a fairly wide range of industries. In an average year, students from the graduate and undergraduate programs find work in over 250 different companies. When interviewing for jobs, Chico students notice that "this school is appreciated by industry," especially in the high-tech sector. In particular, employers seek Chico grads for their strong knowledge of computers and technology, and students agree that "the unique curriculum helps a lot in job hunting."

NEELAM BAHL, BUSINESS GRADUATE PROGRAMS STAFF
BGAD AT CSU, CHICO 041, WEST FIRST AND ORANGE STREET CHICO, CA 95929 UNITED STATES
PHONE: 530-898-4425 • FAX: 530-898-5889
E-MAIL: NBAHL@CSUCHICO.EDU • WEBSITE: WWW.COB.CSUCHICO.EDU

According to Chico's administration, 80 percent of recruiters rate the Chico State curriculum as outstanding or above average compared with other universities at which they recruit. In recent years, the following companies—among others—came to recruit at Chico State: Andersen Consulting, Anixter, Bank of America, Chevron, Deloitte Touche Tohmatsu, Ernst & Young, First Interstate Bank, Hewlett-Packard, Intel, Paine Webber, PricewaterhouseCoopers, Sears, System Integrators, Tandem Computers, Wal-Mart, and Wallace Computer Services.

Student Life and Environment

The undergraduate college at Chico is known throughout California as something of a "party school," and while "most graduate students are not socially active," they say the outgoing vibe definitely rubs off on the business-school community. At Chico, you won't see frowns, complaints, or negative competition. By all accounts, Chico is a "friendly environment with lots of happy students and professors." An MBA student writes, "The college environment—both people and campus—makes the experience here unforgettable." Drawing students from Northern California and across the world, the student body is very "culturally diverse," with a "vastly international student base." In general, the international students attend classes full-time, whereas the majority of California residents "are returning-to-school, working adults" who hold full- or part-time jobs while pursuing their business degree.

Located in idyllic Northern California, hometown Chico is an excellent place to study, as it is "laid-back, small, safe, and affordable." In addition to its excellent atmosphere, Chico is well placed for anyone hoping to work in the greater Northern California region, drawing students from the local community, the San Francisco Bay Area and Sacramento.

Admissions

To apply to Chico's graduate program in business, you must submit a completed application, an application fee, a statement of purpose, three letters of recommendation, and GMAT scores. The minimum acceptable GMAT score is the fiftieth percentile. There is no minimum work requirement to apply to Chico State, and students are accepted from every undergraduate major.

FINANCIAL FACTS

Annual tuition (in-state/ out-of-state)	$4,000/$10,102
Cost of books	$1,500
Room & board	$11,000
% of students receiving aid	65
% of first-year students receiving aid	50
% of students receiving loans	65
% of students receiving grants	10
Average award package	$10,000
Average grant	$1,000

ADMISSIONS

Admissions Selectivity Rating	74
# of applications received	41
% applicants accepted	73
% acceptees attending	63
Average GMAT	530
Range of GMAT	490–570
Average GPA	3.39
TOEFL required of international students	Yes
Minimum TOEFL (paper/computer)	550/213
Application fee	$55
Regular application deadline	Rolling
Regular notification	Rolling
Deferment available	Yes
Maximum length of deferment	1 year
Transfer students accepted	Yes
Transfer application policy Must meet our admissions criteria	
Non-fall admissions	Yes
Need-blind admissions	Yes

Applicants Also Look At
California State University—
Sacramento, San Francisco State
University.

EMPLOYMENT PROFILE

Career Rating		79	Grads Employed by Function	%	Avg. Salary
Primary Source of Full-time Job Acceptances			Finance/Accounting	50	$49,100
School-facilitated activities	18 (82%)		MIS	30	$50,000
Graduate-facilitated activities	4 (18%)		Consulting	10	$60,000
Percent employed	100		General Management	10	$56,000

Top 5 Employers Hiring Grads
BearingPoint; CSU, Chico; Deloitte Touche
Tohmatsu; Ernst & Young; Synopsys Inc.

CALIFORNIA STATE UNIVERSITY—EAST BAY
COLLEGE OF BUSINESS AND ECONOMICS

Academics

The MBA program at California State University—East Bay offers its busy student body an excellent assortment of specializations to choose from: 14 to be exact, including options in accounting, business economics, various computer-related areas, entrepreneurship, management, e-business, international business, computer information systems, marketing management, finance, human resources management, operations and materials management, strategic management taxation, and supply chain management. Most classes here meet in the evenings, making them convenient for a student body comprised mainly of full-time workers.

The CSUEB MBA track includes foundation courses, which can be waived for students who earned undergraduate degrees in business; proficiency requirements in mathematics and statistics; 12 credits in core courses; four credits in international requirements, fulfilled by a course in international business or international economics; a five-credit capstone experience, consisting of either an entrepreneurship practicum or a seminar in strategic management; and course work sufficient to complete an MBA Option (what many schools call a "specialization" or "concentration"). In total, 45 quarter credits are required toward the MBA here.

In all programs, students appreciate the fact that "professors are very sympathetic to family and work issues." They report that "the professors are great in supply chain management," using "case studies that are oriented on real-life situations," and that "the accounting program is superb." Most of all, they love the low cost of attending. Some worry, however, that "the state is reducing its financial support of CSU, and that's caused a reduction in the number of classes offered. This is not a positive trend."

Career and Placement

CSUEB MBAs receive career guidance from the university's Career Development Center (CDC). Individual counseling is available to help students develop a personalized career plan. The school maintains an online resume database, as well as a website with numerous helpful links for MBAs. "Proximity to Silicon Valley" is also a boon to students. Since "this MBA program is catered to working professionals," many students are already involved in a career track.

Student Life and Environment

Those who get involved with campus life at CSUEB tell us that "life at school is dramatically enhanced when participating in campus organizations." Clubs such as the Operations Management Society, for example, "bring in speakers from top companies to address us, and good speakers from outside are sometimes invited to classes to talk about relevant topics." Few here, however, have the time or inclination to pursue such life-enhancing experiences. "This is a commuter school, and there's not too much life on campus," sums up one typical student.

Business school facilities, students tell us, need improvement, but a new building was recently completed. Students appreciate the day-care facility and "a good library full of helpful librarians." "Nice weather and an outstanding view over the bay" also make difficult days a little less stressful.

Nearly half the MBA student population at CSUEB is international, the result of numerous partnerships between the school and overseas business schools. This creates a student body that is "not only from diverse employments, but also from diverse cultures, representing ideas and business methods from all over the world. Everyone shares experiences and everyone is very easy to talk to."

DORIS DUNCAN, DIRECTOR OF MBA PROGRAMS
25800 CARLES BEE BOULEVARD HAYWARD, CA 94542 UNITED STATES
PHONE: 510-885-2419 • FAX: 510-885-2176
E-MAIL: DORIS.DUNCAN@CSUEASTBAY.EDU • WEBSITE: CBEGRAD.CSUEASTBAY.EDU

Admissions

Applications to all graduate business programs at CSUEB are evaluated on the basis of academic transcripts for all undergraduate and post-undergraduate work, and GMAT scores. As the school's website states, "Admission is automatic for applicants with (1) a minimum 1050 'Index Score' and (2) minimum twentieth percentile GMAT Verbal and Quantitative scores. [Index Score = (Upper Division GPA x 200) + Total GMAT]." Some students may be admitted conditionally, pending the completion of nondegree foundation courses. Students must demonstrate writing proficiency prior to enrolling in graduate-level courses; this can be achieved with a score of at least 8 on the university's Writing Skills Test (WST) or a score of at least 4.5 on the GMAT essay. International students must prove proficiency in English in one of a few ways: by earning a TOEFL (Test of English as a Foreign Language) score of at least 550 (paper-based test) or 213 (computer-based test); by earning an IELTS (International English Language Testing System) score of at least 7.0; or by submitting an official transcript verifying receipt of a bachelor's degree from "a U.S. college or university or an international college or university where English is the principal language of instruction."

FINANCIAL FACTS

Annual tuition (in-state/ out-of-state)	$4,736/$11,968
Cost of books	$10,000
Room & board (on/off-campus)	$15,500/$17,500
% of students receiving aid	12
% of first-year students receiving aid	12
% of students receiving loans	8
% of students receiving grants	1
Average award package	$12,943
Average grant	$11,478
Average student loan debt	$25,626

ADMISSIONS

Admissions Selectivity Rating	75
# of applications received	228
% applicants accepted	71
% acceptees attending	88
Average GMAT	530
Range of GMAT	400–630
Average GPA	3.23
TOEFL required of international students	Yes
Minimum TOEFL (paper/computer)	550/213
Application fee	$55
Regular application deadline	6/1
Regular notification	6/21
Non-fall admissions	Yes

Applicants Also Look At

California State University—Sacramento, San Francisco State University, San José State University, University of California—Berkeley, University of California—Davis.

CALIFORNIA STATE UNIVERSITY—FRESNO
CRAIG SCHOOL OF BUSINESS

GENERAL INFORMATION

Type of school	Public
Academic calendar	Semester

SURVEY SAYS . . .
Solid preparation in:
General management
Teamwork
Communication/interpersonal skills
Presentation skills
Entrepreneurial studies

STUDENTS

Enrollment of parent institution	21,000
Enrollment of business school	129
% male/female	75/25
% out-of-state	15
% part-time	100
% minorities	30
% international	20
Average age at entry	26
Average years work experience at entry	4

ACADEMICS

Academic Experience Rating	**82**
Student/faculty ratio	6:1
Profs interesting rating	72
Profs accessible rating	65
% female faculty	33
% minority faculty	6

FINANCIAL FACTS

Annual tuition (in-state/ out-of-state)	$1,811/$6,102
Cost of books	$650
Room & board (off-campus)	$10,700
Average grant	$3,000
Average student loan debt	$20,000

Academics

The MBA program at California State University—Fresno's Craig School of Business is designed with the working student in mind. All weekday classes here meet just once a week, from 6:00 P.M. to 8:45 P.M. Saturday morning classes (usually scheduled from 9:00 A.M. to 11:45 A.M.) are also available.

The Craig MBA consists of 11 classes and a final project. The curriculum commences with six core courses covering such fundamental areas as leadership, MIS, finance, accounting, marketing, and ethics. Students then complete three electives. Electives may be used to create a specialization in agribusiness, entrepreneurship, finance, human resource management, MIS, or marketing; or, students may choose to graduate with a General Management degree. The program concludes with a capstone class in Business Policy and Strategy and a culminating project or thesis.

Up to five introductory foundation courses that do not count toward the graduate degree may be required of some entering students. Students who have earned an undergraduate degree in business from an AACSB-accredited institution within the last seven years generally do not have to take these courses. Those not meeting these criteria may be able to place out of some or all of the introductory courses through examination.

Students identify entrepreneurship and courses dealing with globalization as the program's strengths. Those studying MIS, however, warn that "there currently are not enough professors to offer all of the courses, making it difficult to complete the degree." MBAs here appreciate the fact that the Craig School "has made a point to invest itself into the community for the sake of the community, as well as for the sake of the students. Fresno State feels like a hub of the community, and it's exciting to be affiliated with it." Professors here "are typically passionate about their subject matter, which leads to interesting classes, even when the material isn't what I'd like to be studying (accounting, for example)."

Career and Placement

Career and placement services for Craig MBAs are limited. The school does not have a dedicated Career Services Office; rather, a single Career Services Office serves all undergraduate and graduate students at the university. The office provides a number of recruiting events and other support services, but few are designed to serve the unique needs of MBAs. An MBA Student Association offers additional services, organizing events that "connect MBA students with alumni, faculty, and local community, and business leaders" in order to "build a professional network and lay the foundation for friendships that will last a lifetime." Most Craig students are part-time students with full-time jobs (many attend at their employers' expense), and for them the dearth of career services is not a major drawback.

Student Life and Environment

It's all business (pun intended!) on the Craig MBA campus, as one student expresses: "Extracurricular activities coincide with class times," making participation difficult. While "there are a number of activities available for undergraduate students, it's hard to make these available for graduate students who are busy with work throughout the day."

However, the Craig school is in the process of upgrading its facilities, and many here believe that the "facilities will be amazing in a few years." The library is being remodeled and the university has recently opened a 15,000-seat entertainment and sports center (Savemart Center), the largest of those facilities in California's Central Valley. This

DR. RAFAEL SOLIS, DIRECTOR OF GRADUATE PROGRAMS
5245 NORTH BACKER AVENUE FRESNO, CA 93740 UNITED STATES
PHONE: 559-278-2107 • FAX: 559-278-2572
E-MAIL: MBAINFO@CSUFRESNO.EDU • WEBSITE: WWW.CRAIG.CSUFRESNO.EDU/MBA

venue is used for a variety of sports events ranging from basketball to ice hockey. It has also hosted musical, drama, and dance shows. Hopefully, this new recreation center will cater to graduate students' hectic schedules and provide them with multiple extracurricular options.

The Craig student body "represents a varied mix of industries, allowing for a 'cross-section' view of industries in general" during class discussions and group projects. Many foreign students attend, and "though there are times when language barriers exist, our lives are expanded by their presence." MBAs here report that "although we are so different in terms of age, ethnic background, and work experience, we are all here, going through the same courses and moaning about the same tough professors. There's a feeling of 'We're in this together.'"

Admissions

Admission to the Craig MBA program is determined primarily by the applicant's undergraduate grade point average (GPA) during the final two years of undergraduate work, and GMAT scores. The average admitted student arrives with a GPA of 3.4 and a GMAT score of 566. The quality of undergraduate institution and curriculum pursued are considered when evaluating GPA. Work experience, personal statement, and two letters of recommendation (from employers, professors, or professional peers) also figure into the admissions decision. Because the GMAT score is a major factor in admissions, the admissions office strongly encourages all candidates to prepare for the exam for at least six to eight weeks. International students must have a minimum TOEFL score of 550 (paper-based test) or 213 (computer-based test) to be considered.

ADMISSIONS

Admissions Selectivity Rating	**80**
# of applications received	99
% applicants accepted	63
% acceptees attending	47
Average GMAT	580
Range of GMAT	550–690
Average GPA	3.4
TOEFL required of international students	Yes
Minimum TOEFL (paper/computer)	550/213
Application fee	$55
Regular application deadline	3/1
Regular notification	Rolling
Deferment available	Yes
Maximum length of deferment	1 year
Transfer students accepted	Yes
Transfer application policy	

All foundation courses may be waived through prior course work. Up to 9 units of credit may be transferred into core and elective portion of program. Transfer credit granted on a case-by-case basis through transcript and course syllabus reviews.

Non-fall admissions	Yes
Need-blind admissions	Yes

Applicants Also Look At

Cal Poly State University—San Luis Obispo, Santa Clara University, University of California—Davis.

CALIFORNIA STATE UNIVERSITY—FULLERTON
COLLEGE OF BUSINESS AND ECONOMICS

GENERAL INFORMATION

Type of school	Public
Environment	City
Academic calendar	Semester

SURVEY SAYS . . .

Students love Fullerton, CA
Cutting-edge classes
Happy students
Smart classrooms
Solid preparation in:
Accounting
Quantitative skills

STUDENTS

Enrollment of parent institution	35,921
Enrollment of business school	349
% male/female	100/0
% part-time	100
Average age at entry	27

ACADEMICS

Academic Experience Rating	**74**
Student/faculty ratio	23:1
Profs interesting rating	73
Profs accessible rating	65
% female faculty	22
% minority faculty	20

Prominent Alumni

Kevin Costner, businessman and actor; Maurice Myers, president and CEO, Waste Management, Inc.

FINANCIAL FACTS

Annual tuition (out-of-state)	$8,136
Fees	$3,612
Room & board (on/off-campus)	$5,912/$10,810
Average award package	$4,000
Average grant	$4,000

Academics

The Graduate School of Business at California State University—Fullerton offers "one of only four accredited accounting programs in the state" as well as "a good selection of specializations [at] approximately one-fifth the cost of other MBA programs in the area (UCI, USC, UCLA, Pepperdine)." Students appreciate these assets, as well as the school's "flexible, nonlockstep" curriculum that allows the completely part-time student body to wedge an MBA program into their hectic lives.

CSUF offers three MBA options: the Generalist Plan, the Specialist Plan, and the International Business MBA. The Generalist Plan is designed for students with little or no undergraduate background in business. The program begins with a nine-course foundation sequence (up to three courses can be waived based on equivalent undergraduate work). Students then proceed through seven subject-specific advanced seminars (six prescribed, one elective), a comprehensive capstone course, and a concluding written project or oral examinations. Students with no business background are relieved to find that the program brings them up to speed. One student currently following the foundation sequence writes, "The professors are very helpful and knowledgeable, as well as approachable, which is truly appreciated." MBAs here warn, however, that "the program is long. It could take close to four years to complete on a part-time basis." They also note that "the program allows only elective course for Generalist program. I would prefer the option to have more."

CSFU's Specialist Plan allows students to develop a concentration in accounting, business economics, finance, e-commerce, entrepreneurship, management, management science/information systems, or marketing. The program commences with a 10-course foundation sequence (some or all courses can be waived based on equivalent undergraduate work), then proceeds to six advanced seminars. Students then choose four concentration-related electives before concluding the program with a comprehensive capstone course, and a concluding written project or oral examinations. Students praise this "well-structured program that allows flexibility yet covers all relevant topics," singling out the accounting and finance offerings as "outstanding."

The third option at CSFU is the International Business MBA, which consists of the 10-course foundation sequence (some or all courses can be waived based on equivalent undergraduate work), five advanced seminars, five concentration courses, the comprehensive capstone course, and the concluding written project or oral examinations.

Students in all programs agree that "the faculty consistently challenge us, but make sure we learn the material." Students go on to say that "the academic experience is very beneficial because there is a lot of interaction between students and professors." They also tell us that "the school could improve with some technology . . . like more wireless Internet access, which is limited to a few buildings on campus." For the convenience of those in the south Orange County region, CSUF offers slightly modified versions of the Generalist and Specialist MBA programs at a facility near the Irvine Spectrum.

Career and Placement

The Cal State Fullerton Career Planning and Placement Center provides career services to MBAs at both the Fullerton and Irvine Spectrum locations. Services include walk-in counseling, interview tips, resume review, and job databases. Students may continue to utilize these facilities for up to one year after they graduate for a $25 fee.

PRE-ADMISSION ADVISOR
PO BOX 6848 FULLERTON, CA 92834-6848 UNITED STATES
PHONE: 714-278-3622 • FAX: 714-278-7101
E-MAIL: MBA@FULLERTON.EDU • WEBSITE: BUSINESS.FULLERTON.EDU/GRADUATEPROGRAMS

Student Life and Environment

Don't expect much hand-holding from the folks who run the CSUF MBA program. One student observes, "The school could do a better job in partnering and treating the graduate business students like the professionals that we are, and less like numbers. . . . Except for the milk and cookies that arriving MBA candidates get at the orientation, there are absolutely no mixers hosted by the school whatsoever. It's very clear from the beginning: You're on your own." Not that it matters much to most students, who "tend to work full-time and are not heavily involved in school life." One student explains, "I don't spend much time at school except when there is a group meeting and going to class." But the feeling is that "while I am there, I do enjoy the campus and the people." Students point out, "Some group-project efforts are challenging due to people's schedules and geographic locations. Overall, we always seem to work it out." Students respect each other's schedules and tell us, "These are great people that I love to hang out with."

The MBA program at Fullerton "has a diverse culture, which is great. The students and professors come from a wide variety of countries, backgrounds, and beliefs, which makes the experience even better." Additionally, "almost all MBA students have full-time careers—this is vital for the exchange of ideas." Overall, students tend to be on the youngish side. One student speculates, "Most are in their late twenties or early thirties." The "large international population [includes] a big percentage of Asian nationals."

Admissions

Cal State Fullerton requires the following of all applicants to its MBA program: an "acceptable bachelor's degree from an appropriately accredited institution," with a minimum GPA of 2.5 for the final two years of undergraduate work; GMAT scores reflecting placement in the top 50 percent on the verbal, analytical, and quantitative sections of the exam; a completed background sheet that includes a summary of academic and professional experience and a personal essay; and demonstrated proficiency in calculus and introductory-level computer programming. International students whose first language is not English must score a minimum 570 on the TOEFL paper-and-pencil exam.

ADMISSIONS	
Admissions Selectivity Rating	**83**
# of applications received	447
% applicants accepted	41
% acceptees attending	57
Average GMAT	538
Range of GMAT	490–580
Average GPA	3.28
TOEFL required of international students	Yes
Minimum TOEFL (paper/computer)	570/230
Application fee	$55
Regular application deadline	6/15
Regular notification	Rolling
Transfer students accepted	Yes
Transfer application policy Students must apply as a new student and courses will be evaluated. Students may transfer in up to 9 units.	
Non-fall admissions	Yes
Need-blind admissions	Yes

EMPLOYMENT PROFILE	
Career Rating	74

CALIFORNIA STATE UNIVERSITY—LONG BEACH
COLLEGE OF BUSINESS ADMINISTRATION

GENERAL INFORMATION
Type of school	Public
Environment	City
Academic calendar	Semester

SURVEY SAYS . . .
Students love Long Beach, CA
Happy students
Smart classrooms
Solid preparation in:
Presentation skills

STUDENTS
Enrollment of parent institution	33,000
Enrollment of business school	310
% male/female	58/42
% out-of-state	1
% part-time	70
% minorities	15
% international	30
Average age at entry	28
Average years work experience at entry	5

ACADEMICS
Academic Experience Rating	**70**
Student/faculty ratio	25:1
Profs interesting rating	86
Profs accessible rating	66

Joint Degrees
MBA 1 to 2 years.

FINANCIAL FACTS
Annual tuition (out-of-state)	$7,896
Fees (in-state/ out-of-state)	$1,822/$3,164

Academics

The College of Business Administration at California State University—Long Beach—the "best business school in the California State University system," according to some students here—offers five different MBA programs for the convenience of its students. Most popular among the different options is the Evening MBA, a self-paced program that can be pursued either full- or part-time. Evening classes meet during the week with a curriculum that includes prerequisite courses (which can be waived for students with undergraduate business degrees), core courses, electives (three in one area must be completed for an area of concentration), and a capstone course. Concentrations are offered in information systems, finance, human resources, marketing, general management, accounting, and health care.

Those looking for a more traditional, cohort-based MBA program in a part-time setting will appreciate the Fully Employed MBA (FEMBA) program, a 23-month sequence of four 10-week sessions per year, scheduled on Saturdays for the convenience of full-time workers. FEMBA combines the benefits of a lockstep curriculum and the team-based learning inherent in the cohort system with the expedience of weekend classes. All books and materials are included in the price of the FEMBA program—another plus for those who hate unpleasant surprises.

CSULB also offers three smaller, more specialized MBA programs: the Corporate MBA Program for Boeing, available only to qualified Boeing employees; the Fully Employed MBA Program for Municipal and Public Agency Managers, which focuses on business skills and concepts useful in government and education; and a one-year Accelerated MBA, a full-time program for students anxious to jump-start their business careers.

Students typically choose CSULB for its low tuition rates, which translate into an excellent return on investment. One student writes, "It was the best investment, when you take into account the tuition, the flexible schedule of classes, and the time it generally takes to complete the MBA program." Once admitted, students also enjoy "perfect class sizes that allow all students to contribute to discussions" and professors who "usually come from the private sector and teach more from 'real-world' experience than from theory." Professors here "take an interest in seeing you succeed." Some also describe "a light workload," which could be viewed as a plus or a minus, depending on what a particular student wants from the program.

Career and Placement

CSULB's Career Development Center provides counseling and placement services for all students at the university. The office coordinates career fairs and manages online job postings through BeachLINK, a database accessible only to those with CSULB accounts and passwords. Students report that "the school has a great networking program through mentors in local business."

Student Life and Environment

There are "many different countries represented, including Saudi Arabia and China" in CSULB's student body. One MBA observes, "I rarely have had access to such people before. It is great to meet them in an intellectual environment, which offers a contrast to information provided by the media." Students here are "friendly for the most part and very goal-oriented." In classes, "there seems to be a good mix of married and single students ranging from mid-20s to mid-40s. Some have children, but most don't. Most everyone works at least part-time, if not full-time [because] very few come from a privileged background." One student comments, "I am an older student (48), but found that my age didn't matter as much as I thought it would."

PAULA GLOECKNER, MBA EVALUATOR
1250 BELLFLOWER BOULEVARD LONG BEACH, CA 90840-0119 UNITED STATES
PHONE: 562-985-7988 • FAX: 562-985-5590
E-MAIL: MBA@CSULB.EDU • WEBSITE: WWW.CSULB.EDU

The campus offers "plenty of places to eat" and "is very accommodating of wonderful group meetings and other opportunities to meet fellow students." On the downside, "because this is mostly a commuter campus, there is little or no after-school socializing." Students report that the campus itself "is beautiful and big enough to keep you in shape walking from place to place." Overall, students experience a "very laid-back atmosphere" on campus and point out that despite this, "everyone is still constantly focused on the tasks at hand."

Admissions

Undergraduate GPA and GMAT score are the most important factors in admissions decisions at CSULB. The school requires a minimum GPA of 2.75 for the applicants' final two years' worth of undergraduate credits (either the final 60 semester credits or the final 90 quarter credits). In addition, applicants earn a minimum score of 490 on the GMAT, with a "good balance between the quantitative and verbal sections" and an analytical writing score of at least 3.0. Letters of recommendation, a personal essay, and a resume are also considered in the admissions process. The school notes that "work experience and computer experience are recommended" for all applicants.

ADMISSIONS

Admissions Selectivity Rating	**74**
# of applications received	298
% applicants accepted	85
% acceptees attending	79
Average GMAT	560
Range of GMAT	480-710
Average GPA	3.3
TOEFL required of international students	Yes
Minimum TOEFL (paper/computer)	550/213
Application fee	$55
Regular application deadline	3/30
Regular notification	5/1
Deferment available	Yes
Maximum length of deferment	1 semester
Transfer students accepted	Yes
Must meet our admissions criteria.	
Non-fall admissions	Yes

Applicants Also Look At

California State University—Fullerton, California State University—Los Angeles—Pepperdine University, University of California—Irvine.

CALIFORNIA STATE UNIVERSITY—SAN BERNARDINO
COLLEGE OF BUSINESS AND PUBLIC ADMINISTRATION

GENERAL INFORMATION
Type of school	Public
Environment	City
Academic calendar	Quarter

SURVEY SAYS . . .
Friendly students
Happy students
Smart classrooms
Solid preparation in:
Communication/interpersonal skills
Presentation skills
Quantitative skills

STUDENTS
Enrollment of parent institution	16,479
Enrollment of business school	287
% male/female	63/37
% out-of-state	1
% part-time	38
% minorities	7
% international	62
Average age at entry	29
Average years work experience at entry	5

ACADEMICS
Academic Experience Rating	**72**
Student/faculty ratio	20:1
Profs interesting rating	83
Profs accessible rating	70
% female faculty	12
% minority faculty	9

Joint Degrees
Claremont Graduate University (CGU) has an articulate PhD program in Information Science with CSUSB's MBA Program. As many as 54 CSUSB quarter units can be counted toward your PhD at CGU.

Prominent Alumni
Yuzo Tobisaka, president, Mitsubishi Corp; Larry Sharp, CEO, Arrowhead Credit Union.

Academics

The MBA program at California State University—San Bernardino is "designed for the working professional," with most classes meeting twice weekly in the evenings. Students appreciate the flexibility of the program and also love the way the school "beats the brush establishing student demand for a course. Courses are added when people respond in numbers that they need, and others are deleted based on this same criteria." Best of all, they love the "excellent return on investment" this low-priced program offers. CSUSB operates on a quarterly academic schedule. The MBA program requires 48 quarter units consisting of: seven core courses (accounting, financial theory, information management, organization theory, global corporate strategy, marketing, and operations); and five electives in one of eight concentrations (accounting, finance, entrepreneurship, information assurance, security management, information management, management, marketing management, and supply chain management). In addition, all students must create a portfolio of course work, to be reviewed by faculty, and must complete either a comprehensive project or pass a comprehensive written examination in their area of concentration.

Students speak highly of CSUSB's program in supply chain management, where "students have competed against better-known schools and kick their butts. The small class size and attention to students serves CSUSB well." They also praise the finance and entrepreneurship programs. The latter is strengthened by the College of Business' Inland Empire Center for Entrepreneurship, a research center that promotes entrepreneurship in the surrounding area. Students report that faculty in all areas "seek to challenge the students, and they are more interested in learning rather than quantitative exam scores. They act as facilitators rather than dictators, and that is very motivating." Students also tell us that their "professors are real people who genuinely care about your academic and professional goals. Most professors have 'real-life' business experience and are not entrenched in academia."

CSUSB offers other strengths as well. The computer labs "are open extended hours and 99 percent of the stuff works." With more than 400 computer workstations in the business school facility, students generally have an easy time getting a workstation when they need one. The administration "does a satisfactory job considering the state financial mess." Finally, "the outside-of-class opportunities are very diverse." One student reports, "During my time at CSUSB I took an internship that allowed me face time with the CFO and vice president of a Fortune 500 company."

Career and Placement

The Career Development Center at CSUSB serves all students at the university—undergraduate and graduate. Counselors there offer workshops in interviewing, resume writing, and job-search strategies. The office arranges on-campus interviews and alumni meet-and-greets, and also maintains a database of job listings. A few students feel that "there needs to be more interaction between the school and alumni and businesses in the area to develop more school programs and help students with job placement," but the school's newly formed Business Alliance group should help. For example, the College of Business and Public Administration recently offered a Career Summit covering an array of topics along with a business etiquette luncheon and open networking forum with the business community. Employers likely to hire CSUSB MBAs include Arrowhead Credit Union, GE Transportation, Enterprise Rent-A-Car, American Express Company, ESRI, Arthur Anderson, FEMA, Wells Fargo, and almost all the regional accounting firms, banks, and credit unions.

BETH A. FLYNN, DIRECTOR OF MBA PROGRAM
5500 UNIVERSITY PARKWAY SAN BERNARDINO, CA 92407 UNITED STATES
PHONE: 909-537-5703 • FAX: 909-537-7582
E-MAIL: MBA@CSUSB.EDU • WEBSITE: CBPA.CSUSB.EDU/MBA

Student Life and Environment

The College of Business and Public Administration is located in the 10-year-old Jack H. Brown Hall, a modern facility that suits the needs of the program. Students describe the campus as "a little oasis in San Bernardino. You drive on a smog-filled freeway, and suddenly you see this open landscape in front of you. It is a pleasure walking around on a safe campus when the sun is shining, with the snow-covered mountains as the scenic backdrop." They also regard it as a "quiet, good place to do research because there are not a lot of recreation parks around."

Campus life is available for those with time to enjoy it. One student says, "There are many professional organizations open to MBA students. I belong to the Council of Logistics Management (CLM), Society for Human Resource Management (SHRM), and the American Production and Inventory Control Society (APICS). Our student organizations have visited operations such as Home Depot's cross-dock facility and Unilever's distribution center. The school even provided funding for all the student members of APICS who wished to attend the 2004 International Conference in San Diego." Most students, though, "do not live on or near campus. They are locally employed and attend school during the evenings." This group rarely has time for anything other than class, study, and group work.

CSUSB's student body "is split between a large contingent of foreign students and the rest, who are generally from the Inland Empire. Many students just continued their undergraduate studies and therefore lack any significant experience in the business work environment." The student body also includes "accomplished professionals returning to gain a competitive advantage over their peers due to changing market conditions." Students get along well, as one describes it: "My fellow students are an interesting, diverse group of people that have many experiences different from my own. They are what makes the environment relaxed yet professional all at the same time." Approximately "one-quarter to one-third of students live on campus or in apartments just off campus," with the rest commuting.

Admissions

Applicants to the CSUSB MBA program must first apply for admission to the university, which requires a baccalaureate with a GPA of at least 2.5 for the final two years of undergraduate work. Students clearing this hurdle may then apply for admission to the MBA program. Applicants must submit two sets of official transcripts for all postsecondary academic work; an official GMAT score report; and a personal statement. Three letters of recommendation are recommended but are technically optional. International students must additionally provide an Affidavit of Financial Support and TOEFL scores. The minimum requirement for admission to the program is a formula score of 1050 under the formula [(undergraduate GPA × 200) + GMAT score], with a minimum GMAT score of 470 and a minimum GPA of 2.5. No student may begin MBA work without having earned at least a C grade in the following undergraduate courses or their equivalent at another accredited institution: financial accounting I and II; microeconomics; macroeconomics; business finance; corporate finance; information management; business law; management and organization behavior; strategic management; marketing principles; business statistics; principles of supply chain management; and a grade of B or better in expository writing for administration.

FINANCIAL FACTS

Fees (in-state/ out-of-state)	$4,000/$12,136
Cost of books	$1,500
Room & board (on/off-campus)	$9,000/$12,000
% of students receiving aid	33
% of first-year students receiving aid	33
% of students receiving loans	33
% of students receiving grants	5
Average award package	$6,625
Average grant	$1,000

ADMISSIONS

Admissions Selectivity Rating	**71**
# of applications received	248
% applicants accepted	70
% acceptees attending	57
Average GMAT	510
Range of GMAT	470–650
Average GPA	3.1
TOEFL required of international students	Yes
Minimum TOEFL (paper/computer)	550/213
Application fee	$55
Regular application deadline	7/1
Regular notification	8/1
Early decision program?	Yes
ED Deadline/Notification	2/1 / 6/1
Deferment available	Yes
Maximum length of deferment	1 year
Transfer students accepted	Yes
Transfer application policy	

Only 3 graduate courses may be transferred into the MBA program from approved U.S. universities.

Non-fall admissions	Yes
Need-blind admissions	Yes

Applicants Also Look At

California State Polytechnic University—Pomona, California State University—Fullerton, California State University—Los Angeles, University of California—Riverside.

EMPLOYMENT PROFILE

Career Rating	**66**

CARNEGIE MELLON UNIVERSITY
TEPPER SCHOOL OF BUSINESS

GENERAL INFORMATION
Type of school   Private
Environment   Metropolis
Academic calendar   Mini Semester

SURVEY SAYS . . .
Good peer network
Cutting-edge classes
Smart classrooms
Solid preparation in:
Finance
Teamwork
Quantitative skills

STUDENTS
Enrollment of parent institution	10,120
Enrollment of business school	636
% male/female	78/22
% part-time	53
% minorities	10
% international	29
Average age at entry	28
Average years work experience at entry	5

ACADEMICS
Academic Experience Rating	**97**
Student/faculty ratio	5:1
Profs interesting rating	81
Profs accessible rating	91
% female faculty	16
% minority faculty	3

Joint Degrees
MBA/computational 2.5 years, MBA/software engineering 2.5 years, MBA/law 3 to 4 years, MBA/software engineering 2 years, MBA/environmental engineering 2 years, MBA/civil engineering 2 years, MBA/public policy 2.5 years.

Prominent Alumni
David A. Tepper, CEO and founder, Appalossa Management; David Coulter, managing director and senior advisor, Warburg Pincus LLC; Lewis Hay III, president and CEO FPL; Yoshiaki Fujimori.

Academics

Tepper's MBA program attracts workhorses and future IT and science industry leaders with a "heavily quantitative" emphasis. The program's 20 distinct tracks and concentrations include biotechnology, technology leadership, wealth and asset management, and quantitative analysis. As a result, "Students are just as likely to be able to calculate a discounted cash flow as to identify optimal supply chain quantities and overstock levels" by the time they graduate. But "The program's greatest strength goes deeper than that"; so-called "hard skills" make Tepper students "excellent analytical thinkers."

The Tepper year consists of four mini-semesters, which means that first-year students are straddled with 10 full courses before winter break. Students say that this "grueling" schedule "prepares you extremely well for your internship and beyond." The "class load lightens up" for second-years, and "Students are able to really focus their learning in areas where they are most interested." "This takes the form of corporate-sponsored projects (GM, Bosch, Equitable Resources, Caterpillar), entrepreneurship, and independent academic study with faculty," as well as elective courses that must satisfy distributional requirements in economics, "quant," IT, organizational behavior, strategy, and a concentration of one's choice. The one required second-year course is called Management Game, a team business simulation in which students can draw on a board of real corporate leaders, negotiate labor contracts with real labor leaders, and compete with students from international business schools. "The rigor of our course work is tough but appropriate," says one student. "After going through this, I am fearless about entering the business world." Students would like to see "more detailed courses regarding the markets and where they are going" and "additional courses in foreign languages." For the most part, Tepper's faculty and "attentive" administration "could not be better."

Career and Placement

Tepper has "very strong ties with top management consulting firms," and "The Career Office is good for the traditional areas: finance, consulting, and ops." Indeed, more than half of the Class of 2006 works in finance and consulting alone, with median first-year salaries of $95,000 and $110,000 respectively. (To keep the momentum going, the Career Office recently hired "industry-specific Career Counselors" for these two sectors.) An additional third of 2006 grads work in manufacturing (median salary: $85,100) and technology (median salary: $90,000). Fewer than one percent work in the nonprofit/government arena.

Recruitment comes in many forms, including the credit-bearing kind. Sometimes "large firms come in and literally 'open call' their problems/projects." Faculty also "quietly select" star pupils "to assist them with major consulting projects." One student reports, "For my last mini-semester, I am working on two projects. I will be making just about the same amount over the next 2 months as I will be making over the next 4 months with my permanent employer."

Students would like to see the Career Center diversify, and some progress has been made in the arena. Over the past few years, the career center has continued "working to woo" high-tech California and Silicon Forest firms, and Tepper now hosts "interviews for financial firms . . . en masse" at its "New York campus." In any event, "I think that getting employers to Pittsburgh is no longer an issue," says one student. "The school had a record number of companies recruiting on campus this year." The Career Opportunities Center could further "improve by attracting firms that look for well-rounded employees with quantitative skills instead of [just] for quants."

LAURIE STEWART, EXECUTIVE DIRECTOR OF MASTERS ADMISSIONS
TEPPER SCHOOL OF BUSINESS, 5000 FORBES AVENUE PITTSBURGH, PA 15213 UNITED STATES
PHONE: 412-268-2272 • FAX: 412-268-4209
E-MAIL: MBA-ADMISSIONS@ANDREW.CMU.EDU • WEBSITE: WWW.TEPPER.CMU.EDU

Student Life and Environment

Tepper students describe one another as "team-oriented problem-solvers who work until a task is 100 percent complete." The "atmosphere is obviously competitive but amicable." During the recruitment season, students pull together; someone "who has completed his interview will oftentimes share the questions he received with fellow applicants who are still waiting for their turn. This type of support is amazing." The same is true for exam time, when "Classmates have circulated their self-prepared study guides prior to exams, helping everyone cut down on their prep time." The downside to this team spirit, says one student, is "a lot of cheating."

Typical Tepper students are "bright people who have been extremely successful in their past careers," and are fairly "homogeneous in terms of educational background and pre-MBA experience, targeting a fairly narrow set of post-MBA careers," many of which require the hard skills that Tepper hones. A full 70 percent of the class of 2008 holds undergraduate degrees in engineering, IT, and the sciences; an additional quarter studied economics, accounting, and business. On the other hand, nearly 30 percent of Tepper's approximately 300 students are international, and another tenth are of color. "I thought I knew diversity. . . . "At Tepper, I was awestruck," says one student.

Students like cheap, leafy Pittsburgh. "This area of town is very much centered around the schools," offering a "somewhat laid-back feeling" and plenty of "comfortable, close housing." This means that "most people live close to campus and spend a lot of time there, which fosters a good community." Students maintain "a very active social life." "There is a weekly bar night out, and about twice a month the school sponsors beer and food on Friday night. That is called B**RS and is a great time to hang out with faculty, the PhDs, and fellow MBAs." Because there are events that also include spouses and families, "there is an activity and a social life no matter what stage in life you are" in.

Admissions

Tepper's most recent application required two long essays on professional goals and contribution to the school's diversity. Applicants then answered three out of five short questions about professional background and personal character, with the option to include an additional essay.

Like many schools, Tepper staggers its admission deadlines, with unofficial preference going to early-round applicants. International students must apply no later than March. However, unlike at many schools, rolling admission is available after April for domestic candidates. Most successful applicants have undergraduate GPAs above 3.0 and GMAT scores above 700.

FINANCIAL FACTS

Annual tuition	$41,900
Fees	$388
Cost of books	$2,275
Room & board (off-campus)	$13,500
% of students receiving aid	82
% of first-year students receiving aid	82
% of students receiving loans	82
% of students receiving grants	66
Average award package	$56,847
Average grant	$11,103
Average student loan debt	$64,687

ADMISSIONS

Admissions Selectivity Rating	95
# of applications received	1,343
% applicants accepted	36
% acceptees attending	55
Average GMAT	671
Range of GMAT	620–710
Average GPA	3.31
TOEFL required of international students	Yes
Minimum TOEFL (paper/computer)	600/100
Application fee	$100
Application Deadline/Notification	
Round 1:	11/6 / 12/22
Round 2:	1/8 / 3/12
Round 3:	3/19 / 4/30
Round 4:	4/30 / 6/4
Need-blind admissions	Yes

Applicants Also Look At

Cornell University, Duke University, Massachusetts Institute of Technology, New York University, The University of Chicago, University of Michigan, University of Virginia.

EMPLOYMENT PROFILE

Career Rating	94			
Primary Source of Full-time Job Acceptances		**Grads Employed by Function**	**%**	**Avg. Salary**
School-facilitated activities	89 (68%)	Finance/Accounting	41	$89,997
Graduate-facilitated activities	36 (28%)	Marketing/Sales	12	$75,350
Unknown	5 (4%)	MIS	2	$102,500
Average base starting salary	$93,479	Operations/Production	9	$91,545
Percent employed	95	Consulting	25	$107,248
		General Management	8	$93,889
		Other	3	$88,333

Top 5 Employers Hiring Grads

Bank of America; Booz Allen Hamilton; A.T. Kearney; Amazon; Deutsche Bank.

CASE WESTERN RESERVE UNIVERSITY
WEATHERHEAD SCHOOL OF MANAGEMENT

GENERAL INFORMATION

Type of school	Private
Environment	Metropolis
Academic calendar	Semester

SURVEY SAYS . . .

Happy students
Smart classrooms
Solid preparation in:
Teamwork
Communication/interpersonal skills

STUDENTS

Enrollment of parent institution	9,927
Enrollment of business school	445
% male/female	70/30
% part-time	61
% minorities	51
% international	32
Average age at entry	27
Average years work experience at entry	4

ACADEMICS

Academic Experience Rating	**81**
Student/faculty ratio	9:1
Profs interesting rating	76
Profs accessible rating	83
% female faculty	21
% minority faculty	2

Joint Degrees

MBA/JD 4 years, MD/MBA 5 years, MBA/MS (nursing) 2.5 years, JD/master in nonprofit organizations 4 years, master in nonprofit organizations/MA 2.5 years, MBA/MS (social administration) 2.5 years, MBA/master of international management 2.5 years, MBA/master of accountancy 2 years, MBA/master of public health 2.5 years.

Prominent Alumni

John Breen, CEO (retired), Sherwin Williams; Clayton Deutsch, managing partner, McKinsey & Co.; David Daberko, chairman and CEO, National City Bank; John Neff, CEO (retired) Vanguard Funds.

Academics

Offering the "top organizational behavior program in the world," the Weatherhead School of Management at Case Western University is widely regarded as "one of the country's top graduate business programs," ensuring "brand equity in a Weatherhead degree" to all who succeed here. Students tell us that Weatherhead also excels in entrepreneurship and management information systems and that its finance program "is underrated." "I've been very impressed with it," says one student. A stellar regional reputation makes Case the ideal choice for those who "want to live and work in Ohio."

Weatherhead offers a conventional 2-year, full-time MBA, a "well-regarded" 11-month accelerated MBA, and a part-time program with great flexibility that allows students to work toward their degree at a pace that works for them. All programs include the Leadership Assessment and Development (LEAD) course, a distinctive program feature designed to help students develop long-term career goals and strategies. The Weatherhead MBA also incorporates a Strategic Issues and Applications (SIA) integrative capstone course that centers on case studies and group projects.

Not satisfied to rest on its laurels, Weatherhead is currently in a period of transformation. Students tell us that the "Administration is currently working on focusing our programs to differentiate us" and warn that "some people who came here for a specific reason that is not in the 'plan' anymore may feel they were offered something that wasn't available." A revolving door within the administration further underscores the transition. As far as deans go, one student reports, "We're on something like our fifth one in 4 years" (in reality, it's more like four deans in eight years). Some tell us that "the biggest issue is with the turnover of deans in the School of Management and some faculty leaving because of this." Things are looking up here, though; as one student puts it, "While the school has gone through a lot of change in the last few years, the new staff and administration are remarkably more accessible, transparent, capable, and inclusive in their current roles, as well as in the strategic plan for the school in the future."

Career and Placement

The Career Development Center (CDC) at Case has "a brand-new staff, and students have already been placed for full-time jobs or internships with top companies. . . . For students who haven't found a job, the CDC provides resume reviews; recorded mock interviews with staff, faculty, and alumni professionals who volunteer their time; online mock interviews; Career Fridays, which bring in speakers to give seminars on anything from case interviewing to negotiating a job offer; free access to career websites; access for students to our alumni database; feedback on actual interviews; and a library of career-related books and practice manuals for students to borrow."

Employers who frequently hire Weatherhead MBAs include: Johnson & Johnson, American Greetings, Progressive, Bristol West, Emerson Electric, PNC Bank, Ohio Savings, General Electric Company, Deloitte Touche Tohmatsu, Eaton, Ernst & Young, McKinsey & Company, National City Corporation, Key Corporation, and IBM.

Student Life and Environment

"There is a real sense of community here" among Weatherhead full-timers, who tell us that they "get to know the professors, staff, and students all very well. Many professors go on a first-name basis with students and will attend social events the school has put on." Extracurricular events include "the 'Pull up a Chair' event, which takes place once a month and is put on by professors. There have been ping-pong tournaments, a business fashion show sponsored by Talbots, and a billiards contest." Clubs including the

TIM SLAGER, MBA PROGRAM DIRECTOR
160 PETER B. LEWIS BUILDING, 10900 EUCLID AVENUE CLEVELAND, OH 44106-7235 UNITED STATES
PHONE: 216-368-2030 • FAX: 216-368-5548
E-MAIL: MBAINFO@CASE.EDU • WEBSITE: WWW.WEATHERHEAD.CASE.EDU

Entrepreneurship Venture Association, the Marketing Club, Net Impact, and the Weatherhead Wine Society are all active and allow for outside-the-classroom interaction. Weatherhead is located "in the heart of Cleveland's cultural center," within a couple of blocks of the Botanical Gardens, Severance Hall ("home of the world-renowned Cleveland Orchestra"), Cleveland Museum of Art, The Museum of Natural History, and the Children's Museum.

"There are three types of students at Weatherhead," students tell us: "Engineering/foreign students who typically lack real-world substance; young professionals who maintain work/home/school; and family/parents types who put more energy into their home life, but still contribute with their business expertise." Weatherhead's full-time student body "is about 40 percent international students which makes for an enormous amount of different ideas and backgrounds," says one student. "Each and every one of them brings a lot of experience, creativity, dedication, and ideas to the table." Many tend to be on the youngish side, however, with little in the way of professional background; some American students also find that the shaky English skills of some international students can be a barrier to communication.

Admissions

Applicants to Weatherhead MBA programs must submit the following materials to the Admissions Office: a completed application form; official copies of transcripts for every undergraduate or graduate program attended; an official GMAT score report; two letters of recommendation; a current resume; and essay responses to three questions provided as part of the application package. International students whose transcripts are not in English must have their transcripts translated and interpreted by a professional service. Students whose first language is not English must also submit an official score report for the TOEFL. All international applicants must submit a statement of financial responsibility. The school requires an interview for admission. Weatherhead prefers candidates to submit their applications online. Hard-copy applications may take longer to process, the school warns.

FINANCIAL FACTS

Annual tuition	$32,990
Fees	$1,100
Cost of books	$1,830
Room & board	
(off-campus)	$15,930
% of students receiving aid	80
% of first-year students	
receiving aid	80
% of students receiving loans	35
% of students receiving grants	76
Average award package	$18,414
Average grant	$14,586
Average student loan debt	$43,369

ADMISSIONS

Admissions Selectivity Rating	85
# of applications received	327
% applicants accepted	54
% acceptees attending	38
Average GMAT	614
Range of GMAT	570–650
Average GPA	3.34
TOEFL required of	
international students	Yes
Minimum TOEFL	
(paper/computer)	600/250
Application fee	$50
Regular application deadline	3/1
Regular notification	4/15
Application Deadline/Notification	
Round 1:	12/1 / 1/31
Round 2:	1/15 / 3/1
Round 3:	3/1 / 4/15
Round 4:	3/1 / 6/1
Transfer students accepted	Yes
Transfer application policy	
Maximum number of transferable credits is 6 semester hours from an AASCB-accredited program.	
Non-fall admissions	Yes
Need-blind admissions	Yes

Applicants Also Look At

Carnegie Mellon, The Ohio State University, University of Notre Dame, University of Pittsburgh, University of Rochester, Vanderbilt University, Washington University.

EMPLOYMENT PROFILE		
Career Rating	84	**Top 5 Employers Hiring Grads**
Primary Source of Full-time Job Acceptances		IBM; American Greetings; Eaton; Ernst & Young; Progressive.
School-facilitated activities	41 (30%)	
Graduate-facilitated activities	43 (32%)	
Unknown	51 (38%)	
Percent employed	86	

Catholic University of Leuven/Ghent University
Vlerick Leuven Ghent Management School

Academics

Executive development programs are huge at Vlerick Leuven Ghent: The Belgian business school hosts over 3,000 managers in its open-enrollment seminars and company-specific programs, but the school is also home to a growing MBA program, one whose stature around the world is growing. The school currently offers a full-time English language MBA at its Leuven campus, a part-time Dutch language MBA at its Ghent campus, and a part-time English language MBA at both campuses. The full-time general MBA can be completed in one year, as can master's degrees in marketing and financial management; an MBA in financial services takes two years to complete. In total, about 250 students pursue MBAs at VLG.

Vlerick Leuven Ghent was founded in 1953 by Professor Andre Vlerick; over the years it has developed associations with Ghent University and the Katholieke Universiteit Leuven, and today it serves as the autonomous management school of these prestigious universities, the two largest in Belgium. Association with these two more established schools provides a solid research base; the school's autonomy allows it to "build strong ties with the business community" and "enables it to respond to the development needs of this community in an optimal way," according to the school's brochure. As one student observes, "The fact that the school is backed up by two recognized universities is apparent. It benefits greatly from its location and the support and research of its two parent universities."

MBA programs at Vlerick Leuven Ghent maintain "a strong international focus" derived not only from the curriculum but also from the student body. One student writes, "The basic strength of this program is the dual academic-practical approach. On the one hand, the academic orientation of the professors builds a solid knowledge foundation, while on the other, the experiences of the rest of the multicultural group enrich the whole educational experience." Students tell us that "professors and academics show a lot of respect for the audience, are extremely knowledgeable, and have in many cases extensive personal activity in the fields of management they are covering." MBAs here especially enjoy "the specialization seminars in entrepreneurship and doing business in Europe." Many students feel, however, that "the international MBA could use more international faculty. Most teachers are from Belgium." Students also report that "the workload is extremely heavy," but add that the benefits of the program—good value in a major economic center of the European Union—outweigh any shortfalls.

Career and Placement

The Career Services Office (CSO) at Vlerick Leuven Ghent organizes regular career events on campus; the office also coordinates multi-campus events and online recruiting. In an effort to keep pace with the internationalization of the school's curriculum and student body, the CSO has spent the last few years developing business contacts throughout the world to supplement its already strong base of Belgian businesses. The CSO also offers counseling services and advice on resume writing, interviewing, searching for jobs, and salary negotiation. According to the school's website, "The intention [of the CSO's efforts] is to develop a career management program that throughout the entire year will operate as an integral part of the various courses, with presentations, interactive workshops, and networking events." The office also plans to develop "a lifelong career guidance program, whereby alumni of Vlerick Leuven Ghent Management School will become even more deeply involved in activities organized by the CSO." Students tell us these efforts are working, praising the "great alumni network."

CHARLOTTE DE VOLDER, PROGRAMME COORDINATOR
VLAMINGENSTRAAT 83, 3000 LEUVEN, BELGIUM, REEP 1, 9000 GENT, BELGIUM LEUVEN,
VB 3000 BELGIUM • PHONE: + 32 16 24 88 89 • FAX: + 32 16 24 88 81
E-MAIL: MBA@VLERICK.BE • WEBSITE: WWW.VLERICK.COM

Student Life and Environment

Full-time students at Vlerick Leuven Ghent experience a nonstop academic grind. One student reports, "Life in school starts every day (including exams period, studying for the exams, most of weekends) at 9:00 P.M. and ends at 12:00 A.M. After that, individual work at home is usually required. In this frame, the quality of life can't be good. But then again, this is a commitment well known before the enrollment, so its consistency is remarkable. I personally face time problems and issues with domestic tasks (laundry, house cleaning, nutrition). I skipped visiting my home country at Christmas to catch up with the material I needed to know . . . and this is the situation that I face [at] Easter." Some here manage to squeeze in some free time; they describe "an excellent lifestyle in the very small and safe student town of Leuven, with lots of social, sports, and cultural activities." One student notes, "Belgium is a beer-drinker's paradise. Need I say more?"

Students "represent every continent, which makes participating in the group a very interesting learning experience." They are "active social animals and real team players, and students are very much diversified in professional and academic experience and competencies."

Admissions

Admission to the Vlerick Leuven Ghent Management School requires an undergraduate degree from an institution "recognized by the relevant authorities of the home country." Work experience "is beneficial but not required." Other admissions requirements depend on the method of application; students may choose the "distance procedure" or the "on-campus assessment procedure." Both require a completed application, a resume, a copy of one's passport, and official copies of all postsecondary transcripts and diplomas. The distance procedure requires, in addition, an official GMAT score report, an official TOEFL score report (students whose native language is English are exempted from this requirement), two letters of recommendation, and a personal statement. On-campus assessment "requires your attendance at one of [the school's] in-house admission tests, which consist of an analytical test, a written comprehension test, and two personal interviews (a motivation interview and a management potential/knowledge interview)."

FINANCIAL FACTS

Annual tuition	$18,000
Fees	$18,000
Room & board	
(on/off-campus)	$9,000/$11,000
% of students receiving aid	10
% of first-year students	
receiving aid	10
% of students receiving grants	10
Average award package	$60,000
Average grant	$6,000
Average student loan debt	$5,000

ADMISSIONS

Admissions Selectivity Rating	93
# of applications received	300
% applicants accepted	34
% acceptees attending	53
Average GMAT	636
Range of GMAT	600–650
Average GPA	3.5
TOEFL required of	
international students	Yes
Minimum TOEFL (computer)	255
Application fee	$50
International application fee	$50
Regular application deadline	6/30
Regular notification	7/14
Application Deadline/Notification	
Round 1:	1/22 / 2/1
Round 2:	3/24 / 4/1
Round 3:	6/30 / 7/14
Deferment available	Yes
Maximum length of	
deferment	1 year
Need-blind admissions	Yes

Applicants Also Look At

Bocconi University, Cranfield University, ESADE, HEC School of Management—Paris, IMD (International Institute for Management Development), INSEAD, RSM Erasmus University.

EMPLOYMENT PROFILE

Career Rating	86	Grads Employed by Function	%	Avg. Salary
Primary Source of Full-time Job Acceptances		Accounting	10	$93,000
School-facilitated activities	25 (45%)	Finance/Accounting	15	$93,000
Graduate-facilitated activities	15 (30%)	Marketing/Sales	10	$93,000
Unknown	14 (25%)	Strategic Planning	5	$93,000
Percent employed	90	Consulting	15	$93,000
		Entrepreneurship	20	$93,000
		General Management	10	$93,000
		Venture Capital	5	$93,000
		Internet/New Media	5	$93,000
		Nonprofit	5	$93,000

Top 5 Employers Hiring Grads

Bechtel; Inbev; Belgacom; ING Bank, U.S. Foreign Service.

CHAPMAN UNIVERSITY
THE GEORGE L. ARGYROS SCHOOL OF BUSINESS AND ECONOMICS

Academics

"Chapman may be a small private university, but don't underestimate the quality here. Chapman is as good as, if not better than, many of the larger universities in the U.S.," MBAs in this Orange County program tell us. One student writes, "It was not a surprise to us to see Chapman listed among 'the hidden gems' in the *Washington Post*."

Chapman's MBA program—which can be completed on either a part-time or full-time basis—loads students up with core requirements. A whopping 33 of the 52 credits necessary for graduation are devoted to the core here. Students applaud the core's "strong foundation in concepts needed for today's business" and especially its "focus on business ethics as well as typical business topics." Some here, though, "wish the school allowed [them] to devote more time to majors and concentrations, as other business schools do." Students tell us that "the greatest strengths of [their] business school is in economics and international business." The school adds that the "four research centers represent the strength of the school: the Anderson Center for Economic Research, the Center for Real Estate, the Ralph Leatherby Center for Entrepreneurship and Ethics, and the Walter Schmid Center for International Business." Chapman also offers an Executive MBA program.

Chapman professors "are very accessible outside of class, and they help you to understand ideas or concepts not fully understood during class time. During projects they are helpful in steering you to the right path to get more justifiable solutions." Several students comment that they "would like to see more international faculty at Chapman." One writes, "The whole world is now heading towards globalization. To have international faculty come and teach at Chapman would open entirely new perspectives. This will strengthen Chapman's International Business program even more." Even those who see room for improvement, though, report satisfaction with the school. One MBA explains, "This program is as rigorous as top programs, but, unlike at other larger universities, you won't get lost here at Chapman. Not only do the faculty and staff know you by name but you'll also build a strong bond with the faculty, staff, and other students even after you have graduated, resulting in global networking."

Career and Placement

In response to students' requests, the Argyros School has further invested in the professional success of MBA and EMBA candidates by opening a new MBA Career Management Center in summer 2006. The MBA Career Management Center capitalizes on strong relationships the university has with the Orange County business community and equips students with fundamental skills required to successfully manage options throughout their career. The center provides students with career coaching and a wide variety of career management resources and business networking opportunities.

Student Life and Environment

Chapman University has an enrollment of approximately 5,700, just under one-third of which represents graduate students. The business program is relatively small, with just under 140 MBAs, most attending part-time. The MBA population here is "a good mix, with some really smart and experienced students, and others who are book-smart, funny, nice, friendly, and helpful." Students' ages "run from early 20s to 40s. Ethnic backgrounds and nationalities vary too, as well as types and degree of work experience. The gender mix is about 50–50." MBAs describe "a good, competitive yet friendly atmosphere with students. Everyone pushes fellow students to do better and go that extra mile, and not just to get a good grade but to understand the material."

DEBRA GONDA, ASSOCIATE DIRECTOR
BECKMAN HALL, ONE UNIVERSITY DRIVE, ORANGE, CA 92866 UNITED STATES
PHONE: 714-997-6745 • FAX: 714-997-6757
E-MAIL: GONDA@CHAPMAN.EDU • WEBSITE: WWW.CHAPMAN.EDU/ARGYROS/

Because "Chapman is a commuter school, most people don't relocate to take classes, and not many people are looking for additional friends. Between work, school, and the friends we already have, it doesn't leave much time for classmates." The school does plan occasional events for MBAs, though. One student writes, "The business school usually hosts a get-together event two to three times a semester, whether it's just an hour of eating pizza, sipping coffee, and chatting with the dean, associate deans, and faculty, or a soccer match between the faculty and the business students. Even though each of these events usually doesn't last longer than two hours, these types of activities have helped create a strong bond among the students, faculty, and staff." The school also hosts "a Distinguished Speaker series, where a CEO comes in and talks about their experiences and [students] get free dinner," as well as a dinner program in which students have the opportunity to share a meal and a conversation with highly respected members of Orange County and Southern California. Students appreciate that "the campus is located in a very nice area and has extremely good on-campus facilities, considering the small overall size of the school."

Admissions

The Admissions Office factors "academic performance, leadership ability, work experience, and communication skills" into each of its decisions. The school requires a minimum GPA of 2.5 for the applicants' final two years' worth of undergraduate credits (either the final 60 semester credits or the final 90 quarter credits). All applications must include an official GMAT score report, sealed copies of official transcripts for all postsecondary academic work, two letters of recommendation "from individuals familiar with the applicant's academic or professional abilities," and a completed application with a personal statement "explaining why the applicant is interested in pursuing a graduate degree at Chapman." Two years of business-related work experience is preferred. International applicants must "submit a certified statement demonstrating financial ability to cover all education and living expenses for the full period of time for which the student is applying, [and] all international students, as well as those who attended a university where the language of instruction is English, must take the TOEFL examination and achieve a score of 550 or higher on the paper-based test (or 216 on the computerized version)." Admission to the Executive MBA program requires at least seven years of professional experience and a one-on-one on-campus interview.

FINANCIAL FACTS

Annual tuition	$18,850
Cost of books	$1,750
Room & board (on-campus)	$8,500
% of students receiving aid	77
% of first-year students receiving aid	55
% of students receiving loans	24
% of students receiving grants	32
Average award package	$19,529
Average grant	$5,678

ADMISSIONS

Admissions Selectivity Rating	**75**
# of applications received	116
% applicants accepted	66
% acceptees attending	58
Average GMAT	540
Range of GMAT	440–700
Average GPA	3.18
TOEFL required of international students	Yes
Minimum TOEFL (paper/computer)	550/216
Application fee	$50
Regular application deadline	7/1
Regular notification	Rolling
Deferment available	Yes
Maximum length of deferment	1 year
Transfer students accepted	Yes
Transfer application policy Transfer up to 6 units of course work.	
Non-fall admissions	Yes
Need-blind admissions	Yes

Applicants Also Look At

California State University—Fullerton, Pepperdine University, University of California—Irvine, University of Southern California.

THE CHINESE UNIVERSITY OF HONG KONG
FACULTY OF BUSINESS ADMINISTRATION

Academics

In 1966, The Chinese University of Hong Kong became the first school in China to offer a full-time MBA program. Today, the university boasts one of the most reputable business schools in Asia and the Pacific, attracting students for its "international recognition, good academic reputation, and diverse teacher and student pools." A great entryway for those seeking a professional position in Hong Kong, the school boasts a "strong alumni network" in the city and an excellent reputation in the region. In particular, the school is touted for its programs in finance and marketing, with a special emphasis on Chinese business. Through lecture, case studies, group work, directed research, and discussion, classes are a balance of "individual and group efforts that cultivate teamwork among students that is important for business." Group work is particularly gratifying at CUMBA, where students comprise "a very diverse group from just about every continent. Their combined work experience and life experiences has really contributed to the program."

Maintaining a working relationship with various universities in mainland China and Taiwan, the school's "administration is very dedicated and efficient." The school attracts faculty from all over the world, and the current teaching staff includes professors from Australia, Hong Kong, Europe, New Zealand, mainland China, Southeast Asia, Taiwan, and the United States. Despite their varied origins, CUMBA faculty are deeply engaged in the Hong Kong business culture. A student attests, "Teaching staff are actively involved in the business community in areas of research and consulting. So there are lots of firsthand findings and . . . information [on] local business trends." On the whole, students appreciate the school's progressive outlook, saying professors "stay abreast of the real-life market and keep up to date with their own knowledge."

While Cantonese is the dominant language spoken in Hong Kong, courses at CUMBA are taught in English, with the exception of a few elective courses whose unique nature demands instruction in Chinese. The 54-unit curriculum consists of required core course work, followed by electives. Through electives, students have the option to pursue a concentration in one of three areas: China business, finance, or marketing. The full-time curriculum can be completed in 16 months of study, including internships. Without an internship, the program can be completed as quickly as 12 months. Either way, the program is intense, with a "busy workload and no breaks in between terms." In addition to the traditional MBA programs offered through the school, students may choose to pursue a joint-degree with partner universities in Mainland China or the HEC School of Management in France or the University of Texas at Austin.

Career and Placement

As part of the MBA experience, students at The Chinese University of Hong Kong are expected to develop career goals and design a plan of action to meet those goal. The Career Planning and Development Centre facilitates students looking for summer internship placements, as well as students looking for permanent positions after graduation. The center also hosts an executive development series on presentation, communication, and project management, and a series of career talks and interview workshops.

The school has strong ties in the Hong Kong business community, as well as a large regional alumni network. In recent years, the following companies have recruited CUMBA graduates: Cathay Pacific Airways, Citibank, NA, Deloitte Touche Tohmatsu, Esso HK, Goldman Sachs (Asia), Hang Seng Bank, IBM China/HK, Kimberly-Clark (Hong Kong), KPMG International, Merrill Lynch (Asia), Morgan Stanley, Nestlé HK, PARKnSHOP, Procter & Gamble (HK), The Bank of East Asia, and The Boston Consulting

Group. In 2006, 59 percent of graduating students took positions in Hong Kong (42 percent of whom where not originally from Hong Kong), and another 35 percent accepted positions elsewhere in China. The majority of students took positions in banking and finance.

Student Life and Environment

CUMBA boasts a "beautiful campus" environment, and both part-time and full-time students take classes in the school's MBA Town Centre, a modern and spacious 900-square-meter facility located in the school's central campus. In addition to the extensive computer facilities available via the larger university, MBA students have access to over 100 microcomputers in the Town Centre, connected via LAN network. MBA students have the option of living on campus in the graduate residence halls; they also have access to the school's sports facilities, including three indoor gyms and an Olympic-sized swimming pool.

One of the major attractions of CUMBA is its diverse student population, who bring experience "from a variety of professions and cultures." Totally student run, the MBA Student's Association sponsors a broad range of social and professional events, including executive seminars, company visits, and study tours to mainland China. The school also sponsors various social and recreational events, such as charity and fund-raising activities and sports teams, although some students say "Campus life is not adapted to international students at all." Even part-timers enjoy a sense of community. One says, "I am a part-time student. Fellow students usually have dinner gatherings after school."

Admissions

To be considered for admission to CUMBA, prospective students must hold an undergraduate degree (with at least a B average), have at least 3 yeas of relevant work experience post-graduation, and submit current GMAT scores. The average GMAT score for accepted applicants changes every year; however, the class average usually hovers between 620–640. Interviews are required for all short-listed applicants, either in person or via telephone, as determined by the selection committee.

FINANCIAL FACTS

Annual tuition	$30,460
Cost of books	$11,500
Room & board	
(on/off-campus)	$3,000/$20,500
% of students receiving grants	69
Average grant	$6,793

ADMISSIONS

Admissions Selectivity Rating	89
# of applications received	838
% applicants accepted	56
% acceptees attending	75
Average GMAT	626
Average GPA	3.3
Application fee	$25
Regular application deadline	3/31
Regular notification	6/15
Early decision program?	Yes
ED Deadline/Notification	12/15 / 2/28
Deferment available	Yes
Maximum length of deferment	1 year
Need-blind admissions	Yes

EMPLOYMENT PROFILE

Career Rating	62	Grads Employed by Function	%	Avg. Salary
Primary Source of Full-time Job Acceptances		Finance/Accounting	48	NR
School-facilitated activities	1 (3%)	Human Resources	2	NR
Graduate-facilitated activities	19 (45%)	Marketing/Sales	12	NR
Unknown	22 (52%)	Strategic Planning	2	NR
Percent employed	98	Consulting	7	NR
		Entrepreneurship	10	NR
		General Management	17	NR
		Other	2	NR

Top 5 Employers Hiring Grads

Fortis Bank; JPMorgan; Goldman Sachs; UBS AG; 3M China.

THE CITADEL
SCHOOL OF BUSINESS ADMINISTRATION

GENERAL INFORMATION

Type of school	Public
Environment	City
Academic calendar	Semester

SURVEY SAYS . . .

Students love Charleston, SC
Happy students
Solid preparation in:
Accounting
Communication/interpersonal skills
Presentation skills

STUDENTS

Enrollment of parent institution	3,306
Enrollment of business school	265
% male/female	72/28
% out-of-state	28
% part-time	91
% minorities	12
Average age at entry	25

ACADEMICS

Academic Experience Rating	**69**
Student/faculty ratio	10:1
Profs interesting rating	77
Profs accessible rating	79
% female faculty	23
% minority faculty	4

Joint Degrees

MBA/PharmD 4 years, MBA with concentration in health care management 2 to 6 years, MBA with concentration in sports management, MBA/MD.

FINANCIAL FACTS

Annual tuition (in-state/ out-of-state)	$4,662/$8,676
Fees	$30

Academics

The Citadel offers "the only AACSB-accredited program in Charleston" as well as "a reasonably priced degree"—two features that attract the school's predominantly part-time student body.

The Citadel MBA is a 48-hour program consisting of 24 hours of basic required courses, 12 hours of advanced required courses, and 12 hours of electives. Students who have successfully completed equivalent courses at the undergraduate or graduate level may be permitted to waive some or all of the basic required courses. In order to qualify, students must have completed the work within the previous five years. Electives may be used to develop concentrations in health care administration, hospitality/tourism, or international business. The Citadel also offers two joint degrees: a PharmD/MBA and an MD/MBA.

Students report, "Citadel professors seem incredibly committed to their craft. Most have been at it for decades yet bring verve and enthusiasm to each class." Students appreciate that "professors understand that most of us work over 40 hours per week. They spread out the course load so we can manage it more easily." This spirit of accommodation permeates the entire school. One student writes, "I have found that at any point in my academic career in the Citadel's business school that I have been able to approach all administrators and faculty with ease. Overall, the business school has a family feel, and everyone is looking out for your best interest." In the realm of improvements, some students would like to see the school offer a wider range of electives, and some feel that the faculty needs to be broadened. One student explains, "Many of the core courses are taught by the same professor (i.e., one professor teaches all business law courses, another teaches all the marketing courses, etc.). For someone like me, who has no business background, it seems we receive a very narrow view of the business world."

Career and Placement

The Citadel Career Center provides career services to all students on the Citadel campus. The office provides counseling services; workshops in interviewing, resume building, and job search strategies; career fairs; online job databases; and on-campus recruiting and interviewing. However, much of the office's work is geared toward serving the school's much-larger undergraduate population rather than MBAs and others enrolled in the College of Graduate and Professional Studies.

Student Life and Environment

Citadel MBAs are typically "hardworking individuals juggling full-time jobs, a family, and classes at night." Even so, many try to make time to participate in the school's popular mentoring program, in which "interested students are paired with someone in the community who works or worked in the student's desired career field." The program capitalizes on the fact that "there are many successful retirees in the area who are interested in advising students," but also includes "many accomplished business professionals still working in the field. The program gives the student real insight into that profession rather than the candy-coated version that someone who has never worked in that profession may give."

Students here enjoy other extracurricular options as well. "As part of the Leadership Forum, guest speakers from all over the country come to the Citadel to share their experiences with students," we're told. Plus, "the MBA Association is instrumental in developing relationships among students and professors. It's a great organization to be a part

KATHY JONES, DIRECTOR OF BUSINESS SCHOOL OPERATIONS
171 MOULTRIE STREET CHARLESTON, SC 29409 UNITED STATES
PHONE: 843-953-5089 • FAX: 843-953-7630
E-MAIL: CGPS@CITADEL.EDU • WEBSITE: CITADEL.EDU/CSBA

of." Students also find time in their busy schedules for "occasional social gatherings throughout the year. They range from beers at the local tavern to sit-down dinners in five-star restaurants."

Citadel MBAs "are extremely motivated and resourceful. Everyone greets each other with that wonderful Charleston charm." Commenting on the student body, one student notes that it is "ethnically diverse, in that 10 to 15 percent of my classmates are from other countries and cultures such as Africa, the Middle East, Europe, Asia, and South America." Students "attend classes during the evening either on campus or at a centralized city location called the Low Country Graduate Center. Unlike most undergraduate classes, the students really want to be there and are always eager to participate in class discussions." As one student says, "I only go at night, but I really enjoy the beautiful, quiet campus that's full of diversity and a willingness to learn."

Admissions

Students may apply for admission to the Citadel School of Business Administration for the fall, spring, or summer term. Applicants must submit all of the following materials: a completed application form with application fee; sealed copies of official transcripts for all postsecondary work (transcripts representing work completed outside the U.S. should be translated and evaluated by an academic credential evaluation organization recognized by the Citadel); a sealed official copy of the GMAT score report (a minimum score of 400 is required); two letters of reference from undergraduate professors, business associates, and/or supervisors in government or military service; a resume; and two short personal essays. International students whose first language is not English are required to submit official TOEFL score reports (a minimum score of 550 is required). The school may request an applicant to submit to an interview; otherwise, interviews are not required. The school offers provisional admission to some candidates; provisional status remains in effect until the student has completed all basic courses with a GPA of at least 3.0.

ADMISSIONS

Admissions Selectivity Rating	**60***
# of applications received	71
% applicants accepted	89
Average GMAT	511
Range of GMAT	450–550
TOEFL required of international students	Yes
Minimum TOEFL (paper)	550
Application fee	$30
Regular application deadline	7/20
Regular notification	7/20
Deferment available	Yes
Maximum length of deferment	1 year
Transfer students accepted	Yes

Transfer application policy
A maximum of 6 hours credit for graduate courses from an accredited institution (including consortia and AACSB-accredited institutions) may be approved for transfer (except BADM 635), provided that those courses are determined to be equivalent to one of the advanced or elective courses at The Citadel, that grades of B or better were received in the courses being considered for transfer credit, and that credit for the courses was earned within the five years prior to admission into The Citadel MBA program.

Non-fall admissions	Yes
Need-blind admissions	Yes

Applicants Also Look At
Clemson University, Lander University.

CITY UNIVERSITY OF NEW YORK—BARUCH COLLEGE
ZICKLIN SCHOOL OF BUSINESS

GENERAL INFORMATION

Type of school	Public
Environment	Metropolis
Academic calendar	Semester

SURVEY SAYS . . .

Students love New York, NY
Smart classrooms
Solid preparation in:
Doing business in a global economy

STUDENTS

Enrollment of parent institution	15,500
Enrollment of business school	1,435
% male/female	53/47
% out-of-state	51
% part-time	94
% minorities	7
% international	54
Average age at entry	27
Average years work experience at entry	6

ACADEMICS

Academic Experience Rating	**65**
Student/faculty ratio	35:1
Profs interesting rating	62
Profs accessible rating	80
% female faculty	23
% minority faculty	5

Joint Degrees

JD/MBA 4.5 years.

Prominent Alumni

Larry Zicklin, former managing partner, Neuberger Berman; Marcel Legrand, senior vice president, Monster.com; JoAnn Ryan, president, ConEdison Solutions; William Newman, founder and chairman, New Plan Excel Realty Trust; Hugh Panero, president and CEO, XM Satellite Radio.

Academics

"Baruch is the third-ranked MBA program in New York City, but the tuition is only one-third of NYU or Columbia," students at Baruch's Zicklin School of Business say, spurring many to compare a Zicklin MBA to a value stock and to describe it as "a hidden gem among MBA programs." Accounting and finance are Zicklin's strongest areas; the New York location and the presence of an on-campus simulated trading floor mean finance is also a plus discipline.

Full-time MBA students at Zicklin who participate in an honors program "have a small cohort group within a huge university (Baruch College) and an even larger university system (CUNY), so we get the best of both worlds." Perks include "personalized assistance from full-time honors staff, priority registration for classes, private study areas, numerous career panels and opportunities to meet with executives on campus, and the best professors on campus. Top that, Columbia!" Part-time students may choose between the cohort-based Accelerated Part-Time MBA program, which delivers a degree in just more than 2 years, and the Flex-Time MBA program, a more traditional part-time program in which students schedule evening classes around their typically heavy work schedules.

No matter what program students pursue, they discover that "Zicklin really leverages its New York City location well. We get some great speakers on campus and organize 'treks' to companies." The faculty draws from the city's high-powered business community; one student reports, "Some of the professors are great, and they have real-world experience, e.g., a trader is currently teaching a finance class, and even though his assignments are very long (I've already put [in] 30-plus hours on this project) I am learning a lot." Another adds, "I respect the fact that many professors are current or former executives in their respective fields. This lends an air of authenticity to the lessons and allows you to learn real-life applications, not just about what's written in a textbook." Finally, students appreciate how "Baruch is working hard to promote this school in New York City and on a more national level. This is important because it will draw more companies to recruit here and will continue to attract high-quality students. Baruch is increasing its efforts to get more alumni involved with the school and works hard to increase its presence within the business community in New York."

Career and Placement

Zicklin's Graduate Career Management Center offers business graduate students a broad range of online career development and job search tools, including self assessments and a variety of job boards. The office also schedules regular corporate presentation and information sessions and alumni events and holds regular career management workshops.

Employers who most frequently hire Zicklin graduates include: Citigroup, Colgate-Palmolive, Deloitte Touche Tohmatsu, Goldman Sachs, KPMG International, Lehman Brothers, Ernst & Young, and PricewaterhouseCoopers.

Student Life and Environment

Full-time MBAs report a deluxe graduate school experience at Baruch, telling us that "each day is packed with a wide variety of panels, speakers, and other club activities. There are numerous corporate-sponsored competitions in a variety of fields. . . . The area for the graduate students is nice, with all necessary technology and space to study." Baruch has "fantastic gym and swimming pool facilities, and the campus is very compact, and everything is reachable within minutes." Part-time students are less involved

FRANCES MURPHY, DIRECTOR OF ADMISSIONS
ONE BERNARD BARUCH WAY, BOX H-0820 NEW YORK, NY 10010 UNITED STATES
PHONE: 646-312-1300 • FAX: 646-312-1301 • E-MAIL: ZICKLINGRADADMISSIONS@BARUCH.CUNY.EDU
WEBSITE: WWW.ZICKLIN.BARUCH.CUNY.EDU

with campus life, but not completely shut out. One student writes, "Baruch has some events tailored specifically for grad students, such as the GSA Social, an event where students can meet each other, hang out, and enjoy great food from this Italian restaurant. It's definitely worth going [to], even if only for 1 hour after class."

Students note that "technology, in terms of classroom facilities, is great, especially the simulated trading floor and other career development centers," but warn that "when it comes to administrative duties, the technology is not very integrated. We have some portals that are school specific and others for the statewide requirements. At the beginning of school it was difficult to handle all of the different usernames and passwords to the different sites."

Like the population of its hometown, Zicklin's student body "is diverse and rich in experiences, be it travel, life or work experience. It really makes your classmates interesting." Zicklin has "a lot of international students. There are more than 70 different countries represented at Baruch."

Admissions

All applicants to Zicklin MBA and MS programs must have an accredited bachelor's degree or its international equivalent (official transcripts for all postsecondary academic work required) and must submit an official score report for the GMAT. Students whose first language is not English and who have not graduated from a U.S. undergraduate or graduate school must also submit an official score report for the TOEFL/TWE. Applications must also include a complete application form (hard copy or online), a current resume, two letters of recommendation (at least one should be from a current employer), and an essay describing career goals and explaining why a master's degree in business is important in achieving those goals. In addition to the above, international applicants must also submit translated copies of all transcripts and letters of recommendation; in some cases, applicants may be required to have transcripts evaluated by an independent evaluating agency such as World Educational Services. International applicants must also obtain an F-1 or J-1 visa and must submit a Declaration and Certification of Finances and an Affidavit of Support.

FINANCIAL FACTS

Annual tuition (in-state/ out-of-state)	$8,800/$17,100
Fees	$238
Cost of books	$1,200
Room & board (off-campus)	$20,000
% of students receiving aid	80
% of first-year students receiving aid	95
% of students receiving loans	19
% of students receiving grants	60
Average award package	$9,200
Average grant	$4,100
Average student loan debt	$30,000

ADMISSIONS

Admissions Selectivity Rating	**78**
# of applications received	1,029
% applicants accepted	68
% acceptees attending	57
Average GMAT	582
Range of GMAT	530–620
Average GPA	3.2
TOEFL required for international students	Yes
Minimum TOEFL (paper/computer)	590/243
Application fee	$125
Regular application deadline	4/30
Regular notification	6/15
Deferment available	Yes
Maximum length of deferment	1 year
Transfer students accepted	Yes
Transfer application policy Same application process as all applicants; up to 12 credits from an AACSB-accredited institution may be transferred.	
Non-fall admissions	Yes
Need-blind admissions	Yes

Applicants Also Look At
Columbia University, Fordham University, Hofstra University, New York University, Pace University, Rutgers, The State University of New Jersey, St. John's University.

EMPLOYMENT PROFILE				
Career Rating	**75**	**Grads Employed by Function**	**%**	**Avg. Salary**
Primary Source of Full-time Job Acceptances		Finance/Accounting	73	$76,048
School-facilitated activities	17 (65%)	Human Resources	4	NR
Graduate-facilitated activities	8 (32%)	Marketing/Sales	15	$68,225
Unknown	1 (3%)	General Management	4	NR
Average base starting salary	$74,146	Other	4	NR
Percent employed	86.6	**Top 5 Employers Hiring Grads**		
		Lehman Brothers; Ernst & Young; Citigroup; BlackRock Realty; Colgate-Palmolive.		

CLAREMONT GRADUATE UNIVERSITY
THE PETER F. DRUCKER AND MASATOSHI ITO GRADUATE SCHOOL OF MANAGEMENT

Academics

The Peter F. Drucker and Matatoshi Ito Graduate School of Management at Claremont, known as just "Drucker" for short, finds its basic philosophy in business scholar Peter Drucker's focus on the knowledge economy and in his interest in the management of people and ideas. Flowing from that is an emphasis also on values and ethics as a basis for management and economic decisions. A recently implemented and now-required seminar called the Drucker Difference introduces all beginning MBA students to how the school approaches this—not only through courses in business policy and ethics but also how it plays out in the study of topics including economics and finance.

Students at Drucker are required to complete 32 credits of core courses, comprising slightly more than half of the 60 required for the MBA. That core includes classes in marketing, finance, and operations, as well as advanced study in strategy, and a course in morality and leadership. Students may continue with a general business orientation, select a concentration from Drucker's offerings (in strategy, finance, leadership. marketing, and global business), or choose from topics in the university's other graduate schools and obtain dual majors in fields such as biosciences and cultural management. Drucker also offers an executive MBA program and courses leading to the PhD in business. MBA Students can explore opportunities to study in England, Japan, the Netherlands, and other countries.

Small classes, high standards, and the focus on values are important to students in the program. "Drucker's reputation for ethical responsibility toward the notion of business" was an attraction for many in choosing the school in the first place, and "The intimate environment, which lends itself to a great deal of interaction with the faculty and other students," is another oft-cited strength. "Drucker School professors challenge you to use your whole brain and are always accessible outside of class," students agree . "I get to interact with them rather than a TA," one says. "Course work is extremely relevant and insightful." Professors with professional and academic experience "relate lessons learned into the course work."

The administration earns praise as well. When students hit a snag, "They are there to remedy the problem within the day, a couple of hours actually. Response times are amazing, compared to my undergrad state school," says one student. This supports an academic atmosphere that is "the industry leader in values-centered management training and multidimensional strategic thinking," students say. Here, there is an "emphasis on ethical management" and "on teamwork."

Career and Placement

Nearly three-quarters of Drucker's students attend full-time, and opinion on how helpful the school's Career Center is to both full- and part-time students is mixed. "Career services—although improving—could be more of [a] resource, and the school should arrange for, incorporate, partner, administer, and mandate internships as part of the MBA curriculum," one student reports. "We have our own representative [at the career center] now, which will really change things," another counters. Assisting students with "relationships with employers and networking" is an area that could use a boost, students agree. Ernst & Young, Southern California Edison, Western Asset Management, and Northrup Grumman are among companies that often recruit Drucker graduates.

BRYAN MCSWEENEY, ASSOCIATE DIRECTOR, RECRUITING AND ADMISSIONS
1021 NORTH DARTMOUTH AVENUE CLAREMONT, CA 91711 UNITED STATES
PHONE: 909-607-7811 • FAX: 909-607-9104
E-MAIL: DRUCKER@CGU.EDU • WEBSITE: WWW.DRUCKER.CGU.EDU

Student Life and Environment

"We are very serious, so most of my time spent on campus is in a study room or with a study group" one student says, summing up the "intrinsically driven" but "not competitive" atmosphere that many find at Drucker. "My fellow students show a genuine interest in my success both at school and in life. We help each other through difficult times at school and in our personal lives," adds another. Many students at this school—where "Everyone knows one another by name"—come from international backgrounds, "which I think is terrific," one student notes. "The exchange and learning between people from different business and cultural background[s] has taught me quite a lot." Students agree that diversity is a benefit, but at the same time add that the school "needs more local students" and "should offer a better variety of electives during the 7:00 to10:00 P.M. time frame for students who work full-time." Those who live on campus find that "student housing is a major deficiency, especially for married students." Still, students generally agree that "Claremont is a great place to live. Weather is ideal, mountains are scenic" and the "excellent main street" is within walking distance.

Admissions

In keeping with the school's overall philosophy, the Admissions Office is committed to looking at the whole person when evaluating applicants for admission. GMAT scores are required, as are undergraduate transcripts, three letters of recommendation and a personal statement responding to questions regarding the contributions a student could make to the school's community and how the student has resolved an ethical dilemma that he or she has faced. For the executive MBA program, GMAT scores are not required; instead the school asks for at least 10 years of work experience along with a personal interview. Drucker generally accepts about half of those who apply for the MBA program. In 2006, those students had an average GMAT score of 598, a GPA of 3.27, and averaged 3 years of work experience.

FINANCIAL FACTS

Annual tuition	$38,760
Fees	$250
Cost of books	$1,500
Room & board (on/off-campus)	$12,000/$13,000
% of students receiving aid	67
% of first-year students receiving aid	65
% of students receiving loans	70
% of students receiving grants	50
Average award package	$15,000
Average grant	$6,800
Average student loan debt	$42,686

ADMISSIONS

Admissions Selectivity Rating	85
# of applications received	193
% applicants accepted	50
% acceptees attending	42
Average GMAT	598
Range of GMAT	540–660
Average GPA	3.27
TOEFL required of international students	Yes
Minimum TOEFL (paper/computer)	600/250
Application fee	$60
Application Deadline/Notification	
Round 1:	11/15 / 2/1
Round 2:	2/1 / 4/1
Round 3:	4/1 / 5/15
Round 4:	5/15 / 6/15
Deferment available	Yes
Maximum length of deferment	1 year
Transfer students accepted	Yes
Transfer application policy The maximum number of transferable credits is 10 units.	
Non-fall admissions	Yes
Need-blind admissions	Yes

Applicants Also Look At

Pepperdine University, University of California—Irvine, University of California—Los Angeles (UCLA), University of Southern California.

EMPLOYMENT PROFILE			
Career Rating	84	Grads Employed by Function	% Avg. Salary
Primary Source of Full-time Job Acceptances		Finance/Accounting	22 $67,875
School-facilitated activities	7 (39%)	Human Resources	11 $49,000
Graduate-facilitated activities	8 (44%)	Marketing/Sales	28 $77,800
Unknown	3 (17%)	MIS	5 $62,000
Average base starting salary	$70,361	Operations/Production	6 $95,000
Percent employed	82	Consulting	17 $63,333
		General Management	11 $80,500

CLARK UNIVERSITY
GRADUATE SCHOOL OF MANAGEMENT

GENERAL INFORMATION

Type of school	Private
Environment	City
Academic calendar	Semester

SURVEY SAYS . . .
Friendly students
Solid preparation in:
Finance
General management
Teamwork
Communication/interpersonal skills
Doing business in a global economy

STUDENTS

Enrollment of parent institution	3,071
Enrollment of business school	286
% male/female	53/47
% part-time	44
% minorities	7
% international	55
Average age at entry	27
Average years work experience at entry	5

ACADEMICS

Academic Experience Rating	**72**
Student/faculty ratio	11:1
Profs interesting rating	64
Profs accessible rating	82
% female faculty	40

Joint Degrees
MBA/MSF.

Prominent Alumni
Matt Goldman, co-founder, The Blueman Group; Ralph Crowley, CEO, Polar Beverages; William Aubuchon, CEO, W.E. Aubuchon Co.; Frank Crocetti, vice president, Fidelity Investments.

Academics

A small graduate business program strong in finance (so strong, in fact, that it offers both an MBA with a finance concentration and a Master of Science in Finance), the Graduate School of Management at Clark University offers students "a smaller community" in which they "get to know teachers personally." Clark also excels in international and global studies, an area of study that benefits greatly from the international perspectives of a "diverse student population," of whom nearly three-quarters originate from outside the U.S.

The Clark MBA "is designed to build an excellent foundation in business fundamentals and the critical management judgment needed to analyze complex situations, to plan strategic actions, and to lead people effectively" through a core curriculum of 7- and 14-week classes. Students appreciate the system's flexibility, although some feel that "there are some 7-week courses that should really be a 14-week courses (example: Quantitative Techniques for Derivatives Evaluation), and there are some 14-week classes which should really be 7-week courses (example: CEO Leadership)." Through their choice of electives, students may concentrate in accounting, finance, global business, health care, information systems, or marketing, or they may pursue an MBA in general management without an area of concentration.

The Clark curriculum places a lot of emphasis on "team creation," with students doing "a lot of quality work as a team." One student writes, "The classes are challenging, very interactive, and they give us plenty of opportunity to practice skills, critical decision-making, and business interactions." Professors here "are accessible for concerns or guidance" and are "extremely accommodating and willing to take the time to make sure that we all succeed." Clark's administration is "organized yet flexible."

Career and Placement

The Stevenish Career Management Center at Clark's GSOM provides a range of services, including individual advising, resume and cover letter assistance, online and hardcopy job listings, workshops, internship placement, alumni networking events, alumni professional seminars, career fairs, and on-campus recruiting events. The office also maintains a full career library. Some students still wish it would do more, telling us that "the school definitely needs to improve the career center, helping students to get more jobs and internships." They say that although the center "has gone through significant change [for the better], it still needs to work harder at getting students into the working world."

Employers who hire Clark MBAs include: Analog Devices, Anheuser-Busch, ARAMCO, Bloomberg, LP, Comcast, Dell, Deutsche Bank, EMC, Fallon Healthcare System, the Federal Reserve Bank, Fidelity Investments, General Dynamics, Hewlett-Packard, KPMG International, Lucent Technologies, Public Consulting Group, Staples, Waters Corporation, the World Bank, and the Worcester Art Museum.

Student Life and Environment

At Clark "There are plenty of activities and quality entertainment offered all week long and on weekends." That's why "You are never bored unless you choose to be." Student groups organize numerous events, including international dinners, ski trips, and parties. According to one MBA, "Life is filled with diversity, from the discussions in class to the activities at a social event. Faculty and staff have a very good relationship with students and are very helpful."

Lynn Davis, Director of Enrollment and Marketing, GSOM
950 Main Street, Clark University, Worcester, MA 01610 United States
Phone: 508-793-7406 • Fax: 508-421-3825
E-mail: clarkmba@clarku.edu • Website: www.clarku.edu/gsom

In an effort to improve campus safety, the school provides escorts to students who need to go shopping or otherwise travel within one mile of campus between 4:00 P.M. and 4:00 A.M. Students with cars may find themselves making the 1-hour drive to Boston on nights when they want some big-city entertainment.

Clark's student body includes a large international contingent that "draws heavily from China, India, and Taiwan." "Most of us come from diverse backgrounds," says one student. "I am part of a minority of students who hail from South America. I enjoy working in teams with students from India, the Middle East, and Southeast Asia. It has been a great opportunity to get to know their cultures." One student describes her fellow classmates as "interesting, well traveled, sophisticated, and charming." As a group, though, "There is often a lack of experience" from the professional world before they enter the program.

Admissions

Clark offers applicants an unusual option; the school accepts either the GMAT or the GRE. A 5-year BA/MBA program for Clark undergraduates is available. Clark requires the following of applicants: a completed admissions application; a personal essay; a current resume; two letters of recommendation; and official transcripts from all undergraduate and graduate programs previously attended. Interviews are optional. International applicants must submit all of the above as well as an official score report for the TOEFL (if their native language is other than English) and proof of the financial means to support oneself while attending the program.

FINANCIAL FACTS

Annual tuition	$21,140
Fees	$1,050
Cost of books	$800
Room & board	
(on/off-campus)	$8,400/$9,500
% of students receiving aid	45
% of first-year students	
receiving aid	45
% of students receiving grants	45
Average award package	$10,000
Average grant	$8,000

ADMISSIONS

Admissions Selectivity Rating	**86**
# of applications received	342
% applicants accepted	81
% acceptees attending	40
Average GMAT	530
Range of GMAT	500–570
Average GPA	3.2
TOEFL required of	
international students	Yes
Minimum TOEFL	
(paper/computer)	550/213
Application fee	$50
Regular application deadline	6/1
Regular notification	Rolling
Deferment available	Yes
Maximum length of	
deferment	1 year
Transfer students accepted	Yes
Transfer application policy	
A maximum of two courses may	
be transferred into the program.	
Courses must have been taken at	
an AACSB-accredited school.	
Additional courses taken on the	
graduate level may be applicable	
to course waivers.	
Non-fall admissions	Yes
Need-blind admissions	Yes

Applicants Also Look At

Babson College, Bentley College, Boston University, Brandeis University, Northeastern University, Suffolk University.

EMPLOYMENT PROFILE

Career Rating	**65**
Primary Source of Full-time Job Acceptances	
Percent employed	63

CLARKSON UNIVERSITY
SCHOOL OF BUSINESS

Academics

Clarkson University is best known for its fine engineering programs, so it should come as no surprise that the focus at Clarkson University School of Business is on developing business acumen in engineers. Students recognize what makes their school special, telling us, "Clarkson's academic record is outstanding. It is a competitive engineering school with a growing business program." The curriculum stresses that students approach problem-solving creatively to "focus on the big picture." As one student explains, "Life at Clarkson is academically strenuous but a balance of mind, body, and spirit is encouraged by the business school." Clarkson's history as a "technical school" comes in handy for those students interested in the business side of engineering since "Many technical companies are attracted to the school" and the campus has "strong industry connections" and a "good reputation in the technology world."

Clarkson MBAs are anxious to get their degrees and move on, and the school's accelerated 1-year program suits their needs perfectly. One MBA writes, "After four years of undergrad I don't mind a little extra work load to have a master's in one year." Students agree that "the workload is intense" and places "a strong stress on the team-based experience." All this hard work pays off in the end, though, as students feel that "the group-work emphasis will help in future employment" and "The fast pace and large workload proves [their] ability to work under pressure." Despite this "challenging" atmosphere, students get a break from their studies during the *Globalization and Ethics Week* where corporate executives and alumni speak on various topics.

Clarkson MBAs note that the school's "small size does not sacrifice the quality of most professors." "They are always available and put in every effort to assist students," says one student. Another enthuses, "Professors are incredibly concerned with student progress. They are very accessible outside the classroom and more than willing to start up conversations in the middle of a hallway with any student." However, "They will not tell you the way to succeed. All they will do is guide you in your search to find success." In this way, "The faculty at Clarkson treat their students as equals," which MBAs appreciate.

Career and Placement

Clarkson MBAs receive career services from the Graduate Career Services Office and the university's Career Center, which serves all students at the university. The center schedules career fairs each semester, puts students in contact with Clarkson's alumni network, and provides students with access to the online job database MonsterTrak. MBAs give the office mixed reviews. Some wish it would "attract a more diverse pool of job recruiters in relation to the interests of the students in the program." "They could try to get more business related type firms," adds a student. However, others praise the "many helpful resources such as e-recruiting" that are provided.

Clarkson MBAs most frequently find work with IBM, Accenture, Lockheed Martin, GE, Cooper Industries, Frito-Lay, HSBC, Knowledge Systems and Research, Texas Instruments, and Whiting Turner. While the majority of graduates remain in the Northeast, students are placed throughout the country.

JOSHUA LaFAVE, ASSOCIATE DIRECTOR, GRADUATE BUSINESS PROGRAMS
EIGHT CLARKSON AVENUE, CU BOX 5770 POTSDAM, NY 13699 UNITED STATES
PHONE: 315-268-6613 • FAX: 315-268-3810
E-MAIL: BUSGRAD@CLARKSON.EDU • WEBSITE: WWW.CLARKSON.EDU/BUSINESS/GRADUATE

Student Life and Environment

The majority of Clarkson's student body is full-time, and they report a predictable rhythm to their school days. "You are generally on campus from 8:00 A.M. until 6:00 or 7:00 P.M. There is a lot of work and a lot of meetings to attend with group members," explains one student. As it's a business school, the prevailing mood is businesslike. Students "treat each day as if it were a work day" by dressing "business casual" and acting in "a professional manner." The business school facility follows suit with its "multiple computer labs," "student lounges," and "Learning Development Labs."

Potsdam, of course, is hardly a bustling metropolis. The closest large city is Ottawa, which lies approximately 90 miles and one international border to the north. One student simply states, "It's pretty cold, unless it's summer then it's pretty hot." With "only about three bars in town which are shared with a local SUNY school," students find "not much raucous" about the social scene, saying "It's pretty ho-hum." "Unless you skate or enjoy winter sports, there isn't much else in Potsdam to do," says one student.

Some students, however, manage to see the glass as half full instead of half empty. "A vast diversity of sports, intramurals, and clubs allow students to keep busy outside of class and to socialize with their peers," explains one student. A "majority" of Clarkson students are "involved in an activity of one sort or another." Another adds that the school provides for a "fun environment." Fortunately for all, Clarkson's accelerated 1-year program keeps most students too busy to worry about what type of fun they are, or are not, missing. Students work hard all week long and through much of the weekend as well. One MBA explains, "Weekends are spent doing work all day long. You go out with friends one night a week on the weekend; that's about it."

Admissions

The admissions department at Clarkson University requires that applicants submit an undergraduate transcript, GMAT scores, TOEFL scores (if necessary), and a Test of Spoken English (TSE) (for international students whose native language is not English; the TSE can be administered via telephone), a detailed resume, two one-page personal essays, and three letters of reference. Awards of merit-based scholarships are determined during the admissions process; no separate application is required. Those requiring foundation course work prior to commencing their MBAs "may enroll in the courses at Clarkson before entering the advanced MBA program. For students doing graduate work at another university, they are allowed to transfer in nine credit hours of graduate work."

ADMISSIONS

Admissions Selectivity Rating	**72**
# of applications received	105
% applicants accepted	83
% acceptees attending	71
Average GMAT	544
Range of GMAT	490–583
Average GPA	3.29
TOEFL required of international students	Yes
Minimum TOEFL (paper/computer)	600/250
Application fee	$25
International application fee	$35
Regular application deadline	Rolling
Regular notification	Rolling
Deferment available	Yes
Maximum length of deferment	1 year
Transfer students accepted	Yes
Transfer application policy Graduate students who need to complete foundation course work may enroll in the summer business concepts program at Clarkson before entering the advanced MBA program. For students doing graduate work at another university, they are allowed to transfer in up to 9 credit hours of graduate work from another AACSB-accredited institution.	
Non-fall admissions	Yes
Need-blind admissions	Yes

Applicants Also Look At

Rensselaer Polytechnic Institute, Rochester Institute of Technology, State University of New York at Binghamton, Syracuse University, University of Rochester.

EMPLOYMENT PROFILE

Career Rating	79	Grads Employed by Function	%	Avg. Salary
Primary Source of Full-time Job Acceptances		Finance/Accounting	12	$47,375
School-facilitated activities	8 (24%)	Human Resources	6	$43,000
Graduate-facilitated activities	15 (44%)	Marketing/Sales	9	$48,333
Unknown	11 (32%)	Operations/Production	18	$58,752
Percent employed	90	Consulting	21	$58,000
		General Management	15	$54,500
		Other	13	$52,500
		Nonprofit	6	$42,000

Top 5 Employers Hiring Grads

IBM, Accenture, Lockheed Martin, GE, Central Hudson.

CLEMSON UNIVERSITY
COLLEGE OF BUSINESS AND BEHAVIORAL SCIENCE

Academics

Native South Carolinians seeking the MBA will have a hard time beating the ratio of value to quality that they'll find at Clemson University. Thanks to lower in-state tuition costs, Palmetto State residents can earn a highly regarded business degree for a small fraction of what their peers elsewhere in the country spend. Beautiful weather and first-rate intercollegiate football further sweeten the deal.

Approximately 30 full-time students enter Clemson's MBA program each year; full-timers make up a little less than half the student body. The program, students warn, "moves quickly. We complete 62 graduate-level credits in 21 months." One student explains, "I recommend the program to anyone who is confident that they can keep up with a heavy workload through effective time-management and teamwork skills." The first year is devoted entirely to foundation courses, some taught in a "highly intensive, highly rigorous seven-week format." The second year allows students to choose specializations in one of four designated tracks (innovation and entrepreneurial leadership, supply chain and information management, real estate and marketing management). Double degrees are not uncommon here; one student in our survey was earning an MBA in tandem with an MS in Parks, Recreation, and Tourism Management, while several others noted that "Clemson is strong in engineering and research, so it's a good place for engineers and scientists seeking business education." Students in all areas praise "the reputation of the professors and the school's reputation throughout the Southeast."

Part-time classes meet in the evening at the University Center of Greenville; the program is open only to those with at least two years of work experience. The program consists of five core courses (some or all of which can be waived based on prior academic work or passing a proficiency exam), eight required advanced courses, and three electives. The program offers more flexibility than does the full-time program but also provides fewer opportunities for teamwork and group projects. Participants appreciate the fact that "classes only meet one night per week, which makes it easier on family life." They also tell us that "some professors are fantastic, and others are not so hot. Overall, though, the good outweighs the bad."

Career and Placement

Clemson MBAs benefit from the Office of MBA Career Development, which "assists students and their career development." The office offers career placement support including one-on-one professional coaching, personalized placement assistance as well as a range of self-assessment instruments, job-search counseling, interviewing and resume-writing workshops, seminars, and online job databases. Students praise the value of alumni connections but also feel that the office "needs help with national job-placement services. Clemson is very well connected within the state but not so much outside of the state."

Companies most likely to recruit Clemson MBAs include Accenture, BB&T, Coca-Cola, Datastream Systems Inc., Deloitte Touche Tohmatsu, Duke Power Co., Hewlett-Packard, Hitachi, Lexmark International, Michelin North America, Milliken, PricewaterhouseCoopers, Procter & Gamble, Schlumberger, Sonoco, Trane Co., and Wachovia.

MBA Office—Admissions, Admissions Director, MBA Programs
124 Sirrine Hall, Box 341315, Clemson University, Clemson, SC 29634-1315 United States
Phone: 864-656-3975 • Fax: 864-656-0947
E-mail: mba@clemson.edu • Website: business.clemson.edu/mba/

Student Life and Environment

"'The greatest strength of Clemson University is the 'Clemson Family,'" and MBAs here agree. "The network of alumni and friends is outstanding. Every graduate is more than willing to lend a hand to a fellow Tiger." Community spirit runs especially high during football season, which "is very fun. Enthusiasm generated by the interest in football leads to better community involvement in . . . the university." The surrounding town of Clemson "is dedicated to the university. There is a small downtown area with plenty of bars/restaurants, nearby mountains/lakes, and plenty of other social activities for students to partake in." As one student sums up, "Clemson University is a special place. There are plenty of opportunities for intramural sports, nightlife, guest lectures and speeches, university events, and cultural events."

Clemson MBAs tend to be "laid-back people keeping very rigorous schedules. Small-town life helps because there aren't too many distractions." They are "very supportive of one another. We aid each other through study sessions, workshops, and other methods to ensure that everyone understands the material." One full-time MBA points out, "The other students are truly what make this program excellent. I have built so many friendships that I know I will take with me into the business world. We often take trips together, including spring break, study abroad, professional seminars, etc. Working so closely over the past few years in the classroom has really helped us to become tightly knit and great friends outside of the classroom."

Admissions

Applicants to the MBA program at Clemson must submit a current resume (two years of work experience are required for the Career Accelerator curriculum; work experience is preferred, but not required, for the Career Launch curriculum); one official transcripts representing all undergraduate work (an overall GPA of at least 3.0 in a non-business major is preferred); two letters of recommendation; a one- to two-page personal statement (required of applicants to the Career Launch MBA); phone interview and an official GMAT score report (score of at least 580 preferred for applicants to the full-time program). Non-native English speakers applying to the full-time program must submit TOEFL scores.

FINANCIAL FACTS

Annual tuition (in-state/ out-of-state)	$7,282/$14,570
Cost of books	$1,700
Room & board	$11,480
% of students receiving aid	72
% of first-year students receiving aid	63
% of students receiving loans	54
Average award package	$12,686

ADMISSIONS

Admissions Selectivity Rating	79
# of applications received	174
% applicants accepted	70
% acceptees attending	61
Average GMAT	592
Range of GMAT	558–613
Average GPA	3.2
TOEFL required of international students	Yes
Minimum TOEFL (paper/computer)	580/237
Application fee	$50
Regular application deadline	4/15
Regular notification	4/30
Deferment available	Yes
Maximum length of deferment	1 year
Transfer students accepted	Yes
Transfer application policy Must meet all admission requirements. Can transfer a maximum of 12 semester hours of acceptable course work.	
Need-blind admissions	Yes

Applicants Also Look At
Auburn University, University of South Carolina.

EMPLOYMENT PROFILE

Career Rating	77	Grads Employed by Function	%	Avg. Salary
Primary Source of Full-time Job Acceptances		Finance/Accounting	23	$81,000
School-facilitated activities	6 (43%)	Marketing/Sales	23	$75,600
Graduate-facilitated activities	8 (57%)	General Management	23	$53,700
Unknown	6 (29%)	Operations/Production	23	$60,000
Percent employed	61	Human Resources	8	$73,000

Top 5 Employers Hiring Grads
Bank of America; KPMG International; Michelin; American Express Company; Cap Gemini.

THE COLLEGE OF WILLIAM & MARY
THE MASON SCHOOL OF BUSINESS

GENERAL INFORMATION
Type of school	Public
Environment	Village
Academic calendar	Semester

SURVEY SAYS . . .
Friendly students
Solid preparation in:
Finance
Teamwork
Communication/interpersonal skills
Presentation skills
Quantitative skills

STUDENTS
Enrollment of parent institution	7,500
Enrollment of business school	292
% male/female	73/27
% out-of-state	24
% part-time	57
% minorities	7
% international	30
Average age at entry	26
Average years work experience at entry	3.5

ACADEMICS
Academic Experience Rating	**85**
Student/faculty ratio	2:1
Profs interesting rating	96
Profs accessible rating	98
% female faculty	18
% minority faculty	21

Joint Degrees
MBA/JD 4 years, MBA/MPP 3 years, MIM (with Thunderbird) 3 years.

Prominent Alumni
C. Michael Petters, CEO, Northrop Grumman Newport News; Gary M. Pfeiffer, CFO, E.I. DuPont de Nemours, Inc.; Daniel J. Ludeman, president and CEO, Wachovia Securities; C. Larry Pope, president and COO, Smithfield Foods; James "Buck" McCabe, CFO, Chick-fil-A.

Academics

Students speak highly of the curriculum at the College of William & Mary 's Mason School of Business, but for most it's "the intangibles, particularly the Executive Partners Program, Career Acceleration Modules, and Field Consultancy Programs" that elevate this program and have MBAs declaring it "absolutely wonderful." Mason offers three MBA options, one full-time and two part-time. Part-time options include the flex MBA, a nine-semester sequence consisting of 3-hour, once-weekly classes; and the executive MBA, with classes meeting on alternate weekends.

Full-timers and flex MBAs rave about the school's Executive Partners Program, "a mentorship program for students under the auspice of our Leadership Class" that takes advantage of "Williamsburg's dozens of retired C-level executives who tire of golf and are looking to participate. Those men and women are a huge resource," as they "hold more knowledge than you can access in your time with them (luckily they respond to e-mails and take phone calls as well). They volunteer to come help us and genuinely care about how we do. They are worth their weight in gold."

Mason's Career Acceleration Modes in entrepreneurship, investments and financial services, corporate finance, B2B Marketing, B2C Marketing, and Operations/IT combine training and field projects for companies such as Philip Morris, DuPont, and Hamilton Beach. Field Consultancy Programs puts second-year students to work consulting for the likes of Cox Communications, Sprint, and Blue Cross and Blue Shield Association. Students tell us that both experiences are invaluable.

Mason also shines in the less glamorous task of teaching the MBA curriculum. Professors "are absolutely amazing. They will blow you away with their across-the-board commitment to helping the students completely understand the material." The curriculum itself "puts a strong emphasis on teamwork, leaving no doubt that we will come out extremely well prepared to deal with others both in and out of the workforce." Mason's current facility "is a bit outdated, but we're expecting a brand new state-of-the-art facility in 2009. It would definitely improve the classroom atmosphere and study rooms." One student points out that "prospective students should look at the trajectory of a program. With the expansion of the program and the new building on its way, William & Mary is well on its way to establishing itself as a top-notch MBA program that can reasonably compare itself to Fuqua and Darden."

Career and Placement

Students tell us that recruiting is on the upswing at the Mason School, although "due to the size of the school, there are only certain companies willing to come to campus to recruit." There is, however, a select group that comes here, and it is growing over time. The Executive Partner program has been a recruiting boon, "grooming students to find positions within current recruiting firms and attracting distant companies to campus once they see what students at this little school can do." Students also point out that "when a student decides to pursue an alternative career or company, the Career Services Office is very helpful in developing strategies for that student."

Top employers of Mason MBAs include: Anheuser-Busch, BearingPoint, Booz Allen Hamilton, Capital One, Deloitte Touche Tohmatsu, Dominion Resources, Ernst & Young, Fannie Mae, IBM, Johnson & Johnson, Lafarge, Legg Mason, Landmark Communications, National City Corporation, Rich-Seapak, Target, and Wachovia.

KATHY WILLIAMS PATTISON, DIRECTOR, MBA ADMISSIONS
PO BOX 8795, BLOW HALL, OFFICE 254, WILLIAMSBURG, VA 23187 UNITED STATES
PHONE: 757-221-2900 • FAX: 757-221-2958
E-MAIL: ADMISSIONS@MASON.WM.EDU • WEBSITE: MASON.WM.EDU/MASON

Student Life and Environment

For full-time students at Mason, "The first half of the day is spent in classroom. In the second half, a student ends up partly completing team assignments and partly completing individual assignments." Team projects "create the opportunity to interact with other students" and develop "a great deal of camaraderie, but it is an intense 2 years full of self-improvement and demanding course work." Many students "spend evenings studying late, usually past midnight."

Even so, students do find time to socialize. The opportunities in town are limited, as Williamsburg offers only "a small-town environment. If that's what you want, you will love it here. It is beautiful and safe and loaded with historical activities. Big city it is not. Williamsburg is great, and it is very community based. You will get to know your classmates very well. It is easy to feel very comfortable." Students see an upside to the challenges Williamsburg presents. One student writes, "There are only three bars, and that forces students in the b-school and law school to excel socially. Any large town has a big enough nightlife to seem exciting. We make ours exciting—city social scenes are cake after having fun in such a small environment."

Admissions

Applicants to the full-time, flex, and executive MBA programs must submit official academic transcripts for all undergraduate and graduate work; an official GMAT score report; letters of recommendation; personal essays; and a resume. International applicants whose first language is not English must submit official score reports for either the TOEFL or the IELTS.

FINANCIAL FACTS

Annual tuition (in-state/out-of-state)	$12,550/$26,216
Fees (in-state/out-of-state)	$4,014/$4,148
Cost of books	$1,500
Room & board	$14,481
% of students receiving aid	69
% of first-year students receiving aid	62
% of students receiving loans	42
% of students receiving grants	30
Average award package	$24,090
Average grant	$14,080
Average student loan debt	$36,310

ADMISSIONS

Admissions Selectivity Rating	**81**
# of applications received	208
% applicants accepted	52
% acceptees attending	54
Average GMAT	603
Range of GMAT	540–680
TOEFL required of international students	Yes
Minimum TOEFL (paper/computer)	600/250
Application fee	$100
International application fee	$100
Regular application deadline	4/1
Regular notification	5/1
Deferment available	No
Maximum length of deferment	N/A
Need-blind admissions	Yes

Applicants Also Look At

University of Maryland, University of Virginia, Vanderbilt University, Wake Forest University.

EMPLOYMENT PROFILE

Career Rating	**84**	**Grads Employed by Function**	**% Avg. Salary**
Primary Source of Full-time Job Acceptances		Finance/Accounting	27 $74,042
School-facilitated activities	14 (36%)	Marketing/Sales	42 $72,136
Graduate-facilitated activities	16 (41%)	Operations/Production	8 NR
Unknown	9 (23%)	Consulting	15 $74,500
Average base starting salary	$71,957	Other	8 NR
Percent employed	90	**Top 5 Employers Hiring Grads**	
		BearingPoint; Capital One; Philip Morris USA; Wachovia; Booz Allen Hamilton	

COLORADO STATE UNIVERSITY
COLLEGE OF BUSINESS

GENERAL INFORMATION
Type of school   Public
Environment   City

SURVEY SAYS...
Friendly students
Good peer network
Cutting-edge classes
Helpful alumni
Happy students
Solid preparation in:
Accounting
General management
Teamwork

STUDENTS
Enrollment of
  parent institution   25,090
Enrollment of business school   560
Average age at entry   36
Average years work experience
  at entry   12

ACADEMICS
Academic Experience Rating   **87**
Student/faculty ratio   30:1
Profs interesting rating   89
Profs accessible rating   74
% female faculty   10

Joint Degrees
DVM/MBA 5 years.

FINANCIAL FACTS
Annual tuition (in-state/
  out-of-state) $9,000/$19,000
Fees $45
Cost of books $2,100

Academics

A distance-learning leader, Colorado State University has consistently endeavored to deliver one of the best distance-learning MBAs in the country. Its efforts seem to have paid off. Students in the program agree that "the CSU School of Business is an innovator in distance-learning techniques; it has worked the kinks out both academically and operationally." The school also offers a part-time evening MBA program. Both the evening and the distance-learning MBA are "comprehensive lockstep programs" that are identical in content.

Here's how the CSU MBA works: Part-time MBAs attend classes on campus two evenings for 21 months, and the distance MBA can be completed in the same period of time or extended for up to four years. Classes are taped, burned to DVD, and sent to students in the distance-learning program. Distance learners tell us that their program "seems less 'distancy' because of the recorded lectures on DVD and the fact that we have the identical pace and curriculum as the on-campus students." Students in both programs keep in touch with their professors and each other through a communications software product that allows professors to post assignments and students to complete projects in a virtual meeting space. One student writes, "The program requires extensive use of work teams in a virtual environment, which is 100 percent what a graduate will likely experience in today's business world, because most coworkers will be located in another building, state, time zone, or country."

Whether they complete the program on campus or at home, students enjoy a curriculum that "is not just theory, but very heavy on application. What is taught has immediate applications at my job," comments one working student. CSU professors "are tough and require a heavy workload," but they are also "understanding of the demands on part-time students" and can be "flexible with emergencies." They "teach cutting-edge theory and practice" and are informed by their own experience in the business world. "All professors have worked or are currently working in the industry they are teaching us about. The adjunct professors are also well qualified and put a tremendous amount of time into the students." Accounting, economics, and finance are reportedly the faculty's strongest areas. Perhaps the greatest drawback of the program is that it offers only a general MBA. One student explains, "The school does not offer electives, only core courses." Nearly all students here agree that CSU's strengths far outweigh its weaknesses, however; sums up one MBA, "The school is very ambitious and works hard to create a program that really serves the business students. It is an outstanding program."

Career and Placement

The part-time nature of CSU's MBA program is designed for working professionals, who comprise the vast majority of the student body. The school maintains a College of Business Career Liaison to coordinate activities between the College of Business and the university's Career Center, but the responsibilities of this office are primarily aimed at serving undergraduates. This doesn't have much of an impact on MBAs, however, since most CSU MBAs already have good jobs with such powerhouses as Agilent, Argen, Celestica, Colgate-Palmolive, ConAgra, FedEx, Hewlett-Packard, Honeywell, MCI WorldCom, National Textiles, Parson Group, Siemens, Sun Microsystems, UPS, and Wells Fargo Bank.

ADMISSIONS CONTACT: RACHEL STOLL, GRADUATE ADMISSIONS COORDINATOR
164 ROCKWELL HALL, 1270 CAMPUS DELIVERY, FORT COLLINS, CO 80523-1270 U.S.
PHONE: 970-491-3704 • FAX: 970-491-3481
E-MAIL: RACHEL.STOLL@COLOSTATE.EDU • WEBSITE: WWW.BIZ.COLOSTATE.EDU/MBA

Student Life and Environment

Nestled in the foothills of the Rockies "with a beautiful view," Colorado State University "is a thriving, vibrant community" of 24,000 students, 1,550 faculty, and numerous administrators and employees. The school offers "great access to many academic and social venues, and a pleasant campus atmosphere that supports learning." Taking advantage of these proves "a little tough for older students. Within the MBA program, people are juggling so many balls that they hardly have time to partake." Those who can manage a few free moments enjoy and appreciate the "strong clubs and activities [and] plenty of intramural sports." Many distance students "never visit the campus at all," however.

Among the on-campus student body, "work experiences vary from vet students to engineers in high-tech companies to nurses and general mangers at *Fortune* 100 companies." One MBA writes, "There are even some students who work for not-for-profit firms, which adds yet another level of interest to class discussions and the overall quality of the program at Colorado State University." One student notes, however, that "the program does attract a lot of professional engineers. I wish there were more variety in terms of work experience." A solid mix of international MBAs includes "students from Asia, Latin America, and Canada." Distance learners come "from all types of backgrounds and from all over the place." The average age of students is around 35, and the typical CSU student has about 10 to 15 years of work experience.

Admissions

CSU admits on-campus MBAs in the fall only; distance learners are admitted for either the fall or the spring semester. All applicants must submit a completed application form, a resume, a cover letter, an official GMAT score report, two copies of official transcripts for all postsecondary academic work, and three recommendations. Applicants whose native language is not English must also submit an official TOEFL score report. According to the school's website, CSU looks to "select a richly diverse set of students with various undergraduate degrees and professional experiences. Additional requirements include a minimum of four years post-undergraduate professional work experience, previous academic performance, GMAT scores, work experience, and recommendations are some of the factors considered. In addition, the applicant's personal cover letter should reflect carefully considered reasons for pursuing a business degree at the master's level." Applicants with GPAs below 3.0 must include a letter explaining the circumstances under which they received such grades.

ADMISSIONS

Admissions Selectivity Rating	**79**
# of applications received	206
% applicants accepted	86
% acceptees attending	84
Average GMAT	620
Range of GMAT	530–700
Average GPA	3.20
TOEFL required of international students	Yes
Minimum TOEFL (paper/computer)	565/227
Application fee	$50
Regular application deadline	5/1
Regular notification	6/1
Deferment available	Yes
Maximum length of deferment	1 year
Non-fall admissions	Yes
Need-blind admissions	Yes

Applicants Also Look At

Arizona State University, Florida State University.

COLUMBIA UNIVERSITY
COLUMBIA BUSINESS SCHOOL

GENERAL INFORMATION
Type of school	Private
Environment	Metropolis
Academic calendar	Trimester

SURVEY SAYS . . .
Students love New York, NY
Good social scene
Good peer network
Happy students
Solid preparation in:
Finance
Quantitative skills

STUDENTS
Enrollment of parent institution	24,644
Enrollment of business school	1,242
% male/female	65/35
% minorities	8
% international	36
Average age at entry	28
Average years work experience at entry	5

ACADEMICS
Academic Experience Rating	**88**
Profs interesting rating	64
Profs accessible rating	93

Joint Degrees
MBA/MS (urban planning), MBA/MS (nursing), MBA/MPH (public health), MBA/MIA (international affairs, MBA/MS (industrial or mining engineering, MBA/MS (social work), MBA/MS (journalism), MBA/JD (jurisprudence), MBA/MD (medicine), MBA/DDS (doctor of dental surgery).

Prominent Alumni
Warren Buffett, chairman, Berkshire Hathaway Inc.; Henry Kravis, founding partner, Kohlberg, Kravis; Rochelle Lazarus, chair and CEO, Ogilvy and Mather; Michael Gould, chairman and CEO, Bloomingdales; Sallie Krawcheck, CFO and head of strategy, Citigroup.

Academics

"No other school offers the same caliber of professors, students, varied curriculum, work-life balance, dedication to the local community, and connections and exposure to both the for-profit and nonprofit worlds" as does Columbia, graduate business students at this New York City stalwart tell us. A high-profile program in America's highest-profile city, Columbia offers the kind of MBA program where "it is an everyday occurrence to see a *New York Times* real estate article in which your professor is quoted, learn from a Nobel Prize-winning economist, and attend lectures given by CEOs from *Fortune* 100 companies."

Columbia "excels across academic programs," with solid offerings in finance, marketing, real estate, and management. Students are especially enthusiastic about the unique Social Enterprise program, which places social impact on equal footing with the bottom line; the program provides excellent training for those interested in government or the nonprofit sector. Students also single out the Media program, another unusual offering; the program benefits heavily from the concentration of media outlets in and around New York City.

Columbia's core curriculum occupies most of a student's first year, accounting for 45 percent of credits required for the degree. Some students state that the core is the school's weakest aspect; while appreciating the integrated design of the core, they feel its execution could be better. One student writes, "With the core, the faculty are either extremely talented or extremely poor. There's little consistency and no middle ground. Core professors are generally not as good at teaching the 'soft courses.'" Things improve as students move on to electives, where "at least 80 percent of the professors fall into the 'fully committed' and 'engaging' categories." Through both years of the program, "students are amazingly respectful of each other in the classroom setting and offer real-world experience that enriches every lesson plan." Students also appreciate that "the administration is responsive and attentive to the needs of the student body and tremendously supportive of career and community-service activities."

Career and Placement

The MBA Career Services Office (CSO) at Columbia benefits from a propitious location in the financial capital of the world. The office helps students coordinate internship and employment searches and also provides "a range of complementary resources . . . from intimate workshops on interviewing and presentation skills to a five-part course on different aspects of the job," according to the school's website. The CSO also draws from the region's many business leaders for lectures, seminars, and panel discussions. The school reports that "Hundreds of employers actively recruit at Columbia Business School each year, conducting thousands of on-campus interviews and numerous corporate presentations. Columbia also receives thousands of job postings for off-campus full-time and intern positions."

Nearly half the class of 2004 landed in the finance sector, and basically all graduates enjoyed handsome starting salaries. Top employers include: American Express Company; Bank of America; Booz Allen Hamilton; Citigroup; Deutsche Bank; Goldman Sachs; McKinsey & Company; JPMorgan Chase; Lehman Brothers; and Morgan Stanley.

LINDA MEEHAN, ASSISTANT DEAN, MBA ADMISSIONS
3022 BROADWAY, URIS HALL, ROOM 216, NEW YORK, NY 10027 UNITED STATES
PHONE: 212-854-1961 • FAX: 212-662-6754
E-MAIL: APPLY@GSB.COLUMBIA.EDU • WEBSITE: WWW.GSB.COLUMBIA.EDU

Student Life and Environment

Life at the Columbia Business School is busy, with "a diversity of clubs across all interest areas that, if anything, provide too many options." Then, of course, there's New York City, with its fabulous cultural outlets, world-class eateries, and endless selection of entertainment options. Observes one student, "Since a lot of students are coming from the city, they have lives outside of just the school social scene, which for me is good. We are in New York City so I think it is important to take advantage of that." Sums up another, "Columbia offers its students the greatest work-life balance. We work hard, party hard, volunteer our time in the community, explore New York City, and easily maintain groups of friends both within and outside the business school."

Columbia's campus is located in Morningside Heights, directly north of Manhattan's Upper West Side. The once run-down neighborhood has undergone quite a makeover in the last decade and is now a much more fashionable and expensive address. The enclosed campus runs eight city blocks, small by any standards other than New York's but absolutely expansive compared to, say, NYU. The business-school facilities "don't have enough space, but they're addressing that." Everyone agrees that Columbia's gym "is just terrible;" most prefer jogging in nearby Riverside Park to working out at the gym.

The student body here is "extremely diverse and interesting, international and helpful." The program's high degree of selectiveness ensures that all are accomplished, motivated, and talented. One MBA writes, "The students at Columbia are some of the most well-rounded, worldly, tolerant, intelligent, self motivated, and fun people I've ever met. Beyond all of Columbia's amazing attributes, the students may be the biggest draw to the business school."

Admissions

So you want to be a Columbia MBA? So do a lot of people, making Columbia one of the hardest graduate business schools to gain admission to. In selecting applicants for admission, the school reports that "by design, efforts are made to admit students who add different perspectives to the learning experience. In this way, students are continually learning from the diverse professional experiences and cultural/geographical backgrounds of their classmates. Columbia Business School has also maintained, through a concerted strategic effort, one of the highest enrollments of women and underrepresented minorities among top business schools. The Office of Admissions, in conjunction with the School's Black Business Students Association, Hispanic Business Association, and African American Alumni Association, sponsors information sessions and receptions for prospective students."

FINANCIAL FACTS

Annual tuition	$40,592
Fees	$1,808
Cost of books	$900
Room & board	$18,720

ADMISSIONS

Admissions Selectivity Rating	**99**
# of applications received	5,372
% applicants accepted	17
% acceptees attending	79
Average GMAT	706
Range of GMAT	660–760
Average GPA	3.4
TOEFL required of international students	Yes
Application fee	$215
Regular application deadline	4/20
Regular notification	Rolling
Early decision program?	Yes
ED Deadline/Notification September entry to 10/12 / 12/30	
Non-fall admissions	Yes
Need-blind admissions	Yes

Applicants Also Look At
Harvard University, Stanford University, University of Pennsylvania.

EMPLOYMENT PROFILE			
Career Rating	**96**		
Primary Source of Full-time Job Acceptances		**Grads Employed by Function**	**% Avg. Salary**
School-facilitated activities	282 (51%)	Finance/Accounting	50	NR
Graduate-facilitated activities	91 (17%)	Marketing/Sales	8	$87,272
Unknown	178 (32%)	Operations/Production	1	$82,500
Average base starting salary	$101,428	Strategic Planning	2	$92,550
Percent employed	89	Consulting	21	$108,404
		General Management	4	$91,183
		Venture Capital	5	$116,708
		Other	4	NR

Top 5 Employers Hiring Grads
McKinsey & Company; Lehman Brothers; Citigroup; Goldman Sachs; Booz Allen Hamilton.

CONCORDIA UNIVERSITY
JOHN MOLSON SCHOOL OF BUSINESS

GENERAL INFORMATION
Type of school	Public
Academic calendar	Trimester

SURVEY SAYS . . .
Students love Montreal, QC
Friendly students
Solid preparation in:
Communication/interpersonal skills

STUDENTS
Enrollment of parent institution	44,533
Enrollment of business school	450
% male/female	17/83
% out-of-state	54
% part-time	41
% international	37
Average age at entry	29
Average years work experience at entry	6

ACADEMICS
Academic Experience Rating	**89**
Student/faculty ratio	12:1
Profs interesting rating	80
Profs accessible rating	66
% female faculty	26

Prominent Alumni
Irving Teitelbaum, founder, chairman and CEO, La Senza; Keith Conklin, president and CEO, Nestle Canada; Lawrence Bloomberg, former COO, National Bank; Jean-Yves Monette, executive president and CEO Van Houtte Café.

FINANCIAL FACTS
Annual tuition (in-state/ out-of-state)	$1,668/$12,000
Fees (in-state/ out-of-state)	$945/$1,000
Cost of books	$3,992
Room & board (on/off-campus)	$4,842/$10,688
% of students receiving aid	28
% of first-year students receiving aid	32
Average award package	$9,000
Average grant	$8,111

Academics

Students looking for "a family-like atmosphere with an emphasis on practice and real-world cases" should consider the MBA program at Concordia University's John Molson School of Business (JMSB). At JMSB, students receive a solid general education in business principles as well as the opportunity to specialize in accounting, investment finance, global business, supply chain management, corporate governance, entrepreneurship, marketing, decision sciences/MIS, and management. Private MBA programs such as global aviation and investment management are also offered. There is also an option of an Accelerated MBA or MBA Co-operative Education. The John Molson School of Business operates on a fast-paced, trimester academic calendar. Classes, given in English, are offered in both days and evenings on Mondays through Thursdays "to accommodate both the part-time and full-time student body." Summer classes are offered mainly in the evenings.

With approximately 250 MBAs (split nearly evenly among full-timers and part-timers), JMSB provides each student with the resources they need to maximize their education. One MBA notes, "The greatest strength of the school is its cooperative spirit in the administration, faculty, placement center, and fellow students. Whenever you are looking for something or trying to accomplish something, people here have a can-do attitude." Students agree that at JMSB "you are not just a number, but a person. Everything is more personal here."

One of the high points of the school's academic year is the John Molson MBA Case Competition, held on campus and billed as "the only truly global case competition in the world." JMSB students are extremely passionate about this event and bemoan only the fact that not everyone can participate. "The school should offer the incredible training that the case competition team gets to everyone," writes one student. "That boot-camp intense training is like putting your MBA skills into overdrive." The Concordia Small Business Consulting Bureau offers students another opportunity to flex their business muscles while helping local businesses fine-tune their business plans and reach new consumers.

JMSB MBAs praise the curricular mix of "practical and hands-on education with academics, rather than solely case studies or theories," and give their professors high marks, reporting that they "are keen and sharp with a sense of humor and realism about today's challenges. The professors are tough, and we'll do even better when we graduate because of it." Students are less sanguine about the facilities, which "are old and not very comfortable," but point out that "new facilities are under construction and should be ready by 2006–2007."

Career and Placement

The Career Placement Centre at the John Molson School of Business serves both the undergraduates and graduates. "Graduate student-specific seminars" stand out as a Career Placement Center service in one MBA's opinion. The office provides the standard complement of career counseling, guest lectures, mock interviews, job postings, seminars in networking, resume writing, and salary negotiation. Students surveyed in the past generally agree that it was not enough, complaining about both the number and quality of positions available.

Employers who most frequently hire JMSB MBAs include Abbott Laboratories, Bombardier Aerospace, CIBC, Deloitte Consulting, Dynamic Mutual Funds, L'Oréal, National Bank of Canada, Pratt & Whitney, and RBC Financial Group.

D'ARCY RYAN, DIRECTOR, ADMINISTRATIVE AND ACADEMIC SERVICES
1455 DE MAISONNEUVE BOULEVARD WEST, GM 710 MONTREAL, QC H3G 1M8 CANADA
PHONE: 514-848-2727 • FAX: 514-848-2816
E-MAIL: E_LOBO@JMSB.CONCORDIA.CA • WEBSITE: WWW.JOHNMOLSON.CONCORDIA.CA

Student Life and Environment

JMSB MBAs have opportunities to get involved beyond the classroom, as "there is a minimum of one social activity a month (and up to three per month) for students to relax and have fun, such as a Halloween dance, pub night, an apple-picking trip, or wine-tasting. In addition, sports skills such as golf lessons or intro to scuba lessons and other sports are also offered." There are also "plenty of professional extracurricular activities to take part in, [such as] business leaders who are brought in from the community to share their experiences, past and present, [but] it seems like there is a core of 40 students who are active in everything (i.e., making the most out of their MBA) while the remainder only attend class."

The JMSB campus "is in downtown Montreal, an amazing city in which to live, and off-campus living is great." As a bonus, Montreal is a major player in international finance, pharmaceutical research, and aerospace development, providing lots of internship and placement opportunities for MBAs. The urban setting means that "the campus is not that attractive, but there are lots of possibilities to socialize outside of school. The student life is influenced by the Montreal lifestyle . . . It is not just work." Students complain that the campus "is lacking in open space where the students can sit down together, and the graduate lounge is often overcrowded," but they expect that the new business-school facility will remedy these problems.

"'Multicultural diversity' is the best way to describe what makes the difference in the Concordia MBA program," writes one student, alluding to the UN-style mix that constitutes the JMSB student body. About one-third of the students are Canadian and two-thirds are from around the world. American students typically make up about three percent of the student body. One MBA emphasizes, "The value of the program is greatly enhanced by the cumulative experiences of people coming from all parts of the world. Since people from Montreal are accustomed to this international environment, one feels really welcome here." Students tend to be "intellectually nimble, trustworthy, and respectful, with diverse professional experiences and a willingness to work cooperatively."

Admissions

Concordia admissions officers seek students with "real-world work experience, strong academic backgrounds, clear career objectives, and a commitment to excellence." Applicants must meet the following minimum requirements: undergraduate GPA of 3.0; two years of full-time work experience; a GMAT score of 600; and, for international students, a TOEFL score of 600 (paper-and-pencil) or 250 (computer-based). Career/leadership potential, level of maturity, communication skills, and how closely the student's goals match the program's are also weighed. Complete applications include a personal essay, a resume, official undergraduate transcripts, at least two letters of recommendation, and test scores.

ADMISSIONS

Admissions Selectivity Rating	**89**
# of applications received	458
% applicants accepted	43
% acceptees attending	55
Average GMAT	616
Range of GMAT	620–690
Average GPA	3
TOEFL required of international students	Yes
Minimum TOEFL (paper/computer)	600/250
Application fee	$64
Regular application deadline	Rolling
Regular notification	Rolling
Application Deadline/Notification	
Round 1:	June / NR
Round 2:	Oct / NR
Round 3:	Feb / NR
Early decision program?	Yes
ED Deadline	03/05
Deferment available	Yes
Maximum length of deferment	1 year
Transfer students accepted	Yes
Transfer application policy Applicants may be eligible for advanced standing	
Non-fall admissions	Yes
Need-blind admissions	Yes

Applicants Also Look At

HEC Montreal, McGill University, Queen's University, University of Toronto, York University.

EMPLOYMENT PROFILE			
Career Rating	**76**	**Grads Employed by Function%**	**Avg. Salary**
		Finance/Accounting 14	NR
		Marketing/Sales 24	NR
		Operations/Production 21	NR
		Consulting 34	NR
		General Management 3	NR
		Top 2 Employers Hiring Grads	
		Bombardier; Deloitte Consulting.	

CORNELL UNIVERSITY
JOHNSON GRADUATE SCHOOL OF MANAGEMENT

Academics

Students praise the "variety of MBA programs and areas of study" at Cornell University's Johnson School of Management, where an Accelerated MBA and Executive MBA program complement the traditional 2-year MBA. They also praise the availability of "specialized courses during the first year." The first year consists of eight required courses (Microeconomics for Management, Financial Accounting, Marketing Management, Statistics for Management, Managerial Finance, and Strategy, Managing Operations, and Managing and Leading in Organizations) and a choice of electives or participation in the Immersion Learning program. Eighty percent of students choose to participate in this "well-structured" practicum, which "provides great preparation" to "career switchers" and internship-seekers. Second year students choose an all-elective program. This system, says one student, "allowed me to become a real expert in the field I have selected." Among other strong specializations is the Asset Management track, bolstered by a student-run trading floor with a "$13-million-dollar hedge fund," and an investment studio in the Parker Center for Investment Research. Students also reserve high praise for the Center for Global Sustainable Enterprise, which gives students "amazing access to [top] companies" and schools them in "the strategic advantages a focus on sustainability can offer to innovative private enterprise." Johnson also offers 23 international business courses and study abroad opportunities in numerous countries.

Students say that Johnson's "world-class faculty" is "very accessible." ("I have gotten rides to school by my professors who see me waiting for the bus," says one student.) They also appreciate that the academics allow for more of a work-life balance than at some other schools ("There are no regular courses on Fridays . . . which makes it easier to take short vacations or just relax"). In addition, "The school encourages pursuits outside Johnson," "from cooking classes at the Hotel School to athletic classes (such as sailing on the lake)."

Career and Placement

Johnson alumni "pull us into the top firms," says one MBA candidate. Another affirms, "Cornellians can call any other Cornellian anywhere in the world and we help each other." Where "others care about the consequences of helping, we just do it." In addition, "Our career center is awesome. They really help students find relevant jobs." The top employers of Johnson graduates are American Express, Goldman Sachs, Citigroup, Credit Suisse, General Electric Company, Deloitte Touche Tohmatsu, Lehman Brothers, and UBS. The average starting salary is $94,370, with international students reporting slightly lower salaries than domestic students. Ninety percent of the last graduating class received offers before commencement.

Student Life and Environment

Students say Cornell deserves its reputation as "the 'nice' business school," where "Students get ties out of their locker to help classmates make a great impression at I-banking and consulting corporate briefings." In other words, Cornell students will "gladly help a struggling classmate out anytime." "We hunt as a pack," says one MBA candidate of his "bright and collaborative" peers. As if to underscore the "collegial" climate, Johnson students don't hesitate to praise one other. "My classmates are bright, motivated, genuine people who are all about results," says one student. "People here don't talk about themselves all the time like a lot of business types—they just get the job done." Another adds that Johnson students are "some of the smartest students amongst all schools, but the difference is that Johnson students won't tell you how smart they are." "Students, especially those in the Sustainable Enterprise program, are extremely intelligent nontraditional thinkers and intent on exploring ways new ways of doing business."

Hometown Ithaca is famous for its "beautiful scenery" and "outdoor activities such as cliff climbing, yachting, and hiking." It's also isolated and cold, qualities that foster intimacy among the small student body. "At the Johnson School, it is always 70 degrees and bright . . . in the atrium," jokes one student, a place where "We have frequent social hours." Students are extremely active in nearly 70 organized teams and clubs ("Spouses/partners are welcome and encouraged to join these organizations"), and spend their scanty free time winding down together. "On weekends, there is usually one big social event at night where the majority of the school will gather, and the rest of the weekend is typically spent with smaller groups of friends at a variety of locales." "Whether it's the indoor soccer club playing at 11:00 P.M. on a Sunday night, or the whole lot of us crowding the Palms (a local bar) on Thursday nights, you will always find a group of us out doing something enjoyable." One student warns, "If you enjoy going to dive bars and getting drunk with classmates this is the place for you. If you seek international conversation about global events over wine, look elsewhere."

Admissions

The Johnson application is online only and includes three 400-word essays (two mandatory, one optional). Mandatory topics cover professional achievement and career goals, and the optional essay may be used to detail extenuating circumstances or provide additional bolstering information. Johnson initially reviews applicants through a two-reader system; those who make the cut receive an interview, and only disputed files go to committee. As with other systems, this simply means that it pays to present an extremely strong case for admission. Last year's entering class reported an average GPA of 3.3, average GMAT score of 677, and 4.6 years of work experience.

FINANCIAL FACTS

Annual tuition	$38,800
Fees	$1,560
Cost of books	$1,100
Room & board	$9,500
% of students receiving aid	70
% of students receiving loans	62
% of students receiving grants	28
Average award package	$42,530
Average grant	$2,600
Average student loan debt	$68,500

ADMISSIONS

Admissions Selectivity Rating	**94**
# of applications received	1,797
% applicants accepted	36
% acceptees attending	46
Average GMAT	680
Range of GMAT	600–740
Average GPA	3.33
TOEFL required of international students	Yes
Minimum TOEFL (paper/computer)	600/250
Application fee	$180
Application Deadline/Notification	
Round 1:	10/9 / 11/17
Round 2:	11/9 / 12/18
Round 3:	1/9 / 3/20
Round 4:	3/9 / 4/27
Non-fall admissions	Yes
Need-blind admissions	Yes

Applicants Also Look At
Columbia University, Dartmouth College, Harvard University, Northwestern University, University of Michigan, University of Pennsylvania.

EMPLOYMENT PROFILE

Career Rating	95	Grads Employed by Function	%	Avg. Salary
Primary Source of Full-time Job Acceptances		Finance/Accounting	48	$93,510
School-facilitated activities	122 (49%)	Human Resources	1	NR
Graduate-facilitated activities	129 (51%)	Marketing/Sales	15	$87,530
Average base starting salary	$94,700	Operations/Production	1	NR
Percent employed	95	Consulting	21	$104,260
		General Management	9	$92,570
		Other	5	$91,620

Top 5 Employers Hiring Grads

American Express Company; Credit Suisse; McKinsey & Company; General Electric Company; Lehman Brothers Holdings.

DARTMOUTH COLLEGE
TUCK SCHOOL OF BUSINESS

GENERAL INFORMATION
Type of school	Private
Environment	Village
Academic calendar	Quarters

SURVEY SAYS . . .
Good social scene
Good peer network
Helpful alumni
Solid preparation in:
General management
Teamwork

STUDENTS
Enrollment of parent institution	5,700
Enrollment of business school	490
% male/female	68/32
% minorities	15
% international	31
Average age at entry	28
Average years work experience at entry	5

ACADEMICS
Academic Experience Rating	**98**
Student/faculty ratio	8:1
Profs interesting rating	88
Profs accessible rating	99
% female faculty	24
% minority faculty	15

Joint Degrees
MD/MBA (Dartmouth Medical School), MPH/MBA (public health management with Dartmouth's Center for the Evaluative Clinical Sciences), MEM/MBA offered with (Dartmouth's Thayer School of Engineering), MBA/MALD (Tufts Fletcher School of Law and Diplomacy), MBA/MPA (Kennedy School of Government at Harvard), MBA/MSEL (Vermont Law School's environmental law program), MBA/MA (Paul H. Nitze School of Advanced International Studies at Johns Hopkins University).

Academics

There is no rest for the weary at Tuck, where the "intensive academic core for first-years is accelerated and rigorous." During the elongated (32-week) school year, students take 16 courses, only one of which is elective. One of these is Tuck's trademark First-Year Project, a course in which student teams develop new business ventures or act as consultants in existing ventures, and in which grades rest on the final presentation and other outcomes. This method reflects Tuck's emphasis on "academic deliverables, such as group papers, projects, and presentations." The second year consists of 12 elective courses, which may reflect well-rounded interests or a specialization. For example, Tuck recommends that a student interested in nonprofit and sustainability management take Corporate Social Responsibility, Entrepreneurship in the Social Sector I and II, Ethics in Action, the Tuck Global Consultancy international field study, and Strategic Responses to Market Failure. One student reports, "I feel completely prepared to take on my career post-Tuck. The school does a fantastic job of working students hard in the first year, teaching them the core fundamentals of business, and letting them craft their own paths during the second year." One student notes, "Tuck could update its core curriculum and case study assignments to reflect the current business environment, i.e., more standard courses to better understand the private-market investment climate, corporate ethics, digital media/entertainment, and emerging economies."

Tuck operates through "full immersion." Students "do a lot of work in study groups, which are assigned and required for first-years." Mandatory team rotation forces each student to work closely with a wide swath of his or her peers during the first year. The small class size and isolated location reinforces class cohesiveness and fosters intimacy between MBA students and Tuck faculty and staff. Professors host social "gatherings at their homes and get involved with student organizations." "I have had lunches, dinners, or drinks with the majority of my professors," reports one second-year, "and I am treated with a respect that goes beyond [typical] teacher-student interactions." Administrators are "the nicest people on Earth." Some have even been known to "come in on a Sunday evening and bring food and coffee for us when we have exams." The overall "quality" of faculty and administration alike is "extraordinary."

Career and Placement

Tuck is "very focused on helping students land the jobs they came here to get." "The Career Development Office works tirelessly on behalf of students," though this benefit is most useful for students pursuing "traditional career paths (i.e., consulting, finance, general management)." However, "students interested in other opportunities (i.e., marketing, retail) may need to do more work outside the Career Development Office." Dartmouth is a magnet for recruiters, and "one of the best parts of Tuck is that visiting executives spend meaningful time with us. They don't stop by on their way to another meeting; rather, they have lunch and/or dinner with us, hold individual office hours, and make an effort to share their experiences with members of the class." Recruitment is Northeast focused, but the career office "is continually trying to reach out to West Coast firms"—the ones who often "recruit locally at Stanford and UCLA"—"and does a couple of treks for students interested in returning to the West." The tides may be turning; one student reports seeing "Google, Microsoft, and PG&E on campus this year," a possible "indication that a more diverse lineup of firms [is] coming to Tuck."

Students seeking jobs in "nontraditional" vocations and regions will have better luck with Tuck's extremely strong, supportive alumni network. One student told this story of success: "I e-mailed a Tuck alum who is a managing director at a bulge-bracket investment bank in London, and he called me 5 minutes later to talk. He arranged a personal office visit…and

DAWNA CLARKE, DIRECTOR OF ADMISSIONS
100 TUCK HALL HANOVER, NH 03755 UNITED STATES
PHONE: 603-646-3162 • FAX: 603-646-1441
E-MAIL: TUCK.ADMISSIONS@DARTMOUTH.EDU • WEBSITE: WWW.TUCK.DARTMOUTH.EDU

actually talked HR into sending me straight to second round interviews, because the firm's London office didn't recruit on campus…all because I put 'Tuck' in the subject line."

Tuck's most recent graduating class reports a median total annual compensation of $150,000. Top employers include Booz Allen Hamilton, IBM, Citigroup, The Walt Disney Company, Morgan Stanley, and Starbucks.

Student Life and Environment

Students call posh, pretty Hanover "the quintessential small, New England, Ivy League town," "within a short drive of many great ski resorts" and far removed "from the hustle and bustle of a big city." Unlike many schools, most first-years live on campus. Couples and families live in the Dartmouth-owned Sachem Village housing complex or elsewhere off-campus. The environment is extremely "intimate" and "supportive." Tuckies consider their school very family-friendly, telling us that partners are an integral part of the social scene, and note that "classmates who have children while at Tuck" are surrounded by a "phenomenal support network." Tuck is very inclusive of gay and lesbian students and partners.

The isolated location and clustered housing contribute to "a great deal of school spirit" and "strong camaraderie" in a "work-hard, play-hard environment." "Tuck students really transplant their lives to be here…we make friends quickly here and socialize a lot with our classmates." Students belong to more than 60 clubs, teams, and publications, and attend numerous social functions every week. "The end of the week is typically characterized by social mixers (Tuck Tails), small group dinners…and the occasional full-blown party (winter and spring formals, Tuck Vegas, beach party)." Students report that "sports are very much a part of life at Tuck."

No one gripes about the intimacy, which results in great friendships and means close business ties in the future. "I have had a substantive conversation with each of my 240 classmates and will feel very comfortable calling any of them after graduation for career advice and/or business counsel," reports one Tuckie. Feelings seem to differ when it comes to partying, however. Many students are happy that "ice hockey and beer pong are just as much a part of the Tuck experience as Decision Science and Global Economics," while others aren't wild about "re-living [their] college frat-house experience." The class of 2008 is 34 percent international and an additional 15 percent of color, but students would like to see "more Africans and African Americans" in their class.

Admissions

Like many other schools, Tuck wants to know that you love it for what it is, not only for what it can do for you; show that you have researched the school thoroughly. The class of 2008 reports an average GPA of 3.4 and GMAT score of 710.

Prominent Alumni

Steven Roth, chairman and CEO, Vornado Realty Trust; Elyse Allan, president and CEO, General Electric Canada; Roger McNamee, co-founder and managing director, Elevation Partners; Darryl Green, CEO, Tata Teleservices Limited.

FINANCIAL FACTS

Annual tuition	$40,650
Fees	$240
Cost of books	$3,025
Room & board	
(on/off-campus)	$9,295/$11,030
% of students receiving aid	81
% of first-year students receiving aid	82
% of students receiving loans	88
% of students receiving grants	53
Average award package	$48,682
Average grant	$14,324
Average student loan debt	$77,233

ADMISSIONS

Admissions Selectivity Rating	98
# of applications received	2,276
% applicants accepted	20
% acceptees attending	54
Average GMAT	710
Range of GMAT	660–760
Average GPA	3.4
TOEFL required of international students	Yes
Application fee	$220
International application fee	$220
Application Deadline/Notification	
Round 1:	10/12 / 12/15
Round 2:	11/30 / 2/2
Round 3:	1/11 / 3/23
Round 4:	4/5 / 5/14
Early decision program?	Yes
ED Deadline	10/12
ED Notification	12/15
Deferment available	Yes
Maximum length of deferment	Case-by-case basis.
Need-blind admissions	Yes

Applicants Also Look At

Harvard University, Northwestern University, Stanford University, University of Pennsylvania.

EMPLOYMENT PROFILE

Career Rating	98	Grads Employed by Function	%	Avg. Salary
Primary Source of Full-time Job Acceptances		Finance/Accounting	37	$95,000
Average base starting salary	$100,000	Marketing/Sales	9	$89,000
Percent employed	97	Consulting	40	$108,000
		General Management	6	$99,000
		Other	8	$99,000

Top 5 Employers Hiring Grads
McKinsey & Company; Bain and Company; Lehman Brothers; Morgan Stanley, UBS.

DREXEL UNIVERSITY
BENNETT S. LEBOW COLLEGE OF BUSINESS

GENERAL INFORMATION
Type of school	Private
Academic calendar	July–June

SURVEY SAYS . . .
Students love Philadelphia, PA
Smart classrooms
Solid preparation in:
Accounting

STUDENTS
Enrollment of parent institution	18,466
Enrollment of business school	769
% male/female	79/21
% out-of-state	60
% part-time	68
% minorities	17
% international	50
Average age at entry	30
Average years work experience at entry	8

ACADEMICS
Academic Experience Rating	**80**
Student/faculty ratio	26:1
Profs interesting rating	72
Profs accessible rating	85
% female faculty	26
% minority faculty	29

Joint Degrees
MBA/MS (accounting), MBA/MS (finance), MD/MBA, MBA/MS (television management), JD/MBA.

Prominent Alumni
Raj Gupta, chairman and CEO, Rohm and Haas; Nicholas DeBenedictis, chairman, AquaAmerica; Francis Dunleavy, senior managing director, Bear Energy; Elaine M. Garzarelli, former executie vice president, Lehman Brothers, president Garzarelli Capital Inc.; Dominic J. Frederico, chairman, president and CEO, Assured Guaranty.

Academics

Drexel University is "a top-ranking engineering school," so it should come as no surprise that its LeBow College of Business "has a great reputation for running a hands-on applied program" with "a solid focus on technology." The school's "applied learning philosophy" drives a co-op program "that's one of the best in the country, allowing students to graduate with relevant work experience in their field of study."

LeBow works hard to meet students' needs, offering "a tremendous diversity in the number of programs. There is a program available to meet your individual needs based on your personal and professional lives." These include a 1-year and a 2-year full-time MBA (the former is "the only 1-year program in Philadelphia and includes an international trip in the spring term to provide hands-on international learning"); a 2-year evening cohort MBA (called the LEAD MBA, for LeBow Evening Accelerated Drexel MBA, this program "is very convenient for working professionals, with all classes held on the same 2 nights of the week throughout the program and all classes scheduled by the school"); a more traditional part-time professional MBA; and an online part-time MBA called MBA Anywhere, "which is flexible enough to fit your work schedule, yet has three campus residencies as well, allowing interaction with fellow students." In addition, LeBow also offers an executive MBA and several corporate on-site programs.

Many of the programs offer a broad range of choices in area of concentration (the 1-year program does not offer concentration, only a general MBA). Techie disciplines such as MIS do well here; students also extol offerings in entrepreneurship (the Baiada Center for Entrepreneurship is known as one of the school's many assets), health care systems, and financial management. LeBow also offers a concentration in operations management with a focus on supply chain management. In all disciplines, Drexel professors "are active in research and publishing and are always willing to answer questions about classwork" and are "demanding but fair" in the classroom. "Many are Wharton professors who have simply transferred across the street," students tell us.

Career and Placement

The LeBow Career Services Office is "great with one-on-one sessions and tries hard to be extremely helpful." One MBA writes, "I have found the office very helpful in providing pointers to enhance my resume as well as in providing contact information for companies of interest." Even so, many students feel that "the office could do a better job of bringing recruiters on campus to recruit those of us with 5-plus years of work experience. It seems that the majority of the recruiters that come on campus are primarily recruiting those individuals that have little to no work experience."

Employers most likely to hire LeBow MBAs include: Deloitte Touche Tohmatsu, Guardian, Lockheed Martin, PricewaterhouseCoopers, Citizens Bank, Siemens, Merck, SAP, Rohm & Haas, and Vanguard.

Student Life and Environment

Drexel's location "is excellent, because Philadelphia is a big city with lots of opportunities. Proximity to other big cities like New York City, Baltimore, and Washington, DC is another advantage." University City, the neighborhood in which Drexel is located, provides "lots of great shops and restaurants. Philadelphia has numerous museums, a wide variety of restaurants, theaters, etc. Students have the opportunity to explore the city because downtown is so close."

ANNA SEREFEAS, GRADUATE ADMISSIONS AND RECRUITMENT
3141 CHESTNUT STREET, 207 MATHESON HALL, PHILADELPHIA, PA 19104-2875 UNITED STATES
PHONE: 215-895-6804 • FAX: 215-895-1725
E-MAIL: MBA@DREXEL.EDU • WEBSITE: WWW.LEBOW.DREXEL.EDU

Full-time students enjoy a full slate of extracurricular activities, telling us that The MBA Association is "the greatest asset of the school." "The association has networking events, organizes social outings in Philadelphia, finds professional networking opportunities for fellow students, establishes [and] administers clubs, holds weekly happy hours, liaises between the students and the administration, organizes field trips, and has many other events. Registration into the association is not mandatory, but by the end of the first quarter most students are signed on, because of how the association makes life at Drexel more enjoyable." One student reports that "there seems to be a buzz on campus about the increased student activity in clubs." Part-time students don't participate as heavily outside the classroom since "A lot of activities organized by student groups often conflict with evening class schedules." Those in the LEAD MBA program tell us they "meet twice a week for classes and try to connect via e-mail daily to give each other tips and words of wisdom. Drexel always has a spread of food and drinks for us when we arrive, which is great! After a long day at work and a 3-plus-hour class on finance, it's nice to have a sweet snack to keep you going." LeBow's facilities include "a new business building with a number of computers, a Starbucks, and classrooms that are laid out well for discussions and presentations."

Admissions

Admissions requirements vary by program at LeBow. According to the school's website, LeBow "is interested in well-rounded applicants who have a consistent record of significant achievement and outstanding potential for future success in a variety of areas." Applicants must provide the Admissions Committee with official copies of all college and university transcripts; GMAT scores; letters of recommendation; a personal statement; and a resume. An interview is optional and typically occurs only if the school requests one. Students whose first language is not English and who do not hold an academic degree from a U.S. institution must also submit an official score report for the TOEFL.

FINANCIAL FACTS

Annual tuition	$49,800
Cost of books	$1,200
% of students receiving grants	64
Average grant	$15,500

ADMISSIONS

Admissions Selectivity Rating	**92**
# of applications received	989
% applicants accepted	30
% acceptees attending	58
Average GMAT	610
Range of GMAT	540–660
Average GPA	3.24
TOEFL required of international students	Yes
Minimum TOEFL (paper/computer)	600/250
Application fee	$50
Regular application deadline	8/24
Regular notification	Rolling
Early decision program?	Yes
ED Deadline/Notification	10/1 / 12/1
Summer:	1/1
Deferment available	Yes
Maximum length of deferment	1 year
Transfer students accepted	Yes
Transfer application policy Completed application and all supporting materials to be reviewed by Admissions Committee.	
Non-fall admissions	Yes
Need-blind admissions	Yes

Applicants Also Look At
Temple University, University of Pennsylvania, Villanova University.

EMPLOYMENT PROFILE

Career Rating	72	Grads Employed by Function	%	Avg. Salary
Primary Source of Full-time Job Acceptances		Finance/Accounting	32	$66,800
Percent employed	59	Marketing/Sales	20	$59,530
		MIS	10	$64,400
		Operations/Production	6	$55,667
		Consulting	16	$67,471
		General Management	12	$57,667
		Other	4	$57,750

Top 5 Employers Hiring Grads
Deloitte and Touche; Bristol-Myers Squibb; Lockheed Martin; PriceWaterhouseCoopers; Comcast.

DUKE UNIVERSITY
THE FUQUA SCHOOL OF BUSINESS

GENERAL INFORMATION
Type of school	Private
Environment	City
Academic calendar	Terms

SURVEY SAYS . . .
Good social scene
Good peer network
Solid preparation in:
Marketing
Teamwork
Computer skills

STUDENTS
Enrollment of parent institution	15,806
Enrollment of business school	834
% male/female	74/26
% out-of-state	94
% minorities	8
% international	38
Average age at entry	29
Average years work experience at entry	6

ACADEMICS
Academic Experience Rating	**97**
Student/faculty ratio	8:1
Profs interesting rating	98
Profs accessible rating	88
% female faculty	20
% minority faculty	3

Joint Degrees
MBA/JD 4 years, MBA/master of public policy 3 years, MBA/master of forestry 3 years, MBA/master of environmental management 3 years, MBA/MS (engineering) 3 years, MBA/MD 5 years, MBA/MSN (nursing) 3 years.

Prominent Alumni
Melinda Gates, co-founder, Gates Foundation; Malvinder Singh, CEO and managing director, Ranbaxy; Kerri Anderson, CEO and president, Wendy's International Inc.; Jack Bovender, CEO and chairman, HCA; John Allison, chairman, BB&T.

Academics

Student involvement—not just in academics, but in all facets of extracurricular life—is a hallmark of the MBA program at Duke's Fuqua School of Business. Students here use the term "Team Fuqua" to sum up the collaborative spirit that binds MBAs, professors, and administration. "A strong focus on leadership" is fostered by the school's Center on Leadership and Ethics and "Coach K [Duke basketball coach Mike Krzyzewski, to the uninitiated] takes an active role in this organization and provides an excellent link to real-world leadership."

Fuqua terms are "rapid-paced," lasting only six weeks (classes meet in two two-hour sessions weekly). The curriculum "emphasizes leadership and communication skills," with outstanding offerings in marketing, finance, and health management. Students describe the program as "well-balanced, with strengths in many areas," and boast that it "allows [them] to explore many different options." One MBA student says that the professors are "leaders in their fields. They are engaged in the class, and they are highly passionate about their subjects. It's hard to imagine a professor making basic accounting enjoyable, but my professor has me loving the class because of his energy and passion."

Students and administrators are also on the same team at Duke. "Fuqua is exceptionally responsive to student feedback, and any issue is resolved quickly." For example, "Duke University has made a specific point in the last two years to get its top professors back into teaching core courses after some weakness two years ago in student reviews of core classes. They have been successful, and it has made the core course offerings very strong." Duke MBAs are deeply involved in nearly all aspects of managing the program, which they describe as "almost completely student-run. Almost any event you attend—whether career, speaker, social, or otherwise—is devised, organized, and marketed by students."

Duke also offers three Executive MBA options: an MBA Weekend Program that meets alternate weekends in Durham; an MBA Global Program that combines distance learning and international in-classroom residencies; and the MBA Cross Continent Program that combines week-long international residencies and distance learning. The Global Program requires a minimum of 10 years of professional experience; the Cross Continent Program is designed for less experienced managers.

Career and Placement

Students agree that Fuqua's Career Management Center "has recently taken a huge step forward." The hiring of a new director and additional staff has resulted in improved services and enhanced communication between the CMC and students. "Career counselors are extremely dedicated and have even been known to come in on the weekends to help students/clubs," students tell us. The CMC also boasts "a new online tool that makes the job application and research process a lot simpler and more user-friendly." As a bonus, alumni are "phenomenally loyal. Alums bend over backward to help students find jobs and offer career wisdom."

Employers most likely to hire Fuqua MBAs include Johnson & Johnson, IBM, American Express Company, McKinsey & Company, Kraft Foods, Citigroup, Deloitte Consulting, Bank of America, Bear Sterns, DuPont, and Eli Lilly & Company.

LIZ HARGROVE RILEY, ASSISTANT DEAN AND DIRECTOR OF ADMISSIONS
ONE TOWERVIEW DRIVE DURHAM, NC 27708-0104 UNITED STATES
PHONE: 919-660-7705 • FAX: 919-681-8026
E-MAIL: ADMISSIONS-INFO@FUQUA.DUKE.EDU • WEBSITE: WWW.FUQUA.DUKE.EDU

Student Life and Environment

Duke offers "excellent health care and leadership resources." The Team Fuqua spirit pervades all aspects of life at Duke, including extracurricular activities. On Fuqua Fridays, the school "provides free food, beer, and wine to all Fuqua students, faculty, and their families." One happy student writes, "It's great to see everyone outside of the classroom, and to meet people's wives, husbands, and kids." MBAs also enjoy "regular cultural events," such as "two International Food Festivals each year, International Week, Asian Festival, Latin American/South American events, and events with European business leaders." Students "arrange an annual MBA Games event at which many top-tier business schools compete." The school uses the "monies raised to help the North Carolina Special Olympics athletes to compete." Despite their busy schedules, students also find time to collaborate on FuquaVision, an *SNL*-like parody of life at Fuqua produced "at least once per term. The films are a riot and really show the initiative of students here."

Basketball fanatics could hardly find a happier home, nor could golf enthusiasts; the Duke course is the best of many excellent local facilities available to Duke students. Students point out that "the weather here is great, and the area is outstanding for families." Hometown Durham, although small, "has tons of great restaurants and more to do than most people think." It also offers easy access to Raleigh and Chapel Hill; together the three cities form North Carolina's Triangle region, which offers a decent (if sprawling) approximation of urban amenities. One student sums up, "With 800 like-minded classmates around, a great climate, awesome natural resources, and (Chapel Hill's) Franklin Street only a short drive away, there is plenty to do. The culture and people are great, and school will suck up any ounce of time you give it."

Admissions

Applicants to the Fuqua MBA program must provide the Admissions Department with a one-page business resume, three essays (describe your work experience; describe your career goals; explain what you will contribute to the Fuqua Program), official GMAT scores, official transcripts for all postsecondary academic work, and two recommendations. An interview, though not required, is "strongly encouraged." International students must also provide official TOEFL scores if English is not their first language. To promote recruitment of underrepresented students, Duke conducts MBA Workshops for Minority Applicants, participates in "aggressive minority scholarship programs with partners, including the Toigo Foundation," and hosts the Leadership Education and Development (LEAD) Summer Business Institute. The Weekend Executive MBA prefers at least five years of professional experience; the Global Executive MBA requires a minimum of 10 years' professional experience; the Cross Continent Executive MBA requires three to nine years' experience.

FINANCIAL FACTS

Annual tuition	$39,500
Fees	$1,900
Cost of books	$1,081
Room & board (off-campus)	$13,450
% of students receiving aid	76
% of first-year students receiving aid	75
% of students receiving loans	67
% of students receiving grants	37
Average award package	$44,039
Average grant	$13,798
Average student loan debt	$75,577

ADMISSIONS

Admissions Selectivity Rating	95
# of applications received	2,497
% applicants accepted	37
% acceptees attending	44
Average GMAT	700
Range of GMAT	670–730
Average GPA	3.4
TOEFL required of international students	Yes
Application fee	$185
Application Deadline/Notification	
Round 1:	11/1 / 12/19
Round 2:	1/8 / 3/8
Round 3:	3/21 / 5/1
Deferment available	Yes
Maximum length of deferment	Conditional
Need-blind admissions	Yes

EMPLOYMENT PROFILE

Career Rating	95	Grads Employed by Function	%	Avg. Salary
Primary Source of Full-time Job Acceptances		Finance/Accounting	31	$92,130
School-facilitated activities	210 (69%)	Marketing/Sales	24	$87,360
Graduate-facilitated activities	95 (31%)	Operations/Production	1	$95,000
Average base starting salary	$93,697	Consulting	22	$105,909
Percent employed	89	General Management	21	$90,385
		Other	1	$93,619

Top 5 Employers Hiring Grads

Johnson & Johnson; Citigroup; Bank of America; McKinsey & Company, Deloitte Consulting.

DUQUESNE UNIVERSITY
JOHN F. DONAHUE GRADUATE SCHOOL OF BUSINESS

Academics

"Duquesne is very up-to-date with current business practices, research, and ethics," students at the John F. Donahue Graduate School of Business tell us. Among the distinctive curricular features at this prestigious Pittsburgh university is the "great emphasis on understanding the value chain of a company and how all functions interact within the entire enterprise value chain." Donahue even requires a course in the subject: understanding the value chain is designed to give MBAs unique insight into "how business disciplines work together as a process to create value for customers, employees, and shareholders," according to the school catalog.

The concept that business is a process requiring interdisciplinary analysis is stressed repeatedly throughout the MBA program, which consists of nine core courses and five electives. Students lacking sufficient undergraduate course work in business are typically required to take some or all of an additional nine-course complement of pre-MBA knowledge and skills-related classes. The Donahue School offers a whopping 13 areas of concentration: accounting, business ethics, electronic business, entrepreneurship, environmental management, finance, health care management, human resource management, information systems management, international business, marketing, supply chain management, and taxation. Students may also opt for a general MBA without specialization. Students in our survey singled out offerings in accounting, business ethics, and finance for praise.

Duquesne faculty members "are easily approachable and always available for students outside of class," not only at the downtown campus but also at satellite locations. One student explains, "I am attending school part-time at a satellite campus, yet still we have full, tenured, and even department-heading professors who drive out of their way to instruct us." Professors are also "very professional and knowledgeable about their fields." One student writes, "Most professors are able to provide real-life examples, experiences, and issues. It is not just 'academic perspectives' that only exist in the classroom. Most topics we cover are solutions that could be implemented in a practical setting."

Career and Placement

Duquesne's Career Services Office provides placement and counseling services to all of the university's undergraduate and graduate students. Yet students are "disappointed with the career services program," which they complain "does not do a good job of recruiting potential employers outside of the Pittsburgh region." Some feel the school's top priority should be "to better integrate the students in social/networking situations, and to involve its alumni to assist students as career mentors." Others think the focus should be on marketing. One student comments, "This is a great school, and I think we should take the time to submit the paperwork that needs to get done to rank us as one of the top business schools in the country by those 'Top B-Schools' lists. With greater visibility, more companies would recruit at Duquesne, which would improve our postgraduate job-placement rates, which don't seem to be very strong."

Employers most likely to hire Donohue MBAs include the Mellon Financial Corporation, Management Science Associates, PNC Corporation, U.S. Steel Corporation, Mine Safety Appliance Corporation, Alcoa, Deloitte Touche Tohmatsu, FedEx Ground, and the H. J. Heinz Corporation.

PATRICIA MOORE, MANAGING DIRECTOR
600 FORBES AVENUE, PITTSBURGH, PA 15282 UNITED STATES
PHONE: 412-396-6276 • FAX: 412-396-1726
E-MAIL: GRAD-BUS@DUQ.EDU • WEBSITE: WWW.BUSINESS.DUQ.EDU/GRAD

Student Life and Environment

"The MBA program at Duquesne is really a part-time program," students here explain, with "most of the classes held at night. As a result, you are removed from the rest of the campus." MBAs point out, "Student social clubs do exist, but participation is low due to most students' part-time status. Full-time students do integrate during the day." These full-timers, who make up about 20 percent of the student body, participate in the "many clubs and activities available," which include "MBA happy hours, pizza sessions with speakers, and a Halloween party with a bus trip." The faculty "is very willing to help students establish and advise student organizations."

Students here also enjoy the campus's "modern and well-constructed gym facilities, [the] nice coffee shops and food on campus, [and] the overall safe environment." Because the school is located downtown, students are "not far from professional sports activities. You can walk to Penguins hockey games in five minutes and to Pirates and Steelers games in just a little more." Pittsburgh, most here agree, "is a great city for universities. There is a wealth of knowledge in the area." One student challenges, "For those people who have never been to Pittsburgh, I think they would be surprised as to how great a city it is. It has grown beyond its dark, Steel City image." Students from warmer climes should take note that winters in Pittsburgh are long, cold, and snowy.

"The age range of students is very mixed" at Duquesne. Students observe that "some have just earned their undergraduate degrees, some took a few years off to work, and others are married with kids and coming back to school after many years in the workforce." Quite a few are "middle to upper managers with backgrounds in engineering and manufacturing." Because of "a great international program, [there are] many international students, mostly from Latin America, Eastern Europe, China, and Africa. The diversity adds a lot to classes, as does hearing about the experiences of international classmates."

Admissions

All applicants to the Donahue MBA program must submit official transcripts for all post-secondary academic work, an official GMAT score report, two letters of recommendation, and an autobiographical statement. International students must also submit official TOEFL scores. Work experience is not a prerequisite to entering the program.

FINANCIAL FACTS

Annual tuition	$19,305
Fees	$1,917
Cost of books	$2,500
Room & board (on-campus)	$7,170
% of students receiving aid	70
% of first-year students receiving aid	70
% of students receiving grants	27
Average grant	$19,305

ADMISSIONS

Admissions Selectivity Rating	**65**
Average GMAT	510
Average GPA	3.1
TOEFL required of international students	Yes
Minimum TOEFL (paper/computer)	550/213
Application fee	$50
Regular application deadline	6/1
Regular notification	7/1
Deferment available	Yes
Maximum length of deferment	1 year
Transfer students accepted	Yes
Transfer application policy Will accept up to 15 transfer credits from an-accredited college or university.	
Non-fall admissions	Yes
Need-blind admissions	Yes

Applicants Also Look At

University of Pittsburgh.

EMPLOYMENT PROFILE	
Career Rating	72

EAST CAROLINA UNIVERSITY
COLLEGE OF BUSINESS

Academics

"The greatest strengths of East Carolina University are the many excellent programs that are available, and the fact that most of them are nationally accredited programs," explain students at this state university about 90 miles east of Raleigh. Students also appreciate the availability of online classes that are "better than [they] would have imagined. The professors are computer savvy so you notice little difference between online and a classroom setting."

The ECU MBA is designed to meet the needs of both business and non-business undergraduates. It can also accommodate those without professional experience as well as those who have worked in business, though the school "strongly encourages" those without professional experience "to obtain career-related experience while earning their MBA." Depending on the student's background, the MBA program requires between 10 and 20 courses. For a quick return on investment, the curriculum can be completed in as little as one year by a full-time student with a strong undergraduate background in business.

ECU's MBA program starts with 10 core courses covering material traditionally covered in undergraduate business programs. Some or all of these classes may be waived. Waiver decisions are made on a student-by-student and course-by-course basis. In order for a waiver to be granted, the university requires a minimum grade of B in equivalent undergraduate courses. The core makes up the first half of the program; the second half consists of 10 business breadth courses, seven required and three electives. Elective choices rotate on an annual basis. Those seeking a concentration must take four courses in their chosen area of specialization. The concentrations are pursued in lieu of the three electives. ECU offers concentrations in development and environmental planning, finance, health care management, international management, MIS, school business management, hospitality management, sport management, supply chain management, and security studies. Approximately 20 percent of ECU MBAs choose a specialization.

Students here applaud "the helpfulness of the instructors," whom they regard as "demanding and, at the same time, willing to do anything." One student notes, "Our instructors may not currently be industry leaders, but they have amazing and successful (i.e., enviable) past careers and seem to be here as volunteers to help the future." Another says, "I took away something important from each of them." ECU administrators "do a great job of improving the quality of resources and courses to stay current with business trends."

Career and Placement

Career services are provided to ECU MBAs by the in-house Career Office. The office provides recruiting resources, sponsors on-campus job fairs, organizes seminars and classroom presentations on job-search skills, and offers one-on-one counseling and other advising resources, in addition to internship programs.

LEN RHODES, ASSISTANT DEAN FOR GRADUATE PROGRAMS
3203 BATE BUILDING, GREENVILLE, NC 27858-4353 UNITED STATES
PHONE: 252-328-6970 • FAX: 252-328-2106
E-MAIL: GRADBUS@ECU.EDU • WEBSITE: WWW.BUSINESS.ECU.EDU

Student Life and Environment

Many MBAs at ECU describe a collegiate atmosphere both on campus and within their program, lauding the "school spirit," "[and] excellent sports teams, especially the football team, which receives a lot of support from students." Students also keep busy with more diverse pursuits. One student explains, "We're active in business projects to help local businesses, which is a great way to find local opportunities and learn along the way. Many MBA students are involved with something else at the school, like film, international house, physics, hospital, and volunteering." Students also recommend the campus's Ledonia Wright Culture Center, which "holds interesting events that are fun to go to."

Hometown Greenville is conveniently located less than two hours from both Raleigh and the North Carolina shore. However, there's not a lot of big business in the immediate area.

Students in the MBA program describe themselves as "very open and friendly, and always willing to help you try to understand something or explain a problem you might have in a particular subject." There are "many international students from Asian countries and Africa," with most of the domestic students originating from the eastern part of the state. One-third of the students here are freshly minted college grads, meaning that they don't bring a whole lot in the way of real-world experience to their graduate business classes.

Admissions

To be considered for admission to the MBA program at ECU, applicants must score at least 950 under the formula [(undergraduate GPA × 200) + GMAT score], with a minimum GMAT score of 400. Students who received their undergraduate degrees less than a year before their projected starting date for the MBA program must achieve a score of 950 with a minimum GMAT score of 450. However, if their undergraduate GPA was at least 3.5, they must score at least 400 on the GMAT. Applicants must submit official copies of all postsecondary academic transcripts and official GMAT score reports. International students must exceed the formula-score requirements indicated above by 50 points, as well as score 50 points higher on the GMAT, and must also provide official TOEFL score reports.

FINANCIAL FACTS

Annual tuition (in-state/ out-of-state)	$5,564/$15,880
Cost of books	$500

ADMISSIONS

Admissions Selectivity Rating	**68**
# of applications received	222
% applicants accepted	82
% acceptees attending	85
Average GPA	3.12
TOEFL required of international students	Yes
Minimum TOEFL (paper/computer)	550/213
Application fee	$50
Regular application deadline	Rolling
Regular notification	Rolling
Deferment available	Yes
Maximum length of deferment	1 year
Transfer students accepted	Yes
Transfer application policy Maximum of 9 semester credit hours from AACSB-accredited institution accepted.	
Non-fall admissions	Yes
Need-blind admissions	Yes

EAST TENNESSEE STATE UNIVERSITY
COLLEGE OF BUSINESS AND TECHNOLOGY

Academics

There aren't many choices at the College of Business and Technology at East Tennessee State University—the small program maintains only three business and four technology departments (accounting, economics/finance—urban studies, management/marketing)—but for those who are interested in a general-purpose business degree, ETSU delivers. In addition to the traditional MBA, the school also offers an MAcc (master's of accounting), an MPA (master's of public administration), and a graduate certificate in business administration for "those who seek a basic understanding of business administration but who may not be able to make the commitment of time, effort, and money required to seek a master's degree."

MBAs at ETSU feel that "the administration and faculty here are very student-oriented. Most have set times when they are available outside of class; others excel and really go the extra mile both in class presentation and in their availability to those students that require extra instruction." Professors are regarded as "very knowledgeable in their fields, and many of them are widely recognized as great scholars." One student writes, "Most of them have a work background that can lead to some very good discussions in class, and [the professors present] the applications of the concepts in the real world through their stories." Faculty members are also "easy to work with and understanding about personal matters that can arise."

Students say "We are like a family at ETSU. You go through the same classes with pretty much the same group of students. We are all interested in each other's success. There is low competition." Most students agree that the school does "a very good job of getting the student prepared with the knowledge that is needed in the workplace, but there is just so much that can be taught in the classroom setting." Many students have full-time jobs, and say "true learning from the classroom is applied to the jobs that are obtained after school." But balancing work and school responsibilities can leave some students feeling overextended. One student warns: "Most likely you have one or two people who do not participate in group [projects], leaving the workload for the other two or three people. Those individuals who do not participate always get the same grade." Across the board, students love that "the school is large enough to offer remote-learning facilities, and classes are generally available at convenient times for working adults." Most of all, however, students appreciate that professors "show a major interest in students' ability to understand the work."

Career and Placement

The Career Placement and Internship Services Office at East Tennessee University serves the school's entire undergraduate and graduate student body. The office hosts recruitment visits from various companies, sponsors and participates in career fairs, maintains online job boards and resume books, and offers counseling in interview skills, job search, career match, and resume writing. In the spring of 2004, on-campus recruiters included New York Life, Norfolk Southern, Wachovia, and Wells Fargo. Students are aware that "Johnson City is a small town, which limits the amount of recruiting that is done on campus." Even so, many "believe that [the] school could improve by really showing students what is available out there and helping them find jobs when they get done. It is there right now [at the Career Placement and Internship Services Office], but a student really has to push to find it."

Student Life and Environment

East Tennessee State University is located in Johnson City, a small Appalachian city close to both the North Carolina and Virginia borders. The surrounding area, dubbed the

Dr. Martha Pointer, Director of Graduate Studies

PO Box 70699, Johnson City, TN 37614 United States

Phone: 423-439-5314 • Fax: 423-439-5274

E-mail: business@business.etsu.edu • Website: www.etsu.edu/cbat

Tri-Cities region, also includes Bristol and Kingsport; the charming town of Abingdon, Virginia, is also not too far afield. The area is an outdoor enthusiast's paradise, offering plenty of opportunities for hiking, climbing, skiing, and nature walks. The Tri-Cities area is a rising force in the health care industry, with a developing biotech industry that could bring big players to the region.

With 11,000 students (about 2,000 of whom are graduate students), the ETSU campus has the population to support a busy social scene. MBAs report, "There is a very good social scene, with Thursday nights being the night that most students go out to the clubs. There are not a lot of clubs in the area, but there are many places that one can go and have a beer if they so choose." Students try to find time to support their men's basketball team, the ETSU Bucs, which in the 2003–2004 year won its second consecutive trip to "the Big Dance" (that's the NCAA Tournament to the uninitiated).

ETSU has expanded in recent years, adding several new buildings, including a fitness center (students love the "new, fully equipped athletic facility"). Not all MBAs take the time to enjoy the ETSU campus, however; they note that "the school is a high commuter school. This leads to a low participation level in on-campus clubs" and other activities. Those who do participate recommend the school's several national honor societies. One student touts "the university organization called 'President's Pride.' Through this organization, I am able to socialize with other students, faculty, administrators, and [members of the] community by volunteering for university/community functions."

Through its Adult, Commuter, and Transfer Services (ACTS) Office, ETSU assists its many nontraditional students in adapting to student life. ACTS staff advise students on the nuts and bolts of registration, direct them to the campus's various tutoring services, and help parents find child-care services. This last one can be a problem for MBAs, who typically attend evening classes. One such student comments, "I have a 15-month-old, and I have tried to get some type of care for my child so I can study or attend group meetings, and I have had no luck. This has been the most frustrating part of my school experience."

Admissions

Applications to the College of Business and Technology at East Tennessee State University are considered on a rolling basis. Applicants must submit the following to the Graduate Admissions Office: official copies of transcripts for all undergraduate and graduate work, standardized test scores (GMAT for the MBA or MAcc, GRE for the MPA), TOEFL scores (where applicable; minimum score 550), a personal statement, letters of recommendation, and a resume. Applicants to the MPA program must have a minimum undergraduate GPA of 3.0. All applicants are presumed to be competent with computers and math literate through calculus.

FINANCIAL FACTS

Annual tuition (in-state/ out-of-state)	$5,138/$15,000
Fees	$1,100
Cost of books	$1,000
Room & board (on/off-campus)	$5,000/$6,000
% of students receiving aid	25
% of first-year students receiving aid	25
% of students receiving grants	25
Average award package	$6,000
Average grant	$6,000
Average student loan debt	$10,000

ADMISSIONS

Admissions Selectivity Rating	**75**
# of applications received	70
% applicants accepted	77
% acceptees attending	85
Average GMAT	535
Average GPA	3.30
TOEFL required of international students	Yes
Minimum TOEFL (paper/computer)	550/213
Application fee	$25
International application fee	$35
Regular application deadline	6/1
Regular notification	rolling
Deferment available	Yes
Maximum length of deferment	1 year
Transfer students accepted	Yes
Transfer application policy Up to 9 approved hours may be accepted.	
Non-fall admissions	Yes
Need-blind admissions	Yes

Applicants Also Look At

University of Tennessee, Virginia Tech.

EMPLOYMENT PROFILE				
Career Rating	**66**	**Grads Employed by Function**	**%**	**Avg. Salary**
		Human Resources	10	$30,000
		Marketing/Sales	10	$38,000
		Entrepreneurship	10	$35,000
		General Management	50	$30,000
		Top Employer Hiring Grads		
		Eastman Chemical		

EASTERN MICHIGAN UNIVERSITY
COLLEGE OF BUSINESS

Academics

The MBA program at Eastern Michigan University offers its students "world-class opportunities" complemented by a "small-school feel" and "affordability." EMU emphasizes broad business perspectives through training in hard and soft skill competencies such as leadership and accounting. Students appreciate the curriculum's focus on teaching basic business principles but wish courses would "truly get down to the nitty gritty." The "diversity of international students within the MBA program" brings international perspectives to the classroom. Many students are drawn to EMU because of its "very accessible" evening program which allows students to "work full-time and commute to school for class in the evenings." The core curriculum includes courses in areas such as business communication, quantitative analysis, supply chain management, financial management, and management. Upon completion of the core, students may pursue degrees in general business or specialize in a number of areas including e-business, entrepreneurship, enterprise business intelligence, finance, human resource management, internal auditing, international business, marketing, nonprofit management, and supply chain management.

Students who have undergraduate degrees in business may qualify for an accelerated program, which contributes to the "younger crowd" on campus "who have come right from undergrad." Students say that "the university highly encourages and promotes global/cultural awareness. We have fabulous courses and academic programs abroad courses to enrich student experiences." They also appreciate "the flexibility of the program. Students can either go part-time or full-time depending on their job responsibilities." Describing their "outstanding" professors as "mentors who have a deep investment in seeing us succeed," students appreciate that their professors' teaching skills are complemented by real work experience. "The professors are well-rounded people," and "Most of them worked in the business world before they began teaching." "They are really concerned about [us] doing well," another student observes. Some students would like to see changes, though. "Still too many lectures," says one. "They need to expand on their course offerings. There is a pretty good mix of MBA specializations, but most are general business basics." Another student noted that the school "needs to be more hands-on and get students active in their education."

Student opinion of the administration is mostly positive. As one student explains, "I feel that the faculty and administration is supportive in every way. In addition, they provide one-on-one networking opportunities, advice, [and] mentoring." Another student points out that "advisors and administrators [are] very helpful, knowledgeable, and accessible," and appreciates that "when you need to speak with someone regarding an important issue, it can be handled that day." The "biggest problems [are] with financial aid."

Career and Placement

Eastern Michigan is located in Ypsilanti, ten minutes from the academic hub of Ann Arbor in one direction, and 25 minutes to the metropolis of Detroit in the other. That adds up to a great location for job hunting, and is especially convenient for those students at EMU who are already employed while attending classes. The university's Career Center is available to help graduate students in the College of Business, but most MBA students seem to rely on personal networking, existing job contacts, and student clubs and organizations for employment leads. "I work full-time and commute to school for class in the evenings. I am usually on campus to attend class, conduct research, or meet with a project team" points out one such student. Another adds, "I really enjoy the clubs, connections, special events, and networking opportunities" available on EMU's campus. "Small

DAWN GAYMER, ASSISTANT DEAN, GRADUATE PROGRAMS
404 OWEN, YPSILANTI, MI 48197 UNITED STATES
PHONE: 734-487-4444 • FAX: 734-483-1316
E-MAIL: COB.GRADUATE@EMICH.EDU • WEBSITE: WWW.COB.EMICH.EDU

classes provide great opportunity to make friends and [build a] professional network," says another. Ford Motor Company, Google, Ernst & Young, Target, Comerica Bank, Chase Bank, Proctor & Gamble, and Borders Group are among those who recruit on campus.

Student Life and Environment

Most of Eastern Michigan's classes take place at night and on weekends, which poses some challenges for its student community. "EMU is a commuter school, so it doesn't have the social activities that other business schools may have. I wish there were more social events for business school graduate students," says one. Another student described his peers as "real, honest—not superficial." They are "goal oriented and hard-working. Academics are the first priority for most." As to the student body itself, "Eastern Michigan's students are very diverse. I am Caucasian and I am the minority in almost all of my classes," one says. Another student describes his fellow students as "very open to new experiences; diverse from all areas of the globe, which is special for a smaller business school; hardworking." As a commuter school with night classes, several students wish to see security and safety on campus improved, though others agree with the student who says, "It is located in a great area, 10 minutes from Ann Arbor and 25 minutes from Detroit. Social activities are abundant due to the location of University of Michigan, Wayne State University, and the City of Detroit."

Admissions

GMAT scores, a one-page personal statement describing your plans and goals, and GPA rank, along with TOEFL scores for non-native speakers of English, are required for admission to Eastern Michigan's MBA program. The minimum GMAT score required is 450 and the minimum GPA accepted is 2.5/4.0. In 2006, the average GMAT score was 470, and the average GPA of students accepted into the MBA program was 3.0. Eastern Michigan generally accepts about 60 percent of those who apply to the MBA course, and on average, students have 4 years of work experience.

FINANCIAL FACTS

Annual tuition (in-state/ out-of-state)	$5,448/$10,736
Fees	$1,520
Cost of books	$1,000
Room & board (on-campus)	$8,374
% of students receiving aid	30
% of first-year students receiving aid	38
% of students receiving loans	24
% of students receiving grants	4
Average award package	$10,612
Average grant	$3,889

ADMISSIONS

Admissions Selectivity Rating	71
# of applications received	214
% applicants accepted	57
% acceptees attending	60
Average GMAT	470
Range of GMAT	420–530
Average GPA	3
TOEFL required of international students	Yes
Minimum TOEFL (paper/computer)	550/213
Application fee	$35
International application fee	$35
Regular application deadline	5/15
Regular notification	6/15
Application Deadline/Notification	
Round 1:	5/15
Round 2:	10/15
Round 3:	3/15
Round 4:	4/15
Deferment available	Yes
Maximum length of deferment	1 year
Transfer students accepted	Yes
Transfer application policy 6 credits may be accepted for the core and 6 credits for electives upon approval.	
Non-fall admissions	Yes
Need-blind admissions	Yes

Applicants Also Look At

Central Michigan University, Michigan State University, Oakland University, University of Michigan, University of Michigan—Dearborn, Wayne State University, Western Michigan University.

EMPLOYMENT PROFILE

Career Rating	60*

Grads Employed by Function	%	Avg. Salary
Finance/Accounting	9	$44,500
Human Resources	8	$40,400
Marketing/Sales	15	$61,500
MIS	8	$44,500
Operations/Production	16	$52,600
Consulting	7	$49,600
General Management	18	$57,500
Other	1	$50,000

Top 5 Employers Hiring Grads

Ernst & Young, Target, Comerica Bank, Chase Bank, Procter & Gamble.

EASTERN WASHINGTON UNIVERSITY
COLLEGE OF BUSINESS AND PUBLIC ADMINISTRATION

GENERAL INFORMATION

Type of school	Public
Environment	Town
Academic calendar	Quarter

SURVEY SAYS . . .

Students love Spokane, WA
Friendly students
Solid preparation in:
Teamwork

STUDENTS

Enrollment of parent institution	10,005
Enrollment of business school	950
% male/female	49/51
% out-of-state	12
% part-time	52
% minorities	5
% international	19
Average age at entry	21
Average years work experience at entry	4

ACADEMICS

Academic Experience Rating	**61**
Student/faculty ratio	25:1
Profs interesting rating	61
Profs accessible rating	82
% female faculty	46
% minority faculty	2

Joint Degrees

MBA/MPA 2 years.

Academics

Eastern Washington University offers an MBA that's "cheaper than that offered by other local schools" (namely Gonzaga University) and can be completed in just one year by the extremely diligent. Thanks to the school's active Center for Entrepreneurial Studies, entrepreneurship is among the standout disciplines here. Students praise the school's offerings in health care administration as well, lauding the "great certificate program to accompany the MBA that gives great versatility and unprecedented access in seminar format to professionals active in our community's health care industry."

EWU's MBA program is one of the few anywhere "taught by faculty from more than one department." Instructors here are drawn not only from the Department of Management but also from the Departments of Accounting and Information Systems, ensuring students the opportunity to develop "a unique and interdisciplinary business expertise." Because the business facility also houses the school's Public Administration Program, EWU students have the option to combine an MBA with an MPA.

The EWU MBA consists of 49 credit hours. Core courses constitute 33 hours of required work; electives take up the remaining 16 hours. Foundation courses can add up to an additional 32 hours of required course work, and many or all of these courses can be waived for students with relatively recent undergraduate business degrees. Because EWU operates on a quarterly academic calendar, students who place out of foundation courses may complete the program in one year by taking 10+ credits per semester. Some here feel that "quarters are too short to learn anything" and that "classes spanning two quarters (i.e., with a part I and part II) would be beneficial." Others would like to see "a greater variety of electives offered" as well as "concentrations in areas such as marketing, project management, leadership management, finance, and technology." It should be noted, both of these problem areas are typical of smaller programs. In the asset column, students love "the great evening schedule with convenient hours for working professionals" and praise the "excellent group of well-rounded professionals staff[ing] the program. They are welcoming when you drop by their offices to ask for assistance or guidance."

Career and Placement

The Office of Career Services provides counseling and placement services for the entire EWU student body. The office organizes occasional career fairs and posts notices for other career fairs held in the area. In addition, the office hosts on-campus interviews and other recruitment events and maintains an online placement files service, which provides students' resumes, letters of recommendation, and other documents to prospective employers. Most of Career Services' efforts are directed at the school's substantial undergraduate population. MBAs feel that the school "could definitely improve career services and offer students more opportunities to interact with potential employers."

Cynthia Parker, Program Coordinator
668 North Riverpoint Boulevard, Suite A, Spokane, WA 99202-1677 United States
Phone: 509-358-2248 • Fax: 509-358-2267
E-mail: cparker@mail.ewu.edu • Website: www.ewu.edu/mba

Student Life and Environment

The smallish, predominantly part-time MBA program at EWU consists of "many working professionals and/or students with adequate business experience, [with] a number of younger, less experienced students from Asia" thrown into the mix. The size and part-time nature of the program is not conducive to a cohesive student community. Further exacerbating the situation is the fact that "there's really no organized method of creating social networks with fellow students available. Some students do go out after class to discuss politics, school, etc. all the same, but it's not under the auspices of the school." Students don't even get to tap into the culture of EWU's main campus, since the MBA program "is located on a satellite campus in downtown Spokane, 20 miles from the main campus." While the location can inhibit extracurricular life, it does have the advantage of convenience for those students who work in the downtown area.

Classes convene at the Riverpoint Higher Education Park, located on the banks of the Spokane River. The facility is home to EWU's College of Business and Public Administration, a boon to those seeking a dual degree in those two fields. Riverpoint houses a 200-seat auditorium and a number of state-of-the-art classrooms.

Admissions

Eastern Washington University requires all the following materials from applicants to its MBA program: two copies of the completed application for admission to a graduate program; two copies of official transcripts for all postsecondary academic work; and an official GMAT score report no more than five years old. The MBA program director reserves the right to require additional information. International applicants must provide all of the above materials as well as an official TOEFL score report (if their first language is not English; students must score 580 for admission to the MBA program, 525 to be considered for pre-MBA foundation course work). EWU requires a minimum undergraduate GPA of 3.0 in the last 90 graded quarter credits. The school's website notes, "All students who graduate from the MBA program should have some practical work experience. The majority of students who are accepted into the program are working professionals and meet this requirement. For those students who enter the program lacking professional work experience, an internship should be part of the student's MBA program. Up to four credits earned while in an internship may be used for MBA elective credit."

FINANCIAL FACTS

Annual tuition (in-state/ out-of-state)	$8,114/$15,800
Fees	$75
Cost of books	$1,500
Room & board (on/off-campus)	$6,900/$12,000

ADMISSIONS

Admissions Selectivity Rating	**72**
# of applications received	78
% applicants accepted	64
% acceptees attending	60
Average GMAT	512
Range of GMAT	460–680
Average GPA	3.25
TOEFL required of international students	Yes
Minimum TOEFL (paper/computer)	580/237
Application fee	$100
Regular application deadline	1/1
Regular notification	1/1
Deferment available	Yes
Maximum length of deferment	1 year
Transfer students accepted	Yes
Transfer application policy We will accept up to 12 transfer credits.	
Non-fall admissions	Yes
Need-blind admissions	Yes

ELON UNIVERSITY
MARTHA AND SPENCER LOVE SCHOOL OF BUSINESS

GENERAL INFORMATION
Type of school	Private
Affiliation	United Church of Christ
Academic calendar	Trimester

SURVEY SAYS . . .
Friendly students
Cutting-edge classes
Helpful alumni
Happy students
Smart classrooms
Solid preparation in:
Teamwork
Communication/interpersonal skills
Presentation skills
Doing business in a global economy

STUDENTS
Enrollment of parent institution	5,230
Enrollment of business school	118
% male/female	68/32
% part-time	100
Average age at entry	32
Average years work experience at entry	9

ACADEMICS
Academic Experience Rating	**85**
Student/faculty ratio	20:1
Profs interesting rating	98
Profs accessible rating	82
% female faculty	30
% minority faculty	20

Prominent Alumni
Christina Baker, executive vice president and CFO, Capital Bank; Steven Casey, founder and board secretary, Expression Analysis; Allan Davis, CEO, AllFab Solutions; Bernadette Spong, CFO, Rex Hospital.

FINANCIAL FACTS
Annual tuition	$416 per credit
Average award package	$13,062
Average grant	$3,818
Average student loan debt	$16,807

Academics

Flexible scheduling, an affordable degree, and a "focus on leadership and soft-skill development" earn the praises of MBA students at Elon, a premier regional university in North Carolina's Triad region. Nearly all the part-timers here work full-time in addition to fulfilling their academic responsibilities, so students understandably demand convenience in their program. Elon delivers, scheduling all classes once a week in the evenings (6 P.M. to 9 P.M., Monday through Thursday) during the ten-week fall, winter, and spring terms; classes during the accelerated summer terms meet twice a week. Since the school doesn't have lockstep sequencing, "students can choose the courses they feel fit with their current schedules and timetables." As a result, many finish the program in as brief a period as 21 months—on average, students take slightly more than two years to complete the program.

Elon MBAs can also earn their degrees without putting a significant dent in their bank accounts. One student explains, "What binds most students is the desire to have a strong, valued-added education at a reasonable expense." Many here feel that "the marginal benefits received at schools with higher tuitions aren't worth the extra costs." For the 2006–2007 academic year, courses cost $1,248 each, and students were able to complete their degrees for just under $18,000.

MBAs here praise the "alternative teaching styles and small class sizes." The curriculum "stresses community and teamwork. We do many projects together. The school does not curve the grades in a way such that a portion of the class makes an F; therefore, we all try to work together and not fight for the top position." True to its historic connection to the United Church of Christ, "Elon is as much concerned with producing ethical, trustworthy, and successful leaders as it is with developing students' academic performance." Professors here "are very accessible and actively engage students to improve both the learning experience and the program overall. There is a tremendous opportunity to tailor class projects to individual interests, which enhances the level of enthusiasm and discussion."

Career and Placement

Career-placement services are provided by Elon's Career Development Office, which serves all students in the university. Services offered specifically for MBAs include a battery of self-assessment tools, faculty advising, and seminars with area business leaders. (Through the Legends of Business program, students have met with and learned from Knight Kiplinger, editor-in-chief of the *Kiplinger Letter*; J. Richard Munro, Former Chairman and CEO of Time Warner; and Edward N. Ney, former ambassador to Canada and former Chairman, President and CEO of Young and Rubicam, Inc.) The Love School Board of Advisors meets regularly to work with the administration and faculty to ensure that the program is relevant to the needs of organizations.

Elon MBAs work for some of the area's top employers, including BASF Corporation, Blue Cross & Blue Shield of North Carolina, Cisco Systems, Duke Energy, Labcorp, Dell, GE, Johnson Controls Inc., Sealy, Siemens Medical, Underwriters Laboratories, Volvo, GlaxoSmithKline, IBM, UNC Hospitals, Wachovia, and Wake Med.

ARTHUR W. FADDE, DIRECTOR OF GRADUATE ADMISSIONS
2750 CAMPUS BOX, ELON, NC 27244 UNITED STATES
PHONE: 800-334-8448 EXT. 3 • FAX: 336-278-7699
E-MAIL: ELONMBA@ELON.EDU • WEBSITE: WWW.ELON.EDU/MBA

Student Life and Environment

While students do "study together and occasionally socialize outside of class, most of [them] are older, working, and have active lives apart from the school." Because "the school draws from a large geographic area, it's somewhat hard to mingle with classmates outside of class."

Despite the lack of a "life at school," Elon students sing the praises of their classmates, whom they regard as "an extended family. Students accept each other for who they are and are more than willing to help each other grow and develop in the program." One MBA notes, "I've worked in groups with many strong opinions stemming from a depth of experience and awareness of current events and trends. Many personalities lean towards leadership, and there is a good diversity in both culture and professional background." The student body spans "a wide range of ages, with experienced students helping to educate the less experienced, and the less experienced often assisting the older ones with new perspectives."

In fall 2006, Elon opened the new 60,000 foot Ernest A. Koury Sr. Business Center. This state-of-the-art facility includes the Reed Finance Center, LaRose Digital Theatre, Doherty Center for Entrepreneurial Leadership, computer and research labs, and a variety of specialized classrooms to suit Elon's nationally recognized style of engaged learning.

Elon's central North Carolina location makes it well situated to serve the Triad region, which includes the Greensboro, High Point, and the Winston–Salem metropolitan areas. As a destination, Elon is notable mostly for its proximity to fine dining in Durham, Chapel Hill, and Greensboro; great barbecue in Lexington; the state's best zoo in Asheboro; and some of the finest golf courses in the nation.

Admissions

The Elon MBA requires a minimum of two years' professional experience for all applicants. A completed application must include three letters of recommendation (two from work supervisors), official transcripts from all postsecondary schools attended, and GMAT scores. Students whose native language is not English must also submit TOEFL scores (minimum 550 written, 213 computer). Applicants must exceed a score of 1000 under the formula [(undergraduate GPA $\times$ 200) + GMAT score], and must also have a minimum GMAT score of 470. Undergraduate classes in finance, financial accounting, microeconomics, and statistics are required foundation courses in the MBA program. Students may begin in August or February; applications are assessed on a rolling basis.

ADMISSIONS

Admissions Selectivity Rating	**77**
# of applications received	97
% applicants accepted	78
% acceptees attending	71
Average GMAT	550
Range of GMAT	470–620
Average GPA	3.2
Minimum TOEFL (paper/computer)	550/213
Application fee	$50
Regular application deadline	Rolling
Regular notification	Rolling
Deferment available	Yes
Maximum length of deferment	1 year
Transfer students accepted	Yes
Transfer application policy A student may transfer up to 9 semester hours of credit from another AACSB-accredited school.	
Non-fall admissions	Yes
Need-blind admissions	Yes

Applicants Also Look At

North Carolina State University, The University of North Carolina at Greensboro, Wake Forest University (evening MBA, Winston-Salem).

EMORY UNIVERSITY
GOIZUETA BUSINESS SCHOOL

Academics

With a "great reputation," a "great location" in one of the fastest growing cities in one of the "fastest growing regions in the United States," and the "familial atmosphere" of "a small school with an extremely close-knit community," the Goizueta Business School at Emory University has a large stockpile of assets with which to justify its consistently high national ranking. Goizueta offers a traditional 2-year full-time MBA, an accelerated 1-year MBA, and a part-time evening MBA and Executive MBA.

Nearly everyone here agrees that "the focus on leadership and communications" within the Goizueta curriculum is a tremendous asset and is one of the program's chief drawing cards. "In addition to teaching the basic skills necessary for a career in business, the school is good at fine-tuning students' presentation, leadership, and interpersonal skills," explains one student. MBAs here also tout "one of the top marketing programs in the country." The core curriculum here offers "a mixture of soft and analytical skills" that "develop the needed business skills" in future managers, students report. Students in all disciplines benefit from "the small size" of the program coupled with its "large resources (Emory has a very large endowment)."

Goizueta is "a place full of passionate people," from students on up to the administration. The program's small size means "that everybody knows everybody on a first-name basis, and that includes students, faculty, administrators, Admissions, Career Management, and the Dean. . . . That also means that the students and faculty alike are super approachable and always willing to talk, guide, and discuss. That has been my biggest source of learning at school." Students here enjoy "a high level of involvement in the planning of the program and the strategy of the school," working closely with an administration that is "incredibly responsive to student ideas and requests. If you have an idea, they will help you achieve it. The atmosphere is one of high motivation in a very supportive environment."

Career and Placement

There is some dissatisfaction among students with the Goizueta Career Management Center, and many students complain about the number of companies visiting campus to recruit. "I think that any problems with the career center stem from the size of the school," explains one student. "A school that only graduates about 200 a year just isn't going to attract a ton of companies." Students report that "no one in the administration or student body is complacent" about recruitment. In fact, they feel that "everyone is working diligently to improve the situation." A few even find the office "extremely effective. Any student who makes the effort to seek out assistance is sure to receive answers and support as well as unsolicited follow-ups. Also, various professors and alumni have offered connections or have otherwise offered assistance," helping to mitigate whatever problems exist. "The school has had 100-percent placement for summer internships for as long as I've been here," says one impressed student.

Employers who most frequently hire Emory MBAs include: Adjoined Consulting, A.T. Kearney, Bank of America Securities, Bright House, CHEP International, Deloitte Touche Tohmatsu, Delta Air Lines, Earthlink, Goldman Sachs, The Home Depot, IBM, ING, JPMorgan Chase, Kurt Salmon & Associates, Lehman Brothers, Navigant Consulting, PricewaterhouseCoopers, Sun Trust Bank, UPS, Wachovia, and Zyman Marketing Group.

JULIE R. BAREFOOT, ASSOCIATE DEAN AND DIRECTOR OF MBA ADMISSIONS
1300 CLIFTON ROAD, ATLANTA, GA 30322 UNITED STATES
PHONE: 404-727-6311 • FAX: 404-727-4612
E-MAIL: ADMISSIONS@BUS.EMORY.EDU • WEBSITE: WWW.GOIZUETA.EMORY.EDU

Student Life and Environment

"There is definitely a work-hard, play-hard mentality at Goizueta," where students enjoy "plenty of opportunities to socialize." Favorites include International Potluck—"a great event hosted by the school to learn about other cultures;" "coffee and bagels as a school each Wednesday morning," and "Kegs in the Courtyard and Late Night" on Thursdays. These events "are actively looked forward to by the whole student community." Students tell us that "everyone spends most of first year on campus involved in classes, clubs, social events, recruiting events. There is always something to do. Second year gives you more of an opportunity to create your own schedule. Some people choose to stay actively involved, while others pursue directed study projects, international exchanges, family life, etc." Students appreciate that "spouses are heavily integrated into all campus and off-campus social events."

MBAs at Goizueta "are assigned to sections at the beginning of the year, which become tight groups," but "with only 350 students" in the program, "Everyone knows each other." The school works hard to promote unity. "We have had events like a Halloween Ball and Section Feud (trivia contest)," reports one student, "The Program Office also has a semester-ending town hall meeting to discuss how the year is going and what changes need to be implemented for improvements."

Admissions

Applicants to the Goizueta MBA program must submit the following materials: a completed online application; official transcripts for all undergraduate and graduate schools attended; an official GMAT score report; two letters of recommendation, essay (the first is a narrative resume; the second offers a choice of subjects that center on your sources of inspiration or your career and life aspirations) An interview, while not required, is "strongly recommended." International students whose first language is not English must also submit official score reports for either the TOEFL or the IELTS (minimum acceptable score: 7.0). Candidates for the 1-year program must have an undergraduate degree in a business-related discipline, engineering, or a strong quantitative background and "solid business experience."

FINANCIAL FACTS

Annual tuition	$32,096
Fees	$422
Cost of books	$1,900
Room & board	
(off-campus)	$15,000
% of students receiving aid	82
% of first-year students	
receiving aid	74
% of students receiving loans	57
% of students receiving grants	60
Average award package	$31,542
Average grant	$17,815
Average student loan debt	$54,404

ADMISSIONS

Admissions Selectivity Rating	**95**
# of applications received	1,080
% applicants accepted	37
% acceptees attending	39
Average GMAT	680
Range of GMAT	650–710
Average GPA	3.4
TOEFL required of	
international students	Yes
Minimum TOEFL	
(paper/computer)	600/250
Application fee	$140
Regular application deadline	3/15
Regular notification	Rolling
Deferment available	Yes
Maximum length of	
deferment	1 year
Need-blind admissions	Yes

Applicants Also Look At

Duke University, New York University, Northwestern University, University of Michigan, The University of North Carolina at Chapel Hill, University of Pennsylvania, University of Virginia.

EMPLOYMENT PROFILE			
Career Rating	**91**	**Grads Employed by Function**	**% Avg. Salary**
		Finance/Accounting	33 $78,248
		Marketing/Sales	24 $76,109
		Operations/Production	4 $76,000
		Consulting	21 $89,252
		General Management	4 $74,938
		Other	14 $81,497

ESADE BUSINESS SCHOOL

GENERAL INFORMATION

Type of school	Private
Academic calendar	Annual

SURVEY SAYS . . .

Students love Barcelona, Spain
Solid preparation in:
Marketing
Teamwork
Communication/interpersonal skills

STUDENTS

Enrollment of parent institution	898
Enrollment of business school	431
% male/female	80/20
% part-time	39
% international	72
Average age at entry	28
Average years work experience at entry	5

ACADEMICS

Academic Experience Rating	**90**
Student/faculty ratio	2:1
Profs interesting rating	96
Profs accessible rating	78
% female faculty	21

Prominent Alumni

Enrique Rueda, director of corporate strategy, The World Bank; Ignacio Fonts, general manager, Hewlett-Packard Inkjet; Ferran Soriano, CEO and member of the board, FC Barcelona; Alex Rovira and Fernando Trias de Bes, authors of the best-selling book *The Good Luck*.

Academics

Students at the prestigious ESADE Business School in Barcelona have two full-time MBA options: an 18-month program geared toward students seeking an international dual degree as well as students with non-business backgrounds; and a one-year program, designed for highly experienced students seeking a career boost or a fresh start as international entrepreneurs. Both are bilingual programs (but courses in the one-year program are conducted primarily in English). ESADE also offers a part-time program, taught primarily in Spanish, to local students.

Students report that "ESADE places emphasis on teamwork and collaborative learning." They go on to say, "The workload is significant, but always manageable." The teamwork focus means "half of the learning is done among students through interactions, arguments, and negotiations. These are the skills you will never learn by simply sitting in the classroom, even with the greatest professors teaching you the greatest classes ever." Leadership is also stressed in the "cutting-edge" LEAD (Leadership Assessment and Development) program, in which student groups undertake a challenging business simulation, then review a videotape of their work to analyze which roles were taken by each group member and how successfully each member utilized leadership skills in performing his or her role.

Professors at ESADE sometimes make courses too "heavily lecture-oriented," and some "don't speak good English," but generally professors earn praise for "knowing exactly the material and subjects of the other courses" and for being "accessible after class." Furthermore, students say, "Since class size is small, you can approach professors very casually, and they are friendly and helpful." Students are especially impressed with the marketing program, and they also tell us, "ESADE has one of the best language programs in Europe, which is very important in an International MBA." The administration is very responsive to student input. One MBA writes," It is not uncommon for student suggestions or proposals to change school policy. In this sense, students feel very respected and important at ESADE."

ESADE offers a dual-degree MBA in conjunction with four prestigious U.S. MBA-granting institutions and four equally prestigious Latin American schools; those who complete the program receive degrees from both ESADE and the participating American school.

Career and Placement

ESADE's Career Services office "has only gotten properly started the last couple of years and is not up to par by standards of U.S. schools," observes one American exchange student. However, MBAs report that "the department has made strong improvements in the last few years. There is still room to grow, especially in the connection between employers and students, but they are on their way. They are improving, and this effort must be recognized." Although the school claims contact with more than 1,500 employers, a few students still feel that "ESADE could improve recruiting efforts to companies based in the U.S." and "abroad." The office hosts on-campus forums, recruiting events, corporate presentations, networking and alumni events, workshops, and seminars. It also maintains a Career Resources Center with hard-copy and electronic databases and other reference materials.

Employers most likely to hire ESADE MBAs include Novartis, Citigroup, Bayer, PWC, L'Oreal, GE, BBVA, Accenture, Nike, Deloitte Touche Tohmatsu, Intel, Danone, DuPont, and KPMG International.

NURIA GUILERA, MBA MARKETING AND ADMISSIONS DIRECTOR
AV. D'ESPLUGUES, 92-96 BARCELONA, 08034 SPAIN
PHONE: 011-34-934-952-088 • FAX: 011-34-934-953-828
E-MAIL: MBA@ESADE.EDU • WEBSITE: WWW.ESADE.EDU

Student Life and Environment

"ESADE is a well-balanced school," and it features "individual activities as well as team-work opportunities." While the workload can be demanding, "there is always time to go and have a beer with your friends." Many students enjoy spending each morning "with a cup of café con leche on the sunny terrace of the school overlooking Barcelona." Whether working or playing, ESADE MBAs enjoy a convivial atmosphere. One student comments, "People are very friendly. Even though we may work a lot, social life is very important. I don't see ESADE as an MBA factory like many other business schools, but more like a place to live a once-in-a-lifetime experience."

ESADE "doesn't provide accommodations for students, but the school has an agency that will find you the living space you want. This city is unbeatable and very, very safe." Barcelona, which students call "a very attractive city that has a great social and cultural life," is home to world-renowned art galleries and museums, concert halls, theaters, and international athletic events—not to mention the trippy architectural masterpieces by Antonio Gaudí. It's also a port city and one of the great economic centers of southern Europe.

ESADE's student body is "very diverse, interactive, friendly, creative, and dynamic." One student reports, "My academic team of seven students (which works together the entire first year) has people from Greece, Spain, Puerto Rico, France, Canada, the U.S., and Japan. In terms of business background: corporate finance in a blue-chip company, stock trading in a brokerage, marketing in IT, marketing in biotech, managing a theme park, operations/logistics in the automobile industry, and operations/logistics in meat production. It's a very diverse group." Students go on to say this school "is a very team-oriented and supportive culture and people form very personal and strong relationships."

Admissions

Applicants to the 18-month full-time MBA program must have a minimum of two years' full-time work experience. Applicants to the one-year full-time MBA program must have at least five years of full-time work experience and an undergraduate degree in business or economics (candidates with engineering or mathematics degrees are evaluated in the light of their business experience). Completed applications must include: official transcripts for all undergraduate work, official GMAT and English proficiency scores (ESADE offers its own English proficiency exam), two letters of recommendation, and an application form. Interviews are conducted at the school's request only; all admitted students are interviewed prior to admission. According to the school's website, "Aspects taken into account during the admission process include: the candidate's intellectual abilities; professional potential; maturity; motivation; and ability to work as part of a team."

FINANCIAL FACTS

Annual tuition	$29,575
Cost of books	$200
Room & board (off-campus)	$10,660
% of first-year students receiving aid	40
Average grant	$18,474

ADMISSIONS

Admissions Selectivity Rating	**86**
# of applications received	281
% applicants accepted	63
% acceptees attending	45
Average GMAT	630
Range of GMAT	600–700
Average GPA	3.5
TOEFL required of international students	Yes
Minimum TOEFL (paper/computer)	600/250
Application fee	$100
Regular application deadline	6/30
Regular notification	Rolling
Deferment available	Yes
Maximum length of deferment	1 year
Non-fall admissions	Yes
Need-blind admissions	Yes

EMPLOYMENT PROFILE

Career Rating	85		
Grads Employed by Function		**%**	**Avg. Salary**
Finance/Accounting		16	NR
Marketing/Sales		23	NR
Consulting		23	NR
General Management		34	NR
Other		3	NR
Nonprofit		1	NR

ESSEC Business School
The ESSEC MBA Program

GENERAL INFORMATION
Type of school   Private
Academic calendar   Trimester

SURVEY SAYS . . .
Good social scene
Cutting-edge classes
Solid preparation in:
Finance
General management
Teamwork

STUDENTS
Enrollment of parent institution	3,736
Enrollment of business school	1,818
% male/female	53/47
% international	20
Average age at entry	22
Average years work experience at entry	1

ACADEMICS
Academic Experience Rating	**91**
Student/faculty ratio	19:1
Profs interesting rating	70
Profs accessible rating	84
% female faculty	23

Joint Degrees
ESSEC-Mannheim double-degree MBA, ESSEC-Nanyang Technological University double-degree MBA, ESSEC-Guanghua School of Management double-degree MBA, ESSEC-Seoul National University (double-degree MBA or ESSEC MBA and Seoul MA in international relations), ESSEC-TEC double-degree MBA, European MBA with ESSEC, Mannheim University and Warwick University.

Prominent Alumni
Gilles Pelisson, chairman, Accor Hotel Group; Dominique Reiniche, president Europe, Coca-Cola; Christian Balmes, chairman and CEO, Shell France; Patrick Cescau, chairman, Unilever.

Academics

If you're looking for a "flexible" MBA at "a major player on the international level among European business schools" and one of "the top business schools in France," ESSEC is a school you should consider. After completing seven management fundamentals courses, ESSEC MBAs fashion their own curricula, choosing from more than "200 electives" each semester. Students love the freedom, telling us that "each quarter, we can basically chose to take classes at ESSEC Business School in Paris or Singapore, do an internship with a company in France or abroad, or go on an exchange program abroad with one of ESSEC's 70 academic partners," whose ranks include many prestigious names in the United States and around the world. The school's administration "does a great job of managing this 'a la carte' system," allowing students to "choose almost any courses we want in order to create our specialization and formation."

Because ESSEC believes that students should make "a constant connection between work and the classroom," all students must have at least 18 months of validated professional experience prior to graduation. These internships are easy to find thanks to ESSEC's "great relationship with the business world." The school "has strong links with international finance and consulting companies;" and a campus in Singapore means that opportunities to intern in Southeast Asia are constantly developing. ESSEC's practical philosophy permeates the classroom as well; here "Courses are not just theory. We have a lot of business cases given by corporate partners, and we have a lot of work every week to prepare other business cases in groups (teamwork is very important here)." Throughout the program, there is a "prominent international dimension" bolstered by "the school's ever-increasing partnerships overseas."

The faculty includes "outstanding professors recognized in their fields of specialization, people who publish a lot. They help us get most prepared for our chosen profession and they are also very available and most willing to give us useful insights." Part-time faculty are drawn from "top-notch businesswomen and men and successful entrepreneurs. In any case, they always have a great experience and very useful insights to share."

Career and Placement

Students report that "ESSEC is the best passport to great job opportunities in France and worldwide. The school administration and students are really eager to keep in very close contact with firms. There is a constant exchange between the academic, student and business world. Companies are often involved in student projects too." The school's "excellent relations with European businesses" help students procure the internships required to complete their MBAs. While ESSEC's connections are strongest in France, "Many foreign companies also recruit (largely for their French subsidies), such as the consulting companies McKinsey, BCG, etc. ESSEC is part of their main target schools for recruiting."

Employers most likely to hire ESSEC MBAs include: PricewaterhouseCoopers, L'Oréal, Renault, Societe Generale, Deloitte Touche Tohmatsu, Danone, Michelin, BNP Paribas, Capgemini, Accenture, EDF-GDF, Pinault Printemps Redoute, Procter & Gamble, Deutsche Bank, 3 Suisses International, Pfizer, LVMH, Ernst & Young, Boston Consulting Group, A.T. Kearney, SC Johnson, and Bain.

Student Life and Environment

ESSAC encourages students to participate in extracurricular life, and students respond, forming "about 70 different clubs" that encompass not only business activities but also "theater, a choir, painting, photography, sports, and social groups." The area surrounding ESSAC, Cergy Pontoise, is "an ugly Parisian suburb" located "about an hour from

MR. PHILIPPE REGIMBART, DIRECTOR OF ADMISSIONS
AVENUE BERNARD HIRSCH, B.P. 50105 CERGY-PONTOISE, 95021 FRANCE
PHONE: 011-33-1-3443-3095 • FAX: 011-33-1-3443-3111
E-MAIL: MERIZIO@ESSEC.FR • WEBSITE: WWW.ESSEC.EDU

the center of the city by commuter train." Some describe it as "a modern city with very good amenities, including an artificial lake for sailing or rowing and other water sports, a nearby skating rink, and very good town libraries." Others tell us that "with only two trains to the city per hour, living in Cergy can be a little bit disappointing for those who would prefer the dense atmosphere of Paris to ESSEC school life." Local housing "is pretty easy to find" and "not too expensive."

ESSAC is "undergoing immense changes," students tell us, reporting that "buildings are being built, and new professors are being recruited at an international level. The school is going global and will become internationally known very soon." Some here tell us that "you can stay all day long at ESSEC, and there's always something to do and somewhere to go." Even those who complain that "facilities here could improve" acknowledge that "that is exactly what the school is doing. The current development program aims to double the space available and to upgrade facilities."

Admissions

Students are admitted to ESSEC either as traditional MBAs (this is the way international students enter the program), French MBAs, or as "grande école" students (French students who have attended 1 or 2 years of postsecondary school and are now ready for intensive, focused study in a discipline such as business). Students applying to the traditional MBA program must provide the school with an official GMAT or TAGE-MAGE score report, official transcripts for all postsecondary academic work, an interview, and a resume. Applicants must be under the age of 32; 1 or 2 years of professional experience is highly recommended. French MBA students follow the "Admission sur Titre" admissions path. "Grande école" applicants must meet a variety of requirements, including completion of preparatory undergraduate business classes and completion of at least one 6-month internship.

FINANCIAL FACTS

Annual tuition	$20,200
Cost of books	$565
Room & board (on/off-campus)	$7,500/$11,260
% of students receiving aid	36
% of first-year students receiving aid	33
% of students receiving grants	12
Average award package	$5,822
Average grant	$4,225
Average student loan debt	$25,422

ADMISSIONS

Admissions Selectivity Rating	**97**
# of applications received	4,007
% applicants accepted	23
% acceptees attending	65
Average GMAT	670
Range of GMAT	600–780
TOEFL required of international students	Yes
Minimum TOEFL (paper/computer)	600/230
Application fee	$195
Application Deadline/Notification	
Round 1:	10/14 / 12/1
Round 2:	1/6 / 3/2
Round 3:	2/24 / 4/13
Round 4:	5/5 / 6/15
Deferment available	Yes
Maximum length of deferment	1 year
Need-blind admissions	Yes

Applicants Also Look At

E.M. LYON, ESCP-EAP European School of Management, HEC School of Management—Paris.

EMPLOYMENT PROFILE

Career Rating	87		
Primary Source of Full time Job Acceptances			
Percent employed	80		

Grads Employed by Function	%	Avg. Salary
Accounting	4	NR
Finance/Accounting	11	NR
Human Resources	2	NR
Marketing/Sales	27	NR
MIS	8	NR
Operations/Production	1	NR
Consulting	30	NR
Communications	1	NR
Entrepreneurship	4	NR
General Management	2	NR
Other	9	NR
Nonprofit	1	NR

Top 5 Employers Hiring Grads
Société Générale; PriceWaterhouseCoopers; LVMH; L'Oréal; Accenture.

FAIRFIELD UNIVERSITY
CHARLES F. DOLAN SCHOOL OF BUSINESS

GENERAL INFORMATION
Type of school	Private
Affiliation	Roman Catholic-Jesuit
Environment	Town
Academic calendar	Semester

SURVEY SAYS . . .
Students love Fairfield, CT
Friendly students
Good peer network
Happy students

STUDENTS
Enrollment of parent institution	5,091
Enrollment of business school	165
Average age at entry	29
Average years work experience at entry	6

ACADEMICS
Academic Experience Rating	**71**
Student/faculty ratio	23:1
Profs interesting rating	78
Profs accessible rating	69
% female faculty	36
% minority faculty	2

Prominent Alumni
Dr. E. Gerald Corrigan, managing director, Goldman Sachs; Robert Murphy, Jr., senior vice president, The Walt Disney Company Foundation; Christopher McCormick, president and CEO, LL Bean, Inc.; Dr. Francis Tedesco, president, Medical College of Georgia.

Academics

"Jesuit tenets" guide instruction at the Dolan School of Business, a small, mostly part-time program at Fairfield University that boasts "a fine finance program." Dolan offers graduates an MBA (part-time and full-time), an MS in finance, and an MS in accounting. Qualified professionals may enroll in certificate programs for advanced study in accounting, finance, human resource management, information systems and operations management, international business, marketing, and taxation.

The Dolan MBA curriculum is divided into three components: core courses, breadth courses, and elective specialization or concentration courses. Core classes count toward the graduate degree; they are meant to be functional areas of deficiency in students' academic business backgrounds, and some or all can be waived for students who successfully completed undergraduate courses in the areas these classes cover. Breadth courses account for 18 credits toward the degree and cover important concepts in accounting, finance, information systems, management, business ethics, and marketing. The remainder of the curriculum consists of 12 credits of concentration courses (concentrations are available in accounting, finance, human resource management, information systems and operations, general management, international business, marketing, and taxation), an additional three elective credits, and a three-credit capstone course in global competitive strategy.

The MS in accounting is open to undergraduates in accounting from all undergraduate institutions. Pursued full-time, this program "leads to the MBA and fulfills requirements to sit for the uniform CPA examination" in 12 to 15 months.

Dolan students praise their "very accessible and helpful faculty," telling us that "professors' enthusiasm contributes a lot to the learning experience. The course work is current and interesting." Courses are held between 7:00 and 10 P.M. on weekday evenings for the convenience of employed students; a limited number of weekend courses are also available.

Career and Placement

The Dolan MBA program is a small, predominantly part-time program in which most students already have careers; a number of students actually attend at their employers' expense. This situation creates a relatively small demand for career services within the program; students seeking such services must use the Career Planning Center, which serves the entire student body of the university. The Dolan Graduate Business Association, run by students, is probably the most aggressive advocate for career services within the program. Professors and alumni are also regarded as valuable resources for those seeking internships or careers.

Employers most likely to hire Dolan MBAs include American Skandia, Bayer Corporation, Cendant Corporation, The Common Fund, Gartner, GE, People's Bank, Pitney Bowes, Pfizer, UBS Warburg, Unilever, and United Technologies.

DR. DANA A. WILKIE, ASSISTANT DEAN/DIRECTOR OF GRADUATE PROGRAMS
1073 NORTH BENSON ROAD, FAIRFIELD, CT 06824 UNITED STATES
PHONE: 203-254-4000 • FAX: 203-254-4029
E-MAIL: GRADADMIS@MAIL.FAIRFIELD.EDU • WEBSITE: WWW.FAIRFIELD.EDU/MBA

Student Life and Environment

The Dolan School of Business is housed in a 70,000-square-foot facility that includes a 150-seat amphitheater, a wireless computer network, two high-tech computer labs, eight breakout rooms for meetings and projects, and numerous classrooms and offices. Classrooms are equipped to accommodate all up-to-date teaching technologies. Students here praise the "informal, relaxed atmosphere" and "safe campus" that make the "heavy workload" a little easier to handle. Most agree that extracurricular life is minimal, and that there's "not much for MBAs to do here on campus except go to class."

Dolan students benefit from the school's location near New York City. Nearly 50 *Fortune* 500 companies are headquartered within 50 miles of the school; a little farther afield (in New York City itself and lower Westchester County, all within an hour from campus) approximately 100 *Fortune* 500 companies maintain significant presences. Fairfield County is home to the greatest concentration of U.S. headquarters for foreign multinationals; many of these firms work with the university to provide experiential learning opportunities.

Admissions

Applications may be submitted to Dolan via mail or the Internet. Applications are processed on a rolling basis, and students may commence the program in any term. The Admissions Committee considers applicants' postsecondary academic records, GMAT scores, two letters of recommendation, and resume or other self-evaluation of work experience. International students from non-English-speaking countries must submit TOEFL scores (a minimum score of 550 is required). Applicants to the one-year MBA program in accounting and taxation must meet all the above criteria and must also provide a statement of certification from his/her accounting department faculty and a letter of recommendation from either a former employer or a faculty member outside the discipline of accounting. This program is open only to students who hold, or are in the process of earning, an undergraduate degree in accounting. All entering students in all programs must demonstrate proficiency in microeconomics, macroeconomics, calculus, and statistics. Successful completion of undergraduate work in these areas is the most common way of demonstrating proficiency.

FINANCIAL FACTS

Annual tuition	$18,000
Fees	$100
Cost of books	$1,000
Average grant	$50,000

ADMISSIONS

Admissions Selectivity Rating	**76**
# of applications received	124
% applicants accepted	69
% acceptees attending	86
Average GMAT	537
Range of GMAT	500–650
Average GPA	3.2
TOEFL required of international students	Yes
Minimum TOEFL (paper/computer)	550/213
Application fee	$55
Regular application deadline	Rolling
Regular notification	Rolling
Deferment available	Yes
Maximum length of deferment	1 year
Transfer students accepted	Yes
Transfer application policy	6 credits or Jesuit University Transfer Program
Non-fall admissions	Yes

Applicants Also Look At
Pace University, University of Connecticut, University of Hartford.

FAIRLEIGH DICKINSON UNIVERSITY
SILBERMAN COLLEGE OF BUSINESS

GENERAL INFORMATION
Type of school	Private
Environment	Village

SURVEY SAYS . . .
Students love Teaneck, NJ
Happy students
Solid preparation in:
Communication/interpersonal skills
Presentation skills

STUDENTS
Enrollment of parent institution	12,112
Enrollment of business school	790
% male/female	55/45
% out-of-state	5
% part-time	59
% minorities	15
% international	20
Average age at entry	28

ACADEMICS
Academic Experience Rating	**70**
Student/faculty ratio	25:1
Profs interesting rating	69
Profs accessible rating	81
% female faculty	17

Joint Degrees
MBA/MA (management/corporate and organizational communications), MBA/MA (human resource management/ industrial/organizational psychology).

Prominent Alumni
Michael King, television's leading syndicator, King World; Patrick Zenner, former president and CEO, Hoffman-La Roche, Inc.; Anthony Cuti, chairman, president, CEO, Duane Reade Corporation; George Martin, former NFL Giants captain; John Joyce, CFO, IBM.

Academics

Most of the MBA offerings from Fairleigh Dickinson University are available at both of the school's campuses: the College at Florham campus, located in Madison, and the Metropolitan campus, located in Teaneck. A few specialized programs are available at the Metropolitan campus only; these include the full-time one-year Global Business Management MBA program.

Students appreciate the convenience of the two campuses—although students must enroll at one campus, they are free to take classes at either—and the "flexibility of the program to accommodate working schedules," an important factor for the schools' 463-plus part-time students, most of whom work full-time. Students also appreciate the fact that FDU offers a "well-rounded program" with a "breadth of concentrations." The school offers concentrations in entrepreneurial studies, finance, human resource management, international business, management, management with concentrations in: corporate communications, global business (1-year program), and information systems, marketing, pharmaceutical management, executive MBA programs in management and health and life sciences management, and also MS programs in accounting and taxation. Those in a hurry to finish their degrees especially appreciate the five-week- long Saturday classes. One student explains, "The workload is heavy given the short time period, but without taking some of these classes, I would probably only take one class per semester, and it would have taken me a lot longer to complete the program."

FDU MBAs tell us that "classwork here is fine and moderately challenging." Students enjoy a "good rapport among students" and great professors, especially "the adjuncts who bring a great deal of real-life experience to the classroom." One first-year student says, "I have taken five courses so far. Out of these classes, three of the professors I would rate as top-shelf. I was challenged intellectually and gained a lot from these classes. The other two were introductory classes, yet the professors were always accessible and passionate about their subject. There are definitely some hidden treasures in the faculty." In the past, students have complained that "convoluted processes and unhelpful individuals" have marred their dealings with the school; however, a new administration has been instituted throughout the past two years, and is striving to make things more student centered. Some also feel that "the school needs to upgrade some of the classrooms."

Career and Placement

Each of FDU's campuses maintains its own Career Development Center. Both offices offer self-assessment tools, one-on-one counseling, libraries, resume critiquing, interview and job-search seminars, job listings, on-campus recruitment interviews, co-op and internship services, and career fairs. Past on-campus recruiters have included Advanced Technology Group, Ameriprise Financial, AXA Advisors, the Drug Enforcement Agency, First Investors, Northwest Mutual, ProFinance, Wachovia, and the World Savings Bank, CitiGroup, Deloitte Touche Tohmatsu, KPMG International, Colgate Palmolive, and PricewaterhouseCoopers.

Student Life and Environment

Most of FDU's full-time MBAs (as well as many part-time students) attend the Metropolitan campus in Teaneck, not far from the George Washington Bridge, thus providing easy access to New York City. The program is housed in Dickinson Hall, which offers three microcomputer laboratories, an auditorium, classrooms, and office space. The wooded campus straddles the Hackensack River.

SUSAN NEIHART, DIRECTOR OF GRADUATE RECRUITMENT AND MARKETING
1000 RIVER ROAD, T-KB1-01, TEANECK, NJ 07666 UNITED STATES
PHONE: 201-692-2554 • FAX: 201-692-2560
E-MAIL: GRAD@FDU.EDU • WEBSITE: WWW.FDU.EDU

FDU's College at Florham campus in Madison attracts mostly part-time students. The campus was landscaped by famed architect Frederick Law Olmstead; unfortunately for most MBAs, it's often dark here when they arrive and leave, making it more difficult to appreciate the surrounding beauty. Not that students would have much time to take in their environment anyway, since "most of the MBA students also work full-time. They don't have time for involvement with the school outside the classroom."

At both sites, FDU attracts "a very mixed conglomerate of people" that includes "lots of foreign students." These "intelligent, hardworking, and dedicated" MBAs don't socialize much, but "you meet a lot of people anyway because there are a lot of group assignments." Students are "competitive, but in a friendly way." A considerable number are just starting out in their careers; writes one student who isn't, "I am a mid-career manager and am older than most of the students. However, I do not feel out of place. All of my classes have been great, and the diversity of experiences has resulted in great learning sessions."

Admissions

Applicants to the FDU MBA program must apply to a specific campus; after being admitted, students are permitted to register for classes at either campus. Applications are processed on a rolling basis, with the exception of a few of specialized programs. All applications must include official transcripts for all academic work completed after high school, an official GMAT score report, and a completed application form. Certain programs also require interviews and letters of recommendation; check with the school to learn whether your desired program is included. Students who have not completed all prerequisite courses for the MBA may be admitted conditionally; they may enroll in undergraduate business classes on a nondegree basis in order to qualify for the MBA program. International students whose native language is not English and who have not completed undergraduate degrees in an English-language institution must take the TOEFL and achieve a satisfactory score.

FINANCIAL FACTS

Annual tuition	$16,074
Fees	$608
Cost of books	$2,000
Room & board (on-campus)	$10,390
% of students receiving aid	60
% of students receiving loans	33
% of students receiving grants	33
Average award package	$3,500
Average grant	$5,000

ADMISSIONS

Admissions Selectivity Rating	**84**
# of applications received	515
% applicants accepted	330
% acceptees attending	216
Average GMAT	525
Average GPA	3.5
TOEFL required of international students	Yes
Minimum TOEFL (paper/computer)	550/213
Application fee	$40
Regular application deadline	Rolling
Regular notification	Rolling
Deferment available	Yes
Transfer students accepted	Yes
Transfer application policy	
All core courses can be waived by meeting FDU waiver policy.	
6 credits can be transferred.	
Non-fall admissions	Yes
Need-blind admissions	Yes

FLORIDA ATLANTIC UNIVERSITY
COLLEGE OF BUSINESS

GENERAL INFORMATION
Type of school   Public
Environment   City
Academic calendar   Semester

SURVEY SAYS . . .
Helpful alumni
Solid preparation in:
Teamwork
Communication/interpersonal skills
Presentation skills

STUDENTS
Enrollment of parent institution	25,657
Enrollment of business school	546
% male/female	58/42
% out-of-state	23
% part-time	61
% minorities	24
% international	18
Average age at entry	31
Average years work experience at entry	7

ACADEMICS
Academic Experience Rating	**80**
Student/faculty ratio	14:1
Profs interesting rating	94
Profs accessible rating	71
% female faculty	30

Academics

A wide variety of programs and an equally wide variety of class sites distinguish the MBA programs at Florida Atlantic University's College of Business. Local students are drawn here by the price and convenience; those from farther away come for such distinctive programs as the MBA in Sports Management, which is "one of a handful of such programs in the country that is AACSB accredited," or the Masters of Forensic Accounting—"the oldest program in the nation and one of the few available online." Others come for the MBA in Accounting, "whose students rank among the top ten in CPA Exam passage rates," or the MS in International Business program through which "many students go to Spain and Brazil."

FAU offers MBA classes online as well as on its campuses in Boca Raton, Jupiter, Port Saint Lucie, and two sites in Fort Lauderdale. While students appreciate that "the multiple campuses allow the school to draw students from a wide geographic area," some complain that "the school does not offer a full curriculum at any single location, so you frequently have to drive between campuses that range from 20 to 60 miles apart. Also, courses aren't always offered in the same order as the curriculum requires they are taken." MBAs' praise for the distance-learning program is more unequivocal; they love its convenience and describe it as "a good value." One participant writes, "For those of us in distance learning, the professors are very accommodating and available. I am very pleased with distance delivery."

Students here tell us that FAU professors "are recognized leaders in industry." Several "do consulting, expert-witness, or law-enforcement work outside of the classroom," while others "are solid professors from northern schools that have come to retire in South Florida." One student reports, "Many of my professors have outstanding multidisciplinary knowledge and easiness in sharing it with the students." But another explains, "I come from a top-20 undergraduate school, so I've been disappointed in the ambition of some of the students, but the professors make up for that." Students also tell us that "classes are challenging and involved, and the cases are from real-world scenarios." As at many state schools, the administration "is a nightmare—not at all user-friendly."

Career and Placement

FAU's College of Business houses the Career Resources and Alumni Relations Center to provide undergraduates and graduate business students with "invaluable guidance with interviewing skills, resume preparation, locating employment opportunities, and locating internships." The office also compiles student resumes on a CD-ROM to be distributed to South Florida businesses. Graduate students have exclusive access to the Job Connection, an Internet-based notification system that alerts them to job postings that match their qualifications. FAU participates in a statewide job fair held in the autumn.

Student Life and Environment

FAU attracts students from "a variety of different backgrounds both in business and culture," with "many coming from fields other than business, such as health care, law, and government." There are also a number of freshly minted undergrads in the program. This "diversity of the student body gives students a chance to share different job experiences and look at the business world from many perspectives." International students appreciate that "colleagues are friendly and helpful, which is extremely important for those of us who are separated from family and friends. During my MBA program I have made many friends and I am sure that even after graduation I will be able to maintain good relationships with many of my colleagues."

NICOLE HAMMER, ASSISTANT DIRECTOR OF GRADUATE ADVISING
COB GRADUATE STUDENT PROGRAMS, FW-101, 777 GLADES ROAD, BOCA RATON, FL 33431 U.S.
PHONE: 561-297-2786 • FAX: 561-297-1315
E-MAIL: MBA@FAU.EDU • WEBSITE: WWW.BUSINESS.FAU.EDU

Because so many MBAs are part-time students with full-time jobs, "there is virtually no social activity on campus. It is a great school for students who are married, have children, or are already pursuing a career." One student explains, "The students are focused on getting home after class, since most have been working all day before class. The interaction is limited to what is necessary to get the work done, mostly. People are generally nice, but not very sociable unless they are part of some special group, like sports management or the like." Full-time students enjoy more opportunities to participate in the university community, and they take advantage of them. One writes, "The university gives all students a chance to participate in sport events, concerts, charity actions, religious organizations, and minority clubs. FAU also offers free access to self-defense classes, fitness classes, a gym, and a swimming pool."

Admissions

Admission to a FAU MBA program requires: an undergraduate degree with a GPA of at least 3.0 (on a four-point scale) for the final 60 semester hours of undergraduate course work from an accredited institution. In addition, international students whose first language is not English must also submit official score reports indicating a score of at least 600 on the TOEFL and at least 250 on the Test of Spoken English (TSE). All international applicants must submit Certification of Financial Responsibility and must provide translation and accredited evaluation of their undergraduate transcripts (the latter is necessary only if a grading system other than the American system was used at the degree-granting institution). For all applicants, letters of recommendation, a resume, an interview, and a personal statement are all optional. After undergraduate record and standardized test scores, work history is the most important factor in admissions decisions.

FINANCIAL FACTS

Annual tuition (in-state/ out-of-state)	$5,860/$21,921
Cost of books	$1,200

ADMISSIONS

Admissions Selectivity Rating	**78**
# of applications received	398
% applicants accepted	53
% acceptees attending	72
Average GMAT	520
Range of GMAT	470–580
Average GPA	3.33
TOEFL required of international students	Yes
Minimum TOEFL (paper/computer)	600/250
Application fee	$30
Regular application deadline	7/1
Regular notification	Rolling
Deferment available	Yes
Maximum length of deferment	Up to 1 year.
Transfer students accepted	Yes
Transfer application policy We transfer no more than 6 semester credit hours from an AACSB-accredited program.	
Non-fall admissions	Yes
Need-blind admissions	Yes

Applicants Also Look At

Florida International University, Florida State University, University of Central Florida, University of Florida, University of Michigan—Flint, University of South Florida.

EMPLOYMENT PROFILE	
Career Rating	73

FLORIDA GULF COAST UNIVERSITY
COLLEGE OF BUSINESS

GENERAL INFORMATION

Type of school	Public
Academic calendar	Semester

SURVEY SAYS . . .
Friendly students
Good peer network
Happy students
Solid preparation in:
General management
Teamwork
Doing business in a global economy

STUDENTS

Enrollment of parent institution	8,292
Enrollment of business school	134
% male/female	46/54
% out-of-state	11
% part-time	72
% minorities	41
% international	19
Average age at entry	28
Average years work experience at entry	5

ACADEMICS

Academic Experience Rating	**73**
Student/faculty ratio	3:1
Profs interesting rating	90
Profs accessible rating	77
% female faculty	28
% minority faculty	11

FINANCIAL FACTS

Annual tuition (in-state/ out-of-state)	$4,326/$18,523
Fees (in-state/ out-of-state)	$1,211/$1,873
Room & board (on-campus)	$7,740
% of students receiving aid	95
% of first-year students receiving aid	70
% of students receiving loans	40
% of students receiving grants	57
Average award package	$7,983
Average grant	$1,958
Average student loan debt	$5,746

Academics

Pragmatic concerns—location, affordability, convenience, and the ability to earn a degree quickly—motivate most who select the MBA program at Florida Gulf Coast University, a relatively new institution located two hours' south of Tampa Bay. This predominantly part-time program, which pursues "a clear mission to incorporate the global, national, and local business environment into the curriculum of our specific classes," represents a real bargain for native Floridians who, thanks to a well-developed distance-learning program, can benefit no matter where they live in the state.

FGCU was established in 1997, which means that "the school has new facilities with technology in most classrooms," a major plus in today's tech-driven business world. One student writes, "Technological savvy is important, and we maximize and leverage our position as a new school with new equipment to aid learning, communication, and feedback." The school has quickly developed a reputation among Sunshine State natives. As one put it, "I chose this school because I know that FGCU is going to be the next big university in Florida, and I want to be part of it."

The FGCU MBA "emphasizes the application of analytical, technical, and behavioral tools to solve organizational problems," with "a focus on teamwork and team building so students frequently work closely together." The program consists of 24 hours of foundation courses, 21 hours of core courses, and 9 hours of concentration courses. Students with solid business backgrounds or college transcripts deep in business courses may have some or all of their foundation courses waived. Concentrations are available in finance, general management, marketing, or information systems. There is also an Executive MBA option, which is a two-year lockstep program with a concentration available in real estate development. Or, students may choose to design their own interdisciplinary concentration.

MBAs praise the faculty at FGCU, telling us that professors "are very helpful. They bring a lot of experience and tips with them to the class." One MBA observes, "The generally small size of the program makes the professors very available." Students also appreciate that "FGCU has made a big commitment to online access, not only in distance learning but in having nearly all services online—registration, submitting homework (even for traditional classroom classes), the bookstore, class chat rooms, class-specific e-mail, etc." Although there are still a few bugs in the system, "time should help all of the programs and the campus to become more well-rounded. For being such a new school, FGCU should be commended for where they are now."

Career and Placement

All career services at Florida Gulf Coast University are provided by the school's Career Development Services Office, which assists undergraduates and graduate students in all areas. The office sponsors a variety of events throughout the year, including workshops, seminars, on-campus recruiting visits, and a career fair.

Because the school is relatively new—FGCU welcomed its first students in 1997—its alumni network is in the early stages of development with a major campaign under way to network alum. One student writes, "Over time I hope the university gets more national recognition to reward the staff for their efforts. As alumni become distributed through the national workforce, I hope for more national corporations to recruit from our student ranks."

ANA HILL, ADMISSIONS REGISTRAR OFFICER, GRADUATE ADMISSIONS
10501 FGCU BOULEVARD SOUTH, FORT MYERS, FL 33965 UNITED STATES
PHONE: 239-590-7908 • FAX: 239-590-7894
E-MAIL: GRADUATE@FGCU.EDU • WEBSITE: WWW.FGCU.EDU

Student Life and Environment

FGCU's location, "fifteen minutes from the Gulf of Mexico (Bonita Springs or Fort Myers Beach) in the center of a cypress swamp filled with wildlife," is regarded as one of the school's greatest assets. Students say, "You can't beat the quality of life in southwest Florida. It's still a fairly small town in a beautiful part of the country where it's warm and green all year with great beaches." Better still, the region is "a major growth area, with exciting opportunities for employment in the near future."

FGCU is growing right along with its surroundings. "During the past four years the student population has doubled at FGCU. There have been a number of buildings added," students report. While FGCU "is too young to have a major college sports presence, [the] student athletics program has excellent student athletes who are also great in academics." Greek life "is beginning to become established," and those who live on campus enjoy dorms "located on a lake with water sports (sailing, kayaking, and canoeing). There are always activities available either to the general population or through clubs."

Most students here, however, don't have much time for such diversions. Those who actually attend classes on campus—the school also serves a sizable distance-learning population—generally work full-time. Many have family obligations too, leaving little (make that zero) time for extracurriculars. One MBA explains, "Other than being in class, there really is no campus life for MBA students, as we all have regular full-time jobs, families, and we live scattered around the area in our own homes. Additionally, many of the classes are offered online, so sometimes your 'classmates' might be located in other countries. As for on campus classes, the students are friendly and laid back (this is southwest Florida after all!). But we all go our separate ways to our 'real' lives, home, and our families when class is over." FGCU MBAs "range from students who have just graduated from an undergraduate program to those who have been in the workforce for over 20 years." The types of professions in which these students work range from accounting and real estate to law and the service industry.

Admissions

Admission to the MBA program at FGCU is based on a combination of undergraduate GPA and GMAT scores. To be considered, applicants must have either (1) a minimum GPA of 3.0 for their final 60 credit hours of undergraduate work; or (2) a minimum GMAT score of 500; plus (3) a formula score of at least 1050 under the formula [(undergraduate GPA + 200) + GMAT score], with a minimum GMAT score of at least 400. International students must also submit TOEFL scores (minimum 550 written, 213 computerized). Students may apply for admission to either the Fall or Spring semester. Students may complete a maximum of nine credit hours of graduate-level courses before gaining official admission to the program.

ADMISSIONS	
Admissions Selectivity Rating	**65**
# of applications received	78
% applicants accepted	86
% acceptees attending	76
Average GMAT	500
Range of GMAT	440–550
Average GPA	3.09
TOEFL required of international students	Yes
Minimum TOEFL (paper/computer)	550/213
Application fee	$30
Regular application deadline	6/1
Regular notification	7/1
Deferment available	Yes
Maximum length of deferment	1 semester
Transfer students accepted	Yes
Transfer application policy 6 Credits maybe transfered of approved graduate level course work from a regionally-accredited institution.	
Non-fall admissions	Yes
Need-blind admissions	Yes

FLORIDA INTERNATIONAL UNIVERSITY
ALVIN H. CHAPMAN GRADUATE SCHOOL OF BUSINESS

GENERAL INFORMATION
Type of school   Public
Environment   Metropolis
Academic calendar   Varies

SURVEY SAYS . . .
Cutting-edge classes
Solid preparation in:
OperationsTeamwork
Doing business in a global economy

STUDENTS
Enrollment of parent
  institution   38,097
Enrollment of
  business school   1146
% male/female   55/45
% part-time   86
% minorities   76
% international   22
Average age at entry   30
Average years work
  experience at entry   7

ACADEMICS
Academic Experience Rating   93
Student/faculty ratio   10:1
Profs interesting rating   77
Profs accessible rating   84
% female faculty   30
% minority faculty   33

Joint Degrees
MBA/MSF (Master of Science in
Finance), MBA/MSMIS (Master of
Science in Management Information
Systems), MBA/JD (Jurisprudence
Doctorate), MBA/MALACS (Master
of Arts in Latin American and
Caribbean Studies).

Prominent Alumni
Carlos Alavrez, Mayor, Miami Dade
County; Juan Figuereo, president,
mergers and acquisitions, Wal-
Mart.; Ana Lopez-Blazquez, CEO,
Baptist Health Enterprises; Dennis
Klinger, vice president and chief
information officer, Florida Power &
Light Company; Carlos Migoya,
regional president, Wachovia.

Academics

As its name suggests, Florida International University fixes a steady gaze on global commerce through its Chapman Graduate School of Business. This is especially true for students in FIU's 1-year, full-time International MBA program, but each of the school's varied alternatives stresses international business in its curriculum, with a particular focus on Latin America and the Caribbean (two regions whose populations are well represented in the Miami area). FIU also emphasizes entrepreneurial studies and the development of technological know-how throughout its curriculum. "Overall, a business school student should expect to leave with a very thorough understanding of how changes in business units, companies, industries, and the greater economic ecosystem impact each other," one student says.

In addition to its International MBA program, FIU also offers a 20-month executive MBA featuring an integrated curriculum taught "in cohort format, two classes per quarter" and including a global business trip that provides networking opportunities with corporate leaders abroad; a 20-month professional MBA, with classes also held on Saturdays; a flexible evening MBA, which allows students to choose the number of classes they take per semester while also allowing for a concentration in entrepreneurship, marketing, international business, finance, human resource management, or management information systems; a downtown MBA, a concentrated 18-month program designed for busy professionals who want to study on a convenient schedule at a convenient location; and an MBA for public managers, created specifically to meet the needs of leaders in government and the nonprofit sector.

With all these choices, it is no wonder that students praise the convenience of obtaining an FIU MBA. They also love the relatively low cost of tuition, which, coupled with the "quality of the program," means a great return on investment. Students are uniform in their admiration for an "outstanding faculty" that "is clearly in tune with the theory and practice in their respective fields. They are well versed in international business and rely heavily on current events to stimulate class discussions and case studies, and they do a great job of incorporating advanced technologies into the program." While some here wish the school would "expand the areas of concentration to encompass such disciplines as corporate accounting," most would agree that "this school's strong emphasis on global business is much needed" when a student goes out into the business world.

Career and Placement

Chapman's Career Management Services office provides graduate students and alumni with counseling and placement assistance. The office works closely with the university's Career Services office to coordinate career fairs, on-campus interviews, and other career-related events. Students tell us that FIU's alumni network is large and very helpful.

Top employers of FIU MBAs (including currently employed students attending one of the part time programs) include: American Airlines, Anteon Corporation, Bajaj-Allianz, Bank of America, BAP Developers, Bayview Financial, Caterpillar, CIA, C.R. Bard, Deloitte Touche Tohmatsu, Enterprise Risk Management, Filesx, Florida International University, Halliburton, Humana, Interstate Container, ITESM USA, Microsoft Licensing, Morrison, Brown, Argiz & Farra LLP, Mr. Sake, Novartis, OBM International, Oracle, Paetec, PricewaterhouseCoopers, Proctor & Gamble, Protivity, Sears Holding Corporation, Smith Hanley, The Seminole Tribe, TracFone Wireless, United Motors of America, Wachovia, Weston Financials, Whirlpool Corporation.

PRISCILLA FERREIRA, SENIOR MANAGER, GRADUATE RECRUITING

11200 SOUTH WEST EIGHTH STREET, MARC 230, MIAMI, FL 33199 UNITED STATES

PHONE: 305-348-7398 • FAX: 310-348-3497

E-MAIL: CHAPMAN@FIU.EDU • WEBSITE: BUSINESS.FIU.EDU

Student Life and Environment

Full-time students extol FIU's campus life, telling us that "the Student Government Association at FIU involves all its students, including graduate students, and it's a great environment to learn excellent communication and interpersonal skills." Part-timers, however, tell us that they "are not really involved in any type of campus-life organizations or events." Full-timers and part-timers alike agree that academic life "fosters a very collegial environment. This works very well to create an atmosphere of learning."

FIU's student body "represents a truly international class, with students coming from many different countries. It is great experience to be a part of such a student body." Students include "businesspeople with different industrial backgrounds, different cultures, and with a lot of experience in their respective industries." The programs "have people from both corporate American and from the public sector, and they bring different strengths to the table." They are typically "amicable and are always putting maximum effort," making them "great people to be friends with."

Admissions

Admissions requirements to FIU's MBA programs vary somewhat from program to program. As a general rule, students with the best combination of grade point average (GPA), applicable test scores, and pertinent work experience who also meet specific program requirements will have the first opportunity to enter the programs, according to the school's website. Applicants to the school's popular International MBA program must submit the following materials: an official copy of an undergraduate transcript, with a GPA of at least 3.0 in upper-division course work strongly preferred, official proof of undergraduate degree; a current resume; a personal statement; and an official GMAT or GRE score report. In addition to the above documents, international students whose primary language is not English must also provide an official score report for the TOEFL (minimum score: 550, paper-based test; 213, computer-based test) or the IELTS (minimum score: 6.3 overall). They must also submit their transcripts to a translation agency, to be forwarded to FIU, and they must provide the following documents: Declaration of Certification of Finances (DCF); a bank letter; a sponsor letter if applicable; and an F-1 transfer if they already have an F-1 Visa.

FINANCIAL FACTS

Annual tuition (in-state/ out-of-state)	$27,500/$31,500
Cost of books	$1,800
Room & board (on/off-campus)	$12,000/$18,000
% of students receiving aid	91
% of first-year students receiving aid	91
% of students receiving loans	45
% of students receiving grants	6
Average award package	$16,350
Average grant	$5,000
Average student loan debt	$20,000

ADMISSIONS

Admissions Selectivity Rating	92
# of applications received	1,970
% applicants accepted	51
% acceptees attending	75
Average GMAT	539
Range of GMAT	420–710
Average GPA	3.28
TOEFL required of international students	Yes
Minimum TOEFL (paper/computer)	550/213
Application fee	$30
Regular application deadline	Rolling
Regular notification	Rolling
Deferment available	Yes
Maximum length of deferment	1 year
Transfer students accepted	Yes
Transfer application policy	

A student may receive permission to transfer up to 6 semester hours of graduate credit towards his or her degree program if the courses were taken at the graduate level at an-accredited college or university, the courses were not introductory or "survey" in nature, the student earned grades of "B" or higher in the courses, the courses are judged by the department chair, college dean, graduate school dean and program manager to be relevant to the student's degree program, the courses were not core courses, the credits were not used toward another degree.

Non-fall admissions	Yes
Need-blind admissions	Yes

Applicants Also Look At

Florida State U., U. of Florida, U. of Miami, U. of South Carolina.

EMPLOYMENT PROFILE

Career Rating	67	Grads Employed by Function	%	Avg. Salary
Primary Source of Full-time Job Acceptances		Finance/Accounting	20	$71,667
School-facilitated activities	8 (50%)	Human Resources	7	$50,000
Graduate-facilitated activities	7 (44%)	Marketing/Sales	33	$51,600
Unknown	1 (6%)	Consulting	20	$61,000
Average base starting salary	$60,333	General Management	13	$52,500
Percent employed	18	**Top Employer Hiring Grads**		
		Bank of America.		

FLORIDA STATE UNIVERSITY
COLLEGE OF BUSINESS

GENERAL INFORMATION

Type of school	Public
Environment	City
Academic calendar	Semester

SURVEY SAYS . . .
Happy students
Smart classrooms
Solid preparation in:
Finance
Presentation skills
Computer skills

STUDENTS

Enrollment of parent institution	38,000
Enrollment of business school	180
% male/female	90/10
% out-of-state	12
% part-time	77
% minorities	8
% international	5
Average age at entry	26
Average years work experience at entry	3

ACADEMICS

Academic Experience Rating	**87**
Student/faculty ratio	30:1
Profs interesting rating	97
Profs accessible rating	78
% female faculty	13
% minority faculty	3

Joint Degrees
JD/MBA 4 years.

Prominent Alumni
Gary Rogers, president and CEO, GE Plastics; Craig Wardlaw, executive vice president and CIO, Bank of America; Craig Ramsey, partner, Accenture; Chuck Hardwick, senior vice president, Pfizer.

Academics

"Florida State University's MBA program is comparatively small," which students tell us "has many advantages." One student reports, "Every person within the admissions and administrative offices knows each student's name and a little about each person. We say 'hello' in the halls and their doors are never closed. They assist each student not only with academic affairs and support but also with personal issues if needed." The small size of the program also means that "professors are easily accessible to help with any questions or concerns that may arise. The size of the program also allows them to act on their concern for the progress of the students." On the downside, "as a smaller program, they don't receive much national recognition."

For most of the school's current students, national recognition is not their main concern anyway. They are mostly local and predominantly part-time, looking to advance in jobs they already hold or make an upward move within the local job market. What students here generally want most is affordability, convenience, and a solid reputation within the state. FSU scores big on all three counts. A low, in-state tuition suits most MBAs' budgets, while a selection of part-time and full-time options presents an unusually wide range of choices for a program of this size. This all adds up to make an "MBA program that is a hidden treasure waiting to be discovered." Both the full-time program and the part-time program on the main campus in Tallahassee offer concentrations in finance and marketing and supply-chain management. Part-time programs at branch campuses, "though completely served by the faculty of the main campus, offer only general MBAs. There is no real area of concentration offered because electives are inconsistent." The school also offers an online MBA that students can complete "from anywhere in the world." The online program allows for a general MBA, as well as concentrations in hospitality administration and real estate finance and analysis.

Career and Placement

Even though FSU's MBA program is small and largely part-time, the school maintains a separate career services office for graduate students in business. It also sponsors a mentoring program that "connects protégés with mentors who can share their experience and wisdom concerning general business leadership skills, professional success factors, management skills, team building, and communication skills," according to the school's website.

Employers most likely to hire FSU MBAs include Raytheon, Harris, and BB&T. The school reports that 33 percent of its graduates find work in operations (average salary $70,000), 25 percent find work in finance ($42,500), and 17 percent in marketing ($51,250).

Student Life and Environment

Students love FSU's "amazing, beautiful campus" with its "enthusiastic students and diligent professors." They also love hometown Tallahassee, which they describe as "a small town, but big enough to have malls and good restaurants. It's also close to the beach, which is great." Those interested in government careers should find plenty to interest them here, as "Tallahassee is a very political city with thousands of state employees, providing a unique opportunity to take advantage of many state employment positions."

LISA BEVERLY, ADMISSIONS DIRECTOR
GRADUATE PROGRAMS, COLLEGE OF BUSINESS, FSU TALLAHASSEE, FL 32306-1110 UNITED STATES
PHONE: 850-644-6458 • FAX: 850-644-0588
E-MAIL: GRADPROG@COB.FSU.EDU • WEBSITE: WWW.COB.FSU.EDU/GRAD

The mostly part-time students here "usually attend evening classes twice a week and meet with small groups outside of class whenever we can. That's about it for campus involvement." Full-timers get more involved in the life of the university, which of course includes "outstanding athletics programs. The FSU football and baseball teams are constantly in the national championship race, so it makes for a very exciting sports atmosphere." One student writes, "The best time is during football season when students can get to know each other at tailgates and other events." Another claims that for students here, "the nightlife is second to none. There's nothing like going to Bullwinkle's after a tough exam!"

FSU MBAs tell us the school runs "a smooth operation" all around. They enjoy "a friendly atmosphere that allows for positive group cohesiveness during teamwork exercises." Students benefit from each others' "diverse backgrounds. We have people who have just graduated from undergraduate programs, people returning to school after a few years of work experience, and people with previous experience in the military. Overall, we have a very tight-knit group of students." Students speculate that their classmates have, "on average, about five years of work experience."

Admissions

The Admissions Office at Florida State University requires all of the following from applicants to its MBA program: official copies of transcripts for all postsecondary academic work; an official GMAT score report; three letters of recommendation from former professors and/or employers; a resume; and a personal statement. Students must have proficiency working with PCs. International students whose first language is not English must also submit an official score report for the TOEFL (minimum score of 600 paper-based test or 250 computer-based test required). All test scores must be no more than five years old. The school lists the following programs designed to increase recruitment of underrepresented and disadvantaged students: the FAMU Feeder Program, FAMU Graduate & Professional Days, GradQuest, MBA Advantage, Minority Student Orientation Program, Leslie Wilson Assistantships, the Delores Auzenne Minority Fellowship, and the University Fellowship.

FINANCIAL FACTS

Annual tuition (in-state/ out-of-state)	$9,600/$36,153
Cost of books	$5,750
Room & board (on/off-campus)	$13,000/$15,000
% of students receiving aid	32
% of first-year students receiving aid	32
% of students receiving grants	28
Average award package	$10,000
Average grant	$2,500

ADMISSIONS

Admissions Selectivity Rating	87
# of applications received	476
% applicants accepted	44
% acceptees attending	85
Average GMAT	550
Range of GMAT	500–600
Average GPA	3.43
TOEFL required of international students	Yes
Minimum TOEFL (paper/computer)	600/250
Application fee	$30
Regular application deadline	2/1
Regular notification	Rolling
Deferment available	Yes
Maximum length of deferment	1 year
Transfer students accepted	Yes
Transfer application policy Transfer applicants must complete the same application process as all other applicants.	
Non-fall admissions	Yes
Need-blind admissions	Yes

Applicants Also Look At

University of Florida, University of North Florida, University of South Florida.

EMPLOYMENT PROFILE		
Career Rating	60*	**Top 5 Employers Hiring Grads**
		Wachovia; U.S. Staffing; CSX Corporation; Harris; Avaya.

FORDHAM UNIVERSITY
GRADUATE SCHOOL OF BUSINESS ADMINISTRATION

Academics

With top-dog competitors like Columbia University and NYU just a short subway ride away from its Manhattan campus, Fordham's Graduate School of Business Administration has quite a crowd to elbow its way through in order to get the attention it deserves. The school faces a "catch-22": Located anywhere else in the country, Fordham's program would be much better known and much more highly regarded. But at the same time, if it were located anywhere else it couldn't piggyback on the world's business center or the faculties of its competitors, from which it sometimes draws adjunct professors.

Students at Fordham recognize that they have a good thing going, and they have faith that the rest of the world will soon catch on. The school already has a solid reputation in accounting and tax. Its finance department enjoys "a strong reputation on Wall Street," and for good reason: "Professors in Finance are like the drill sergeants in the Marines. They make you work, and they make you think. It is all very practical. They touch on theory here and there, but mostly help you to understand why you need to know this, and then you learn it inside and out. They are also very open to questions. They never force you to just accept that this is the way it is done." Fordham also boasts "the only communications and media management concentration in New York City," a program that sets students up for careers with the city's many broadcast giants.

Fordham caters to part-time students with a "great, flexible schedule" that "allows students to switch between full- and part-time attendance just by taking more or fewer classes. Other schools require you to withdraw and reapply; you don't have to go through that process here." Students who live or work in Westchester County may wish to take advantage of the program's satellite campus in Tarrytown, at which all required courses and select electives are offered. The many full-time employed students here appreciate these conveniences. As one student explains, "The greatest strength of the school is the flexibility it offers. It has core courses and a minimum number of credits to be taken, but you can choose which core courses you want to start with and with what professors. You can also take some elective courses in the first year. It allows you to do internships outside of the summer months because you can regulate your class hours yourself, and there are many evening classes."

Career and Placement

The Fordham MBA Career Services Office provides placement and counseling to the school's business graduate students. The office benefits greatly from the school's location in a world finance center; one student observes, "Although not a Top 10 school—yet— Fordham still attracts some of the top 200 businesses located in the New York metro area to recruit for employment." Even so, students are aware that their student body is at best the third choice of most big recruiters in New York. One MBA writes, "Honestly, campus recruitment is difficult. Top companies do not invest enough money in recruiting the very talented, best, and brightest students at Fordham." The perception that "career services and a larger, better-equipped staff for career services are needed" does not help matters though the school is enhancing career services and training for students. On a positive note, "the school is currently getting more involved with the alumni," which should improve networking opportunities. Full-timers also benefit from their interactions with part-time students, "most of whom work for prestigious companies in New York City. Networking with the part-time students can lead to jobs and internships."

Cynthia Perez, Director
33 West 60th Street, 4th Floor, New York, NY 10023 United States
Phone: 212-636-6200 • Fax: 212-636-7076
E-mail: admissionsgb@fordham.edu • Website: www.bnet.fordham.edu

Student Life and Environment

Life in Fordham's MBA program "is very social, with Thursday happy hours every week where you can meet full-time and part-time students and network. There are also many opportunities to join clubs and actively participate in the many activities arranged by the different clubs. You don't have time to do everything!" The school's Lincoln Center location means that fine dining and upscale shopping are just outside the school's doors. One student notes, "We're in the heart of New York City, just off of Central Park at Lincoln Center. It's a great place to enjoy the spring and summer weather. Catching up in Central Park on a Wi-Fi-enabled computer is definitely one of the perks."

About the only criticism of Fordham's facilities is that MBAs feel a little crowded out by other students. One MBA observes, "They need to separate the graduate business school from the other graduate schools located on the campus. The law school feels separate, but the business school shares many resources with both undergraduate and other graduate programs. A graduate business lounge and special study areas within the library that facilitate discussion groups would really help."

Admissions

Admission to the Fordham MBA program is competitive. Applicants must submit all of the following materials: a completed application, either hard copy or online; copies of all postsecondary transcripts; an official GMAT score report; two letters of recommendation, preferably from current supervisors, managers, clients, and/or coworkers; a personal statement of length 500 to 1,000 words; and a current resume. International applicants whose first language is not English must also submit an official TOEFL score report. Interviews are not required, but can be granted at the applicant's request. Interview availability is limited; those wishing to interview are encouraged to make their request early in the admissions process. The median GMAT score among admitted students is 600 in the full-time program, 575 in the part-time program.

FINANCIAL FACTS

Annual tuition	$32,775
Fees	$444
Cost of books	$1,040
Average grant	$3,000

ADMISSIONS

Admissions Selectivity Rating	82
# of applications received	1,000
% applicants accepted	65
% acceptees attending	60
Average GMAT	600
Range of GMAT	540–670
Average GPA	3.15
TOEFL required of international students	Yes
Minimum TOEFL (paper/computer)	600/250/100
Application fee	$65
Regular application deadline	6/1
Regular notification	Rolling
Deferment available	Yes
Maximum length of deferment	1 year
Transfer students accepted	Yes
Transfer application policy ACCSB-accredited school; prerequisite and core courses can be waived based on course work taken at other institution.	
Non-fall admissions	Yes
Need-blind admissions	Yes

Applicants Also Look At

Boston University, City University of New York—Baruch College, Columbia University, New York University, Pace University, Rutgers, The State University of New Jersey, St. John's University.

EMPLOYMENT PROFILE

Career Rating	83	Grads Employed by Function	%	Avg. Salary
Primary Source of Full-time Job Acceptances		Finance/Accounting	32	$100,000
Percent employed	80	Human Resources	2	$72,000
		Marketing/Sales	27	$130,000
		MIS	4	$72,500
		Operations/Production	3	$105,000
		Strategic Planning	2	$103,000
		Consulting	4	$95,000
		Communications	6	$75,000
		General Management	7	$85,000
		Nonprofit	1	$72,000

Top 5 Employers Hiring Grads

Citigroup; Ernst & Young; Bear Stearns; Microsoft; Dannon, Inc.

FRANCIS MARION UNIVERSITY
SCHOOL OF BUSINESS

Academics

The School of Business at South Carolina's Francis Marion University offers a "convenient" MBA program "scheduled in the evening to accommodate working students." Since FMU is a state school, it does so at a price that doesn't break the bank.

This small school—one of the smallest state universities to earn AACSB accreditation, according to the university view book—affords "plenty of good one-on-one time with teachers" to its almost exclusively part-time student body. FMU offers both a general MBA and an MBA with a concentration in Health Management. The former is designed to serve the general business population of the Pee Dee region and beyond; the latter is directed toward individuals currently employed in the health care field and/or those with backgrounds in health care. The Health Management Degree is delivered to FMU students through online classes and resources.

All FMU MBAs must complete courses in accounting for management control, managerial economics, financial theory and applications, management science and statistics, marketing, and finance. Students in the general MBA program must also complete classes in financial accounting, information systems, international business, production management, entrepreneurship, and strategic management. Students pursuing a health concentration must also complete classes in health policy, health economics, health care delivery systems, financial management for health care organizations, and health law and risk management. Students in health management may also take three hours of elective course work. At the conclusion of the program, students must pass comprehensive final examinations covering 10 of 12 functions.

MBAs tell us that the program meets their needs, although some feel that "there is too much busywork" and others complain that "some classes are too easy, more suitable to undergraduates than MBAs." One student suggests, "Tailor the program to the real jobs graduates will get." Many also feel that "the school needs to offer more and a wider variety of MBA classes." Most, however, tell us that the convenience and cost of the degree are strong positives.

Career and Placement

FMU's MBA program is too small to support career services dedicated exclusively to its students. MBAs receive career assistance from the university's Office of Career Development, which serves undergraduates and graduates in all divisions. Students here also benefit from an active Alumni Association, whose newest chapter is the MBA Alumni Chapter.

BEN KYER, DIRECTOR
BOX 100547, FLORENCE, SC 29501-0547 UNITED STATES
PHONE: 843-661-1436 • FAX: 843-661-1432
E-MAIL: ALPHA1@FMARION.EDU • WEBSITE: ALPHA1.FMARION.EDU

ADMISSIONS	
Admissions Selectivity Rating	**62**
# of applications received	33
% applicants accepted	85
% acceptees attending	93
Average GMAT	400
Average GPA	3
TOEFL required of international students	Yes
Minimum TOEFL (paper/computer)	550/213
Application fee	$25
Regular application deadline	Rolling
Regular notification	Rolling
Deferment available	Yes

Student Life and Environment

Life in the FMU MBA program "can be hectic," especially toward the end of the semester. "It seems like all projects and exams are due at the same time," writes one student. Most students are "intelligent and hardworking . . . professional adults trying to obtain a common goal" while juggling careers and family obligations along with their academic responsibilities. As a result, few participate in extracurricular activities.

To enhance campus life, FMU hosts regular artists and lecture series. The school also houses an art gallery that displays student and faculty work as well as traveling exhibitions, film series, a planetarium and observatory, concerts, and festivals. FMU's Patriots compete in Division II of the NCAA. Popular spectator sports include basketball, soccer, men's baseball, women's softball, and women's volleyball.

FMU is located just outside of Florence, SC, a city of 33,000 that offers movie theaters, malls, restaurants, a symphony orchestra, and professional hockey (the Pee Dee Pride skate in the East Coast Hockey League). The city is located at the intersections of I-95 and I-20, making travel in all four cardinal directions a snap. Columbia, Charleston, Myrtle Beach, and Fayetteville, NC, are all within 100 miles.

Admissions

Applicants to the FMU MBA program must submit a completed application; official transcripts for all postsecondary academic work, in a sealed envelope addressed to the applicant from the awarding school; official GMAT scores; two letters of recommendation; and a personal statement of purpose. All materials must be delivered to the school in a single envelope or package. In addition, international applicants must submit official TOEFL scores and a Confidential Financial Statement form demonstrating their ability to pay all expenses related to an FMU MBA. All successful applicants meet the following minimum guidelines: a score greater than 950 under the formula [(undergraduate GPA × 200) + GMAT score] or a score greater than 1000 under the formula [(GPA for final 60 hours of undergraduates work × 200) + GMAT score]. Applicants with non-business undergraduate degrees are generally required to complete the business foundation sequence prior to beginning work on their MBA. The sequence is an 18-hour, 8-course curriculum covering the basics of accounting, economics, statistics, business law, management, information systems, finance, and marketing. Students with undergraduate business degrees typically have this requirement waived.

THE GEORGE WASHINGTON UNIVERSITY
SCHOOL OF BUSINESS

Academics

For many aspiring business school students, The George Washington University School of Business is simply too good to pass up. First, there's hometown Washington, DC, with its international flavor and job opportunities in "all three sectors," not to mention the school's "tremendous" diversity of academic options. In addition to a popular program in international business, GW offers concentration options in environmental management, science management, tourism and entertainment management, and an "increasingly popular" real estate and urban development specialization. Joint-degrees with the law school and Elliott School of International Affairs provide another powerful draw.

"Teamwork during the first year is a priority," and entering MBA students are challenged by the cohort-oriented core curriculum emphasizing principles in general management. Second-year students have the opportunity to select a specialization and choose from a broad set of electives whose "breadth and depth" are universally appreciated. This means that prospective GW students should anticipate exposure to a wide variety of courses, such as Energy Management, Management of the Acute Care Hospital, Sports Law, and Business Representation and Lobbying, many of which would not even be available at most b-schools. Second-year students also complete a capstone course, Strategy Formulation and Implementation, which deals with the developing world and culminates in a lengthy team report on environmental strategic management.

Students say that professors at GW "are feast or famine," noting that "a few are spectacular" and "always accessible," while others appear not to "care about their students or classes and are much more concerned with their own work." Luckily, "The small size of the program results in individual attention from the faculty and administration." While some students take a dim view of the administration ("Politics rule the place, and it is hard to get [the] proper attention the full-time MBA program deserves"), they also appreciate some of its upsides, such as "supportive" funding of "academic extracurricular activities such as business case competitions." Students also love the "much-needed and appreciated" "new business building" on campus, which "drastically improved the quality of facilities and technology for teaching the MBA program."

Career and Placement

The F. David Fowler Career Center "was totally revamped" recently, and most students are ecstatic about the changes. "The school hired professional consultants, and they are absolutely fantastic!" says one student. "I can't say enough about the advisors or the resources they provide!" Another student is disappointed that there is now only "one Career Center for business school undergrads and grads," and says that "faculty in specific departments" and "connections with alumni" are "much more helpful in sharing opportunities."

Fortunately, "Employers love GW and GW students," and "Many GW grads are working in the field in DC." While nearly half of grads go into consulting and finance, GW is also something of a feeder school for the public sector, sending 13 percent of its graduates into government positions. More than a tenth accept positions in the nonprofit sector. Top recruiters on campus include BearingPoint, U.S. government agencies, the World Bank, Friedman Billings Ramsey, Freddie Mac, BB&T, Nextel Communications, International Finance Corporation, Riggs Bank, and the National Committee for Quality Assurance.

Student Life and Environment

You "can't beat" GW's "ideal location" in downtown DC, which gives students "access to all the resources of the greater Washington, DC area. This includes cultural events like plays

VALERIA BELLAGAMBA, DIRECTOR, DATA AND ENROLLMENT MANAGEMENT
2201 G STREET NW, SUITE #550, WASHINGTON, DC 20052 UNITED STATES
PHONE: 202-994-7710 • FAX: 202-994-3571
E-MAIL: GOSBGRAD@GWU.EDU • WEBSITE: WWW.BUSINESS.GWU.EDU

and concerts, speakers, and social events." The school's location also provides an "outstanding environment to get internship or work at international organizations, NGOs, government, or other outstanding firms." The school's "very diverse" community includes "many international and minority students," who represent "a wealth of culture [and] ideas." The first-year curriculum's cohort setup "fosters a sense of unity" among GW students, who call their peers "driven, motivated," and "always willing to help one another." "I loved the feeling of community at GW," says one student. Another student concurs: "It is small enough so I am known or recognized by program faculty and students, but large enough that everyone doesn't know everyone else's business." "Students and alumni are extremely involved and helpful in academic and club events," and students appreciate that they "are able to be very entrepreneurial in starting clubs and hosting panels." On "Thursday night, we have IPOs (informal public outings) [in which] people from school gather for drinks and a good time." Students complain, however, that the MBA Association "must keep in mind [that] some students can't afford $10 beers and $20 cover charges for IPOs."

Admissions

Recently admitted MBA students at The George Washington University had an average GMAT score of 625 and 5 years of full-time work experience. As at most b-schools, applicants straight out of college face tough obstacles when it comes to the admissions process and to fitting in among their peers, but some do overcome these obstacles. GW does not accept 3-year degrees; to be accepted, grads of such programs must earn 2-year master's degrees.

By offering some merit scholarships and endowed scholarships for which international students are eligible, GW flouts the b-school convention of bleeding students dry financially. Many students, both domestic and international, cited generous scholarships as a deciding factor in their choice of GW.

FINANCIAL FACTS

Annual tuition	$29,670
Fees	$30
Cost of books	$2,530
Room & board (off-campus)	$16,380
% of students receiving aid	75
% of first-year students receiving aid	40
% of students receiving loans	50
Average award package	$25,000
Average grant	$10,000
Average student loan debt	$42,254

ADMISSIONS

Admissions Selectivity Rating	**96**
# of applications received	1,064
% applicants accepted	34
% acceptees attending	89
Average GMAT	625
Range of GMAT	570–710
Average GPA	3.6
TOEFL required of international students	Yes
Minimum TOEFL (paper/computer)	600/250
Application fee	$60
Regular application deadline	4/1
Regular notification	Rolling
Deferment available	Yes
Maximum length of deferment	1 year
Transfer students accepted	Yes
Transfer application policy Standard application procedures.	
Non-fall admissions	Yes
Need-blind admissions	Yes

Applicants Also Look At

Boston College, Boston University, Georgetown University, New York University, Thunderbird, University of Maryland, Vanderbilt University.

EMPLOYMENT PROFILE			
Career Rating	**85**	**Grads Employed by Function**	**% Avg. Salary**
Primary Source of Full-time Job Acceptances		Finance/Accounting	31 $68,333
Average base starting salary	$72,000	Human Resources	2 NR
Percent employed	86	Marketing/Sales	12 $57,000
		Operations/Production	7 $70,000
		Consulting	36 $74,000
		General Management	7 $59,000
		Other	5 $53,000

GEORGETOWN UNIVERSITY
MCDONOUGH SCHOOL OF BUSINESS

GENERAL INFORMATION
Type of school   Private
Affiliation   Roman Catholic-Jesuit
Environment   Metropolis
Academic calendar   Module

SURVEY SAYS . . .
Students love Washington, DC
Friendly students
Good peer network
Helpful alumni
Solid preparation in:
Doing business in a global economy

STUDENTS
Enrollment of parent institution	13,652
Enrollment of business school	470
% male/female	64/36
% minorities	10
% international	30
Average age at entry	28
Average years work experience at entry	5

ACADEMICS
Academic Experience Rating	**90**
Student/faculty ratio	7:1
Profs interesting rating	83
Profs accessible rating	94
% female faculty	32
% minority faculty	16

Joint Degrees
MBA/MSFS 3 years, MBA/MA (physics) 3 years, MBA/JD 4 years, MBA/MPP 3 years, MBA/MD 5 years, MBA/PhD (physics) 5 years.

Academics

Offering "a diverse global environment in the world's greatest capital city," the McDonough School of Business at Georgetown University offers an MBA with a strong international focus bolstered by "its international enrollment" and the second-year Global Integrative Experience, a course that culminates in a mandatory 9-day, international consulting experience. The school's location in the nation's capital—a magnet for diplomats and international business reps—further enhances the school's global scope.

McDonough's "innovative curriculum" capitalizes on the university's many strengths by "integrating other elements of the Georgetown University, such as the Public Policy Institute and the School of Foreign Service," thereby exploiting an advantage to "merge public and private interests to create well-rounded, business-minded individuals." The MBA program also benefits from "access to Georgetown University-related activities, such as speakers and workshops," and a "highly responsive alumni" who are "very receptive to networking with MBA students."

McDonough's full-time program operates on a 6-week modular calendar, a system many here wish the school would abandon. Students tell us that "five classes crammed into 6-week modules is too much," not allowing students "to delve into course material." Another student agrees: "Many feel like I do, overwhelmed by the breadth and depth of the work that we must complete in 6 weeks." Students who would love to see an upgrade to facilities will not have to wait much longer; "a gorgeous brand-new building in the center of campus" will be dedicated to the business school in 2008. The school introduced a part-time evening program during the 2006–2007 academic year.

MBAs at Georgetown benefit from "small class sizes" because it "encourages a great deal of interaction." Also, students appreciate "a faculty that is very dedicated to teaching, which is clearly distinct from many schools that are more research focused." While international business is McDonough's greatest strength, it isn't its only standout discipline; students laud the "strong management" offerings and note that the school is "a hidden gem for investment banks." Students also appreciate the school's Jesuit underpinnings, which stress ethics, immersion in the liberal arts and philosophy, and the importance of community service.

Career and Placement

McDonough students have complained about career services in the past, but many now emphatically tell us that "there has been considerable improvement" in this area, and "Whereas there was a time when the Career Management Center could have stepped up its efforts, this is no longer the case." The addition of a new Dean and a new Director of Career Management sparked the transformation; today, "Career Management is very dedicated. The office is extremely helpful in providing advice and consultation. Furthermore, the quality of the companies and the job opportunities that are made available to students are outstanding."

Employers who most frequently hire McDonough graduates include: Citigroup, Booz Allen Hamilton, Credit Suisse, Merrill Lynch, AES, America Online, Lehman Brothers, International Finance Corporation (IFC), 3M, American Express Company, Avaya, Bank of New York, Deloitte Touche Tohmatsu, Ford Motor Company, and JPMorgan Chase.

MONICA GRAY, DIRECTOR OF ADMISSIONS
PO BOX 571148, WASHINGTON, DC 20057-1148 UNITED STATES
PHONE: 202-687-4200 • FAX: 202-687-7809
E-MAIL: MBA@GEORGETOWN.EDU • WEBSITE: WWW.MSB.EDU/PROSPECTIVE/GRADUATE/MBA

Student Life and Environment

"The workload is intense" at McDonough, with the module system rushing classes along to the point that "it can interfere with the internship/job search. Even so, students who are driven find ways to make it work." Because full-timers attend classes in four separate cohorts, "There isn't much opportunity for you to interact with the three-fourths of the class not in your own cohort," but the "Significant amounts of group work help foster teamwork skills and force people to deal with uncomfortable or unfamiliar situations within their cohorts." Students do get to interact with folks outside their cohorts through "a decent number of clubs and social activities."

Georgetown University is a hub of political and intellectual activity; its many schools host "lectures and activities . . . that are extremely interesting. There are many opportunities to attend lectures with prominent speakers, such as Kofi Anan, [the] President of Afghanistan, etc., who are visiting town." Washington, DC offers even greater diversions, with "many cultural outlets that are unique to DC such as restaurants, nightlife, a great zoo, and museums."

McDonough MBAs enjoy a "highly cooperative environment. Classmates are not at all competitive." The student body "is extremely diverse in both background and professional experience. Even a student without a strong business/financial background would feel comfortable studying here." Part-time evening students "tend to have full-time jobs. Many are married and have kids; they have absolutely no time to socialize."

Admissions

McDonough students report that "the admission process is smooth here because Georgetown likes to meet individually with each student." Applicants must submit all of the following materials: an application form (online application is preferred); a resume; a personal statement of affiliations, community contributions, and personal interests; three required essays; official transcripts for all postsecondary academic work; two evaluations, preferably from professional supervisors; and an official GMAT score report. Interviews are encouraged but are conducted only at the invitation of the school after December 15. International students must submit official score reports for the TOEFL or IELTS in addition to the above materials. McDonough requires a minimum of 2 years of post-collegiate professional experience (and prefers 3 or more) prior to admission.

FINANCIAL FACTS

Annual tuition	$35,328
Fees	$2,303
Cost of books	$2,134
Room & board (off-campus)	$13,000
% of students receiving aid	76
% of first-year students receiving aid	38
% of students receiving loans	80
% of students receiving grants	26
Average award package	$45,000
Average grant	$12,000
Average student loan debt	$58,000

ADMISSIONS

Admissions Selectivity Rating	91
# of applications received	1,515
% applicants accepted	41
% acceptees attending	36
Average GMAT	665
Range of GMAT	620–720
Average GPA	3.2
TOEFL required of international students	Yes
Minimum TOEFL (paper/computer)	600/250
Application fee	$140
Regular application deadline	2/9
Regular notification	3/29
Application Deadline/Notification	
Round 1:	12/1 / 1/25
Round 2:	2/9 / 3/29
Round 3:	4/20 / 5/24
Need-blind admissions	Yes

EMPLOYMENT PROFILE

Career Rating	90		
Primary Source of Full-time Job Acceptances		**Grads Employed by Function**	**% Avg. Salary**
School-facilitated activities	109 (67%)	Finance/Accounting	43 $91,089
Graduate-facilitated activities	53 (33%)	Human Resources	1 NR
Unknown	32	Marketing/Sales	19 $82,576
Average base starting salary	$87,985	Operations/Production	2 $84,333
Percent employed	89	Consulting	24 $90,185
		General Management	6 $91,055
		Other	3 $60,000

GEORGIA INSTITUTE OF TECHNOLOGY
COLLEGE OF MANAGEMENT

GENERAL INFORMATION

Type of school	Public
Environment	Metropolis
Academic calendar	Semester

SURVEY SAYS . . .
Students love Atlanta, GA
Friendly students
Happy students
Smart classrooms
Solid preparation in:
Operations
Quantitative skills

STUDENTS

Enrollment of parent institution	15,576
Enrollment of business school	140
% male/female	75/25
% out-of-state	37
% minorities	24
% international	24
Average age at entry	27
Average years work experience at entry	4

ACADEMICS

Academic Experience Rating	**92**
Profs interesting rating	79
Profs accessible rating	87
% female faculty	17

Joint Degrees
Dual degree programs with any Masters or PhD degree at Georgia Tech.

Prominent Alumni
David C. Garrett, Jr, retired chairman and CEO, Delta Airlines; George C., president and CEO, Federal Reserve Bank of Atlanta; Tom A. Fanning, executive vice president, CFO, The Southern Co.

Academics

As part of a university that is home to one of the best-known engineering schools in the United States, it's not surprising that the MBA program at Georgia Institute of Technology focuses on the quantitative aspects of business. During the first year of the program, students are required to take core courses in areas such as accounting and management, while the second year is taken up with concentrations within the business school or from other areas of the university. Full-time students participate in an internship between the first and second years of the program. Fifty-four credits are required for the MBA, with concentrations available in accounting, finance, information technology management, marketing, organizational behavior, operations management, strategic management within the business school. Dual-degree programs with any other subjects offered by the university is a popular option. Georgia Tech also offers an Executive Master of Science in Management of Technology, Global Executive MBA, Master of Science in Quantitative and Computational Finance, and courses leading to the PhD in Business. Institutes of Entrepreneurship, New Venture Development, and International Business allow for advanced study in those areas, and students may study abroad in Argentina, Brazil, China, Colombia, Denmark, France, Germany, Japan, Mexico, Netherlands, South Korea, Spain, and Turkey.

In Fall 2007, Georgia Tech began offering a part-time evening MBA program for the first time. It is expected to take 3 years to complete rather than the full-time program's 2 years, with students attending classes 2 nights a week. Course offerings and admissions standards are expected to be similar to those of the full-time day program.

Students are drawn to the emphasis on technology, and to the costs at Tech, which arelower than some comparable business schools in the South. "Georgia Tech's MBA program has the same quality as higher-ranked programs, and with a much better return on investment," students say. The school, which is "known for technology," offers "one of the best entrepreneurship opportunities in the country," with "strong operations and IT management programs," they add. The quality of teaching is generally well regarded, too, as is the administration. "The administration is student focused, the professors challenge you, and the academic experience helps because it mirrors the real business experience" at Georgia Tech. "Extremely knowledgeable and very helpful," professors make themselves available to all students. "I have sat down with professors I have never taken a class from to solicit their feedback on industry projects," one student tells us.

Career and Placement

The Jones Career Center offers MBA career-guide materials, job-bank databases, and participation in a nationwide interviewing consortium with 15 other business schools, as well as career fairs and assistance targeted to international students.

Atlanta's big-city locale is a plus for students in their job search, as are the "amazing" career services offered at the business school. "The location in the heart of Atlanta can't be beat in terms of access to companies," one student points out. Meanwhile, the staff at the Career Center "get outstanding companies to come to the school and really work to get you in front of any company you are pursing," another adds. "They will help you tremendously," one student sums up. Among the companies recruiting at Georgia Tech are Bank of America, BearingPoint, BellSouth, Delta Airlines, Microsoft, Siemens, Turner Broadcasting System, and The Home Depot.

Student Life and Environment

Most of Georgia Tech's MBA students have academic and professional backgrounds in engineering, the hard sciences, and business. Women outnumber the men in this program. While there are areas for improvement, students appreciate their classmates who "are fun, friendly, smart, and insightful. The size of the class makes it possible to really get to know them," and overall they are "supportive. I have learned just as much from my classmates as I have from my classes," says one student. Many would like to see better "alumni relations, [and more] domestic student geographical diversity" along with "better inclusion of spouses and children into school activities." As one student puts it, "I've heard some fellow students comment that it's not quite as family friendly as they might like since the majority of the students don't have kids (although many are married)," but at least students have taken it upon themselves to plan more activities that include significant others. Most students agree that there's a great camaraderie here. "Every student adds value, and no one is admitted just to improve numbers," says one satisfied student. "The learning occurs in and out of the classroom," and "It feels like we are a team, not competing against each other, but challenging ourselves to be better," says another. One sums up: "My classmates are open, personable people who truly try to help one another out. I feel as though our class is building the strong network that will last for years to come."

Admissions

GMAT scores, undergraduate GPA, work experience, and the results of a personal interview are factors than weigh most heavily with those who evaluate applicants for Georgia Tech's MBA program. Personal essays and recommendations are also important, with extracurricular activities carrying less weight. A class in business calculus is a required prerequisite for enrollment, and familiarity with probability theory is suggested as well. A TOEFL score of 550 is required of those whose first language is not English. In 2006, the average GMAT score of those admitted was 669, with a range of 630 to 710, and the average GPA was 3.41. Georgia Tech generally accepts around 40 percent of those who apply. Enrolling students average 3 and half years of work experience, with many coming from engineering backgrounds.

FINANCIAL FACTS

Annual tuition (in-state/ out-of-state)	$6,248/$24,994
Fees	$1,034
Cost of books	$1,400
Room & board	$12,000
% of students receiving grants	30
Average grant	$6,000
Average student loan debt	$16,000

ADMISSIONS

Admissions Selectivity Rating	95
# of applications received	292
% applicants accepted	39
% acceptees attending	66
Average GMAT	669
Range of GMAT	630–710
Average GPA	3.41
TOEFL required of international students	Yes
Minimum TOEFL (paper/computer)	600/250
Application fee	$50
International application fee	$50
Regular application deadline	3/15
Regular notification	Rolling
Deferment available	Yes
Maximum length of deferment	1 year
Need-blind admissions	Yes

Applicants Also Look At

Emory University, Indiana University—Bloomington, Purdue University, University of Maryland, The University of North Carolina at Chapel Hill, Vanderbilt University, Wake Forest University (evening MBA, Winston-Salem).

EMPLOYMENT PROFILE

Career Rating	90	Grads Employed by Function	%	Avg. Salary
Primary Source of Full-time Job Acceptances		Finance/Accounting	13	$65,000
School-facilitated activities	58%	Human Resources	2	NR
Graduate-facilitated activities	27%	Marketing/Sales	11	$72,500
Unknown	15%	MIS	14	$81,916
Percent employed	92	Operations/Production	16	$72,571
		Consulting	24	$89,350
		General Management	9	$91,000
		Other	11	$70,312

Top 5 Employers Hiring Grads
IBM; Honeywell; The Home Depot; PriceWaterhouse Coopers; GE.

GEORGIA SOUTHERN UNIVERSITY
COLLEGE OF BUSINESS ADMINISTRATION

GENERAL INFORMATION
Type of school	Public
Environment	Village
Academic calendar	Semester

SURVEY SAYS . . .
Happy students
Smart classrooms
Solid preparation in:
General management
Teamwork
Communication/interpersonal skills
Computer skills
Doing business in a global economy

STUDENTS
Enrollment of parent institution	16,425
Enrollment of business school	187
% male/female	59/41
% out-of-state	32
% part-time	57
% minorities	54
% international	25
Average age at entry	27

ACADEMICS
Academic Experience Rating	**75**
Student/faculty ratio	7:1
Profs interesting rating	85
Profs accessible rating	70
% female faculty	26
% minority faculty	7

Joint Degrees
MBA (with a concentration in accounting, health services administration, information systems, international business) 2 years.

Prominent Alumni
Dan Cathy, president/CEO, Chick-fil-A; James Kennedy, director, NASA John F. Kennedy Space Flight Center; Karl Peace, president, Biopharmaceutical Research Consultants; Steven Cowan, novelist; Tony Arata, singer/songwriter.

Academics

The College of Business Administration at Georgia Southern University serves a predominately local student population with a general MBA, as well as MBAs with concentrations in accounting, health services administration, information systems, and international business. A Master of Accounting Degree is also available, and students in our survey speak especially highly of the accountancy programs. The MAcc degree offers a concentration in forensic accounting.

Less than half of Georgia Southern's MBAs are full-time students; others attend part-time, usually on top of a full-time work schedule. Well aware of this noble act, the school works hard to accommodate the varied lifestyles of its students. One part-timer writes, "The administration at Georgia Southern has been very helpful. My schedule has been hectic, but they have worked with me to graduate in a timely manner." Many of the full-timers are students who "got their BAs here and just stuck around." One such student explains, "I completed my undergraduate degree at Georgia Southern, and when the MBA program started a concentration in Information Systems, I took the opportunity to continue my education in a field that I am very interested in."

Convenience, cost, and comfort are the three main reasons so many undergraduates choose to remain on at GSU. One student writes, "I love the faculty here. Because Georgia Southern is a teaching institution, the professors are very accessible and willing to help. They have time to work with students and to teach classes." Another notes, "There's no academic Darwinism here, no weed-out courses. Unlike other schools, GSU professors support and assist students, and seem genuinely interested in their success." Students also appreciate "that the quality of the courses offered is equivalent to those at larger business schools, but there is no 'big school mind-set.'" One drawback students point out is that "there are sometimes difficulties getting into classes. This is due to a sudden boom in business-school students. Currently, the student/professor ratio is fairly high."

Full-time students attend classes at GSU's Statesboro campuses. Part-timers may attend classes in Statesboro or Savannah, or they may participate in the distance-learning program by attending classes in Brunswick. A Web-exclusive collaborative MBA is offered in conjunction with five other schools in the University of Georgia system.

Career and Placement

Georgia Southern's small MBA program is served by a satellite office of the university's central Career Services Office. Many career-oriented events, such as workshops and recruitment events, serve the university at large rather than business students exclusively. According to the school's website, the COBA Satellite Office houses "literature on academic majors, career information . . . handouts and other resources to help prepare you for professional employment and graduate school."

Nearly 100 employers visit the Georgia Southern campus each year. Top employers of graduating MBAs include: Gulfstream Aerospace, Inc.; Memorial Medical Hospital; Great Dane Trucking, Inc.; and Sun Trust Bank.

Student Life and Environment

GSU's MBA program boasts "a highly diverse" student body. Students tell us that they "vary widely in terms of race, sex, and culture. Most are working in a related business field, but there are also students who have recently completed their undergraduate degrees and have no related experience to contribute. They range in ages between 23 and 53." More than 10 percent of the student body is international.

Dr. Michael McDonald, Graduate Program Director
PO Box 8050 Statesboro, GA 30460-8154 United States
Phone: 912-486-7240 • Fax: 912-486-7480
E-mail: gradschool@georgiasouthern.edu • Website: coba.georgiasouthern.edu/mba

With a small student body (and an even smaller full-time population), GSU lacks the makings of an active extracurricular scene. Even so, one student reports that "there are many different functions and activities to attend. For example, this year I attended an evening dinner that was directed at teaching students how to maintain etiquette in a professional setting. There were different companies that sponsored tables and either one or two representatives would also participate at each table." The school also hosts major-related organizations. Students tell us they feel "a lot of pressure from the faculty to achieve and to remain active in school-sponsored events. There are incentives (positive and negative) that encourage participation."

Hometown Statesboro "is a small town in southeast Georgia where the college and Wal-Mart are pretty much all that's going on. Because GSU is the attraction in Statesboro, life here is all about studying and working. Most people go to Savannah or Atlanta on weekends." At least it's good to know that "the area surrounding the campus is primarily geared toward serving the needs of students, producing a 'college town' atmosphere. The facilities provided (gyms, computer labs, student center, etc.) are of a quality usually only seen at much larger schools."

Admissions

Admission to the Georgia Southern MBA program is determined through the application of the formula [(undergraduate GPA × 200) + GMAT score]. A score of at least 1000 ensures admission. Applicants may receive provisional admission with a score between 950 and 1000, with an undergraduate GPA of at least 2.80, or with a GMAT score of at least 470. A minimum GMAT score of 430 is required for admission to the MBA or MAcc.

An alternate formula applies to students who do not qualify under the formula above but who excelled during their final two years of undergraduate work. This formula, called the upper-level formula, is [(undergraduate GPA for final 60 semester hours × 200) + GMAT score]. A score of at least 1050 qualifies. Students who have not taken the GMAT may also gain admission if their undergraduate GPA is at least 3.25, or their GPA for their final 60 semester hours is at least 3.5. Students in this category must submit an acceptable GMAT score by the time they complete their second graduate-level course.

FINANCIAL FACTS

Annual tuition (in-state/out-of-state)	$3,044/$12,172
Fees	$1,052
Cost of books	$1,000
Room & board (on/off-campus)	$6,500/$2,680
% of students receiving aid	75
% of first-year students receiving aid	74
% of students receiving loans	38
% of students receiving grants	59
Average award package	$9,930
Average grant	$5,864

ADMISSIONS

Admissions Selectivity Rating	70
# of applications received	95
% applicants accepted	77
% acceptees attending	79
Average GMAT	495
Range of GMAT	460–510
Average GPA	3.13
TOEFL required of international students	Yes
Minimum TOEFL (paper/computer)	530/213
Application fee	$50
Regular application deadline	6/1
Regular notification	7/1
Deferment available	Yes
Maximum length of deferment	1 year
Transfer students accepted	Yes
Transfer application policy	

No more than 6 semester hours of graduate credit may be transferred to a graduate program at Georgia Southern. Only grades of B or higher will be accepted for transfer.

Non-fall admissions	Yes
Need-blind admissions	Yes

Applicants Also Look At

Georgia State University, Kennesaw State University, University of Georgia.

GEORGIA STATE UNIVERSITY

J. MACK ROBINSON COLLEGE OF BUSINESS

GENERAL INFORMATION

Type of school	Public
Environment	Metropolis
Academic calendar	Semester

SURVEY SAYS . . .

Students love Atlanta, GA
Cutting-edge classes
Happy students
Smart classrooms
Solid preparation in:
Accounting

STUDENTS

Enrollment of parent institution	26,134
Enrollment of business school	1,099
% male/female	66/34
% part-time	67
% minorities	33
% international	21
Average age at entry	29
Average years work experience at entry	6

ACADEMICS

Academic Experience Rating	**81**
Student/faculty ratio	25:1
Profs interesting rating	82
Profs accessible rating	93
% female faculty	31
% minority faculty	21

Joint Degrees

MBA/JD Full-time 2 to 6 years to complete the JD degree and 8 years to complete the MBA degree, MBA/MHA 2.8 to 5 years to complete program.

Prominent Alumni

James E. Copeland, Deloitte Touche Tohmatsu; A.W. Bill Dahlberg, chairman, Mirant; Kenneth Lewis, chairman and CEO, Bank of America; Richard H. Lenny, chairman, Hershey Foods; Mackey McDonald, chairman, president and CEO, VF Corp.

Academics

Georgia State University offers four types of MBAs through its J. Mack Robinson College of Business: the Flexible MBA, a full-time or part-time program that allows students to begin during any semester and to schedule classes around other obligations; the Global Partners MBA, a full-time, 14-month program that includes six-week residencies in Paris and Rio, a two-week residency in China, three days in Washington, DC, and the remaining time in Atlanta and at an internship or field-experiment site; the Professional MBA, a 24-month, lockstep Thursday-and-Saturday program based on the Flexible MBA curriculum, for high-potential professionals with at least three years of management experience; and the Executive MBA, an 18-month, lockstep, Friday-and-Saturday program focusing on international business and leadership. The Executive MBA program is open only to applicants with at least seven years of work experience and a minimum of five years at the management level.

In all programs, students report that "professors at GSU are highly qualified. Many of them either work or have worked outside academia, giving them a much fuller understanding of business and the pressures students face. Additionally, the professors seem to be enthusiastic about teaching. They seem to genuinely enjoy class and stimulate class discussions." One student notes, "The top-quality instructors have enabled me to quickly turn business theory into real-world results for my employer." Students are especially high on the finance program, which they tell us is "super hard, but super good!" Programs in accounting and actuarial science also receive MBAs' praise. In all disciplines, students report that "the workload is challenging, but it all is very relevant," although a few students complain that "some of the case studies seem a little dated." In the best classes, professors "really focus on drawing course work right out of the *Wall Street Journal*. The professor never even touched the textbook. It was great, but I understand why everyone doesn't do it; it's a lot of additional work for the professor."

Career and Placement

The Office of Graduate Career Management (GCM) at GSU offers a full range of services, including career advising, career workshops, the career leader self-assessment service, assistance with internships, resume review, resume referral, alumni contacts, a career library, recruitment events, on-campus interviews, and online job databases. While students "would like to see some bigger names recruiting on campus, especially in banking," most agree that the GCM does a solid job serving a large clientele.

In 2004, the top 10 recruiters of GSU MBAs were: BB&T; Chick-fil-A; ChoicePoint; Cox Communications; GE Power Systems; KPMG International, LLP; PricewaterhouseCoopers; Radiant Systems; Reznick, Fedder & Silverman; and Wachovia. Three-tenths of recent graduates found work in accounting (average starting salary $58,000). About one in four found work in finance ($55,000); one in six was employed in marketing ($51,500).

Student Life and Environment

The MBAs at Georgia State are "mostly older students with more work experience. Many have families. All are very intelligent and hardworking." Most attend part-time while working full-time jobs and are "very willing to share job experiences that relate to classroom material. They talk a lot in class, which is helpful." "Many are international students," all of them full-timers. Because most students have substantial obligations

KARL ADAMS, SENIOR ACADEMIC ADVISOR
PO BOX 3988, ATLANTA, GA 30302-3988 UNITED STATES
PHONE: 404-463-4568 • FAX: 404-651-2721
E-MAIL: MASTERSADMISSIONS@GSU.EDU • WEBSITE: ROBINSON.GSU.EDU

outside school, "there is no real sense of a student body here. It's every wo/man for her/himself." One student writes, "I wish there is something that we could do to make life more communal, but given that so many attendees work, this is difficult. This is one of the drawbacks from going to part-time school. If I could do it over, I may have quit work and gone to school full-time. But on the other hand, I have continually been able to apply, in real-time, the things that I learn in school to my work. In retrospect, [this experience] has probably reinforced this work more than anything."

Students love hometown Atlanta, which "offers great resources" both for career opportunities and for fine living. The city is home to a number of *Fortune* 500 companies, including Coca-Cola, The Home Depot, and Delta Airlines. On campus, GSU's MBA Centers "are immaculate and well thought out in terms of their design to facilitate class discussion and student/teacher interaction."

Admissions

Applicants to GSU MBA programs must submit all of the following materials to the Office of Admissions: official copies of transcripts for all postsecondary academic work; an official GMAT score report; a resume (at least two years of full-time professional experience is preferred); and two personal essays. Letters of recommendation are not required but are considered for those candidates who submit them. International students must submit, in addition to the above materials, evidence of sufficient financial resources to fund their MBA studies; an independent evaluation of all academic transcripts for work completed abroad; and, for students whose first language is not English, an official score report for the TOEFL. International students are required to carry a full-time course load.

FINANCIAL FACTS

Annual tuition (in-state/ out-of-state)	$7,868/$28,532
Fees	$988
Cost of books	$1,200
Room & board	$11,060
% of students receiving aid	15
% of first-year students receiving aid	15
% of students receiving loans	11
% of students receiving grants	2
Average award package	$16,889
Average grant	$4,500
Average student loan debt	$35,667

ADMISSIONS

Admissions Selectivity Rating	**88**
# of applications received	373
% applicants accepted	54
% acceptees attending	79
Average GMAT	610
Range of GMAT	570–650
Average GPA	3.39
TOEFL required of international students	Yes
Minimum TOEFL (paper/computer)	610/255
Application fee	$50
International application fee	$50
Regular application deadline	5/1
Regular notification	6/15
Deferment available	Yes
Maximum length of deferment	2 semesters
Non-fall admissions	Yes
Need-blind admissions	Yes

Applicants Also Look At

City University of New York—Baruch College, Clark Atlanta University, Emory University, Georgia Institute of Technology, Kennesaw State University, University of Florida, University of Georgia.

EMPLOYMENT PROFILE

Career Rating	68	Grads Employed by Function	%	Avg. Salary
Primary Source of Full-time Job Acceptances		Finance/Accounting	50	$49,333
School-facilitated activities	5 (63%)	Marketing/Sales	12	NR
Graduate-facilitated activities	3 (37%)	Consulting	25	NR
		Other	12	$0

Top 5 Employers Hiring Grads

Deloitte Touche Tohmatsu; PricewaterhouseCoopers; Cherry, Bekaert and Holland; Equifax; Evergreen Management, Inc.

GONZAGA UNIVERSITY
GRADUATE SCHOOL OF BUSINESS

Academics

With its "Jesuit tradition in which ethics are strongly emphasized," Gonzaga University serves up a solid AACSB-accredited MBA to its predominantly part-time working professional student body. Accounting is among the school's strongest areas, as "Gonzaga has an excellent reputation for preparing students to take the CPA exam, of which the pass rate among Gonzaga students is high." Number-crunchers here may opt for an MAcc, an MBA with a concentration in accounting, or a combined MBA/MAcc. Gonzaga offers concentrations in finance, health care management, and marketing. In Fall 2005, concentrations in entrepreneurship, ethics, sports management and supply-chain management were added. Students may also opt to design an individualized concentration.

Gonzaga's MBA curriculum consists of 22 credits in core courses (11 two-credit classes) and 11 credits in electives, through which students may develop a concentration if they so desire. Students who did not major in business as undergraduates are typically required to complete a series of foundation requirements prior to beginning work on their MBA. Overall, students appreciate the program's "very integrated approach [and the] accessible teachers who are friendly and intelligent and have created a great learning environment." For the most part, students report that they find the professors and administration members "wonderful to work with." Some, however, complain about a "heavy emphasis on examination-based measurement. It can be too much like the undergraduate experience. There is little emphasis on writing papers and research, and thus little opportunity for creativity."

In the past, the MBA respondents to our survey saw improvements on the horizon, however, referring to some of the problems they encountered as mere "growing pains." Gonzaga's Graduate School of Business has experienced a dramatic increase in enrollment from 166 students in 2000 to 229 students in 2004. To ensure that quality was not sacrificed as a result of this growth, Gonzaga embarked on a major expansion to Jepson Center, added nine new professors, and expanded the curriculum to include eight areas of concentration. Class sizes remain small, and the program has maintained its reputation for high quality and flexibility. One MBA elaborates: "The administration of the university and the business school are both very forward-thinking. Both have been expanding and upgrading the programs at the school. I know that I am at a school that is continuing to grow and gain in national prominence."

Career and Placement

The Gonzaga Career Center and the School of Business Administration staff and faculty provide career counseling and placement services to MBAs here, including 301 seminars covering self-assessment, career planning, resume writing, and conducting a successful job search; mock interviews and interview critiques; on-campus recruiting and interviewing; a career resources library; alumni events; and internship placement assistance. Some would like to see "more internship" opportunities, but students have few complaints.

Employers of Gonzaga business graduates include Accenture, Bank of America, Boeing, Empire Health, Ernst & Young, Itron, KPMG, Nordstrom Corporate, Merrill Lynch, Microsoft, Nike, Pitney Bowes, Potlatch, Washington Trust, and Wells Fargo.

STACEY CHATMAN, GRADUATE PROGRAMS SPECIALIST FOR ADMISSIONS
502 EAST BOONE AVENUE, SPOKANE, WA 99528-0009 UNITED STATES
PHONE: 509-324-4622 • FAX: 509-323-5811
E-MAIL: CHATMAN@JEPSON.GONZAGA.EDU • WEBSITE: WWW.GONZAGA.EDU/MBA

Student Life and Environment

MBAs mention that there are two types of students in the Graduate School of Business: There are "those who graduated from GU as an undergrad; most of these students are straight out of the undergrad program. There are also those who are new to the university; most of them have work experience and are a few years older than the students who have their undergrad degree from GU." In general, "Students here are friendly and intelligent." There are a fair number of international MBAs, including "students from places like Nepal, China, the Ukraine, the UK, India, Lebanon, and Latin America." Women make up just under 40 percent of the student body. (One female respondent would like to see the school place a "greater emphasis on women in business.") Students call their fellow MBAs "warm, intelligent, [and] hardworking" and are quick to sing the praises of the "friendly" atmosphere at GU.

Life at GU is great for those who spend time around campus (though part-timers generally don't, as many work full-time). "There are all sorts of activities and club sports for students to participate in (including Young Republicans and Young Democrats clubs, philosophy clubs, business clubs, and sports teams in hockey, lacrosse, and much more)." Gonzaga's nationally ranked men's basketball team is the source of much GU student pride. One MBA writes, "Going to the games is fun, and it builds camaraderie within the student body." While "the curriculum is challenging, there is still plenty of free time to work or enjoy life outside of school," a fact of GU life that students appreciate. While a few report that they opted to pursue their degrees at GU because of the "Jesuit educator emphasis," most don't comment at all on the school's religious affiliation.

Admissions

Applicants to the MBA program at Gonzaga must submit two official copies of all post-secondary academic transcripts, official GMAT scores, two letters of recommendation, a professional resume, three short essays, and a completed application. International students must also submit official TOEFL scores (if English is not their first language) and a financial declaration form. Work experience is not required, "although the majority of students who enter the program have 4 or 5 years prior work experience." A minimum GMAT score of 500 is strongly preferred by the Admissions Committee.

FINANCIAL FACTS

Annual tuition	$11,055
Room & board	$8,250
% of students receiving aid	90
% of first-year students receiving aid	90
% of students receiving loans	30
% of students receiving grants	70
Average grant	$7,000
Average student loan debt	$10,404

ADMISSIONS

Admissions Selectivity Rating	**76**
# of applications received	143
% applicants accepted	81
% acceptees attending	87
Average GMAT	572
Range of GMAT	500–610
Average GPA	3.4
TOEFL required of international students	Yes
Minimum TOEFL (paper/computer)	570/230
Application fee	$45
Regular application deadline	Rolling
Regular notification	Rolling
Deferment available	Yes
Maximum length of deferment	4 years
Transfer students accepted	Yes
Transfer application policy	
Transcripts are evaluated to ensure that desired learning objectives have been fulfilled. Up to 6 credits can be transferred in.	
Non-fall admissions	Yes

Applicants Also Look At

Montana State University, Seattle Pacific University, Seattle University, University of Montana—Missoula, University of Portland, Washington State University, Willamette University.

EMPLOYMENT PROFILE

Career Rating	77	Grads Employed by Function	%	Avg. Salary
		Finance/Accounting	20	NR
		Human Resources	10	NR
		Marketing/Sales	10	NR
		MIS	5	NR
		Strategic Planning	5	NR
		Consulting	5	NR
		Entrepreneurship	5	NR
		General Management	10	NR
		Venture Capital	10	NR
		Other	5	NR
		Nonprofit	5	NR

GRAND VALLEY STATE UNIVERSITY
SEIDMAN COLLEGE OF BUSINESS

Academics

With a newly renovated campus, state-of-the-art facilities, and a solid regional reputation, the Grand Valley State University MBA program has quite a lot to offer its working-professional student body. MBAs here appreciate what they have, bragging that "technologically, the campus has no equal when it comes to wireless Internet access and computer resource availability." They also praise the "affordability" and "flexibility" of the program as well as the "quality of instruction."

Most students are part-timers, and thus take advantage of the aforementioned flexible scheduling options, which include evening and weekend courses delivered in seven- or 14-week modules. Students wishing to fast-track can complete the program in as few as 16 months. Most students here are from the area, and as a result, many are familiar with the local business leaders who "work with the school and take interest in the curriculum being offered. Their input also lends real-world examples to classroom material and theory." Students' work experiences similarly enrich the classroom experience.

Seidman professors "are often active in the business world, maintaining the edge to pass on to the students." Their involvement with more than 400 local and national companies generates opportunities for students to work on projects in area organizations under the supervision of the faculty and establish "connections with the West Michigan business community." One MBA reports, "I have had accounting instructors who were former Securities and Exchange Commission executives. My global competitiveness class was taught by a former director of the World Bank. My auditing professor was an adjunct professor who also happened to be a Partner at BDO Seidman. Overall, of the 11 classes taken to earn my MBA, nine were taught by PhDs and two of those PhDs were also CPAs." Many students single out faculty in finance and accounting for praise; of the latter, they note, "The Seidman School of Business has always had a very high pass rate on the CPA exam. I was able to pass in two attempts after having been out of school for a number of years and then brushing up through the Becker Review. The accounting courses definitely gave me a good background to draw from."

Career and Placement

Career placement and counseling services are provided through the university's Career Services Office, which offers a variety of online resources, seminars and workshops, individual counseling services, and recruitment events. "The Business School office has been incredible in supporting student goals," and someone is "always available."

Student Life and Environment

The Seidman MBA program is housed in the DeVos Center on GVSU's downtown Grand Rapids campus, which students tell us is "nearly new and maintained with incredible focus and attention." Assets include "beautiful courtyards and facilities to accommodate a person who wants to relax, [and a] great new high-tech library." Although a few express past parking woes, some also praise the "new parking garage with lots of spots." The DeVos Center also features "many open gathering spaces, which increase the experiences of interacting with other students inside and outside of the business school," as well as "great technology, with free wireless Internet for laptops and PDAs." Students report that "classrooms are all up-to-date with equipment and lighting," and mention that they "are invited to use the technology for presentations and lectures during many activities."

CLAUDIA BAJEMA, GRADUATE BUSINESS PROGRAMS DIRECTOR
401 WEST FULTON GRAND RAPIDS, MI 49504 UNITED STATES
PHONE: 616-331-7400 • FAX: 616-331-7389
E-MAIL: GO2GVMBA@GVSU.EDU • WEBSITE: WWW.GVSU.EDU/BUSINESS

MBAs enjoy "strong ties with the balance of the university to keep students in touch with the rest of college life." Students tell us, "Strong athletic programs also serve as an avenue to bring students together for a common, energetic experience" Even so, most students here spend little extracurricular time on campus. One explains, "The MBA program is pretty nonsocial, as most people are working full-time. The undergrad campus has a more active life." Some would like to see more of "a community for graduate students," while others are happy with the status quo.

"GVSU pulls from a fairly wide geographic area for business graduate students, and many commute 40 minutes to an hour for classes and library use. With strong family commitments, many students return home after class, but there is networking between students that live in similar areas, which is very helpful." The post-work environment can be very comforting as "occasionally a portion of the class will gather at a local establishment following class or an exam." Students represent "a diverse base coming from various sectors, including teaching, accounting, health sciences, engineering, and law. The students have strong ties, ranging from local, small businesses to international conglomerates, located here in the area." They are "career oriented, driven, experienced people who are often balancing an active family, social, and business life."

Admissions

Completed applications to the Grand Valley State MBA program include official transcripts for all previous postsecondary academic work, an essay describing the applicant's goals and objectives, GMAT scores, and, for non-native English speakers, TOEFL scores. Students who have previously completed graduate programs may apply for a waiver of the GMAT requirement. Students who have not previously completed course work in core business disciplines may be admitted to the program conditionally, pending completion of foundation courses in financial and managerial accounting, data analysis, finance, business law, macro- and micro-economics, marketing, and operations. Students can place out of foundation courses through school-administered examinations.

FINANCIAL FACTS

Annual tuition (in-state/ out-of-state)	$5,850/$10,800
Fees	$90
Cost of books	$1,500
Room & board (on/off-campus)	$6,500/$5,000

ADMISSIONS

Admissions Selectivity Rating	**76**
# of applications received	146
% applicants accepted	82
% acceptees attending	85
Average GMAT	566
Range of GMAT	520–680
Average GPA	3.3
TOEFL required of International students	Yes
Minimum TOEFL (paper/computer)	550/213
Application fee	$30
Regular application deadline	12/1
Regular notification	Rolling
Deferment available	Yes
Maximum length of deferment	1 year
Transfer students accepted	Yes
Transfer application policy Students may transfer up to 9 credits with B or better at discretion of program director.	
Non-fall admissions	Yes
Need-blind admissions	Yes

Applicants Also Look At
Western Michigan University.

HARVARD UNIVERSITY
HARVARD BUSINESS SCHOOL

Academics

A "tried-and-true General Management focus with no concentrations or majors and no published GPAs," a "pedagogical approach that relies strongly on the case method," and most of all "a reputation as the best business program in the country" make Harvard Business School one of the top prizes in the MBA admissions sweepstakes. Applicants lucky enough to gain admission here rarely decide to go elsewhere.

The school's full-time-only program is relatively large; approximately 900 students enter the program each year. Students tell us, "Despite its large size, the school feels surprisingly small" thanks to a combination of factors. First is an administration that "could be a role model for any enterprise. This place is very well run." Second is the subdivision of classes into smaller sections of 90 students, who together attack approximately 500 case studies during their two years here. Finally, there's a faculty that "is obviously committed to excelling at teaching and developing relationships with the students. Each faculty member loves being here, regardless of whether they are a superstar or not, and that makes a difference. Faculty guide discussion well and enliven the classroom."

The case method predominates at Harvard; explains one student, "I sit in my section of 90 students every day and debate business topics. My section mates come from all walks of life and all of them are incredibly successful. I prepare my 13 cases per week so that I can contribute to this environment." Students love the approach, although they point out that "the case method is not as great for quantitative courses such as finance." Numerous field-study classes supplement the program, especially during the second year, which is devoted to elective study. School-wide initiatives—combinations of interdisciplinary classes, field study, contests, and club work—encourage research and provide added focus in the areas of social enterprise, entrepreneurship, global issues, and leadership.

Ultimately, though, HBS' strength resides in the quality of its instructors. One student notes, "HBS is one of the few schools where a large part of the professor's evaluation is based on classroom teaching. The professors at HBS are wonderful teachers and take great interest in their students." As one first-year puts it, "If first semester is representative of the whole experience, I'll be a happy grad. My accounting professor managed to make accounting my favorite class (seems unimaginable!), and I'll definitely take whatever he teaches during the second year of elective courses."

Career and Placement

Harvard Business School hardly needs a Career Development Center, any more than Rolls Royce needs salesmen to move its cars. The school maintains a robust career services office all the same, providing a full range of counseling and internship- and career-placement services. Over 800 companies pay recruiting visits to the HBS campus each year in search of full-time hires; another 400 come looking for summer interns. Nearly half of all MBAs remain on the East Coast after graduation, about half of whom take jobs in New York City. Twenty percent find international placements; half work in Europe and about a quarter work in Asia.

Student Life and Environment

Life at HBS "is as hectic as you want it to be." One student writes, "My life is pretty much moving along at breakneck speed. I wouldn't want it any other way because the school offers an incredible amount and array of activities, from volunteer consulting to running conferences." Because Harvard University is a magnet for innovative and prestigious thinkers in all disciplines, "This place is like a candy store for a five-year-old; you want to eat a lot more than what's good for you. You can spend all your time on studies, lectures from academics/politicians from all over the world, visiting business leaders, conferences, sports, or the nightlife. A 60-hour day would be appropriate."

Students generally manage to find the time to enjoy "a very social and outgoing environment" at HBS. One married student writes, "Most weekends my husband and I have a choice: the 'college scene' where we can hit up the Harvard or Central Square bars with the singles, or the 'married scene' where we have dinner, play goofy board games, and drink with our 'couple friends.' Either can be a great escape from the other, and both are always a lot of fun!" Close relationships are easy to forge here, as "the section system means you have 89 close friends in the program, which makes learning and being here fun. It also means in the business world there will always be 89 incredibly smart, connected people who will go to bat for me no matter what."

The population of this program is, unsurprisingly, exceptional. As one MBA explains, "The quality of people here is unlike anything I've experienced. For the first time in my adult life, I'm surrounded by people whose interests and abilities fascinate and inspire me. All religions, nationalities, cultures, and sexual orientations exist here, happily, and together. I think Boston cultivates this kind of 'meshing of all thoughts' in such a way that everyone is comfortable, and everyone learns. The city and the school are both comfortable in their own skins, and the students take on that characteristic here."

Admissions

Applicants to Harvard Business School must submit a "complete HBS application portfolio, including personal essays, academics transcripts, and three letters of recommendation." In addition, students must provide scores from the GMAT, and applicants from non-English-speaking countries must submit scores for either the TOEFL or the IELTS (scores must be no more than two years old). Applications must be submitted online. Academic ability, leadership experience, and unique personal characteristics all figure prominently into the admissions decision. The school's viewbook notes that "because our MBA curriculum is fast-paced and rigorously analytical, we strongly encourage all applicants to complete introductory courses in quantitative subjects such as accounting, finance, and economics before coming to HBS. For some candidates, we may make admission contingent upon their completing such courses before they enroll." Good luck!

FINANCIAL FACTS

Annual tuition	$39,600
Fees	$2,606
Cost of books	$3,850
% of students receiving aid	71
% of first-year students receiving aid	71
% of students receiving loans	66
% of students receiving grants	52
Average award package	$51,900
Average grant	$19,200
Average student loan debt	$83,310

ADMISSIONS

Admissions Selectivity Rating	99
# of applications received	6,716
% applicants accepted	15
% acceptees attending	90
TOEFL required of international students	Yes
Minimum TOEFL (computer)	267
Application fee	$235
Application Deadline/Notification	
Round 1:	10/12 / 1/17
Round 2:	1/3 / 3/28
Round 3:	3/7 / 5/9
Need-blind admissions	Yes

EMPLOYMENT PROFILE

Career Rating	99	Grads Employed by Function	%	Avg. Salary
Primary Source of Full-time Job Acceptances		Finance/Accounting	41	NR
Average base starting salary	$100,000	Marketing/Sales	13	NR
Percent employed	98	Strategic Planning	5	NR
		Consulting	22	NR
		General Management	12	NR
		Other	2	NR

HEC Montreal
MBA Program

Academics

HEC Montreal, the "little school that could," has truly ascended the ranks of international MBA programs in recent years. A relatively obscure school until the 1990s, HEC Montreal launched a curriculum overhaul midway through the decade that yielded dramatic results: Within a decade, the school had become the first North American institution to earn accreditation from EQUIS (the European Foundation for Management Development), AMBA (the Association of MBAs of the United Kingdom), and AACSB International.

HEC Montreal offers both a full-time and a part-time MBA program. International students are eligible for the full-time program only; this program, aptly named 'the Intensive MBA,' "is really a full two-year program condensed into 53 weeks. If you are motivated and disciplined, then you will succeed in this environment." Students warn that "it is very intensive and there is a solid workload throughout the program, with very few breaks in between." Cohort-based education and an emphasis on team projects helps students develop an esprit de corps to weather the program's challenges; explains one MBA, "We, all 180 students, take all the same classes for the first six months, which makes for great understanding amongst ourselves. We all know what the others are going through regarding workload and projects." While most here praise the full-time program, a few complain that "sometimes the pace is a bit too fast and we don't have time to sit back and reflect on what we've learned. Also, the pace does not allow much time for extracurricular seminars." Students may choose between French-only instruction and English-only instruction; roughly 60 percent of students opt for the English-only program.

The part-time program at HEC Montreal, called the MBA in Action, takes three years to complete. The curricula for the full-time and part-time programs are virtually identical; the major difference is that part-time students are exempted from the requirement to complete a field project. Part-timers warn that "occasionally we get professors who are low-level outsiders rather than the mostly experienced professors who teach the entire full-time program, and some of them are not such great teachers." They also point out that the program's team-learning format is hampered by the fact that "lots of students drop out or don't show up for meetings because of work obligations. Not enough effort is put into restoring team spirit when that happens." Students in both programs agree that the school "makes good use of classroom technology" and that "teaching methods tend to be very participative and pragmatic."

Career and Placement

The HEC Montreal Career Centre provides career and placement services to undergraduates, graduates, and alumni. According to the school viewbook, "The Centre is well known for its personalized approach, and provides constant support for students as well as recent and past graduates: helping them prepare for interviews and draw up their résumés, providing information on the labor market, job-search strategies, conducting psychometric assessments (academic guidance and skills profiling), and career planning, assessment and redirection."

Companies that recruit on campus include Accenture, Air Canada, Bell Canada, Bombardier, CIBC World Markets, Cirque du Soleil, Deloitte Touche Tohmatsu, Emirates National Oil Company, Ernst & Young, GE Commercial Finance, IBM, Johnson & Johnson, L'Oreal, Matrox, McKinsey & Company, Merck Frosst, Pratt & Whitney, Procter & Gamble, RBC Financial Group, Scotiabank, TD Financial Group, Toyota, UPS.

IVANA BONADUCE, IVANA.BONADUCE@HEC.CA, STUDENT ADVISOR
3000 CHEMIN DE LA COTE STE-CATHERINE, MONTREAL, QC H3T 2A7 CANADA
PHONE: 514-340-6957 • FAX: 514-340-5640
E-MAIL: MBA@HEC.CA • WEBSITE: WWW.HEC.CA

Student Life and Environment

The MBA program at HEC Montreal is "very well located in Montreal, near the subway with access to all the Université de Montreal complex for other classes, if wanted." Facilities include "a new building that is aesthetically very nice, with lots of services for students," and "the biggest business library on campus." Students appreciate that the school is situated on "a nice, open space and that everything you need—food, lodging, subway, sports—is available on site." The gym facilities, students tell us, "are considered to be the best in Montreal."

For both full-time and part-time students, "the compressed six-week course terms (including exam period) makes the work pace fast and heavy," so "there is not necessarily a lot of time for social activities. However, the student association does try very hard to coordinate activities for" students, including "cinq à sept happy hours, a Quebec tradition that is alive and well at HEC Montreal. Every other Thursday, the student association takes over the campus lounge and we blow off a little steam! The parties are so much fun that the undergraduates try to sneak in, no doubt attracted by the dancing on the bars!" One student observes, "Our MBA association aims to involve all students in deciding what types of activities are provided. They concentrate on providing social activities that encourage the integration of English- and French-speaking students, as well as the international student community of HEC Montreal. Events such as the Magic of the Lanterns in the Botanical Gardens and an International Potluck dinner are perfect ways of opening up cultural barriers and introducing a broader, more international environment, where students are encouraged to share experiences and learn from each other."

Admissions

Applicants to HEC Montreal must hold a baccalaureate earned "with a satisfactory average." Students must also demonstrate "at least two years of relevant full-time work experience" subsequent to completing undergraduate study. Applications must also include an official score report for the GMAT and two letters of recommendation (at least one from an employer). Non-native English speakers applying to the English-only program must pass the HECTOPE business English test (administered by HEC Montreal) or submit scores for either the TOEFL or IELTS. Non-native French speakers applying to the French-only program must complete the Test de français international (an ETS-administered exam). Applicants who are not citizens of Canada must obtain a certificat d'acceptation du Québec (C.A.Q.) and a document attesting to their right to reside in Canada (Student Authorization or Ministerial Permit). The school recommends that accepted students apply for these documents as soon as they receive confirmation of their admission to the program.

FINANCIAL FACTS

Annual tuition (in-state/ out-of-state)	$3,700/$18,000
Cost of books	$1,700
Room & board (off-campus)	$15,000
% of students receiving grants	73
Average grant	$4,160

ADMISSIONS

Admissions Selectivity Rating	79
# of applications received	421
% applicants accepted	63
% acceptees attending	66
Average GMAT	613
Range of GMAT	530–710
TOEFL required of international students	Yes
Minimum TOEFL (paper/computer)	600/250
Application fee	$65
Regular application deadline	3/15
Regular notification	4/1
Deferment available	Yes
Maximum length of deferment	1 year
Need-blind admissions	Yes

EMPLOYMENT PROFILE

Career Rating	81	Grads Employed by Function	%	Avg. Salary
Primary Source of Full-time Job Acceptances		Finance/Accounting	15	$58,000
School-facilitated activities	30%	Marketing/Sales	21	$48,300
Graduate-facilitated activities	50%	MIS	11	$72,400
Unknown	20%	Operations/Production	8	$57,200
Percent employed	77	Consulting	20	$58,400
		General Management	14	$58,700
		Other	11	$62,400

Top 5 Employers Hiring Grads

Deloitte Touche Tohmatsu; Air Canada; Bell Canada; TD Bank Financial Group; L'Oreal Canada.

HEC School of Management—Paris
HEC MBA Program

GENERAL INFORMATION
Type of school	Public
Academic calendar	Quarter

SURVEY SAYS . . .
Friendly students
Good peer network
Happy students
Solid preparation in:
Marketing
Accounting
Teamwork

STUDENTS
Enrollment of parent institution	2,700
Enrollment of business school	201
% male/female	72/28
% international	80
Average age at entry	30
Average years work experience at entry	6

ACADEMICS
Academic Experience Rating	**98**
Student/faculty ratio	4:1
Profs interesting rating	82
Profs accessible rating	69
% female faculty	15

Joint Degrees
Nine double-degree programs are available as an option. These include NYU Stern School of Business, the London School of Economics, The Fletcher School of Law and Diplomacy, Tsinghua (SEM), The Chinese University of Hong Kong, FGV (Brazil), ITESM (Mexico), UTDT (Argentina) and PUC (Chile). Study periods vary between programs.

Prominent Alumni
Sidney Taurel, president and CEO, Eli Lilly and Co; Fumiaki Maeda, managing director, Mitsubishi Bank; Daniel Bernard, CEO, Carrefour; Pierre Danon, senior advisor, JP Morgan; Pascal Cagni, vice president, Apple.

Academics

"The sense of community [and] the focus on creating international managers [are] amazing" at the HEC School of Management, whose full-time, 16-month MBA program is offered in both an English-only and bilingual format. Because of its generalist approach, the HEC MBA "enables students to understand and participate in all functions of a business." Students tell us that "there is heavy emphasis on general skills as well as the human, personal interactions that are necessary in order to be successful in business, particularly in a multicultural and multilingual environment." Arithmophobes, take note: "Because it focuses on creating general management skills, the school does not focus on developing in-depth quantitative skills."

At HEC, "teamwork is stressed among the students, faculty, and administration to build a memorable MBA family, [especially] during the early phases of the program. The latter part of the course is more individual." The classroom atmosphere, students agree, is convivial. Students report, "The academic workload and class schedule are challenging but workable" and appreciate the duration of the program, which "is neither too short nor too long."

HEC instructors are "a diversified group of professors, with differing talents and competencies. The differentiation in styles and backgrounds is as apparent in the faculty as in the student body, which adds to the international experience of adapting to new cultures and environments." Students note, "Open communication and willingness to cooperate is a strong forte among all faculty, [and] professors' contacts in the business community make the classroom interactive." HEC's name carries considerable weight in Europe, allowing the school to "attract excellent speakers." One student writes, "During my 15 months of class, HEC had the pleasure of welcoming the prime minister, some of his team of ministers, and CEOs of global and French companies (Airbus, Nissan, Renault, Dassault)."

Of course, the school's location also means that the school has "a French public-service-type administration," which catches more than a few foreign students off-guard. American students, in particular, have little patience for the "completely rigid, bureaucratic, and inefficient structure [that] needs to be completely overhauled." Some, however, see a silver lining to this dark cloud: "The advantage is that you get a much better understanding of French society than you would if there was a non-French-style administration."

Career and Placement

The Career Development Office at HEC provides counseling services, workshops, and seminars in job-search skills and interview techniques, access to online self-assessment instruments, contact to the school's 25,000-plus alumni worldwide, four major job fairs per year, and "privileged access to firms actively supporting HEC." The office sponsors regular corporate presentations and recruitment programs that bring over 200 employers to campus each year. Thirty-eight percent of all non-European members of the class of 2004 found employment in Europe; 88 percent found positions "of international scope." Nearly half used their degree to change both the sector and function of their careers.

Students see both strengths and weaknesses in the career office. One writes, "If you want to work in France, the name of HEC will help you for life. This is a fantastic networking opportunity in France, and it is growing on the international scale." However, many feel that career services are "currently too focused on French companies or French divisions of international companies. Efforts need to be made to improve the relationship with other international companies." Employers most likely to hire HEC MBAs include

Isabelle Cota, Director of Student Services and Development
One rue de la Liberation Jouy-en-Josas cedex, 78351 France
Phone: 011 33 0)139 67 95 46 • Fax: 011 33 0)139 67 74 65
E-mail: admissionmba@hec.fr • Website: www.mba.hec.edu

Barclays Capital; BT Retail; Hilti; Johnson & Johnson; L'Oréal; Michelin; Nestlé; and Société Générale.

Student Life and Environment

The first term at HEC is grueling, students tell us, and during that initial period, "life centers around the campus and the MBA building. Students are getting involved in one or two extracurriculars that are important to them, but it is difficult to get involved in much more because of the workload." Things ease up afterwards, allowing students a little more time to enjoy all that the campus and Paris have to offer. Throughout the school year, "there are never two days without an event organized by one of the clubs, either a professional club or sports club." Every Wednesday night brings "Happy Hour at the Piano Bar, a chilled-out bar with wood floors, glass walls that overlook campus, candles, and good beer." Beer? Not for everyone. Many here "love kicking back after a hard day's work and enjoying a glass of Bordeaux."

HEC "offers the advantage of being part of a larger institution and as such is not insulated within its own self-absorbed environment," which students appreciate. They also praise the campus, which is "located in a beautiful forest, not far from Versailles and Paris." The 250-acre campus provides plenty of space to kick the soccer ball (i.e., football) around. The campus also features tennis courts, basketball courts, a climbing wall, and a nine-hole golf course. The proximity to Paris "adds a cultural and artistic flavor to the experience."

HEC's student body is 80 percent international, representing over 40 countries. The setting is "incredibly international [and] intellectually stimulating. Everyone has unique and insightful insights into not just business, but politics, society, and culture."

Admissions

HEC requires the following of applicants: an electronically filed application form; official undergraduate transcripts, transcripts for all graduate work; GMAT scores (and TOEFL scores, where appropriate); two letters of recommendation; four passport-size photos and a copy of one's passport or birth certificate; and the application fee. An interview is required as its results are given serious consideration in the admissions decision. The school's literature states, "The admissions process for the HEC MBA program is a rigorous one. The MBA experience is an interactive one, and each participant is called upon to contribute to the learning process through his or her personal and professional experience." As a result, past academic, professional, and personal experience are all important factors. The ability to perform well in teamwork situations is also considered essential.

FINANCIAL FACTS

Annual tuition	$46,000
Cost of books	$1,100
Room & board	
(on/off-campus)	$15,000/$20,000
% of students receiving aid	70
% of students receiving loans	60
% of students receiving grants	33
Average grant	$9,000

ADMISSIONS

Admissions Selectivity Rating	97
# of applications received	888
% applicants accepted	21
% acceptees attending	58
Average GMAT	660
Range of GMAT	590–750
Average GPA	3.65
TOEFL required of	
international students	Yes
Minimum TOEFL	
(paper/computer)	600/250
Application fee	$100
International application fee	$100
Regular application deadline	4/27
Regular notification	5/31
Deferment available	Yes
Maximum length of	
deferment	1 year
Non-fall admissions	Yes
Need-blind admissions	Yes

Applicants Also Look At
IMD(International Institute for Management Development), INSEAD, London Business School, New York University.

EMPLOYMENT PROFILE

Career Rating	81	Grads Employed by Function	%	Avg. Salary
Primary Source of Full-time Job Acceptances		Finance/Accounting	15	$94,475
School-facilitated activities	36 (35%)	Human Resources	1	NR
Graduate-facilitated activities	47 (46%)	Marketing/Sales	22	$94,097
Unknown	19 (19%)	MIS	3	NR
Average base starting salary	$93,838	Operations/Production	3	NR
Percent employed	16	Consulting	27	$90,934
		General Management	23	$97,149
		Other	6	NR

Top 5 Employers Hiring Grads
McKinsey & Company; Areva; Capgemini; PWC; Société Générale.

HHL—Leipzig Graduate School of Management

GENERAL INFORMATION

Type of school	Private
Academic calendar	Term

SURVEY SAYS . . .

Students love Leipzig, Germany
Friendly students
Happy students
Solid preparation in:
Teamwork
Doing business in a global economy
Entrepreneurial studies

STUDENTS

Enrollment of business school	45
% male/female	80/20
% part-time	50
% international	68
Average age at entry	31
Average years work experience at entry	7

ACADEMICS

Academic Experience Rating	**92**
Student/faculty ratio	5:1
Profs interesting rating	97
Profs accessible rating	66
% female faculty	25

Prominent Alumni

Jack Artman, manager, MandA;
Bodo Marr, manager, MandA;
Thomas Ludwig, investment banking professional.

Academics

HHL—Leipzig Graduate School of Management offers German and international business students an appealing mix of a well-established name and modern innovation. Founded in 1898, HHL is the oldest business school in Germany, and its students benefit from its deserved reputation as a solid training ground for European managers. The MBA program, however, is relatively new, having only graduated its first class in 2001. Because the program is still in its nascent stages, students tell us, "It is striving to achieve more in the global ranking, so they really make an effort, as opposed to many established schools that expect their reputation to work for them." Since the program runs its course in a scant 15 months, it also appeals to the cost-conscious and to those in a hurry to climb the corporate ladder of success.

The HHL curriculum is divided into three categories. Core courses cover the basics in management; this segment of the program is particularly well-suited to the German students "whose prior academic training was not focused on business but rather was in the natural sciences, humanities, or social sciences" and whom the Admissions Office targets. Specialization courses in accounting, finance, marketing, business organization, and strategy allow students to hone a particular skill set. Students tell us that specializations in finance, marketing, and strategy "are the tops, especially finance and marketing with very well-known professors who publish a lot in their field and are on boards of corporations." Application courses in such areas as entrepreneurship, innovation management, and corporate-government relations keep students abreast of contemporary issues in the business world.

HHL professors "can be contacted almost 24 hours a day," and "those who are comfortable with English can even be fun in classes." Internships, study abroad, and independent study options are all available. A high-quality education at a reasonable price is cited by students as one of the main reasons they chose the school.

Career and Placement

HHL MBAs report with satisfaction that "one of the big strengths of this program is its excellent contact to companies. Almost all top companies in consulting, banking, and industry come for presentation and recruiting. Companies react surprisingly positively when saying that you are from our school." One student comments, "Concerning placement, there is a huge database of direct contact people. Rather than applying over a 'website' one can contact people or alumni. This helps to stay away from the crowd that applies over recruiting websites of companies."

According to HHL, the school "has a record of placing graduates with prominent international firms—including Arthur Andersen, BASF, Bayer, BGG, Bertelsmann, BDO, Booz Allen and Hamilton, Boston Consulting Group, Daimler-Chrysler, Deutsche Bank, E.ON, Ernst & Young, Ford, Henkel, Kirch-Gruppe, KPMG International, McKinsey & Company, Nestlé, PricewaterhouseCoopers, Procter & Gamble, Siemens, Tui, and Volkswagen—as well as with many German 'Mittelstand' companies." Other companies that recruit on campus include A.T. Kearney, Accenture, Allianz AG, BMW, Citibank, FairAd, Goldman Sachs, Horváth & Partner, Lufthansa Cargo, OnVista, Porsche, Sachsen LB, and Wellington.

PETRA SPANKA, EXECUTIVE DIRECTOR
JAHNALLEE 59, LEIPZIG, 04109 GERMANY
PHONE: 01149341- 9851734 • FAX: 01149341- 9851 731
E-MAIL: PETRA.SPANKA@HHL.DE • WEBSITE: WWW.HHL.DE

Student Life and Environment

An accelerated academic schedule at HHL means that "life is somewhat focused on the courses. There is a lot of pre-work and post-work to do for almost all courses. Most courses integrate a high amount of applied case studies and group work. In some weeks/months the balance of studying and doing other things is bad (i.e., a lot of studying)." One student notes, "Classes in finance are especially tough, but teach a lot that you need later in respective jobs." Even so, there is some time leftover to socialize. One MBA writes, "The school organizes a lot of parties and integrates in social life staff (i.e., professors) and students. The professors and students are almost on a friendship level and they help the students where they can."

Many students were attracted to the school because it represents "a somewhat wild mixture of nations, ages, and backgrounds," with about one third hailing from Germany and the rest "from different countries in Asia, South and North America, Europe, etc. Also, they have different working experiences; some of them are businessmen, some are engineers. Some worked for law firms, some served in the Navy as IT engineers." What they all share in common is that they "are ready to help, ready to work, and ready to party." As one student observes, "They are very interesting and challenging to work with. I can't imagine better fellow students!"

Leipzig is "a great town [with] a long academic record [and] many sports facilities," students tell us. Bach and Schumann put this ancient trade center on the musical map, and their traditions are carried on today in the city's many concert halls, theaters, cafés and cabarets, jazz clubs, and discos. The city is conveniently located for travel to and from Berlin, Dresden, and Weimar, as well as to major Czech and Polish cities.

Admissions

All applicants to HHL's MBA program must submit GMAT scores (according to the school, students with scores of at least 650 "are more likely to be offered admission than applicants with lower scores"), proof of undergraduate degree and transcripts, two recommendations, a resume, and a completed application. Non-native English speakers must also submit proof of English proficiency. HHL accepts TOEFL scores to fulfill this requirement. The admissions committee convenes once a month to consider all completed applications, at which point it decides either to accept, reject, or wait-list each candidate.

FINANCIAL FACTS

Annual tuition	$27,477
Cost of books	$300
Room & board (off-campus)	$7,500
% of students receiving aid	15
% of first-year students receiving aid	10
Average grant	$100,000

ADMISSIONS

Admissions Selectivity Rating	88
# of applications received	130
% applicants accepted	54
% acceptees attending	64
Average GMAT	610
Range of GMAT	550–780
Average GPA	3.5
TOEFL required of international students	Yes
Minimum TOEFL (paper/computer)	600/250
Regular application deadline	6/1
Regular notification	6/14
Application Deadline/Notification	
Round 1:	4/1 / 4/14
Round 2:	5/1 / 5/14
Round 3:	6/1 / 6/14
Deferment available	Yes
Maximum length of deferment	1 year
Transfer students accepted	Yes
Transfer application policy	
Course work and examinations in an economic degree program at another university or college of equal status.	
Need-blind admissions	Yes

Applicants Also Look At
GISMA Business School.

EMPLOYMENT PROFILE			
Career Rating	**81**		
Primary Source of Full-time Job Acceptances		**Grads Employed by Function**	**% Avg. Salary**
School-facilitated activities	12 (30%)	Accounting	3 NR
Graduate-facilitated activities	10	Finance/Accounting	3 NR
Unknown	17	Human Resources	5 NR
Percent employed	85	Marketing/Sales	12 NR
		MIS	5 NR
		Operations/Production	12 NR
		Consulting	12 NR
		Communications	7 NR
		Entrepreneurship	5 NR
		General Management	12 NR
		Global Management	5 NR
		Other	5 NR
		Internet/New Media	12 NR

HOFSTRA UNIVERSITY
FRANK G. ZARB SCHOOL OF BUSINESS

GENERAL INFORMATION

Type of school	Private
Environment	City

SURVEY SAYS . . .
Cutting-edge classes
Smart classrooms
Solid preparation in:
Teamwork
Presentation skills
Computer skills

STUDENTS

Enrollment of parent institution	12,550
Enrollment of business school	569
% male/female	63/37
% out-of-state	3
% part-time	71
% minorities	25
% international	24
Average age at entry	30
Average years work experience at entry	3

ACADEMICS

Academic Experience Rating	**61**
Student/faculty ratio	11:1
Profs interesting rating	61
Profs accessible rating	83
% female faculty	18
% minority faculty	25

Joint Degrees
JD/MBA 4 years, BBA/MBA 5 years, BBA/MS 5 years.

Prominent Alumni
Patrick Purcell, president and publisher, *Boston Herald*; James Campbell, president and CEO, GE Consumer and Industrial; Ellen Deutsch, senior vice president and chief growth officer, The Hain Celestial Group; Bruce Gordon, CFO and senior vice president, Walt Disney Internet Group; Kathy Marinello, CEO, The Ceridian Corp.

Academics

Hofstra is "the school with the best academic reputation on Long Island," an ideal location (bucolic, close to NYC, and near most students' homes and jobs) for the vast majority of its students. Excellent professors and technological resources round out the picture. "My academic experience so far has been very pleasurable," reports one Zarb student. "Professors treat you like a customer, doing their best to meet [and] satisfy your needs [and] concerns. The campus is beautifully maintained, and the university has devoted a lot of resources to improvement [and] expansion of infrastructure and technology on campus." "The business school is making an effort to stay abreast of industry trends, inviting industry leaders as guest speakers, [and] maintaining technologically up-to-date classrooms." Moreover, "The campus is mostly wireless, and every classroom is equipped with SMART Board and AV." To top it off, "The administration is accessible and friendly. They work with each student one-on-one and have the best interests of the student in mind."

Zarb's MBA students must ascend five academic stepping-stones to earn the 48-credit degree. Residency workshops (noncredit classes on such topics as library resources, calculus, and statistics), core competency courses (survey economics, business, and ethics classes), and the advanced core (set courses in accounting, business computer information systems, finance, international business, management, marketing, and quality management) make up the bulk of the program. Well-prepared students can place out of a limited number of courses in these three areas, but those longing for electives must simply console themselves with the quality of teaching within the requirements. "The professors are very engaging and dynamic. I don't find myself getting bored in class but really interested, and [I'm] learning new ideas," says one student. Another adds, "There are no strict lectures, and students always offer comments, ideas, and opinions. Debates have even formed from time to time. Class is quite stimulating." A five-course concentration allows students considerably more freedom in pursuing their passions—from finance to health services management to international business to sports management. One finance major says, "I learned a great deal about finance . . . and business management overall. My professors were great. Most had industry experience and were up to date with current industry trends." The final component is an integrative capstone revolving around teamwork and management simulation.

Zarb's 2.5-year MBA curriculum is broad, deep, and somewhat flexible, allowing students to place out of a limited number of classes and focus on their passions. But Zarb doesn't offer the guidance to match. Students gripe that requirements "aren't clear" and recommend that school administrators "help students choose better classes and inform students about certain classes not offered in the next semester so students can choose other classes."

Career and Placement

The "excellent career center" connects MBAs with jobs in what students call "quality companies in the areas of investment banking, private equity, and institutional finance." Nearly all students take jobs in the Northeast, and the finance and accounting industries account for more than half of students' first jobs post-graduation. Top employers are Integrated Business Systems, Citigroup, Goldman Sachs, Canon USA, Deloitte Touche Tohmatsu, GE, Ernst & Young, Cablevision, Protiviti, BDO Seidman, MSC Direct, Computer Associates, Hain Celestial, Marcum and Kliegman LLP, and ADP.

Student Life and Environment

"Hofstra is mostly a commuter school," explains one Zarb student. "The problem is that it could be more than that, but it doesn't try." But other students see it differently. "[Students] are very involved in clubs and activities," declares one student. Students enjoy "home sporting events [and] drama productions." "The campus is vibrant and beautiful. It feels like a second home to me." Suburban Hempstead is "close to NYC" near the Long Island Railroad which makes for an easy commute into the city, but quiet enough to "allow [students] to concentrate on studying."

Students describe one another as "hardworking, driven"—indeed, most "are working full-time while attending classes"—"cooperative," and "very friendly." Though they "tend to be single and in the early stages of their careers," Zarb students do "represent a wide range in ages" and backgrounds, and, as a result, they "bring different opinions" and "life/work experience" "to each [classroom] discussion." Nearly half of the "very diverse" student body is female, and the full-time cohort is one-fourth international and one-fourth students of color. The vast majority "are already employed full-time," most "in the particular field they would like to be in." As a result of having concrete goals, students are very "motivated" and "focused on their education."

Admissions

Hofstra "has a good reputation, and its entrance requirement is not as high as some other top-tier schools in the city," says one student happily, although another student sees this more as a cause for gripes: "The school could be more selective in who it accepts and, thus, raise some of the academic standards." Indeed, Zarb's 85 percent acceptance rate paints a rosy picture for determined applicants who may not have stellar academic credentials or extensive work experience. The average entering student reports a 3.09 GPA, 505 GMAT, and 3 years of work experience.

FINANCIAL FACTS

Annual tuition	$13,860
Fees	$930
Cost of books	$3,666
Room & board (on/off-campus)	$9,800/$11,760
% of students receiving aid	68
% of first-year students receiving aid	75
% of students receiving loans	49
% of students receiving grants	33
Average award package	$16,668
Average grant	$8,500
Average student loan debt	$38,717

ADMISSIONS

Admissions Selectivity Rating	65
# of applications received	347
% applicants accepted	85
% acceptees attending	64
Average GMAT	505
Range of GMAT	450–570
Average GPA	3.09
TOEFL required of international students	Yes
Application fee	$60
Regular application deadline	Rolling
Regular notification	Rolling
Deferment available	Yes
Maximum length of deferment	1 year
Transfer students accepted	Yes
Transfer application policy Number of transferable credits is limited to a maximum of 9 credits.	
Non-fall admissions	Yes
Need-blind admissions	Yes

Applicants Also Look At

City University of New York—Baruch College, New York University, Pace University, St. John's University.

EMPLOYMENT PROFILE

Career Rating	74	Grads Employed by Function	%	Avg. Salary
Primary Source of Full-time Job Acceptances		Finance/Accounting	63	$65,850
School-facilitated activities	12 (34%)	Marketing/Sales	22	$56,450
Graduate-facilitated activities	10 (29%)	Consulting	4	$54,000
Unknown	13 (37%)	General Management	7	NR
Average base starting salary	$62,652	Other	4	$60,000
Percent employed	77	**Top 5 Employers Hiring Grads**		
		Integrated Business Systems; Citigroup; Deloitte Touche Tohmatsu; GE; Goldman Sachs.		

HONG KONG U. OF SCIENCE AND TECHNOLOGY
HKUST BUSINESS SCHOOL

GENERAL INFORMATION
Type of school   Public
Academic calendar   Semester

SURVEY SAYS . . .
Students love Kowloon, Hong Kong
Solid preparation in:
Finance
Accounting
Teamwork

STUDENTS
Enrollment of
  business school   1,004
% male/female   56/44
% part-time   67
% international   80
Average age at entry   28
Average years work
  experience at entry   5

ACADEMICS
Academic experience rating   63
Profs interesting rating   78
Profs accessible rating   68
% female faculty   13

Joint Degrees
MBA/MSc (financial analysis)
3 years, MBA/MSc (investment
management) 3 years, MBA/MSc
(information systems management)
3 years.

Prominent Alumni
Edmund Ho, director, Citigroup
Global Markcts Asia; Rebecca Chan,
partner, PricewaterhouseCoopers;
Marco Elli, president and CEO,
Pirelli Japan KK; Jackson Ng, CFO
and director, Modern Terminals Ltd.;
SC Liu, chairman, Evergreen Real
Estate Consultant.

Academics

"You can't learn about a region from a distance. You need to experience it personally." So say the international students drawn to the MBA program at the Hong Kong University of Science and Technology; they come here looking for "easy access to the Chinese culture for Western students," and they know that this is the place to get it. One MBA writes, "There is no way a school in Europe or the U.S. could teach you about this region as well as HKUST can. There is no other school in Asia that can touch it in that respect." Another agrees, "HKUST has the best Chinese faculty in the world catering to business in China."

Full-time students can choose from two curricular options at HKUST: a 12-month option that minimizes the student's time away from work, and a 16-month option that allows for participation in exchange programs with one of 51 overseas business schools. The school also offers a part-time MBA. Students tell us that "the finance faculty is top-notch, as it needs to be for a financial center of the world like Hong Kong," and that "the school is also excellent in accounting and IT." Consulting, strategy, and marketing reportedly "could be stronger." The faculty has strong credentials. One MBA reports, "It's a very strong research faculty who present their findings at the international level. They are also, for the most part, very capable of imparting with their insights in a compelling and engaging manner."

MBAs also praise the program's "emphasis on teamwork, [the] good balance of practical case-based teaching and theory" in the classroom, and a curricular structure that ensures students are prepared to participate in class. "There are compulsory assignments to hand in before class, which is good to force students to prepare for class and also arrive on time. The professors also count participation towards the grade, so students are encouraged to raise questions."

HKUST is also home to a part-time MBA program, which takes two years to complete. Part-time students complete the same required courses as do full-timers but have fewer elective requirements; the school admits about 120 part-timers each year, dividing them into two cohorts of 60. The program is scheduled "to meet the special needs of working professionals and managers."

Career and Placement

HKUST maintains a dedicated MBA Career Services Office for its graduate students in business. The office offers career counseling, a variety of self-assessment tools, workshops in job-search and interview skills, recruiting events, internships, resume books, and job listings. Students feel that they "need closer relationships or partnerships with companies, especially large companies in mainland China and other important countries or cities outside Hong Kong." MBAs also tell us that "this is still a young program," which they see as both an impediment and an asset. "Our alumni network is still relatively small; however, there is no doubt that the people we are studying with are the future of China and this region. So it's a small network, but a very useful one indeed," writes one student.

Employers who most frequently hire HKUST MBAs include Citigroup, Monitor Group, Watson Wyatt, HSBC. Nearly half of HKUST grads wind up in the finance and consulting sectors.

Student Life and Environment

Full-time students at HKUST constitute "a small group with around 60 students, yet with diversity in cultural, background, and working experience. We are friendly, helpful, active, and full of creative ideas!" Students come here from all around the world; as one student reports, "The range of nationalities present spans from Thai, Korean, Israeli, Indian, and Filipino to New Zealander, Swiss, Irish, French, and Canadian." There are a lot of students from mainland China here; international students appreciate how "their background provides invaluable input into the program."

The HKUST campus "on a hill overlooking the ocean [is] an oasis that is only 20 minutes by MTR from the heart of the central business district." Students enjoy "numerous activities after class. Every Friday noon, students, faculty, and some staff of MBA office will have a self-service lunch together. It is a small family atmosphere, and we chat with each other casually. After the lunch, there will be a country presentation by one or a group of students from a certain country." Students spend leisure time together too, "hiking the trails beside the sea, boating, enjoying nightlife on the famous bar street of Hong Kong, attending concerts, [or] shopping." One MBA writes, "School life cycles between periods of intense work and pure fun."

Students love Hong Kong, "a very international city" of seven million. As one MBA puts it, "Hong Kong is Asia's world city. If you don't have a life here, you just don't have a life." The "nightlife, food, entertainment are all world-class," the city is "super-safe," and the "public transportation is excellent." The school's location "is convenient to visit the Hong Kong stock exchange or other big companies. You are even able to do some field study in mainland China."

Admissions

HKUST expects all applicants to hold "a good bachelor degree from a recognized university" and to have strong GMAT scores, full-time work experience (at least three years for the part-time program, at least one year for the full-time program), and to be proficient in English. All applicants must provide two letters of reference along with official copies of their transcripts and GMAT score reports. Students whose first language is not English must also provide TOEFL scores. An interview, scheduled at the school's behest, is required prior to admission; it can be conducted by telephone if a face-to-face interview is impractical. The online application is required by the school.

FINANCIAL FACTS

Annual tuition	$32,750
Cost of books	$1,000
Room & board	
(on/off-campus)	$4,600/$6,200

ADMISSIONS

Admissions Selectivity Rating	**60***
Range of GMAT	560–710
Minimum TOEFL	
(paper/computer)	600/250
Application fee	$64
International application fee	$64
Regular application deadline	3/31
Regular notification	6/15
Application Deadline/Notification	
Round 1:	12/15 / 2/28
Round 2:	3/31 / 6/15
Deferment available	Yes
Maximum length of	
deferment	1 year

EMPLOYMENT PROFILE

		Grads Employed by Function	%	Avg. Salary
Career Rating	**80**			
Primary Source of Full-time Job Acceptances		Finance/Accounting	20	NR
Percent employed	95	Marketing/Sales	8	NR
		Strategic Planning	25	NR
		Consulting	25	NR
		General Management	17	NR
		Other	5	NR

HOWARD UNIVERSITY
SCHOOL OF BUSINESS

Academics

Students who want "a school with great recruitment" that will challenge them academically turn to Howard University, one of the nation's most prestigious Historically Black institutions. With a full-time day program, an accelerated part-time program, and a conventional part-time program, Howard has options to accommodate a wide range of students.

The entire MBA program is relatively small, with the majority of students enrolled full-time. The size of the program nurtures "a positive and supportive atmosphere." Students appreciate the "support and mentoring that is actively given by the administration. . . . They really do root for the success of their students." They help students in other ways as well. One MBA tells us that one of the university's strengths lies in the "availability of financial aid. Howard University has a legacy of being benevolent, which is followed diligently by the School of Business."

Students praise Howard for its "good supply chain management program," for its entrepreneurship program, and for offering a combined JD/MBA. Concentrations are available in entrepreneurship, finance, human resources management, information systems, international business, marketing, and supply chain management. Professors here "have this zeal" that is "refreshing." They also employ "some very up-to-date teaching styles." Students mention that their professors "all seem to not only have working knowledge of how the business world operates, but also seem genuinely passionate the subject matters they teach." The academics are "challenging" but students believe that means they will be "helpful in the workplace."

MBAs here warn that the full-time program is still ironing out some kinks. "I have seen steady progress; however, additional full-time staff is needed to move the full-time day program to the next level," says one MBA. "The next few years will determine the commitment from the university in regards to the MBA program." They also feel that "Howard could stand to improve on having better technological facilities." Fortunately, the administration "seems actively involved in ensuring that its students are well prepared for the world of management," suggesting that the program's shortcomings will soon be addressed.

Career and Placement

Students tell us that "the biggest strength of the school is the networking aspect of the curriculum. No one can say that Howard is not a highly visible program, especially when it comes to recruiting minorities." Indeed, many choose to attend Howard "because of the number and quality of companies recruiting MBAs from Howard University." With "several career fairs and numerous companies that come to interview and hire" the students, Howard works hard to provide each student with ample recruitment opportunities.

Employers that frequently hire Howard MBAs include: Bear Stearns, Citigroup, Dell, Clark Construction, Deloitte Touche Tohmatsu, Dewey Ballantine LLP, Eaton Corporation, Ernst & Young, Hartford Financial Services, IBM, Intel, KPMG International, Liberty Mutual Group, MetLife, Merrill Lynch, Microsoft, PricewaterhouseCoopers, Shapiro Morin & Oshinsky LLP, Sprint, SunTrust, Stockamp and Associates, Tyco, United Technologies Corporation, and Wachovia. Accenture, Bank of America, Honeywell, ING, Johnson & Johnson, MetLife, Procter & Gamble, Roche Pharmaceuticals.

MBA Admissions, Office of Graduate Programs
2600 Sixth Street Northwest, Suite 236, Washington, DC 20059 United States
Phone: 202-806-1725 • Fax: 202-986-4435
E-mail: MBA_BSCHOOL@HOWARD.EDU • Website: WWW.BSCHOOL.HOWARD.EDU

Student Life and Environment

Life at Howard "is a balancing act between getting all the course work [done] and networking with the companies that often visit our campus." Fortunately, "the school ensures that there is no lack of support or resources, thus making it possible for us to take advantage of all there is to be offered." Students also try to make time for the "many activities Howard has to offer. Our Graduate Business Student Council (GBSC) sponsors a variety of events such as happy hours, ice skating, and clothes drives." They "attempt to keep students active in the community while offering them a social environment to express themselves on the weekend." Then, of course, there's Washington DC, a vibrant metropolis with opportunities on both the career and extracurricular fronts.

Howard's academically demanding MBA program is undoubtedly "time consuming. Some of the professors really want us to get into depth about the subject matter," says one MBA. "Many of our classes require group projects," which is "one of the challenges at Howard, especially with such a diverse mix of students. The students look out for each other, though. There are informal study groups and networks to help." That looking out doesn't end in the classroom. At Howard, students "interact with each other like family and care about each other like family. This relationship makes studying and even partying together easy and fun." Facilities "are somewhat adequate for what needs to be done." Students "have [their] own computer lab and lounge where we meet and socialize between classes. The lab is where we spend most our day studying, having group meetings, or just taking care of things before we head home for the evening."

Admissions

Applicants to the Howard MBA program must submit the following materials to the Admissions Office: a completed application form; an up-to-date resume; an official score report for the GMAT (taken no more than 5 years before date of application); official transcripts for all undergraduate and graduate course work; three completed evaluation and recommendation forms, completed by at least one academic and one professional supervisor (the school encourages students to submit letters of recommendation in addition to these forms); a personal statement describing the applicant's abilities, experiences, and goals in pursuing the MBA; and proof of at least 1 year of significant post-collegiate professional or managerial experience. Applicants must have completed advanced college algebra and/or calculus in order to be admitted. International applicants must submit all of the above plus a Statement of Financial Resources. International students who attended a non-English speaking undergraduate institution must have their transcripts translated and interpreted by a professional service. They must also submit an official score report for the TOEFL.

FINANCIAL FACTS

Annual tuition	$14,065
Fees	$805
Cost of books	$2,400
Room & board (on/off-campus)	$12,224/$17,000
% of students receiving aid	85
% of first-year students receiving aid	80
% of students receiving loans	58
% of students receiving grants	54
Average award package	$23,355
Average grant	$10,234
Average student loan debt	$32,573

ADMISSIONS

Admissions Selectivity Rating	**76**
# of applications received	161
% applicants accepted	59
% acceptees attending	78
Average GMAT	522
Range of GMAT	410–730
Average GPA	3.12
TOEFL required of international students	Yes
Minimum TOEFL (paper/computer)	550/213
Application fee	$65
Regular application deadline	4/1
Regular notification	5/1

Application Deadline/Notification

Round 1:	11/15 / 1/1
Round 2:	2/1 / 3/1
Round 3:	4/1 / 5/1
Round 4:	5/15 / 6/1
Early decision program?	Yes
ED Deadline/Notification	11/15 / 1/1
Deferment available	Yes
Maximum length of deferment	2 semesters
Transfer students accepted	Yes

Transfer application policy
Must meet Howard's MBA program admission criteria. Students can only transfer a maximum of 6 credit hours from an AACSB-accredited graduate business program.

Non-fall admissions	Yes
Need-blind admissions	Yes

Applicants Also Look At

American University, Clark Atlanta University, George Mason University, Georgetown University, The George Washington University, University of Maryland.

EMPLOYMENT PROFILE

Career Rating	**87**	**Grads Employed by Function**	**% Avg. Salary**
Primary Source of Full-time Job Acceptances		Finance/Accounting	32 $73,333
School-facilitated activities	19 (68%)	Human Resources	3 NR
Graduate-facilitated activities	7 (25%)	Marketing/Sales	3 NR
Unknown	2 (7%)	Operations/Production	29 $79,625
Percent employed	76	Consulting	13 $78,000
		General Management	3 $60,000
		Other	16 $114,250

Top 5 Employers Hiring Grads
Dell; Dewey-Ballentine, LLP; Intel; IBM; UTC.

IAE Universidad Austral
Management and Business School

GENERAL INFORMATION
Type of school   Private

SURVEY SAYS . . .
Good peer network
Happy students
Solid preparation in:
Marketing
Finance
General management

STUDENTS

Enrollment of business school	48
% male/female	69/31
% minorities	15
% international	35
Average age at entry	28
Average years work experience at entry	5

ACADEMICS

Academic Experience Rating	87
Profs interesting rating	95
Profs accessible rating	77
% female faculty	9
% minority faculty	16

Academics

Future MBAs choose IAE Universidad Austral's intensive one-year program because of the school's "excellent reputation in Argentina and throughout Latin America" as well as for the speed with which it delivers results. The bilingual program (classes are taught in Spanish and English), which runs from January to December, has been honed over time to provide a quality education to its students. As the school's website states, the one-year MBA program "is the result of the 25-year experience IAE has acquired in providing part-time Executive MBA programs and the contributions of many years of delivering full-time programs supplied by the Harvard Business School and the IESE of Barcelona."

IAE's "intensive" program is "a one-year hardworking MBA. The schedule runs from 9:00 A.M. to 6:00 P.M., with only a two-hour break in the middle of the day (from 12:30 P.M. to 2.30 P.M.) for sports and eating." The program begins with a month-long "leveling course," during which students are reacquainted with fundamental quantitative skills in statistics, mathematics, and accounting. The second module of the program consists of an extensive core curriculum that focuses on three areas: "technical skills in marketing, finance, etc.; critical thinking skills that teach you new ways to approach both professional problems and personal problems; and teamwork skills." During the third module, students choose from a selection of electives. The fourth and fifth modules of the program are devoted to interdisciplinary analysis of business problems, fieldwork, networking, and developing management skills.

Students speak highly of the program, reporting that "professors are all very good. Most of them have PhDs, and they have a lot of patience. They always are able to help you inside and outside the class." The program runs smoothly, and this ease is especially important given the amount of work piled on students; no one here has time to wade through bureaucratic red tape. As one MBA notes, "The administration provides exceptional service. It is well prepared for the needs of its classmates: Everything we need is available for us." And perhaps most important, "IAE has very good contacts with businesses in Latin America, and a very important aspect is that it provides us with internal and external mentors."

Career and Placement

The Career Services Department at IAE works with students and companies to facilitate recruitment and placement. Students report, however, that "the department is underdeveloped, especially in the international job market." The alumni network, on the other hand, "is unbelievable," according to students; one reports, "I could speak to many important executives from the best companies of my country because they were alumni." Employers who have worked with IAE include Alto Parana SA, Arthur D. Little, Banco Galicia, Belise & Asociados, Bodegas Lagarde, CCBA SA, Citibank NA, Fiat Argentina, Ford Argentina, GE Capital Cia, Global Praxis, Hart Casares, Johnson & Johnson Medical SA, KPMG Consultores, Kraft Food Argentina, McKinsey & Company, Nestlé Argentina SA, Novartis Argentina SA, Sade Skanska Ingeniería y Construcciones SA, and The Walt Disney Company.

Casilla de Correo Nº49, Mariano Acosta s/nº y Ruta Nac. 8 Pilar, Bs. As., 1629
Argentina
Phone: 011 54.2322.48.1000 • Fax: 011 54.2322.48.1050
E-mail: ffragueiro@iae.edu.ar • Website: www.iae.edu.ar/web2005_eng/home/home.html

Student Life and Environment

IAE's campus "is located in Pilar, 50 kilometers from the capital" of Argentina, in a beautiful setting "with a lot of trees, grass, and greenery everywhere." Despite the bucolic setting, "you can find everything near the campus: a mall, restaurants, supermarkets, movies, gas stations, etc." Campus facilities include areas where students "can play soccer, tennis, and rugby during the two-hour lunch break." Big-city life isn't too far off, as "the campus is one hour away from Buenos Aires." Students note, however, that "since IAE's program is a one-year MBA, the workload is so heavy that there is very little time to do activities outside the classroom." Classes convene from 9:00 A.M. to 6:00 P.M.; most students "study until 9:00 P.M., then have some dinner with friends," and then call it a day.

About 70 percent of IAE's students are Argentine; the remaining students come from other parts of Latin America, Europe, and the United States. Students are drawn from all sectors: marketing, banking, consulting, engineering, services, and even agriculture are represented here. About half the students consider themselves "young entrepreneurs," and nearly as many see themselves as "young, socially oriented professionals." Students generally "have great senses of humor, don't hesitate to help one another, and enjoy hanging out, drinking beer and wine, and watching movies."

Admissions

Applicants to the full-time MBA program at IAE must have at least three years of post-undergraduate work experience. The admissions department requires all of the following materials: official transcripts for all postsecondary academic work; an official GMAT score report (minimum acceptable score 550; IAE also offers its own skills exam which can be taken in lieu of the GMAT); a resume; personal essays; letters of recommendation; a completed application form; and, for students whose first language is not English, a minimum TOEFL score of 570 (paper-based test) or 230 (computer-based test). The admissions committee uses the above materials to screen candidates. Those deemed possible candidates for the program must undergo an admissions interview with an IAE professor and members of both the admissions and career management departments.

FINANCIAL FACTS

Annual tuition	$17,000

ADMISSIONS

Admissions Selectivity Rating	**84**
# of applications received	111
% applicants accepted	57
% acceptees attending	76
Average GMAT	618
TOEFL required of international students	Yes
Minimum TOEFL (computer)	230

EMPLOYMENT PROFILE

Career Rating	67	Grads Employed by Function	%	Avg. Salary
		Accounting	2	NR
		Finance/Accounting	4	NR
		Human Resources	4	NR
		Marketing/Sales	13	NR
		Operations/Production	6	NR
		Consulting	11	NR
		Communications	2	NR
		Entrepreneurship	2	NR
		Nonprofit	6	NR

ILLINOIS INSTITUTE OF TECHNOLOGY
STUART GRADUATE SCHOOL OF BUSINESS

Academics

The Stuart Graduate School of Business at Chicago's Illinois Institute of Technology recognizes the diverse needs of its student body and works hard to accommodate them all.
Those looking to expedite their MBAs, for example, can enroll in the school's full-time
program; about one-third of the students here do just that. Those who want to pursue
their degrees contemporaneously with their careers have a number of part-time options,
including the lockstep "two-year part-time fast-track MBA" (offered at the school's Rice
Campus in Wheaton) and the "customizable world-class MBA." Classes are scheduled
during weekdays, evenings, and weekends for the convenience of all of Stuart's con-
stituencies. All MBA programs consist of a minimum of 16 classes; specialization is available in all but the fast-track program and requires an additional four classes.

IIT is a world-class research institution, and, not surprisingly, Stuart MBAs benefit from
the presence of the high-powered academics here. Three research centers—the Center for
Financial Markets, the Chicago Geospatial Exchange, and the Center for Sustainable
Enterprise—offer unique options to adventurous MBAs. There is even an optional specialization in sustainable enterprise that trains students "to identify, develop, communicate, and help implement practical and equitable business strategies that advance the
ecological sustainability of the Chicago area while fostering current and future economic viability." Stuart was recently ranked among the world's leaders in incorporating environmental management.

Many here, however, prefer more traditional fare. Stuart MBAs laud the school's entrepreneurship program as well as offerings in finance and marketing. Some extol the
advantages conferred by the presence of a health care concentration, and quite a few full-
timers take advantage of dual-degree programs in law or public administration.
Throughout the curriculum, students praise "the use of technology and real-life examples, and the application of business problems." Stuart professors "are always willing to
help and provide out-of-the-classroom tutorials and further explanations," plus "their
experience and techniques are outstanding." Similarly, administrators "are extremely
helpful and go out of their way to get to know each student personally and help anyone."
With IIT's small cohorts, "there is no crowding in the libraries, computer labs, etc. And,
we get to learn a lot from group discussions." For many, though, "the school's greatest
strength is its strategic location. It is because of its location that we are able to get internships and other opportunities to work." About the only weakness here, students tell us,
is that "the school's image needs to be improved. The rankings need improvement and
people need to know about IIT a lot more."

Career and Placement

The Office of Career Services at the Stuart MBA program provides students with one-on-
one career counseling, workshops in interviewing and resume preparation, and research
on companies and opportunities appropriate to each student's goals. A self-assessment,
conducted as students enter the program, helps the office tailor its services to the individual needs of each MBA. The university at large conducts career fairs through its
Career Development Center.

Employers who most frequently hire Stuart MBAs include Bank One, Northern Trust,
Bank of America, ABN-Amro, Lucent Technologies, JPMorgan, Navistar, Johnson &
Johnson, Capitol One, Vankampen, US EPA, Reuters, Cantor Fitzgerald, McLagan
Partners, Motorola, Inc., and Akamal Trading. About half of all Stuart MBAs remain in
the Midwest after graduation; most of the rest head to one of the two coasts.

BRIAN JANSEN, DIRECTOR OF ADMISSIONS
565 WEST ADAMS STREET CHICAGO, IL 60661 UNITED STATES
PHONE: 312-906-6567 • FAX: 312-906-6549
E-MAIL: ADMISSIONS@STUART.IIT.EDU • WEBSITE: WWW.STUART.IIT.EDU

Student Life and Environment

IIT's main MBA programs are located "in a separate building in downtown Chicago. That building houses law and business school students only, so there isn't much activity there really, just serious-looking students walking to and fro. The main campus has more life, and there is a free shuttle to transport you between campuses. I appreciate the peace and quiet of our building, though. It's very easy to find a nook to study in without constant interference," remarks one student. MBAs participate in "lots of study groups. We also have socials every Wednesday, and students often go out into town in small groups." Despite these opportunities, many here feel that they "need more organizations, activities, a bigger career center, and more seminars and activities with others outside the school (i.e. businesses, other universities, etc.)."

The student body includes many who have considerable work experience, as well as "a lot of diversity in terms of nationality and occupation." One student observes, "The diverse population aids in creating a learning experience unlike any other. Students learn as much (if not more) outside the classroom than in the classroom, just by interacting with everyone around them." When they can find the time, students love to take advantage of "the world's biggest financial city," which also offers plenty in the way of culture, entertainment, fine dining, and nightlife. Again, it comes back to location. "Stuart is located near the Chicago loop in the midst of big-name business companies, allowing for excellent networking and job opportunities. It's also very close to public transportation."

Admissions

The IIT Stuart Graduate School of Business requires applicants to submit GMAT scores, official undergraduate transcripts for all schools attended, two letters of recommendation from people "who can attest to your academic or professional qualifications," two required essays (personal statement and career goals) with the option to submit additional essays (describe a difficult challenge you have faced, describe your ideal company), and a resume. International students must also submit TOEFL scores no more than two years old. Undergraduate transcripts in languages other than English must be accompanied by an English translation.

FINANCIAL FACTS

Annual tuition	$24,333
Fees	$960
Cost of books	$1,000
Room & board	
(on/off-campus)	$10,600/$14,000
% of students receiving aid	47
% of first-year students	
receiving aid	27
% of students receiving loans	43
% of students receiving grants	47
Average award package	$6,249
Average grant	$6,249
Average student loan debt	$40,000

ADMISSIONS

Admissions Selectivity Rating	73
# of applications received	222
% applicants accepted	70
% acceptees attending	21
Average GMAT	565
Range of GMAT	510–600
Average GPA	3
TOEFL required of	
international students	Yes
Minimum TOEFL	
(paper/computer)	550/213
Application fee	$75
Regular application deadline	8/15
Regular notification	Rolling
Deferment available	Yes
Maximum length of	
deferment	1 year
Transfer students accepted	Yes
Transfer application policy	
With advisor approval may transfer up to 4 core courses and 2 elective courses.	
Non-fall admissions	Yes
Need-blind admissions	Yes

EMPLOYMENT PROFILE

Career Rating		86	Grads Employed by Function	%	Avg. Salary
Primary Source of Full-time Job Acceptances			Finance/Accounting	22	$68,000
School-facilitated activities	3 (13%)		Marketing/Sales	22	$94,333
Graduate-facilitated activities	5 (21%)		MIS	11	NR
Unknown	16 (66%)		Operations/Production	11	$55,000
Percent employed	80		Consulting	6	$53,500
			General Management	17	$52,000
			Other	11	$64,500
			Top 5 Employers Hiring Grads		
			Intel; Bank of America; Morningstar; Fidelity; Johnson & Johnson.		

ILLINOIS STATE UNIVERSITY
COLLEGE OF BUSINESS

Academics

With a new $30 million College of Business building that students describe as "state-of-the-art" and "absolutely amazing," the College of Business at Illinois State University is clearly making a big investment in the future of undergraduate and graduate business studies. The school's MBA program is tailored toward the needs of part-time students: Classes convene once a week, always starting at 6:00 P.M. About one-quarter of the student body attends full-time, typically taking three classes per semester. Part-time students usually enroll in one or two classes per semester.

With a total of 200 students, the MBA program at ISU is small enough to allow "individualized attention from professors." Students praise the "big university resources with a small classroom focus" here. One MBA writes, "Although the atmosphere is challenging, the professors are available to assist students outside of class periods, and I believe they are personally vested in the success of their students. I believe I am getting the quality of education one would only expect to find at nationally known private colleges." The size of the program has its drawbacks as well: Several students in our survey complained that "electives are few and far between. Almost all electives are only offered every two years." To clarify, of the 23 MBA electives offerings, 8 are offered every year and 15 are offered every other year.

The ISU curriculum is divided into three segments: foundation work, core courses, and electives. Seven foundation courses cover the material typically covered in an undergraduate business program; students with undergraduate business degrees typically are allowed to forego all of these classes. Nine core courses and three electives must be completed by all MBAs. Students may use their electives to develop an area of concentration in accounting, finance, international business, management, marketing, or fine arts administration. The arts program is relatively unique, helping the school draw students from outside the immediate region.

Career and Placement

Illinois State University's career services include resume and job posting through eRecruiting. Other services are provided by the Career Center, which serves the entire undergraduate and graduate population of the university. Students report that the university's "affiliation with such local companies as State Farm, Caterpillar, Mitsubishi, and Country Companies" translates into "great internship opportunities." Students also feel that "getting more diversity in corporate recruiters from different areas of business other than finance and insurance to appeal to a broader MBA group" should be a major priority of the MBA program. The school reports that 94 percent of its MBAs are employed at the time of their graduation.

SJ Chang, Associate Dean for MBA and Undergraduate Programs
Campus Box 5570, MBA Program, Normal, IL 61790-5570 United States
Phone: 309-438-8388 • Fax: 309-438-7255
E-mail: isumba@exchange.cob.ilstu.edu • Website: www.mba.ilstu.edu

Student Life and Environment

"You are able to become as involved as you would like" in the MBA program at ISU. Students report that "various activities take place on campus, and it is up to each student to get involved. Clubs, events, sports, and plays are just a few of the options that students have to choose from." Students enjoy "a great social network with the MBAs. We all have a lot of classes together as it is a relatively small group. We build homecoming floats and meet for drinks regularly. There seems to be a very good balance between learning, getting our work done, and sharing our experience."

Not everyone gets involved, of course. Many of the students here are part-time students with full-time jobs, and many just want to fulfill their academic obligations and get home. One student explains: "School life is spent with three-hour classes per week for each course. Group meetings for projects, research, case studies, and homework assignments: This is very much the pattern for 90 percent of the courses." While "the workload can be tough," most here agree that "the homework load is fair, and expectations are fair. The culture is typically Midwestern, with values of accountability for oneself and helping out others. This starts with the professors and is imparted to the students."

While the school reports that the average work experience of full-time MBA students is 2.59 years, some of our survey respondents find their full-time peers' lack of work experience troubling. As one puts it, "I have noticed a tremendous difference between those students [with little work experience] and the ones with careers. It can be very frustrating to work with full-time students because they do not exert as much effort or have strong time-management or leadership skills." They also "cannot speak from experience or relate real-life stories to the class." Large local companies such as State Farm, Country Companies, and Mitsubishi contribute many students to the part-time program.

Admissions

Applicants to the ISU MBA program must submit applications to both the graduate college of the university and the MBA program. To receive priority in the admissions process, applications should be received February 1; applications for spring entry are due by September 1. All applications must include two official copies of transcripts for all academic work completed beyond high school; GMAT scores; a resume; two personal essays; and two letters of reference. GPA for the final 60 credit hours of undergraduate work and GMAT scores are the primary determining factors in the admissions decision. In recent years, successful applicants have posted an average GPA of 3.4 and an average GMAT score of 545. International students whose first language is not English must submit TOEFL scores. A minimum score of 600 on the paper-and-pencil test or 250 on the computer-based test is required. Work experience is considered "beneficial" and is "strongly encouraged," but is not required.

FINANCIAL FACTS

Annual tuition (in-state/ out-of-state)	$2,610/$5,454
Fees	$778
Cost of books	$825
Room & board (on/off-campus)	$5,576/$5,834
% of students receiving aid	94
% of first-year students receiving aid	89
% of students receiving loans	53
% of students receiving grants	95
Average award package	$14,110
Average grant	$6,889
Average student loan debt	$20,439

ADMISSIONS

Admissions Selectivity Rating	**72**
# of applications received	50
% applicants accepted	86
% acceptees attending	67
Average GMAT	545
Range of GMAT	500–580
Average GPA	3.46
TOEFL required of international students	Yes
Minimum TOEFL (paper/computer)	600/250
Application fee	$40
International application fee	$40
Regular application deadline	9/1
Regular notification	8/15
Early decision program?	Yes
ED Deadline/Notification	2/1 / 2/15
Deferment available	Yes
Maximum length of deferment	1 year
Transfer students accepted	Yes
Transfer application policy Must be in good academic standing and complete all regular application requirements, maximum 9 hours transfer credit accepted.	
Non-fall admissions	Yes
Need-blind admissions	Yes

IMD INTERNATIONAL
INTERNATIONAL INSTITUTE FOR MANAGEMENT DEVELOPMENT

Academics

A highly selective one-year MBA program with a strong focus on leadership skills, the IMD MBA is an "intense" but "worthwhile" program in which "the development of leadership and team skills in a demanding environment gets everyone ready for the real world beyond the MBA program." Students appreciate the "real-world, real-learning" focus at IMD, where "classes feel more practical than academic, which is suitable for the average student, who is 31 years old with seven years of work experience."

IMD starts its program in January with a five-month sequence called Building Blocks, combined with start-up projects. It is the toughest part of the program, students tell us, in which "14-hour days are the norm [and] just about everything is done in teams that work under high time pressure. This brings out all the colors of team members very quickly, so you learn much about people and teamwork, even those of us already experienced with it." MBAs warn that the "class and teams are expected to self-manage their priorities and meet all program goals." The school does a good job of selecting students who can handle these responsibilities; as one MBA explains, "We receive a ton of information in a short period of time, and it works because the students and faculty are both up for the challenge to be the best."

The second portion of the MBA program commences in June, when students prepare for a field-learning experience in Argentina, a country facing a difficult business environment. After a summer break, students return to undertake long-term (two months) international consulting projects, then return to school for electives and a weeklong leadership program. With so many strands to coordinate, it's fortunate that "this school is run in the traditional Swiss way; in other words, like clockwork. Everything is very structured and it works, (although it can, at times, be perceived as inflexible)."

IMD professors "bring many real-life situations into the classroom and share with us the latest thinking." Students report approvingly that "there is no tenure for the faculty, which makes people listen to the feedback from the MBA class. This is taken very seriously." Students only wish the school were better known in the U.S.; one student remarks, "We are not very well known outside of Europe, and there needs to be work done to raise the awareness of IMD."

Career and Placement

Career Development Services at IMD are provided by the school's career services team, faculty members, a corporate development team that "works closely with IMD clients to solve their corporate development needs through IMD public and in-company programs," a "learning network" of 150 affiliated international companies, and alumni. Self-assessment, individual counseling, workshops, and on-campus recruiting are all available to IMD MBAs. Employers most likely to hire IMD graduates include DuPont, Medtronic, Philip Morris, GE Capital, Shell International, Novartis International AG, McKinsey & Company, Indesit Company, and the Samsung Global Strategy Group.

Student Life and Environment

IMD's MBA program is intensive. One student warns, "The first six months are like bootcamp: classes eight hours a day, 5 and a half days a week, and group work another six hours a day minimum. Everything is closed when we are free, so there is very little interaction with the city during the first semester of work." Fortunately, "that first semester is not just all about working hard. The bonds and friendships you develop here last a lifetime, and the alumni networks are a great testament to that." Also, "it gets a bit better the last five months, [when] life changes dramatically" and travel becomes an integral part of the program. Students first take a one-week Discovery Expedition to Argentina, then "become consultants to international companies for two months. This involves extensive traveling for most and exciting exposure."

Because of the nature of the program, students see precious little of hometown Lausanne, but when they can get out they find a small, lovely European city that provides ready access to Lac Léman and the mountains. Geneva is close by to provide big-city diversions and access to international banks and corporations, government agencies, and NGOs.

The "small group of 90 students [at IMD] enables MBAs to really get to know each and every one of the participants in the program very well. Also, the student environment promotes a real sense of shared purpose and makes people actively contribute not only to courses but also in extracurricular activities." Students are competitive, but in a healthy way— "competition is between teams, not individuals"—and appreciate that "you will never find arrogant know-alls in this program, despite the high level of experience students have. You will find brilliant people with an exceptional sense of curiosity to learn from your experiences. The strict selection convinces everyone that each student is here for a reason." Over 35 nationalities are represented within the student body, bringing a "wide diversity of student backgrounds from a cultural and nationality point of view as well as work experiences, which bring great value during discussions."

Admissions

"The admission process is probably the longest and toughest among all the top business schools," students at IMD tell us, and they may well be right. The first stage of the application process is pretty standard: applicants send in an application, 10 short essays, official transcripts, GMAT scores, three letters of recommendation, and a resume (showing a minimum three years' professional experience that includes "some international exposure"). The next stage, though, is unusually rigorous; it's a by-invitation-only interview day that includes not only a personal interview with an admissions committee member but also an impromptu presentation and a case-study discussion with a group of other interviewees. The school uses this multistage review process to cull from its applicant pool a group of 90 students who are not only bright, accomplished, and innovative but who also demonstrate both leadership potential and strong interpersonal skills.

FINANCIAL FACTS

Annual tuition	$44,110
Fees	$16,000
Room & board (off-campus)	$10,400
% of students receiving aid	21
% of students receiving loans	13
% of students receiving grants	11
Average award package	$32,293
Average grant	$22,000

ADMISSIONS

Admissions Selectivity Rating	97
# of applications received	375
% applicants accepted	28
% acceptees attending	86
Average GMAT	680
Range of GMAT	650–720
Application fee	$230
Regular application deadline	9/1
Regular notification	Rolling
Application Deadline/Notification	
Round 1:	4/1 / rolling
Round 2:	6/1 / rolling
Round 3:	8/1 / rolling
Round 4:	9/1 / rolling
Non-fall admissions	Yes
Need-blind admissions	Yes

Applicants Also Look At

Columbia University, Harvard University, IESE Business School, INSEAD, Stanford University, University of London, University of Pennsylvania.

EMPLOYMENT PROFILE

Career Rating	89		
Primary Source of Full-time Job Acceptances		**Grads Employed by Function**	**% Avg. Salary**
School-facilitated activities	46	Finance/Accounting	18 NR
Graduate-facilitated activities	23	Human Resources	1 NR
Unknown	7	Marketing/Sales	23 NR
Percent employed	93	MIS	1 NR
		Operations/Production	3 NR
		Consulting	19 NR
		General Management	35 NR
		Top 5 Employers Hiring Grads	
		Firmenich; DuPont; Alcan; GE Europe; McKinsey & Company.	

Indiana State University
College of Business

Academics

Mainly geared toward students early in their business careers, the MBA program at Indiana State University offers graduate-level preparation to aspiring managers and business professionals. "You get a lot of value for the money" at ISU, where small class sizes and public-school tuition combine to deliver plenty of bang for your buck. With fewer than 100 students in the MBA program, the school offers a friendly and caring environment in which to study. Students repeatedly report that the "faculty is very knowledgeable," but also "very friendly, always willing to help, and very supportive." The school's administration also earns praise for its accessibility. The result is a school community in which "everyone works together to achieve a common goal: allowing us to get our MBA in an excellent environment. The whole school—including the dean—recognizes the MBAs and appreciates what they do for the school."

The Indiana State MBA consists of 33 semester units (plus foundational course work for students who did not study business as an undergraduate), which can be completed in one year and four months of full-time study. Students wishing to continue to work while they earn their MBAs may also choose to study part-time. Part-time students tell us that the school's small and intimate environment is particularly beneficial for them, as "the small size of the university and of the MBA program is advantageous in getting to know fellow students, even if one works full-time." Through core course work and electives, the program emphasizes strategic thinking, problem-solving skills, organizational change, international business, and group dynamics.

The program's emphasis on critical thinking means that "students come out of school without the idea that they already know everything. Students are more than willing to learn and can think outside the box." But students also have plenty of access to hands-on projects: Business students have the opportunity to assist faculty in real-world research projects through programs such as the Small Business Development Center (SBDC), which provides business planning assistance to start-up companies, and through consulting services to existing small businesses. In addition, the school offers excellent Graduate Assistantship programs, which cover the cost of tuition and give participants the opportunity to "work with faculty on a daily basis."

Career and Placement

In 2004, the College of Business opened the Career Experience Center (CEC), where students can research positions using the Sycamore CareerLink electronic database, attend career-building workshops, and prepare for interviews. A premier institution in the tri-state area, students at Indiana State University say their school "provides opportunities in the region which otherwise would not exist;" however, they also point out that the school could provide more internship and job fairs to improve the career development opportunities available to students.

DALE VARBLE, DIRECTOR, MBA PROGRAM
INDIANA STATE UNIVERSITY, TERRE HAUTE, IN 47809 UNITED STATES
PHONE: 812-237-2002 • FAX: 812-237-8720
E-MAIL: MBA@INDSTATE.EDU • WEBSITE: WEB.INDSTATE.EDU/SCHBUS/MBA.HTML

Student Life and Environment

Like many business schools, ISU tends to attract two types of students: recent graduates and older, returning students, "many of whom are part-time." Not surprisingly, part-time students tend to limit their campus activities to class and have little interest in extracurricular socializing. The full-time students tend to be more social. As many have recently graduated from college, they share a general camaraderie and sense of campus culture. In fact, many of the full-time students "live in the same housing, so they have gotten to know each other well." Moreover, the faculty and staff help to promote unity and spirit amongst the MBA population: For example, a second-year student tells us, "I am VP of our MBA Association and try to plan social events in which the faculty participates. We have had decent turnout considering the fact that professors do have lives outside of ISU." Campus culture in general is welcoming, and "students are generally very friendly with one another and accepting of new students from varied backgrounds."

For those looking for a typically collegiate experience, the ISU campus is home to over 10,000 students. The active college community provides a wide variety of clubs, organizations, and activities for interested students, so "there is plenty to do as long as students make an attempt to get involved in student organizations such as fraternities, sororities, or any other social club." The school's "many international students" provide the student body with a diversity of backgrounds and experiences. The school's location in downtown Terre Haute, Indiana, also provides students with plenty of off-campus opportunities to amuse themselves.

Admissions

In considering applicants for the MBA program, Indiana State University considers the following criteria: acceptance to the School of Graduate Studies; successful completion of undergraduate degree; GPA of at least 2.5; basic computing skills; GMAT scores; and prerequisite competency. Prerequisite course work for the program includes micro- and macroeconomics, financial and managerial accounting, finance, principles of marketing, principles of management, management science, and statistics. Potential students must display a GMAT-GPA admissions index of 1050 or higher (the admissions index numbers are calculated by multiplying GPA by 200 and adding GMAT scores). However, the school states that "applicants with an index between 950 and 1050, or whose grade point average is less than 2.5 on a 4-point scale, will be considered on a case-by-case basis."

FINANCIAL FACTS

Annual tuition (in-state/ out-of-state)	$4,170/$8,280
Fees	$74
Cost of books	$900
Room & board	$7,800
% of students receiving aid	30
% of first-year students receiving aid	30
% of students receiving grants	30
Average award package	$12,210
Average grant	$6,210

ADMISSIONS

Admissions Selectivity Rating	**70**
# of applications received	136
% applicants accepted	73
Average GMAT	522
Range of GMAT	400-750
Average GPA	3.16
TOEFL required of international students	Yes
Minimum TOEFL (paper/computer)	550/213
Application fee	$35
Regular application deadline	Rolling
Regular notification	Rolling
Deferment available	Yes
Maximum length of deferment	2 years
Transfer students accepted	Yes
Transfer application policy Will only accept 6 credit hours from AACSB-accredited universities.	
Non-fall admissions	Yes

Applicants Also Look At

Ball State University, Illinois State University, Indiana University—Kokomo, Indiana University—Purdue University Indianapolis, McMaster University, Purdue University, The University of Texas at Austin.

EMPLOYMENT PROFILE			
Career Rating	**60***		
	Grads Employed by Function	**%**	**Avg. Salary**
	Human Resources	10	NR
	Marketing/Sales	10	NR
	MIS	10	NR
	General Management	30	NR

INDIANA UNIVERSITY—BLOOMINGTON
KELLEY SCHOOL OF BUSINESS

GENERAL INFORMATION

Type of school	Public
Environment	Town
Academic calendar	Semester

SURVEY SAYS . . .
Good peer network
Happy students
Smart classrooms
Solid preparation in:
Marketing
Quantitative skills

STUDENTS

Enrollment of parent institution	37,958
Enrollment of business school	678
% male/female	75/25
% out-of-state	78
% part-time	41
% minorities	15
% international	38
Average age at entry	28
Average years work experience at entry	5

ACADEMICS

Academic Experience Rating	**96**
Student/faculty ratio	26:1
Profs interesting rating	99
Profs accessible rating	99
% female faculty	33
% minority faculty	13

Joint Degrees
MBA/JD 4 years, MBA/MA (area studies) 3 years, MBA/MA (telecommunications) 3 years, MBA/JD 3 years.

Prominent Alumni
John T. Chambers, president and CEO, Cisco Systems, Inc.; Phillip Francis, chairman and CEO, PetSmart; Jeff M. Fettig, chairman and CEO, Whirlpool Corporation; Hideo Ito, chairman, CEO, Toshiba; Bradley Alford, president and CEO, Nestlé Brands Co.

Academics

Not many top 20 MBA programs earn accolades for their "down-to-earth culture," but the Kelley School of Business at Indiana University—Bloomington isn't just any top-20 MBA program. Maybe it's the school's distance from the nation's economic epicenters, or maybe it's just the confidence that comes from having "a phenomenal faculty" and a highly innovative, highly respected curriculum, but whatever the reason, students here leave the program with not only a first-rate education but also a singularly warm and fuzzy feeling about the school and their experiences there.

The Kelley MBA commences with a 15-week integrated core curriculum "consisting of eight subjects taught by eight faculty. It's an amazing learning experience." Students tell us that "the core is frustrating, challenging, and fun all at the same time. The integrated curriculum helps students make connections between business functions." It helps that "core faculty are excellent teachers although most also have extensive research backgrounds." The core and a leadership/professional/career development module consume most of the first semester; the second allows students to begin major and elective work, enhanced by industry-focused, week-long 'academies' that provide concentrated exposure to a business sector through guest speakers, seminars, field trips, and case competitions. Many students make key business contacts through their academy experiences; one student reports, "Everyone in the Investment Management Academy got their jobs through alumni, who took special interest in helping us succeed at their companies."

Students tell us that it's difficult to find a weak discipline here; Indiana "is strong across all core disciplines," providing a "great all-around business education covering marketing, operations, finance, and entrepreneurship." But it's the friendly and supportive atmosphere that impresses students most; they report glowingly of "faculty who are always willing to help students outside of class, for career searches, school projects, internships and even full-time work issues." One MBA sums up, "The greatest strength of the school is the collaborative environment fostered by the administration, faculty, and students. I truly feel like people try to help each other as much as possible."

Career and Placement

Top b-schools rarely have recruiting woes, and although Indiana isn't exactly a hop, skip, and jump from Wall Street, Kelley has little trouble attracting top recruiters to campus. One student reports, "There are approximately 100 companies that come to recruit 200 MBA grads. For finance majors, there are substantially more jobs than students." Indiana's famously loyal alumni network is also helpful when it comes time to find a job.

Not content with being merely excellent, the school works hard to broaden its recruiting profile. Students tell us that "over the past several years, many new companies have started to recruit on campus. Because Kelley is so strong in marketing, finance, and general management, most of the companies had a focus in one of those areas. Recently, the Career Placement Center has renewed its focus on consulting, investment banking, and investment management firms."

Top recruiters of Kelley MBAs include: Cummins, Target, Kraft Foods, Eli Lilly and Company, 3M Company, Ford Motor Company, Procter & Gamble, Intel, General Electric Company, Banc of America Securities, Guidant Corporaton, IBM, Microsoft, Northwest Airlines, PricewaterhouseCoopers.

James Holmen, Director of Admissions and Financial Aid
1275 East Tenth Street, Suite 2010, Bloomington, IN 47405-1703 United States
Phone: 812-855-8006 • Fax: 812-855-9039
E-mail: MBAOFFICE@INDIANA.EDU • Website: WWW.KELLEY.INDIANA.EDU/MBA

Student Life and Environment

The Kelley program is quite labor intensive, especially during the first semester of first year. One first-semester student says, "If I am not preparing for the next day's classes, I am working with my team on a deliverable or . . . participating in mock interviews." The school's excellent facilities, which include breakout rooms and "a great student lounge where students mingle and work," provide a study-friendly environment. When students have free time, they "hit a rotation of four or five bars, tailgate during football season, and, of course, participate in school-sponsored activities," as well as join professional and social groups. Because most students live within five miles of campus, "You will often run into fellow students at the grocery store, out at restaurants, or at the mall. Life here is pleasant, uncrowded, and affordable." Even jaded urbanites find Bloomington agreeable as well as "surprisingly forward-thinking and modern. There are new and high-end apartments opening up . . . within walking distance to downtown Bloomington, making the school car-optional (in the right locations)." Students with significant others happily report that "a Partners Club supports current students' family members and partners. It's been a tremendously positive experience for my wife and me," writes one student.

Kelley students enjoy "great school spirit" in "a very collaborative environment. Students are not competitive. We have student-led review sessions and feel that we have achieved a goal when our colleagues succeed." They are the type of "very driven, hardworking, extremely bright people" you would expect to find at a top program. Most are "are from the Midwest and plan on staying in the Midwest. Perhaps for this reason, they don't have the egos you may find at other business schools (perhaps in bigger cities)."

Admissions

The Kelley MBA program is highly selective. The Admissions Office considers all the following factors: academic record, including cumulative grade point average, area of concentration, balance of electives, and trend of grades; GMAT scores; work experience (2 or more years strongly recommended); evidence of leadership ability; two letters of reference; and personal essays. Successful applicants need not have majored in business as undergraduates but should understand algebra and statistics and have some facility with spreadsheets. Calculus is important for some majors. Kelley has four separate application deadlines, with separate screening for each batch of applicants. In general, your chances are better if you apply early; however, it is better to wait for a later deadline if doing so will improve your application. Those seeking merit scholarships should try to apply by the January 15 deadline.

FINANCIAL FACTS

Annual tuition (in-state/ out-of-state)	$14,234/$29,056
Fees	$1,403
Cost of books	$1,900
Room & board	$8,750
% of students receiving aid	95
% of first-year students receiving aid	95
% of students receiving loans	90
% of students receiving grants	60
Average award package	$28,550
Average grant	$15,500
Average student loan debt	$36,000

ADMISSIONS

Admissions Selectivity Rating	92
# of applications received	1,056
% applicants accepted	40
% acceptees attending	48
Average GMAT	645
Range of GMAT	610–710
Average GPA	3.3
TOEFL required of international students	Yes
Minimum TOEFL (paper/computer)	600/250
Application fee	$75
Regular application deadline	3/1
Regular notification	4/30
Application Deadline/Notification	
Round 1:	11/15 / 2/1
Round 2:	1/15 / 3/30
Round 3:	3/1 / 4/30
Round 4:	4/15 / 5/30
Deferment available	Yes
Maximum length of deferment	1 year
Need-blind admissions	Yes

Applicants Also Look At

Purdue University, University of Michigan, The University of North Carolina at Chapel Hill, Vanderbilt University, Washington University.

EMPLOYMENT PROFILE

Career Rating	90	Grads Employed by Function	%	Avg. Salary
Primary Source of Full-time Job Acceptances		Finance/Accounting	35	$83,934
School-facilitated activities	126 (80%)	Human Resources	1	NR
Graduate-facilitated activities	31 (19%)	Marketing/Sales	36	$81,110
Average base starting salary	$83,875	MIS	1	NR
Percent employed	90	Operations/Production	5	$79,055
		Consulting	12	$98,921
		General Management	5	$86,428
		Other	2	NR

Top 5 Employers Hiring Grads

Cummins; Johnson & Johnson; Citigroup; Procter & Gamble; GE.

INDIANA UNIVERSITY—KOKOMO
SCHOOL OF BUSINESS

GENERAL INFORMATION
Type of school	Public
Environment	Village
Academic calendar	Semester

SURVEY SAYS . . .
Friendly students
Cutting-edge classes
Happy students
Smart classrooms
Solid preparation in:
Marketing

STUDENTS
Enrollment of parent institution	2,735
Enrollment of business school	114
% male/female	94/6
% part-time	81
% minorities	1
% international	2
Average age at entry	31
Average years work experience at entry	8

ACADEMICS
Academic Experience Rating	**75**
Student/faculty ratio	7:1
Profs interesting rating	77
Profs accessible rating	84
% female faculty	43
% minority faculty	21

Academics

The predominantly part-time, local student body of the MBA program at Indiana University—Kokomo love the convenience, the affordability, and the prestige of their graduate business program. A public school that is one of only a dozen AACSB-accredited MBA programs in the state of Indiana, Kokomo, represents the best option for businesspeople seeking an affordable career advancement opportunity in and around this city of 50,000.

IU Kokomo's program is "attuned to the regional industry base" of north-central Indiana but is also flexible enough to "foster effective management of resources in diverse organizational units and settings." Students tell us that the program is well designed "to meet the overall aspirations of the employees of the local companies," which they appreciate. Because nearly all its students work full-time, the program offers flexible scheduling. All required classes are held during the week in the evening hours; electives are offered either during the day or in the evenings. Classes are alternately offered in 8- and 16-week formats, accommodating both those in a hurry to complete course work and those who wish to learn at a (somewhat) less frantic pace. In either format, "MBA classes emphasize frequent presentations and assignments, so the pace of classes is hectic and challenging." Except for a capstone course, classes may be taken in any order, another accommodation to the convenience of IU's busy students. Part-time students generally complete the 30-credit program in four years.

Students love the IU faculty, which is comprised of many "active researchers published in peer-review journals," some of whom also happen to be "excellent instructors with teaching awards." One MBA writes, "We have an excellent group of professionals who constantly strive to improve themselves and their students by seeking new challenges." Most professors "are extremely knowledgeable and very eager to help students and offer advice or guidance, [and they] are understanding of working students, especially when work requires us to travel." MBAs also appreciate how Kokomo's smaller campus "offers an intimate learning environment."

There are also drawbacks to a small program on a small campus, MBAs note. Many feel that they "need more diverse business classes. The school needs to offer more electives and concentration areas." One MBA opines, "More major choices like finance and accounting and IT in the MBA would be welcome. Also, the school needs to offer electives on entrepreneurship. Right now it's only available as an independent study." Also on students' wish list remain "opportunities to work with local companies and industries and participate on projects with them."

LINDA FICHT, MBA DIRECTOR
PO BOX 9003, KOKOMO, IN 46904-9003 UNITED STATES
PHONE: 765-455-9465 • FAX: 765-455-9348
E-MAIL: LFICHT@IUK.EDU • WEBSITE: WWW.IUK.EDU/MBA

Career and Placement

IU Kokomo does not aggressively promote its career services for MBA students. Because most students in the program "are employed full-time in positions of responsibility," few actually require placement services or career counseling, and those who do generally rely on the assistance of their professors. MBAs may take advantage of the university's Office of Career Services, which maintains job boards, a Career Library and Resource Center, and online career-related databases. Those actively seeking work complain that "the quality of on-campus recruiting employers, the placement facilities, and the connections to alumni and businesses in the community all need improvement."

Kokomo MBAs are "a very diverse group with a wide range of industry backgrounds." Their employers include DaimlerChrysler, Delphi Delco, First National Bank, First Source Bank, Star Financial Bank, General Motors, Haynes International, Howard Community Hospital, St. Joseph Hospital, Subaru-Isuzu, and other smaller local businesses. Students regard their peers as "friendly, and more importantly, they submit assignments [on] time and are well prepared for tests. They value teamwork."

Student Life and Environment

"There's not much to do on campus" at IU Kokomo, which provides "a good learning environment [but] no social aspects." The situation doesn't bother most MBAs, who barely have time for their classes and study groups, much less extracurricular activity. The school offers child care services, which students greatly appreciate. Additionally, it is worth highlighting the efforts of the MBA Association (MBAA), which organizes social and intellectual events for those students who do spend time on campus. The school invites business leaders as part of its distinguished lecture series, enabling students to learn from some of the business world's top players.

Admissions

Admission to the MBA program at IU Kokomo requires a bachelor's degree from an accredited college or university (business major not required); a completed application to the program; a personal statement; and official transcripts for all postsecondary academic work. Most applicants must also submit GMAT scores; those already holding graduate degrees from accredited institutions, however, are exempted from this requirement. An admission index (AI) of at least 1000 under the formula [(undergraduate GPA × 200) + GMAT score] is required of all applicants who submit GMAT scores. Successful completion of undergraduate-level courses in calculus, statistics and composition, and a background in microcomputer applications are prerequisites to beginning the MBA program; however, these courses can be completed after admission to the program. International applicants must meet the aforementioned requirements and must also submit TOEFL scores. The school reports that "admission decisions are based on an overall assessment of the applicant's academic capability, professional achievement, and potential. The MBA program admits students for Fall, Spring, and Summer semesters."

FINANCIAL FACTS

Annual tuition (in-state/ out-of-state)	$7,110/$15,930
Fees	$420
Cost of books	$850

ADMISSIONS

Admissions Selectivity Rating	**74**
# of applications received	32
% applicants accepted	84
% acceptees attending	100
Average GMAT	543
Average GPA	3.4
TOEFL required of international students	Yes
Minimum TOEFL (paper/computer)	550/213
Application fee	$40
International application fee	$60
Regular application deadline	8/1
Regular notification	Rolling
Deferment available	Yes
Transfer students accepted	Yes
Transfer application policy 6 credits from AACSB-accredited schools.	
Non-fall admissions	Yes
Need-blind admissions	Yes

Applicants Also Look At

Indiana University—Bloomington, Purdue University.

INDIANA UNIVERSITY OF PENNSYLVANIA
EBERLY COLLEGE OF BUSINESS AND INFORMATION TECHNOLOGY

GENERAL INFORMATION
Type of school   Public
Academic calendar   Semester

SURVEY SAYS . . .
Friendly students
Smart classrooms

STUDENTS
Enrollment of parent institution	14,248
Enrollment of business school	238
% male/female	61/39
% out-of-state	69
% part-time	52
% minorities	5
% international	68
Average age at entry	27
Average years work experience at entry	2

ACADEMICS
Academic Experience Rating	**83**
Student/faculty ratio	11:1
Profs interesting rating	90
Profs accessible rating	87
% female faculty	23
% minority faculty	33

Joint Degrees
MBA 1 year, MBA (with concentration) 1.5 years.

Prominent Alumni
Richard B. Clark, president and CEO, Brookfield Financial Properties LP; Terry L. Dunlap, president, Allegheny Ludlum; Regina Dressel Stover, senior vice president, Mellon Financial Corporation; Timothy W. Wallace, CEO, FullTilt Solutions; Jeffrey R. DeMarco, director of human resources, KPMG International.

Academics

"Affordable and away from the hustle and bustle of the city," the Eberly College of Business and Information Technology at Indiana University of Pennsylvania

offers a "high-quality education at a very affordable price." Thanks to the school's numerous partnerships with overseas schools, Eberly also provides "international exposure" and is "a great fit for international students, since it offers a diverse academic program and environment with the opportunity to interact with students from different parts of the world."

Students appreciate that "IUP's MBA program is large enough to be widely recognized by employers yet small enough to allow for many one-on-one learning experiences." Professors here "are diverse in background, culture, and work experience" and "have a handle on the real world." "One of my management professors serves as an external consultant for the World Bank and the United Nations, and it has been a pleasure to interact with her and participate in her class," reports one MBA. My marketing professor has been an advisor/consultant of the government of the former Czechoslovakia Republic during the country's transition from state-owned and planned to marketing economy. I was impressed by his vast experience and passion for teaching marketing." IUP's "tough but helpful" instructors bring "a myriad of global, real-world experiences" to the classroom. Sure, they "expect a lot from you, but that is a good thing. The environment is very focused on helping you succeed." Students also appreciate the program's "top-notch" technological capabilities that include "multiple computer labs, computers, projectors, and document readers in every classroom, campus wide Wi-Fi, and the availability of almost any software program you might encounter in the workforce."

Students see their program as "strongly geared toward manufacturing." Some feel the program "could benefit from introducing more service-industry scenarios and case studies," while others would like to see "more concentrations like entrepreneurship, supply chain management, and statistics." Those days may not be that far off if the "growing popularity of IUP" leads to an expansion of the program. Currently the school offers concentrations only in accounting, finance, human resource management, international business, management information systems, and marketing.

Career and Placement

IUP's Office of Career Services provides counseling and placement services to the university's undergraduates, graduate students, and alumni. Assistance in resume writing, interviewing, and job-hunting skills is available. The office maintains an extensive library, provides hard-copy and online job postings, and organizes recruiting events both on and off campus. Students wish the office would "get more recruiters to come onto campus so the students would not have to travel off campus for interviews."

Companies recruiting on the IUP campus include: Alcoa, American Express, Bristol-Myers Squibb Company, Champion International, CIGNA, DuPont Company, Eddie Bauer, EDS, ExxonMobil, Federated Investors, General Motors, Georgia Pacific, IBM, JC Penney, K-Mart, Mellon Bank, PepsiCo, PNC Bank, Sony Electronics, Sun Microsystems, Wal-Mart, The Walt Disney Company, and Westinghouse. All the major public accounting firms including Deloitte Touche Tohmatsu; Ernst & Young; PricewaterhouseCoopers; KPMG International; and Arthur Andersen LLP, recruit annually on campus.

KRISH KRISHNAN, DIRECTOR OF ADMISSION
664 PRATT DRIVE, ROOM 402, INDIANA, PA 15705-1081 UNITED STATES
PHONE: 724-357-2522 • FAX: 724-357-4862
E-MAIL: IUP-MBA@IUP.EDU • WEBSITE: WWW.EBERLY.IUP.EDU/MBA

Student Life and Environment

IUP is located in Indiana, Pennsylvania, "a very attractive town with a very friendly atmosphere" that, for many, makes it "the perfect atmosphere to explore business at a comfortable pace to understand the basics before being thrown into a very rapid workforce. This town and school give the students an opportunity to learn at their own pace." While many appreciate that the "pretty" school is isolated "from many of the dangers city campuses must deal with," some bemoan the fact that "there are not too many attractions around," even if it does have a "very nice environment for study." Some see the remote location as an impediment to increased on-campus job recruiting.

Campus life includes "many clubs that one could get involved in" as well as lots of events, meetings, and projects, to the point that "there isn't much time for anything else." Explains one student, "IUP encourages students to network with one another and to become involved to get the most out of our graduate school experience. I know I will be leaving this program with a group of people located all around the world that I will be able to contact throughout my career."

IUP's MBA program is home to "an extremely diverse population of international students with a wide array of real-world knowledge that allow for an eye-opening education, especially in the international field of business." Most are young, as "Older students attend classes at a satellite location."

Admissions

All students in the MBA program at IUP must have completed an undergraduate degree at an accredited college or university with a grade point average of at least 2.6. The school requires official transcripts from all postsecondary schools attended, an official GMAT score report (minimum score of 450 required), two letters of recommendation from professors (for those completing undergraduate study) or from employers/supervisors (for those with at least 4 years of professional experience), a completed resume, and a one-page personal statement of goals in pursuing an MBA. In addition to the above, international students must also submit a Foreign Student Financial Affidavit. Those who attended undergraduate institutions at which English is not the primary language must have their transcripts translated and interpreted by a professional service. International students whose first language is not English must submit an official TOEFL score report (minimum score of 200 on the computer-based test, 533 on the paper-based test).

FINANCIAL FACTS

Annual tuition (in-state/ out-of-state)	$6,048/$9,678
Fees (in-state/ out-of-state)	$1,069/$1,132
Cost of books	$900
Room & board	$5,160
% of students receiving aid	36
% of first-year students receiving aid	22
% of students receiving loans	72
% of students receiving grants	5
Average award package	$8,100
Average grant	$8,100

ADMISSIONS

Admissions Selectivity Rating	74
# of applications received	274
% applicants accepted	70
% acceptees attending	70
Average GMAT	532
Range of GMAT	450–620
Average GPA	3.17
TOEFL required of international students	Yes
Minimum TOEFL (paper/computer)	550/213
Application fee	$30
International application fee	$30
Regular application deadline	7/30
Regular notification	Rolling
Deferment available	Yes
Maximum length of deferment	1 year
Transfer students accepted	Yes
Transfer application policy	
Written request for transfer required of transfer applicants. Maximum of six credits transfer.	
Non-fall admissions	Yes
Need-blind admissions	Yes

Applicants Also Look At

Duquesne University, University of Pittsburgh, West Virginia University

EMPLOYMENT PROFILE

Career Rating	71	Grads Employed by Function	%	Avg. Salary
Primary Source of Full-time Job Acceptances		Other	72	$49,250
Percent employed	72			

Indiana University—South Bend
School of Business and Economics

GENERAL INFORMATION

Type of school	Public
Academic calendar	Semester

SURVEY SAYS . . .

Friendly students
Cutting-edge classes
Happy students
Smart classrooms
Solid preparation in:
Finance

STUDENTS

Enrollment of parent institution	7,420
Enrollment of business school	223

ACADEMICS

Academic Experience Rating	**61**
Student/faculty ratio	17:1
Profs interesting rating	70
Profs accessible rating	67
% female faculty	15
% minority faculty	33

Academics

The School of Business and Economics at Indiana University—South Bend gears its MBA program toward the needs of the part-time student. Here, "classes meet once a week in the evening, making it easy to attend school and work full-time." Most classes begin at 7:00 P.M., accommodating students who have to travel some distance after work in order to get to class. MBA students here typically take two classes in each of the fall and spring semesters and one class during each summer session; this allows most students who hold business undergraduate degrees to complete the program in just two years.

Phase I of the IUSB MBA covers skills prerequisite to advanced business study. Classes in economics, financial accounting, financial management, marketing, mathematics, organizational behavior, and statistics cover material typically covered in undergraduate business programs. Students with undergraduate business degrees typically place out of these courses; other students may place out by passing a competency examination in each field. Phase II consists of seven core courses in buyer behavior, international business, legal and ethical issues in business, management information systems, managerial price theory, production management, and strategic financial management. Phase III covers advanced subjects and allows for students to take two electives. Phase IV consists entirely of a capstone course. Students must pass a final comprehensive exam in order to receive their degrees.

Students here praise the "excellent MIS/MIT offerings" and the "small classes with friendly, approachable professors" who "have a wealth of experiences in the business world. The whole experience is very student-centered here." A "great library and facilities" and "strength in the high-technology area" help students handle the heavy burden of the program, and international students enjoy "strong support in housing, counseling, etc." Many here, however, feel that "the program needs to allow for specialization" and wish that "the school could offer more choices for specific strategic business classes and project management classes."

Career and Placement

The Career Services Office at IUSB serves the entire student and alumni population of the school. The office is primarily dedicated to undergraduates, although its services are also available to MBAs. The office provides the standard complement of job-search services, skills seminars, personal assessments, and one-on-one counseling. The following is a partial list of employers who attended IUSB's spring job fair in 2006: First Source Bank, AM General, Ave Maria Press, Bankers Life and Casualty Company, Becker Professional Review, Cintas, Citigroup, Craighead, Lange and Hough, Crowe Chizek and Company, Fastenal, Fastsigns, JPMorgan Chase, John Hancock Financial Network, Lippert Components Inc., Menards, Northwestern Mutual Finance Network, Peoplelink Staffing Solutions, Productivity Management, Inc., SCORE, Spyglass Search, and the Teachers Credit Union.

SHARON PETERSON, GRADUATE BUSINESS RECORDS REPRESENTATIVE
1700 MISHAWAKA AVENUE, PO BOX 7111, SOUTH BEND, IN 46634-7111 UNITED STATES
PHONE: 574-520-4138 • FAX: 574-520-4866
E-MAIL: GRADBUS@IUSB.EDU • WEBSITE: WWW.IUSB.EDU/~BUSE/GRAD

Student Life and Environment

The IUSB MBA program caters to part-time students, the majority of whom are "full-time employed, mostly with children, working to improve their situation." Full-time students "tend to be international students" representing "a wide mix of nationalities from Africa, Asia, the Americas, etc." This "mostly friendly and helpful" population includes individuals from "a wide range of ages, from the 20s to the 50s." Students note that "all the diversity in the student body helps us see things from different perspectives."

Don't expect to pal around with your classmates here, though, as "going to class at night and working all day leaves little time for socializing during the week." IUSB MBA students "have mostly a commuter attitude. They only spend time on campus to attend class."

IUSB is a midsize state university with an undergraduate population of approximately 6,400 and a graduate population of about 1,100. South Bend is a substantial city, with a population of over 100,000. Major employers in the metropolitan area include IUSB, the University of Notre Dame, Memorial Hospital, St. Joseph Regional Medical Center, ADP, AG Edwards, Bosch, Coachman Industries, FedEx, Honeywell, Liberty Mutual, and State Farm. The advertising, aviation, biotechnology, engineering, finance, and nonprofit sectors all have a strong presence in the region. South Bend's location offers relatively easy access to Indianapolis and Chicago.

Admissions

The MBA program at Indiana University—South Bend requires applicants to submit all of the following: a completed application and data sheet, available online; official transcripts for all postsecondary academic work; two letters of recommendation (recommendation form available online); a personal statement describing one's background, outlining one's goals in the program, and recounting an experience that led to personal growth; and an official score report for the GMAT. International students whose native language is not English must submit all of the above as well as an official score report for the TOEFL; minimum required score for consideration is 550 (paper-based test) or 213 (computer-based test). Applications are accepted for admission commencing with the Fall, Spring, or Summer semesters. IUSB admits students at two levels: Full Admission and Probationary Admission. Full Admission requires a minimum GMAT score of 450 and an undergraduate business degree from an AACSB-accredited school with a minimum GPA of 2.75. Probationary Admission is granted to applicants "whose GPA does not quite meet minimum standards." Such students must maintain an in-program GPA of at least 2.75 in order to remain in the program.

FINANCIAL FACTS

Annual tuition (in-state/ out-of-state)	$4,050/$9,720
Cost of books	$700
Room & board (on/off-campus)	$5,000/$8,000

ADMISSIONS

Admissions Selectivity Rating 60*

# of applications received	49
% applicants accepted	100
% acceptees attending	69
Range of GMAT	430–690
TOEFL required of international students	Yes
Minimum TOEFL (paper/computer)	550/213
Application fee	$45
International application fee	$55
Regular application deadline	7/1
Regular notification	Rolling
Deferment available	Yes
Maximum length of deferment	1 year
Non-fall admissions	Yes

Applicants Also Look At

University of Notre Dame, Western Michigan University.

INDIANA UNIVERSITY—SOUTHEAST
SCHOOL OF BUSINESS

GENERAL INFORMATION

Type of school	Public
Environment	Village
Academic calendar	Semester

SURVEY SAYS . . .
Cutting-edge classes
Happy students
Smart classrooms
Solid preparation in:
Operations

STUDENTS

Enrollment of parent institution	6,164
Enrollment of business school	203
% part-time	99
Average age at entry	28
Average years work experience at entry	6

ACADEMICS

Academic Experience Rating	**83**
Student/faculty ratio	15:1
Profs interesting rating	83
Profs accessible rating	70
% female faculty	22
% minority faculty	16

Joint Degrees
MBA/MSSF 3 to 4 years.

Academics

The MBA program at Indiana University—Southeast is designed to be a part-time program; students must petition the MBA Policies Committee to take more than the normal course load of six credit hours per semester and three credit hours per each of two summer sessions. That suits most students here fine. They're largely a full-time working, part-time degree-seeking group ready to put in at least two years' work to earn their degrees.

IUS's MBA curriculum is divided into four phases. The first "emphasizes the development and mastery of the fundamental tools of decision-making," while the second focuses on communication skills, ethical issues, and functioning within the business environment. The third phase consists of advanced courses as well as an integrative class in decision-making; the fourth includes a strategic management class and two electives. Students with non-business undergraduate degrees typically must complete up to eight foundation classes before beginning their MBA work. Some students tell us that "course work doesn't seem to 'build' and there are no academic concentrations, which is a major disappointment." Most, however, focus on the positives, which include "good technology integration into curriculum, . . . small classes that can be very attractive to someone wanting more one-on-one interaction with their professor, [and the] challenging workload."

A community service requirement of 20 hours "in projects such as volunteering for Big Brothers/Big Sisters, providing tax assistance to the elderly or disadvantaged, or participating in a United Way agency" is a unique aspect of this program. "Services such as directing or participating in a community cleanup sponsored by the Rotary Club or chairing a church clothing drive for the needy are acceptable projects because they serve a need of the greater community." Once students have completed their service, they must submit a one- to two-page summary of their role in the experience to the MBA director.

Career and Placement

The Office of Career Services and Placement at IUS serves all undergraduate and graduate students at the school. It offers all the standard services: "opportunities for career exploration, clarification, and professional growth, thereby increasing career awareness, instilling personal confidence, providing enhanced employment opportunities, and encouraging [students and alumni] to achieve their personal and professional career-related goals"—in other words, counseling, job fairs, workshops, and online job boards. MBAs here would like to see "better networking and job-search opportunities. Because nearly every student already has a job, there is not much in the way of recruitment or networking through the school."

Student Life and Environment

IUS "is a commuter campus," so "students come to class and leave." Classes are also offered at an off-campus site in Jeffersonville, IN, at the IU Southeast Graduate Center; this is very convenient for students who are coming in from nearby Louisville, KY. A typical student writes, "I tend to go straight to my class, which meets once a week, am engaged in it for three hours, then go right home. I have a family at home, and it is my preference to not participate in the limited school activities." Those limited activities include "various meetings to help students network with other students, teaching staff, and other business professionals." Some here feel "more clubs and/or activities geared specifically toward MBA students would be nice."

Jay White, PhD, Director of Graduate Business Programs
Hillside Hall 117, 4201 Grant Line Road, New Albany, IN 47150 United States
Phone: 812-941-2364 • Fax: 812-941-2581
E-mail: iusmba@ius.edu • Website: www.ius.edu/MBA

The IUS curriculum requires some teamwork, and fortunately "there are many locations available to meet with groups or teams." The school also boasts "a brand-new, state-of-the-art library that is almost completed, which will offer many more meeting rooms and high-tech equipment available for student use."

MBAs at IUS are a "diverse group. Some students are younger and the MBA program represents an extension of their undergraduate degree, while others have been in the workforce for at least ten years prior to returning to the classroom." One MBA writes, "The diversity (minority, work experience, life experience) in the student population is what contributes so much to the academic excellence at the school. Students learn from each other." The preponderance of professionals here means students are "generally more cooperative, as the vast majority hold full-time jobs and competition is really a non-factor."

Admissions

Completed applications to the IUS MBA program must include an official GMAT score report, official copies of all undergraduate transcripts, and a resume. The school uses the following formula to evaluate candidates: [(undergraduate GPA × 200) + GMAT score]. IUS looks for candidates with a formula score of at least 1050, with GMAT scores of at least 470. Students with undergraduate degrees in business are likely to place out of some or all of the school's eight foundation courses in business; all other admitted students must complete these foundation courses before beginning work on the actual MBA.

FINANCIAL FACTS

Annual tuition (in-state/ out-of-state)	$240/$540 per credit hour

ADMISSIONS

Admissions Selectivity Rating	**82**
# of applications received	89
% applicants accepted	57
% acceptees attending	76
Average GMAT	558
Range of GMAT	513–603
Average GPA	3.24
TOEFL required of international students	Yes
Minimum TOEFL (paper/computer)	550/213
Application fee	$35
International application fee	$55
Regular application deadline	Rolling
Regular notification	Rolling
Deferment available	Yes
Maximum length of deferment	Indefinite
Transfer students accepted	Yes

Transfer application policy
Students may transfer a maximum of 6 graduate credit hours (with no gradoc below B) from another AACSB-accredited MBA program to count toward the 36 credit hour MBA curriculum at IU Southeast. Students may request that graduate credit not meeting this criterion be reviewed for transfer approval. The final disposition of all transfer course work is determined by the Graduate Business Policies Committee.

Non-fall admissions	Yes
Need-blind admissions	Yes

Applicants Also Look At

Bellarmine University, University of Louisville.

INSEAD

GENERAL INFORMATION

Type of school	Private
Academic calendar	Sept.–July

SURVEY SAYS . . .
Good social scene
Good peer network
Solid preparation in:
General management
Doing business in a global economy
Entrepreneurial studies

STUDENTS

Enrollment of parent institution	
Enrollment of business school	887
% male/female	76/24
% international	89
Average age at entry	29
Average years work experience at entry	5

ACADEMICS

Academic Experience Rating	**74**
Student/faculty ratio	7:1
Profs interesting rating	98
Profs accessible rating	84
% female faculty	15

Prominent Alumni
Lindsay Owen-Jones, CEO, L'Oreal; Helen Alexander, CEO, The Economist Group; Patrick Cescau, CEO, Unilever; Paul Desmarais ,Jr., CEO, Power Corp. Canada.

Academics

To some INSEAD MBAs, their school is "the only truly international MBA" available. With two campuses located halfway around the globe from each other—one in Singapore, the other outside Paris—and the option to study at both during the "very accelerated" one-year program offered here, INSEAD truly has an advantage over other pretenders to the title. A student body "from all over the world, with no nationality represented by more than 10 percent of the intake" in any give term, further bolsters INSEAD's claim to primacy. Students may apply to either INSEAD campus; more than half choose to take their core requirements in one location, and then travel to the other for at least one of the curriculum's three elective segments. Exchange with Wharton is also available during the fourth and fifth segments of the curriculum. The program begins with two two-month core sequences covering basic business principles and functional skills. The final three two-month segments include courses in global and IT management issues plus 10 electives, chosen from a portfolio of 80. Students tell us that the program "is really well designed. It is probably the most dynamic and innovative school in the world." While some say "it's too intensive, with not enough time to digest sufficiently before graduation," others tell us "it suits [our] ambitions perfectly. We learn fast and there is never a lull, but the workload is manageable and [we]'ve learned a great deal that I think [we] can apply directly." INSEAD professors are "a mix of stars and some clouds of dust. The stars can make a lecture blow your mind, while the clouds of dust can leave you stranded in a boring space. Fortunately there are more stars." An exchange student from Wharton reports, "INSEAD professors are much better prepared for classes—evident in the depth of material covered in the allotted time—than professors I had at Wharton." Students identify consulting, finance, and entrepreneurship as the faculty's strongest areas. INSEAD's administration is a tale of two campuses—or, more accurately, a tale of two countries. One student explains, "In France, the day-to-day administration is poor, as is the IT. The country is not efficient, nor particularly friendly." In Singapore, on the other hand, "The administration is extremely efficient. Everyone knows your name—the food servers, the office personnel, sometimes even the receptionist. The campus has about 100 students and it is very intimate." Basically, "the Singapore campus runs like a Ferrari while the Fontainebleau campus runs like a Peugeot."

Career and Placement

INSEAD maintains Career Services offices on both its European and Asia campuses. The offices promote students to employers around the globe while providing MBAs with one-on-one counseling and coaching, job-search strategies, and on-campus recruiting events. Students generally feel that "Career Services could improve. The school has a great record of top companies coming on campus, and the alumni network is very efficient, but sometimes INSEAD Career Services could be more proactive in connecting students with companies who are not on-campus recruiters." Students in Asia complain that "the Career Services is not yet connected to all major Asian companies here in Singapore," but they also point out that "additional resources recently allotted to Career Services here is a good start." An "alumni network so huge you find them wherever you go [is] extremely accessible and supportive." Employers most likely to hire INSEAD MBAs include McKinsey & Company; American Express Company; Booz Allen Hamilton; GE; The Boston Consulting Group; Johnson & Johnson; Bain & Company; A.T. Kearney; Honeywell; and Royal Dutch Shell.

Student Life and Environment

Dealing with "a one-year program that leaves everyone fully focused on school life" means "life at school is very hectic" for students on both INSEAD campuses. The school mandates some fun time by declaring about 15 "National Weeks" per school year, during which "each country 'owns' a specific week and activities are organized around a country theme. Students are given specific names related to the country and the professors use them, which make interactions really funny. One of my friends was called Albert Einstein all through German Week." Students also participate in "twenty or so different clubs. The school is MBA-only, so clubs are all with MBAs. This puts pressure on MBAs to organize clubs in an already hectic year, but it also means that the networking with your classmates is that much better." When they can find time, students in Fontainebleau organize small group dinners or "blowout parties in elegant French country chateaus with professional DJs, dancers, and always an open bar." Students experience "good French cuisine, good wine, enjoyable social activities, a great forest, and the pleasure of living in a nice and typical French town." Coming along with the territory is a "bureaucracy and inefficiency impossible to experience elsewhere." Students organize "fewer activities in Singapore but more group travel and barbecues. Indeed, most participants tend to stay in the same two buildings near the campus," which is "fabulous" with its "modern facilities," and is contrasted by escapes to Bali or Thailand. INSEAD students "are definitely the greatest asset at the school," according to their peers. One explains, "You will not find a more international group at any school in the world. I've been to other schools that boast an 'international' student body. That usually means the occasional token Asian. Here you have equal numbers of Chinese, Indians, French, Brits, Americans, etc. To top it off, every one of those people is from the top of their respective classes before coming here." Even though "students are graded on a forced z-curve, so there are people who will fail a class," INSEAD MBAs "are helpful to each other and most tend to do fine." One student says, "This year has been truly unforgettable—I would recommend the program to anyone who wants to meet talented, fantastic people from literally every corner of the world."

Admissions

INSEAD has two intake points, in September and January. Students may apply to begin the program at either time; application is online only. All applicants must provide a personal profile, resume, five personal essays, two recommendations attesting to leadership potential and management capacity, a photograph, an official GMAT score report, and official transcripts for all postsecondary academic work. In addition, all students must enter the program with proficiency in English and a second language. Non-native English speakers may submit results from the TOEFL, TOEIC, CPE, or IELTS. English speakers must provide certification of a second language. A third commercially useful language (sorry, no Latin!) is required to graduate. While language instruction is available through INSEAD, the intensity of the MBA program is such that the school recommends students get a start on their third language before the program begins. While most admitted students have "several years of meaningful professional experience and demonstrate clear management potential," work experience is not a hard-and-fast prerequisite to admission. The applicant's choice of campus is not taken into account in the admission decision; however, placement at one's campus of choice is not fully guaranteed.

FINANCIAL FACTS

Annual tuition	$63,400
Cost of books	$1,500
Room & board (off-campus)	$28,500
% of first-year students receiving aid	50
Average grant	$15,000

ADMISSIONS

Admissions Selectivity Rating 60*

Average GMAT	702
Range of GMAT	620–790
Average GPA	4
TOEFL required of international students	Yes
Minimum TOEFL (paper/computer)	620/260
Application fee	$250
Regular application deadline	3/23
Regular notification	6/24
Application Deadline/Notification	
Round 1:	3/23 / 6/24
Round 2:	5/18 / 9/9
Round 3:	6/29 / 10/14
Non-fall admissions	Yes
Need blind admissions	Yes

EMPLOYMENT PROFILE				
Career Rating	90	**Grads Employed by Function%**	**Avg.**	**Salary**
Primary Source of Full-time Job Acceptances		Finance/Accounting	21	NR
Percent employed	88	Marketing/Sales	12	NR
		Operations/Production	4	NR
		Strategic Planning	10	NR
		Consulting	38	NR
		General Management	10	NR
		Other	5	NR

IONA COLLEGE
HAGAN SCHOOL OF BUSINESS

GENERAL INFORMATION
Type of school	Private
Affiliation	Roman Catholic
Environment	City
Academic calendar	Trimester

SURVEY SAYS . . .
Cutting-edge classes
Solid preparation in:
Presentation skills

STUDENTS
Enrollment of parent institution	4,242
Enrollment of business school	266
% male/female	47/53
% out-of-state	24
% part-time	87
% minorities	15
% international	9
Average age at entry	27
Average years work experience at entry	3

ACADEMICS
Academic Experience Rating	**72**
Student/faculty ratio	6:1
Profs interesting rating	78
Profs accessible rating	81
% female faculty	20
% minority faculty	5

Prominent Alumni
Alfred F. Kelly, Jr., group president, American Express Company; Robert Greifeld, president, NASDAQ; Randel A. Falco, chairman and CEO, AOL; Fran Nolan, executive vice president, TIAA-CREF; Catherine R. Kinney, president and Co-COO, NYSE Group Inc.

Academics

The Hagan School of Business at Iona College enjoys "a solid reputation in New York." That, and "the flexibility of the program"—it "offers many distance learning and hybrid courses so that you can take lecture classes with your peers, or web-based classes on your own time"—appeal to the predominantly part-time student body here. Hagan also fits the needs of those in a hurry to complete their degrees; explains one MBA, "The classes are on a trimester basis, meaning the overall length of the program is shorter, allowing you to graduate faster." Students tell us that "the trimester schedule of classes seems to be designed with working individuals in mind."

Hagan has a relatively small graduate business program, creating a "small-school setting that allows a sense of community amongst the students and the teachers." Students may attend classes on the main campus in New Rochelle or at the Rockland Graduate Center in Pearl River. Online classes are available. The school also offers onsite MBA at Wyeth Ayert Pharmaceutical offices; the on-site option is also available to employees of Ford Motor Company, Jaguar Cars, Land Rover Group, and Volvo Cars. Regardless of the option, Iona works hard to accommodate working students and their employers. One student writes, "The cooperation between the school and the company in which I was an employee was great. The school facilitated many factors for the students including parking, general access, registering, paying, and having small classes. They also provide classes through distance learning."

Iona professors "are savvy in all areas and tend to be knowledgeable and available when needed." They are demanding, but they "are great as long as you do the work and pay attention to what they are talking about." Students appreciate that "it seems like [professors] are all very involved in their fields, consulting or running their own businesses, [which] allows them to stay current and apply real experience to academic theory." Iona offers concentrations in finance, human resource management, information decision technology management, marketing, and management. The school also offers certificate programs in international business and e-commerce.

Career and Placement

The Gerri Ripp Center for Career Development handles counseling and placement services for all Iona students and alumni. Students tell us that "Iona has several career guidance and placement programs and several academic and community social justice programs in the Catholic tradition. Iona is one of the most respected colleges in the greater New York metropolitan region." Even so, many here feel the office needs to improve its game. One student says, "Career services are important to many MBA students who are looking to leave their current employer after completing the MBA program. There are limited resources in the area of career services for these individuals, however."

Student Life and Environment

"There is life constantly on campus" at Iona's main campus in New Rochelle, MBAs tell us. "Even after 5:00 [P.M.], which could be considered off peak, there are always students milling about. We frequently get together after classes to meet and talk. Many graduate students belong to clubs and athletic teams, which brings a strong sense of community." One student adds, "It's fast paced because everyone is involved in something, from clubs to athletics to on-campus jobs. It's a very friendly environment and not too small or not too big." Students at the satellite campuses tell us that "the majority of clubs, activities, etc., occur at the New Rochelle campus." These students "pretty much attend class and then go home. Students do not hang out at the Rockland Graduate Center. Most go to

VERONICA-JAREK-PRINZ, DIRECTOR OF MBA ADMISSIONS
715 NORTH AVENUE, NEW ROCHELLE, NY 10801 UNITED STATES
PHONE: 914-633-2289 • FAX: 914-637-7720
E-MAIL: HAGAN@IONA.EDU • WEBSITE: WWW.IONA.EDU/HAGAN

their classes and then go home to their families. However, everyone is friendly, and you do get to know your classmates."

Iona MBAs are a mixed group. On the New Rochelle campus, "Many are young, fresh from getting their undergraduate degree." In fact, some are recent graduates of Iona, taking advantage of course waivers to speed through their MBAs. However, "There are also many who are older, with children, trying to balance their school, career, and life. It is a diverse group in terms of ethnicity, experiences, and personality." A number of Iona's full-timers are international students who "are able to give international insight into the very globally focused business courses."

Admissions

Applicants to the Hagan MBA program must submit the following materials: a completed Hagan School of Business application form, along with a $50 application fee; copies of official transcripts from each undergraduate and graduate institution attended; two letters of recommendation; and an official score report for the GMAT reflecting a score no more than 5 years old (the GMAT requirement may be waived for applicants with at least 7 years of post-undergraduate professional experience). International applicants must submit all of the materials listed above, as well as an official score report for the TOEFL, WES, and cash support affidavit. Transcripts in languages other than English must be translated and interpreted by an approved service. Applications are processed on a rolling basis and are valid for 1 full year from the day they are received by the school. Applicants may request an interview, which the school recommends but does not require.

FINANCIAL FACTS

Annual tuition	$17,955
Fees	$150
% of students receiving aid	68
% of first-year students receiving aid	90
% of students receiving loans	44
% of students receiving grants	29
Average award package	$10,723
Average grant	$1,937
Average student loan debt	$22,118

ADMISSIONS

Admissions Selectivity Rating	**69**
# of applications received	96
% applicants accepted	84
% acceptees attending	84
Average GMAT	430
Range of GMAT	300–600
Average GPA	3.25
TOEFL required of international students	Yes
Minimum TOEFL (paper/computer)	550/213
Application fee	$50
Regular application deadline	Rolling
Regular notification	Rolling
Deferment available	Yes
Maximum length of deferment	1 year
Transfer students accepted	Yes
Transfer application policy Max of 6 upper-level credits accepted. 30 credit minimum required to earn a degree at Iona.	
Non-fall admissions	Yes
Need-blind admissions	Yes

Applicants Also Look At
Fordham University, Pace University.

ITHACA COLLEGE
SCHOOL OF BUSINESS

GENERAL INFORMATION
Type of school	Private
Academic calendar	Semester

SURVEY SAYS . . .
Happy students
Solid preparation in:
General management
OperationsTeamwork
Communication/interpersonal skills

STUDENTS
Enrollment of parent institution	6,412
Enrollment of business school	640
% male/female	47/53
% out-of-state	32
% part-time	32
% minorities	5
% international	5
Average age at entry	24
Average years work experience at entry	1

ACADEMICS
Academic Experience Rating	**76**
Student/faculty ratio	1:1
Profs interesting rating	80
Profs accessible rating	79
% female faculty	32
% minority faculty	20

Joint Degrees
MBA 10 months, MBA (professional accountancy) 10 months.

Academics

MBA students in Ithaca College's small graduate program may choose between two programs: an MBA in business administration and an MBA in professional accountancy. Both degrees require 35 credit hours and can be completed by full-time students in 12 months—and this is the selling point of the program. As one student explains, "A 1-year program offered me a faster track to my post-MBA life."

The curriculum for Ithaca's Business Administration MBA starts with function-level analysis of firms. Once students have mastered the workings of an individual business, the focus grows wider to encompass entire industries, finally concluding with a project in which students analyze an industry of their choice and assess individual firms within that industry. Classes emphasize "a balance between building technical and interpersonal skills," and students praise professors for their "hands-on teaching philosophy." "The faculty is always willing to bend over backwards to meet students' academic and professional needs," says one student. "While the professors remain rather rigid in their expectations of students, most will work tirelessly with students to ensure they succeed." Another student notes, "The school does a good job offering elective courses that are in line with students' career aspirations. Since the program is small, faculty surveys students prior to each semester. The result is a course offering that honestly reflects the interests of students. I see this adaptability as Ithaca's greatest strength because it can help overcome the obstacles often associated with a smaller business school."

Ithaca's Professional Accountancy MBA primarily functions as the culmination of a 5-year undergraduate/graduate program for students in the college's undergraduate accounting program, although candidates from other schools can gain admission. Most here agree that although "many students that graduated from Ithaca as undergrads" are now part of the MBA program, there are also "older" or "married" students in attendance.

The curriculum includes a thorough review of principles of business administration as well as advanced instruction in financial accounting and reporting, managerial and cost accounting, auditing, taxation, and principles of business law. Students in both programs are full of praise for the school. "Overall, I think the school is really starting to take off. Ithaca worked hard to receive AACSB accreditation, [and] since that happened the school has retained high standards for both students and faculty." Another adds, "Tuition is high, but you can definitely see where the money went. Everything from the smart boards in the classrooms—which help make articulating difficult accounting concepts much easier—to the trading room is state-of-the-art."

Students note that the 1-year duration of the program helps offset the relatively high cost of attending. That said, while it had been a "little pricey" in the past, "Prices have come down." They also appreciate the fact that the business school administration "welcome(s) comments and suggestions from the grad students on what could help better the program. If you have any problems, they do their best to help you solve the issues." The future's looking good here, so bring your shades. As one student points out, "When the new business building is constructed (which should be soon), the program will get bigger and become better known."

Career and Placement

The Ithaca College Career Services Office provides self-assessment inventories, e-Recruiting tools, one-on-one advising, mock interviews, workshops, a library, and on-campus recruiting. The school also hosts a graduate school job fair and other special recruiting events. Though despite all this, some students find that "Ithaca could do a better job attracting recruiters from upper-tier businesses." While they appreciate the "many local recruiters on campus" and "ample alumni network and mentoring program," some still find a dearth of businesses at which they're "trying to get [their] foot in the door."

Employers who recruit on the Ithaca campus include Lockheed-Martin, Merrill Lynch, PricewaterhouseCoopers, Ernst & Young, Deloitte & Touche Tomastu, KPMG International, and an active alumni recruiting network.

Student Life and Environment

MBA students at Ithaca College enjoy "a great community atmosphere" at a school that "is just the right size, so that you can go anywhere and know somebody, and meet somebody new." One student writes, "All students are easygoing and approachable. The small size of the program means that many people have identical course schedules. This makes for a tight-knit group of students and strong, long-lasting friendships."

The demands of the program keep MBA students "pretty detached from the rest of the campus. You never deal with grad students from any of the other programs (unless they happen to take a business elective)." However, "Students work hard and play hard" when their schedule allows. "Most weekends I find myself in one or more bars or restaurants eating and drinking with classmates," says one student. Ultimately, "Life at Ithaca is good."

Admissions

Applicants to Ithaca's MBA program must have completed either a bachelor's program in business or accounting, or a bachelor's program in any field along with having taken Ithaca's Pre-MBA Modules. Post-undergraduate work experience is not required; in fact, many students enter the program immediately after completing work on their bachelor's degree. Successful applicants typically have "an undergraduate GPA of 3.0 or higher and a minimum GMAT score of 500." All applications must include official undergraduate transcripts, official GMAT scores, and two letters of recommendation in addition to the essay. Merit-based academic scholarships are also available from the program.

FINANCIAL FACTS

Annual tuition	$21,875
% of students receiving aid	43
% of first-year students receiving aid	48
% of students receiving grants	43
Average grant	$4,700

ADMISSIONS

Admissions Selectivity Rating	**70**
# of applications received	36
% applicants accepted	83
% acceptees attending	77
Average GMAT	515
Range of GMAT	460–590
Average GPA	3.36
TOEFL required of international students	Yes
Minimum TOEFL (paper/computer)	550/213
Application fee	$40
Regular application deadline	8/1
Regular notification	8/15
Deferment available	Yes
Transfer students accepted	Yes
Transfer application policy Transfer credits from AACSB-accredited institutions accepted on case-by-case basis.	
Non-fall admissions	Yes
Need-blind admissions	Yes

EMPLOYMENT PROFILE

Career Rating	60*
Primary Source of Full-time Job Acceptances	
Unknown	20 (100%)

JACKSONVILLE STATE UNIVERSITY
COLLEGE OF COMMERCE AND BUSINESS ADMINISTRATION

GENERAL INFORMATION
Type of school	Public
Environment	Village

SURVEY SAYS . . .
Friendly students
Cutting-edge classes
Happy students
Solid preparation in:
Finance
General management
Communication/interpersonal skills

STUDENTS
Enrollment of parent institution	9,100
Enrollment of business school	90
% male/female	50/50
% out-of-state	10
% part-time	70
% minorities	10
% international	75
Average age at entry	30
Average years work experience at entry	3

ACADEMICS
Academic Experience Rating	**69**
Student/faculty ratio	15:1
Profs interesting rating	75
Profs accessible rating	73
% female faculty	33

Academics

The College of Commerce and Business Administration at Jacksonville State University offers a small, predominantly part-time AACSB-accredited MBA program that students praise for its convenience, affordability, and "personalized attention." The school serves the city of Jacksonville and the eastern Alabama region.

JSU offers both full-time and part-time MBA tracks. JSU's undergraduate program generally provides the majority of full-time students, as most continue directly from their bachelor's degree on to earn their master's. The part-time program is the almost-exclusive domain of area residents "who are working full-time and trying to get ahead in their careers by getting an MBA."

A sequence of foundation courses makes the JSU MBA available to everyone, even students with no previous academic experience in business. The eight-course foundation track covers business organization and administration; statistics; principles of financial accounting; macroeconomics; business; finance; business law and ethics; operations and technology; and marketing. Students with undergraduate course work in these areas may place out of the courses and begin immediately on degree-related course work, which consists of 10 courses: seven required courses, one organization class chosen from a group of three, one international business class chosen from a group of three, and an elective. Students may choose to pursue a concentration in accounting, which requires an additional six hours of course work.

All candidates for a master's degree at JSU must pass comprehensive oral examinations at the end of their program, which some here find stressful and unnecessary. "I do not agree with the oral exams policy. If instructors believe that a student knows the material and that student makes the grade on exams and projects, that should be sufficient," writes one student. Otherwise, students generally express satisfaction with the program, praising the school's administration ("It has a good vision and is focused") and the "well-read, detail-oriented, and dedicated" professors who "have good experience in the fields in which they teach." While most here applaud the school's efforts to provide distance-education options, they also anxiously await the day when the school works the bugs out of the system. One MBA warns, "The school often puts too many students in the distance-learning classes. Also, we lose 20 minutes on average per class due to technical difficulties."

Career and Placement

JSU's Office of Career Placement Services is oriented primarily toward serving the school's undergraduate programs, although it also offers services to graduate students and alumni. The office coordinates career fairs, referrals, on-campus job interviews, and job listings. It also maintains a reference room, conducts mock interviews, and offers workshops in resume writing. Students can sign up for an e-mail service that notifies them whenever new jobs are posted with the school. Individual career counseling is offered through the Office of Counseling and Career Services.

Dr. Jean Pugliese, Associate Dean
700 Pelham Road North Jacksonville, AL 36265 United States
Phone: 256-782-5329 • Fax: 256-782-5321
E-mail: pugliese@jsucc.jsu.edu • Website: www.jsu.edu

Student Life and Environment

Students describe their peers as "academically curious, energized, competitive, and sociable." While "there are a lot of activities from student organizations Monday to Thursday" available to MBAs on the FSU campus, most students are "way too busy balancing personal lives (jobs, spouses, kids, volunteer work, church) and school to worry about clubs!" Once Friday rolls around, "most residents go home, and the campus is a ghost town on weekends." The school could "improve school spirit and attendance at school activities" but so many students only have time to be on campus for class that the point might be moot.

JSU is the largest employer in Jacksonville, an eastern Alabama town of approximately 8,000. Other major employers in the area include the Anniston Army Depot, the Regional Medical Center, and a number of manufacturing and distribution concerns. Jacksonville is less than 100 miles from Atlanta and Birmingham.

Admissions

Applicants to the JSU MBA program must meet one of the following minimum requirements to be considered for unconditional admission: a score of at least 950 under the formula [(undergraduate GPA × 200) + GMAT score]; or a score of at least 1000 under the formula [(undergraduate GPA for final 64 hours of course work taken toward undergraduate degree × 200) + GMAT score]. Scores of 850 (entire undergraduate GPA) or 900 (final 64 hours) are sufficient to qualify students for conditional admission. Students admitted conditionally must earn a GPA of at least 3.0 for their first 12 hours of graduate course work and must complete the course work within a time frame established by the Graduate Committee. All applicants must first seek admission to the College of Graduate Studies; only after gaining admission to the college are they admitted to a particular program. Applicants must then provide the college of Graduate Studies with official copies of all postsecondary academic transcripts and three Graduate Reference forms completed by people who can assess the applicant's potential for success in the MBA program. Applicants whose native language is not English must provide an official TOEFL score report.

FINANCIAL FACTS

Annual tuition (in-state/ out-of-state)	$4,050/$8,100
Cost of books	$1,500
Room & board (on/off-campus)	$2,500/$8,500
Average grant	$1,000

ADMISSIONS

Admissions Selectivity Rating	**71**
# of applications received	19
% applicants accepted	68
% acceptees attending	100
Average GMAT	462
Range of GMAT	410–490
Average GPA	3.26
TOEFL required of international students	Yes
Minimum TOEFL (paper/computer)	500/173
Application fee	$20
Transfer students accepted	Yes
Transfer application policy 6 hours of approved courses with grade of A or B.	
Non-fall admissions	Yes
Need-blind admissions	Yes

JOHN CARROLL UNIVERSITY
THE BOLER SCHOOL OF BUSINESS

GENERAL INFORMATION

Type of school	Private
Affiliation	Roman Catholic-Jesuit
Environment	Metropolis
Academic calendar	Semester

SURVEY SAYS . . .

Students love University Heights, OH
Friendly students
Cutting-edge classes
Helpful alumni
Happy students
Solid preparation in:
Communication/interpersonal skills

STUDENTS

Enrollment of parent institution	3,830
Enrollment of business school	193
% male/female	89/11
% out-of-state	1
% part-time	86
% minorities	1
Average age at entry	26
Average years work experience at entry	3

ACADEMICS

Academic Experience Rating	**73**
Student/faculty ratio	17:1
Profs interesting rating	88
Profs accessible rating	77
% female faculty	12
% minority faculty	1

Joint Degrees

Communications management 2 to 3 years, nonprofit adminstration 2 to 3 years.

Academics

Accountancy is the strongest area at the Boler School of Business at John Carroll University, a Jesuit institution on the outskirts of Cleveland. One JCU student reports, "The people in this program are predominantly accounting students. The emphasis in many of the classes, even non-accounting classes, has a strong focus on accounting." Through the Accountancy Department, students can receive either an MBA with a concentration in accountancy or an MSAcc. Beyond this specialization, Boler also offers MBA concentrations in finance, marketing, human resource management, and international business.

Designed to meet the needs of part-time students, the Boler MBA offers a great degree of "flexibility of scheduling." Students may proceed through the program at their own pace, taking as few as one or as many as four courses per term (the latter option allows students with undergraduate business degrees to graduate in one year). Boler's membership in the 23-school Jesuit MBA network also affords students who relocate mid-program the opportunity to transfer all their credits to a Jesuit MBA program in or near their new hometown.

The Boler MBA is divided into four blocks. The first block consists of eight foundation courses, some or all of which can be waived on the basis of undergraduate academic achievement. Required courses covering fundamental business functions constitute the second block. The third block consists of three electives, one of which must be among a group of international business classes. The final block consists of two integrative courses covering business ethics and corporate strategic management. The school's Jesuit foundations ensure that ethics are stressed throughout the curriculum.

MBAs at Boler report that "the greatest strength of JCU is its culture. The students, faculty, staff, and administrators are all friendly and helpful. The focus is always on developing the whole person though academics and ethics discussions." Instructor access is the subject of much praise. One student writes, "I didn't think I would be able to meet and speak with my professors with the same frequency as my undergraduate experiences, but every time I've requested to meet or speak with one of my professors, it has always been a smooth process." Professors "are able to bring experience as well as theory to their classes [and] are very well known in their fields—in many cases considered experts." Some MBAs here feel that the school "needs to develop more concentrations and focus the program toward those concentrations" in order "to become more competitive with leading business schools." Campus technology also needs an upgrade, students report.

Career and Placement

Boler MBAs seeking career guidance and placement services may use the Center for Career Services, which attends to the needs of the entire university population. Services provided include online job and resume posting, counseling, and interview scheduling. The office also functions as a clearinghouse for alumni network contacts and employer inquiries. An annual business-related job fair, open to both graduates and undergraduates in the business school, draws more than 100 recruiters to the campus.

GAYLE BRUNO-GANNON, ASSISTANT TO THE DEAN ADMISSIONS AND RECRUITING
20700 NORTH PARK BOULEVARD, UNIVERSITY HEIGHTS, OH 44118-4581 UNITED STATES
PHONE: 216-397-1970 • FAX: 216-397-1833
E-MAIL: GGANNON@JCU.EDU • WEBSITE: BSOB.JCU.EDU/GRADUATEBUSINESS

Student Life and Environment

Because "about half the MBA students have jobs and are extremely busy; a good portion are married; [and] most students here attend part-time and only come to campus for class once a week, it is more difficult to bond here than it would be in a full-time program, and most people are mainly focused on their lives/jobs outside of school." School thus functions as "a complement to that life." Some wish the school offered "more graduate-student activities, clubs, and more opportunities for career planning, mentoring, and meeting with successful alumni." They see the formation of a Graduate Student Association, which "is working on developing a graduate-student life and addressing graduate-student issues," as a step in the right direction.

The "hardworking, busy professionals" who populate most of the part-time ranks stand in stark contrast to the majority of full-timers, who "have just completed their undergraduate degrees and have no relevant real-world work experience." Some feel that "the school caters to these students a great deal; the classes are more like advanced undergraduate classes rather than graduate classes for working professionals." Others approve of both the pacing and the classroom mix, telling us that their peers "come from a variety of academic and work backgrounds. Many are entry-level and midlevel management. The program is somewhat competitive, but not a cutthroat environment."

Admissions

Applicants to John Carroll University's MBA program must provide the school's admissions department with a completed graduate school application form, an official GMAT score report, official transcripts for all postsecondary academic work, at least one letter of recommendation, a resume, and a statement of purpose essay titled, "Graduate business education: Enabling me to achieve my personal goals and become a leader." International students must also provide TOEFL scores, appropriate financial documentation, and, when applicable, an English translation of all documents submitted in a language other than English. Academic record and GMAT scores are the most important factors in the admissions decision; letters of recommendation, the essay, and work experience are also considered important. According to the school's website, previous work experience "is not required, but having professional experience provides a frame of reference for classroom discussion, and is therefore encouraged."

FINANCIAL FACTS

Annual tuition	$14,274
Cost of books	$800
% of students receiving aid	44
% of first-year students receiving aid	23
% of students receiving loans	61
% of students receiving grants	12
Average award package	$18,500
Average grant	$5,300

ADMISSIONS

Admissions Selectivity Rating	**78**
# of applications received	126
% applicants accepted	54
% acceptees attending	57
Average GMAT	544
Range of GMAT	450–640
Average GPA	3.2
TOEFL required of international students	Yes
Minimum TOEFL (paper/computer)	550/215
Application fee	$25
International application fee	$35
Regular application deadline	Rolling
Regular notification	Rolling
Deferment available	Yes
Maximum length of deferment	1 year
Transfer students accepted	Yes
Transfer application policy	

Applicants from members of the Network of MBA programs at Jesuit universities and colleges will have all credits transferred. Otherwise, applications are reviewed on a case-by-case basis.

Non-fall admissions	Yes
Need-blind admissions	Yes

Applicants Also Look At
Case Western Reserve University, Cleveland State University.

KENNESAW STATE UNIVERSITY
MICHAEL J. COLES COLLEGE OF BUSINESS

GENERAL INFORMATION

Type of school	Public
Environment	Town
Academic calendar	Semester

SURVEY SAYS . . .

Cutting-edge classes
Helpful alumni
Happy students
Solid preparation in:
Accounting
Communication/interpersonal skills
Computer skills

STUDENTS

Enrollment of parent institution	19,854
Enrollment of business school	755
% male/female	55/45
% part-time	100
Average age at entry	31
Average years work experience at entry	8

ACADEMICS

Academic Experience Rating	**78**
Student/faculty ratio	6:1
Profs interesting rating	76
Profs accessible rating	83
% female faculty	35
% minority faculty	12

Academics

Prospective MBAs at the Michael J. Coles College of Business at Kennesaw State University may choose from three program options: the Coles MBA, offered in Kennesaw, Dalton, and the Cobb Galleria scheduled for the convenience of its predominantly part-time student body; a WebMBA, which allows more experienced students to complete the degree in 18 months with only a single visit to campus (the rest of the program can be completed from home); and an MBA for Experienced Professionals, an 18-month Executive MBA program in which classes meet one weekend per month. Coles also offers a Master of Accounting (MAcc) degree.

Students in the Coles MBA program, the most popular of the options, appreciate the "flexibility it gives students who work full-time" and the "excellent curriculum that lets you choose from courses that are actually applicable to your career." Professors here "are knowledgeable and supportive [and] have extensive experience in their fields. They usually have more than one graduate degree and are very involved in the business community in Atlanta." One MBA tells us, "Never have I experienced such a committed group of individuals." Some students complain that "there are many excellent classes in the catalog. However, most are rarely offered." But most focus on positive aspects of the program. One student sums up, "The challenge of this program has shown me what I'm truly made of! I've done things that I never would have dreamed of doing. As a result, I have a tremendous amount of confidence in my personal ability. This experience has and will open hundreds of doors, not just in the workplace, but most importantly, in my mind."

Career and Placement

KSU's Career Services Center coordinates a number of events and provides a range of services to the school's graduate business students. Events and services include career fairs, internship fairs, a statewide job fair, and ongoing on-campus interviews, as well as OwlTRAK, an online job- and resume-posting database. The CSC regularly updates its website to keep students informed of upcoming events.

In addition, KSU has contracted Career Beam to provide students with assessments and counseling services, access to exclusive databases, and resume, cover letter, and career-planning counseling. (Call it outsourcing if you like.) Students give the service good marks, and especially like the fact that the services are provided at no additional cost to them.

Student Life and Environment

With over 19,000 students, Kennesaw State is the third-largest school in the University System of Georgia. Located just 20 miles northwest of downtown Atlanta, KSU is conveniently located to benefit from the wealth of the big city. The school draws faculty and guest lecturers from the metropolitan area and full-time students find it easier to secure meaningful internships because of the city's many opportunities.

The Coles College is located in the Burruss Building, a modern business facility complete with tiered and traditional classrooms, seminar rooms, meeting areas, and networked computer labs. All classrooms are equipped to accommodate modern presentation technology. Burruss is also the site of the Tetley Lectures, an endowed series that regularly brings business leaders to campus to lecture and interact with Coles students.

DAVID BAUGHER, DIRECTOR OF ADMISSIONS
1000 CHASTAIN ROAD, #132, KENNESAW, GA 30144 UNITED STATES
PHONE: 770-420-4377 • FAX: 770-423-6885
E-MAIL: KSUGRAD@KENNESAW.EDU • WEBSITE: WWW.COLESMBA.COM

Most Coles MBAs are part-time students with jobs and families, and accordingly, most "show up, do [their] work, discuss some issues with classmates, and head home." To accommodate these students, "classes are mainly at night. The people here are friendly; it is not a competitive program at all since people are usually already employed." A "significant number of foreign students adds to [the] diverse mix," though students detect "a couple of distinct groups of students. There is one group of people who have plenty of work experience and are building upon this. The other group has little work experience and doesn't add as much to group activities. The first group seems to be taking harder classes and harder professors to learn more from this experience. The second group targets less challenging professors just to get out." Full-time students report "a diverse environment that is set up to promote interaction between students. There are many activities designed to bring the school together. The athletics give the school the national recognition that they deserve."

Admissions

Applicants to the Coles MBA and MACC programs at Kennesaw State must submit the following to the Office of Graduate Admissions: a completed application (hard copy or on-line); one official transcript for each school attended, including the school that awarded the baccalaureate (a minimum undergraduate GPA of 2.8 is required for admission); and an official report of GMAT score. In addition, international applicants must also provide TOEFL scores (if their native language is not English); a sponsor letter; a bank letter certifying sufficient support funds; a copy of a valid passport; an evaluation of all transcripts for academic work completed outside the U.S.; and proof of immigrant status. The Graduate Business Office reserves the right to request, in addition, a resume, statement of objectives, and two letters of recommendation from all candidates. At least two years of full-time professional business experience is strongly preferred for candidates to all programs. Applicants for the Coles Executive MBA should contact that Office for Admissions requirements, procedures, selectivity, and fees. 1.   Applicants for the Coles Executive MBA should contact that Office for Admissions requirements, procedures, selectivity, and fees.

FINANCIAL FACTS

Annual tuition (in-state/ out-of-state)	$2,926/$11,704
Fees	$606
Cost of books	$1,300
Room & board (on/off-campus)	$4,000/$6,000

ADMISSIONS

Admissions Selectivity Rating	**81**
# of applications received	192
% applicants accepted	47
% acceptees attending	78
Average GMAT	520
Range of GMAT	480–550
Average GPA	3.19
TOEFL required of international students	Yes
Minimum TOEFL (paper/computer)	550/213
Application fee	$50
International application fee	$50
Regular application deadline	Rolling
Regular notification	Rolling
Deferment available	Yes
Maximum length of deferment	1 year
Transfer students accepted	Yes
Transfer application policy Transfer credit from AACSB-international-accredited universities is possible. Limits and restrictions apply.	
Non-fall admissions	Yes
Need-blind admissions	Yes

Applicants Also Look At
Georgia State University, University of Georgia.

KENT STATE UNIVERSITY
THE COLLEGE OF BUSINESS ADMINISTRATION AND GRADUATE SCHOOL OF MANAGEMENT

GENERAL INFORMATION

Type of school	Public
Environment	Village
Academic calendar	Semester

SURVEY SAYS . . .
Students love Kent, OH
Good social scene
Helpful alumni
Happy students
Smart classrooms
Solid preparation in:
Computer skills

STUDENTS

Enrollment of parent institution	22,697
Enrollment of business school	261
% male/female	55/45
% out-of-state	10
% part-time	60
% minorities	5
% international	21
Average age at entry	24
Average years work experience at entry	1

ACADEMICS

Academic Experience Rating	**63**
Student/faculty ratio	25:1
Profs interesting rating	89
Profs accessible rating	61
% female faculty	22
% minority faculty	5

Joint Degrees
MBA/MS (nursing) 3 years,
MBA/Master of Library Science 3
years, MBA/Master of Architecture 3
years.

Prominent Alumni
Yank Heisler, CEO, Key Bank
Corporation; Leigh Herington, Ohio
State Senator; M. R. Rangaswami,
co-founder, Sand-Hill Venture
Capital LLC; Richard Ferry, chair-
man, Korn-Ferry International;
George Stevens, Dean, College of
Business, Kent State University.

Academics

The Graduate School of Management at Kent State University offers both a full-time MBA and a part-time professional MBA, with the ratio of part-time students to full-time students being roughly two to one. The school also offers three dual-degree options (in conjunction with the Nursing program, the Library Science program, and the Architecture program), as well as opportunities to study abroad. Finally, the Kent State GSM offers an Executive MBA to candidates with the prerequisite amount of work experience and the support of their employers.

A Kent State MBA requires between 39 and 54 hours of course work. It can be completed by a full-time student in 15 months, though many students take two years to finish. The number of required credits depends upon the student's undergraduate work in business. A core course can be waived, for example, for students who have previously taken two undergraduate courses or one graduate course in the core subject and earned a grade of B or better. The entire core curriculum consists of 30 credit hours of classwork; the remainder of the program is made up of executive modules, integrative management courses, and electives. The school offers concentrations in accounting, finance, human resource management, information systems, international business, and marketing.

Students here tell us that the majority of professors "are very passionate about their fields." Most have deep real-world experience. They are "also lawyers and businesspeople and everything else, so they know what it's like to have a heavy workload, and they demand excellence without letting the class get so stuffy that you don't want to be there." Some excel at "incorporating new computer-based learning tools and keeping up with technology," although they can be stymied in their efforts by the resources of the university. "Many of the classrooms are not equipped with multimedia connections, and some professors still rely on overheads instead of PowerPoint presentations," one student warns. Students here do appreciate that the "tutoring possibilities are fabulous."

Career and Placement

The Kent State Career Services Center provides "comprehensive employment search services" for the GSM graduate students, as well as workshops in interviewing, resume writing, and job-search strategies. The CSC posts employment opportunities and coordinates on-campus interviews, and the office reports that approximately 500 employers visit the campus to hire for business and government positions each year.

Employers most likely to hire Kent State MBAs include Ernst & Young, Progressive Insurance, Key Bank, Little Tikes, Jo-Ann Stores Inc., Summa Health System, FedEx Systems, The Timken Company, and Diebold Inc.

LOUISE DITCHEY, DIRECTOR, MASTER'S PROGRAMS
PO BOX 5190, KENT, OH 44242-0001 UNITED STATES
PHONE: 330-672-2282 • FAX: 330-672-7303
E-MAIL: GRADBUS@BSA3.KENT.EDU • WEBSITE: BUSINESS.KENT.EDU/GRAD

Student Life and Environment

Kent State is a large university where "there is always something going on, whether it is a sports event or a speaker on campus. Kent gives its students many opportunities to get out of their rooms and meet people." Many agree that the school is "very large but very friendly." Full-time students here tend to be either international students or recent undergraduates. In either case, they are typically closer in age to undergraduates than to the older part-time students in their program, and they are more likely to enjoy collegiate recreation. Many work out regularly, taking advantage of "the 52,000-square-foot student recreation center, which houses an enormous weightlifting facility and cardio machines. There is a three-story rock wall, a one-sixth-mile indoor track, racquetball courts, basketball courts, volleyball courts, and badminton courts. It is the best part of campus."

Students report that Kent has "a beautiful campus" with "nice dorms" but that its "classrooms are older and not aesthetically pleasing or comfortable. The rooms are too hot in the winter and cold in the summer. The chairs are connected to the tables and when you move yours, you may move your neighbor as well." Commuters appreciate that "if you have a night class, you have the opportunity to have a member of campus security walk you to your class. Also, the bus system here is very helpful."

Kent's part-time students are typically "blue-collar managers or individuals working in small- to medium-size manufacturing and financial institutions. Most are married with children." It is "harder for those students to make time for the group projects that teachers frequently assign," we're told, which sometimes creates tension between the "older, nontraditional students" and the younger ones with fewer outside commitments. But, for the most part, full-time and part-time students get along well here. International students "are from so many different countries and walks of life, it gives an extremely diverse learning environment. Everyone learns from one another's experiences."

Admissions

Applicants to the MBA program at Kent State must provide the school with official transcripts from all postsecondary institutions attended; an official GMAT score report; a resume; letters of recommendation (three for the full-time program, two for the Professional MBA program); and a personal statement. International students must additionally provide TOEFL scores (if English is not their native language) and must complete an international student application to the school.

FINANCIAL FACTS

Annual tuition (in-state/ out-of-state)	$8,968/$15,980
Cost of books	$1,200
Room & board (on/off-campus)	$8,300/$8,000
% of students receiving aid	33
% of first-year students receiving aid	19
Average award package	$15,476

ADMISSIONS

Admissions Selectivity Rating	**69**
# of applications received	89
% applicants accepted	81
% acceptees attending	58
Average GMAT	521
Range of GMAT	420–600
Average GPA	3.35
TOEFL required of international students	Yes
Minimum TOEFL (paper/computer)	550/213
Application fee	$30
Regular application deadline	4/1
Regular notification	4/15
Deferment available	Yes
Maximum length of deferment	1 year
Transfer students accepted	Yes
Transfer application policy AASCB-accredited program; less than 6 years old by the time Kent degree is conferred; 12 credit hours maximum; approved by graduate committee and dean.	
Non-fall admissions	Yes
Need-blind admissions	Yes

Applicants Also Look At

Case Western Reserve University, Cleveland State University, John Carroll University, The Ohio State University, The University of Akron, Youngstown State University.

EMPLOYMENT PROFILE			
Career Rating	**71**	**Grads Employed by Function**	**% Avg. Salary**
		Finance/Accounting	52 $45,278
		Marketing/Sales	12 $36,500
		MIS	6 $52,500
		General Management	12 $57,500
		Other	18 $42,500

Top 5 Employers Hiring Grads
Key Bank; KMPG International; Deloitte Touche Tohmatsu; First Energy Corporation; PPG Industries.

LAMAR UNIVERSITY
COLLEGE OF BUSINESS

Academics

The MBA program at Lamar University's College of Business serves a predominantly local population drawn to the school by "convenience, affordability, and the reputation of the program." Small class sizes providing a "personal" feel, and lots of "access to professors" creates "opportunities for individuals to get involved and shine." Two of Lamar's greatest assets are its "faculty-to-student ratio and the individualized attention that the school provides," one student writes.

Lamar offers a Cohort MBA, a full-time evening program that includes several experiential learning opportunities. The program is intense; classes meet 4 nights a week, and the curriculum goes pretty much nonstop for 16 months, but those who tough it out are rewarded with an MBA earned in a relatively short time for relatively little money. Cohort MBA participants must have earned an undergraduate degree in business. The school also offers a traditional MBA, which also meets in the evenings, but it allows for part-time attendance. The traditional MBA program is open to all college graduates; those who lack the requisite academic business background must complete a series of leveling courses before commencing the MBA proper.

Both programs earn praise for "being convenient to professionals in the area and working to meet the needs of the students." University staffers "make a point to know each student personally" and the administration "is very accommodating. Schedules and special circumstances result in solutions, not brick walls. This attitude of working together applies in class and administration." One MBA adds, "The Dean encourages all of the faculty to be available to students for questions. They are always available when I need them either by their office hours, e-mail, or special appointment." Students also appreciate that "this is a growing program. As a student, I can see many opportunities for future MBA students." As for now, students are already enjoying a great "hometown feeling" that helps students manage "the stress of returning to school while raising a family and performing at work."

Career and Placement

The Career Center at Lamar has "great resources," but because the MBA program is relatively small, "MBA students must work hard to get career placement advice. More recruiters for MBA students would be a great help. The school brings in many speakers and alumni specifically for MBA students, and that is a great help." Students are satisfied that "the school is working on and needs to continue working on developing the Placement Office and networking for MBA students." Students who can get to the school during the day have a more positive outlook on the office, as many of its services and events—such as lunchtime Executive in Residence seminars—are available primarily during standard business hours. The Career Center offers one-on-one career advising, personal assessments, and online job search resources.

Employers who most frequently hire graduates include: Ernst & Young, Melton & Melton LLP, Merrill Lynch, and Chase.

DEBBY PIPER, GRADUATE ADMISSIONS OFFICE
PO BOX L0078, BEAUMONT, TX 77710 UNITED STATES
PHONE: 409-880-8356 • FAX: 409-880-8414
E-MAIL: GRADMISSIONS@HAL.LAMAR.EDU • WEBSITE: MBA.LAMAR.EDU

Student Life and Environment

"There are a lot of events to participate in around the Lamar campus," and "With the campus being smaller it is actually easier to be involved in several different groups. There are tons of leadership opportunities." Administrators and student groups "are working to involve students in networking opportunities such as socials, a mentoring program with alumni, and through guest speakers." How many MBAs get involved is another question entirely; most attend classes in the evenings and have little time to spare. One student writes, "I work 50 to 60 hours a week and attend class at night, study when I can during the week, and commit most of the weekend to school other than coaching a soccer team. As a father of four, this commitment takes time away from my family, but with an understanding wife, we are managing. The long and short of it is I don't have time for a social life on campus."

Regardless of how many hours students spend there, the Lamar campus "offers a great atmosphere for learning. This campus has traditionally been a commuter school, but it is now transitioning to a campus-centered institution. There is campus day care and increasing opportunity for extracurricular and social participation." Lamar "is adding new state-of-the-art facilities such as the dining facility, residence halls, and recreational sports facilities" in its effort to make the campus more homey and accommodating. A student adds, "The school is also working to clean up the surrounding area by buying vacant property surrounding the campus." Hometown Beaumont is "a wonderful place to raise a family. The economy is booming, and the university contributes by providing a skilled workforce to meet the expanding labor force in the area."

Admissions

Lamar University requires all applicants to provide GMAT scores, undergraduate transcripts, essays, and TOEFL scores (for students whose native language is not English). An interview, letters of recommendation, personal statement, resume, and evidence of computer experience are all recommended but not required; all are taken into account in rendering an admissions decision. Applicants must earn a score of at least 950 under the formula (200 multiplied by GPA plus GMAT) or a score of 1000 under the formula (200 multiplied by GPA for final 60 semester hours of undergraduate work plus GMAT). In both cases, a minimum GMAT score of 450 is required for unconditional admission; students with scores between 400 and 450 qualify for conditional admission. International applicants must provide proof of financial support.

FINANCIAL FACTS

Annual tuition (in-state/ out-of-state)	$3,672/$10,272
Fees	$1,104
Cost of books	$1,328
Room & board (on/off-campus)	$5,888/$6,660
% of students receiving aid	45
% of first-year students receiving aid	33
% of students receiving loans	19
% of students receiving grants	37
Average award package	$5,018
Average grant	$1,545
Average student loan debt	$720

ADMISSIONS

Admissions Selectivity Rating	64
# of applications received	48
% applicants accepted	92
% acceptees attending	66
Average GMAT	509
Range of GMAT	440–560
Average GPA	3.11
TOEFL required of international students	Yes
Minimum TOEFL (paper/computer)	525/200
Application fee	$25
International application fee	$75
Regular application deadline	5/1
Regular notification	Rolling
Deferment available	Yes
Maximum length of deferment	1 year
Transfer students accepted	Yes
Transfer application policy Accept 6 hours from another AACSB MBA program.	
Non-fall admissions	Yes
Need-blind admissions	Yes

EMPLOYMENT PROFILE

Career Rating	75	Grads Employed by Function	%	Avg. Salary
Primary Source of Full-time Job Acceptances		Finance/Accounting	30	$45,000
School-facilitated activities	20%	Human Resources	5	$40,000
Graduate-facilitated activities	80%	Marketing/Sales	20	$65,000
Percent employed	99	MIS	5	$60,000
		Operations/Production	5	$75,000
		Consulting	5	$40,000
		General Management	30	$50,000

LONG ISLAND UNIVERSITY—C.W. POST CAMPUS
COLLEGE OF MANAGEMENT

GENERAL INFORMATION
Type of school   Private
Academic calendar   Trimester

SURVEY SAYS . . .
Students love Brookville, NY
Friendly students
Cutting-edge classes
Happy students
Smart classrooms
Solid preparation in:
Teamwork

STUDENTS
Enrollment of parent
  institution   8,500
Enrollment of
  business school   271
% male/female   86/14
% out-of-state   2
% part-time   71
% minorities   4
% international   15
Average age at entry   27
Average years work
  experience at entry   6

ACADEMICS
Academic Experience Rating   65
Student/faculty ratio   15:1
Profs interesting rating   73
Profs accessible rating   64
% female faculty   23
% minority faculty   23

Joint Degrees
JD/MBA 4.5 years, BS/MBA 5 years.

Academics

One of only two AACSB-accredited MBA programs on Long Island, the College of Management at Long Island University—C.W. Post Campus serves the area's sizable population by providing a prestigious graduate degree accessible to full-timers and part-timers alike.

The vast majority of graduate students here are part-timers, attending classes in the evenings and/or on Saturdays. The college offers two programs to satisfy students' needs: the Campus MBA, with classes that meet weekly Monday through Thursday (there are two time slots for classes each night: 6:40 to 8:30 P.M., and 8:40 to 10:30 P.M.); and the Saturday MBA, which features intensive five-week classes (meeting from 9:00 A.M. to 3:30 P.M.) to allow students with the requisite undergraduate background in business to earn their degrees in 15 to 23 months. Students in the Campus MBA program may supplement their curricula with Saturday classes.

Students here extol the "excellent academic experience" and "professors who understand and are willing to accommodate students." Students complain that "the school should offer a wider range of elective courses" and wish that it would offer more "independent study [classes] to better accommodate students' interests and their graduation time frames." All students here may supplement their degrees by combining four 700-level electives to earn an advanced certificate in any of the following areas: accounting and taxation, finance, international business, management, management information systems, and marketing.

Career and Placement

The Office of Professional Experience & Career Planning at C.W. Post handles counseling and placement responsibilities for all students. The office provides self-assessment diagnostics, career counseling, resume and job-search advisement, mock interviews, job fairs, recruiting events, and online databases. An MBA association supplements these services by "helping students network with each other and exchange ideas and information helpful for career advancement in our competitive business world," according to the College's *MBA Bulletin*.

BETH CARSON, DIRECTOR OF GRADUATE AND INTERNATIONAL ADMISSIONS
720 NORTHERN BOULEVARD, BROOKVILLE, NY 11548 UNITED STATES
PHONE: 516-299-3952 • FAX: 516-299-2418
E-MAIL: BETH.CARSON@LIU.EDU • WEBSITE: WWW.LIU.EDU/POSTMBA

Student Life and Environment

Unlike most New York area schools, the Post campus of LIU boasts a "beautiful campus" spread out across 300+ acres of prime real estate. Twenty acres of the campus are devoted to an arboretum; the entire campus is heavily wooded, with over 4,000 trees that include some of the largest trees on Long Island. Students love the campus but warn that "it's hard to find many buildings the first few times on campus because it's so big" and that "there is definitely a parking problem around the most heavily used buildings."

College of Management facilities include "an excellent library and computer labs." Students appreciate that the school "is willing to spend the money necessary to upgrade facilities and classrooms, which, as a result, tend to be in great shape." Unfortunately, "the resources are not geared toward returning adult students, so things like the bookstore hours and campus facilities are not open when we're usually here." The part-timers who make up the majority of the student body note that "this is a commuter school, so there are very few clubs or activities geared toward graduate students, especially those of us who work. There is the occasional function during business hours, but many of us can't make it to them."

Post's "extremely friendly and helpful" MBA students include many students hit by the nation's recent economic woes; "There are a number of students who are here because they were not able to get a job after graduation," explains one student. Others "are working toward getting another job." Overall, "there is a range of experience levels, from significant work experience to none at all."

Admissions

Prerequisites to admission to the Post MBA include competence in business communications, mathematics, and computers, as demonstrated through undergraduate work, successful completion of a related workshop, or successful completion of a waiver exam. All applicants must submit a completed application form, an official GMAT score report, two copies of official transcripts for all postsecondary academic work, a resume, a personal essay explaining one's purpose in pursuing an MBA, and two letters of recommendation. Students whose first language is not English must also submit official results for the TOEFL (minimum score of 527 on the paper-based test, 197 on the computer-based test); students who completed undergraduate degrees from institutions that teach primarily in English are exempted from this requirement.

FINANCIAL FACTS

Annual tuition	$14,220
Fees	$630
Cost of books	$1,850
Room & board	$9,100
% of students receiving aid	80
% of students receiving loans	80
% of students receiving grants	2
Average grant	$3,000

ADMISSIONS

Admissions Selectivity Rating	**72**
# of applications received	192
% applicants accepted	65
% acceptees attending	38
Average GMAT	492
Range of GMAT	420–620
Average GPA	3.13
TOEFL required of international students	Yes
Minimum TOEFL (paper/computer)	527/197
Application fee	$30
Regular application deadline	8/7
Regular notification	8/7
Deferment available	Yes
Maximum length of deferment	1 year
Transfer students accepted	Yes
Transfer application policy	Maximum of 6 credits within the last five years (grades of B or better). AACSB-accredited school.
Non-fall admissions	Yes
Need-blind admissions	Yes

Applicants Also Look At

Hofstra University, St. John's University.

LOUISIANA STATE UNIVERSITY
E.J. OURSO COLLEGE OF BUSINESS

GENERAL INFORMATION
Type of school	Public
Environment	Metropolis
Academic calendar	Aug.–Aug.

SURVEY SAYS . . .
Friendly students
Good social scene
Happy students
Smart classrooms
Solid preparation in:
Presentation skills

STUDENTS
Enrollment of parent institution	26,229
Enrollment of business school	299
% male/female	70/30
% out-of-state	11
% minorities	9
% international	11
Average age at entry	23
Average years work experience at entry	1.5

ACADEMICS
Academic Experience Rating	**96**
Student/faculty ratio	1:1
Profs interesting rating	88
Profs accessible rating	74
% female faculty	24
% minority faculty	2

Joint Degrees
JD/MBA (also awards a BS in civil law) 4 years.

Prominent Alumni
Harry Hawks, executive vice president and CEO, Hearst-Argyle Television; D. Martin Phillips, senior managing director, EnCap Investments, LLC; Ross Centanni, chairman, president and CEO, Gardner Denver, Inc.; Richard F. Gill, executive vice president, Shaw Group, Inc.; John H. Boydstun, president of the Power Group, Capital One's banking segment and member of Capital One's executive committee.

Academics

A "world-renowned internal audit program, very intense and real-world driven," and a great football team are two of the main attractions of the Flores MBA program at the E.J. Ourso College of Business—and not necessarily in that order. Sure, students here take their schoolwork and careers very seriously, but there's something about the school's location in Baton Rouge that reminds MBAs there's more to life than case studies and presentations. They get the job done here, and they do it well, but they also remember to save time to enjoy the gorgeous campus, the accommodating hometown, the darn good food, and their convivial classmates.

Although the marquee feature at Ourso is the internal audit program—its graduates have won the International CIA Student High Achievement Award on the Certified Internal Auditor Examination 15 times in the last 18 years—the school is hardly a one-trick pony. Other standouts include the entrepreneurship program ("consistently one of the top in the nation") and a solid concentration in finance. All students here must complete "a strong core curriculum" that provides "a good academic foundation, but without the cutthroat competition that I think could be harmful to the learning environment," writes one MBA. Another notes, "The combination of case studies and current-events discussions that have been integrated into the course work provide the chance to see exactly how the lessons from lectures and text are implemented in today's fluid business environment."

Professors "really try to connect in-class concepts with real-world application. Also, students are exposed to professional panels, presentations by industry leaders, and in-state trips to prominent businesses. Trips to foreign countries are offered for international business classes." Students also love the administration, praising it as "second to none. They provide students with a place to go if they need to resolve a problem or just have someone to speak to." "The only drawback here is the brick-and-mortar facilities, [which] are old and deteriorating."

Career and Placement

Flores MBAs are served in their career pursuits by a number of offices and programs, including the LSU Career Services Center, the MBA Placement Program, the Center for Internal Audit Placement Services, and the school's MBA specialization advisors.

Of 68 graduating members of the class of 2003, 41 had full-time employment at commencement. Eighteen MBAs found work at *Fortune* 500 companies (Altria Group, Inc; Chevron; Eli Lilly and Company; Entergy Corporation; ExxonMobil; FedEx; Hartford Financial Services; IBM; International Paper; Lockheed Martin; Schering-Plough; The Shaw Group; and Wal-Mart). Employers that most consistently hire the greatest number of Flores MBAs include Accenture, Chevron, Deloitte Touche Tohmatsu, Entergy Corporation, ExxonMobil, Ernst & Young, Eli Lilly, FedEx, IBM, KPMG International, Lockheed Martin, LSU, PricewaterhouseCoopers, and Shell Oil Company. Nearly 350 companies recruit for full-time employees each year on the LSU campus; just over 100 seek summer interns here.

Student Life and Environment

You'd be hard pressed to find an MBA student here who will badmouth the quality of life at LSU. Students praise the "great social scene," the campus ("one of the most attractive available"), and the "many clubs and organizations that one can join, so that there is always some type of activity going on for the general school public." One student

KATHLEEN BOSWORTH, ASSOCIATE DIRECTOR, FLORES MBA PROGRAMS
E. J. OURSO COLLEGE OF BUSINESS, 3176 CEBA BUILDING, BATON ROUGE, LA 70803 U.S.
PHONE: 225-578-8867 • FAX: 225-578-2421
E-MAIL: BUSMBA@LSU.EDU • WEBSITE: MBA.LSU.EDU

reports, "The MBA Association is always having a gathering or some service activity. The students are always getting together for trips to the bar after a particularly tough day at school." Extracurricular life peaks during the fall, when football dominates the entire campus. One MBA explains, "No matter where you're at on campus or what's going on in your classes or life, you can't ignore the electricity of what's happening each Saturday night. You have to fight the RV's to park for class . . . on Thursday! Anticipating the Golden Band from Tigerland marching through campus, watching the games at Death Valley . . . there's nothing like it."

Students also love hometown Baton Rouge, where "there are lots of places to go out, from the Chimes, with a beer menu of over 120 [varieties], to multiple dance clubs around town. The downtown area is beginning to see more life brought to it, which adds more flavor to the mix." Even the pigskin-averse can't resist the allure of "walking through campus amongst the newly bloomed azaleas, under the stately oaks that have adorned the banks of the Mississippi for over 200 years. Friends and professors alike stroll down Highland Road, just a few miles from plantations as old as sugar, all the while getting an education that anyone would be proud of."

The "true Southern ladies and gentlemen" who attend LSU "take advantage of the opportunity to socialize during and after class. This small class size has ultimately allowed us to become a close-knit class," notes one MBA. The class includes "quite a few highly technical engineers, because of the proximity to large oil refineries" and some other professionals. However, "the majority do not have work experience, and this means there are strong differences between the objectives that everyone has. Married students and older students with more work experience tend to have better focus toward their career objectives."

Admissions

All applicants to Flores must submit a complete set of undergraduate transcripts (minimum 3.0 GPA required), GMAT scores, letter of recommendation, a personal statement, and a professional resume. An interview is required but previous work experience, while preferred, is not. Admissions officers study the application for evidence of "community work, demonstrated leadership potential, career direction and purpose, personal qualities and interpersonal skills, and academic performance and promise." International applicants must also submit the TOEFL (minimum score: 550 written, 213 computer-based).

FINANCIAL FACTS

Annual tuition (in-state/ out-of-state)	$2,992/$11,292
Cost of books	$1,500
Room & board (on/off-campus)	$6,498/$10,768

ADMISSIONS

Admissions Selectivity Rating	**96**
# of applications received	130
% applicants accepted	66
% acceptees attending	82
Average GMAT	611
Range of GMAT	570–650
Average GPA	3.36
TOEFL required of international students	Yes
Minimum TOEFL (paper/computer)	550/213
Application fee	$25
Transfer students accepted	Yes
Transfer application policy	

Applicants must have attended an AACSB-accredited school and meet the entrance requirements for the Flores MBA Program.

Need-blind admissions	Yes

Applicants Also Look At

Loyola University New Orleans, Mississippi State University, Tulane University, University of Alabama—Tuscaloosa, University of Georgia, University of New Orleans, The University of Texas at Austin.

EMPLOYMENT PROFILE

Career Rating	60*	Top 5 Employers Hiring Grads
		Deloitte Touche Tohmatsu; ExxonMobil; Hibernia/CitiBank; KPMG International; Entergy.

LOYOLA COLLEGE IN MARYLAND
SELLINGER SCHOOL OF BUSINESS AND MANAGEMENT

GENERAL INFORMATION

Type of school	Private
Affiliation	Roman Catholic-Jesuit
Environment	Village
Academic calendar	Semester

SURVEY SAYS . . .
Students love Baltimore, MD
Good peer network
Helpful alumni
Happy students
Smart classrooms

STUDENTS

Enrollment of parent institution	6,035
Enrollment of business school	791
% male/female	100/0
% part-time	100
Average age at entry	28

ACADEMICS

Academic Experience Rating	**78**
Student/faculty ratio	12:1
Profs interesting rating	87
Profs accessible rating	71
% female faculty	28
% minority faculty	10

Academics

Students at the Sellinger School of Business and Management at Loyola College in Maryland love the school's "solid reputation in the Baltimore/Washington, DC, area" as well as the program's "great flexibility for part-time MBAs." Sellinger's self-paced curriculum suits the lifestyles of its busy students, allowing them to schedule classes around their other commitments. Sellinger's two campuses (Timonium and Columbia) that "offer most of the same courses," further augment students' options.

Loyola's MBA program requires between 33 and 53 credits, depending on one's undergraduate background in business. Those eligible to waive preprogram competencies and foundation courses can complete the program in as little as 12 months. The Sellinger curriculum is organized around five integrated areas of study: leadership and teamwork, social responsibility and ethics, IT, global markets, and learning through reflection. MBAs here appreciate the "strong focus on ethics throughout the curriculum." They also tell us that international business studies here are greatly enhanced by "mini-mester courses that involve traveling to a foreign country. There is a two-week trip to Europe and a one-week trip to Chile. It's a nice bonus, and a great way to pick up credits between semesters." Concentrations are offered in accounting, finance, general business, international business, management, MIS, and marketing. Loyola also has an Executive MBA program.

Students give the academics here an "A+" and report that Sellinger "uses people who are well-established in business to teach the core courses. This means there is no gap between what is taught in the classroom and what the 'real world' is doing. The businesspeople who teach these classes greatly enjoy teaching, and it shows." Classes are interactive, too. One MBA candidate explains, "We don't just read the text and do the homework from the book. We read the text, relate it to our business and personal lives, and apply models to help us comprehend what we just learned." When things get rough, "there are tutors available, with the ability to focus on individual needs." Advisors, on the other hand, "are very hands-off. If you want to find out about resources such as programs, you might not be aware these things exist unless you dig for them yourself."

Career and Placement

Loyola students tell us that "because this is a part-time program, almost all students have full-time jobs, and the school does not offer a lot of resources in career counseling and placement." One student writes, "I only know about the career counseling program because I went to this school for my undergraduate degree. Most graduates are probably not aware we have one." Those who are aware of the service would like to see it beefed up. "Yes, we have jobs. However, this does not mean students are not looking for a job change upon graduation," points out one student. A "strong local alumni network" is Loyola's greatest asset in this area.

Scott Greatorex, Graduate Admissions Director
4501 North Charles Street, Baltimore, MD 21210 United States
Phone: 410-617-5020 • Fax: 410-617-2002
E-mail: graduate@loyola.edu/mba@loyola.edu • Website: sellinger.loyola.edu

Student Life and Environment

The Sellinger MBA program is entirely part-time, which students say "creates an atmosphere similar to a community college. There is really no life at school," which actually suits students just fine. Students explain, "Obtaining an MBA is an extremely hard thing to do when working full-time, and the students are very respectful of each other and the teacher because of that. We are all here to strengthen our educational background and move up in the world. School life in a part-time MBA program centers around academics." Fortunately, "the administration and faculty are sensitive to student work/school balance issues. They work to strike a balance between maintaining a top-quality curriculum and providing some flexibility when needed by students."

Occasional extracurricular events do occur here, and students make the most of them. For example, "the school sponsors an alumni night every semester where current students and alumni can network in a relaxed atmosphere. It also sponsors a student appreciation night every semester with refreshments before class." Students socialize on a more casual basis as well. "During evening classes, students are able to meet for a cup of coffee at Starbucks, relax in the lounge and read a book, or catch a show on one of its many flat-screen televisions," explains one student.

The Sellinger student body "is a vibrant population of many young professionals, many with type-A personalities." There is "an intense, yet friendly and productive, sense of competition at Loyola," with students generally "more concerned with learning and networking than being the best at the expense of other classmates." Some here observe that "due to the recent economic environment, there is a noticeable percentage of students right out of undergrad, who decided to get more education before jumping into the market." Overall, though, there is "definitely a diverse group here. There are younger students and older students; married students and single students; students completing the MBA program to move up at their current job; and students completing the MBA program to move to a different company."

Admissions

A complete application to the Loyola College MBA program includes: a completed application form; a personal statement; a resume; an official GMAT score report; official transcripts for all degree work and for any postsecondary academic work completed within five years of application; as well as international documents, where appropriate. Applicants with a 3.25 undergraduate GPA and five years of work experience may waive the GMAT requirement, as may students with an advanced degree in any other discipline (e.g., an MA, a PhD, a JD, etc.). Interviews and letters of recommendation are optional.

FINANCIAL FACTS

Annual tuition	$9,450
Fees	$50
Cost of books	$630
Room & board (off-campus)	$13,365
% of students receiving aid	38
% of first-year students receiving aid	62
% of students receiving loans	33
% of students receiving grants	12
Average award package	$16,120
Average grant	$10,920
Average student loan debt	$26,550

ADMISSIONS

Admissions Selectivity Rating	74
# of applications received	558
% applicants accepted	81
% acceptees attending	85
Average GMAT	536
Range of GMAT	440–680
Average GPA	3.34
TOEFL required of international students	Yes
Minimum TOEFL (paper/computer)	550/215
Application fee	$50
Regular application deadline	Rolling
Regular notification	Rolling
Deferment available	Yes
Maximum length of deferment	1 year
Transfer students accepted	Yes
Transfer application policy	
Only classes from another AACSB-accredited school will be counted.	
Non-fall admissions	Yes
Need-blind admissions	Yes

LOYOLA MARYMOUNT UNIVERSITY
COLLEGE OF BUSINESS ADMINISTRATION

GENERAL INFORMATION

Type of school	Private
Affiliation	Roman Catholic-Jesuit
Environment	Metropolis
Academic calendar	Semester

SURVEY SAYS . . .

Loyola Marymount University - MBA Program
Students love Los Angeles, CA
Happy students
Smart classrooms
Solid preparation in:
Teamwork

STUDENTS

Enrollment of parent institution	8,582
Enrollment of business school	298
% male/female	60/40
% part-time	70
% minorities	30
% international	37
Average age at entry	26
Average years work experience at entry	4

ACADEMICS

Academic Experience Rating	**82**
Student/faculty ratio	22:1
Profs interesting rating	94
Profs accessible rating	79
% female faculty	20
% minority faculty	21

Joint Degrees

MBA/JD 4 years, MBA/SELP (systems engineering) 4 years.

Academics

Loyola Marymount University capably serves its largely part-time student body with an extremely accommodating program that allows students to enter in either the Fall or Spring semester, take as many classes as they can handle, and choose from "a cafeteria-style of elective courses in which a variety of subjects are offered."

Students love LMU's "unbelievable" entrepreneurship program taught by "renowned professors." They also love the international business program and the unique Comparative Management Systems (CMS) option, "where you research issues in foreign countries and then travel to those countries to do hands-on research and interviews. CMS is a great alternative to a traditional thesis." Dual-degree options such as the Systems Engineering Leadership Program (MBA and MS in Systems Engineering) and the JD/MBA program also earn praise.

Students love the "teamwork-oriented and friendly" vibe, with "none of that backstabbing you hear about on other campuses. It's like *The Apprentice* for the winning team, not the losing team." Classwork involves "going to class and participating, not just sitting there and listening to the professor lecture. There is a lot of group work, so you really get to know your peers through large projects and presentations." MBAs also appreciate the Jesuit influence on the curriculum, which translates to "a lot of emphasis on ethics." Professors, we're told, are the school's "greatest strength. They challenge us and push our ideas and we get our money's worth for our education." They also "do a great job of applying real-world situations to theory [and] are a great networking resource."

Career and Placement

LMU serves two distinct student bodies: a majority of part-timers who already have full-time jobs, and a minority who attend full-time and will be looking for job placement post-MBA. The MBA Career Services Office (CSO) doesn't see much of the former, whose employers frequently foot the bill for their MBAs. The latter benefit from resume and cover-letter seminars; interview and salary-negotiation workshops; and career counseling. An MBA Mentor program pairs students with area execs, while the annual Meet the Firms event brings employers to campus to meet with prospective employees and interns.

The CSO also offers the CareerLeader assessment tool and access to Vault.com and Monstertrak.com. The office maintains an online bulletin board for job postings. Students feel that "the school could improve in its ability to attract top-notch companies to the career fair. This would allow LMU grads to compete on a more level playing field with the likes of USC and UCLA." They also "would like to see LMU's alumni association have the power and prestige of a USC."

Student Life and Environment

All students, full-time and part-time, attend classes together at LMU. Classes begin at 4:25 P.M. and continue through the evening. MBAs appreciate that the "beautiful campus" is "very safe," that "faculty and staff are usually available from 9:00 A.M. to 7:00 P.M.," and that "the business building remains open after classes end at 10:00 P.M., allowing students to work." They warn, however, that parking is extremely difficult.

MARIA MCGILL, MBA COORDINATOR
ONE LMU DRIVE, MS 8387, LOS ANGELES, CA 90045-2659 UNITED STATES
PHONE: 310-338-2848 • FAX: 310-338-2899
E-MAIL: MBAPC@LMU.EDU • WEBSITE: MBA.LMU.EDU

LMU offers "many organized social and networking activities" to its business students, but many are too busy with work, class assignments, and family obligations to take advantage. Those who do speak highly of the opportunities; as one reports, "The school provides weekday and weekend activities that encourage students, faculty, and alumni to mingle. From yacht cruises to a day at the horse-races, LMU has a great social culture." Students add, "We have multiple Food 'n' Schmooze nights each semester, which give us the opportunity to get to know our fellow students before and after class over dinner. We also do First Fridays by meeting at different bars on the first Friday of every month." Even so, this "is an evening program, so I don't think we have the same intensity of community as full-time MBA programs might have," concedes one MBA. Another explains, "Because the program is geared towards working adults, most students are part-time and thus come to class and leave immediately afterwards. It's almost like a commuter school in that sense. I wish the program would offer day courses and not just evening courses."

The typical LMU professional is "an aerospace or entertainment industry professional who is very smart and highly motivated." In recent years, an increasing proportion of the student body has arrived with little or no professional experience. One student explains, "The student body is changing in that many students used to come from local engineering companies, but they have cut tuition subsidies so students are now younger." Another observes, "About 25 percent of students are recent college grads. They don't participate much in class discussions. About 75 percent are over 24. This group is the most vocal in class, participate more, and are engaging."

Admissions

LMU implements a relatively lenient admissions policy. Work experience, for example, is not required; while most students have worked post-baccalaureate an average of four years, some students arrive here with little or no professional experience. The school enforces no minimum undergraduate GPA or GMAT score, although the average GPA of 3.29 among admitted students bespeaks an academically accomplished student body. No prerequisite courses are required of enrollees; however, students must show evidence of college-level math proficiency (i.e., business math or intermediate algebra) before enrolling in quantitative courses. Applicants may be admitted for fall or spring semesters. Applications are processed on a rolling basis.

FINANCIAL FACTS

Annual tuition	$24,165
Fees	$400
Cost of books	$1,300

ADMISSIONS

Admissions Selectivity Rating	**78**
# of applications received	260
% applicants accepted	66
% acceptees attending	61
Average GMAT	562
Average GPA	3.29
TOEFL required of international students	Yes
Minimum TOEFL (paper/computer)	600/250
Application fee	$50
Regular application deadline	Rolling
Regular notification	Rolling
Deferment available	Yes
Maximum length of deferment	1 year
Transfer students accepted	Yes

Transfer application policy
Students from other Jesuit MBA programs may transfer core and electives through the Jesuit Transfer Network. Students who attend an AACSB-accredited MBA program (not Jesuit) with equivalent course work of B or better may only transfer in 6 units of upper division course credit, but may be eligible for core course waivers.

Non-fall admissions	Yes
Need-blind admissions	Yes

Applicants Also Look At
Pepperdine University, University of California, Los Angeles (UCLA), University of Southern California.

LOYOLA UNIVERSITY—CHICAGO
GRADUATE SCHOOL OF BUSINESS

Academics

Like many big-city business schools, Loyola University of Chicago capitalizes on its location. Chicago, students here agree, has "a first-rate business environment . . . there is no better city." The city not only provides students with opportunities unthinkable at schools in more isolated locations but also serves to attract "top-notch faculty" who are "among the top in the country. Professors come from diverse backgrounds. Many have worked internationally and have valuable insight to provide in class. Others have been at top executive positions with top global companies." It's possible to find a faculty this strong in Podunk, but it's not likely.

A Jesuit university, Loyola is institutionally committed to "teaching how to think, rather than teaching mechanics" as well as to a curricular "emphasis on ethics and ethical leadership." The idea is to train students who are flexible enough to adapt; as one student puts it, "We live in a world where change is the norm, so to be able to navigate change and apply what we learn to new situations is critical." Flexibility is also a hallmark of the design of Loyola's part-time program, which is frequently ranked among the nation's top 20. Students tell us that Loyola's classes "fit my busy work schedule" while the quarterly calendar with relatively few required courses "allows flexibility to take courses that are of interest across disciplines rather than requiring specific courses."

Loyola offers a broad range of graduate business degrees. Students tell us that "the accounting department is very strong," that the MS in human resources is "all encompassing," and that the MS in integrated marketing communications "offers a holistic approach to advertising, marketing, PR and the customer experience." A good student/faculty ratio "provides for closer contacts of students with their professors" while a curricular emphasis on teamwork develops skills "important in modern business environments." Students also appreciate the "integration of high technology courses in the graduate programs, which introduces prospective graduates to situations likely to be encountered in the real world of business or administration."

Career and Placement

The Business Career Center at Loyola is dedicated exclusively to undergraduate and graduate students in business. Some here recount good experiences with the office; one student writes, "They have hooked me up with two great internships, and I have been talking to multiple companies about full-time work which was done through the BCC." Others aren't as impressed. As one puts it, "With the wealth of great companies in the area and Loyola alumni out in the workforce, I was often underwhelmed by the opportunities presented to the GSB students at Loyola. Many companies had events with DePaul and other campuses but were not recruiting at Loyola. My best career help came directly from professors." Some wonder how much the BCC can accomplish on its own, noting that "While LUC is a fine school, holding its own against many of the other schools located in Chicago . . . with close proximity to U of Chicago and Northwestern, most companies choose to recruit there. In line with the outdated thinking 'You'll never get fired for buying IBM,' most firms feel the same way about those two schools. This is unfortunate, but the truth."

Employers who most frequently hire Loyola MBAs include: Northern Trust, Federal Reserve Bank, Deloitte Touche Tohmatsu, Eli Lilly and Company, Sara Lee, Grant Thornton, Crain's Chicago Business, Archdiocese of Chicago, and Solo Cup.

OLIVIA HEATH, ENROLLMENT ADVISOR
ONE EAST PEARSON CHICAGO, IL 60611 UNITED STATES
PHONE: 312-915-6124 • FAX: 312-915-7207
E-MAIL: GSB@LUC.EDU • WEBSITE: WWW.GSB.LUC.EDU

Student Life and Environment

Loyola's Graduate School of Business "is located in the heart of Chicago" and "has two buildings where classes are held" where "the facilities are great. Classrooms are equipped with the latest technology, costing the university thousands per classroom. The libraries are very large and have resources that you need." A "new dorm building right next to the GSB" is very convenient for those who choose to live in school housing; students report that "the campus is safe" and that security is good. Those who live off campus report that the location "is easily accessible. There is good public transportation and regular shuttle services between the two campuses at downtown Chicago."

Business classes at Loyola "take place in the evening" (with a few weekend classes), so "Sometimes it feels like a commuter school in the sense that the students come to class and then leave to focus on their own personal/work lives. However, if you seek out clubs and organizations, a social life is available." Indeed, "there has, in the last year, been a significant increase in the school's coordinating activities for the students to network. Lots of mixers, several outings to local sport events and an increase in a sense of 'community' as opposed to 'just school.'" Full-time students even report "more opportunities than I can take advantage of. There are lectures, guest speakers, networking events, career fairs, study abroad programs, and social outings."

Admissions

Applicants to Loyola's Graduate School of Business must submit the following materials: a completed application form; one set of official transcripts for all completed undergraduate and graduate course work; an official GMAT test score report (applicants with a minimum of 10 years' managerial experience may submit an essay requesting a GMAT waiver); two letters of recommendation; a personal statement of goals; and a current resume. International applicants must submit all of the above materials as well as a Declaration and Certification of Finances form. International students whose first language is not English must submit official score reports for either the TOEFL or IELTS exams. Applicants whose transcripts are in a language other than English must have the transcripts translated and analyzed by an outside credentialing service.

FINANCIAL FACTS

Annual tuition	$27,180
Fees	$300
Cost of books	$800
Room & board	
(on/off-campus)	$11,000/$12,000
% of students receiving aid	70
% of first-year students	
receiving aid	63
% of students receiving loans	65
% of students receiving grants	8
Average award package	$15,302
Average grant	$7,102
Average student loan debt	$39,908

ADMISSIONS

Admissions Selectivity Rating	71
# of applications received	602
% applicants accepted	85
% acceptees attending	62
Average GMAT	550
Range of GMAT	500–640
Average GPA	3.34
TOEFL required of	
international students	Yes
Minimum TOEFL	
(paper/computer)	550/213
Application fee	$50
Regular application deadline	8/6
Regular notification	Rolling
Deferment available	Yes
Maximum length of	
deferment	1 year
Transfer students accepted	Yes
Transfer application policy	
Up to 9 hours of B or better course work can transfer from AACSB-accredited institutions.	
Non-fall admissions	Yes
Need-blind admissions	Yes

Applicants Also Look At

DePaul University, Illinois Institute of Technology, Northern Illinois University, Northwestern University, The University of Chicago, University of Illinois, University of Illinois at Chicago.

EMPLOYMENT PROFILE

Career Rating	64	Grads Employed by Function	%	Avg. Salary
Primary Source of Full-time Job Acceptances		Finance/Accounting	17	$66,000
School-facilitated activities	10 (11%)	Human Resources	5	$67,800
Graduate-facilitated activities	57 (64%)	Marketing/Sales	5	$52,000
Unknown	22 (25%)	MIS	1	$66,560
Percent employed	19	Strategic Planning	1	$110,000
		General Management	6	$88,209
		Other	14	$70,320
		Nonprofit	3	$48,000

LOYOLA UNIVERSITY—NEW ORLEANS
JOSEPH A. BUTT, S.J. COLLEGE OF BUSINESS ADMINISTRATION

GENERAL INFORMATION

Type of school	Private
Affiliation	Roman Catholic-Jesuit
Environment	City
Academic calendar	Semester

SURVEY SAYS . . .
Good peer network
Cutting-edge classes
Solid preparation in:
General management

STUDENTS

Enrollment of parent institution	4,874
Enrollment of business school	70
% male/female	75/25
% out-of-state	19
% part-time	77
% minorities	31
% international	38
Average age at entry	24
Average years work experience at entry	2

ACADEMICS

Academic Experience Rating	**76**
Student/faculty ratio	13:1
Profs interesting rating	89
Profs accessible rating	89
% female faculty	25
% minority faculty	15

Joint Degrees
MBA/JD 4 to 5 years.

Academics

With a program small enough to provide a "family-like environment," Loyola University—New Orleans serves a largely local student body seeking a "personalized education experience" at an institution with "a solid academic reputation." Just how comfortable is it? Many of the students we surveyed happily identified themselves as former Loyola undergrads who couldn't wait to get back here to pursue graduate work.

Loyola offers both a general MBA and an MBA with concentration in any of the following areas: finance, international business, or marketing. The school also offers a combined MBA/JD, which typically takes 4 to 5 years to complete. The MBA is divided into four components: a basic core, designed for the needs of students with little undergraduate background in business (business majors can place out of some or all of these courses); an advanced core; electives; and a capstone course called Global Strategy, which emphasizes case study and integrative analysis. Flexibility "to accommodate working students" is the key in this program. Students may attend on either a part-time or full-time basis and, since classes meet only once weekly in the evening, have some latitude in fashioning their class schedules. The curriculum is designed to "challenge you to think and think of things from different perspectives."

Students report that their "outstanding" professors "are very enthusiastic about the subject matter, which makes class time so much more valuable. It is clear that the priority of professors is teaching and working with the students." Better still, small class sizes mean "You get one-on-one time to discuss issues at length with your professors." The scale of the program also allows administrators to provide more personalized service. Students tell us that they are "really active and helpful in assisting students to achieve their academic goals. They try to accommodate students as best as possible to ensure that the proper classes are offered and that there are interesting business electives to take."

Career and Placement

Loyola maintains a Counseling and Career Services Center to serve all undergraduate and graduate students of the university. Services include self-assessment instruments, career counseling, internship and job placement services, and guidance in resume writing, interviewing, job search, and salary negotiation skills. The office organizes on-campus recruiting events. Students remind us that "we don't only use the Career Center on the main campus; we all network with each other and recent alumni to pass on applicable contacts to each other." The MBA Association also contributes by organizing networking events.

In recent years, Loyola MBAs have been placed with: AmSouth Bank, BearingPoint, Clear Channel Radio, Entergy, Freeport-McMoRan, Harrah's, Hibernia Bank, Northrop Grumman, Prudential Financial Services, Qualified Health Services, Ritz Carlton, Trumpet Advertising and Marketing, U.S. Department of Commerce, and Whitney Bank.

STEPHANIE MANSFIELD, MBA MARKETING AND COMMUNICATIONS
6363 ST. CHARLES AVENUE, CAMPUS BOX 15, NEW ORLEANS, LA 70118 UNITED STATES
PHONE: 504-864-7965 • FAX: 504-864-7970
E-MAIL: SMANS@LOYNO.EDU • WEBSITE: CBA.LOYNO.EDU/MBA

Student Life and Environment

Loyola's MBA program is a small evening program in which students are "supportive and friendly." "Everyone wants to see everyone else succeed." It's not as close as your typical cohort-based daytime program, however—in part because students simply don't spend as much time together and in part because "The school doesn't do enough to foster camaraderie between students. They have bar parties, which are pretty routine and the same people go" every time. "More barbeques and [other] functions would help." Even if the school did step up the level of activities, though, there's no guarantee it would foster greater student involvement. Attendance at events reflects students' "level of commitment to the program," observes one MBA.

Loyola is located in the fashionable uptown section of New Orleans. The campus sustained no flooding during Hurricane Katrina. In fact, damage to the campus was relatively minor, with the school Recreational Complex taking the biggest hit. The school was closed during the Fall 2005 semester but reopened in January 2006. More than 90 percent of its undergraduate population returned. Students today report that the campus is small but pretty and that "the library is the best! The school understands that a library isn't just about books any more and offers lots of technical resources that can help you find any kind of information you need."

Loyola draws a student body representing "diverse backgrounds." One MBA writes, "I have really enjoyed getting to know the other students. Everyone's background is so different that we are able to learn from many different perspectives. There is some noticeable difference between the older, experienced students and the younger, straight-out-of-school students in both their personal and academic styles, but nothing that is impossible to work with." Students here tend to be "intellectually curious team players as opposed to cutthroat competitors." Many have full-time jobs.

Admissions

Loyola requires the following of applicants to its MBA program: official transcripts for all past postsecondary academic work; an official score report for the GMAT; two letters of recommendation; a 400-word personal statement of purpose; and a resume. International students whose first language is not English must also submit TOEFL scores (the minimum acceptable score is 237; scores can be no more than 2 years old); all international students must provide an affidavit demonstrating sufficient financial resources to support themselves during their tenure at the university. Work experience, though not required, is strongly recommended. Interviews are optional.

FINANCIAL FACTS

Annual tuition	$24,800
Fees	$1,056
Cost of books	$1,500
Room & board (off-campus)	$8,000
Average grant	$5,000

ADMISSIONS

Admissions Selectivity Rating	**74**
# of applications received	33
% applicants accepted	82
% acceptees attending	67
Average GMAT	555
Range of GMAT	430–760
Average GPA	3.2
TOEFL required of international students	Yes
Minimum TOEFL (paper/computer)	580/237
Application fee	$50
Regular application deadline	6/15
Regular notification	Rolling
Deferment available	Yes
Maximum length of deferment	1 year
Transfer students accepted	Yes
Transfer application policy	

If an applicant comes from an AACSB-accredited program, the foundation work may apply to our program. Also, a maximum of 6 credit hours may be applied to the advanced level. Only B's or better are accepted.

Non-fall admissions	Yes
Need-blind admissions	Yes

Applicants Also Look At

Louisiana State University, Tulane University.

EMPLOYMENT PROFILE	
Career Rating	72

MARIST COLLEGE
SCHOOL OF MANAGEMENT

GENERAL INFORMATION
Type of school	Private
Academic calendar	Semester

SURVEY SAYS . . .
Solid preparation in:
General management
Operations
Quantitative skills
Computer skills
Doing business in a global economy

STUDENTS
Enrollment of parent institution	5,877
Enrollment of business school	210
% male/female	100/0
% part-time	100
Average age at entry	31
Average years work experience at entry	7

ACADEMICS
Academic Experience Rating	**68**
Student/faculty ratio	20:1
Profs interesting rating	79
Profs accessible rating	80

Academics

For more than 30 years, Marist College has offered working professionals the opportunity to pursue an MBA degree on a part-time basis. Today, the school continues to operate a part-time, campus-based program, while also distinguishing itself as "one of the few AACSB-accredited graduate schools that offered an MBA program fully online, while being affordable." While part-time students in other MBA programs complain about the difficulties of balancing home life, work, and school, the Marist "program [is] tailored to those working long hours and still offer[s] a strong reputation with a decent curriculum." The flexibility of the program is perhaps its most attractive feature, allowing students to take traditional or online courses, or a blend of the two. Indeed, students tell us that "being able to mix online courses as well as traditional in-class courses is very beneficial for students who also work full time."

The curriculum at Marist is divided into foundation courses, core courses, and electives; however, foundation courses may be waived for students who have an undergraduate degree in business. Taking two courses per semester and one course in the summer, many students are able to earn their MBA in just 2 years. To accommodate the schedule of working professionals, traditional classroom courses are scheduled one evening per week, Monday through Thursday, on the Marist College campus, as well as in off-site classrooms. Online classes are available 24 hours a day, 7 days a week, and have no on-campus requirement whatsoever. "The high quality of the program and professors" draws many students to the school, and online students are welcome to meet with faculty in person while taking the course. Students say Marist professors are, on the whole, "accessible and very helpful."

The school is technologically and organizationally equipped to help online students plan and execute a quality educational program. A student shares, "Enrollment is a breeze, and the Assistant Dean who works with online students is very helpful." Another adds, "The administration was very helpful in getting [me] access to courses to meet my academic plan." Online classes are very similar to classroom courses in that students must be prepared to turn in assignments, take exams, participate in class, and meet deadlines. Course work is fully multimedia and includes group projects, case studies, computer simulations, and presentations. Students insist that they build a sense of community via the Internet, and "Group projects illuminate personalities pretty well even over the web." A current student enthuses, "I completed my program completely online. I have found many students to be actively engaged and willing to collaborate via online chat, e-mail, and over the phone."

Whether online or in the classroom, students say the program is high quality and challenging. One shares, "I started here after moving away from Chicago, where I attended a top-10 MBA program (Kellogg). I find the classes to be rigorous and academically competitive. I was worried that the courses would seem much easier than Kellogg['s], but my fears were misplaced." Even so, the program is fairly structured, and some students say they'd like to have the option of "more concentrations within the program" that are "structured to specific disciplines" while "removing some courses that aren't as beneficial to one's future goals."

Career and Placement

Ninety-five percent of Marist students work full-time while completing their MBA. Ranging from relatively young professionals to senior managers, most students plan to stay with their current company upon termination of the program. For those who are

ANU R. AILAWADHI, DIRECTOR OF GRADUATE ADMISSIONS
3399 NORTH ROAD, POUGHKEEPSIE, NY 12601 UNITED STATES
PHONE: 845-575-3800 • FAX: 845-575-3166
E-MAIL: GRADUATE@MARIST.EDU • WEBSITE: WWW.MARIST.EDU/MANAGEMENT/MBA

looking for a new position, MBA students have access to the Marist College Career Services Office, which hosts career-building workshops, career conferences, career fairs, and a host of online resources. The 2007 Spring Career Conference at Marist included a number of regional employers, including: Affinity Group/Mass Mutual, Aldi, CVS Pharmacy, First Investors Corporation, Gap, Gunn Allen Financial Corporation, Household Finance, IBM, MetLife, Morgan Stanley, Northwestern Mutual Financial Network, Ryder Transportation, Target, United Parcel Service, Wells Fargo, and Worldwide Express.

Student Life and Environment

Because a large percentage of Marist courses are taught via the Internet, the student community is largely virtual. Even so, Marist students have the opportunity to get to know their classmates through the phone and Internet, describing them as "hardworking, intelligent [people], with work and family obligations." Those who attend classes on campus tell us the school promotes a "good sense of community" and "attracts people who are just plain nice and helpful both to work and teach and as students." While the business school is located on Marist's lively undergraduate campus, there aren't many social or recreational activities targeted at business students. Indeed, some would like to see "more opportunities for socializing, networking, out-of-classroom learning (speakers, etc.)."

Marist is located in Poughkeepsie, New York, a small city about 90 minutes from both New York City and Albany. A picturesque campus environment, the school is located near the Catskill Mountains, and the surrounding area is a paradise for hiking, cross-country skiing, mountain biking, and other outdoor activities. There are also a number of attractions in the town of Poughkeepsie, including the historic Barhadon Theater and Mid-Hudson Civic Center, which show opera, ballet, Broadway shows, and popular performers.

Admission

To apply to the graduate program at the Marist School of Management, students must possess an undergraduate degree in any discipline. Whether applying to the online or on-campus program, all applicants must submit a completed graduate school application, an application fee, two letters of recommendation, responses to the essay questions, official GMAT scores, and official transcripts from undergraduate study.

FINANCIAL FACTS

Annual tuition	$11,340
Fees	$60
Cost of books	$1,348
% of students receiving aid	22
% of first-year students receiving aid	13
% of students receiving loans	18
% of students receiving grants	14
Average award package	$10,726
Average grant	$1,633

ADMISSIONS

Admissions Selectivity Rating	68
# of applications received	80
% applicants accepted	89
% acceptees attending	72
Average GMAT	543
Range of GMAT	508–550
Average GPA	3.15
TOEFL required of international students	Yes
Minimum TOEFL (paper/computer)	550/213
Application fee	$50
Regular application deadline	7/1
Regular notification	7/15
Deferment available	Yes
Maximum length of deferment	1 year
Transfer students accepted	Yes
Transfer application policy No more than six credit hours of core courses accepted from AACSB-accredited programs.	
Non-fall admissions	Yes
Need-blind admissions	Yes

Applicants Also Look At

Fairfield University, Pace University, University of Connecticut.

EMPLOYMENT PROFILE

Career Rating	79	Grads Employed by Function	%	Avg. Salary
Primary Source of Full-time Job Acceptances		General Management	92	$65,000
Percent employed	92			

MARQUETTE UNIVERSITY
COLLEGE OF BUSINESS ADMINISTRATION

Academics

A strong reputation like "the best business school in the area," a "superior faculty," and "a strong international focus in the curriculum" all appeal to the MBA students at Marquette University's College of Business Administration, a nationally known Jesuit-run school in Milwaukee. Marquette belongs to the Network of MBA Programs at Jesuit Colleges and Universities. This means all credits here transfer to any other participating Jesuit MBA program, a significant convenience in today's fluid employment environment. Jesuit sponsorship also ensures a strong curricular focus on ethics.

Marquette offers a part-time and full-time MBA, an Executive MBA, and MS degrees in accounting, applied economics, engineering management, and human resources. The MBA is offered in three locations: Downtown, Waukesha, and Kohler. Programs operate on a semester calendar, which makes for a demanding academic load. But part-time students here—who constitute the majority of the student body—report, "Professors understand the challenges that a working professional faces when going back to school. They are friendly and supportive and really help the transition back into school." Similarly, the administration "offers an impressive level of assistance. They know that most of us have busy lives so they make registering for class simple. If there is a problem, you call and it is taken care of. And they know your name, which is remarkable for a school our size."

MBAs at Marquette may specialize in e-business, economics, finance, human resources, international business, management information systems, marketing, or total quality management. Offerings are especially broad in human resources. Across the curriculum, students commend Marquette professors for "keeping up with new technological trends." MBAs also appreciate "Marquette's focus on teaching. You can tell that, for the most part, professors are here because they like to teach. They like students, people, and helping out. They want to challenge you and make sure that you've learned something along the way. It's a nice balance." Instructors also incorporate "a good balance of text, case work, and projects" to give students a wide range of learning experiences.

Career and Placement

The Career Services Center at Marquette provides counseling and placement services to all undergraduates and graduate students at the university. The office organizes workshops, one-on-one counseling sessions, on-site recruiting events, and job databases. In addition, the College of Business offers career-management services. Students are happy to report that the MBA program provides "a number of opportunities to interview with the Big Four firms as well as a number of local and regional firms," and also praise the "strong alumni and business connections in Milwaukee/southern Wisconsin."

Student Life and Environment

Most MBA students at Marquette are part-time students with full-time jobs. They generally "go to class and go home. That's it." One MBA explains, "I feel about as connected to Marquette as one does to, say, a parking garage at work: You're there all the time and it's very useful, but you wouldn't notice any difference if you had to park somewhere else one day, and you wouldn't miss it." There are also about 90 full-time students here, however, who involve themselves in the life of the university. One reports, "Marquette offers about 80 clubs and organizations—everything from athletics to cultural groups to arts to academic organizations and honor societies. Athletics (especially basketball) is strongly supported. In addition, the College of Business/MBA program hosts events. There is a strong sense of identity and belonging to a great, dynamic group." The program "tries to include the family when possible," which students appreciate.

DR. JEANNE SIMMONS, ASSOCIATE DEAN
PO BOX 1881, STRAZ HALL, SUITE 275, MILWAUKEE, WI 53201-1881 UNITED STATES
PHONE: 414-288-7145 • FAX: 414-288-8078
E-MAIL: MBA@MARQUETTE.EDU • WEBSITE: WWW.MARQUETTE.EDU/GSM

Students at Marquette see Milwaukee as another asset, one that provides "many activities, connections, and opportunities that come from being near a large city." Some worry about safety on the downtown campus, although others report that "the campus is becoming more enclosed," reducing safety issues. Chicago is less than a two-hour drive to the south.

Marquette's student body consists "mostly of career people who are working toward their MBA part-time. They are friendly and enthusiastic, are good in group work situations, [and] provide a collegial attitude to the program." Because "they come from many different large corporations in the Milwaukee area," they offer "good insight into the economic environment of Milwaukee." Some, though, "are not from business backgrounds. They come from engineering, health care, public service, or not-for-profits. The problem with this mix is that these students do not have the ability to offer many strategic business insights because they are just learning the concepts." For many at this Jesuit institution, "spiritual life takes a priority, which is a healthy change from state institutions."

Admissions

Applicants to the Marquette MBA program must provide the Admissions Office official transcripts for all previous postsecondary academic work, an official GMAT score report, a personal essay, and a resume. International students are additionally required to submit three letters of recommendation and an official score report for the TOEFL or another acceptable English proficiency exam. Marquette encourages applicants to apply for full admission but also offers a temporary-admission option for noninternational applicants, good for one semester only. Students applying to campuses other than the downtown campus must specify their campus of choice on their application.

FINANCIAL FACTS
Annual tuition	$13,500
Cost of books	$750

ADMISSIONS
Admissions Selectivity Rating	**74**
# of applications received	323
% applicants accepted	86
% acceptees attending	74
Average GMAT	572
Average GPA	3.26
TOEFL required of international students	Yes
Minimum TOEFL (paper)	550
Application fee	$40
Regular application deadline	Rolling
Regular notification	Rolling
Deferment available	Yes
Maximum length of deferment	Usually one year
Transfer students accepted	Yes
Transfer application policy We accept transfers from other Jesuit schools. We will also accept up to 6 approved credits from AACSB schools.	
Non-fall admissions	Yes

Applicants Also Look At
DePaul University, Loyola University—Chicago, University of Wisconsin—Milwaukee.

MASSACHUSETTS INSTITUTE OF TECHNOLOGY
SLOAN SCHOOL OF MANAGEMENT

Academics

Students tell us that MIT Sloan "is the very best school for innovation in business," pointing to "the absolute best operations research people in the world;" the fact that "today's leaders in finance and economics were all either educated at Sloan or teach here;" and the university's role as one of the nation's leading engineering, tech, and science research centers. They also cite the Sloan Innovation Period, a week wedged in the middle of each semester during which, along with leadership workshops, "Students learn from faculty about their current research interests."

Sloan's quant-intensive, two-year, full-time program commences with a rigorous core that involves a large measure of "friendly, team-based learning" as well as "a combination of videos, cases, group exercises, etc. The classes are extremely engaging, and I expect to retain a lot more due to the variation in styles of learning," says one student. Requirements can largely be dispensed with during the first semester here, after which "the design of students' MIT Sloan education is mostly in their own hands, provided they acquire appropriate credits in leadership, research, and practice," according to the school's website.

Students speak highly of MIT's Entrepreneurial Program, noting that it benefits greatly from the research taking place throughout the university. In the past year, a new pilot course was rolled out called the Entrepreneurship and Innovation option which allows students to engage in a seminar and more structured curriculum focused on the realm of entrepreneurship. One writes, "Sloan students visit various MIT labs, assessing the marketability of technology projects. They also write business plans and help start-up ventures emerging from MIT's labs, and are heavily involved in supporting new businesses—both locally and globally—through the entrepreneurial department." Another adds, "The environment is very entrepreneurial and with the opportunities students have to take initiative to shape the extracurricular and academic life here, Sloan is a fantastic place to develop your leadership skills."

Other special programs singled out for praise include the Leaders for Manufacturing Program: "The best of its kind, it tailors the MBA experience toward people interested in working for a manufacturing company in the future." Another is the MIT Sloan Fellows Program in Innovation and Global Leadership, "clearly the best program for a mid-career executive due to the intensity of the one-year program." The Cambridge address means "students have many opportunities to network with the school and beyond by cross-registering with other MIT schools or Harvard."

Career and Placement

Sloan's Career Development Office provides MBAs with a range of career management resources, including seminars, self-assessment tools, library materials, and online databases. The CDO hosts on-campus recruiting events throughout the school year to much success. The school reports that approximately 60 percent of students seeking a career change achieve their goal through such events, with the remainder finding new jobs through alumni connections, faculty recommendations, job postings, and other similar methods. Students tell us that the CDO is supportive but could stand to improve in some areas; "Career placement services are nonexistent for special programs, like the Biomedical Enterprise Program," writes one student. To make up for it, the "supportive nature of the student body" means "people try to use their network to help other students find jobs." 2. However, there has been a strong focus on enhancing services in the CDO.

Employers most likely to hire Sloan MBAs include Boston Consulting Group, Citigroup, Bain and Company, IBM Corporation, Lehman Brothers, McKinsey Co., Merrill Lynch, Unilever, Goldman Sachs, and United Technologies Corporation.

Rod Garcia, Admissions Director
50 Memorial Drive, E52-101, Cambridge, MA 02139 United States
Phone: 617-258-5434 • Fax: 617-253-6405
E-mail: mbaadmissions@sloan.mit.edu • Website: mitsloan.mit.edu/mba

FINANCIAL FACTS

Annual tuition	$44,766
Fees	$230
Cost of books	$4,000
Room & board	$27,690
% of students receiving aid	75
% of first-year students receiving aid	69
% of students receiving loans	70
% of students receiving grants	22
Average award package	$51,126
Average grant	$17,588
Average student loan debt	$56,389

ADMISSIONS

Admissions Selectivity Rating	99
# of applications received	2,943
% applicants accepted	20
% acceptees attending	62
Average GMAT	710
Range of GMAT	610–740
Average GPA	3.5
Minimum TOEFL (paper)	600
Application fee	$230
Regular application deadline	11/2
Regular notification	1/31
Application Deadline/Notification	
Round 1:	11/1 / 1/29
Round 2:	1/10 / 4/2
Need-blind admissions	Yes

Student Life and Environment

"The tough part of MIT Sloan is balancing your time to take advantage of all that the school and community offer," students tell us. This is especially true during the first semester core, which students describe as "intense." One first-semester MBA writes, "People work real hard, and at the same time, companies are coming to campus and there are a lot of clubs. This semester is an exercise in prioritization and balancing tasks." One confesses, "There is so much work that you have to make choices as to which review sessions you can attend." Fortunately, "although there is a lot of work, very little of it is useless or busy work." The MBA continues, "When it's all over, I'll be very happy that I was made to do this much at the beginning of my busines-school experience." Students tell us that "After first semester, the pressure is off and life consists of an even mix of schoolwork, socializing, career exploration, and personal time." Administration meanwhile is doing its part to try and alleviate pressure in the core semester.

MIT offers "a plethora of social activity options. A large portion of students play in various intramural sports, [and] there are actually routine options for each weeknight: 'Muddy Mondays' at the on-campus pub, 'Thirst Quenchers' moves the happy hour location each Tuesday, each Wednesday Sloan students gather at the BHP (Beacon Hill Pub), and have 'Consumption Functions' each Thursday night." Clubs "are all student-driven, and there are quite a number of them." One student sums up, "I end every night complaining to myself, 'Why does the day only have 24 hours?'"

Sloan MIT students are "very diverse and extremely impressive with respect to what they did before business school. Many were entrepreneurs who had their own companies." One writes, "What really impresses me is how humble they are. Though most have made remarkable and sometimes extraordinary accomplishments, they rarely speak of them." Although "Students are, by nature, competitive and put a lot of effort into winning intramural athletic events, [they are] very collaborative and helpful" in the classroom.

Admissions

Completed applications to the Sloan MBA program include two letters of recommendation, postsecondary transcripts (self-reported prior to interview; if called for an interview, applicants must provide official transcripts), a resume, four personal essays, supplemental information, and GMAT scores. The school requires additional materials from applicants to the Leaders for Manufacturing

Overmatter because of inserts

Program and the Biomedical Enterprise Program. Sloan is extremely competitive; the school's website points out that "Nearly all the applicants to the MIT Sloan School of Management have noteworthy academic records, competitive GMAT scores, and an average of five-plus years of professional experience."

EMPLOYMENT PROFILE

Career Rating	96	Grads Employed by Function	%	Avg. Salary
Primary Source of Full-time Job Acceptances		Finance/Accounting	28	$96,545
School-facilitated activities	222 (79%)	Marketing/Sales	9	$96,946
Graduate-facilitated activities	52 (19%)	Operations/Production	10	$97,667
Unknown	6 (2%)	Consulting	30	$108,398
Average base starting salary	$101,988	General Management	6	$103,389
Percent employed	94	Other	13	$104,865

Top 5 Employers Hiring Grads

McKinsey & Company; Bain and Company; The Boston Consulting Group; Lehman Brothers; Microsoft.

MCMASTER UNIVERSITY
DeGroote School of Business

Academics

The DeGroote School of Business at McMaster University offers conventional full-time and part-time MBAs, but its co-op program (with paid work terms) truly distinguishes it from the competition. It is a program that, in the words of one student, is "vital to the school's differentiation factor." Through co-op, students with no business experience can enter DeGroote and 2 years later emerge with an MBA and significant professional experience.

DeGroote's co-op program is especially "friendly to young grads," as it carries no prerequisite of professional experience though 46 percent have some work experience. Students appreciate that the program "offers a great way for fresh graduates to gain specialized work experience while concurrently completing their degree. The ability to simultaneously learn theory and apply it in the business world is priceless." The program also suits some already in the midst of their careers. One student revels in the fact that co-op offers "the best way to get a job in a different field" than his experience was in.

DeGroote also offers an accelerated MBA program for individuals with an undergraduate business degree. Students enter at what is traditionally the program's second year and have eight months of intensive study. Students tell us that DeGroote offers "good networking" with the biotech and pharmaceutical industries, and they praise the "innovative" curriculum for its emphasis on "leadership and ethical culture." The program also stresses "team building and cross-functional teamwork," thereby building necessary business communication skills. Some here lament that "quantitative material is afforded seemingly little attention . . . the material covered is cursory," while others observe that "first-year courses are too much like undergraduate [business] courses." Qualified students can enter the MBA program from any undergraduate discipline.

Even those who see problems, however, agree that the school is headed in the right direction. One student commends, "I have been tremendously impressed with the direction [the Dean] has taken the school in recent years." Another agrees, "No question about it, the leaders of our program are putting it on the map." Students like that the current Dean "is not from the academic world and has brought a practical perspective to the school and courses. . . . He knows what he is talking about." They also love that "the price of the program (compared to other programs in the Ontario area) is low." Sums up one MBA, "Given . . . the cost of the program, I felt that McMaster offered a far superior return on investment than most business schools."

Career and Placement

DeGroote's Centre for Business Career Development "is an excellent resource for students." The center shows an "aggressive ambition" that "is necessary in this job market, and is beginning to pay dividends" for students. The office provides counseling and placement services throughout the MBA program and partners with many high end and notable Canadian employers to "deliver seamless, on-campus company information sessions and career recruiting," according to the school's website. Some here feel that "more diverse career opportunities would be nice. Currently, our on-campus recruitment is very focused on accounting and finance jobs, and they do this very well. However, opportunities in other areas such as consulting and marketing leave something to be desired."

Employers most likely to hire DeGroote MBAs include: Abbott Laboratories, Accenture, Bank of Montreal, Bank of Nova Scotia, Bell Canada, Bell Mobility, BMO, Canadian Tire, CIBC World Markets, Dofasco, Eli Lilly and Company, Gennum Corporation, Hydro One, Janssen-Ortho, the Ministry of Health, PricewaterhouseCoopers, Scotia Capital Markets, Sprint Canada, TD Securities, and Telus.

BEN CHAPDELAINE/DENISE ANDERSON, RECRUITING ADMINISTRATOR
MGD A114, 1280 MAIN STREET, WEST HAMILTON, ONTARIO, ON L8S 4M4 CANADA
PHONE: 905-525-9140 • FAX: 905-521-8995
E-MAIL: MBAINFO@MCMASTER.CA • WEBSITE: WWW.DEGROOTE.MCMASTER.CA

Student Life and Environment

Students enjoy a "very social atmosphere" at DeGroote. One reports, "We all spend a lot of time with each other, whether it's outside of school or just grabbing coffee. You can always find someone to get coffee within Innis (our business library) at any time of day or night." They also tell us that "life on campus is excellent. It is a home away from home for anyone who wants to make it so. Facilities are open at all hours, the environment is comfortable, and the school has gone out of its way to make MBAs a priority (e.g., the entire top floor of the building is now an MBA study space)."

Academics here "are challenging but still provide us with free time to pursue other interests as well." A new recreation center that opened recently "is state of the art" while classrooms are "modern and well equipped." The DeGroote MBA Association "plans frequent events and activities"; "There are several MBA intramural sports teams" and "opportunities to participate in case competitions." No wonder students tell us that life here is "quite busy" and things move at a "fast pace. Fortunately, there is always help when you need it."

Hometown Hamilton "is not the most attractive place to live in general, but the location of the school in the west end of the city is quite safe and attractive. The mid-range size of the school in comparison to other Canadian universities gives it the best of both worlds: small-school networking with larger-school sports and community involvement." McMaster University is located within close proximity to the vibrant and diverse city of Toronto.

Admissions

The Admissions Staff at DeGroote focuses primarily on applicants' final 2 years of undergraduate work (minimum 3.0 GPA strongly preferred) and their GMAT scores in assessing candidates. The process is highly holistic in nature. Work experience and demonstrated community leadership skills are also considered, as are evidence of ethical maturity and business aptitude. Applicants to the co-op program are assessed by interview for communication skills, initiative, leadership potential, and general experience. Applicants must submit official transcripts for all previous undergraduate and graduate work, an official score report for the GMAT, two letters of recommendation, and a current resume. One year of post-collegiate work experience is required of applicants to the full-time and part-time programs; applicants to the co-op program need not have prior professional experience. International students whose first language is not English must submit an official score report for the TOEFL (minimum score:100, internet-based test; 250, computer-based test; or 600, paper-based test strongly preferred).

FINANCIAL FACTS

Annual tuition	$10,300
Cost of books	$1,500
Room & board	
(on/off-campus)	$5,500/$4,300
% of students receiving aid	30
% of first-year students	
receiving aid	38
% of students receiving grants	27
Average award package	$3,400
Average grant	$2,500

ADMISSIONS

Admissions Selectivity Rating	**85**
# of applications received	387
% applicants accepted	60
% acceptees attending	66
Average GMAT	620
Average GPA	3
TOEFL required of	
international students	Yes
Minimum TOEFL	
(paper/computer)	600/250
Application fee	$135
Regular application deadline	6/15
Regular notification	Rolling
Non-fall admissions	Yes

Applicants Also Look At

University of Toronto, Wilfrid Laurier University (Canada), York University.

EMPLOYMENT PROFILE

Career Rating	81	Grads Employed by Function	%	Avg. Salary
Primary Source of Full-time Job Acceptances		Finance/Accounting	35	$51,500
School-facilitated activities	31 (52%)	Human Resources	2	$46,750
Graduate-facilitated activities	29 (48%)	Marketing/Sales	27	$53,682
Average base starting salary	$52,873	MIS	2	$58,650
Percent employed	82	Operations/Production	8	$53,465
		Consulting	23	$49,664
		General Management	3	$74,375

Top 5 Employers Hiring Grads

Bank of Montreal; Courtyard Group; Janssen-Ortho; Scotia Bank; CIBC.

MERCER UNIVERSITY—ATLANTA
EUGENE W. STETSON SCHOOL OF BUSINESS AND ECONOMICS

GENERAL INFORMATION

Type of school	Private
Affiliation	Baptist
Academic calendar	Semester

SURVEY SAYS . . .

Students love Atlanta, GA
Friendly students
Good peer network
Cutting-edge classes
Happy students
Smart classrooms

STUDENTS

Enrollment of parent institution	7,188
Enrollment of business school	324
% male/female	54/46
% out-of-state	8
% part-time	44
% minorities	37
% international	12
Average age at entry	30
Average years work experience at entry	6

ACADEMICS

Academic Experience Rating	**73**
Student/faculty ratio	20:1
Profs interesting rating	74
Profs accessible rating	75
% female faculty	38
% minority faculty	19

Joint Degrees

MBA/Doctor of Pharmacy 4 years,
MBA/Master of Divinity 3 years.

Prominent Alumni

Karen Romaine Thomas, vice president, CFO, Schwan's Bakery, Inc.; John F. Hough, health scientist administrator, NIH; William Astary, senior vice president of sales, Acuity Brand Lighting; Paul Gianneschi, mananging principal and founder, Hatch Medical, LLC; Joann Herold, vice president, marketing, Honey Baked Ham Company.

Academics

Designed for the convenience of its predominantly professional student body, Mercer University in Atlanta offers a number of accommodations to suit busy MBAs. Classes here meet only once a week, on weekday evenings or on Saturday. Eight-week sessions help students proceed through the program at a steady pace, while five separate admissions entry points mean students can begin the program at virtually any time of the year. As the school's website asserts, "The program is tailored to meet the needs of individuals already employed as managers," as well as those "preparing for advancement into middle-management and administrative levels."

Mercer is a Baptist university with its main campus an hour south of Atlanta, in Macon, Georgia, and a graduate and professional campus in Atlanta. The school draws on its roots to provide a program that "focuses on ethical leadership and problem-solving skills" in order to give students a "competitive edge" in today's business world. This goal is further achieved through "the establishment of a real-world experience base by maintaining continuous interaction with community organizations, profit and non-profit, through seminars and special programs for practicing managers and administrators." The school's location in a major metropolis is a great asset in achieving this goal.

The heart of the Mercer MBA in Atlanta is a core curriculum covering managerial economics, managerial accounting, marketing, management information systems, corporation finance, operations management science, and ethics. A concluding simulation student seminar and electives are also part of the program. Prior to beginning core course work, incoming Mercer students may be required to complete a sequence of four non-graduate-level foundation courses covering micro- and macro-economics, accounting and finance, management and marketing, and business law. Equivalent courses previously completed at the undergraduate level may allow students to place out of these requirements.

Mercer MBAs appreciate their "professional" and "personable" professors who are "helpful outside the class, open to feedback, [and] truly care that the students are learning." One respondent exclaims, "They push you!" Students also love "the timeliness of the program" and the "state-of-the-art equipment in the lecture rooms," but wish that "more class options were available throughout the school year."

Career and Placement

The Office of Career Services at Mercer "provides support to students and alumni in the areas of decision-making and networking," according to the school catalog, which also notes that "students and alumni can view and be informed of ongoing full-time, part-time, and internship opportunities by registering online with SUCCESSTRAK. Annual career days, an academic majors fair, a senior kick-off event, and presentations on resume design and other job-search topics" are all offered here. Students here tell us that "recruiting and corporate partnerships" all could use improvement.

Karen Goss Herlitz, Assistant Vice President for Admissions
Mercer University, 3001 Mercer University Drive, Atlanta, GA 30341-4155 United States
Phone: 678-547-6417 • Fax: 678-547-6367
E-mail: atlbusadm@mercer.edu • Website: www.mercer.edu/business

Student Life and Environment

Mercer's Atlanta campus is "primarily a commuter campus" where classes "are held in the evenings to accommodate working individuals." Although most students spend very little time on campus, a few would like to see a stronger MBA community and call for "more graduate associations, especially for minorities and women."

Mercer MBAs are "mostly full-time workers in the professional world" who "generally have substantial real-world experiences to contribute." This mélange of professionals makes for "good networking because there's lots of different people in different fields." Students also appreciate the "diverse mix of cultural ethnicities" drawn to Mercer's Atlanta campus.

Hometown Atlanta is one of the great cities of the Southeast, a corporate and cultural mecca that is home to Coca-Cola, The Home Depot, Delta, and a slew of other business giants. The city is awash in restaurants, clubs, live music venues, theaters, culture of every shape and form, and great professional athletics. Top that off with the fact that the weather's fantastic.

Admissions

Applicants to the Stetson MBA program at Mercer must provide the school with a completed application form, two sets of official transcripts from each postsecondary academic institution attended, a resume, and an official GMAT score report showing test results no more than five years old. In addition, international applicants whose first language is not English must demonstrate English proficiency through TOEFL scores. All students who received undergraduate degrees abroad must, at their own expense, provide an independent evaluation (and, where appropriate, a translation) of their undergraduate records. International students must additionally demonstrate the ability to finance their education at Mercer.

FINANCIAL FACTS

Annual tuition	$13,776
Fees	$160
Cost of books	$1,000
Room & board (off-campus)	$9,450
% of students receiving aid	60
% of first-year students receiving aid	60
% of students receiving loans	60
% of students receiving grants	1
Average award package	$12,666
Average grant	$1,140
Average student loan debt	$20,000

ADMISSIONS

Admissions Selectivity Rating	73
# of applications received	165
% applicants accepted	62
% acceptees attending	73
Average GMAT	503
Range of GMAT	450–610
Average GPA	3.00
TOEFL required of international students	Yes
Minimum TOEFL (paper/computer)	550/213
Application fee	$50
International application fee	$100
Regular application deadline	7/1
Regular notification	Rolling
Deferment available	Yes
Maximum length of deferment	5 years past GMAT
Transfer students accepted	Yes
Transfer application policy	Will consider up to two courses (6 semester hours) in transfer within past five years.
Non-fall admissions	Yes
Need-blind admissions	Yes

Applicants Also Look At

Georgia State University, Kennesaw State University, University of Georgia.

EMPLOYMENT PROFILE

Career Rating	82	Grads Employed by Function	%	Avg. Salary
Primary Source of Full-time Job Acceptances		Finance/Accounting	11	$69,000
Percent employed	86	Human Resources	2	$83,000
		Marketing/Sales	21	$79,781
		MIS	5	$76,833
		Operations/Production	12	$80,281
		Consulting	2	$112,000
		General Management	10	$69,528
		Other	27	$69,953

MERCER UNIVERSITY—MACON
EUGENE W. STETSON SCHOOL OF BUSINESS AND ECONOMICS

Academics

Baptist-affiliated Mercer University provides its MBAs a program that "focuses on ethical leadership and problem-solving skills" in order to give students a "competitive edge" in today's business world. Nearly all the students in this program attend part-time while working full-time. According to the school, "The program is tailored to meet the needs of individuals already employed as managers," as well as those "preparing for advancement into middle-management and administrative levels."

Incoming Mercer students should have at least 18 hours of undergraduate work in business with a grade of C or better; those lacking these credentials will need to complete an additional nine hours of graduate electives. All students must demonstrate mastery in statistics, microeconomics, and principles of finance, either through examination or successfully completed undergraduate work. Students lacking these credentials are required to take the appropriate foundation classes before beginning work on their MBA.

The heart of the Mercer MBA is a 12-course core curriculum covering financial reporting, operations management, applied microeconomic analysis, global macroeconomic environment, management and business law, corporate finance, accounting, leadership, and ethics. A seminar in strategic management, an integrative capstone class, and electives (available in accounting, economics, general business, management, MIS, and marketing) are also part of the program.

Students praise the MBA program for providing "lots of individual attention," an outcome of the school's choice to "keep class sizes small." The "solid faculty make themselves available," which is helpful since "some of the course work is hard for people who work full-time to get done." A surprising number of students here warn that class times are too often inconvenient for full-time workers, and some suggest class time could be used more wisely ("Lectures are too long!" says one). They also point out that "it would be nice to have a wider selection of classes," although they recognize that "at so small a school, it would be hard to offer more without increasing costs."

Career and Placement

The Office of Career Services at Mercer "provides support to students and alumni in the areas of decision-making and networking," according to the school catalog, which also notes that "students and alumni can view and be informed of ongoing full-time, part-time, and internship opportunities by registering online with SUCCESSTRAK. Annual career days, an academic majors fair, a senior kick-off event, and presentations on resume design and other job-search topics" are all offered here. Students in the MBA program would like to see the services improved.

ROBERT (BOB) HOLLAND, JR., DIRECTOR OF ACADEMIC ADMINISTRATION
1400 COLEMAN AVENUE, SSBE, MACON, GA 31207 UNITED STATES
PHONE: 478-301-2835 • FAX: 478-301-2635
E-MAIL: HOLLAND_R@MERCER.EDU • WEBSITE: WWW2.MERCER.EDU

Student Life and Environment

"Most people in the MBA program work," so "there is limited outside contact" among Mercer MBAs, "but everyone is very close in class." The pace of life here is always a little frantic because most students are juggling full-time jobs and school obligations, but "it is especially frantic around finals and midterms, in part due to the number of classes each professor teaches."

Mercer students include "a mix of people from off campus who have full-time jobs and graduate assistants, as well as other Mercer employees." They "contribute a vast array of experience that enriches the program," students tell us. The school's Baptist affiliation tends to help the school attract minorities.

Hometown Macon, a city of about 125,000, is home to three other colleges and universities, making it a serious college town. The city offers all the typical school-town prerequisites, including clubs, bowling alleys, bars, cheap eats, and plenty of shopping. Medicine is big business here, as is education; insurance is another major player, as both GEICO and the Georgia Farm Bureau Federation maintain major operations in Macon.

Admissions

Applicants to the Stetson MBA program at Mercer must provide the school with a completed application form, two sets of official transcripts from each postsecondary academic institution attended, a resume, and an official GMAT score report showing test results no more than five years old. In addition, international applicants whose first language is not English must demonstrate English proficiency both through TOEFL scores and, upon arrival at the school, a test administered by the English Language Institute of Mercer University. All students who received undergraduate degrees abroad must, at their own expense, provide an independent evaluation (and, where appropriate, a translation) of their undergraduate records. International students must additionally demonstrate the ability to finance their education at Mercer.

FINANCIAL FACTS

Annual tuition	$17,000
Fees	$483
Cost of books	$2,000
Room & board (off-campus)	$7,000

ADMISSIONS

Admissions Selectivity Rating	**67**
# of applications received	15
% applicants accepted	100
% acceptees attending	100
Average GMAT	520
Range of GMAT	450–600
Average GPA	3.5
TOEFL required of international students	Yes
Minimum TOEFL (paper/computer)	550/213
Application fee	$50
Regular application deadline	Rolling
Regular notification	Rolling
Non-fall admissions	Yes
Need-blind admissions	Yes

MIAMI UNIVERSITY (OH)
RICHARD T. FARMER SCHOOL OF BUSINESS

Academics

The Richard T. Farmer School of Business at Miami University has completely revamped its MBA program over the last few years, and it finally rolled out its new-and-improved program for the 2005–2006 academic year. The new Farmer MBA is an accelerated 14-month full-time-only program (the school will introduce its new part-time program in 2006–2007) that emphasizes practical experience: All participants complete a nine-month extended internship and a capstone international field study. Early reviews are extremely positive. In one student's opinion, "This has to be one of the most progressive and relevant program designs available."

Miami's MBA program kicks off with a four-month "Summer Boot Camp," an intensive survey of graduate-level material in accounting, economics, information systems, marketing, organizational behavior, and statistics. Boot Camp lays the groundwork for the "highly integrated" classes of the Fall and Spring semesters. Fall semester focuses on internal enterprise by "investigating processes and functions within the business itself," according to the school's website. External enterprise, "those relationships or factors which affect the business but which are not found within the company itself, such as supply-chain management, vendor partnerships, and capital acquisition," is the focus of Spring classes. Throughout both semesters, students participate in an extended internship that sends them off-campus one day per week.

Students here brag that "our administration is of the highest quality—comprised of seasoned businesspeople who understand what the market's needs are for skills and qualities of tomorrow's MBA." They also appreciate the fact that "the program utilizes a group of consulting business partners (some of the most seasoned and recognized business leaders in their fields) who advise on the program design and career opportunities for its students. The program offers a unique opportunity for all of its students to mentor under these respectable business leaders, where a rapport can be built and subsequent networks can be expanded." Instructors also earn high praise for "always being willing to help. They are enthusiastic and passionate about their subjects, whether customer acquisition or strategy or new product development and integration."

Career and Placement

Miami's Office of Career Services "does an exceptional job bringing a diverse group of *Fortune* 500 companies in for recruiting," students report, observing that "the setup of the interviewing schedule allows each student a fair opportunity to interview for any position with any company on campus, but also requires responsibility, research, and awareness on the student's part." The office provides a number of other standard career-placement services, but students tell us that their careers receive their greatest push from the internships and mentoring relationships incorporated into the MBA program itself. One writes, "The exposure to top executives (Jeff Immelt, Brad Alford, John Faraci), the Mentorship program, and the integrated internship—it's all great. No other school places you with a *Fortune* 25 company for a whole year, but that's what this school did for me."

Judy Barille, MBA Director
Laws Hall, Oxford, OH 45056 United States
Phone: 513-529-6643 • Fax: 513-529-2487
E-mail: miamimba@muohio.edu • Website: mba.muohio.edu

Student Life and Environment

Miami has upgraded its MBA program in recent years. It hasn't upgraded its facility yet, but it is in the process of doing just that. The school breaks ground on the $30 million Farmer Hall in the summer of 2006 and expects to have the new business center open for the Fall semester of 2008.

Students love the Miami campus, which one describes as "among the nicest I've seen." Hometown Oxford "is pretty nice. It is a college town so something is always going on, but the town is still very laid-back and residents are quite friendly. The atmosphere is light, young, vibrant, and active." The city is "also only 45 minutes away from Cincinnati, and with so many people commuting, the city is very accessible."

The Miami MBA student body "seems to be split. Half are very involved in the program, half are here to get their degree." Regardless of their level of commitment, everyone here "grows really close because of the small size of the class. We get along very well and know what to expect from one another."

Admissions

Admission to the MBA program at Miami University requires a minimum undergraduate GPA of 2.75, with a minimum GPA of 3.00 for the final two full years (i.e., four semesters) of undergraduate study; applicants must provide two official transcripts of all postsecondary academic work. GMAT scores are also required. Miami admissions officers also consider work experience (a minimum of three years post-undergraduate professional experience is typically required) and personal qualities as reflected in the essays, two letters of recommendation, and an interview. International students must meet all of the above requirements and must, in addition, demonstrate English competency through the TOEFL and the Test of Written English (TWE). Transcripts in languages other than English must be translated and must bear the official seal of the issuing institution.

FINANCIAL FACTS

Annual tuition (in-state/ out-of-state)	$15,755/$34,050
Fees	$1,382
Cost of books	$1,000
Room & board	$6,000
% of students receiving aid	25
% of first-year students receiving aid	80
Average grant	$2,000

ADMISSIONS

Admissions Selectivity Rating	86
# of applications received	102
% applicants accepted	41
% acceptees attending	74
Average GMAT	552
Range of GMAT	520–580
Average GPA	3.2
TOEFL required of international students	Yes
Minimum TOEFL (paper/computer)	550/220
Application fee	$35
Regular application deadline	2/1
Regular notification	Rolling
Deferment available	Yes
Maximum length of deferment	2 years
Non-fall admissions	Yes

Applicants Also Look At

Bowling Green State University, Indiana University—Bloomington, The Ohio State University, University of Cincinnati, University of Dayton.

EMPLOYMENT PROFILE

Career Rating	82	Grads Employed by Function	%	Avg. Salary
		Finance/Accounting	42	$45,000
		Marketing/Sales	42	$61,670
		MIS	16	$52,333

MILLSAPS COLLEGE
ELSE SCHOOL OF MANAGEMENT

GENERAL INFORMATION

Type of school	Private
Affiliation	Methodist
Environment	Metropolis
Academic calendar	Semester

SURVEY SAYS . . .
Solid preparation in:
Teamwork
Communication/interpersonal skills
Presentation skills

STUDENTS

Enrollment of parent institution	1,146
Enrollment of business school	53
% male/female	58/42
% part-time	60
Average age at entry	25
Average years work experience at entry	4

ACADEMICS

Academic Experience Rating	**84**
Student/faculty ratio	12:1
Profs interesting rating	96
Profs accessible rating	85
% female faculty	39
% minority faculty	5

Prominent Alumni
Bo Chastain, CEO, MS State Hospital; John Stupka, former CEO, Skytel; Richard H. Mills, Jr., CEO, Tellus Operating Group; Will Flatt, CFO, Parkway Properties; Sharon O'Shea, president and CEO, e-Triage.

Academics

Reflecting the spirit and friendliness of the Millsaps undergraduate institution, the Else School of Management at Millsaps College offers a rigorous MBA program in a refreshingly intimate atmosphere. The student/faculty ratio at Millsaps is very low, with many classes taught in teams by two or more professors. In fact, "in class sizes of less than 20, we often have 2 PhDs or 1 PhD and a JD." These numbers allow for an engaging and productive classroom experience: "Classes focus on participation and discussion," and "students are eager to learn as well as participate in class."

While professors at Millsaps actively engage in research and professional activities, they "really love teaching and their students," and "are available outside of class through e-mail or meetings. They give students the one-on-one attention that you'd expect at a small school." For students who are struggling with course work or wish to solicit professional advice, professors "always have an open-door policy and are very open to questions, comments, or suggestions." No matter what subjects they teach, "all the professors know a lot about their fields, but they also know about other fields so they help us relate all aspects of business together." According to one student, "they prepare us for the real world, not just the academics."

While the academic atmosphere at Millsaps is friendly and supportive, students make it clear that "the course work is challenging." Overall, students value the preparation this workload gives them; in particular, students appreciate the fact that "the program really focuses on effective oral and written communications skills." In fact, "several weekend communications seminars are part of the core curriculum." A current student tells us that applicants should "expect to write, write, and then write some more!"

Working students say that Millsaps is particularly suited to their unique needs: "The classes are conveniently scheduled and the school's proximity to the downtown central business district makes it very easy to get to classes easily and on time." In fact, 90 percent of the MBA classes at the Else School are offered in the evening to accommodate work or internships. The library is also "open at all hours to facilitate all schedules." "Professors understand that working students have obligations other than school and exert every effort to help students who have missed class."

Career and Placement

"Millsaps has an excellent academic reputation within the state and certainly within the local community," making it a great choice for students who wish to launch or promote their careers in the Jackson region. One second-year student explains, "I chose this school based on three factors: its reputation, the kind of students that it produces, and the respect that a degree from Millsaps garners." Many students who attend Millsaps are already working in Jackson and have chosen to pursue an MBA at Millsaps to increase their opportunities at their current companies. For recent college grads who want to build their professional experience, Millsaps offers academic credit for internship experiences in a professional environment. Students may receive additional assistance through the Millsaps College Career Center, which offers resume and interview counseling, career-development services, and internship placement. The school also organizes a variety of career-development opportunities, community-service activities, and professional development seminars.

BILL BRISTER, DIRECTOR OF GRADUATE BUSINESS ADMISSIONS
1701 NORTH STATE STREET, JACKSON, MS 39210 UNITED STATES
PHONE: 601-974-1253 • FAX: 601-974-1260
E-MAIL: MBAMACC@MILLSAPS.EDU • WEBSITE: WWW.MILLSAPS.EDU/ESOM

Student Life and Environment

A "friendly, very Southern atmosphere" permeates the Else School campus, whose location in Jackson makes for plenty of social and cultural opportunities. While most students hail from the state of Mississippi, the student body is nevertheless "a diverse bunch that has the utmost respect for individuals from various backgrounds." Given the school's flexible evening schedule and supportive academic environment, it's not surprising that many Millsaps students are older professionals; however, there is also a decent population of younger students, of whom "quite a few are actually right out of undergraduate [programs]."

There are several business honoraries chartered at Millsaps College, including Beta Gamma Sigma, Beta Alpha Psi, and the Financial Management Association. For those looking for a little fun, the Else School hosts several annual events for MBAs: "The dean attempts to pull the MBA students into the school activities; for example, we had a tailgating party for homecoming." However, since the program is largely part-time, students admit that "working full-time and being in school part-time doesn't leave much time for social activities." In general, "most of the students go to class and then go home to their families." A second-year student admits, "Besides group work and the occasional holiday party or community-service activity, there is not as much social interaction as I would like."

Admissions

Admission to Millsaps is rolling. To apply, prospective students must submit an application form, GMAT scores, two letters of recommendation, and official transcripts from all previously attended graduate and undergraduate institutions. Along with their application materials, students must submit an essay detailing their reasons for pursuing an MBA. The Else School also requires a personal interview for all applicants. Prospective students do not need to have studied business as an undergraduate, but students with no background in accounting may be required to take undergraduate courses to catch up. There is no minimum GMAT score requirement for admission to the MBA program, although a score of 500 or better is preferred.

FINANCIAL FACTS

Annual tuition	$23,520
Cost of books	$550
% of students receiving aid	85
% of first-year students receiving aid	100
% of students receiving grants	90

ADMISSIONS

Admissions Selectivity Rating	**73**
# of applications received	69
% applicants accepted	80
% acceptees attending	71
Average GMAT	540
Range of GMAT	510–640
Average GPA	3.4
TOEFL required of international students	Yes
Minimum TOEFL (paper/computer)	550/230
Application fee	$25
Deferment available	Yes
Maximum length of deferment	1 year
Transfer students accepted	Yes
Transfer application policy Student in good standing; 6 hours from a non-AACSB program; 12 hours from a AACSB-accredited program	
Non-fall admissions	Yes
Need-blind admissions	Yes

EMPLOYMENT PROFILE

Career Rating	64	Grads Employed by Function	%	Avg. Salary
Primary Source of Full-time Job Acceptances		Finance/Accounting	2	NR
Percent employed	8	Marketing/Sales	2	NR
		MIS	2	NR
		Global Management	1	NR
		Nonprofit	1	NR

MINNESOTA STATE UNIVERSITY—MANKATO
COLLEGE OF BUSINESS

GENERAL INFORMATION

Type of school	Public
Academic calendar	Semester

SURVEY SAYS . . .
Students love Mankato, MN
Friendly students
Smart classrooms

STUDENTS

Enrollment of parent institution	14,000
Enrollment of business school	32
% male/female	67/33
% out-of-state	16
% part-time	40
% minorities	2
% international	20
Average age at entry	27
Average years work experience at entry	4

ACADEMICS

Academic Experience Rating	**83**
Student/faculty ratio	12:1
Profs interesting rating	81
Profs accessible rating	71
% female faculty	25

Academics

The MBA program at Minnesota State University—Mankato's College of Business employs an unusual calendar. Each semester here is divided into two eight-week modules, during which students complete two-credit courses that meet once a week. The school's goal in creating this system is to afford maximum flexibility to the school's busy students. MBAs here can take one or two classes per module, and they can skip a module entirely when necessary without losing too much ground. A student who takes the maximum number of classes per module can complete the program in about two years. One student writes, "The most attractive part of this program was the class schedule. I am a working individual, so classes from 6:00 to 9:00 P.M. are a great option for me, because I don't have to take off from work to attend classes!"

MSU Mankato's MBA program allows students to concentrate in international business (international study opportunities are available) or leadership and organizational change. Students may also fashion their own concentrations in consultation with a faculty advisor. An executive lecture series and executive seminars give students the chance "to learn from, as well as interact with, top executives." Students appreciate that the curriculum "places more emphasis on real life. Theories are great, but theories won't get you through life. Tying current business trends to course work makes the material applicable to life today and allows business students to use course information in their current jobs." They also approve of the school's "attempts to teach course-work fundamentals as well as up-to-date problems, situations, and changes that are currently affecting businesses today."

Mankato MBAs report that "most classes have moderate reading, and many use case studies. The class formats are split between lecture and interactive learning. The class sizes are just great, and the level of feedback from the professors and from the other students' insights really makes a difference." The financial burden of attending is lessened by the "many great opportunities for graduate assistantships, which pay for tuition while giving you work experience."

Career and Placement

MSU Mankato's Career Development Center serves all undergraduate students, graduate students, and alumni of the school. The MBA program is relatively new, with its first graduating class being Spring 2006 so there is still plenty of room for growth. The College of Business has recently partnered with CareerBeam which allows MBA students to access more than 20,000 business sources across 50 job categories. Students here should consider mining another valuable resource: the faculty. One student explains, "I am sure not every student takes advantage of this, but I have talked with many professors regarding career path, industry insight, corporate contacts, etc., and they all have been extremely useful developing postgraduate career prospects. I have about five months left in the program and have secured numerous interviews and a few job offers."

LIZ OLMANSON, DEPARTMENT ASSISTANT
MSU MBA PROGRAM, 150 MORRIS HALL MANKATO, MN 56001 UNITED STATES
PHONE: 507-389-2967 • FAX: 507-389-5497
E-MAIL: MBA@MNSU.EDU • WEBSITE: WWW.COB.MNSU.EDU

Student Life and Environment

Mankato, students tell us, is "a great college town with a warm and friendly community, and a growing university with a vast support system from local businesses and leaders." The town of 45,000 is located about 65 miles southwest of Minneapolis. The surrounding region is "the health care, commercial, and cultural center of south-central Minnesota," according to the school's website. Residents have easy access to parks and ski facilities; outdoor activities are very popular here. MSU's athletic teams, which compete in the North Central Conference, enjoy strong support from area residents. The Twin Cities can be reached in less than one and a half hours by automobile.

MSU Mankato's MBAs generally work full-time in addition to attending school, so they "don't have any time to enjoy campus life. Most of us try to spend as little time on campus as possible." Some students complain that "there are few programs outside of class to provide learning and application experiences. Groups, clubs, or other opportunities focused toward the graduate student body would enrich the graduate experience." Most, however, acknowledge that they wouldn't take advantage of such opportunities because they lack the time to do so.

Admissions

Applicants to the MBA program at MSU Mankato's College of Business must submit all of the following materials to the College of Graduate Studies: a completed application form; two official transcripts from one's degree-granting institution(s); and official score reports for the GMAT and, if applicable, the TOEFL. International applicants must also complete a Financial Statement Form demonstrating that they have sufficient funds to pay for the program. Most international applicants are required to have their undergraduate transcripts evaluated by a well-regarded credential evaluation service. All applicants must also submit a separate MBA program application form, a resume, and two letters of reference to the College of Business. Admission to the MBA program is competitive. Applicants are assessed holistically. Relevant factors include test scores (a score of at least 500 on the GMAT and 550 on the paper version of the TOEFL are recommended), undergraduate GPA, work experience, and quality of letters of reference.

FINANCIAL FACTS

Annual tuition (in-state/ out-of-state)	$7,903/$10,812
Fees	$368
Cost of books	$650
Room & board (on-campus)	$8,600
% of students receiving aid	10
% of students receiving loans	10
Average award package	$15,000

ADMISSIONS

Admissions Selectivity Rating	**79**
# of applications received	27
% applicants accepted	74
% acceptees attending	100
Average GMAT	560
Range of GMAT	480–680
Average GPA	3.36
TOEFL required of international students	Yes
Minimum TOEFL (paper/computer)	550/210
Application fee	$40
Regular application deadline	6/1
Regular notification	7/15
Deferment available	Yes
Maximum length of deferment	1 year
Transfer students accepted	Yes
Transfer application policy Students may transfer up to six credits from a regionally-accredited institution.	
Non-fall admissions	Yes
Need-blind admissions	Yes

MISSOURI STATE UNIVERSITY (FORMERLY SW MISSOURI STATE U.)
COLLEGE OF BUSINESS ADMINISTRATION

Academics

With a solid reputation in its home state and a growing reputation throughout the country, the College of Business Administration (COBA) at Missouri State University provides a "highly affordable" MBA to a diverse mix of local and international students. Students agree the college is "consistently recognized as a strong business school, especially in technology management." They also love the management and accounting departments at MSU.

Through an arrangement with both the International School of Management Studies in Chennai (Madras), Indian students can complete their "foundation" courses in India, and then complete the remainder of the program (33 credit hours) in Missouri. One of the many Indian students attending MSU writes, "The arrangement allowed me to do my prerequisite courses in India and the regular MBA in the U.S." About one third of the full-time MBA student body is international.

The college offers "true diversity among the faculty. There are conservatives as well as liberals here." Professors earn high marks for "always being willing to take extra time to help a student understand a difficult concept. They expect a lot of preparation and in turn will work their hardest to help you succeed." Most here feel that "this school is definitely headed in the right direction. Class selection is expanding, and the student population is becoming increasingly diverse. The school keeps fairly up-to-date on technology as well."

Career and Placement

MSU hosts "many career fairs, with many companies from the surrounding states recruiting here." Respondents to our survey are satisfied with the school's career center, praising its "commitment to helping students find internship opportunities during school and permanent employment after school." Nearly 400 companies visit the campus looking for full-time hires each year; a little over 100 recruit summer interns on campus. These figures apply to the entire university; the figure for how many of these companies specifically recruit MBAs is unknown.

A little more than half of MSU's MBAs remain in the region after graduation. About a third find work overseas, an unsurprising figure given the large international population. Top employers of MSU MBAs include Wal-Mart, Payless, Hallmark, Samson, FedEx, Anheuser Busch, DataTronics, Edward Jones, State Farm, Caterpillar, Occidental, Petroleum Renaissance Financial, John Hancock, Boeing, State Street, Gateway Financial, the Federal Reserve Bank, Cerner, Target, Toys R Us, Federated Insurance, Enterprise, Archer Daniels Midland, KPMG, Baird Kurtz & Dobson, Deloitte Touche Tohmatsu, Kirkpatrick, Phillips & Miller, CPAs, Sherwin Williams, AG Edwards, and Koch Industries.

Student Life and Environment

MBAs love the "nice and quiet city" of Springfield, with its "unique 'small town' atmosphere with all the amenities of a major city. You get the best of both worlds!" The city boasts "outdoor recreation that is second to none, with several area lakes [and state and national parks], two regional medical centers, a regional shopping mall, and minor league baseball, football, and hockey teams, and even a professional tennis team." Other amenities include "over 300 different churches to attend, plenty of nightlife in the Jordan Valley Park area, [and] several golf and racquet clubs, as well as one of the largest

TOBIN BUSHMAN, GRADUATE COLLEGE COORDINATOR
901 SOUTH NATIONAL AVENUE, SPRINGFIELD, MO 65897 UNITED STATES
PHONE: 417-836-5335 • FAX: 417-836-6888
E-MAIL: GRADUATECOLLEGE@MISSOURISTATE.EDU • WEBSITE: WWW.COBA.MISSOURISTATE.EDU

equestrian communities in this region of the country." With "plenty of low-cost housing available [and] Branson, one of the entertainment capitals of the world, only 45 minutes away," what's not to love about Springfield?

Best of all, students needn't even leave school grounds to find something to do because "the campus is always brimming with activity." Student organizations "regularly conduct events to keep students involved." Students advise, "Whether you get involved or not is completely up to you. You are accepted if you want to be, and never shunned." Either way you'll feel secure on this "very well-lit and safe campus. A number of safety features are offered throughout [the] campus, including a service where the Safety & Transportation officials will walk you back to your car or residence hall at night." No wonder MBA students agree that "this university is really student-oriented. Everything is done here to create good atmosphere for learning and having fun at the same time."

The rhythm of life in the COBA is such that "life goes on smoothly, and with lots of fun." There is "lots of reading and preparing for classes during the week. Every class has a group project and individual assignments. The midterm times are silent with the libraries full of studies." The weekends, on the other hand, "are crowded with students playing and cheering up." The student body here is drawn "from all different countries, which offers a vast knowledge of other cultures on top of the knowledge of business." Many come from India, where MSU participates in a twinning program to facilitate exchange students. Everyone here enjoys "a very friendly atmosphere where everyone is very helpful toward each other."

Admissions

The admissions office at MSU makes the following minimum requirements of applicants: a GPA of at least 2.75 for the final two years (60 semester hours) of undergraduate work; a minimum GMAT score of 400, with at least a 20-percentile ranking in both verbal and written portions of the test; and a minimum GPA–GMAT score of 1000 based on this formula: (undergraduate GPA in last 60 hours of undergraduate work × 200) + GMAT score. International students who do not initially meet the verbal or written requirements may be admitted conditionally and subsequently required to demonstrate English proficiency through additional testing and/or course work. For these students, a minimum score of 550 on the paper-based TOEFL is also generally required.

FINANCIAL FACTS

Annual tuition (in-state/ out-of-state)	$4,536/$9,072
Fees	$508
Cost of books	$875
Room & board (on/off-campus)	$4,806/$5,200
% of students receiving aid	55
% of students receiving loans	53
% of students receiving grants	34
Average award package	$8,909
Average grant	$3,112
Average student loan debt	$16,500

ADMISSIONS

Admissions Selectivity Rating	66
# of applications received	160
% applicants accepted	98
% acceptees attending	98
Average GMAT	510
Range of GMAT	440–570
Average GPA	3.4
TOEFL required of international students	Yes
Minimum TOEFL (paper/computer)	550/213
Application fee	$30
Regular application deadline	Rolling
Regular notification	Rolling
Deferment available	Yes
Maximum length of deferment	Semester
Transfer students accepted	Yes
Transfer application policy	with advisor permission.
Non-fall admissions	Yes

Applicants Also Look At

Arkansas State University, Central Missouri State University, Southeast Missouri State University, University of Arkansas at Little Rock, University of Missouri—Columbia, University of Missouri—Kansas City, University of Missouri—St. Louis.

EMPLOYMENT PROFILE			
Career Rating	74	**Grads Employed by Function**	**% Avg. Salary**
Primary Source of Full-time Job Acceptances		Accounting	10 $47,265
School-facilitated activities	30%	Finance/Accounting	9 $41,875
Graduate-facilitated activities	20%	Human Resources	3 $33,456
Unknown	50%	Marketing/Sales	12 $43,667
		MIS	12 $48,920
		Operations/Production	10 $41,000
		Consulting	12 $39,810
		General Management	20 $40,988
		Other	12 $43,210
		Top 5 Employers Hiring Grads	
		BKD; State of Missouri; Missouri State University; Boeing; Wal-Mart.	

Monmouth University
School of Business Administration

Academics

"The administration and professors at Monmouth University are always looking out for students' best interests," MBAs at this private institution an hour south of New York City tell us. One student observes, "Monmouth keeps up with the changing business world. For example, it added a health care program, and it is constantly updating its courses with new practices and techniques." Monmouth may not be the school for everyone—students warn that "the breadth of the subject matter offered is narrow, as there are only two concentrations, real estate and health care administration"—but for those looking for a general degree or with interest in those specific areas, Monmouth may well fit the bill. Monmouth also offers an MBA track in accounting. The program is designed to fulfill New Jersey's requirement of 150 credit hours prior to sitting for the CPA exam.

Monmouth's general MBA requires a minimum of 30 credit hours. Note, however, that students with deficiencies in their undergraduate business educations may be required to take core courses that can increase the requirement to up to 48 hours. The accounting track requires a minimum of 33 credit hours, as does the concentration in real estate. The health care concentration requires 36 credit hours. All tracks conclude with an integrative capstone course. Students report that required courses for all MBAs provide "a good foundation in the history and evolution of a business concept." They warn that elective options are scant. One writes, "Of the many nonrequired courses listed in the catalog, very few are offered each semester. For example, there are only two finance courses offered for the Spring 2005 term!" Even more worrisome is that "required courses fill up quickly, and are packed full with 30 students. Sometimes a new section is added, and sometimes it isn't." Starting in fall 2007, Monmouth is offering an Accelerated MBA, which is a one-year, 30-credit fast-track program. Applicants must have earned a bachelor's degree in business within the last seven years.

On a positive note, "professors at Monmouth have a vast amount of business experience related to the courses they teach." One student offers, "I feel confident I am learning about how things work in the real business world along with the prevalent academic thinking on a given subject." Teachers also "seem to always be available for consultation before class and many other hours as well. It's nice being able to talk to the professors about concepts you may be trying to relate to the current working world, as well as concepts with which you may struggle." Students inform us that "the library is very good, with many valuable resources, both print and electronic." One MBA remarks, "The computer labs are good too. Wi-fi service is a plus; I hope they continue adding more coverage."

Career and Placement

Career services are provided to Monmouth MBAs by the Life and Career Advising Center, which serves the entire university. The office administers aptitude tests and career inventories, and provides a contact point between students and alumni and businesses. One-on-one counseling services are also available. Additionally, Monmouth has an Accounting Honors Employment Program.

Student Life and Environment

Monmouth has "an absolutely beautiful campus with lovely historical buildings of import" located "one mile from the beach," a location that provides "a lot of places to go and things to do outside the classroom." Those who stick around campus long enough to socialize report, "Life at Monmouth is very active. While the school is very quiet on weekends, the weekdays are filled with fun, educational activities. There is great school

KEVIN ROANE, DIRECTOR, GRADUATE ADMISSION
400 CEDAR AVENUE, WEST LONG BRANCH, NJ 07764-1898 UNITED STATES
PHONE: 732-571-3452 • FAX: 732-263-5123
E-MAIL: GRADADM@MONMOUTH.EDU • WEBSITE: WWW.MONMOUTH.EDU

spirit" fostered by "university sporting events, which the majority of students attend." Between classes, students often head for "the Java Coffee Cafe at the student center." These same students get the most out of "a wide range of clubs and a very helpful Career Advising Center staff."

For the many part-time MBA students here with major commitments outside of school, participation in extracurriculars is a rarity. One such student explains, "In part-time MBA programs, students don't really get to socialize much with their classmates. Most graduate students come to school, put their time in for classes, and then go home to their work and families. We rarely see each other outside of class. It's not the same as a full-time experience." Part-time or full-time, "the majority of graduate students at Monmouth are very friendly and are always looking to share experiences and network with new students."

Campus amenities include "plenty of study areas on campus. Recently the school added two 24-hour computer labs." Students' still would like more classrooms and some on-campus housing for graduate students.

Admissions

Minimum requirements for admission to the Monmouth MBA program include: a GMAT score of at least 450; a formula score of at least 1000 under the formula [(undergraduate GPA × 200) + GMAT score]; and an overall undergraduate GPA of at least 2.75. Regular admission generally requires a minimum GMAT score of 500. For those whose undergraduate degree is more than eight years old, a GMAT score of 450 is acceptable, provided the applicant has sufficient managerial experience and produces two letters of recommendation and a detailed resume. Students who hold graduate degrees in other areas (PhD, EdD, MD, JD, CPA) may be exempted from the above admissions requirements. International students whose native language is not English must submit official TOEFL score reports in addition to all required documents listed above. Foreign language documents and transcripts must be notarized and translated (Monmouth recommends World Education Service in New York). International students must demonstrate sufficient funds to support at least their first year of study at Monmouth University and sufficient additional resources to fund completion of their degree.

FINANCIAL FACTS

Annual tuition	$12,132
Fees	$620
Cost of books	$900
Room & board (off-campus)	$13,375
% of students receiving aid	85
% of first-year students receiving aid	68
% of students receiving loans	54
% of students receiving grants	67
Average award package	$12,974
Average grant	$2,991
Average student loan debt	$27,294

ADMISSIONS

Admissions Selectivity Rating	65
# of applications received	125
% applicants accepted	88
% acceptees attending	60
Average GMAT	507
Range of GMAT	460–540
Average GPA	3.18
TOEFL required of international students	Yes
Minimum TOEFL (paper/computer)	550/225
Application fee	$50
Regular application deadline	7/15
Regular notification	Rolling
Deferment available	Yes
Maximum length of deferment	1 year
Transfer students accepted	Yes
Transfer application policy Must complete at least 30 credits at Monmouth.	
Transfer credits must be within 7 years and with acceptable grade.	
Non-fall admissions	Yes
Need-blind admissions	Yes

MONTCLAIR STATE UNIVERSITY
SCHOOL OF BUSINESS

GENERAL INFORMATION

Type of school	Public
Environment	Town
Academic calendar	Year-round

SURVEY SAYS . . .

Students love Montclair, NJ
Friendly students
Good peer network
Helpful alumni
Solid preparation in:
Doing business in a global economy

STUDENTS

Enrollment of parent institution	16,076
Enrollment of business school	302
% male/female	44/56
% out-of-state	26
% part-time	82
% minorities	16
% international	10
Average age at entry	29
Average years work experience at entry	8

ACADEMICS

Academic Experience Rating	**68**
Student/faculty ratio	25:1
Profs interesting rating	64
Profs accessible rating	62
% female faculty	30
% minority faculty	28

Joint Degrees

MBA/MS (chemistry) 62 semester hours.

Prominent Alumni

Steve Adubato, anchor, WNET NY, PBS; Paul Weber, MD, director global medical affairs, Schering-Plough; Annette Catino, president and CEO, QualCare, Inc.; Thomas P. Zucosky, CIO, Discovery Capital Management; A. J. Khubani, president and CEO, Telebrands.

Academics

Affordability, "proximity to New York City," and "a program that caters to part-time students" are the main attractions at the MBA program at Montclair State University. The school offers a full-time program, with classes in the evenings and Saturdays; a part-time evening program; and an accelerated Saturday program. Approximately one-quarter of the student body attends full-time.

The Montclair MBA is a 48-credit sequence including nine credits of introductory management classes, a 15-credit functional core (covering accounting, finance, marketing, and information management), 9 credits of advanced business courses, 12–18 credits of electives (some of which may be used to create an area of concentration), and a three-credit capstone course in advanced strategic management. Up to 15 hours of these classes can be waived based on prior academic work or through challenge examinations. Concentrations are available in accounting, economics, finance, international business, management, marketing, and MIS.

Montclair professors "have a good amount of practical knowledge and integrate current topics well, without going into overkill mode. The program design offers a good balance of individual and group assignments, papers, exams, and presentations." Instructors earn praise for being "understanding of students' other obligations, but without being pushovers," and for "bringing great real-world experience to [the] classroom." Administrators earn praise for soliciting student evaluations of their professors, and for actually listening to these comments: students claim that "some professors have actually been removed from the program upon student request." Administrators are also very approachable; one student states, they "hold lunches that are a great environment for conversation. They're really good at listening to students."

Career and Placement

The MSU Career Development Center serves all undergraduates and graduates at the school. MBAs are not impressed; one writes, "We need to establish an alumni club or organization and a career/campus recruiting office." Another agrees, "It would be nice to have a career services center active for MBAs. In all my years attending I have yet to have anyone from the MBA office or career office offer a meeting, discussion, or follow-up on my studies." Living near New York City, "the greatest free market in the world," makes it a little easier for students to find internships and jobs on their own. Most MSU MBAs attend while pursuing full-time careers; their employers include Abbott Laboratories, ADP, AT&T Wireless Services, Bank of New York, Con Edison, Deloitte Consulting, Goldman Sachs, Gucci, Kodak, the *New York Times*, the Office of the New Jersey Attorney General, PricewaterhouseCoopers, Prudential Financial, Sodexho USA, Thomson Financial, United Parcel Service, and Wyeth-Ayerst Research.

Student Life and Environment

Montclair is "mostly a commuter campus," with "about 75 percent of the students attending part-time and working full-time." As a result, "Most people don't get involved in activities because there are higher priorities (work, family, the rest of life)." The part-time student body arrives with "an interesting array of backgrounds and work experiences," we're told. The large number of part-time commuters means "group work can be difficult because we all have different schedules, but we figure out how to work together."

Ms. Jennifer O'Sullivan, Admissions Coordinator
College Hall, Room 203, One Normal Avenue, Montclair, NJ 07043 United States
Phone: 973-655-5147 • Fax: 973-655-7869
E-mail: GRADUATE.SCHOOL@MONTCLAIR.EDU • Website: WWW.MONTCLAIR.EDU/MBA

The town of Montclair has several major parks and lots of quiet streets. It boasts four movie theaters, an art museum and several art galleries, lots of artisan shops, two off-Broadway theater companies, a host of funky restaurants, and an abundance of coffee shops. Students remark that they often see no need to venture into New York City proper, as they are able to partake in a range of cultural activities without ever leaving the Montclair vicinity. Cross-town public transportation is also pretty good, and access to and from NYC is frequent, easy, and cheap.

Those MBAs who live on campus and attend full-time "tend to be the international students." They tell us that "overall, campus life is good. We have many graduate- and undergraduate-level clubs and organizations to choose from. There is something for everyone at MSU." Full-timers and commuters alike appreciate the fact that "there is a diner on campus, proof that this is a Jersey school."

Admissions

Applicants to the MSU/MBA program "must have at least earned a bachelor's degree from a regionally accredited college or university (or the foreign equivalent)" and must submit two official copies of transcripts for all academic work completed after high school; an official score report for the GMAT (applicants holding a terminal degree—a PhD, MD, or JD, for example—are exempt from the GMAT requirement); a personal statement of professional goals; two letters of recommendation from "persons qualified to evaluate the applicant's promise of academic achievement and potential for professional growth;" and a completed application form. International students whose first language is not English must submit an official score report for the TOEFL. Of these elements, the undergraduate GPA and the GMAT score are among the most important factors that the Admissions Department considers. The average GMAT score of the 2005 entering class was 500, and the average GPA was 3.24. Prior work experience is "strongly recommended" but is not required.

FINANCIAL FACTS

Annual tuition (in-state/ out-of-state)	$9,466/$12,778
Fees	$1,143
Cost of books	$3,600
Room & board (on/off-campus)	$8,250/$12,500
% of students receiving aid	26
% of first-year students receiving aid	32
% of students receiving loans	22
% of students receiving grants	6
Average award package	$12,862
Average grant	$2,596
Average student loan debt	$26,629

ADMISSIONS

Admissions Selectivity Rating	72
# of applications received	146
% applicants accepted	63
% acceptees attending	65
Average GMAT	490
Range of GMAT	435–580
Average GPA	3.12
TOEFL required of international students	Yes
Minimum TOEFL (paper/computer)	550/213
Application fee	$60
International application fee	$60
Regular application deadline	Rolling
Regular notification	Rolling
Deferment available	Yes
Maximum length of deferment	1 year
Transfer students accepted	Yes

Transfer application policy
Through prior academic experience, graduate transfer credits, and/or challenge examinations, the MBA degree requirements may be reduced by up to 15 credits (SH) of core courses. Waiver assessments are made after candidates are accepted to the MBA program, at an initial advising appointment with the MBA Director.

Non-fall admissions	Yes
Need-blind admissions	Yes

Applicants Also Look At
Farleigh Dickinson University, Metropolitan, Rutgers, The State University of New Jersey, Seton Hall University.

EMPLOYMENT PROFILE

Career Rating	62	Grads Employed by Function	%	Avg. Salary
Primary Source of Full-time Job Acceptances		Finance/Accounting	28	$60,000
School-facilitated activities	10	Marketing/Sales	16	$75,000
Graduate-facilitated activities	90	MIS	8	$60,000
Percent employed	15	Operations/Production	4	$65,000
		Consulting	4	$50,000
		General Management	40	$80,000

Top 5 Employers Hiring Grads
Roche Laboratories; Schering-Plough; Morgan Stanley; Johnson & Johnson; Prudential.

MONTEREY INSTITUTE OF INTERNATIONAL STUDIES
FISHER GRADUATE SCHOOL OF INTERNATIONAL BUSINESS

GENERAL INFORMATION

Type of school	Private
Environment	Town
Academic calendar	Semester

SURVEY SAYS...

Students love Monterey, CA
Friendly students
Solid preparation in:
Teamwork
Communication/interpersonal skills
Doing business in a global economy

STUDENTS

Enrollment of parent institution	766
Enrollment of business school	71
% male/female	55/45
% part-time	1
% minorities	14
% international	35
Average age at entry	28
Average years work experience at entry	4

ACADEMICS

Academic Experience Rating	**70**
Student/faculty ratio	5:1
Profs interesting rating	87
Profs accessible rating	72
% female faculty	13
% minority faculty	17

Joint Degrees
MBA/MA 3 years MBA/MA 3 years, MBA/MA 3 years, MBA/MPA 3 years, MBA/MA 3 years, MBA/MA 3 years.

Prominent Alumni
Fumio Matsushima, head of private banking, HSBC Japan; J.R. Williams, vice president, Prudential Securities; Elizabeth Powell, vice president of customer service, Motorola; Naoko Yanaghara, vice president, AT&T Japan; Venkatesh Baggubati, actor.

Academics

With its "truly international focus," the Fisher Graduate School of International Business at the Monterey Institute of International Studies prepares students for "an exciting future [in] a world of business that is going global." At MIIS, "every course places emphasis on international aspects, from case studies to projects, and everyone speaks at least two languages." MBAs appreciate that "everyone here, from faculty to students, has international experience." Nearly half the student body is international.

The school's Monterey, CA, location is a huge advantage, allowing it to "play upon the wealth of business in the San Francisco Bay area. Many top executives and CEOs frequently visit as guest speakers and offer mentorship to students." It also allows the school to "pull professors from Stanford and Berkeley for once-weekly classes and weekend-long seminars." And lastly (it almost goes without saying) Monterey provides an idyllic setting in which students can relax and devote themselves to study.

"The workload is very heavy here," MBAs report, with "lots of simulation, oftentimes in other languages so you don't always understand what is going on—much like in the real world. In these instances we have to rely on each other for translations and try alternative ways of contributing to teamwork." In addition to the curriculum, one student notes the benefits from "a great workshop series [that runs] 15 hours over one weekend, exploring a specific topic in-depth with acknowledged leaders. I love the workshops. Plus, the school lets you audit them if your workload doesn't permit you to take the class for a grade." The workshops are frequently led by "visiting professors who are great resources for future career contacts and have a wealth of knowledge in their chosen field of expertise." MIIS's full-time faculty receives similarly high praise. Students say, "We are all on a first-name basis. Not only are the professors very experienced in instruction, but they are also still heavily involved in outside, real-world consulting and/or professions. They are very eager to help, but unwilling to spoon-feed."

Career and Placement

The Career Management Center (CMC) for the Fisher MBA program offers "a customized approach to each individual's goals, skill set, and educational and personal background," according to the school. The office "acts as an 'executive search firm'" to help students "target potential employers and enhance their added value" through online career assessments, one-on-one consultations, and workshops in interviewing skills, salary negotiation, internships, and networking.

Many of the students in our survey tell us, however, that they would like to see "more active company involvement in recruiting at the school." They concede that the CMC faces a tough challenge: The school is too small to attract many on-campus recruiters and too new to have much in the way of an alumni network. Most recruiters, we're told, are drawn from within a 30-mile radius, and big international players are unfortunately absent. (The exceptions are NGOs and U.S. government agencies, which do recruit here.) About one-third of Monterey's MBAs move on to jobs in the nonprofit sector. Consulting gobbles up another 20 percent. About half remain on the Pacific coast, while one in five finds work outside the United States.

Student Life and Environment

"The Business School at Monterey is very small," students point out, noting that "the entire institute has only about a thousand students at the most." Full-time MBAs number less than 100, so "students tend to be fairly tight and there is a lot of interaction

CAROLINE MANSI, ENROLLMENT MANAGER
460 PIERCE STREET, MONTEREY, CA 93940 UNITED STATES
PHONE: 831-647-4123 • FAX: 831-647-6405
E-MAIL: ADMIT@MIIS.EDU • WEBSITE: FISHER.MIIS.EDU

between cohorts." MBAs also mix with graduate students in other programs. An MBA reports, "We have institute-wide happy hours every other Friday. There are always opportunities to socialize with fellow students, but no pressure to do things you don't feel comfortable with." Most do feel comfortable, though. As one MBA put it, "It's such a great way to get to know classmates and students in other schools, even the bookworms find a way to make it. It is a good time!"

As you might expect at a school this size, social and extracurricular life isn't exactly buzzing. However, MBAs here point out, "for graduate students wanting to study and focus, that can be a plus." Also in the plus column, "Monterey is a beautiful place to go to school." [Monterey] provides excellent additional resources, as there are two military academic institutions with libraries and research utilities that are accessible to students. Home not only to MIIS but also to the Defense Language Institute, the Navy Postgraduate School, three postsecondary schools, and Language Line Services (a provider of telephone-based interpretation), Monterey has earned its nickname of "the language capital of the world." The benefit is that this combination of schools and businesses "brings an incredible mix of people to the peninsula."

Many of those people can be found on the MIIS campus, where "about half the students are international while the Americans have all spent significant amounts of time abroad and are competent in another language." This makes it "very easy to find a conversation partner to foster an interest in many languages, including Korean, Mandarin Chinese, Arabic, French, Spanish, Italian, Japanese, and many more." Students describe the setting as "a very accurate representation of the future of the global business village. You can be exposed to and appreciate the cultures and behaviors of businesspeople from all over the world—you're interacting with them, not just reading about it in a book." Students "tend to be more collaborative than competitive, more socially responsible than purely financially motivated." The drawback: They're "inexperienced overall in business, [and] lack practical experience."

Admissions

MIIS will consider any applicant with at least a 3.0 undergraduate GPA, provided the applicant speaks English and at least one other language at an advanced (i.e., third-year undergraduate) level. Applicants must also submit GMAT scores, letters of recommendation, and a personal statement. A resume and an interview, while not required, are strongly recommended.

FINANCIAL FACTS

Annual tuition	$26,500
Fees	$200
Cost of books	$900
Room & board (off-campus)	$8,400
% of students receiving aid	84
% of first-year students receiving aid	87
% of students receiving loans	58
% of students receiving grants	82
Average award package	$24,193
Average grant	$7,716
Average student loan debt	$31,726

ADMISSIONS

Admissions Selectivity Rating	**72**
# of applications received	94
% applicants accepted	86
% acceptees attending	53
Average GMAT	572
Range of GMAT	460–630
Average GPA	3.21
TOEFL required of international students	Yes
Minimum TOEFL (paper/computer)	550/213
Application fee	$50
Regular application deadline	3/15
Regular notification	5/1
Transfer students accepted	Yes
Transfer application policy	
Credits must be from an AACSB-accredited college or university, must be with a B or better. Possible to transfer up to 25% of total program. Dean makes final determination.	
Non-fall admissions	Yes
Need-blind admissions	Yes

Applicants Also Look At

Pepperdine University, Thunderbird, University of California—San Diego, University of South Carolina

EMPLOYMENT PROFILE	
Career Rating	**70**
Primary Source of Full-time Job Acceptances	
School-facilitated activities	12 (22%)
Graduate-facilitated activities	7 (13%)
Unknown	35 (65%)
Average base starting salary	$65,339
Percent employed	73

NATIONAL UNIVERSITY OF SINGAPORE
BUSINESS SCHOOL

GENERAL INFORMATION
Type of school   Public

SURVEY SAYS . . .
Students love Singapore
Smart classrooms

STUDENTS
Enrollment of	
business school	251
% male/female	80/20
% out-of-state	57
% part-time	38
% international	57
Average age at entry	29
Average years work	
experience at entry	6

ACADEMICS
Academic Experience Rating	**84**
Student/faculty ratio	3:1
Profs interesting rating	73
Profs accessible rating	89
% female faculty	21
% minority faculty	25

Joint Degrees
NUS-Peking University IMBA 24 months, UCLA-NUS executive MBA 15 months.

Prominent Alumni
Janet Ang, vice president, Lenovo; Wong Ah Long, CEO, Pacific Star Investments and Development Pte. Ltd.; Hsieh Fu Hua, CEO, Singapore Exchange Ltd.; Peter Seah, Chairman, Singapore Technologies Engineering Ltd; Pratap Nambiar, regional partner, KPMG Asia Pacific.

Academics

"Asia is fast becoming the center of global business activity," students at the National University of Singapore Business School remind us, and "NUS is one of the best schools, both to learn about how business is conducted in Asia and to network with corporations established in the region." The school is "considered one of the best universities in the world and the topmost business school in Asia." The school's location "offers a strategic advantage," because Singapore "is the financial hub of Asia and the hub of all Asian business. "NUS Business School gives the best possible value" and prepares students for a solid business career overall, "where the regional job market, especially for a career in finance, is quite good."

NUS' graduate business programs offer "a global perspective with an Asian outlook" augmented by "the ability to be part of a multicultural society in Singapore. You can enhance your understandings of, and contacts within, the Chinese, Indian, and Southeast Asian business cultures here." Students also extol "the excellent facilities, especially the libraries and auditoriums," the "very strong faculty," and the excellent "value."

NUS has long offered a part-time program. It recently added a full-time program that "has increased class sizes; the school administration has been able to handle it very well and there have been no logistical or administrative issues." Students have the option to pursue a general MBA or one with a specialization in either real estate management or health care management. Either way, they must complete a 10-course core module that "provides a holistic view of the entire business world" while giving us "exposure to all different fields of management." All of the modules "are very important, the type of courses you'd take even if they were electives."

Students also tell us that the program and the entire environment are very flexible. "We are free to do what we want (obviously within the parameter of rules), which helps us in being as creative as we want. Professors are eager to help us in various international events and competitions. This is a great impetus for students that brings out the best in them." The administration received an upgrade a few years ago "when we got our new Dean from the London Business School." Students tell us that "administrators are open to discussion on improving the course and integrates new business concepts in the curriculum," which they appreciate.

Career and Placement

The Career Services Office (CSO) "is a strong point of the NUS Business School," students report. One writes, "I was surprised to see so many companies coming over for on-campus recruitment." Another adds, "The CSO is changing so fast and for the better. Many job postings" are available to choose from. Some here feel that the office could do a better job bringing recruiters to campus; others counter that those who complain mostly "come from places where the placement cells actually ensure that companies come and recruit on the same day. That is not the way it works in Singapore and most of rest of the world."

Companies most likely to hire NUS MBAs include: ExxonMobil Asia Pacific, Hewlett-Packard Singapore, International Enterprise Singapore, KPMG International, Ministry of Trade and Industry, National Computer Board, NEC Singapore PTE LTD, Proctor & Gamble, Philips Electronics, Shell Eastern Petroleum, Singapore Police Force, Sony Systems Design International, and Swiss Bank Corporation.

PROFESSOR KULWANT SINGH, VICE DEAN (GRADUATE STUDIES)
BIZ 2 BUILDING, 1 BUSINESS LINK, LEVEL 5, SINGAPORE, 117592 SINGAPORE
PHONE: 011-65-65168871 • FAX: 011-65-68724423
E-MAIL: MBA@NUS.EDU.SG • WEBSITE: BSCHOOL.NUS.EDU

Student Life and Environment

The NUS program carries a moderate workload, allowing for a "fantastic balance between studies and fun." The workload also means that "students have time to think about career moves, take part in business plan competitions and do some job searching." Extracurricular events include "lots of competitions, amazing speakers from the industry, lots of different activities with student clubs," and "wonderful parties like International Day and the Deepawali celebration." An annual Graduate Business Conference "brings us all together." In the past, the conference has featured such noteworthy keynote speakers as Jimmy Carter and former GM Chairperson John Smale.

On campus, "The MBA lounge is the place to be if you [want to] be a part of the 'in' group. Discussions . . . range from politics, business ethics, case studies, and the venue for the next 'jam' session (basically music, booze, and fun)." Some students complain that "the layout of the school is not ideal, because it is spread out over too many buildings."

NUS draws a "mature and serious" student body of professionals "who are obviously occupied with how their careers are going and who are earnest in wanting to learn." These "well-traveled" MBA candidates are highly international; India and China are heavily represented, while students from the United States, Switzerland, Norway, Korea, and other far-flung locations fill out the student body. In terms of background, students "come from engineering, commerce, medicine, architecture, and many more fields. As the median work experience is about 4 years, there is a good quality of contribution that people make in the class."

Admissions

NUS seeks applicants who "have leadership capabilities and the strong desire and drive for academic and management excellence" and who are "motivated, mature, focused and have a desire to make a positive impact on business and society," according to the school's website. Applicants to the NUS School of Business must provide the Admissions Office with transcripts for all undergraduate and graduate work, GMAT scores, TOEFL or IELTS scores (for non-native English speakers), two letters of recommendation, and a resume demonstrating at least 2 years of post-baccalaureate professional experience. An interview and/or further written assessments may be required of some borderline candidates.

FINANCIAL FACTS

Annual tuition	$11,100
Cost of books	$600
Room & board	
(on/off-campus)	$8,625/$5,625
% of students receiving grants	16
Average grant	$17,000

ADMISSIONS

Admissions Selectivity Rating	84
# of applications received	712
% applicants accepted	61
% acceptees attending	57
Average GMAT	653
Range of GMAT	620–680
TOEFL required of international students	Yes
Minimum TOEFL (paper/computer)	620/260
Regular application deadline	5/31
Regular notification	6/1
Deferment available	Yes
Maximum length of deferment	1 year
Transfer students accepted	Yes
Transfer application policy Admission and credit transfer applications are evaluated on a case-by-case basis, depend on the student's record and performance within the MBA program, and the quality of the program and school.	
Non-fall admissions	Yes
Need-blind admissions	Yes

EMPLOYMENT PROFILE

Career Rating	71	Grads Employed by Function	%	Avg. Salary
Primary Source of Full-time Job Acceptances		Finance/Accounting	21	$48,696
School-facilitated activities	20 (48%)	Human Resources	2	$26,667
Graduate-facilitated activities	22 (52%)	Marketing/Sales	38	$40,175
Percent employed	86	MIS	2	$23,333
		Operations/Production	10	$39,667
		Consulting	5	$43,333
		General Management	17	$34,142
		Other	5	$38,333
		Top 5 Employers Hiring Grads		
		National University of Singapore; Synovate; Citibank; BP; Frost and Sullivan.		

NEW JERSEY INSTITUTE OF TECHNOLOGY
SCHOOL OF MANAGEMENT

Academics

The New Jersey Institute of Technology MBA program "offers a technology-focused curriculum" that "is best suited for future managers/leaders in the technical/IT field." Students enrolled in this "affordable, convenient" program tell us that an "interesting curriculum focused on practical knowledge" "provides a very good blend of business and technology management" supplemented by "first-rate facilities." The school offers a 48-credit MBA that can be completed in two years by full-timers or four years by part-timers. An 18-month accelerated Executive MBA is open to managers and professionals; the program meets on alternate Saturdays. The availability of "both in-class and online course options makes the school very flexible."

NJIT's curriculum focuses on the development and interrelation of four themes: the transition toward a knowledge-based economy, the emergence of the digital firm, the increasing globalization of business, and the primacy of innovation in gaining a competitive advantage in the modern business world. All students here complete a 27-credit core curriculum, followed by a six-credit module in knowledge and information management, a six-credit module in technology and innovation, and nine credits to be applied toward a concentration. Concentrations are available in e-commerce, finance, infrastructure management, marketing, MIS, operations management, and transportation and logistics. The school also offers "appealing independent study opportunities."

Students report that the faculty is mixed in quality. As one of them notes, "Most professors I've encountered are decent to good. Some professors are outstanding. The overall academic experience has been very solid so far." Another explains, "There are professors who have demanding workloads that keep you up all night trying to meet deadlines and grade incredibly hard and there are those that give moderate workloads and demand far less." Many agree that "the only area that the graduate degree program can improve in is the diversification of classes. Many classes in the later modules are not available for various reasons. Most of these reasons are very valid, but when you want to take one class and it won't be offered until two semesters from now, it can leave you scrambling for another class that can take its place." EMBA students tell us that their program "is well administered and continues to get better. The program is extremely aggressive in its schedule and scope and the professors and administrators are cognizant of the fragile balance between work, family, and school."

Career and Placement

NJIT maintains a Career Resources Center to serve all undergraduates and graduates at the university. The center includes a library, self-assessment exams, and online job postings. Counseling services are also available. Some of the companies recruiting MBAs on the NJIT campus in 2005 included ASCO Power Technologies, BAE Systems CNIR, IBM, Keyence Corporation of America, Lucent Technologies, Peri Software Solutions Inc., Schindler Elevator Corporation, Sensor Products, Sozoh Technologies, Inc, Stryker Orthopaedics, Telcordia Technologies, and Vonage.

Student Life and Environment

Students who take their classes on the NJIT campus tell us that "academic life here consists of a strong learning culture. The supporting facilities are excellent. There is less emphasis on extracurricular activities." One MBA adds, "Commuters will find themselves driving to school and home with the lack of fun things to do after hours. Living on campus is another story. You can find things to do almost all the time. However, most grad students don't live on campus."

NJIT is located in Newark, NJ, meaning that it is not much more than a stone's throw from downtown New York City. Thus, students have access not only to endless entertainment opportunities but also to an equally robust supply of business resources.

NJIT's student body consists of "an ethnically diverse group of working professionals ranging in age from 30 to 45. Most are married with children and have extremely active lives. The range of professional business experience varies greatly. The majority of the students have low to middle-management positions. However . . . the class is committed to learning and to the overall objective of career development through the program. In general, students are friendly and helpful. The classroom dynamic is robust and healthy and as a result lends itself to thoughtful discussion."

Admissions

All applications to the NJIT MBA program must, at minimum, include complete transcripts for all work done at the undergraduate level and an official score report for the GMAT (although applicants who already hold a master's or doctoral degree from an accredited university are exempt from the GMAT requirement). Students entering the program must also demonstrate competency in economics, finance, information systems, and quantitative methods; these requirements may be met with undergraduate work or through completion of pre-degree foundation courses. International students whose first language is not English are required to submit scores for the TOEFL exam. All students may provide supplemental application materials, including up to three letters of recommendation, a personal statement, and a description of work experience or a resume, if they wish

FINANCIAL FACTS

Annual tuition (in-state/ out-of-state)	$10,506/$17,264
Fees	$1,440
Cost of books	$1,400
Room & board	$8,980
% of students receiving aid	65
% of first-year students receiving aid	70
% of students receiving loans	55
% of students receiving grants	35
Average grant	$10,000
Average student loan debt	$10,000

ADMISSIONS

Admissions Selectivity Rating	**86**
# of applications received	256
% applicants accepted	37
% acceptees attending	80
Average GMAT	522
Range of GMAT	480–550
Average GPA	3.5
TOEFL required of international students	Yes
Minimum TOEFL (paper/computer)	525/213
Application fee	$60
Regular application deadline	Rolling
Regular notification	Rolling
Non fall admissions	Yes

NEW MEXICO STATE UNIVERSITY
COLLEGE OF BUSINESS

Academics

The College of Business at New Mexico State University is "extremely technologically savvy," a quality that serves it well in a state that is home to several air force bases, major NASA operations, two national laboratories, Spaceport America, and several big tech players (Intel, for one, has a large manufacturing plant in Albuquerque). The tech sector is, in fact, the fastest-growing employer in the Las Cruces area.

NMSU incorporates technology in all disciplines, and has developed several specialized degrees. The school also "concentrates on entrepreneurs because of its abundant resources. It's planning new ways to convert these resources into products." NMSU is a participant in the Space Alliance Technology Outreach Program (SATOP), "which creates interactions between students and the corporate people and gives a very good exposure to the aerospace industry."

Many students simply appreciate the convenience of the program, praising its "wonderfully located campus with a very unique and culturally diverse academic program." The school serves both full-time and part-time MBAs, and fully understands and meets the needs of traditional and nontraditional students when it comes to education. NMSU has even "created an MBA cohort program for the Los Alamos National Laboratory. Every other weekend a NMSU professor comes to Los Alamos. We are enrolled in two classes per semester and each class meets once a month for two 5-hour sessions. This schedule is wonderfully convenient, and communication is ongoing throughout the months." A school that comes to you—you can't beat that for convenience.

Instructors at NMSU "are well respected in their fields and apply real-world applications to their lectures and assignments," while "The administration is always very responsive whenever a conflict arises." A "socially and ethnically diverse student population" informs class discussion. One student sums up, "I have had a very positive overall academic experience. Every single administrator and faculty member has treated me with the utmost respect and professional courtesy."

Career and Placement

NMSU's Placement and Career Services Office provides university students with on-campus employment, internship listings, career listings, workshops, advising, job fairs, and online research tools. The school holds a number of job fairs and other recruiting events throughout the year, but all are primarily targeted toward undergraduates. As a result, relatively few of the many companies that visit campus seek MBAs.

Recent employers of NMSU MBAs include: Accenture, ElPaso Electric, Ernst & Young, Agilent Technologies, ConocoPhilips Company, General Motors, Hewlett-Packard, IBM, Intel, KPMG International, NASA, Los Alamos National Laboratories, Qwest, Sandia National Laboratory, TXU Energy, and Wells Fargo.

DR. BOBBIE GREEN, DIRECTOR, MBA PROGRAM
114 GUTHRIE HALL, MSC 3GSP, LAS CRUCES, NM 88003-8001 UNITED STATES
PHONE: 505-646-8003 • FAX: 505-646-7977
E-MAIL: MBA@NMSU.EDU • WEBSITE: BUSINESS.NMSU.EDU/MBA

Student Life and Environment

NMSU "is a great place to continue your education and the Las Cruces area is second to none," students report, adding that "Las Cruces is a very slow-paced, small-town type environment. It is, however, slowly changing due to this area being designated as one of the top-10 places to retire in the nation." The school is located "in its own private corner of the city, and it is very safe, clean, and spirit oriented."

Many who attend the MBA program work part-time as well; one such student writes, "This is a focused and relevant MBA that meets my needs as a nontraditional student who holds down a full-time civil engineering job." When they can manage to take a break from their responsibilities, they "enjoy attending college sporting events and special events at the Pan American Center on campus. The campus is also a nice place to take a long walk for exercise or leisure, strolling from pond to pond." The campus includes excellent facilities for workouts and for study. Some here point out that "NMSU could definitely improve in how it caters to students with families. Child care is only available to students with very low incomes, or at the standard child care rates in this city. There also don't seem to be any family-oriented extracurricular activities."

The NMSU MBA population includes "a large portion of international students, who come because of the affordability and friendly environment. Classes with widely diversified cultures and nations contribute to the discussions related to international trade and global business management." Students "have diverse work experience, which makes interaction between students interesting and useful" and results in "a very professional approach to problem-solving case studies or application of curriculum covered in course material."

Admissions

Applicants to the NMSU MBA program must apply for admission to the university's graduate school before they can be admitted to the GMAT program. Admission to the graduate school requires that the applicant hold a 4-year undergraduate degree from an accredited institution with a GPA of at least 3.0 (some exceptions to the GPA requirement are possible; contact school for details). International applicants must earn at least a 530 on the paper-based TOEFL or a 197 on the computer-based TOEFL. Applicants to the MBA program must meet one of the following criteria: a minimum GMAT score of 400 and a minimum score of 1400 under the formula (GPA multiplied by GMAT); possession of a graduate degree from an accredited institution; or completion of at least 4 years of full-time professional work and an undergraduate GPA of at least 3.25.

FINANCIAL FACTS

Annual tuition (in-state/ out-of-state)	$3,624/$11,550
Cost of books	$1,000
Room & board (on/off-campus)	$5,200/$7,000
% of students receiving aid	22
% of first-year students receiving aid	10
% of students receiving loans	30
% of students receiving grants	8
Average award package	$350,000
Average grant	$30,000

ADMISSIONS

Admissions Selectivity Rating	**75**
# of applications received	102
% applicants accepted	69
% acceptees attending	100
Average GMAT	500
Range of GMAT	480–760
Average GPA	3.25
TOEFL required of international students	Yes
Minimum TOEFL (paper/computer)	530/197
Application fee	$30
International application fee	$50
Regular application deadline	7/1
Regular notification	8/4
Deferment available	Yes
Maximum length of deferment	1 year
Transfer students accepted	Yes
Transfer application policy A maximum of 12 semester credits from AACSB schools.	
Non-fall admissions	Yes
Need-blind admissions	Yes

EMPLOYMENT PROFILE			
Career Rating	63	**Grads Employed by Function% Avg. Salary**	
		Finance/Accounting	2 NR
		Marketing/Sales	5 NR
		Operations/Production	2 NR
		Consulting	2 NR
		General Management	7 NR
		Quantitative	2 NR

NEW YORK UNIVERSITY
LEONARD N. STERN SCHOOL OF BUSINESS

Academics

In name, culture, and spirit, the Stern School of Business at New York University is defined by the city that surrounds it. "Smack in the middle of all the great New York industries," students at NYU tell us that "the city and its offerings are as much a part of the program as is its course curriculum." Traditionally recognized as a powerhouse in the field of finance, students say you can't beat NYU's financial and accounting programs: "I started with no knowledge of how capital markets work and I now consider myself well above average, even in NYC!" In fact, academics are "of the highest caliber" in almost every field and are spearheaded by a talented teaching staff that includes "a Nobel laureate, the preeminent bankruptcy expert, and a financial statements professor who literally wrote the CFA book on the subject." Promoting an equal emphasis on theory and practice, the teaching staff is a "good balance between tenured academic (i.e., research oriented) professors and clinical (i.e., practical, real-world experience) professors." "The faculty and administration have tailored the course load so that MBA students are not overwhelmed by the combination of academics and the job search."

The evening program at NYU is "the highest ranked part-time MBA program in the nation," benefiting students with its stellar reputation as well as its diverse and accomplished student body. As one student explains, "Everyone is working so there are always new viewpoints on the business world being interjected into our conversations. Also, rather than meeting only future bankers and consultants, there's been a wide range of careers represented." The school also offers a weekend MBA program, called the Langone Program, though some feel "The quality of offerings, professors, and administrative help is higher for the weekday night classes than for the Saturday classes."

Despite the intensity of the urban environment, the atmosphere at Stern is surprisingly friendly and noncompetitive. On the whole, NYU students are "hardworking, driven, diverse, and above all, incredibly friendly and helpful." Faculty are "very accessible" and willing to help students grow personally and professionally. A current student shares, "The professors are generally very approachable. Professor Damodaran teaches a class on valuation with over 250 students but he always finds time to answer my most mundane questions." Even the higher-ups are described as responsive and easily accessible; for example, "The Dean knows all of us by name and has had lunch with each of us throughout our time here."

Career and Placement

Bright, well trained, and ready for action, NYU grads are in high demand. A current student marvels, "First-years only have a few weeks to adjust to academic demands before companies start flooding campus. In the meantime, the Office of Career Development prepares them for the job search by refining their networking and interviewing skills and by polishing their resumes." Thanks to "Stern's strong ties with finance recruiters in the area," many students have employment offers by the end of their first year; however, "For those who are still looking for a full-time position, the second-year job search begins earlier than the first-year internship search, but it is over for many before the Christmas break." Be warned, however, that "Part-time students do not have much access to recruiting events. The administration has been working to better meet part-time students' needs."

Hundreds of companies recruit at Stern. Some of the top companies are: American Express, Banc of America Securities, Booz Allen Hamilton, Citigroup, Colgate, Deloitte Touche Tohmatsu, Deutsche Bank, Ernst & Young, General Electric Company, Goldman

ANIKA DAVIS PRATT, ASSISTANT DEAN, MBA ADMISSIONS
44 WEST FOURTH STREET, SUITE 6-70, NEW YORK, NY 10012 UNITED STATES
PHONE: 212-998-0600 • FAX: 212-995-4231
E-MAIL: STERNMBA@STERN.NYU.EDU • WEBSITE: WWW.STERN.NYU.EDU

Sachs, IBM, JPMorgan Chase, Johnson & Johnson, Lehman Brothers, L'Oréal, McKinsey & Company, MTV Networks, Pfizer, Standard & Poor's, and Unilever.

Student Life and Environment

Located downtown and just a few paces from Wall Street, the city's high-energy atmosphere seeps into the student body at Stern. As one student explains, "Going to Stern is all about a cultural fit. Students have very well-balanced lives; we work hard and play harder." On campus, students are involved in the school community, taking advantage of the "limitless opportunities to be involved and take leadership roles in clubs." More than your typical college town, "Being in the heart of the city makes student life at Stern completely unique." Not surprisingly, the school boasts a "great social atmosphere," and students get together for myriad extracurricular events, from the Thursday evening "beer blast" to more refined events such as "dinners at Japanese restaurants organized by the Japan Business Association, the Global Business Conference organized by the Emerging Markets Association, and happy hours organized by a number of clubs."

Even part-time students (many of whom have families or preexisting social lives) say Stern makes an effort to keep them in the loop. Attests a current part-timer, "Since I am only on campus for 2 nights a week, a lot of the social interaction with my peers occurs at events on weekends. However, there have been many events and conferences which have allowed me to interact with other part-time students as well as the full-time student community."

Admissions

NYU's Admission's Committee strives to create a business school community that is as vibrant and diverse as New York City itself. In addition to having a strong academic background, Stern students are leaders in a wide range of fields, bringing diverse expertise and experiences to the program. The entering class of 2008 numbers just over 400 and boasts an average undergraduate GPA of 3.4. The class's average GMAT score was 700, with a range of 640–750.

FINANCIAL FACTS

Annual tuition	$37,900
Fees	$1,890
Cost of books	$1,404
Room & board	$18,560
% of students receiving aid	66
% of first-year students receiving aid	73
% of students receiving loans	63
% of students receiving grants	48
Average award package	$45,600
Average grant	$13,950
Average student loan debt	$66,682

ADMISSIONS

Admissions Selectivity Rating	**98**
# of applications received	3,613
% applicants accepted	20
% acceptees attending	47
Average GMAT	700
Range of GMAT	650–750
Average GPA	3.4
TOEFL required of international students	Yes
Application fee	$175
Application Deadline/Notification	
Round 1:	12/1 / 2/15
Round 2:	1/15 / 4/1
Round 3:	3/15 / 6/1
Non-fall admissions	Yes
Need-blind admissions	Yes

EMPLOYMENT PROFILE

Career Rating	97	Grads Employed by Function	%	Avg. Salary
Primary Source of Full-time Job Acceptances		Finance/Accounting	62	$143,208
School-facilitated activities	216 (69%)	Marketing/Sales	19	$118,120
Graduate-facilitated activities	69 (22%)	MIS	2	$124,667
Unknown	3 (9%)	Operations/Production	2	$108,333
Percent employed	92	Consulting	13	$139,724
		General Management	1	$104,927
		Venture Capital	1	$144,750

Top 5 Employers Hiring Grads

Lehman Brothers; Citigroup; Bank of America Securities; American Express Company; Goldman Sachs.

NORTH CAROLINA STATE UNIVERSITY
COLLEGE OF MANAGEMENT

Academics

"The greatest strength of the MBA program at North Carolina State is its focus on technology," many students at this small, new graduate business program in Raleigh tell us. NCSU's program is tailor-made to fit the needs of businesses in nearby Research Triangle Park, where communications, technology, and pharmaceutical firms are always looking to hire "the engineers and scientists to whom this program caters."

NCSU's focus on technology and engineering allows it to offer some unique areas of concentration. The school is "very strong in the integration of marketing and technical knowledge" thanks to its "unique Product Innovation Management program," for example. A biotechnology and pharmaceutical program is another standout; both the faculty and student body benefit from the school's proximity to GlaxoSmithKline, Novartis, and other big regional pharmaceutical players. Students here also boast about the "outstanding supply-chain management program, which carries a great reputation in the region."

Students describe NCSU professors as "hit and miss," but with more hits than misses. They're generally "very energetic about the subjects they teach," "have a wealth of experience from the real world that they use to help teach," and "are easy to contact outside of class and quick to return phone calls." Students appreciate a pedagogical approach across the curriculum that is "focused more on practical team projects and less on business case study." "Strong emphases on communications and presentations skills" and "cross-functional insight into business" are also highly valued. On the downside, "being at a state-funded school [means] budget crunches have hit hard and cut back a lot of nice extras" here.

About two-thirds of all students attend part-time. Full-timers find internships between their first and second year. As one second-year full-time student observes, "Having done an internship this past summer and continued it part-time into the school year, I can definitely say that school is much tougher than real life. I don't know what other scale I can use, other than to say that school appears to be preparing me for difficult situations I may face in the future."

Career and Placement

The program at NCSU "has some very strong industry connections, so students have very well-known companies to choose from for employment," MBAs tell us. In 2005, internship placements included positions with CAT, Chevron Texaco, Cree, Delphi, Duke Energy, Heard & Associates, IBM, Halliburton, the Hoop Group, Last Mile, MCNBC, MTS Sensors, Murphy Family SAS, Ventures, Northrop Grumman, Progress Energy, Red Hat, Starquest Dance, Talecris, and VF Corporation. Graduating MBAs found work with BB&T, Bechtel, Boston Scientific, Capital One, Chevron Texaco, Cisco, Credit Suisse, Duke Energy, First Boston, IBM, John Deere, Last Mile, Nortel, RBC Centura, Red Hat, SAS, Sigmon, Team Pharma, Tech Engage, Teleflex, and Withers.

PAM BOSTIC, MBA PROGRAM DIRECTOR
MBA PROGRAM OFFICE, CAMPUS BOX 8114, RALEIGH, NC 27695-8114 UNITED STATES
PHONE: 919-515-5584 • FAX: 919-515-5073
E-MAIL: MBA@NCSU.EDU • WEBSITE: WWW.MBA.NCSU.EDU

Student Life and Environment

The majority of NCSU's MBAs are part-time students, most of whom work in addition to attending school. One such student explains, "We don't have a lot of free time. We enjoy the experience of being in school, but work, classes, and the constant group meetings for classes limit the amount of free time." Full-time students "generally do not work at the same time" and so "usually have more free time to concentrate on things outside of school." As one of these students explains, "Our academic work and social life is well balanced. Almost every fortnight the entire class has a party. All the students in the class are constantly working on group projects and we have formed good study groups, which help us a lot by dividing the work among ourselves and thus making us able to accomplish everything."

Full-timers and part-timers alike agree that "Raleigh, NC, is a great city. The weather here is outstanding. And there are plenty of available activities, such as attending NC State football and basketball games." Located in central North Carolina, Raleigh allows for easy escapes to the beach (about two hours away by car) or the mountains (about three hours away, in the other direction). Raleigh is part of a greater metropolitan area known as the Triangle that is also home to University of North Carolina, Duke University, and numerous other smaller colleges and universities.

The MBA program at NCSU draws a "friendly, professional, mature, experienced, and extremely helpful" student body. A "strong sense of sharing our experience and supporting each other as we face many challenges" helps students survive the sometimes intense demands of the program. China, Belarus, India, Turkey, Romania, Bulgaria, and Jamaica are among the nations represented in the student body here.

Admissions

Admission to NCSU's MBA program is "highly competitive." Successful candidates typically have strong undergraduate academic records and solid GMAT scores, work experience "demonstrating management potential, leadership skills, creativity," the ability to work in teams, and a genuine interest in technology as it relates to management issues. Interviews are required prior to admission; the school contacts applicants who are deemed potential candidates for the program.

Cost of books	$1,000
Room & board	
(on/off-campus)	$6,000/$10,000
% of first-year students receiving aid	81
Average award package	$14,519
Average grant	$9,139
Average student loan debt	$31,122

ADMISSIONS

Admissions Selectivity Rating	88
# of applications received	139
% applicants accepted	43
% acceptees attending	57
Average GMAT	597
Range of GMAT	560–640
Average GPA	3.23
TOEFL required of international students	Yes
Minimum TOEFL (paper/computer)	600/250
Application fee	$55
International application fee	$65
Regular application deadline	3/3
Regular notification	4/3
Application Deadline	
Round 1:	10/12
Round 2:	1/7
Round 3:	3/1
Early decision program	Yes
ED Deadline	10/12
ED Notification	11/12
Deferment available	Yes
Maximum length of deferment	1 year
Transfer students accepted	Yes
Transfer application policy	

The NC State MBA program can accept up to 12 hours of transfer credit from another AACSB-accredited MBA program. The grade received for a transfer class must be a B or better, and the class must have been taken no more than 6 years prior to the applicant's projected graduation date from the MBA program at NC State's College of Management.

Need-blind admissions	Yes

Applicants Also Look At

University of Maryland, The University of North Carolina at Chapel Hill, University of North Carolina at Charlotte, University of South Carolina, Wake Forest University–Babcock.

EMPLOYMENT PROFILE

Career Rating	77	Grads Employed by Function	%	Avg. Salary
Primary Source of Full-time Job Acceptances		Finance/Accounting	19	$71,250
School-facilitated activities	18 (67%)	Marketing/Sales	5	$60,000
Graduate-facilitated activities	9 (33%)	Operations/Production	33	$78,715
Percent employed	19	Consulting	19	$68,750
		General Management	10	$41,000
		Other	14	$68,333

Top 5 Employers Hiring Grads

Chevron Texaco; IBM; Nortel; Bank of America; Cree.

NORTHEASTERN UNIVERSITY
COLLEGE OF BUSINESS ADMINISTRATION

Academics

Northeastern University has long been known as a leader in the field of cooperative education, and full-time MBAs here benefit from the school's expertise through a six-month corporate residency program that "puts students with brand-name corporations. The program provides a venue for students to apply and prove themselves in the industry they desire." Students love both the idea and the execution of corporate residency—it is the number one reason cited by full-time students for choosing Northeastern. They report that "The six-month corporate residency opportunity allows students to graduate with measurable real-world experience, unlike schools that offer six-week internships. NEU has strong relationships with a lot of Boston's biggest companies. Especially if you are looking to gain experience in a new field, this program is great." As an added bonus, it "pays pretty well, too!"

Approximately one-third of MBAs at NEU enroll in the full-time MBA program, which can be completed in 24 months. The curriculum consists of foundation courses, in a career management course, a globalization requirement, elective work (concentrations are available in finance, marketing, and supply-chain management), and a corporate residency (optional, but most students opt in). Students report that "the required full-time courses tend to be more challenging than the electives (which are offered in the evenings to accommodate both the full- and part-time students)" and praise their professors, telling us that they are "very well-regarded in their field." One student notes, "Several professors have produced highly influential research studies, and many are accomplished professionals in the private/public sectors." Another mentions, "All of my professors have been Ivy-League educated, and have taught at many of the leading business schools around the country. The administrators are very accessible as well, and all of my concerns have been addressed promptly."

Northeastern also offers an evening MBA consisting of 12 core courses and nine electives. Evening MBA students typically take between two and seven years to finish the degree, taking one or two classes per semester in evening sessions. Other degree options at Northeastern include a High Tech MBA (for tech experts seeking business acumen), an Executive MBA, master's programs in accounting, finance, and taxation, and certificate programs in advanced study of business administration, supply- chain management, and taxation.

Career and Placement

Northeastern's full-time program necessitates that the school forge strong connections to Boston-area businesses, and these relationships pay dividends for the efforts of the school's Career Center. "Our Career Center's corporate residency placement efforts and relationships with companies for that purpose are outstanding," explains one student. Employers in 2006 included Carrier, Procter & Gamble, IBM, Ocean Spray Cranberries, Inc., Raytheon Corporation, Sovereign Bank, State Street, Staples, Inc., Thermo Fisher Scientific, and W.R. Grace & Co. NEU students agree the corporate residency program definitely provides students with a leg up when it comes time for their corporate residency companies to hire new full-timers.

All told, more than 50 companies typically recruit MBAs on campus each year; another 80 come looking for summer interns and corporate residency employees. Employers most likely to hire Northeastern MBAs after graduation include Bayer, Citigroup, Fidelity Investments, Procter & Gamble, Lindt & Sprungli, MasterFoods USA, Raytheon Corporation, State Street, TJX Corporation, and W.R. Grace & Co.

EVELYN TATE, DIRECTOR, RECRUITMENT AND ADMISSIONS
350 DODGE HALL, 360 HUNTINGTON AVENUE, BOSTON, MA 02115 UNITED STATES
PHONE: 617-373-5992 • FAX: 617-373-8564
E-MAIL: GSBA@NEU.EDU • WEBSITE: WWW.MBA.NEU.EDU

Student Life and Environment

Full-time students in Northeastern's MBA program describe a "very close-knit group" of students who "go out with each other every week and often have get-togethers outside of school. The business school also sets up weekly events that we all go to." The program helps, as "classes stress group work, and students have a chance to bond and form life-time friendships" through group work. So too does life in Boston, a city that "is good fun. You can live, shop, and go to school in the best parts of Boston. Newbury, Commonwealth, and Marlborough Streets are all only a couple of blocks away." Part-time students are also invited to these events but sometimes find it difficult to participate due to work and family commitments.

The Northeastern student body "is very diverse with students from all areas. Aside from U.S. students, there are international students from Asia, Africa, Europe, Central/South America, and the Caribbean represented. This gives students a global business perspective and a chance to share different ideas." MBAs observe that "the student body is a happy medium of older students who are more career-focused and younger students who want to enjoy the grad-school lifestyle."

Admissions

All applicants to the Northeastern MBA program must provide the Admissions Office with the following: a completed application (preferably online); sealed copies of official transcripts for all postsecondary schools attended; a current resume; three essays; two professional letters of recommendation; and an official GMAT score report. In addition, international students whose first language is not English must submit TOEFL results. All international students must submit transcripts that have been translated with U.S. grade equivalents assigned for work completed, as well as a certified Declaration and Certification of Finances Statement. Successful candidates will have a minimum of two years' work experience (postgraduate), demonstrated leadership ability or potential, and a strong undergraduate academic preparation.

FINANCIAL FACTS

Annual tuition	$31,500
Fees	$395
Cost of books	$1,500
Room & board (off-campus)	$14,250
% of students receiving aid	59
% of first-year students receiving aid	94
% of students receiving loans	38
% of students receiving grants	51
Average award package	$24,686
Average grant	$15,042
Average student loan debt	$66,793

ADMISSIONS

Admissions Selectivity Rating	**86**
# of applications received	342
% applicants accepted	41
% acceptees attending	45
Average GMAT	584
Range of GMAT	538–620
Average GPA	3.31
TOEFL required of international students	Yes
Minimum TOEFL (paper/computer)	600/250
Application fee	$100
Regular application deadline	4/15
Regular notification	5/15
Application Deadline/Notification	
Round 1:	11/30 / 2/15
Round 2:	2/1 / 3/30
Round 3:	3/15 / 4/15
Round 4:	4/15 / 5/15
Transfer students accepted	Yes
Transfer application policy	
We may award a limited number of transfer credits for MBA courses taken at AACSB-accredited institutions.	
Need-blind admissions	Yes

Applicants Also Look At

Babson College, Boston College, Boston University, University of Massachusetts Amherst.

EMPLOYMENT PROFILE

Career Rating	80	Grads Employed by Function	%	Avg. Salary
Primary Source of Full-time Job Acceptances		Finance/Accounting	33	$68,333
School-facilitated activities	16 (40%)	Marketing/Sales	36	$59,788
Graduate-facilitated activities	20 (50%)	MIS	3	$95,000
Unknown	4 (10%)	Operations/Production	3	$62,500
Average base starting salary	$68,357	Consulting	11	$90,900
Percent employed	67	Other	11	$70,000

Top 5 Employers Hiring Grads
Fidelity; Proctor & Gamble/Gillette; Liberty Mutual; Perot Systems; Technology Business Research Inc.

NORTHERN ARIZONA UNIVERSITY
THE W.A. FRANKE COLLEGE OF BUSINESS

GENERAL INFORMATION

Type of school	Public
Environment	Town
Academic calendar	July–May

SURVEY SAYS . . .
Good peer network
Solid preparation in:
Marketing
Accounting
Presentation skills
Computer skills
Doing business in a global economy

STUDENTS

Enrollment of parent institution	19,147
Enrollment of business school	13
% male/female	61/39
% out-of-state	39
% minorities	39
Average age at entry	25
Average years work experience at entry	2

ACADEMICS

Academic Experience Rating	**79**
Student/faculty ratio	12:1
Profs interesting rating	99
Profs accessible rating	99
% female faculty	20
% minority faculty	10

Academics

Whether you're in a hurry or in a big hurry to collect your MBA, Administration at Northern Arizona University can accommodate you. The school's MBA program for students with undergraduate degrees in business takes a mere 10 months to complete. Even those who lack a business background can hustle through the NAU MBA, however, thanks to an accelerated foundation course program (called the Common Body of Knowledge) that allows students to earn an MBA in 18 months or less.

NAU offers two graduate options: the MBA and the MBA-ACC. In the MBA program, students can emphasis in accounting, finance, general management, marketing analysis and distribution management, geographic information systems, or a custom emphasis. Geographic information systems is the specialty of the house, students tell us; MBAs also tell us that "the accounting department is fantastic." Throughout the program, teamwork and an integrative cross-disciplinary approach to the material are stressed.

Students here report that the program is "intense and fun at the same time," leaving them "better prepared and more knowledgeable in regards to the major business functions, such as marketing, management, finance, and accounting." Professors "offer challenging work, but they are always available for further instruction beyond classroom hours." One MBA writes, "Our professors strive to enrich students' professional and business skills to prepare them for success in the work force. Professors are welcoming and know students on a first-name basis, which makes communication easier and more fluid." Administrators are "helpful and resourceful when meeting student needs." On the downside, some feel the school's small size can narrow students' options too much; "The school could . . . provide more variety of elective courses to differentiate student skills," writes one student.

Career and Placement

The Gateway Student Success Center at NAU provides career services to all students at the university through counseling and placement services. Students also work directly with the MBA Director in their efforts to find career opportunities. The school reports that average starting salaries for graduates are up 28 percent since 2004. Still, some here complain that "the school could improve on providing a stronger network of alumni to connect graduates with potential job opportunities."

In the past, NAU MBAs have gone on to work at such major corporations as American Express, American Management Systems, AT&T, the Federal Reserve Bank, General Dynamics, Hewlett-Packard, Honeywell, IBM, Intel, Intuit, Motorola, Nestlé, Rockwell International, Safeway Stores, Sandia National Laboratory, State Farm Insurance, Walgreen Co., and W.L. Gore & Associates. Others have signed on with smaller firms and still others have pursued academic careers. The school currently reports that employers who most frequently hire graduates include: Vanguard Investments, Intel, Pulte Homes, Countrywide Bank, and Shea Homes.

Student Life and Environment

Students in the NAU MBA program are the beneficiaries of a "wonderful" new building that "offers all the students a great place to study." The "modern-yet-retro" facility includes plenty of open space, designed to encourage students to linger after class in order to break off into study groups or simply to hang out and socialize.

Student life here "is balanced between schoolwork and activities outside of school." One MBA observes, "During the week, school comes first along with opportunities to go to

JERI DENNIS, PROGRAM COORDINATOR
PO BOX 15066, FLAGSTAFF, AZ 86011-5066 UNITED STATES
PHONE: 928-523-7342 • FAX: 928-523-7996
E-MAIL: MBA@NAU.EDU • WEBSITE: WWW.CBA.NAU.EDU/MBA

the gym or engage in other recreational activities. Some weekends are full of schoolwork, but most weekends include time to go outside and engage in recreational activities," which typically include "lots of outdoor recreation (skiing, hiking, fishing, running, and visiting the Grand Canyon)" thanks to the school's "superb" location amid the San Francisco peaks. MBAs point out that "the emphasis is really placed on undergraduates at NAU," explaining why many grad students "engage in activities that we set up outside the student-run clubs."

NAU MBAs "come from a variety of backgrounds," which gives students a chance "to meet so many different people" and, as a result, "learn quite a bit about other cultures and how they function." Most here "like to share their opinions, and there is a lot of respect among classmates," who are "supportive and help to create a culture of helpfulness, professionalism, and team orientation."

Admissions

All applicants to the MBA program at NAU must complete an application for graduate admission as well as a supplemental application to the MBA program. They must also submit official transcripts for all postsecondary academic work, an official GMAT score report, a personal essay describing the applicant's background and career ambitions, and three letters of recommendation. In addition to the above, international students must submit an official TOEFL score report and an official Test of Spoken English score report. Successful applicants should score a minimum of 450 on the GMAT, with both verbal and quantitative scores above the twenty-fifth percentile. Under the formula [GMAT score multiplied by (GPA for final 64 undergraduate semester hours multiplied by 200)] applicants should score at least 1050. Incoming students must be proficient in mathematics through introductory calculus, must have mastery of basic business-related computer applications, and must have either completed an undergraduate degree in business or complete the school's Common Base of Knowledge course sequence before commencing work on the MBA.

FINANCIAL FACTS

Annual tuition (in-state/ out-of-state)	$6,516/$16,198
Fees	$3,500
Cost of books	$1,295
Room & board	$7,520
% of students receiving aid	80

ADMISSIONS

Admissions Selectivity Rating	**80**
# of applications received	31
% applicants accepted	65
% acceptees attending	80
Average GMAT	506
Range of GMAT	470–580
Average GPA	3.27
TOEFL required of International students	Yes
Minimum TOEFL (paper/computer)	600/250
Application fee	$50
Regular application deadline	5/1
Regular notification	6/1
Early decision program	Yes
ED Deadline/Notification	11/1 / 12/1
Deferment available	Yes
Maximum length of deferment	1 year
Transfer students accepted	Yes
Transfer application policy 9 hours toward electives only.	
Non-fall admissions	Yes
Need-blind admissions	Yes

EMPLOYMENT PROFILE

Career Rating	61	Grads Employed by Function	%	Avg. Salary
Primary Source of Full-time Job Acceptances		Finance/Accounting	3	NR
School-facilitated activities	5 (42%)	Human Resources	10	NR
Graduate-facilitated activities	10 (83%)	Marketing/Sales	3	NR
Percent employed	35	General Management	3	NR
		Other	1	NR

NORTHERN KENTUCKY UNIVERSITY
COLLEGE OF BUSINESS

GENERAL INFORMATION
Type of school	Public
Environment	Metropolis

SURVEY SAYS...
Solid preparation in:
Presentation skills
Doing business in a global economy

STUDENTS
Enrollment of parent institution	14,000
Enrollment of business school	235
% male/female	58/42
% out-of-state	16
% part-time	85
Average age at entry	27
Average years work experience at entry	5

ACADEMICS
Academic Experience Rating	**70**
Student/faculty ratio	20:1
Profs interesting rating	78
Profs accessible rating	87

Joint Degrees
MBA/JD 2.8 + years.

Academics

Its location "10 minutes from downtown Cincinnati, Ohio" and "affordable [overall cost] relative to other AACSB-accredited schools in the area" draws enthusiastic students to Northern Kentucky University's College of Business. About 85 percent of the students here attend part-time, and those who do appreciate that "classes are offered in the evenings"—most courses meet from 6:00 to 9:00 P.M. once a week—"so that [students] can attend all required classes without cutting into [their] work schedules." NKU also offers two 7-week summer sessions that run on accelerated evening schedules. While class times are convenient, students say that NKU's "greatest strength" is "the course work itself. NKU is very challenging and very strict with academics. Although it is not so easy to prepare for class at times, this has helped prepare me well for my professional career by pushing me to the limit." Class sizes are "small," and professors are "passionate about their subject areas" and "always willing to stay [after class] with you and meet whenever you need to." They're also, for the most part, "flexible and understand that most graduate students also work full-time and have a family." Many have "very relevant real-life experience to impart," and their ranks "include the former director of human resources of a major public utility, a consultant who specializes in turning businesses around, and a finance professor who works as a Certified Financial Planner on the side. No, Jack Welch does not teach here, but those [who] do are knowledgeable and do a good job." Students love that NKU "allows specialization of the MBA" and cite its Entrepreneurship Institute, International Business Center, and finance programs as major strengths.

Overall, students find NKU to be a place where "The student is the top priority." "The staff has always been quick [when] answering my questions and available when I need them," a student writes.

Career and Placement

"There is a wonderful Career Center on campus, but it is primarily focused on meeting the needs of undergraduates," NKU business students tell us. That being said, students admit that, for the most part, they "already have jobs, so career placement is not a large need." Most are looking to move up the ranks with their current employer; those looking to jump ship turn to their fellow students for job leads. Which isn't to say there aren't those who'd like a little more help in the area of job placement: "I think we need more career counselors within the MBA program for those of us who do not come from a traditional business background," one student tells us. Another would like NKU to "improve job [placement] opportunities through alumni relations."

Student Life and Environment

Many at NKU are "on the 'slow' track to finish because of the demands of family and jobs." As such, the school differs from institutions that "have the same students begin and end the program together"; most here "meet different students each semester." Despite this, students report that their "classmates are great people who, through this MBA program, have become real friends." Such friendships are forged largely without the assistance of clubs or activities geared toward graduate students: "I'm a commuter, so most of my time at school is in class, in the library, or meeting to do group work," a typical student writes. While NKU's campus "has food/coffee stands in almost every building" and "computers everywhere with free printing," drawbacks include a "mostly concrete" aesthetic and difficult parking "at certain times of the day."

Students describe their "hardworking" peers as "friendly" but "competitive." NKU strongly recommends that potential applicants obtain 2 years of work experience before applying, and, by all accounts, its student body is "very diverse" in employment backgrounds. "Most [students here] are mid-20s to mid-30s," but "age ranges from 20 to 50." "Quite a few are married with children" and "Most have significant work experience." When students seek common ground, they need look no further than their objective: "We are all here for the same reason: to get an MBA," one student writes. That being said, most students are "eager to learn and get the most from their MBA experience, not just a credential."

Admissions

To gain admission to NKU, applicants must obtain a bachelor's degree from a regionally accredited institution and possess a cumulative undergraduate GPA of at least 2.50 on a 4.00 scale; he or she must also obtain a score of at least 450 on a GMAT taken within the last 5 years and, if applicable, obtain a score of at least 550 on the paper version of the TOEFL (or at least 213 on the computer version of the test). Applicants will be admitted if he or she obtains at least 1,000 points via the formula 200 multiplied by GPA plus GMAT score. In lieu of admission via the formula above, a student will be admitted if he or she obtains at least 1,050 points via the formula 200 multiplied by GPA for student's last 60 semester hours plus GMAT score.

FINANCIAL FACTS

Annual tuition (in-state/ out-of-state)	$346/377
	per semester hour
% of students receiving aid	33
% of students receiving loans	23
% of students receiving grants	10
Average award package	$8,356
Average grant	$3,359
Average student loan debt	$27,880

ADMISSIONS

Admissions Selectivity Rating	**75**
# of applications received	109
% applicants accepted	66
% acceptees attending	72
Average GMAT	529
Range of GMAT	440–630
Average GPA	3.28
TOEFL required of international students	Yes
Minimum TOEFL (paper/computer)	550/213
Regular application deadline	8/1
Regular notification	rolling
Deferment available	Yes
Transfer students accepted	Yes
Transfer application policy A maximum of 9 hours from regionally-accredited institutions.	
Non-fall admissions	Yes
Need-blind admissions	Yes

Applicants Also Look At

University of Cincinnati, Xavier University.

NORTHWESTERN UNIVERSITY
KELLOGG SCHOOL OF MANAGEMENT

Academics

At the Kellogg School of Management at Northwestern University, you can almost feel the cooperation in the air. "It's the kind of atmosphere that even if you don't know people, you will say 'hi' in the halls," reports one student. This "collaborative," "collegial," and "student-led environment" at Kellogg means that students' input is always sought, and their voices and desires have a huge impact on the course the school takes both academically and socially. According to one student, "Kellogg almost doesn't have a formal administration. Students run everything." Other students agree that this crash-course in democracy is "the best way to train tomorrow's business leaders" and note that it also lends the school "a certain energy around the campus that brings excitement to each and every day."

One facet of the cooperative spirit is that both professors and students receive regular performance evaluations. For professors, the pressure is on at mid- and end-of-quarter when the reviews are administered, especially since "Year-end bonuses are based on their ratings from students." However, it seems the results are rarely negative as the majority of students here praise them as "bright, accomplished, fair, and engaging." Students aren't exempt from the scrutiny of their peers, either. Through a web-based program called TeamNet, Kellogg students are able to receive "confidential, detailed, and honest feedback on how they work in teams" from fellow students, faculty, and staff. According to the school, this produces an unparalleled ability to "respond to and give confidential peer feedback, something excellent managers do well."

Another major draw to the program is the school's 1-year MBA program that allows students to earn their MBAs in just 12 months. "Kellogg's 1-year program is one-of-a-kind," one student says. "It's the best return on investment and offers great flexibility combined with small classes and highest quality students." There is, of course, the traditional 2-year program available as well. For either program, the core curriculum classes consist of nine courses in the "fundamental areas of accounting, management and organizations, marketing, finance, decision sciences, and management and strategy." In addition to the 1-year MBA program, another unique facet at Kellogg is the Master of Management and Manufacturing (MMM), offered in conjunction the McCormick School of Engineering and designed to aid students who wish to pursue "management roles in product-driven companies."

Kellogg offers a lengthy list of majors in which students can specialize, from biotechnology to technology industry management, though some students feel that "application of technology is a little slow compared to other schools." Conversely, students single out the "breadth of the marketing, strategy, and finance departments."

Overridingly, students feel confident in regards to their prospective futures thanks to Kellogg's "overall atmosphere, solid reputation and ranking, [and] strength across academic disciplines."

Career and Placement

Recent recruiters with a presence at Kellogg include Merrill Lynch, Microsoft, UBS, JPMorgan Chase, and Booz Allen Hamilton; most students are confident that their school has a "sterling reputation among corporate recruiters." It helps, too, that professors are "student focused" and fellow students are "willing to go out on a limb to help . . . with recruiting, career advice, and schoolwork." While students agree that the team-focused environment ensures that "networking at Kellogg is tremendous," many would like to see the Career Center focus more on locating smaller job opportunities. Others worry that the center "is not focused enough on helping out international students get jobs—either in the U.S. or internationally."

BETH FLYE, ASSISTANT DEAN, ADMISSIONS AND FINANCIAL AID
2001 SHERIDAN ROAD, EVANSTON, IL 60208 UNITED STATES
PHONE: 847-491-3308 • FAX: 847-491-4960
E-MAIL: MBAADMISSIONS@KELLOGG.NORTHWESTERN.EDU
WEBSITE: WWW.KELLOGG.NORTHWESTERN.EDU

Student Life and Environment

Kellogg is situated in Evanston, Illinois, along the shores of Lake Michigan, with only a short commute on the El (elevated train) to downtown Chicago. Most here appreciate this proximity since there aren't "a lot of activities in the city of Evanston." However, don't confuse the city for the campus as "There is a lot going on [at] school." One student explains, "There are dozens, maybe hundreds of clubs at school—special interest, sports, academic, career, spouse/children, politics and government, nonprofit, gay and lesbian, etc." Though the student body is "alive and energetic," some find that diversity, "both ethnically and in terms of people from industries other than consulting," could be improved.

The school has been steadily undergoing multiple renovations to its facilities over the years, including "new classrooms wired for network access," "group study rooms," "quiet study rooms," a "computer training facility" and "expanded computer lab," "free-standing computer terminals," a "student lounge," "lockers," and a "sky-lit atrium." Despite this, some would rather have "a new, more modern building" than spend time "renovating the old one." Others note that "off-campus living facilities are outdated, but they're working on it!"

Admissions

Admissions Officers at Kellogg have the unenviable job of whittling a pile of approximately 4,500 applications down to an admitted class of just less than 700. During this process, they look for work experience, academic excellence, and personality. The school's Admissions Board conducts thousands of interviews each fall. For the entering class of 2006, the average GMAT score was 703. The average amount of employment time was just over 5 years for admitted students. In addition, 28 percent of Kellogg students hail from outside of the United States, and for those applicants, TOEFL scores are required. The average TOEFL score for enrolled students is 279 on the computer-based exam.

FINANCIAL FACTS

Annual tuition	$41,115
Room & board	$13,515
% of students receiving aid	69
Average award package	$42,207
Average grant	$11,212
Average student loan debt	$71,221

ADMISSIONS

Admissions Selectivity Rating	98
# of applications received	4,072
% applicants accepted	24
% acceptees attending	57
Average GMAT	702
Average GPA	3.45
TOEFL required of international students	Yes
Application fee	$225
Regular application deadline	1/5
Regular notification	3/26
Application Deadline/Notification	
Round 1:	10/20 / 1/8
Round 2:	1/5 / 3/26
Round 3:	3/9 / 5/7
Deferment available	Yes
Maximum length of deferment	case by case
Non-fall admissions	Yes
Need blind admissions	Yes

EMPLOYMENT PROFILE

Career Rating	95	Grads Employed by Function	%	Avg. Salary
Primary Source of Full-time Job Acceptances		Finance/Accounting	23	NR
School-facilitated activities	254 (56%)	Human Resources	1	NR
Graduate-facilitated activities	199 (44%)	Marketing/Sales	29	NR
Percent employed	94	Operations/Production	2	NR
		Consulting	36	NR
		General Management	8	NR
		Other	1	R

Top 5 Employers Hiring Grads

McKinsey & Company; Boston Consulting Group; Microsoft; Johnson & Johnson, Bain and Company.

THE OHIO STATE UNIVERSITY
MAX M. FISHER COLLEGE OF BUSINESS

Academics

Ranked among the nation's top-25 MBA programs and among the top 10 such programs at public universities, the Fisher MBA program at Ohio State University offers both "great value" and "high-quality classroom training." With a student/faculty ratio of 5 to 1, Fisher is able to offer "a lot of personal attention" as well. One student writes of a factor that convinced him to attend: "The students and faculty seemed on very familiar terms."

OSU excels in a broad range of disciplines. Students agree that Fisher is "one of the best schools in the operations and supply department" and also that the school has "great finance and logistics programs" and is strong in marketing. MBAs here appreciate "the flexibility within the curriculum to design [one's] own major" as well as the "emphasis on group learning" that serves as the program's pedagogic foundation. While the "smaller program size . . . allows the students to get to know each other, as well as the professors, far more intimately than at most business schools," students also benefit from being on "a large university campus," which "lets students tap many resources available at large schools such as OSU."

Fisher operates on a quarterly academic calendar, which makes for a fast-paced learning environment. Some find it overwhelming, revealing that "if you don't have knowledge of a subject before coming into the class, you're screwed because you don't have time to learn it." "If you want to hide behind a laptop or sit in the back row, you have every opportunity to do it." Others handle the system better. The fact that many find time for extracurriculars (see "Student Life and Environment" below) indicates that, for most students, the workload is manageable. Professors' teaching skills "vary greatly . . . but the administration seems very anxious and willing to adjust the line-up from year to year based off our recommendations. For each quarter there is a formal Fisher-driven evaluation on each professor. . . . The great majority of professors seems to be very receptive to this system and will alter their teaching styles if necessary and/or possible." It's also "not uncommon for Fisher to replace one or two 'core' faculty teachers each year if students overwhelmingly feel that he or she is not working out." Students add that professors, regardless of their teaching ability, make themselves available and that "most, if not all, are tightly integrated into the Columbus/outside business community. All of them are known and respected by managers of the companies" that students interview with.

Career and Placement

Fisher's "second-to-none" Career Services Office attracts "a large number of companies in and around Columbus." Students tell us that "operations is the one field that the best companies come to Fisher for." Some here regret that while regional recruiting is quite good, "There are almost no companies from other parts of the country." Others, however, counter that "there is ample support for students interested in positions outside of the Midwest. Many of the finance students are pursuing investment banking opportunities in the Northeast with great success." Students here also benefit from "a fantastic alumni base that is always willing to help out current students."

Companies most likely to extend offers to OSU MBAs in 2006 included: American Greetings, Capital One, Defense Finance and Accounting Services, Emerson, Johnson & Johnson, Kimberly-Clark, Limited Brands, Motorola, Nationwide, Nestlé, Oracle Consulting, PricewaterhouseCoopers, Procter & Gamble, and United Stationers.

Student Life and Environment

"Many students are active in various organizations" and extracurricular projects at Fisher, including "the Fisher Board Fellows, which allow you to interact with members from the Board of Directors of various companies large and small within Columbus . . . the Initiative for Managing Services, whereby students from the first year full-time program get an

DAVID SMITH, EXECUTIVE DIRECTOR, GRADUATE PROGRAMS OFFICE
100 GERLACH HALL, 2108 NEIL AVENUE, COLUMBUS, OH 43210-1144 UNITED STATES
PHONE: 614-292-8511 • FAX: 614-292-9006
E-MAIL: MBA@FISHER.OSU.EDU • WEBSITE: FISHERMBA.OSU.EDU

insight into diverse fields of business management from marketing to human resources, way before their summer internship actually starts . . . and Fisher Professional Services, which provides consulting services to various companies in and around Columbus (predominantly) and is growing rapidly. Students, both first and second year do these consulting projects and assignments along with their regular course work and internships." One MBA adds, "Student organizations are very active. The Finance Club took students interested in a Wall Street career to New York to network with a variety of investment banks. The Marketing Association organized a networking trip to Chicago and Milwaukee. Most career-type organizations provide students a large number of opportunities to interact with companies."

Fisher's facilities are "brand new and all resources are state of the art." "The school is well equipped technologically, and the professors definitely utilize the tech resources. Notes and all other materials are available in hard copy and digital format. Communications are frequent and through e-mail from them as well." Prospective students should know that the OSU campus is a bit sports crazed. One student explains, "Being a Buckeye is like a religion, and you're quickly indoctrinated upon arrival. People have a lot of fun going to all kinds of Buckeye sports events. We also have an event of the week that brings together everyone for a moment of relaxation—much needed after a tough week!" "Students and faculty all seem to love, not just like, being Buckeyes and working alongside one another," one MBA says. Another agrees: "The administration keeps a close ear to student feedback and takes quick action to mend issues. And the students themselves are a joy to learn from."

Admissions

The Admissions Office at Fisher requires applicants to provide two official copies of transcripts for all undergraduate and graduate institutions attended, GMAT scores, three letters of recommendation, essays, and a resume of work experience. Interviews are conducted at the request of the Admissions Department. In addition to the above, international applicants whose first language is not English must provide proof of English proficiency (the school accepts several standardized tests, including the TOEFL, MELAB, and IELTS; minimum acceptable scores are 600 on the paper-based TOEFL, 250 on the computer-based TOEFL, 86 on the MELAB, and 8 on the IELTS) and an affidavit of financial support.

FINANCIAL FACTS

Annual tuition (in-state/ out-of-state)	$18,696/$32,049
Fees	$783
Cost of books	$2,586
Room & board (on/off-campus)	$6,378/$7,200
% of students receiving aid	74
% of first-year students receiving aid	84
% of students receiving loans	57
% of students receiving grants	61
Average award package	$26,409
Average grant	$17,609

ADMISSIONS

Admissions Selectivity Rating	94
# of applications received	559
% applicants accepted	42
% acceptees attending	54
Average GMAT	669
Range of GMAT	630–700
Average GPA	3.44
TOEFL required of international students	Yes
Minimum TOEFL (paper/computer)	600/250
Application fee	$60
International application fee	$70
Regular application deadline	Rolling
Regular notification	Rolling
Deferment available	Yes
Maximum length of deferment	1 year
Need-blind admissions	Yes

Applicants Also Look At
Duke University, Indiana University—Bloomington, Michigan State University, Northwestern University, Purdue University, The University of North Carolina at Chapel Hill, University of Michigan.

EMPLOYMENT PROFILE

Career Rating	89	Grads Employed by Function	%	Avg. Salary
Primary Source of Full-time Job Acceptances		Finance/Accounting	27	$84,667
School-facilitated activities	77 (74%)	Marketing/Sales	27	$78,813
Graduate-facilitated activities	27 (26%)	Operations/Production	12	$75,486
Average base starting salary	$84,674	Consulting	23	$81,567
Percent employed	96	General Management	10	$87,643
		Top 5 Employers Hiring Grads		
		Limited Brands; Nationwide; American Greetings; Capital One; Oracle.		

OLD DOMINION UNIVERSITY
COLLEGE OF BUSINESS AND PUBLIC ADMINISTRATION

Academics

The MBA program at Old Dominion University serves a predominantly local student population for whom cost and convenience are major priorities. Students here also appreciate that "program options are deeper here than at others in the area."

Choices are indeed myriad in the ODU College of Business and Public Administration. Students may pursue a traditional MBA or an MS in Accounting, an MA in Economics, an MPA, a Master of Urban Studies, an MS in Computer Science, along with two PhD options. Furthermore, they may take classes part-time or full-time; in the daytime, evenings, or weekends; and at the main campus in Norfolk, at any of several satellite campuses; or in virtual classrooms at the Northern Virginia Higher Education Center, where students participate in a lockstep, cohort program. MBA students may choose a concentration in financial analysis and valuation, international business, public administration, information technology and enterprise integration, business and economic forecasting, or maritime and port management, or they may opt for a general MBA without a concentration. A variety of study abroad options and independent research projects round out the choices here.

Whatever option they pursue, students praise the program's many conveniences. They appreciate the way in which "Electronic communication allows submittal of questions and assigned work, as well as distribution of reference material. The system is set up well to allow easy contact with the instructors and classmates." Because so many are employed, students are especially grateful that "the school works very well with people who work full-time, with great class schedules on nights and weekends." Professors here "are a truly outstanding group, with many who have been successful professionally and are now teaching. Their combination of real-world experience and academic theory allows for a richness of education." Professors are also easily accessible "7 days a week," while administrators "always return telephone calls." As one student aptly asks, "What more can you expect from a school?"

Career and Placement

Old Dominion offers career services to its MBA through the university Career Development Center. The university dedicates one counselor in the CDC Office to serve MBAs; she assists students in finding both internship and full-time positions, helps with resume and cover letter preparation, and provides individual career consultation. MBA students also benefit from an MBA Association comprised of both current students and alumni. The association organizes numerous career-promoting events over the course of the school year, including seminars, forums, social events, community service, and an annual dinner.

Student Life and Environment

ODU's MBA program is located in Constant Hall, a thoroughly renovated facility that features 21 mediated wireless classrooms, executive education facilities, and a computer lab dedicated to business students. The new facilities are just part of a plan "to help transform this school from a commuter-oriented school to a traditional urban university." The university is "expanding by adding other facilities" as well, but students report that ODU is still a long way from becoming a conventional residential school with a full and active campus life.

For now, the ODU MBA "is very commuter oriented," meaning that most students "don't spend a lot of time at school." One student says, "Unfortunately, I don't have enough time to experience much of what the school has to offer due to full-time work

MRS. RHYANNE HENLEY, MBA PROGRAM MANAGER
CONSTANT HALL, 1026, NORFOLK, VA 23529 UNITED STATES
PHONE: 757-683-3585 • FAX: 757-683-5750
E-MAIL: MBAINFO@ODU.EDU • WEBSITE: WWW.ODU-MBA.ORG

along with school requirements," and another adds, "I don't spend a lot of time at school because I am married with kids." Most students live in and around Norfolk, a naval town with a population of approximately a quarter-million. Surrounding cities and suburbs including Virginia Beach, Newport News, Hampton, and Chesapeake make this a substantial metropolitan area. Top regional employers include the military, Sentara Health Care, American Systems Engineering, Amerigroup, Manpower, Geico Direct, Gold Key Resorts, Stihl, Norfolk Southern, and the Christian Broadcasting Network.

ODU's MBA program attracts "many current and former military personnel" (military personnel who receive any form of tuition assistance are charged the in-state rate for all tuition charges regardless of their home state), as well as students who "run a broad range of race, age, experience, and sociopolitical background." Students are "generally likeable, easygoing, and friendly, and willing to help out in a team effort."

Admissions

All applicants to the MBA program at ODU must submit the following materials: a completed application (paper or online) including statement of personal objectives and resume; an official GMAT score report; official transcripts for all undergraduate and graduate work; a letter of recommendation (from a professor if you are currently a student; from a supervisor if you are currently employed); and a tuition-rate-determination form (to determine eligibility for in-state tuition). International students whose first language is not English must also submit an official score report for the TOEFL. Applications generally take 4 to 6 weeks to process once all materials have arrived at the Admissions Office. Incoming students who have not completed college-level calculus are required to complete an equivalent undergraduate course during their first semester of MBA work. ODU considers the trend of undergraduate grades as well as overall cumulative GPA; those who showed marked improvement in junior and senior years can overcome poor performance as underclassmen. Returning adults with considerable work experience may earn up to six credits toward the MBA for skills and knowledge accrued through work; credits are awarded on the basis of evaluation, examination, certifications, or portfolio.

FINANCIAL FACTS

Annual tuition (in-state/ out-of-state)	$6,840/$17,160
Fees	$185
Cost of books	$800
Room & board (on/off-campus)	$6,500/$7,500
Average grant	$14,500

ADMISSIONS

Admissions Selectivity Rating	**75**
# of applications received	235
% applicants accepted	74
% acceptees attending	77
Average GMAT	546
Average GPA	3.15
TOEFL required of international students	Yes
Minimum TOEFL (paper/computer)	550/213
Application fee	$40
Regular application deadline	6/1
Regular notification	Rolling
Application Deadline/Notification	
Round 1:	11/1 / 12/1
Round 2:	3/1 / 4/1
Round 3:	6/1 / 7/1
Deferment available	Yes
Maximum length of deferment	1 year
Transfer students accepted	Yes
Transfer application policy We accept up to 12 credit hours from AACSB-accredited MBA programs only.	
Non-fall admissions	Yes
Need-blind admissions	Yes

PACIFIC LUTHERAN UNIVERSITY
SCHOOL OF BUSINESS

GENERAL INFORMATION

Type of school	Private
Affiliation	Lutheran
Environment	City
Academic calendar	4-1-4-3

SURVEY SAYS . . .

Cutting-edge classes
Smart classrooms
Solid preparation in:
General management
Doing business in a global economy

STUDENTS

Enrollment of parent institution	3,640
Enrollment of business school	80
% part-time	8
% international	17
Average age at entry	32
Average years work experience at entry	10

ACADEMICS

Academic Experience Rating	**73**
Student/faculty ratio	8:1
Profs interesting rating	78
Profs accessible rating	86

Academics

With an average of 15 students per class, the School of Business at Pacific Lutheran University offers "classes size small enough to actually get personal attention and learn from other students as well as the faculty members." This, a strong local reputation, and a "school schedule [that] really caters to working professionals" are among the top reasons students choose the MBA program at PLU.

PLU accommodates a broad swath of the professional world through a wide range of offerings. Students may pursue an accelerated 16-month MBA for the Knowledge Economy, which focuses on technology and innovation management, or they may pursue the same degree through the conventional part-time evening program. They may opt for an MBA in Health Care Management, or they may pursue an MBA in Entrepreneurship and closely held business. An MBA in general management is also offered. The curriculum includes 36 credit hours of required core courses and 9 credit hours of electives. It can be completed in 20 months, although most students take longer. Students appreciate "the emphasis on leadership" in this "robust curriculum." Busy professionals also love that "the curriculum is set up so you can graduate very quickly with only 9 units a semester and 2 nights a week. This is probably the quickest legitimate MBA program in Washington."

A unique feature of the PLU MBA is the 10-day international experience, the cost of which is covered largely by tuition. (Students may be responsible for one or two meals per day; travel and hotel are included.) The program may include a trade mission trip organized by the Tacoma World Trade Center, or may involve travel to an international destination to meet with foreign business leaders to study global business best practices.

As one student sums up, "The administration, faculty, and academic experience are why I chose PLU. The past 2 years have strengthened my overall skills and provided me an educational experience I will never forget. The school impressed me on my first visit and impresses me even more today with their skill and knowledge base."

Career and Placement

The Career Development Office at PLU provides placement and counseling services for all undergraduates, graduate students, and alumni. The office acts as a liaison between current students and alumni in order to establish mentoring relationships. It also assists students with internship and career placement, and it works with the PLU Business Network, an alumni association, to schedule social events throughout the school year. Another significant networking opportunity is the MBA Executive Leadership Series, a series of addresses delivered by area execs. Among recent speakers are Belo Corp. President Ray Heacox and Pyramid Breweries CEO Scott Barnum.

Employers who most frequently hire Pacific Lutheran MBAs include Boeing, Microsoft, Weyerhaeuser, State Farm Insurance, and Intel.

ABBY WIGSTROM-CARLSON, DIRECTOR OF GRADUATE PROGRAMS AND EXTERNAL RELATIONS
OFFICE OF ADMISSIONS, PACIFIC LUTHERAN UNIVERSITY TACOMA, WA 98447 UNITED STATES
PHONE: 253-535-7151 • FAX: 253-536-5136
E-MAIL: PLUMBA@PLU.EDU • WEBSITE: WWW.PLU.EDU/MBA

Student Life and Environment

The MBA program at PLU is unusually small; only 65 students were enrolled for the 2005–2006 academic year. Although most attend full-time, classes are scheduled at the convenience of part-time students during weekday evenings, resulting in "flexible evening schedules for working professionals." Students tell us that "classes go by fairly quickly and they are set up on a rotational schedule so you only have each class once every 10 days or so. This allows a good amount of prep time. The reading is fairly light, but most of the projects are group assignments, which can be tough for [those with] busy lives."

Students appreciate that PLU "is committed to making the school better. Many great changes have happened since my arrival, including a new, modern, updated facility; free Wi-Fi access; outstanding, well-equipped rooms; and real-life practical experience from the faculty. I am getting a better education than I had expected, and my expectations coming in were high," declares one student. They also enjoy a homey environment; one student notes, "It is a small school, [and] there are always people looking out for your safety."

As part of the PLU student body you'll find "accountants, doctors, bankers, and lawyers" who together form "a big family and enjoy spending time together." Students tell us that "the age range is broad, and the experience they bring adds to the learning experience." Most "are working professionals with families" along with "a few international students who do not work outside of school." Students also remark on noticing "a higher percentage of school employees enrolled in the program than one might expect."

Admissions

According to the school, Admission Officers of the PLU MBA program look for candidates who "have demonstrated proven success in a challenging undergraduate or master's-level program," "desire academic, personal, and career challenges," "communicate clearly and demonstrate leadership capability in a variety of settings," "serve in their community, workplace, church, or school," and "bring a unique perspective to the classroom environment." Applicants must provide the school with the following materials: official transcripts covering all undergraduate and graduate work; an official GMAT or GRE score report; a current resume; a completed application form; two letters of recommendation; and a 300-word statement of personal goals. Candidates whose native language is other than English must also submit an official TOEFL or IELTS score report. International transcripts must be submitted to Educational Perspectives for evaluation. All international applicants are required to submit an I-20 as well as a Declaration of Finances.

FINANCIAL FACTS

Annual tuition	$17,625
Cost of books	$1,800
Room & board	$6,765
% of students receiving aid	30
% of students receiving grants	19
Average grant	$2,575

ADMISSIONS

Admissions Selectivity Rating	**70**
# of applications received	35
% applicants accepted	86
% acceptees attending	83
Average GPA	3.23
TOEFL required of international students	Yes
Minimum TOEFL (paper/computer)	573/230
Application fee	$40
Regular application deadline	Rolling
Regular notification	Rolling
Deferment available	Yes
Maximum length of deferment	1 year
Transfer students accepted	Yes
Transfer application policy Minimum of 24 semester hours in residence.	
Non-fall admissions	Yes
Need-blind admissions	Yes

Applicants Also Look At
Seattle Pacific University, Seattle University, University of Washington.

EMPLOYMENT PROFILE	
Career Rating	83

PENNSYLVANIA STATE UNIVERSITY
SMEAL COLLEGE OF BUSINESS

GENERAL INFORMATION
Type of school	Public
Environment	Town
Academic calendar	7-1-7 week modules

SURVEY SAYS . . .
Good social scene
Good peer network
Smart classrooms
Solid preparation in:
Communication/interpersonal skills
Presentation skills

STUDENTS
Enrollment of parent institution	41,289
Enrollment of business school	150
% male/female	74/26
% out-of-state	65
% minorities	19
% international	34
Average age at entry	28
Average years work experience at entry	5

ACADEMICS
Academic Experience Rating	**98**
Student/faculty ratio	2:1
Profs interesting rating	93
Profs accessible rating	97
% female faculty	15
% minority faculty	20

Joint Degrees
BS/MBA 5 years, quality and manufacturing management 2 to 3 years, JD/MBA 4 years.

Prominent Alumni
John Arnold, chairman and CEO, Petroleum Products Corporation; J. David Rogers, chairman and CEO, JD Capital Management; James R. Stengel, CMO, Procter & Gamble.

Academics

Many factors combine to convince MBAs at Penn State's Smeal College of Business that their program offers "one of the best returns on investment in the world." The "reasonable tuition and amazing financial assistance from the program" certainly play a large part, not to mention the school's small-town location, which provides "a cheap place to live and study, so costs are minimal." There's also "the world-class education provided by professors who are extremely respected in their industry," and, last but not least, "the benefit of the Penn State network with the largest active alumni base in the country." One student describes the alumni as "rabidly loyal to the school and very willing to help current students. . . . They also come back for football tailgates, so students have a great opportunity to connect with many alumni in person."

The Smeal MBA is "a very small program" (between 75 and 110 students in each incoming class) that "facilitates a more personalized education" through "great access to professors and professional development opportunities." Students love the "many opportunities to build close relationships with a world-class faculty." One student explains, "MBAs are on a first-name basis with all faculty and staff. Everyone really goes out of their way to make sure you are on the right path in virtually everything." Administrators "join the students daily for coffee and are tremendously responsive to our needs. They also join us for social events and attend outside events." Students are especially pleased that "the new Dean is committed to transforming this program into a national powerhouse."

Smeal excels in supply chain management; students tell us that finance is another strength of the program, as is business-to-business marketing (a product of Smeal's Institute for the Study of Business Markets, which "brings the thought leaders from around the world together to face the challenges in today's B2B markets"). They warn that "the first year at Smeal is packed. Students coming into the program should expect to be in class 16 hours a week and working outside the classroom around 20 hours." Things don't let up that much during the second year, but students don't mind; they tell us that the program "prepares students for the challenges they will face once they re-enter the workforce in a management capacity. Students develop both technical and leadership skills and are well positioned to lead business in the future. In addition, the collaborative culture of the program translates well into successful behaviors in the business world."

Career and Placement

Career Services is a mixed bag at Penn State. Students grumble that "due to the small size of our MBA program, the school struggles to bring in a large number of recruiters in various disciplines." However, they also point out that "career services have been upgraded recently." They also point out that "the school sponsors treks to Philadelphia and New York City to enable/facilitate students to connect with recruiters and alumni," and that "through a school database, you can quickly identify key alumni contacts at every major company in the world." Overall, most agree the placement picture here is pretty good.

Companies most likely to employ Smeal MBAs include: Air Products & Chemicals, Amazon.com, Avaya, Bank of America Corporation, Bear Stearns, CIGNA, Citigroup, Dell, DuPont, ExxonMobil, Ford Motor Company, Hewlett-Packard, Honeywell International, IBM, Intel, Johnson & Johnson, Kennametal, KPMG International, Pfizer, Praxair, PricewaterhouseCoopers, Solectron, and Time Inc.

Ms. Carrie Marcinkevage, Director, MBA Admissions
220 Business Bldg., Pennsylvania State University—University Park, PA 16802-33603 U.S.
Phone: 814-863-0474 • Fax: 814-863-8072
E-mail: smealmba@psu.edu • Website: www.smeal.psu.edu/mba

Student Life and Environment

State College, Pennsylvania, may not have Manhattan's glitz and glamour, but it is "a beautiful town and a fantastic place to spend 2 challenging years of your life." The town provides "great nightlife and a downtown bar scene," while the school provides the football beloved by so many here. Major events such as Thon and Arts Fest pepper the academic calendar, and students report that "outside of the classroom, opportunities abound for cross-cultural learning (student organizations host numerous events), philanthropic involvement (Habitat for Humanity, etc.), and social events (we went skydiving at the beginning of the semester!)." The business school "has just moved into a new, state-of-the art $68 million building that takes advantage of cutting-edge technology available today. The building helps strengthen a sense of community that is already very evident at Penn State." On the downside, students tell us that "activities can be limited due to the small size of the school. There are always demands for more clubs, but not always enough students available. Several students and spouses started a partners club this year, which should help new students with domestic partners."

Admissions

The Smeal admission's website notes that Admissions Officers work hard to optimize class composition for each entering class. Diverse backgrounds in terms of both professional and life experience are sought so that a wide range of perspectives inform group work and class discussion. Applicants to the program must submit the following materials: a completed online application form; official copies of all transcripts for all postsecondary academic work; an official GMAT score report; two letters of recommendation from individuals who can assess your past professional performance; personal essays; a resume; and an interview. In addition to all of the above, international applicants must also submit an official score report for the TOEFL; and evidence of sufficient funds to cover at least 1 year's expenses while in the program (approximately $40,000 to $45,000). The school admits some students directly from undergraduate programs, but most students enter with at least 4 years of professional experience.

FINANCIAL FACTS

Annual tuition (in-state/ out-of-state)	$16,222/$27,380
Fees	$530
Cost of books	$1,500
Room & board	$12,650
% of students receiving aid	89
% of first-year students receiving aid	88
% of students receiving loans	34
% of students receiving grants	84
Average award package	$15,033
Average grant	$9,365
Average student loan debt	$29,997

ADMISSIONS

Admissions Selectivity Rating	93
# of applications received	511
% applicants accepted	34
% acceptees attending	48
Average GMAT	651
Range of GMAT	560–730
Average GPA	3.3
TOEFL required of international students	Yes
Minimum TOEFL (paper/computer)	600/250
Application fee	$60
Regular application deadline	4/15
Regular notification	5/31
Early decision program	Yes
ED Deadline/Notification	12/1 / 1/31
Deferment available	Yes
Maximum length of deferment	1 year
Need-blind admissions	Yes

Applicants Also Look At

Indiana University—Bloomington, Michigan State University—College of Law, Purdue University, The Ohio State University, University of Illinois, University of Maryland.

EMPLOYMENT PROFILE

Career Rating	90	Grads Employed by Function	%	Avg. Salary
Primary Source of Full-time Job Acceptances		Finance/Accounting	34	$83,553
School-facilitated activities	41 (75%)	Human Resources	2	NR
Graduate-facilitated activities	14 (25%)	Marketing/Sales	22	$78,834
Average base starting salary	$81,071	Operations/Production	18	$84,000
Percent employed	95	Consulting	3	NR
		General Management	13	$86,571
		Other	7	$67,000

Top 5 Employers Hiring Grads

Intel, DuPont, Air Products & Chemicals, Citigroup, Standard & Poors.

PENNSYLVANIA STATE UNIVERSITY—ERIE, THE BEHREND COLLEGE
SAM AND IRENE BLACK SCHOOL OF BUSINESS

GENERAL INFORMATION
Type of school	Public
Environment	Village
Academic calendar	Semester

SURVEY SAYS . . .
Cutting-edge classes
Solid preparation in:
General management
Teamwork
Communication/interpersonal skills

STUDENTS
Enrollment of parent institution	3,996
Enrollment of business school	163
% male/female	64/36
% out-of-state	7
% part-time	66
% minorities	9
% international	4
Average age at entry	26
Average years work experience at entry	4

ACADEMICS
Academic Experience Rating	**72**
Student/faculty ratio	6:1
Profs interesting rating	77
Profs accessible rating	82
% female faculty	22
% minority faculty	22

Academics

Thanks to its "good institutional name and reputation," Penn State—Behrend draws an "intelligent, diverse, competitive" group of students to its comprehensive and broad-based MBA program. A general degree that aims to develop the critical-thinking skills necessary for a career in mid- and upper-level management, the MBA curriculum consists of 48 units, or 14 courses. Of these, 18 units form the foundation core courses, comprised of four introductory classes: Business, Government, and Society; Costs, Competition, and Market Performance; Demand, Operations, and Firm Performance; and Integrated Business Analysis. After completing these courses, students must complete 18 credits of advanced required courses and 12 credits of elective course work. For those who have already taken business courses, the program can be streamlined through the omission of certain foundation courses.

Depending on their previous academic preparation, full-time students can usually complete the MBA curriculum in three semesters, whereas part-time students usually require 3 to 4 years to complete the program. You'll find a pretty decisive split on the Penn State campus between "those who are relatively fresh out of undergrad with little/no work experience," and returning students "who are married with children and have 10-plus years of work experience (often in a technical background)." In fact, many of the younger students have come to the program directly out of the undergraduate college, as the school offers talented business majors the opportunity to complete an MBA with one additional year of study. A lively mix, students enjoy the diversity within the student body, telling us, "My fellow students are intelligent people. We learn a lot off of each other due to our diverse professional and undergraduate backgrounds."

Professors join the Penn State faculty from a variety of distinguished professional and academic backgrounds, and "The majority are outstanding" in the classroom. There is no predominant teaching methodology at the school, and "Professors are different, but each is able to teach a particular course in a dynamic way." The result is a diversified and useful academic experience. A second-year student adds, "Each class has given me valuable information, especially those that I thought were not relevant in my profession. Those particular classes have pushed me beyond my comfortable boundaries and allowed me to succeed." Enrolling roughly 90 new students annually, the program is fairly small, and the school prides itself on establishing supportive relationships between professors and students. A current student attests, "The professors are a pleasure to be around, and they understand that the student body is not only diverse in its gender and race but its work experience and age as well."

While the program has historically maintained a limited enrollment, many students mention that the program has grown considerably in recent years, increasing average class sizes and causing some administrative distress. However, many feel "The program is moving in the right direction," reassuring us that school officials are "always looking for ways to improve" and will probably have "all the bugs worked out in a few years."

Career and Placement

A high percentage of Penn State students are currently employed in a professional position and are pursuing an MBA with the intention of improving their career opportunities at their current company. In fact, a considerable number of Penn State students receive tuition assistance from their employers. Even so, "A significant portion of those students desires a career change upon graduating." For those, the Penn State—Behrend Academic Advising and Career Development Center serves both the undergraduate and graduate

ANN M. BURBULES, GRADUATE ADMISSIONS COUNSELOR
4701 COLLEGE DRIVE, ERIE, PA 16563 UNITED STATES
PHONE: 814-898-7255 • FAX: 814-898-6044
E-MAIL: PSBehrendMBA@PSU.EDU • WEBSITE: WWW.BEHREND.PSU.EDU

population at Penn State, including students in the MBA program. The CDC hosts career fairs, on-campus recruiting and interview events, seminars, and workshops. A growing number of organizations participate in Penn State Behrend career fairs each year. In 2005, the MBA graduates who responded to the CDC's placement survey reported an average salary of $59,214, with a salary range between $42,000 and $65,000.

Student Life and Environment

In the Sam and Irene Black School MBA program, students are "interesting, easy to work with, helpful, and enjoyable to be around," making class time and study groups a pleasure rather than a chore. A current student shares, "I have a lot of fun with classmates working on projects and activities although I am only there 2 days a week." While there are plenty of student organizations and activities associated with the larger university, a majority of MBA students "are commuters who have difficulty scheduling classes and meeting time commitments around work and family obligations." These students "only spend time at school for class time and group work/study time" and generally do not participate in extracurricular clubs or activities. As a result, "Getting to know everyone is difficult" and students admit, "There is little social interaction other than going out for 2 hours at the very end of the semester." Life at Penn State is nonetheless agreeable, boasting a "very friendly atmosphere, very amicable personnel and students, very attractive campus setting." Currently, the school is located in a new $30-million Research and Economic Development Center, and students agree that "the new business building is a great asset to the MBA program."

Admissions

Students may apply to begin study at Penn State in the fall, spring, or summer semester. Admissions decisions are made on a rolling basis. To apply, students must submit two official transcripts, official GMAT scores, a statement of purpose, an application fee, and three recommendation forms. Candidates with the highest GMAT scores and GPA are given priority in admissions. Candidates are evaluated based on the strength of their combined GMAT score and GPA; therefore, a lower GMAT score can be compensated for by a higher GPA, or vice versa.

FINANCIAL FACTS

Annual tuition (in-state/ out-of-state)	$10,836/$16,866
Fees	$478
Cost of books	$1,075
Room & board (on/off-campus)	$0/$8,262
% of students receiving aid	50
% of first-year students receiving aid	68
% of students receiving loans	58
% of students receiving grants	4
Average award package	$15,565
Average grant	$1,800

ADMISSIONS

Admissions Selectivity Rating	69
# of applications received	74
% applicants accepted	85
% acceptees attending	87
Average GMAT	511
Range of GMAT	450–560
Average GPA	3.16
TOEFL required of international students	Yes
Minimum TOEFL (paper/computer)	550/213
Application fee	$45
Regular application deadline	7/10
Regular notification	Rolling
Deferment available	Yes
Maximum length of deferment	2 years
Transfer students accepted	Yes
Transfer application policy	

Up to 10 credits of relevant graduate work completed at an accredited institution. Credits earned to complete a previous graduate degree may not be used to fulfill MBA degree requirements. Transferred graduate work must have been completed no more than 5 years before the student is fully admitted as a degree candidate at Penn State Erie. Course work must be of at least a B quality and appear on the graduate transcript of a regionally-accredited institution. Pass/Fail grades are not transferable.

Non-fall admissions	Yes
Need-blind admissions	Yes

EMPLOYMENT PROFILE

Career Rating	68	Grads Employed by Function	%	Avg. Salary
		Finance/Accounting	40	$48,500
		Marketing/Sales	20	$45,000
		MIS	20	$55,000
		Operations/Production	20	$55,000

PEPPERDINE UNIVERSITY
GRAZIADIO SCHOOL OF BUSINESS AND MANAGEMENT

Academics

Pepperdine's Graziadio School of Business and Management offers a range of program options for full-time students, working individuals, and accomplished execs. Full-time programs include a traditional MBA, an international program, and two joint-degree programs: an MBA/Master of Public Policy and an MBA/JD. About three in four students here attend part-time, and those looking to schedule their education around a full-time job can do so with either morning or evening classes. The school encourages mid-level managers to take advantage of its executive MBA program and senior-level executives to take advantage of its presidential and key executive MBA program; both programs meet on weekends. The school's Master of Science in Organization Development is also geared toward those with significant professional experience and is composed of eight 1-week sessions at various locations in California and abroad.

Across programs, the Graziadio curriculum focuses on "keeping up with the changing global economy while doing business in an ethical manner." Course work on organizational behavior is "very strong," though students tell us that "employers aren't so worried about that if you want to do something like high finance." "Small class sizes" are the norm here, and "Most grades are based on group presentations and papers rather than testing." While most students enjoy this setup, a few gripe that "people can get by without doing much work at all if others in the group do the work" and describe the atmosphere as "too nonchalant." By all accounts, Graziadio "professors genuinely care" about students and "have tons of real-world experience." Staff members are reportedly "helpful," though some here describe the overall administration of the school as "slightly disjointed." A few students would also like Graziadio to recruit students with "higher GMAT" scores in order to boost its standing in the b-school community.

Career and Placement

Graziadio boasts the largest b-school alumni network in Southern California; the school has over 30,000 alumni, and over 3,600 of them occupy prominent positions at major organizations. It is not surprising, then, that students cite the opportunities the school provides to "network" as one of its major strengths. However, many students also characterize the school's Career Services as a significant weakness. As one student explains, "The current staff is helpful in identifying alumni whom [students] can connect with, but is little help in . . . helping students target employers that fulfill their desired profession." A few Graziadio students tell us that "Recruiting/Career Services is improving." A multipurpose online tool provided by the school allows students to manage most of their job search in a single place.

Employers who frequently hire Graziadio graduates include: NASA, Mattel, Countrywide Financial, KPMG International, AT&T, Boston Consulting Group, Nestlé, Princess Cruises, The Walt Disney Company, Wellpoint, Wells Fargo, Farmer's Insurance, Cintas, and Wilmington Trust. Students here, however, maintain that few "great companies actively recruit—I have to go to those companies myself and bang on [their] door."

DARRELL ERIKSEN, DIRECTOR OF ADMISSIONS
6100 CENTER DRIVE, LOS ANGELES, CA 90045 UNITED STATES
PHONE: 310-568-5535 • FAX: 310-568-5779
E-MAIL: GSBM@PEPPERDINE.EDU • WEBSITE: WWW.BSCHOOL.PEPPERDINE.EDU

Student Life and Environment

Students at Graziadio report that "all classes have a group project element so we spend a lot of time outside of class with other students," adding that these interactions "usually go beyond academic levels; classmates usually hang out together outside of school." Of the "well-educated" and "energetic" students here, a sanguine student writes: "I know these are people I will keep in contact with for the rest of my life." A student in the financial industry adds: "We have so many international students; I'll have friends all over the world now." "It is challenging, rewarding, and fun," a student coming from the field of pharmaceutical marketing writes. "Days are long, and I work hard, but I enjoy being at school. I look forward to seeing my classmates. I usually have one or two meetings in a day—for team projects and/or extracurricular activities. I generally spend all day on campus."

Just which Pepperdine campus a Graziadio student calls home, however, varies. The university's primary campus is in Malibu, but it also maintains graduate campuses in West Los Angeles, Encino, Irvine, Long Beach, Pasadena, Santa Clara, and Westlake Village; each of Graziadio's different programs is offered on one or more of these campuses. Students on the primary campus in Malibu describe it as "beautiful and peaceful." "It's a great place to come study, but it's so secluded that you end up wanting to actually leave Malibu and head into areas where there's more life." To that end, some here claim that "hitting the bars and clubs in Santa Monica and Hollywood happens at least once a week, if not twice a weekend." "Talks by industry professionals" (including "some fairly big-time CEOs"), "information sessions by local companies for recruitment purposes, and, sometimes, club events" also mix things up. Students believe, however, that the school could provide "more social activities" for students in the different programs "to network better [and] to build a better sense of school unity for the business school."

Admissions

The Admissions staff at Graziadio provides prospective applicants with one on-one consultations regarding their suitability for its programs. This acts as a prescreening process; therefore, the school is more selective than its admit rate would suggest.

FINANCIAL FACTS

Annual tuition	$32,804
Fees	$585
Cost of books	$1,000
Room & board (off-campus)	$14,000
% of students receiving aid	58
% of students receiving loans	31
% of students receiving grants	35
Average award package	$27,800
Average grant	$21,311
Average student loan debt	$62,374

ADMISSIONS

Admissions Selectivity Rating	**80**
# of applications received	371
% applicants accepted	72
% acceptees attending	37
Average GMAT	627
Range of GMAT	580–700
Average GPA	3.2
TOEFL required of international students	Yes
Minimum TOEFL (paper/computer)	600/250
Application fee	$50
Regular application deadline	5/1
Regular notification	Rolling
Early decision program	Yes
ED Deadline/Notification	12/15 / 1/15
Deferment available	Yes
Maximum length of deferment	1 year
Transfer students accepted	Yes
Transfer application policy	
No more than 2 courses may be transferred, contingent upon approval of policy committee.	
Need-blind admissions	Yes

EMPLOYMENT PROFILE

Career Rating	79	Grads Employed by Function	%	Avg. Salary
Primary Source of Full-time Job Acceptances		Finance/Accounting	42	$75,123
Percent employed	76	Human Resources	1	$73,000
		Marketing/Sales	27	$76,313
		Operations/Production	9	$71,185
		Consulting	9	$75,867
		General Management	9	$56,600

Top 5 Employers Hiring Grads

Warner Bros.; Homestore; Yahoo!; Wells Fargo; Countrywide.

PITTSBURG STATE UNIVERSITY
GLADYS A. KELCE COLLEGE OF BUSINESS

GENERAL INFORMATION

Type of school	Public
Environment	Village
Academic calendar	Semester

SURVEY SAYS . . .
Happy students
Smart classrooms
Solid preparation in:
General management
Presentation skills
Quantitative skills
Computer skills

STUDENTS

Enrollment of parent institution	6,500
Enrollment of business school	136
% male/female	55/45
% out-of-state	53
% part-time	27
% international	43
Average age at entry	25
Average years work experience at entry	1

ACADEMICS

Academic Experience Rating	**81**
Student/faculty ratio	25:1
Profs interesting rating	86
Profs accessible rating	78
% female faculty	15
% minority faculty	10

Prominent Alumni
Lee Scott, president and CEO, Wal-mart; John Lampe, president and CEO, Firestone/Bridgestone; John Lowe, executive vice president, ConocoPhillips Company; Orvil Bicknell, CEO, NPC International; Richard Colliver, executive vice president, American Honda.

Academics

Students choose the MBA program at Pittsburg State University because "it's reasonably priced, convenient to home, [and perhaps most importantly,] because it is one of the best in the state of Kansas." In fact, the school's reputation is such that—despite its relatively remote location—PSU's MBA program attracts a substantial international student population on a consistent basis. This "strong international student community" contributes significantly to classroom instruction here.

Students may attend PSU on either a full-time or part-time basis; part-time classes are offered in Kansas City as well as on the Pittsburg campus. Either program requires a minimum of 34 course hours beyond foundation courses; some or all of the 30 hours of foundation courses may be waived for students with undergraduate degrees in business. A waiver of all 30 hours of foundation classes makes it possible to receive an MBA in 12 months. The part-time program requires a minimum of two and a half years to complete.

PSU's professors are "accessible and approachable [and] dedicated to making you work hard and learn, but doing it in a caring and fun way." One student writes, "A high ratio of PhDs teach the core courses." Like the students, "Professors come from a variety of different countries." Classes at PSU "are relatively small, allowing for good interaction between instructors and the class," which students appreciate. They also appreciate how "the administration is very supportive of the MBA program and interested in the views of the students."

PSU MBAs may earn concentrations in accounting and general administration. Although no concentration is offered in marketing, students single the discipline out for praise, telling us the school is "famous for its marketing section."

Career and Placement

According to PSU's website, the university's relationship with area businesses and its reputation for applying high admissions standards result in "an excellent record of placement of [the school's] MBA candidates." Students confirm this assertion; one writes, "I chose PSU because of its reputation for being a great business school and because of the many job opportunities that are available through PSU's career service after you graduate."

Career services are provided through the university's Career Services Office. Employers who most frequently hire PSU MBAs include Deloitte Touche Tohmatsu, PricewaterhouseCoopers, Payless ShoeSource, Core-Mark, Sprint, Hallmark, Cessna, Koch Industries, Inc., Wal-Mart, and Allstate.

Student Life and Environment

"Located in a peaceful small town," Pittsburg State offers students a lifestyle that "is pretty laid back." The university at large "not only offers excellent academic programs but also excellent entertainment programs, such as outdoor movies [and] comedians." Besides "various clubs and organizations to join for nearly any student's taste or major" and a recently remodeled student center, the school offers events such as "recitals at the music school building. There are also plays at the theater department to attend, and there are about five art exhibits, both student and traveling, per school year."

The majority of Pittsburg MBAs attend full-time, although there is also a sizable part-time population here. One student notes a distinction between the two groups: "The majority of the full-time students at my school are international students, and they tend to stick together in their own groups. Most of the American students work during the day and go to class at night." Students are typically "hardworking, goal-oriented, [and]

Jaime Vanderbeck, Administrative Officer, Graduate Studies
1701 South Broadway, Pittsburg, KS 66762-7540 United States
Phone: 620-235-4222 • Fax: 620-235-4219
E-mail: grad@pittstate.edu • Website: www.pittstate.edu/kelce

very friendly." With just over 100 MBAs in the entire program, "students know virtually everyone in the MBA program, which is nice." An MBA Association promotes the goals of MBA students and helps organize recruiting events.

Pittsburg is a town of just under 20,000. It is situated in the southeast corner of Kansas, 120 miles to the south of Kansas City. The region's rolling prairies attract outdoor enthusiasts; hunters, fishers, and hikers are all welcome. The university occupies a central role in the life of the community, providing entertainment as well as employment to the town's citizens. PSU's athletic teams, the Gorillas, receive enthusiastic support from sports fans throughout the area.

Admissions

Applicants to Pittsburg's MBA program must provide the admissions department with official copies of transcripts for all postsecondary academic work, official GMAT score reports, and a completed application to the Graduate School of PSU. International students whose first language is not English must also submit TOEFL scores. All applicants must achieve a minimum GMAT score of 400 and must receive a formula score of at least 1,050 under the formula [(undergraduate GPA × 200) + GMAT score]. Students with undergraduate degrees in non-business areas are typically required to complete foundation courses in statistics; organizational theory; marketing; business law; production management; financial and managerial accounting; MIS; business finance; and micro and macro economics prior to beginning the MBA program. Such applicants may be admitted to the program conditionally, pending successful completion of these courses.

FINANCIAL FACTS

Annual tuition (in-state/ out-of-state)	$4,288/$10,546
Cost of books	$1,200
Room & board (on/off-campus)	$4,844/$7,266
% of students receiving aid	50
% of first-year students receiving aid	25
% of students receiving loans	25
% of students receiving grants	15
Average award package	$8,500
Average grant	$3,500

ADMISSIONS

Admissions Selectivity Rating	72
# of applications received	270
% applicants accepted	76
% acceptees attending	67
Average GMAT	510
Range of GMAT	400-710
Average GPA	3.5
TOEFL required of international students	Yes
Minimum TOEFL (paper/computer)	550/213
Application fee	$35
International application fee	$60
Regular application deadline	7/15
Regular notification	8/1
Deferment available	Yes
Maximum length of deferment	1 year
Transfer students accepted	Yes
Transfer application policy Up to 9 semester hours may be transferred from another accredited program.	
Non-fall admissions	Yes
Need-blind admissions	Yes

EMPLOYMENT PROFILE

Career Rating	62	Grads Employed by Function	%	Avg. Salary
Primary Source of Full-time Job Acceptances		Marketing/Sales	24	$44,000
School-facilitated activities	43 (72%)	MIS	22	$45,000
Unknown	17 (28%)	General Management	54	$45,000
Percent employed	25	**Top 5 Employers Hiring Grads**		
		Deloitte Touche Tohmatsu; Sprint; Wal Mart; AllState.		

PORTLAND STATE UNIVERSITY
SCHOOL OF BUSINESS ADMINISTRATION

GENERAL INFORMATION
Type of school   Public

SURVEY SAYS . . .
Students love Portland, OR
Cutting-edge classes
Solid preparation in:
Accounting
General management

STUDENTS
Enrollment of parent institution	24,015
Enrollment of business school	373
% male/female	54/46
% out-of-state	16
% part-time	82
% minorities	19
% international	22
Average age at entry	30
Average years work experience at entry	5

ACADEMICS
Academic Experience Rating	**75**
Student/faculty ratio	35:1
Profs interesting rating	81
Profs accessible rating	80
% female faculty	36

Prominent Alumni
Gary Ames, former president/CEO, U.S. West; Gerry Cameron, chairman of the board (retired), U.S. Bancorp; Scott Davis, chief financial officer, UPS; Ray Guenther, northwest operations director, Intel; Darrell Webb, president, Fred Meyer/Kroger.

Academics

MBA students choose Portland State, "the acknowledged leader in MBA education in this area," for its "interdisciplinary approach to sustainable development," "location and low costs," and flexible options for "working professionals," including "evening classes" and part-time and eMBA programs. These students are not disappointed. They remark that the "well-designed" and "well-run" new MBA-plus program, which has replaced the traditional MBA, represents "a very innovative approach to developing the students' soft skills as well as technical skills." The 72-credit program consists of seven foundation courses in business perspectives and leadership development, seven courses in business disciplines including financial management and organizational management, three integrated application courses that include opportunities for business simulation and real-world consultancy, and 16 elective credits that may constitute a specialization such as finance or lead to a certificate in sustainability, real estate development, or food marketing and logistics. Some students would prefer an even "broader range of specialization areas," including a "marketing specialization program." One degree candidate says, MBA-plus "courses link together across topics very well. . . . Themes repeat across marketing, finance, accounting, operations, etc." Credits may also be accrued at study abroad programs in Marseille, Copenhagen, and Asolo, Italy. The Graduate School of Business also offers the 49-credit MSFA (Master of Science in Financial Analysis) and 65-credit, East Asia–focused MIM (Master of International Management) degrees.

Unlike at many other schools, students say they are "happy" with administrators and faculty. "On-campus operations are well run" (although "The school is still sorting out how best to run the online courses") and "Professors are intelligent, caring role models." The "few who share administrative and teaching roles" are especially "inspiring." In particular, Graduate Director and Professor Carolyn McKnight "is phenomenal. . . . She has very innovative ideas for the department based on [her] professional and academic experience," and is a proponent of the "managerial intelligence" training that characterizes the new MBA-plus program. Students differ, however, in their satisfaction with the school's material resources. Several gripe that the "aging" "facilities need updating" and the program should "streamline the technology a bit more." Others praise the technology available to students, noting, "All classrooms support multimedia presentations, and many support broadcast to and interaction with remote students."

Student Life and Environment

Student life at the School of Business Administration is defined by the cohort system in which students take all classes with a set group of peers. MBA candidates call the SBA environment "the antithesis of the Ivy: experience trumps intellect; cooperation trumps competition." The typical student, if such a person exists, is a "good-natured," youngish West Coaster with a science or techie background and "a desire to better" himself or herself rather than crush others on the way to the top. The "bright, fun, challenging, and fabulous" students do, however, reflect substantial diversity in interests and experience: "To my left is a nonprofit executive director with a donut shack on the side," demonstrates one student, and "To my right [is] a drag-show-producing math savant." Going against the grain, there are even "at least five kids in my cohort who could make—and rock—*The Apprentice*."

This high level of individuality and creativity reflects the mood and character of PSU's "great location." A small Pacific Rim city whose residents are "focused on the environment and sustainability" and attuned to their neighbors across the ocean, Portland is also the hub of Silicon Forest, a prominent high-tech region that boasts Intel and IBM corpo-

PAM MITCHELL, GRADUATE PROGRAMS ADVISOR
631 SOUTHWEST HARRISON STREET, PORTLAND, OR 97201 UNITED STATES
PHONE: 503-725-8001 • FAX: 503-725-5740
E-MAIL: MBAINFO@PDX.EDU • WEBSITE: WWW.MBA.PDX.EDU

rate garrisons. The housing costs, anything-goes lifestyle, and lush scenery compare favorably to what you'd find in Palo Alto, and SBA's Food Industry Leadership Center thrives on the agricultural wealth of the region.

Career and Placement

In order to facilitate the connections that power student job searches, the school's business-only Career Center presides over internships, mentorships with local corporate leaders, and other pre-graduation opportunities that smooth the way to job offers. One of the school's most interesting networking programs is embedded in the curriculum itself: BA 506: Business Project places MBA candidates as consultants in Portland-area businesses for an average of 4 months and average profit of about $50,000 to the organizations. Students may request projects that fulfill a particular area of specialization, such as finance or sustainability. Not surprisingly, SBA-minted MBAs often head to surrounding high-tech companies such as IBM, Intel, and Xerox.

Admissions

The program requires a bare-minimum 2.75 undergraduate GPA and 470 GMAT score, but students with numbers this low are unlikely to be admitted in the absence of substantial graduate work and/or business experience. A more realistic (and typically successful) application would include a GMAT score in the mid-600s and GPA between 3.0 and 3.5, as well as work experience. In many ways, the application requirements are more hassle-free than you might expect: For instance, PSU requires only a one-page statement of intent rather than the multiple short essay questions that fill other schools' forms.

Because PSU is a public university, residents of Oregon and bordering Washington counties receive more than 25 percent off their tuition bills. Residency criteria are strict, excluding those who have moved to Oregon to attend school; be sure you meet them before banking on in-state prices.

FINANCIAL FACTS

Annual tuition (in-state/ out-of-state)	$9,468/$15,696
Fees	$1,050
Cost of books	$1,300
Room & board	$12,000

ADMISSIONS

Admissions Selectivity Rating	**78**
# of applications received	237
% applicants accepted	76
% acceptees attending	77
Average GMAT	597
Range of GMAT	550–610
Average GPA	2.97
TOEFL required of international students	Yes
Minimum TOEFL (paper/computer)	550/213
Application fee	$50
Regular application deadline	4/1
Regular notification	5/30
Early decision program	Yes
ED Deadline/Notification	1/1 / 4/1
Transfer students accepted	Yes
Transfer application policy Maximum of 1/3 of the total number of PSU credits may transfer from a U.S.-accredited university.	
Need blind admissions	Yes

Applicants Also Look At
Oregon State University, University of Oregon, University of Portland, Willamette University.

EMPLOYMENT PROFILE			
Career Rating	**76**	**Grads Employed by Function%**	**Avg. Salary**
Primary Source of Full-time Job Acceptances		Finance/Accounting 35	$56,400
Percent employed	73	Marketing/Sales 18	$55,400
		Consulting 18	$60,000
		General Management 18	$60,000
		Other 11	$57,000

PURDUE UNIVERSITY
KRANNERT SCHOOL OF MANAGEMENT

Academics

If you are looking for a technical and progressive MBA program with strong ties to the Midwestern business community, you'll find a good match at the Krannert School of Management at Purdue University. While the program provides a thorough education in all aspects of business and management, Krannert attracts many students for its "strength and rankings of finance, operations, and quantitative methods programs." A 60-unit course of study, roughly half the MBA program is comprised of core course work. Maintaining a "strong quantitative focus" throughout the first year, students appreciate the fact that "core classes are taught by professors [who] are nationally and internationally respected in their fields." However, be prepared for the fact that the program is extremely rigid at first, as "All but two core classes occur in first year with little opportunity for electives." On top of that, students warn us that "the workload is tremendous, especially in the core classes, and there is an air of competitiveness."

Despite the challenges, don't be scared away. Students reassure us that "Krannert's program through the first year is challenging," mostly due to a heavy course load. "But as a rule, the teachers are effective in teaching the material and preparing students for the real world." Another adds, "Professors are top-notch in their fields and very approachable outside of the classroom. In fact, students routinely take advantage of a program that allows students to take their favorite professors out to lunch." On top of that, a friendly and laid-back vibe permeates the campus, despite the curricular demands. Students promise us that the program is "competitive to a point," but that most are "more concerned about getting the most out of the program than beating everyone else for the grades."

Once they have survived the core curriculum, the norm reverses in the second year, during which the "schedule is almost completely electives and is designed around the individual." Within their elective choices, students are encouraged to pursue a specialization in an area such as accounting, finance, marketing, strategic management, operations management, information systems, e-business, or human resource management. With dynamic and progressive course offerings, "Krannert also does a great job of adapting the curriculum to meet the needs of the dynamic corporate world." A student elaborates, "The leadership of the Krannert program is very much in tune with the needs of corporate America and is quick to implement necessary changes to accommodate those needs." However, some lament the fact that "no course work is aimed at not-for-profit or green learning; most material taught is aimed at manufacturing." In addition to the standard curriculum, Krannert runs a variety of special programs to keep abreast of current trends in business, including the Friday Management Development Series.

Career and Placement

Students can prepare for interviews, contact employers, research companies, and career counseling through Krannert Graduate Career Services. Students say "The companies recruiting at Purdue now are primarily the 'heavy hitters' you'd like to see;" although some international students say they could use more support in looking for positions. The mean base salary for last year's Purdue graduates was $83,661. Seventy-three percent of students also received a signing bonus with their offer of employment, averaging an additional $14,114.

CARMEN CASTRO-RIVERA, DIRECTOR OF ADMISSIONS
RAWLS HALL, ROOM 2020, 100 SOUTH GRANT STREET, WEST LAFAYETTE, IN 47907 U.S.
PHONE: 765-494-0773 • FAX: 765-494-9841 • E-MAIL: MASTERS@KRANNERT.PURDUE.EDU
WEBSITE: WWW.KRANNERT.PURDUE.EDU/PROGRAMS/MASTERS

The top employers for the class of 2006 were: Air Products, American Axle & Manufacturing, Analog Devices, Bank of America, Citigroup, Cummins, Dell, Discover Financial, Eaton, EchoStar, Eli Lilly and Company, Ford Motor Company, General Electric Company, Guidant, Hewlett-Packard, Honeywell, IBM, Intel, Johnson & Johnson, Kimberly-Clark, Liberty Mutual, Motorola, Northrop Grumman, Praxair, Procter & Gamble, Raytheon, Roche Diagnostics, United Technologies.

Student Life and Environment

At Krannert School of Management, students are "kind, smart, open and very team oriented." Students love the fact that "everyone in the program seems to follow the 'Work Hard, Work Together, Work Right' mantra that Krannert advertises." The environment is further enhanced by the professional diversity within the program, as students hail from "many different work backgrounds, including those from engineering and the sciences." A current student explains, "My peers also bring a wealth of experiences to the classroom. I have several friends in the program that served in Iraq, one who worked at a nuclear power plant, and one who ran his own business in California."

During the week, most students are busy keeping up with the heavy workload. However, they say it's not too unpleasant because "The common areas provide a great place to study and share ideas with other students. . . . There's always someone around to help you out with whatever course you're working on." When is time to relax, they don't have to look far: "Since it is a smaller program, students are all very close. There are bowling leagues, athletic clubs, and numerous social outings." In fact, "Starting Thursday night the schedule becomes a little more relaxed. There are usually group meetings over the weekends but there is still plenty of time to get recharged for the next week." On top of that, West Lafayette, Indiana, is a "small but safe college town" with "many outdoor activities" in the surrounding area.

Admissions

To apply to Krannert School of Management, all candidates must submit an official undergraduate transcript, GMAT scores, a resume, letters of recommendation, and several admissions essays. In 2006, the entering class had a mean GPA of 3.27 on a 4.0 scale, and a mean GMAT score of 661. Women comprised 29 percent of the entering class. While some students have significantly more or less professional experience before the class of 2006, the average post-college work experience was 4.4 years.

FINANCIAL FACTS

Annual tuition (in-state/ out-of-state)	$15,276/$30,010
Fees	$500
Cost of books	$1,900
Room & board (off-campus)	$7,500
% of first-year students receiving aid	54
Average award package	$18,268
Average grant	$5,500

ADMISSIONS

Admissions Selectivity Rating	87
# of applications received	765
% applicants accepted	56
% acceptees attending	34
Average GMAT	661
Range of GMAT	620–700
Average GPA	3.3
TOEFL required of international students	Yes
Minimum TOEFL (paper/computer)	575/230
Application fee	$55
Regular application deadline	3/1
Regular notification	4/15
Application Deadline/Notification	
Round 1:	11/1 / 12/15
Round 2:	1/1 / 3/1
Round 3:	3/1 / 4/15
Round 4:	5/1 / 6/15
Early decision program	Yes
ED Deadline/Notification	11/1 / 12/15
Deferment available	Yes
Maximum length of deferment	1 year
Need-blind admissions	Yes

Applicants Also Look At

Indiana University—Bloomington, The Ohio State University, The University of Chicago, University of Michigan, The University of North Carolina at Chapel Hill, University of Southern California, The University of Texas at Austin.

EMPLOYMENT PROFILE

Career Rating	88	Grads Employed by Function	%	Avg. Salary
Primary Source of Full-time Job Acceptances		Finance/Accounting	32	$80,035
Percent employed	96	Marketing/Sales	17	$82,792
		MIS	4	$82,703
		Operations/Production	17	$89,358
		Consulting	19	$87,154
		General Management	5	$85,625
		Other	2	NR

Top 3 Employers Hiring Grads
Intel; Discover Financial; Proctor & Gamble.

QUEEN'S UNIVERSITY
QUEEN'S SCHOOL OF BUSINESS

Academics

Queen's University quickly burst onto many prospective MBAs' radars in 2004, when *BusinessWeek* magazine named it the number one international MBA program. The school was no secret to Canadian and international employers, though; in fact, their high regard for Queen's MBAs contributed substantially to the lofty BW ranking.

Queen's has taken a unique route to the top: specialization. The Queen's MBA is officially called the "Queen's MBA for Science and Technology," a designation that accurately indicates the program's focus. Although the curriculum looks like that of a standard MBA program, all students and professors here have considerable backgrounds in science, mathematics, technology, and/or engineering. Their backgrounds inform every aspect of instruction and class discussion here. "The analytical strength in the class is unbelievable," students agree.

Queen's offers a great return on investment, thanks to a 12-month calendar that allows students "to return to the work force faster." Like most one-year MBAs, the Queen's MBA "is very intense and the course load is pretty heavy." A "very strong team-based learning" approach permeates all classes. All students here are assigned to a single team for the duration of the program, and "a significant portion of a student's overall marks is derived from group work." The idea is to model the team atmosphere in which students will work throughout their careers.

With between 60 and 80 students each year, Queen's runs "a very small program" that "allows the administration and students to get to know each other very well." The result is a happy student body: MBAs tell us that the "amazing administration couldn't be more helpful. It is amazingly receptive to any requests." Likewise, professors are regarded as "warm-hearted, committed, responsible, open-minded, and talented." Most of all, students appreciate the school's "excellent reputation, which is on the upswing across the world."

Career and Placement

Career and placement services to MBA students at Queen's University are provided by personal career managers, who offer "one-on-one coaching to help you explore your career options and chart your career path." Career managers assist students with practice interviews, resume counseling, and self-assessment instruments. Numerous online job postings are available through the Student Career Services Office, which also coordinates student-alumni contacts. Students appreciate the office's hard work but feel that "on-campus recruitment companies lack variety and this needs to improve." Some note that "Kingston is a small town, and that may be why we have fewer connections with companies compared with schools in big cities."

Typically, about one-fourth of Queen's MBAs find their first post-degree jobs in finance. The same number take positions with high tech and telecommunications firms. Around 16 percent go into management consulting, and just under 10 percent find work in manufacturing and bio-pharmaceuticals. About half the graduating class typically has a position by graduation day.

Student Life and Environment

Queen's one-year curriculum means "a hectic academic schedule" that leaves little free time. As one student notes, "Despite efforts to balance our lifestyles as students, our lives are school. Since the program is only one year long, our friends and families are very accepting of this fact." Life here generally consists of "classes followed by preparation assignments, exams, projects, and presentations."

There are opportunities to blow off steam, however: "the school organizes numerous social events such as a cruise and hockey games," for example. Most popular of all is the "Point Four" club, a "tradition that has the whole class going out for drinks every Thursday night. This tradition is continued in numerous cities in Canada after graduation." The origin of the club's name, incidentally, is the notion that "going out one day a week will only reduce your grade by 0.4 percent."

MBAs in this high-caliber program are "very bright and intelligent" and the community "friendly and close-knit," qualities that are assets to the team-oriented approach to learning. While some feel that "the science and technology background sometimes hinders the very technical ones who cannot think out of the box," few would argue with the assertion that everyone here is "very strong analytically and mathematically." The international nature of the student body means that "people can talk about issues in North America as easily as issues in Africa or Asia."

Admissions

Minimum requirements for admission to the Queen's MBA for Science and Technology program include: a four-year undergraduate degree in an engineering, technology, or science discipline, plus two years of relevant work experience; or, a four-year undergraduate degree in some other discipline, plus two years work experience in a science- or technology-related area. Most admitted students have an undergraduate grade point average (GPA) of at least 3.3 and a GMAT score of at least 600. Students whose first language is not English must submit a score for the TOEFL, IELTS, or MELAB. A cover letter and resume, three letters of reference, and three short-answer essays—all of which can be completed online—are also required. Applicants from the USA must obtain a student visa from the Canadian government in order to attend the school; the school warns that this process can take up to three months.

FINANCIAL FACTS

Annual tuition (in-state/ out-of-state)	$48,944/$53,161
Fees (in-state/ out-of-state)	$736/$746
Room & board	$17,340
% of students receiving aid	15
% of students receiving grants	70
Average grant	$10,000

ADMISSIONS

Admissions Selectivity Rating	60*
Average GMAT	660
Range of GMAT	560–770
TOEFL required of international students	Yes
Minimum TOEFL (paper/computer)	600/250
Application Deadline	
Round 1:	11/30
Round 2:	1/15
Round 3:	3/23
Deferment available	Yes
Maximum length of deferment	1 year
Non-fall admissions	Yes
Need-blind admissions	Yes

Applicants Also Look At
Harvard University, IMD (International Institute for Management Development), INSEAD, Massachusetts Institute of Technology, University of Toronto, University of Western Ontario Richard Ivey School of Business, York University.

EMPLOYMENT PROFILE

Career Rating	85	Grads Employed by Function	%	Avg. Salary
Primary Source of Full-time Job Acceptances		Finance/Accounting	35	$64,158
School-facilitated activities	48%	Consulting	26	$80,630
Graduate-facilitated activities	52%	Other	39	$61,557
Percent employed	87			

QUINNIPIAC UNIVERSITY
SCHOOL OF BUSINESS

Academics

The School of Business at Quinnipiac University capably serves both a part-time and a full-time MBA population. Part-time students make up about three-quarters of the MBA program and are primarily full-time working professionals, while one-quarter of the program is comprised of full-time students. The School of Business offers "extraordinary resources [and] small classes with ample instructor attention" to its MBAs.

Full-time students can complete the Quinnipiac MBA—which can be taken with either a thesis or non-thesis option—in as little as 15 months. Students who opt for the six-credit thesis research project must complete a thesis paper over the course of two semesters, under the supervision of a faculty member. Thesis topics must be approved by the department head and the director of the MBA program; theses are reviewed by the student's thesis advisor and a second faculty member. Students choosing the thesis option complete two additional electives to reach the required 12 credits of electives.

Quinnipiac offers concentrations in accounting, computer information systems, economics, finance, health care management, international business, management and marketing, as well as a new MBA Chartered Financial Analyst track and an MBA in Health Care Management. While most are "more than pleased with the learning environment and the pro-student attitude from the faculty and administrative personnel, some complain that the program is "much easier and less time consuming" than they expected, and wish for a "more competitive/demanding program." Students tell us that the faculty across departments is "very well rounded. Every teacher at the MBA level has a PhD from a top business school and business experience in the given course." They are "generally accessible and great teachers," leading to "a good all-around experience."

Career and Placement

The School of Business now has its own Career Services Office, with the Assistant Dean of Career Services specifically designated to assist students with career-related matters. Many of Quinnipiac's part-time students are concurrently employed by such prominent area concerns as Aetna, Anthem, AT&T, Blue Cross/Blue Shield, General Electric Company, the Hospital of St. Raphael, JPMorgan Chase, United Technologies, Yale New Haven Hospital, .

Student Life and Environment

Quinnipiac's MBA program makes its home in the Lender School of Business Center, whose assortment of classroom styles (tiered, semicircular, and conventional) accommodates a wide range of teaching and presentation styles. The facility also includes six breakout rooms for small meetings, two LAN rooms equipped with 24 workstations, wireless Internet access, and television monitors continually broadcasting CNBC and CNN. The school's network makes business databases available to students both on campus and at home, via the Internet. Quinnipiac's 47,000-square-foot Arnold Bernhard Library boasts a high-tech infrastructure that allows for access to numerous digital archives and online business resources. The newest resource is The Terry W. Goodwin '67 Financial Technology Center. The Center is a 1,500 square foot simulated trading room with 31 dual-monitor computer workstations. This state-of-the-art facility allows students to access real-time financial data, practice analytical finance methods, conduct trading simulations, analyze economic databases, and develop financial models.

JENNIFER BOUTIN, ASSISTANT DIRECTOR OF GRADUATE ADMISSIONS
275 MOUNT CARMEL AVENUE, AB-GRD, HAMDEN, CT 06518-1940 UNITED STATES
PHONE: 203-582-8672 • FAX: 203-582-3443
E-MAIL: GRADUATE@QUINNIPIAC.EDU • WEBSITE: WWW.QUINNIPIAC.EDU/X197.XML

Working students make up most of the part-time program; one student writes, "Each group has a different approach to course work. Those students who I have been involved with on group projects rely heavily on the more experienced students, in part because their course load is too heavy." They also rely on more experienced students because "they are young and inexperienced, and they are in graduate-level courses which require business experience to participate. They are unprepared." Fortunately, "everyone seems to support each other within the framework of a healthy competitive environment. There is diversity, respect, and always something enriching to the learning experience." Part-timers note that "there is very little social activity offered for graduate students, especially those of us who attend part-time. The school life is really focused on the undergraduate campus community." Hopefully, the relatively new Graduate Student Council will continue remedying this dearth of events

The Quinnipiac campus, set amid 400 wooded acres on the periphery of Sleeping Giant State Park, "is very beautiful. The setting of the state park sells itself; it creates a beautiful atmosphere." The bucolic location is very convenient to New Haven, which is eight miles away. New York City is one and a half hours away by train or by automobile. Boston is about two hours to the Northeast.

Admissions

Quinnipiac processes MBA applications on a rolling basis. A complete application includes official transcripts for all postsecondary academic work, a recent resume, an official GMAT score report, two letters of recommendation, and a completed application form. The Admissions Office screens applicants using the formula [(undergraduate GPA × 200) + GMAT score], with a minimum acceptable score of 1,100, a minimum undergraduate GPA of 2.7, and a minimum GMAT score of 500 generally required. Not all applicants who meet these criteria are admitted to the program. The school notes that "work experience and recommendations also are strongly considered in the process." Many Quinnipiac MBAs enter through the BS/MBA program, which is open to Quinnipiac undergraduates only; the school expects such students to have a minimum undergraduate GPA of 3.0 with at least a 3.25 GPA in their major. BS/MBA applicants with a cumulative GPA less than 3.0 are required to submit GMAT scores. International applicants must provide an official statement of sufficient financial support and, if their native language is not English, TOEFL scores.

FINANCIAL FACTS

Annual tuition	$15,525
Fees	$540
Cost of books	$600
Room & board (off-campus)	$12,798
% of students receiving aid	69
% of first-year students receiving aid	72
% of students receiving loans	57
% of students receiving grants	19
Average award package	$24,102
Average grant	$12,262
Average student loan debt	$21,578

ADMISSIONS

Admissions Selectivity Rating	79
# of applications received	93
% applicants accepted	61
% acceptees attending	95
Average GMAT	540
Range of GMAT	500–570
Average GPA	3.11
TOEFL required of international students	Yes
Minimum TOEFL (paper/computer)	575/233
Application fee	$45
International application fee	$45
Regular application deadline	Rolling
Regular notification	Rolling
Deferment available	Yes
Maximum length of deferment	1 year
Transfer students accepted	Yes
Transfer application policy 9 transfer credits allowed with equivalent graduate courses.	
Non-fall admissions	Yes
Need-blind admissions	Yes

Applicants Also Look At

Fairfield University, Rensselaer Polytechnic Institute, University of Connecticut, University of Hartford, University of New Haven.

RADFORD UNIVERSITY
COLLEGE OF BUSINESS AND ECONOMICS

Academics

The College of Business and Economics at Radford University is home to a large undergraduate population; nearly one in four RU undergrads majors in a business-related area. The much smaller MBA program capitalizes on the resources and strengths of the school's undergraduate program to provide a solid generalist graduate degree. As one student assessed the program says, "The school is affordable, and it is good for someone who does not plan on conquering the world, but rather [someone who] wants to stay in their community and better themselves," though some grads do go on to work for major firms around the world.

Because of the size of the program, MBAs at Radford enjoy "small classes with plenty of personal attention." One student notes, "after only one semester, I am already convinced going to this school was the right decision for future endeavors. Professors are easily accessible and responsive to students' needs, and the administration is very attentive." Radford's curriculum focuses on "the presentation experience" and a large dose of writing; "there are lots of challenging papers assigned," students warn. Because of the nature of the program (classes are held almost exclusively in the evening), the program tends to be a little more lecture-based and academic than others. Some feel that "they need more opportunities to work with outside companies and more real-life examples of local companies and speakers" in order to gain more practical experience within the program.

What Radford isn't is a place to forge a high degree of expertise in one area. That's because "it is a basic MBA program that does not allow for specialization." Some students see this as a drawback; one writes, "I would like more marketing courses because I would like to go into the marketing field upon graduation. This program only offers one marketing course." Others feel they are best served by the program's broad approach; one student explains, "My analytical business-diagnosing skills and presentation skills have been greatly enhanced by this MBA program." Radford's curriculum consists of eight required courses and two electives; the greatest number of electives are available in economics, finance, and management. Aggressive students can complete the degree in as little as 12 months, although some students work full-time and accordingly attend the program on a part-time basis. MBA courses are offered in two locations: the main campus in Radford, Virginia, and the Roanoke Higher Education Center in Roanoke, Virginia.

Radford's "tough but fair" professors "are excellent and even inspiring. Students find that they want to do their best work for all of them." They also "have a good sense of humor," which comes in handy during those long three-hour classes following a full work day.

Career and Placement

The Center for Experiential Learning and Career Development at Radford University offers a variety of resources to undergraduates, graduates, and alumni. These include a virtual resume, internship, and job database "where students and employers come together to post and view resumes and position openings," as well as workshops in resume and portfolio development, career fairs, and career-assessment tools. On-campus recruiters include Ameriprise Financial, DMG Securities, Ferguson Enterprises, Northwestern Mutual, State Farm, Wachovia, and the federal government.

Dr. Clarence Rose, Director, MBA Program
MBA office, Box 6956 Radford, VA 24142 United States
Phone: 540-831-5185 • Fax: 540-831-6655
E-mail: rumba@radford.edu • Website: cobe-web.asp.radford.edu

Student Life and Environment

Radford's MBA program serves two identifiable populations. One consists of full-time workers who live in the area or in nearby Roanoke. The second, which is also substantial, is made up of "students fresh from Radford undergraduate programs." Wrote one of the professional students of his younger peers, "Some of their writing skills have not been up to graduate-level quality, which can be a real problem in team situations. All of these issues should be taken care of through the admissions process."

The Radford campus "has many formally organized activities," but most students are too busy to participate. The campus is small and pretty, attributes appreciated by the school's MBAs. Those who attend classes at the Roanoke Higher Education Center tell us that "the RHEC is a newly remodeled, high tech, and comfortable facility more suited to providing an appropriate atmosphere for educating older MBA students." Students at both campuses praise the school's "excellent website, telecommunications equipment, [and] library."

Hometown Radford is a small town in the Blue Ridge Mountains; Roanoke is about 45 miles away. The area is most amenable to outdoor enthusiasts, as it provides easy access to the Appalachian Trail, the New River, and Clayton Lake. Shopping, restaurants, nightlife, and such are not in great supply, students warn, although the proximity of Roanoke helps to make up for this deficiency. Charleston, West Virginia, and Greensboro, North Carolina, are also within a reasonable driving distance.

Admissions

Admission to Radford's MBA program requires successful completion of an undergraduate degree with a minimum GPA of 2.75. Applicants must also submit an official report of GMAT scores, TOEFL scores (international students), two letters of recommendation, a resume of work experience, a personal statement of purpose, and "evidence of creativity and leadership." Also, "applicants must also have taken accredited collegiate preparation in the following foundation areas (or equivalents): fundamentals of financial accounting, fundamentals of managerial accounting, principles of economics I and II, organizational behavior, essentials of marketing, introduction to business finance, business statistics, and business calculus." Students can earn credit for some of these prerequisites through CLEP testing. Competency with computers is also a prerequisite.

FINANCIAL FACTS

Annual tuition (in-state/ out-of-state)	$7,800/$14,340
Cost of books	$1,000
Room & board	$6,218

ADMISSIONS

Admissions Selectivity Rating	**83**
# of applications received	70
% applicants accepted	65
% acceptees attending	90
Average GMAT	500
Range of GMAT	400–680
Average GPA	3.14
TOEFL required of international students	Yes
Minimum TOEFL (paper/computer)	550/213
Application fee	$40
Regular application deadline	Rolling
Regular notification	Rolling
Deferment available	Yes
Maximum length of deferment	1 year
Transfer students accepted	Yes
Transfer application policy Maximum of 6 credit hours.	
Non-fall admissions	Yes
Need-blind admissions	Yes

Applicants Also Look At
Virginia Tech.

RENSSELAER POLYTECHNIC INSTITUTE
LALLY SCHOOL OF MANAGEMENT AND TECHNOLOGY

Academics

The Rensselaer Polytechnic Institute Lally School of Management and Technology is located in Troy, New York, a historic town along the Hudson River. Once a major center of the Industrial Revolution (during the 1800s), Troy now finds itself at the center of a technological revolution. Rensselaer's sterling reputation as a school that turns out technical superstars has influenced Lally's direction. The Lally MBA program combines technological innovation and a focus on entrepreneurship in a team-oriented curriculum that cuts across all business functions.

The 50 students enrolled in the Lally MBA program appreciate being in an "entrepreneurship program friendly to those with technical backgrounds." Rensselaer's state-of-the-art facilities include the Center for Entrepreneurship, the Business Incubator Program, and the RPI tech-park, so it's no surprise that the Lally School's strength is in technological entrepreneurship. The school's mantra is that "technology creation and commercialization do not occur in an ivory tower; they happen in a competitive, increasingly global marketplace. Our students and faculty have a passion for taking ideas and turning them into real-world products." Students here concur: "Everybody at Rensselaer thinks about initiating a company." One student adds, "This makes it one of the best schools in providing a technology-driven MBA."

A few years ago, Lally introduced a dynamic new MBA curriculum that identifies five critical areas for advancing business through innovation and mimics real-world decision making. The curriculum is based on "streams of knowledge" and modeled after their signature course, "Developing Innovative Products and Services," in which student teams develop a new product or service, write a business and marketing plan, and learn how to market and sell it. Students love this program, arguing that it "prepares future business leaders and strategic thinkers. Most courses incorporate projects that are applied to real businesses in the community." Some of the groups have even taken their products to compete in the "Tech Valley Collegiate Business Plan Competition" sponsored by the school's own Severino Center for Technological Entrepreneurship. There, teams compete for the money to make their theoretical venture a reality. Some groups from these classes have "actually now established themselves as startups!" Some students point out that "even if you don't have a desire to start your own company, the experiences you gain can be used in established tech companies."

However, none of this means that traditional business school curriculum is lacking. The school has a strict core curriculum, which takes up the entire first year of the MBA program, and a summer internship is encouraged. In the second year, there are only three required classes; that year is primarily dedicated to specialization. While professors are "hit or miss" pedagogically, they're always focused on the student: "Even in the larger classes, you can tell that the professors really know who everyone is." At the moment, students would like to be allowed "more freedom to take electives" and would like to see "more seminars and more of a focus on financial market topics." And despite the assurances of most students that all the Rensselaer facilities boast top-of-the-line technology, some students would like to see Lally "upgrade some of its classrooms." Fortunately, the administration here is "bend-over-backward supportive of students and their needs. This program at Lally is growing and developing, so our input is extremely valuable. I don't know of any other school where [student] input is acted on within a semester."

PEDRO GONZALEZ, DIRECTOR OF MBA/MS ADMISSIONS AND CAREER RESOURCES
110 EIGHTH STREET, PITTSBURGH BUILDING 5100, TROY, NY 12180-3590 UNITED STATES
PHONE: 518-276-6565 • FAX: 518-276-2665
E-MAIL: LALLYMBA@RPI.EDU • WEBSITE: LALLYSCHOOL.RPI.EDU

Career and Placement

Though the emphasis at Lally is so much about creating jobs rather than looking for them, Career Services reports that they've managed to place plenty of their students. The average salary for Lally's MBA graduates in 2006 was around $66,400; 43 percent of those who completed the MBA were employed in the Northeast region of the United States; iconic companies such as IBM, GE, and 3M frequently hire Lally graduates. According to some students, the weakest link in the employment chain is Lally's "circle of alumni," which is not as involved as most current students would like.

Student Life and Environment

Including Lally's "interesting mix of nationalities, talents, and backgrounds," Troy is home to just about 55,000 people. The city benefits from its proximity to Albany, which, despite what New York City likes to believe, is still the capital of the state. And students who manage to make time in their hectic academic schedule point out that there are "tons of cultural opportunities like readings, speakers, and music on campus and in town. We have a brewpub in town making great beer. There is a good live music scene." The school, along with student-run groups, tries to facilitate student interaction as well. "We have regular social functions that get both classes together and try to involve faculty as well. Since it's a smaller program, it's pretty close knit, and a lot of students organize social activities and invite the entire class."

Admissions

Though the majority of Lally's admitted students come from some sort of technical background, 35 percent do not. The average age for an admitted student is 28, the average work experience is about 4 years, the average GMAT is 629, and the average undergraduate GPA is 3.41.

FINANCIAL FACTS

Annual tuition	$34,900
Fees	$1,802
Cost of books	$1,802
Room & board	$9,000

ADMISSIONS

Admissions Selectivity Rating	87
# of applications received	102
% applicants accepted	55
% acceptees attending	40
Average GMAT	629
Average GPA	3.41
TOEFL required of international students	Yes
Minimum TOEFL (paper/computer)	600/250
Application fee	$75
Regular application deadline	7/1
Regular notification	Rolling
Early decision program?	Yes
ED Deadline/Notification Fall semester, 1/15 / 2/15	
Deferment available	Yes
Maximum length of deferment	1 year
Need-blind admissions	Yes

Applicants Also Look At

Baboon College, Carnegie Mellon, Georgia Institute of Technology, Massachusetts Institute of Technology, New York University, State University of New York at Albany, University of Rochester.

EMPLOYMENT PROFILE

Career Rating	79	Grads Employed by Function	%	Avg. Salary
Primary Source of Full-time Job Acceptances		Finance/Accounting	20	$77,500
School-facilitated activities	3 (15%)	Marketing/Sales	20	$54,677
Graduate-facilitated activities	16 (80%)	MIS	10	$91,000
Unknown	1 (5%)	Operations/Production	5	$80,000
Percent employed	70	Consulting	25	$73,960
		General Management	10	$52,500
		Other	10	$44,000
		Top 5 Employers Hiring Grads		
		American Express Company; IBM; Xerox; Accenture; Becton-Dickinson.		

RICE UNIVERSITY
JESSE H. JONES GRADUATE SCHOOL OF MANAGEMENT

Academics

The Jones Graduate School of Management at Rice University is "one of the top schools in the world for finance" as well as "a core school for [recruiting by] most of the world's top energy companies," students in this prestigious program brag. That latter distinction has much to do with Rice's location in Houston, America's oil capital. One student explains, "If I could pick up Rice and put it anywhere in the country, I would put it right back in Houston. There are more MBA-level jobs in Houston than in many other states combined. The demand for Rice graduates in this area is incredible."

The MBA program at Rice has undergone a makeover recently, with "curriculum changes and changes to the module system. Classes are structured in 6-week modules with two modules per semester. This has reduced the pace and amount of the workload" over the previous system "and has allowed students a greater opportunity to explore extracurricular activities" In addition to its stellar offerings in finance, Rice also has "a strong entrepreneurship program" and a "great" strategy curriculum, and it "excels in accounting as well as communication." Overall this is "a very technical, quantitatively rigorous MBA" with "unbelievable facilities." One unique feature here is "the Rice Alliance program, which integrates business/science/engineering disciplines in the areas of new technology and entrepreneurship such as nanotechnology, which is a strong discipline at Rice."

Rice "is a small program, so you get the personal attention that you need," and students get to enjoy "the feel of a well-knit community. When I walk down the hall, I have to say hello to 95 percent of the people I see because I know them from somewhere or another," says one MBA. The faculty here includes "CEOs, CFOs, and board members of *Fortune* 500 companies in Houston" who "are very accessible and helpful outside of class." What's more, "The professors continue to get better" here, as "The program office and the Dean have a strong role in attracting new profs to Jones." "The new program office is very interested in the students' needs and [is] committed to working with students to make their experience better." It helps that "the administration is readily available to partner with students" on whatever they need. The administration also works hard to attract "highly touted keynote speakers" who "routinely visit the Jones school to give us the latest in business planning, experience, and analytics."

Career and Placement

The Career Management Center at Jones "has come a long way in the last couple of years. Top investment banks like Goldman Sachs, Lehman Brothers, and other bulge brackets are recruiting more Rice MBAs each year. The majority of students have two to three offers for full-time positions" upon graduation. If there is a weakness here, it is that "there is heavy emphasis on the energy industry. I would like to see more technology companies from California and financial institutions from cities like New York and Boston to come and recruit at Rice," says one MBA. In the asset column, "Recruitment from real estate firms has picked up due to word of the technical nature of the program." Students tell us "The alumni network is wonderful, and both undergrads of Rice and Rice MBA alums are more than happy to help with a job search."

Employers who most frequently hire Rice MBAs include: Citigroup, ConocoPhillips Company, Continental Airlines, Dell, Deloitte Touche Tohmatsu, Hewlett-Packard, Intel Corporation, JPMorgan Chase, Merrill Lynch, and TXU.

LISA W. ANDERSON, DIRECTOR OF ADMISSIONS
MBA ADMISSIONS, 6100 MAIN STREET, MS 531, JONES SCHOOL, PO BOX 2932,
HOUSTON, TX 77005-2932 US. • PHONE: 888-844-4773 • FAX: 713-348-6147
E-MAIL: RICEMBA@RICE.EDU • WEBSITE: WWW.JONESGSM.RICE.EDU

Student Life and Environment

"Rice doesn't feel like school, it feels like a family," students tell us, reporting that "every week, we have social network events where the faculty and professors all unwind. It's a great balance between social life and school." Those events include Partios, which are "parties on the patio every Thursday, often sponsored by recruiting companies" that draw a crowd with "free beer (yes, beer) and pizza." Another fave is the Coffee Colloquium, a free breakfast every Monday and Wednesday morning that provides "a chance to meet professors and other students. and get the latest news." Students get involved here in the "variety of student activities and professional clubs that truly contribute to the overall student experience."

Aside from the fun stuff, first-year students must deal with a "mountain of assignments, case studies, and teamwork projects" that can be "overwhelming" because "They all have to be done now!" First-year course work, in particular, can be "rough, with little available time to socialize or network off campus." "If you think your communication and presentation skills are excellent, be prepared for a lesson in humility," warns one student. The workload eases up during the second year of the program, allowing students more time to devote to such opportunities as the Wright Fund, "a student-run fund with market value of over $850,000" that gives them "hands-on and real-world knowledge in investment management."

The Jones School "is also located in the most beautiful building on the Rice University campus. With its technology, the school is a wonderful place to be stuck in working on a team project for hours on end." Students want you to know that "the general perception that Houston is an ugly city" is accurate, but also that Rice is located "in the nicest, most beautiful part of Houston, with 100-year-old oak trees that line the roads, and within walking distance to the Museum District and Rice Village. This is the ritzy, old-money area of Houston."

Admissions

Applicants to the Jones school must provide the Admissions Committee with official copies of all undergraduate and graduate transcripts, GMAT scores, two letters of recommendation, two personal essays, and a resume. An interview is also required. The school considers "leadership experience and team-based experiences" in evaluating candidates and seeks "unique qualities that the candidate will contribute to the program." International applicants must also demonstrate English proficiency and provide proof of sufficient financial support to pay for their education and expenses while studying at the Jones School. While post-undergraduate professional experience is not required, the school prefers candidates with at least 2 years of such experience.

Prominent Alumni

James S. Turley, chairman and CEO, Ernst & Young; Subha Barry, first vice president, Merrill Lynch; Keith Anderson, vice chair, BlackRock, Inc.; Doug Foshee, president and CEO, El Paso Corporation; Gretchen Lash, former president and CEO, Engemann Asset Management.

FINANCIAL FACTS

Annual tuition	$32,150
Fees	$2,058
Cost of books	$1,500
Room & board	
(on/off-campus)	$10,200/$15,000
% of students receiving aid	81
% of students receiving loans	64
% of students receiving grants	64
Average grant	$12,748
Average student loan debt	$55,222

ADMISSIONS

Admissions Selectivity Rating	89
# of applications received	437
% applicants accepted	48
% acceptees attending	50
Average GMAT	632
Range of GMAT	590–670
Average GPA	3.27
TOEFL required of	
international students	Yes
Minimum TOEFL	
(paper/computer)	600/250
Application fee	$100
Regular application deadline	3/26
Regular notification	5/1
Application Deadline/Notification	
Round 1:	11/13 / 12/22
Round 2:	1/22 / 3/15
Round 3:	3/26 / 5/1
Deferment available	Yes
Maximum length of	
deferment	1 year
Need-blind admissions	Yes

Applicants Also Look At

Boston University, Georgetown University, Southern Methodist University, Texas A&M University System Health Science Center, The University of Texas at Austin, Vanderbilt University, Wake Forest University—Babcock.

EMPLOYMENT PROFILE

Career Rating	92	Grads Employed by Function	%	Avg. Salary
Primary Source of Full-time Job Acceptances		Finance/Accounting	52	$88,121
School-facilitated activities	54 (49%)	Marketing/Sales	13	$80,826
Graduate-facilitated activities	55 (51%)	Operations/Production	4	$89,150
Percent employed	86	Consulting	17	$94,812
		General Management	14	$78,138

Top 5 Employers Hiring Grads

Chevron; FMC Technologies; BearingPoint; ExxonMobil; DataCert.

ROCHESTER INSTITUTE OF TECHNOLOGY
E. PHILIP SAUNDERS COLLEGE OF BUSINESS

GENERAL INFORMATION

Type of school	Private
Environment	City
Academic calendar	Quarter

SURVEY SAYS . . .
Cutting-edge classes
Smart classrooms

STUDENTS

Enrollment of parent institution	15,557
Enrollment of business school	304
% male/female	62/38
% out-of-state	22
% part-time	39
% minorities	8
% international	38
Average age at entry	26
Average years work experience at entry	4

ACADEMICS

Academic Experience Rating	**66**
Profs interesting rating	72
Profs accessible rating	85
% female faculty	19
% minority faculty	5

Academics

Rochester Institute of Technology is among the nation's top engineering/science schools, so it should come as no surprise that the RIT MBA "concentrates on both business and technology," with a "practical, rather than theoretical, structure and philosophy" that students find appealing. RIT's "blend of engineering and business for the MBA program" results in "course material that is highly applicable to existing industry issues," students tell us.

RIT's approach to getting students in and out of the program is every bit as practical as its approach to curriculum. One MBA reports, "The school has practices in place that allow you to get your degree more quickly. It recognizes undergraduate course work for waiving courses, for example, and it has programs in place where you can get your degree in 1 year (full-time). Also, the program is structured in a way that makes it easier for people who are working full-time to get their degree" by allowing them to place out of foundation courses through examination. Part-timers tell us the program "is very well structured to our needs. Almost all classes are in the evening (or at least offered in the evening), and because other students are in a similar situation, professors and teammates are used to being flexible with meeting times." The only impediment to total convenience, students tell us, is that required courses for concentrations aren't offered as frequently as they might be. "Many are only offered once a year, making it difficult to schedule them," warns one MBA.

RIT's MBA curriculum "heavily utilizes case studies, which is nice." A quarterly academic schedule "is fast, competitive, and very challenging," but students generally like the way it keeps the curriculum moving quickly forward. Students also appreciate "the heavy focus on technology" (RIT has "great facilities with first-rate technology" to support this focus) and "the almost endless possibilities to combine concentrations and classes." Entrepreneurship and market research earn students' approval; unique offerings here include environmentally sustainability management, software project management, and telecommunications.

Career and Placement

RIT provides placement and counseling services through the university-wide Office of Cooperative Education and Career Services. Students tell us that their job searches are abetted by the school's great reputation; one MBA reports, "I am getting calls for jobs because I have RIT on my resume. I was hired for my current job by an RIT alum (didn't know it before the interview, though)." The alumni network is universally praised for its assistance during and after the program. Students are less uniform in their praise of the placement office, telling us that job fairs "are too heavily weighted toward tech and government employers looking for only one or two hires. Not enough companies [are] looking for business employees."

Employers who recently hired RIT MBAs include: Bausch & Lomb, Bose, Capital One Financial Services, Cypress Semiconductor Corporation, Danka Office Imaging Company, Deloitte Touche Tohmatsu, Eastman Kodak, Fluor, Frontier Corporation, General Electric Company, Global Crossing, Heidelberg Digital, Hewlett-Packard, IBM, Lockheed Martin, Motorola, Paychex, PricewaterhouseCoopers, Proctor & Gamble, Prudential Securities, RCN Telecom Services, and Xerox.

DIANE ELLISON, DIRECTOR, PART-TIME AND GRADUATE ENROLLMENT
105 LOMB MEMORIAL DRIVE, ROCHESTER, NY 14623 UNITED STATES
PHONE: 585-475-7284 • FAX: 585-475-5476
E-MAIL: GRADINFO@RIT.EDU • WEBSITE: WWW.RITMBA.COM

Student Life and Environment

Under RIT's quarterly calendar, "The general course load is three classes. Some people take four, but that makes it hard to really learn the stuff without getting overworked." Classes here "are generally taught at night (6:00 P.M. to 9:20 P.M.) once a week. Some courses are also taught during the daytime, and some are even offered online." The school's facility "has recently been extensively remodeled and is beautiful. It has a lot of glass on the front of the first floor, new computer labs, new wall coverings and flooring, and more solid oak trim." Students "meet before class and socialize in the lounge on the first floor or in the graduate student lounge on the second floor. Students also gather before class around the lounge chairs that are interspersed in the upstairs hallways and discuss course work." They also bond through "the many clubs that are available to all," although many are too busy with work and personal obligations to participate. Hometown Rochester "is a lot of fun" with "a great downtown life," although "The local weather is awful." Diversions include "skiing, bars, parks, casinos, and day trips" to Buffalo and Canada.

RIT students include a large number who come "straight from undergraduate programs, meaning they are not always able to contribute that much practical knowledge to class discussion." They are "smart, friendly, and motivated without being overly competitive." The program is "evenly split between full-time and part-time, evenly split between men and women, and evenly split between American and international."

Admissions

RIT accepts applications to its MBA program for all four quarters; most full-time students enter the program in the fall. Online application is available. All applicants must have an undergraduate degree from an accredited university or college and must be able to demonstrate proficiency in algebra, statistics, and computer literacy. A completed application includes an official copy of the applicant's undergraduate transcript, an official GMAT score report, a current resume, and a personal statement. International students whose transcripts are not in English must have their transcripts translated and interpreted by an accredited service. They must also submit an official score report for the TOEFL.

FINANCIAL FACTS

Annual tuition	$26,901
Fees	$483
Cost of books	$1,500
Room & board (on-campus)	$10,000
% of students receiving aid	24
% of first-year students receiving aid	32
% of students receiving grants	24
Average grant	$10,644

ADMISSIONS

Admissions Selectivity Rating	**75**
# of applications received	254
% applicants accepted	84
% acceptees attending	62
Average GMAT	598
Range of GMAT	540–650
Average GPA	3
TOEFL required of international students	Yes
Minimum TOEFL (paper/computer)	580/237
Application fee	$50
Regular application deadline	8/1
Regular notification	Rolling
Deferment available	Yes
Maximum length of deferment	1 year
Transfer students accepted	Yes
Transfer application policy Transfer up to 3 courses if relevant to program; grade of B or better.	
Non-fall admissions	Yes
Need-blind admissions	Yes

ROLLINS COLLEGE
CRUMMER GRADUATE SCHOOL OF BUSINESS

GENERAL INFORMATION

Type of school	Private
Environment	Town
Academic calendar	Semester

SURVEY SAYS . . .

Cutting-edge classes
Solid preparation in:
Presentation skills
Quantitative skills
Computer skills

STUDENTS

Enrollment of parent institution	3,478
Enrollment of business school	526
% male/female	65/35
% out-of-state	28
% part-time	72
% minorities	12
% international	16
Average age at entry	26
Average years work experience at entry	3

ACADEMICS

Academic Experience Rating	**86**
Student/faculty ratio	20:1
Profs interesting rating	89
Profs accessible rating	97
% female faculty	13
% minority faculty	13

Academics

With an "excellent reputation" in the region, a "great alumni network" and "strong connections to central Florida businesses including Walt Disney World, Darden Restaurants, Morgan Stanley, SunTrust and Universal Orlando," and "numerous global projects," the Rollins MBA has a lot to offer America's future business tycoons. And with four separate programs—each geared to the needs of a distinct demographic—just about anyone and everyone, from the business neophyte to the experienced manager, can benefit.

Rollins' sole full-time MBA program is its early advantage MBA (EAMBA), which is aimed primarily at recent college grads with little or no work experience—although working stiffs on sabbatical are also welcome. The school also offers three part-time programs: the professional MBA, open to anyone currently employed full-time; the Saturday MBA, designed for mid- to senior-level professionals (minimum 5 years of work experience required); and the executive MBA, which meets on alternate Fridays and Saturdays and is open only to those with at least 10 years of professional experience.

Students in all programs praise the "wonderful faculty," who bring a lot to the table with "a high level of professionalism, competence, and real-world experience," as well as their "down-to-earth personalities. They're willing to go the extra mile to assist students." MBAs also appreciate that the curriculum "allows business students to be creative. How often do you get to hear of students having fun and being creative at business school? At Rollins it happens." International business is one of the program's main focal points; each year about 130 students participate in 12-week international consulting projects.

Crummer promotes "numerous presentations and meetings with business leaders" to the great benefit of students; those in the part-time programs, however, note that these events typically occur at times inconvenient to students with full-time jobs. In the EAMBA, students tell us they benefit from "a team environment that helps prepare students for the real world." Team spirit is built from the beginning of the program, as students endure the grueling core curriculum in cohorts. MBAs also praise "the wide range of available courses and a good number of concentrations for a school of this size. Academics are rigorous."

Career and Placement

The Career Management Center handles placement services for Rollins MBAs, offering a variety of in-person and online counseling and recruiting services. In 2006, the mean salary for a graduating EAMBA was $60,000; the median salary was $50,000. That's not bad for a group that typically enters the program with no real work experience.

Top employers of Crummer MBAs include: The Walt Disney Company, Radiant, CNL Group, FedEx, Harris Corporation, Johnson & Johnson, Marriott International, Darden Restaurant Group, AT&T, Siemens Westinghouse, CIA, Dynetech, Citigroup, Universal Studios, General Mills, Tupperware, and SunTrust Bank. Students are generally satisfied with the school's ties to the business community, its alumni connections, and its recruiting efforts, although some complain that "we don't get enough recruiting companies outside of banking, financial services, and Disney."

STEPHEN GAUTHIER, ASSOCIATE DEAN
1000 HOLT AVENUE, #2722, WINTER PARK, FL 32789-4499 UNITED STATES
PHONE: 407-646-2405 • FAX: 407-646-2522
E-MAIL: MBAADMISSIONS@ROLLINS.EDU • WEBSITE: WWW.CRUMMER.ROLLINS.EDU

Student Life and Environment

Full-time students at Crummer report that "there is a real sense of belonging and inclusion at the business school. Through the wide range of student-run organizations, our students network with business professionals, volunteer in the community, develop themselves professionally, and socialize with each other." The school provides "plenty of activities and speakers on campus," most often "scheduled around lunchtime so students do not have to leave the business school." Students tell us that "these are great networking events, as well as being informative." Once classes are over, students enjoy "a very social atmosphere on and around campus. Rollins is located on a beautiful campus in a great town where there is lots of shops, restaurants, and fun things to do. It's a great environment to be in."

Part-time students, naturally, are not as involved in campus life, since "Everyone in our program has a full-time job and does not have a lot of time for outside the classroom activities. Still, most students have found ways to get involved in one way or another." Part-timers tell us that many of them "try to get to class early, sometimes even 30 minutes early to set up our computers and chat with the professors, who are always around. This helps with networking and camaraderie." Regardless of their program, students tell us that "classes are intense but interesting. You really need to be prepared, or you can easily get called out by your professor or fellow students for not putting the needed prep work in. Even subjects like accounting are taught from the perspective of the skills a business executive would need to use."

Admissions

Applicants to Crummer's EAMBA program must provide the school with the following: official transcripts for all undergraduate, graduate, and professional school work; an official GMAT score report; personal essays; two 'confidential evaluations' (letters of recommendation); and a resume. Interviews are conducted at the school's invitation only. Applicants to the executive MBA program must meet all of the above requirements in addition to a required interview, and they must also submit proof of their employer's support for their participation. PMBA and SMBA applicants must interview as part of the application process as well.

FINANCIAL FACTS

Annual tuition	$26,800
Fees	$60
Cost of books	$2,200
Room & board (off-campus)	$15,000
% of students receiving aid	50
% of first-year students receiving aid	48
% of students receiving grants	50
Average award package	$15,154
Average grant	$15,154
Average student loan debt	$28,900

ADMISSIONS

Admissions Selectivity Rating	80
# of applications received	190
% applicants accepted	62
% acceptees attending	67
Average GMAT	571
Range of GMAT	510–650
Average GPA	3.2
TOEFL required of international students	Yes
Application fee	$50
Regular application deadline	Rolling
Regular notification	Rolling
Deferment available	Yes
Maximum length of deferment	1 year
Transfer students accepted	Yes
Transfer application policy	
The school accepts up to 6 credits transferred from an MBA program that is accredited by the AACSB.	
Non-fall admissions	Yes
Need-blind admissions	Yes

Applicants Also Look At

Florida State University, Stetson University, University of Central Florida, University of Florida, University of Miami, Vanderbilt University, Wake Forest University.

EMPLOYMENT PROFILE

Career Rating	78	Grads Employed by Function	%	Avg. Salary
Primary Source of Full-time Job Acceptances		Finance/Accounting	52	$53,800
School-facilitated activities	68%	Marketing/Sales	25	$50,000
Graduate-facilitated activities	32%	MIS	5	NR
		Operations/Production	2	$60,000
		Consulting	7	NR
		General Management	5	$300,000
		Other	4	$51,000

ROWAN UNIVERSITY
THE ROHRER COLLEGE OF BUSINESS

GENERAL INFORMATION
Type of school	Public
Academic calendar	Semester

SURVEY SAYS . . .
Cutting-edge classes
Solid preparation in:
Communication/interpersonal skills
Presentation skills

STUDENTS
Enrollment of business school	79
% male/female	56/44
% part-time	80
% international	13
Average age at entry	29

ACADEMICS
Academic Experience Rating	**74**
Student/faculty ratio	16:1
Profs interesting rating	76
Profs accessible rating	86
% female faculty	40
% minority faculty	32

Academics

Rowan University's MBA program, the school tells us, "offers a variety of course scheduling options for both part-time and full-time students." "As working adults, we have been treated like valued customers," one student notes, pointing out that the once-a-week, three-hour classes (mostly week nights, with some classes held on Saturday mornings) best fit her busy work schedule. Because most students attend part-time, a Rowan degree usually takes between three and six years to complete; those enrolled full-time have the option of completing the program in a single year.

The Rowan MBA curriculum commences with 27 hours of required core courses covering fundamental general-management skills and concludes with an integrative capstone seminar. The curriculum also leaves room for nine hours of electives; students may choose to take a variety of courses that match their career needs or may use these courses to specialize in finance, accounting, management marketing, or entrepreneurship. MBAs tell us that "every class involves group work, which teaches students to work well with each other and share work. This skill set has helped in the workforce as well." They also wish the school would expand its selection of electives; one student observes, "Rowan could offer specializations in some different tracks, such as human resources and marketing. This would help the program grow."

The program has been growing in recent years, a fact that students acknowledge and appreciate. The school recently earned AACSB accreditation, placing it among the nation's top programs. Students tell us that "there has been an increase in the quality of the program, and [they] were delighted when the Rowan program was accredited in 2003. Enrollment has increased, and [they] see a great future for Rowan's MBA program." One graduating BA/MBA student told us that "although the program started at a low level, it is now getting tougher and tougher to get into." The increased standards, we're told, have paid dividends in more challenging classes and more illuminating in-class discussions.

Rowan MBAs love that "we are able to access the library's databases from our home computers. It's great to be able to look up material 24/7. Also, online and tele-registrations have reduced the hassle of registering to zero." Technology remains in the spotlight in the classroom; "Rowan teaches computer skills that have proven invaluable in the workforce," students tell us, although they also complain that "the audiovisual capabilities are terrible in all but one classroom. It is a very limiting feature when trying to receive information or do presentations." Overall, students feel that Rowan "is a great regional school whose current programs and commitment to expansion of the program will continue to take great strides in drawing students from outside this region."

Career and Placement

Rowan maintains a Career and Academic Planning Center "to provide developmental advising" to all students in their pursuit of academic and professional goals. The CAPC serves the entire school; there is no office dedicated specifically to MBAs or to business students on the undergraduate and graduate levels. CAPC Services include one-on-one counseling, workshops, online self-assessment and job databases (CampusRecruiter, Career Key), career publications, and employer directories. Services are available to alumni as well as to current students. It should be noted that most current students are full-time workers looking to advance within their current places of work; relatively few students seeking MBAs are actively searching for new jobs.

Student Life and Environment

Because Rowan serves mostly part-time students almost exclusively, its student body is more "a collection of people that get together in the evening for three hours" than a coherent and cohesive community. That's not to say the opportunities to socialize and network aren't there; as one BA/MBA student explains, "As an undergraduate, I found many activities that were available to students who lived on and off campus. I enjoyed my four years living on campus. Rowan had activities for everyone, including day and evening events, student government, community-service efforts, fraternities, and campus-wide events. As a graduate student, however, I am a working professional, so I do not have any time to participate in the activities available."

Rowan's suburban New Jersey home town of Glassboro is a mere half-hour's drive from Philadelphia; the Jersey shore is less than an hour to the east, and Atlantic City is only 50 miles away. New York; Washington, DC; and the Chesapeake are all within easy travel distances. The Rowan campus is in the middle of an ambitious expansion program, with makeovers planned for most facilities and several new buildings going up. Students praise the new athletic center and enjoy watching Rowan's Division III excellent men's and women's basketball teams.

Admissions

Rowan's graduate b-students are required to complete seven foundation courses, or their undergraduate. Those courses are foundations of accounting, statistics I, principles of finance, principles of marketing, calculus, operations management, and global perspective on economics. Applicants to the MBA program must submit official transcripts for all undergraduate work (with a minimum GPA of 2.5. overall or 2.8 for final 60 semester hours), GMAT or GRE scores, two letters of recommendation, a personal statement of career objectives, evidence of computer proficiency, and a resume. International students whose first language is not English must also provide TOEFL (or equivalent) scores.

FINANCIAL FACTS

Annual tuition	$9,882
Fees	$1,888
Cost of books	$700
Room & board (on-campus)	$6,044

ADMISSIONS

Admissions Selectivity Rating	**75**
# of applications received	58
% applicants accepted	71
% acceptees attending	78
Average GMAT	534
Range of GMAT	460–650
Average GPA	3.28
TOEFL required of international students	Yes
Minimum TOEFL (paper/computer)	550/213
Application fee	$50
Regular application deadline	Rolling
Regular notification	Rolling
Deferment available	Yes
Maximum length of deferment	1 year
Transfer students accepted	Yes
Transfer application policy Student may transfer up to 9 credit hours.	
Non-fall admissions	Yes
Need-blind admissions	Yes

Applicants Also Look At

Rutgers, The State University of New Jersey.

RSM Erasmus University

Academics

Future international business moguls choose RSM Erasmus for two simple reasons: The school provides "the most international MBA" experience in the world, and Rotterdam is in the heart of the EEC, with "easy access" to Germany and the "EU labor market." RSM provides a "very challenging, positive learning environment," but its intensive 15-month MBA program is not for the faint of heart. The "workload is heavy," and the curriculum is front loaded (students take 11 general management courses in the first two semesters). During this period, the day "starts at 9:30 A.M. with classes and ends at 7:00 P.M. with some group work or . . . [an] assignment." Overworked students take comfort in the fact that their professors are "excellent! They clearly enjoy teaching their subject matters, and because they are from all over the world, we get different perspectives in class." Students also point out that "the small class size means we have more opportunities to form close relationships with the program staff." During the third semester, students choose an advanced course from one of four areas of specialization (finance, marketing, strategy, or IT), then plunge into a summer associateship. The final semester is an elective curriculum; about a third of students fulfill these credits in one of 30 international exchange programs. All academic work in residency at RSM is conducted in English.

With one eye trained on the executive job market and the other on skill development and business knowledge, Rotterdam is what "b-school should be"; that is, "practical and academic at the same time." The Personal Leadership Development program, a mandatory 15-month experiential course, adds additional value. One student sums it up: "In hindsight I would not have gone to any other business school. RSM offers the right balance of soft and hard skills." "The school [also] has a strong sense of social responsibility." "I am now equipped to be a stronger and more sensitive businessperson," writes one satisfied student.

Career and Placement

Students say RSM's "Career Services Department is currently understaffed. They are encouraging, but they lack manpower." For less-motivated students, this might "be an issue." Regardless, RSM Erasmus MBAs can look forward to bright and lucrative careers. While the school is responsible for connecting students with about three-quarters of internships and half of post-MBA jobs, students also find significant career opportunities within the alumni network and elsewhere. Top employers of RSM grads are ABN Amro, Barclays Capital, Campina, Coca-Cola, Eli Lilly and Company, General Electric Company, Hewlett-Packard, ING, Interbrand, Johnson & Johnson, KPN, L'Oréal, McKinsey & Company, Novartis, Orange, Philips, Reckitt Benckiser, Roland Berger, Strategy Consultants, Shell Oil Company, and Siemens Business Services. Newly minted grads report a mean base salary of $104,426, with women earning slightly more than men.

Student Life and Environment

RSM "Students form a strong and very connected group," students say. "Everyone is automatically a member of every club. It's your responsibility to contribute as much or as little to the events. For example, though you may not be in any entrepreneurial courses, you are automatically invited to [hear] every entrepreneurial speaker on campus. And once you arrive, you are welcome in the room." The collegial atmosphere is "perfect and wonderful," says one MBA candidate. "I'd like to go back to the first semester and to start again." Even so, students are "extremely driven." "Almost half want to be entre-

RICK RUDOLPH, SENIOR MARKETING AND ADMISSIONS MANAGER
BURGEMEESTER OUDLAAN 50, J BUILDING 3062 PA ROTTERDAM, NETHERLANDS
PHONE: 011-31-10-4082222 • FAX: 011-31-10-4529509
E-MAIL: MBA.INFO@RSM.NL • WEBSITE: WWW.RSM.NL/MBA

preneurs or have owned businesses." RSM's "inspiring and challenging" students don't shrink from competition or from giving "positive and constructive criticism."

Diversity is no afterthought here—it's the reason MBA candidates choose RSM. Students say that the "international perspective was a big draw. Several other [schools] claimed to be international, but mostly had over 50 percent from one or two backgrounds." RSM, on the other hand, "has 42 nationalities and only small clusters from the same backgrounds." This means that students learn "a lot from classmates," and "There is no ruling racial group in our class." "It is just great!" enthuses one student. "A mix of cultures brings so many good things out of each student that it is almost like magic. The amount of kindness that I've experienced is just overwhelming." Demographically speaking, students are overwhelmingly European and Asian, with large Indian and Taiwanese communities; the average student is in his or her late 20s, with an undergraduate background in business or economics and more than 5 years of pre-MBA work experience. A quarter of MBA candidates are women. Partners and spouses "have banded together" to form "a supportive network," "and routinely have nights out on the town."

Admissions

RSM Erasmus admits more than half of all its applicants—good news to the self-selected pool of MBA candidates whose passion for international business and culture brings them to RSM. Admission is no cakewalk—successful applicants report an average GMAT score of 620 and a minimum of 2 years' work experience—but the numbers give good reason for optimism. The most recent application requires essays on career goals, hobbies and interests, and difficult decisions—slightly more personal topics than appear on American applications. Submit translations of your academic transcripts if they are written in languages other than Dutch and English, and prepare for an interview if you make the first cut. Admission is rolling.

FINANCIAL FACTS

Annual tuition	$46,752
Cost of books	$800
% of students receiving aid	35
% of first-year students receiving aid	35
% of students receiving loans	16
% of students receiving grants	19
Average award package	$22,645
Average grant	$12,440

ADMISSIONS

Admissions Selectivity Rating	83
# of applications received	447
% applicants accepted	53
% acceptees attending	47
Average GMAT	620
Range of GMAT	580–720
Minimum TOEFL (paper/computer)	600/250
Application fee	$50
Regular application deadline	7/15
Regular notification	Rolling
Need-blind admissions	Yes

EMPLOYMENT PROFILE

Career Rating	87	Grads Employed by Function	%	Avg. Salary
Primary Source of Full-time Job Acceptances		Finance/Accounting	22	NR
School-facilitated activities	37 (49%)	Human Resources	1	NR
Graduate-facilitated activities	35 (47%)	Marketing/Sales	25	NR
Unknown	3 (4%)	MIS	4	NR
Average base starting salary	$104,426	Operations/Production	5	NR
		Consulting	32	NR
		General Management	10	NR
		Other	1	NR
		Top 5 Employers Hiring Grads		
		ABN Amro; McKinsey & Company; Mittal Steel; A.T. Kearney; Accenture.		

RUTGERS, THE STATE UNIVERSITY OF NEW JERSEY
RUTGERS BUSINESS SCHOOL—NEWARK AND NEW BRUNSWICK

GENERAL INFORMATION
Type of school	Public
Academic calendar	Trimester

SURVEY SAYS . . .
Friendly students
Good peer network
Helpful alumni
Happy students
Smart classrooms
Solid preparation in:
Communication/interpersonal skills
Presentation skills

STUDENTS
Enrollment of parent institution	50,000
Enrollment of business school	1,494
% male/female	65/35
% out-of-state	9
% part-time	75
% minorities	17
% international	28
Average age at entry	27
Average years work experience at entry	4

ACADEMICS
Academic Experience Rating	**83**
Student/faculty ratio	15:1
Profs interesting rating	76
Profs accessible rating	93
% female faculty	23
% minority faculty	4

Joint Degrees
MPH/MBA, MD/MBA, JD/MBA,
MS/MBA (Biomedical Sciences)
MPP/MBA, MCRP/MBA.

Prominent Alumni
Thomas A. Renyi, chairman and
CEO, The Bank of New York; Gary
Cohen, president, Becton-Dickinson
Medical; Irwin M. Lerner, chairman
of the board (retired), Hoffmann-La
Roche; Nicholas J. Valeriani, world-
wide chairman, Johnson &
Johnson; Ralph Izzo, president and
COO, PSE&G.

Academics

A "renowned international business program," "marketing professors who are well-known in their respective fields," and perhaps most of all "a top-rated pharmaceutical MBA program" draw a strong applicant pool to the MBA program at Rutgers Business School. The school's location "in a metropolitan area with easy access to New York City and Philadelphia" is another one of Rutgers' prized assets. But for many New Jersey natives, the low in-state tuition is the greatest attraction; coupled with the quality of the program, the cost of attending RBS allows Garden Staters to realize a substantial return on investment here.

A full-time Rutgers MBA requires a minimum of 60 class-hour credits. The newly revised full-time curriculum being introduced in fall 2007 includes 19 credits of core courses, 6 credits of foundation courses, 3 credits in interfunctional management, and 32 credits of electives. The part-time curriculum varies slightly from the full-time curriculum but follows the same general approach. Concentrations are available in six primary disciplines, including finance, management and global business, information technology, marketing, pharmaceutical management and supply chain management.

Students love the fact that Rutgers offers "terrific professors who know real-life situations and bring that experience to the classroom," and "an administration that is constantly active and involved." "Proximity to New York City" and "connections within the pharmaceutical industry" translate into plenty of job opportunities for graduates. The school's website boasts that the region "has the highest concentration of corporate headquarters for U.S. metro areas of comparable size." Part-time students appreciate that "the workload is perfect—not too overwhelming, but still substantial. We learn a lot and I feel that we will be well prepared when we graduate."

Career and Placement

The Office of Career Management provides counseling and placement services to Rutgers' full-time and part-time MBAs as well as to alumni of the program. Students report that the office provides "great career forums that network students with alumni." In 2005, students completing their first year in the program found summer internships in the following industries: pharmaceutical, 50 percent; finance and health care, 10 percent each; manufacturing, technology, and telecommunications, 6 percent each; consumer goods, government, nonprofit, and real estate, 3 percent each. Recent employers of Rutgers MBAs include The Bank of New York, Becton Dickinson, Bristol-Myers Squibb, Celgene Corp., Citigroup, Church & Dwight, Daiichi Sankyo, Deloitte Touche Tohmatsu, Dendrite International, Ethicon, Inc., Hoffman-La Roche, Johnson & Johnson, Kraft Foods, KPMG International, Lockheed Martin, Merrill Lynch, Novartis, Pfizer, Praxair, Reckitt Benckiser, Sanofi-Aventis, Siemens Corp., Strategyx, Stryker, Tyco International USA.

RITA GALEN, DIRECTOR OF ADMISSIONS
190 UNIVERSITY AVENUE, NEWARK, NJ 07102-1813 UNITED STATES
PHONE: 973-353-1234 • FAX: 973-353-1592
E-MAIL: ADMIT@BUSINESS.RUTGERS.EDU • WEBSITE: WWW.BUSINESS.RUTGERS.EDU

Student Life and Environment

Rutgers Business School boasts an extremely diverse student body. Women constitute more than one-third the population here—an unusually high proportion for an American MBA program. The international population is substantial: 40 countries are represented among the graduate business student population. Students tell us that their peers "come from greatly diverse backgrounds, both culturally and professionally" and that "although they are competitive, they are always willing to help one another." Approximately 25 percent of the student body attends full-time. The majority part-timers tell us that "social contact is limited, as people are tired after work and want to go home. We are very busy juggling work, school, and family (those of us who have one). Involvement outside of class is usually limited to one study group per class per week."

Full-time classes are offered at the Rutgers' Newark campus; part-time classes are available at the two main campuses in Newark and New Brunswick and also at satellite sites in Jersey City, Morristown, and Princeton. New Brunswick is among the nation's premier health care centers, providing an optimal setting for the school's health-related programs. Newark is a large city located about a half hour away from central Manhattan by train. New Jersey Transit makes travel to and from New York City relatively easy, convenient, and affordable. It certainly beats driving in the area.

Admissions

The admissions committee serving the Rutgers MBA program gives primary consideration to evidence of academic promise. Undergraduate transcripts and transcripts for any graduate work are scrutinized both for the student's performance in class and for the quality and rigor of the program pursued. GMAT scores also figure into the committee's assessment of a candidate's readiness. Admissions officers also consider applicants' professional history, recommendations from supervisors, evidence of leadership and civic involvement, and the personal essay. The school "seeks a diverse student body to bring to the classroom varying experiences and backgrounds;" appraisal of students' personal histories allows it to achieve this goal. Applicants must submit a completed application form, official transcripts for all postsecondary academic work, an official GMAT score report, a current resume, two letters of professional reference, and an essay. International applicants must meet all of the above requirements and must submit an official score report for the TOEFL, professional translations of all transcripts not in English, and appropriate financial documentation.

FINANCIAL FACTS

Annual tuition (in-state/ out-of-state)	$18,930/$31,494
Fees	$1,448
Cost of books	$3,000

ADMISSIONS

Admissions Selectivity Rating	88
# of applications received	229
% applicants accepted	52
% acceptees attending	49
Average GMAT	639
Range of GMAT	590–690
Average GPA	3.3
TOEFL required of international students	Yes
Minimum TOEFL (paper/computer)	600/250
Application fee	$60
Regular application deadline	5/1
Regular notification	Rolling
Deferment available	Yes
Maximum length of deferment	1 year
Transfer students accepted	Yes
Transfer application policy Students may transfer a maximum of 18 applicable credits earned in an MDA program at an AACSB-accredited school with a B or better.	
Non-fall admissions	No
Need-blind admissions	Yes

Applicants Also Look At

City University of New York—Baruch College, Fordham University, New York University, Pennsylvania State University, Seton Hall University.

EMPLOYMENT PROFILE

Career Rating	69	Grads Employed by Function	%	Avg. Salary
Primary Source of Full-time Job Acceptances		Finance/Accounting	31	$71,455
School-facilitated activities	23 (62%)	Marketing/Sales	37	$83,254
Graduate-facilitated activities	14 (38%)	MIS	3	$110,000
Average base starting salary	$78,852	Operations/Production	23	$77,625
Percent employed	90	Consulting	3	$85,000
		General Management	3	$75,000

Top 5 Employers Hiring Grads

Johnson & Johnson; Hoffman-La Roche; Bristol-Meyers Squibb; StrategyX; Church and Dwight.

RUTGERS, THE STATE UNIVERSITY OF NEW JERSEY—CAMDEN
SCHOOL OF BUSINESS

Academics

Located just across the Benjamin Franklin Bridge from Philadelphia, the School of Business MBA program at Rutgers—Camden offers a convenient and affordable graduate degree option for both Garden State and City of Brotherly Love residents. This small program consists almost entirely of part-time students pursuing degrees while simultaneously engaging in careers and, quite often, starting families.

Fortunately for these busy students, "Professors and administrators bend over backward for the students to ensure they are achieving their educational goals" by "making themselves very accessible. Their main priority is ensuring that we understand everything gone over in class and can apply it to the real world." Students here also appreciate that "classes are well organized and there are many opportunities to enroll in unique courses that include exposure to industry professionals." On the downside, some here feel that "expectations for student performance are too low in general and the amount of material covered is not enough to feel really comfortable in a number of areas."

The Rutgers MBA consists of 57 credits, 36 devoted to the core curriculum and 21 to electives. The school website notes, "Some course requirements may be waived based upon prior knowledge gained at the undergraduate level." Students may combine three electives to create a concentration in one of the following disciplines: accounting, e-commerce technology, finance, international business, health care management, management, operations management/management science, or marketing. Concentrations in international business and health care management piggyback on other divisions of the university, allowing students to gain exposure to the School of Law and the Department of Public Policy and Administration. Students are not required to concentrate in an area; they may opt instead for a general MBA. Thanks to "institutional relationships with universities and companies in Namibia and South Africa," Rutgers MBAs have the opportunity to study abroad and "experience firsthand the issues facing emerging global markets." The business school also offers classes in Voorhees, Mt. Laurel, Cherry Hill, and Atlantic City.

Career and Placement

The Career Center at Rutgers University/Camden handles counseling and placement services for all undergraduate and graduate students. The office provides all the following services: assessment inventories, career counseling, a career library, job fairs, on-campus recruiting events, resume critique, skills seminars, and Web-based resume posting. More than one hundred recruiters visit the Camden campus each year. Top recruiters include: Bally's Park Place Casino and Resort, Bristol-Myers Squibb, Campbell Soup Company, Commerce Bank, Galaxy Scientific, J&J Snack Foods, Lockheed Martin, Merck, Mobil, Okidata, PaineWebber, PHH Mortgage, PSE&G, Rohm and Haas, and the U.S. Air Force.

Ms. Joany McCracken, MBA Program Administrator
MBA Program, Business and Science Building, Camden, NJ 08102-1401 United States
Phone: 856-225-6452 • Fax: 856-225-6231 • E-mail: mba@camden-sbc.rutgers.edu
Website: camden-sbc.rutgers.edu/ProspectiveStudent/grad

Student Life and Environment

Most Rutgers-Camden MBAs "are married with children and work full-time. In spite of this, they show up to class regularly, have their work done on time, and participate a lot in class. We do a lot of group work, and most people are easy to work with." One student observes, "Everyone is really nice and willing to help you out with knowledge from other classes they may have taken already. Throughout the semester you get real close with your classmates. The business school is really like a family here." Rutgers' on-the-go grads appreciate how "The campus is specifically geared toward the busy professional who wants to jump start his or her career. The library is open late during the regular semesters, although it closes early in the summer and winter intermission sessions."

Those who seek opportunities on this campus usually find them. One MBA explains, "The business school has connected me with a lot of great employers and I have been doing a lot of interviews. The campus offers a lot of activities and events that are open to all students regardless of what school they are in." Students love the convenience of Camden, which can be easily accessed via public transportation (the PATCO Hi-Speed train line) or automobile. They warn that "there's not a lot to do in Camden," but with Philadelphia so close by (and Atlantic City an easy drive or bus ride away), there's always plenty to do within a reasonable travel distance.

Admissions

Applicants to the School of Business MBA program at Rutgers—Camden must submit the following materials: an online application form, an official score report for the GMAT (the average score is approximately 560), two official copies of transcripts for all postsecondary academic work (minimum undergraduate GPA of 2.5 required), three letters of recommendation, a personal statement, and a resume. International students must also submit appropriate financial documentation, those whose first language is not English must submit official score reports for the TOEFL (minimum acceptable score of 550 paper-based test or 230 computer-based test) or IELTS (minimum acceptable score of Band 7).

FINANCIAL FACTS

Annual tuition (in-state/ out-of-state)	$15,921/$24,067
Fees	$1,438
Room & board (on-campus)	$6,716

ADMISSIONS

Admissions Selectivity Rating	**78**
# of applications received	228
% applicants accepted	52
% acceptees attending	55
Average GMAT	560
Average GPA	3.2
TOEFL required of international students	Yes
Minimum TOEFL (paper/computer)	550/230
Application fee	$60
Deferment available	Yes
Maximum length of deferment	1 semester
Transfer students accepted	Yes
Transfer application policy Students must complete at least 36 credits in our program. We will transfer courses from AACSB-accredited schools with a grade of D or better.	
Non-fall admissions	Yes
Need-blind admissions	Yes

Applicants Also Look At

Drexel University, Rowan University, Temple University, University of Delaware.

EMPLOYMENT PROFILE		
Career Rating	**71**	**Top 5 Employers Hiring Grads**
		Lockheed Martin; Aramark; Deloitte Touche Tohmatsu; JPMorgan Chase; Computer Sciences Corporation.

SACRED HEART UNIVERSITY
JOHN F. WELCH COLLEGE OF BUSINESS

GENERAL INFORMATION

Type of school	Private
Affiliation	Roman Catholic
Academic calendar	Trimester

SURVEY SAYS . . .

Cutting-edge classes
Solid preparation in:
General management
Doing business in a global economy

STUDENTS

Enrollment of parent institution	5,775
Enrollment of business school	183

ACADEMICS

Academic Experience Rating	**70**
Profs interesting rating	87
Profs accessible rating	88

Academics

The John F. Welch College of Business at Sacred Heart University "has a great reputation" and is making "strides . . . to make it one of the best business schools" in the area. SHU has built its MBA program on the back of its "amazing" undergraduate business program, reproducing the "small class size and personal attention" that mark the undergrad experience here. Students believe this combination leads to "a successful graduate experience as well." "As an undergraduate at Sacred Heart University, I was impressed with the quality of education," relates one of the BA/MBA students. "The professors are highly educated individuals who apply real-world material to the subject matter. In addition, the faculty is highly focused on teaching each individual student and does not consider the students only numbers."

The Welch school offers a number of MBA options. BA/MBA students can complete both their undergraduate and graduate degrees in business in 5 years. An MBA for liberal arts majors allows nonbusiness majors to complete their BA and MBA in 6 years' time. A part-time evening program serves area professionals. The school also offers MBA studies overseas at its campus in Luxembourg. Students on the Fairfield campus may pursue concentrations in accounting, finance, and general management; on the Luxembourg campus, concentrations in finance and general management are available. Students report that "course offerings in the areas of international business, accounting, finance, and marketing show that the curriculum taught at our business school reflects the changing nature of business in the world. I think the school is well equipped to develop MBAs for the twenty-first century, where doing business across borders and cultures is going to be the deciding factor for success of future enterprises."

Students are also bullish on the school's future, praising the "dedication to growth, which can be seen in the recent AACSB accreditation and naming ceremony with Jack Welch."

Career and Placement

SHU's Office of Career Development offers a range of services to MBA students. Staff provides assistance in resume creation and critique, conducts seminars in interview skills, maintains online job postings, and organizes on-campus job fairs and interview sessions. The content of the office's website suggests that services are designed primarily for undergraduate students. However, Career Development is in the process of hiring a full-time Assistant Director whose primary focus will be on MBA student internships and job placement. The site indicates that the following employers interviewed on campus during the fall of 2006: Affinion Group, Enterprise Rent-A-Car, Ernst & Young, The Hartford, PricewaterhouseCoopers, SureSource, Vertrue.

MEREDITH WOERZ, DIRECTOR OF GRADUATE ADMISSIONS
5151 PARK AVENUE, FAIRFIELD, CT 06825 UNITED STATES
PHONE: 203-365-7619 • FAX: 203-365-4732
E-MAIL: GRADSTUDIES@SACREDHEART.EDU • WEBSITE: WWW.SACREDHEART.EDU

Student Life and Environment

Students find plenty to do, telling us that "there are many activities for students to participate in" along with "clubs such as Graduate Counsel, Commuter Counsel, cultural clubs, business-related clubs (such as Students in Free Enterprise), and much more." One full-time student adds, "There are plenty of events such as committee meetings, alumni events, and public speaking events that students can attend." Best of all, according to some, is that "professors participate in extracurricular activities along with students and provide mentoring in an informal setting."

Students on the Luxembourg campus "all work 40-plus hours a week," darting on campus only "for evening and Saturday courses." On the Fairfield campus, students "are mostly from Fairfield and New Haven counties, but some of them drive all the way from New York State." Students tell us that their classmates challenge them "to work harder, especially when you work in groups, because you want to do your part."

Admissions

Applicants to the MBA program at SHU's Welch College of Business must submit the following materials: a completed application form; official transcripts from all undergraduate institutions attended; a personal statement of career and academic goals; two letters of recommendation; a current professional resume; and an official GMAT score report. International applicants, including applicants to the MBA program in Luxembourg, must submit transcripts in English; foreign language transcripts must be translated and analyzed by an approved professional service. Applicants whose first language is not English (except those with a degree from an English-language institution) must submit an official score report for the TOEFL. Students should anticipate at least a 3-month wait in the issuance of student visas for the Luxembourg program. The Luxembourg program runs approximately nine 6-week sessions per year; students may apply for admission and begin the program during any session. The Fairfield campus operates on a trimester calendar.

FINANCIAL FACTS
Annual tuition	$24,000

ADMISSIONS
Admissions Selectivity Rating	65
TOEFL required of international students	Yes
Minimum TOEFL (paper/computer)	550/213
Application fee	$50
International application fee	$100
Deferment available	Yes
Maximum length of deferment	1 year
Transfer students accepted	Yes
Transfer application policy Transferred credits are reviewed by the program director.	
Non-fall admissions	Yes
Need-blind admissions	Yes

Applicants Also Look At
Fairfield University, University of Connecticut.

SAGINAW VALLEY STATE UNIVERSITY
COLLEGE OF BUSINESS AND MANAGEMENT

GENERAL INFORMATION
Type of school	Public
Academic calendar	Year round

SURVEY SAYS . . .
Friendly students
Helpful alumni
Smart classrooms
Solid preparation in:
General management
Communication/interpersonal skills
Presentation skills
Computer skills
Doing business in a global economy

STUDENTS
Enrollment of parent institution	9,543
Enrollment of business school	66
% male/female	68/32
% part-time	67
% minorities	9
% international	40
Average age at entry	27
Average years work experience at entry	4

ACADEMICS
Academic Experience Rating	**67**
Student/faculty ratio	5:1
Profs interesting rating	71
Profs accessible rating	63
% female faculty	24
% minority faculty	12

Academics

Students cite convenience, affordability, and AACSB accreditation as their main reasons for choosing the MBA program at Saginaw Valley State. Most students attend the school part-time while holding down full-time jobs. That's why they appreciate the flexibility of the program, which allows them to complete their degree at their own pace. Full-timers here are typically international students or accounting undergraduates participating in the 3/2 BBA/MBA degree program.

The MBA program at SVSU begins with a three-course business and management foundation sequence taught online and covering the basic principles of statistics, business law, and MIS. Students with related undergraduate course work are generally allowed to waive these courses taught using a hybrid method of half in class and half online, and proceed directly to the business core, a nine-course curriculum of required courses. The business core courses focus on global business, business ethics, managerial accounting, macroeconomics, managerial finance, organizational behavior and leadership, business process design, integrated marketing management, and management of global corporations. Students must also complete three elective courses. If all three electives are in the same functional area, they will have a concentration. Additionally, the school offers an international business concentration.

Students at SVSU say, "Most of the professors have taught us through real-life experiences of their own, which is a definite plus." (Though some students remark that several professors could "use even more real life experience to teach from.") Another plus is that "professors make themselves available more than I would have imagined. Sometimes e-mail is most convenient, and they seem to be quick at getting back with me," one student notes. Students also praise the school's "relatively new equipment and facilities," the "small class size," and "the option to take a class as an independent study for some classes." Their complaints generally derive from the size of the program, which limits options. One student writes, "There are limited electives every term and it's hard to wait until one is offered that looks interesting, so sometimes you have to take one just because it is the only class available for you during the term."

Career and Placement

Though Saginaw Valley State's Career Planning and Placement Office primarily serves undergraduates, MBA students also receive assistance and counseling in the areas of online databases, counseling, mock interviews, and coordination between students and alumni. For MBAs, professors are generally more helpful; many are, or recently were, active in the area business community and can provide contacts and recommendations to students. A recent SVSU internal survey showed that 93 percent of its MBA holders were employed full-time; 83 percent were employed in fields related to their major. Of the many students who attended SVSU while working full-time, 61 percent received a promotion from their employer after completing the degree.

JILL WETMORE, ASSISTANT DEAN, COLLEGE OF BUSINESS AND MANAGEMENT
7400 BAY ROAD, UNIVERSITY CENTER, MI 48710 UNITED STATES
PHONE: 989-964-4064 • FAX: 989-964-7497
E-MAIL: CBMDEAN@SVSU.EDU • WEBSITE: WWW.SVSU.EDU/CBM

Student Life and Environment

SVSU's 782-acre campus is located in east central Michigan's tri-city area and serves the communities of Bay City, Midland, and Saginaw. The MBA program makes its home in Curtis Hall, a facility that also houses the University Conference and Events Center. As a result, students needn't leave the building to attend plays, conferences, and lectures.

Most SVSU MBA students have full-time commitments beyond school—work, family, community, often all three—and thus have time to visit campus only for classes, study, group meetings, and meetings with professors. Students are relieved to find that "the environment has worked out well" to meet their busy schedules, noting that "professors are very accommodating." One student writes, "Most of the group projects have team members who are willing to meet to get the project done and they are flexible in meeting times."

Although they don't spend as much time with each other as do their peers in predominantly full-time programs, SVSU MBAs manage to bond through classes and projects. One explains, "Classes encourage interaction and we get to know most of our fellow students because the average class size is relatively small." They tell us that their classmates "tend to be here because of a desire to be more competitive in the professional world, but do not tend to be overly competitive with each other." SVSU "seems to attract a large percentage of its students from the professional world, and a fair number of students internationally. The number of international students is surprising because SVSU is a smaller school in a smaller community."

Admissions

The admissions department applies a formula to establish a floor for all applicants. To be considered for admission, students must score above 1,050 under the formula [(undergraduate GPA for final two years of four-year undergraduate program × 200) + GMAT score], and must have a GMAT score of at least 450. Applicants must also submit a current resume, a one-page personal essay (statement of goals), two letters of reference, and official copies of all undergraduate and graduate transcripts. International students also need to demonstrate sufficient finances to support themselves while studying in the United States; additional documents are also required of them. Applicants whose first language is not English must submit official TOEFL scores. Undergraduates in the SVSU Accounting Program may opt for a 3/2 option at the end of their junior year—successful completion of which results in a BBA and MBA at the end of five years' study.

FINANCIAL FACTS

Annual tuition (in-state/ out-of-state)	$5,419/$10,416
Fees	$248
Cost of books	$1,500
Room & board	$6,538
% of students receiving aid	45

ADMISSIONS

Admissions Selectivity Rating	**63**
# of applications received	50
% applicants accepted	90
% acceptees attending	44
Average GMAT	501
Range of GMAT	450–530
Average GPA	3.17
TOEFL required of international students	Yes
Minimum TOEFL (paper/computer)	525/197
Application fee	$25
International application fee	$60
Regular application deadline	Rolling
Regular notification	Rolling
Deferment available	Yes
Maximum length of deferment	7 semesters
Transfer students accepted	Yes
Transfer application policy may transfer 0 credits	
Non-fall admissions	Yes
Need-blind admissions	Yes

Applicants Also Look At

Central Michigan University, Michigan State University—College of Law, Northwood University, University of Michigan—Flint.

EMPLOYMENT PROFILE	
Career Rating	73

SAINT JOSEPH'S UNIVERSITY
ERIVAN K. HAUB SCHOOL OF BUSINESS

Academics

The Erivan K. Haub School of Business at Saint Joseph's University "has a great and long tradition of being a place for the top students in the Philadelphia area. At Saint Joe's you know you are getting one of the best educations available," due in part to "the Jesuit mission of cura personalis, or care for the whole person" which imbues the program with "the Jesuit philosophy of duty and service to others. This is extremely positive. There is high attention to ethics." A "great faculty and good facilities" are also part of the mix here.

The vast majority of Saint Joe's MBAs attend on a part-time basis, and these Philly-area professionals love the flexibility of the program, which allows students to complete the program at their own pace. Strength in a variety of areas broadens students' choices; we're told that Haub is home to "a great accounting department" and that the Master of Science in Financial Services offered here is quite useful because it "covers all required course work to permit sitting for the Certified Financial Planning exam. " Students also tell us that the school has "the best MS in Human Resource Management program available to working adults in the region." Some here, however, complain that "the curriculum isn't as flexible as it needs to be, especially for part-time students who work for a living. Some also feel that the school "should update the curriculum for some courses (the MBA Information Technology and Empowering Human Potential core required courses come immediately to mind)" to bring content in line with twenty-first-century business realities.

Saint Joe's keeps MBA classes small to "allow interaction on many levels. You can't hide from the teacher or your classmates." Professors "are knowledgeable and surprisingly accessible." One MBA elaborates, "I have trouble with math, and both professors helped to ensure that any questions I had about concepts or theory were answered. The course work is intriguing, challenging, and applicable to the problems facing society today. . . . I have been able to apply 90 percent of what I learn in class to my job and personal life." Saint Joe's offers concentrations in 10 areas: accounting, decision and system sciences, finance, health and medical services, human resource management, international business, international marketing, management, marketing, and nonprofit management.

Career and Placement

The Career Development Center at Saint Joe's serves all undergraduates, graduate students, and alumni. Students tell us the office is "typical of parochial Philadelphia colleges like La Salle and Temple," with a recruiting base largely from the Philadelphia area. While some wish for a broader range of recruiters, others "think SJU caters to its students' wants, and most want to stay in the Philly area. That's why they came to school here in the first place. If you are unsure about what you want to do after MBA, Career Services has a great assessment system, where they meet and counsel you on where you would be a good fit." Saint Joe's MBAs also benefit from "tremendous alumni networking."

ADELE FOLEY, DIRECTOR
5600 CITY AVENUE, MANDEVILLE HALL, #284, PHILADELPHIA, PA 19131 UNITED STATES
PHONE: 610-660-1690 • FAX: 610-660-1599
E-MAIL: SJUMBA@SJU.EDU • WEBSITE: WWW.SJU.EDU/HSB

Student Life and Environment

Saint Joe's offers its MBA program in two locations. The school's main campus is located "on the outskirts of the city, so you have that city feel without the dangers of a city." Students love the "small campus in a big city" and report that "the decor of the architecture and the outlay of the campus are inviting and serene. Students all smile and are genuinely happy and safe." A satellite site is located at Ursinus College in Collegeville; students here describe a conventional evening-program experience, with little extracurricular life on and around campus.

Saint Joe's graduate business programs "sponsor events throughout the semester to encourage networking." An esprit de corps is further enhanced by the fact that "the school has a very fanatical sports fan base." While extracurricular agendas are relatively light, most students here are good with that. One student writes, "Life at school is fine. It does not interfere with professional or family commitments. The program is very understanding that there are other commitments at this juncture of life."

Admissions

Applicants to the Haub MBA program must submit the following materials to the school: an official transcript from each undergraduate and graduate institution at which credits were earned; an official GMAT score report (not more than 7 years old); two letters of recommendation; a current resume; and a personal statement of 250 to 500 words outlining career objectives and the value of an MBA in reaching those objectives. International applicants must submit all of the following as well as a statement of financial support. International applicants who attended undergraduate institutions at which English was not the language of instruction must have their transcripts translated and interpreted by World Education Service. Students whose first language is not English must submit an official TOEFL score report. Saint Joe's admits MBA students for fall, spring, and summer terms.

FINANCIAL FACTS

Annual tuition	$15,603
Cost of books	$800
Average award package	$15,603

ADMISSIONS

Admissions Selectivity Rating	**76**
# of applications received	237
% applicants accepted	65
% acceptees attending	79
Average GMAT	526
Average GPA	3.23
TOEFL required of international students	Yes
Minimum TOEFL (paper/computer)	550/213
Application fee	$35
Regular application deadline	Rolling
Regular notification	Rolling
Deferment available	Yes
Maximum length of deferment	1 year
Transfer students accepted	Yes
Transfer application policy They must provide a completed application including original test scores.	
Non-fall admissions	Yes
Need-blind admissions	Yes

Applicants Also Look At

Drexel University, La Salle University, Pennsylvania State University—Great Valley Campus, Temple University, Villanova University.

SAINT LOUIS UNIVERSITY
JOHN COOK SCHOOL OF BUSINESS

GENERAL INFORMATION
Type of school   Private
Affiliation   Roman Catholic
Environment   Metropolis
Academic calendar   Semester

SURVEY SAYS . . .
Students love St. Louis, MO
Happy students
Smart classrooms
Solid preparation in:
General management
Teamwork
Presentation skills

STUDENTS
Enrollment of parent
  institution   12,034
Enrollment of
  business school   349
% male/female   61/39
% part-time   80
% minorities   9
% international   6
Average age at entry   26
Average years work
  experience at entry   2

ACADEMICS
Academic Experience Rating   **84**
Student/faculty ratio   15:1
Profs interesting rating   84
Profs accessible rating   70
% female faculty   10

Joint Degrees
MBA/JD 3.5 years, MBA/Master of
Health Administration 2 years,
MBA/MD 5 years.

Prominent Alumni
August A. Busch, IV, president,
Anheuser-Busch, Inc.; Mark
Lamping, president, St. Louis
Cardinals; Robert Ciapciak, general
partner, Edward Jones; Alison
Talbot, vice president of operations,
Miss Elaine; Patrick J. Sly, executive
vice president, Emerson Electric Co.

Academics

The John Cook School of Business at Saint Louis University offers both a full-time and a part-time Professional MBA (PMBA) program. A substantial majority of the students here attend the part-time program, usually while working full-time jobs in the St. Louis area.

The "enhanced, flexible" curriculum of the PMBA program, which was first introduced in the fall of 2004, is designed to allow working professionals to take as many or as few courses as they want, when they want. The sequence of 11 to 15 courses (four foundation courses may be waived, depending on the student's undergraduate and professional qualifications) can be completed in as little as two years. All classes are offered in the evenings, typically once a week from 6 P.M. to 9 P.M. Besides the foundation courses, the PMBA curriculum includes five breadth courses; a capstone course; a course covering business law, business ethics, and career management; and four electives.

The SLU full-time MBA is also a relatively recent arrival, with its first classes convening in 1999. The one-year program covers the same fundamental business functions covered in the PMBA program, but also "emphasizes oral and written communications, teamwork skills, and other leadership competencies, linked with a practical, working knowledge of business ethics and a global perspective," according to the school's website. The 48–54-credit curriculum, offered primarily during the day, includes up to 6 electives, allowing students to specialize in accounting, economics, entrepreneurship, finance, international business, management, marketing, MIS, or operations and supply chain management. The one-year program also includes a two-week study abroad tour.

"Because of the relatively small class size" in both MBA programs, "professors are able to interact with students easily and frequently" at SLU. One student explains, "The school is like a tight-knit community where faculty, staff, and administration make students the first priority. This is obvious in every aspect of campus interaction." Students praise offerings in finance and international business, telling us that the latter benefits from "excellent study-abroad opportunities." A few here complain that "some professors lack the necessary real-world experience to teach graduate students" and feel that "the school could upgrade the technology in the classroom. Lectures should be taped and made available online."

Career and Placement

The Career Resources Center at the John Cook School of Business provides Career Services and counseling for all MBAs. The center offers self-assessments, personal advising, resume assistance, mock interviews, and access to multiple online and hard-copy databases and reference sources. Students tell us that the school's regional reputation and alumni network are its most effective career-enhancing assets. One writes, "I chose the school for its regional name recognition and the quality associated with the education given here. In the St. Louis area, this school opens many doors in the business field. The school is also well-networked in the community." Another adds, "The variety and reputations of the companies at which SLU alums and faculty currently work or have worked at in the past are impressive. I know that when I am close to graduating, I will have no trouble finding a great job."

Student Life and Environment

SLU's "beautiful campus" is a park-like setting peppered with sculptures, fountains, archways, and verdant open spaces. Because the Jesuit tradition seeks to educate the whole person, SLU brings numerous cultural events to campus. Through the campus

NANCY BISCAN, PROGRAM COORDINATOR
3674 LINDELL BOULEVARD, SUITE 132, ST. LOUIS, MO 63108 UNITED STATES
PHONE: 314-977-6221 • FAX: 314-977-1416
E-MAIL: GRADBIZ@SLU.EDU • WEBSITE: GRADBIZ.SLU.EDU

ministry, opportunities for service and spiritual growth are readily available. SLU competes in 16 NCAA Division I sports; the men's basketball and soccer teams both draw hefty crowds. The school's midtown location provides students easy access to the Fox Theatre, the Sheldon Concert Hall, the Grandel Square Theatre, and the Powell Symphony Hall.

"On-campus activities are readily available and student-driven," MBAs report, although many part-timers have difficulty making time to take advantage of them. One first semester, part-timer writes, "I plan to join various business clubs eventually, such as the Marketing Club and/or MIS Club, after I have chosen a concentration in the program." The student body here includes "new college graduates and seasoned professionals. Some are single while others have kids and are married. Some have business backgrounds while others have engineering and other backgrounds. It is a fairly diverse cross section of people." Students are "competitive, friendly, smart, anxious to learn," yet "always willing to help each other out."

Admissions

Saint Louis University accepts both online and paper-and-pencil applications; an Adobe Acrobat file of the application can be downloaded at the school's website. All applications must include a completed application form, personal statement, two letters of recommendation (at least one professional), official transcripts for all postsecondary academic work, and an official GMAT score report. International applicants must provide all of the above plus certification of financial support and, for non-native English speakers, an official TOEFL score report. According to the school, "Work experience plays a large role [in the admissions decision]. For applicants with limited or no work experience, the GMAT and GPA become very important." Interviews are required for the one-year MBA program.

FINANCIAL FACTS

Annual tuition	$47,785
Fees	$190
Cost of books	$1,250
Room & board (off-campus)	$11,000
% of students receiving aid	95
% of first-year students receiving aid	95
% of students receiving grants	95
Average grant	$9,000

ADMISSIONS

Admissions Selectivity Rating	85
# of applications received	74
% applicants accepted	49
% acceptees attending	72
Average GMAT	559
Range of GMAT	500–610
Average GPA	3.42
TOEFL required of international students	Yes
Minimum TOEFL (paper/computer)	550/250
Application fee	$90
Early decision program	Yes
ED Deadline/Notification	11/1 / 12/1
Deferment available	Yes
Maximum length of deferment	1 year
Transfer students accepted	Yes
Transfer application policy Part-time MBA only; 6 credit hours from another AACSB-accredited school; member of Jesuit MBA Consortium.	
Non-fall admissions	Yes
Need-blind admissions	Yes

Applicants Also Look At
Washington University.

EMPLOYMENT PROFILE

Career Rating	76	Grads Employed by Function	%	Avg. Salary
Primary Source of Full-time Job Acceptances		Finance/Accounting	7	$50,000
School-facilitated activities	13 (68%)	Marketing/Sales	14	$70,000
Graduate-facilitated activities	3 (16%)	Operations/Production	14	$62,000
Unknown	3 (16%)	General Management	29	$61,000
Percent employed	83	Other	36	$69,000

SAN DIEGO STATE UNIVERSITY
GRADUATE SCHOOL OF BUSINESS

GENERAL INFORMATION
Type of school   Public
Environment   City
Academic calendar   Semester

SURVEY SAYS . . .
Students love San Diego, CA
Happy students

STUDENTS
Enrollment of parent
  institution   32,693
Enrollment of
  business school   700
% male/female   60/40
% out-of-state   12
% part-time   55
% minorities   15
% international   19
Average age at entry   28
Average years work
  experience at entry   5

ACADEMICS
Academic Experience Rating   84
Student/faculty ratio   35:1
Profs interesting rating   84
Profs accessible rating   72
% female faculty   14
% minority faculty   3

Joint Degrees
MBA/MA (Latin American studies)
3 to 4 years, MBA/JD 4 years.

Academics

A solid return on investment—especially for California natives—and a "great reputation in international business and entrepreneurship" are among the major attractions at San Diego State University's Graduate School of Business. Entrepreneurship is a particular strength, with the prestigious Entrepreneurial Management Center helping SDSU earn a "high ranking among all entrepreneurship programs." A sports business MBA program "that partners with Major League Baseball, National Football League, and National Basketball Association teams" is another big draw.

Potential SDSU business grads have a number of choices to consider. The conventional MBA program here presupposes that students did not study business as undergraduates. Thus, it includes 19 foundation credits that cannot be waived (because the program is cohort-based). Students who studied business as undergraduates, however, are more suitable candidates for the MSBA program. Students "really like the way it is set up. It allows you to finish in one year and specialize in an area." The Sports Business Management MBA has its own separate program. SDSU also offers an MS in accounting ("one of the few accredited accounting programs in the state," one student writes) and an Executive MBA program.

Students praise SDSU as an "efficient school" where "the faculty is very attuned with latest trends in the business world, and professors can offer very practical experience in the classroom based on their consulting work." Faculty instruction is supplemented by "guest lecturers who are well-respected and powerful." Throughout the curriculum, students here "do a lot of group work, which facilitates good student relationships and teamwork." Students appreciate that "classes are taught in an open and participatory environment" that fortunately is "not overly competitive. Quality of life is important to the people attending and working in the community, and they aim to balance academic achievement with living well." The school's city of San Diego location also means that a steady supply of local business leaders are always on hand, whether as mentors or potential employers.

Career and Placement

Career and placement services for SDSU MBAs are handled through the Career Services Office of the university; there is no dedicated Career Services Office for the MBA program. Supplemental services are provided through the MBA Association and the Entrepreneurial Management Center. Students see Career Services here as a weak area, with comments that "on-campus recruiting needs to be improved." As far as the effectiveness of the alumni network goes, students are split. Some see it as a strength, while others feel the school should work harder to "foster better communication between the students and alumni for employment purposes."

S. SCOTT, ASSOCIATE DIRECTOR OF THE MBA PROGRAMS
5500 CAMPANILE DRIVE, SAN DIEGO, CA 92182-8228 UNITED STATES
PHONE: 619-594-8073 • FAX: 619-594-1863
E-MAIL: SDSUMBA@MAIL.SDSU.EDU • WEBSITE: WWW.SDSU.EDU/BUSINESS

Student Life and Environment

SDSU "provides an interesting, active environment, allowing students to be as involved or as isolated as they choose." Business students at this school are presented with "an incredible array of options to create the ultimate experience." Most important to business students, "There are many clubs to join that are great networking, social and career opportunities." In addition to these "great clubs" are "large events and a variety of cultural activities to participate in" while enjoying a "nice campus. . .that seems always to be striving for continual improvement."

The city of San Diego brings a lot to the table as well. It's "an outstanding place to live" with plenty of opportunity for those who wish to stick around after they graduate. Biotechnology, software development, and wireless communications industries all thrive here. The city is widely regarded as a leading laboratory for entrepreneurial development, and the U.S. military has a huge presence.

SDSU attracts "a great mix of enthusiastic people who are excited about furthering their education." This "intelligent, multi-cultural, driven, diverse" population includes "some who have many years of work experience and others who have only recently finished their undergraduate degrees." True to the Californian character, "Many here don't appear to be very competitive, which makes the atmosphere pretty relaxed and easy going. Still, the students are often the quietly successful type, so you never know what they are capable of until you ask them."

Admissions

Nearly 1,500 potential MBAs apply to SDSU's "highly competitive" program every year. The Admissions Committee considers a number of factors, including GMAT score (minimum score of 540 is required; the average score of an admitted student is 609); GPA for the final sixty course hours of undergraduate academic work (minimum 2.85 for American students, 3.0 for international students (for their entire four year degree); average GPA for admitted students was 3.3); letters of recommendation, resume (work experience is preferred but not required); and personal statement. None of the final three is required, but each "can enhance an application," according to the school's website. International students whose first language is not English must also submit official TOEFL scores; a minimum paper-and-pencil test score of 550 or an Internet-based test score of 79 is required. Applications are accepted for both the Fall and Spring terms. They are processed on a rolling basis, so it's best to apply as early as possible.

FINANCIAL FACTS

Annual tuition (in-state/ out-of-state)	$3,758/$11,894
Cost of books	$1,260
Room & board	$9,391

ADMISSIONS

Admissions Selectivity Rating	**88**
# of applications received	807
% applicants accepted	48
% acceptees attending	61
Average GMAT	609
Range of GMAT	560–620
Average GPA	3.3
TOEFL required of international students	Yes
Minimum TOEFL (paper/computer)	550/213
Application fee	$55
Regular application deadline	4/15
Regular notification	5/15
Transfer students accepted	Yes
Transfer application policy They apply through the normal admissions process and then will transfer SDSU's courses according to our discretion.	
Non-fall admissions	Yes
Need-blind admissions	Yes

Applicants Also Look At

University of California, San Diego, University of San Diego.

SAN FRANCISCO STATE UNIVERSITY
COLLEGE OF BUSINESS

GENERAL INFORMATION
Type of school   Public
Environment   Metropolis

SURVEY SAYS . . .
Students love San Francisco, CA
Happy students
Solid preparation in:
Accounting
Quantitative skills
Computer skills
Doing business in a global economy

STUDENTS
Enrollment of parent institution	29,000
Enrollment of business school	498
% male/female	48/52
% out-of-state	1
% part-time	65
% minorities	25
% international	35
Average age at entry	28
Average years work experience at entry	3

ACADEMICS
Academic Experience Rating	**77**
Student/faculty ratio	24:1
Profs interesting rating	82
Profs accessible rating	61
% female faculty	36
% minority faculty	40

Prominent Alumni
Mohan Gyani, CEP and president, AT&T Wireless Group; Gordon Hoff, vice president of international deposit services, Bank of America; Jo Malins, vice president of international conformance, Citibank.

Academics

The College of Business at San Francisco State University offers a range of MBA options to satisfy the needs of every student. A conventional MBA, the most popular of the school's choices, is offered on both a full-time and part-time basis and includes a thorough complement of foundation courses for those with little undergraduate or practical business experience (such courses may be waived for students with a deeper academic background in business). An Executive MBA program is offered both on-campus and at an off-site location. This is a fixed curriculum cohort program where students attend class seven hours per week and finish the program in 23 months. SFSU also offers a Master of Science in Business Administration, the MSBA, for students seeking a personalized curriculum that allows for in-depth specialization in one or more areas, such as accounting, finance, and information systems.

Students at SFSU appreciate "the flexibility of the program" and praise its "strong accounting department, [the] great faculty in the decision sciences department, [and the] access to great professors, contacts, and networking in the field of marketing." San Francisco itself is seen as a tremendous asset. One student explains, "Many top-quality professors want to live in the San Francisco Bay area, but there are only so many jobs at Stanford and Berkeley, so SFSU benefits from the overflow of top-quality professors. Overall, I feel that I'm getting Stanford-level instruction at community college-level prices. The professors and the program structure are excellent. It's like getting a Porsche at Hyundai prices." Another student agrees, "This could be the best value MBA program in the country, and it's in a great city with a great professional environment, including Silicon Valley and the San Francisco financial district nearby."

Like many state-run schools, SFSU is sometimes a little deficient in administrative functions. Students tell us that the program "needs to provide more advising time, especially for new students, at the beginning of the semester. We also need clearer guidelines in terms of classes that the students need to take." One student reports, "The staff is very knowledgeable, yet they can provide different answers to the same questions, which causes confusion among the students."

Career and Placement

SFSU College of Business offers career workshops in resume writing, job search, strategies, salary negotiation, networking facilitated by a career management consultant. The university career services provides career counseling services, organizes job fairs, and assists students in internship searches. Online services include job databases and an alumni networking site. Students are unimpressed, "career placement is non-existent here. Students are on their own when it comes to the job/internship search. Although students ask for job-placement assistance, the school provides no valuable help at all," writes one student. Another MBA observes, "In exchange for the low tuition, one cedes the network that would have come from attending a UC or private school."

Student Life and Environment

The MBA program at SFSU has relocated to the historic site of the old San Francisco Emporium. This dynamic new environment in the heart of downtown is directly on the Powell Street BART and Muni lines and surrounded by ample parking. The new location is equipped with 10 classrooms, 5 break out rooms, 2 conference rooms, a library resource center, computer lab, student lounge, printing/copying room, and faculty and staff offices. Part-timers applaud the move, telling us that "the development of the downtown

ARMAAN MOATTARI, ASSISTANT DIRECTOR OF ADMISSIONS
835 MARKET STREET, SUITE 550, SAN FRANCISCO, CA 94103 UNITED STATES
PHONE: 415-819-4310 • FAX: 415-817-4340
E-MAIL: MBA@SFSU.EDU • WEBSITE: MBA.SFSU.EDU

campus will make the program extremely convenient for those of us who work in the financial district." A few opponents ask, "What about the people who don't work downtown? There is no parking and I don't want to take public transportation home after a night class. The current location is excellent. People working downtown can easily hop on the M streetcar to arrive at the front door of the school in 20 minutes." Regardless of how they feel about the move, nearly everyone here agrees that "the school's greatest strength is that it's located in San Francisco, where there are lots of opportunities around."

Because SFSU "is a commuter school," MBAs "come on campus only to go to their classes or meet with other students to work on group projects." Students feel that "more social functions to connect fellow MBA students with each other would be a plus." One student writes, "There is not a lot of time for social interaction. The group work assignments help compensate for this deficiency and is something I have, eventually, learned to appreciate, despite the added onus of making time." Students also love such high-tech campus amenities as "Wi-Fi throughout the building and great online research possibilities through the library."

SFSU draws a large international population, "especially from Asia and Europe, although I also know people from Georgia (former USSR), Turkey, Egypt, Venezuela, Chile, [and] Brazil," observes one student. Another notes, "Having received my undergraduate degree from a small private college that touted its 'diversity,' I was unsure what to expect from a larger state school. But the diversity of the students in my classes is amazing. This is what my private undergrad college was trying to accomplish. We have all types, colors, background—married, unmarried, old, young, you name it. It makes for a very interesting and stimulating learning environment." Many students here "have worked for high-tech companies in Silicon Valley," although the general impression is that most international students arrive with little work experience.

Admissions

The admissions office at SFSU requires all of the following materials of applicants: a completed application (pencil-and-paper or computer-based); one sealed copies of official transcripts from all postsecondary programs attended; a sealed official GMAT score report; and a letter of intent (i.e., personal statement of purpose). Letters of recommendation are optional. International students whose first language is not English must submit sealed official TOEFL score reports. All international students must submit a financial statement demonstrating that the student has at least $20,000 to cover the cost of the program, and a signed form indicating agreement to purchase medical health insurance. The minimum GMAT score for all applicants is 500; a minimum rank of 25th percentile on the verbal, math, and writing sections is also required.

FINANCIAL FACTS

Annual tuition (in-state/ out-of-state)	$6,498/$14,634
Cost of books	$2,000
Room & board (on-campus)	$10,000

ADMISSIONS

Admissions Selectivity Rating	**84**
# of applications received	892
% applicants accepted	45
% acceptees attending	57
Average GMAT	574
Range of GMAT	500–700
Average GPA	3.13
TOEFL required of international students	Yes
Minimum TOEFL (paper/computer)	570/230
Application fee	$55
Regular application deadline	5/1
Regular notification	5/15
Transfer students accepted	Yes
Transfer application policy Applicants need to apply to the program and waive out our foundation requirements.	
Non-fall admissions	Yes

Applicants Also Look At
California State University, East Bay, San José State University.

EMPLOYMENT PROFILE	
Career Rating	86
Primary Source of Full-time Job Acceptances	
Percent employed	90

SAN JOSE STATE UNIVERSITY
LUCAS GRADUATE SCHOOL OF BUSINESS

Academics

Students at the AACSB-accredited Lucas Graduate School of Business at San Jose State University tell us that their school offers "part-time convenience" in the "center of the Silicon Valley" and a "workload that is manageable for full-time professionals." In addition, students enjoy a "high-quality academic program" whose hallmarks are "affordability" and "flexibility."

San Jose State's full-time, 1-year MBA program is just one of four Master of Business Administration degrees that the school offers, and is "designed for non-working individuals who prefer an intensive, cohort style of learning" and who want to complete the MBA degree in less time than it would normally take. San Jose State also offers a traditional on-campus MBA program that is designed for "students who prefer the educational atmosphere provided by a university setting." The on-campus program provides semester-length courses that meet once a week and a limited number of 6-week courses are available during the summer. An accelerated, off-campus program is usually preferred by students who want an "executive" style of learning. Classes are delivered year-round in six 8-week sessions, which allows students to complete six (or more) courses in a year's time. Finally, a Master's of Business Administration/Master's of Science in Engineering dual-degree program is tailored to working students and may be completed in 32 months.

The MBA program at San Jose State combines "case studies, lecture, research, team projects, computer analysis, student presentations, and presentations by members in the business community" to "provide 'simply the best' business education to a diverse, talented group of individuals from all over the world." Students in all programs benefit from "awesome" professors who are "knowledgeable and humorous." A "smooth administration" is available to answer students' questions. Students love that "guest speakers from over 100 Silicon Valley firms address College of Business classes" and say the school "takes advantage of its Silicon Valley location by hiring local professionals to teach part-time." "No courses are taught by teaching assistants." Overall, students say San Jose State is a "good value for the money."

Career and Placement

One of the obvious strengths of attending a school close to so many "high-tech companies" is that "most of the students work for companies like Oracle, Google, and Juniper Networks," which creates "great social networks and contacts" as well as a short commute to class for the "bulk" of students. The school claims that "80 percent of [its] graduate students are full-time business professionals in Silicon Valley companies." There is also an entrepreneurial culture evident amongst San Jose's graduate students. Many have start-up experience, work for start-ups, or have begun their own companies after graduation.

Additionally, San Jose provides students in the 1-year accelerated program with "direct exposure to Silicon Valley companies" and a challenging "curriculum [that] includes a 'consulting' course in which a team of students works with a 'client' firm to solve a particular, real-time problem for the company." Students say the program is "very geared toward the Pacific Rim business climate," and wish for more "career assistance" landing jobs outside Silicon Valley. Other areas in which students said the school could improve include the school's "standing with local companies," and frequency of "alumni events."

Employers who have hired San Jose MBAs include Abercrombie & Fitch, Adobe Systems, AltaVista, AMD, American Red Cross, Apple, AT&T, Charles Schwab, Chevron,

MARGARET FARMER, ADMISSIONS COORDINATOR
ONE WASHINGTON SQUARE, BUSINESS TOWER 350, SAN JOSE, CA 95192-0162 UNITED STATES
PHONE: 408-924-3420 • FAX: 408-924-3426
E-MAIL: MBA@COB.SJSU.EDU • WEBSITE: WWW.COB.SJSU.EDU/GRADUATE

Citibank, Cisco, Disneyland, Dow Jones & Company, eBay, Eastman Kodak, General Electric Company, Goodyear, HP, H&R Block Financial Advisers, Compaq, Intel, Lucent Technologies Merrill Lynch, Microsoft, Morgan Stanley, Netscape, Nordstrom, PepsiCo, Sprint, Staples, Starbucks, Symantec Corporation, T-Mobile, Texas Instruments, Toyota, Toys "R" Us, Visa, Wells Fargo, Xerox, Yahoo!.

Student Life and Environment

Students are "diverse," "highly intelligent," and "professionally experienced" at San Jose State. Student life is "busy, busy!," and because so many students work full-time and attend classes on one of the off-campus sites, there is the opinion among the student body of feeling scattered. "I do not spend much time on campus," one commuter says. Students recommend "integrating the 1-year MBA with the main campus," and they would also like to see more electives and more "interactive activities." Students appreciate the MBA Association's efforts to "promote social interaction among all MBA students, their families, faculty, and administrators" by organizing a variety of activities, including workshops, lectures, social mixers, and an annual BBQ lunch. When students want to head off campus, San Jose State's "downtown setting [makes] for an exciting" and "social atmosphere" full of interesting diversions.

Admissions

Applicants to Lucas must submit the following materials: official transcripts covering undergraduate work; an official GMAT score report; and a completed application form. Candidates who have earned a degree from a university in which the language of instruction was not English must submit an official TOEFL score report. Priority for admission will be given to applicants with better than a 3.0 GPA (on a 4.0 scale) in their last 60 semester units or 90 quarter units of course work and a score of at least 500 on the GMAT, with scores in the verbal and quantitative sections in the 50th percentile or above. Recently admitted had an average undergraduate GPA of 3.22 and an average GMAT score of 555.

FINANCIAL FACTS

Annual tuition (in-state/ out-of-state)	$3,858/$9,960
Cost of books	$1,314
Room & board (on/off-campus)	$9,096/$9,225
% of students receiving aid	1
% of first-year students receiving aid	10
% of students receiving loans	1
% of students receiving grants	2
Average award package	$12,226
Average grant	$2,427

ADMISSIONS

Admissions Selectivity Rating	81
# of applications received	448
% applicants accepted	55
% acceptees attending	58
Average GMAT	555
Range of GMAT	510–600
Average GPA	3.22
TOEFL required of international students	Yes
Minimum TOEFL (paper/computer)	550/213
Application fee	$55
Regular application deadline	5/1
Regular notification	7/1
Transfer students accepted	Yes
Transfer application policy Applicant must meet admission requirements; up 20% of units can be transferred from AACSB-accredited Institution.	
Non-fall admissions	Yes
Need-blind admissions	Yes

Applicants Also Look At

California State University, East Bay, San Francisco State University, Santa Clara University, University of California, Berkeley.

EMPLOYMENT PROFILE

Career Rating	76	Grads Employed by Function	%	Avg. Salary
Primary Source of Full-time Job Acceptances		Finance/Accounting	29	$67,500
School-facilitated activities	6 (86%)	Marketing/Sales	14	$65,000
Unknown	1 (14%)	Operations/Production	14	$65,000
Percent employed	67	Communications	14	NR
		General Management	14	$85,000

SANTA CLARA UNIVERSITY
LEAVEY SCHOOL OF BUSINESS

GENERAL INFORMATION
Type of school	Private
Affiliation	Roman Catholic-Jesuit
Environment	City
Academic calendar	Quarters

SURVEY SAYS . . .
Students love Santa Clara, CA
Friendly students
Good peer network
Cutting-edge classes
Helpful alumni
Happy students
Solid preparation in:
General management
Teamwork

STUDENTS
Enrollment of parent institution	8,397
Enrollment of business school	1,126
% male/female	66/34
% part-time	82
% minorities	15
% international	22
Average age at entry	30
Average years work experience at entry	7

ACADEMICS
Academic Experience Rating	**84**
Student/faculty ratio	16:1
Profs interesting rating	85
Profs accessible rating	70
% female faculty	18
% minority faculty	10

Joint Degrees
JD/MBA 4 years.

Academics

The Leavey School of Business at Santa Clara University combines "Jesuit values, primarily in the quality of education and the emphasis on high integrity," with a Silicon Valley location that draws "the cream of the crop to the faculty, such as the former 3Com CEO." The result is a unique MBA program that "caters to part-time students" but also has plenty to offer full-timers.

Customer service is the name of the game at Leavey, where "the dean runs the school as if it was a company in itself. He provides quarterly reports of the progress of school and reviews student evaluations as a measure of the progress." Administrators "do everything they can to keep up with the changing trends in business and business schools. For example, this year, they introduced international exposure for the student. Every summer, one or two student groups visit another country to meet with business leaders and financial institutions to understand how business is done in that country. This year, the group went to China. Next year, one group will go to China and another, to Germany." Professors take a similar student-first approach; they are "eager to help students in the classroom and to introduce them to colleagues for future employment opportunities. They are always available for personal/professional consultation."

Leavey's curriculum employs "a great case-study approach" that "is structured to maximize teamwork abilities." Students find this pedagogical approach immediately applicable to their professional lives. MBAs also "love the 'experimental' classes that students can choose as electives, such as Spirituality and Leadership, which really gets you to focus on your inner self and become a better, less stressed person." Students tell us the school excels in accounting, general management, and marketing. Asked where the school should improve, one student comments, "For some reason, the school is not so well recognized as other schools in the area, namely Stanford and Berkeley. But I have been quite impressed with SCU so far. The campus is good and the academic standards are excellent. I think the school will stand to gain if marketed better."

Career and Placement

Students appreciate the "great Bay Area network" connected to SCU; MBAs here benefit from "a terrific level of interaction with leaders and innovators in Silicon Valley." The Graduate Business Career Services Office capitalizes on these connections to help students procure internships ("The quarter system allows for some interesting internship opportunities in the area because local employers know some students can be available part-time or full-time for a quarter or two," explains one student) and post-graduation jobs. Even so, students feel the service isn't all it could be. As one observes, "Since most students are working, there are limited resources devoted to the internship/career placement program. Also, SCU also does not do enough promotion of the program out in the business community. Its reputation is only good regionally, despite its high ranking as a part-time business program."

The top ten employers of graduates of the class of 2004 were Applied Materials, Inc.; Cisco Systems, Inc.; eBay; Hewlett-Packard; KLA-Tencor Corporation; Silicon Valley Bank; Sun Microsystems; VERITAS Software; Wells Fargo; and Xilinx.

JENNIFER TAYLOR, DIRECTOR, GRADUATE BUSINESS ADMISSIONS
223 KENNA HALL, 500 EL CAMINO REAL, SANTA CLARA, CA 95053-0001 UNITED STATES
PHONE: 408-554-4539 • FAX: 408-544-4571
E-MAIL: MBAADMISSIONS@SCU.EDU • WEBSITE: WWW.SCU.EDU/BUSINESS

Student Life and Environment

MBAs report that SCU "provides a safe, clean, study environment coupled with a very caring and personal staff. The school really treats students as 'customers' and caters to their needs, offering extended library hours during exams. The staff wants the students to succeed." Part-timers also appreciate that "the schedule is really terrific [and] works for working folks as well as commuters." A new facility is in the works, we're told, which is a good thing; students agree that "the current facility is old and cramped."

SCU's "gorgeous and safe campus" offers a number of top amenities, including "a state-of-the-art gym and pool, great recreation areas, and a late-night venue called The Bronco with a pool table and a large television and several couches," as well as "campus-wide wireless access, [and] a peaceful rose garden and a church for when you need serenity." Although most students are part-timers with numerous other commitments outside school, MBAs here do occasionally socialize. One writes, "There are quarter-end bar nights which are great for relaxing after your last final with current classmates, catching up with past classmates, and meeting new people." Another student points out that "life at school can be great for those who do the work to get involved. It can be a commuter school if that is all a student wants to get out of it. [But] there is always something social to do on the weekends, either sponsored by the school or just going out with other MBA students."

"Many students here have jobs," which "provides the best opportunity for networking and recruiting after graduation, as you have gained so many resources at numerous organizations," students here tell us. MBAs range from the mid 20s to the mid 40s. Their "backgrounds are extremely diverse; they come from such areas as financial services, banking, semiconductors, software, technology management, finance, and human resources, to name a few." Engineers from the Silicon Valley are the single most visible contingent.

Admissions

Applicants to Leavey MBA programs at SCU must provide the Admissions Office with all of the following: official transcripts for all postsecondary academic work; official GMAT score reports reflecting scores no more than five years old; a completed application and a copy of same; two letters of recommendation; and personal essays. A third essay is optional. Candidates whose first language is not English must also submit official score reports for the TOEFL (minimum required score: 600 paper-based test, 250 computer-based test). Work experience is not a prerequisite to admission, although a minimum of two years of experience is recommended; on average, admitted students have between five and seven years of post-undergraduate professional experience. All applicants must demonstrate competency in four areas: college algebra, calculus, and oral communications. SCU uses targeted advertising and recruiting events to enhance its minority and disadvantaged populations.

FINANCIAL FACTS

Annual tuition	$19,278
Fees	$165
Cost of books	$1,000
Room & board (off-campus)	$13,000

ADMISSIONS

Admissions Selectivity Rating	79
# of applications received	395
% applicants accepted	80
% acceptees attending	64
Average GMAT	624
Range of GMAT	540–720
Average GPA	3.28
TOEFL required of international students	Yes
Minimum TOEFL (paper/computer)	600/250
Application fee	$75
International application fee	$100
Regular application deadline	6/1
Regular notification	Rolling
Early decision program?	Yes
ED Deadline/Notification	3/1 / 4/15
Deferment available	Yes
Maximum length of deferment	2 quarters
Transfer students accepted	Yes
Transfer application policy Apply as all others	
Non-fall admissions	Yes
Need-blind admissions	Yes

Applicants Also Look At

San José State University, University of California—Berkeley, University of California—Davis, University of San Francisco.

EMPLOYMENT PROFILE	
Career Rating	86
Primary Source of Full-time Job Acceptances	
School-facilitated activities	4 (12%)
Graduate-facilitated activities	30 (88%)
Average base starting salary	$88,680
Percent employed	64

SEATTLE PACIFIC UNIVERSITY
SCHOOL OF BUSINESS AND ECONOMICS

GENERAL INFORMATION

Type of school	Private
Affiliation	Free Methodist
Environment	Metropolis
Academic calendar	Quarters

SURVEY SAYS . . .
Students love Seattle, WA
Friendly students
Happy students
Smart classrooms
Solid preparation in:
Teamwork

STUDENTS

Enrollment of parent institution	3,830
Enrollment of business school	137
% male/female	60/40
% part-time	88
% international	8
Average age at entry	28
Average years work experience at entry	6

ACADEMICS

Academic Experience Rating	**73**
Student/faculty ratio	17:1
Profs interesting rating	87
Profs accessible rating	81
% female faculty	25
% minority faculty	5

Academics

Students in the Puget Sound region looking for a "great local school" with a "positive atmosphere" would be wise to investigate the School of Business and Economics at Seattle Pacific University, which runs two programs for graduate students: an MBA and a Master of Science in Information Systems Management (MSISM). The school offers a variety of concentrations for students in its MBA program, including: management of business processes, finance, e-business, human resource management, and information systems management. Most classes here meet one evening each week, and students can fill up or scale back on classes as their outside responsibilities fluctuate. A first-year student writes, "The flexibility that the school offered in setting my class schedule was a major selling point. The school also offered two classes in Christian ethics that I thought would be interesting considering some of the recent corporate scandals." SPU introduces "ethical considerations" into "all" b-school classes, which, students tell us, is something the school has done "since long before it was a trendy issue."

Students say their professors are, for the most part, "very impressive." "Most of them have had or still have a successful business" and can provide "concrete examples" of the "theories taught in class." Their ranks include several "former CEOs," and "Many are still very connected." While one student cautions that "not all professors are top-notch—I had a Managerial Communications course in which we studied junior-high grammar," most here focus on the positive: "I've only had one or two course experiences where I felt the instructor wasn't helping me learn at the highest level," a third-year student avows. Professors "bend over backwards to provide a positive learning experience" and are "very accessible" outside of the classroom. They're also "understanding of the fact that most students in the program are also working full-time as well as juggling family commitments."

SPU is unusual in that its administration draws even greater praise than its professors, with one student describing it as "the best-administered school I have ever seen or heard about." By all accounts, it's "really easy to get things taken care of" here. Not only is it "easy to sign up for classes," but also the administration "will add class sections if interest is high for a particular class," which allows students to "take the classes and go back to work." That being said, students still harbor a few complaints; specifically, the school "could do better getting big-name CEOs to speak" at its speaker series, and "The business school computer lab [should be] open more hours."

Career and Placement

SPU has great connections with area businesses, and students cite "mentorship and internship opportunities" as a major strength. The school, however, does not leverage its connections for jobs at graduation. Students tell us that "placement services are intentionally restricted" as "many companies [are] paying tuition for their employees [to] attend SPU," and "SPU would not want to discourage [such] companies from [doing so] by giving the impression that it supported career transition[s] for employed students at graduation." Students say that "those of us who attend full-time without working are at a disadvantage versus those who attend schools without this limitation." Most here believe that, "given the large percentage of students who plan career transitions after graduation anyway," SPU's stance on placement "is not valid and should be abandoned in favor of a strong placement assistance program to include the invitation of interested companies to recruit on campus."

DEBBIE WYSOMIERSKI, ASSOCIATE GRADUATE DIRECTOR
3307 THIRD AVENUR W., SUITE 201, SEATTLE, WA 98119-1950 UNITED STATES
PHONE: 206-281-2753 • FAX: 206-281-2733
E-MAIL: MBA@SPU.EDU • WEBSITE: WWW.SPU.EDU/SBE

Student Life and Environment

"Exceedingly helpful and accommodating" students who are "interested in getting to know you" "create a great learning environment" at SPU. Students describe their peers as "high-integrity people" who are both "supportive and competitive. They expect and bring the best out of one another." SPU students represent "a good variety of ages," though most are "married with children" and "trying to balance full-time work and a graduate program." Across the board, students here are "very driven and dedicated to getting the most out of the program at SPU." "A large portion of the students are employed at Boeing," the result of cross-pollination with the on-site MBA SPU offers at Boeing's nearby Everett, Washington, facility.

Many students "just go to classes and go back home," so "At school it is all work. There is limited time to socialize outside of class. This is the nature of [having a] full-time job and school [commitments]." Fortunately, the campus is "attractive" and "There are plenty of good options for eating" in the vicinity.

Admissions

When reviewing applicants, SPU's School of Business and Economics looks for an undergraduate GPA of 3.0 on a 4.0 scale and at least 1 year of continuous, full-time work experience. In addition, applicants to the MBA program should obtain a score of 490 or greater on the GMAT, and applicants to the MSISM program should obtain a score of 450 or greater on the verbal section of the GRE as well as a score of 525 or greater on the quantitative section of the test. A GPA or standardized test score that does not meet the guidelines listed above will be considered and may be accepted if other areas of the application are strong. Domestic students may apply for the fall, winter, spring, or summer term; international students may apply for any term with the exception of Summer.

FINANCIAL FACTS

Annual tuition	$14,160
Cost of books	$1,200
Room & board (off-campus)	$10,829
Average grant	$1,200

ADMISSIONS

Admissions Selectivity Rating	**71**
# of applications received	37
% applicants accepted	76
% acceptees attending	64
Average GMAT	514
Range of GMAT	460–550
Average GPA	3.32
TOEFL required of international students	Yes
Minimum TOEFL (paper/computer)	565/225
Application fee	$50
Regular application deadline	8/1
Regular notification	8/31
Deferment available	Yes
Maximum length of deferment	2 quarters
Transfer students accepted	Yes
Transfer application policy	
Regular Admission Process	
Non-fall admissions	Yes
Need-blind admissions	Yes

Applicants Also Look At

Seattle University, University of Washington.

SEATTLE UNIVERSITY
ALBERS SCHOOL OF BUSINESS AND ECONOMICS

Academics

The MBA program at Seattle University offers full-time and part-time degrees, but students here agree that the school "caters to the working student, maintaining a stronger focus on its evening MBA program than other schools that have day and evening programs." It's an approach that makes good sense, given that four-fifths of the students here are part-time students who typically have full-time jobs.

Students here appreciate that SU's curriculum "allows a tailored approach (as opposed to a track program), meaning that you can take the courses that are most meaningful to you and your future." Many evening programs offer a rather Spartan spread of options, but Seattle University bucks that trend; it provides "a good selection of electives" to evening students. Also, because the program is not lockstep, "Students can take a quarter off or take fewer credits when professional obligations make that necessary." The quarterly schedule is also a convenience in this regard, although it does mean that course material must be mastered over a relatively short period. Fortunately, "Professors here balance the workload, knowing that most of us have full-time jobs." One student sums up, "The school's culture is to treat students as customers and to deliver excellent customer service."

A Jesuit school, Seattle University incorporates "a focus on social justice" and "a push toward ethics and ethical business practices" into the curriculum and also has "community service opportunities built into the program," an aspect students here find very appealing. One student notes, "I want an all-encompassing education—not just a textbook knowledge about how to be a good manager. I want to be a good, well-rounded corporate citizen. Seattle University has all the right ingredients." MBAs here also love "the study abroad program, with its trips to China, Korea, Japan, Italy, and France." But perhaps most of all, they love the engaged faculty who "are very down-to-earth and willing to go the extra mile to make sure the students understand the materials. No matter whether it's meeting outside of class, staying after class late, or an endless e-mail correspondence, the professors have a caring mindset."

Career and Placement

When it comes to career advancement, "The greatest strength of this program is probably the reputation SU has in the business community in the Seattle area." There are lots of high-powered employers in the city, so that's a major plus. Students' enthusiasm is tempered; they tell us that "career and placement services are not as visible as they could be, and often the jobs that are publicized are with a limited group of employers or require much more experience than the standard younger MBA student has. Additionally, all the jobs are very near the campus while students come from all over, some as far as 60 miles away. An expanded geographical offering of available jobs would be helpful."

Top employers of Seattle University MBAs include: Washington Mutual, Paccar, Expeditors, PricewaterhouseCoopers, Deloitte Touche Tohmatsu, Amazon.com, Weyerhaeuser, Wells Fargo, Boeing, Moss Adams, InfoSpace, Holland American Line, Russel Investment, Microsoft, GMI, T-Mobile, Banner Bank.

JANET SHANDLEY, DIRECTOR, GRADUATE ADMISSIONS
901 TWELFTH AVENUE, PO BOX 222000, SEATTLE, WA 98122-1090 UNITED STATES
PHONE: 206-296-2000 • FAX: 206-296-5656
E-MAIL: GRAD-ADMISSIONS@SEATTLEU.EDU • WEBSITE: WWW.SEATTLEU.EDU / ASBE

Student Life and Environment

Most students at Albers "work full-time and attend school part-time, which means the environment is very different from that of a mostly full-time student base. For those who work and go to school it's great; you get to go to school with people who understand what you're going through, and everyone is very supportive of each others' busy schedules." Many here "try to gather before classes in the Atrium. I know of some students who come early from work to 'hang out' with their fellow MBA students before class. Professors are there too. It is a friendly environment that makes you feel like you are . . . more than a number in the school." While the administration allocates "the majority of its funding to undergraduates," Albers' Graduate Student Council "has been working to increase funding in order to increase graduate student activities and functions. We have talks about the different business environments by leaders in that environment. They help students understand the problems and potential of those industries."

SU maintains a satellite campus in Bellevue, which students say is "a bit drab and not as full of life as the Seattle campus but is darn convenient for those who work on the East Side." One student who attends classes there notes, "With the volume of people that we meet through our leadership courses and study abroad trips. I think that the East Side campus can be a great place to take classes and to network with students that you meet through other parts of the program. And the East Side campus really isn't that bad. It has a computer lab and wireless Internet as well as a place to grab something to eat" before class, with "coffee or vending-machine snacks."

Admissions

Applicants to the MBA program at the Albers School must submit the following materials: an official undergraduate transcript reflecting at least the final 2 years (60 semester credits/90 quarter credits) of academic work; transcripts reflecting any post-baccalaureate academic work, regardless of whether it led to a degree; an official GMAT score report; a current resume; and a completed application form. International students whose first language is not English must also submit an official TOEFL score report (237 minimum computer-based score for unconditional admission; students with scores of 227 to 233 may be admitted but must complete a Culture Language Bridge Program). Minimum standards for admission are typically a GMAT score of 500 and an undergraduate GPA of 3.0; students who do not meet these minimums are encouraged to submit personal statements and/or letters of reference in support of their applications.

FINANCIAL FACTS

Annual tuition	$16,794
Cost of books	$1,107
Room & board (on-campus)	$7,158
% of students receiving aid	36
% of first-year students receiving aid	48
% of students receiving loans	30
% of students receiving grants	5
Average award package	$19,088
Average grant	$9,433
Average student loan debt	$31,650

ADMISSIONS

Admissions Selectivity Rating	78
# of applications received	272
% applicants accepted	69
% acceptees attending	72
Average GMAT	563
Range of GMAT	480–660
Average GPA	3.36
TOEFL required of international students	Yes
Minimum TOEFL (paper/computer)	580/237
Application fee	$55
Regular application deadline	8/20
Deferment available	Yes
Maximum length of deferment	1 year
Transfer students accepted	Yes
Transfer application policy	Applicants must meet standard admission requirements. The university will accept 9 quarter credits from AACSB-accredited schools. Students transferring from an-accredited Jesuit MBA program (JEBNET) may transfer up to 50% of credits.
Non-fall admissions	Yes
Need-blind admissions	Yes

Applicants Also Look At

Pacific Lutheran University, San Francisco State University, Seattle Pacific University, University of Washington, Washington State University, Western Washington University.

SETON HALL UNIVERSITY
STILLMAN SCHOOL OF BUSINESS

Academics

Stillman School of Business at Seton Hall University offers students a location close to New York City along with "high academic standards," a "wonderful reputation," "comfortable class size," a streamlined course plan, and a Catholic tradition of service to community. It also offers one of the few MBA level concentrations in sports management in the country.

The MBA program at Seton Hall requires "42 credits rather than traditional 60." One student claims, "There are great opportunities for learning at a challenging pace and level." Four "hub" courses covering business basics such as marketing, economics, management, and finance are required, along with one course each in international perspectives and social responsibility. One student says, "Social responsibilities and morals are a vital part of the curriculum." This focus, students believe, "sets Seton Hall apart from the rest of institutions out there." Another student adds, "Group projects . . . tend to be a focus at the school and are often illuminating of the human condition—interesting!" There's also a capstone course, integrating ideas and topics studied across the business disciplines. In addition to sports management, students may concentrate in accounting, finance, financial markets, institutions and instruments, health care administration, information systems, international business, management, marketing, and pharmaceutical management. Students may also pursue double concentrations combining two of these areas. In addition, students must complete 20 hours of volunteer work with a community organization of their choice as a graduation requirement for the MBA.

In keeping with the streamlined nature of Seton Hall's programs, study abroad opportunities are offered as 10-day immersion experiences, rather than whole semesters. In recent years students have studied in countries including Italy, China, Poland, Czechoslovakia, France, and Spain. In addition, at the New Jersey campus, the school maintains several practically oriented Centers for Excellence, in areas such as entrepreneurship, securities trading, international business, sports polling, and sports management, which students are encouraged to explore. Programs combining the MBA with a JD or a Master of Science in Nursing are also offered.

Students, most of whom work full-time and attend part-time, appreciate the quality of teaching at Seton Hall, the scheduling choices, and the atmosphere. The administration "has made accommodations for me and my wife to enroll in classes that would have exceeded our allowable credits in a single semester. Additionally, [the] request of a professor has opened an independent study class in business leadership," says one individual. The professors "exemplify a good balance between academic scholarship and practical experience. They are approachable, down-to-earth, serious, and passionate about their disciplines," many students agree, and "They are very embracing and always willing to help in any way possible." One definite strong point of the program is the "very personalized attention by the faculty."

Career and Placement

The Career Center at Stillman School of Business offers help with career assessment and planning, tips on interviewing and networking, and a mentoring program. Given that most students already work full-time and that the school is located just 14 miles from the business hub of New York City, students find that personal networking and being near an active business city often is more useful. "The location of the school is excellent because it is close to the city and other areas where major corporations are based," one student points out. "Since most students are working, it seems like the Career Center for-

Catherine Bianchi, Director of Graduate Admissions
Graduate Admissions, Stillman School of Business, 400 South Orange Avenue,
South Orange, NJ 07079-2692 United States • Phone: 973-761-9262 • Fax: 973-761-9208
E-mail: bianchca@shu.edu • Website: www.business.shu.edu

gets about MBA students," many feel. "The Stillman School could improve on its alumni network," one students says. "There are a lot of very [wealthy,] successful alumni who have lost touch with the school due to the fact that no one has reached out to them," and "The school should do more to get the word out about how good it is."

Merrill Lynch, the New Jersey Nets, PricewaterhouseCoopers, Prudential Financial, Madison Square Garden, the New York Yankees, and Tiffany & Co. are among those who have employed Seton Hall graduates.

Student Life and Environment

Most students in the MBA program are busy with family and commitments off campus. "Business school students go to class and then go home," says one student, and others agree with the students who say, "I feel like I am part of a community when I go to Seton Hall." That community is, most agree, centered around classwork and academic projects. Students are "motivated professionals at all stages of their career who ask questions, make great comments, and stay engaged in class," who are "diverse" as well as "determined, disciplined, dedicated, freethink[ing], gregarious-natured [individuals with] dynamic personalities. They are "friendly, helpful, competitive, motivating, and adaptive," as well as "not afraid of a heavy workload, looking to share and learn experiences, and [looking for] an education [that will] challenge ideas and processes."

The Catholic tradition of service to and engagement with the community plays out as an inclusive aspect of the college atmosphere, as well. "Being Jewish in a Catholic school worried me at first, but I never had an issue, and people accepted me from the beginning," one student admits.

Admissions

Scores on the GMAT, letters of recommendation, a personal essay about background and goals, and copies of transcripts are required for admission to Stillman School of Business at Seton Hall. The TOEFL is also required for all international applicants. In 2006, the average GMAT score among accepted applicants was 565, with the range of scores for those accepted running between 500 and 700. The average GPA was 3.30. Seton Hall accepted slightly more than half of those who applied in that year, and those students averaged 4 years of work experience in addition to their academic credentials.

FINANCIAL FACTS

Annual tuition	$20,328
Fees	$610
Cost of books	$1,458
Room & board (off-campus)	$10,200
% of students receiving aid	10
% of first-year students receiving aid	5
% of students receiving grants	3
Average grant	$20,328

ADMISSIONS

Admissions Selectivity Rating	**77**
# of applications received	271
% applicants accepted	110
% acceptees attending	77
Average GMAT	555
Range of GMAT	510–600
Average GPA	3.22
TOEFL required of international students	Yes
Minimum TOEFL (paper/computer)	607/254
Application fee	$75
Regular application deadline	6/1
Regular notification	Rolling
Deferment available	Yes
Maximum length of deferment	1 academic year
Transfer students accepted	Yes
Transfer application policy	

Students must submit a formal application and satisfy all requirements for admission. In addition to graduate transcripts, it is suggested that the student also submit a course description and syllabus for the courses he/she intends to transfer. Upon gaining admission to the MBA program, the associate dean for academic services will review the student's transcripts to determine which graduate courses may be transferred. Students are eligible to transfer up to a maximum of 12 credits.

Non-fall admissions	Yes
Need-blind admissions	Yes

Applicants Also Look At

Columbia University, Farleigh Dickinson University, Fordham University, Montclair State University, New York University, Pace University, Rutgers, The State University of New Jersey.

SHIPPENSBURG UNIVERSITY
JOHN L. GROVE COLLEGE OF BUSINESS

GENERAL INFORMATION
Type of school   Public

SURVEY SAYS . . .
Friendly students
Cutting-edge classes
Happy students
Smart classrooms
Solid preparation in:
Finance
Accounting

STUDENTS
Average age at entry   32
Average years work
    experience at entry   5

ACADEMICS
Academic Experience Rating   **61**
Profs interesting rating   61
Profs accessible rating   62

Academics

The MBA program at the Shippensburg University's John L. Grove College of Business exploits twenty-first century technology to the great convenience of its busy student body. Two-thirds of each course in the program is taught in an electronic classroom; videoconferencing technology allows the classes to be broadcast to remote sites so that students and professors in different locations can interact. Area employers may even have their electronic conference rooms added to the school's roster of videoconferencing sites, thus allowing employees to complete the program from their workplaces. The other third of the course content is presented via the Internet, which permits students to complete the work at their own pace. For added convenience, all classes are recorded on digital video and uploaded to the program's website so that students may later stream the classes online.

The Shippensburg MBA consists of 30 credits, meaning "You can do the whole program in one year," which is exactly what some students here are after. Most students attend part-time though, taking two or more years to earn the degree. Students whose undergraduate degree was in an area other than business typically must take up to six prerequisite under-graduate-level courses (in accounting, economics, finance, operations, organizational behavior, and marketing) prior to beginning course work on the MBA proper. The MBA curriculum consists of eight required classes (managerial accounting, global manage-ment finance, entrepreneurship, international business, organizational leadership, information management, supply chain, and strategic management) and two electives.

Students tell us that Shippensburg professors "tend to be very friendly and like to see success. They bond well with successful students who show that they are interested in doing well and learning the material." Some concede that "It takes money to keep really, really good professors here and we do not have it!" but quickly add that "The professors that we do have are very good and dedicated." The online component of the program stresses independent learning, which many students appreciate; as one student explains, "Because we have to teach ourselves, we end up learning a lot." Students also love the convenience of taking classes in remote locations; many attend a learning center in Harrisburg near their places of employment. Students also note approvingly that "because this is a new program, the administration takes suggestions seriously. And the technology is great, when it works."

Career and Placement

The Career Development Center (CDC) of Shippensburg University serves current stu-dents and alumni of the university. The office offers counseling services, organizes job search programs, provides seminars in job-search skills, and publishes a bi-weekly newsletter announcing upcoming on-campus interviews. Employers who have recruited on the Shippensburg campus in the past include Advantica, Allegis Group, CACI International, Capital Blue Cross, Citibank, Edward Jones Investments, Ernst & Young, Federated Mutual Insurance, Fulton Bank, G E Fanuc Automation, Highmark, Inc., IBM, Integrated Management Solutions, KPMG International, LLP, Lockheed Martin, Nationwide Insurance, Northwestern Mutual Financial Network, the Pennsylvania Department of Revenue, PricewaterhouseCoopers, Raytheon, The Vanguard Group, Vectron International, and Wells Fargo.

GRADUATE ADMISSIONS OFFICE,
1871 OLD MAIN DRIVE, SHIPPENSBURG, PA 17257 UNITED STATES
PHONE: 717-477-1213 • FAX: 717)477-4016
E-MAIL: GRADUATE@SHIP.EDU • WEBSITE: WEBSPACE.SHIP.EDU/MBA

Student Life and Environment

Shippensburg is a public university that is home to over 6,500 undergraduate students and about 1,000 graduate students. The campus, spread over 200 acres, is located 40 miles southwest of Harrisburg, not far from the Pennsylvania Turnpike. The school is accredited by the AACSB. Many MBA students attend the Dixon University Center in Harrisburg, where they participate in Shippensburg-based classes via teleconferencing technology.

Most students in the MBA program attend part-time and have little time for extracurricular involvement. While some feel "the department needs to have more clubs and social events for the students to join," most are happy to restrict their involvement to class-related activities. The majority of students here are "older, married adults who are employed full-time." They share the common bond of "all working toward the same goal" and "don't feel in competition with each other in the least." In fact, there's a "definite sense of community within the school." Some here tell us that "the students who take classes on campus at Ship tend to be more immature than those at Harrisburg. The Harrisburg people tend to be working professionals, whereas Shippensburg has more students who came straight from undergrad to the MBA program."

Admissions

The Admissions Office at Shippensburg University requires applicants to submit official copies of transcripts for all undergraduate work and a current resume. GMAT scores are required only for applicants whose undergraduate GPA is below 3.0; students required to take the GMAT must submit an official GMAT score report. In addition, applicants must either have work experience or undergraduate credits in computer usage, oral and written communication, and quantitative analysis. A personal statement and letters of recommendation are both optional. International applicants must not only meet all of the above requirements, but must also submit an international student application, an evaluation of their transcripts by a professional evaluating service (either Educational Credential Evaluators (ECE) or World Education Services (WES)); an official score report for the TOEFL; and an affidavit of support accompanied by a current bank statement. Applicants who do not meet Shippensburg's admissions requirements may seek special consideration. Some such students do receive provisional admissions status, which allows them to enter the program and continue contingent upon success in their initial MBA course work.

FINANCIAL FACTS

Annual tuition (in-state/ out-of-state)	$3,024/$4,839
Fees (in-state/ out-of-state)	$63/$94

ADMISSIONS

Admissions Selectivity Rating 60*

Minimum TOEFL (paper/computer)	550/213
Application fee	$30
Regular application deadline	Rolling
Regular notification	Rolling
Deferment available	Yes
Maximum length of deferment	1 year
Transfer students accepted	Yes
Transfer application policy Up to 9 credits may transfer.	
Non-fall admissions	Yes

SOUTHEAST MISSOURI STATE UNIVERSITY
DONALD L. HARRISON COLLEGE OF BUSINESS

GENERAL INFORMATION

Type of school	Public
Environment	Town
Academic calendar	Semester

SURVEY SAYS...
Solid preparation in:
Computer skills

STUDENTS

Enrollment of parent institution
10,000

Enrollment of business school	79
% male/female	55/45
% out-of-state	11
% part-time	35
% minorities	5
% international	13
Average age at entry	27

ACADEMICS

Academic Experience Rating	**77**
Student/faculty ratio	19:1
Profs interesting rating	66
Profs accessible rating	88
% female faculty	40
% minority faculty	10

Joint Degrees

MBA/Masters in International
Business and Economics (with
University of Applied Sciences,
Schmalkalden, Germany).

Academics

The Donald L. Harrison College of Business at Southeast Missouri State University (SEMO) offers students plenty of "bang for their buck." In 2003, *U.S. News & World Report* reported that the school produces some of the "least indebted students" in the nation. As one MBA student says, "It's not Kellogg, but it's as good as you'll find for the money. I was an MBA at another university for a semester and transferred because the education there was not up to par with the tuition charged. SEMO, which charges much less, has provided a much better value." Harrison MBAs can choose from seven different degree options: accounting, environmental management, finance, general management, industrial management, international business, and a recently added concentration in health administration. MBAs praise "the variety of available disciplines of study, given the size of the institution," although they also warn that "there should be a wider variety of courses offered each semester." One student adds, "Sometimes you may be very limited to what [courses] you will be able to take. For instance, I can't take any summer courses because the courses that will be offered are ones that I have already taken." Internships play an integral role in the Harrison MBA—at least for its younger full-timers. The school notes, "Students have the opportunity to participate in internship assignments (and receive full credit as an elective course) that bring our graduate students into contact with the managerial practice of business. Our students have benefited from internships with American Express Financial, Coca-Cola, KPMG International, Merrill Lynch, [and] Northwestern Mutual Life, to name just a few." Many Harrison MBAs have jobs (they attend evening classes), and so, do not participate in the internship program. Students love Harrison's small classes and the focus on in-class discussion. One older MBA student writes, "As a nontraditional student with over 30 years [of] business experience, my reflections and experiences were sometimes sought [after] and discussed as another means to broaden the overall picture of the real work place. I felt valued as a contributor by most professors and younger students. Diversity and variety seemed to be positive influences in most of my classes. Students were supportive of each others' efforts." However, some other students feel that "some professors do not demand enough from students, especially in the area of presentation and revision of work. Overall, this school's MBA program should be more challenging."

Career and Placement

Harrison placement services are provided by SEMO's Career Services Office, which serves all undergraduates and graduate students at the university. In conjunction with the Alumni Affairs office, Career Services has established the Southeast Career Alumni Network to facilitate job searches. The office also offers the standard array of services including counseling, workshops, and online support. Students are unimpressed; they feel that "the biggest area the MBA administration must improve on is the career center. The business school doesn't have a career center. We must use the undergraduate career center that focuses on attracting jobs for undergraduates. Obtaining a job through the career center at Southeast is nearly impossible. All work must be self-initiated and completed." Harrison MBAs who seek new jobs after graduation most often find themselves working for Accenture, Bausch & Lomb, Dow Jones & Company, PricewaterhouseCoopers, TG Missouri, and Texas Instruments. About one in ten students finds a job outside the United States.

Student Life and Environment

"Life at school is good!" one Harrison MBA reports. The student body is tight and the surrounding town of Cape Girardeau is pleasant and quiet. Another student explains, "Cape Girardeau is a fairly small town, so there are some limitations on recreational activity. In

ADMISSIONS CONTACT: DR. KENNETH HEISCHMIDT, DIRECTOR, MBA PROGRAM
MBA PROGRAM, SOUTHEAST MISSOURI STATE UNIVERSITY, 1 UNIVERSITY PLAZA, MS 5890,
CAPE GIRARDEAU, MO 63701 UNITED STATES
PHONE: 573-651-5116 • FAX: 573-651-5032
E-MAIL: MBA@SEMO.EDU • WEBSITE: WWW6.SEMO.EDU/MBA

warm months, there are many lakes, parks, and trails nearby to enjoy. The people in the community are friendly overall." One MBA student says, "Even though Cape Girardeau is a relatively small town, there is actually quite a lot to do, and it is close to Memphis and St. Louis for people who want to get to a city every once in a while." Campus life centers on the MBA Association, which "has holiday parties, happy-hour gatherings, intramural sports teams, [and] sponsors speakers." One student says, "I must give credit to the MBA Association because they work hard to create a positive social atmosphere for students." However, other MBAs believe that is pretty much the only school-related extracurricular. One student writes, "It seems the only student organization that MBA students are a part of is the MBA Association. This may be because MBA students have busy schedules." Other students feel that "the administration needs to work at creating more community. Although the student-run MBA Association does well, the administration does little to make new students feel welcomed." Students agree that "[SEMO's campus] is nice and fairly attractive [with] good facilities on-campus for student recreation, exercise, leisure, activities, and so on. The library resources are adequate and [continue to] improve—considering the budget crisis of the past couple years. The surrounding community is fairly supportive of the university and recognizes the impact it plays on its economy." Although one student comments, "For those who work during the day and study at night, some of the facilities are not open (for example, the bookstore). Sometimes the working student just simply cannot get to campus before it closes and has to take time off work to get necessary books for class." Students agree, "[The Harrison student body] comes from a wide array of backgrounds: rural, urban, suburban, international, and so on. The mix of such a diversity of students offers a relatively interesting student population." The school notes, "Approximately 16 percent of our MBA students and half of our alumni are international students. Since Southeast Missouri State University launched its MBA program in fall 1996, students from more than 25 countries have studied in the program. Currently, students from more than eight countries represent their nations and bring the world to the classroom."

Admissions

Harrison admissions officers use a formula to establish a floor for all MBA applicants: (200 × GPA [on a four-point scale] + GMAT score). Applicants must score at least 1,000 to be considered for admission. In addition, applicants must score at least 400 on the GMAT and must have earned at least a C in all required foundation courses for the GMAT program. These foundation courses are applied calculus, financial management, introductory statistics, management and organizational behavior, management information systems, principles of financial accounting, principles of macroeconomics, principles of managerial accounting, principles of marketing, and principles of microeconomics. Students without the requisite undergraduate work may place out of foundation courses through local and/or CLEP exams.

FINANCIAL FACTS

Annual tuition (in-state/ out-of-state)	$5,064/$8,952
Cost of books	$500
Room & board	$4,800
Average award package	$11,200
Average grant	$11,200

ADMISSIONS

Admissions Selectivity Rating	71
# of applications received	62
% applicants accepted	85
% acceptees attending	79
Average GMAT	515
Range of GMAT	410–620
Average GPA	3.56
TOEFL required of international students	Yes
Minimum TOEFL (paper/computer)	550/213
Application fee	$20
International application fee	$100
Regular application deadline	Rolling
Regular notification	Rolling
Deferment available	Yes
Maximum length of deferment	1 year
Transfer students accepted	Yes
Transfer application policy	May transfer 9 hours authorized by director of MBA program.
Non-fall admissions	Yes
Need-blind admissions	Yes

Applicants Also Look At

Missouri State University (formerly SW MSU), Saint Louis University, Southern Illinois University, University of Missouri—Columbia, University of Missouri—St. Louis.

EMPLOYMENT PROFILE			
Career Rating	92	Top Employer Hiring Grads	
Primary Source of Full-time Job Acceptances		Boeing.	
Unknown	1		
Percent employed	95		

SOUTHERN ILLINOIS UNIVERSITY—CARBONDALE
COLLEGE OF BUSINESS AND ADMINISTRATION

Academics

The College of Business and Administration at Southern Illinois University—Carbondale offers both a traditional MBA and off-campus EMBA options in Hong Kong, Singapore, and Taiwan. All programs are AACSB-accredited. About half the graduate students at SIUC attend full-time. While part-time students can manage the program as well, the mixed schedule of daytime and nighttime classes limits their options somewhat.

SIUC MBAs report that "the school is famous for its finance department" and that it offers "good courses in the Management of Information Systems." Classes here "are very interactive, with only 20 to 30 students in a class," and "professors work to extend the understanding of the discipline in all classes. Also, most professors seek to design classes in an unorthodox manner to develop skills needed for business." Many students cite the low cost of attending as their primary reason for choosing SIUC; relatively low tuition rates are made effectively lower by the availability of "a lot of assistantships for students." SIUC maintains a relationship with ESC-Grenoble, which allows SIUC MBAs to study for a Masters of International Business (MIB) in France.

Entering students who lack the required knowledge base for an MBA program are required to complete up to 37 hours of foundation courses prior to beginning work on their MBA. It helps that students with degrees outside business may receive credit for any equivalent undergraduate business classes in which they earned a grade of C or better. Such students must present both a transcript and a course syllabus for each course in order to be considered for the exemption. Students with undergraduate degrees in business generally are exempt from all foundation course work.

Full-time students who arrive with undergraduate business degrees under their belt can finish the 33-semester hour MBA program in 12 months. The MBA curriculum includes seven core courses and four electives. Students may also pursue electives in finance, marketing, international business, management information systems, and organizational behavior. Those who wish to concentrate in a particular area can opt to take all of their electives in one discipline.

Career and Placement

Southern Illinois University maintains a separate Business Placement Center to serve the College of Business and Administration. The office serves undergraduates, graduates, and alumni of the school. The office coordinates an annual job fair, maintains e-recruiting resources, and provides career counseling to students. Some here feel that "The career center could use a more hands-on effort with graduates. The only contact I had was through e-mail notices of career center activities." On-campus recruiters include 7-Eleven, Aldi, Archer Daniels Midland (ADM), CBIZ Business Solutions, Deloitte Touche Tohmatsu, Disney, Ernst & Young, Federated Insurance, KPMG International, MB Financial, MMP&W, PricewaterhouseCoopers, Regions Financial Corporation, State Farm Insurance, Swink, Fiehler & Company, Watkins Uiberall, and Woodbury Financial.

Dr. Don Gribbin, MBA Program Director

Rehn Hall 133, 1025 Lincoln Drive, Mail Code 4625, Carbondale, IL 62901 United States

Phone: 618-453-3030 • Fax: 618-453-7961

E-mail: mbagp@cba.siu.edu • Website: www.cba.siu.edu

Student Life and Environment

An overall student population of more than 20,000 keeps the SIUC campus hopping. As one MBA student explains, "There are lots of things to do here, such as [hearing] guest speakers and seminars to attend. The school often has forums for students to express their opinions on politics. They also offer fun events like concerts, and many students are avid sports fans, so sporting events are social gatherings." The campus recreation center "is very good, with basketball courts, swimming pools, racquetball courts, etc. There are also weight rooms and many cardiovascular fitness machines, and the staff that works at the Rec Center is very helpful." As if all that weren't enough, "The Student Center is an excellent facility for throwing pots, woodworking, and metal smithing." Even the surrounding campus "is beautiful, with forests all around where you can go hiking if the weather allows."

The city of Carbondale has a population of about 26,000, and the surrounding county is home to nearly 60,000 Illinoisans. St. Louis is the closest big city; it's less than 100 miles to the west. Both Chicago and Kansas City are just over 300 miles away. Major employers in the area include Nascote Industries, West Teleservices, Southern Illinois Healthcare, and the Maytag Corporation.

SIUC MBAs include "many international students. There are more young students than in many MBA programs, but not at the expense of competence." To some "it seems that almost every other student in the MBA program is a recent graduate of SIUC. Although they come from varied backgrounds…they are very similar," especially in that "few seem to have undergraduate degrees in business."

Admissions

All applicants to the MBA program at SIUC must provide the admissions department with a completed application to the university's graduate school; a separate application to the College of Business; official transcripts for all postsecondary academic work; an official score report for the GMAT; and three letters of recommendation. International applicants must also provide an official score report for the TOEFL (minimum score: 550 paper, 213 computer), a financial statement for graduate international students, and a photocopy of their passport. Work experience is not required; however, students with work experience do receive special consideration. All applications are assessed individually and holistically. Admission to the program requires a minimum undergraduate GPA of 2.7 (on a four-point scale) over the applicant's most recent 60 semester hours.

FINANCIAL FACTS

Annual tuition (in-state/ out-of-state)	$5,760/$11,520
Fees	$1,414
Cost of books	$840

ADMISSIONS

Admissions Selectivity Rating	**73**
# of applications received	78
% applicants accepted	69
% acceptees attending	63
Average GMAT	507
Range of GMAT	440–570
Average GPA	3.4
TOEFL required of international students	Yes
Minimum TOEFL (paper/computer)	550/213
Application fee	$35
Regular application deadline	3/15
Regular notification	6/1
Deferment available	Yes
Maximum length of deferment	1 year
Transfer students accepted	Yes
Transfer application policy Maximum number of transfer credits accepted for core curriculum is 6.	
Non-fall admissions	Yes

Applicants Also Look At

Eastern Illinois University, University of Illinois, University of Missouri—Columbia, Western Illinois University.

SOUTHERN ILLINOIS UNIVERSITY—EDWARDSVILLE
SCHOOL OF BUSINESS

GENERAL INFORMATION
Type of school   Public
Environment   Village

SURVEY SAYS . . .
Helpful alumni
Happy students
Solid preparation in:
General management
Computer skills

STUDENTS
Enrollment of parent
  institution   13,449
Enrollment of
  business school   178
% part-time   100
Average age at entry   27
Average years work
  experience at entry   2

ACADEMICS
Academic Experience Rating   **77**
Student/faculty ratio   5:1
Profs interesting rating   83
Profs accessible rating   61
% female faculty   37
% minority faculty   16

Prominent Alumni
Fernando G. Aguirre, president and CEO, Chiquita Brands International; John Shimkus, U.S. Representative, 19th District; Ralph Korte, president, Korte Construction Company; Deanna L. Daughhetee, president, American Equity Mortgage, Inc.; Dion C. Joannou, president, Nortel North America.

Academics

Students are drawn to the business programs at Southern Illinois University—Edwardsville by "the cheapest tuition in the St. Louis metro area," the convenience of "a lot of night and weekend classes," and "the good reputation" of the program, bolstered by its AACSB accreditation. SIUE offers a general MBA as well as specialized master's programs in accountancy, marketing research, economics, finance, and computer management and information systems.

SIUE's MBA program commences with a sequence of seven foundation courses covering basic principles of business and management. Students with undergraduate degrees in business generally place out of all these courses, provided they earned a grade of at least C in the corresponding undergraduate course. Nonbusiness majors who completed related undergraduate courses may place out of individual foundation courses. Foundation courses are not credited toward the MBA.

Credit-bearing MBA course work consists of 30 semester hours, half devoted to required courses and half to electives. Electives are available in accounting, economics, finance, international business, management, computer management and information systems, marketing, and production. A student may elect to write an independent thesis in order to fulfill some of the elective requirements. All students must complete a comprehensive examination.

MBA students at SIUE tell us that "professors are very knowledgeable and well-prepared for classes." Overall, they "are very interested in providing an excellent learning environment." While "the administration of the School of Business is first-rate," the "administration of the university as a whole is not as impressive." Students warn that "There is far too much red tape and far too many walls built into the system." Some here also feel that "the physical classroom environment needs an overhaul for the MBA student. We need something much different than the kindergarten desks-in-a-row. Some professors have made efforts to improve this, but for the most part it is very poor, not conducive for most adults who work all day at a desk." Students also would like to see the program incorporate online classes.

Career and Placement

Business students at SIUE are served by the university's Career Development Center, which provides career counseling and placement services for all students and alumni. Services include individual counseling, resume referral, on-campus interview sessions, workshops on various career-related skills, and a Career Resources Center with both online and hard-copy materials. SIUE holds two annual career fairs, one in the fall and one in the spring.

Student Life and Environment

SIUE is located in Edwardsville, a city of 22,000 strong that's just twenty miles northeast of St. Louis, Missouri. St. Louis provides copious opportunities for work, shopping, and entertainment. The school's location in a major metropolitan area also means that it serves a potential market of nearly three million people. Major employers in the area include the Bank of Edwardsville, Keller Companies, Richards Brick, and SIUE.

The university is home to more than 13,000 students and sits on a meandering campus that features woodlands, lakes, and rolling hills. Students note that "the campus is very nice and has all the amenities you could need." Most business students "don't spend a lot of time on campus," though, as "We commute and attend evening and weekend classes. This is very helpful to those of us in the working world" but it dampens student participation in the school community at large.

SIUE business students "come from impressively diverse backgrounds," are "pleasant to work with," and "have a great deal of real-world knowledge to share." Most "have children and full-time jobs, yet they have decided to come back to school and finish their degrees. Their commitments outside the classroom force them to be creative with their time-management skills and this, in turn, becomes a valuable tool that they can use in the business world." The student body includes "people from various cultures, which makes class interesting. They are also very easy to talk to!"

Admissions

Applicants to the MBA program at SIUE must apply for admission to the Graduate School. Applications are processed in two stages: During the first, admissions officers consider only the applicant's undergraduate GPA (as indicated by official copies of transcripts for all postsecondary academic work) and GMAT score. Applicants who meet one of the following minimum requirements are admitted to the program: an admission score of at least 950 under the formula [(undergraduate GPA $\times$ 200) + GMAT score], or a GMAT score of at least 400 with a minimum raw score of at least 20 on both the verbal and quantitative portions of the exam and an analytical writing score of at least 4.0. The average admitted student greatly exceeds both of these minimum criteria, boasting an undergraduate GPA of 3.28 and a GMAT score of approximately 518. In the second review stage, candidates who fail to meet the minimum requirements are reviewed individually by a faculty committee, which considers the quality of the applicant's undergraduate curriculum and program, evidence of business skills, work experience, and writing sample. The faculty committee admits those who, in its estimation, demonstrate the promise to succeed in the program. International applicants must submit official TOEFL score reports and provide proof of financial means to support themselves while enrolled in the program.

FINANCIAL FACTS

Annual tuition (in-state/ out-of-state)	$5,200/$12,043
Fees	$629
Cost of books	$1,000
Room & board (on-campus)	$7,000
% of students receiving aid	43
% of first-year students receiving aid	5
% of students receiving loans	22
% of students receiving grants	12
Average award package	$8,386
Average grant	$2,773
Average student loan debt	$15,050

ADMISSIONS

Admissions Selectivity Rating	**76**
# of applications received	166
% applicants accepted	59
% acceptees attending	77
Average GMAT	495
Range of GMAT	440–550
Average GPA	3.28
TOEFL required of international students	Yes
Minimum TOEFL (paper/computer)	550/213
Application fee	$30
Regular application deadline	Rolling
Regular notification	Rolling
Deferment available	Yes
Maximum length of deferment	1 year
Transfer students accepted	Yes
Transfer application policy Up to 9 hours from an AACSB-accredited school.	
Non-fall admissions	Yes
Need-blind admissions	Yes

Applicants Also Look At

Saint Louis University, University of Missouri—St. Louis, Washington University.

SOUTHERN METHODIST UNIVERSITY
COX SCHOOL OF BUSINESS

Academics

A contemporary and challenging business program situated in a lively, commerce-oriented city, Southern Methodist University's Cox School of Business is touted by students as the "best program offered in Dallas/Fort Worth area" in its balance of "course offerings, rankings, network ability and recognition, and faculty quality." All MBA students are initially enrolled in the general management concentration, taking a series of courses that provide a thorough introduction to business theory, including "very deep and modernized topics in the area of finance and accounting." Once they have finished the core curriculum, students may tailor their education through one or two academic concentrations, including leadership, marketing, information technology, and accounting. Students appreciate the fact that SMU is highly focused on the latest trends and on a practical approach to business education, saying "Teachers bring relevant material to the class and challenge students every day."

Responding to the increasingly global economy, Cox offers a "forward-thinking, cutting-edge program with a strong focus on the international marketplace." In 2000, Cox inaugurated the Global Leadership Program, a partnership with more than 90 leading businesses and government organizations throughout Asia, Latin America, and Europe. Students participating in the Global Leadership Program take a seminar in their first semester, which provides a comprehensive study of the culture, politics, and business in Asia, Latin America, or Europe. At the end of the second semester, these students travel to the region for a 2-week, hands-on immersion into global commerce and culture. For those who wish to further enhance their international acumen, the school operates a number of international exchange programs with universities in China, Japan, Singapore, Australia, Belgium, Denmark, Spain, Argentina, Brazil, and Mexico, among others.

In addition to the traditional, 2-year, full-time MBA, the school offers two part-time programs: the professional MBA for students who wish to work full-time while pursuing the MBA and the executive MBA for students who already have advanced business experience. Students in the part-time programs appreciate the camaraderie they feel among their classmates as well as the support of the faculty. One student assures, "They realize that we are all working professionals, and [they] are always there to lend a hand." Whether full-time or part-time, many say the greatest benefit of the program is "the way the b-school administration cares about the individual students." A current student shares, "Before I was even accepted, the Admissions staff and administration made me feel as if I was a part of the school."

Career and Placement

For those hoping to work in Texas or the Southwest region, Southern Methodist University is an excellent choice; the school maintains a "great reputation and alumni network in the Dallas/Fort Worth area, Texas, and the Southwestern U.S. cities." In fact, 80 percent of graduates took jobs in the Southwest last year, many in hometown Dallas. Since Dallas itself is a "very corporate city," many stay put after graduation. However, some feel the school is too Dallas-centric and "would improve the value to its graduates by increasing the number of companies recruiting for positions in Houston, Austin, and San Antonio."

Cox graduates have a high job-placement rate, and the majority of students take finance/accounting or marketing/sales positions, comprising 36.6 percent and 20.3 percent of last year's graduates, respectively. In 2006, the average salary of a Cox graduate was $76,902, of which 45 percent also received signing bonuses.

PATTI CUDNEY, DIRECTOR, MBA ADMISSIONS
P.O. BOX 750333 DALLAS, TX 75275 UNITED STATES
PHONE: 214-768-1214 • FAX: 214-768-3956
E-MAIL: MBAINFO@MAIL.COX.SMU.EDU • WEBSITE: WWW.COXMBA.COM

Student Life and Environment

On the Cox campus, you'll find "a great group of people, most in their 20s, some in their 30s, with different backgrounds and interests, but all outgoing." Conversation and camaraderie are not limited to the classroom, and "The school makes a strong effort to have students interact outside the classroom. They host events all the time to mingle with fellow students, professors, alumni, and even guests that people bring." For those who wish to augment the academic experience through a club or recreational activity, "there are plenty of chances for anyone who wishes to get involved with extracurricular activities to do so." However, many part-time students say the demands of work and study are overwhelming. A second-year student laments, "Being in the professional MBA program I wish I had more time to take advantage of all the school offers."

Located in Dallas, Texas, the campus is within striking distance of every form of entertainment imaginable, including restaurants, museums, shopping, and seven major sports teams. On the flip side, the school's pleasant campus offers relief from the bustling city. A current student enthusiastically sums it up: "The campus is beautiful—shady tree-lined streets with really attractive people in one of the most pro-business cities with an awesome nightlife. Seriously, who could ask for anything more!?"

Admissions

Successful applicants to SMU have leadership experience, a strong academic record, and competitive scores on the GMAT. Last year, the average GMAT score for accepted applicants was 644. Personal qualities are also heavily weighed, and Cox admits students with a history of professional and personal growth, demonstrated achievements, proven academic abilities, and leadership potential. Although an academic background in business is not a requirement for admission, SMU recommends students enter the program with a working knowledge of calculus, accounting, statistics, and microeconomics. Qualified applicants are offered the opportunity to interview with the Admissions staff.

Admissions criteria differ slightly for students seeking admission to Cox's part-time programs. In addition to the aforementioned, applicants to the PMBA program must have at least 2 years of professional work experience and a strong basic knowledge of accounting, statistics, and microeconomics. Applicants to the executive MBA program are expected to have a minimum of 8 years of experience in mid- to upper-level management and to currently hold a senior-level title.

FINANCIAL FACTS

Annual tuition	$33,360
Fees	$3,230
Cost of books	$2,000
Room & board (off-campus)	$10,000
% of students receiving grants	73
Average grant	$23,000

ADMISSIONS

Admissions Selectivity Rating	**88**
# of applications received	315
% applicants accepted	51
% acceptees attending	52
Average GMAT	643
Range of GMAT	610–680
Average GPA	3.19
TOEFL required of international students	Yes
Minimum TOEFL (paper/computer)	600/250
Application fee	$75
Regular application deadline	4/15
Regular notification	6/1
Application Deadline/Notification	
Round 1:	11/15 / 1/15
Round 2:	1/15 / 3/15
Round 3:	3/1 / 5/1
Round 4:	4/15 / 6/1
Early decision program?	Yes
ED Deadline/Notification	11/15 / 01/15
Deferment available	Yes
Maximum length of deferment	1 year
Need-blind admissions	Yes

Applicants Also Look At

Georgetown University, Rice University, Texas A&M University System Health Science Center, Texas Christian University (TCU), The University of Texas at Austin, Vanderbilt University, Washington University.

EMPLOYMENT PROFILE

Career Rating	83	Grads Employed by Function	%	Avg. Salary
Primary Source of Full-time Job Acceptances		Finance/Accounting	37	$74,750
School-facilitated activities	21 (50%)	Human Resources	5	NR
Graduate-facilitated activities	20 (48%)	Marketing/Sales	29	$75,327
Unknown	1 (2%)	Operations/Production	2	NR
Average base starting salary	$76,902	Consulting	12	$88,800
Percent employed	70	General Management	5	NR
		Other	10	$55,900

Top 5 Employers Hiring Grads

American Airlines; Behringer Harvard Real Estate Investments; Frito-Lay; FTI Consulting; Johnson & Johnson.

ST. JOHN'S UNIVERSITY
THE PETER J. TOBIN COLLEGE OF BUSINESS

GENERAL INFORMATION
Type of school	Private
Affiliation	Roman Catholic
Environment	Metropolis
Academic calendar	Semester

SURVEY SAYS . . .
Students love Queens, NY
Happy students
Smart classrooms
Solid preparation in:
Teamwork
Presentation skills

STUDENTS
Enrollment of parent institution	20,348
Enrollment of business school	663
% male/female	55/45
% out-of-state	40
% part-time	68
% minorities	15
% international	37
Average age at entry	26
Average years work experience at entry	3

ACADEMICS
Academic Experience Rating	**78**
Student/faculty ratio	12:1
Profs interesting rating	79
Profs accessible rating	72
% female faculty	18
% minority faculty	10

Joint Degrees
JD/MBA (full-time enrollment required) 4 years.

Prominent Alumni
Kathryn Morrissey, president, global wholesale markets, AT&T; Richard Carbone, CFO, Prudential Financial; Joseph Garcia, CFO, Spanish Broadcasting System.

Academics

"New York City is the financial capital of the world," one MBA student at St. John's Tobin College of Business correctly observes, "and SJU's proximity to the city is one of its greatest strengths." Indeed, Tobin offers three location options to students seeking an MBA at New York, the university's main campus in Jamaica, Queens; a small campus in the financial district of Manhattan (the focus here is primarily on risk management, insurance, and financial services); and another small campus on Staten Island (most courses here are in accounting-related fields). A fourth campus gives students yet another fabulously urban option: Rome, Italy, where international business and finance are in the spotlight.

Access to New York means access to great faculty, and MBAs at Tobin tell us that St. John's has recruited a solid core of teachers. "Most of my accounting/tax professors have graduated from prestigious law schools and have had successful careers. Learning from them has been a huge benefit," writes one accounting student. Students also praise the faculty in insurance and marketing. MBAs here appreciate the fact that "New York City is known throughout the world as a financial hub. This can provide many opportunities for employment, or even education experiences for students."

Students love how Tobin "is currently updating curriculum, constantly improving teaching methods, implementing new technology, and hiring new professors educated in the academic and professional fields. The result is a positive and worthwhile experience." The program "places a lot of emphasis on team-building and presentation skills," which students find useful. One writes, "Most classes are presented, in full or in part, as seminars, requiring students to work in groups and presenting to the class. These activities are helpful in developing needed skills." Students also approve of "the strong emphasis the school places on ethics in business practice." The administration scores high marks in the helpfulness department. Asked where SJU needs an upgrade, students suggest that Tobin "could further improve by continuing the technology program currently being undertaken to encompass the entire campus, with emphasis on including wireless capabilities in lecture halls and on laptop computers in standard course procedures for the MBA program." Some even feel that "the emphasis on technology within the program will allow SJU to propel the MBA program years ahead of other comparable universities."

Career and Placement

The Career Center at St. John's University provides placement and counseling services for Tobin MBAs as well as for all other students of the university. Students remind us that St. John's location is a great boon to their career searches. Being in New York provides "great networking opportunities with companies long before you start working through clubs and departmental events."

Employers most likely to hire Tobin MBAs include Accenture, American Express Company, Citigroup, City of New York, JPMorgan Chase, Merrill Lynch, and Revlon.

SHEILA RUSSELL, ASSISTANT DIRECTOR OF MBA ADMISSIONS
8000 UTOPIA PARKWAY, 111 BENT HALL, QUEENS, NY 11439 UNITED STATES
PHONE: 718-990-1345 • FAX: 718-990-5242
E-MAIL: MBAADMISSIONS@STJOHNS.EDU • WEBSITE: WWW.STJOHNS.EDU / TOBIN

Student Life and Environment

The Tobin MBA program "is mostly designed for those who work during the day, so classes are only offered at night." One full-time student writes, "The schedule took some getting used to, but once I got used to it, I began to appreciate it, as I can spend my days studying and doing research for my graduate assistant program." Full-timers are otherwise "very active and very proactive on campus. Within the past year, many students have combined their efforts to implement clubs and activities that provide networking opportunities, academic opportunities, and social gatherings." Even the campus itself "is an active one. Due to the NYC area and the fast-paced environment, the campus is always fluttering with excitement, from sports events to guest lectures by individuals such as Spike Lee and Cornell West." The majority of MBA students, however, experience little of this excitement; they're here as part-timers who come to campus for class, then leave. One MBA explains, "Unfortunately, my work and school schedule do not provide me with many opportunities to participate in campus activities. I attend St. John's on a part-time basis while working full-time."

One look at the student body here tells you that Tobin is "a real New Yorker school" with "type-A MBA students in abundance,"—and they wouldn't have it any other way. "Their aims are clear, their motivations are apparent, their goals are attainable, and their willingness to increase the level of competition in the program produces professionals uniquely qualified and highly valued in their particular professional fields," explains one student. With its main campus in Queens, Tobin needn't look far to attract an international student body, one of the world's most international populations lives within a 10-mile radius of the school. Students "come from different countries and bring their business experience to the table." One student comments, "It has also been a pleasure meeting such a diverse group of students and having the opportunity to study and prepare group projects with them while surrounded by the energetic city of New York."

Admissions

Tobin requires all applicants to provide the admissions with: official transcripts for all undergraduate, graduate, and professional school academic work attempted; an official GMAT score report for an exam taken within the past five years; letters of recommendation; a personal statement; and a resume. Students whose native language is not English must also submit an official TOEFL score report. Work experience is not required for admission to the program, although it is preferred. Informal on-campus interviews are available for prospective students but are not required, except in special cases.

FINANCIAL FACTS

Annual tuition	$23,850
Fees	$250
Cost of books	$3,000
Room & board	
(on/off-campus)	$12,000/$15,000
% of students receiving aid	30
% of first-year students	
receiving aid	14
Average award package	$14,914
Average grant	$1,812

ADMISSIONS

Admissions Selectivity Rating	76
# of applications received	644
% applicants accepted	59
% acceptees attending	62
Average GMAT	530
Range of GMAT	440–630
Average GPA	3.2
TOEFL required of	
international students	Yes
Minimum TOEFL (paper)	580
Application fee	$40
Regular application deadline	6/1
Regular notification	Rolling
Deferment available	Yes
Maximum length of	
deferment	1 year
Transfer students accepted	Yes
Transfer application policy	
Must use regular application;	
individual review of transfer	
credits.	
Non-fall admissions	Yes
Need-blind admissions	Yes

Applicants Also Look At

City University of New York—Baruch College, Fordham University, Hofstra University, New York University, Pace University.

EMPLOYMENT PROFILE

Career Rating	85	Top 5 Employers Hiring Grads
		Merrill Lynch; PricewaterhouseCoopers; Citigroup; Deloitte Touche Tohmatsu; Goldman Sachs.

ST. MARY'S UNIVERSITY
BILL GREEHEY SCHOOL OF BUSINESS

GENERAL INFORMATION

Type of school	Private
Affiliation	Roman Catholic
Environment	Metropolis
Academic calendar	Semester

SURVEY SAYS . . .
Students love San Antonio, TX
Friendly students
Cutting-edge classes
Happy students
Solid preparation in:
Teamwork

STUDENTS

Enrollment of parent institution	3,904
Enrollment of business school	91
% male/female	60/40
% part-time	81
% minorities	10
Average age at entry	33
Average years work experience at entry	3

ACADEMICS

Academic Experience Rating	**83**
Student/faculty ratio	10:1
Profs interesting rating	80
Profs accessible rating	67
% female faculty	36
% minority faculty	4

Joint Degrees
JD/MBA.

Prominent Alumni
Bill Greehey, CEO, Valero Energy.

Academics

There are big days ahead for the MBA program at St. Mary's University. Thanks to a $25 million donation from Valero Energy chairman Bill Greehey, the university has planned major upgrades to the faculty, curriculum, and student scholarship support in the business school. The school of business—renamed in Greehey's honor in March of 2006—is one of the major beneficiary of the local philanthropist's largesse. Whatever improvements are made will only add to some already commendable assets here, including "a unique international entrepreneurship program" a "solid financial planning curriculum," and a professional accounting curriculum.

Prerequisites to MBA study at Greehey begin with the completion of six undergraduate-level fundamentals courses. Students arriving with undergraduate degrees in business can place out of these courses, as can students who demonstrate proficiency through CLEP and DANTES examinations. After completing or placing out of these fundamentals courses, students must complete a 30 semester-hour program that includes five core courses (in human resources, accounting/finance, international business, informational technology, and marketing). Tracks are offered in financial planning, professional accountancy and general management as well as a joint JD/MBA. (Note that the financial planning concentration requires two additional classes, meaning that students who choose this option must complete 36 semester hours to graduate.) All students must pass a written examination at the end of the program.

MBAs here praise the faculty for "focusing on teaching and understanding" and "providing real-life experience. They bring a lot of outside experience to the classroom." St. Mary's has always been known for its personal touches, and students confirm that "classes are small and the program as a whole is small. This allows for a lot of individual attention from professors and administrators." Students here appreciate this "laid- back program with not too much pressure" but wish that the administration was sometimes a little less laid back. They tell us that administrators "are very disorganized. They lose papers way too often."

Career and Placement

The Career Services Center at St. Mary's University serves all undergraduate students, graduate students, and alumni of the school. The office provides one-on-one advisement with career counselors, a library of career-related materials including hard-copy and online job search databases, special events (Resume Drive, Business Etiquette Dinner, Mock Interview Day), a career fair, and connections to an alumni mentoring program. Students tell us that "the strong alumni network" is one of the biggest attractions of a St. Mary's degree. Employers interviewing on the St. Mary's campus in the spring of 2006 included BNSF Railway; Fisher, Herbst, & Kemble; USAA; Valero Energy; and Walgreens.

Dr. Richard Menger, MBA Program Director

One Camino Santa Maria, San Antonio, TX 78228-8507 United States

Phone: 210-436-3101 • Fax: 210-431-2220

E-mail: lbagley@stmarytx.edu • Website: www.stmarytx.edu/business

Student Life and Environment

St. Mary's student body includes "many Hispanic women working toward improving their careers." The school has traditionally served the Hispanic community well; over half of all undergraduates here are Hispanic. On the whole, students "are diverse in age and cultures, all striving toward a common goal." Many "have careers and a family." Their classmates describe them as "team-oriented, hard-working, and friendly."

With over one million residents within city limits and almost as many living in the metropolitan area, San Antonio is the third-largest city in Texas and one of the larger cities in the country. The military and the petroleum industry both have major presences here. With nearly 20 million visitors every year, San Antonio is also a major player in the nation's tourism trade. Students speak highly of the city, although they warn that "the school is located in a very rough part of town."

Admissions

Applicants to the MBA program at St. Mary's must apply to the graduate school for admission. Applications are reviewed by the MBA program director, who makes recommendations to the Graduate Council. The council is then responsible for the final admissions decisions. Candidates must submit all of the following materials to the graduate admissions office: a completed application form; an official score report for the GMAT; two sets of official transcripts for all postsecondary academic work; two letters of recommendation "from individuals well acquainted with your academic/professional ability" (graduates of St. Mary's University are exempt from this requirement); and a completed health form (required by Texas State Law). An interview may also be required; candidates for whom an interview is required will be notified by the school. International applicants must provide all of the above materials as well as a signed financial statement; and, an official score report for the TOEFL (minimum acceptable score: 570 paper-based, 230 computer-based, 67 Internet; students with lower TOEFL scores may be allowed to attend the English Language School in order to meet minimum language proficiency requirements). Admitted students may receive regular admission, which is unconditional. Students may also receive conditional admission, which allows them to enroll in no more than nine hours of classes, after which their admission status is reappraised; or they may receive special admission as a nondegree seeking student. They may also receive auditor status, which is a noncredit option for students who are not working toward a graduate business degree.

FINANCIAL FACTS

Annual tuition	$18,240
Fees	$500
Cost of books	$750
Room & board (on/off-campus)	$6,000/$7,500
% of students receiving grants	2
Average grant	$24,000

ADMISSIONS

Admissions Selectivity Rating	**86**
# of applications received	59
% applicants accepted	63
% acceptees attending	100
Average GMAT	572
Range of GMAT	560–650
Average GPA	3.72
TOEFL required of international students	Yes
Minimum TOEFL (paper/computer)	570/230
Application fee	$30
Regular application deadline	Rolling
Regular notification	Rolling
Deferment available	Yes
Maximum length of deferment	1 year
Transfer students accepted	Yes
Transfer application policy On recommendation of the graduate program director may accept a maximum of 6 semester hours from AACSB-accredited programs.	
Non-fall admissions	Yes
Need-blind admissions	Yes

Applicants Also Look At

University of Texas Health Science Center at San Antonio.

STANFORD UNIVERSITY
STANFORD GRADUATE SCHOOL OF BUSINESS

Academics

Students are attracted to Stanford's "culture of entrepreneurship and social welfare," as well as its "strength in general management" and finance. "It's simply the best," explains one student, and the numerous students who turned down Harvard Business School for Stanford presumably agree. Anticipation runs high for the "exciting new curriculum," which debuts this year and will feature "a high degree of customization," mandatory "overseas experience," and a "leadership development program." The new second-year program offers a choice to take 16 out of more than 100 electives, ranging from "Strategy and Global Supply Networks" to "Entrepreneurial Design for Extreme Affordability," "Biodesign Innovation," "Managing Talent," and "Urban School System Reform." Overseas work encompasses international internships known as the Global Management Immersion Experience (GMIX), study trips ("Trips for 2007/2008 include Australia, Brazil, China, Ghana, Italy, Korea, Middle East, Russia, Scandinavia, Singapore/Malaysia, South Africa, and U.K./Ireland"), International Service Learning trips through the Public Management Program, and an exchange program with China's Tsinghua University School of Economics and Management. "This new curriculum is a huge differentiation point versus other b-schools, as Stanford is truly integrating new business trends and practices into not just course offerings but the entire methodology of education." "I wish I could reapply and start all over," comments one second-year.

"The weakest part of the school" may be the "overly bureaucratic" administration. Although one student sees administrators as "out of touch" and "cold-hearted," another says that the new curriculum proves they are "open to new ideas." As for faculty, "There's a highly academic culture among professors that places less value on teaching," says one student, "but it frankly hasn't affected the quality of my academic experience at all. My professors have mostly been very good and very accessible." "The professors are outstanding," affirms another student. "If you want to learn from accomplished, extremely successful businesspeople, . . . this is where they teach!" Another says, "I regularly eat lunch with one of the most successful venture capitalists in the Valley, who happens to be teaching my entrepreneurship elective."

Career and Placement

As far as job placement, there really is a Stanford difference. "If you want to learn how to effectively start and/or run a business, I would be hard pressed to find a school with more resources and a better network," says one student. Sure enough, about 10 percent of the class goes into entrepreneurship immediately after graduation. Stanford's outstanding relationship with high tech, private equity, and venture capital means that 21 percent of grads go into these fields. Location is everything—a slight majority of students stay on the West Coast, and more than a tenth go abroad, while only about a fifth work in the MBA-saturated Northeast. The median first-year salary for grads is $110,000. Students tell us that Stanford creates "a sense of perspective in its students that extends past their future professional lives. Stanford graduates well-rounded MBAs who will likely do well in many aspects of life, not just their job."

Student Life and Environment

Students describe the Stanford environment as a "cooperative culture" of "excellence without the arrogance," and are awed by the talent and diversity of their classmates. "My peers come from backgrounds in everything from international development to finance to consulting to education to entrepreneurship. Hearing their experiences and working with them is what has made the program." Students are more likely to have undergraduate

DERRICK BOLTON, DIRECTOR OF MBA ADMISSIONS
518 MEMORIAL WAY STANFORD, CA 94305-5015 UNITED STATES
PHONE: 650-723-2766 • FAX: 650-725-7831
E-MAIL: • WEBSITE: WWW.GSB.STANFORD.EDU

degrees in the humanities and social sciences and to possess advanced degrees than students at many other schools. They "are not just competent in one area but they are also intellectuals and athletes and musicians and entrepreneurs and board members and highly socially adept. Stanford GSB is a beautifully humbling experience because you are truly amongst the best of the best." Grades are not disclosed, and students are "collaborative"; they "reach out to help each other without being asked." Social life here is very active. These students "know how to juggle academic work with other club activities and partying," and many "want to spend the 2 years getting to know their classmates as well as possible."

The spacious campus has the feel and many of the luxuries of an exclusive resort. Gardens and palm trees surround university buildings, the weather is fine, sports facilities are excellent, and few strangers venture onto campus. "This morning I had a breakfast meeting with a designer from the design firm IDEO about a business I am working on with classmates, then went to the pool for a workout with some friends who are doing the Wildflower Triathlon with me," reports one student. Stanford is the hub of Silicon Valley, "a perfect location for someone looking to get into high tech," and for many entrepreneurs-in-training, that's excitement enough. One student tells us that "everyone talks about starting their own ventures." If neighboring Palo Alto feels "a bit boring and yuppity, . . . fortunately, San Francisco is only 30 minutes away" by car.

Admissions

The GSB Admissions Office says that candidates should not include academic recommendations unless they reflect work experience (as a TA or research assistant, for example). The top criteria for admission are "intellectual vitality," "demonstrated leadership potential," and "personal qualities and contributions"—Stanford looks for community leaders—so the "impact [you made] on [your] workplace" matters much more than your job responsibilities. Students report a broad range of GMAT scores, with a median of 720 (the GRE is also acceptable in some cases), and a median TOEFL score of 283.

FINANCIAL FACTS

Annual tuition	$45,921
Cost of books	$2,816
Room & board	
(on/off-campus)	$19,044/$19,809
% of students receiving aid	72
% of first-year students receiving aid	71
% of students receiving loans	62
% of students receiving grants	54
Average award package	$47,351
Average grant	$12,368
Average student loan debt	$80,937

ADMISSIONS

Admissions Selectivity Rating	99
# of applications received	4,868
% applicants accepted	10
% acceptees attending	79
Average GMAT	720
Range of GMAT	690–750
Average GPA	3.61
TOEFL required of international students	Yes
Minimum TOEFL (paper/computer)	600/250
Application fee	$245
Application Deadline/Notification	
Round 1:	10/25 / 1/18
Round 2:	1/10 / 4/5
Round 3:	3/14 / 5/10
Deferment available	Yes
Maximum length of deferment	Very limited
Need-blind admissions	Yes

Applicants Also Look At
Harvard University.

EMPLOYMENT PROFILE

Career Rating	**99**	**Grads Employed by Function**	**% Avg. Salary**
Primary Source of Full-time Job Acceptances		Finance/Accounting	37 $123,442
School-facilitated activities	132 (53%)	Marketing/Sales	18 $101,904
Graduate-facilitated activities	119 (47%)	Operations/Production	2 $97,500
Percent employed	94	Strategic Planning	6 $107,607
		Consulting	25 $108,282
		General Management	6 $99,286
		Venture Capital	2 $171,250
		Other	4 $100,500

Top 5 Employers Hiring Grads
Amazon.com; Genentech; Lehman Brothers; McKinsey & Company; T. Rowe Price.

STATE UNIVERSITY OF NEW YORK AT BINGHAMTON
SCHOOL OF MANAGEMENT

GENERAL INFORMATION
Type of school	Public
Environment	Town
Academic calendar	Semester

SURVEY SAYS . . .
Friendly students
Cutting-edge classes
Helpful alumni
Smart classrooms
Solid preparation in:
Teamwork
Presentation skills

STUDENTS
Enrollment of parent institution	14,716
Enrollment of business school	102
% male/female	69/31
% out-of-state	7
% part-time	8
% minorities	5
% international	38
Average age at entry	23
Average years work experience at entry	2

ACADEMICS
Academic Experience Rating	**77**
Student/faculty ratio	6:1
Profs interesting rating	86
Profs accessible rating	68
% female faculty	18
% minority faculty	1

Joint Degrees
BS/MBA (Watson School of Engineering) 5 years,
BA/MBA (Harpur College of Arts and Sciences) 5 years.

Academics

The School of Management at SUNY Binghamton (Binghamton University to the locals) piggybacks on the university's "world-renowned Center for Leadership Studies" to offer a highly regarded concentration in HRM/consulting and leadership. Finance is another strong area at SOM; the *Journal of Finance* recently ranked the faculty twenty-third out of 330 finance departments in terms of research productivity per faculty member. MBAs here also speak highly of Binghamton's accounting program.

That's not a bad trifecta for a program as small as this one (fewer than 130 MBAs attend, most full-time); the presence of a large research university with a big undergraduate business program certainly helps a lot here. Despite their high profile as research heavyweights, professors earn praise for being "very approachable. Many prefer to be on a first-name basis with students [and] are available for hours each day and very willing to work with students. They can be flexible with workload if there is a week with an inordinate amount of projects due and/or tests." As at many research-intensive institutions, not all are great teachers. "Most present their ideas clearly, some less so diplomatically," offers one MBA.

Students especially appreciate that "the SOM is constantly trying to improve. That means administrators are open to student suggestions and they support students as much as they can in academics and job searching." One MBA observes, "Everyone, including the Dean and Associate Dean, has an open-door policy." MBAs are less enthusiastic about the pervasiveness of team-based study throughout the curriculum. One student laments, "So many of my international colleagues are dependent on my assistance for understanding the basic information being presented in class that it greatly hampers my ability to learn as an individual."

Despite this drawback, most here feel that this same "diversity (of interests and backgrounds) among students and faculty" is actually one of Binghamton's strengths. Best of all, it's an MBA that can be acquired for the proverbial song. As one student explains, "Considering the price of an MBA here, you get a great education for your money!"

Career and Placement

Like most small programs, Binghamton lacks a powerhouse Career Development Center; it's simply too hard to attract lots of recruiters to a campus this remote to interview so few MBAs. The office does what it can, offering counseling services, career workshops, resume-development services, resume-referral services, a career-resource library, and access to the alumni network.

Top employers of Binghamton MBAs include Ernst & Young, Estée Lauder, Wal-Mart, Canon, American Express Company, BAE Systems, State Street, KPMG International, and First Capital. About two-thirds of all graduates remain in the Mid-Atlantic states or New England. Approximately one in eight lands a job overseas.

Student Life and Environment

Binghamton MBAs "focus heavily on academics. One MBA says, "Many of us are teaching as well as pursuing our own degree. For many of us, there is little time for clubs or other activities." Which works out just fine, since there aren't many, anyway. The program is simply too small to sustain much in the way of MBA-specific extracurricular clubs. The university at large, however, is another matter. It's home to "many undergraduate-organized clubs (over 250) that accept any student as a member." One MBA explains, "Because Binghamton has such a large undergraduate population, there are

ALESIA WHEELER-WADE, ASSISTANT DIRECTOR MBA/MS PROGRAM
SCHOOL OF MANAGEMENT, PO BOX 6000, VESTAL PARKWAY, E. BINGHAMTON, NY 13902-6000 U.S.
PHONE: 607-777-2317 • FAX: 607-777-4872
E-MAIL: SOMADVIS@BINGHAMTON.EDU • WEBSITE: SOM.BINGHAMTON.EDU

clubs for many activities, sports, intellectual interests, and nationalities. If you're outdoorsy, this is a great place to be." So long as you own a raincoat, that is. As one MBA warns, "The weather is very overcast and it rains a lot," making "the town seem worndown and lethargic."

Indeed, students agree that hometown Binghamton "doesn't have much going on, but it's a quiet, inexpensive place to concentrate on studies. And the graduate student population is large and diverse, providing opportunities to meet people." On another positive note, "The areas surrounding campus are very safe" and the downtown area has "a number of college bars." There's also an "excellent transportation system run by students (grad and undergrad) that specifically targets the off-campus locations where most students live. It also provides jobs for students." For those so inclined, "the athletic facilities on campus are very nice, and very usable to every student."

Binghamton's "enthusiastic, outgoing, very diverse" student body includes a sizable aggregation of international students who "share what they have learned through life experience." Most here "are very studious and competitive," which "fosters an intellectually stimulating environment." They're not cutthroat, however. They "enjoy commiserating with each other over [their] workloads" and when it comes down to it are "more cooperative than competitive, which helps create a friendly learning environment for everyone."

Admissions

Applicants to the Binghamton MBA program must submit two copies of official undergraduate transcripts for all college work, two letters of recommendation, a personal statement, and GMAT scores. Work experience, while preferred, is not required. Additionally, international students must submit a certified statement of financial responsibility and TOEFL scores (minimum acceptable paper-and-pencil score is 580).

To attract minority applicants, the School of Management offers the Clifford D. Clark Graduate Fellowship Program for Underrepresented Minority Students. According to the school, "These fellowships are granted to students entering both master's and doctoral degree programs and carry stipends of between $6,800 and $12,750 (depending on discipline) for the academic year plus a full-tuition scholarship. Renewals or graduate assistantships may be awarded in subsequent years, depending upon availability of funds.

FINANCIAL FACTS

Annual tuition (in-state/ out-of-state)	$7,100/$11,340
Fees	$1,019
Cost of books	$1,500
Room & board (on/off-campus)	$0/$6,800
% of students receiving aid	50
% of first-year students receiving aid	45
% of students receiving loans	34
% of students receiving grants	20
Average award package	$8,275
Average grant	$8,275
Average student loan debt	$23,047

ADMISSIONS

Admissions Selectivity Rating	84
# of applications received	262
% applicants accepted	57
% acceptees attending	45
Average GMAT	614
Range of GMAT	590–640
Average GPA	3.33
TOEFL required of international students	Yes
Minimum TOEFL (paper/computer)	580/237
Application fee	$60
Regular application deadline	3/15
Regular notification	Rolling
Deferment available	Yes
Maximum length of deferment	1 year
Need-blind admissions	Yes

Applicants Also Look At
City University of New York—Baruch College, State University of New York at Albany, State University of New York—University at Buffalo, SUNY—College at Geneseo, Syracuse University.

EMPLOYMENT PROFILE

Career Rating	80	Grads Employed by Function	%	Avg. Salary
Primary Source of Full-time Job Acceptances		Finance/Accounting	27	$64,666
School-facilitated activities	17 (77%)	Marketing/Sales	9	$36,250
Unknown	5 (23%)	MIS	5	$55,000
Average base starting salary	$55,409	Consulting	45	$55,400
Percent employed	95	General Management	9	$45,000
		Other	5	$59,500

Top 5 Employers Hiring Grads
Ernst & Young; KPMG International; Protiviti; Bloomberg.

STATE UNIVERSITY OF NEW YORK—OSWEGO
SCHOOL OF BUSINESS

Academics

Students who enroll in the School of Business at SUNY Oswego can expect several things: excellent value for their money, intimate classes, knowledgeable professors, state-of-the-art facilities, and an excellent hockey team. As one student puts it, "In most areas, the school of business is at the top of its class. The classes are challenging and worthwhile. Most professors are really good at their areas. They are also widely available to help students both inside and out of class." According to most of the students, the "very small classes promote learning and student-professor interaction."

Designed as a degree in general management, an MBA from SUNY Oswego provides a solid grounding in the basics of modern business organization. The school says that "this program is intended to be equally applicable to private, public, and governmental sectors of management." The core subjects required of students include management, accounting, marketing, organization, law, and finance. In addition, students can choose to specialize in a specific field such as international management, manufacturing management, organizational leadership, or financial services. Core requirements include management information systems, managerial finance, marketing management, management science I, international business, global perspectives on organizational management, and management policy. A wide range of electives is also available to students at SUNY Oswego, including management economics, database development, collective bargaining, industrial and organizational psychology, industrial sociology, principles of forecasting, business research, futures and options markets, database development, project management, public-sector accounting, and advanced auditing.

Students find their course work both rigorous and exciting. As one puts it, "the professors are excellent and the classes are fun and challenging." Another says, "the course load is challenging, requiring solid communication and organization skills. Many professors are conducting research on global trade, accounting, and management science. My academic experience has been very positive. I would suggest Oswego to all prospective business students (undergraduate or graduate)."

Career and Placement

Although Oswego has a lot to offer—lovely campus, low cost, quality education, intimate program—most students wish it would go further in strengthening its Career Services department. There is little aid specifically for prospective MBAs, and the job search is often directed almost entirely by the student. As one puts it, "Connecting with employers is a difficult task. Linking up with quality employers looking for graduates with postgraduate degrees needs to be addressed."

ADMISSIONS CONTACT, GRADUATE OFFICE, DAVID W. KING, DEAN OF GRADUATE STUDIES
ADDRESS: 602 CULKIN HALL, SUNY OSWEGO, OSWEGO, NY 13126 UNITED STATES
PHONE: 315-312-3692 • FAX: 315-312-3577
E-MAIL: MBA@OSWEGO.EDU • WEBSITE: WWW.OSWEGO.EDU/BUSINESS/MBA

Student Life and Environment

Students at SUNY Oswego rave about their "beautiful campus," which, they proudly point out, is also extremely "technologically advanced and mostly wireless." The typical MBA's social life is strong, and there are "plenty of bars around for an active nightlife." As one student says, "At Oswego, I had the opportunity to make new friends from all over the world. The social life is active and I consider myself lucky." For the most part, students claim to be "very active on campus. There is a multitude of clubs and organizations to choose from." Students enjoy their "great gyms to work out in or play a game of racquetball." Plus—as is typical in upstate New York—the school's athletic life centers on their "excellent hockey team, instead of football." As one student puts it, "what's excellent about living on campus here is that there is every resource that you could possibly need available on campus. There are new buildings and renovations, from a new student center to the newly renovated freshman residence hall and new business center with technology classrooms."

Admissions

To be considered for admission to the small MBA program at the School of Business at SUNY Oswego, a candidate must have a minimum GPA of 2.6 out of 4.0. The minimum required score for the GMAT is 450, unless the applicant's native language is not English, in which case the minimum score is 400. Taking the TOEFL test is also required for students whose native language is not English.

FINANCIAL FACTS

Annual tuition (in-state/ out-of-state)	$7,100/$11,340
Fees	$721
Cost of books	$800
Room & board (on-campus)	$8,840
% of students receiving aid	45
% of first-year students receiving aid	14
% of students receiving loans	29
% of students receiving grants	18
Average award package	$13,650
Average grant	$533
Average student loan debt	$30,120

ADMISSIONS

Admissions Selectivity Rating	63
# of applications received	86
% applicants accepted	90
% acceptees attending	29
Average GMAT	520
Range of GMAT	310–750
Average GPA	3.00
TOEFL required of international students	Yes
Minimum TOEFL (paper/computer)	560/220
Application fee	$50
Regular application deadline	4/15
Regular notification	6/1
Deferment available	Yes
Maximum length of deferment	1 year
Transfer students accepted	Yes
Transfer application policy 2 classes may be transferred into the program.	
Non-fall admissions	Yes
Need-blind admissions	Yes

Applicants Also Look At

State University of New York at Albany, State University of New York—University at Buffalo.

EMPLOYMENT PROFILE

Career Rating	68	Grads Employed by Function	%	Avg. Salary
		Finance/Accounting	10	$38,000
		Human Resources	5	NR
		MIS	5	NR
		Operations/Production	10	NR
		General Management	5	NR
		Quantitative	5	NR
		Nonprofit	10	NR

STATE UNIVERSITY OF NEW YORK—UNIVERSITY AT ALBANY
SCHOOL OF BUSINESS

Academics

Students in the MBA programs at State University of New York—University at Albany School of Business love that the school "constantly updates the curriculum to mirror current business trends." In its full-time and various part-time programs, Albany uses "a combination of classroom instruction and applied experience" to prepare students for the business world of tomorrow.

About one in four MBA students at Albany attend the program full-time. This number includes the majority of international students, who account for approximately 20 percent of the student body. The full-time program takes two years to complete. The first year is dedicated to core competencies; students undertake in-depth study in accounting, economics, finance, human resources, information systems, and marketing. Case studies play a central role in classroom study, as do reading assignments and classes that divide time between lectures and discussions. Group projects supplement the curriculum and offer students opportunities to develop important teamwork skills. The first year culminates in a one-week integrative course that addresses social, legal, and political issues in international business. According to students, the first-year curriculum "is heavily weighted toward global business and the changing economy."

The second year of the full-time program—which also allows students to develop an area of specialization—focuses on technology, an area in which Albany excels. Students praise the school's "cutting-edge use of technology and IT knowledge" and note that "everyone learns IT here." Students' work in this area reaches its high point in an information systems-based field project during which students provide consulting services to such organizations as the Albany Medical Center, DuPont, GE, KeyCorp, PepsiCo, Tiffany & Co., Towers Perrin, and a variety of regional nonprofits. The field project consumes one-third of the second-year curriculum, with a hands-on approach that prepares students for full-time employment.

Albany also offers several part-time options. In the Evening MBA Program, classes convene once a week in three-hour sessions. The program is "extremely flexible" and allows students to enter during the Fall, Spring, or Summer semester. Evening MBA program students may use elective classes to develop a specialization in management information systems, management, marketing, finance, new venture development, or tax. A Weekend MBA Program is also available; its classes meet every other weekend, with classes held on Friday afternoons and all day Saturday. It now also includes a one-week international business experience. This program meets off campus at a satellite facility in Saratoga. Students may enter the program in the fall only, and enrollment is limited to 24 students per year.

Career and Placement

Albany's School of Business maintains its own Career Services Office, whose work is supplemented by the school's Career Development Center, which serves the entire university. The Career Services Office provides workshops on cover letter writing, resume writing, interviewing, developing job-search skills, and honing business-related social skills. MBAs who graduate from Albany receive job offers from many small and medium-sized businesses as well as from such business giants as Accenture, Bear Stearns, Deloitte Consulting, Deutsche Bank, Ernst & Young, Goldman Sachs, IBM, KPMG & International, Merrill Lynch, and PricewaterhouseCoopers. Results from a recent survey indicate that MBAs typically receive initial offers in the $60,000 range.

Student Life and Environment

Most students in the Albany MBA program attend part-time; they have little time to

ZINA LAWRENCE, DIRECTOR, GRADUATE STUDENT SERVICES
1400 WASHINGTON AVENUE BA 361 ALBANY, NY 12222 UNITED STATES
PHONE: 518-442-4961 • FAX: 518-442-4975
E-MAIL: BUSWEB@ALBANY.EDU • WEBSITE: WWW.ALBANY.EDU/BUSINESS

devote to extracurricular life because of their commitments to course work, careers, and family. The program attracts "many area IT professionals and their coworkers," but the student body is fairly diverse, with participants "from many different fields, industries, career levels, and cultural backgrounds." Students tell us that "it is a wonderful experience to be in a classroom with people that have very diversified backgrounds."

Nearly 17,000 students are enrolled in the nine degree-granting schools and colleges at the State University of New York at Albany. Like all large state universities, it pursues the mission of offering an affordable education to state residents while also providing the state and country with cutting-edge research. The university was founded in 1844; undergraduate business study was not added to the curriculum until 1970. Graduate business programs began a few years later. Facilities include classrooms and computer labs equipped with the latest high-tech accoutrements; these serve the program's focus on technology well. Students appreciate the facilities but note that "the campus buildings should be spruced up a bit. The buildings are old and unattractive."

Admissions

Applicants to the MBA program at the State University of New York at Albany School of Business must provide the graduate admissions department with all of the following: official copies of transcripts for all postsecondary academic work, an official score report for the GMAT, a resume, three letters of recommendation, and a personal statement of purpose. International applicants must provide all of the above plus an official score report for the TOEFL (minimum acceptable score: 600 paper-based; 250 computer based); and a financial affidavit accompanied by appropriate supporting documentation to demonstrate the applicant's "ability to meet all educational and living expenses for the entire period of intended study." Furthermore, international academic transcripts in languages other than English must be accompanied by a certified English translation.

FINANCIAL FACTS

Annual tuition (in-state/ out-of-state)	$7,100/$11,340
Fees	$1,028
Cost of books	$1,000
Room & board (on/off-campus)	$9,000/$7,500
% of students receiving aid	60
% of first-year students receiving aid	50
% of students receiving loans	75
% of students receiving grants	10
Average award package	$14,200
Average grant	$15,000
Average student loan debt	$20,000

ADMISSIONS

Admissions Selectivity Rating	79
# of applications received	282
% applicants accepted	56
% acceptees attending	73
Average GMAT	542
Range of GMAT	450–640
Average GPA	3.24
TOEFL required of international students	Yes
Minimum TOEFL (paper/computer)	600/250
Application fee	$75
Regular application deadline	3/1
Regular notification	6/6
Deferment available	Yes
Maximum length of deferment	1 year
Transfer students accepted	Yes
Transfer application policy Students are allowed up to 6 transfer credits.	
Need-blind admissions	Yes

Applicants Also Look At
State University of New York at Binghamton, State University of New York—University at Buffalo.

EMPLOYMENT PROFILE

Career Rating	74	Grads Employed by Function	%	Avg. Salary
Primary Source of Full-time Job Acceptances		Finance/Accounting	4	$40,000
School-facilitated activities	70%	Human Resources	26	$56,500
Graduate-facilitated activities	20%	MIS	27	$52,600
Unknown	10%	Consulting	41	$63,000
Average base starting salary	$54,200	Nonprofit	2	$42,000
Percent employed	87	**Top 5 Employers Hiring Grads**		

Top 5 Employers Hiring Grads
Deloitte Consulting; KPMG International; GE; E and Y; New York State.

STATE UNIVERSITY OF NEW YORK—UNIVERSITY AT BUFFALO
SCHOOL OF MANAGEMENT

GENERAL INFORMATION
Type of school   Public
Environment   Metropolis
Academic calendar   Semester

SURVEY SAYS . . .
Smart classrooms
Solid preparation in:
Teamwork
Communication/interpersonal skills
Quantitative skills

STUDENTS
Enrollment of parent institution	27,220
Enrollment of business school	479
% male/female	55/45
% out-of-state	3
% part-time	43
% minorities	3
% international	40
Average age at entry	25
Average years work experience at entry	2

ACADEMICS
Academic Experience Rating	**79**
Student/faculty ratio	9:1
Profs interesting rating	71
Profs accessible rating	86
% female faculty	20
% minority faculty	30

Joint Degrees
JD/MBA, MD/MBA
MBA/Architecture, MBA/Pharmacy,
MBA/Geography, BS/MBA (Business
or Engineering), MBA/MSW,
AuD/MBA, MBA/MPH.

Prominent Alumni
Robert W. Black, senior vice president and chief strategy officer, Kimberly-Clark; Jeremy Jacobs, Sr., CEO, Delaware North Cos.; Millard Drexler, chairman and CEO, J. Crew; Margaret Hempling McGlynn, president-Merck Vaccines, Merck and Co., Inc.; John Q. Doyle, president, American Home Assurance Co. (an AIG Co.).

Academics

Students come to the "very affordable" and "reputable" State University of New York—University at Buffalo School of Management to get a great education at a great price. Teamwork defines the Buffalo experience. First-year students spend 8–12 hours a week in their assigned study groups, a commitment that represents "the second most important aspect of the program next to class attendance," according to the university. One student warns that the "UB business school is highly dedicated to working in teams. If you are an individualistic individual you will most likely not like this environment." Ten study groups make up a cohort. The members of a cohort take core management courses together during the first year. Of these courses, students say statistics arguably "has the heaviest workload." Students take "one or two [additional] electives each semester."

For most students, the second year is about specialization. "University at Buffalo was one of the few schools I found that had the biotechnology [management] concentration," says one student. Specialization in this field means mandatory courses in entrepreneurship, intellectual property or FDA law, project management or product design, database management or medical statistics, and general management, as well as opportunities to take related classes outside the School of Management. UB's highly regarded finance major is bolstered by semesters and workshops at SUNY's Levin Institute in Manhattan. Much of the faculty is simply "outstanding," and "Most courses are of moderate workload." Students also rate the administration as "one of the best," willing to "bend over backward to help current students." MBA candidates wish for improved operations and marketing courses ("Everything I learned about marketing I learned from my internship," grumbles one second-year), a dedicated library, and increased "course offerings," made possible by "more teachers."

Career and Placement

Student opinion is divided on the helpfulness of UB's Career Resource Center (CRC). Enthusiastic students say the office "goes beyond the requirements to make sure that students are totally prepared for all aspects of the recruiting process. From the minute that you walk in the door, they have a checkpoint system to make sure that you are on track for obtaining a job after graduation." Alumni networking events such as a "cruise on Lake Erie" "allow MS/MBA students to discuss real-world industry experiences and how best to prepare for the job market."

Detractors contend that while the CRC "is great for students with [fewer] than 5 years of work experience" and its "technological resources are excellent," it doesn't draw "big recruiters outside the accounting discipline" and is too focused on the local area. Additionally, students say the CRC "does a poor job of prepping companies for on-campus job fairs; many company reps come unprepared to discuss opportunities with MS/MBA students." "I know many people who submitted resumes through the CRC for internships and did not get phone calls. However, when they later submitted them themselves, they did get phone calls," says a second-year. Average starting salary for the class of 2006 was $55,149. Top employers include Deloitte Touche Tohmatsu, Ernst & Young, M&T Bank, PepsiCo, and PricewaterhouseCoopers

JAIMIE FALZARANO, ASSISTANT DIRECTOR OF GRADUATE PROGRAMS
203 ALFIERO CENTER, BUFFALO, NY 14260 UNITED STATES
PHONE: 716-645-3204 • FAX: 716-645-2341
E-MAIL: SOM-APPS@BUFFALO.EDU • WEBSITE: MGT.BUFFALO.EDU

Student Life and Environment

The collegiality of the classroom environment at SUNY Buffalo spills over into the social life on campus, and the "competitive, cheerful" students spend their weekends "unwinding and getting to know each other" better. A bevy of organized activities exist for just this purpose. "The Graduate Management Association has a free happy hour each Friday to make sure students interact outside of the classroom. Additionally, they host at least one major social every month." "There are lots of student clubs and athletic activities, so [students] can get to know people with similar interests." The city of Buffalo, which boasts a conveniently "low cost of living," offers diversions like "Buffalo Sabres and Bills" games. Students say "There is always something to do at UB."

Buffalo's "hardworking and diverse" MBA students often come in "fresh," i.e., "with no [full-time] work experience." Some students gripe that this makes for "a challenging team environment when someone with years of experience enters" a study group. The cultural expertise of international students, who make up approximately 40 percent of the class, is highly valued: "We have country forums every month where students from a particular country can talk about their culture, traditions, and most importantly, the business practices in their country." American students tend to be "from the local area," and students say the school should "make a stronger effort to recruit minorities not represented in the business profession." One student notes that the school "needs more effort in European and Latin American recruitment," and recommends that the School of Management "offer financial aid for international students whose global experiences are not represented."

Admissions

Average GMAT and TOEFL scores for the class of 2008 were 595 and 256 respectively; the average student holds 2 years of work experience. International students must also take the SPEAK/TSE exam and (except in the case of a limited list of 16 Indian universities) must supplement 3-year degrees with an additional year of scholarship. The Admissions Office warns that criteria will become more selective for its next class, which will be 43 percent smaller at just 100 students.

FINANCIAL FACTS

Annual tuition (in-state/ out-of-state)	$7,100/$11,340
Fees	$1,315
Cost of books	$1,025
Room & board	$9,300
% of students receiving aid	25
% of first-year students receiving aid	20
% of students receiving grants	25
Average award package	$14,000
Average grant	$5,000

ADMISSIONS

Admissions Selectivity Rating	**85**
# of applications received	495
% applicants accepted	55
% acceptees attending	54
Average GMAT	595
Range of GMAT	568–669
Average GPA	3.3
TOEFL required of international students	Yes
Minimum TOEFL (paper/computer)	573/230
Application fee	$50
Regular application deadline	6/1
Regular notification	Rolling
Deferment available	Yes
Maximum length of deferment	1 year
Need-blind admissions	Yes

Applicants Also Look At

Boston University, Canisius College, City University of New York—Baruch College, State University of New York at Binghamton, The University of Texas at Dallas, University of Pittsburgh, University of Rochester.

EMPLOYMENT PROFILE

Career Rating	77
Primary Source of Full-time Job Acceptances	
School-facilitated activities	43 (57%)
Graduate-facilitated activities	33 (43%)
Average base starting salary	$55,149
Percent employed	75

Grads Employed by Function	%	Avg. Salary
Finance/Accounting	37	$59,408
Marketing/Sales	17	$51,000
MIS	7	$65,000
Operations/Production	19	$51,777
Consulting	7	$54,800
General Management	12	$62,778
Other	1	NR

Top 5 Employers Hiring Grads
Ernst & Young; Citigroup; Deloitte Touche Tohmatsu; HSBC; M&T Bank.

STETSON UNIVERSITY
SCHOOL OF BUSINESS ADMINISTRATION

GENERAL INFORMATION
Type of school	Private
Environment	Town
Academic calendar	Semesters

SURVEY SAYS . . .
Cutting-edge classes
Solid preparation in:
Finance
Quantitative skills
Doing business in a global economy

STUDENTS
Enrollment of parent institution	2,700
Enrollment of business school	205
% male/female	64/36
% out-of-state	15
% part-time	60
% minorities	9
% international	8
Average age at entry	26
Average years work experience at entry	2

ACADEMICS
Academic Experience Rating	**79**
Student/faculty ratio	15:1
Profs interesting rating	89
Profs accessible rating	88
% female faculty	25
% minority faculty	4

Joint Degrees
MBA/JD 3 years.

Academics

One of the advantages of small programs like the Stetson University School of Business Administration—which sometimes hosts fewer than 20 students—is that you really "get to know each other." As one student says, "The faculty and administration at Stetson are easily accessible and extremely supportive. Everyone is on a first-name basis, and the individual attention makes me feel as if my money was well spent." Many claim that the "nicest thing is that the school is small, and class sizes are small." One student says, "I have had a great experience at Stetson and am glad that I chose this school for my graduate-level classes. The professors always have time to talk to you and help you [and]. . . the administration is great and will help you whenever you need it."

The school, which is located on campuses throughout central Florida, "offers classes in three locations to serve the needs of not just the full-time student but also the working student." The locations are situated "throughout central Florida, including Orlando and Tampa, two of the largest metropolitan areas in Florida and two major job markets." Other students point out that "the proximity of the school to major job markets like Orlando, Tampa, and Jacksonville is a major strength of the program" that helps to draw "Many international students and working professionals with a passion for business!"

Stetson's MBA offers a general business management degree, though students can choose to specialize in a number of different areas. According to the school, "[The] programs are designed not to make you a technical specialist, but rather to provide you with a range of knowledge needed by the professional manager." The MBA program is divided into two parts: the business foundation and the advanced-level courses. Students appreciate the focus of the program along with its "current curriculum" taught by "very knowledgeable" and "concerned" professors. Others have been extremely impressed by "the professional experience that the faculty brings from their diverse backgrounds" and how "Everyone is encouraged to work in teams and [to] get to know each other."

Stetson also offers several special programs for its business students including the Family Business Center, the Joseph C. Prince Entrepreneurial Program, and the Roland George Investments Program. Stetson also has a summer school abroad program in Innsbruck, Austria, that is open to students in all majors and concentrations. Still, many students would like to see "an entrepreneurship program for students interested in that field" as well as more offerings in "economics" and "stock market overview." Another complaint is the uneven distribution of classes among the campuses. Though DeLand houses the main campus, many students complain that "the course offerings at the Celebration campus in Orlando and the Law School campus in Gulfport are not as plentiful as in DeLand."

Career and Placement

Stetson's Career Management Office offers a variety of services to its MBA students including "individual career counseling, career planning and development in the classroom, resume referrals, internship development, full-time placement, on-campus recruiting, mock interviews, and the Business and Industry Speaker Series presentations." However, some students still express dissatisfaction with the office, feeling it "needs improvement."

DR. FRANK A. DEZOORT, DIRECTOR, GRADUATE BUSINESS PROGRAMS
421 NORTH WOODLAND BOULEVARD, UNIT 8398, DELAND, FL 32723 UNITED STATES
PHONE: 386-822-7410 • FAX: 386-822-7413
E-MAIL: JBOSCO@STETSON.EDU • WEBSITE: WWW.STETSON.EDU/BUSINESS

Student Life and Environment

With campuses in DeLand (20 minutes north of Orlando), Celebration (located in Orlando), and Gulfport (near St. Petersburg), Stetson University has the advantages of pleasant weather, active campus life, vital student athletics, and an extremely friendly student body. As a "values-centered, comprehensive, private liberal arts university," Stetson promises on its website that all of its students will be "challenged by [the] academic programs in more than 40 disciplines. Just as importantly, [students] will learn about life and all the opportunities it holds." As one student says, "We have a well-rounded class with a global perspective. The facilities are modern, and the campus is beautiful. The class sizes are small, and the competition is stiff." Many note the wide variety of activities on campus. "The school has so many clubs, sororities, fraternities, and intramurals," enthuses one student, while another explains his reasons for staying out of the fray: "The market keeps me plenty busy (and fishing on my boat)."

Besides the fact that "the student body feels like a small community where most people know each other," students are impressed that they've "met so many wonderful people while going to Stetson." To take a break from MBA stress, students decompress with their peers at beaches, bars, restaurants, and clubs. And then there's the omnipresent Disney World, "conveniently located less than 30 minutes from Daytona, which offers students wonderful, inexpensive nightlife and vacation spots."

Admissions

All applicants to Stetson's MBA program must have received a BA from an accredited college or university. Stetson is quick to point out that "the undergraduate degree need not be in business administration" since "the course of study is specifically designed to accommodate the non-business as well as the business degree holder." (According to the school, this combination of an "MBA with a non-business undergraduate degree is considered outstanding career preparation in many fields.") MBA applicants must submit GMAT scores, undergraduate transcripts, three letters of recommendation, a medical report, and a recent photograph of themselves in order to be considered.

FINANCIAL FACTS

Annual tuition	$16,500
Cost of books	$1,400

ADMISSIONS

Admissions Selectivity Rating	70
# of applications received	209
% applicants accepted	90
% acceptees attending	83
Average GMAT	529
Range of GMAT	425–690
Average GPA	3.5
TOEFL required of international students	Yes
Minimum TOEFL (paper/computer)	550/213
Application fee	$25
Regular application deadline	5/31
Regular notification	6/30
Application Deadline/Notification	
Round 1:	1/1 / 1/11
Round 2:	3/1 / 3/15
Round 3:	5/1 / 5/15
Round 4:	8/1 / 8/12
Early decision program?	Yes
ED Deadline/Notification	Fall
8/1,Spring 10/15,summer	
	4/15 / 6/15
Deferment available	Yes
Maximum length of deferment	1 year
Transfer students accepted	Yes
Transfer application policy Maximum 6 credit hours from AACSB-accredited school.	
Non-fall admissions	Yes
Need-blind admissions	Yes

EMPLOYMENT PROFILE	
Career Rating	71

SUFFOLK UNIVERSITY
SAWYER BUSINESS SCHOOL

Academics

When singing the praises of their Boston-based business school, Suffolk University students immediately mention the kindness and quality of their professors. Among the school's talented teaching staff "Most—over 95 percent—hold PhDs, and all are extremely passionate about the subject they are teaching." However, they aren't just knowledgeable; they are also dedicated educators. One current student adds, "One word describes Suffolk faculty: that is 'commitment.' Rain, snow, or sunlight, professors are available at any time through e-mail, phone, or by appointment." In fact, the entire institution is very student oriented. In addition to seeking help from their professors, Suffolk offers "many mentoring programs, networking programs, and advisors who are willing to help."

Boasting a sizable part-time population, many students choose Suffolk University because of its flexible scheduling options, which allows students to take courses at the main campus, at one of the many "satellite locations outside of Boston," or via the Internet. In that and many ways, Suffolk, "really caters to creating the optimal experience for someone who is working full-time and going to school part-time." Whether studying full-time or part-time, all Suffolk MBAs are required to take three introductory courses, plus 24 units of core course work in areas such as management, economics, and marketing. After completing these requirements, Suffolk students have a great deal of liberty in planning their educations, because the school offers more than 100 electives in areas such as accounting and finance, entrepreneurship, health administration, information systems, international business, and marketing.

A large percentage of the school's full-time students hail from outside the United States, which adds a "fresh, firsthand, and global intelligence to the classroom." Students appreciate the international angle, describing themselves as "a business-focused 'United Nations'—working together to learn about business and our place it." The school further demonstrates its commitment to an international business education through core and elective course work, including a series of global-travel seminars. These week-long courses are conducted in a foreign country and "At least two professors attend and really take part in the learning experience with the students."

Students further praise Suffolk's "commitment to group work and real business cases/studies," saying the teaching methodology reflects the fact that "important business decisions are not made [by] taking a written exam but by how you react in a situation and under pressure." Students have the chance to stretch their wings in the classroom thanks to "smaller class sizes, typically 25 to 35, where I . . . have the opportunity to share my working and leadership experiences as well as hearing about my peers'." Because of the practical focus, Suffolk students feel they are well prepared to start or to advance in their career after graduation. A student sums it up: "What will set a Suffolk University MBA grad apart from the others is the in-depth training we receive on crucial skills such as networking and follow-up protocols, self-assessment and self-evaluation skills, goal setting, speech and presentation skills, resume writing, interviewing skills, and business etiquette. The expertise and confidence gained from this knowledge is well worth the tuition."

Career and Placement

Suffolk prides itself on preparing students for the real world, and effective, long-term career planning is a major piece of the puzzle. In fact, every student at Suffolk must take an introductory course aptly named Effective Career Planning, designed to help students evaluate their professional skills and career paths and to make a solid plan for what they

JUDITH L. REYNOLDS, DIRECTOR OF GRADUATE ADMISSIONS
EIGHT ASHBURTON PLACE, BOSTON, MA 02108 UNITED STATES
PHONE: 617-573-8302 • FAX: 617-305-1733
E-MAIL: GRAD.ADMISSION@SUFFOLK.EDU • WEBSITE: WWW.SUFFOLK.EDU/BUSINESS

wish to accomplish with an MBA. In addition, the Suffolk MBA EDGE offers professional development events throughout the academic year. These events run the gamut from seminars on power lunches and the professional image to MBA networking week and Technology Day. MBA EDGE also hosts a number of career services events such as workshops on resume writing and salary negotiations.

Ideally located in downtown Boston, "There are numerous top Boston-based businesses that recruit at Suffolk University." However, some suggest that the school could broaden its scope of opportunities. "I would like to see the school bring in top recruiters in the investment banking and private equity sectors, and I know I am not alone in that desire. A Suffolk MBA can get a job in these sectors but it requires a great deal of leg work," explains a student.

Student Life and Environment

Whether you call it networking or socializing, "Suffolk stresses getting to know your peers and receiving the best education at the same time." With an admissions process that emphasizes personal qualities as well as academic excellence, "Suffolk University does an excellent job of handpicking the candidates for this program," admitting students who are "inquisitive travelers, inventive thinkers, creative problem-solvers and just plain down-to-earth." Thanks to the international focus and part-time programs, the school boasts a "very diverse culture with respect to age, ethnicity, gender, and employment background."

In addition to the friendships they make within the school of business, Suffolk MBAs also participate in "a graduate school association that often holds events at neighboring pubs and restaurants." Located in the heart of downtown Boston, "The campus has a constant buzz about it." A few blocks from Boston Commons and all the downtown restaurants, nightlife, and public transportation, the "terrific location" is what attracts many students to Suffolk in the first place.

Admissions

To apply to Suffolk University Sawyer School of Business, students must submit undergraduate transcripts, a resume, and a completed application, including essays. Those applying to the full-time program must have at least 1 year of work experience; however, the average admit has logged 3 years in a professional position. Part-time applicants are expected to have spent more time in the professional world and average 5 to 7 years of work experience. Applicants must also submit GMAT scores, though exceptions may be made for practicing CPAs, and attorneys.

FINANCIAL FACTS

Annual tuition	$29,490
Fees	$20
Cost of books	$1,010
Room & board (off-campus)	$12,000
% of students receiving aid	63
% of first-year students receiving aid	67
% of students receiving loans	34
% of students receiving grants	27
Average award package	$18,048
Average grant	$6,957

ADMISSIONS

Admissions Selectivity Rating	67
# of applications received	464
% applicants accepted	74
% acceptees attending	45
Average GMAT	502
Range of GMAT	450–650
Average GPA	3.19
TOEFL required of international students	Yes
Minimum TOEFL (paper/computer)	550/213
Application fee	$50
Regular application deadline	6/15
Regular notification	Rolling
Deferment available	Yes
Maximum length of deferment	1 year
Transfer students accepted	Yes
Transfer application policy Same as for regular applicants.	
Non-fall admissions	Yes
Need-blind admissions	Yes

Applicants Also Look At
Babson College, Bentley College, Boston College, Boston University, Northeastern University.

EMPLOYMENT PROFILE

Career Rating	84	Grads Employed by Function	%	Avg. Salary
Primary Source of Full-time Job Acceptances		Finance/Accounting	54	$67,100
School-facilitated activities	5 (31%)	Operations/Production	15	$75,000
Graduate-facilitated activities	11 (69%)	Consulting	8	$90,000
		General Management	15	$45,000
		Other	8	$135,000

Top 5 Employers Hiring Grads
PricewaterhouseCoopers; Ernst & Young; Fidelity Investments; IBM; Thomson Financial.

SYRACUSE UNIVERSITY
MARTIN J. WHITMAN SCHOOL OF MANAGEMENT

GENERAL INFORMATION
Type of school	Private
Environment	City
Academic calendar	Semester

SURVEY SAYS . . .
Smart classrooms
Solid preparation in:
OperationsTeamwork
Entrepreneurial studies

STUDENTS
Enrollment of parent institution	19,082
Enrollment of business school	349
% male/female	71/29
% part-time	80
% minorities	10
% international	50
Average age at entry	26
Average years work experience at entry	3

ACADEMICS
Academic Experience Rating	**86**
Student/faculty ratio	8:1
Profs interesting rating	65
Profs accessible rating	84
% female faculty	13

Joint Degrees
MBA/JD 4 years, MBA/Master of Public Administration 3 years, with any other degree-bearing graduate program offered at Syracuse University.

Prominent Alumni
Martin J. Whitman, founder, Third Avenue Value Fund; Dick Clark, chairman and CEO, Dick Clark Productions; Dan D'Aniello, founding partner, Carlyle Group; Alfonse D'Amato, former U.S. Senator; Arthur Rock; venture capitalist, Arthur Rock and Company.

Academics

A tiny MBA program at a "great, nationally recognized" university, the Whitman School of Business at Syracuse University provides a thorough business education in an intimate academic setting. With fewer than 30 students per entering class, students benefit from uniformly small class sizes, and "the opportunity to develop relationships with every classmate as well as professors." These relationships are incredibly valuable, as "Professors get to know students on a personal level and help out in every way they can." One student elaborates, "By talking with faculty and administration, I have been put in close personal contact with a number of prominent alumni and have even been offered internship positions at some of the top firms in their respective fields due to these alumni relationships."

Whitman's challenging 54-unit curriculum includes a year of core course work in essentials like economics and finance. Core courses extend into the second year; however, by the final semester, course work is comprised entirely of electives, and students may complete a concentration in accounting, entrepreneurship, finance, general management, supply chain management, or marketing management. In addition to the traditional program, the school offers an accelerated MBA for students with a business background. Students may also pursue a joint-degree with any other graduate department at the university, including "a great JD/MBA program with a lot of connections in and around New York City."

Mixing traditional lectures with hands-on projects, Whitman's curriculum introduces Syracuse students to both the practical and theoretical sides of business. A student shares, "Our leadership class was mostly lectures and reading and more of an in-class discussion that did not require intensive study. Our GEM class [involved] creating a whole new business from scratch, presenting to a venture capitalist and having a certain number of deliverables ready in 3 months." As a result of this variety, "The workload can be anywhere from easy to killer depending on deadlines and classes." Fortunately, students find lots of support: "Professors are regularly available, but especially on days they know students will need them—they are in their offices later than most students remain at school."

A great option for those early in their careers, Syracuse does not require previous professional experience for entry into the MBA program and "The majority of the MBA students in my class have had less than 5 years work experience, so [they] are fairly young." As one student explains, "I had internship experiences but no professional work experience. Syracuse University was one of the only universities that allowed me to get a quality MBA earlier in life when I have the time to go to school versus later in life when family and work become a higher priority than education."

Career and Placement

Career placement is taken seriously at Syracuse. During their studies, students hone their skills through internships at local companies, and "Every week there is some event for students to take part in, whether it is a guest speaker or networking reception." When it comes to permanent placements, "The school's strong accounting and supply chain [management] programs are well recognized nationally, and students in those fields get good job offers." However, with a young and largely international student body, placements can occasionally be more difficult. A current student explains, "Part of the problem is that because they accept students with little to no work experience, it is also tougher to place those MBA students in jobs, specifically international students in finance and marketing fields."

CAROL J. SWANBERG, DIRECTOR OF ADMISSIONS AND FINANCIAL AID
721 UNIVERSITY AVENUE, SUITE 315, SYRACUSE, NY 13244-2450 UNITED STATES
PHONE: 315-443-9214 • FAX: 315-443-9517
E-MAIL: MBAINFO@SYR.EDU • WEBSITE: WHITMAN.SYR.EDU

In 2006, 71 percent of students were employed within 3 months of graduation. Companies that offered positions to graduates include: Bear Stearns, ChinaTrust Commercial Bank, Citigroup, Deloitte Touche Tohmatsu, Ellis Deming Development, Ernst & Young, Health Net, JPMorgan Chase, PricewaterhouseCoopers, Rockefeller & Co., Samsung SDI, and Verizon Wireless. Another nice perk is that the school "pays for CFA testing and travel expenses for job interviews."

Student Life and Environment

You might be surprised how much you'll learn from your classmates on this tiny but diverse campus. A student praises, "Many of the students have international backgrounds and offer an international/alternative perspective to traditional North American ways of thinking." Despite students' cultural differences, the environment is noncontentious and friendly, and "People here really care for others, especially new students." There are many ways to fill your free time at Syracuse, and students say the "Many academic, social, and cultural activities to choose from [make] the experience rewarding." When they aren't hitting the books, students "plan trips together (to national and international destinations), events together (i.e., bowling night, international day), and involve the faculty as well (i.e., student versus faculty softball)."

While the city of Syracuse isn't the most happening location, students reassure us that communities outside Syracuse are "clean, crime-free, and cater to professionals. We have golf courses and ski resorts around the area that cater to people with those interests. There is also plenty to do in term of hiking, camping canoeing." In addition, many Syracuse students "take part in charity work around the city, offering their business skills and acumen to small business owners who may not always have a solid business background."

Admissions

Admission to Syracuse is competitive. Last year's entering class (for the full-time program) had an average GMAT score of 619, with a range of 560–700 and an average undergraduate GPA of 3.3. To apply to the accelerated program, students must have an undergraduate degree in business, a GMAT score of 650 or better, and 4 or more years of professional work experience. Reviews are made on a rolling basis and students are notified of their acceptance or nonacceptance within 4 to 6 weeks.

FINANCIAL FACTS

Annual tuition	$28,200
Fees	$890
Cost of books	$1,325
Room & board	$12,490
% of students receiving aid	61
% of first-year students receiving aid	78
% of students receiving loans	23
% of students receiving grants	35
Average award package	$28,284
Average grant	$19,514
Average student loan debt	$51,942

ADMISSIONS

Admissions Selectivity Rating	89
# of applications received	227
% applicants accepted	37
% acceptees attending	33
Average GMAT	619
Range of GMAT	570–670
Average GPA	3.33
TOEFL required of international students	Yes
Minimum TOEFL (paper/computer)	600/250
Application fee	$65
Application Deadline/Notification	
Round 1:	1/15 / 2/15
Round 2:	3/1 / 4/1
Round 3:	5/1 / 6/1
Deferment available	Yes
Maximum length of deferment	1 year
Need-blind admissions	Yes

Applicants Also Look At

Boston University, Cornell University, New York University, Pennsylvania State University, University of Illinois, University of Rochester, University of Wisconsin.

EMPLOYMENT PROFILE

Career Rating	78	Grads Employed by Function	%	Avg. Salary
Primary Source of Full-time Job Acceptances		Finance/Accounting	49	$60,042
Percent employed	71	Marketing/Sales	14	$63,071
		Operations/Production	4	NR
		Consulting	2	NR

Top 5 Employers Hiring Grads
Rothstein Kass; PricewaterhouseCoopers; KPMG International; Deloitte Consulting; ChinaTrust Commercial Bank.

TEMPLE UNIVERSITY
THE FOX SCHOOL OF BUSINESS AND MANAGEMENT

Academics

Temple University's Richard J. Fox School of Business and Management boasts more than 5,500 students and 154 full-time faculty, making it one of the largest business schools in the world. Despite its large size, the MBA program is an intimate one with "only 30 full-timers." The small size of the full-time program has many benefits, particularly when it comes to access to the faculty. As one student explains, "The administration is readily available, and you get lots of individualized attention." The "outstanding, very dedicated, [and] extremely knowledgeable" professors are central to students' satisfaction with program, and students appreciate that "the course work and curriculum are organized well." Very few students have gripes about the administration, but even those who do felt that they were heard. As one student says, "They do a great job [of] soliciting and acting on feedback from students to improve the program. They are very committed to the MBA program and its continued success."

Working students can take advantage of Fox's part-time MBA, and the executive MBA and international MBA programs cater to more seasoned professionals interested in a specific focus. The IMBA and health care programs are known for being particularly strong at Fox, but students also have many positive things to say about some of the school's other curricular offerings. The Finance Department earns great reviews, with students citing "professors who have years of industry experience behind them," who modify the course structure to address "needs and changes in the industry."

Students routinely say that a combination of price and reputation is what drew them to Fox. Most feel that the quality of instruction is "comparable to any top business school in the country." The school's integrated approach to the core curriculum is thought to be "highly beneficial," with each course building on content learned in earlier classes. One student notes that professors "communicate with each other [and] work hard to integrate the courses with each other." After completing core and elective courses, degree candidates get some real-world experience by participating in the Enterprise Management Consulting Practice (EMC). Students say this "consulting practicum in the second year of the program will help [students] apply all of the skills learned through the program." Students are assigned to teams to assist on a real-life consulting project for some influential start-ups, corporations, and nonprofit organizations.

Career and Placement

Students may be thrilled with the academics at Fox, but they are less enthusiastic about the career services resources. Many students complain that the Career Services Office "has little external experience in order to guide students who are looking to change careers." Others feel that the absence of a large recruiting presence is a matter of brand recognition, with "very few companies aware of the strength of the full-time Temple program." Despite the school's large alumni network, students feel that alums were hampered by their companies' recruiting policies. One student explained that "if the company doesn't recruit at Temple, then the Temple alum is not likely to help current Temple students in their internship and career search." The school is aware of the shortcomings within Career Services, and many students concede that the "administration is trying very hard to improve in this area."

Although students may feel that Career Services leaves something to be desired, this certainly doesn't hinder them in their pursuit of employment. Last year, 66 percent of students looking for a job had received and accepted offers by graduation; 3 months after graduation, 88 percent had received and accepted offers. Most graduates entered the financial or consulting industries, and the mean base salary (not including bonuses) was $77,936.

WILLIAM MCDONALD, DIRECTOR, ENROLLMENT MANAGEMENT
1515 MARKET STREET, SUITE 400, PHILADELPHIA, PA 19102 UNITED STATES
PHONE: 215-204-5890 • FAX: 215-204-1632
E-MAIL: FOXINFO@TEMPLE.EDU • WEBSITE: WWW.FOX.TEMPLE.EDU/MBAMS

Student Life and Environment

Fox touts its Philadelphia location as one of its major benefits; certainly the school's location in the center of the Northeast Corridor puts it within easy reach of a host of multinational companies, and public transportation provides easy access to the business hubs of New York and Washington, DC. Fox has facilities on two campuses, the Main Campus and the Center City Campus; however, most students say that they spend the majority of their time at Center City.

Most students at Fox are enrolled in the part-time program and "just come for class and then leave." However, the full-time program is made up of a "tight group of students who work well together in class and outside of class." Fox's full-time students especially appreciate the school's supportive, teamwork-focused environment, particularly when "compared to the competitive nature found [at schools] across town." "We share job leads and help each other network," says one full-time student. "This cohort has really bonded." The full time students are the most socially active outside of class, and there are "many opportunities to party hard." However, there aren't as many student organizations on campus as some would like, mostly because it's hard to maintain student involvement: "The part-time students . . . do not participate in activities, and full-time students are only in school for 2 years."

Admissions

In a recently admitted class the average undergraduate GPA hovered around 3.5, and the average GMAT was approximately 651. Students had an average of 3.5 years of work experience. TOEFL scores for international applicants are required.

FINANCIAL FACTS

Annual tuition (in-state/ out-of-state)	$15,390/$23,640
Fees	$750
Cost of books	$1,200
Room & board	$15,000
% of students receiving aid	63
% of first-year students receiving aid	58
% of students receiving loans	82
% of students receiving grants	41
Average award package	$450,000
Average grant	$5,000
Average student loan debt	$36,000

ADMISSIONS

Admissions Selectivity Rating	88
# of applications received	310
% applicants accepted	55
% acceptees attending	68
Average GMAT	642
Range of GMAT	600–680
Average GPA	3.28
TOEFL required of international students	Yes
Minimum TOEFL (paper/computer)	575/230
Application fee	$50
Regular application deadline	6/1
Regular notification	Rolling
Deferment available	Yes
Maximum length of deferment	1 year
Transfer students accepted	Yes
Transfer application policy	Reviewed on a case-by-case basis for the professional MBA (part-time) program.
Non-fall admissions	Yes
Need-blind admissions	Yes

Applicants Also Look At

Drexel University, The Garvin School of International Management (Distance Learning MBA), Pennsylvania State University, Saint Joseph's University, Thunderbird, University of Maryland, University of Pennsylvania, Villanova University.

EMPLOYMENT PROFILE

Career Rating	83	**Grads Employed by Function**		**%**	**Avg. Salary**
Primary Source of Full-time Job Acceptances		Finance/Accounting		28	$63,118
School-facilitated activities	39 (70%)	Marketing/Sales		17	$79,273
Graduate-facilitated activities	13 (23%)	Consulting		33	$92,333
Unknown	4 (7%)	General Management		9	$87,000
Average base starting salary	$77,936	Other		13	$64,474
Percent employed	88	**Top 5 Employers Hiring Grads**			
		Bank of America; Blackrock Financial; Ernst & Young; GlaxoSmithKline; Campbell's Soup Company.			

TENNESSEE TECHNOLOGICAL UNIVERSITY
COLLEGE OF BUSINESS

Academics

Accessibility and convenience are the most frequently cited attributes of the MBA program at Tennessee Tech, a midsize state university located halfway between Nashville and Knoxville. Students here may take classes on campus or at home through the school's distance-learning option. The program actually allows students to exercise both options simultaneously, so it's not either/or. In fact, MBAs are encouraged to find the ideal combination of on- and off-campus classes to suit their personal schedules. Students may attend part-time or full-time (more than half are part-timers), and may enter the program in the fall, spring, or summer. The program is also accessible to most students' budgets, especially those who reside in the state of Tennessee.

Enrollees love the distance program. One MBA writes, "The DMBA (Distance MBA) is a big strength of TTU. It allows students to get their MBA without ever stepping foot on campus. This is very valuable to out-of-state students and to those of us who work full-time." Despite the novelty of the program, most report that it runs smoothly. One student writes, "My graduating class is the first class of the Distance MBA program, and we have had an excellent experience. Our professors are very flexible and the staff is top-notch. The course work is the same for the on-campus program, so we are fully prepared to succeed in today's business environment." Lectures are delivered on a set of CD ROMs, providing students with a rare and valuable permanent record. Class interaction is facilitated through WebCT; students log on to a site that provides access to e-mail, a course calendar, bulletin boards, quizzes and exams, and chat rooms, as well as downloadable PowerPoint presentations.

Even the campus-based courses incorporate "some online components," which students appreciate, noting the school's "total commitment to staying current with technological trends, which ensures Tech students have the latest tools for use in their jobs." Professors here represent "a good mix. Some are more traditional, others very technological. Some are really laid back and may have a class meeting at a downtown restaurant during happy hour. Some bring things to life by presenting research in an understandable form. For example, did you know that just the smell of fresh-baked cookies can increase productivity? There's a little bit of everything to keep it interesting." Administrators are "very approachable. They are always willing to go the extra mile to help the students. They truly care about giving us a quality education, and they do it with a smile."

TTU offers concentrations in accounting and MIS. The MBA program, which consists of seven, three-hour core courses and nine hours of electives, can be completed in one year by a full-time student.

Career and Placement

Career Services at Tennessee Tech are of interest primarily to the school's full-time MBAs, since most of the part-timers and distance-learning enrollees are currently employed. Placement services are handled through the university's Career Services Office; there is no career office dedicated solely to the MBA program or to the College of Business. The MBA office does provide some supplemental career counseling and placement assistance. The school's website states that "the key to placement is flexibility. We generally place all MBAs who are seriously looking for a position."

Nearly all graduates remain in the Tennessee region following graduation. A few find work in the Southern Atlantic states, while a few others relocate to the Southwest. On average, 136 employers recruit each year on the Tennessee Tech campus.

Dr. Bob Wood, Assistant Dean of Graduate Studies
Box 5023, TTU, 1105 N. Peachtree, Cookeville, TN 38505 United States
Phone: 931-372-3600 • Fax: 931-372-6544
E-mail: mbastudies@tntech.edu • Website: www.tntech.edu/mba

Student Life and Environment

The MBA program at Tennessee Tech provides a "small school environment within a larger university" for the cadre of students who attend classes on campus. Full-timers tell us that "life at Tech is thoroughly enjoyable. There is enough diversity to offer something for everyone as well as being small enough that you don't get lost in the crowd." Students "can join the MBA society and get involved in the panel discussions" to fill out their extracurricular schedules. Part-timers, on the other hand, "do not get very involved with the student activities that are offered" but they can still "enjoy going to Tech because," as one says, "I can go to on-campus courses as opposed to taking them online."

Many Tech MBAs do take the courses online, however, and for them "there is not any face-to-face contact with classmates." Even so, one distance learner reports that "the WebCT experience has been more enriching for me than my on campus classes. I do miss the amenities found on campus, such as the library, help desk, and fitness center, though." In the plus column, distance learners needn't cope with a parking situation that "will give you a headache."

Hometown "Cookeville and the surrounding area provide many outdoor activities. With major cities like Nashville and Knoxville within 100 miles, many students leave for the weekend." The student body is a mix of people who "just graduated from Tech as under-grads and are somewhat insular" and professionals "with strengths in various fields: some financial, some technology, some creative." One student writes, "I can't count the times I've leaned on my fellow classmates for support and vice versa. The morale here is wonderful." Full-timers form a tight group, saying they "study together, get our work done, and then go out and have a couple of drinks. Even though we're in the heart of the 'Bible Belt,' we know how to have a good time."

Admissions

Successful applicants to the Tennessee Tech MBA program must have a minimum under-graduate GPA of 2.5, a minimum GMAT score of 450, and a minimum formula score of 1,000 using the formula [(undergraduate GPA × 200) + GMAT score] or 1050 using the formula [(undergraduate GPA for final 60 semester hours × 200) + GMAT score]. Applicants must also provide a statement of computer proficiency attesting to aptitude in word processing, spreadsheet, and presentation software. Students whose native language is not English must provide TOEFL scores (minimum 550 paper-and-pencil, 213 computer-based). Entering students who have not completed an undergraduate business core are required to complete pre-MBA foundation modules in accounting, business law, economics, finance, management, marketing, and business statistics/quantitative methods. Special minority fellowships and graduate assistantships are offered to attract students from underrepresented populations.

FINANCIAL FACTS

Annual tuition (out-of-state)	$12,220
Fees	$7,746
Cost of books	$1,500
Room & board (on/off-campus)	$5,270/$6,000
% of students receiving aid	50
% of first-year students receiving aid	45
% of students receiving grants	25
Average award package	$15,594
Average grant	$1,500
Average student loan debt	$5,000

ADMISSIONS

Admissions Selectivity Rating	69
# of applications received	102
% applicants accepted	84
% acceptees attending	66
Average GMAT	526
Range of GMAT	450-760
Average GPA	3.27
TOEFL required of international students	Yes
Minimum TOEFL (paper/computer)	550/213
Application fee	$25
International application fee	$30
Regular application deadline	Rolling
Regular notification	Rolling
Deferment available	Yes
Maximum length of deferment	1 year
Transfer students accepted	Yes
Transfer application policy TTU will transfer 9 hours or less from an AACSB-accredited school.	
Non-fall admissions	Yes
Need-blind admissions	Yes

Applicants Also Look At

Middle Tennessee State University, University of Tennessee.

EMPLOYMENT PROFILE			
Career Rating	**75**		
Primary Source of Full-time Job Acceptances		**Grads Employed by Function**	**% Avg. Salary**
Average base starting salary	$46,178	Finance/Accounting	50 NR
Percent employed	95	Marketing/Sales	10 NR
		MIS	5 NR
		General Management	20 NR
		Other	15 NR

Texas A&M International University

College of Business Administration

Academics

The College of Business Administration at Texas A&M International University "is dedicated to the delivery of a high quality professional and internationalized education to a graduate student population that is drawn from a wide variety of countries and cultures," according to the college's website, which also points out that "these programs [are intended to] contribute to the students' success in leadership positions in both domestic and international settings." This AACSB-accredited school offers a general MBA, an MBA in international banking (MBA-IBK), an MBA in international trade (MBA-IT), and a PhD in International Business Administration.

All MBA programs at TAMIU require mastery of eight foundation areas: accounting, information systems, quantitative methods, economics, finance, management, marketing, and operations. Students may fulfill these requirements by completing corresponding undergraduate courses at TAMIU, by showing evidence of equivalent course work at another undergraduate institution, or by having earned an undergraduate business degree from an AACSB-accredited program. Waivers are only granted for course work completed within the previous seven years.

TAMIU's general MBA is taught in both English and Spanish. The 30-hour program allows students to concentrate in one of the following areas: accounting, information systems, international business, international finance, international trade economics, logistics, and management marketing. The strong international focus of the program "gives students the opportunity to immerse themselves in an international environment in which we can analyze situations of different countries. The diversity of the student body helps." Students also praise the "extremely optimistic" professors who "honestly care about their students and are always willing to offer a helping hand." One student writes, "Teachers are very good and highly cooperative, with great academic ability. They have the knowledge to impart, help the students and, offer their valuable suggestions to guide their further course of action."

Students also point out that "the small size of the program is a great strength. The student population is not big, so there is enough opportunity to interact with your professors and get to know everyone in your college." MBAs here appreciate how "professors acknowledge that the majority of the class works full-time and also goes to school, so they make the assignments challenging, but not impossible." In addition to the above-mentioned degrees, TAMIU also offers a master of professional accountancy (MPAcc), a master of science in international logistics (MS/IL), a master of science in information systems (MS/IS), and a doctorate in international business administration (PhD/BA).

Career and Placement

The Texas A&M International Career Services Office provides counseling and placement services to the entire undergraduate and graduate student body. The office organizes on-campus recruiting events, career expos, and job fairs. It also offers one-on-one counseling, workshops, library services, and resume review.

IMELDA LOPEZ, GRADUATE ADMISSIONS ADVISOR
5201 UNIVERSITY BOULEVARD, LAREDO, TX 78041 UNITED STATES
PHONE: 956-326-2485 • FAX: 956-326-2479
E-MAIL: LOPEZ@TAMIU.EDU • WEBSITE: WWW.TAMIU.EDU/COBA

Student Life and Environment

Around 40 percent of TAMIU's MBA students attend full-time, providing a sizeable base for clubs, organizations, and extracurricular activity. Students tell us that "campus life offers a diverse field of organizations. New clubs and sports are always developing." They also report that "seminars provided by the school are good. Many important speakers visit the campus to deliver inspirational speeches on important current topics, including politics, finance, economics, and health." Part-timers generally "don't get to spend much time on campus, but rather just get here for class at night and leave once classes are done." They "visit the computer labs and library to do research and work," but otherwise spend little extra time socializing.

Hometown Laredo "is poised at the gateway to Mexico," placing it "at an enviable crossroads of international business and life." 156 miles south of San Antonio and 153 miles north of Monterrey, Mexico, this city of over 150,000 is the fastest growing in the state of Texas. The area's growth has been spurred by Laredo's increasing role as a center for international manufacturing and trade. Top employers in the area, outside of education and government, include the Laredo Medical Center, the H-E-B Grocery Company, Doctor's Hospital, Laredo Candle, and area banks.

TAMIU's "friendly, frank, cheerful and helpful" students "enjoy the challenge of studying in a foreign country and expect the experience to give them a better professional future." More than half the MBAs here are international students; most of whom are Mexican and Latin American. Almost twenty percent of the international student body comes from Asia.

Admissions

Applying to the TAMIU MBA program is a two-step process, as applicants must be admitted to both the university at large and the College of Business in order to enroll in the MBA program. Applicants must submit the following materials to the Office of Graduate Admission: a completed application; an official copy of transcripts for all postsecondary academic work undertaken; and an official score report for the GMAT. Applicants must also provide a statement of purpose, a resume, and two letters of recommendation. The TOEFL is required of all students who completed undergraduate study in a country where English is not the language of instruction; a minimum score of 550 paper-based or 213 computer-based is required. International students must also submit documentation demonstrating the ability to support themselves financially while studying at TAMIU.

FINANCIAL FACTS

Annual tuition (in-state/ out-of-state)	$1,170/$6,120
Fees	$2,109
Cost of books	$2,161
Room & board (on/off-campus)	$6,500/$5,700
% of students receiving aid	22
% of first-year students receiving aid	19
% of students receiving loans	12
% of students receiving grants	18
Average award package	$4,000
Average grant	$1,000

ADMISSIONS

Admissions Selectivity Rating	61
# of applications received	59
% applicants accepted	98
% acceptees attending	83
Average GMAT	430
Range of GMAT	350–490
Average GPA	3.3
TOEFL required of international students	Yes
Minimum TOEFL (paper/computer)	550/213
Application fee	$25
Regular application deadline	4/30
Deferment available	Yes
Maximum length of deferment	1 year
Transfer students accepted	Yes

Transfer application policy
In terms of the application process, this remains the same as first-time applicants. However, for F1 applicants, it is critical these applicants be in-status at their current institution.

Non-fall admissions	Yes
Need-blind admissions	Yes

Applicants Also Look At
Texas A&M University—Corpus Christi, Texas A&M University—Commerce, The University of Texas—Pan American.

EMPLOYMENT PROFILE	
Career Rating	69

TEXAS A&M UNIVERSITY—COLLEGE STATION

MAYS BUSINESS SCHOOL

Academics

The top-ranked Mays Business School at Texas A&M University—College Station combines a one-size-fits-all approach with specialization options to provide its small student body a cost-effective and streamlined, yet flexible, MBA degree. This inexpensive public school offers one of the 10 quickest returns on investment, according to *BusinessWeek*. *Financial Times* ranked it the fourth best value in U.S. graduate business education. One MBA agrees, "The education you receive is top notch for the cost."

All Mays students complete a 49-credit core sequence over a 16-month period. This core covers accounting, business communication, finance, global management, information and operations management, marketing, negotiations, and management, all with "an emphasis on character and ethics, a very appealing aspect of the program." This mandatory curriculum that combines "business competencies, communications, international issues, teamwork, and ethics" means all Mays MBAs "are prepared to be strategic thinkers, effective communicators, and accountable team members and leaders in today's global marketplace," according to the school.

Those seeking specialization are welcome to remain at Mays for an additional semester, participate in study abroad, or undertake other enrichment opportunities. The school offers specialization in 11 predefined areas (students speak most highly of accounting, marketing, management, and real estate). MBAs may also design specializations of their own. Other unique aspects of the program include the Technology Transfer Challenge, in which MBAs compete to develop commercial applications for promising new technologies. The school writes, "The Challenge's design is based on state-of-the-art knowledge management theory, demonstrating how knowledge management principles can be used to help evaluate the potential of patents and other raw technologies. It demands a level of creativity not possible with traditional case competitions."

Students here love the "low cost and excellent financial aid," as well as the school's vision. One MBA exclaims, "The school continues to replace weak faculty in an effort to improve. And the program is definitely improving, with great faculty leading the way." They also appreciate that it's a "conservative, strong program with high starting salaries and great recruiting companies." Naturally, though, a few see its small size as a drawback. One such student opines, "The Mays MBA Class of 2006 is only 70 students strong. If the school is ever to be mentioned amongst Harvard, Texas, and Michigan, then it will have to expand to upwards of 500 students."

Career and Placement

A&M's legendary alumni network works its magic for MBAs. Students exploit this valuable asset through publications, a website, newsletters, and on- and off-campus events. The Mays Graduate Business Career Services (GBCS) Office also provides one-on-one counseling, online assessment tools, and frequent workshops on crafting resumes and cover letters, networking, interviewing, and negotiating your salary.

Hundreds of companies recruit on the College Station campus each year—just how many come for the purpose of interviewing MBAs is less clear. What counts is that the results are pretty impressive. Employers of Mays MBAs include BP, CattleSoft, Chevron Phillips, China National Petroleum Corp, CIA, Citibank, Citigroup, DuPont, Eagle Pass Winery, the Federal Reserve Bank, First Houston Mortgage, Ford, Hewlett-Packard, Johnson-Lancaster & Associates, Procter & Gamble, Smith Barney, Solutions Inc., Sovico Trading Ltd., USAA, Wal-Mart, and World Savings. In 2004, the mean starting salary of a Mays MBA was $77,153. One student sums up, "One of the greatest facets of a Texas A&M education is the high salary upon graduation with relatively low tuition costs."

WENDY FLYNN, DIRECTOR OF MBA ADMISSIONS
4117 TAMU, COLLEGE STATION, TX 77843-4117 UNITED STATES
PHONE: 979-845-4714 • FAX: 979-862-2393
E-MAIL: MAYSMBA@TAMU.EDU • WEBSITE: MBA.TAMU.EDU

Student Life and Environment

Although "school requires much of a student's time" at A&M, "the lifestyle in College Station is still very enjoyable." Furthermore, "those who wish to participate in social activities will not be disappointed," MBAs write, since "there are weekly events organized, as well as plenty of hot spots to frequent." It will come as no surprise to anyone who knows anything at all about the school that "football is the major activity" and that A&M is "big into traditions, and it really enhances the life here." Lesser-known but popular diversions also include "rollerblading, volleyball, tennis, and other sports." Overall, MBAs here agree that "Texas A&M is very conservative and an excellent environment to learn quality business practices."

With a substantial international population, Mays' student body is "very diverse in ethnicity, education, and experience," although not so much in gender. MBAs tend to be "boisterous in class, friendly and intelligent, [and] proactive in regards to career advancement and networking." All "have some special skills which make them unique. If one is good in math, another is very good in communications." One MBA observes, "Fellow students are like good coworkers at the office: During class and study time they work hard, but after class, they know how to have fun."

Admissions

With a limited number of slots available, the Mays MBA program can keep admissions very competitive. Successful applicants typically have at least two years of post-college, full-time work experience, good GMAT scores ("quant and verbal sections must have scores at least at the 50th percentile for consideration," notes the Admissions Office), and evidence of leadership and professional skill. All applicants must submit a current resume, three letters of recommendation from professional sources, and application essays. International students must provide TOEFL scores (minimum 600 on the paper-and-pencil test, 250 on the computerized test for admission). A&M "aggressively seeks to enhance diversity on all levels in the program, and has programs in place to recruit all students who will bring diversity to our program."

FINANCIAL FACTS

Annual tuition (in-state/ out-of-state)	$7,045/$18,745
Fees	$7,903
Cost of books	$1,428
Room & board (off-campus)	$9,679
% of students receiving aid	75
% of first-year students receiving aid	75
% of students receiving loans	65
% of students receiving grants	75
Average award package	$17,281
Average grant	$4,968
Average student loan debt	$26,300

ADMISSIONS

Admissions Selectivity Rating	93
# of applications received	372
% applicants accepted	35
% acceptees attending	58
Average GMAT	643
Range of GMAT	600–690
Average GPA	3.44
TOEFL required of international students	Yes
Minimum TOEFL (paper/computer)	600/250
Application fee	$50
International application fee	$75
Application Deadline	
Round 1:	11/1
Round 2:	1/4
Round 3:	2/28
Round 4:	4/15
Deferment available	Yes
Maximum length of deferment	1 year
Need-blind admissions	Yes

Applicants Also Look At

Arizona State University, Brigham Young University, Rice University, The University of Texas at Austin, University of Maryland, University of Notre Dame, Vanderbilt University.

EMPLOYMENT PROFILE

Career Rating	89	Grads Employed by Function	%	Avg. Salary
Primary Source of Full-time Job Acceptances		Finance/Accounting	29	$83,929
School-facilitated activities	43%	Marketing/Sales	18	$79,525
Graduate-facilitated activities	57%	MIS	6	$84,825
Average base starting salary	$81,685	Operations/Production	11	$81,842
Percent employed	98	Consulting	16	$83,580
		General Management	18	$75,133

Top 4 Employers Hiring Grads
Citigroup; FTI Consulting; Dell; BearingPoint.

TEXAS A&M UNIVERSITY—CORPUS CHRISTI
COLLEGE OF BUSINESS

GENERAL INFORMATION

Type of school	Public
Environment	Village
Academic calendar	Semester

SURVEY SAYS . . .

Solid preparation in:
Marketing
Computer skills

STUDENTS

Enrollment of parent institution	8,584
Enrollment of business school	131
% male/female	49/51
% part-time	66
% minorities	7
% international	58
Average age at entry	28

ACADEMICS

Academic Experience Rating	**63**
Profs interesting rating	82
Profs accessible rating	86
% female faculty	27
% minority faculty	21

Academics

"Cost and location," along with strong word of mouth—students hear "very good reviews from previous MBA students in comparison to other schools"—drive MBA traffic toward the College of Business at Texas A&M University—Corpus Christi (TAMUCC), an AACSB-accredited MBA program. Convenience is another important factor. One student offers that the school is "flexible with my work schedule"; another agrees that with all MBA classes held at night, it is "easy to integrate school and work."

The school offers two areas of concentration: international business, and health care management. While students tout TAMUCC's "strong accounting program" (the school offers a Master of Accounting in addition to the MBA), some feel that "it would be great to have more management or operations electives" here. As a general rule, "A lot of courses are in the catalog but are not offered and have not been for several years (according to my advisor)." Those with undergraduate degrees in business can complete the TAMUCC MBA in 30 semester hours. Those with degrees in other areas must also complete some or all of six foundation courses covering material typically taught at the undergraduate level.

TAMUCC professors "are available to the students. If you can't meet at their office time, they are always available for an appointment." "I have had profs give me their home number for questions on projects," one student says. Students appreciate the "strong real-life academic instruction" that professors impart. Most "are able to incorporate real-life skills in all aspects of their courses. The things we learn we can actually apply in our jobs," one student relates. To keep students competitive in the job market, professors here "generally try to incorporate many teaching methods that are in use at top business schools like Harvard," by requiring students "to perform many case studies in addition to textual readings. There is a strong emphasis on preparing us to be great oral and written communicators by requiring presentations and papers weekly in multiple classes."

Career and Placement

The TAMUCC Career Services office provides counseling and placement services for all undergraduates, graduate students, and alumni of the university. Frequent seminars and presentations are offered on such topics as "How to Job Search in the 'Hidden Market,'" "The Second Interview and Salary Negotiation," and "How to Get a Federal Job." The office also provides career counseling, computer-based self-assessments, job search advisement, online and hard-copy job postings, a career resource library and computer lab, videotaped mock interviews, and job fairs and on-campus recruiting events. Students tell us that the program would benefit from even more "job fairs and more actively getting companies to recruit here." Top employers in the area include the Naval Air Station Corpus Christi, Christus Spohn Health System, the Corpus Christi Army Depot, H-E-B Grocery Co., Bay Limited, SSP Partners/Circle K, Driscoll Children's Hospital, APAC, First Data, and Gulf Marine Fabricators.

Student Life and Environment

"Most graduate students work full-time, have families, and attend school part-time" at TAMUCC, "so their involvement with the school and school activities is minimal." Even so, students report that "group projects are usually done on campus." Those who do have time to participate in campus activities will find that "there is much to do here other than schoolwork." One student explains, "Our calendar is full of events and opportunities. I cannot stress how friendly and happy the ambiance is at TAMUCC."

TAMUCC "has a great campus" located on a 240-acre island surrounded by Corpus

SHARON POLANSKY, DIRECTOR OF MASTER'S PROGRAMS
6300 OCEAN DRIVE, CORPUS CHRISTI, TX 78412 UNITED STATES
PHONE: 361-825-2655 • FAX: 361-825-2725
E-MAIL: SHARON.POLANSKY@TAMUCC.EDU • WEBSITE: WWW.COB.TAMUCC.EDU

FINANCIAL FACTS

Annual tuition (in-state/ out-of-state)	$2,439/$7,389
Fees	$972

ADMISSIONS

Admissions Selectivity Rating	**64**
# of applications received	46
% applicants accepted	89
% acceptees attending	93
Average GMAT	475
Range of GMAT	400–550
Average GPA	3.08
TOEFL required of international students	Yes
Minimum TOEFL (paper/computer)	550/213
Application fee	$40
International application fee	$70
Regular application deadline	7/15
Regular notification	Rolling
Deferment available	Yes
Maximum length of deferment	1 year
Transfer students accepted	Yes
Transfer application policy Possibility of transferring in 6 credits from-accredited school with grade of D or above.	
Non-fall admissions	Yes
Need-blind admissions	Yes

Christi Bay and Oso Bay; downtown Corpus Christi is about 10 miles away. Students "are all over the place before classes. You can hear them talking and sharing ideas and enjoying the atmosphere" of this "island university." The library "has plenty of computer labs that are adequate for the campus size and . . . subscribes to many online research databases," which can be used extensively in b-school. Students tell us that "many new buildings are being built and lots of money is pouring into the school." As a bonus, "the university is closely linked with" the surrounding community.

Corpus Christi has a population of about a quarter-million. Its seaside location makes it a popular destination for vacationers and tourists; the city receives 5 million visitors annually. TAMUCC itself attracts a "very diverse group," made up of "young, old, Hispanic[s], foreigners, and your typical Texan[s]." One student reports, "My accounting class has almost 50 percent international students from South Korea, China, Japan, Thailand, Phillipines, Russia (Moscow), Turkey, and France." Students here are, "in general, smart people who choose to pursue their master's at night, while working during the day. Everyone is extremely friendly, and you get to know each other because of the small class sizes, which range from 6 to 44. The median class size is probably around 18." There are "a lot" of military personnel in the program, not surprising, given the large military presence in Corpus Christi.

Admissions

All applicants to the TAMUCC MBA program must submit the following materials: official transcripts for all undergraduate and graduate work, an official score report for the GMAT (test score can be no more than 5 years old); two letters of recommendation; a current resume or curriculum vitae; a personal essay stating your reasons for pursuing the MBA; and a completed application form. In addition, international students whose first language is not English must submit an official score for the TOEFL (minimum score: 550, paper-based test; 213, computer-based test) and an evaluation of non-English language transcripts executed by Education Credential Evaluators, Inc., International Education Research Foundation, Inc., or World Education Services. All international applicants must submit an I-34 form or other notarized confirmation of adequate financial support, a copy of their current visa, and proof of medical insurance.

TEXAS CHRISTIAN UNIVERSITY
THE M. J. NEELEY SCHOOL OF BUSINESS

Academics

Students at Texas Christian University's M.J. Neeley School of Business have at least four MBA degree programs to choose from. There's the full-time program, in which students generally attend day classes and which requires 54 credit hours to complete, and the evening or professional MBA, which requires students to attend class 2 nights a week for 48 credit hours. For those who hold a bachelor's degree in business, there is an accelerated MBA option requiring just 36 credits, and for students who have substantial work experience TCU offers an executive MBA option with classes meeting on Fridays and Saturdays. Joint-degrees in education and physics are also offered, along with a 2-year master's program in international management. Citing "the value of their education versus the cost," students laud the breadth of academic options offered and note that TCU has "great resources to customize programs to individual needs."

The core MBA curriculum focuses on both strategic and analytical management skills, with managing financial resources, managing people, and market-driven strategy among the topics covered. Integrative team projects that combine the skills learned in these classes are required, and about 20 credit hours are available for concentrations and electives which may include work at the school's centers for excellence in leadership, supply chain management, professional communication, and capital management. Study abroad opportunities are also offered in Germany, Mexico, Italy, and Chile. Overall, students say "The first-year experience is great," but some students feel "The second year has left a lot to be desired." "If the first year can be described as having a lot of overlap and being tightly integrated, the second year is sort of anarchic." "A lot of the courses like global strategy, ethics, [and] information technology strategy are almost complete jokes. The school just does not put forward the best or right professors to teach these courses at a graduate level."

Throughout the curriculum, "a great deal of emphasis is placed on real-world experience. Consulting projects are offered and students are encouraged or required to participate. And the faculty is generally flexible to accommodate your work schedule if you decide to work an internship during the academic year." In fact, most students find that "the M.J. Neeley School staff and faculty are helpful, willing, energetic, smart people who enjoy students' questions." Neeley's "excellent" professors "are easily accessible and are eager to help you achieve your goals." As one student says, "The faculty places many challenges before us." Students also laud the "great administration" for being "very helpful and interested in your individual success and experience." Both faculty and staff "[show] so much care toward each student to make sure his/her experience is fulfilling."

Career and Placement

Neeley's location in the heart of Fort Worth, close to the center of the vibrant Dallas/Fort Worth metroplex, is an asset students value when it comes time to launch their post-MBA job search. The school does its part too, with "an excellent Career Services" staff available for individual consultations and access to a database of job openings for MBAs online. The Career Center also conducts targeted career management seminars on topics such as networking, writing a cover letter, developing leadership skills, and the like. The Career Services staff is "very helpful and interested in your individual success and experience," students say. These "supportive and helpful Career Counselors," along with a good reputation among area businesses, are a formidable combination when it comes to job placement. In 2006, nearly 90 percent of graduating MBAs had received at least one job offer

PEGGY CONWAY, DIRECTOR OF MBA ADMISSIONS
PO BOX 298540, FORT WORTH, TX 76129 UNITED STATES
PHONE: 817-257-7531 • FAX: 817-257-6431
E-MAIL: MBAINFO@TCU.EDU • WEBSITE: WWW.MBA.TCU.EDU

before graduation. Sabre Holdings, Frito Lay, PepsiCo., Alcan Labs, and Goldman Sachs are among those who hire TCU graduates.

Student Life and Environment

Students say that Neeley has the "best facilities in the area," a "beautiful" campus, and "easy" parking, all of which complement campus life. Student opinion about their classmates is split, with some students describing the vibe on campus as a "very friendly, good, team-based atmosphere" with "classmates [who are] more like family. We all look out for each other." Other students observe "young, immature, bright, resilient party people with a strong 'beer factor'" who are "inexperienced in team environments." One student remarks that most of his classmates "are looking for a piece of paper with three letters on it: MBA. There is definitely a lack of effort overall." While most students agree that "the top students are extremely motivated and intelligent," they also observe that "there is a steep decline after the top 25 percent in terms of work ethic and intellectual capability." Unsurprisingly, then, "getting better MBA candidates" was an area cited as being in need of improvement by many. Academic differences notwithstanding, campus life and life in Fort Worth in general, garnered praise from students across the board. Dallas/Fort Worth is "very fun, [with] lots of activities for all students. Good athletic events, churches, and nightlife. [There's] something for everyone," students agreed.

Admissions

GMAT scores, undergraduate GPA, personal statements, letters of recommendation, a resume, and TOEFL scores for students whose native language is not English are all required to apply for admission at TCU. According to the school's website, TCU looks for "a history of setting and achieving challenging goals in every aspect of your life" when making admissions decisions. In 2006, accepted students had an average GMAT score of 624 with an average GPA of 3.22, plus 4 years of work experience. Those pursuing the executive MBA option had an average of 16 years of work experience.

FINANCIAL FACTS

Annual tuition	$26,700
Fees	$2,700
Cost of books	$1,600
Room & board (off-campus)	$12,000
% of students receiving aid	98
% of first-year students receiving aid	100
% of students receiving loans	53
% of students receiving grants	97
Average award package	$30,571
Average grant	$21,157

ADMISSIONS

Admissions Selectivity Rating	84
# of applications received	105
% applicants accepted	64
% acceptees attending	57
Average GMAT	624
Range of GMAT	510–760
Average GPA	3.22
TOEFL required of international students	Yes
Minimum TOEFL (paper/computer)	550/213
Application fee	$75
Application Deadline/Notification	
Round 1:	11/30 / 12/15
Round 2:	1/31 / 2/28
Round 3:	3/15 / 4/13
Round 4:	4/30 / 5/31
Early decision program?	Yes
ED Deadline/Notification	11/30 / 12/15
Deferment available	Yes
Maximum length of deferment	1 year
Transfer students accepted	Yes
Transfer application policy Maximum transferable credits are 6 semester hours from an AACSB-accredited institution.	
Need-blind admissions	Yes

Applicants Also Look At

Baylor University, Rice University, Southern Methodist University, Texas A&M University Tulane University, The University of Texas at Austin.

EMPLOYMENT PROFILE

Career Rating	79	Grads Employed by Function	%	Avg. Salary
Primary Source of Full-time Job Acceptances		Finance/Accounting	36	$67,000
School-facilitated activities	61%	Marketing/Sales	10	$78,666
Graduate-facilitated activities	39%	Operations/Production	16	$68,400
Average base starting salary	$69,550	Consulting	20	$68,583
Percent employed	92	General Management	10	$76,000
		Other	6	NR

Top 5 Employers Hiring Grads
American Airlines; AT&T; Accenture; Citigroup; Sabre Holdings.

TEXAS SOUTHERN UNIVERSITY
JESSE H. JONES SCHOOL OF BUSINESS

GENERAL INFORMATION
Type of school   Public

SURVEY SAYS . . .
Solid preparation in:
Finance
General management
OperationsTeamwork
Doing business in a global economy
Entrepreneurial studies

ACADEMICS
Academic Experience Rating   **61**
Profs interesting rating   70
Profs accessible rating   66

Academics

Students at the Texas Southern University's Jesse H. Jones School of Business have a lot of great things to say about their program, not the least of which is the school's focus on "diversity and entrepreneurship." Students enrolled in the MBA program at this historically black college have four degree tracks to choose from. JHJ offers an MBA degree with a general business concentration, an MBA with a health care administration concentration, a dual MBA/JD degree, and a Master's of Science degree in Management Information Systems. Whatever degree program they ultimately choose, students across the board speak of a "very intense program with very friendly and accessible staff members" and a "challenging" curriculum. "Professors are awesome," students say, and they "love the relationship between students and professors." In fact, one of the most common reasons that students choose Texas Southern is because of the school's visionary and "awesome" professors. Of these luminaries, students say, "They are highly competitive and knowledgeable about their professions," and students appreciate the "quality of their experience and expertise." Also, as one student points out, the professors show a distinct "ability to steer students' creativity and innovation." Despite these accolades, a few students commented that there could be "more professors" and that the "administration needs major work."

Beyond the "convenience" and "academic excellence" along with "a unique perspective" that Texas Southern offers, other strengths cited by students were the school's "location, cost, [and] small classes." "My MBA class is like a small family," one student said. While the small class sizes are a boon when it comes to gaining access to faculty, students say it can also be a limitation, especially when it comes to course selection. "We need more marketing courses," one student says. One student believes the problem is that "the business school does not fully challenge the academic potential of the students." Another adds that the school needs to "broaden the curriculum and course offerings," and that the administration should "design classes around the application of curriculum." But on the whole, however, student comments lean more toward the positive. "My overall academic experience has been great," one student says. "It's a good school," another sums up.

Career and Placement

According to the school, Texas Southern is a "major historically black college and university located in a leading international business environment." Located in Houston, Texas, the school prides itself—and students enjoy the benefits of—its "location, location, location," which any business student knows is a key component to landing the right job post-graduation. Hometown Houston offers "good career and placement" according to students. The largest city in Texas and the fourth largest city in the United States, Houston and its "booming economy" attract "31,000 new jobs among the 18 *Fortune* 500 companies and thousands of energy-related firms headquartered here," according to the school's website.

The Cooperative Education and Placement Services Center at Texas Southern University works every year to capitalize on the school's great location, and bring more companies on campus to recruiting events. The center hosts information sessions throughout the year where students can meet with company representatives to learn more about opportunities with their firm. Some of the companies that have conducted sessions recently are: Black & Decker, CITGO, Continental Airlines, Shell Oil Company, Target, Pfizer, and Kraft Foods. Other companies have visited the campus as part of a career development series, and they include: Wells Fargo, JPMorgan Chase, American Express Company, Merrill Lynch, and ING.

FINANCIAL FACTS

Annual tuition (in-state/ out-of-state)	$5,856/$13,266
Room & board (on/off-campus)	$6,056/$6,336

ADMISSIONS

Admissions Selectivity Rating 60*

Regular application deadline   7/15

Student Life and Environment

When it comes to student life at Texas Southern, it's literally all about the students. Given Texas Southern's small class size and "intimate" learning environment, it's no wonder that student life at the school is characterized by a sense of "community" and a "welcoming" atmosphere. In fact, the "intimacy of the students in the program" is a common theme running throughout student comments about Texas Southern. Students say the class is like a "tight-knit family," characterized by "supportive instructors" and "diverse," "open communications." Students here appreciate the "unique perspective" their peers bring to the campus, and note that they "cut across every strata—social, economic, business experience, [and] age." Despite their differences, these "talented," and "career-oriented" students "have similar goals and objectives," commonalities that are bolstered by the school's "encouragement of teamwork" and "smart, competitive, and fun" learning environment. It helps that students in the program are "nice and professional" and "encouraging and compassionate about education." It's clear that Texas Southern's "professional, career-focused, results-driven, friendly, and down-to-earth" MBAs feel they are in good company.

Admissions

Students seeking admission to any of Texas Southern's four degree programs will need to submit, along with the application fee and completed application, official transcripts from all colleges and universities previously attended; GRE, GMAT and TOEFL scores; a personal statement; a current resume; and two letters of recommendation. There is an English Proficiency Requirement. Each graduate student who is admitted must have an analytical writing score of 3.5 or higher on the GRE or GMAT exam or enroll in a graduate-level English class. Admission is for the fall semester only. Conditional admission may be offered to students who do not meet all of the application requirements but demonstrate promise and ability.

TEXAS TECH UNIVERSITY
JERRY S. RAWLS COLLEGE OF BUSINESS ADMINISTRATION

GENERAL INFORMATION

Type of school	Public
Environment	City
Academic calendar	

SURVEY SAYS . . .

Good social scene
Cutting-edge classes
Solid preparation in:
Teamwork
Communication/interpersonal skills
Presentation skills

STUDENTS

Enrollment of parent institution	27,996
Enrollment of business school	412
% male/female	75/25
% out-of-state	11
% part-time	84
% minorities	6
% international	11
Average age at entry	24
Average years work experience at entry	2

ACADEMICS

Academic Experience Rating	**71**
Student/faculty ratio	8:1
Profs interesting rating	70
Profs accessible rating	85
% female faculty	11
% minority faculty	1

Joint Degrees

MD/MBA 4 years, JD/MBA 3 years, MBA/MA (foreign language) 2 years, MBA/MA (architecture) 2.5 years, dual MBA programs with Universidad Anahuac/Mexico 2 years, Sup de Co Montpellier 2 years.

Prominent Alumni

Jerry V. Smith, president, J. V. Smith Professional Corporation-CPA; Robert C. Brown, director, Wayne and Gladys Valley Foundation; James C. Wetherbe, PhD, TTU Bobby G. Stevenson chair in information technology.

Academics

"Academics are on the rise" at Texas Tech University's Rawls College of Business, where the main attraction is a slew of special concentrations and unique joint-degree programs. One future attorney says, "Texas Tech is one of the few schools that offers a 3-year joint JD/MBA program, [in] which I am currently enrolled. Most schools offer these degrees in a minimum of 4 years." The health organization management specialization and MD/MBA are also huge draws for many students (not to mention the school's "great facilities" and "reasonable price"). Rawls's proximity to the School of Law and School of Medicine facilitate these partnerships. Joint-degrees are also available in architecture, foreign languages, personal financial planning, and environmental toxicology. The "energy commerce department is excellent" and provides a rare training opportunity for future oil execs. Other notable concentrations include agribusiness, entrepreneurship, and statistics. Students gave less than rave reviews to the accounting department, which one student says "has completely ruined my chances of becoming CPA-eligible, as I am an MBA student, and they no longer allow MBA students to take graduate accounting courses."

The Rawls faculty consists of many "well-published, tenured, and highly regarded members of the academic community"—"passionate" teachers who "are interested in the students, not just [in] the research." The faculty "comes from all parts of the world," and "Their experiences and industry knowledge bring a complete understanding to the subject matter." One student cautions that "some male professors are still outdated in their ideas about women. They are not against women in power positions, but they sometimes make assumptions about women." Professors are "accommodating" to students who "lack a business background" and "are always willing to put in the extra hour for anyone who needs extra help." Students had mostly positive things to say about the administration, noting that it has done "everything possible to ensure that students can be enrolled in their appropriate classes. It has made registration a breeze." Some students wish the administration would make "more inclusion of other cultures, ethnicities, and women" in the faculty and classroom a priority.

Career and Placement

"TTU has a strong alumni base that tries to hire new graduates," students say. "It is not uncommon for several alumni to be employed at the same company." The new Career Management Center serves both undergraduates and graduates, and "Many students, even graduate students, find jobs" thanks to the center's services. Some students complain that the CMC "does not put much effort into obtaining job opportunities for [international students]" and that when grad students ask about working in companies with little or no relationship to Rawls, "We are often told that . . . it is out of the question." Eighty percent of Rawls MBAs take jobs in Texas and the Southwest. The vast majority of grads enter the finance industry, but the highest-paid grads are the 5 percent who go into manufacturing jobs. Top employers include Cintas, Deloitte Touche Tohmatsu, Enterprise Rent-A-Car, ExxonMobil, Halliburton, JPMorgan Chase, Lockheed Martin, National Instruments, Plains Capital, PricewaterhouseCoopers, Rolled Alloys, Sherwin Williams, Southwest Bank of Texas, Texas Bank, Texas Tech, USAA, Wal-Mart, and Wells Fargo.

CINDY BARNES, DIRECTOR, GRADUATE SERVICES CENTER
RAWLS COLLEGE OF BUSINESS, GRADUATE SERVICES CENTER, LUBBOCK, TX 79409-2101 U.S.
PHONE: 806-742-3184 • FAX: 806-742-3958
E-MAIL: MBA@TTU.EDU • WEBSITE: MBA.BA.TTU.EDU

Student Life and Environment

"Texas Tech has the best people in the world, hands down," students say. "People are very laid-back, friendly, and always willing to help. That is what I love about Texas Tech and Lubbock." Another student agrees, "You can't walk across campus without someone saying 'hello.' Everyone is always smiling, which makes life on campus much more enjoyable." One student asks, "Where else can you meet a total stranger on campus who is willing to walk you to the building that you just cannot seem to locate?!"

"Due to the accelerated MBA for TTU undergrads, the graduate students do not really differ from undergraduate students," says one MBA candidate. Grad students tend to be "conservative," "friendly, charismatic" Texas Tech grads who "are still in their early 20s and [enjoy] partying and going out" and often have little work experience. Some students say "The social scene is much more important than working." While this is great news for students who fit the party mold, one student complains, "I went Greek in undergrad and I loved my sisters in the Tri-Deltas, but I don't want to relive those days again."

Rawls students love the "secluded west Texas" city of Lubbock, "a very social town" where everyone is "supportive of Texas Tech and the students." Students say that "nightlife around the campus is great for after-school networking." Lubbock may be "in the middle of nowhere," which makes landing internships difficult, but most students feel the advantages far outweigh any inconveniences. In particular, "The cost of living is extremely cheap", "three bedroom/two-bath homes rent for under $1000 a month." In addition, "The weather is fair, which makes for a lot of outdoor activities."

Admissions

The outlook is good for applicants to Rawls, which has an 82-percent MBA acceptance rate. Successful candidates boast a mean GMAT score of around 528, a mean GPA of 3.4, and 2 years' average work experience. Those who'd like to get a taste of Rawls before committing can take up to 12 credit hours as nonmatriculated students.

FINANCIAL FACTS

Annual tuition (in-state/ out-of-state)	$4,440/$11,040
Fees	$2,966
Cost of books	$1,500
Room & board	$6,000
% of students receiving aid	100
% of first-year students receiving aid	100
% of students receiving grants	100
Average grant	$2,000
Average student loan debt	$12,318

ADMISSIONS

Admissions Selectivity Rating	**72**
# of applications received	378
% applicants accepted	82
% acceptees attending	78
Average GMAT	528
Range of GMAT	480–570
Average GPA	3.4
TOEFL required of international students	Yes
Minimum TOEFL (paper/computer)	550/213
Application fee	$50
International application fee	$60
Regular application deadline	Rolling
Regular notification	Rolling
Deferment available	Yes
Maximum length of deferment	1 year
Transfer students accepted	Yes
Transfer application policy Up to six hours may transfer.	
Non-fall admissions	Yes
Need-blind admissions	Yes

Applicants Also Look At

Texas A&M University System Health Science Center, The University of Texas at Austin.

EMPLOYMENT PROFILE

Career Rating	70	Grads Employed by Function	%	Avg. Salary
Primary Source of Full-time Job Acceptances		Finance/Accounting	45	$48,333
Unknown	20 (100%)	Marketing/Sales	5	$54,000
Average base starting salary	$45,215	MIS	5	NR
Percent employed	69	Operations/Production	5	$45,000
		Consulting	10	$51,000
		General Management	10	$35,500
		Other	20	$38,025

Top 5 Employers Hiring Grads

Ryan and Co.; Pfizer; Bank of America; Comerica Bank; Walgreens.

THUNDERBIRD
SCHOOL OF GLOBAL MANAGEMENT

Academics

There is one overriding reason to pursue an MBA at Thunderbird: it is "the single most globally oriented program in the United States, bar none." In today's business environment, "having specialized knowledge of the global business is a must," and Thunderbird's consistently high rankings in international business draws a community of talented students from across the world. At a school where "over 60 percent of students were born outside the United States or have worked outside the United States," students compare the environment to "a mini U.N. or maybe mini LA," where cultural exchange is highly encouraged. A current student enthuses, "The students and faculty are passionate about international business, and it creates this overwhelming and awe-inspiring feeling of community and an 'Oh my God! I can't believe there is a school like this' feeling."

When it comes to the teaching staff, "Professors are as global as the students," and the "learning opportunities from both faculty and students are outstanding." More than just your average professionals, professors at Thunderbird are veritable experts in their fields, and "Textbooks for many subjects are written by professors at this school." What's more, they consistently are described as student oriented, "really solid, accessible, and for the most part, 'on your side.'" A student elaborates, "They manage to hold their expectations high, while also taking personal responsibility for how well students understand the material."

Students warn that the "workload is heavy," especially in the first year; however, the atmosphere isn't cutthroat. A student assures, "Student collaboration is common and encouraged—there is not the sense that ego-driven, competitive students prevail here." Throughout the core MBA curriculum, course material maintains its focus on global business, and "All of my classes have in some way or form integrated this purpose and help reinforce the materials from other courses." In addition, Thunderbird offers a range of special, internationally focused course offerings on topics such as international market and country analysis. Before graduating, all MBA candidates must be proficient in one foreign language in order to confer their degree.

Many students note that the school has been going through some administrative changes in recent years, which has "resulted in academic class changes, professor departures, and other jarring events that the students were, overall, not informed of and not prepared for." However, most feel that the rocky road will smooth over shortly; and they are quick to point out that the academic programs remain top-notch.

Career and Placement

The Career Management Center at Thunderbird is actively involved in a student's career choices from day one—in fact, students meet with a Career Counselor before they even begin the program. Students note that "the administration seems very focused on finding employment for students," which they demonstrate through more than 150 corporate visits annually, including government, NGO, and intelligence organizations. The CMC also hosts a series of career-related events, including the October career fair and spring career week. It further helps that "the alumni network is also very strong," with many Thunderbird graduates retaining great memories of and respect for their alma mater. However, the region isn't necessarily the best fit in terms of career opportunities, as "Phoenix does not offer much in terms of a multitude of activities or jobs for international business students." Fortunately, should your dream job materialize on campus, "The student body is so diverse concerning employment interests that it is very rare for two students to be competing for the same employment position."

Judy Johnson, Dean of Admissions
15249 North 59th Avenue, Glendale, AZ 85306-6000 United States
Phone: 602-978-7100 • Fax: 602-439-5432
E-mail: admissions@thunderbird.edu • Website: www.thunderbird.edu

For the 2005–2006 academic year, Thunderbird MBAs were offered jobs with an average salary of $105,413 (an aggregate of the average base salary of $77,065, an average signing bonus of $12,283, plus an average for other guaranteed compensation of $16,065.) Thirty-four percent chose to work outside the United States. The top employers of 2005–2006 graduates were Hilti, Cisco, Intel, Deutsche Post World Net, Bristol-Myers Squibb Company, Honeywell, Johnson & Johnson, ACNielsen, HSBC, and IBM.

Student Life and Environment

While Thunderbird is a graduate-only program, campus life might feel something like undergrad. Most Thunderbird students live on campus (many without a car), and "All students are involved in campus clubs or other activities." In addition, students gather for "multiple parties every week," rugby games with the school team, and a plethora of ongoing social and cultural events. A student says, "Culture nights here are the bomb: Korean drums, Capoeira, Thai and Indian dances, cultural[ly] based fashion shows, and abundant food. Learning to love the fabulous cultures around us is one of the great pleasures of Thunderbird." Believe it or not, students say the cafeteria food isn't half bad, and many note that "we also have a pub on campus, which is a great place to meet students that you probably wouldn't meet in class."

While they hail from across the world and every imaginable background, Thunderbird students can nonetheless be characterized as "friendly, collaborative, lively, and highly motivated," or alternately as "worldly, traveled, sophisticated." They take their studies seriously, but Thunderbird students also know when its time to relax, and "friendly discussion over a beer is more likely to be about climbing a mountain in Japan or teaching English in Italy than it is to be about high finance." When they aren't dedicating themselves to school-related activities, "Weekend trips to nearby attractions are common, and even in the busiest of times, students find time to help in the community and to treat themselves to dinners out."

Admissions

To apply to Thunderbird, students must submit a completed application including three personal essays, GMAT scores and (for international students) TOEFL test scores, two letters of recommendation, official transcripts, and a resume. Before entering the program, students are also required to complete course work in macroeconomics and microeconomics. Because a large portion of Thunderbird course work is driven by case studies and practical, hands-on examples, students must have at least 2 years of professional work experience to be considered for the program.

FINANCIAL FACTS

Annual tuition	$34,950
Cost of books	$1,420
Room & board (on/off-campus)	$3,900/$7,200
% of students receiving aid	68
% of first-year students receiving aid	68
% of students receiving loans	47
% of students receiving grants	36
Average award package	$27,387
Average grant	$16,613
Average student loan debt	$24,993

ADMISSIONS

Admissions Selectivity Rating	80
# of applications received	581
% applicants accepted	71
% acceptees attending	61
Average GMAT	602
Range of GMAT	560–640
Average GPA	3.3
TOEFL required of international students	Yes
Minimum TOEFL (paper/computer)	600/250
Application fee	$125
Application Deadline/Notification	
Round 1:	12/30 / Rolling
Round 2:	2/28 / Rolling
Round 3:	4/15 / Rolling
Round 4:	6/30 / Rolling
Deferment available	Yes
Maximum length of deferment	1 year
Non-fall admissions	Yes
Need-blind admissions	Yes

Applicants Also Look At

Babson College, Southern Methodist University, University of Notre Dame, University of South Carolina, University of Southern California.

EMPLOYMENT PROFILE

Career Rating		75		Grads Employed by Function	%	Avg. Salary
Primary Source of Full-time Job Acceptances				Finance/Accounting	23	$83,205
School-facilitated activities		108 (50%)		Human Resources	2	$77,500
Graduate-facilitated activities		109 (50%)		Marketing/Sales	33	$72,076
Average base starting salary		$77,297		Operations/Production	11	$77,164
Percent employed		48		Consulting	14	$81,080
				General Management	11	$81,039
				Other	6	$67,728

Top 5 Employers Hiring Grads

Hilti; Cisco; Intel; Bristol-Meyers Squibb; Johnson & Johnson.

TULANE UNIVERSITY
FREEMAN SCHOOL OF BUSINESS

GENERAL INFORMATION

Type of school	Private
Environment	City
Academic calendar	Semester

SURVEY SAYS . . .
Friendly students
Good social scene
Good peer network
Happy students
Smart classrooms
Solid preparation in:

STUDENTS

Enrollment of parent institution	11,256
Enrollment of business school	210
% male/female	74/26
% out-of-state	79
% part-time	34
% minorities	18
% international	26
Average age at entry	26
Average years work experience at entry	4

ACADEMICS

Academic Experience Rating	**80**
Student/faculty ratio	22:1
Profs interesting rating	80
Profs accessible rating	84
% female faculty	38
% minority faculty	5

Joint Degrees
MBA/MD 5 years, MBA/JD 4 years, MBA/MA (Latin American studies) 2.5 years, MBA/MA (health administration) 2.5 years, MBA/MA (political science) 2.5 years, MACCT/JD 4 years, MACCT/MBA 2 years, MACCT/JD 3.5 years, MBA/MEng 2.5 years.

Prominent Alumni
Burdon Lawrence, chair, Kirby Corp.; Wayne Downing, National Director, Deputy National Security Adviser; Ray Nagin, Mayor, City of New Orleans; Larry Gordon, film producer, former president, 20th Century Fox.

Academics

A lot has changed but also stayed the same for MBA students at Tulane. Students note that being "part of the first class in a new curriculum following Hurricane Katrina," they can "see the value in the changes that were made even though there have been a few bumps in the road while the changes have been implemented." "Class size" is still "one of the strong points about Tulane," with sizes "around 50 students." And many happily report that "Tulane has . . . recovered from Hurricane Katrina as [has] New Orleans." "Courses in finance, international business, and entrepreneurship" are strong—particularly finance (many here take "at least a supporting concentration in finance") and entrepreneurship (which is "nationally ranked")—though some find "a limitation of course variety because of the small enrollment."

MBAs appreciate the "at-home atmosphere" at Tulane's Freeman School between students and their "knowledgeable, outgoing, and sometimes brilliantly innovative" professors. They "want students to ask questions and visit them in their office," explains one student. Despite a general feeling of administrative uncertainty after the hurricane, students are confident that "once the faculty turnover has settled down, things will be excellent." But until then, they note, "The professors we have had, are top-notch." And this helps to keep the stress low during the school's intensive 7-week academic terms. Be warned: the heavy course work starts on day one and doesn't let up until exam day.

Before the hurricane, Tulane had experienced impressive growth, and while there are no plans to change that outlook, "enrollment has been lower." Despite this, Tulane is rising with the city. As one student explains, "Some of my classmates decided to transfer to other schools after they evacuated, [but] most of them came back to New Orleans," proving that "the attractiveness of the city and the school" are tough to resist. In light of all this, the school has been "very responsive and receptive to students" who acknowledge that "change is a part of life here." One thing that probably will not change is Freeman's overriding mission of "providing the skills that will be directly applicable to your career."

Career and Placement

Career prep begins as soon as students arrive at the Freeman School; orientation includes training in the use of eRecruiting, Tulane's online student information-management system. Subsequent training in interviewing, resume building, internship hunting, and salary negotiation follows and is offered throughout the program. Tulane also maintains a database (called the Career Consultants Network) of Freeman alumni willing to counsel current students. Job fairs and other recruiting events pepper Freeman's academic calendar.

The school's best efforts notwithstanding, students are less than 100-percent satisfied with their Career Office. One MBA explains that although "the CMC has a horrible reputation . . . it is what the students make of it." Most students concede that "the New Orleans economy is a drawback, but with aggressive . . . networking students have the opportunity to land very good jobs." "Many students in my class have landed great jobs in New York, Houston, Dallas, and a few in New Orleans, among other places," says one student.

Companies most likely to hire Freeman MBAs include Bank of America, Citibank, Credit Suisse, D&T Management Solutions, Entergy, FedEx, First Union Securities, Jackson & Rhodes, JPMorgan Chase, PA Consulting, Reliant Energy, Towers Perrin, and TXU.

Bill D. Sandefer, Director of Graduate Admissions and Financial Aid
Seven McAlister Drive, Suite 401, New Orleans, LA 70118 United States
Phone: 504-865-5410 • Fax: 504-865-6770
E-mail: freeman.admissions@tulane.edu • Website: freeman.tulane.edu

Student Life and Environment

In 2003 the school completed building Goldring/Woldenberg Hall II and the facility earned top marks from all students, who found it "attractive and technologically advanced—amazing." With all the "latest and greatest technology, including a trading floor, digital media theater, 60-inch plasma TVs . . . [and] a number of breakout rooms for students to use for group work," students found plenty of room to host speakers, club meetings, and social functions. And even after all that's gone on, students still report that "the facility is state of the art and has recovered from damage of the hurricane." Students also enthusiastically agree that "New Orleans is a great place to live, and our alumni are great." We have several school-sponsored events that are usually well organized, though in New Orleans style," MBAs report. They add, "Social functions are extremely fun and occur quite often. We usually have a great turnout for each and every one, which makes for great friendships and networking opportunities within the MBA program."

Students here are "very outgoing socially and creative in applying their skills towards real life." One student explains, "For example, we meet every Thursday for 'Think and Drink' and have a 'Social Chair' as a VP position in student government. We also consult with businesses, volunteer, and network more than any other school I see at conferences." One student approvingly notes, "Student organizations also invite speakers [and] do community consulting and other helpful jobs for the communities in New Orleans." "Being in New Orleans, Tulane offers outstanding life outside of the classroom," says one student. "Great food, great music, great festivals, great easygoing people . . . who could ask for anything better?"

Admissions

Freeman reviews applications to its graduate programs in three separate rounds, and the school encourages students to apply as early as possible to maximize their chances of gaining admission. The following is required to apply: an undergraduate transcript, an affidavit of support, GMAT scores, TOEFL scores (for international students), two letters of recommendation, a current resume, personal statement, and interview. Minority recruitment efforts include Destination MBA, the National Black MBA Association Career Fair, targeted GMASS searches, and minority fellowships.

FINANCIAL FACTS

Annual tuition	$33,750
Fees	$1,600
Cost of books	$1,600
Room & board	$11,000
% of students receiving aid	80
% of first-year students receiving aid	74
% of students receiving loans	42
% of students receiving grants	47
Average award package	$41,055
Average grant	$9,350
Average student loan debt	$67,010

ADMISSIONS

Admissions Selectivity Rating	89
# of applications received	159
% applicants accepted	61
% acceptees attending	72
Average GMAT	656
Range of GMAT	540–730
Average GPA	3.26
TOEFL required of international students	Yes
Minimum TOEFL (paper/computer)	600/250
Application fee	$125
Regular application deadline	5/1
Regular notification	6/1
Application Deadline/Notification	
Round 1:	11/15 / 12/15
Round 2:	1/15 / 2/15
Round 3:	3/15 / 4/15
Round 4:	5/1 / 6/1
Need-blind admissions	Yes

Applicants Also Look At

Emory University, Rice University, Southern Methodist University, The University of North Carolina at Chapel Hill, The University of Texas at Austin, Vanderbilt University, Washington University.

EMPLOYMENT PROFILE

Career Rating	84	Grads Employed by Function	%	Avg. Salary
Primary Source of Full-time Job Acceptances		Finance/Accounting	55	$71,417
School-facilitated activities	54%	Marketing/Sales	14	$80,000
Graduate-facilitated activities	46%	Consulting	10	$70,000
Average base starting salary	$73,375	General Management	20	$63,333
Percent employed	93	Other	1	$115,000
		Top Employer Hiring Grads		
		TXU corporation.		

THE UNIVERSITY OF AKRON
COLLEGE OF BUSINESS ADMINISTRATION

GENERAL INFORMATION
Type of school   Public
Environment   City

SURVEY SAYS . . .
Friendly students
Cutting-edge classes
Smart classrooms

STUDENTS
Enrollment of parent institution	22,636
Enrollment of business school	245
% male/female	60/40
% out-of-state	2
% part-time	53
% minorities	3
% international	52
Average age at entry	26
Average years work experience at entry	4

ACADEMICS
Academic Experience Rating	**63**
Student/faculty ratio	23:1
Profs interesting rating	64
Profs accessible rating	80
% female faculty	18
% minority faculty	18

Joint Degrees
MBA/JD, MTax/JD, MSM-HR/JD.

Prominent Alumni
Gary Taylor, founder, president and CEO, Infocision Management Group; Anthony Alexander, president and CEO, FirstEnergy Corporation; Richard Marsh, senior vice president and CFO, First Energy Corporation; David Grubb, partner/senior executive, Accenture; Andrew Platt, vice president and CIO, The J.M. Smucker Company.

Academics

Offering a flexible and comprehensive MBA program and boasting an "excellent reputation for business," The University of Akron attracts students from Ohio and beyond who wish to augment their undergraduate degrees or professional experiences with an MBA. The school's low tuition combined with a generous scholarship program makes the program affordable; in fact, "The school supports a lot of students financially," making it a highly appealing choice for many qualified students.

Before they begin their studies, the university conducts a one-on-one consultation with future business students to help them tailor the program to their needs. For those with a more limited business background, the program begins with a series of eight foundational courses. These courses form the cornerstone of the MBA program, establishing a common background and introducing students to the vocabulary they will share throughout their studies. Foundational courses are followed by core courses, which are designed to create breadth within the program, in areas such as leadership and international business. After that, students add depth to their studies by choosing an area of concentration. For the particularly ambitious types, "The University of Akron offers great opportunities through a joint-degree program with its law school. Students can pursue a JD/MBA, JD/MTax, or a JD/MSM-HR simultaneously!"

Thanks to the school's sizable international population, "Group work at The University of Akron presents a valuable opportunity to not only meet diverse people, but also to explore the unique perspective and immense knowledge that others can contribute." A satisfied second-year student shares, "The class discussions require everyone's input, and the respect [shown] for other's opinions is extremely professional. I will actually miss the classes after graduation . . . but not the long weekends writing case studies." Promoting a friendly atmosphere inside and outside the classroom, "Professors are outstanding to talk to outside of class." However, students mention that the program tends to take an academic (rather than practical) approach to business education."

Working students find the program at The University of Akron particularly amenable, as "There is a lot of flexibility in terms of the timings of courses offered and also variety." On the whole, students report that the school is run smoothly, saying the university's "new Dean seems very dynamic and a person who would bring about far-reaching changes in a place that is already full of life and enthusiasm." They also give kudos to the Academic Advising Office, "which is always available to help students with scheduling classes and other problems that we as students encounter on a daily basis."

Career and Placement

The University of Akron Center for Career Management serves the school's undergraduate and graduate community; however, there is no job placement office associated with the business school in particular. As a result, some complain that "there is no serious networking or career counseling or job placement structure here." However, through the CCM, business students can get help with cover letters and resumes, research corporations and positions, and receive one-on-one counseling with career advisors. The CCM also hosts a number of career fairs and on-campus recruiting events annually. Among the companies who recruited at The University of Akron this year are: Allstate Insurance Company, Ameriprise Financial, Bank of America, CareerBuilder.com, Charles Schwab, CVS/Pharmacy, Diebold, Enterprise Rent-A-Car, Northwestern Mutual Finance Network, PERI Software Solutions, Rite Aid, the U.S. Social Security Administration, Target, UPS, Ernst & Young, FedEx, Frito-Lay, INROADS, Linens 'n Things, Lone Star Steel, and

MYRA WEAKLAND, ASSISTANT DIRECTOR
THE UNIVERSITY OF AKRON, CBA 412 AKRON, OH 44325-4805 UNITED STATES
PHONE: 330-972-7043 • FAX: 330-972-6588
E-MAIL: GRADCBA@UAKRON.EDU • WEBSITE: WWW.UAKRON.EDU/CBA/GRAD

National Interstate Insurance Company. The school's large international population also suggest that the "university should strive to bring those companies on campus which could sponsor international students to work for them."

Student Life and Environment

The student body at The University of Akron is "culturally diverse, friendly, and competitive," creating a laid-back but stimulating atmosphere on campus. Business students enjoy the university's "beautiful and green campus" and appreciate the modern amenities in the business building. A student elaborates, "The wireless computer network is extremely fast and reliable, and all of the classrooms have brand-new multimedia systems." Due to the school's active evening program, a large number of students are "part-time, have day jobs, and are married. A lot of them have children too." Balancing a demanding career and family life with the demands of an MBA program is obviously a challenge. As a result, a large percentage of students say, "There is not a whole lot of time for socialization with other students because of everything else going on."

Full-time students, on the other hand, enjoy the "lively" campus atmosphere and say you'll be "surprised to see how many full-time students there are in the grad program." In the past few years, the larger university "offers students many improved resources for both academic and leisure activities." For example, there are "lots of frats and sports activities," and "The gym/wellness center is a great place to burn off steam." Many students say they chose The University of Akron because they are already based in the area; however, this does not prevent them from recognizing the benefits of this laid-back town. A current student tells us, "The downtown area provides several different types of bars and restaurants. Highland Square and Fairlawn areas also provide shops and different activities to do during time away from classes and studying."

Admissions

To apply to The University of Akron's MBA program, prospective students must submit a completed application, undergraduate transcripts, GMAT scores, and, if English is a second language, TOEFL scores. Be sure to double check your application: Admissions Officials remind us that these materials make a lasting impression and "Spelling errors are noted." Currently, The University of Akron requires a GPA of at least 2.75 for entry, though some successful applicants with significant professional experience have been admitted with lower grades. The previous incoming class presented average GMAT scores of 570 and an average of 5 years of professional experience.

FINANCIAL FACTS

Annual tuition (in-state/ out-of-state)	$14,481/$23,302
Fees	$798
Cost of books	$1,200
Room & board	$10,000
% of students receiving aid	23
% of first-year students receiving aid	10
Average award package	$25,679

ADMISSIONS

Admissions Selectivity Rating	71
# of applications received	180
% applicants accepted	80
% acceptees attending	52
Average GMAT	535
Range of GMAT	480–580
Average GPA	3.3
TOEFL required of international students	Yes
Minimum TOEFL (paper/computer)	550/213
Application fee	$30
International application fee	$40
Regular application deadline	8/1
Regular notification	8/15
Deferment available	Yes
Maximum length of deferment	2 years
Transfer students accepted	Yes
Transfer application policy	Up to 24 credits of foundation courses may be waived. 9 credits of the core may transfer from AACSB-accredited schools if approved by the director.
Non-fall admissions	Yes
Need-blind admissions	Yes

Applicants Also Look At

Case Western Reserve University, Cleveland State University, John Carroll University, Kent State University, The Ohio State University, University of Cincinnati, Youngstown State University.

EMPLOYMENT PROFILE

Career Rating	68	Grads Employed by Function	%	Avg. Salary
Primary Source of Full-time Job Acceptances		Finance/Accounting	14	$49,900
School-facilitated activities	3 (7%)	Marketing/Sales	5	$55,000
Graduate-facilitated activities	4 (9%)	General Management	19	$44,000
Unknown	37 (84%)	Other	14	$45,830
Percent employed	46	**Top 5 Employers Hiring Grads**		
		Diebold, Inc.; National City Bank; Ernst & Young; Gojo Industries; Western Reserve Systems Group.		

THE UNIVERSITY OF ALABAMA AT BIRMINGHAM
SCHOOL OF BUSINESS

GENERAL INFORMATION

Type of school	Public
Environment	Metropolis
Academic calendar	Semester

SURVEY SAYS . . .
Cutting-edge classes
Solid preparation in:
Accounting

STUDENTS

Enrollment of parent institution	16,000
Enrollment of business school	398
% male/female	56/44
% out-of-state	5
% part-time	66
% minorities	5
% international	17
Average age at entry	27
Average years work experience at entry	4

ACADEMICS

Academic Experience Rating	**73**
Student/faculty ratio	30:1
Profs interesting rating	87
Profs accessible rating	83
% female faculty	16
% minority faculty	12

Joint Degrees
MBA/MPH 2 to 3 years, MBA/MS (Health Administration) 2 to 3 years, MBA/MS (Nursing) 2 to 3 years.

Prominent Alumni
John Bakane, CEO, Mills; Daryl Byrd, CEO and president, Iberia Bank; Susan Story, CEO and president, Gulf Power Company; James Woodward, chancellor, University of North Carolina at Charlotte; Stephen Zelnak, CEO and president, Martin Marietta Materials.

Academics

The School of Business at the The University of Alabama at Birmingham offers its students concentrations in finance, information technology management, and health care management. "It's a great program" with a "metropolitan" location. Generally known for its medical and health sciences—with highly respected and well-funded research programs, and for strong schools of medicine and nursing—UAB offers in the School of Business several combined degree programs, including MBA/Master of Public Health, MBA/Master of Science in Health Administration and MBA/Master of Science in Nursing. In 2005 the school also launched a program known as MBA for scientists, aimed at helping those who hold advanced degrees in the sciences learn the tools of life science entrepreneurship practices.

All students are required to take foundational courses in subjects including organizational behavior, corporate finance, marketing concepts, and microeconomic analysis. These comprise 21 of the 51 credits required for graduation. Five advanced courses in specific areas including a seminar in marketing policy and at least one course relating to international business are also required, and the remaining classes focus on the student's area of specialization. There are opportunities for study abroad during the program through agreements with schools in Spain, Italy, and England.

Students praise the "strong academics," the flexible scheduling, and especially the quality of their professors "who have a great deal of academic and real-world experience." The program also has an "excellent reputation as a quality MBA program," and students agree that "the school's prestige," which is based on solid teaching and good administration, "is growing." "The professors really know their field. They bring real-world experience to the classroom." The administration also is a "very solid team, focused on improving the business school."

The university points with pride to the high ranking of its graduates when taking CPA and CFA exams—finance graduates of UAB pass the CFA exam at a rate 20 percent higher than the national average, for example—but some students feel that there may be too much emphasis on the numbers side of business practice. "The experience has been great in reference to understanding the mathematical side of business," but "I would like to have some classes that focus on terminology with not so much math work," one student says.

Career and Placement

There is a Career Services Office located in the School of Business building at UAB, which offers career counseling, coaching, practical workshops on areas such as resume writing and job searching, and an online database of jobs as well as a database to which students may upload their resumes. About three quarters of UAB's MBA student are working professionals, and most candidates for the degree have several years of work experience, so perhaps it's not surprising that they ask for "better recruitment programs for business. The career fairs are heavy in sciences and social sciences," one student believes. However, "location in a metro setting in the Southeast," is a plus: Birmingham is the largest city in Alabama and one of the largest cities in the Southeast. "It is a good state university, and it is located in a great city," which are factors that students agree are helpful in their job searches.

AmSouth Bank, Alabama Power, Wal-Mart, Baptist Health Systems, BellSouth; and Blue Cross and Blue Shield Association are among those who have hired UAB graduates.

ADMISSIONS CONTACT: CHRISTY MANNING, MBA PROGRAM COORDINATOR
ADDRESS: 1530 THIRD AVENUE SOUTH, BEC 210 BIRMINGHAM, AL 35294-4460 UNITED STATES
PHONE: 205-934-8815 • FAX: 205-934-9200
E-MAIL: CMANNING@UAB.EDU • WEBSITE: WWW.BUSINESS.UAB.EDU/MBA

Student Life and Environment

Most students pursuing an MBA take classes in the late afternoons and evenings at UAB. Opinions are mixed on whether this allows them the opportunity to connect with campus life and their fellow students or if it's more of a hindrance. "I'm part-time so I don't really have a chance to attend activities for full-time students. I'm at campus for school, group meetings, and study time," explains one student. Happy with the level of activity and interaction or not, most find their fellow students "friendly and enjoyable to be around," and "good, hardworking people" who are also "very diverse. "Extremely intelligent, but not very socially oriented," says another student. "Most of all our students have lots of work experience." In common with many MBA programs, UAB appeals to those who already live nearby: "Most work full-time. Most live full-time in [the] community," one student reports.

Birmingham itself has changed over the years from a center for manufacturing, once known as the Pittsburgh of the South for its steel industry, to a center for the information technology business, and for medical research, with a quality of life that ranks it high on most national surveys.

Admissions

Academic GPA rank and scores on the GMAT are considered very important by those making admissions decisions for the graduate business programs at UAB, followed by work experience and personal essays. A minimum score of 480 on the GMAT is required. In 2006 the average score for those admitted is 553, and the average GPA is 3.2. Non-native English speakers must score at least 550 on the TOEFL, and all students are required to have passed a course in business calculus with a grade of C or better in the 5 years preceding admission, or to pass a proficiency exam or, once admitted, to schedule a course in it. At least 2 years of work experience is required for admission; the average student admitted has 4 years.

FINANCIAL FACTS

Annual tuition (in-state/ out-of-state)	$170/$425 per credit

ADMISSIONS

Admissions Selectivity Rating	**74**
# of applications received	276
% applicants accepted	81
% acceptees attending	77
Average GMAT	553
Range of GMAT	510–600
Average GPA	3.2
TOEFL required of International students	Yes
Minimum TOEFL (paper/computer)	550/213
Application fee	$50
International application fee	$75
Regular application deadline	7/1
Regular notification	8/1
Deferment available	Yes
Maximum length of deferment	1 year
Transfer students accepted	Yes
Transfer application policy Must meet UAB MBA admission requirements. Transfer courses must be from AACSB-accredited program and equivalent to our required courses. We will accept up to 25% of the degree program in transfer work with a minimum B grade.	
Non-fall admissions	Yes
Need-blind admissions	Yes

Applicants Also Look At
Samford University.

EMPLOYMENT PROFILE	
Career Rating	74

THE UNIVERSITY OF ALABAMA AT TUSCALOOSA
MANDERSON GRADUATE SCHOOL OF BUSINESS

GENERAL INFORMATION
Type of school	Public
Environment	City
Academic calendar	Semester

SURVEY SAYS . . .
Good peer network
Smart classrooms
Solid preparation in:
Marketing
Accounting
Teamwork
Computer skills

STUDENTS
Enrollment of parent institution	22,000
Enrollment of business school	116
% male/female	75/25
% out-of-state	39
% minorities	10
% international	13
Average age at entry	25
Average years work experience at entry	2

ACADEMICS
Academic Experience Rating	**95**
Student/faculty ratio	12:1
Profs interesting rating	92
Profs accessible rating	89
% female faculty	13
% minority faculty	10

Joint Degrees
MBA/JD 4 years, MBA/MA (modern languages) 3 years, MBA/MSN (nursing) 3 years, MBA/MS (engineering).

Prominent Alumni
Don James, chairman and CEO, Vulcan; Samuel D. DiPiazza, vice chairman, PricewaterhouseCoopers; Richard Anthony, CEO, Synovus; Ben Jenkins, vice chair, Wachovia; Gary Fayard, senior vice president and CFO, Coca-Cola.

Academics

Offering a unique combination of "national reputation and Southern hospitality," the Manderson Graduate School of Business at the The University of Alabama at Tuscaloosa treats its MBAs to a small and rigorous program that "stresses the technical aspect of many of the fields covered in the curriculum." The school is well positioned to do so, given that "facilities are fantastic" here, with "a high level of technology in the classroom. Every student has a laptop, and there is a wireless cloud for the business school. You can log on anywhere inside or outside the facilities." Manderson's tech emphasis means that "those with highly quantitative abilities will almost certainly enjoy many of the classes and do quite well, and will quickly acclimate to the workplace upon graduation."

The MBA program at Tuscaloosa is full-time only, with concentrations offered in five areas. Students speak highly of the finance and enterprise consulting programs; several (who apparently don't require sleep) praised the joint JD/MBA program. Professors here are "fantastic. Most write leading textbooks in their subject areas. Better still, they are highly accessible and willing to work as hard as students, and they passionately desire to help students grow as leaders." The program itself is "very rigorous, with high levels of interaction with students and a strong team atmosphere." Some students told us that the workload "sometimes seems impossible."

Administrators here "respond to changes in the marketplace, totally dropping something or taking on something new full force because they know that it will be needed for success in the marketplace." The school also does a great job of keeping "the greatest alumni in the country" in the loop, an endeavor students especially appreciate when it comes time to find a job.

Career and Placement

Students tell us that "currently, the Manderson program is very regional as far as career placement. However, the administration recognizes this weakness and is working to fix that issue in a variety of creative ways. Given their dedication and gung-ho attitudes, expect the program to see quick results." The school has the proper building blocks; MBAs report that "career administrators are awesome, sending constant correspondence regarding our progress and upcoming events." Underrepresented/underprivileged students are further served by the Capstone MBA Fellows program, which "seeks to place underrepresented students in the private sector for 10 to 20 hours per week for the duration of the 2-year MBA program." Top employers of Manderson MBAs include the AEA Group, Southern Company, Capgemini, Lithonia Lighting, Mercedes-Benz, Proctor & Gamble, International Paper, FedEx, Johnson & Johnson, and AmSouth.

Student Life and Environment

"Life as an MBA student is busy" at Tuscaloosa, as students "have 15 credit hours per semester, and the work is challenging." Students tell us that "although classes usually only last for half the day, the rest of the afternoon and much of the evening in spent going over material. Most of the material is so detailed and comprehensive that it takes tremendous effort at times to meet professors' expectations." In addition, "Team projects are a key part of our grade," and they, too, demand time. The heavy workload helps build a tight campus community; students "go out together, study together, and end up being involved in most aspects of each others' lives." Even when the school day is done, they continue to hang out; "On the evenings and weekends, the MBAA Association, Net Impact, and NAWMBA offer events and socials. Well-known speakers are brought in on almost a weekly basis."

Ms. Pam Vickers, Manager, Admissions and Student Services
Box 870223, Tuscaloosa, AL 35487-0223 United States
Phone: 205-348-9122 • Fax: 205-348-4504
E-mail: MBA@CBA.UA.EDU • Website: WWW.CBA.UA.EDU/MBA

UA Tuscaloosa students fully embrace the school's football program, "which is very much an essential part of the experience at the university and is a huge part of the traditions. This is a school that is heavily involved in its athletics." Students also tell us that "the school has a beautiful campus that offers countless opportunities to get involved" and that "Tuscaloosa is a great college town, incredibly fun," with "restaurants and bar/grill locations as well as retail and a grocery store on 'the Strip,' which is within walking distance of the b-school complex." The larger city of Birmingham is close enough to provide occasional nights out as well as internship opportunities and professional contacts.

Manderson MBAs tend to be "young, unmarried, and straight out of college," meaning that "many have never worked full-time out of school. This results in a relatively immature class with little appreciation for the opportunity cost of being here." Fortunately, students are "highly intelligent and motivated," so they're capable of managing the challenging work required of them. They're also "competitive yet willing to lend a helping hand at a moment's notice. It's a friendly atmosphere."

Admissions

Applicants to the Manderson MBA program must submit three copies of the completed application form; two copies of a personal statement detailing their past accomplishments and future ambitions; a copy of their current resume; an official GMAT or GRE score report (score must be less than 5 years old); three letters of recommendation; and two official transcripts from each postsecondary institution attended. International applicants must also supply an immigration and visa information form; certification of finances; and, for those applicants whose first language is not English, an official TOEFL score report (score must be less than 2 years old). The Admissions Committee occasionally requests an admissions interview but otherwise no interview is required. The school reports that it formulates each incoming class "to represent a diversity of academic, work, cultural, and international experiences that reflects today's workplace. An applicant's background that has the potential to make a unique or missing contribution to an incoming MBA class's make-up can be the deciding admissions factors that supercedes other factors." Incoming students are expected to know how to use Microsoft Office software.

FINANCIAL FACTS

Annual tuition (in-state/ out-of-state)	$5,278/$15,294
Fees	$2,000
Cost of books	$2,000
Room & board	$9,000
% of students receiving aid	70
% of first-year students receiving aid	100
% of students receiving loans	25
% of students receiving grants	65
Average award package	$14,522
Average grant	$7,956
Average student loan debt	$13,424

ADMISSIONS

Admissions Selectivity Rating	89
# of applications received	185
% applicants accepted	46
% acceptees attending	62
Average GMAT	620
Range of GMAT	550–690
Average GPA	3.4
TOEFL required of international students	Yes
Minimum TOEFL (paper/computer)	550/213
Application fee	$35
Regular application deadline	4/15
Regular notification	Rolling
Application Deadline/Notification	
Round 1:	1/5 / 1/20
Round 2:	2/15 / 3/1
Round 3:	4/15 / 5/1
Round 4:	7/1 / 7/15
Early decision program	Yes
ED Deadline/Notification	Rolling
	up to 1/5 / 01/20
Deferment available	Yes
Maximum length of deferment	1 year renewable
Transfer students accepted	Yes
Transfer application policy	
Rare, but up to 12 credit hours accepted for transfer from AACSB-accredited programs subject to committee approval.	
Need-blind admissions	Yes

Applicants Also Look At

Auburn University, Louisiana State University, University of Florida, University of Georgia, University of Mississippi, University of Tennessee.

EMPLOYMENT PROFILE

Career Rating	82		
Primary Source of Full-time Job Acceptances			
School-facilitated activities	29 (75%)		
Graduate-facilitated activities	7 (18%)		
Unknown	3 (7%)		
Percent employed	86		

Grads Employed by Function	%	Avg. Salary
Finance/Accounting	19	$58,484
Marketing/Sales	15	$60,700
MIS	27	$56,562
Operations/Production	15	$52,000
Consulting	12	$59,250
General Management	6	$56,250
Other	6	$57,500

Top 5 Employers Hiring Grads
Accenture; KPMG International; Deloitte Touche Tohmatsu; Procter & Gamble; Southern Company.

UNIVERSITY OF ALBERTA
SCHOOL OF BUSINESS

GENERAL INFORMATION

Type of school	Public
Environment	City
Academic calendar	Sept.

SURVEY SAYS . . .
Friendly students
Solid preparation in:
Accounting
General management
Quantitative skills
Doing business in a global economy

STUDENTS

Enrollment of parent institution	36,435
Enrollment of business school	276
% male/female	67/33
% part-time	57
% international	37
Average age at entry	30
Average years work experience at entry	7

ACADEMICS

Academic Experience Rating	**86**
Student/faculty ratio	4:1
Profs interesting rating	74
Profs accessible rating	87
% female faculty	18

Joint Degrees
MBA/LLB 4 years, MBA/MEng
(Engineering) 2 years, MBA/MAg
(Agriculture) 2 years, MBA/MF
(Forestry) 2 years.

Academics

With only 60 students admitted per year, the University of Alberta's 2-year MBA program is highly selective. Students spend the majority of their first year completing core requirements in accounting, business strategy, economics, finance, management science, marketing, and organizational behavior. Teamwork is a central part of the program, and students are assigned to teams at orientation so that they can get to know each other "without the demands of the program that will soon be upon them." In their second year, students are allowed to take elective courses and pursue a specialization in natural resources and energy, international business, technology commercialization, leisure and sports management, or public management. Alberta's diverse offerings are what draw many students to the campus. In fact, Alberta is the "only program in Canada to offer a specialization in leisure and sport management" and "The natural resources and energy specialization is one of only a couple in the world." However, in order to complete a specialization, students must submit a letter of application during the first semester. Alberta offers several MBA joint-degree programs, including MBA/Master of Agriculture, MBA/Master of Engineering, MBA/Master of Forestry, and an MBA/LLB.

Students have rave reviews for their professors, a group of "brilliant academics" who "really care about your performance" and "obviously enjoy teaching MBA students." Students characterize the support provided by the MBA Office as "unbelievable." "We are always aware of what upcoming deadlines are upon us," one student says. "And when we need help with finding courses that work best for us, the staff is extremely helpful."

Although some students feel the school had a tendency to be bureaucratic, one student cites "the welcoming experience I had by the administrative staff" as a "significant motivating factor for me to attend this program." MBA candidates appreciate the small class sizes, particularly in the second-year specialization courses, but some say there's a disconnect between theory and real-world practice.

Part-time students say "The school is really geared to full-time students who have access to the administration during the day and who can attend daytime tutorials." Other part-time students feel there could be "better adaptations and accommodations," as the program's demands on their time are often "extreme." Many students mentioned facilities as an area that could be improved, mostly as a result of the "rapid growth at the university." Students say the facilities are "old" and often "cramped," and that study facilities need upgrading. However, the university is working to address these problems, and "new buildings are on the way!" Overall, students are happy with life at Alberta; as one student put it, "I could not have made a better personal choice."

Career and Placement

The University of Alberta has the highest job-placement rating in Canada, with 93 percent of graduates finding employment within 3 months of graduation. Students praise the "the strength of the networks" built by the school. A wide variety of companies have a presence on campus, including HSBC, KPMG International, Caterpillar, ATCO Electric, the Alberta Government, and the Canadian Soccer Association.

Students accepted jobs in many different industries, with equal percentages going to marketing/sales, consulting, general management, and finance/accounting. The average salary for students who accepted employment 3 months after graduation was $58,373. Some students mentioned that the school could provide "more not-for-profit/arts management information," but, by and large, the students were pleased with the services provided by the Career Office.

JOAN WHITE, EXECUTIVE DIRECTOR, MBA PROGRAMS
2-30 BUSINESS BUILDING, EDMONTON, AB T6G 2R6 CANADA
PHONE: 780-492-3946 • FAX: 780-492-7825
E-MAIL: MBA@UALBERTA.CA • WEBSITE: WWW.MBA.NET

Student Life and Environment

Students at Alberta are nothing if not busy. Life on campus is described as "hectic but fun," with "no shortages of extracurricular activities to get involved in." Among other things, the university organizes holiday get-togethers, and hosts a very popular intra-mural sports league, and for students who like to party, "There's no shortage of that, either!" The campus, "large in both area and in students," is situated in Edmonton, "one of the most dynamic and red-hot economies in North America." Although Edmonton provides many opportunities for eager MBA students, the "booming economy" can be problematic when it comes to housing, as there is more demand than supply.

The student body is "all ages, and from all over the world." Described as "helpful, intelligent, friendly," the students at Alberta are "high-achieving people willing to work with and help each other." The student body is also very diverse, with almost 50 percent international enrollment. Classes are "very tightly knit," a closeness that starts "right from the orientation." Although the students are "very competitive," most describe their classmates as "very willing to take time to help other students." As with most MBA programs, there is a dividing line between the full-time and part-time students. The full-time students "tend to be younger and have less work experience" than the part-timers, who generally work full-time and take classes at night. However, whether full-time or part-time, most students agreed that their fellow degree candidates were "genuinely nice people."

Admissions

In a recently admitted class, students at the 25th percentile had GPAs of 3.0 and GMAT scores of 550. Students at the 75th percentile had GPAs of 3.5 and a GMAT score of 610. Students had an average of 7 years of work experience.

FINANCIAL FACTS

Annual tuition (in-state/ out-of-state)	$8,800/$18,300
Fees	$670
Cost of books	$1,300
Room & board (on/off-campus)	$7,000/$9,500
% of students receiving aid	60
% of first-year students receiving aid	84
% of students receiving grants	60
Average grant	$3,650

ADMISSIONS

Admissions Selectivity Rating	**84**
# of applications received	200
% applicants accepted	51
% acceptees attending	44
Average GMAT	575
Range of GMAT	550–610
Average GPA	3.4
TOEFL required of international students	Yes
Minimum TOEFL (paper/computer)	600/250
Application fee	$88
Regular application deadline	4/30
Regular notification	Rolling
Deferment available	Yes
Maximum length of deferment	1 year
Need-blind admissions	Yes

Applicants Also Look At

McGill University, The University of British Columbia, University of Calgary, University of Toronto, University of Western Ontario Richard Ivey School of Business, York University.

EMPLOYMENT PROFILE

Career Rating	77	Grads Employed by Function	%	Avg. Salary
Primary Source of Full-time Job Acceptances		Finance/Accounting	15	$54,517
School-facilitated activities	23 (43%)	Marketing/Sales	19	$47,398
Graduate-facilitated activities	25 (46%)	Operations/Production	7	$57,670
Unknown	6 (11%)	Consulting	19	$53,976
Percent employed	93	General Management	19	$44,785
		Other	21	$85,354

Top 5 Employers Hiring Grads

Alberta Government; Finning; Sierra Systems; HSBC; Royal Bank.

UNIVERSITY OF ARIZONA
ELLER COLLEGE OF MANAGEMENT

Academics

Getting your MBA at The University of Arizona is a warm and sunny experience. With 120 graduate students in the full-time program, "Eller is well known for its close-knit community with a small class size" as well as for a high ranking for its entrepreneurship, MIS, and finance programs. The intimate academic setting really pays off at Eller, where the student body brings its own unique cultural and professional experiences to the classroom. A student says, "People ranging from 22 to 45 (age) are enrolled in the MBA program. They include army personnel, farmers, and lawyers, and over half the students are international. The experiences they bring to the table are phenomenal."

The Eller curriculum provides a rigorous business education, with an "emphasis on group work and case studies." Since a majority of the teaching staff joins Eller with a blend of academic credentials and real-world know-how, they lend practical insight to theoretical topics. Students explain, "We have knowledgeable professors who have prepared us well for the business world, including former executives with a great deal of experience." Academics are manageable but the "time commitment is challenging" especially for students who work while attending school; however, students reassure that when the going gets rough, professors are "extremely helpful and go out of their way to assist students." A current student exclaims, "Most of the professors work from home on weekends and reply to e-mails almost instantaneously—this surprises me!"

A startup spirit pervades the campus, and many students come to The University of Arizona for the high-ranked entrepreneurial program. Through the McGuire Entrepreneurship Center, students can pursue a nine-unit concentration in entrepreneurship, with course work in new venture finance, competitive advantage and industry analysis, and venture development. Those looking for a special, diversified education have also found a good match at Eller, as it "is surrounded by strong schools in the university, and it has made a good effort of providing dual degrees between MBA and other science/law-based programs." These dual-degree programs allow students to "further customize their educations and [the programs] provide [students] with additional assets in today's working world." Eller doubles its appeal with a low, public school price tag, as well as a "generous scholarship program," which makes an Eller MBA highly affordable.

Career and Placement

The Office of Career Development aims to provide highly personalized service to each individual student, helping them to plan and achieve their career goals. The office further supports students in their job search through professional development workshops, interview preparation, resume preparation, and professional mentoring. In 2006, 89 percent of students were placed upon graduation, making an average salary of $59,250. Last year, the biggest employers were Intel, China Trust Bank, Dial, Raytheon, and US Airways. In 2005, the largest employers of U of A students were Advanced Micro Devices, Burlington Northern, Santa Fe Railway, Ernst &Young, IBM, and Intel.

Located in the heart of Tucson, Arizona, Eller is "really close to the companies and lots of job opportunities." Despite the excellence of the MBA program, some students are disheartened because it's "hard to get recruiters from top companies interested because we do not have the brand name of some schools." However, the Eller administrators are aware of this limitation, and the "Challenges associated with being small and not well recognized nationally are being handled on an ongoing basis." In fact, "New Career Officers have recently been hired," and students believe that career placement opportunities will continue to improve.

MARISA COX, DIRECTOR OF MBA ADMISSIONS
McCLELLAND HALL 210, BUILDING 108, 1130 E HELEN STREET, PO BOX 210108, TUCSON, AZ
85721-0108 UNITED STATES
PHONE: 520-621-4008 • FAX: 520-621-2606
E-MAIL: MBA_ADMISSIONS@ELLER.ARIZONA.EDU • WEBSITE: ELLERMBA.ARIZONA.EDU/

Student Life and Environment

Between work, school, networking, and socializing, "life's hectic" at Eller. Blending work with pleasure, Eller "is academically challenging yet provides a lot of social activities allowing students to interact and form firm friendships." A student adds, "Every day there is something new that I look forward to. I spend more time in school than at home, and I just love doing that!" For friendship and future business purposes, the Eller student body is appealing, as "students are friendly, organized, and very culturally diverse, creating a strong sense of global awareness in the environment. Also, I have noticed that they have a high level of business integrity, and many of them have an entrepreneurial nature."

In the pleasant, low-cost, Southwestern city of Tucson, Arizona, the warm and sunny Eller campus is an ideal location for graduate students on a tight budget. Close to the Saguaro National Forest and surrounded by beautiful desert scenery, Eller students further benefit from low-cost "great outdoor activities, such as hiking and cycling." The charming and laid-back college campus also boasts a "great recreation center."

Admissions

The admissions process at The University of Arizona is highly quantitative, analyzing each applicant's ability to handle the analytic portions of the program as evidenced by their GMAT scores, undergraduate record, and work experience. The Admissions Committee carefully evaluates each applicant's intellectual capacity, professional experience and career progression, and personal qualities that demonstrate leadership, integrity, initiative, and potential.

In most cases, students must have a GPA of at least 3.0 to be considered for admission; however, the Class of 2006 presented much higher averages, with an average undergraduate GPA of 3.5 and an average GMAT score of 624. There are three rounds of admissions deadlines at Eller, with rolling admissions in the interviewing periods, though students are highly encouraged to apply in first round, especially if they are international students or scholarship applicants. All qualified applicants are interviewed by an Admissions Official, either in person or via telephone.

FINANCIAL FACTS

Annual tuition (in-state/ out-of-state)	$15,044/$25,851
Fees	$224
Cost of books	$800
Room & board	$8,400
% of students receiving grants	70
Average grant	$17,939

ADMISSIONS

Admissions Selectivity Rating	87
# of applications received	224
% applicants accepted	53
% acceptees attending	47
Average GMAT	624
Range of GMAT	533–707
Average GPA	3.49
TOEFL required of international students	Yes
Minimum TOEFL (paper/computer)	600/250
Application fee	$50
Regular application deadline	4/15
Regular notification	5/15
Application Deadline/Notification	
Round 1:	11/15 / 12/15
Round 2:	2/15 / 3/15
Round 3:	4/15 / 5/15
Early decision program?	Yes
ED Deadline/Notification	11/15 / 12/15
Deferment available	Yes
Maximum length of deferment	1 year
Need-blind admissions	Yes

Applicants Also Look At

Arizona State University, Babson College, Thunderbird, University of California—Irvine, University of Colorado, The University of Texas at Austin, Wake Forest University.

EMPLOYMENT PROFILE

Career Rating	76	Grads Employed by Function	%	Avg. Salary
Primary Source of Full-time Job Acceptances		Finance/Accounting	38	$53,805
School-facilitated activities	28 (56%)	Human Resources	2	NR
Graduate-facilitated activities	22 (44%)	Marketing/Sales	29	$54,521
Average base starting salary	$59,250	MIS	6	$75,000
Percent employed	89	Operations/Production	6	$64,333
		Consulting	13	$70,333
		Other	6	$60,923

Top 5 Employers Hiring Grads

Intel Corporation; China Trust Bank; Dial Corporation; Raytheon; US Airways.

UNIVERSITY OF ARKANSAS—FAYETTEVILLE
SAM M. WALTON COLLEGE OF BUSINESS

GENERAL INFORMATION
Type of school	Public
Environment	Town

SURVEY SAYS . . .
Students love Fayetteville, AR
Cutting-edge classes
Happy students
Smart classrooms
Solid preparation in:
Finance
Quantitative skills

STUDENTS
Enrollment of parent institution	17,929
Enrollment of business school	126
% male/female	70/30
% out-of-state	25
% part-time	76
% international	33
Average age at entry	27
Average years work experience at entry	5

ACADEMICS
Academic Experience Rating	**89**
Student/faculty ratio	24:1
Profs interesting rating	80
Profs accessible rating	82
% female faculty	19
% minority faculty	17

Joint Degrees
MBA/JD 4 years.

Prominent Alumni
S. Robson Walton, chair, Wal-Mart Stores Inc.; William Dillard Sr., chair, Dillards Inc.; Jack Stephens, Stephens Inc.; Thomas F. McLarty, former White House Chief of Staff.

Academics

From the moment you arrive, it's clear that students at the University of Arkansas' have a prime location "next to the largest retail corporation in the world." And that's a good thing, since "with Wal-Mart headquarters just a few miles away and multiple vendor offices in the vicinity," the school can easily fulfill its mission of "providing students with real world experiences—especially in supply chain and marketing at Wal-Mart." Students can't resist drawing comparisons to their neighbor and benefactor; one student writes, "The school offers good quality at low cost. It's the Wal-Mart of schools." And Wal-Mart money, students agree, has made Walton College "the most technologically advanced of any school in the U of A system. The classrooms and facilities are second to none."

In order to maximize return on students' investment, Walton offers a 16-month MBA program. Though 4 months longer than the previous version, students find this "better than the old 1-year program" since it "now includes a summer internship, study abroad, or corporate consulting project." Also, one student adds, "The extra time in the program helps give you more time to find a job that is a good fit." The core is covered in two 8-week integrated modules in the fall and the spring starts with a 5-week strategic management course followed by an 11-week consulting project, during which students apply classroom lessons to the real-world problems of local companies ("There are many employment opportunities with Fortune 500 companies in the local area who are eager to hire from the U of A").

MBAs report that "the classes are challenging, and you are expected to work hard." They love the school's "local reputation and contacts, especially if you want to get involved in the retail/Wal-Mart vendor industry." Students also appreciate how "The administration is dedicated to bringing the best teachers together with the best students. They want us to succeed in the class and in life." Accordingly, most students agree that the faculty is "way more knowledgeable, professional, helpful, and approachable than I ever expected." Another explains, "Most of the classes are very interactive, and a top-notch faculty applies and teaches the most current tools to solve today's business problems. They really do challenge us to think outside the box." They also have high hopes for the program's future; as one student comments, "Unlike Wal-Mart right now the stock of a Walton School of Business Diploma is growing at an exponential rate. I think you will find that the people leading business into the future will be from the U of A's Walton College of Business. And let me tell you they are sharp, very sharp. They don't call us Razorbacks for nothing!"

Career and Placement

Since the U of A is so "well known" within the business world, Career Development wouldn't have to do much to help students. However, the Career Center at Walton offers students a number of job fairs each year, some aimed specifically at a particular function (supply chain management, engineering, IT), and others that are open to the entire campus. Students single out the "exceptional" paid graduate assistantship program which allows them to work "on or off campus in offices of international companies, research labs, or with professors." "The work experience you gain through the graduate assistantship program is priceless," says one student.

Top employers of Walton MBAs include J.B. Hunt, Masterfoods, Tyson Foods, Unilever, and, of course, Wal-Mart. About three in five graduates remain in the area; approximately 10 percent find jobs outside of the United States.

Michele Halsell, Assistant Dean for Graduate Programs
475 Business Building, Fayetteville, AR 72701 United States
Phone: 479-575-2851 • Fax: 479-575-8721
E-mail: gsb@walton.uark.edu • Website: gsb.uark.edu

Student Life and Environment

The old real estate cliché holds true; it's all about "location, location, location." In Fayetteville, students enjoy a "close proximity to Wal-Mart headquarters and 'Vendorville' (all Wal-Mart suppliers, including Newell-Rubbermaid, Procter & Gamble, and Unilever, have offices here) in one of the fastest-growing region in the country (according to the Milken Institute)," both of which create "great opportunities for newly minted MBAs." In addition, students agree, "Fayetteville is a great town to be in. There is plenty to do socially after hours," says one student. Check out Dixon Street, a near-doppelganger for Bourbon Street, that lines the way to the U of A with bars, shops, and restaurants. And then there are always the football games.

According to students, MBAs form a tight-knit and "unique" community at the university. The rigors of the accelerated academic program also help forge an esprit de corps, but there's more to it than that. One student explains, "The students in the Walton College of Business have formed a collegial and cohesive group. The small size of the program and efforts of the MBA program administration have fostered a supportive and team-oriented approach to our business education." Add into the mix a healthy dose of diversity with "many" students hailing from "China, India, South Korea, Bulgaria, and various states in the U.S." and coming from backgrounds in "engineering, business, law, and arts and sciences." In addition, "Some students have owned their own businesses or worked for large corporations" and "almost everyone . . . has worked or studied abroad."

Admissions

The Walton Admissions Committee reports that successful applicants on average have undergraduate GPAs of 3.4, GMAT scores of 620, and, for international students, TOFEL scores of 550 (paper-based test) or 213 (computer-based test). Preference is given to those with at least 2 years of work experience (or substantial extracurricular involvement in their undergraduate programs). In addition, aim for three letters of recommendation and a compelling personal statement. The school mentions that "underrepresented minorities are encouraged to apply, and special financial assistance is available to minority students."

FINANCIAL FACTS

Annual tuition (in-state/ out-of-state)	$16,847/$39,855
Fees	$2,224
Cost of books	$1,500
Room & board (on/off-campus)	$6,127/$9,700
% of students receiving aid	100
% of first-year students receiving aid	100
% of students receiving grants	100
Average award package	$17,000
Average grant	$17,000
Average student loan debt	$18,500

ADMISSIONS

Admissions Selectivity Rating	91
# of applications received	207
% applicants accepted	50
% acceptees attending	84
Average GMAT	625
Range of GMAT	560–640
Average GPA	3.47
TOEFL required of international students	Yes
Minimum TOEFL (paper/computer)	550/213
Application fee	$40
International application fee	$50
Regular application deadline	9/15
Regular notification	10/15
Deferment available	Yes
Maximum length of deferment	1 year
Transfer students accepted	Yes
Transfer application policy Max 6 hours, electives from an AACSB-accredited school, A or B grades.	
Non-fall admissions	Yes
Need-blind admissions	Yes

Applicants Also Look At

Oklahoma State University, Texas A&M University System Health Science Center, University of Georgia, University of Mississippi, University of Oklahoma, University of Tennessee, The University of Texas at Austin.

EMPLOYMENT PROFILE

Career Rating	78	Grads Employed by Function	%	Avg. Salary
		Finance/Accounting	9	NR
		Marketing/Sales	19	NR
		MIS	13	NR
		Operations/Production	9	NR
		Consulting	3	NR
		Other	47	R

Top 5 Employers Hiring Grads
J.B. Hunt; Wal-Mart, Inc.; IBM; Dial; Google.

THE UNIVERSITY OF BRITISH COLUMBIA
SAUDER SCHOOL OF BUSINESS

GENERAL INFORMATION
Type of school   Public

SURVEY SAYS . . .
Students love Vancouver, BC
Happy students
Smart classrooms
Solid preparation in:
Accounting
Teamwork

STUDENTS
Enrollment of parent institution	45,000
% international	44
Average age at entry	31
Average years work experience at entry	6

ACADEMICS
Academic Experience Rating	**89**
Student/faculty ratio	20:1
Profs interesting rating	98
Profs accessible rating	86
% female faculty	17

Joint Degrees
MBA/LLB 4 years, MBA/MAPPS
(Master of Arts, Asia Pacific Policy
Studies) 2 years, MBA/CMA 2 years.

Academics

Students in this prestigious 15-month, full-time MBA program at Vancouver's University of British Columbia report that "Sauder professors look for an integrated approach that develops every student's overall understanding of each facet of business, using relevant materials and current events. This results in ensuring that Sauder students are ready for the challenges of today's business world without burdening them with outdated business concepts." Through "a mix of theory and concepts, case studies, real-project analysis, and internships," students agree, "this program provides [them] with very good opportunities [to develop] practical, useful management practices."

"The most valuable part of the Sauder MBA program is the integrative core," students report. The core, an intensive 13-week sequence, is taught as a single course rather than as a set of discrete disciplines, an approach befitting Sauder's focus. Because of both the sheer quantity of work and the level of complex thinking required, the core is extremely challenging. One student explains, "I feel I'm going through the business equivalent of Navy Seal training. Surviving the core is the toughest thing I've ever done...but I can honestly say I've never laughed this hard nor had so much fun." Students happily note that "after solving so many cases, analyzing so many businesses, and critically tearing apart complex business theories, you come out of the core thinking you can do almost anything. It really is inspiring." Another benefit of the workload is that "it prepares students to cope with demanding deadlines and timelines in their chosen careers." But such preparation results from rigorous training, including "twenty-four hours a week of class lectures, case studies and presentations, assignment submissions, course readings to catch up on, and multiple submissions due on some days."

The remainder of the program post-core is devoted primarily to specialization and professional development. Students tell us that finance is "by far" the school's strongest area, although supply chain management, entrepreneurship, and international business also earn praise. Administrators here "do their job and more. They are service-oriented and very focused in addressing students' needs." When students find spare time to put down the business books, they "can learn about the interesting research happening in other faculties, because the school has so much interesting research-oriented stuff happening all the time."

Career and Placement

UBC's Business Career Centre offers both personal consultation as well as a structured program to help students identify goals and then develop strategies to meet those goals. Its services include self-assessment assistance, coaching sessions, skills training programs (in resume writing, interviewing, and networking), recruiting events (which bring "corporate recruiters from prominent companies" to interview job candidates), and job postings. Students wish the office could do more to attract companies from the east coast, and many emphasize that "UBC needs to continue to build its alumni network, and its Business Career Centre needs more resources to attract recruiters and companies to come to UBC to find qualified MBA grads in all areas, not just finance," the school's strongest discipline.

Employers likely to hire UBC MBAs include Accenture, Bank of Montreal, Bombardier, Citibank, General Motors of Canada, Genome BC, Ledcor Industries, MacDonald Dettwiler & Associates, the Ministry of Energy & Mines, the PepsiCo, Procter & Gamble, Westport Innovations, and Xantrex Technology.

MBA Programs Office, MBA Programs Office
#160 - 2053 Main Mall, Vancouver, BC V6T 1Z2 Canada
Phone: 604-822-8422 • Fax: 604-822-9030
E-mail: mba@sauder.ubc.ca • Website: www.sauder.ubc.ca/mba

Student Life and Environment

It's impossible to separate the quality of life at UBC from its hometown of Vancouver, which students unanimously proclaim "one of the best places on earth." This "vibrant city [is] a great place to live. It's very safe, and there's always so much to do. Whistler Mountain is on your doorstep, so lots of ski trips are planned, with hiking in the Rockies during the summer. The wineries aren't too far away, either!" Vancouver's "strategic location—facing directly into the Asian market"—provides excellent internship and career opportunities for UBC MBAs. Non-Canadian students happily report that "our spouses can work here legally for the duration of our courses! In the U.S., my wife would have had to do nothing for two years." About the only downside is that "because Vancouver is a great place to live, people are willing to take lower wages. There are a lot of excellent-quality people looking for jobs in Vancouver too, so the competition is tough. It is difficult to get a really high-paid job in Vancouver, but your quality of life makes [taking a lower-paying job] worth it!"

UBC's "park-like campus" is located "on a peninsula with vistas of mountains and oceans." The facilities are "excellent. The commerce building is wireless-enabled, the MBA lounge is a great place to hang out, and there are adequate restaurants for all tastes." Furthermore, "the facilities include pools and gyms, and a movie theater located in the university. There's also a graduate bar on campus that provides a beautiful view of Vancouver, and the school has a great 18-hole golf course." Students can participate in "tons of different clubs" that help them network while developing business-related or recreational skills. "There is a good balance between the workload and time for yourself," with "plenty and diverse social and development events."

Admissions

Admission to the Sauder MBA program is extremely competitive. All applicants must submit official transcripts for undergraduate work (students who attended schools where English was not the primary language must arrange for a literal translation of their transcripts to be delivered to UBC), official GMAT score reports, evidence of English proficiency (TOEFL scores for students whose first language is not English), a resume, and three letters of reference. Interviews are by invitation only; the school interviews roughly half of its applicant pool. The school's viewbook notes that "only under exceptional circumstances will applicants with less than two years of full-time work experience be admitted to this program." On average, students enter the program with between six and eight years' full-time professional experience. Applications are processed on a rolling basis; admitted students may not defer admission.

FINANCIAL FACTS

Annual tuition	$24,500
Cost of books	$1,200

ADMISSIONS

Admissions Selectivity Rating	82
# of applications received	304
% applicants accepted	69
% acceptees attending	49
Average GMAT	620
Range of GMAT	590–680
Average GPA	3.3
TOEFL required of international students	Yes
Minimum TOEFL (paper/computer)	600/250
Application fee	$125
Regular application deadline	4/30
Regular notification	Rolling
Need-blind admissions	Yes

EMPLOYMENT PROFILE

Career Rating	87	Grads Employed by Function	%	Avg. Salary
Primary Source of Full-time Job Acceptances		Finance/Accounting	25	$73,000
Percent employed	90	Human Resources	1	NR
		Marketing/Sales	9	$70,000
		MIS	6	$75,000
		Operations/Production	2	$60,000
		Consulting	17	$94,000
		General Management	10	$80,000
		Other	30	NR

UNIVERSITY OF CALGARY
HASKAYNE SCHOOL OF BUSINESS

Academics

The University of Calgary's Haskayne School of Business boasts more than 3,000 full- and part-time students enrolled in bachelor's, master's, PhD, and executive education programs. Despite its large size, intimacy is the name of the game with the MBA program. "It is a relatively small-sized MBA program—around 30 full-time," says one candidate, "so it is good for students." Haskayne is one of the top business schools in the world, and has received top rankings from several sources. Students echo these accolades, describing their classmates as "knowledgeable," the administration as "friendly and helpful," and the professors as having "strong academic backgrounds." One student says, "I am very happy with the close support" provided by the faculty.

Aside from the traditional MBA, Haskayne offers many degrees, including the Alberta/Haskayne Executive MBA (offered jointly with the University of Alberta), a PhD, and an interdisciplinary Master of Science in Sustainable Energy Development in Quito, Ecuador. Students praised the school's "focus on the oil and gas industry," as well as their "expertise in finance." Haskayne also offers several joint-degrees with other faculties within the University of Calgary, including the MBA/MBT, JD/MBA, MD/MBA, and MSW/MBA. Some students wish that "the Haskayne school would be more strict with academic enrollment." "The class age is getting younger and those coming in have very little tangible work experience."

The Haskayne MBA is a 20-course program, which consists of 10 core courses, 2 integrative courses, and 8 electives. Up to two electives can be taken outside the School of Business with approval from the MBA office. Students appreciate the program's flexibility, and the "ability to tailor your course work, activities, [and] job searches to your future career field." Another says: "Coming from an engineering background and wanting to transition into investment banking, I have found this school very accommodating." Students also have an opportunity to engage in a mentorship program in their second year, and 43 senior executives from 32 companies were participating as mentors in 2006–2007. One student who benefited from the program said, "This was the most helpful career development opportunity I have taken advantage of while at Haskayne. My mentor was an ideal match for me and highly networked into the business community."

Career and Placement

Students are very enthusiastic about the career opportunities afforded by Haskayne's "close ties to the business community," and the Career Center earns praise for its "help concerning resume writing and interview skills." In surveys, the school's location is consistently listed as one of its major benefits. It's "in the heart of the current hottest (economically speaking) city in Canada," and the city is in "close proximity to major companies' headquarters." Another student said, "There are plenty of quality jobs available for MBA students . . . high-profile oil and gas companies and investment banks are a staple at recruitment drives."

There is a strong multinational recruiting presence on campus, and students enjoy a great deal of "opportunity upon graduation," particularly in the energy and financial sectors, where "salary and benefits are far superior to many other industries." Companies that frequently hire graduates include Nexen, Enbridge, Suncor Energy, CIBC World Markets, Scotia Bank, Shell Canada, Imperial Oil, and Deloitte Touche Tohmatsu. The mean base salary (without bonus) is $95,351, and 93 percent of students reported accepting offers by three months after graduation. As one student said, "It is an MBA employee's market right now."

Michael McKinlay, Admissions Coordinator
2500 University Drive, NW Calgary, AB T2N 1N4 Canada
Phone: 403-220-3808 • Fax: 403-282-0095
E-mail: mbarequest@mgmt.ucalgary.ca • Website: www.haskayne.ucalgary.ca/mba

Student Life and Environment

Students tout the "diversity of the class" and the lack of "the hostile competitive environment" at Haskayne, which has "made for a better learning experience." Because of the small class size, students know each other well and "spend many hours outside of class together." Others echoed that sentiment, describing their classmates as "like family." Life in Calgary is described as "on the go," and although the MBA Society plans social events for students like skiing and bowling, some students note that the heavy workload makes it difficult to get involved with extracurricular activities.

The biggest complaint among students is the scarce housing, which is described as "difficult (and expensive!)" and "a nightmare." Students praise the facilities, particularly the "great gym at the school with modern equipment" and the MBA Lounge, where "most of the students spend the whole day." There are always people there "to help you or just to chat." As is the case with many other schools, the part-time students feel segregated from the full-time students. "As a part-time student, I am little involved in campus life," one student says. Other part-timers agree, explaining that "you attend your courses and go home."

Admissions

Fall 2006, the average GMAT score for Haskayne first-years was 614, and the average GPA was 3.30. Students had an average of 6 years of work experience. The average age of the Fall 2006 entering class was 30.

FINANCIAL FACTS

Annual tuition (in-state/ out-of-state)	$1,450/$20,350
Fees	$843
Cost of books	$1,702
Room & board	$12,000
% of first-year students receiving aid	75
Average grant	$5,000

ADMISSIONS

Admissions Selectivity Rating	**84**
# of applications received	200
% applicants accepted	60
% acceptees attending	54
Average GMAT	614
Range of GMAT	550–680
Average GPA	3.3
TOEFL required of international students	Yes
Minimum TOEFL (paper/computer)	600/250
Application fee	$100
International application fee	$130
Regular application deadline	5/1
Regular notification	Rolling
Application Deadline/Notification	
Round 1:	11/15 / 1/15
Round 2:	1/15 / 3/1
Round 3:	3/1 / 5/1
Round 4:	5/1 / 6/15
Deferment available	Yes
Maximum length of deferment	1 year
Transfer students accepted	Yes
Transfer application policy	
We can accept up to 9 courses.	
Need-blind admissions	Yes

Applicants Also Look At

Queen's University, University of Alberta, The University of British Columbia, University of Western Ontario, York University.

EMPLOYMENT PROFILE				
Career Rating	**91**	**Grads Employed by Function**	**%**	**Avg. Salary**
Primary Source of Full-time Job Acceptances		Finance/Accounting	31	NR
School-facilitated activities	44%	Human Resources	3	NR
Graduate-facilitated activities	56%	Marketing/Sales	11	NR
Percent employed (within 3 months)	93	MIS	3	NR
		Operations/Production	36	NR
		Consulting	14	NR
		Other	2	NR

UNIVERSITY OF CALIFORNIA—BERKELEY
HAAS SCHOOL OF BUSINESS

Academics

The Haas School of Business at the University of California—Berkeley offers students "a truly interactive environment," one in which "professors learn from the students as well as the other way around" thanks to students' substantial input into the program. The full-time program in particular is designed to provide students with an unusual degree of autonomy; explains one student, "Student initiative comes into play in every aspect of the program, from scheduling speakers to career search." Students here also design and run, with faculty oversight, a number of electives every semester. The result of all this freedom is that "students are forced to become entrepreneurs as part of their education." The small size of the program (only 250 full-time students and about as many part-timers) contributes to the experience by "forcing a collaborative environment where competition is put aside in order to help one another."

Haas backs up its unique approach to graduate business education with a strong curriculum and a solid faculty. The school excels in social entrepreneurship, corporate social responsibility, general management, and technology; this last area capitalizes on Berkeley's location "across the bay from San Francisco and just one hour from Silicon Valley." The faculty includes a number of stars; boasts one MBA, "Our finance professor is serving as the president of the San Francisco Federal Reserve. Our Dean was on leave as [Governor] Arnold Schwarzenegger's Finance Director. They don't get better than this." Better still, "not only are the professors outstanding in their fields, but they are also highly approachable and willing to make changes to the class to meet the students' needs." Semesters move along quickly here; "The academic pace is very fast," students observe, "but the workload is not overwhelming." While the core "is solid," most here prefer the "awesome electives that give you some great opportunities outside the classroom."

Career and Placement

When it comes time to find a career, Berkeley MBAs benefit from their program's high profile and sound reputation. As is often the case at such schools, the Haas Career Center provides a broad range of excellent services. Students here benefit from one-on-one advisement, access to numerous online job databases, industry clubs, workshops, seminars, and a mentoring program in which second-year students counsel first years in their search for internships.

Employers most likely to hire Haas MBAs include Bank of America; the Clorox Company; Deloitte Touche Tohmatsu; Gap, Inc.; Johnson & Johnson; LeapFrog Enterprises, Inc.; McKinsey & Company; Microsoft; Samsung Group; and Wells Fargo.

Student Life and Environment

For full-time students, "student clubs are at the heart of the school" because they help organize student input to the program. Explains one MBA, "Nothing happens at Haas without student involvement. Just about every full-time student is heavily involved in all aspects of the school. From student government to admissions to industry clubs to sports and wine clubs, everyone is able to express their interests and tap their fellow students for more information or just someone to share a good meal." The administration "fully supports club activities and has our needs on their minds continuously. It is only with their aid that we have been able to accomplish so much in our short time here."

PETER JOHNSON, EXECUTIVE DIRECTOR OF INTERNATIONAL ADMISSIONS
430 STUDENT SERVICES BUILDING, #1902 BERKELEY, CA 94720-1902 UNITED STATES
PHONE: 510-642-1405 • FAX: 510-643-6659
E-MAIL: MBAADM@HAAS.BERKELEY.EDU • WEBSITE: WWW.HAAS.BERKELEY.EDU

Between classes, clubs, and other extracurricular options, "live is very busy" for full-time students at Haas. There are "groups constantly getting together to go to arts festivals, AIDS walks, golfing, cycling, surfing, skiing, attending seminars, hearing guest lecturers, and hiking, to name just a few activities. The opportunities are endless and everyone loves being here." Thursday nights "are a tradition at Haas. We have BoW (Bar of the Week) in Berkeley and San Francisco, so there are always fun places to check out as you get to know the area." Students also appreciate their "access to the Bay Area's business, culture, natural beauty, and geographic diversity. Networking opportunities abound because so many business and thought leaders either live in the area or pass through here."

The "great, resourceful, creative, and mellow" students of Haas are "warm, but with a competitive edge—in the best sense of the word." Students speculate that "Haas' long-standing 'no grade-disclosure' policy" results in "students who are extremely helpful to each other, making certain that learning is truly a collaborative process." Indeed, our survey respondents all agree that "students at Haas are extremely team-oriented. They very much work together to get things done. The Berkeley MBA attracts top-notch students from all over the world and we mutually benefit from one another's experiences." Adds one student, "Given how diverse the work experiences are here, I find myself learning from those around me every day. These are truly the type of people I want to work with and for after graduation."

Admissions

Applicants to Haas graduate programs must submit all the following materials to the admissions department: official copies of transcripts for all postsecondary academic work, an official GMAT score report, letters of recommendation, a personal statement, and a resume. Interviews are conducted on an invitation-only basis. In addition to the above materials, international applicants whose first language is not English must also submit official score reports for the TOEFL (minimum score of 570 for the paper-based test, 230 for the computer-based test). The school considers all of the following in determining admissions status: "demonstration of quantitative ability; quality of work experience, including depth and breadth of responsibilities; opportunities to demonstrate leadership, etc.; strength of letters of recommendation; depth and breadth of extracurricular and community involvement; and strength of short answer and essays, including articulation of clear focus and goals."

FINANCIAL FACTS

Annual tuition (in-state/ out-of-state)	$26,880/$37,949
Fees (in-state/ out-of-state)	$23,984/$22,930
Cost of books	$2,500
Room & board	$19,356

ADMISSIONS

Admissions Selectivity Rating	98
# of applications received	2,727
% applicants accepted	17
% acceptees attending	51
Average GMAT	707
Range of GMAT	680–740
Average GPA	3.51
TOEFL required of international students	Yes
Minimum TOEFL (paper/computer)	570/230
Application fee	$175
Regular application deadline	3/12
Regular notification	5/14
Application Deadline/Notification	
Round 1:	11/6 / 1/29
Round 2:	12/11 / 3/19
Round 3:	1/31 / 4/30
Round 4:	3/12 / 5/14
Need-blind admissions	Yes

Applicants Also Look At

Columbia University, Harvard University, New York University, Northwestern University, Stanford University, University of California, Los Angeles (UCLA), University of Pennsylvania.

EMPLOYMENT PROFILE

Career Rating	98	Grads Employed by Function	%	Avg. Salary
Primary Source of Full-time Job Acceptances		Finance/Accounting	29	$93,911
School-facilitated activities	1	Marketing/Sales	24	$100,608
Average base starting salary	$98,977	Operations/Production	2	$90,200
Percent employed	21	Consulting	25	$106,045
		General Management	17	$96,598

University of California—Davis
Graduate School of Management

Academics

With a class size of fewer than 60 students, the full-time daytime MBA program at UC—Davis "is the closest thing to a private education, combined with all the resources of the University of California." It's a combination students here appreciate. One student says, "UC—Davis Graduate School of Management is based on a team-oriented and collaborative environment. I didn't feel that a school focused on . . . intense competition was truly reflective of the qualities that would serve me well in my post-MBA career. The GSM's emphasis on ideas to action through teamwork has been everything I hoped for."

UC—Davis excels in a surprising range of disciplines, given the size of the program. Students describe a "renowned organizational behavior program" and say the school is especially strong in finance. Also, "If you want to be an entrepreneur, there is no other school you should even consider applying to. There are more opportunities for viable startups moving through the UC—Davis campus than the GSM can even handle!" The school's Consulting Center "allows students to take on real-life projects for credit," while recent changes to the curriculum have created "a strong and quickly evolving focus area (via classes, concentrations, centers of excellence, student organizations, and dual degrees) in corporate social responsibility and business sustainability."

The Davis business faculty "is top-notch. Their expertise is almost always available for students to draw on. We have a formal student-faculty mentoring program, most professors have an open-door policy, and their offices are in our building. They have been willing to sponsor clubs, teach new courses that students request, aid in job searches, employ students as research and teaching assistants, attend social events, etc." Students love how "The administration eagerly pursues feedback from students and then implements effectual change. We work together to better the school based on changing business and social trends and the goals of the current student body. It is very encouraging to see a suggestion implemented quickly that improves the quality of our educational experience."

Career and Placement

Students report that "as a small school, our Career Services resources are more limited than other programs," so "Finding a post-MBA career takes more student initiative than may be required at bigger schools." While the office "is excellent for finding finance jobs," it "leaves a little to be desired in other areas." Also, "Being in the Sacramento area really hurts our ability to recruit companies. Services are improving, though." On another positive note, "While being a small program limits the breadth of alumni contacts, the value of the contacts derived from our small feel far outweighs the downside."

Employers that most frequently recruit Davis MBAs include: AT&T, Blue Cross and Blue Shield Association, CalPERS, CalSTRS, Clorox, Deloitte Touche Tohmatsu, eBay, E&J Gallo Winery, Gartner Consulting, Hewlett-Packard, IBM, Intel, Kaiser Permanente, MRSI Consulting, National Forest Service, PricewaterhouseCoopers, and Wells Fargo.

Student Life and Environment

At the top of Davis MBAs' wish list is a new facility, as the program currently is housed "in a small older building." A new building has been promised for some time, but students report that ground had yet to be broken as of February 2007, and that the new building "will not be ready until at least 2008 or 2009." When it arrives, the new facility "will include a conference center, restaurant, etc., and will be located across from the famous Mondavi Center."

JAMES STEVENS, ASSISTANT DEAN, STUDENT AFFAIRS
GRADUATE SCHOOL OF MANAGEMENT, ONE SHIELDS AVENUE, AOB IV, DAVIS, CA 95616 U.S.
PHONE: 530-752-7658 • FAX: 530-754-9355
E-MAIL: ADMISSIONS@GSM.UCDAVIS.EDU • WEBSITE: WWW.GSM.UCDAVIS.EDU

Davis MBAs "are given the opportunity to become involved in a large number of clubs," thanks to the small size of the program. One student writes, "As the leader of the UC—Davis chapter of Challenge for Charity, I know that I can literally call 30 to 50 percent of my classmates on the weekend for help with an event or project and they'd be willing to help. I think that would be extremely difficult to find at bigger schools." Extracurricular events "range from career/academic panels to wine appreciation classes to flag football games. We work hard and play hard here, and everyone is included." While "there are no specific activities for partners/spouses, they are always encouraged to join in and come to events."

Davis "is a growing midsize city. It is called 'bike town U.S.A.' because there is no need to own a car (this is rare in California). . . . There is a diverse mix of restaurants, including Thai, Chinese, Japanese, Mexican, Czech, Bavarian, French, European, Indian, American fare, and others." The city is located "20 minutes from downtown Sacramento, 90 minutes from San Francisco, and 2 hours from Lake Tahoe." Another student says, "The environment in Davis is awesome. It has high quality of life, elementary schools are great, everybody bikes around, there's no violence," and there's "huge diversity."

Admissions

Admissions Officers for the full-time MBA program at UC—Davis consider the following factors in assessing candidates: academic potential, professional potential, and personal qualities. Full-time work experience is not required for admission. Applicants must submit the following materials: a completed application form (online or hard copy); a current resume; a list of outside activities and honors; three personal essays; official transcripts from each undergraduate and graduate institution attended; two letters of recommendation; and an official GMAT score report. Applicants whose native language is not English must submit an official TOEFL score report reflecting a score no more than 2 years old. Applications to the full-time program are accepted for the fall semester only.

FINANCIAL FACTS

Annual tuition	$10,244
Fees (in-state/ out-of-state)	$22,163/$34,408
Cost of books	$1,665
Room & board	$13,024
% of students receiving aid	80
% of first-year students receiving aid	82
% of students receiving loans	54
% of students receiving grants	72
Average award package	$21,448
Average grant	$12,777
Average student loan debt	$34,723

ADMISSIONS

Admissions Selectivity Rating	96
# of applications received	316
% applicants accepted	28
% acceptees attending	62
Average GMAT	671
Range of GMAT	590–770
Average GPA	3.4
TOEFL required of international students	Yes
Minimum TOEFL (paper/computer)	600/250
Application fee	$100
Application Deadline/Notification	
Round 1:	11/15 / 1/31
Round 2:	1/17 / 3/31
Round 3:	3/14 / 5/31
Round 4:	5/16 / 6/30
Early decision program?	Yes
ED Deadline/Notification	11/15 / 1/31
Deferment available	Yes
Maximum length of deferment	1 year
Need-blind admissions	Yes

Applicants Also Look At

Stanford University, University of California—Berkeley, University of California—Irvine, University of California—Los Angeles (UCLA), University of Southern California, The University of Texas at Austin, University of Washington.

EMPLOYMENT PROFILE

Career Rating	88	Grads Employed by Function	%	Avg. Salary
Primary Source of Full-time Job Acceptances		Finance/Accounting	56	$69,527
School-facilitated activities	23 (56%)	Human Resources	8	$74,633
Graduate-facilitated activities	18 (44%)	Marketing/Sales	17	$75,631
Average base starting salary	$73,028	Consulting	13	$84,000
Percent employed	91	Entrepreneurship	2	NR
		Venture Capital	2	$65,000
		Internet/New Media	2	$70,000

Top 5 Employers Hiring Grads
Intel; E&J Gallo Winery; Mervyn's; Gartner Consulting; AT&T.

UNIVERSITY OF CALIFORNIA—IRVINE
THE PAUL MERAGE SCHOOL OF BUSINESS

GENERAL INFORMATION

Type of school	Public
Environment	City
Academic calendar	Sept. to June

SURVEY SAYS . . .

Students love Irvine, CA
Friendly students
Good peer network
Cutting-edge classes
Smart classrooms
Solid preparation in:
Teamwork
Computer skills

STUDENTS

Enrollment of parent institution	24,000
Enrollment of business school	800
% male/female	67/33
% part-time	74
% international	30
Average age at entry	28
Average years work experience at entry	5

ACADEMICS

Academic Experience Rating	**86**
Student/faculty ratio	7:1
Profs interesting rating	65
Profs accessible rating	86
% female faculty	25

Joint Degrees

MD/MBA 5 to 6 years.

Prominent Alumni

Lisa Locklear, vice president, Ingram Micro; Darcy Kopcho, executive vice president, Capital Group Companies; George Kessinger, president and CEO, Goodwill Industries International; Norman Witt, vice president community development, The Irvine CO.

Academics

At the University of California—Irvine's Paul Merage School of Business, "The buzz is growing so quickly you can just feel that UC—Irvine is about to explode." Students across the board had rave reviews for the school, calling it "a great experience." Students praise an "intimate environment" that includes monthly lunches with the Dean, and "faculty and staff who actually remember you." The "experienced professors" all are "very knowledgeable in their fields. Some are not as good teachers but [are] great research[ers]. We also have professors [who] are full-time professionals" that "provide valuable insights" and are "very committed to teaching first-year students the basic skills needed to succeed." Students also reserved high praise for the administration, which is "very involved in our day-to-day needs." As one student put it, "They really make us feel wanted."

Aside from the full-time MBA, Merage offers a fully employed MBA, an executive MBA, and a health care executive MBA. Merage also offers a doctoral program, with degrees available in accounting, finance, information systems, marketing, operations and decision technologies, organization and management, and strategy. The full-time MBA program has 13 core courses, after which students are allowed to take a range of elective courses to tailor their program to their specific career goals. Students say the school excels at disciplines like finance and marketing, but that it's "missing out on the opportunity to really expand the course offerings to include topics like CSR [corporate social responsibility] and globalization."

Unique elements of the Merage experience include the opportunity to study abroad at one of 10 different business schools throughout Europe, South America, and Asia, as well as the Merage MBA Field Project. Available to second-year students, the Field Project is a 10-week corporate program in which student teams work directly with company managers while receiving guidance from a faculty expert. Students appreciate the school's heavy focus on teamwork, commenting that "it's common to see groups of students working together on campus," and that "it's not a competitive environment like other MBA programs." As one student gushed, "The school is in an upswing . . . everything is great. I really love it here!"

Career and Placement

UC—Irvine students have a "special advantage" when it comes to employment opportunities because of their proximity to University Research Park, which is located next to the campus. Host to a slew of big-name corporations like America Online, Cisco Systems, and McKinsey & Company, the park "attracts companies interested in hiring UCI students and collaborating with faculty on research projects." Although students appreciate the wide variety of companies that recruit for summer internships (149 in 2006), some students mentioned that the career center could do a better job of "helping students with their job search outside of Southern California." However, many students saw "dramatic improvement" in the university's support of the Career Center, as well as the recent overhaul of its strategy.

Many large companies have a recruiting presence on campus, including Microsoft, KPMG International, Intel, Buena Vista Home Entertainment, Accenture, Bristol-Myers Squibb Company, and Honda Motor Company. Almost half of the 2006 graduates went into the finance/accounting industry, and the remaining students went into either marketing or consulting. Fifty-eight percent of students had a job offer by graduation, and 83 percent had accepted an offer within 3 months after graduation.

CHRISTINE HOYT, SENIOR RECRUITMENT AND ADMISSIONS OFFICER
SB 220, IRVINE, CA 92697-3125 UNITED STATES
PHONE: 949-824-4622 • FAX: 949-824-2235
E-MAIL: MBA@MERAGE.UCI.EDU • WEBSITE: WWW.MERAGE.UCI.EDU

Student Life and Environment

It's all about the location at UC—Irvine. Nestled in famous Orange County, Merage students truly feel that "you can't beat the O.C." Although Irvine itself is described as a "safe and quiet town," the nearby beach cities of Newport and Laguna are "awesome destinations" for "sunny days and wild nights." With "nearby beach, golf courses, and relatively close places to ski/snowboard," students have plenty of ways to blow off steam and hang out with their classmates.

Student life at Merage is very social, and the students describe each other as "proactive [about] socializing together outside of school" and, a little more bluntly, "party animals, smart and friendly." Students can take advantage of the abundance of extracurricular activities on campus. With a range of activities that include "functional/career clubs to corporate social responsibility clubs," students have "many opportunities to get involved." Outside of clubs, students mentioned the weekly happy hours, which are well attended and give "everyone a chance to get to know each other better."

For most of the students, housing is "a very special aspect" of the Merage experience. With plenty of space on campus, "most MBAs will get housing if they want it," at a cost that is "lower than private market." First-years are usually assigned to live in the same apartment complex, which students describe as "gorgeous" and beneficial to students' social lives. Students say the housing situation contributes to "a family atmosphere that really strengthens the community bonds."

Admissions

The average undergraduate GPA of recently admitted students was 3.37, and their average GMAT score was 687. The average age of the students was 20, and most had around 5 years of work experience. International students make up 34 percent of the student body.

FINANCIAL FACTS

Annual tuition (in-state/ out-of-state)	$25,176/$36,451
Cost of books	$2,729
Room & board (on/off-campus)	$11,039/$14,425
% of students receiving aid	80
% of first-year students receiving aid	84
% of students receiving loans	54
% of students receiving grants	67
Average award package	$22,500
Average grant	$10,784
Average student loan debt	$45,500

ADMISSIONS

Admissions Selectivity Rating	93
# of applications received	600
% applicants accepted	40
% acceptees attending	41
Average GMAT	670
Range of GMAT	600–730
Average GPA	3.3
TOEFL required of international students	Yes
Minimum TOEFL (paper/computer)	600/250
Application fee	$150
Regular application deadline	11/1
Regular notification	2/1
Application Deadline/Notification	
Round 1:	11/1 / 1/15
Round 2:	12/15 / 3/1
Round 3:	2/1 / 4/1
Round 4:	4/15 / 6/15
Non-fall admissions	Yes
Need-blind admissions	Yes

Applicants Also Look At

University of California—Berkeley, University of California—Davis, University of California—Los Angeles (UCLA), University of Southern California, University of Washington.

EMPLOYMENT PROFILE

Career Rating	76	Grads Employed by Function	%	Avg. Salary
Primary Source of Full-time Job Acceptances		Finance/Accounting	42	$68,934
School-facilitated activities	36 (58%)	Human Resources	2	NR
Graduate-facilitated activities	26 (42%)	Marketing/Sales	22	$72,286
Average base starting salary	$72,263	MIS	3	$72,000
Percent employed	31	Operations/Production	3	$67,000
		Consulting	21	$74,650
		General Management	5	$74,333
		Other	2	$75,000

Top 5 Employers Hiring Grads
PricewaterhouseCoopers; CBH Consulting; IBM; Buena Vista Home Entertainment; PIMCO.

UNIVERSITY OF CALIFORNIA—LOS ANGELES
ANDERSON SCHOOL OF MANAGEMENT

GENERAL INFORMATION

Type of school	Public
Environment	Metropolis
Academic calendar	Quarters

SURVEY SAYS . . .

Students love Los Angeles, CA
Friendly students
Good social scene
Good peer network
Happy students

STUDENTS

Enrollment of parent institution	38,000
Enrollment of business school	1,332
% male/female	70/30
% out-of-state	26
% part-time	48
% minorities	19
% international	28
Average age at entry	28
Average years work experience at entry	5

ACADEMICS

Academic Experience Rating	**97**
Student/faculty ratio	8:1
Profs interesting rating	83
Profs accessible rating	88
% female faculty	18
% minority faculty	25

Joint Degrees

MBA/JD, MBA/MD, MBA/DDS, MBA/MPH, MBA/Master of Latin American Studies, MBA/Master of Urban Planning, MBA/Master of Computer Science, MBA/Master of Public Policy, MBA/Master of Library and Information Science, MBA/Master of Nursing, MBA/Master of Public Health.

Prominent Alumni

Jeff Henley, chairman, Oracle Corporation; William Gross, founder and chief investment officer, PIMCO; Chris Zyda, international CFO, Amazon.com.

Academics

Future business mavens show their innate decision-making powers when choosing to pursue an MBA at UCLA Anderson School of Business, an institution touted as the "best school in Southern California as far as reputation" that has the added benefit of being a "great value since it's a public school." Among its many advantages, UCLA boasts a prime location in Los Angeles, offering access to Hollywood and the entertainment industry, as well as "greater exposure to Asia and greater name recognition in Asia" than is typically found in East Coast schools. Students also choose Anderson for the "emphasis on entrepreneurial topics in the curriculum" and the fact that a "culture of leadership and cooperation is reinforced throughout the courses and student activities."

Students report that the school's "intellectually top-notch faculty," make learning engaging as well as useful, as professors are "well respected in their fields and effective in class." In addition to their skill in the classroom, UCLA professors are lauded as friendly, accessible, and "committed to our learning experience." But don't mistake the affable atmosphere for an easy ride. The pace is "fast and furious" especially at the beginning, as there is an "extremely heavy workload the first quarter of the first year."

Throughout the program's rigorous core courses and elective offerings, Anderson strives to make "theoretical material relevant to real-world situations." Professors are "on top of current industry trends and have interesting/dynamic lectures reflecting their specialized industry knowledge." Applying classroom concepts to practical scenarios, the culmination of an Anderson MBA is a 20-week course entitled Applied Management Research, through which students work in groups to build a business plan, conduct a management field study, or collaborate on a special project.

Through the school's numerous research centers, students have access to specialized academic and extracurricular activities, classes, and association with expert faculty. The various student-run clubs and academic organizations further enhance the curricular experience through events and seminars. For example, "150 events, from hosted dinners to strategy workshops, are hosted by the Entrepreneur Association each year." Anderson also operates several international exchange programs, through which students earn course credit at universities in Asia, Europe, Australia, and Latin America.

Career and Placement

With the reputation as the "best in the West," UCLA students have full "access to top recruiters in entertainment and technology" and can look for a job during the plethora of "on-site recruiting events with all the top firms." Offering "amazing placement services," the Parker Career Management Center brings more than 300 companies to recruit on campus each year.

In 2006, a whopping 97 percent of UCLA students who were looking for a job had received an offer within 3 months of graduation, and 93.4 percent had accepted an offer. A second-year student attests, "I already have several very competitive job offers from the top-tier firms in the industry in which I wish to work." Consulting was the most popular career choice (as it has been for several years at UCLA), drawing 14 percent of graduates. The next most popular fields were entertainment, with 11.8 percent of graduates, and real estate, with 10.5 percent of graduates. The average salary for a new graduate was $92,011.

Linda Baldwin, Director of Admissions
110 Westwood Plaza, Gold Hall, Suite B201, Los Angeles, CA 90095-1481 United States
Phone: 310-825-6944 • Fax: 310-825-8582
E-mail: mba.admissions@anderson.ucla.edu • Website: www.anderson.ucla.edu

Student Life and Environment

Although it is a competitive, top-tier school, UCLA "has a reputation as having a laid-back student body where there's not a lot of competitiveness/mean-spiritedness among the students." Does it live up to its image? Absolutely. UCLA business students are "friendly, social, outgoing, intellectually curious and have amazing pedigrees—minus the egos that are often associated with top backgrounds." Others describe them as "brilliant party animals" who are "fun loving yet have very high standards for the quality of their work." A lively collegiate environment, "social events, networking events, study groups, classes, lunch, clubs meetings" are well attended; and "Most activities are student run with minimal support from administration," a situation well suited to entrepreneurial graduate students.

If you want to blow off steam with your classmates, "There are social activities every week, multiple times a week," including a "social party for the whole business school every Thursday evening." However, given the school's demanding workload, "Some people attend every one of them, and some people attend very few." A second-year student admits, "It can be a 'fun in the sun' school to some extent, but I spend a whole lot more time with formulas and models than I do with a surfboard." Even so, students are sure to take advantage of their fabulous location. A current students shares, "Weekends are filled with more than waves and beer. Sunshine affords great hiking all year long, such as Runyon Canyon, and many of us escape at least once per quarter to nearby sunny San Diego or up north for a weekend of cultural exuberance in San Francisco."

Admissions

UCLA receives thousands of applications for an entering class of just 360 students. Admissions Officials insist that there is no specific skill set or "cookie cutter" profile for a successful applicant to Anderson. Rather, the Admissions Committee evaluates each applicant's unique ability to be a leader in management and to contribute to the community at UCLA. As such, there are no minimum requirements for GMAT scores or undergraduate GPA, and there is no minimum requirement for previous work experience—though these factors are heavily considered in an admissions decision. Other factors that influence an admissions decision are TOEFL scores (when applicable), achievements, awards, letters of recommendation, college and community involvement, and previous leadership experience. Prospective students also have the option of scheduling an interview at UCLA.

FINANCIAL FACTS

Annual tuition (in-state/ out-of-state)	$12,245
Fees (in-state/ out-of-state)	$26,932/$23,836
Cost of books	$7,500
Room & board	$12,927
% of students receiving aid	70
% of first-year students receiving aid	75
% of students receiving loans	70
% of students receiving grants	60
Average award package	$51,930
Average grant	$15,000
Average student loan debt	$87,000

ADMISSIONS

Admissions Selectivity Rating	**97**
# of applications received	2,609
% applicants accepted	29
% acceptees attending	48
Average GMAT	710
Range of GMAT	640–750
Average GPA	3.55
TOEFL required of international students	Yes
Minimum TOEFL (paper/computer)	600/260
Application fee	$175
Regular application deadline	4/28
Regular notification	6/23
Application Deadline/Notification	
Round 1:	11/3 / 1/26
Round 2:	1/5 / 3/24
Round 3:	2/21 / 5/19
Round 4:	4/28 / 6/23
Early decision program	Yes
ED Deadline/Notification	11/3 / 1/26
Deferment available	Yes
Maximum length of deferment	Case-by-case basis
Need-blind admissions	Yes

Applicants Also Look At

Duke University, Harvard University, Northwestern University, Stanford University, University of California—Berkeley, University of Pennsylvania.

EMPLOYMENT PROFILE

Career Rating	94	Grads Employed by Function	%	Avg. Salary
Primary Source of Full-time Job Acceptances		Finance/Accounting	35	$93,192
School-facilitated activities	167 (66%)	Human Resources	1	$79,333
Graduate-facilitated activities	87 (34%)	Marketing/Sales	28	$82,000
Unknown	1	Consulting	16	$107,107
Average base starting salary	$92,011	General Management	4	$85,420
Percent employed	93	Other	15	$94,914

Top 5 Employers Hiring Grads

Deloitte Consulting; Intel; The Boston Consulting Group; Lehman Brothers; Toyota Motor Corporation U.S.A.

UNIVERSITY OF CALIFORNIA—RIVERSIDE
A. GARY ANDERSON GRADUATE SCHOOL OF MANAGEMENT

Academics

Combine the Southern California climate with a "fantastic school" and it's easy to understand why the A. Gary Anderson Graduate School of Management at UC—Riverside gets such high marks from students. One raves, "I am having the time of my life [and] . . . feel very privileged to be here." Many MBA candidates here are taking their first steps in the business world, as applicants are not required to have work experience—which can be a good or bad thing depending on who you talk to. One thing students do agree on is the "challenging" classes, bolstered by the "very accessible" professors who "care very much about their students' learning and understanding of the course material." However, some students would like to see them "chase the new trends of business aggressively."

The six components of an MBA from AGSM are the core courses, an internship, the communication workshop, the electives, a "capstone course," and a case project or thesis. Though the core courses take up more time than any other single component, students are most enthusiastic about the "wide diversity of electives," which are all seminar size and designed to "encourage participative learning." One student explains, "I love coming to a small school like UCR's AGSM. You get real interaction with professors, and all of the students know each other, which allows for tighter bonds and networks." There are 10 areas of electives, and students are allowed to take up to nine courses from any area, such as accounting, entrepreneurial management, finance, general management, human resources management/organizational behavior, international management, management information systems, management science, marketing, and production and operations management.

Most students agree that "discussion is greatly encouraged" in class. A fair number of courses "require presentation with business formal attire" and some "even require group debate." One student notes, "It gives you some pressure, but it's fun." Some lament the feeling that the university "does not attach [enough] importance to our business school," and hope for this to change in the near future. Others, though conscious that the school is a "research-oriented university," wouldn't mind getting more "attention from some professors" who they find to be "mostly researchers and not lecturers."

Career and Placement

Aside from recent budget cuts, the thing that has most students at AGSM are up in arms about is the Career Resources Center. As one student says, "The school desperately needs a stronger Career Counseling Center designed just for the MBA students." Another adds, "I really think the school should begin to target the school's alumni more. There are many UCR MBAs in the industry and they could be a real resource and asset to the school." The MBA now has its own Career Services, which should help alleviate many of the students' concerns regarding "job placement," "internships," and "professional networking."

CINDY ROULETTE, MBA STUDENT AFFAIRS OFFICER
ANDERSON HALL, RIVERSIDE, CA 92521-0203 UNITED STATES
PHONE: 951-827-4551 • FAX: 951-827-3970
E-MAIL: MBA@UCR.EDU • WEBSITE: WWW.AGSM.UCR.EDU

Student Life and Environment

In recent years Riverside, California has undergone both something of a renaissance and an influx of people. Gone are the days of quiet orange groves, and in their place resides the veritable capital of the Inland Empire. Whether your tastes run to the great outdoors or to great shopping, students find "plenty of unique hangouts, interesting shopping, and a wide variety of eats to fit anyone's desires (and budget)." Some MBA students feel that they "lack social activities" within the program, though in many instances this could be blamed on the large amount of "homework" these students undertake. That said, as the university (and those that surround it) continue to grow, students can expect more avenues to their social outlets to open.

The school itself is housed in a 30,000-square-foot building that features "state-of-the-art research and teaching facilities." MBA students agree that their "computer lab is very nice" and relish that they, as MBAs, "have priority over all computers in the lab." Other students gripe that they're stuck in "a small building that consists of one lecture room and one classroom. Our school has suffered greatly from the previous budget cuts." Still, the building must have something going for it because "MBA students rarely venture onto the main campus at [UC Riverside], unless it's to go to the library or bookstore."

Students report that "most people are very nice, and it is easy to meet new people if you try." These "very laid-back and friendly" students have formed "a tight-knit community here because our graduate program is so small." "I pretty much know and am friends with every other MBA student," says one. Due to the proximity of students, there is "a level of competition between students during academic competitions and presentations," but most happily note that "it is healthy and in good fun."

Admissions

At AGSM, students from all undergraduate majors and levels of business experience are eligible for admission. In fact, more than 30 percent of all incoming students come from a background other than business and have little—if any—experience in the business world. According to the school, "There is no minimum GPA or GMAT requirement for MBA admission consideration." However, they also say "Satisfying minimal standards does not guarantee admission, since the number of qualified applicants far exceeds the number of places available," meaning that you'd best do your best. It is worth noting that because the school doesn't require prior work experience, all prospective MBAs must complete an internship "to ensure your success upon graduation."

FINANCIAL FACTS

Annual tuition (out-of-state)	$12,245
Fees	$23,455
Cost of books	$1,650
Room & board (on/off-campus)	$8,954/$8,954
% of students receiving aid	45
% of first-year students receiving aid	46
% of students receiving grants	45
Average award package	$21,573
Average grant	$14,276

ADMISSIONS

Admissions Selectivity Rating	78
# of applications received	263
% applicants accepted	59
% acceptees attending	28
Average GMAT	569
Range of GMAT	540–610
Average GPA	3.35
TOEFL required of international students	Yes
Minimum TOEFL (paper/computer)	550/213
Application fee	$60
International application fee	$75
Regular application deadline	5/1
Regular notification	6/1
Transfer students accepted	Yes
Transfer application policy A maximum of 8 graduate units taken in residence may be transferred.	
Non-fall admissions	Yes
Need-blind admissions	Yes

Applicants Also Look At

California State Polytechnic University—Pomona, California State University—Fullerton, Pepperdine University, University of California—Irvine, University of California—San Diego.

EMPLOYMENT PROFILE

Career Rating	62	**Grads Employed by Function % Avg. Salary**	
Primary Source of Full-time Job Acceptances		Finance/Accounting	30 $44,900
School-facilitated activities	12 (30%)	Human Resources	10 $31,200
Graduate-facilitated activities	29 (70%)	Marketing/Sales	20 $30,900
Percent employed	47	**Top 4 Employers Hiring Grads**	
		Deloitte Touche Tohmatsu; Ernst & Young; Cathay Bank–Taiwan; IEHP.	

UNIVERSITY OF CENTRAL ARKANSAS
COLLEGE OF BUSINESS ADMINISTRATION

GENERAL INFORMATION

Type of school	Public
Environment	Town
Academic calendar	Semester

SURVEY SAYS . . .
Friendly students
Happy students
Solid preparation in:
Finance
Presentation skills

STUDENTS

Enrollment of parent institution	12,300
Enrollment of business school	88
% male/female	77/23
% out-of-state	26
% part-time	56
% minorities	23
% international	20
Average age at entry	26
Average years work experience at entry	4

ACADEMICS

Academic Experience Rating	**62**
Student/faculty ratio	28:1
Profs interesting rating	65
Profs accessible rating	64
% female faculty	19
% minority faculty	19

Academics

Affordability, location, the flexibility of the program, and the opportunity to complete a degree in one year are the primary reasons students choose one of the MBA programs at the University of Central Arkansas. UCA offers both a standard MBA and an International MBA. A Pre-MBA Certificate program is also available for students who lack the necessary related undergraduate course work.

UCA's conventional MBA requires 30 credit hours, making it possible for full-time students to complete the program in one year. The program is comprised of 10 three-credit classes offered in the afternoons and evenings. Courses cover information systems, accounting, managerial economics, communication, financial decision making, business law, entrepreneurship, marketing, and strategic management. The program concludes with an integrative class. Elective and specialization options are not available.

The International MBA program requires 36 credit hours, meaning that, too, can be completed in one year by full-time students. The program is comprised of 12 three-credit classes offered in the afternoons and evenings. Courses cover information systems, accounting, managerial economics, financial decision making, business law, global entrepreneurship, marketing, international strategic management, and multicultural communications. In addition, students must take an integrative capstone class and two graduate-level electives in business, international culture, or foreign language. Students may complete an internship with a global company in lieu of the two electives.

Students wishing to receive an MBA but who lack the necessary undergraduate course work in business may complete that course work through the Pre-MBA Certificate program. Applicants to the program must meet the same requirements as applicants to the MBA program; completion of the Pre-MBA program does not guarantee admission to the MBA program. The program consists of six courses covering basic concepts in accounting, economics, finance, management, marketing, and quantitative analysis.

Professors get mixed reviews here. More than one respondent points out, "We have some very good professors, but some are unorganized and have a hard time communicating their subjects to students."

Career and Placement

Because UCA's MBA program is so small and many of the students are part-timers who already have jobs, the school offers few career and placement services directed exclusively to MBAs. Still, several students express a desire for better relations with local companies and overall "better job placement." Students may use the Career Services Office, which serves the entire university; the office provides counseling, training, mock interviews, workshops, access to online job databases, and school-wide career fairs and other recruiting events. Only a handful of employers visit the campus each year for the express purpose of recruiting MBAs. Employers most likely to hire UCA MBAs include Acxiom, ALLTEL, Entergy, First Security Bank, and Kimberly-Clark.

DAVID KIM, MBA DIRECTOR
COLLEGE OF BUSINESS, UNIVERSITY OF CENTRAL ARKANSAS CONWAY, AR 72035 UNITED STATES
PHONE: 501-450-5316 • FAX: 501-450-5302
E-MAIL: DAVIDK@UCA.EDU • WEBSITE: WWW.UCA.EDU/DIVISIONS/ACADEMIC/MBA

Student Life and Environment

The University of Central Arkansas is located in Conway, one of the state's fastest growing cities. The city is home to a number of industries, including Kimberly-Clark, AmTran, Virco, and Baldwin Piano. Database magnate Acxiom makes its headquarters in Conway. A number of government headquarters are located in Conway as well. Besides UCA, the city is also home to Hendrix College and Central Baptist College.

The UCA campus is "a unique mix of Georgian-style architecture and up-to-date technology," according to the school's view book. The school has a long and proud tradition in intercollegiate athletics—Scotty Pippin played his college ball here—and the school's 10,000-plus students regularly turn out to cheer on their Bears and Sugar Bears. The MBA program is located in the Burdick Business Administration building, which was built in 1973.

Because of the International MBA program, the student body here includes "fairly diverse nationalities, which is good." Not so good is the fact that "many American students seem to have come directly from undergraduate programs" and thus lack the practical business experience necessary to contribute meaningfully to classroom discussion.

Admissions

All applicants to the MBA program at UCA must have earned an undergraduate degree from an accredited U.S. institution or its overseas equivalent, with a minimum GPA of 2.7, or a minimum GPA of 3.0 for the final 60 hours of undergraduate study. Applicants must also submit official GMAT scores; the admissions committee requires a minimum GMAT score of 450 from all applicants. UCA uses formulas to create minimum cut offs for applicants. Applicants must have a minimum formula index of 1,000 under the formula [(undergraduate GPA × 200) + GMAT score], or a minimum formula index of 1,050 under the formula [(undergraduate GPA for the final 60 hours of study × 200) + GMAT score]. International applicants whose first language is not English must also submit TOEFL scores.

FINANCIAL FACTS

Annual tuition (in-state/ out-of-state)	$5,592/$10,308
Fees	$202
Cost of books	$1,000
Room & board (on/off-campus)	$6,260/$6,000

ADMISSIONS

Admissions Selectivity Rating	**65**
# of applications received	36
% applicants accepted	100
% acceptees attending	83
Average GMAT	523
Range of GMAT	470–580
Average GPA	3.32
TOEFL required of international students	Yes
Minimum TOEFL (paper/computer)	550/213
Application fee	$25
International application fee	$40
Deferment available	Yes
Maximum length of deferment	3 years
Transfer students accepted	Yes
Transfer application policy A maximum of 6 graduate hours is transferrable from a AACSB-accredited institution.	
Non-fall admissions	Yes

Applicants Also Look At

University of Arkansas at Little Rock, University of Arkansas—Fayetteville.

UNIVERSITY OF CENTRAL FLORIDA
COLLEGE OF BUSINESS ADMINISTRATION

Academics

Students pursing an MBA at the University of Central Florida have three options: the traditional MBA, a part-time evening program designed for working professionals; the full-time one-year MBA, a daytime program for freshly minted BAs as well as mid-career professionals looking to jumpstart their careers; and an Executive MBA, designed for current executives and managers. The school also offers MS degrees in accounting, economics, taxation, information systems, and sports business management. Additionally, they have two new certificate programs in entrepreneurship and technology commercialization.

UCF offers concentrations in accounting, economics, finance, entrepreneurship, environmental management and policy, human resources and change management, international business, and management information systems. Both the full-time and part-time MBA programs require between 39 and 51 course hours, depending on one's undergraduate background in business. The school reports that its greatest strengths lie in applied economics, environmental economics, MIS, hi-tech marketing, and entrepreneurship. In addition, students appreciate "the school's focus on technology, which gives it a leg up over more traditional institutions," as well as the program's "strong emphasis on leadership, integrity, academia, and community involvement."

Students interested in the popular Sports Business Management Track must apply for separate admission to the Master in Sports Business Management Program. The program, which awards an MBA as well as the master's degree, requires a 10-week internship.

While students love both the cost and convenience of UCF's graduate business programs, they tell us that the programs are not without their faults. Some complain that "electives aren't clearly laid out, and many of the classes aren't focused enough, making them a repeat of undergraduate business courses." Just as many believe that "the school has more research-oriented teachers than teachers who can actually teach," and that too many professors "lack real-world experience. They are so focused on theory that they do not focus enough on practice." On the other hand, others point out that "professors are generally very experienced in their fields and have a great deal of related knowledge to share."

Career and Placement

UCF's Career Resource Center operates a satellite office at the College of Business Administration to serve business graduates and undergraduates. The office includes a Career Information Library stocked with job binders, salary surveys, employer databases, and other reading materials. Workshops are offered in resume writing, job search strategies, interviewing techniques, and federal employment opportunities. Students have free access to MonsterTrak during their tenure at the school and for one semester following graduation.

Employers who most frequently hire UCF MBAs include AmSouth Bank, Darden, SunTrust, Citibank, Coca-Cola, Aventis, Cendant, Dynetech, IRS, Intersil, and Marriott Vacation Clubs.

Judy Ryder, Director of Graduate Admissions
PO Box 161400, BA I, Room 240, Orlando, FL 32816 United States
Phone: 407-823-4723 • Fax: 407-823-0219
E-mail: cbagrad@bus.ucf.edu • Website: www.bus.ucf.edu

Student Life and Environment

Students in UCF's traditional MBA program attend classes in the evenings, as most are working during the day. These students typically "go to classes and then leave" without participating in the university's extracurricular life. Students in the one-year full-time program, on the other hand, do immerse themselves in the UCF environment. One writes, "You could actually live your whole life on campus—it is almost its own town! We have absolutely everything so you don't even need a car! The gym is spectacular, the food selection is extensive, and there are hundreds of clubs doing great things in the community as well as encouraging students to network." Facilities are equally edifying; one MBA observes, "There are computers everywhere. The dorms are very nice and clean, most even have individual bedrooms and common rooms with kitchens." Everyone here appreciates that "the environment is relatively safe. The campus is well-lit at night and there is a free escort service anywhere on campus if you don't want to walk alone."

Students love Orlando, "a city known throughout the world and one that everyone would like to visit at some point in their lives." The city is an excellent resource for students seeking internships and post-degree jobs. The campus is located "on the outskirts of the city," which some feel is a "great location." Others complain that "it is difficult to access the campus from downtown Orlando. Drive time is between 40 minutes and one hour."

The UCF College of Business Administration attracts "mostly younger professionals or those who are recent graduates and are looking to get a start in a career field," along with "some older students with families and long-time careers. Many students are married." They tend to be "warm and cordial, competitive, yet also good team players who are willing to help others in need." Some feel that "many of the non-business students in the MBA program seem to lag behind, dragging classes to a lower level. More stringent requirements should be implemented for acceptance into the MBA program, possibly including prior business experience."

Admissions

Applicants to the UCF College of Business MBA program must complete an online application to the UCF School of Graduate Studies. Additionally, applicants must submit official transcripts for each university or college attended, an official GMAT score, a personal essay, a resume, and three letters of recommendation. International students whose first language is not English must also submit TOEFL scores. All international students need to provide translations of non-English documents and an accredited course-by-course evaluation of transcripts from institutions that do not employ the American system. UCF requires a minimum GMAT score of 540 (550 for the one-year full-time program) for its MBA programs; requirements for other master's programs are less restrictive. An undergraduate GPA of at least 3.0 is also required.

FINANCIAL FACTS

Annual tuition (in-state/ out-of-state)	$6,168/$22,800
Fees	$158
Cost of books	$1,500
Room & board (on/off-campus)	$7,000/$10,000
% of students receiving aid	6
% of first-year students receiving aid	22
% of students receiving grants	4
Average award package	$12,000
Average grant	$10,000

ADMISSIONS

Admissions Selectivity Rating	78
# of applications received	244
% applicants accepted	71
% acceptees attending	87
Average GMAT	560
Range of GMAT	510–690
Average GPA	3.3
TOEFL required of international students	Yes
Minimum TOEFL (paper/computer)	575/233
Application fee	$30
Regular application deadline	6/15
Regular notification	Rolling
Early decision program	Yes
ED Deadline/Notification	Fall only: 4/15 / 5/15
Transfer students accepted	Yes
Transfer application policy Transfer applicants must be from a regionally or nationally-accredited university. Students may transfer in up to 9 hours.	
Need-blind admissions	Yes

Applicants Also Look At
Florida State University, Rollins College, University of Florida, University of South Florida.

EMPLOYMENT PROFILE

Career Rating	73			
Primary Source of Full-time Job Acceptances		**Grads Employed by Function**	**%**	**Avg. Salary**
School-facilitated activities	9 (35%)	Finance/Accounting	41	$51,388
Graduate-facilitated activities	17 (65%)	Marketing/Sales	41	$57,500
Average base starting salary	$53,295	MIS	13	$57,500
		Operations/Production	5	$55,000
		Top 5 Employers Hiring Grads		
		GlaxoSmithKline; Lockheed Martin; UCF Executive Development Center; Embarq; Fairwinds Credit Union.		

THE UNIVERSITY OF CHICAGO
GRADUATE SCHOOL OF BUSINESS

GENERAL INFORMATION
Type of school	Private
Environment	Metropolis
Academic calendar	Quarter

SURVEY SAYS . . .
Students love Chicago, IL
Good peer network
Cutting-edge classes
Happy students
Smart classrooms
Solid preparation in:
Finance
Accounting
Quantitative skills

STUDENTS
Enrollment of parent institution	13,400
Enrollment of business school	3,180
% male/female	73/27
% part-time	58
% minorities	10
% international	30
Average age at entry	28
Average years work experience at entry	5

ACADEMICS
Academic Experience Rating	**72**
Student/faculty ratio	15:1
Profs interesting rating	95
Profs accessible rating	88
% female faculty	16
% minority faculty	2

Joint Degrees
MBA/AM (Area Studies), MBA/AM International Relations, JD/MBA, MD/MBA, MBA/MPP (Public Policy Studies), MBA/AM (Social Service Administration).

Prominent Alumni
Timothy Chen, CEO, Microsoft Greater China; Frederic de Bure, managing director, eBay, Singapore; Robert Lane, chairman and CEO, Deere and Company; Joe Mansueto, CEO/founder, Morningstar; John Corzine, Govenor, New Jersey.

Academics

"The emphasis on [students] learning the basics rather than some predigested goo" along with "an unbeatable faculty" are "what make the University of Chicago's Graduate School of Business (GSB) one of the best, especially in hard-core areas such as finance and accounting," students tell us. A "rigorous quantitative program that compels students to think critically and analytically" is the hallmark of a Chicago MBA, although students hasten to add that GSB also "emphasizes persuasion, communication, and negotiation skills."

Chicago offers a full-time, part-time evening, part-time weekend, and executive MBA program. All three tracks share "top-notch" faculty, wide-ranging academic options, and an approach that "doesn't chase new trends in business but instead relies on teaching sound fundamentals that can then be applied to any situation." The programs differ in some details; full-time students, for example, enjoy a grade nondisclosure policy that creates a conducive environment for "teamwork and sharing of ideas." Full-time students must also complete the Leadership Exploration and Development (LEAD) program, which "provides analytic frameworks for leadership that are very helpful in determining the best way to use [one's] strengths and where to improve." While neither grade nondisclosure nor LEAD is included in the part-time curriculum, part-timers enjoy "great flexibility," noting that "most classes have several sessions taught by the same professor during the same quarter, enabling students to make up class sessions if for some reason they cannot attend their normal session." GSB's weekend executive and regular MBAs have "students flying to Chicago from across the U.S. and world to attend classes on Saturdays. This connects a much broader and more diverse group of people than other MBA programs can."

Chicago's faculty includes Nobel laureates and cutting-edge researchers "who also excel in the classroom." One accounting student reports, "Both my corporate tax strategy professor and my M&A accounting professor consult for corporate and government clients, so they have intimate knowledge of how to apply what they teach in the real world." GSB is best known for its faculty in finance, economics, and accounting, but students note that the school should work to "increase awareness of its excellence in marketing, entrepreneurship, and general management disciplines." Many students also "do a one-term or full-year exchange program at a foreign business school," and "These international career development opportunities are a big part of the experience for many GSB students."

Career and Placement

The GSB Career Services Office doesn't have too work hard; as one student explains, "The network and doors that open up to a graduate from Chicago GSB are outstanding. Gaining an MBA from this school carries a lot of weight and in the job market no one will question your education." That doesn't mean that Career Services slacks off, however; on the contrary, it "is an excellent resource and deserves praise," and does a good job attracting recruiters in consulting, accounting, and finance including McKinsey & Company, Lehman Brothers, Citigroup, The Boston Consulting Group, UBS, A.T. Kearney, Credit Suisse, Goldman Sachs, Merrill Lynch, Bear Stearns, and Booz Allen Hamilton.

Chicago GSB also excels at "preparing career changers. You learn from the best faculty in the world to attain the skills you need to succeed in your given career. The alumni, and especially second-year students at the school, are available to answer any questions.

ROSEMARIA MARTINELLI, ASSOCIATE DEAN, STUDENT RECRUITMENT AND ADMISSIONS
5807 SOUTH WOODLAWN AVENUE, CHICAGO, IL 60637 UNITED STATES
PHONE: 773-702-7369 • FAX: 773-702-9085
E-MAIL: ADMISSIONS@ChicagoGSB.edu • WEBSITE: ChicagoGSB.edu

Career Services does an excellent job of helping you identify your transferable skills to your new targeted career . . . I would highly recommend the school for people looking to change careers."

Student Life and Environment

"The social aspect of University of Chicago is often overlooked," students in the full-time program tell us, reporting that "There are all kinds of opportunities to get together with other students in social or more formal settings, including school-sponsored happy hours, etc." Although "MBAs here work as hard as students at any other b-school, we know how to have fun too." One student writes, "If anything, there are too many programs and opportunities to be involved. You need to carefully consider them all to properly juggle [your] schedule." And with "the great city of Chicago is at our doorstep," students don't have to look far to find a wide range of fun diversions.

The school is located on Chicago's South Side in the Hyde Park neighborhood, which "is too often made out to be a scary place when, in fact, it's not. There is a pretty unique mixture of socioeconomic groups here, so you can drive by a building with three poor families living in it and four blocks later be at a stop sign next to a million-dollar (or more) home. The fact is that it's on the South Side of Chicago so people automatically say, 'bad, scary neighborhood.'" Part-time students attend classes at the Gleacher Center, "a beautiful building" in downtown Chicago, just off the Magnificent Mile. For students whose activities keep them in the Hyde Park area, GSB's Charles M. Harper Center boasts a "winter garden," a "dramatic foyer in the center of the building" where "People can catch up, do work, or just relax for a moment."

Admissions

Admission to Chicago's Graduate School of Business is extremely competitive. Admissions Officers scrutinize a wide array of qualifications, including academic record (quality of curriculum, scholarships, special honors, etc.), work experience (quality as well as quantity), and overall "fit"(interpersonal skills, unique experiences, philanthropic activity). Applicants must provide the Admissions Office with transcripts for all postsecondary academic work, an official GMAT score report, letters of recommendation, personal essays, and TOEFL/IELTS scores (for international students only). Interviews are required for all candidates for the evening and weekend MBA programs; applicants to the full-time program interview on a "by invitation only" basis.

FINANCIAL FACTS

Annual tuition	$41,600
Fees	$612
Cost of books	$2,100
Room & board	$18,900
% of students receiving aid	85
% of first-year students receiving aid	79
% of students receiving loans	85
% of students receiving grants	25
Average award package	$38,669
Average grant	$20,203
Average student loan debt	$83,480

ADMISSIONS

Admissions Selectivity Rating	60*
Average GMAT	703
Average GPA	3.5
TOEFL required of international students	Yes
Minimum TOEFL (paper/computer)	600/250
Application fee	$200
Application Deadline/Notification	
Round 1:	10/18 / 1/04
Round 2:	1/10 / 3/28
Round 3:	3/14 / 5/16
Deferment available	Yes
Maximum length of deferment	1 year
Need-blind admissions	Yes

EMPLOYMENT PROFILE

Career Rating		99
Primary Source of Full-time Job Acceptances		
School-facilitated activities	425 (87%)	
Graduate-facilitated activities	63 (13%)	
Percent employed	95	

Grads Employed by Function	%	Avg. Salary
Finance/Accounting	59	$96,972
Marketing/Sales	11	$87,636
Consulting	22	$107,247
General Management	6	$95,641
Other	2	$103,000

Top 5 Employers Hiring Grads
McKinsey & Company; Deutsche Bank; Lehman Brothers; Citigroup; Merrill Lynch.

UNIVERSITY OF CINCINNATI
COLLEGE OF BUSINESS

GENERAL INFORMATION

Type of school	Public
Environment	Metropolis
Academic calendar	Quarter

SURVEY SAYS . . .
Good peer network
Cutting-edge classes
Solid preparation in:
Accounting
General management
Teamwork

STUDENTS

Enrollment of parent institution	35,527
Enrollment of business school	329
% male/female	62/38
% out-of-state	15
% part-time	84
% minorities	9
% international	34
Average age at entry	28
Average years work experience at entry	4

ACADEMICS

Academic Experience Rating	**86**
Student/faculty ratio	4:1
Profs interesting rating	91
Profs accessible rating	81
% female faculty	29
% minority faculty	3

Joint Degrees
MBA/JD 4 years, MBA/MA (Arts Administration) 3 years, MBA/MD 5 years, MBA/Nursing 3 years, MBA/MS (Accounting, Finance, Information Systems, Marketing or Quantitative Analysis) 2 years.

Prominent Alumni
Robert Taft, former governor, Ohio; John F. Barrett, president and CEO, Western-Southern Life; Myron E. Ullman, III, CEO, JCPenney; Dr. Candace Kendle, chairman and CEO, Kendle International; Richard E. Thornburgh, vice chairman, Credit Suisse.

Academics

Future MBAs may choose from multiple options at the University of Cincinnati's College of Business. For full-timers in a hurry, UC offers a full-time 12-month MBA; a 15-month degree that packs the course work just as tightly but adds a three-month internship; and a 21-month degree that, along with a three-month internship, combines an MBA and MS for those "seeking a high degree of rigorous specialization in addition to an applied general management education." UC's full-time programs take advantage of their ability to sequence classes, allowing advanced classes to build on concepts taught in previous classes.

UC also offers part-time options at a variety of sites, including the Clifton Campus, the Blue Ash Professional Development Center (both evening programs) and Wright Patterson Air Force Base (a mid-afternoon program). The part-time program is by necessity more flexible than its full-time counterpart, but is otherwise similar, employing the same professors and providing the same support services. In both the full-time and part-time programs, concentrations are available in construction management, finance, information systems, international business, management, marketing, operations management, quantitative analysis, and commercial real estate.

The UC MBA program stresses teamwork, which students appreciate. One writes, "The team structure that is fostered from day one is instrumental in making our program unique and successful. The teams are organized in such a way that no one gets left behind. There is almost an imperative that everyone graduates; an instilled sense of community and support, which has been so refreshing. Coming from Procter & Gamble, I recognize the necessity of teaching a team-based structure. It's remarkable." The small size of the program "means students get a lot of attention, something you can never have too much of." However, for many, "the greatest strength of UC is its focus on global business. The College of Business stresses to every student the need to look at business from a global perspective. There are study-abroad opportunities. There are also many foreign students in class with us to give us a different viewpoint of a situation." Offerings in quantitative analysis and commercial real estate also receive high marks.

Career and Placement

Students tell us that "the MBA Career Office puts extensive effort into assuring us that we have the tools to find a job and brings in various employers for recruiting activities." The office's efforts include one-on-one counseling meetings; career development workshops; career days; online recruiting and contact databases; videotaped mock interviews; and on-campus recruiting events.

Employers most likely to hire UC MBAs include Fifth Third Bank, Procter & Gamble, The ARS Group, Toyota Motor Manufacturing, L'Oreal, Cincinnati Bell, Sara Lee, Cintas, Eli Lilly and Company, Burke, Inc., Steak 'n Shake, and Charter Consulting.

Student Life and Environment

The "driven and intelligent" MBAs at UC enjoy a "diverse mix" that includes a one-quarter international population, a range of experience levels ("we have students right out of undergraduate schools, as well as students well into their careers"), and backgrounds ("a lot of the students are engineering undergrads looking to utilize an MBA for the opportunity of advancement in the engineering field; most others are business undergrads looking for career advancement"). The program has an unusually even gender split as well. One student sums up, "UC doesn't recruit a specific mold of what is perceived as

DAWN OWENS, ASSOCIATE DIRECTOR ADMISSIONS
CARL H. LINDNER HALL, SUITE 606, PO BOX 210020, CINCINNATI, OH 45221-0020 U.S.
PHONE: 513-556-7024 • FAX: 513-558-7006
E-MAIL: GRADUATE@UC.EDU • WEBSITE: WWW.BUSINESS.UC.EDU/MBA

'the MBA Student.' They recruit a diverse mix that makes the experience surprisingly worldly in decidedly Midwestern Cincinnati." The mix "adds a lot of value to the classes."

"The majority of students are commuters" in the UC MBA program, "and it is challenging to have graduate students involved in on-campus activities. We do enjoy the academic strength and fellow classmates, but not all of us feel fully integrated into the campus." The opportunities are there, though, and full-time students generally take advantage of them, reporting that "the administration is focused on activities and connecting students to the university and community. We have weekly networking dinners or happy hours with people from GE, Procter & Gamble, and Cincinnati Bell. The MBA Association has been active in organizing social activities for students as well." In addition, "we have a lot of free lunches associated with training sessions and academic and career development sessions. They are wonderful. And we have all kinds of recreational facilities and free movies to broaden our view of the world." UC's men's basketball team is "amazing, and everyone rallies around it. As one student puts it, "For being a mostly commuter campus, there are plenty of opportunities to get involved on campus."

Admissions

Applicants to the UC MBA program must submit an official GMAT score report, official copies of all postsecondary academic transcripts, two essays, two letters of recommendation, a resume, and a completed application form. Applicants need not have earned undergraduate degrees in business; in fact, only half the students here have. The rest are primarily split among engineering and liberal arts majors, with a few science majors thrown in to the mix. Completion of a college-level calculus course is required of all applicants. International applicants must also submit results for the TOEFL exam and certification of finances. In an effort to increase the population of underrepresented students, "UC offers the Albert C. Yates Scholarships and Fellowships to candidates from underrepresented groups. The scholarships cover full tuition and fees and the fellowship additionally provides a stipend each quarter."

FINANCIAL FACTS

Annual tuition (in-state/ out-of-state)	$20,800/$26,204
Fees	$2,004
Cost of books	$3,500
Room & board (on/off-campus)	$13,500/$15,000
% of students receiving aid	78
% of first-year students receiving aid	78
% of students receiving loans	47
% of students receiving grants	51
Average award package	$20,799
Average grant	$11,355

ADMISSIONS

Admissions Selectivity Rating	**79**
# of applications received	189
% applicants accepted	83
% acceptees attending	65
Average GMAT	574
Range of GMAT	510–640
Average GPA	3.23
TOEFL required of international students	Yes
Minimum TOEFL (paper/computer)	600/250
Application fee	$40
Regular application deadline	5/31
Regular notification	Rolling
Early decision program	Yes
ED Deadline/Notification	Fall, 2/15/ 3/30
Deferment available	Yes
Maximum length of deferment	1 year
Transfer students accepted	Yes
Transfer application policy Applicants must be transferring from an AACSB-accredited institution, have no more than 12 credit hours, and a 3.0 in class.	
Non-fall admissions	Yes
Need-blind admissions	Yes

Applicants Also Look At

Indiana University—Bloomington, Miami University Ohio, Northern Kentucky University, The Ohio State University, University of Dayton, Wright State University, Xavier University.

EMPLOYMENT PROFILE

Career Rating	69	Grads Employed by Function	%	Avg. Salary
Primary Source of Full-time Job Acceptances		Finance/Accounting	30	$53,933
Graduate-facilitated activities	31 (100%)	Human Resources	5	$80,000
Percent employed	30	Marketing/Sales	30	$61,750
		MIS	10	$76,250
		Operations/Production	10	$52,500
		General Management	15	$52,167

Top 5 Employers Hiring Grads
Target; Procter & Gamble; Fifth Third Bank; A.C. Nielsen; Citigroup.

UNIVERSITY OF CONNECTICUT
SCHOOL OF BUSINESS

GENERAL INFORMATION
Type of school	Public
Environment	Town
Academic calendar	Semester

SURVEY SAYS . . .
Smart classrooms
Solid preparation in:
Finance
Accounting
Computer skills

STUDENTS
Enrollment of parent institution	28,481
Enrollment of business school	1,040
% male/female	63/37
% out-of-state	18
% part-time	86
% minorities	13
% international	38
Average age at entry	27
Average years work experience at entry	4.8

ACADEMICS
Academic Experience Rating	**76**
Student/faculty ratio	13:1
Profs interesting rating	68
Profs accessible rating	86
% female faculty	14
% minority faculty	28

Joint Degrees
MBA/JD, MBA/MD, MBA/MSW, MBA/MA (International Studies), MBA/Master of International Management, MBA/MS (Nursing) 4 years.

Prominent Alumni
Robert W. Crispin, chairman and CEO, ING Investment Management Americas; Robert E. Diamond, CEO, Barclays Capital; Penelope A. Dobkin, portfolio manager, Fidelity Investments; John Y. Kim, president, Prudential Retirement and Investment Services; Denis Nayden, managing partner, Oakhill Capital.

Academics

An "innovative curriculum" that emphasizes experiential learning is the hallmark of the MBA program at the University of Connecticut, providing students with "tremendous opportunities to integrate classroom learning with real-life business problem-solving." No wonder students tell us that UConn "offers a high-level education at state school cost, along with many highly appealing academic programs." To top it all off, a "premium location close to financial centers such as Boston, New York City, and Hartford" makes the job-search process at the end of the program that much easier.

Experiential learning opportunities at UConn include various "learning accelerators," which include "consulting assignments for a variety of Connecticut firms"; the Student Managed Fund, which "provides students an opportunity to put their financial skills into practice by investing $1 million of real cash"; and the GE edgelab, which partners the university with GE to "leverage the expertise and research backgrounds of distinguished UConn School of Business faculty and MBAs to provide unbiased perspective and strategic insights to GE businesses."

UConn's strengths include "an exceptional real estate department," a "highly rated operations and information management department," a "terrific marketing department," and a solid finance program. Students also report that "new initiatives in entrepreneurship are being implemented," and that "an international concentration is under discussion." Students in all areas benefit from small classes that promote "individualized attention from faculty and the opportunity to build a closer network with peers."

The school supplements this with "excellent facilities." The program is growing, and students say "The school's administration is handling the business school's expansion very well. I am constantly surprised by their accessibility and by the fact that they know everyone's name."

Career and Placement

Connecticut MBAs agree that their Career Services Office does a good job of bringing insurance industry and finance recruiters to campus, but in other areas they see shortcomings. One student writes,: "The school needs to improve placement in larger investment banking firms. Not enough is done to help students contact alumni [who] would be willing to help them. They only just now got an alumni database together that students can access." For others, placement in internships is "the issue many people are facing right now. More needs to be done to ensure that first-years have a summer internship and second-years have a job." Some here feel that "the Career Services Office is "overworked," and that the office "needs a larger staff that can recruit companies to recruit students on campus."

Employers who most frequently hire Connecticut MBAs include United Technologies, CIGNA, IBM, Travelers, GE, The Hartford, Citigroup, ESPN, Aetna, General Dynamics and PricewaterhouseCoopers.

Student Life and Environment

"Facilities are excellent within the business school" at UConn, which recently relocated its MBAs to "a brand-new building with state-of-the-art equipment." Students tell us that "food selection on campus is great, group meeting space is great, and there is plenty of easily accessible space to meet for team projects." A "new student union is great and provides lots of activities for commuter students."

SURESH NAIR, ASSOCIATE DEAN
2100 HILLSIDE ROAD, UNIT 1041, STORRS, CT 06269-1041 UNITED STATES
PHONE: 860-486-2872 • FAX: 860-486-5222
E-MAIL: UCONNMBA@BUSINESS.UCONN.EDU • WEBSITE: WWW.BUSINESS.UCONN.EDU

Life on campus in Storrs "is very fun. People help each other out, there aren't really any cliques, and everyone talks to everyone. We are one big happy 'family.' Every Thursday night our whole class goes to happy hour together, and it's a great way to unwind after a week of classes." Also, the program's Graduate Business Association "works hard and provides many events." The active campus life helps make up for the fact that Storrs "is in the middle of nowhere" and is "pretty small, so if anyone wants big-city style, this may not be the place for them." Students say they feel "very safe around campus."

UConn provides on-campus housing for some MBAs. Students love the convenience, telling us that "the shuttle comes right to the door, the apartments are clean, and the building is quiet." Not all students live on or near campus, of course. Many "have a long commute or are married and/or have children, and they tend to be less involved in activities on campus, but those that live on campus or are younger/single socialize a lot." UConn draws MBAs "from all over the world, and they make the program ethnically diverse. UConn has a great engineering program, a law school, and a medical school. Many of those students cross over into the MBA program. It makes for a wonderful experience in the classroom."

Admissions

UConn classifies its MBA admissions as "highly competitive." Applicants typically have GMAT scores of at least 560 and an undergraduate GPA of at least 3.0. They have at least 2 full years of post-undergraduate professional experience and have completed a college-level calculus course. Students who don't meet these standards are nonetheless encouraged to apply, particularly if their professional or life experiences will enrich the classroom experience. Applicants must submit the following materials: an application form, completed online; official transcripts from the student's degree-granting undergraduate institution and from any graduate programs attended; an official GMAT score report; two letters of recommendation from professional supervisors or mentors; and a current resume.

International applicants must meet the above requirements and must also submit professional translations and interpretations of transcripts in languages other than English. Students whose native language is not English must submit an official TOEFL score report (minimum score: 575, paper-based test; 233, computer-based test; 90–91, Internet-based test).

FINANCIAL FACTS

Annual tuition (in-state/ out-of-state)	$7,992/$20,772
Fees	$1,518
Cost of books	$3,000
Room & board (on/off-campus)	$8,684/$9,500
% of students receiving aid	57
% of first-year students receiving aid	66
% of students receiving loans	21
% of students receiving grants	37
Average award package	$23,000
Average grant	$14,000

ADMISSIONS

Admissions Selectivity Rating	83
# of applications received	305
% applicants accepted	61
% acceptees attending	48
Average GMAT	603
Range of GMAT	560–660
Average GPA	3.4
TOEFL required of international students	Yes
Minimum TOEFL (paper/computer)	575/233
Application fee	$65
Regular application deadline	4/15
Regular notification	Rolling
Deferment available	Yes
Maximum length of deferment	1 year
Transfer students accepted	Yes
Transfer application policy	

All students requesting to transfer are required to meet with the director of the MBA program. A maximum of 15 credits are accepted.

Need-blind admissions	Yes

Applicants Also Look At

Boston University, Yale University, New York University, University of Pittsburgh, SUNY Buffalo, University of Massachusetts—Amherst.

EMPLOYMENT PROFILE

Career Rating	82	Grads Employed by Function	%	Avg. Salary
Primary Source of Full-time Job Acceptances		Finance/Accounting	37	$70,364
School-facilitated activities	1 (2%)	Marketing/Sales	12	$66,875
Graduate-facilitated activities	24 (98%)	MIS	15	$67,000
Percent employed	86	Operations/Production	2	NR
		Consulting	7	$62,333
		Other	10	NR

Top 5 Employers Hiring Grads
The Hartford; GE; PricewaterhouseCoopers; ING; Bank of America.

UNIVERSITY OF DAYTON
SCHOOL OF BUSINESS ADMINISTRATION

GENERAL INFORMATION

Type of school	Private
Affiliation	Roman Catholic
Environment	City
Academic calendar	Semester

SURVEY SAYS . . .
Friendly students
Smart classrooms
Solid preparation in:
General management
Teamwork

STUDENTS

Enrollment of parent institution	10,200
Enrollment of business school	455
% male/female	67/33
% part-time	80
% minorities	10
Average age at entry	29
Average years work experience at entry	6

ACADEMICS

Academic Experience Rating	**80**
Student/faculty ratio	7:1
Profs interesting rating	86
Profs accessible rating	74
% female faculty	21

Joint Degrees
MBA/JD 3 to 4 years.

Prominent Alumni
Keith Hawk, vice president, Lexis-Nexis; Phil Parker, president and CEO, Dayton Area Chamber of Commerce; Mike Turner, U.S. Congressman, OH.

Academics

An "exceptional integrated core curriculum," "excellent faculty," a "strong alumni base," and "a marvelous Marianist-centered campus life" attract students to the MBA program at the University of Dayton, a mid-size Catholic university in southwestern Ohio. Students here assure us that their School of Business Administration offers "one of the best kept secrets in the world of MBA programs."

They are especially enthusiastic about the program's "exceptional process-oriented 'integrated' approach to the core curriculum," which they deem "extremely unique." This integrated approach "allows students to break out of the strict mold of marketing and management," and enroll in "courses involving the integration of two major disciplines (i.e. operations management paired with managerial accounting)." In doing so, students get "the opportunity to have two (or more) senior faculty teaching a class rather than just one (not to mention possibly one executive-in-residence or more)." "Class participation is expected" in all of these classes, forcing "students to think about the interaction between different disciplines, and how decisions or actions in one will affect another."

Dayton MBAs also love the "guaranteed real-world consulting project experience" that, coupled with the school's "integration of its entire curriculum with area industry and its leveraging of professors with industry experience," ensures that students confront "real-life examples in class and elsewhere." Facilities "are terrific," and professors are "a diverse group made up of career teachers, professionals who teach part-time, and retired business leaders. All are accessible and offer a lot to the program." Students busy with careers appreciate that "the program is organized well" and UD "allows for a great amount of flexibility, so you can complete it at your own pace." The Dayton MBA curriculum consists of the integrated core, electives, and a two-semester capstone segment. Students may use their electives to develop a concentration in accounting, entrepreneurship, finance, international business, management information systems, operations management, marketing, and technology-enhanced business/e-commerce. The school is especially noted for its work in finance (driven by the Davis Center for Portfolio Management) and entrepreneurship (Dayton houses the Crotty Center for Entrepreneurial Leadership).

Career and Placement

MBAs at University of Dayton are served by the Career Services Office, which assists undergraduates, graduates, and alumni in their development and placement needs. The office provides graduate students with the following services: career advisement; job search and résumé critiquing workshops, career fairs, online résumé referral, on-campus recruiting events, and contact with the alumni career network. Employers who typically recruit on the Dayton campus include ACNielsen, Deloitte Touche Tohmatsu, Xerox, Ernst & Young, Ethicon Endo-Surgery, Federal-Mogul, Fifth Third Bank, FM Global, GE, Georgia-Pacific, NCR, NVR/Ryan Homes, PricewaterhouseCoopers, Procter & Gamble, Sherwin Williams, and USG Corporation.

Student Life and Environment

The degree to which a student is involved in extracurricular life at Dayton "depends on whether you are a full-time or part-time student. Full time students are still connected to undergraduates and the university, while part-time students don't feel as connected." As one part-timer explains, "If someone were interested in getting involved, there are plenty of opportunities, but MBA students typically do not take advantage of these due to a lack of time. Many of us have full-time jobs." Those who can indulge in campus fun report

JANICE GLYNN, DIRECTOR MBA PROGRAM
300 COLLEGE PARK AVENUE, DAYTON, OH 45469-2234 UNITED STATES
PHONE: 937-229-3733 • FAX: 937-229-3882
E-MAIL: MBA@UDAYTON.EDU • WEBSITE: WWW.SBA.UDAYTON.EDU/MBA

that they enjoy "a very modern gym that contains a pool, track, climbing wall, free weight room, aerobic room, and numerous other things" as well as "a tremendous amount of school spirit at the University of Dayton. Here, I feel like part of a family. I believe UD has struck the perfect balance of being an extremely social campus while upholding academic excellence." Full-timers and part-timers alike note that "the campus is very inviting. There are several places to study before and after class and also places to meet with groups, with plenty of resources for graduate students." Students also report that the school "recently implemented a graduate student social networking event that was very well received. Several more are planned for the upcoming year."

The Dayton MBA program consists of "a diverse mix of individuals from many different walks of life: Some are right out of college, some have been out for 25 years, some have 10-plus years work experience, some have none. In general people are able to share real life examples [that] make the learning environment better."

Admissions

All applications to the University of Dayton MBA program must include official transcripts for all postsecondary academic work, an official GMAT score report, a completed application form, and a current resume or curriculum vita. Personal statements are encouraged but not required. Letters of recommendation from employers or professors are not required either; however, the admissions committee will consider them if they are submitted. International applicants must meet all of the above requirements and must also provide a translation of any non-English language transcripts and official scores for the TOEFL (minimum score of 550 paper exam, 213 computer exam required for unconditional admission; students with lower scores may be admitted under the condition that they successfully complete English as a Second Language training).

FINANCIAL FACTS

Annual tuition	$15,720
Fees	$75
Cost of books	$600
Average grant	$1,000

ADMISSIONS

Admissions Selectivity Rating	**75**
# of applications received	315
% applicants accepted	80
% acceptees attending	80
Average GMAT	556
Average GPA	3.18
TOEFL required of international students	Yes
Minimum TOEFL (paper/computer)	550/213
Regular application deadline	Rolling
Regular notification	Rolling
Deferment available	Yes
Maximum length of deferment	1 year
Transfer students accepted	Yes
Transfer application policy Students may request up to 6 semester hours of approved graduate transfer credit of course work of B or better graded quality.	
Non-fall admissions	Yes
Need-blind admissions	Yes

Applicants Also Look At

Miami University Ohio, University of Cincinnati, Wright State University, Xavier University.

UNIVERSITY OF DENVER
DANIELS COLLEGE OF BUSINESS

GENERAL INFORMATION
Type of school   Private
Environment   Metropolis
Academic calendar   Quarter

SURVEY SAYS . . .
Students love Denver, CO
Cutting-edge classes
Solid preparation in:
Teamwork
Communication/interpersonal skills

STUDENTS
Enrollment of parent institution	10,791
Enrollment of business school	538
% male/female	66/34
% out-of-state	36
% part-time	43
% minorities	6
% international	30
Average age at entry	26
Average years work experience at entry	5

ACADEMICS
Academic Experience Rating	**77**
Student/faculty ratio	30:1
Profs interesting rating	80
Profs accessible rating	85
% female faculty	18
% minority faculty	5

Joint Degrees
JD/MBA, JD/IMBA, JD/MSRECM 3
to 4 years, IMBA/MA (Global
Finance, Trade, and Economic
Integration) 2 to 3 years. Flexible
dual degree offered with any other
approved University of Denver
degree, combined degree with any
other approved Daniels degrees.

Prominent Alumni
Peter Coors, chairman, Coors
Brewing Company; Andrew Daly,
former president, Vail Resorts;
Condoleezza Rice, U.S. Secretary of
State; Gale Norton, former U.S.
Secretary of the Interior.

Academics

At the University of Denver's Daniels College of Business, future business leaders benefit from an excellent combination of "academic rigor, high-quality faculty, and values-based and ethically focused curriculum." The Daniels MBA provides a balanced educational experience and is nationally renowned for its focus on business ethics. Students say the school lives up to its good reputation: "Ethics and values are emphasized in every class," giving "every student at Daniels a strong sense of purpose and challenging us to examine our motivation and action in our daily lives and careers."

Students appreciate the school's practical approach to learning, telling us that "the professor's at DU work hard to keep things focused on business applications." A current student confirms, "I am learning things that I take back to work immediately and feel well prepared to contribute at a higher level at my company." The program also maintains "high expectations and focus on writing and communication in all subject areas," which can make the course work particularly time consuming. Even so, students assure us that "class work, depending on the class, ranges from easy to moderately hard, but the environment is certainly not cutthroat."

As the reputation of the Daniels MBA grows, the school continually strives to strengthen the quality of its education along with its program rankings. As a result, "The professors and administration are always asking for feedback, and new programs are continuously presenting themselves." Students appreciate the school's commitment to the student experience, saying professors "genuinely care about their students and want us to succeed." In fact, ambitious MBA candidates are pleased to report that "professors eagerly take students on as a graduate assistants to help them with research and to further augment what they are learning."

In addition to attracting a large number of international students, the University of Denver operates a program that "gives high-achieving undergraduate business students the opportunity to continue on to get their MBA in only 1 extra year." As a result, the student body includes a number of younger students, some of whom have yet to enter the workforce. However, with a student population of over 950, there is plenty of diversity on the Daniels campus. A current student attests, "DU is a well-rounded school with diversity in race, ethnicity, and age. This diversity, especially in age, offers me perspectives on business in more ways than I could have ever found anywhere else."

Career and Placement

Boasting the "best reputation in the Denver area," students at Daniels say they enjoy a competitive edge in the local business community. To maximize that edge, The Suitts Center for Career Services provides a variety of resources for job seekers, including professional development workshops, career advising, company tours and career shadowing, alumni and executive mentoring, as well as extensive print and online job search tools. As one student explains, "They have programs to help anyone willing to put the time and energy into perfecting a resume, mock interview, etc. They will go as far as you need them to."

Fifty-four percent of last year's graduating class (both U.S. citizens and international students) had accepted a job offer within 3 months of graduation at a mean base salary of about $56,000. Twenty-five percent took jobs in sales/marketing, and another 25 percent of the class accepted jobs in finance/banking. The following companies are among those who hired Daniels MBA students in 2006: AIMCO, Allstate Insurance Company, Axcent Sports, Booz Allen Hamilton, Edward Jones, Ernst & Young, Fast Enterprises, G2

GREG GRAUBERGER, DIRECTOR OF ADMISSIONS - ACTING
2101 SOUTH UNIVERSITY BLVD. #255, RIFKIN CENTER FOR STUDENT SERVICES, DENVER, CO 80208 U.S.
PHONE: 303-871-3416 • FAX: 303-871-4466
E-MAIL: DANIELS@DU.EDU • WEBSITE: WWW.DANIELS.DU.EDU

Analytics, Hitachi Consulting, Northwest Airlines, Oppenheimer Funds, Pitney Bowes, Starbucks, and United Parcel Service.

Student Life and Environment

With a large student body comprised of "dedicated, hardworking, interesting, fun, intelligent, friendly people," the University of Denver boasts an incredibly dynamic and vibrant campus atmosphere. In addition to their studies, Daniels students enjoy a lively social scene: "Because so many of the students are young and unmarried, Daniels has a collegiate feel which gives you a chance to meet and become friends with a lot of new people."

Networking is practically built into the program as, "the school provides various social events for students to gather outside of class which helps to enrich the relationships." For example, "Bar nights for grad students are frequent and the Graduate Board (GBSA) does a wonderful job of getting involvement in activities from students." Many students also mention that a "bimonthly happy hour is held for all business students," which is not only a reliable stress-buster but a great career opportunity, as "Many of these happy hours are also hosted by regional companies that use them as a marketing and recruiting opportunity."

Hometown Denver is a great place to work and study, with "fantastic weather," ample recreation and outdoor activities, and plenty of business and industry. University of Denver's campus is similarly first rate, boasting a "wonderful recreation center and tremendous facilities." With the school's enviable location right at the foot of the Rocky Mountains, it's no surprise that in addition to work and studies, "everybody skis."

Admissions

Daniels admits students who demonstrate a commitment to advanced learning, leadership potential, and strong ethical standards. Admissions are selective, and decisions are based on a qualitative review of a candidate's personal, professional, and intellectual preparedness. Last year's entering class submitted a mean GMAT score of 597 and had an average undergraduate GPA of 3.18. Full-time students entered with an average of 5 years professional work experience, whereas part-time students had 11 years of relevant professional experience, on average. Once a completed application is submitted, candidates receive a response in 3 to 6 weeks.

FINANCIAL FACTS

Annual tuition	$29,628
Fees	$744
Cost of books	$1,300
Room & board	$9,900
% of students receiving aid	81
% of first-year students receiving aid	95
% of students receiving loans	50
% of students receiving grants	50
Average award package	$9,250
Average grant	$7,000

ADMISSIONS

Admissions Selectivity Rating	82
# of applications received	467
% applicants accepted	59
% acceptees attending	40
Average GMAT	597
Range of GMAT	550–640
Average GPA	3.18
TOEFL required of international students	Yes
Minimum TOEFL (paper/computer)	600/250
Application fee	$50
Regular application deadline	3/15
Regular notification	5/1
Application Deadline/Notification	
Round 1:	1/15 / 3/1
Round 2:	3/15 / 5/1
Round 3:	5/15 / 7/1
Deferment available	Yes
Maximum length of deferment	1 year
Transfer students accepted	Yes
Transfer application policy 8 quarter hours (6 semester hours) toward electives.	
Need-blind admissions	Yes

Applicants Also Look At

American University, Arizona State University, Boston University, Brigham Young University, Thunderbird, University of Arizona, University of Colorado.

EMPLOYMENT PROFILE

Career Rating	68

Primary Source of Full-time Job Acceptances

School-facilitated activities	17 (30%)
Graduate-facilitated activities	38 (68%)
Unknown	1 (2%)
Average base starting salary	$55,994
Percent employed	30

Grads Employed by Function	%	Avg. Salary
Finance/Accounting	34	$53,736
Marketing/Sales	25	$55,336
MIS	4	$57,500
Operations/Production	4	$73,000
Consulting	14	$58,268
General Management	16	$54,278
Other	3	$70,000

Top 5 Employers Hiring Grads

Aimco; Oppenheimer Funds, Inc.; The Interger Group; Sun Microsystems; Hitachi Consulting Corp.

UNIVERSITY OF FLORIDA
WARRINGTON COLLEGE OF BUSINESS

GENERAL INFORMATION

Type of school	Public
Environment	City
Academic calendar	Semester

SURVEY SAYS . . .
Good social scene
Good peer network
Solid preparation in:
Finance
Communication/interpersonal skills
Quantitative skills

STUDENTS

Enrollment of parent institution	50,000
Enrollment of business school	827
% male/female	70/30
% out-of-state	31
% part-time	86
% minorities	8
% international	15
Average age at entry	27
Average years work experience at entry	5

ACADEMICS

Academic Experience Rating	**95**
Student/faculty ratio	13:1
Profs interesting rating	87
Profs accessible rating	95
% female faculty	14
% minority faculty	19

Joint Degrees
MBA/JD 4 years, MBA/MS (Medical Sciences, Biotechnology), MBA/PhD (Medical Sciences, Biotechnology), MBA/BS (Industrial and Systems Engineering), MBA/Doctor of Pharmacy, MBA/PhD (Medical Sciences), MBA/MD, MBA/Master of Exercise and Sport Science 3 years.

Prominent Alumni
John Dasburg, chairman and CEO, ASTAR Air Cargo; Cesar Alvarez, CEO, managing partner, Greenberg Traurig LLP; William R. Hough, president, William R. Hough and Co. and WRH Mortgage.

Academics

Offering "a wide range of ways to earn an MBA, including a 1-year program, a 2-year program, an executive MBA, an online degree, and the South Florida program," the Warrington College of Business at the University of Florida "not only serves different types of students but also allows students to expand their professional alumni network" through interaction with a wide variety of peers. Students here also appreciate the relatively small size of the program, which ensures "small class sizes" and "great interaction with professors, resulting in more individualized attention from faculty." And, as a state school, Florida delivers it all "at a low cost," resulting in "a great return on investment."

Students report that Warrington boasts "excellent finance and real estate programs." One student explains, "The real estate department offers not only an excellent curriculum but also has additional mentorship opportunities and networking trips outside of the standard MBA program," while "The finance professors are some of the most intelligent individuals I have ever had the pleasure of meeting." Students here also tout a "very strong management program" and an "underrated program in marketing." Across disciplines, "The wide variety of courses and concentrations can tailor to anyone's needs or interests," a benefit of students' access to "the resources of a monstrous learning institution."

Florida boasts "a strong faculty who facilitate learning and are very approachable" and are also "often leaders in their respective fields and are willing to speak with you about industry experiences and contacts." A "great alumni network" shepherded by a "helpful Director of Alumni Affairs" is "very helpful in providing mentoring opportunities and contacts for potential job opportunities." While "some of the facilities here are somewhat outdated," a "recent gift to the graduate business school" means that "a multimillion-dollar facility will be built in the next year or two and will provide a substantial boost to an already world-class program."

Career and Placement

The Graduate Business Career Services office at Florida "works hard to help students with their career search" and "tries to be as innovative as possible to assist students with their search" through such programs as 'Day in the Life,' which "allows MBAs to go to UF business partners' offices and experience a day at that business. This allows the students the ability to get an inside track to making contacts at potential employers, to make good impressions, and to get a feel for corporate culture." Some here wish the office did a better job of attracting on-campus recruiters; some see this as the result of the program's size. One MBA explains, "One of GBCSO's challenges is the size of the graduate program. Even though UF is one of the largest universities in the nation, the MBA program is one of the smallest. Therefore, it is a little more difficult to get recruiters to come to see a smaller group of potential recruits."

Employers who most frequently hire Florida MBAs include: Pulte Homes, Accenture, IBM, Wachovia, Bank of America, Jabil Circuits, Lennar Homes, Pratt & Whitney, Lockheed Martin, Cintas, CSX, Johnson & Johnson, ExxonMobil, Ryder, Deloitte Touche Tohmatsu, Raymond James, BB&T, Citicorp, Ernest & Young, Capital One, and Target.

MICHELLE LOVELL, ASSOCIATE DIRECTOR OF ADMISSIONS
134 BRYAN HALL, PO BOX 117152, GAINESVILLE, FL 32611-7152 UNITED STATES
PHONE: 877-435-2622 • FAX: 352-392-8791
E-MAIL: FLORIDAMBA@CBA.UFL.EDU • WEBSITE: WWW.FLORIDAMBA.UFL.EDU

Student Life and Environment

"Campus life is great" at Florida, where in 2006 "We won the football national championship, and may repeat as basketball champs too." It isn't just about sports here, though; "There are constantly social events and alumni events around the state for us to attend," and the Gainesville area is "a terrific place to go to school," with "a diverse range of things to do. If you're a runner, you can run almost anywhere in town or on campus with great weather year round. If you enjoy nature, there are many great resources and activities to enjoy in the area from springs and lakes to beaches not too far away. There's always something exciting happening on campus from plays, concerts, and lectures to Gator athletics—which are reason enough to go to UF." All in all, students enjoy "an incredible split of academics and fun" with "great opportunities to network and socialize both in and out of school."

Academic life at UF "is hectic, as our courses are organized into 7-week modules. Most of the assignments are team-based, requiring additional time to schedule meetings and develop a single document." As a result, "the MBA lounge is always full of working teams." Fortunately, the close-knit nature of the student body makes "creating study groups and seeking help extremely easy. The relationship between the students and the faculty and staff make it a unique place to study"; students are catered to "as customers of their product." Students here also benefit from "the great diversity among the prior work experiences of classmates. We have engineers, linguistics majors and lawyers in addition to many business majors."

Admissions

Applicants to Florida MBA programs must submit the following materials to the Admissions Office: official copies of transcripts for all undergraduate and graduate programs attended; an official score report for the GMAT (scores may be no more than 5 years old); a resume showing meaningful post-undergraduate professional experience (at least 2 years for the full-time MBA, at least 8 years for the executive MBA; two letters of recommendation from those in a position to evaluate professional performance; and essays. Interviews are conducted by invitation only. International applicants whose first language is not English must submit an official score report for the TOEFL (minimum score: 600 on the written version; 250 on the computer version). The school conducts a Graduate Minority Campus Visitation program, a 'Women in Business' Recruiting Day, and a Diversity Recruitment Day in its efforts to attract underrepresented demographics.

FINANCIAL FACTS

Annual tuition (in-state/ out-of-state)	$6,827/$21,951
Fees	$500
Cost of books	$2,630
Room & board (on/off-campus)	$7,530/$7,640
% of students receiving aid	85
% of first-year students receiving aid	93
% of students receiving loans	42
% of students receiving grants	58
Average award package	$12,600
Average grant	$8,773
Average student loan debt	$11,372

ADMISSIONS

Admissions Selectivity Rating	**92**
# of applications received	277
% applicants accepted	49
% acceptees attending	62
Average GMAT	675
Range of GMAT	650–700
Average GPA	3.38
TOEFL required of international students	Yes
Minimum TOEFL (paper/computer)	600/250
Application fee	$30
Regular application deadline	4/15
Regular notification	Rolling
Deferment available	Yes
Maximum length of deferment	1 year
Non-fall admissions	Yes
Need-blind admissions	Yes

Applicants Also Look At

Emory University, Georgetown University, University of Georgia, The University of North Carolina at Chapel Hill, University of Notre Dame, University of Southern California, The University of Texas at Austin.

EMPLOYMENT PROFILE

Career Rating	82	Grads Employed by Function	%	Avg. Salary
Primary Source of Full-time Job Acceptances		Finance/Accounting	44	$68,714
School-facilitated activities	17 (36%)	Marketing/Sales	9	$49,333
Graduate-facilitated activities	15 (32%)	MIS	9	$64,767
Unknown	15 (32%)	Operations/Production	9	$56,000
Average base starting salary	$66,333	Consulting	19	$74,500
Percent employed	93	General Management	9	$76,667

Top 5 Employers Hiring Grads

CSX; Citigroup; Johnson & Johnson; Wachovia.

University of Georgia
Terry College of Business

GENERAL INFORMATION
Type of school	Public
Environment	City
Academic calendar	Semester

SURVEY SAYS . . .
Good social scene
Good peer network
Smart classrooms
Solid preparation in:
Finance
Accounting
Communication/interpersonal skills

STUDENTS
Enrollment of parent institution	33,660
Enrollment of business school	500
% male/female	66/34
% out-of-state	52
% minorities	13
% international	18
Average age at entry	27
Average years work experience at entry	4

ACADEMICS
Academic Experience Rating	**89**
Student/faculty ratio	25:1
Profs interesting rating	85
Profs accessible rating	86

Joint Degrees
JD/MBA 4 years, MACC 5 years.

Prominent Alumni
Mason Hawkins, chair and CEO, Southeastern Asset Management; George Slusser, president, Coldwell Banker Commercial.

Academics

You'll get a lot of bang for your buck at the University of Georgia's Terry MBA program. Despite small class sizes, world-class faculty, and top-ranked programs in insurance/risk management, real estate, MIS, and accounting, UGA tuition is inexpensive, and the school is "very generous with financial aid." All totaled, University of Georgia is an incredible value. A student jokes, "Compared to Wake or Vandy, UGA might as well be free."

Spearheaded by professors who are "accessible, understanding, progressive, and committed," UGA students describe the academic program as "challenging and relevant." Joining the faculty from a range of impressive backgrounds, UGA students are taught "statistics by the ex-CFO of Kodak, economics by the nation's best economist, entrepreneurship by an MS, MBA, PhD, and doctorate holder all from Harvard, and law by America's best property-rights favoring lawyer." Attesting to the thoroughness and strength of the program, a current student shares, "I have 8 years of experience in my career and, so far, many of my experiences have been taught, or at least simulated, in most of my classes." While their credentials are undisputable, Terry professors are "very helpful, and most make time readily for students with questions or needs."

University of Georgia operates two full-time MBA programs: a 2-year, program for students who do not have an undergraduate degree in business, and an accelerated, 11-month program for students holding a business degree from an AACSB-accredited institution. For 2-year students, the first year consists of foundational course work, followed by a summer internship. In the second year, students tailor their studies through elective course work. Students on the 11-month track take a crash course/review of business topics during the summer months before joining 2-year students in the second year of electives.

While UGA provides thorough training on business essentials, it is not a hard-nosed, quantitative program; rather, professors at Terry "place a tremendous value on the soft skills and the development of a well-rounded individual" through "a strong leadership and personal development component." The academic curriculum is further enhanced by "requirements that allow us to build our skills both inside and outside of the classroom including community-service hour requirements, club activity requirements, career coaching, and leadership training seminars." Through the Terry International Business program, the school runs week-long international trips during spring break, with lectures, company visits, and cultural exposure.

Career and Placement

The Terry MBA Career Resource Center recently partnered with Stanton Chase International, an executive search firm that is ranked in the top 1 percent of firms nationwide. Through Stanton Chase, students have access to two on-site career consultants four days a week, as well as access to Stanton Chase's 56 offices in 34 countries.

In addition to recruiting, the Career Resource Center works individually with MBA students to develop an effective strategy to target the companies and positions that are in line with each student's career goals. Last year the placement rate within 3 months of graduation was 92 percent, and the mean base salary was $68,791 with an average signing bonus of $8,302. While UGA students certainly feel that their school cares about placing them in top positions, they say that UGA could improve by offering "more diverse jobs, not just finance and accounting."

Student Life and Environment

This school sustains a tight-knit intellectual and social community. "The caliber of the individuals and the cohesion within the program are what truly brings value to the MBA

ANNE C. COOPER, DIRECTOR, FULL-TIME MBA ADMISSIONS
361 BROOKS HALL, ATHENS, GA 30602-6264 UNITED STATES
PHONE: 706-542-5671 • FAX: 706-542-5351
E-MAIL: TERRYMBA@TERRY.UGA.EDU • WEBSITE: WWW.TERRY.UGA.EDU/MBA

experience" at UGA. "My classmates range in age from 22 to 39, and the relationships I have built with them are ones that will last for years to come," says a current student. Hailing from "diverse backgrounds," the student body includes "deep-sea divers, army officers who served in Afghanistan, a geography professor, a chemist, lawyers, engineers, hoteliers, entrepreneurs, CPAs, finance professionals, consultants, real estate professionals, CNN/CNBC media professionals, logisticians, fresh undergrads, and many more." Generally speaking, students are social and friendly, and "regularly hang out" outside of the classroom.

Through the MBA program, there is always something happening on campus, and "The business program has linked arms with the music, education, and law schools during different events to provide more networking opportunities." Through the university, there are "football games, night life, community service, arts and exhibitions, cultural interactions" and more. Surrounding Athens offers "great nightlife, culture, weather, sports, and restaurants." In fact, some say, "There are so many really good activities to get involved in that . . . 2 years is just too short." Even "Beyond those activities, we have an active group of students who enjoy being around one another and are a close-knit group," sums up one student.

Admissions

Applicants to UGA are evaluated for academic and intellectual ability, personal qualities, professional experience, and management potential. The school evaluates these factors based on a student's academic transcripts, admissions essays, GMAT scores, professional resume, honors and activities, letters of recommendation, and, for international students, TOEFL scores. In addition, because personal factors are highly important to the program, personal interviews with Admissions Staff are highly encouraged, though not mandatory. Current students take note of the stellar community at UGA, saying, "Our Admissions Office is very good at bringing the right group of people together to benefit both the school and the students."

UGA usually receives about 400 applications for the MBA program. Last year's entering class had an average GMAT score of 651 and a GPA of 3.3, with professional work experience of 4.4 years. Work experience is very important and heavily weighed in an application. If a student has less than 2 years of experience, chances of admission are limited. University of Georgia admits students on a rolling basis, so students (especially those seeking scholarships and assistantships) are encouraged to apply early.

FINANCIAL FACTS

Annual tuition (in-state/ out-of-state)	$8,268/$26,364
Fees	$1,072
Cost of books	$1,000
Room & board (on/off-campus)	$12,400/$16,500
% of students receiving aid	95
% of first-year students receiving aid	75
% of students receiving grants	90
Average grant	$23,500

ADMISSIONS

Admissions Selectivity Rating	**89**
# of applications received	285
% applicants accepted	51
% acceptees attending	57
Average GMAT	651
Range of GMAT	560–700
Average GPA	3.34
TOEFL required of international students	Yes
Minimum TOEFL (paper/computer)	577/233
Application fee	$62
Regular application deadline	5/12
Regular notification	Rolling
Deferment available	Yes
Maximum length of deferment	1 year
Non-fall admissions	Yes
Need-blind admissions	Yes

Applicants Also Look At

Emory University, Georgia Institute of Technology, The University of North Carolina at Chapel Hill, The University of Texas at Austin.

EMPLOYMENT PROFILE

		Grads Employed by Function	%	Avg. Salary
Career Rating	**87**	Finance/Accounting	45	$71,426
Primary Source of Full-time Job Acceptances		Marketing/Sales	10	$61,100
School-facilitated activities	27 (39%)	MIS	3	NR
Graduate-facilitated activities	25 (36%)	Operations/Production	1	NR
Unknown	17 (25%)	Consulting	25	$75,901
Average base starting salary	$72,484	General Management	12	$87,500
Percent employed	92	Other	4	NR

Top 5 Employers Hiring Grads
Bank of America; Accenture; The Home Depot; Oracle; Booz Allen Hamilton.

UNIVERSITY OF HARTFORD
THE BARNEY SCHOOL OF BUSINESS

Academics

Convenience and a marketable degree are the chief drawing cards for most graduate students at the University of Hartford's Barney School of Business. This predominantly part-time population comes here because the school is local to their homes and employment, flexible to their scheduling needs, and able to deliver a prestigious degree recognized throughout the Northeastern business community.

The Hartford MBA has achieved the gold standard of excellence—AACSB accreditation. The program owes a large measure of its success to an excellent faculty who "are a wealth of knowledge in their areas and are usually very willing to ensure that students get the knowledge they desire." One student says that instructors "come from very diverse backgrounds with a wide array of previous work experience, which I feel helps creates an extremely interesting learning environment." Plus, they know how to teach; according to students, "The professors' methods of class delivery is outstanding. Maintaining interest after [a] full day of work can be difficult. Operations management—amazing. Accounting, which can be so boring—quite the eye-opener. Even the dry statistics were enjoyable."

None of this would do students any good, of course, if it weren't offered in a form adaptable to their busy work schedules. Hartford accommodates its students by scheduling classes once a week on evenings and weekends. Professors here are "very accessible and also understand the demands of the work-school balance," offering "great flexibility to help those who have constraints in both time and money." The administration has pitched in by formulating its "no-hassle" approach which makes books and other curricular materials, identification cards, and parking permits (included in the cost of tuition) available at the same site in which MBA classes are held.

The Hartford MBA consists of 17 three-credit courses. Six core courses cover material mastered by undergraduates with business majors and may be waived on that basis. All other courses—five breadth courses (leadership, managing technology, managing customer interfaces, business law, and performance analysis), five electives, and a capstone course that "integrates functional approaches and environment issues by having students make strategic business decisions" are mandatory. MBAs praise the curriculum's "emphasis on group-based assignments and its emphasis on practical cases and examples in classes."

Career and Placement

Placement and Career-counseling Services are provided to Barney MBAs by the Career Services Office, which serves the entire undergraduate and graduate student body of the university. Services include resume and cover-letter writing workshops, seminars on networking and interviewing strategies, job banks, on-campus interviewing, and job fairs.

Student Life and Environment

Nearly all part-timers at the Barney MBA program arrive on campus as classes begin and leave as soon as they end; if they spend any more time there, it's to study, meet with a professor, or participate in a study group. MBA Association, major-related clubs, and pub nights simply aren't part of the equation here. As a typical student explains, "I am a commuter with children at home; therefore, hanging out at the school is not in my schedule. Barbecues and networking get-togethers I do attend, and they are very good." Full-time students benefit from such campus programs as the Lunch and Learn Series, which brings in executives to address students, and non-credit enrichment workshops.

CLAIRE SILVERSTEIN, DIRECTOR OF MBA PROGRAM
200 BLOOMFIELD AVENUE, CENTER FOR GRADUATE AND ADULT SERVICES, CC231, WEST
HARTFORD, CT 06117 UNITED STATES
PHONE: 860-768-4444 • FAX: 860-768-4821
E-MAIL: ADMISSIONS@HARTFORD.EDU • WEBSITE: BARNEY.HARTFORD.EDU

The business school makes its home in Beatrice Fox Auerbach Hall, which recently received a partial makeover to renovate its entry hall. The facility houses a "newly refurbished reading room with daily newspapers and periodicals" and two information technology centers on the wireless campus are loaded with computers complete with flat screens. Students appreciate the effort, but many agree that the school needs a more dramatic technological upgrade.

Hartford benefits from its location in one of the nation's insurance centers. The school attracts students from "a wide variety of business and even engineering specialists" whose experiences add to instruction. The school's proximity to "the biggest financial industry in the world—New York City" is also an asset, allowing for guest speakers, internship opportunities, and day trips for interviews and recruiting.

Hartford MBAs "range in age from recent college graduates up to their 50s and higher. It is good, particularly during group projects, to have such diversely experienced co-group members." With about "half the class made up of international students native to foreign countries, the MBA student body is quite diverse, and not just ethnically. Our working backgrounds are so different: engineers, stockbrokers, chemists, a physicist, insurance, business administrators, accountants—oh, boy. You get all of us in a working group [and] it is quite the experience, especially for a class project," notes one MBA.

Admissions

The Barney admissions office requires all MBA applicants to submit official transcripts from all previously attended postsecondary schools, two letters of recommendation, official GMAT results, a resume, a letter of intent describing the applicant's academic and career goals, and a completed application. Applicants with at least three years of continuous work experience may apply for a GMAT waiver. International students must submit TOEFL scores and a Guarantor's Statement of Financial Support in addition to the above.

FINANCIAL FACTS

Annual tuition	$9,900
Room & board (on-campus)	$9,922
% of students receiving aid	17
% of first-year students receiving aid	50
% of students receiving loans	15
% of students receiving grants	4
Average award package	$13,368
Average grant	$3,667

ADMISSIONS

Admissions Selectivity Rating	**72**
# of applications received	159
% applicants accepted	70
% acceptees attending	75
Average GMAT	510
Range of GMAT	450-720
Average GPA	3
TOEFL required of international students	Yes
Minimum TOFFL (paper/computer)	550/213
Application fee	$45
International application fee	$60
Regular application deadline	Rolling
Regular notification	Rolling
Deferment available	Yes
Maximum length of deferment	1 year
Transfer students accepted	Yes
Transfer application policy Based on individual cases.	
Non-fall admissions	Yes

UNIVERSITY OF HOUSTON
C.T. BAUER COLLEGE OF BUSINESS

GENERAL INFORMATION
Type of school   Public
Environment   Metropolis
Academic calendar   Semester

SURVEY SAYS . . .
Students love Houston, TX
Happy students
Smart classrooms
Solid preparation in:
Accounting
Quantitative skills

STUDENTS
Enrollment of parent institution	34,334
Enrollment of business school	499
% male/female	64/36
% out-of-state	28
% part-time	94
% minorities	14
% international	18
Average age at entry	28
Average years work experience at entry	7

ACADEMICS
Academic Experience Rating	**75**
Student/faculty ratio	3:1
Profs interesting rating	72
Profs accessible rating	67
% female faculty	26
% minority faculty	20

Joint Degrees
MBA/JD 4 to 6 years, MBA/MIE (Industrial Engineering 2 to 5 years, MBA/MA (Spanish) 2 to 5 years), MBA/MS (Hospitality Management) 2 to 5 years, MBA/MSW 3 to 5 years, MBA/Masters in International Management 3 to 5 years.

Prominent Alumni
Fran Keeth, president and CEO, Shell Chemical, LP; Karen Katz, president and CEO, Neiman Marcus Stores; David McClanahan, president and CEO, CenterPoint Energy; Harry Lambroussis, president, International Paper–Latin America.

Academics

The University of Houston is riding high from a $40 million donation from Charles T. Bauer—so high, in fact, that they renamed the business school in his honor. Bauer's gift, the largest in university history, has spurred the school to greater heights, allowing it to attract top-line faculty, upgrade facilities, and fuel cutting-edge research at its many centers and institutes. Yet, to the delight of students, the school remains "reasonably priced."

Despite the emphasis on big names and research, students at Bauer tell us that "the MBA from UH is definitely a real-life, practical MBA that will be useful in the real world" and that "the best professors are not always the academics, but rather the practitioners of business who bring to the table a lot of relevant real-life experience." Students point out that "some of these teachers are not regular faculty but are rather designated 'Executive Professors' who teach only one or two classes per semester." These teachers "are often drawn from such big-name businesses as ExxonMobil, Royal Dutch Shell, PricewaterhouseCooper."

Bauer's students, two-thirds of whom attend part time, extol the program's "focus on meeting the needs of part-time students who are working full-time." The school offers "cohort scheduling with night classes [and] low tuition costs compared to other schools in the area,"—both high priorities for the school's aspiring MBAs. In addition, the Bauer College has introduced a new full-time day program for Fall 2006 that allows students to complete almost all their required core classes in their first year of study. Bauer's 'mini-lockstep' 30-hour core curriculum helps create cohesion even among the part-time student body. It also allows the school to organize material in thematically related modules, each culminating in an integrative capstone course. This ensures that students learn and apply multiple skills to solve problems and improve their understanding of the business world. MBAs praise the "extensive use of case histories and research papers" in their classes and appreciate the "good selection of advanced electives." The curriculum allows for six electives over the course of the program. In addition to concentrations in accounting, finance, decision and information sciences, management, and marketing, five new specialized concentrations in energy have been added to provide students with industry-specific knowledge in key areas of the energy business. Bauer students' main desire is for the "administration to be more open to change."

The Bauer College also offers an Executive MBA program as well as graduate certificate programs such as Energy Risk Management, Energy Finance, Energy Investment Analysis, and Economics of the Energy Value Chain. Upcoming certificate program offerings will include Sales Leadership, Product Management, Business Consulting, and Marketing Analysis. Graduate certificate program offerings include energy accounting, energy risk management, and financial services management.

Career and Placement

Bauer students may employ the services of the Rockwell Career Center. The center offers a number of career-readiness workshops in such areas as resume writing, interviewing strategies, networking, and developing a professional image. The office also assists students in finding jobs and internships, and organizes career fairs. Career counseling services are provided at the Rockwell Center, and students may use the office to access proprietary online job databases. Bauer students may also use a variety of online services free of charge; other career assessment tools are also available through the Rockwell Center.

ALBA VILLEGAS, PROGRAM COORDINATOR
334 MELCHER HALL, ROOM 330, HOUSTON, TX 77204-6021 UNITED STATES
PHONE: 713-743-0700 • FAX: 713-743-4807
E-MAIL: HOUSTONMBA@UH.EDU • WEBSITE: WWW.BAUER.UH.EDU/MBA

Employers most likely to take on Bauer MBAs include AIM Management Group, Spectra Energy, Hewlett-Packard, ExxonMobil, Shell Services International, Deloitte Touche Tomatsu, CenterPoint Energy, Continental Airlines, and Merrill Lynch.

Student Life and Environment

The Bauer College of Business is housed in Melcher Hall on the east end of the University of Houston campus. The facility includes the AIM Center for Investment Management, a $5-million learning laboratory that students use to manage a mutual fund called The Cougar Fund. The facility is also home to several of Bauer's research institutes, including the Global Energy Management Institute and the Center for Entrepreneurship & Innovation, and programs that serve the Houston business community (e.g., the Center for Executive Development, the Program for Excellence in Selling).

Prior to the introduction of the new full time program in Fall 2006, students describe Bauer as"a commuter school" that "is not really comparable with a conventional MBA program. This one is geared towards working professionals who already live and are working in Houston. We barely have time to handle school and work, much less social activities. Those activities that are scheduled here are geared more towards the international students, many of whom attend full-time." When school is done, "there is no 'Let's hit the bars' attitude. Students generally are tired—they want to go home to their families after class. If we meet on the weekends, it is to do work on group projects, not for fun." MBAs report that "fellow students bring to the table a diversity of experience and background. This makes for really rich discussions."

Admissions

Applicants to the Bauer MBA program must submit all of the following materials: a completed application; official transcripts for all undergraduate work; an official GMAT score report; a resume; two letters of reference; and a short, personal essay explaining the student's choice of the Bauer MBA program. International students whose first language is not English must also submit official score reports for the TOEFL or IELTS, unless they have already earned a degree in the U.S. Those with transcripts from overseas must provide translations but need not provide evaluations, as Bauer prefers to make its own assessment of the transcripts. The school admits students for Fall and Spring semesters.

FINANCIAL FACTS

Annual tuition (in-state/ out-of-state)	$5,760/$10,710
Fees	$3,309
Cost of books	$1,400
Room & board (on-campus)	$7,300
% of students receiving aid	52
% of first-year students receiving aid	52
% of students receiving loans	45
% of students receiving grants	38
Average award package	$17,942
Average grant	$3,462
Average student loan debt	$29,229

ADMISSIONS

Admissions Selectivity Rating	81
# of applications received	395
% applicants accepted	67
% acceptees attending	68
Average GMAT	585
Range of GMAT	540–620
Average GPA	3.21
TOEFL required of international students	Yes
Minimum TOEFL (paper/computer)	603/250
Application fee	$75
International application fee	$150
Regular application deadline	5/1
Regular notification	6/1
Deferment available	Yes
Maximum length of deferment	1 year
Non-fall admissions	Yes
Need-blind admissions	Yes

Applicants Also Look At

Rice University, Texas A&M University System Health Science Center, University of Houston—Clear Lake, The University of Texas at Austin, Texas A&M—College Station.

UNIVERSITY OF HOUSTON—VICTORIA
SCHOOL OF BUSINESS ADMINISTRATION

GENERAL INFORMATION

Type of school   Public

SURVEY SAYS . . .

Students love Victoria, TX
Happy students
Solid preparation in:
General management
Quantitative skills

STUDENTS

Enrollment of parent institution	2,491
Enrollment of business school	522
% male/female	43/57
% out-of-state	2
% part-time	78
% minorities	75
% international	16
Average age at entry	31
Average years work experience at entry	2

ACADEMICS

Academic Experience Rating	**71**
Student/faculty ratio	18:1
Profs interesting rating	88
Profs accessible rating	67
% female faculty	15
% minority faculty	67

Academics

The options are abundant for MBAs at the University of Houston—Victoria. Students here can pursue a traditional MBA, or they can also choose from among several other degree options: a Global MBA, with a focus on international business and management; a Master's of Economic Development and Entrepreneurship, with a focus on start-ups and entrepreneurial enterprises; and a fourth-year bridge MBA, designed for ultra-ambitious undergraduates who want to spend their fourth year of school prepping for an MBA program. UHV also allows students several choices of venue: Many programs are available not only at the main campus in Victoria but also at satellite campuses in Sugar Land and Katy (the Cinco Ranch campus). All classes are available to distance learners online.

The highlight of the UHV MBA curriculum, students agree, is the MBA Conference; it's "the culmination of everything that has been learned in the MBA program and applied to an original team case. Each team is competing for top honors and must present its findings at the MBA conference to faculty and students. It is truly a team effort." The competition "really helps us to recapture all the concepts that we have learned through out the program," students say.

Many students—especially those with full-time jobs—opt to take advantage of the well-supported distance-learning options here. Explains one, "Because the course material was online, and because my work in the oil business carried me to very remote locations (e.g., jungles of the Amazon, the Andes mountains, the Caribbean, offshore on a drilling platform), I was always 'present and accounted for.' I could not have finished the MBA if it had not been for the use of technology at UHV." Distance learning allows such students to participate in their courses "while literally working in the global economy, making it easy to learn how the MBA material integrates with the real world." Even those who don't have to trot around the globe appreciate how "we don't waste the time commuting to and from campus, and that results in much more time to devote to researching and studying the material."

Career and Placement

UHV's MBA program maintains a Career Opportunities Center that houses a collection of job-search resources. Students here also have access to the Career Planning and Placement Office, which serves the entire university community. Students note, however, that the school "is clearly lacking many elements in MBA career placement services. As a relatively new program, they are still working to develop contacts and organize this aspect." As this is a nontraditional program, on-campus recruiting is minimal. However, several employers including 3M, AXA Financial Advisors, Banco Popular, Colgate-Palmolive, DuPont, GE, Goldman Sachs, Johnson & Johnson, JPMorgan Chase, PricewaterhouseCoopers, the United States Securities and Exchange Commission, and Wachovia.

LINDA PARR, ADMISSIONS COORDINATOR
3007 NORTH BEN WILSON STREET, VICTORIA, TX 77901 UNITED STATES
PHONE: 361-570-4119 • FAX: 361-570-4114
E-MAIL: PARRL@UHV.EDU • WEBSITE: WWW.UHV.EDU/BUS

Student Life and Environment

UHV holds MBA classes on three campuses. As one student explains, "The UHV main campus is located in Victoria, Texas. There are also large satellite campuses located in South Houston and West Houston. All facilities have state-of-the-art equipment and all campuses offer online courses that run concurrently with the face-to-face classes." Classes "are scheduled at convenient times, and most of the lecturers are understanding in extending our assignment deadlines during personal emergencies. Most of the heavy workload is in a few courses in the second year, but otherwise it is easy to keep up with the classwork." One student sums it up like this: "Life at UHV is unique. You can be as involved or uninvolved as you choose. The technology resources are wonderful, especially the online research tools. The facilities are always clean and attractive inside and out."

Students describe their peers as "mature, experienced, leaders in their communities, smart, current, and well-respected." Many are hard-working professionals with families who still find time and energy to make school a priority. Team projects aren't a problem here, as "it is easy to form teams with enthusiastic students that are willing to share the work together. The diversity of the students allows different views of attacking business problems." One student tells us that the school "is a good fit for students that really want to learn, but not for students who just want to check the box that an MBA was completed."

Admissions

Applicants to the UVH MBA program are eligible for unconditional admission to the program if they have a four-year undergraduate degree from an accredited institution, earned a GPA of at least 2.5. Students with an admissions index of at least 1,400—calculated under the formula (GPA x 200) + (GMAT x 2)—also qualify for unconditional admission. Students who fail to meet these requirements may qualify for conditional admission. Those students who have previously earned a graduate or professional degree (e.g. MD, PhD, JD) are generally exempted from the GMAT requirement. Under certain circumstances, the school will accept a recent (i.e., less than 5 years old) GRE score in lieu of a GMAT score; a combined verbal-quantitative score of at least 900 is required. A GMAT waiver may also be granted to applicants who meet all the following requirements: an undergraduate GPA of at least 3.0; a grade of B or better in two qualifying courses offered by UVH; and at least two years of relevant professional experience. Such students must submit a personal statement describing their career objectives.

FINANCIAL FACTS

Annual tuition (in-state/ out-of-state)	$1,920/$4,632
Fees	$1,164
Cost of books	$1,200
% of students receiving aid	57
% of first-year students receiving aid	48
% of students receiving loans	43
% of students receiving grants	43
Average grant	$1,281
Average student loan debt	$31,498

ADMISSIONS

Admissions Selectivity Rating	61
# of applications received	244
% applicants accepted	99
% acceptees attending	82
Average GMAT	444
Range of GMAT	390–510
Average GPA	3.1
TOEFL required of international students	Yes
Minimum TOEFL (paper/computer)	550/213
Deferment available	Yes
Maximum length of deferment	1 year
Transfer students accepted	Yes
Transfer application policy Up to 6 hours of graduate business course work may be accepted with approval.	
Non-fall admissions	Yes
Need-blind admissions	Yes

Applicants Also Look At

University of Houston, University of Houston—Clear Lake.

EMPLOYMENT PROFILE

Career Rating	**88**
Primary Source of Full-time Job Acceptances	
Percent employed	79

UNIVERSITY OF ILLINOIS—CHICAGO
LIAUTAUD GRADUATE SCHOOL OF BUSINESS

GENERAL INFORMATION

Type of school	Public
Environment	City
Academic calendar	Semester

SURVEY SAYS . . .

Students love Chicago, IL
Friendly students
Good social scene
Cutting-edge classes
Solid preparation in:
Accounting

STUDENTS

Enrollment of parent institution	26,000
Enrollment of business school	412
% male/female	65/35
% out-of-state	4
% part-time	60
% minorities	4
% international	36
Average age at entry	29
Average years work experience at entry	6

ACADEMICS

Academic Experience Rating	**74**
Profs interesting rating	69
Profs accessible rating	82
% female faculty	18
% minority faculty	18

Joint Degrees

MBA/MSA 2.5 to 6 years, MBA/MPH 2.5 to 6 years, MBA/MSN 2 to 6 years, MBA/MA (Economics) 2.5 to 6 years, MS/MIS 2.5 to 6 years, MBA/MD 5 years, MBA/PharmD 5 years.

Prominent Alumni

Ray Roman, senior vice president, Motorola; Bill Merchantz, president and CEO, Lakeview Technologies, Inc.; Kay Schwichtenberg, president and CEO, Central Life Sciences; Peter Gillespie, senior vice president, JPMorgan Chase.

Academics

Offering an "affordable," "socially progressive" MBA program in the stellar city of Chicago, the University of Illinois at Chicago's Liautaud Graduate School of Business is an "outstanding value" in graduate business education. The program consists of 54 credit hours—roughly 13 or 14 courses—half of which are dedicated to the school's core curriculum. These six courses lay the foundation for the Liautaud MBA and are generally taken during the first two semesters of course work. After completing the core course work," Liautaud students take up to 30 credit hours of advanced electives. Due to the school's "flexibility and the option of various concentrations," students have the opportunity to focus their studies on one or two areas of interest—including a "highly ranked" entrepreneurship program—allowing them to graduate with targeted business savvy. Students may also take two courses in the Professional Topics Series, which address emerging trends in business. Some recent offerings include Cross-Functional Teams, The Chicago Exchanges, and Corporate Strategy.

There are a wide variety of professors and teaching styles at Liautaud and "Like any school, some professors are much better than others." Students across the board, however, are "very impressed with the level of personal attention available with professors and administrators," especially "for a large school." The curriculum is enhanced by considerable group work and case studies; students praise the fact that "course projects have been very challenging and have given [us] hands-on experience in real-life [business] situations." Moreover, students say their classmates contribute to the overall learning experience since "Most of them are experienced and knowledgeable in their field and bring professionalism to the class."

Liautaud students rave about the school's prime location in the commerce-friendly city of Chicago. In addition to the opportunities they gain in the classroom, students benefit from the fact that the school is "tied closely into the Chicago business community and successful Chicago business people." Noteworthy businesspeople often come to the campus, though "Visiting speakers are often scheduled prohibitively for part-time students." All students appreciate the myriad advantages that come with being in a "huge urban city with lots of learning opportunities," although some note that the "facilities could be upgraded/updated" and are "not conducive to learning." As one student jokes, "[The] library is louder than a heavy metal concert."

Career and Placement

Through Liautaud's Career Services Office, students have access to a number of professional development seminars on topics such as salary negotiation, personal branding, resume building, networking, and on-campus interviews. The center also offers advising, career development assistance (like mock interviews), and alumni and employer contacts, including an alumni mentor program, roundtable recruiting, and career fairs. Students' experiences with the Career Services Office is a mixed bag. Some observe that the school fails to tap into local resources and "needs to do better job of facilitating alumni interaction," while others claim that "the new Career Center is excellent in partnering students with potential employers and taking students through resume preparation, mock interview."

RITA BIELIAUSKAS, ADMISSIONS DIRECTOR
815 WEST VAN BUREN, SUITE 220, CHICAGO, IL 60607 UNITED STATES
PHONE: 312-996-4573 • FAX: 312-413-0338
E-MAIL: MBA@UIC.EDU • WEBSITE: WWW.MBA.UIC.EDU

While the school continues to "work on providing better career opportunities" for students, the following companies have recently hired LGSB graduates: Abbott Laboratories, Allstate Insurance Company, Information Resources, Baxter, Caterpillar, Deloitte Touche Tohmatsu, Hewitt Associates, Morningstar, State Farm, Lockheed Martin, Nuveen Investments, UBS Financial, HSBC, Caremark, and Navigant Consulting.

Students Life and Environment

Because a large percentage of Liautaud students commute to school, there is something of a split amongst the student body and their perception of campus life. Part-time students are more likely to jet home rather than hang out after class, making it "difficult to foster a sense of community." Full-time students take a more active role in the campus community, participating in case competitions, conferences, and activities put on by the MBA Student Association. When it comes to their peers, students appreciate their classmates for being "friendly and intellectual without being overly competitive." "Minority groups are strongly represented" on campus, as are part-time students, "which aids in making contacts." As one student reports, "Overall, it is a campus filled with fun and academic activities. There is always something to do at Liautaud. The campus life is never boring here."

When students need to head off campus, "all of the amenities of Chicago [are] just beyond the campus perimeter." One student attests, "Apart from academics, I have always enjoyed hanging out with my fellow classmates for a bar night, movie night, or even a casual dinner." With a plethora of restaurants, bars, shopping, and cultural activities just a stone's throw away, there is always something to do after class—and usually someone ready and willing to join you.

Admissions

To apply to the University of Illinois at Chicago's Liautaud Graduate School of Business, you must submit a completed application (including several essay questions), an application fee, official transcripts from your undergraduate institution, GMAT scores, a current resume, two letters of recommendation, and, for international students, TOEFL test scores. Liautaud looks for candidates who demonstrate academic ability and strong management potential. The ideal candidate possesses the ability to lead, work in a team, conceptualize and analyze complex problems, and formulate solutions. To be considered for admission, Liautaud requires a B average on the last 60 hours of undergraduate course work (3.0 on a 4.0 scale). When analyzing an applicant's academic record, the school looks for evidence of analytic and quantitative skills.

FINANCIAL FACTS

Annual tuition (in-state/ out-of-state)	$13,788/$25,786
Fees	$2,512
Cost of books	$1,389
Room & board (on-campus)	$11,250
% of students receiving aid	22
% of students receiving loans	96
% of students receiving grants	50

ADMISSIONS

Admissions Selectivity Rating	88
# of applications received	444
% applicants accepted	36
% acceptees attending	57
Average GMAT	585
Range of GMAT	500–740
Average GPA	3
TOEFL required of international students	Yes
Minimum TOEFL (paper/computer)	570/230
Application fee	$50
International application fee	$60
Regular application deadline	5/15
Regular notification	Rolling
Deferment available	Yes
Maximum length of deferment	1 semester
Transfer students accepted	Yes
Transfer application policy	Need to apply and be accepted to the UIC MBA program. Can submit transcripts from previous course work with a grade of B or better and a course description. Must be from an AACSB-accredited institution. Maximum of 12 semester hours may transfer.
Non-fall admissions	Yes
Need-blind admissions	Yes

Applicants Also Look At

DePaul University, Loyola University Chicago, Northwestern University, The University of Chicago.

UNIVERSITY OF ILLINOIS AT URBANA-CHAMPAIGN
COLLEGE OF BUSINESS

GENERAL INFORMATION
Type of school	Public
Environment	City
Academic calendar	Semester

SURVEY SAYS . . .
Friendly students
Smart classrooms
Solid preparation in:
Teamwork
Communication/interpersonal skills

STUDENTS
Enrollment of parent institution	41,342
Enrollment of business school	203
% male/female	65/35
% part-time	19
% minorities	15
% international	56
Average age at entry	27
Average years work experience at entry	4

ACADEMICS
Academic Experience Rating	**71**
Student/faculty ratio	3:1
Profs interesting rating	87
Profs accessible rating	89
% female faculty	23
% minority faculty	11

Joint Degrees
MBA/MA 3 years, MBA/MS 3 years,
MBA/MS 3 years, MBA/MS 3 years,
MBA/MS 3 years, MBA/MS 3 years,
MBA/MD 5 years, MBA/MS 3 years,
MBA/JD 4 years, MBA/MS 3 years,
MBA/ILIR 3 years.

Prominent Alumni
Mike Tokarz, chairman, The Tokarz Group, Tom Siebel, founder, chairman and CEO, Siebel Systems, Inc.; Jan Klug Valentic, executive vice president, Young and Rubicam; Alan Feldman, president and CEO, Midas, Inc., Bruce Holecek, CEO, Hobbico.

Academics

You get a lot of bang for your buck at University of Illinois at Urbana-Champaign. Despite the school's low price tag, UIUC's College of Business offers an unbeatable mix of "strong academics, intimate class sizes, and a tight-knit, community environment." The unique, first-year curriculum takes a decidedly integrated approach to business education. Instead of taking individual courses in accounting, finance, and marketing, students march through a series of intensive, interdisciplinary courses that progressively cover all business essentials. The result is "a well-rounded experience that ensures the basics within each discipline are mastered." Be forewarned: The program is intense. Students caution, "This school is by no means a walk in the park—we have four 7-week semesters in the first year, which makes the curriculum that much more rigorous under the time constraints." However, they also reassure us that the heavy workload is eased by the fact that "the professors are very accommodating and accessible, while the MBA administration is also very accessible."

In their second year at UIUC, students identify a professional concentration in finance, marketing, information technology, operations management, general management, or a customized concentration. After the broad-based approach in the first year, the second year allows students to add depth and specificity to their studies. A unique component of the curriculum is the "Illinois Business Consulting, which gives students the opportunity to work with actual clients while in school." Through this student-run and faculty-supported consulting business, students have the chance to work on projects for a range of clients, from major players like the Ford Motor Company to new ventures to nonprofit organizations.

Peers are an important part of the educational experience at UIUC, as group assignments are a major component of the curriculum. Fortunately, students describe their classmates as interesting, diverse, and "very hardworking due to the rigorous workload, but also not as competitive or 'type A' as in other programs." Thanks to the prevalence of international students, "Every day is a class in international culture and customs!" While the cultural differences have been known to cause some stress during group assignments, most savvy business students see these challenges as an excellent opportunity to hone key social and negotiation skills. In the words of a current student: "This program offers an amazing opportunity—for someone that takes it—to learn about other cultures in a very informal setting."

Career and Placement

Through the MBA Career Services Office, students at University of Illinois have access to extensive online job-search resources, on-campus interviews, and a variety of professional development activities, including mock interviews, resume critiques, and workshops. The Career Services Office hosts two annual campus career fairs as well as special trips to Chicago, where students have the opportunity to meet with recruiters and UIUC alumni.

Ideally located and well respected in the region, students at UIUC say they benefit from "great networking, especially in Chicago and the Midwest." In fact, 94 percent of last year's graduates received a job offer within 3 months of graduation. The mean base salary for UIUC grads after graduation was $77,185 per year, with a range between $52,000 and $125,000. The most popular career fields were finance/accounting and marketing, which drew 30 percent and 18 percent of graduates, respectively. In 2006, the top hiring companies were: AT&T, BearingPoint, Capital One, Capgemini, Flowserve, Ford Motor Company, IBM, IllinoisVENTURES, Ingersoll Rand, Intel, International Truck and Engine Corporation, LG Electronics, Mercer Human Resource Consulting, Samsung, and

JAQUILIN WILSON, DIRECTOR OF ADMISSIONS
405 DAVID KINLEY HALL, 1407 WEST GREGORY DRIVE, URBANA, IL 61801 UNITED STATES
PHONE: 217-244-7602 • FAX: 217-333-1156
E-MAIL: MBA@UIUC.EDU • WEBSITE: WWW.MBA.UIUC.EDU

Walgreen Co.

Student Life and Environment

Part of a large university and located in lively college town, UIUC's College of Business feels a little like returning to college. Taking advantage of the rich campus environment, business students enjoy tailgating and football games, replete with a beautiful main quad that "gives you that all-American feeling of 'college life.'" The fun doesn't stop there. Within the business school, "There are a lot of activities to choose from." "Scheduled weekly events include intramural sports, bowling, and social events at local establishments." Students warn, however, "with schoolwork and all the activities" available on campus, the UIUC experience "teaches you the true meaning of 'time management.'"

While many UIUC students take advantage of the school's proximity to Chicago (just a 2-hour drive away), they also exclaim, "It is surprising how much there is to do at a campus in the middle of the corn fields of central Illinois!" In fact, "Downtown Champaign (near the bus/train station) has been completely revitalized and has a number of trendy bars that would do Chicago proud. The selection of ethnic restaurants is similarly impressive with an amazing array of Japanese, Korean, Thai, and Chinese restaurants." Drawing friendly, young professionals, the student body at UIUC "is a social bunch who gather weekly to strengthen their ties and networks." Students also enjoy a small bonus within their busy schedule: "Since there's no class on Fridays, everyone convenes at a local establishment on Thursday nights to celebrate the end of a long, 4-day week."

Admissions

The Admissions Committee at the University of Illinois at Urbana-Champaign begins reviewing completed applications in December and will notify applicants of a decision within 4 to 6 weeks. Last year's entering class had an average undergraduate GPA of 3.4 and an average GMAT score of 652. Forty percent of entering students were business majors in college, and had more than 4 years of professional work experience before entering the program. UIUC does not have a minimum required GMAT score or GPA for admission. If you have taken the GMAT more than once, the Admissions Committee will only consider your highest score. There are no academic prerequisites for the program.

FINANCIAL FACTS

Annual tuition (in-state/ out-of-state)	$16,500/$24,400
Fees	$2,410
Cost of books	$2,500
Room & board (on/off-campus)	$14,196/$11,000

ADMISSIONS

Admissions Selectivity Rating	60*
# of applications received	495
Average GMAT	652
Range of GMAT	640–690
Average GPA	3.4
TOEFL required of international students	Yes
Application fee	$50
International application fee	$60
Regular application deadline	3/15
Regular notification	Rolling
Early decision program	Yes
ED Deadline/Notification	12/15 / 2/15
Need-blind admissions	Yes

Applicants Also Look At

Indiana University—Bloomington, Northwestern University, Purdue University, The University of Chicago, University of Michigan, University of Wisconsin, Washington University.

EMPLOYMENT PROFILE			
Career Rating	88	Top 5 Employers Hiring Grads	
Primary Source of Full-time Job Acceptances		Samsung; LG; IBM; AT&T; Walgreen Co.	
School-facilitated activities	25 (69%)		
Graduate-facilitated activities	9 (25%)		
Unknown	2 (6%)		
Percent employed	94		

THE UNIVERSITY OF IOWA
HENRY B. TIPPIE SCHOOL OF MANAGEMENT

GENERAL INFORMATION

Type of school	Public
Environment	City
Academic calendar	Semester

SURVEY SAYS . . .

Students love Iowa City, IA
Friendly students
Smart classrooms
Solid preparation in:
Finance

STUDENTS

Enrollment of parent institution	29,979
Enrollment of business school	943
% male/female	75/25
% out-of-state	65
% part-time	87
% minorities	2
% international	43
Average age at entry	26
Average years work experience at entry	3

ACADEMICS

Academic Experience Rating	**89**
Student/faculty ratio	5:1
Profs interesting rating	69
Profs accessible rating	94
% female faculty	26
% minority faculty	16

Joint Degrees

MBA/JD 4 years, MBA/Hospital and Health Administration 2.5 years, MBA/Library Science 3 years, MBA/Nursing 3 years, MBA/MD 5 years.

Prominent Alumni

Chris Michel, HR manager, Ford Motor Co.; Kathleen A. Dore, president, TV and radio, CanWest Mediaworks; Kerry Killinger, chair, president and CEO, Washington Mutual Savings Bank; Michael Maves, MD, executive vice president and CEO, American Medical Association; Ted E. Ziemann, president, Cargill Health and Food.

Academics

"Quality, location, and price" combine to make the MBA program at the University of Iowa's Henry B. Tippie School of Management an exceptional value. So exceptional, in fact, that "the school is ranked number one by Forbes in terms of speed of payback [on investment]." Students know how good they have it; one writes, "The Tippie School of Management at the University of Iowa appeared to be the complete package: passionate professors, rigorous academics, individual attention, ambitious yet inclusive student body, and a successful Career Services Department. When recruiting, Tippie treats you first class, and this does not change once you enter the program!"

Finance is the area in which Tippie's reputation is the strongest; marketing is another of the school's strengths. Both full-time and part-time students complete a comprehensive core curriculum before undertaking a concentration. Students report that instruction is best in concentration courses but that, throughout the curriculum, "Academics are strenuous and relevant. There is meaning in what we learn." The program is "very focused on the core skills and knowledge set rather than on chasing fads or flights of fancy." The relatively small size of the program means that it's a very personalized experience. "Professors, administrators, and classmates know one another personally and service is given on a one-on-one basis." Students also recognize drawbacks to the size of their program, telling us that "it prevents us from being ranked highly by publications that rely heavily on feedback from a random pool of potential employers because we don't send a great deal of people to California or New York."

Tippie professors "are both good teachers and cutting-edge researchers." Professors typically "have business experience through consulting, owning consulting companies, or [working] in business before teaching. They are not afraid to challenge you to work to your potential. Most really care about preparing you and try to give you the edge to be successful." They also "concentrate on our learning; an A is great, but learning the material is more important than a grade." Administrators "are passionate about the success of this program, and are in touch with students' needs."

Career and Placement

Tippie's MBA Career Services Office is "committed" to students and is "very strong in helping [students] find a job or internship," given the constraints created by the relatively small size of the MBA program. Many students feel that Tippie "needs to be a larger program so that we can attract more company representatives to campus for interviewing." As one student puts it, "Many companies don't want to come to campus for 65 students per class."

Employers who most frequently hire Tippie MBAs include: AEGON USA, Allsteel, Best Buy, Federal Home Loan Bank, Freddie Mac, Galliard Capital Management, General Electric Company, Goldman Sachs, HNI Corporation, John Deere Credit Company, Lancaster Pollard & Co., Millward Brown, Northwest Airlines, Pearson Education, and Wells Dairy.

Student Life and Environment

Because the Tippie MBA is "a small program at a large university, everyone is encouraged to get involved in many different things. There is a great sense of community among those in the program." Full-time students, in particular, are "really involved with campus activities like case competitions, social nights out, international celebrations, volunteer opportunities, sporting events, cultural and performing arts events, and more." Because "Iowans love their football . . . for most home games the MBA Association has a

MARY SPREEN, DIRECTOR OF MBA ADMISSIONS AND FINANCIAL AID
E442 POMERANTZ CENTER, HENRY B. TIPPIE SCHOOL OF MANAGEMENT, THE UNIVERSITY OF IOWA,
IOWA CITY, IA 52242-1000 UNITED STATES
PHONE: 319-335-1039 • FAX: 319-335-3604
E-MAIL: TIPPIEMBA@UIOWA.EDU • WEBSITE: WWW.BIZ.UIOWA.EDU/MBA

company-sponsored tailgate. The tailgates are fun and also allow for some networking with the sponsoring company."

Thank God It's Thursday (there are no MBA classes held on Fridays) is a tradition here that "typically involves going to bars, but we also use TGIT events to build ourselves professionally. For example: We hold a wine tasting and invite the medical, law, and pharmacy students; we take private tours at the Museum of Art; students participate in golf lessons; or we have an occasional Texas Hold 'Em tournament (you never know when you'll have to entertain an important client in Vegas)."

The MBA program "holds most of its classes in a brand-new building across from the fairly new general business building." Students say, "It's very nice, and there is almost always something going on besides classes, whether it is an executive speaker, alumni event, awards ceremony, or a student organization function." Because Tippie "has a tremendous international community," students enjoy "social activities that include dinners for events like Diwali, Lunar New Year, and Thanksgiving where we share our cultures."

Admissions

Applicants to the Tippie MBA program must submit official transcripts for all completed postsecondary academic work; an official GMAT score report; a current resume; two personal essays (topics provided in application packet); and three letters of recommendation. International students whose first language is not English must submit an official score report for either the TOEFL or the IELTS. Full-time students may apply for admission in the fall only; part-time students may begin study in either the fall or spring semesters. An admission interview is required of all full-time candidates. The school recommends, but does not require, a minimum of 2 years of postundergraduate professional experience for applicants to the full-time program.

FINANCIAL FACTS

Annual tuition (in-state/ out-of-state)	$13,162/$24,142
Fees	$943
Cost of books	$2,200
Room & board	$11,900
% of students receiving aid	57
% of first-year students receiving aid	63
% of students receiving grants	57
Average award package	$17,746
Average grant	$3,892
Average student loan debt	$35,114

ADMISSIONS

Admissions Selectivity Rating	94
# of applications received	235
% applicants accepted	43
% acceptees attending	62
Average GMAT	655
Range of GMAT	600–720
Average GPA	3.52
TOEFL required of international students	Yes
Minimum TOEFL (paper/computer)	600/250
Application fee	$60
International application fee	$85
Regular application deadline	7/15
Regular notification	Rolling
Deferment available	Yes
Maximum length of deferment	1 year
Transfer students accepted	Yes
Transfer application policy Maximum number of transferable credits is 9 (from AACSB-accredited programs only).	
Non-fall admissions	Yes
Need-blind admissions	Yes

Applicants Also Look At

Indiana University—Bloomington, Michigan State University—College of Law, Purdue University, The Ohio State University, University of Illinois, University of Minnesota, University of Wisconsin.

EMPLOYMENT PROFILE

Career Rating	88
Primary Source of Full-time Job Acceptances	
School-facilitated activities	26 (79%)
Graduate-facilitated activities	7 (21%)
Average base starting salary	$72,884
Percent employed	94

Grads Employed by Function	%	Avg. Salary
Finance/Accounting	36	$77,564
Marketing/Sales	36	$68,930
MIS	11	$68,870
Operations/Production	10	$76,400
Consulting	7	NR

Top 5 Employers Hiring Grads
AEGON USA; Best Buy Co. Inc.; Discover Financial Services; HNI Corporation; Meredith Corporation.

UNIVERSITY OF KANSAS
SCHOOL OF BUSINESS

GENERAL INFORMATION

Type of school	Public
Environment	City
Academic calendar	Semester

SURVEY SAYS . . .
Students love Lawrence, KS
Happy students
Solid preparation in:
Doing business in a global economy

STUDENTS

Enrollment of parent institution	27,890
Enrollment of business school	165
% male/female	95/5
% out-of-state	5
% part-time	37
% minorities	10
% international	10
Average age at entry	26
Average years work experience at entry	5

ACADEMICS

Academic Experience Rating	**75**
Student/faculty ratio	8:1
Profs interesting rating	71
Profs accessible rating	85
% female faculty	30
% minority faculty	2

Joint Degrees
MBA/JD 3 years, MBA/Petroleum Management 2 years, MBA/MA (Russian and Eastern European Studies) 2 years, MBA/MA (Latin American Studies) 2 years, MBA/Masters in Management 2 years.

Academics

Students at the University of Kansas' School of Business describe their institution as "the best business school in the Midwest," and they have good reason to be so complimentary. "Positive, up-tempo, friendly, and lots of work," the Kansas program is "vastly underrated" and a "truly wonderful" grad school experience. The students characterize the professors as "second to none" and are impressed with their academic and professional backgrounds." KU profs, who are "active in the business world within their fields," exhibit "a great blend of teaching skills and real-world experience."

Students are held to a high standard and are "expected to be well prepared, well read, and well spoken in course discussions." The "fantastic" administration receives high praise as well. One MBA candidate reported that "if you want to try something different or want to attend a conference, they support you 100 percent of the time." Students also mention the administration's constant efforts "to improve facilities, encourage student involvement and input, and expand the faculty and curriculum."

On top of the full-time MBA offered at KU, the school also offers an evening-professional MBA, a Master's in Accounting, Master's in Finance, and several dual-degree MBAs, including a JD/MBA, MBA/MIM, MBA-PharmD, MBA/PM (petroleum management), as well as three international-themed dual degrees involving Latin American, European, and Asian studies. KU also has an extensive PhD program in which students can concentrate in accounting, information systems, finance, marketing, decision sciences, and management. KU's "focus on the global business environment" is a huge draw for many applicants, who feel that the school provides "an exceptional international business program for being in the middle of the United States and far from the coasts." Reasonable fees also are a major plus, and many students feel they're receiving a great deal of value for their money.

As one might expect from a school that focuses a great deal on international business, KU has an international program that allows students to obtain real-world experience in the global marketplace. The KU School of Business partners with the Center for International Business Education and Research to facilitate study abroad with an array of businesses across the globe. In the past few years students have traveled to India, China, Germany, France, Brazil, and Mexico as part of the program. With these types of experiences available to students, it's no wonder they describe the KU program as a "good value for the money that offered many options in terms of international experience."

Career and Placement

On its website the school boasts that "KU Business alumni are chief officers and senior executives of dozens of Fortune 500 companies." Fortunately for KU students who aspire to such heights, Kansas City is home to many large corporations, including Sprint and Hallmark, and the metropolitan area was named one of the "Top 20 Areas to Start and Grow a Company" by Inc.com. KU also has a second campus (Edwards Campus) located in nearby Overland Park, which was named one of the top 10 cities for doing business by Business Development Outlook.

Students give glowing reviews to the school's Career Services Department, which does a "fantastic job of preparing students for the job-search process and facilitating that process through two massive career fairs, many interview and resume workshops, one-on-one counseling, and more." One student says, "I already have a job waiting for me when I complete the master's program, thanks to the business school's Career Services and KU's strong reputation in the region."

DEE STEINLE, ADMINISTRATIVE DIRECTOR OF MASTER'S PROGRAMS
206 SUMMERFIELD HALL, 1300 SUNNYSIDE AVENUE LAWRENCE, KS 66045 UNITED STATES
PHONE: 785-864-7596 • FAX: 785-864-5376
E-MAIL: BSCHOOLGRAD@KU.EDU • WEBSITE: WWW.BUSINESS.KU.EDU

Approximately 47 percent of Kansas students accepted job offers before graduating in 2006, and by 3 months after graduation, that number had grown to 88 percent. The average salary for graduates was $50,667 (not including bonus). The majority of students accepted jobs in marketing and finance, although there were quite a few who went into operations and consulting. A range of companies recruit on campus, and the ones who hire graduates most frequently include Deloitte Touche Tohmatsu, Payless Shoe Source, Sprint, Capgemini, Ernst & Young, and KPMG International.

Student Life and Environment

KU students enjoy life on campus, which many describe as "great." The only complaint is that "there are really more things that I'd like to be able to participate in than I have time to do!" One student described life at KU as "filled with a variety of activities, including extracurriculars (Net Impact, MBA Ambassadors), social events put on by MBA student organizations, working for the MBA Admissions Office, and of course, course work."

Although the majority of the class is "ambitious and concentrated on their future," students are also "very fun people." There is diversity among the MBA candidates, and the students "vary from people straight out of undergrad to people 35 years old, and they all have different goals and lifestyles, but they communicate well and make the classes enjoyable by opening up discussion without judging others." Some say their classmates "are the very best part about my experience in the KU MBA program." Overall, students are more than satisfied with their experiences at KU. As one student said, "I cannot thank KU enough for preparing me to excel in my future endeavors."

Admissions

Applications are accepted at anytime, up until posted application deadlines. KU is now accepting applications for all programs for the Fall 2007 semester. In a recently admitted class, students' average undergraduate GPA was around 3.3, and the average GMAT was approximately 600. Students had an average of 5 years of work experience.

FINANCIAL FACTS

Annual tuition (in-state/ out-of-state)	$19,102/$34,575
Cost of books	$2,000
Room & board (on-campus)	$10,435
% of students receiving aid	50
% of first-year students receiving aid	50
% of students receiving grants	25
Average grant	$1,500

ADMISSIONS

Admissions Selectivity Rating	78
# of applications received	268
% applicants accepted	73
% acceptees attending	85
Average GMAT	600
Range of GMAT	540–690
Average GPA	3.3
TOEFL required of international students	Yes
Minimum TOEFL (paper/computer)	53/20
Application fee	$60
Regular application deadline	6/1
Regular notification	Rolling
Deferment available	Yes
Maximum length of deferment	1 year
Transfer students accepted	Yes
Transfer application policy Maximum number of transferable credit hours is 6.	
Non-fall admissions	Yes
Need-blind admissions	Yes

Applicants Also Look At

Iowa State University, University of Iowa, University of Missouri—Columbia, University of Nebraska—Lincoln, University of Oklahoma.

EMPLOYMENT PROFILE

Career Rating	63	Grads Employed by Function	%	Avg. Salary
Primary Source of Full-time Job Acceptances		Finance/Accounting	28	$33,500
School-facilitated activities	4 (29%)	Marketing/Sales	24	$43,700
Graduate-facilitated activities	10 (71%)	Operations/Production	12	$40,000
Average base starting salary	$50,667	Consulting	12	$69,000
Percent employed	76	Other	24	$80,000

UNIVERSITY OF KENTUCKY
GATTON COLLEGE OF BUSINESS AND ECONOMICS

GENERAL INFORMATION

Type of school	Public
Environment	City
Academic calendar	Semester

SURVEY SAYS . . .
Students love Lexington, KY
Good social scene
Cutting-edge classes
Solid preparation in:
Teamwork
Communication/interpersonal skills

STUDENTS

Enrollment of parent institution	26,545
Enrollment of business school	179
% male/female	68/32
% out-of-state	12
% part-time	58
% minorities	13
% international	6
Average age at entry	25
Average years work experience at entry	2

ACADEMICS

Academic Experience Rating	**82**
Student/faculty ratio	3:1
Profs interesting rating	70
Profs accessible rating	86
% female faculty	15
% minority faculty	5

Joint Degrees
MBA/JD 4 years, BS (Engineering)/MBA 5 years, MD/MBA 5 years, PharmD/MBA 4 years, MBA/MA (International Relations) 3 years.

Prominent Alumni
Chris Sullivan, chairman of the board, Outback Steakhouse; Paul Rooke, executive vice president, Lexmark International, Inc.; Gretchen Price, vice president, Finance and Accounting, global operations, PandG; Greg Burns, chairman and CEO, O'Charley's, Inc..

Academics

Educating business students for more than 80 years, the Gatton College features bachelor's, master's and doctoral degrees within three academic units: the School of Management, the Von Allmen School of Accountancy, and the Department of Economics. There are three majors offered in the MBA program: marketing, finance, and IT.

Students praise Gatton's "approachable" faculty and staff, describing support from them as "top-notch." "They go above and beyond to make sure every student is given the resources to succeed," says one MBA candidate. "Having an MBA center dedicated to us has been one the best academic experiences I've had." The professors are leaders in their field and are "published in respected journals." They are "very dedicated to helping us learn the course work," and are remarkably open with the candidates. "They give us access to their published, unpublished, and even working papers. They have done this without making their own material the main basis of assignments and exams, which I like, because it lets them be more unbiased," one student says. Several students say the program would benefit greatly from the professors and administrators doing "a better job of working together and becoming a cohesive unit," because the "lack of communication between the two groups causes some problems for the students."

Gatton has undergone a major change recently, making the transition to an 11-month immersion MBA. The new program is designed "for both business and non-business students but is much more challenging for those without a business background." The arduous program boasts "a unique structure and opportunities for PDMA and Six Sigma certification." Because the program is only a year long, students do not have a summer off to participate in an internship. To address this, the school has implemented a program called Project Connect, which pairs teams of students with a company to work on real-world projects during the course of the year. In 2006, participating companies included Lexmark, Humana, Fifth Third, Tempur-Pedic, and United Technologies.

The part-time students aren't that thrilled with the program's transition, expressing concern that "working professionals seeking an MBA from Gatton aren't provided the same opportunities and resources as those students in the 11-month program." However, there's agreement that all of the students are "driven, intelligent, hardworking, studious."

Career and Placement

There are 103 students in Gatton's MBA program, and 229 companies participated in recruiting last year, so it's no wonder students say "Career placement is getting better." However, some feel the Career Center needs to "focus more on separating undergrad recruiting from MBA recruiting."

Career services at the University of Kentucky are based in the James W. Stuckert Career Center. Among other services, the Career Center hosts a mentoring program and specialized MBA workshops. The mentoring program provides students with networking contacts, including alumni, friends of UK, and employers. Through mentoring contacts, students can participate in informational interviews and shadowing, as well as ask for career advice. The Career Center also hosts several career fairs throughout the year, with the Business Career Fair held in the fall semester, followed by the Spring Career and Internship Expo. To help students prepare for these events, Gatton offers MBA workshops whose topics include resume writing, interviewing, networking, salary negotiations, etiquette, and more.

BEVERLY KEMPER, MBA ACADEMIC COORDINATOR
145 GATTON, COLLEGE OF BUSINESS AND ECONOMICS, LEXINGTON, KY 40506-0034 UNITED STATES
PHONE: 859-257-7722 • FAX: 859-323-9971
E-MAIL: KEMPER@UKY.EDU • WEBSITE: GATTON.UKY.EDU

Last year the average salary for a Gatton graduate was $50,098. Recruiting employers included Humana, the Department of Labor, Proctor & Gamble, Ryder, and Toyota. Finance is the most popular of the three Gatton majors, with almost half of graduates taking jobs in finance. Fifty-eight percent of candidates accepted offers before they graduated, and by 3 months after graduation, 75 percent had accepted offers.

Student Life and Environment

Located on a 687-acre campus near downtown Lexington, the University of Kentucky has an enrollment of 26,000 students and is a nationally recognized research institution. Students enjoy life in Lexington, and among Gatton's strengths they list "the local area, local quality of life, temperate climate, [and] good facilities." Lexington is the second largest city in Kentucky and has an international reputation for its bluegrass horse farms, and is home to the renowned Keeneland Race Track. Another big draw for Lexington residents is the UK men's basketball team, a perennial powerhouse. The student body isn't particularly diverse, with students describing their peers as "mostly middle-class White Americans, with a majority being conservative." However, despite "not [being] an extremely diverse group," students are tolerant and "very accepting of differences."

Gatton students tend to form close bonds because of the short duration of the program. As one student says, "The program is only 11 months, so we spend a lot of time around each other." The result is a "family atmosphere" that's conducive to collaboration. "Everyone I have interacted with has been very friendly and willing to offer advice or any help they could," one MBA candidate says. "I was happily surprised to discover this, as I assumed classmates would be more cutthroat."

Admissions

In the fall of 2006, the average undergraduate GPA was 3.4, and the average GMAT was 598. Sixty-seven percent of the student population was male, out of a class of 94, and 17 states and 4 countries were represented. Students had an average of 2.6 years of work experience, and their average age was 26.

FINANCIAL FACTS

Annual tuition (in-state/ out-of-state)	$7,652/$15,678
Fees (in-state/ out-of-state)	$6,000/$7,000
Cost of books	$2,500
Room & board (on/off-campus)	$8,250/$9,100
% of students receiving aid	19
% of first-year students receiving aid	19
% of students receiving grants	19
Average award package	$9,817
Average grant	$9,817

ADMISSIONS

Admissions Selectivity Rating	89
# of applications received	192
% applicants accepted	68
% acceptees attending	72
Average GMAT	598
Range of GMAT	500–750
Average GPA	3.39
TOEFL required of international students	Yes
Minimum TOEFL (paper/computer)	550/213
Application fee	$40
International application fee	$55
Regular application deadline	6/1
Regular notification	Rolling
Transfer students accepted	Yes
Transfer application policy File must be completed and applicant is considered as a regular applicant only for evening program.	
Need-blind admissions	Yes

Applicants Also Look At

Eastern Kentucky University, Indiana University—Bloomington, The Ohio State University, University of Cincinnati, University of Louisville, University of Tennessee, Xavier University.

EMPLOYMENT PROFILE

Career Rating	69	Grads Employed by Function	%	Avg. Salary
Primary Source of Full-time Job Acceptances		Finance/Accounting	47	$48,998
School-facilitated activities	28 (55%)	Marketing/Sales	6	$42,333
Graduate-facilitated activities	23 (45%)	Operations/Production	6	$45,500
Percent employed	75	Consulting	10	$48,240
		General Management	17	$49,261
		Other	14	$61,571

Top 5 Employers Hiring Grads
Humana; Department of Labor; Procter & Gamble; Ryder; Toyota.

UNIVERSITY OF LOUISIANA—LAFAYETTE
B. I. MOODY III COLLEGE OF BUSINESS

GENERAL INFORMATION
Type of school	Public
Environment	City
Academic calendar	Semester

SURVEY SAYS . . .
Cutting-edge classes
Solid preparation in:
General management
Computer skills

STUDENTS
Enrollment of parent institution	16,800
Enrollment of business school	176
% male/female	53/47
% out-of-state	4
% part-time	80
% minorities	8
% international	4
Average age at entry	27
Average years work experience at entry	6

ACADEMICS
Academic Experience Rating	**73**
Student/faculty ratio	20:1
Profs interesting rating	71
Profs accessible rating	83
% female faculty	40
% minority faculty	12

Prominent Alumni
Mike DeHart, Stuller Management Services, Inc.; Stefni Lotief, UL women's softball coach; Greg Roberts, director of aviation, Lafayette Airport; Dr. Ross Judice, EVP and CMO, Acadian Ambulance Service and Air Med.

Academics

Convenience and local reputation are the reasons most aspiring businesspeople choose the Moody MBA program at the University of Louisiana—Lafayette. The majority of Moody students work full time in the area and attend classes in the evenings, thus limiting their choices of programs in which to enroll. Few mind though, as Moody is "a really good school," especially "for students who work full-time," and offers a "cozy college atmosphere" where "just about everyone knows everyone else," and the faculty "really cares about the students."

Students at Moody report that the school has a "great reputation in the computer sciences" and is "the best and closest" when it comes to the health care industry. In fact, ULL offers an MBA with a concentration in health care administration, an appealing option to the area's many health care professionals. Professors have a lot of experience in their fields and "can relate to what we need better than those who just teach us with no experience to back it up." Among students' few complaints was that the relatively small size of the program limits course selection. "Schedule conflicts are common, and this is causing me to graduate at a later date than I anticipated," writes one student.

The Moody MBA requires students to complete 33 semester hours consisting of 27 hours of required core courses and 6 semester hours of electives (the health care MBA also consists of 33 semester hours but divides those hours between business and health care administration classes). Students who did not major in business as undergraduates are typically required to complete an additional 15 semester hours in foundation courses; these courses are prerequisite to, but do not count toward, the graduate degree.

Career and Placement

The Moody MBA program coordinates with the university's Career Services Center and the Internship Office to offer MBA N-Work, a service dedicated to finding jobs for past and current students. The Career Services Center offers Moody students on-campus job fairs and other placement services, but its primary mission is to serve undergraduates. The MBA Association is probably students' most effective conduit to employment. It should be noted that many Moody MBAs are currently employed, often by companies funding their graduate education, and thus are not actively seeking jobs. Top employers of Moody MBAs include Stuller, Lafayette General Medical Center, The Schumacher Group, Schlumberger, Acadian Ambulance Service and Air Med Services, Our Lady of Lourdes Regional Medical Center, Chevron, Texaco, and Louisiana Health Care Group Lafayette.

Student Life and Environment

Most students in the Moody MBA program attend part time, with lives so full of family and work obligations that they rarely linger unnecessarily on campus. Don't expect the hustle and bustle of a Northeastern b-school here, however; even the busiest MBAs tell us that "the school has a very laid-back attitude." That's simply the way life is in this section of Louisiana, known as Acadiana; students tell us that "in this part of the state, things are very relaxed and fun, and school is no different. We work hard, of course, but the overall feeling is more relaxed than, I assume, other business schools to be." Hometown Lafayette is "a great place to live" with an "excellent culture" that is "very attractive" to students. Students who can find time for campus events tell us that the schools "provide great opportunities to network and learn more about specific fields of work and study" and that the MBA Association does an especially good job "hosting socials and banquets and helping students and faculty get to know each other."

Dr. C. Eddie Palmer, Dean of the Graduate School
Martin Hall, Room #332, PO Box 40200, Lafayette, LA 70504-0200 United States
Phone: 337-482-6965 • Fax: 337-482-1333
E-mail: Gradschool@louisiana.edu • Website: moody.louisiana.edu

Moody MBAs are "are competitive and, for the most part, have a positive attitude toward learning," although "Some are happy to settle for B's and socialize too." Students note that the school draws "an ethnically diverse" population and that "the 'joie de vivre' of the Cajun students at UL promotes a friendly but competitive atmosphere that you won't find elsewhere." While most students here are "older people coming back to school," Moody also has a number of students "just out of undergraduate school." Most feel their classmates "are mature and very helpful," a good thing since "In this program there are a lot of group projects. In every group I have been in, everyone pulls their own weight."

Admissions

Applicants to the Moody MBA program must meet the following minimum requirements for admission: a bachelor's degree from an accredited U.S. college or university or an equivalent degree from a foreign school; a minimum overall undergraduate GPA of 2.75; an "acceptable" score on the GMAT (average score for the 2006 entering class was approximately 500; analytical writing scores are also considered); three letters of recommendation from people capable of assessing your academic ability and potential to succeed in a graduate program; a written personal statement (up to 750 words describing why you wish to pursue an MBA); a current resume (include degrees earned, employment history, honors and awards received, summary of computer skills, and list of overseas travel and foreign language abilities); and, for international students, TOEFL scores. The school prefers but does not require previous work experience. The school accepts electronically submitted applications.

FINANCIAL FACTS

Annual tuition (in-state/ out-of-state)	$3,104/$9,284
Cost of books	$1,000
Room & board (on/off-campus)	$3,750/$6,750
% of students receiving aid	60
% of students receiving loans	40
% of students receiving grants	25
Average grant	$8,605
Average student loan debt	$5,000

ADMISSIONS

Admissions Selectivity Rating	**79**
# of applications received	150
% applicants accepted	57
% acceptees attending	78
Average GMAT	537
Range of GMAT	470–610
Average GPA	3.24
TOEFL required of international students	Yes
Minimum TOEFL (paper/computer)	550/213
Application fee	$20
International application fee	$30
Regular application deadline	6/30
Regular notification	8/1
Early decision program	Yes
ED Deadline/Notification	Applications processed as soon as received
Deferment available	Yes
Maximum length of deferment	1 year
Transfer students accepted	Yes
Transfer application policy	Can transfer in a maximum of 9 credit hours; must apply through regular process.
Non-fall admissions	Yes
Need-blind admissions	Yes

Applicants Also Look At

Louisiana State University, Louisiana Tech University, Loyola University New Orleans, McNeese State University, Nicholls State University, Tulane University, University of New Orleans.

EMPLOYMENT PROFILE	
Career Rating	72

UNIVERSITY OF LOUISVILLE
COLLEGE OF BUSINESS

Academics

The College of Business at the University of Louisville offers two primary MBA options. The first is the new Professional MBA, a two-year accelerated program offered in two formats (two nights per week and occasional Saturdays, or all-day Saturday), and taught in six-week modules across 14 terms, including a consecutive two-term capstone project, five professional development Saturdays per year, and six elective choices. The second is the IMBA, an integrated, two-year lockstep program that focuses primarily on entrepreneurship. The IMBA is also scheduled for the convenience of working students, meeting twice weekly in the evenings. The university also offers a number of joint-degree MBA programs. Both MBA programs offer a cohort-based team learning environment in a two year, year-round format, and guarantee no tuition increase for students who complete the program with their cohort.

Students tell us that "Most of the professors have an innovative approach to teaching, and they look for ways to make their classes better. If I were to restart the program three years after graduating, I am sure it would be a unique experience." Students appreciate that this approach "is essential given the ever-changing business environment," adding that "We may not be a Harvard or Wharton, but we still produce some of the world's leaders in business. In addition, the program offers a great work/life balance." Students praise their professors for "demonstrating meaningful real-world knowledge through prior experiences. The course work they present is very applicable to situations I face as a manager at a bank each day."

Louisville's IMBA is a lockstep program with an entrepreneurial focus. All courses and meeting times are mandatory. This approach allows for greater integration within the curriculum; classes can be team-taught to highlight the interconnectedness of two or more business disciplines, for example. It also allows the school to vary course lengths. Because all students are taking all courses together, scheduling need not be restrained by traditional semester intervals, and students love the results. One participant writes, "I feel that it's designed to give me everything I wanted in a graduate business program. Everything that I have learned thus far has been applied in my professional life."

Career and Placement

Louisville MBAs receive career counseling and placement services from the Ulmer Career Management Center, an all-new, state-of-the-art, 3,800 square foot facility that includes a career management resource library, conference rooms, and interview rooms. The office provides resume assistance, training seminars on interviewing skills, and on-campus recruiting events supported by CareerLeader tools and Symplicty software. Students confess that "the career center is just beginning to get off the ground" and that "the school still needs to improve in its career management for graduate students. Although some jobs have been posted, the majority are geared towards undergraduates or students who have graduated from the MBA program and already have several years of experience." On the bright side, students find that attending Louisville creates "many networking opportunities. Most classmates have full-time jobs and experience in the 'real world.' You can make connections with students throughout Louisville that will stay with you a long time." Opportunities to network are also enhanced in the Professional MBA through the capstone project, which is a team-based, external consulting project.

KEVIN KANE, ADMINISTRATIVE DIRECTOR, MASTERS PROGRAMS
COLLEGE OF BUSINESS, LOUISVILLE, KY 40292 UNITED STATES
PHONE: 502-852-3969 • FAX: 502-852-4901
E-MAIL: K0KANE01@GWISE.LOUISVILLE.EDU • WEBSITE: BUSINESS.LOUISVILLE.EDU/MBA

Student Life and Environment

Most MBAs at Louisville "have little involvement with the rest of campus (library, gym, etc.) because most work full-time and attend classes in the evenings." Students spend so little time on campus that "they are secluded from other graduate students and, to a certain extent, from the other MBA students," though the recent creation of the Professional MBA program should offer more opportunities to network and utilize campus facilities with other members of their cohort. Even the busiest MBAs, however, know that "our basketball team is nationally recognized and dominates both the school and the town during the season." Those who find time to spend on campus boast that it is "very accommodating, with a recently renovated state-of-the-art library and a great athletic program (activities MBAs can attend when not studying!)." One student notes, "Although it's an urban campus, you would never know it given the quaint, friendly atmosphere." MBA 'campus life' will be enhanced in 18-24 months with the planned relocation of the College's graduate business programs to the heart of downtown Louisville.

The metropolitan Louisville area is home to over one million people. Students describe it as "a city full of opportunities for recent or upcoming MBA grads. Openings for MBAs are frequently e-mailed to students by school officials, which is a great service." A recent Wall Street Journal supplement ranked Louisville "the nation's fourth best city for job opportunities for recent graduates." Papa John's, YUM!, Humana Health Insurance, UPS Worldport, and GE all have a large presence in the city; some are headquartered here. Students report that the area surrounding the school "is not the best residential area, it's not good housing. There is good, safe housing about 15 minutes from campus, though, over in the Highlands."

Admissions

Admission to the University of Louisville MBA program is, without a doubt, competitive. Students in the program rank in the top third of MBA candidates nationwide. Applicants must submit all of the following to the Admissions Office: a completed application; an official copy of all undergraduate transcripts; an official GMAT score report; a one-page personal statement; two letters of recommendation from professors (or employers for applicants who have been out of school for a substantial period); and a current resume. International students must provide, in addition to the above, an official TOEFL score report (minimum score: 170 computer-based test, 550 paper-and-pencil test). All candidates must be proficient in computer and quantitative skills prior to the commencement of their MBA work.

FINANCIAL FACTS

Annual tuition	$25,000
Cost of books	$1,000
Room & board	
(on/off-campus)	$9,620/$12,000
Average award package	$11,569
Average grant	$3,314
Average student loan debt	$33,139

ADMISSIONS

Admissions Selectivity Rating	92
# of applications received	264
% applicants accepted	91
% acceptees attending	90
Average GMAT	548
Range of GMAT	500–700
Average GPA	3.3
TOEFL required of	
international students	Yes
Minimum TOEFL	
(paper/computer)	530/170
Application fee	$50
Regular application deadline	5/31
Regular notification	Rolling
Deferment available	Yes
Maximum length of	
deferment	case by case
Transfer students accepted	Yes
Transfer application policy	
Up to 6 credits are accepted from an AACSB-accredited MBA program.	
Non-fall admissions	Yes
Need-blind admissions	Yes

Applicants Also Look At
Bellarmine University, Indiana University Southeast.

UNIVERSITY OF MARYLAND—COLLEGE PARK

ROBERT H. SMITH SCHOOL OF BUSINESS

Academics

The Robert H. Smith School of Business at the University of Maryland—College Park places "an extraordinary emphasis on technology in business," refocusing traditional disciplines such as finance, management, and marketing on the emerging world of e-business. Thanks to the largesse of the school's namesake—an area real estate developer who recently donated $30 million to the university—the Smith School has the resources necessary to maintain and develop the state-of-the-art facilities its curriculum requires.

Smith MBAs commence their work with a core curriculum that "is very comprehensive and prepares students well with a solid foundation." Students report that "it is fast-paced and challenging, but the professors make sure the students keep pace." To ensure that students can tailor their MBAs to the areas that interest them most, Smith sets aside "a huge portion of degree requirements for elective courses." Electives can be used to fashion an area of specialization in one of 18 disciplines; students are especially enthusiastic about Smith's offerings in entrepreneurship and information technology. A general management degree without specialization is also an option here. In addition to the traditional curriculum, MBAs may also pursue Experiential Learning Modules (ELMs), such as case competitions, which "provide a great opportunity to continue learning and applying it outside of the classroom."

Smith professors, students agree, "are great. They are genuinely interested in our progress. Very approachable and down-to-earth, too." Observes one student, "Subjects I hated in my undergraduate university—economics and statistics, for example—I enjoy taking at Smith just because of the professors who teach them."

Career and Placement

Smith's Office of Career Management (OCM) offers MBA students the full complement of career-related services, including a number of high-tech interviewing and job-search facilities. They also tell us that OCM "brings a good number of companies to campus, although more would certainly be better." International students would love to see "at least one officer devoted exclusively to helping [us] find jobs." These students will be happy to hear that in April 2005 the school retained a leading immigration law firm, McCandlish Holton PC, to help recruiters hire international students.

Employers most likely to hire Smith MBAs include: Avaya; Citigroup; Constellation Power Source; Deloitte Touche Tohmatsu; Delta; Fannie Mae; IBM; Intel; Johnson & Johnson; Navigant; PepsiCo; PricewaterhouseCoopers; UBS; Wachovia; and World Bank.

Student Life and Environment

Life at Smith is hectic, as "the pressure of the MBA is always looming overhead, with generally two case studies, one to two tests per week, and exams around the corner." Even so, "people still find time to enjoy themselves and hang around with friends." There's "Happy Hour every Thursday, sports clubs for those who like to play intramurals, and cultural clubs (Black, Hispanic, Indian, Asian, Chinese, International, and Jewish) that are very active within the school organizing dinners and fund raising." Students also like to "hit the DC club and bar scene on weekends, and any night of the week you can usually find someone who's willing to join you for a few beers at a local watering hole." One student observes, "There are enough activities inside and outside of the classroom to keep anyone occupied. Formals, tailgates, sporting events, speakers, forums, career development—you name it, we have it." Maryland's part-time students

LeAnne Dagnall, Associate Director, MBA and MS Admissions
2308 Van Munching Hall, University of Maryland College, Park, MD 20742-1871 U.S.
Phone: 301-405-2278 • Fax: 301-314-9862
E-mail: mba_info@rhsmith.umd.edu • Website: www.rhsmith.umd.edu

are, of course, much less intimately integrated into extracurricular life. These students, who attend on evenings and weekends, generally spend the minimum amount of time necessary on campus.

Smith MBAs include "a large number of international students" and "a diverse blend of backgrounds, nationalities, ethnicities, and experience. Despite these differences, there is an amazingly strong team-oriented feeling here at Smith School." This "sense of community" is all the more amazing when you realize that "the student body is naturally fragmented by the fact that we live everywhere from Baltimore to Northern Virginia, not just in suburban Maryland and DC."

Admissions

All applicants to Smith MBA programs at College Park must submit the following to the School: two official copies of transcripts for all postsecondary academic work; an official GMAT score report; personal essays; two letters of recommendation; and a completed application form. Interviews are required for full-time applicants. International students must also provide an official TOEFL score report (minimum required score: 600 paper-based test, 250 computer-based test) and a financial certification form, with supporting documents. The school lists the following outreach programs for minority and disadvantaged students: Kaleidoscope: Advancing Diversity at Smith, a Fall semester recruitment event for underrepresented minority students; Women and the MBA, a symposium oriented to educating women about the advantages of the MBA; Management Leadership for Tomorrow: a partnership that focuses on guiding minority students through the MBA application preparation process; online chats for prospective MBA students from underrepresented groups (Africa, South America, Women, African American, and Hispanics); and participation at conferences of minority professional organizations, including the Society for Hispanic Professional Engineers, the Women's Information Network, Graduate Women in Business, the National Society for Black Engineers, and the Black MBA Association."

FINANCIAL FACTS

Annual tuition (in-state/ out-of-state)	$14,454/$23,814
Fees	$13,384

ADMISSIONS

Admissions Selectivity Rating	87
# of applications received	1,349
% applicants accepted	55
% acceptees attending	59
Average GMAT	619
Range of GMAT	570–660
Average GPA	3.35
TOEFL required of international students	Yes
Minimum TOEFL (paper/computer)	600/250
Application fee	$60
Regular application deadline	Rolling
Regular notification	Rolling
Application Deadline/Notification	
Round 1:	11/1 / 1/15
Round 2:	12/15 / 2/1
Round 3:	1/15 / 3/15
Round 4:	3/15 / 5/01
Early decision program	Yes
ED Deadline/Notification	11/1, 12/15 / 2/1
Need-blind admissions	Yes

Applicants Also Look At

Carnegie Mellon, The George Washington University, Georgetown University, Rochester Institute of Technology, The University of North Carolina at Chapel Hill, The University of Texas at Austin, University of Virginia.

EMPLOYMENT PROFILE				
Career Rating	90	**Grads Employed by Function**	**%**	**Avg. Salary**
Primary Source of Full-time Job Acceptances		Finance/Accounting	42	$81,670
School-facilitated activities	93 (79%)	Marketing/Sales	23	$79,286
Graduate-facilitated activities	24 (21%)	MIS	3	$78,666
Average base starting salary	$83,165	Operations/Production	4	$78,000
Percent employed	95	Consulting	18	$93,850
		General Management	10	$81,909
		Top 5 Employers Hiring Grads		
		IBM; Citigroup; W.R. Grace & Co. Black & Decker; Intel.		

UNIVERSITY OF MASSACHUSETTS—AMHERST
ISENBERG SCHOOL OF MANAGEMENT

Academics

Bargain hunters can't say enough about the full-time MBA program at UMass—Amherst's Isenberg School of Management. As a state school, UMass already charges relatively low tuition, but the deal gets even better here as "Tuition is waived for most students" as part of a graduate assistantship program. This program pays double dividends by allowing students "to work with professors on a regular basis and learn information that is not easily taught in a classroom setting. Many of the faculty [members] are engaged in great research projects that the assistants are able to take part and aid in."

UMass keeps its MBA program trim, and "The small class size certainly promotes camaraderie and special relationships among classmates. Everyone, especially the faculty, knows who we are and is generally very happy to help us out with anything," comments one student. The program accommodates a high degree of individualization through "a great system of double MBA majors, in which full-time MBAs are allowed to interact with other people with a variety of interests and take advantage of other academic resources." The school offers dual-degree programs in sports management, hospitality and tourism management, public policy and administration, and four different engineering fields (industrial, mechanical, civil, and environmental).

Isenberg's full-time program "is structured in such a way so that the cohort works together as a unit instead of pitting us against each other." The first year of the program is "very intense" while the second year is "flexible." Instruction is targeted at "practical application of concepts, not for memorization."

Career and Placement

Students report that the MBA Career Management Office at UMass "needs some improvements, but it was reorganized at the beginning of this school year. We now have a career person dedicated to the MBA students. The benefit of this is already being felt, and I expect it to continue to improve in the coming year or two," one student informs us. Currently, "Many venture capitalists visit campus and will hold seminars or lunch meetings for the students," but "Larger corporations are underrepresented in the area of recruiting." Some acknowledge that the program's size presents a potential stumbling block to improvement. One student explains, "While the small class sizes allow for the high personal attention, it's hard to get recruiters to come to campus. The small size also seems to work against the school in some of the ranking systems, which is unfortunate as the program has been outstanding so far."

Employers who most frequently hire UMass—Amherst MBAs include MassMutual Financial Group, United Technologies Corporation, PricewaterhouseCoopers, Carrier Corporation, Babson Capital, Baystate Medical Center, and Deloitte Touche Tohmatsu.

Student Life and Environment

The full-time program at Isenberg "is very busy," as it operates on a quarter system instead of semesters. "It seems that there are always papers, projects, or homework to do, but due to our numerous study groups the work is less formidable," says one student. MBAs "work very hard but find time to unwind as well. Some get to speaker presentations, some catch hockey games, some enjoy the bar scene." Students appreciate that "the first-year track program creates an instant community, providing a working and social environment that make the transition from work to school that much easier through the added resource of peers experiencing the same thing." The b-school facility "is well-equipped with breakout rooms for group work and study sessions." Students often "find themselves weaving in and out of several breakout rooms, finding answers and helping each other out. We may be divided into groups, but we still value others' help," one tells

CARI CAPENTER, DIRECTOR OF MBA ADMISSIONS
305 ISENBERG SCHOOL OF MANAGEMENT, UNIVERSITY OF MASSACHUSETTS, AMHERST, MA 01003 U.S.
PHONE: 413-545-5608 • FAX: 413-577-2234
E-MAIL: GRADPROG@SOM.UMASS.EDU • WEBSITE: WWW.ISENBERG.UMASS.EDU/MBA

us. The program hosts "a fair number of clubs, such as the Graduate Business Association, the Graduate Student Senate, Women in Business, Net Impact, etc. that are active and putting on events monthly. There are many ways for people to be involved if they want to be."

UMass is "a large university within a small town" with "good sporting events, interesting restaurants, and big cities not too far" away. Hartford is about an hour's drive to the south; Boston and New York City are both close enough for day trips. The town of Amherst "is very liberal," and much of the surrounding area "is very gay-friendly." The town has "a few good places for night activities." Northampton, for example, which is "the next town over, has even more locations for nightlife and is only a free short bus ride for anyone without a car."

Admissions

Applicants to the full-time MBA program at the Isenberg School must submit all of the following materials to the Admissions Department: a completed application form; a personal statement; an official GMAT score report; two official copies of transcripts of all undergraduate and graduate institutions attended at which at least six credits were completed; two letters of recommendation; and a current resume. International applicants whose first language is not English must submit an official TOEFL score report (minimum score: 600, paper-based test; 250, computer-based test). The Admissions Department reports that it seeks students with "demonstrated academic ability, personal drive, self-confidence and enthusiasm, potential to thrive in a small personal program, and 2 to 4 years of professional work experience." To attract underrepresented demographics, the school offers "a mentoring program for diverse graduate students, participation in the National Black MBA and National Society of Hispanic MBA conferences," and "coordination with university ALANA and GLBT representatives to continually promote and improve our program."

Prominent Alumni
Eugene M. Isenberg, chairman and CEO, Nabors Industries, Ltd.; Michael G. Philipp, chairman, Credit Suisse Inc.; Nancy S. Loewe, CFO, GE Industrial Consumer and Industrial Division; Jeffrey C. Taylor, founder, monster.com, founder and CEO, aeons.com; Vivek Paul, partner, Texas Pacific Group Ventures.

FINANCIAL FACTS
Annual tuition (in-state/out-of-state)	$2,640/$9,937
Fees (in-state/out-of-state)	$7,242/$8,969
Cost of books	$2,000
Room & board (on/off-campus)	$7,050/$8,500
% of students receiving aid	74
% of first-year students receiving aid	56
% of students receiving loans	48
% of students receiving grants	1
Average award package	$25,951
Average grant	$25,951

ADMISSIONS
Admissions Selectivity Rating	97
# of applications received	247
% applicants accepted	22
% acceptees attending	63
Average GMAT	648
Range of GMAT	610–690
Average GPA	3.44
TOEFL required of international students	Yes
Minimum TOEFL (paper/computer)	600/250
Application fee	$40
International application fee	$65
Regular application deadline	2/1
Deferment available	Yes
Maximum length of deferment	1 year
Need-blind admissions	Yes

Applicants Also Look At
Boston College, Boston University, Northwestern University, Pennsylvania State University, University of Connecticut, The University of North Carolina at Chapel Hill.

EMPLOYMENT PROFILE
Career Rating	85	Grads Employed by Function	%	Avg. Salary
Primary Source of Full-time Job Acceptances		Finance/Accounting	42	$87,000
School-facilitated activities	2 (10%)	Marketing/Sales	5	$69,000
Graduate-facilitated activities	15 (80%)	Consulting	5	$80,000
Unknown	2 (10%)	General Management	26	$78,500
Percent employed	95	Other	21	$62,500

UNIVERSITY OF MASSACHUSETTS—BOSTON
GRADUATE COLLEGE OF MANAGEMENT

GENERAL INFORMATION
Type of school	Public
Environment	Metropolis
Academic calendar	Semesters

SURVEY SAYS . . .
Cutting-edge classes
Solid preparation in:
Teamwork
Communication/interpersonal skills
Presentation skills

STUDENTS
Enrollment of parent institution	12,000
Enrollment of business school	274
% male/female	48/52
% out-of-state	30
% part-time	65
% minorities	10
% international	27
Average age at entry	29
Average years work experience at entry	6

ACADEMICS
Academic Experience Rating	**87**
Student/faculty ratio	13:1
Profs interesting rating	86
Profs accessible rating	88
% female faculty	35
% minority faculty	38

Prominent Alumni
Thomas M. Menino, Mayor, Boston; Joseph Abboud, fashion designer; James Kantelis, CEO, Sprague Energy Corporation; Mark Atkins, CEO, Invention Machine; Joseph P. Kennedy, U.S. Congressman.

Academics

"Bang for the buck" is hardly the only reason for choosing the MBA program at UMass—Boston, but it's such a huge perk that few students can resist citing it as one of their primary motivations for attending. Many chose this program over more prestigious but also more expensive private school alternatives. One MBA tells us he is getting an "education similar to programs [that cost] two to three times more money." Students don't have to sacrifice quality to get value here, since "we can tap into the best educational resources in the world with professors from BC, BU, Northeastern, Harvard, and all the other schools in the Boston area."

Students report that UMass—Boston boasts "strong" human resources and information technology concentrations as well as "a strong accounting program with lots of accounting firms who recruit here." The school also offers "a tremendous international program focusing on leadership, integrity, and diplomacy." Throughout the program the quality of instruction is "very high"; professors are "accessible, helpful, and challenge their students." "All are knowledgeable," and although "A few do not have the gift of teaching," most are generous with their time outside of class and are available by e-mail just about any time."

UMass—Boston offers both a full-time and part-time MBA. Students rave that they have found "the most convenient part-time program and the best value in Boston." "Flexible class schedules" are enhanced by "sympathy for, empathy with, and accommodations made for [students'] full-time employment status by faculty and administration." They also point out that "being in downtown Boston and convenient to public transportation makes this an excellent environment." Students of all types appreciate how the low cost "yields a diverse group" of "highly qualified" students, "many of whom have undergraduate degrees from universities with competing business schools." On the downside, "The campus and facilities are outdated," meaning that "the physical plant is in desperate need of an overhaul."

Career and Placement

Students tell us that "the administration is extremely helpful and offers a lot of extra networking events throughout the year with area employers" at UMass—Boston. Students in finance are especially well served, as the school is "networked in with leadership of the largest institutions in Boston's financial district." Students in other disciplines, on the other hand, sometimes feel that the school could "improve by building a strong network of alumni" and by "providing more placement opportunities after graduation." The College of Management Career Center serves both undergraduates and graduate students in business. The school offers graduate students placement services as well as advice on salary negotiation.

Employers most likely to hire UMass—Boston MBAs include: Bank of America, Fidelity Investments, Investor Bank and Trust, Raytheon, and State Street.

Student Life and Environment

UMass—Boston "is a commuter school" with "most of the campus life geared toward undergraduates," but there are opportunities for students (especially full-time students) to get involved outside of classes. There are the recently implemented "international celebrations," which are "great for cultural awareness and fun" along with numerous clubs (although many meetings are at 5:00 P.M., hardly ideal for working students). Still, "Life at UMass is fun. It is relaxed and so diverse that everyone fits in. The campus is located

WILLIAM KOEHLER, GRADUATE PROGRAM DIRECTOR
100 MORRISSEY BOULEVARD, MBA OFFICE, BOSTON, MA 02125-3393 UNITED STATES
PHONE: 617-287-7720 • FAX: 617-287-7725
E-MAIL: MBA@UMB.EDU • WEBSITE: WWW.MANAGEMENT.UMB.EDU

on Boston Harbor, so it is not unusual to see students studying outside by the harbor. There are lots of activities at the university covering almost all fields and interests."

Unfortunately, students refer to UMass—Boston's facilities as "problematic." "The classrooms are very outdated and uncomfortable" and "are not that clean" with furniture that "is very old and not well maintained." As one MBA here observes, "The facilities do not match the level of the professors. Hopefully over time this discrepancy will get smaller." Students tell us that the Graduate Center at Healey Library is an excellent resource.

Students here "all come from different ethnic and social backgrounds, and our work experience varies. But our goals are all the same: educational achievement and the desire to learn." One student explains, "Our Director of Admissions is very keen on bringing in a diverse background of students, from various professional and academic backgrounds. My class is not overloaded with one type of student." Most here "are full-time employees. But there are full-time students also. I like the diversity of my classes because my fellow students are from different countries, religions, cultures, backgrounds and have different work experience, so you learn a lot."

Admissions

Applicants to the University of Massachusetts—Boston MBA program must submit all of the following materials: a completed online application; official transcripts from all higher education institutions attended, undergraduate and graduate, whether you received a degree or not; official GMAT scores; three letters of recommendation from employers, professors or character references; and two essays as described in the university graduate admission packet, one describing why you chose UMass—Boston and a second describing your professional objectives and the role of an MBA in achieving them. The first (approximately one page in length) should describe why you have chosen to apply to UMass—Boston. International applicants must submit all of the above plus: bank statements (in English) showing $31,034 in available cash; a letter of support if another party is providing your funds, a Declaration and Certification of Finances (DCF) form, and official TOEFL scores.

FINANCIAL FACTS

Annual tuition (in-state/ out-of-state)	$2,590/$9,758
Fees (in-state/ out-of-state)	$6,322/$9,011
Cost of books	$1,000
Room & board (off-campus)	$10,000
% of students receiving aid	45
% of first-year students receiving aid	40
% of students receiving loans	62
% of students receiving grants	22
Average grant	$14,000
Average student loan debt	$19,500

ADMISSIONS

Admissions Selectivity Rating	86
# of applications received	263
% applicants accepted	44
% acceptees attending	66
Average GMAT	570
Range of GMAT	520–640
Average GPA	3.31
TOEFL required of international students	Yes
Minimum TOEFL (paper/computer)	600/250
Application fee	$40
International application fee	$60
Regular application deadline	6/1
Regular notification	7/1
Application Deadline/Notification	
Round 1:	3/1 / 3/15
Round 2:	6/1 / 7/1
Deferment available	Yes
Maximum length of deferment	1 semester
Transfer students accepted	Yes
Transfer application policy Same applicant procedure. Transfer credits and waivers will be considered.	
Non-fall admissions	Yes
Need-blind admissions	Yes

Applicants Also Look At

Babson College, Bentley College, Boston College, Boston University, Northeastern University, Suffolk University, University of Massachusetts Amherst.

EMPLOYMENT PROFILE

Career Rating	85	**Top 4 Employers Hiring Grads**
Primary Source of Full-time Job Acceptances		State Street; Bank of America; Gillette (P&G);
Average base starting salary	$71,000	Investors Bank and Trust.

UNIVERSITY OF MASSACHUSETTS—DARTMOUTH
CHARLTON COLLEGE OF BUSINESS

GENERAL INFORMATION

Type of school	Public
Environment	Town
Academic calendar	Sept.–May

SURVEY SAYS . . .

Students love North Dartmouth, MA
Helpful alumni
Happy students
Smart classrooms
Solid preparation in:
Accounting
Presentation skills

STUDENTS

Enrollment of	
business school	250
% male/female	50/50
Average age at entry	26
Average years work	
experience at entry	6

ACADEMICS

Academic Experience Rating	**61**
Profs interesting rating	72
Profs accessible rating	62
% female faculty	10
% minority faculty	16

Joint Degrees

JD/MBA (in conjunction with
Southern New England School
of Law).

Academics

The AACSB-accredited MBA program at the University of Massachusetts—Dartmouth is "building its reputation, giving students a great deal of pride in feeling that they are part of something that will be much bigger in the future." For the present, UMass Dartmouth excels at providing its mix of local part-timers and international full-timers a convenient MBA program that can be completed in as little as one year or as many as five years.

All students here must complete a eight-course sequence of core requirements that cover fundamental concepts in accounting, information technology, finance, organization, operations, strategy, and marketing. Four electives are also required; students completing all three electives in a single "concentration stream" may earn an MBA with a concentration. Concentrations are available in accounting, business information, e-commerce, finance, international business, management, marketing, and operations. Students without concentrations graduate with a general MBA.

Entering students who have not satisfactorily completed undergraduate classes in business may be required to complete up to three foundation courses prior to enrolling in any of the 12 courses credited toward the MBA. Completion of an equivalent undergraduate course with a grade of at least a B typically qualifies students to skip a foundation course. Students with undergraduate degrees in business are generally exempt from foundation requirements.

UMass Dartmouth MBA students praise their program's "fine academic facilities and equipment" as well as the school's "favorable student-professor ratio." Administrators and professors are "very helpful and nice" and have a way of "making everything easier to understand." The net result of these positive factors is a "satisfying academic experience."

Career and Placement

The Career Resource Center at UMass Dartmouth serves all students and alumni of the university. The center provides counseling services, job postings, access to job search engines, and workshops in interviewing, resume writing, and career search. The CRC also maintains the Alumni Career Network and organizes on-campus recruiting events. MBA students receive additional career counseling from the MBA program coordinator. The majority of UMass Dartmouth MBAs attend while working full-time; the primary goal of many is to advance at their current place of employment rather than to find a new career. Thus, many MBAs here do not utilize the university's Career Services.

Student Life and Environment

Part-time students constitute the majority in UMass Dartmouth's MBA program, and they are drawn almost exclusively from the surrounding area. These "motivated, interesting and intelligent individuals" include a number of students who are "relatively older, with years of experience in the professional world. Many of them bring their experiences to bear in our classroom discussions." The school also hosts a number of full-timers, many of them "international students with different backgrounds, most of whom are younger than 30." Their ranks include "lots of scholarship students from Germany." MBAs from both populations bond well. As one explains, "I have found my fellow students to be team-oriented and I have made lasting friendships. We have formed informal study groups and we have helped each other through difficult class times."

All classes at UMass Dartmouth are offered in the evenings in order to accommodate students with jobs. Many part-timers juggle family and career responsibilities with work and accordingly spend as little time on campus as possible. "Generally, because the school is

NANCY LUDWIN, MBA COORDINATOR
285 OLD WESTPORT ROAD, NORTH DARTMOUTH, MA 02747-2300 UNITED STATES
PHONE: 508-999-8543 • FAX: 508-999-8776
E-MAIL: GRADUATE@UMASSD.EDU • WEBSITE: WWW.UMASSD.EDU/CHARLTON

oriented toward commuter students and people who take night classes, there really is no campus life for MBA students per se," explains one part-time student. Full-timers socialize more often; they "come together before and after class and perform some teamwork and long discussions. Outside the classroom, there are many social activities, from karate courses to chess, from sport activities to art. It is easy to find many things (to do)."

The main UMass Dartmouth campus is located in the southeast corner of the state, about one hour's drive from Boston and about a half hour away from Providence, Rhode Island. Wholesale trade helps fuel the local economy, as do fishing, cranberry farming, retail, and the remnants of the region's once-robust manufacturing industry.

Admissions

UMass Dartmouth considers all of the following in evaluating candidates for its MBA program: previous undergraduate and graduate academic record; GMAT scores or scores on an equivalent test; two letters of recommendation (one from a faculty member and one from an employer preferred); a personal statement of 200 to 300 words describing one's academic and career goals; and employment experience. TOEFL scores are required of all international applicants whose first language is not English. UMass Dartmouth offers certificate programs that, for some, provide a backdoor entry to the MBA program. One such student writes, "I came here because they offer certificate programs. I entered a certificate program first, then applied again to be a formal MBA student."

Students already in possession of a master's degree may apply for a post-master's certificate. Students complete five classes in one of the following: e-commerce, finance, general management, leadership, marketing, or supply chain management.

FINANCIAL FACTS

Annual tuition (in-state/ out-of-state)	$9,173/$17,536

ADMISSIONS

Admissions Selectivity Rating	**60***
Average GMAT	540
Average GPA	3.4
TOEFL required of international students	Yes
Application fee (in-state/ out-of-state)	$35/$55
Regular application deadline	Rolling
Regular notification	Rolling
Deferment available	Yes
Maximum length of deferment	1 semester
Need-blind admissions	Yes

UNIVERSITY OF MASSACHUSETTS—LOWELL
COLLEGE OF MANAGEMENT

Academics

Cost and convenience are the reasons students most often cite for choosing the MBA program at the University of Massachusetts—Lowell (UML) College of Management. They also have faith in its quality. As one student declares, "I know I will feel confident and proud to receive my MBA/IT from UML." Lowell MBAs may attend the program full-time; most, however, attend part-time. Distance-learning options are available for nearly all classes offered here. Classes meet after 6:00 P.M. on weekdays.

The UML MBA commences with 12 hours of foundation courses in subjects traditionally covered in undergraduate business programs. Students who have completed equivalent undergraduate classes within the last 5 years and have earned at least a B may receive a waiver for some or all of these courses; alternately, students may attempt to place out of these classes through written exams. The curriculum also includes seven core courses in accounting, finance, analysis of customers and markets, MIS, operations, managing organization design and change, and strategy. The program concludes with three electives, which students may use to develop a concentration in accounting, finance, or information technology. They may also take an MBA in general business. Students speak highly of the IT offerings here, telling us that "if you're interested in business in a technology- or engineering-based company, UMass—Lowell is perfect."

UML professors "are firm but fair, available, and they have real-world experience." Just understand that "the curriculum is not easy." One MBA observes, "Some professors are much more in tune with current events and practices than others. The ones who can make their topics relevant to current topics tend to have the most stimulating classes. I have been able to use much of what I've learned already and apply it to my company, and it's paid off in a big way in some cases. If I left today without the degree, I can tell you that what I've learned has already had a positive impact in my professional life." Students appreciate that "most of the professors and the curriculum are practical for people who work full-time and also have families."

Career and Placement

The UML Career Services Office provides counseling and placement services to all undergraduates, graduates, and alumni of the university. The office organizes a variety of job fairs throughout the school year. It also provides practice interviews, counsels students on resume writing and job-search skills, schedules corporate information sessions on campus, and offers access to online job search engines such as MonsterTRAK. The office coordinates the efforts of the University Career Advisory Network, which is essentially an online community of alumni and current students.

Employers who most frequently hire UMass—Lowell MBAs include: Bank of America, Banknorth, Fidelity, Putnam Investments, Raytheon, Wyeth, Gillette (P&G), U.S. Air Force, U.S. Government, Dana Farber Cancer Institute, and CR Bard.

Student Life and Environment

UML MBAs largely fall into the category of "working professionals [who] take classes at night" who "have no idea (and don't care, frankly) what activities [are available] on campus." They're "just interested in taking classes, not joining clubs or spending time with other students." Those who do spend time on campus tell us that "the campus and student facilities are comfortable. A lot of effort has been made to make UML a nice place to be. Ten years ago it wasn't anything special, but now it is." One MBA adds, "The gym and coffee shop are excellent."

GARY M. MUCICA, DIRECTOR, GRADUATE MANAGEMENT PROGRAMS
ONE UNIVERSITY AVENUE, LOWELL, MA 01854-2881 UNITED STATES
PHONE: 978-934-2848 • FAX: 978-934-4017
E-MAIL: KATHLEEN_ROURKE@UML.EDU • WEBSITE: WWW.UML.EDU/MBA

Despite the upgrades to the university at large, some here feel that the MBA facilities are in need of a makeover. One student explains, "The school needs to improve facilities. A lot of the equipment is old and outdated, and classrooms are not set up for students to have a laptop at their desk (no electrical plugs)." They also warn that "the new online computer program for scheduling, fees, bills, etc. leaves a lot to be" desired. It's set up to be "self-service" but is simply "not easy to work with." Students who take online classes say UML "could improve by offering interactive audio and video," which would "remove the feeling of isolation you sometimes feel when taking online classes." One student tempers his comment by adding, "This is true with most universities today; but as an IT professional, I am sure it will change in the near future."

Plenty of MBAs here chose the business school because they "really enjoyed" their undergraduate experience here. Among the "working professionals" at UML are some who "are back in school after a long layoff." Overall, the "motivated, friendly, and engaging" folks are generally "a pleasure to interact with on an intellectual and personal basis." Most "are understanding of personal needs/issues when it comes to professional or family conflicts and are able to work around them when it comes to group projects."

Admissions

The MBA program at the University of Massachusetts—Lowell requires applicants to submit the following materials: an official transcript of undergraduate grades; an official GMAT score report; three letters of recommendation from "employment-related sources" demonstrating a minimum of 2 years of relevant work experience; a current resume; and a one-page essay describing academic and career objectives. Applicants must complete prerequisite courses in microeconomics and statistics prior to entering the program. According to the school's website, "An aptitude for management decision-making and demonstrated academic ability are the most important qualifications for admission." International students whose first language is not English must submit an official score report for the TOEFL; a minimum score of 550 on the paper-based exam is required. UMass—Lowell admits new students for both the fall and spring terms.

FINANCIAL FACTS

Annual tuition (in-state/ out-of-state)	$1,637/$6,425
Fees (in-state/ out-of-state)	$6,070/$9,050
Cost of books	$1,000
Room & board	$6,311
% of students receiving aid	10
% of first-year students receiving aid	10
% of students receiving loans	10

ADMISSIONS

Admissions Selectivity Rating	**83**
# of applications received	80
% applicants accepted	51
% acceptees attending	85
Average GMAT	540
Range of GMAT	480–610
Average GPA	3.29
TOEFL required of international students	Yes
Minimum TOEFL (paper/computer)	600/250
Application fee	$20
International application fee	$35
Regular application deadline	Rolling
Regular notification	Rolling
Deferment available	Yes
Maximum length of deferment	1 year
Transfer students accepted	Yes
Transfer application policy	
Must be from an AACSB-accredited program; maximum of 12 tranfer credits.	
Non-fall admissions	Yes
Need-blind admissions	Yes

Applicants Also Look At

Bentley College, Boston College, Boston University, Northeastern University, Suffolk University, University of Massachusetts Amherst, University of Massachusetts Boston.

EMPLOYMENT PROFILE			
Career Rating	**61**		
Primary Source of Full-time Job Acceptances		**Grads Employed by Function**	**% Avg. Salary**
Percent employed	6	Finance/Accounting	21 NR
		Marketing/Sales	8 NR
		MIS	13 NR
		Operations/Production	28 NR
		General Management	10 NR
		Other	12 NR
		Nonprofit	8 NR

UNIVERSITY OF MEMPHIS
FOGELMAN COLLEGE OF BUSINESS AND ECONOMICS

Academics

Fogelman College of Business and Economics at the University of Memphis is a no-non-sense professional MBA program designed for working people "from all walks of business life" who are looking to further their careers but who don't have a lot of time or energy to waste. The school has a solid reputation among locally based businesses like FedEx. One student holds Memphis in such high regard that she has two degrees from there: "The University of Memphis is where I received my BBA in accounting. I liked my experience there, and I knew that an MBA from there would open many doors in the company that I work for."

Students say their "very knowledgeable" professors "present concepts completely" and help them relate the course material to practice. "Each of them has done extensive research in their field and [is] noted to be among the best in the country for their area of expertise." Another student says: "Every professor is interested in the development of each student into future managers and business leaders." The administration does not receive the same ringing endorsement, however. Some take issue with the allocation of funds in certain areas. One student was succinct and blunt: "Solid professors, good academic experience, but really bad administration that spends money" excessively.

Some students also have difficulty with course selection and enrollment; many required or desired classes are offered only once per semester under limited enrollment, and these courses "often conflict with each other." Since pretty much all of the courses take place in the evenings to accommodate the vast majority of students who have day jobs, there's very little leeway in terms of scheduling. But these night classes also give part-time and full-time students the opportunity to interact with each other through "small classes and heavy teamwork," something not found in a lot of MBA programs. "A lot of projects are team based, so you get to know classmates very well." One student takes away warm feelings about the camaraderie he felt at the school: "I have a new set of best friends. I never thought it was possible after reaching age 40."

In keeping with the no-frills approach to the program, however, the facilities tend toward the sparse side. Several students expressed disdain for the academic buildings and equipment and spoke of the need for "more technology in the classroom." One student said the classrooms "need better seating. The desks were made for 4th graders."

Career and Placement

Some students say the program needs better ties to "big industries" to provide those students seeking out new or nonlocal careers with better job prospects. Fortunately for the students looking to stay in the area (and there are many), "There are several excellent companies in the area, also, that recruit heavily," and since the student body is, as one student puts it, "not nearly as competitive as I expected," everyone is "very supportive" and happy to help each other land available positions. Another boon to the school's local reputation is the recently formed partnership with the Leadership Academy. The partnership, known as the Community Internship, gives MBA students the chance to team with Leadership Academy fellows on projects designed to benefit the community.

Student Life and Environment

The school is located in the midtown area of Memphis, which "is great for students because there are a lot of social establishments nearby" offering "a lot of things for students to do recreationally." Of course, there are the well-traveled destinations like Graceland (check out Elvis' gaudy yellow and black rec room), Sun Studios, and the famous Beale Street, with its string of live-music joints and soul food. And the National

GREGORY W. BOLLER, DIRECTOR OF MASTER'S PROGRAMS
GRADUATE SCHOOL ADMINISTRATION BUILDING, ROOM 216, MEMPHIS, TN 38152-3370 U.S.
PHONE: 901-678-2911 • FAX: 901-678-5023
E-MAIL: GRADSCH@MEMPHIS.EDU • WEBSITE: FCBE.MEMPHIS.EDU

Civil Rights Museum, located at the old Lorraine Motel where Martin Luther King, Jr., was shot to death in 1968, is a haunting must-see for tourists and locals alike. Overall, "The University of Memphis, like the city of Memphis, is greatly underrated," one student says.

Since "Most graduate students work and commute," little time is left for a social life outside of the classroom, but there's a foundation for friendship and networking among the "outgoing" and "friendly" individuals that attend Fogelman. Though some think "The school could put more effort into organized activities for students outside of class," the "busy" nature of the student body doesn't lend itself to much free time anyway, so complaints are few. Everyone is in agreement over the variety of backgrounds provided by their classmates: "The graduate population is very diverse, which makes things more interesting." "You have a great opportunity to meet people from various backgrounds (educational and ethnic)," another student says.

Admissions

Admittance to the professional MBA program at the Fogelman College of Business and Economics is not terribly selective, and the admissions requirements are fairly standard. Applicants to the school's professional MBA program must submit the following materials: a completed application (either online or via mail); an official copy of undergraduate transcripts from all colleges and universities attended (even if you did not graduate); a copy of your current resume; a statement of personal interest; a 1,000-word essay answering one of the acceptable questions provided on the school's admissions website; two letters of recommendation; and an official GMAT or GRE score report. Interviews and previous work experience are optional. In addition to the above documents, international students whose primary language is not English must also provide an official score report for the TOEFL (minimum score: 550, paper-based test; 213, computer-based test).

FINANCIAL FACTS

Annual tuition (in-state/ out-of-state)	$6,720/$17,372
Fees	$88
Cost of books	$10,000
Room & board	$6,000

ADMISSIONS

Admissions Selectivity Rating	78
# of applications received	113
% applicants accepted	62
% acceptees attending	100
Average GMAT	530
Range of GMAT	530–700
Average GPA	3.2
TOEFL required of international students	Yes
Minimum TOEFL (paper/computer)	550/213
Application fee	$35
International application fee	$60
Regular application deadline	7/1
Regular notification	Rolling
Deferment available	Yes
Maximum length of deferment	1 year
Non-fall admissions	Yes

EMPLOYMENT PROFILE	
Career Rating	72

UNIVERSITY OF MIAMI
SCHOOL OF BUSINESS ADMINISTRATION

GENERAL INFORMATION
Type of school	Private
Environment	Town
Academic calendar	Aug. to May

SURVEY SAYS . . .
Good social scene
Smart classrooms
Solid preparation in:
General management
Quantitative skills

STUDENTS
Enrollment of parent institution	15,670
Enrollment of business school	265
% male/female	64/36
% out-of-state	21
% part-time	1
% minorities	20
% international	28
Average age at entry	25
Average years work experience at entry	2

ACADEMICS
Academic Experience Rating	**82**
Student/faculty ratio	6:1
Profs interesting rating	95
Profs accessible rating	77
% female faculty	28
% minority faculty	19

Joint Degrees
JD/MBA 3.5 to 4.5 years.

Prominent Alumni
Raul H., president and COO, McDonald's Corporation; Matthew Evan Rubel, CEO, Payless Shoe Source; Jack Creighton, Jr., strategic director, Madrona Venture Group; Martin E. Zweig, president and chair, Zweig-DiMenna.

Academics

A rigorous MBA program with a strong international focus, the University of Miami School of Business Administration prides itself on attracting a diverse and multinational faculty and student body, and on offering challenging and relevant course work for today's global professional. For students who did not study business as an undergraduate, the school offers a full-time, two-year, 48-credit program, which must be completed over the course of two years. Those with an undergraduate business degree within the last five years may apply for the accelerated one-year program, which requires the completion of 32 credits over the course of two semesters. Each of these programs is targeted individuals who want to advance their career. Since there are no summer courses in either program, students are encouraged to do an internship.

Both the one-year and two-year programs boast a lockstep curriculum, in which the entire entering class moves through required course work in unison. As a result, students form strong professional, scholarly, and social relationships with their classmates. On this campus, a third of students hail from outside the United States and comprise "a wide range of ages," so these relationships form an integral part of the learning experience at the University of Miami. A current student enthuses, "fellow classmates interest me, challenge me, and contribute to a productive class/team environment." With a "small student to teacher ratio," the environment is truly collaborative and "people work together on every aspect of education and life."

Elective classes are available to students in both programs. While students say the program is excellent, some feel it could be improved by becoming "much more challenging" and incorporating a heavier workload. Students in the two-year program may choose to focus their electives to receive a concentration in accounting, computer information systems, finance, international business, management, management science, or marketing. In general, students have high praises for University of Miami professors, especially for those in their area of concentration. One student reports, "The professors in my chosen concentration of management science are outstanding and have prepared me very well for my career post-graduation. The school has afforded me opportunities within management science that are not available elsewhere and has helped me to pursue different career paths."

Career and Placement

The Ziff Graduate Career Service Center at the University of Miami is available to graduate business students only and offers career advising, online and on-campus recruiting, a career library, and periodic workshops on resume writing and job search strategy. Boasting the sixth largest alumni network in the world, University of Miami students have access to a large, international employment base. As the program is targeted toward younger students who graduated from college within the past five years, "work experience is, for all practical purposes, nonexistent" within the business school student body. Therefore, the career office tends to focus their efforts on placing recent grads in entry-level management positions. Students report that, "on-campus recruiting is sufficient for students with no real work experience," while more advanced professional positions are harder to come by.

DANIELA M. VINALS, ASSOCIATE DIRECTOR
PO BOX 248505, CORAL GABLES, FL 33124-6524 UNITED STATES
PHONE: 305-284-4607 • FAX: 305-284-1878
E-MAIL: MBA@MIAMI.EDU • WEBSITE: WWW.BUS.MIAMI.EDU/GRAD

Student Life and Environment

For a business student, you couldn't ask for a more comfortable lifestyle and environment than at the University of Miami. With a "perfect location" on the university's Coral Gables campus, the business school is housed in an "absolutely beautiful" $24-million facility, in which, "Each classroom has big, comfy leather executive chairs for the students and great computers for the professor." There is even "a lounge for graduate business students that has free coffee and bagels every morning."

The campus vibe is highly social, as "most everyone moved to Miami from different states/cities, and it was very easy to make new friends who will last a lifetime." On top of that, "There is a great student run organization, Graduate Business Student Association, that arranges and sponsors many events. It is easy to meet new people and make many friends." For those who like to get involved, "There are clubs for every concentration plus a few others. A lot of the students form intramural teams for flag football, soccer, and softball." Students are quick to mention that "The football team is a big deal here and everyone goes to the games together, and the business school always has a tailgate before the games." Situated in Miami, the party capital of the Southeast, "there is a very active social life both on and off campus," as students further enjoy world-class cultural and recreational opportunities—not to mention, perfect weather—in their immediate vicinity.

Admissions

To apply to the MBA program, students must submit a completed application, official transcripts from any undergraduate and postgraduate course work, a current resume, one letter of recommendation, official GMAT score reports, and TOEFL test scores for non-native speakers of English. Students are evaluated on the strength of all application materials. Students wishing to enter the two-year program do not need to have undergraduate business degrees. However, those wishing to enter the accelerated one-year program must have an undergraduate business degree within the last five years from an accredited university. Admissions decisions are made on a rolling basis until the class is full, though students are encouraged to apply at least three months before the beginning of the term. Students who wish to be considered for scholarships, fellowships, or graduate assistantship are advised to apply early, as they are available for fall applicants only.

FINANCIAL FACTS

Annual tuition	$30,720
Fees	$194
Cost of books	$1,080
Room & board (off-campus)	$9,278
% of students receiving aid	59
% of first-year students receiving aid	64
% of students receiving loans	37
% of students receiving grants	42
Average award package	$29,353
Average grant	$17,322
Average student loan debt	$52,124

ADMISSIONS

Admissions Selectivity Rating	78
# of applications received	393
% applicants accepted	68
% acceptees attending	42
Average GMAT	600
Range of GMAT	560–633
Average GPA	3.18
TOEFL required of international students	Yes
Minimum TOEFL (paper/computer)	550/213
Application fee	$50
Regular application deadline	Rolling
Regular notification	Rolling
Deferment available	Yes
Maximum length of deferment	1 year
Non-fall admissions	Yes
Need-blind admissions	Yes

EMPLOYMENT PROFILE

Career Rating	64	Grads Employed by Function	%	Avg. Salary
Primary Source of Full-time Job Acceptances		Finance/Accounting	29	$64,888
School-facilitated activities	43 (59%)	Marketing/Sales	12	$56,833
Graduate-facilitated activities	28 (38%)	MIS	2	$64,238
Unknown	2 (3%)	Operations/Production	6	$66,667
Average base starting salary	$65,519	Consulting	1	$62,000
Percent employed	34	General Management	8	$71,563

Top 5 Employers Hiring Grads
Lennar Corporation; Norwegian Cruise Line; DHL; Capital One; Gabelli Asset Management.

UNIVERSITY OF MICHIGAN—ANN ARBOR
STEPHEN M. ROSS SCHOOL OF BUSINESS

GENERAL INFORMATION

Type of school	Public
Environment	City
Academic calendar	Semester

SURVEY SAYS . . .
Good social scene
Good peer network
Cutting-edge classes
Happy students
Solid preparation in:
General management
Teamwork
Doing business in a global economy

STUDENTS

Enrollment of parent institution	39,533
Enrollment of business school	609
% male/female	70/30
% out-of-state	92
% part-time	31
% minorities	11
% international	35
Average age at entry	29
Average years work experience at entry	5

ACADEMICS

Academic Experience Rating	**96**
Student/faculty ratio	15:1
Profs interesting rating	85
Profs accessible rating	98
% female faculty	26
% minority faculty	26

Joint Degrees
For a list of all joint degree programs please visit www.bus.umich.edu/Academics/Mb aProgram/JointDegreesMba.htm.

Prominent Alumni
John M. Devine, vice chair and CFO, General Motors Corporation; Mary Kay Haben, group vice president, Kraft North America, president, Kraft Cheese; John W. Madigan, chair and CEO, Tribune Company; Stephen W. Sanger, chair and CEO, General Mills.

Academics

After the 2004 $100 million donation from Stephen M. Ross—the largest gift ever bestowed upon any U.S. business school—the school has been witness to an exponential increase in both construction and curriculum, including a new $145 million facility and a revised MBA curriculum whose benefits include carefully sequenced core courses, more electives, and the opportunity to focus on specific areas of interest prior to internship interviews. Most students agree that the program "ranks high in everything," but note that it is "extremely strong in corporate strategy, entrepreneurial studies, management accounting, marketing, organizational behavior, nonprofit organizations, social venturing, and venture capital/private equity/entrepreneurial finance."

Much of the program's strength comes from the "great professors who respond to the individual classes' needs and interests." Students appreciate that the "helpful and challenging" faculty "push you to think," adding that "classes are a great mix of lecture and performance." Because the business school does not require students to specialize, MBAs "have a lot of flexibility in the second-year schedule to focus on the classes [they] want." Just keep in mind the rigorous core curriculum must be completed before students can take on the multitude of electives the school has on offer. (Some of these courses are so "popular" that the administration works "with the professor to expand the number of sections they teach in order to give the most opportunity to people to take the class.)

MBAs add that the workload is fairly heavy, but "That's what we're paying for." One student explains, "We take five classes per semester, and each class usually meets twice a week for 1 and a half hours at a time. For every 1-and-a-half-hour class, there's probably about that much preparation time that is put in outside of class." As a major research institution, Michigan gives its MBAs access to world-class research facilities. And don't forget about the "breadth and depth" of the "second-to-none" opportunities offered, such as "dual degrees, academic programs, International Multidisciplinary Action Projects, and [access to] institutes such as The William Davidson Institute for International Studies and the Zell Lurie Institute for Entrepreneurial Studies."

On the aesthetic front, many note that "classrooms need to be upgraded" and that "facilities could be improved." The good news in this is that the school's administration "is driven to improve the school" and has "a strategic plan for the school." And that $100 million mentioned earlier has come a long way to make these students' hopes for the campus become a foreseeable reality.

Career and Placement

The university is home to a "powerful and active alumni movement," meaning that MBA graduates have exceptional access to career opportunities; "Alums seem to go out of their way to help you." U of M's Student Career Services Office at the Ross School of Business, serves both undergraduates and graduate students, and reports that an impressive 90.6 percent of recent MBA graduates received their first job offer within 3 months of graduating.

Top employers of Michigan MBAs include Citigroup, Booz Allen Hamilton, Dell, McKinsey & Company, American Express Company, JPMorgan Chase, A.T. Kearney, Eli Lilly and Company, Bain & Company, Ford Motor Company, Medtronic, 3M, Cummins, General Mills, Guidant Corporation, Intel, Kraft Foods, Lehman Brothers, Microsoft, National City Corporation, and SC Johnson.

James P. Hayes, Director of Admissions
701 Tappan Street, Ann Arbor, MI 48109-1234 United States
Phone: 734-763-5796 • Fax: 734-763-7804
E-mail: rossmba@umich.edu • Website: www.bus.umich.edu

Student Life and Environment

"If you like college towns, you will love Ann Arbor," students at U of M agree. In addition, on campus you'll find the "friendliest group of people I've ever met," says one student. "This is my new extended family." And this family has no shortage of social opportunities. "There's happy hour every Thursday, tailgates every Football Saturday, and numerous club parties in between," explains one student. "You can't beat Michigan football, hockey, and basketball." With "jazz [clubs], dance clubs, and restaurants" in the city, students find a "heck of a lot of fun" everywhere they go. Some even venture to Detroit. But beware the winter months, warn students: "The weather is cold . . . and students do spend too much time studying because there's not much else to do when it's 15 degrees out."

The MBA program offers "abundant opportunities to get involved, from professional to social clubs, newspaper, admissions, and career counseling. There's even a wine-tasting club." One student mentions that "without the energy the other students provide, many of the clubs/activities would not happen and our experience here would not be as rich." And students work together here to find a "good work-life balance." "We work quite hard, but on Thursday evenings, practically all MBAs flock to the b-school happy-hour bar, Mitch's," says one. "No weekend goes by without lots of prep for class, several group meetings, and at least one party or social/fun activity." The program also "provides lots of opportunities for spouses to get together. It also has joint programs with other schools in the university, which provide meaningful activities."

Admissions

Applications to the University of Michigan MBA program must include undergraduate transcripts, GMAT test scores (on average, successful applicants score 700), TOEFL test scores (for international students), letters of recommendation, a personal statement, and a resume. The school also looks at an applicant's record of success, clarity of goals, and management and leadership potential. The program does require previous work experience and, though not required, interviews are "highly recommended." There are many minority recruitment efforts, such as the Consortium for Graduate Study in Management, Robert F. Toigo Fellowships in Finance, National Society of Hispanic MBA Conference, National Black MBA Conference, and many more.

FINANCIAL FACTS

Annual tuition (in-state/ out-of-state)	$33,800/$38,800
Fees	$189
Cost of books	$7,730
Room & board	$9,752
% of students receiving aid	75
% of first-year students receiving aid	75
% of students receiving loans	47
% of students receiving grants	48
Average award package	$56,655
Average grant	$11,044
Average student loan debt	$61,600

ADMISSIONS

Admissions Selectivity Rating	96
# of applications received	2,067
% applicants accepted	32
% acceptees attending	63
Average GMAT	690
Range of GMAT	640–740
Average GPA	3.3
TOEFL required of international students	Yes
Minimum TOEFL (paper/computer)	600/250
Application fee	$180
Regular application deadline	11/4
Regular notification	1/5
Application Deadline/Notification	
Round 1:	11/1 / 1/15
Round 2:	1/7 / 3/15
Round 3:	3/1 / 5/15
Deferment available	Yes
Maximum length of deferment	1 year
Transfer students accepted	Yes
Transfer application policy	
Transfer applicants are welcome to apply, but no credits will transfer into our program.	
Need-blind admissions	Yes

Applicants Also Look At
Duke University, Northwestern University, The University of Chicago, University of Pennsylvania.

EMPLOYMENT PROFILE

Career Rating	98	Grads Employed by Function	%	Avg. Salary
Primary Source of Full-time Job Acceptances		Finance/Accounting	34	$90,850
School-facilitated activities	244 (68%)	Marketing/Sales	24	$85,378
Graduate-facilitated activities	110 (31%)	Operations/Production	3	$90,000
Unknown	4 (1%)	Strategic Planning	3	$84,679
		Consulting	22	$104,267
		General Management	6	$90,059
		Other	8	$84,810

Top 5 Employers Hiring Grads
Citigroup; Lehman Brothers; Deloitte Consulting; A.T. Kearney; Kraft Foods.

UNIVERSITY OF MICHIGAN—FLINT
SCHOOL OF MANAGEMENT

GENERAL INFORMATION
Type of school	Public
Environment	City
Academic calendar	Semesters

SURVEY SAYS . . .
Cutting-edge classes
Solid preparation in:
Communication/interpersonal skills
Presentation skills
Quantitative skills

STUDENTS
Enrollment of parent institution	6,527
Enrollment of business school	167
% part-time	100
Average age at entry	31
Average years work experience at entry	3

ACADEMICS
Academic Experience Rating	**78**
Student/faculty ratio	11:1
Profs interesting rating	82
Profs accessible rating	80
% female faculty	24
% minority faculty	19

Academics

Offering two programs designed with the needs of working students in mind, the University of Michigan—Flint satisfies MBAs with a winning combination of convenience, "excellent professors," and the "name recognition" that comes with a University of Michigan degree. Prospective MBAs choose between a traditional evening MBA program, in which cohorts convene for weekly classes, and the *NetPlus!* a mixed mode MBA program, complemented by "weekend residencies every 6 weeks in order to receive some classroom interaction and perspective." One student writes, "The mixed media *NetPlus!* program available at the University of Michigan—Flint is unsurpassed by any other program. It offers the best of both worlds for my busy life." UM—Flint's traditional MBA is typically completed in 20–32 months; the *NetPlus!* program takes 15–24 months to complete.

No matter which program they choose, students will find a curriculum that "focuses on the importance of international business" while requiring "lots of projects and case studies." Each program commences with four foundation courses (waivers are available for those who have completed equivalent undergraduate or graduate courses, followed by eight core courses (three functional, four external environment/managerial support, and one capstone class), two general electives, or three concentration-specific electives. Flint offers six areas of concentration: accounting, health care management, lean manufacturing, international business, organizational leadership, and finance.

Professors here, we're told, "are exceptional. One cannot say enough about their knowledge in terms of course work and their real world application." In terms of workload, professors "are demanding but very understanding of working professionals. They pile the work on, but know when it's pushing to the limit. Grading is fair, an A is not automatic, but if solid work is put in you aren't beat up on minor things." The administration is "outstanding." One student reports, "Although I live over an hour from campus, I have never had a problem getting help from someone in the MBA office, with everything from financial aid to contacting a professor in an emergency."

Career and Placement

UM—Flint's Career Development Center focuses primarily on serving the school's undergraduate population. Limited services, including resume posting, online job boards, and counseling are available to Flint's MBAs, but few use them. Some here complain that the school "needs to develop contacts with recruiting companies and hold job fairs," but many simply don't care; they have jobs and see the MBA as a means to improve their current situation, not as a stepping stone to a new career.

D. NICOL TAYLOR-VARGO, MBA, MBA PROGRAM DIRECTOR
SCHOOL OF MANAGEMENT, UM—FLINT, 3180 WILLIAM S. WHITE BUIDLING, 303 EAST KEARSLEY
STREET, FLINT, MI 48502-1950 UNITED STATES
PHONE: 810-762-3163 • FAX: 810-237-6685
E-MAIL: UMFLINTMBA1@UMICH.EDU • WEBSITE: MBA.UMFLINT.EDU

FINANCIAL FACTS

Annual tuition	$9,036
Fees	$334
Cost of books	$270
Average award package	$15,472
Average grant	$2,273

ADMISSIONS

Admissions Selectivity Rating	**71**
# of applications received	72
% applicants accepted	85
% acceptees attending	87
Average GMAT	528
Range of GMAT	460–590
Average GPA	3.18
TOEFL required of international students	Yes
Minimum TOEFL (paper/computer)	550/213
Application fee	$55
Regular application deadline	Rolling
Regular notification	Rolling
Deferment available	Yes
Maximum length of deferment	1 year
Transfer students accepted	Yes
Transfer application policy	AACSB-accredited; B or better; grad level; 9 credit hours only; not part of any other degree program.
Non-fall admissions	Yes
Need-blind admissions	Yes

Student Life and Environment

For students attending all MBA classes on campus, "The life of the school is fast paced, requiring lots of classmates to work in teams to finish projects. The program focuses a lot of time on projects and case studies." Because "Most professors want a lot out of you," the pace here "can be kind of hectic." For the many students who work full-time and manage family obligations in addition to their graduate work, "Life at school is limited to what is required in the classroom."

Students in the *NetPlus!* program participate in "weekend residencies every 6 weeks to receive some classroom interaction and perspective." They tell us that "the residencies are great because they provide more interaction. The group studies and chances to work with a diverse group of people is a benefit." MBAs note that "the campus is beautiful," "safe, and brightly lit," but it is "located in the middle of downtown Flint," a "bad city." Some complain that "the campus is sort of spread out." Campus facilities earn high marks from all students.

Flint MBAs are "professional, ambitious, and intelligent," not to mention "friendly, helpful, and funny." Most "are working adults returning to school in order to learn management techniques because either they are new managers, or want to move up the corporate ladder." According to at least one international student, the student body can be a little "provincial." "Many students are from the counties surrounding Flint, and not many have international experience." Not only does this sometimes impede class discussion, but it also "can make it hard for a foreign student to make contacts with fellow students. They've lived in Michigan all their lives and have all their friends at arm's reach. They have little need and incentive to make more contacts other than in the study groups."

Admissions

All applicants to the School of Management at the University of Michigan—Flint must provide the school with official copies of all undergraduate and graduate transcripts, GMAT scores, TOEFL scores (international students), three letters of recommendation (preferably from employers and/or professors), a statement of purpose (in response to the question: "What are your career objectives and how will an MBA contribute to achieving those goals), and a resume. Work experience is preferred; the average student arrives with 3 years of professional experience. The school catalog notes that "admission decisions are guided by a desire to draw participants from diverse organizations and backgrounds, balancing class composition to ensure diverse, wide-ranging experiences and perspectives." An online application is available.

UNIVERSITY OF MISSISSIPPI
SCHOOL OF BUSINESS ADMINISTRATION

GENERAL INFORMATION

Type of school	Public
Environment	Village
Academic calendar	Semester

SURVEY SAYS . . .

Students love University, MS
Friendly students
Solid preparation in:
Quantitative skills

STUDENTS

Enrollment of parent institution	14,000
Enrollment of business school	59
% male/female	72/28
% out-of-state	37
% part-time	22
% international	6
Average age at entry	26
Average years work experience at entry	2

ACADEMICS

Academic Experience Rating	**69**
Student/faculty ratio	30:1
Profs interesting rating	86
Profs accessible rating	66
% female faculty	18

Academics

The University of Mississippi—known affectionately as "Ole Miss" to its many students and supporters—offers students two MBA options. The first is an intensive, one-year full-time MBA, which does not require post-undergraduate professional experience for admission; the other is the two-year professional MBA for working adults, which gives strong preference to students with at least two years of post-undergraduate business-related employment.

Ole Miss' one-year program runs 11 months, commencing in July and ending in May. The curriculum consists of 13 prescribed courses, taught cohort-style with an emphasis on "the integration of subjects into real business applications." Students warn that the program is intense. As one explains, "Overall, you have to be very serious if you want to be in a one-year program. Don't let the kind recruiters fool you: You are in for hell if you are not 100 percent committed...There is hardly any time to breathe. This is only for the extremely serious." Instructors "expect a lot out of us," and even "The administration is concerned with our performance and takes measures to continually monitor our progression through the classes. Overall, the academic experience is rigorous." One student concurs, "The program could use more breaks. Or, they could lengthen it to ease the stress."

The part-time MBA at Ole Miss is more flexible, using "alternate methods of delivering course content" that include interactive CD-ROMs, DVDs, videoconferencing, conference calls, and Internet learning. Some on-campus sessions are required, but most of the program can be completed remotely. In both the part-time and full-time program, "Professors all have business backgrounds and have been tenured for a long time, or they have short academic careers and long, successful business careers in the fields they teach." Instructors typically employ "real-world examples and tie your education from them into your own work experiences. Dictation seldom happens. Discussion of the assigned readings is the primary classroom focus."

Career and Placement

Ole Miss MBAs receive career support from the university's Career Center. Students report that many of the best career opportunities come via the alumni network, which is "very supportive. The Ole Miss 'brand' is well-respected in the Southeast." Employers that recruit on the Ole Miss campus include Acxiom, Allstate, Bancorp South, FedEx, Harrah's, IBM, International Paper, Regions Bank, and the Tennessee Valley Authority.

Student Life and Environment

The swift pace of the full-time MBA program means that many students "study so much that it is hard to have a life. But when there are small breaks, the potential to have a great time is definitely there." First and foremost, is Ole Miss football and the requisite tailgate parties beforehand, but there's much more to the social scene than sports. The school "offers a wide variety of activities socially and academically that you can become involved in. This place has a lot of great traditions." Students appreciate the Ole Miss grounds, which one describes as "a walking campus that promotes and produces beautiful people!"

DR. JOHN HOLLEMAN, DIRECTOR OF MBA ADMINSTRATRION
319 CONNER HALL, UNIVERSITY, MS 38677 UNITED STATES
PHONE: 662-915-5483 • FAX: 662-915-7968
E-MAIL: JHOLLEMAN@BUS.OLEMISS.EDU • WEBSITE: WWW.OLEMISSBUSINESS.COM

Hometown Oxford is a small, Southern college town distinguished by the university and the residences of several famous writers, including John Grisham. The town has become a travel destination for many, not only for Ole Miss sporting events but also for festivals such as the Double Decker Arts Festival and conferences as the Faulkner & Yoknapatawpha Conference (named after the author William Faulkner, who made his home in Oxford, and the fictional county in which much of his work is set). The city of Memphis is just 70 miles to the north.

Full-timers at Ole Miss tend to be "very young. The majority are 22 years old. Some have had internships, but none have actually worked. It's very difficult to have a discussion about business if you've never been involved in one. The few students with work experience talk 95 percent of the time." The student community is close. As one student explains, "One thing about going through an MBA 'boot camp' like this is that you come together very quickly. Because you're all suffering together, people are very friendly and quick to help you out."

Admissions

All applicants to the full time MBA program at Ole Miss must provide an official transcript of undergraduate work showing a minimum 3.0 GPA for the final 60 semesters hours of academic work; an official GMAT score report (the school lists 550 as the cut-off for "acceptable" scores); two letters of recommendation; and a 400-word personal statement of purpose. Students who have not completed prerequisite course work in undergraduate business disciplines will be required to complete such courses successfully before commencing work on their graduate degrees. International students must meet all of the above requirements and submit TOEFL scores (minimum acceptable score is 600). Applicants to the professional MBA program "with two or more years of post-baccalaureate degree professional work experience" receive "particular consideration" from the Admissions Committee. The professional MBA program is "very competitive."

FINANCIAL FACTS

Annual tuition (in-state/ out-of-state)	$7,000/$13,000
Cost of books	$5,000
Room & board (on/off-campus)	$8,800/$10,000
Average grant	$1,469

ADMISSIONS

Admissions Selectivity Rating	**82**
# of applications received	189
% applicants accepted	54
% acceptees attending	45
Average GMAT	562
Range of GMAT	500–610
Average GPA	3.65
TOEFL required of international students	Yes
Minimum TOEFL (paper)	600
Application fee	$25
Regular application deadline	3/1
Regular notification	4/1
Non-fall admissions	Yes
Need-blind admissions	Yes

EMPLOYMENT PROFILE

Career Rating	70	Grads Employed by Function	%	Avg. Salary
		Finance/Accounting	15	NR
		Marketing/Sales	15	NR
		MIS	20	NR
		Consulting	10	NR
		Entrepreneurship	5	NR
		General Management	5	NR
		Internet/New Media	25	NR

UNIVERSITY OF MISSOURI—COLUMBIA
COLLEGE OF BUSINESS

Academics

Boasting modern facilities, a cool campus culture, talented students, and superbly friendly faculty and staff, the University of Missouri—Columbia is a great place to earn a degree while enjoying the best aspects of academic life. With just 200 graduate students in the business program each year, "class sizes are kept low so there is a lot of student-teacher interaction." As a result, the academic environment is highly supportive, and "the professors are wonderful at providing help outside of the classroom for both class-related items and professional development." In addition, students dole out praise for the school's super-friendly administrators, whom they describe as "very congenial and efficient" as well as highly responsive to student needs. A current student attests, "The administration has a great flow of communication. I can go to them when I need assistance with class work or if I simply want advice."

While the majority of students focus on management, marketing, finance, or management information systems, "Mizzou" likes to stay on top of the trends—"Whenever a new market trend emerges, it is incorporated into the classroom environment, either in a class or in a seminar." Course work is just one component of this highly integrated program, which also draws heavily on teamwork, networking, and hands-on projects. For example, the school boasts "something called the Integrated Functional Perspective project, [where] students work together without a classroom setting and do a case analysis that involves several functions, instead of simply the one that you are studying." In general, Mizzou's "programs are designed to encourage networking between students, alumni, and faculty"; work outside the classroom is as important as work within it. Students dole out endless praise for the caliber of their talented classmates, whom they characterize as "very active in the program, extremely bright, hardworking, and [possess] diverse talents and career aspirations that make for a great learning environment."

Given the focus on extracurricular learning, Mizzou "strikes a great balance between exceptional in-class learning while not making the workload too rigorous." Students feel they are definitely learning techniques that will be essential outside the classroom. "However, the reasonably manageable workload provides the opportunity to do outside research and independent study that pertain to my niche interests." Even so, don't expect to coast through the program. Mizzou MBAs definitely keep busy with "a great amount of networking, socializing, teamwork, and career development activities outside of the classroom. So, when you factor in all the MBA-related events, classes, studying, and outside events, you will spend 40 hours a week involved with the program."

Career and Placement

The MBA program at Mizzou "does a great job of polishing young businesspeople into professionals," and students at the University of Missouri feel confident entering the workforce after graduation. In addition to course work, "professional development opportunities add the finesse that is needed to succeed in a competitive business environment."

Through the Career Services Office, students have access to career and internship fairs, career-building workshops, and online job databases. The office also maintains contact with a number of recruiting firms across the United States. The school has an especially excellent reputation in the Columbia area and the state of Missouri, and "several recruiters are discovering the value of students who come out of this university, so the on-campus recruiting opportunities are phenomenal!" Some students, however, feel that the school is still too regionally focused, and that "Career Services could offer more [recruiting opportunities with] companies outside of Missouri."

BARBARA SCHNEIDER, COORDINATOR RECRUITING AND ADMISSIONS
213 CORNELL HALL, COLUMBIA, MO 65211 UNITED STATES
PHONE: 573-882-2750 • FAX: 573-882-6838
E-MAIL: MBA@MISSOURI.EDU • WEBSITE: MBA.MISSOURI.EDU

Student Life and Environment

A MBA at Mizzou is "not only about academics; it's also about socializing, networking, and finding out who you really are." The students form a "very tight-knit" group. Most hail from Missouri yet come from "very diverse backgrounds ethnically and educationally." After class, students are enthusiastic to "kick back and relax together"; they also "love to celebrate the diversity of the program with special international days, language partner programs, and impromptu dinners and cultural activities."

Extracurricular opportunities are ample, and "about half of the students are involved in the MBA Association. Through this organization, students participate in philanthropy activities (such as Big Brothers, Big Sisters, and Relay for Life), professional development activities (networking receptions, workshops, and alumni events), and social events (weekly happy hours, parties, and wine tastings)." Students with families should take note, however: The programs primarily cater to a younger set, and while "some spouses come to MBA events, most are left out."

On campus, MBA students enjoy "an outstanding library, tons of cultural events, beautiful architecture, and lots of brand new student housing," as well as a state-of-the-art rec center. On top of that, "The business school is housed in a brand-new, technologically-advanced building that is full of resources for the students." According to students here, there's no better location than Columbia, Missouri, which many characterize as "a very forward-thinking city, perfect for both families and younger singletons." The consummate college town, Columbia is home to a host of "schools, parks, libraries, hike-and-bike trails, and arts programs, as well as standard college-town nightlife and activities."

Admissions

The University of Missouri evaluates prospective students based on the strength of their undergraduate work, leadership skills, and GMAT scores. Work experience is not a requirement of the program, but is a factor that is considered in the admissions decision. In the previous year, successful applicants to University of Missouri—Columbia's graduate business program submitted an average GPA of 3.38 and an average GMAT score of 625. Applicants must submit an MU Graduate School Application and MBA Department Application. Admissions decisions are made on a rolling basis, and students are usually notified of a decision within three weeks of submitting all of the necessary application materials. Students can enter in the Fall, Winter, or Summer terms and graduate in three or four semesters depending upon their academic background.

FINANCIAL FACTS

Annual tuition (in-state/ out-of-state)	$8,292/$21,411
Fees	$800
Cost of books	$908
Room & board (off-campus)	$7,848
% of students receiving aid	55
% of first-year students receiving aid	45
% of students receiving grants	16
Average award package	$13,000
Average grant	$4,800

ADMISSIONS

Admissions Selectivity Rating	87
# of applications received	366
% applicants accepted	54
% acceptees attending	51
Average GMAT	623
Range of GMAT	590–650
Average GPA	3.41
TOEFL required of international students	Yes
Minimum TOEFL (paper/computer)	550/213
Application fee	$45
International application fee	$60
Regular application deadline	Rolling
Regular notification	Rolling
Deferment available	Yes
Maximum length of deferment	1 year
Transfer students accepted	Yes
Transfer application policy	
Students may waive up to 27 credit hours and may transfer 6 credit hours from an AACSB MBA program.	
Non-fall admissions	Yes
Need-blind admissions	Yes

EMPLOYMENT PROFILE

Career Rating	80	Grads Employed by Function	%	Avg. Salary
Primary Source of Full-time Job Acceptances		Finance/Accounting	43	$48,970
School-facilitated activities	27 (63%)	Human Resources	3	$43,000
Graduate-facilitated activities	12 (28%)	Marketing/Sales	17	$57,857
Unknown	4 (9%)	MIS	10	$58,625
Percent employed	86	Consulting	13	$54,700
		General Management	7	$52,833
		Other	7	$63,441

Top 5 Employers Hiring Grads
Cerner; MarketSphere Consulting; Sprint; KeyBank.

UNIVERSITY OF MISSOURI—KANSAS CITY
HENRY W. BLOCH SCHOOL OF BUSINESS AND PUBLIC ADMINISTRATION

GENERAL INFORMATION
Type of school	Public
Environment	Metropolis
Academic calendar	Semester

SURVEY SAYS . . .
Students love Kansas City, MO
Happy students
Smart classrooms
Solid preparation in:
Teamwork
Communication/interpersonal skills

STUDENTS
Enrollment of parent institution	14,221
Enrollment of business school	360
% male/female	60/40
% part-time	100
Average age at entry	30
Average years work experience at entry	4

ACADEMICS
Academic Experience Rating	**79**
Student/faculty ratio	14:1
Profs interesting rating	66
Profs accessible rating	69
% female faculty	16
% minority faculty	8

Joint Degrees
JD/MBA, JD/MPA.

Prominent Alumni
Mark Funkhouser, Mayor, Kansas City, MO; Terry Dunn, President and CEO, Dunn Industries, Inc.; Bob Regnier, president, Bank of Blue Valley; Tom Holcom, president, Pioneer Financial Services, Inc.

Academics

"A convenient location" and "a strong reputation" in the region attract students to the Henry W. Bloch School of Business and Public Administration at the University of Missouri—Kansas City, a large public institution serving nearly 15,000 undergraduates and graduate students. As you would expect of a school named after a founder of tax-preparation giant H & R Block, accounting is among the strongest programs here. Many also praise the finance emphasis, pointing out that "many of the professors [in this discipline] are distinguished and have impressive backgrounds in publications."

The Bloch MBA requires a minimum of 30 semester hours of course work, and students who enter the program with deficiencies in core skills (e.g. students who did not satisfactorily complete a business major at the undergraduate level) may be required to complete up to 18 additional semester hours as well as introductory classes in mathematics and computer applications. All students must complete a minimum of 18 semester hours outside their area of emphasis. Twelve semester hours are required to complete an emphasis; emphases are available in entrepreneurship, finance, general management, international business, leadership and change in human systems, management information systems, marketing, and operations management.

Students appreciate the "availability of experiential learning" throughout the program and observe that "the quality of the faculty is very high and the overall program is quite thorough." Small class sizes encourage strong relationships between students and teachers—a boon for those MBAs hoping to develop a mentor while here. UMKC's administration "is not very noticeable, which is a good thing. They don't get in the way. They are accessible, though."

Career and Placement

UMKC's Career Services Center, which serves the entire university population, recently opened a satellite office at the Bloch School to serve business graduates and undergraduates. Unfortunately, the office only stays open until 5:00 P.M., making it difficult for Bloch's many part-time students who hold full-time jobs to benefit from its services. It's only an issue for some—many students here have little interest in leaving their current employers—but it is a nuisance for those it affects. Employers who recruit on the UMKC campus include Ameriprise Financial Services, Inc., Cerner, Commerce Bank, Eli Lilly & Company, Etelligent Consulting Inc., the Farmers Insurance Group, the Federal Bureau of Investigation, First Investors Corp., the Internal Revenue Service, John Hancock Financial Services, State Street, US Bank, Wells Fargo, and Zen Infotech.

Student Life and Environment

"Most MBA students are working professionals during the day and students at night" at UMKC. "Many are married and have kids, most are hard working and competitive," and nearly all are "looking for more out of their careers." This population is supplemented by "a significant international presence" and "some executive students. UMKC is an urban school that fits the mold." For the most part, students' careers and familial obligations leave them "minimal time for extracurricular interaction." They attend classes, participate in team projects, and try to make time for study groups. Aside from that, they do not spend much time on campus.

JENNIFER DEHAEMERS, DIRECTOR OF ADMISSIONS
5100 ROCKHILL ROAD, KANSAS CITY, MO 64110 UNITED STATES
PHONE: 816-235-1111 • FAX: 816-235-5544
E-MAIL: ADMIT@UMKC.EDU • WEBSITE: WWW.BLOCH.UMKC.EDU

The Bloch School is located in a renovated and expanded facility that is also one of the city's historic mansions. The building has been updated to meet the requirements of twenty-first century business education. Students have access to modern classrooms and to computer and research laboratories.

The Kansas City metropolitan area sprawls over six counties in two states, Missouri and Kansas. The region is home to nearly two million residents, placing it among the 30 largest metropolitan regions in the country. Naturally, numerous companies and national organizations are headquartered in the city. They include American Century, Applebee's, Aquila, Black and Veatch, Ferrallgas, Hallmark, H & R Block, Interstate Bakeries, Russell Stover, and Sprint.

Admissions

Applicants to the MBA program at the University of Missouri—Kansas City must submit official copies of transcripts for all academic work completed after high school and an official score report for the GMAT. The school will consider graduate-level admissions tests other than the GMAT (e.g. LSAT, GRE) so long as scores exceed the fiftieth percentile in all parts of the exam. Candidates must also provide the admissions committee with all of the following: a completed application form (available online); a current resume showing both work history and professional certifications; a personal statement of purpose in pursuing the MBA; and a summary of the candidate's current commitments to work (i.e., hours of work per week, amount of business travel). International students must provide all of the above and must also provide an official score report for the TOEFL; a minimum score of 550 on the paper-based exam or 213 on the computer-based exam is required.

FINANCIAL FACTS

Annual tuition (in-state/ out-of-state)	$5,634/$13,804
% of students receiving aid	37
% of first-year students receiving aid	36
% of students receiving loans	32
% of students receiving grants	13
Average award package	$14,091
Average grant	$2,944
Average student loan debt	$28,976

ADMISSIONS

Admissions Selectivity Rating	**82**
# of applications received	246
% applicants accepted	58
% acceptees attending	85
Average GMAT	548
Range of GMAT	510–580
Average GPA	3.29
TOEFL required of international students	Yes
Minimum TOEFL (paper/computer)	550/213
Application fee	$35
International application fee	$50
Regular application deadline	5/1
Regular notification	Rolling
Deferment available	Yes
Maximum length of deferment	1 year
Transfer students accepted	Yes
Transfer application policy We will accept up to 6 hours of grad credit from an AACSB-accredited institution.	
Non-fall admissions	Yes
Need-blind admissions	Yes

Applicants Also Look At
Rockhurst University, University of Kansas.

UNIVERSITY OF MISSOURI—ST. LOUIS
COLLEGE OF BUSINESS ADMINISTRATION

GENERAL INFORMATION
Type of school	Public
Environment	Metropolis
Academic calendar	Semester

SURVEY SAYS . . .
Cutting-edge classes
Smart classrooms
Solid preparation in:
Operations
Doing business in a global economy

STUDENTS
Enrollment of parent institution	12,100
Enrollment of business school	462
% male/female	62/38
% out-of-state	18
% part-time	72
% minorities	1
% international	15
Average age at entry	29
Average years work experience at entry	5

ACADEMICS
Academic Experience Rating	**72**
Student/faculty ratio	12:1
Profs interesting rating	74
Profs accessible rating	84
% female faculty	22
% minority faculty	4

Academics

Students looking to earn one of the three "affordable" MBAs (evening, professional, and international) offered at the University of Missouri—St. Louis's College of Business Administration will find themselves doing so at the largest AACSB-accredited business school in the St. Louis region, and the only AACSB-accredited business school to offer an online MBA. The predominantly part-time program is completed through mostly night courses, and with a large population of older students returning to school after several years in the workplace, "most have become very efficient in time management."

The course of study in the evening MBA provides a solid foundation in the functional areas of business with emphasis areas available in accounting, finance, information systems, logistics and supply chain management, management, marketing, and operations management. The professional MBA program is a much smaller cohort of working individuals who take all of their classes together. One student says this arrangement allows her "to feel more comfortable and enables me to take more risks (presenting, sharing ideas) than in a traditional class setting." Another value-add is the school's reputable program in logistics/supply chain management. The International MBA is a unique two-year program in which students spend the first year studying overseas at a partner institution and the second year on campus at UM-St. Louis.

The "accessible" professors at UMSL get fairly positive reviews, though the instruction methods are not without their detractors. Many remain unchallenged by the courses, which tend to "overlap," "They are pretty much doing Finance 101, Marketing 101, etc.," one student grumbles. Another doesn't like what he sees as an overemphasis on group projects, which must be coordinated outside the classroom: "This is night school for people with jobs and families; we don't have time to do group projects in every class . . . once or twice is enough to teach teamwork concepts!"

Another gripe is the lack of "real-world interaction" opportunities offered by the school, such as required internships and more business leaders in the classroom. "I think my academic experience will be pure[ly] academic, without any real business insight," one student says. But another thinks the "strong international presence" at UMSL "contributes to my understanding of the global marketplace. If I have a question about how to effectively penetrate the European market and capture the broadest consumer base possible, I ask my classmate from France." The school's strong reputation in the St. Louis area allows for numerous internships, and students say the faculty members are willing to use their connections with top local employers and alumni channels to help students put their knowledge to use in more practical settings. Criticisms aside, students here recognize that they're getting a "quality education for a reasonable price."

Career and Placement

The counseling at the Career and Placement Center at UMSL is "very limited," with an annual subscription fee for benefits one typically finds included in the cost of tuition (i.e., resume critics, job postings). One student finds that "there is virtually no placement assistance that is geared toward grad students that already have some experience," with most career events featuring recruiters looking for undergraduate (and sometimes MBA) students only. "It doesn't seem like our Career Services Department has contacts in the real world other than to collect and post job descriptions and availability," says a graduating student.

THOMAS EYSSELL, ASSOCIATE DEAN AND DIRECTOR OF GRADUATE STUDIES
ONE UNIVERSITY BOULEVARD, 250 UNIVERSITY CENTER, ST. LOUIS, MO 63121-4499 UNITED STATES
PHONE: 314-516-5885 • FAX: 314-516-7202
E-MAIL: MBA@UMSL.EDU • WEBSITE: MBA.UMSL.EDU

Student Life and Environment

Life in St. Louis, "a baseball town," is pretty much what you make of it, and since the majority of (American) students here have lived in the area for a while, they're typically pretty settled in. "The most popular question asked at a party: 'What high school did you go to?'" says a student. The breakdown of students tends to divvy up into "married working professionals," international and exchange students who "are likely to have their own community (friendship) within their origin or with other international students," and the smallest subset, full-time American students.

Though everyone is easy to talk to, "even though ages of the students may vary widely," "Social unity is not a characteristic" of the college, and there's no doubt that the primary focus for most students at UMSL is to go to class and then leave. This is just as well for the school, which isn't exactly chomping at the bit to provide activities that most students wouldn't attend anyway. "I don't think students even know what organizations UMSL has," says a student, and for those that do, most events are not grad student–specific, so people show only "marginal student involvement." The facilities, while functional, are "not aesthetically pleasing," and the gym and parking situations leave much to be desired.

Admissions

Though professional experience is not required for admittance into the traditional MBA program, it does play a factor in admissions decisions. In order to gain nonrestricted admittance to any of the school's MBA programs, an applicant must submit a GMAT score of at least 500 (50th percentile) overall and must have an undergraduate GPA of at least 3.0. Applicants who score below the 30th percentile on either the verbal or quantitative component of the GMAT generally are not accepted. Applicants also must submit an official copy of undergraduate transcripts from all institutions where course work was completed (this should come directly from the schools themselves); a current resume; an official GMAT score report; a personal statement; and two letters of recommendation.

In addition to the above documents, international students whose primary language is not English must also provide an official score report for the TOEFL (minimum score: 550, paper-based test; 213, computer-based test).

FINANCIAL FACTS

Annual tuition	$6,316
Fees	$1,287
Cost of books	$3,000
Room & board (on/off-campus)	$5,600/$6,180
% of students receiving aid	53
% of first-year students receiving aid	48
% of students receiving loans	32
% of students receiving grants	24
Average award package	$10,139
Average grant	$6,159
Average student loan debt	$5,933

ADMISSIONS

Admissions Selectivity Rating	74
# of applications received	106
% applicants accepted	80
% acceptees attending	71
Average GMAT	550
Range of GMAT	470–590
Average GPA	3.2
TOEFL required of international students	Yes
Minimum TOEFL (paper/computer)	550/213
Application fee	$35
International application fee	$40
Regular application deadline	7/1
Regular notification	Rolling
Deferment available	Yes
Maximum length of deferment	1 year
Transfer students accepted	Yes
Transfer application policy	
Transcripts are evaluated for relevant course work; maximum of 9 hours of acceptable graduate credit allowed to transfer in.	
Non-fall admissions	Yes
Need-blind admissions	Yes

EMPLOYMENT PROFILE			
Career Rating	65	Grads Employed by Function	% Avg. Salary
		Finance/Accounting	50 $51,600
		Consulting	17 $42,500
		Communications	16 $43,000
		Other	17 $48,000

UNIVERSITY OF NEVADA—LAS VEGAS
COLLEGE OF BUSINESS

GENERAL INFORMATION
Type of school   Public
Environment   Metropolis
Academic calendar   Semesters

SURVEY SAYS . . .
Students love Las Vegas, NV
Friendly students
Good social scene
Good peer network
Happy students
Solid preparation in:
Quantitative skills

STUDENTS
Enrollment of parent
  institution   27,912
Enrollment of
  business school   297
Average age at entry   28
Average years work
  experience at entry   6

ACADEMICS
Academic Experience Rating **74**
Student/faculty ratio   30:1
Profs interesting rating   70
Profs accessible rating   65
% female faculty   23
% minority faculty   21

Joint Degrees
MBA/MS Hotel Administration 2.5 years,
JD/MBA 4 to 5 years, MBA/DDM (Dental Medicine).

Academics

The College of Business at the University of Nevada—Las Vegas offers both a full-time day and full-time and part-time evening MBA as well as a cohort-based weekend Executive MBA program for more experienced professionals. Roughly half the students in these programs attend the college full time.

UNLV's evening MBA consists of 48 credit hours, 33 of which are devoted to core courses. Students must devote five electives to a single area in order to achieve a concentration; the college offers concentrations in finance, management information systems, service marketing, and venture management. An accelerated program is open only to evening students who score at least a 600 on the GMAT (with a score exceeding the 50th percentile in both verbal and quantitative skills) and an undergraduate business degree from an AACSB-accredited university. Students who meet these conditions may be allowed to waive up to six of the ten required core courses.

The 18-month Executive MBA program offers a general management degree; in order to preserve the program's cohort-based approach to learning, all students follow the same curriculum. The program begins with a week of intensive work; afterwards, students meet every Friday and Saturday from 8:30 A.M. to 5:30 P.M. Applicants to the program must have at least seven years of professional experience, at least three of which have been spent in "a key decision-making role."

UNLV also offers combined-degree programs in hotel administration, dental medicine, management information system and a JD/MBA. Students point out that the "hotel concentration feeds off the Las Vegas resort market."

Career and Placement

The UNLV College of Business Career Services Center serves only graduate students in business. According to the College's website, the office seeks to help students define career goals, develop a career plan, market themselves, develop job-search skills, sharpen interviewing skills, and contact alumni. The office serves as a liaison to the local business community, maintains a number of hard-copy and online job databases, and organizes lectures and on-campus recruiting events.

Employers most likely to hire UNLV MBAs include Bechtel Nevada, Bechtel SAIC, Citibank, Harrah's Entertainment Inc., Pulte Homes, US Bank, and Wells Fargo. A plurality of the class of 2004 wound up in the finance sector, and almost everyone had found employment by graduation.

ROBERT CHATFIELD, MBA PROGRAMS DIRECTOR
4505 MARYLAND PARKWAY, BOX 456031, LAS VEGAS, NV 89154-6031 UNITED STATES
PHONE: 702-895-3655 • FAX: 702-895-3632
E-MAIL: COBMBA@UNLV.EDU • WEBSITE: BUSINESS.UNLV.EDU

Student Life and Environment

Las Vegas is one of America's top tourist destinations, primarily because "it's fun every single night." Those who live here know that Vegas has a lot more to offer than just gambling, over-the-top floor shows, and cheap buffets. The Las Vegas metropolitan region is home to 1.5 million residents, many of whom never set foot inside a casino. The city boasts all the amenities of a midsize metropolis and adds to the mix a perennially sunny climate and proximity to plenty of outdoor fun; Lake Mead, the Colorado River, and the Hoover Dam are all within a half-hour's drive of the city. Some fabulous skiing and hiking awaits residents on Mount Charleston, less than an hour northwest of Sin City.

UNLV does its part to keep things interesting, providing "new cultural and entertainment attractions to the community every day," according to the college's website. Prominent lecturers and touring performing artists regularly stop by this desert campus.

Admissions

Applicants to the MBA program at UNLV must submit the following to the Admissions Committee: official transcripts for all postsecondary academic work undertaken; an official score report for the GMAT; two letters of recommendation; a personal essay; and a resume. An interview is required for admission to the Executive MBA program, but not for other graduate programs. The TOEFL is not required of students who completed degree programs conducted in English or the U.S., U.K., Australia, Canada, or New Zealand. All international applicants must provide financial certification documents.

FINANCIAL FACTS

Annual tuition	
(in-state)	$172.25 per credit
Annual tuition (out-of-state)	$8,674
Fees	$456
Cost of books	$800
Room & board	
(on/off-campus)	$5,000/$7,000
% of students receiving aid	55
% of students receiving loans	25
% of students receiving grants	3
Average award package	$16,633
Average grant	$2,954
Average student loan debt	$34,309

ADMISSIONS

Admissions Selectivity Rating	**92**
# of applications received	177
% applicants accepted	38
% acceptees attending	96
Average GMAT	597
Range of GMAT	550–630
Average GPA	3.24
TOEFL required of	
international students	Yes
Minimum TOEFL	
(paper/computer)	550/213
Application fee	$60
International application fee	$75
Regular application deadline	6/1
Regular notification	7/1
Deferment available	Yes
Maximum length of	
deferment	1 semester
Transfer students accepted	Yes
Transfer application policy	
Total of 6 credits from an AACSB-accredited school.	
Non-fall admissions	Yes
Need-blind admissions	Yes

EMPLOYMENT PROFILE

Career Rating	67	Grads Employed by Function	%	Avg. Salary
		Finance/Accounting	40	$52,000
		Human Resources	2	$50,000
		Marketing/Sales	20	$45,000
		MIS	3	$50,000
		Operations/Production	2	$65,000
		Consulting	3	$60,000
		General Management	10	$70,000
		Other	10	$35,000

UNIVERSITY OF NEVADA—RENO
COLLEGE OF BUSINESS ADMINSTRATION

Academics

The University of Nevada—Reno's College of Business offers graduate business programs designed to serve the needs of its largely local and mostly part-time student body. As high tech, distribution, hospitality, tourism, and gambling dominate western Nevada's business landscape, UNR's business school curriculum takes note of this, offering specializations in accounting, finance, gaming management, international business, and supply chain management. All MBA students are required to follow a core curriculum intended to provide them with a foundation in statistics, marketing, economics, and finance; the core curriculum takes up roughly half the credits required for the degree.

Students must also take classes in managing computer-based systems and understanding changing business environments, and must choose courses from several other areas of business before moving into their area of specialization. Specialized classes make up about one quarter of the credits required for the degree.

UNR's ranking as one of the top 150 research institutions in the U.S. attracts business professors who are "very accessible and helpful" as well as "skilled in blending real-world experience with academic theory," with an ability "to promote critical thinking and teamwork." Nearly three-quarters of the students are in part-time programs, but that "doesn't mean that the course material is less rigorous," students agree. In fact, "This program challenges you since the classes are condensed" and "Some classes have overloaded us with homework and projects," one student grumbles. If they were to make improvements, some students would start with what they describe as a limited class selection, offering "too many accounting/finance classes and not enough other subjects." Fortunately, faculty and administration are "always willing to listen to your goals and dreams, and help to custom design the MBA program you need to follow." In fact, "The greatest strength of the school is its practical, hands-on curriculum." One student echoes the sentiments of his classmates when he says, "I am getting a great education at such a bargain!"

Career and Placement

In 2005, 3 months after graduation, an impressive 99 percent of the College of Business MBA holders at UNR were employed, with an average starting salary of $50,000. While some students do not find the Career Connections Center very active ("I didn't even know we had one," said one), others take advantage of career fairs, recruiting appointments, and networking among fellow students to find jobs. A reported snag in the process is that "students do not have much of an opportunity to mingle with one another due to the late-night classes and the fact that most students work at least part-time," one points out. The Career Connections Center does offer a variety of workshops targeted to the general university population on topics such as resume writing, effective networking, and developing interviewing skills in which MBA student may participate. The school's 2006 graduates were recruited by the following companies: Gentech, The Peppermill Casinos, Wells Fargo, the Bureau of Land Management, Coventry Health Care, and International Game Technology.

VICKI KRENTZ, COORDINATOR OF GRADUATE PROGRAMS
MAILSTOP 0024, RENO, NV 89557 UNITED STATES
PHONE: 775-784-4912 • FAX: 775-784-1773
E-MAIL: VKRENTZ@UNR.EDU • WEBSITE: WWW.COBA.UNR.EDU/MBA

Student Life and Environment

UNR College of Business students are a "very diverse group of people, racially, cultural-ly, and in the range of experiences they have had prior to school." "About 50 percent have a science or engineering background; about 50 percent have a business or liberal arts background," students say. This range of experience is a real benefit both inside and outside the classroom: "I have had the opportunity to meet many people from various backgrounds. The diverse student body makes attending classes well worth the time."

UNR's campus sits on a hill north of downtown, and the original campus design (it's the oldest university in Nevada) was modeled on Thomas Jefferson's ideal of an academic village. But students here—"mostly married with children, employed full-time, non-career changers who are looking for advancement within their current organization"—rarely have time to take in the scenery. Despite their busy schedules, UNR's "friendly" students help create a welcoming atmosphere on campus. "My fellow students are mature and respectful. They are always willing to help anyone who is unsure about any-thing," says one student.

Since "students commute to the campus, live off campus and tend to be local profes-sionals," students say it's sometimes difficult to build connections. However, "I like the fact that the restaurants and coffeehouse are open late for night students. They really try!" pointed out one such student, echoing the thoughts of many of his classmates.

Admissions

Two or more years of work experience, a minimum GPA of 2.75 on a 4.0 scale, and a GMAT score of at least 500 are required for admission to the College of Business at UNR. A resume, two letters of reference, and a two- to three-page personal statement concern-ing background and goals are also needed. A minimum TOEFL score of 550 is required from non-native English speakers. In 2006, the average GMAT score for those admitted was 522, and the average length of work experience was six years. A full 85 percent of those who applied were accepted, and about three-quarters of them pursued their degrees on a part-time basis. Of the 69 students enrolled in graduate programs in 2006, approximately 51 percent were women.

ADMISSIONS	
Admissions Selectivity Rating	**71**
# of applications received	88
% applicants accepted	85
% acceptees attending	93
Average GMAT	522
Average GPA	3.1
TOEFL required of international students	Yes
Minimum TOEFL (paper)	550
Application fee	$60
Regular application deadline	3/15 & 10/15
Regular notification	Rolling
Deferment available	Yes
Maximum length of deferment	1 year
Non-fall admissions	Yes

EMPLOYMENT PROFILE	
Career Rating	**63**

UNIVERSITY OF NEW HAMPSHIRE
WHITTEMORE SCHOOL OF BUSINESS AND ECONOMICS

GENERAL INFORMATION
Type of school	Public
Environment	Village
Academic calendar	5 terms

SURVEY SAYS . . .
Friendly students
Helpful alumni
Smart classrooms
Solid preparation in:
Teamwork
Communication/interpersonal skills
Presentation skills

STUDENTS
Enrollment of parent institution	13,957
Enrollment of business school	259
% male/female	39/61
% out-of-state	28
% part-time	61
% minorities	6
% international	15
Average age at entry	28
Average years work experience at entry	5

ACADEMICS
Academic Experience Rating	**74**
Student/faculty ratio	4:1
Profs interesting rating	71
Profs accessible rating	68
% female faculty	16
% minority faculty	4

Joint Degrees
Current UNH seniors can apply early admission to MS accounting program and count 1 graduate course toward both degree requirements.

Prominent Alumni
Dan Burnham, president (retired), Raytheon; Terry Tracy, managing director, Citigroup; Garrett Ilg, president, Adobe Japan; David Cote, chairman/president/CEO, Honeywell; Arthur B. Learmonth, president, Magtag Service Business Unit.

Academics

Things are changing at the University of New Hampshire's Whittemore School of Business and Economics: In 2005–2006, the school introduced a brand-new MBA program designed to streamline the degree-earning process. The new program hustles full-time students through in less than one year (through an "intense program" that leaves "little time for anything else," according to the school's website), while part-timers graduate in fewer than two years. Students here frequently cite the speed with which the program can be completed as one of its biggest draws.

Whittemore's full-time program begins in late August with a five-week term, during which students study management, accounting, and organizational behavior. The second term, which runs for three months, consists entirely of required courses in economics, marketing, information systems and enterprise integration, and financial management. Term three is split between two required courses (one in organizations and leadership, the other in managerial decision making) and two electives. Term four consists of two required courses covering operations management and business strategy, and electives. This provides student teams the opportunity to work on a real-world project with a major company, such as Fidelity Investments or Liberty Mutual Life. The program concludes with term five, during which students complete a consulting project. Students can take electives in marketing and supply chain management, entrepreneurial venture creation, or financial management. Many students single out the entrepreneurship classes as a highlight of the program.

Whittemore's part-time program follows a similar curriculum to the full-time program, although it replaces the consulting project with two electives. The part-time program offers the same selection of concentrations as the full-time program.

MBAs at Whittemore detect an "an emphasis on academic greatness that fosters a great study environment." They report approvingly that "the faculty is always willing to help out" and that "the school offers lots of resources for going into the workplace," and "professors are, for the most part, very good and have extensive experience and research in their fields. The experience from the Whittemore School of Business and Economics is one of academic intensity as well as a lot of fun."

Career and Placement

Business students at UNH have their own placement service which works in partnership with the university-at-large placement office, the University Advising and Career Center. Placement staff work with business undergraduates, graduates, and alumni to forge career strategies, identify potential employers, and navigate the recruitment process. Recent employers of Whittemore School graduates include Anthem Blue Cross Blue Shield, AT&T, Boise Cascade, Chubb Life-America, Cigna, Credit Suisse, Fidelity Investments, GE, IBM, LL Bean, Inc., The McGraw-Hill Companies, Osram Sylvania, Pfizer, Raytheon, Sprague Energy, Timken Aerospace, Verizon, and Westinghouse.

GEORGE ABRAHAM, DIRECTOR, GRADUATE AND EVECUTIVE PROGRAMS
116 McCONNELL HALL, 15 COLLEGE ROAD, DURHAM, NH 03824 UNITED STATES
PHONE: 603-862-1367 • FAX: 603-862-4468
E-MAIL: WSBE.GRAD@UNH.EDU • WEBSITE: WWW.MBA.UNH.EDU

Student Life and Environment

"Most of us are in the same boat here: all fresh out of undergrad with no business knowledge whatsoever," explains one full-time student. "This alone gives us a strong bond. But add myriad team-building exercises and an intense workload, and we've become very close in our time together thus far." MBAs here describe themselves as "overachievers—we were hand-picked by the program's creator—but we manage to maintain a balance between our academic lives and our social lives." Outside the classroom, students participate in international competitions, such as I2P Idea to Product and the NASA Means Business Competition. Discipline-related clubs are also available. Like full-timers, part-timers tend to be young; however, they typically have full-time jobs, and their extracurricular experiences are more limited.

The UNH campus and surrounding area provide "a fun, beautiful environment to be in. The seasons are amazing, and the skiing is great." Durham is "a small college town" with "a few bars, three or four pizza places, and a cell phone service provider," but fortunately "Portsmouth and the beaches are close by." Students tell us that "it is desirable to take trips down to Boston for some excitement."

Admissions

Applicants to the MBA program at UNH's Whittemore School must provide the Admissions Department with all of the following: official copies of transcripts for all postsecondary academic work; an official score report for the GMAT; three letters of reference focusing on the candidate's "strengths, weaknesses, and potential for academic and managerial success"; responses to essay questions, which the school deems a "crucial" aspect of the application; a current resume; and any evidence of leadership skills that the applicant wishes to provide. Applicants to the Executive MBA program must undergo an admissions interview. Applicants to other MBA programs may request an interview but are not required to do so. (It is, however, "strongly recommended" that such applicants who have "one or more weak components in their profile" schedule an appointment.) Two years of work experience is "recommended but not required" for the full-time and part-time MBA programs; a minimum of seven years of professional experience is required for the Executive MBA program. International applicants must meet all of the above requirements and must submit an official score report for the TOEFL (minimum required score: 550 paper-based test, 213 computer-based test).

FINANCIAL FACTS

Annual tuition (in-state/ out-of-state)	$14,000/$25,000
Fees	$1,343
Cost of books	$2,100
Room & board (on/off-campus)	$7,900/$8,800
% of students receiving aid	77
% of first-year students receiving aid	77
% of students receiving loans	44
% of students receiving grants	54
Average award package	$14,535
Average grant	$5,915
Average student loan debt	$18,405

ADMISSIONS

Admissions Selectivity Rating	79
# of applications received	209
% applicants accepted	62
% acceptees attending	78
Average GMAT	554
Range of GMAT	490–610
Average GPA	3.2
TOEFL required of international students	Yes
Minimum TOEFL (paper/computer)	550/213
Application fee	$60
Regular application deadline	7/1
Regular notification	Rolling
Early decision program?	Yes
ED Deadline/Notification	4/1 / 05/15
Deferment available	Yes
Maximum length of deferment	1 year
Transfer students accepted	Yes
Transfer application policy A maximum of 9 credits may be considered for transfer credit.	
Non-fall admissions	Yes
Need-blind admissions	Yes

Applicants Also Look At
Babson College, Bentley College, Boston University, Suffolk University.

EMPLOYMENT PROFILE

Career Rating	78	Grads Employed by Function	%	Avg. Salary
Primary Source of Full-time Job Acceptances		Finance/Accounting	20	$57,950
School-facilitated activities	9 (40%)	Marketing/Sales	25	$41,700
Graduate-facilitated activities	11 (50%)	MIS	10	$93,000
Unknown	2 (10%)	Operations/Production	5	$40,000
Percent employed	91	General Management	35	$50,788
		Other	5	$42,000

Top 5 Employers Hiring Grads
Liberty Mutual; Fidelity Investments; Lindt Sprungli; Citizen's Advisors; Newport Computer Services.

THE UNIVERSITY OF NORTH CAROLINA AT CHAPEL HILL
KENAN-FLAGLER BUSINESS SCHOOL

GENERAL INFORMATION
Type of school	Public
Environment	Town
Academic calendar	Semester

SURVEY SAYS . . .
Friendly students
Good social scene
Good peer network
Solid preparation in:
Teamwork

STUDENTS
Enrollment of parent institution	23,000
Enrollment of business school	567
% male/female	73/27
% out-of-state	76
% minorities	12
% international	27
Average age at entry	28
Average years work experience at entry	5

ACADEMICS
Academic Experience Rating	**94**
Student/faculty ratio	5:1
Profs interesting rating	89
Profs accessible rating	99
% female faculty	17
% minority faculty	1

Joint Degrees
MBA/JD 4 years, MBA/master of regional planning 3 years, MBA/master of health care administration 3 years, MBA/master of science in information sciences 3 years.

Prominent Alumni
Paul Clayton, president and CEO, Jamba Juice; Brent Callinicos, vice president and treasurer, Google, Inc.; Donna Dean, chief investment officer, The Rockefeller Foundation; Thomas M. Belk, Jr., president and CEO, Belk, Inc.; Daryl Brewster, president and CEO, Krispy Kreme Doughnuts Inc.

Academics

The University of North Carolina at Chapel Hill's Kenan-Flagler Business School offers a practical and progressive MBA program, with a faculty and staff "committed to making sure the curriculum reflects what students need to be successful after graduation." The program begins with a rigorous core curriculum that covers the full cycle of running a business. With an emphasis on case study and group work, students appreciate a core curriculum that is "extremely well-integrated, so that what you learn in one class will show up in a different context in another class." They also appreciate their school's staunch commitment to education, explaining, "When the core faculty is teaching, that's all they are doing—no research or travel—so they are available and willing to talk with students as much as needed." Consistently small class sizes further ensure that the "personal attention you receive from administrative staff and faculty is outstanding." A current student reassures, "On several occasions, I've been working late and had a question—there was always someone to help me out."

In the second semester, students begin to take elective course work, gaining "more in-depth knowledge of emerging business issues." The school is noted for "extremely strong marketing, entrepreneurship, and real estate programs," and for its unique sustainable energy concentration. Committed to innovation, 20 percent of the school's elective offerings change annually in response to new business trends. An excellent choice for those considering a career change or looking to expand upon their current professional experience, "The Kenan-Flagler MBA is not targeted [at] individuals who just want a generic management degree, but [at] those who want a degree tailored to their area of specialization." Students can further specialize their studies through courses "taken from other graduate programs within the broader university."

A former CEO, Kenan-Flagler's Dean Steve Jones runs the school like a well-oiled business venture, and consequently the administration is surprisingly responsive to student suggestions and concerns. UNC's administrators "take action when requests are made to change curriculum and administrative situations." When it comes to academics, "Student feedback is taken in the middle and at the end of the course. The feedback is incorporated into the new version of the course quickly."

Career and Placement

Boasting a stellar reputation "coupled with one of the best startup/tech communities on the East Coast," Kenan-Flagler students enjoy great job-placement opportunities through the school's Career Management Center. The CMC also lends a hand with one-on-one career counseling, peer counseling, and group training sessions on topics such as writing a resume, salary negotiations, and how to work a career fair. Students also have access to the school's alumni base, which is "strong and actively participates in recruiting and networking."

Last year, the mean base salary for Kenan-Flagler grads (U.S. citizens) was $90,984, with a high of $140,000. Eighty percent of graduates also received signing bonuses. Real estate, marketing, investment banking, and consulting are the most popular career choices, and a plethora of companies recruit on the UNC campus. Here is an abbreviated list of companies who hired three or more Kenan-Flagler students last year: Amazon.com, Bain & Company, Bank of America, Bear Stearns, Black & Decker, Booz Allen Hamilton, The Boston Consulting Group, Citigroup, Credit Suisse, CSE Consulting, Deloitte Touche Tohmatsu, DuPont, Goldman Sachs, The Hershey Company, Hewlett-Packard, The Home Depot, IBM, Johnson & Johnson, Kenan Institute Asia, Kraft Foods, Last Mile Communications, Lehman Brothers, Lowe's Companies, McKinsey & Company, McNeil Consumer & Specialty Pharmaceuticals, Morgan Stanley, PepsiCo, Pulte Homes, TIAA-CREF.

SHERRY WALLACE, DIRECTOR, MBA ADMISSIONS
CB #3490, McCOLL BUILDING, CHAPEL HILL, NC 27599-3490 UNITED STATES
PHONE: 919-962-3236 • FAX: 919-962-0898
E-MAIL: MBA_INFO@UNC.EDU • WEBSITE: WWW.KENAN-FLAGLER.UNC.EDU

Student Life and Environment

Located in a beautiful college town and blessed with an extraordinarily affable student body, life is good at UNC Chapel Hill. "Everyone goes the extra mile to help and contribute to the overall atmosphere," says one student. Another student observes, "The one word I'd have to use to describe the students at KFBS is 'dynamic.' I've been really impressed with the depth and diversity of their backgrounds, work experiences, and what they contribute to class."

While the workload is considerable, the life of a UNC MBA student is "very busy but very balanced." In addition to schoolwork, "Students at UNC are very involved in extracurricular and community activities." For example, "The Business School has its own Habitat House at which students volunteer every weekend." Students assure us that the social life outside of class is "vibrant, including tailgating on the lawn, black-tie casino night, and MBA Olympics against Duke." Off campus, "The Chapel Hill area is a great place for outdoors activities and the town has lots of bars and nightlife." Going out with fellow students is a popular pastime, and "Chapel Hill is especially great for single students because there's so much to do and so many people to meet." However, those who have already tied the knot are happy too: "I'm married, and I've found that KFBS is very accepting and helpful for the married students."

Admissions

The Kenan-Flagler School of Business admits students who demonstrate leadership and organizational skills, communication ability, interpersonal skills, teamwork ability, analytic and problem-solving skills, drive and motivation, prior academic performance, career progression, and career goals. The school recommends at least 2 years of full-time work experience before entering the program. No specific course work is necessary, but students must have knowledge of financial accounting, statistics, macroeconomics, and calculus. Last year's entering class had a median GMAT score of 660, a median GPA of 3.3, and professional work experience averaging 5.3 years. Qualified candidates are invited to interview from September through April.

FINANCIAL FACTS

Annual tuition (in-state/ out-of-state)	$18,375/36,749
Fees	$2,817
Cost of books	$4,540
Room & board	$16,300
% of students receiving aid	77
% of first-year students receiving aid	75
% of students receiving loans	71
% of students receiving grants	64
Average award package	$39,540
Average grant	$8,376
Average student loan debt	$70,366

ADMISSIONS

Admissions Selectivity Rating	90
# of applications received	1,338
% applicants accepted	47
% acceptees attending	45
Average GMAT	664
Range of GMAT	640–700
Average GPA	3.27
TOEFL required of international students	Yes
Minimum TOEFL (paper/computer)	600/250
Application fee	$130
Regular application deadline	3/2
Regular notification	4/27
Application Deadline/Notification	
Round 1:	10/27 / 12/11
Round 2:	12/1 / 2/5
Round 3:	1/5 / 3/12
Round 4:	3/2 / 4/27
Early decision program	Yes
ED Deadline/Notification	10/27/12/11
Deferment available	Yes
Maximum length of deferment	1 year (emergency only)
Need-blind admissions	Yes

Applicants Also Look At

Duke University, Northwestern University, University of Michigan, University of Virginia.

EMPLOYMENT PROFILE

Career Rating	92	Grads Employed by Function	%	Avg. Salary
Primary Source of Full-time Job Acceptances		Finance/Accounting	52	$89,935
School-facilitated activities	150 (70%)	Marketing/Sales	19	$83,615
Graduate-facilitated activities	65 (30%)	Operations/Production	1	$92,666
Average base starting salary	$89,494	Consulting	16	$99,281
Percent employed	91	General Management	5	$75,790
		Other	6	$88,793

Top 5 Employers Hiring Grads

Bank of America; Deloitte Consulting; Johnson & Johnson; Lehman Brothers; Citigroup.

THE UNIVERSITY OF NORTH CAROLINA AT CHARLOTTE
BELK COLLEGE OF BUSINESS

Academics

A large part-time program "allows working professionals to earn their degree in the evening without interrupting their careers" at the University of North Carolina at Charlotte, a state school located in one of the nation's major banking centers. MBAs in this "incredibly flexible program" can take one to four courses per term at two convenient locations, and as long as they're North Carolina residents, they can do it for a remarkably low price. "I think it's probably one of the top five business schools in terms of return on investment," one Tar Heel tells us.

Belk offers a whopping 9 areas of concentration (business finance, information & technology management, international business, management, marketing, economics, real estate finance and development, supply chain management, and financial institutions/commercial banking), as well as the option to design one of your own. Banking and finance-related disciplines are strong, benefiting from the school's location. Other disciplines also benefit from Charlotte's status as a business center. One MBA explains, "Many of the professors are very active within their fields as well as in the community, and often run their own businesses. They bring valuable knowledge and experience into the classroom, and keep current events in the forefront of class discussion." The program has recently intensified its focus on international business, employing technology to run joint learning ventures with students in Mexico, Europe, Asia, and Latin America.

Students here warn that "Most of the time, the course load is very heavy, but that's the only way you learn a lot from a master's program." Fortunately, when work becomes overwhelming, the professors "are very helpful and knowledgeable" and administrators "are willing to meet one-on-one and they respond to your e-mails almost immediately, even during registration week." Best of all, the school's leaders are "very committed to implement students' input and develop a stronger program." No wonder MBAs express a high degree of satisfaction with Belk, telling us that "it offers a well-diversified and challenging program that's most likely as good as any."

Career and Placement

Belk students receive career and placement assistance from both the administration of their program and the university's Career Center. The Career Center maintains a list of job postings and recruiting schedules; conducts workshops and counseling sessions in resume writing, interviewing, and networking; and provides assistance in employment searches. A total of 37 companies visit the UNC at Charlotte campus each year to recruit MBAs for full-time employment; another seven recruit summer interns here. Many students attend part-time on their employer's dime and do not use the school's career services.

Top employers of Belk MBAs include AG Edwards, Bank of America, BB&T, Belk Stores Services, Carolina Health Care System, Cisco Systems, Compass Group, Duke Energy, IBM, Ingersoll-Rand, Northwestern Mutual, TIAA-CREF, and Wachovia.

Student Life and Environment

Belk MBAs "are very career-focused . . . working adults" who "spend very little time on campus," and accordingly "Many do not have time for much outside of class." When attending classes, students appreciate the "clean, safe, new buildings, and well-kept grounds," but they rarely stick around long once classes end. Full-timers note that "there are a lot of activities which are cocurricular [and] a lot of extracurricular activities, like

JEREMIAH NELSON, ASSOCIATE DIRECTOR OF THE MBA PROGRAM
9201 UNIVERSITY CITY BOULEVARD, CHARLOTTE, NC 28223-0001 UNITED STATES
PHONE: 704-687-2569 • FAX: 704-687-2809
E-MAIL: MBA@UNCC.EDU • WEBSITE: WWW.MBA.UNCC.EDU

plays, dramas, and movies to watch together on weekends here on campus. There are also a few international festivals organized by UNC at Charlotte each year." Even so, most feel that "the MBA program needs to be more involved in the community and more active in sponsoring seminars, etc. The school in general should do more to make it a 'non-commuter' school." They report optimistically, "The association representing business school students is trying to bring about these changes."

Students see great benefit in attending school in Charlotte, a "growing city" with "diverse companies that allow UNC at Charlotte to attract students who could go to better schools." Charlotte is a major global banking center and is the U.S. headquarters to over 400 global corporations (among which are nine *Fortune* 500 companies). Health care and technology are also major players in the employment market here. The program's thousand-acre main campus is both beautiful and easily accessible. Students may also attend classes at the uptown campus in the Mint Museum of Craft & Design.

The Belk student body consists primarily of "two general types of students. One type is the recent undergraduate who has either not found employment or is not ready to commit to a full-time job yet. The other type is the achieving professional, typically with four or more years of experience and family commitments that prevent him or her from attending a 'name school' full-time. Thankfully, UNC at Charlotte is devoting its resources to attracting the second type of student." Of the latter, MBAs agree that "Full-time employment gives students excellent working experience to bring to class, probably more so than in a full-time program." Wachovia, Bank of America, Duke Energy, IBM, and Bell South are all major feeders into the program, but over 210 companies are represented here, including nonprofits, real estate developers, and sole proprietorships.

Admissions

Belk prefers students with at least three years of professional experience. Eighty percent of its students are part-timers who also work full-time. Applicants must provide the school with two official copies of all transcripts for postsecondary-school work, GMAT scores, a personal essay "describing the applicant's experience and objectives in undertaking graduate study," a resume, and three evaluations from "persons familiar with the applicant's personal and professional qualifications." International applicants must provide TOEFL scores (minimum 557 paper-and-pencil, 220 computer-based), IELTS scores (minimum overall band score 6.5), or MELAB scores (minimum 78), as well as a statement of sufficient financial resources to cover the cost of education and living in Charlotte.

FINANCIAL FACTS

Annual tuition (in-state/ out-of-state)	$9,274/$19,481
% of students receiving aid	53
% of students receiving loans	16
% of students receiving grants	15

ADMISSIONS

Admissions Selectivity Rating	**91**
# of applications received	431
% applicants accepted	69
% acceptees attending	67
Average GMAT	578
Range of GMAT	530–610
Average GPA	3.1
TOEFL required of international students	Yes
Minimum TOEFL (paper/computer)	557/220
Application fee	$55
Regular application deadline	Rolling
Regular notification	Rolling
Deferment available	Yes
Maximum length of deferment	1 year
Transfer students accepted	Yes
Transfer application policy	

All students have to complete the graduate application materials and submit official test scores. With permission, it may be possible to transfer graduate level work from an AACSB-accredited university. This will be considered when the application materials are officially reviewed. At least 30 hours of graduate level course work must be completed in residence at UNC Charlotte.

Non-fall admissions	Yes
Need-blind admissions	Yes

EMPLOYMENT PROFILE

Career Rating	81	Grads Employed by Function	%	Avg. Salary
		Finance/Accounting	35	NR
		Human Resources	2	NR
		Marketing/Sales	7	NR
		MIS	5	NR
		Operations/Production	14	NR
		Consulting	12	NR
		General Management	5	NR
		Other	18	NR

THE UNIVERSITY OF NORTH CAROLINA AT GREENSBORO
JOSEPH M. BRYAN SCHOOL OF BUSINESS AND ECONOMICS

GENERAL INFORMATION
Type of school	Public
Environment	City
Academic calendar	Semester

SURVEY SAYS . . .
Economics
Helpful alumni
Happy students
Smart classrooms
Solid preparation in:
Computer skills
Doing business in a global economy

STUDENTS
Enrollment of parent institution	16,632
Enrollment of business school	195
% male/female	56/44
% out-of-state	22
% part-time	77
% minorities	13
% international	19
Average age at entry	26
Average years work experience at entry	3

ACADEMICS
Academic Experience Rating	**74**
Student/faculty ratio	19:1
Profs interesting rating	87
Profs accessible rating	67
% female faculty	11
% minority faculty	5

Joint Degrees
MSN/MBA 2 to 5 years, MBA/MS (gerontology) 2 to 5 years.

Prominent Alumni
Gary Smith, executive vice president and CFO, International Textile Group; Joe K. Pickett, chairman and CEO, HomeSide International, Inc.; Lee McGehee Porter III, managing director, Weiss, Peck and Greer, L.L.C.; Dean Priddy, CFO and vice president of administration, RF Micro Devices.

Academics

Most of the students in the Bryan MBA program at The University of North Carolina Greensboro are part-timers, and the school accordingly tailors its evening program to their needs. MBAs tell us that their school gets the job done, praising the flexible scheduling system that allows them to shoehorn schoolwork into their busy lives. They also appreciate a "very affordable price" that doesn't impinge on the "outstanding quality of the program" and technological assets that are "a huge plus for UNCG," including a wireless network that supports "a variety of computing environments and provides access to a wide range of software to support instructional and research activities," numerous computer labs, and modern computing and projection equipment in classrooms.

Classes for experienced students at Bryan are offered in the evening, a system that "allows maximum flexibility for working students, and allows daytime internship opportunities for full-time students." In addition to prerequisite courses (which can be waived for students with appropriate academic or professional backgrounds) and foundation courses, Bryan offers electives in advanced accounting, finance, management information systems, marketing, international business, and economics. Students may also take electives through the masters of textile design and marketing program, a program that capitalizes on Greensboro's historic role as a textile manufacturer. All classes "are taught in seven-week increments, so the pace of the courses is fast. Having this type of class enables you to learn quickly and then apply that knowledge to the next layer of classes you take."

Bryan "does well in pulling experts from the field to teach one or two courses, including CEOs from top firms. Some still practice in their field but most are on a 'second' career as a teacher." The professors "demand that students set high standards ethically, professionally, and academically," but are also "understanding of the multitude of priorities in life in addition to course work. It takes self-motivation to excel in this program," in which "class interaction is encouraged and stressed." The MBA program introduced a full-time day MBA option in August 2004 to attract recent graduates with little or no work experience. The course structure is similar to the evening option but more emphasis is placed on practical learning experiences through summer internships, study abroad, and a capstone consulting course. The students in the daytime option go through "Boot camp"—a four day skill and team building program before they begin graduate level course work.

Career and Placement

The office providing Career Services to Bryan MBAs is new and dedicated to providing service to MBA and MS in information technology and management students. It will assist current students and alumni, at no charge, in career and internship placement services.

Top employers of Bryan MBAs include BB&T, Wachovia, VF Corporation, Sara Lee, Volvo, American Express Company, Gilbarco Veeder-Root, Syngenta, the Moses Cone Health Care System, the Center for Creative Leadership, Eveready, Degussa Inc., Dow Corning, Labcorps, Banner Pharmacaps, North Carolina Baptist Hospital, Deloitte Touche Tohmatsu, Procter & Gamble, Reynolds American, Dixon Hughes PLLC, Merck, and a variety of regional organizations.

Student Life and Environment

Because the Bryan MBA is largely a part-time evening program, "Most of the students work a full week and attend classes at night. Add to that the pressures of family and basic household responsibilities, and there's not much time for social clubs and organizations." Even so, the program makes "some attempts at activities, but it's hard because most of us work and go to school." On a positive note, "a lot of the MBA social events

DR. CATHERINE HOLDERNESS, ADMINISTRATIVE DIRECTOR, MBA PROGRAM
PO BOX 26165, GREENSBORO, NC 27402-6165 UNITED STATES
PHONE: 336-334-5390 • FAX: 336-334-4209
E-MAIL: MYBRYANMBA@UNCG.EDU • WEBSITE: WWW.MYBRYANMBA.COM

try to include alumni, which is important and helps with networking for jobs when you get out." The university at large is busy, with plenty of athletic events, theatrical productions, and lectures. As one MBA puts it, "Many of us in the MBA program are too tired to take advantage of all that's offered by the university."

Bryan students enjoy a genial classroom atmosphere in which "the environment is competitive, but students look out for one another and try to help one another out." Full-timers "tend to stick together. Almost any time of day you can find a group of them in the business school studying, conversing, eating, etc." Full-timers also note that "the recreational facilities are outstanding [and] the campus is well-lit and safe." All students complain that "parking is an issue, due to the increased enrollment in the MBA program."

Students tell us that hometown Greensboro, a midsize city with a small-town feel, "is full of entertainment options." The city is part of North Carolina's Triad metropolitan region (which also includes High Point and Winston-Salem), home to 11 colleges and universities as well as a 24,000-seat arena (home of the ACC basketball tournaments), minor-league baseball, and numerous theaters, galleries, and restaurants. The location provides easy access to mountain getaways, Sandhills golf, and North Carolina's two largest cities, Charlotte (a major banking center) and Raleigh (the state capital).

"There is a large group of international students" in the Bryan MBA program, "which enables U.S. students to understand the global business world more clearly." Students come from Germany, France, Italy, China, India, Japan, Thailand, and Holland, we're told. Local students "are a good mix of younger students who recently graduated from undergrad school and students in their 30s or 40s (or higher) who have been in the work force for some time." Many "are technically oriented by degree and experience."

Admissions

Applicants to the Bryan MBA program must provide the admissions office with a completed application, two sets of official undergraduate transcripts, GMAT scores, a personal essay, and three letters of recommendation from coworkers and/or current/former instructors. International students must also submit TOEFL scores and an affidavit of financial support. The school reports that the average successful applicant has a GMAT score of 552 and an undergraduate GPA of 3.4. Note, however, that half of all successful applicants fail to meet at least one of those benchmarks. Previous work experience is preferred but not required. Bryan fellowships, scholarships, and graduate assistantships are available to outstanding and well-deserving students.

FINANCIAL FACTS

Annual tuition (in-state/ out-of-state)	$4,372/$15,422
Fees	$1,505
Cost of books	$1,200
Room & board (on/off-campus)	$5,297/$8,066
% of students receiving aid	37
Average grant	$6,000

ADMISSIONS

Admissions Selectivity Rating	72
# of applications received	218
% applicants accepted	80
% acceptees attending	34
Average GMAT	570
Range of GMAT	530–600
Average GPA	3.3
TOEFL required of international students	Yes
Minimum TOEFL (paper/computer)	550/213
Application fee	$45
Regular application deadline	7/1
Regular notification	Rolling
Deferment available	Yes
Maximum length of deferment	1 year
Transfer students accepted	Yes
Transfer application policy They must be in good standing at a fellow AACSB-accredited MBA program and may transfer no more than 12 semester credit hours of approved course work.	
Non-fall admissions	Yes
Need-blind admissions	Yes

Applicants Also Look At
North Carolina State University, The University of North Carolina at Chapel Hill, Wake Forest University (evening MBA, Winston-Salem).

EMPLOYMENT PROFILE	
Career Rating	83
Primary Source of Full-time Job Acceptances	
Percent employed	85

THE UNIVERSITY OF NORTH CAROLINA AT WILMINGTON
CAMERON SCHOOL OF BUSINESS

GENERAL INFORMATION

Type of school	Public
Environment	City

SURVEY SAYS . . .
Students love Wilmington, NC
Solid preparation in:
Finance
Accounting

STUDENTS

Enrollment of parent institution	10,300
Enrollment of business school	120
% male/female	61/39
% part-time	100
% minorities	3
Average age at entry	31
Average years work experience at entry	8

ACADEMICS

Academic Experience Rating	**76**
Profs interesting rating	63
Profs accessible rating	81

Academics

The Cameron School of Business at UNC Wilmington offers a part-time evening and weekend program leading toward the MBA. In the fall of 2007, the school began a full-time international degree program, which offers dual degrees with several universities in Spain, Russia, and other countries. It requires residency abroad, and is open to those with undergraduate degrees in business.

Students from any undergraduate background may enroll in the evening MBA program, and in recent years approximately 70 percent of those students have come from academic fields other than business. "The administration understands the pressures involved with full-time employment and classwork," one student says. "The administration and professors are willing to help ease this stress, but still require a high level of participation and learning."

Though the program is part-time in the sense that classes meet in the evenings and on weekends, Cameron requires courses to be taken in sequence, and it employs an integrated-project model. Students are assigned to groups to work on exercises and practical presentations, and "Students will generally hang around after class meetings with assigned work teams to discuss upcoming projects or deadlines."

The evening MBA program consists of 49 credit hours, which, with the exception of three courses in special topics toward the end of the program, are mainly in prescribed courses. These include subjects such as macroeconomics, business law, and behavioral management. Communications, decision making, teamwork, organizational change, and ethics are stressed in cross-disciplinary activities, which require students to integrate the skills they're learning, both in strategic exercises and real-world problems posed by local business partners.

Special topics may include study in new product development, technology management, investment analysis, and strategic information systems. An executive challenge situation designed to test students' leadership skills is required near the end of the course work.

"Practical application with actual business" is a strength of the curriculum at Cameron, students say, and "Projects with local small businesses are . . . very beneficial in helping the students tie all the classroom materials in to real-life situations." But one student complains that "the quality of instruction has ranged from excellent to awful." Several students echo the concern that "at times, especially for experienced students, some professors still act like they are teaching undergrads," although, "Overall, the professors are very helpful and accessible."

One student says that "the program is small enough for faculty to really care about you and your success, as opposed to some of the larger schools that appear to be about status alone." Many feel the administration could benefit from some reorganization, but "The MBA program administrators can best be typified as supportive and student focused," and that "the program is evolving and changing as the needs of students change."

Career and Placement

There is a dedicated Career Services representative at the school of business at UNCW, and MBA students may also use the general university's career services, such as online databases, career workshops, and career fairs. Almost all Cameron students work full-time while earning their degrees, and many are sponsored by local employers. Those who do seek career assistance would like "more interaction with the business community to

KATHY ERICKSON, GRADUATE PROGRAMS ADMINISTRATOR
601 SOUTH COLLEGE ROAD, WILMINGTON, NC 28403-5920 UNITED STATES
PHONE: 910-962-3903 • FAX: 910-962-3815
E-MAIL: GRADSTUDIES@UNCW.EDU • WEBSITE: WWW.CSB.UNCW.EDU/MBA/INDEX.STM

assist in job placement," and a Career Services Office that is "more ambitious about marketing itself" to business.

General Electric Company, Corning, International Paper, New Hanover Regional Medical Center, the U.S. Coast Guard, United Parcel Service, and First Citizens Bank are among the employers who have recruited Cameron School graduates.

Student Life and Environment

Students at the Cameron School of Business seem to appreciate both town and gown, not surprising as most work full-time in the region.

"Wilmington is a great city for families," one man points out, and "There is plenty of life outside of schoolwork here." Another student praises the "friendly people, beautiful beaches, and [the] tons of restaurants and things to do." As one student explains, "Learning at UNCW takes place in a very laid-back atmosphere." Another notes that although "lacking in racial diversity, there is strong diversity in experience levels, age, and industry segment, coupled with an extremely collaborative and supportive environment." Life in the program isn't "cutthroat . . . everyone wants to see each other do well and graduate."

What would students like to see improved? "Job placement, parking, class-time child care!" is the resounding cry, in addition to "more [academic] specialization. The program is currently a general MBA program." But students agree with their classmate who says "UNCW offers a good 2-year evening program in a great area, with a beautiful campus, and a fine reputation."

Admissions

GMAT scores, transcripts, letters of recommendation, a resume, TOEFL scores for those who need prove fluency in English, and a year of work experience are required for admission to the MBA program at UNCW. The program also requires a three-semester hour course in introductory calculus, or its equivalent, and while the school would prefer that students have this before admission, arrangements can be made to take the classes during the student's first term at the university. In 2006 the average GMAT score for those accepted was 555, and the average GPA was 3.50; students had more than 6 years of work experience on average.

FINANCIAL FACTS

Annual tuition (in-state/ out-of-state)	$4,696/$9,267

ADMISSIONS

Admissions Selectivity Rating	**88**
# of applications received	147
% applicants accepted	44
% acceptees attending	92
Average GMAT	555
Average GPA	3.5
TOEFL required of international students	Yes
Minimum TOEFL (paper/computer)	500/213
Application fee	$45
International application fee	$45
Regular application deadline	2/1
Regular notification	Rolling
Deferment available	Yes
Maximum length of deferment	1 year
Non-fall admissions	Yes

THE UNIVERSITY OF NORTH DAKOTA
COLLEGE OF BUSINESS AND PUBLIC ADMINISTRATION

GENERAL INFORMATION

Type of school	Public
Environment	Town

SURVEY SAYS . . .
Friendly students
Happy students
Smart classrooms
Solid preparation in:
Communication/interpersonal skills
Presentation skills
Computer skills

STUDENTS

Enrollment of parent institution	11,300
Enrollment of business school	106
% male/female	60/40
% out-of-state	30
% part-time	60
% minorities	15
% international	10
Average age at entry	27
Average years work experience at entry	5

ACADEMICS

Academic Experience Rating	**76**
Student/faculty ratio	3:1
Profs interesting rating	75
Profs accessible rating	69
% female faculty	23
% minority faculty	20

Academics

Affordability, convenience, a "solid reputation in the area," and a popular 3/2 combined bachelor's-MBA program draw students to the College of Business and Public Administration at the University of North Dakota, one of only two AACSB-accredited programs in the state. More than half the students here attend full-time, many under the Combined Model that yields a baccalaureate in business and a MBA in five years' time. The part-time population include a number of distance learners; UND has offered long-distance learning for more than 10 years through IVN, the state-run interactive video network.

The UND MBA consists of 32 hours of course work (35 hours for students pursuing a concentration). Twenty-four hours are committed to core classes, two hours are set aside for independent study, and the remaining hours are allotted to electives. Because this is a small program, concentrations are available in two areas only: accounting, and international business. The former program can be used to help fulfill the 150-hour requirement for taking the CPA exam; the latter program requires students to complete nine hours of course work at the Business Institute University of Norway. Students here praise the "outstanding accounting concentration" and also love the college's courses in entrepreneurship. In all areas, classes at UND are "small and discussion based," leading to "a more intimate student-teacher relationship." Sums up one student, "This is the best school in the state of North Dakota. It's also great having a Division I hockey team. It helps with recruiting, believe it or not."

Career and Placement

The UND Career Services Office provides counseling and placement services for all enrolled students of the university. The office organizes career fairs and on-campus recruiting events. On average, about 25 companies visit the campus to recruit MBAs each year; another three visit to recruit summer interns. Employers most likely to hire UND MBAs include Cargill, Deloitte Touche Tohmatsu, PricewaterhouseCoopers, Honeywell, Microsoft Great Plains, Eide Bailley, and McGladdrey Pullen.

Student Life and Environment

The College of Business and Public Administration building at UND boasts a number of high-tech facilities, including the A. Kirk Lanterman Investment Center, which "provides students access to real-time financial market data and research information, which augments student education at the graduate and undergraduate levels," according to the college's website. The Page Family Marketing Center provides marketing students with a research lab, breakout rooms, a conference room, and a focus group area equipped with video cameras for taping focus-group sessions. Students appreciate these assets, but are most pleased that "all the classes are in the same building, which means we don't have to go outside in the winter!"

Students can make their extracurricular lives at UND as busy as they want. The program hosts a solid complement of professional groups and student organizations. There are plenty of opportunities for physical activity, both indoor and out: students have access to an Arnold Palmer-designed golf course, parks, swimming pools, and a gym. The university's hockey team draws large crowds of winter sports enthusiasts. The area is also ideal for skaters, sledders, snowmobilers, and cross-country skiers. Students report that "the various seasons provide a diverse climate" in Grand Forks, but warn that "the Winter session is very harsh because of the weather."

DR. SUSAN NELSON, MBA DIRECTOR
GAMBLE HALL, PO BOX 8098, GRAND FORKS, ND 58202 UNITED STATES
PHONE: 701-777-4853 • FAX: 701-777-2019
E-MAIL: MBA@UND.NODAK.EDU • WEBSITE: WWW.BUSINESS.UND.EDU/MBA

"Many students come straight out of undergraduate school and into the program" at UND, but the student body as a whole is drawn "from all different backgrounds and all different locations." Nearly one-third of the student body originates from outside North Dakota. Students form a "friendly community" of "smart and self-sufficient" future MBAs.

Admissions

Admissions requirements to the MBA program at UND include: an undergraduate degree from an accredited institution, with a GPA of at least 2.75 for the full four years or 3.00 for the final two years of undergraduate work (a 3.00 GPA is required for admission under the Combined Model, which allows students to begin their MBA work after three years of undergraduate work); and demonstrated proficiency in basic accounting, administrative process, economics, functional areas of business, mathematics, and quantitative methods. Applicants who do not meet this final requirement may be admitted conditionally, pending completion of course work in the prescribed areas. International students whose first language is not English must additionally demonstrate language mastery through the TOEFL.

FINANCIAL FACTS

Annual tuition (in-state/out-of-state)	$254/$583 per credit hour
Cost of books	$3,300
Room & board (on-campus)	$3,932
% of students receiving aid	40
% of first-year students receiving aid	25
% of students receiving grants	2
Average grant	$7,000

ADMISSIONS

Admissions Selectivity Rating	77
# of applications received	36
% applicants accepted	64
% acceptees attending	70
Average GMAT	545
Range of GMAT	390-680
Average GPA	3.2
TOEFL required of international students	Yes
Minimum TOEFL (paper/computer)	550/213
Application fee	$35
Regular application deadline	Rolling
Regular notification	Rolling
Deferment available	Yes
Maximum length of deferment	Up to 1 year.
Transfer students accepted	Yes
Transfer application policy	
Up to 9 credits of approved course work can be transferred.	
Non-fall admissions	Yes
Need-blind admissions	Yes

Applicants Also Look At
North Dakota State University,
University of Minnesota.

EMPLOYMENT PROFILE

Career Rating	64		
		Grads Employed by Function	**% Avg. Salary**
		Accounting	25 $50,000
		Finance/Accounting	20 $45,000
		Human Resources	15 $38,000
		Marketing/Sales	20 $45,000
		MIS	5 $40,000
		Consulting	5 $42,000
		Communications	5 $37,000
		General Management	5 $40,000

University of North Florida
Coggin College of Business

GENERAL INFORMATION

Type of school	Public
Environment	Metropolis

SURVEY SAYS . . .

Students love Jacksonville, Fl
Happy students
Smart classrooms
Solid preparation in:
Accounting
Teamwork
Doing business in a global economy

STUDENTS

Enrollment of parent institution	16,084
Enrollment of business school	417
% male/female	56/44
% out-of-state	2
% part-time	71
% minorities	15
% international	6
Average age at entry	27

ACADEMICS

Academic Experience Rating	**85**
Student/faculty ratio	9:1
Profs interesting rating	96
Profs accessible rating	72
% female faculty	17
% minority faculty	6

Joint Degrees

Global MBA.

Prominent Alumni

David A. Smith, president and CEO, PSS World Medical, Inc.; Catherine Reynolds, chair, Catherine Reynolds Foundation; Mark Vitner, chief economist, Wachovia; Steve Perez, CFO, Nextran, Inc.; Donna Harper, founder, SystemLogics.

Academics

When you consider the cost-benefit ratio, The University of North Florida Coggin College of Business is an excellent choice for the sensible business student, as it offers "quality instructors and overall programs at an affordable price." Intended for students with a bachelor's degree in any field, Coggin offers general graduate level course work in a wide range of business topics, including accounting, finance, international business and e-commerce. As a vast majority of the school's 450 graduate students are working professionals, the school offers a flexible evening schedule, and classes are also offered on the weekends.

Coggin has a strong "focus on application-based learning." All UNF professors join the faculty with real world experience, and students are expected to take a hands-on, practical approach to their education. A student reports, "I have been very pleased with my professors at UNF. A majority of them have published several books, journal articles, and have also been part of corporate America, such as Dun & Bradstreet and *Fortune* 500 companies. They have brought valuable corporate experience into the classroom." Another student adds, "I have seen a direct correlation between my performance at work and the additional knowledge gained through my MBA courses. Most professors have done an excellent job relating the course material to real-world business examples."

A distinguishing characteristic of the Coggin MBA program is its strong focus on international business. In particular, Coggin offers the unique GlobalMBA program, a business school exchange operated in conjunction with three partner universities in France, Germany, and Poland. The GlobalMBA brings "a ton of international students" to the UNF campus each year, a benefit to the entire student community. "The GlobalMBA attracts students from across the world," writes one student. "My current cohort has nationalities of Greece, Iran, Bulgaria, Germany, France, Poland, and the U.S.A. This makes for a great intercultural experience, as well as a wonderful interactive learning environment." For students in the regular MBA program, "There are several opportunities for UNF students to study abroad all over the world."

Coggin offers a number of concentrations for those who wish to focus their education on a specific business field. Currently, the faculty has approved concentrations in the following fields of study: accounting, construction management, e-commerce, economics, finance, human resource management, international business, logistics, or management application. Students also point out that UNF offers the unique "opportunity to be selected in the Osprey Financial Group, the student run investment portfolio" that manages a $600,000 portfolio of equity and fixed income securities. Still, many students believe Coggin could offer "more options for electives." Many tell us that the research facilities need to be updated; "Really, the biggest improvement [is] the library. It is dated and the material is lacking. You have to go to your local library or order the book you need from another university," writes a second-year student. Luckily, a library extension is underway.

Career and Placement

Coggin students "mostly consist of local Jacksonville residents who intend to continue their careers in the area." As such, the school is an excellent choice for those interested in finding quality employment in the burgeoning Jacksonville region, as it is "well regarded in the community." This is mainly due to that fact that faculty and administrators work "diligently at keeping their business school on the cutting edge and involving the local business community."

MICHELLE MOUTON, THE GRADUATE SCHOOL COORDINATOR
4567 ST JOHN'S BLUFF ROAD SOUTH, BUILDING 10, JACKSONVILLE, FL 32224 UNITED STATES
PHONE: 904-620-1360 • FAX: 904-620-1362
E-MAIL: MMOUTON@UNF.EDU • WEBSITE: WWW.UNF.EDU/COGGIN

Student Life and Environment

With its international focus and active part-time program, Coggin attracts "a very diverse group of students. Some with families, some...straight out of undergrad." Satisfied part-time students praise the fact that "for the working student, UNF is a great university that allows you to balance your educational objectives." While the campus vibe is low-key and friendly, most business students "have busy lives and would really like to minimize the time spent on campus." Therefore, most are uninterested in participating in campus clubs or social activities. In fact, "many of us only attend functions that are mandatory on campus or for our group work."

Nonetheless, UNF still also manages to appeal to full-time students. For those who want a more traditional college experience, "The campus housing is pretty good," and "UNF has tons of clubs, sororities, and sports" in which MBA students are free to participate. Students also note that "the weather, the people, the campus are all wonderful." In fact, "The city itself is full of activities from the beach to NFL football games, to clubs to hockey games. You can't get bored!"

Admissions

To apply to the Coggin School of Business, you must submit a completed application, an application fee, undergraduate transcripts, and GMAT scores. Admission to the regular MBA program is based on undergraduate GPA and GMAT scores. To be admitted, a minimum 1,000 index must be obtained on the formula (GPA x 200) + GMAT total score. GMAT: In addition to the minimum 1,000 index, a minimum 20 Verbal and 22 Quantitative GMAT sub-score and a 450 score total are required for graduate admission. Currently, the Analytical Writing Analysis sub-score is not used as an admission criterion.

Students must apply separately for the GlobalMBA program. To apply to the GlobalMBA, students must submit a completed application and fee, undergraduate transcripts, and GMAT scores. The minimum GMAT score for the GlobalMBA is 500. These documents are carefully reviewed and qualified candidates are then invited for personal interviews with the admissions committee. All applications for the GlobalMBA must be submitted by April 1.

FINANCIAL FACTS

Annual tuition (in-state/ out-of-state)	$6,020/$20,212
Cost of books	$800
Room & board (on/off-campus)	$6,268/$8,300
% of students receiving aid	24
% of first-year students receiving aid	29
% of students receiving loans	20
% of students receiving grants	7
Average award package	$3,407
Average grant	$1,064

ADMISSIONS

Admissions Selectivity Rating	81
# of applications received	267
% applicants accepted	52
% acceptees attending	76
Average GMAT	538
Range of GMAT	490–570
Average GPA	3.24
TOEFL required of international students	Yes
Minimum TOEFL (paper)	550
Application fee	$30
Regular application deadline	7/1
Regular notification	Rolling
Deferment available	Yes
Maximum length of deferment	1 semester
Transfer students accepted	Yes
Transfer application policy on a case-by-case basis.	
Non-fall admissions	Yes
Need-blind admissions	Yes

EMPLOYMENT PROFILE

Career Rating	60*	Grads Employed by Function	%	Avg. Salary
Primary Source of Full-time Job Acceptances		Finance/Accounting	33	$48,125
School-facilitated activities	2 (11%)	Human Resources	13	$52,300
Graduate-facilitated activities	16 (89%)	Marketing/Sales	12	$37,300
		Operations/Production	21	$49,800
		General Management	8	$43,500
		Other	13	$35,600

Top 5 Employers Hiring Grads

KPMG International; CSX Transportation; PricewaterhouseCoopers; Ernst & Young.

UNIVERSITY OF NORTHERN IOWA
COLLEGE OF BUSINESS ADMINISTRATION

GENERAL INFORMATION

Type of school	Public
Environment	Town
Academic calendar	Trimester

SURVEY SAYS . . .
Friendly students
Good peer network
Happy students
Solid preparation in:
General management
Teamwork

STUDENTS

Enrollment of parent institution	12,260
Enrollment of business school	74
% male/female	71/29
% out-of-state	43
% part-time	91
% minorities	14
% international	29
Average age at entry	29
Average years work experience at entry	6

ACADEMICS

Academic Experience Rating	**89**
Student/faculty ratio	25:1
Profs interesting rating	89
Profs accessible rating	76
% female faculty	17
% minority faculty	19

Prominent Alumni
Nancy Aossey, CEO, International Medical Corporation; Mark Baldwin, CEO, Iowa Laser Technology; Kevin Lentz, senior vice President, Cuna Mutual Insurance; Gary Rolling, president and CEO, J-Tec Associates, Inc.; Kyle Selberg, vice president marketing, Principal Financial Group.

Academics

Combining state-of-the-art facilities, "impossibly friendly" faculty, and a low, public school price tag, it's no wonder that University of Northern Iowa students feel theirs is "the best business program in the Midwest." A friendly environment is balanced with a high caliber of academics creating "a small-college feel and university opportunities" at UNI. Professors are "knowledgeable, efficient, friendly, concerned, creative, and provide a learning- and result-oriented atmosphere with as little psychological pressure as possible." One current student tells us, "Most of the professors are above standard academically speaking and are willing to help the students as much as possible." Another adds, "It's a great value and the faculty are very accessible. They are passionate about their work and strive to continually improve programs." On that note, the university is dedicated to offering course work that addresses current issues in business, and one of the school's greatest strengths is "the diversity of the classes and the desire to incorporate current issues and trends into the various classes."

Committed to providing a thorough but expeditious education, the University of Northern Iowa's curriculum can be tailored to fit the objectives and needs of each individual student. In fact, before beginning the program, every student's educational and professional background is evaluated to determine which foundational courses he/she will be required to take in order to complete the degree. As a result, students entering the program with business experience may be able to complete the program more quickly, and thereby save on tuition costs. In this and other ways, the school's "great and efficient administration," displays its' commitment to students' needs. By all accounts, "the school is running smoothly" and "the administration is very active in making sure all students have the resources they need to succeed in the program and beyond."

All courses in the graduate program at the University of Northern Iowa are offered in the evening to accommodate students who work full-time or who wish to pursue an internship during business hours. Of UNI master's students, "The majority are working or have work experience" and are able to directly integrate their course work into their current positions. In terms of practical, hands-on components, the MBA at UNI culminates in the business capstone experience, a one-credit course in which the student serves as a consultant to a local company under the advisement of a UNI faculty member. In addition, students may gain real-world experience through one of the school's two-week international programs in Hong Kong and Paris, France.

Career and Placement

In the Cedar Falls area, UNI is "well known for its finance and business degrees," giving graduates a step-up in the local market. For extra support, the Academic Advising and Career Services Center at UNI offers workshops, resume reviews, cover letter advice, mock interviews, and Internet resources for job seekers. Recruiters visit the campus throughout the year, and the school also hosts the Fall Career Fair Day and the Spring Job and Internship Fair for job seekers.

NANCY L. HOFFMAN, MBA PROGRAM ASSISTANT
COLLEGE OF BUSINESS ADMINISTRATION, CURRIS BUSINESS BUILDING 325, CEDAR FALLS, IA 50613-0123 UNITED STATES • PHONE: 319-273-6243 • FAX: 319-273-6230 • E-MAIL: MBA@UNI.EDU
WEBSITE: WWW.CBA.UNI.EDU/DBWEB/PAGES/PROGRAMS/GRADUATE-BUS-ADMIN.CFM

Student Life and Environment

UNI's MBA Program offers "excellent facilities and technology," to undergraduate and graduate business students. A surprisingly diverse community, "MBA students at the University of Northern Iowa represent a wide variety of ethnic, cultural and educational backgrounds, as well as a breadth of future endeavors. The diversity helps to create a dynamic and intellectually challenging learning environment." As one current student enthuses: "I was amazed at the diversity of students in the MBA program (in regards to) marital status, age, ethnicity, and work experience. This was great for classroom discussion." Despite the diversity within the student body, everyone finds a place, as "Life at the University of Northern Iowa is well suited to a variety of needs."

Outside the classroom, "There are a wide variety of activities offered through the university at large. In addition, there are a large number of extracurricular and social activities offered." Students note that "the athletic teams are spectacular at UNI" and a source of pride for the whole school community. A number of academic organizations are represented on campus, including the Economics Club, Accounting Club, American Marketing Association, as well as honor organizations such as Beta Gamma Sigma and Mu Kappa Tau, among others. However, the level of extracurricular involvement is laid back and entirely up to each student. "If a student is interested in community or campus involvement, there are numerous groups to join. If the student would rather not be involved, there is no pressure to join extracurricular activities."

Admissions

Applicants to the University of Northern Iowa must submit official GMAT scores, transcripts from all colleges and universities attended, and three essays that address the applicant's professional and personal background. The Admissions Committee selects applicants based on their communication skills, demonstrated leadership potential, intellectual capability, and academic success during undergraduate and graduate work. The Admissions Committee considers each applicant's particular accomplishments individually, and admissions essays are strongly weighted in a decision. Applicants must have a bachelor's degree from an accredited university or college. In the past three years, successful applicants have submitted GMAT scores averaging 560–580.

FINANCIAL FACTS

Annual tuition (in-state/ out-of-state)	$5,936/$14,074
Fees	$1,026
Cost of books	$1,500
Room & board	$6,100

ADMISSIONS

Admissions Selectivity Rating	**85**
# of applications received	66
% applicants accepted	50
% acceptees attending	76
Average GMAT	572
Range of GMAT	500–680
Average GPA	3.2
TOEFL required of international students	Yes
Minimum TOEFL (paper/computer)	600/250
Application fee	$30
International application fee	$50
Regular application deadline	7/20
Regular notification	Rolling
Deferment available	Yes
Maximum length of deferment	1 year
Transfer students accepted	Yes
Transfer application policy Students may transfer up to 11 hours of AACSB-accredited graduate credit.	
Non-fall admissions	Yes
Need-blind admissions	Yes

Applicants Also Look At

Iowa State University, University of Iowa, University of Minnesota, University of Nebraska—Lincoln.

EMPLOYMENT PROFILE

Career Rating	93
Primary Source of Full-time Job Acceptances	
Percent employed	100

UNIVERSITY OF NOTRE DAME
MENDOZA COLLEGE OF BUSINESS

Academics

Students come the University of Notre Dame to become part of the "Notre Dame family," and few leave disappointed; the MBA program at the Mendoza College of Business fosters a strong sense of community that, coupled with the campus-wide school spirit, quickly makes Notre Dame feel like home. Add "outstanding professor-student interaction" and "great potential for alumni networking" and you understand why student satisfaction levels are so high here.

The Mendoza MBA program "excels at providing an overall business understanding," students tell us. The school offers a 2-year full-time program that "is perfect for non-business undergraduate majors to gain a well-rounded understanding of business fundamentals," as well as a 1-year program for those with exceptionally strong business backgrounds. Students say, "Ethics is a hallmark of the school and it can be seen in every course," and "The school's reputation for producing ethical graduates is more important in recent years than ever before."

Mendoza implemented a modular curriculum a few years back, and "The 2007 class is the first to complete our entire course work under the current 'module' system. The module system will allow Notre Dame MBAs to be better prepared than were previous classes. Although "There was some negative press after the transition," "now that the transition is completed, Notre Dame will move quickly [back] up the rankings." The faculty here "is top-notch." Their research, publications, work experience, and generally great personalities inspire confidence in their ability to prepare [students] for the business world."

Career and Placement

"The majority of recruiting is Midwest based" at Notre Dame, and while some complain about the dearth of New York finance-sector recruiters, most students feel that "the Career Office does a good job of locating companies from various regions." Mendoza MBAs recognize that "our small class size hinders our ability to get a large selection of companies from each region, but they are represented." However, "The situation is greatly improving, with some bulge-bracket and many middle-market banks already recruiting on campus. This will improve over time as the school moves toward its long-term mission of improving rank."

Of course, Notre Dame's storied alumni network helps with placement. Students tell us that "the Career Development Office recently made it easier for current MBA students to get in contact with alumni. Prior to this, it was a very prolonged process that involved Career Development responding to individual student's requests for alumni contact information in their respective field." These contacts can be invaluable. As one student reports, "I went to a conference with several classmates for the weekend where we met a ND alum recruiter for a major corporation. . . .We were invited over his house to talk and have a couple of drinks. This is what you get at Notre Dame: family. And our family is everywhere in every kind of position." No wonder students brag that "becoming a member of the alumni network is worth more than the cost of tuition."

Companies recruiting Mendoza MBAs include: Avaya Systems, DaimlerChrysler, Deloitte Touche Tohmatsu, Ernst & Young, Ford Motor Company, GE, Hewlett-Packard, Honeywell, IBM, Intel, Johnson & Johnson, Kraft Foods, PricewaterhouseCoopers, SAP, Sandler O'Neill, Sprint, Textron Financial, The Gallup Organization, Western & Southern Life, and Whirlpool.

BRIAN LOHR, DIRECTOR OF ADMISSIONS
276 MENDOZA, COLLEGE OF BUSINESS, NOTRE DAME, IN 46556-4656 UNITED STATES
PHONE: 574-631-8488 • FAX: 574-631-8800
E-MAIL: MBA.1@ND.EDU • WEBSITE: WWW.ND.EDU/~MBA

Student Life and Environment

There's no doubt that Notre Dame is a very social campus, but the extent to which MBAs can partake in that social life depends on whether they're in their first or second year of the program. First year is "very difficult" with a massive workload. Many students "spend twice as much time on schoolwork" during their first year, and find it difficult to "juggle [classes] with career pursuits." Those who can carve out some leisure time agree that "Notre Dame has a culture that is contagious! It's not hard to keep yourself busy with a broad range of activities, whether it's class, a group meeting, intramural game, community-service event, or a football tailgate. There's never a dull moment." Football unites the campus and provides more than mere entertainment; it also "lures large corporations for networking events." Also, alumni return to campus for football games "for years after graduation and usually for life." Hometown South Bend is a small town, with only a "few good places to go out." The "students make up for it, though. We host a lot of social gatherings."

Mendoza MBAs benefit from "a strong esprit de corps" built on team projects and "an ethical foundation that is reinforced constantly so that it actually has an effect." Most are "married, with families and children, and have been working in industry for 7 to 10 years." They represent "more diverse backgrounds than some of the 'big' schools back East, meaning we have folks from engineering, the public sector, and other nontraditional or non-business backgrounds. These are very sharp people who may have had the 'wrong' undergrad pedigree but are every bit as bright as those at any b-school anywhere."

Admissions

Applicants to Mendoza's 2-year MBA program must provide the Admissions Department with all of the following: proof of an undergraduate degree from an accredited college or university; official transcript(s); GMAT scores; a current resume; three essays (topics provided by school); and two letters of recommendation. Transcripts and/or resume must demonstrate familiarity with basic quantitative processes and accounting methods. A background in statistics is strongly recommended. International students must also provide TOEFL scores and visa documentation. Applicants to the 1-year program must present academic transcripts showing successful completion of 6 credit hours each of mathematics, accounting, and economics and 3 credit hours each of marketing and MIS. All applicants must have at least 2 years of meaningful work experience.

FINANCIAL FACTS

Annual tuition	$35,905
Fees	$575
Cost of books	$1,550
Room & board (on/off-campus)	$7,650/$12,936
% of students receiving aid	83
% of first-year students receiving aid	81
% of students receiving loans	58
% of students receiving grants	68
Average award package	$37,405
Average grant	$15,538
Average student loan debt	$53,095

ADMISSIONS

Admissions Selectivity Rating	91
# of applications received	582
% applicants accepted	47
% acceptees attending	50
Average GMAT	667
Range of GMAT	560–740
Average GPA	3.21
TOEFL required of international students	Yes
Minimum TOEFL (paper/computer)	600/250
Application fee	$100
International application fee	$100
Regular application deadline	1/15
Regular notification	2/15
Application Deadline/Notification	
Round 1:	11/15 / 12/15
Round 2:	1/15 / 2/15
Round 3:	3/15 / 4/15
Round 4:	5/1 / 6/1
Early decision program?	Yes
ED Deadline/Notification	11/15/12/15
Deferment available	Yes
Maximum length of deferment	1 year
Non-fall admissions	Yes
Need-blind admissions	Yes

Applicants Also Look At
Georgetown University, Northwestern University, University of Michigan, The University of Texas at Austin, Vanderbilt University.

EMPLOYMENT PROFILE

Career Rating	88	Grads Employed by Function	%	Avg. Salary
Primary Source of Full-time Job Acceptances		Finance/Accounting	37	$80,487
School-facilitated activities	67 (54%)	Human Resources	2	NR
Graduate-facilitated activities	28 (22%)	Marketing/Sales	17	$78,947
Unknown	30 (24%)	MIS	3	$81,000
Average base starting salary	$79,855	Operations/Production	3	$64,832
Percent employed	97	Consulting	23	$81,421
		General Management	10	$80,880
		Other	5	$80,400

Top 5 Employers Hiring Grads
KPMG International; GE; Accenture; DaimlerChrysler; IBM.

University of Oklahoma
Michael F. Price College of Business

Academics

With "great facilities," a low student/faculty ratio, and "a connection to the Oklahoma City market," the Price College of Business at the University of Oklahoma "offers great value" to Midwestern students, particularly if they're interested in working in the energy or banking sectors. Students tell us that Price's size is a good fit for all, offering "the feel of a very small school with small classes fostering interaction with professors, [while] at the same time you are attending a large university with great traditions, outstanding athletic programs, and a very strong and loyal network of alumni across the United States."

Price offers both a full-time MBA and a part-time professional MBA with evening classes held from 6:00 P.M. to 9:40 P.M. Monday through Thursday. Both programs offer concentrations in entrepreneurship, corporate finance, investment management, business process integration, risk management, management information systems, and supply chain management. Students speak especially highly of the school's offerings in entrepreneurship, finance, and MIS.

MBAs here report that "the faculty is very intelligent, but many are focused on research." As one student puts it, "A lot of the teachers for required courses are too 'academic.' The entrepreneurship teachers are the exception. They give real-life lessons and bring great personal experience to the students." Another student adds, "Some departments are better than others at integrating industry into teaching. The best provide students opportunities to work on projects with local companies as well as major corporate sponsors for practical concept application." On a positive note, "The staff and resources provided at the University of Oklahoma are unmatched! They are dedicated in equipping students with information and knowledge that will help provide opportunities that aren't found elsewhere." Students also tell us that "the business communication center is wonderful."

Career and Placement

Primary responsibility for career counseling and placement services falls to the MBA Student Support Center at Price. The center provides one-on-one mentoring, assistance with resume preparation and interviewing skills, and contacts with corporate recruiters. Students tell us that "our school has a very strong alumni network that cares about current and past students" and that the school does a good job of attracting recruiters in the field of finance; other areas are not as well served, they complain. One MBA warns, "Any students not interested in working in finance for an oil company or local bank should not count on the student support center in their job search." Summer internship programs like the Price Scholars program (which sends students to New York City) and International Internship programs "are good, but relatively few students are selected, and the others are really left to fend for themselves."

Employers who most frequently hire Price MBAs include: ExxonMobil, Bank of Oklahoma, OGE, RiskMetrics, ConocoPhillips Company, SBC, American Airlines, Devon Energy, Schlumberger, KPMG International, Ernst & Young, and Liquidnet.

Student Life and Environment

The Price MBA program "is housed in the new wing of the business school, a facility nicer than those of most Fortune 500 companies. The classrooms have computers, dual projectors, [and] DVD and audio systems." As if all that wasn't enough, "The business school is right next to the football stadium, which provides covered parking for faculty and students. Graduate student housing is brand new, and the Student Fitness Center is huge and has all of the latest equipment." Extracurricular life here is subdued; part-

GINA AMUNDSON, DIRECTOR OF GRADUATE PROGRAMS
1003 ASP AVENUE, PRICE HALL, SUITE 1040, NORMAN, OK 73019-4302 UNITED STATES
PHONE: 405-325-4107 • FAX: 405-325-7753
E-MAIL: GAMUNDSON@OU.EDU • WEBSITE: PRICE.OU.EDU/MBA

timers and full-timers with jobs tell us that the MBA program is "round the clock," with "not much time for extracurricular activities." Many here make time for football, because "Everybody here loves it. It brings people and the town together."

Students tell us that OU's campus "is beautiful and well manicured" and in the process of a major revitalization. "I have lost count of the number of construction projects due to donations," writes one student. OU is located in Norman, "a great town: small but not too small. People are friendly, and the living expenses are very low. It is true that the town dies out during the summer, but as an MBA student you will hold an internship, and you probably will not be in town." Furthermore, Norman is "just 20 minutes from downtown Oklahoma City."

Admissions

Applicants to the Price MBA program must submit the following materials to the Office of Admissions and Records: an application for admission to the university; an official transcript from every undergraduate and graduate institution attended; and, for international applicants, a financial statement as well as an official TOEFL score report (minimum score: 213, computer-based test; 550, paper-based test) if English is not their first language. In addition, all applicants must also submit the following materials to the MBA Admissions Office: a completed supplemental application for graduate study in business; an official score report for the GMAT; a current resume; a personal statement of career and educational goals; and three letters of recommendation. Applicants to the full-time program must have an undergraduate GPA of at least 3.2 and a GMAT score of at least 600. Two years of work experience is preferred but not required.

FINANCIAL FACTS

Annual tuition (in-state/ out-of-state)	$5,801/$14,989
Fees	$4,780
Cost of books	$1,099
Room & board	$7,654

ADMISSIONS

Admissions Selectivity Rating	**81**
# of applications received	98
% applicants accepted	71
% acceptees attending	66
Average GMAT	604
Range of GMAT	540–690
Average GPA	3.46
TOEFL required of international students	Yes
Minimum TOEFL (paper/computer)	550/213
Application fee	$40
International application fee	$90
Regular application deadline	7/1
Regular notification	Rolling
Deferment available	Yes
Maximum length of deferment	1 year
Transfer students accepted	Yes
Transfer application policy Students may transfer into our part-time MBA program from other AACSB-accredited institutions.	
Need-blind admissions	Yes

Applicants Also Look At

Oklahoma State University, Texas A&M University System Health Science Center, The University of Texas at Austin.

EMPLOYMENT PROFILE

Career Rating	81	Grads Employed by Function	%	Avg. Salary
Primary Source of Full-time Job Acceptances		Finance/Accounting	10	$57,125
School-facilitated activities	16 (76%)	MIS	4	$56,000
Graduate-facilitated activities	5 (24%)	Consulting	4	$64,750
Average base starting salary	$60,633	General Management	2	$70,000
Percent employed	95	Other	1	$67,500

Top 5 Employers Hiring Grads

KPMG; Chesapeake; RiskMetrics; Devon; Deloitte.

UNIVERSITY OF OREGON
CHARLES H. LUNDQUIST COLLEGE OF BUSINESS

Academics

Despite its small size and off-the-beaten-path location, the Charles H. Lundquist College of Business MBA program at the University of Oregon is quickly developing a national reputation. Credit lies primarily with two nationally recognized programs. The first, in sports business, provides MBAs with "invaluable connections in the sports industry" through "course work and opportunities to meet and work with top execs." The other program, in entrepreneurship, thrives thanks to its excellent faculty, who "have propelled this small program into many national top 25 lists over the past three years. This program gives Oregon MBAs unique access to, and preparation for, the top domestic and international business plan competitions." Oregon also offers programs in corporate finance, financial analysis, marketing, MIS, and supply chain management.

No matter what area students choose, they agree that "the greatest strengths of this school are the faculty and small class size. The staff and faculty go out of their way to help students, and the small class size makes them very accessible to each and every student." All 110 MBAs here are full-time students, a situation that fosters a close academic community. This makes it easier for students to face down "a rigorous presentation-skills module that runs for the entire first year" as well as "challenging, team-based projects such as SPP (the Strategic Planning Project), in which students gain experience in planning marketing strategy." Professors earn high marks for "trying very hard to ride the forefront of thought in marketing, strategy, and sustainable business. It is the strength of the institution that the desire is so strong and resources are available to us," vouches one student.

MBAs also benefit from the university at large ("We are encouraged to draw from other schools in the university in order to meet our own needs, which allows great flexibility," writes one student) and "facilities and classroom technology that are highly superior."

Career and Placement

Success in recruitment faces two hurdles at the University of Oregon. First is the small class size, which many companies see as a disincentive to visit the campus. Second is the school's relatively out-of-the-way location, which is not ideal for a quick visit. One student explains, "Eugene, Oregon is not easily accessible for business recruiters, but there is nothing that can fix that. It is especially difficult to get companies from outside the Northwest to visit the school."

There are other factors, too. One student writes, "In comparative average salary rankings, the Oregon MBA often ranks below other schools for two reasons: 1) Many students interested in nonprofit and competitive sports marketing careers attend the program. 2) Regional unemployment rates have affected salaries in many areas for graduating students." Fortunately, "the Oregon MBA also has a great network of alumni who are willing to work with current students."

All told, 18 employers typically visit campus each year to seek full-time employees; another 7 come looking for summer interns. Top employers include Hewlett-Packard, Intel, Tektronik, ESPN, and Bear Creek. An interesting stat: nearly one in four Oregon MBAs finds his/her first job outside the U.S.

Student Life and Environment

Even if the location isn't always recruiter-friendly, it is absolutely friendly to the MBAs who attend school here. "Located in one of the most beautiful parts of the country," the University of Oregon bestows an extremely high quality of life on its students. "The town and campus are amazing," and beyond both are abundant natural resources in which

PERRI McGEE, ADMISSIONS ASSISTANT

1208 UNIVERSITY OF OREGON, EUGENE, OR 97403-1208 UNITED STATES

PHONE: 541-346-1462 • FAX: 541-346-0073

E-MAIL: INFO@OREGONMBA.COM • WEBSITE: WWW.OREGONMBA.COM

"outdoor activities abound." While "the workload is heavy" in the program, students here usually find time to unwind. One MBA explains, "Life at the U of O is all about having a healthy environment to support your hard work. I put in a good 60-plus hours a week on school, but when we have free time, students get together and take advantage of what the area has to offer. For example, I had class all morning, then went for a quick hike to reenergize to study until 8 or 9, and then I'll be off to meet classmates for a beer at a local microbrewery. That's a 10-hour day of studying, but I can avoid burning out." MBAs don't have to worry about driving home from the bars, either, since "students enjoy free public bus transportation, which is more than ample."

MBAs don't even need to leave campus to enjoy themselves. "In the university at large, there are plenty of events to go to," such as lectures, performances, movies, and sporting events. MBAs within the program say they enjoy "great team-building activities, rafting trips, golf outings, and bagel lunches. There are also football games and low-key and informal social events where we interact with fellow students and faculty." The Lundquist facility is homey and comfortable, a "beautiful new building that serves as a hub for the MBA students and others taking business classes. And it has all the latest technology." One MBA sums up, "The outdoor and on-campus activities are endless, which makes it very easy to get a good balance of schoolwork and social interaction."

Because of the small class size, Oregon MBAs "all know each other after only three weeks. It makes the experience much more enjoyable." Broadening the social circle is the fact that "the MBA and JD programs have good and frequent interaction, attending each other's events." The program has a "very strong Asian population," but otherwise "there is little racial diversity." Students are "very friendly [and] are very willing to use and share their experiences for the benefit of the class." Although "everyone is competitive, there are no egos."

Admissions

With a program that is small by design, Oregon allows itself the luxury to hand-pick each student admitted. Students are chosen for their potential in the business world and for their fit with the program. Admissions officers look for those who are eager for experiential learning, who have good team skills, and who are comfortable with complexity and uncertainty. In addition, successful applicants typically have a minimum GMAT score of 600 (and at least a 60th percentile rank on the quantitative section), an undergraduate GPA of at least 3.0, and two years of full-time, post-undergraduate work experience. Prior to enrollment, students must complete one term each of microeconomics and macroeconomics.

FINANCIAL FACTS

Annual tuition (in-state/ out-of-state)	$11,055/$15,591
Fees (in-state/ out-of-state)	$1,650/$1,650
Cost of books	$1,000
Room & board (on/off-campus)	$10,569/$11,020
% of students receiving aid	65
% of first-year students receiving aid	70
% of students receiving loans	58
% of students receiving grants	39
Average award package	$25,109
Average grant	$7,000
Average student loan debt	$32,119

ADMISSIONS

Admissions Selectivity Rating	88
# of applications received	152
% applicants accepted	53
% acceptees attending	55
Average GMAT	628
Range of GMAT	585–650
Average GPA	3.39
TOEFL required of international students	Yes
Minimum TOEFL (paper/computer)	600/250
Application fee	$50
Regular application deadline	3/15
Regular notification	4/15
Application Deadline/Notification	
Round 1:	11/15 / 12/15
Round 2:	2/15 / 3/15
Round 3:	3/15 / 4/15
Early decision program?	Yes
ED Deadline/Notification	11/15 / 12/15
Deferment available	Yes
Maximum length of deferment	1 year
Need-blind admissions	Yes

Applicants Also Look At

Arizona State University, University of Colorado, University of Washington.

EMPLOYMENT PROFILE				
Career Rating	**79**	**Grads Employed by Function**	**%**	**Avg. Salary**
Primary Source of Full-time Job Acceptances		Finance/Accounting	27	$58,857
School-facilitated activities	22 (67%)	Human Resources	3	$69,700
Graduate-facilitated activities	7 (21%)	Marketing/Sales	36	$51,125
Unknown	4 (12%)	Operations/Production	15	$61,000
Average base starting salary	$59,073	Consulting	9	$60,667
Percent employed	83	General Management	9	$95,000
		Top 5 Employers Hiring Grads		
		Intel Corporation; NIKE; Harry and David; Hewlett-Packard; Textronix.		

UNIVERSITY OF OTTAWA
TELFER SCHOOL OF MANAGEMENT

GENERAL INFORMATION
Type of school	Public
Academic calendar	Aug.–Aug.

SURVEY SAYS . . .
Students love Ottawa, ON
Solid preparation in:
General management
Presentation skills
Doing business in a global economy

STUDENTS
Enrollment of parent institution	34,362
Enrollment of business school	3,300
% male/female	58/42
% part-time	64
% international	29
Average age at entry	31
Average years work experience at entry	8

ACADEMICS
Academic Experience Rating	**83**
Student/faculty ratio	3:1
Profs interesting rating	68
Profs accessible rating	91
% female faculty	27

Joint Degrees
MBA/LLB 40 months.

Prominent Alumni
Paul Desmarais, chairman of the executive committee, Power Corporation; Robert Ashe, president and CEO, Cognos Inc.; Guy Laflamme, vice president marketing and commerce, National Capital Commission; Mark R. Bruneau, executive vice president and chief strategy officer, Bell Canada Enterprises; André Marcheterre, president, Merck Frosst Canada; Ian Telfer, chairman, Goldcorp Inc.

Academics

The MBA program at the University of Ottawa's Telfer School of Management is well integrated with top area employers. Students tell us, "The school has a very strong reputation with the federal government," as well as "close links with the Canadian high-tech industry. Ottawa is considered 'Silicon Valley North.'" MBAs here "interact with business leaders on a regular schedule, are encouraged to consult with governmental organizations, and never feel 'isolated in a classroom' from the real world." A "wide alumni network" also "provides excellent and current knowledge in all areas," keeping the program grounded in real-world issues and strategies.

Ottawa offers both a "12-month intensive" full-time program and a part-time program. Both teach "a broad, cross-functional curriculum" that places "a focus on leadership and performance management" and "reflects private and public sector influences." All students participate in a consulting project in which they "deal with a real project provided and coordinated by a real company, along with [a] senior professor and a mentor who is a certified consultant." Students tell us that throughout the curriculum, "There's a lot to learn, and, definitely, you have to learn it more on your own. The Greek way [of] teaching, i.e., having a mentor that spoon feeds, is nonexistent in this school, so [you] can get very respectable professors, but they will not give you everything; you have to go out on your own and dig for at least 50 percent of what you should learn."

Ottawa is a bilingual school, with instruction available in English and French. The Telfer School of Management offers a general management MBA, with a consulting project chosen by the student group.

Career and Placement

Ottawa's School of Management Career Centre offers one-on-one counseling, supplemented with an intensive self-assessment program. The office has access to online job search tools and exclusive job postings.

Employers who most frequently hire Ottawa MBAs include Accenture, Bank of Nova Scotia, Bell Canada, BMO Nesbitt, Business Development Bank of Canada, Canada Mortgage and Housing Corporation (CMHC), Canadian Commercial Corporation (CCC), CIBC, Clarica, Costco, Deloitte Touche Tohmatsu, Ernst & Young, IBM Canada, KPMG International, Kraft Foods, Labatt, Laurentian Bank of Canada, L'Oréal, National Bank of Canada, Natural Research Council of Canada (NRC), Nortel, PepsiCo, PricewaterhouseCoopers, Primerica Financial Services, Public Service Alliance of Canada, RBC Royal Bank, SwiftTrade Securities, TD Waterhouse Investment, Toyota Canada, Veritaaq Technology House, and Xerox Canada.

Student Life and Environment

The Telfer MBA is a cohort based with English, French, full-time and part-time cohorts. It also has an exchange program with some of the top schools in France. We get really good students who bring a totally different perspective of the world. The American way of doing things surprises them, and the European way surprises us." Starting in September 2007, the Telfer School of Management will move into their state-of-the-art Desmarais Building. Named in honor of Paul G. Desmarais, a University of Ottawa alumnus and one of Canada's most distinguished corporate leaders, the 12-story structure offers management students an unparalleled learning environment.

DANIELLE CHARETTE, ADMISSION AND REGISTRATION OFFICER
TELFER SCHOOL OF MANAGEMENT, UNIVERSITY OF OTTAWA, DESMARAIS BUILDING, 55 LAURIER
AVENUE EAST, OTTAWA, ON K1N 6N5 (CANADA) PHONE: 613-562-5884 • FAX: 613-562-5912
E-MAIL: MBA@MANAGEMENT.UOTTAWA.CA • WEBSITE: WWW.TELFER.UOTTAWA.CA

"Life is easy to manage" in Ottawa. The campus "is located downtown and within easy reach [of] parking for the students. It is absolutely safe and friendly. There are two gyms and several pubs and cafes located nearby." The school "truly feels like home." Not that the students, even the part-timers, have much time to go out. A full-timer tells us that "academics always take precedence" and that "social life is not very strong, since the program is a 1-year intensive program." Part-timers, meanwhile, are typically too busy with work, family, and schoolwork on top of all that to play an intramural sport or hit the happy hours. One part-timer writes, "The course workload is quite heavy, given that I'm part of the part-time cohort. School was not flexible for those who needed to lighten their course load because of work or family obligations during the first two-thirds of the program. [There is] more flexibility for the elective courses."

Admissions

All applicants to the Ottawa MBA program must submit the following materials to admissions: a completed online application form, printed out; official academic transcripts from all postsecondary institutions attended; a current resume reflecting at least 2 years' professional or managerial experience; two letters of recommendation (at least one from a recent employer); a 500-word personal statement describing goals in pursuing the MBA; an official GMAT score report demonstrating at least 50th percentile performance, with a strong showing in each subsection and a minimum score of 4.5 on the analytical writing section; proof of language proficiency for the applicant's desired program (English or French). English proficiency may be demonstrated through the TOEFL (minimum score of 250 on the computer-based test; minimum score of 5 on the Test of Written English; minimum score of 50 on the Test of Spoken English), IELTS (minimum score of 7 in at least three of four categories and minimum score of 6 in the fourth category), or CANTEST (minimum score of 14, with no individual test score below 4.0 and a minimum score of 4.5 on the oral section). The school reserves the right to request an interview of applicants.

FINANCIAL FACTS

Annual tuition (in-state/ out-of-state)	$13,680/$22,549
Fees	$891
Cost of books	$1,300
Room & board (on/off-campus)	$4,625/$5,760
Average grant	$6,692

ADMISSIONS

Admissions Selectivity Rating   84

# of applications received	231
% applicants accepted	64
% acceptees attending	72
Average GMAT	607
Range of GMAT	550–740
Average GPA	3.15
TOEFL required of International students	Yes
Minimum TOEFL (paper/computer)	600/250
Application fee	$68
Regular application deadline	4/1
Regular notification	Rolling
Transfer students accepted	Yes
Transfer application policy A maximum of 24 credits could be retained for graduate courses in management completed in a Canadian MBA program or AACSB-accredited program.	
Need-blind admissions	Yes

EMPLOYMENT PROFILE

Career Rating	88	Grads Employed by Function	%	Avg. Salary
		Finance/Accounting	8	NR
		Marketing/Sales	4	NR
		MIS	13	NR
		Operations/Production	4	NR
		Consulting	12	NR
		General Management	48	NR
		Other	8	NR
		Nonprofit	1	NR

UNIVERSITY OF THE PACIFIC
EBERHARDT SCHOOL OF BUSINESS

GENERAL INFORMATION

Type of school	Private
Affiliation	Non-denominational
Environment	City
Academic calendar	Semester

SURVEY SAYS . . .
Friendly students
Good social scene
Helpful alumni
Solid preparation in:
Teamwork
Communication/interpersonal skills
Presentation skills

STUDENTS

Enrollment of parent institution	6,251
Enrollment of business school	51
% male/female	52/48
% out-of-state	18
% part-time	22
% minorities	38
% international	18
Average age at entry	24
Average years work experience at entry	2

ACADEMICS

Academic Experience Rating	**87**
Student/faculty ratio	9:1
Profs interesting rating	82
Profs accessible rating	69
% female faculty	25
% minority faculty	14

Joint Degrees
MBA/JD 4 years, MBA/Peace Corps 3.5 years, MBA/PharmD 4 years.

Prominent Alumni
A.G. Spanos, real estate development; David Gerber, MGM/UA; Dave Brubeck, jazz composer/ musician; Jaime Lee Curtis, actress; Chris Isaak, rock musician/actor.

Academics

At the Eberhardt School of Business at the University of the Pacific, a small cohort of MBAs enjoys a surprising range of degree options, including an 18-month accelerated full-time program, and joint-degree programs in law and pharmacology. The school also offers a unique master's international Peace Corps/MBA, which includes two years of on-campus study and a two-year Peace Corps assignment.

In all programs, "small class sizes that allow professors to engage students in their education" and a "strong emphasis on field experience" distinguish an Eberhardt degree. Field experience opportunities include participation in an annual global business couse that has taken students to South Korea, Singapore, Chile, Malaysia, Spain, Ireland, France, England, Finland, and Estonia.

Eberhardt offers specialization in four areas: finance, marketing, management, and entrepreneurship. Classes are taught by professors who "have great experience in different industries and apply their experiences to the applications of the course." Students appreciate how "the team aspect of business is stressed within the classroom. The students here apply it to all aspects of Pacific. They have made this a great learning experience." They also give the administration a thumbs up, telling us that administrators "have always been helpful in achieving goals, as well as providing solutions to any problems faced in the past. They've always been reliable."

Career and Placement

Eberhardt MBAs receive career assistance through the Career Management Center, which serves both undergraduates and graduates in business. Services include monthly career development seminars, one-on-one career counseling, e-recruiting tools, and access to alumni and employers. Many here commend the office's "major push on networking and finding a job before you graduate. The ESB Career Management Center is very helpful."

More than seventy-five employers visit the Pacific campus to recruit MBAs each year, and may hire interns for career positions. Another 25 recruit here for summer interns. Employers who most frequently hire Eberhardt MBAs include Boboli International, Deloitte Touche Tohmatsu, Ernest & Julio Gallo Winery, Ernst & Young, Accenture, Clorox, and state and federal government agencies.

Student Life and Environment

Both the size and the nature of the Eberhardt MBA contribute to a low-key extracurricular scene. The small student body is subdivided into one-year and two-year students, full-timers and part-timers, and joint-degree/non-joint-degree MBAs. With many classes held at night and many students commuting to campus, there can be a lack of social activity, but as the school is moving to a single cohort of full-time students, this will likely change. One MBA comments, "It's easy for students to feel isolated, as it seems we aren't as unified outside school as [we] are in class." The MBA Association does its best, "trying to gather students every Thursday for socializing, wine tasting, movie nights, bar nights, trips, and other community services as a means of helping others and getting together." An MBA reports, "About half the MBA population goes to these events. They're usually fun."

The Pacific community at large offers a great deal more, and MBAs are welcome to partake. One student writes, "Within the university, there are many different schools which include pharmacy, education, engineering, and music (to name a few). By being in a

CHRISTOPHER LOZANO, ESB DIRECTOR, STUDENT RECRUITMENT AND ADMISSIONS
MBA PROGRAM OFFICE, 3601 PACIFIC AVENUE, STOCKTON, CA 95211 UNITED STATES
PHONE: 800-952-3179 • FAX: 209-946-2586
E-MAIL: MBA@PACIFIC.EDU • WEBSITE: WWW.PACIFIC.EDU/MBA

diverse environment, business students can meet other students who come from a wide variety of backgrounds." The campus "has a strong Greek influence, as well as lots of clubs and organizations. If anyone wants to get involved, one does not need to look hard." Another agrees, "Overall, I'm having a great experience at Pacific. Clubs provide a great opportunity to get involved in the community and meet other students. The school also has a lacrosse team that I joined and really enjoy." MBAs approve of the beautiful campus, which "is built much like many of the campuses on the East Coast: brick buildings and ivy-covered walls." The campus so closely follows the Ivy League model, in fact, that moviemakers often use it as a stand-in for Harvard or Yale. On campus, "Students have access to many facilities including the Conservatory, Pacific Theatre, an Olympic swimming pool, track, and many others." The only downside: "While the campus is generally a safe place to be, the surrounding area can be dangerous at night. Campus police do a good job of keeping the university safe, but an escort service would be nice."

Eberhardt MBA's tend to be "young and excited, eager sharks waiting to venture into the depths of the unknown [but] with little to no experience in the work field." Their shark-like qualities notwithstanding, students tend to be "very supportive and enthusiastic about the program." A considerable number "come from other countries such as France, Brazil, and the Philippines, and they bring a wide array of experiences to the education."

Admissions

Applicants to Eberhardt must submit official transcripts for all undergraduate, graduate, and professional schools attended; two letters of recommendation (one from an instructor, one from a work supervisor); GMAT scores; a completed application; and an interview. The Admissions Committee studies grade trends and ranks students by formula score, applying the formula [(undergraduate GPA × 200) + GMAT score] and looking for scores of at least 1,200. International students must also submit TOEFL scores (minimum 550 paper-and-pencil, 213 computer-based) and a Certification of Finances. Prior to beginning the MBA program, students must have completed the following prerequisite courses: intro microeconomics, intro macroeconomics, probability and statistics, and calculus.

FINANCIAL FACTS

Annual tuition	$26,260
Fees	$450
Cost of books	$1,500
Room & board	$11,500
% of students receiving aid	68
% of first-year students receiving aid	80
% of students receiving loans	35
% of students receiving grants	47
Average award package	$18,752
Average grant	$7,394
Average student loan debt	$16,033

ADMISSIONS

Admissions Selectivity Rating	**85**
# of applications received	94
% applicants accepted	52
% acceptees attending	76
Average GMAT	570
Range of GMAT	550–600
Average GPA	3.35
TOEFL required of international students	Yes
Minimum TOEFL (paper/computer)	550/213
Application fee	$75
Regular application deadline	3/1
Regular notification	Rolling
Deferment available	Yes
Maximum length of deferment	1 year
Transfer students accepted	Yes
Transfer application policy	
Students may transfer up to 2 advanced courses from another AACSB-accredited MBA Program.	
Need-blind admissions	Yes

Applicants Also Look At
California State University—Sacramento, California State University, East Bay, San Francisco State University, Santa Clara University, University of California—Davis, University of San Francisco, University of Southern California.

EMPLOYMENT PROFILE

Career Rating	81	Grads Employed by Function	%	Avg. Salary
Primary Source of Full-time Job Acceptances		Finance/Accounting	50	$52,250
School-facilitated activities	7 (77%)	Marketing/Sales	30	$45,500
Graduate-facilitated activities	2 (24%)	MIS	10	NR
Average base starting salary	$50,438	Consulting	10	$51,500
Percent employed	90	**Top 5 Employers Hiring Grads**		
		Accenture; PriceWaterhouse Coopers; Ernst & Young; Pulte Homes; Clorox of the West.		

UNIVERSITY OF PENNSYLVANIA
WHARTON SCHOOL GRADUATE DIVISION

GENERAL INFORMATION
Type of school	Private
Environment	Metropolis
Academic calendar	Semester

SURVEY SAYS . . .
Good social scene
Good peer network
Cutting-edge classes
Smart classrooms
Solid preparation in:
Finance
Accounting
Quantitative skills

STUDENTS
Enrollment of parent institution	23,236
Enrollment of business school	1,702
% male/female	64/36
% minorities	26
% international	38
Average age at entry	28
Average years work experience at entry	6

ACADEMICS
Academic Experience Rating	**99**
Student/faculty ratio	5:1
Profs interesting rating	79
Profs accessible rating	92
% female faculty	20
% minority faculty	11

Joint Degrees
MBA/JD, MBA/MD, MBA/DMD (dental, MBA/MSE (engineering), MBA/MA, MBA/MSW, MBA/PhD, MBA/animal health economics training program, MBA/VMD (vetrinary), MBA/MSN (nursing).

Prominent Alumni
J.D. Power III, founder and chairman, JD Power and Associates; Klaus Zumwinkel, chairman and CEO, Deutsche Post AG; Lewis Platt, former chairman, Hewlett-Packard; Arthur D. Collins, president and CEO, Medtronic, Inc.

Academics

The University of Pennsylvania's Wharton School, one of the premier MBA programs in the world, is best known for its "strong finance reputation," but the curriculum's "strong emphasis on quantitative analysis" extends "across many disciplines, not just finance but marketing, entrepreneurship, operations, international business, real estate, etc." as well. All areas present a "holistic program with a mix of case studies, traditional lecture formats, experiential learning opportunities, and strong co-curricular programs."

Students brag that Wharton "provides all the resources necessary for us to succeed, and then some," reporting that "the difficult part here is deciding between which resources—lectures, seminars, simulations, clubs, special events—one can fit into one's schedule." Writes one student, "The breadth and depth of the academic curriculum and the extracurricular activities is so huge that I would need at least six MBA years to experience 20 percent of it all." A heavy workload, described as "difficult for everyone but the most brilliant to manage," makes those choices even tougher. But what impresses students most here is the degree to which students themselves contribute to the learning experience. Wharton uses a "co-production model of learning" that "requires engagement from all participants in the Wharton community." One MBA observes, "Students sometimes add more value than assigned readings. Students make Wharton. 'Student-run' is an understatement." Another agrees, "The 'co-production model' is not just a buzz word; it really exists here."

Under the Wharton pedagogic system, "Classes build on each other. Professors are known to coordinate timing of discussing certain topics to ensure that the student has mastered the concept in another class." Much work here is done in teams. To promote cooperation and reduce competitiveness, Wharton policy currently forbids grade disclosure to recruiters. Students report that the policy "fosters an environment of helping at the school." Nondisclosure apparently has little impact on students' motivation to work. One notes, "The school has high expectations for each admit, and the overall performance of the students rises to that expectation."

Career and Placement

Wharton is a brand that pretty much sells itself, so it's no surprise that the school's career services are highly regarded and widely appreciated by students. Each year brings the following career placement services to the campus: over 200 employer information sessions; almost 300 recruiting companies; and, more than 5,000 job-board postings. Wharton's Career Management Services Office also offers resume review and distribution, mock interviews, internship placement, one-on-one counseling, and over 25 career treks both in and outside the U.S. No wonder students praise the "fantastic career opportunities and resources." About 40 percent of Wharton MBAs take jobs in the finance sector; 28 percent wind up in consulting; and 5 percent find jobs in the health care/pharma/biotech arena.

THOMAS CALEEL, DIRECTOR OF ADMISSIONS AND FINANCIAL AID
420 JON M. HUNTSMAN HALL, 3730 WALNUT STREET, PHILADELPHIA, PA 19104-6340 U.S.
PHONE: 215-898-6183 • FAX: 215-898-0120
E-MAIL: MBA.ADMISSIONS@WHARTON.UPENN.EDU • WEBSITE: WWW.WHARTON.UPENN.EDU/MBA

Student Life and Environment

Life at Wharton offers "an amazing number of choices in terms of classes, activities, clubs, etc." It's an atmosphere students tell us is filled with a constant stream of unique opportunities they wouldn't otherwise have. One student cites these personal examples: "At Wharton I have done a four-week study trip to greater China; a consulting project to an Israeli company that wanted to enter the U.S. market; a marketing consulting project for AOL for the mobile location-based services product; a leadership venture to Ecuador next spring to learn about teamwork through a mountain climbing expedition; dozens of fantastic speakers; and finally, some great parties." MBAs appreciate that their "partners are involved in almost all campus-related activities here." One reports, "My wife and one-year-old daughter enjoy going to activities every Wednesday and Friday with the Wharton Kids Club. This has proved to be very helpful in providing an environment where my wife can make lots of friends in a new city, and my daughter can play with other kids her own age."

Hometown Philadelphia "is underrated but still needs work." One Bay Area native notes, "I was worried about Philadelphia after living in San Francisco, but I have been pleasantly surprised by the depth of culture, fun, and good food." Wharton's new facility, Huntsman Hall, is "top-of-the-line" but MBAs gripe that "sharing the building with undergraduates leads to scarce group study rooms. Most students do not use the library because it is overrun with undergrads." Still, Wharton does most things right. You realize this when you ask students what most needs improving here and all they can think to mention is "full-size lockers for each student."

Admissions

Wharton is among the most selective MBA programs in the country. On average, the school receives between 7 and 10 applications for each available slot. The school's website notes that "approximately 75 to 80 percent of all applicants are qualified for admission." Applicants are evaluated holistically by at least three members of the Admissions Committee. All prior academic experience, including graduate work and certifications, is considered. GMAT scores also figure into the decision. Quality of professional experiences, career choices, and stated goals for entering the program are all carefully reviewed. Committee members also look for evidence of leadership, interpersonal skills, entrepreneurial spirit, and good citizenship. International students must demonstrate competency in English through essays and interviews. Applying as early as possible is strongly advised.

FINANCIAL FACTS

Annual tuition	$39,835
Fees	$5,900
Cost of books	$2,478
Room & board (on-campus)	$14,200
% of students receiving aid	87
% of first-year students receiving aid	60
% of students receiving loans	60
% of students receiving grants	40
Average award package	$35,000
Average grant	$5,000
Average student loan debt	$85,000

ADMISSIONS

Admissions Selectivity Rating	**99**
# of applications received	6,189
% applicants accepted	19
% acceptees attending	69
Average GMAT	713
Range of GMAT	660–760
Average GPA	3.5
TOEFL required of international students	Yes
Application fee	$215
Regular application deadline	
Regular notification	
Application Deadline/Notification	
Round 1:	10/12 / 12/21
Round 2:	1/4 / 3/22
Round 3:	3/1 / 5/17
Deferment available	Yes
Maximum length of deferment	case by case
Need-blind admissions	Yes

EMPLOYMENT PROFILE			
Career Rating	97	**Grads Employed by Function**	**% Avg. Salary**
		Consulting	21 $120,000

UNIVERSITY OF PITTSBURGH
JOSEPH M. KATZ GRADUATE SCHOOL OF BUSINESS

GENERAL INFORMATION
Type of school   Public
Environment   City

SURVEY SAYS . . .
Students love Pittsburgh, PA
Happy students
Solid preparation in:
Teamwork
Quantitative skills

STUDENTS
Enrollment of parent
  institution   33,574
Enrollment of
  business school   649
% male/female   67/33
% out-of-state   15
% part-time   69
% minorities   1
% international   15
Average age at entry   25
Average years work
  experience at entry   3

ACADEMICS
Academic Experience Rating   **82**
Student/faculty ratio   10:1
Profs interesting rating   81
Profs accessible rating   83
% female faculty   18
% minority faculty   24

Joint Degrees
MBA/MS-MIS (management of
information systems), MBA/MSIE
(industrial engineering), MBA/MS
(bioengineering), JD/MBA,
MBA/MPIA (public and international
affairs), MBA/MIB (international
business) MBA/MID (international
development) MBA/MA (in areas of
specialization such as East Asia,
Latin America, and Eastern Europe).

Prominent Alumni
Kevin Woods Sharer, chair and CEO,
AMGEN, INC.; Raymond William
Smith, Rothschild N. America;
Charlotte Ann Zuschlag, president
and CEO, ESB Financial Corporation.

Academics

Boasting a "good hometown reputation," ample elective offerings, and a "team-building approach to learning," the University of Pittsburgh's Joseph M. Katz Graduate School of Business is an excellent MBA program for both full-time students and working professionals. Stressing real-world applications of academic theory, Katz professors "are in tune with issues being faced out there, which they incorporate into their classes or target their research towards." In addition to classroom instruction, "The school is very big on scheduling guest speakers to share real world examples with the students." "Recently a woman from Deloitte's consulting section came to speak about being a woman in the business world."

In 1963, Katz became the first university to offer a 1-year MBA program. Designed for students with a strong background in economics or business, the 1-year MBA continues to draw students. Katz also operates a part-time program, through which business professionals can complete an MBA during the evening. According to students in the part-time program, professors are "accommodating to the needs of part-time students and try to manage the course in a manner that will not overwhelm." This includes "spreading apart their due dates and exams to make sure students aren't incredibly overloaded." Students say, "The high caliber of people who are in the part time program really make the class time so much more contextual and rewarding because we're directly applying the information we're learning to work circumstances." The 2-year, full-time program, on the other hand, is designed for students who need a longer and more thorough introduction to business, and the program incorporates highly individualized coaching and mentoring. Whether studying part-time, full-time, or on the accelerated track, Katz students quickly discover that "the academics are quite challenging"; however, the school maintains a "friendly learning atmosphere," and struggling students are pleased to find that "professors are always willing to work with students."

When it comes to the school's higher-ups, many students report that "the administrative team is very good and are able to help tackle any student issues or problems," while others feel that "the administration does not value part time students very much." However, "The arrival of the new dean last year has been the turning point," marking a new and more positive era in the school's management, and "creating a new sense of unity" between part-time and full-time students. Other non-academic staff also received kudos from students: "The advisor staff and Admissions Office personnel are almost bend-over-backwards friendly."

Career and Placement

All students at Katz receive one-on-one personalized mentoring to help them develop their "soft skills" within a managerial context. Through Career Services, students can seek further career preparation, including assistance researching positions, interviewing, negotiating offers, and seeking promotions. Career opportunities are enhanced by the fact that "the school has very strong ties with many companies in Pittsburgh and the western Pennsylvania region in general," and by all reports the "Career Counselors are very helpful if you engage them."

Last year, 71 percent of students seeking employment had received an offer by graduation, and 95 percent had received an offer within 3 months of graduating. Jobs in the manufacturing industry have been the most popular for several years, drawing 28 percent of last year's class. Another 19 percent of graduates took jobs in the financial services industry. The following companies are among the many that hired 2006 Katz grads:

KELLY R. WILSON, ASSISTANT DEAN AND DIRECTOR
276 MERVIS HALL, ROBERTO CLEMENTE DRIVE, PITTSBURGH, PA 15260 UNITED STATES
PHONE: 412-648-1700 • FAX: 412-648-1659
E-MAIL: MBA@KATZ.PITT.EDU • WEBSITE: WWW.KATZ.PITT.EDU

Bayer Healthcare, Capital One, Cisco Systems, Del Monte Foods, Deloitte Touche Tohmatsu, Deutsche Bank, Ford Motor Company, General Electric, GlaxoSmithKline, H.J. Heinz Company, Hewlett-Packard, JPMorgan Chase, NBC, Northrop Grumman, Samsung, SBI Holdings, St. Clair Hospital, U.S. Patent and Trademark Office, Washington Mutual, Wilshire Associates, and Wyeth Pharmaceuticals.

Student Life and Environment

There is "a good work/life balance" at Katz, where the friendly atmosphere and reasonable workload allow students to succeed academically while maintaining a healthy extracurricular and social life. There is always something happening on campus, as "The school has a golf club, ski/snow sports club, various academic clubs and a Student Executive Board to arrange activities to benefit the student body as a whole." Students in the part time program find their time is more limited, as most "are busy juggling careers, family, and the MBA." However, Katz students appear to be comfortable with their hectic lifestyle, as one student explains: "Most are working full-time and understand how busy life can get, but still find time socialize with classmates after class during the week or on weekends."

On campus, Katz students enjoy a beautiful, three-story building, often a hub of activity thanks to "a small cafe located in the main building. Students come here straight from work to eat and socialize before class." The surrounding city of Pittsburg offers plenty of restaurants and nightlife, especially for sports fans: "Pittsburgh is a sports-loving community with the Steelers, the Penguins, and the Pirates, as well as all the Pitt teams."

Admissions

Applicants to the Joseph M. Katz Graduate School of Business are evaluated for admission based on their undergraduate GPA, GMAT scores, and previous work experience. In addition, the Admissions Committee evaluates qualitative parts of the application, including career goals, recommendations, admissions essays, management potential, leadership skills, and community-service experience. While an interview is not required, 97 percent of last year's entering class was interviewed. Students are encouraged to enter the program with at least 2 years of professional work experience.

FINANCIAL FACTS

Annual tuition (in-state/ out-of-state)	$13,934/$21,252
Fees	$5,160
Cost of books	$1,050
Room & board (off-campus)	$13,200
% of students receiving aid	23
% of first-year students receiving aid	41
% of students receiving grants	N/A
Average award package	$13,000

ADMISSIONS

Admissions Selectivity Rating	87
# of applications received	521
% applicants accepted	48
% acceptees attending	49
Average GMAT	620
Range of GMAT	540–700
Average GPA	3.23
TOEFL required of international students	Yes
Minimum TOEFL (paper/computer)	600/250
Application fee	$50
Regular application deadline	1/15
Regular notification	3/15

Application Deadline/Notification

Round 1:	11/1 / 12/15
Round 2:	12/1 / 2/1
Round 3:	1/15 / 3/15
Round 4:	3/1 / 4/15
Transfer students accepted	Yes

Transfer application policy
Matching course work; accepting up to 17 credits from an AACSB MBA program provided that credits were not used to complete a previous MBA degree.

Need-blind admissions	Yes

Applicants Also Look At

Carnegie Mellon, Duquesne University, Pennsylvania State University, The Ohio State University, University of Illinois, University of Maryland, University of Pennsylvania.

EMPLOYMENT PROFILE

Career Rating	87	Grads Employed by Function	%	Avg. Salary
Primary Source of Full-time Job Acceptances		Accounting		N/A
School-facilitated activities	37 (56%)	Finance/Accounting	39	$72,000
Graduate-facilitated activities	29 (44%)	Human Resources	2	N/A
Average base starting salary	$69,000	Marketing/Sales	23	$64,850
Percent employed	94	MIS	6	$63,300
		Operations/Production	8	$84,250
		Consulting	11	$60,000
		Other	13	N/A

Top 4 Employers Hiring Grads
Ford Motor Co., KPMG INternational; GlaxoSmithKline; Deloitte Touche Tohmatsu.

UNIVERSITY OF PORTLAND
PAMPLIN SCHOOL OF BUSINESS ADMINISTRATION

GENERAL INFORMATION

Type of school	Private
Affiliation	Roman Catholic
Environment	Metropolis
Academic calendar	Semester

SURVEY SAYS . . .
Students love Portland, OR
Happy students
Smart classrooms
Solid preparation in:
Teamwork
Entrepreneurial studies

STUDENTS

Enrollment of parent institution	3,500
Enrollment of business school	144
% male/female	60/40
% out-of-state	44
% part-time	55
% minorities	7
% international	37
Average age at entry	29
Average years work experience at entry	5

ACADEMICS

Academic Experience Rating	**74**
Student/faculty ratio	13:1
Profs interesting rating	74
Profs accessible rating	62
% female faculty	20
% minority faculty	15

Prominent Alumni
Dr. Robert B. Pamplin. Jr., philanthropist and entreprenuer; Fidele Baccio, co-founder, Bon Apetite.

Academics

The Pamplin MBA at the University of Portland is structured to suit the needs of its largely part-time student body. A flexible schedule built around evening classes accommodates a student body that typically is also part of the full-time work force of Portland. About 30 percent of the students here have full-time status; their numbers primarily include international students and students in the five-year BBA/MBA program.

For students with undergraduate degrees in non-business areas, the Pamplin MBA begins with a Foundation Core, a series of college-level courses covering basic principles of economics, marketing, finance, and accounting. Students who majored in business during college skip the Foundation Core and proceed directly to the Integration Core, a cross-disciplinary sequence focusing on "solving common business problems." The Advanced Core, covering advanced analysis of statistics, information systems, finance, marketing, and international business follows. Students may use electives to establish a concentration in entrepreneurship, finance, global business, health care, management, or marketing. Alternatively, students can design their own concentrations in consultation with a faculty advisor. Students may also choose electives from a variety of disciplines and graduate with a degree in general management.

Students praise the Pamplin School for its willingness to experiment and innovate. The school "has the flexibility to allow students to take classes in any area of business," writes one student, adding that she is "working on earning a CPA and CMA licenses in addition to my MBA. There were no other programs in this area that offered all of this!" Another student approvingly notes that "UP seems to always hire guest professors to offer new classes, such as special 'Summer only' classes in areas like real estate or nonprofit accounting and management." Participation in JEBNET, "a network of 30 universities nationwide," allows students who must relocate to complete their MBAs at another school without losing credits.

Portland business professors "are very good. They all have their doctorates, have decades of professional experience in their fields, know other professionals in their respective fields, and invite these professionals into class to give real-world examples of what we are learning." Students also value the school's "great local reputation." The program is "administered extremely well, with regular communications from the school, including schedules, a newsletter, etc. The same cannot be said for the university at large, unfortunately."

Career and Placement

The University of Portland's Office of Career Services provides career and placement services for the school's undergraduate students, graduate students, and alumni. Office staff maintain job and internship listings, company research, and lists of alumni contacts. The office also organizes resume-writing and interviewing workshops, job fairs, and networking events. Students feel that the office, like much of the university, "sees UP primarily as an undergraduate institution and provides services accordingly" and believe that the school "should network better with local companies to get them to recruit on campus." Employers that recruit on campus include Black and Veatch, Deloitte Touche Tohmatsu, Ernst & Young, KPMG, and PricewaterhouseCoopers.

MELISSA MCCARTHY, MBA PROGRAM COORDINATOR
5000 N. WILLAMETTE BOULEVARD, PORTLAND, OR 97203 UNITED STATES
PHONE: 503-943-7225 • FAX: 503-943-8041
E-MAIL: MBA-UP@UP.EDU • WEBSITE: BUSINESS.UP.EDU

Student Life and Environment

"There are no real clubs on campus" for Pamplin MBAs, "and no one seems to care. Because of the scheduling—classes are from 4:00 P.M. to 7:00 P.M. or 7:00 P.M. to 10:00 P.M. Monday through Thursday—it is almost impossible to get out into the community and attend business-related events, or even most school events, since they are scheduled right during the middle of most of our classes." One student observes, "The University of Portland's MBA program is mostly attended by working professionals who are only on campus long enough to go to class and then go home to their families. While there is not really a sense of community with this group, there is a strong sense of pride that we are attending the best MBA program in the city, and one of the best in the Northwest."

The average Pamplin student "is about 29 years old. There are a few of us with a couple of years of work experience but the majority of the students have been out for four or five years and there are also others who have been out for eight to fifteen years." The program is "diverse both ethnically and financially, populated by people who are always willing to help while at the same time are very competitive."

The city of Portland is among the most appealing in the Pacific Northwest. An arts Mecca, the city also hosts numerous fine restaurants, great shopping, and major-league professional basketball. The city's location provides easy access to numerous locations ideal for outdoor activity.

Admissions

Applicants to the MBA program at the University of Portland must meet the following minimum requirements: an undergraduate GPA of at least 3.0; a GMAT score of at least 500; and an "admission index" of at least 1,100 under the formula [(undergraduate GPA x 200) + GMAT score]. Work experience, though strongly recommended, is not required; applicants with at least three years of post-baccalaureate professional experience are considered optimal candidates for the program. International students must score at least 570 on the TOEFL paper test or 230 on the computer-adaptive version of the TOEFL. All applications to the University of Portland must include a completed application form, a personal statement of goals, official transcripts for all postsecondary academic work, an official GMAT score report, and two letters of recommendation. International students must submit all of the above as well as an official TOEFL score report and a financial statement that indicates they will have adequate support throughout the duration of study. This is required before the I-20 form will be issued to them.

FINANCIAL FACTS

Annual tuition	$26,208
Fees	$480
Cost of books	$600
% of students receiving aid	90
% of first-year students receiving aid	60
% of students receiving grants	20
Average award package	$18,500
Average grant	$4,500

ADMISSIONS

Admissions Selectivity Rating	**71**
# of applications received	73
% applicants accepted	82
% acceptees attending	57
Average GMAT	540
Average GPA	3.39
TOEFL required of international students	Yes
Minimum TOEFL (paper/computer)	570/230
Application fee	$50
Regular application deadline	Rolling
Regular notification	Rolling
Deferment available	Yes
Maximum length of deferment	1 year
Transfer students accepted	Yes
Transfer application policy	6 semester hours of transfer credit from AACSB-accredited program, or all credits in the Jesuit Transfer Agreement.
Non-fall admissions	Yes
Need-blind admissions	Yes

Applicants Also Look At
Portland State University.

UNIVERSITY OF RHODE ISLAND
COLLEGE OF BUSINESS ADMINISTRATION

GENERAL INFORMATION
Type of school	Public
Environment	Village
Academic calendar	Semesters

SURVEY SAYS . . .
Friendly students
Happy students
Smart classrooms
Solid preparation in:
Accounting

STUDENTS
Enrollment of parent institution	15,095
Enrollment of business school	174
% male/female	76/24
% out-of-state	52
% part-time	88
% international	38
Average age at entry	29

ACADEMICS
Academic Experience Rating	**77**
Student/faculty ratio	4:1
Profs interesting rating	87
Profs accessible rating	69
% female faculty	24

Joint Degrees
MBA/PharmD 7 years, MBA/engineering 5 years.

Academics

The College of Business Administration at the University of Rhode Island offers a one-year, full-time MBA program with "a very compact curriculum that focuses on the most important fields." Students "like the one-year aspect," noting that "it costs less and is more efficient" than traditional two-year programs. The school also offers a part-time program, which is favored by area students who wish to continue their careers while attending school. The full-time program convenes on URI's main campus in Kingston, while the evening classes for part-time students meet at the Allen Shawn Feinstein College of Continuing Education in Providence. URI's relatively small graduate business program—fewer than 200 students pursue MBAs here—allows students to forge close relationships with their professors.

URI's one-year full-time MBA is a non-thesis program consisting of 48 class-hour credits. The entire curriculum is integrated, with only six credits of electives allowed. Students love how the program is "designed to have us working with real-life small businesses" by "setting up consulting relationships with local companies." They also tell us that "the program incorporates teamwork into every aspect of the program, which is a great strength," and that "all the professors are very competent and demand student participation in class." Some wish that "the core curriculum would offer a little more flexibility" so that "we could develop concentrations for our MBAs," or that faculty would "do a better job of creating a competitive atmosphere and challenging the students to improve the overall quality of the program." Some also feel that "the focus of the program is too regional, preparing you for working in Rhode Island (vs. NYC or Boston)" and that "a greater focus on global business would improve the program."

Part-time MBA students must complete at least 36 class-hour credits. Students lacking in foundation skills may be required to take up to 17 additional credits of prerequisite classes covering undergraduate business material. The part-time curriculum is similar to the full-time curriculum, although it allows students a few more elective options.

Career and Placement

Career and placement services are provided to URI MBAs by the university's Career Services Office, which serves the entire university population. All MBA students receive a BEACON ("Become Employed at Career Online Network") account in order to access the university's online recruitment system, which is powered by MonsterTRAK. BEACON notifies students by e-mail when opportunities that fit their skill set are posted; it also enables students to monitor the on-campus interviewing schedule and to search a database of job postings. Other services available to grad students include one-on-one counseling; personal assessments; workshops on resume writing, interviewing, and job search skills; mock interviews; resume review; job and internship fairs; and networking events.

Lisa Lancellotta, Coordinator, MBA Programs
7 Lippitt Road, Ballentine Hall, Kingston, RI 02881 United States
Phone: 401-874-5000 • Fax: 401-874-4312
E-mail: mba@uri.edu • Website: www.cba.uri.edu/mba

Student Life and Environment

URI's College of Business has "great technology in the classrooms." Larger classes are held in a tiered-seating facility equipped with touch-screen controls, a computer, a projector, audiovisual equipment, and both wired and wireless Internet access. Smaller classrooms boast many of the same amenities. The business facility also has two computer labs with 40 computers each, a seminar room, and two conference rooms. Wireless service is supported throughout Ballentine Hall, home to the College of Business.

URI is located in Kingston, where "the beach is close" and "apartments are clean and spacious as well as low cost." It's not hard to find housing close to campus. Many students "live in houses on the beach, the type of places that are rented to vacationers in the summer." The school itself makes up a large portion of the town of Kingston, but larger cities and big-city fun are within easy reach. Providence sits a short drive from campus, and Boston, MA and New Haven, CT are both easily reachable by car or train.

URI's campus "is mostly populated by undergrads," and students in the MBA program also "are mostly young—either recent grads or only a few years out of school. Everyone is very nice and social, easy to talk to, and willing to work as a team." "Some are married" and "many have an international background or are exchange students," although "there are also plenty of local kids here, too."

Admissions

URI offers many components of its application online and encourages applicants to submit materials online whenever possible. Students may provide all of the following materials via the Internet: a current resume, a personal statement of purpose, and letters of recommendation (applicants e-mail referees, who then send their recommendations directly to the school). Students must also provide the admissions office with official transcripts for all postsecondary academic work and an official score report for the GMAT (scores must be no more than five years old). International applicants must provide all of the above plus an official TOEFL score report (scores must be no more than five years old); the minimum required score for admission is 575 on the paper-based test, 233 on the computer-based test. The school notes that applicants with a GPA below 3.0 and GMAT scores below the 50th percentile "have a low probability of admission," but allows that grades and test scores are not the sole criteria for admission. The school seeks candidates with demonstrated strength in quantitative skills, work experience ("valued," but not required, according to university materials), leadership potential, motivation, and communication skills.

FINANCIAL FACTS

Annual tuition (in-state/ out-of-state)	$11,057/$31,688
Fees	$2,905
Cost of books	$3,500

ADMISSIONS

Admissions Selectivity Rating	**74**
# of applications received	68
% applicants accepted	76
% acceptees attending	75
Average GPA	3.21
TOEFL required of international students	Yes
Minimum TOEFL (paper/computer)	575/233
Application fee	$50
Regular application deadline	4/15
Regular notification	Rolling
Deferment available	Yes
Maximum length of deferment	1 year
Transfer students accepted	Yes
Transfer application policy Can take up to 20% of total credits from another AACSB-accredited college/university.	
Non-fall admissions	Yes
Need-blind admissions	Yes

Applicants Also Look At

Babson College, Boston College, Boston University, Bryant University, Northeastern University, Suffolk University, University of Connecticut.

UNIVERSITY OF RICHMOND
ROBINS SCHOOL OF BUSINESS

GENERAL INFORMATION
Type of school	Private
Environment	Metropolis
Academic calendar	Semester

SURVEY SAYS . . .
Friendly students
Good peer network
Happy students
Smart classrooms
Solid preparation in:
Accounting

STUDENTS
Enrollment of parent institution	4,494
Enrollment of business school	148
% male/female	56/44
% part-time	100
Average age at entry	28
Average years work experience at entry	5

ACADEMICS
Academic Experience Rating	**87**
Student/faculty ratio	3:1
Profs interesting rating	92
Profs accessible rating	76
% female faculty	20
% minority faculty	4

Joint Degrees
MBA/JD 3 to 4 years.

Prominent Alumni
David Beran, senior vice president, Philip Morris USA; Lyn McDermid, chief information officer, Dominion Resources; Larry Marsh, managing director, Lehman Brothers; Bruce Kay, vice president, Markel Corporation.

Academics

Offering "an excellent MBA program for part-time working students," the University of Richmond is ideal for business professionals looking to expand their skill set and advance their career opportunities. The curriculum is "geared toward business in the real world and not just conceptual skills" and, from the first day of classes, practical applications of business issues are stressed. In fact, the program begins with the opening residency, a case-based course that introduces students to business topics through a "live" case.

In the classroom, professors "are not strict academics, but bring an extensive amount of background from the professional world;" "classes focus on cases and discussions more so than on lectures and books." Group work and student participation is encouraged, and the classroom environment is characterized by "rich discussions and a laid back atmosphere that fosters contributions from all points of view." Students tell us that "the atmosphere is collaborative and genuinely friendly" and "the professors are terrific and interested in learning from us as we learn from them."

"The past two associate deans of the school have been very progressive," one student asserts, "and as a result they have been able to create a strong, relevant, and current MBA program." This program includes course work in current topics such as leadership, ethics, and international business. A unique requirement of the Richmond MBA is that all students must participate in the international residency, a weeklong consulting project in a foreign country in Asia, Latin America, or Central or Eastern Europe.

Given the program's focus on working students, professors are sensitive to the needs of part-time students. All classes are taught at night and students "can even meet with some faculty on Sunday afternoons." Even so, students warn us that the "workload is slightly overboard given that 95 percent of us are trying to juggle school with very demanding day jobs." However, one student contests: "The school is academically challenging but not busy work; it is work that actually helps me to be more successful at work. I feel more knowledgeable regarding the global economy and trends than ever before."

Career and Placement

Many students choose University of Richmond based on the advice of their colleagues and employers, as it has a "fine reputation for being a challenging program that allows its graduates to advance in their careers." While the school is very efficient at accomplishing this goal, students complain that "because the program is part-time and most students go through the program while continuing to work full-time during the day, there is no career office to help in a job search besides the general one that's focused on undergraduate students." In fact, "the careers services branch is strong for undergrads and the law school," but "the school has made little effort to attract area employers to campus to target MBA students or program graduates." Many suggest that while "a formal office may not be needed, it would be nice to have a few faculty members who function as career counselors and are able to attract employers to campus specifically for MBAs when appropriate." Even so, students say they benefit immensely from the school's strong standing in the local community, as well as its "great reputation throughout the Southeast with a growing national reputation."

Dr. Richard S. Coughlan, Associate Dean for Graduate and Executive Programs
MBA Office, Robins School of Business, University of Richmond, Richmond, VA 23173 U.S.
Phone: 804-289-8553 • Fax: 804-287-1228
E-mail: mba@richmond.edu • Website: business.richmond.edu/mba

Student Life and Environment

With a lovely academic environment—even for graduate students screeching in after a long day of work—the University of Richmond's "campus is beautiful and the classrooms have the latest in technology tools." Generally speaking, the Richmond MBA caters to "very hard working professionals from the Richmond area." However, professionally speaking, students hail from a wide variety of backgrounds, "from the military to corporate America to government and nonprofit."

As the program is primarily part-time, there "is not much campus activity associated with the program. Its classes and that's it." Even so, you might be surprised to learn that U of R students "are relatively social, so they gather on their own a great deal." A student explains: "We don't have all the bells and whistles of a normal, full-time MBA program, such as student clubs and organizations. That's not to say we're not social and never get together after classes, though." Another adds, "We have a good time with each other, get to know each other really well, and enjoy our experience." Even those who have little time outside the program find that "the international residency program, where you spend a week abroad with your classmates working on a business case [in] a foreign company, is a great bonding experience." However, some would like to see "more activities catered to families with children. I have not seen any such activities advertised by the business school; if they are, they aren't very noticeable."

Admissions

Applicants to the Robins School of Business must submit a completed application form, official GMAT scores, official transcripts from each college and university attended, and a current resume. As the program is designed for working professionals, students are required to have at least two years of relevant work experience after completion of their bachelor's degree, though the average student applies with more than 4 years of experience. There are no minimum GPA or GMAT requirements. As a point of reference, in the past year accepted students had an average GMAT score of 587 and an average undergraduate GPA of 3.15. While the majority of students attend part-time, students may apply to complete the program full-time, or apply to the JD/MBA joint-degree program. Applicants to either the full-time or joint-degree program may be considered without prior work experience.

FINANCIAL FACTS

Annual tuition	$27,590
Cost of books	$4,835
Room & board	
(off-campus)	$9,000
% of students receiving aid	36
% of first-year students	
receiving aid	39
% of students receiving loans	21
% of students receiving grants	22
Average award package	$13,945
Average grant	$9,720
Average student loan debt	$56,750

ADMISSIONS

Admissions Selectivity Rating	**77**
# of applications received	78
% applicants accepted	77
% acceptees attending	72
Average GMAT	587
Range of GMAT	560–630
Average GPA	3.15
TOEFL required of	
international students	Yes
Minimum TOEFL	
(paper/computer)	600/250
Application fee	$50
International application fee	$50
Regular application deadline	5/1
Regular notification	6/1
Deferment available	Yes
Maximum length of	
deferment	1 year
Transfer students accepted	Yes
Transfer application policy	
Maximum of 12 hours of transfer	
credit accepted from other AACSB-	
accredited schools.	
Need-blind admissions	Yes

Applicants Also Look At
College of William and Mary, University of Virginia, Wake Forest University—Babcock.

UNIVERSITY OF ROCHESTER
WILLIAM E. SIMON GRADUATE SCHOOL OF BUSINESS ADMINISTRATION

GENERAL INFORMATION
Type of school	Private
Environment	City
Academic calendar	Quarter

SURVEY SAYS . . .
Helpful alumni
Solid preparation in:
Finance
Accounting
Quantitative skills

STUDENTS
Enrollment of parent institution	8,730
Enrollment of business school	800
% male/female	70/30
% out-of-state	66
% part-time	46
% minorities	33
% international	42
Average age at entry	27
Average years work experience at entry	4

ACADEMICS
Academic Experience Rating	**93**
Student/faculty ratio	10:1
Profs interesting rating	89
Profs accessible rating	89
% female faculty	12

Joint Degrees
MBA/master of public health 3 years, MD/MBA 5 years.

Prominent Alumni
Andy Thomas, CEO, Heineken USA; Ronald Fielding, senior vice president, OppenheimerFunds; Robert Keegan, CEO, Goodyear Tire Company; Mark Grier, vice chairman, Prudential Insurance Co.; Mark Ain, founder and CEO, Kronos Incorporated.

Academics

One student sums it up perfectly: Simon is "definitely a school on the rise." Though founded in the 1960s under an already well-established parent institution, it's only been in recent years that the school has started to make the strides necessary to become a world-class institution. Students here say the "rigorous" academic workload is as heavy as you make it out to be, though "If you don't stay on top of your work, you will get lost very quickly." It's this flexibility and trust on the part of the school of which students speak most highly: "You have the unique ability to [tailor] your education to whatever way you see fit by utilizing all of the resources and opportunities available," one student said.

The "top-notch" faculty at Simon is a high point for students, and "To be able to speak directly with some of the leaders in their various fields is really impressive." Another student adds: "The small class size, combined with professor quality/availability, is an unbelievably strong combination." However, a few others caution that accessibility doesn't always translate into helpfulness when it comes to making students understand material they might have trouble understanding. And some professors aren't as successful as others when it comes to venturing or teaching outside of their field.

Students enjoy their classes and find them "challenging," but one notes that "there is not a wide variety offered after the core is complete." A robust program in finance and accounting is highly regarded, and the school's "economics-based approach to analyzing all business problems" is an invaluable tool for students as they prepare to enter the workforce.

At this up-and-coming school, the administration has the difficult task of increasing the breadth of the program and generating buzz, while simultaneously acting to keep things running smoothly, a job they have more than proven themselves up to. Those who attend Simon rave about its administration, which is "quick to fix any problem." Also praised is the "awesome" Dean ("an invaluable resource for networking and personal guidance"), who holds several town hall-style meetings per quarter "to find out what the students want."

Career and Placement

On the whole, Career Services at Simon generally is well received for what the office provides students, but there's no question that more diversity in recruiting (in terms of both the number of companies interviewing on campus and the number of cities in which programs are available) would be welcome. International and more experienced students also feel that more could be done to aid them in their search for employment. Boston and New York are heavily favored areas for recruitment, but the school's biggest asset tends to be the alumni: "In recent years, alumni have been responsible for opening up big hiring pipelines with major firms such as Citibank and J&J. This trend is continuing with openings to major players such as McKinsey."

Other companies that typically hire Simon grads include M&T Bank, Deloitte Touche Tohmatsu, and Xerox.

GREGORY V. MacDONALD, EXECUTIVE DIRECTOR FOR MBA ADMISSIONS AND ADMININSTRATION
305 SCHLEGEL HALL, ROCHESTER, NY 14627-0107 UNITED STATES
PHONE: 585-275-3533 • FAX: 585-271-3907
E-MAIL: ADMISSIONS@SIMON.ROCHESTER.EDU • WEBSITE: WWW.SIMON.ROCHESTER.EDU

Student Life and Environment

It's an "academically competitive" crowd here; "intelligent," "friendly," and "helpful to a point, but it is business school, so when crunch time hits, if you're all in the same class and they're not your immediate friends, you might have to search harder for help." Simon is home to a very large number of international students, many of whose language and writing skills leave something to be desired in team projects, where they can be a "burden," according to one student. She adds, "I would not have come to this school had I fully understood the impact of this."

However, since it's a small school, the overall crowd tends to be very "close-knit" and familiar with each other, students say. Although some are wholly focused on school and their career search, many are very social outside of classroom, either in the "active bar/club atmosphere" or at school-sponsored events. As a younger crowd, "There are very few people at the school who are married or have a significant other," and many people socialize with students from neighboring grad schools and universities. Rochester "could never be called a charming town," and the cold weather and heavy snow can be an unpleasant surprise for many non-Northeasterners, but the city does have an ample night life and great cultural activities, including fairs, festivals, theater, films, music, and art galleries.

Admissions

As a general rule, students with the best combination of GPA, applicable test scores, and relevant team/leadership experience (either through internships, post-baccalaureate work, or extracurricular activities) will have the first opportunity to enter the programs, according to the school's website. Applicants to the school's MBA program must submit the following materials: an online application, including three required essays; an official copy of undergraduate transcripts from all institutions where course work was completed; two letters of recommendation; a current resume; an official GMAT score report; and an interview (if requested by the Admissions Committee). In addition to the above documents, international students whose primary language is not English must also provide an official score report for the TOEFL, unless they have studied for at least one full academic year in a college or university where English is the language of instruction.

FINANCIAL FACTS

Annual tuition	$36,840
Fees	$950
Cost of books	$1,800
Room & board	$10,215
% of students receiving grants	65

ADMISSIONS

Admissions Selectivity Rating	94
Average GMAT	667
Range of GMAT	640–700
Average GPA	3.46
TOEFL required of international students	Yes
Application fee	$125
Application Deadline/Notification	
Round 1:	12/1 / 2/15
Round 2:	1/8 / 3/30
Round 3:	4/1 / 5/15
Round 4:	6/1 / 7/15
Early decision program?	Yes
ED Deadline/Notification	11/1 / 1/15
Transfer students accepted	Yes
Transfer application policy	
No more than 9 credit hours; may not be core courses.	
Non-fall admissions	Yes
Need-blind admissions	Yes

Applicants Also Look At
Carnegie Mellon, Columbia University, Cornell University, Indiana University—Bloomington, New York University.

EMPLOYMENT PROFILE

Career Rating	87	Grads Employed by Function	%	Avg. Salary
Primary Source of Full-time Job Acceptances		Finance/Accounting	59	$79,336
School-facilitated activities	67 (66%)	Marketing/Sales	19	$75,358
Graduate-facilitated activities	35 (34%)	Operations/Production	6	$72,480
Percent employed	91	Consulting	10	$83,953
		General Management	6	$86,424

Top 5 Employers Hiring Grads

Citigroup; Procter & Gamble; Johnson & Johnson; Deloitte Touche Tohmatsu; Xerox Corporation.

UNIVERSITY OF SCRANTON
KANIA SCHOOL OF MANAGEMENT

GENERAL INFORMATION
Type of school	Private
Affiliation	Roman Catholic-Jesuit
Environment	City

SURVEY SAYS . . .
Helpful alumni
Happy students
Smart classrooms
Solid preparation in:
Quantitative skills
Computer skills

STUDENTS
Enrollment of parent institution	5,353
Enrollment of business school	93
% male/female	60/40
% part-time	57
% minorities	2
% international	35
Average age at entry	30
Average years work experience at entry	2

ACADEMICS
Academic Experience Rating	**66**
Student/faculty ratio	12:1
Profs interesting rating	95
Profs accessible rating	76
% female faculty	36
% minority faculty	2

Academics

Offering one of Northeast Pennsylvania's only AACSB-accredited MBA programs, The University of Scranton delivers graduate business study that not only "emphasizes a set of skills and perspectives needed to succeed in the increasingly fast-paced, global and technology-oriented business environment" but does so within the ethical framework of a Catholic education. Typical of Jesuit institutions, The University of Scranton expects its professors to dedicate themselves to teaching. Apparently they meet that expectation; students report, "The faculty here is outstanding. Our professors are very accessible outside the classroom to review course material and offer career guidance."

For students with little academic or professional background in business, the Scranton MBA begins with qualifying modules covering basic concepts in statistics, management, information management, finance, accounting, and marketing. Qualified students may skip these modules and proceed directly to 10 extending courses of their choosing, including at least one international course. The extending courses advance the basic functional areas of business: accounting, enterprise management technology, marketing, management, managerial economics, organizational behavior, financial management, management information systems, and operations management.

The Scranton MBA curriculum also allows for four advanced electives, at least one of which must cover material pertaining to international business. Students may fashion a field of specialization by taking no more than four extending courses in one of the following areas: accounting, finance, international business, marketing, operations management, management information systems, and enterprise management technology. Students may also complete a dual specialization by taking four unique courses in each of the two specialization areas. Specialization is not required; students may choose instead to earn a general MBA degree.

To complete the MBA degree, Scranton students must take two mission specific courses. business policy, which is designed to "synthesize the knowledge students have gained in every other extending course in the program." In this course, MBAs "develop, present, and defend their own policy recommendations in case studies which require an understanding of all areas of business to make sound judgments." The other required course is responsibility, sustainability, and justice, which reflects upon the relationship between sustainable development, business, and all affected stakeholders.

In recent years, The University of Scranton has entered into a unique relationship with the Beijing International MBA program held on the campus of Peking University in Beijing. Through their arrangement, Scranton sends professors to teach in China. Professors return to Scranton with new insights about the world's fastest-growing economy, to the benefit of all Scranton MBAs.

Career and Placement

Scranton MBAs receive career and placement services from the school's Office of Career Services, which serves the university at large. The office, "guided by the principles of Jesuit education and aware of the need to impart knowledge that has immediate and long-term value," seeks to "assume the roles of advisor, teacher, and mentor" for MBAs seeking postgraduation employment. Many do not; full-timers are the minority here, and the majority of part-time students are already employed and looking to advance within their companies.

JAMES L. GOONAN, DIRECTOR OF ADMISSIONS, CGLE
UNIVERSITY OF SCRANTON, 800 LINDEN STREET, SCRANTON, PA 18510-4631 UNITED STATES
PHONE: 570-941-7600 • FAX: 570-941-5995 • E-MAIL: GRADUATESCHOOL@SCRANTON.EDU
WEBSITE: ACADEMIC.SCRANTON.EDU/DEPARTMENT/GRADSCH/GMBA.HTM

Student Life and Environment

Scranton's MBA program is a small one, "scheduled specifically for students who work full-time." Approximately seven in ten Scranton MBAs attend part-time. Because many Scranton MBAs are full-time workers/part-time students, the school offers all classes in the early evening and at night; all classes meet once per week.

Due to the demands of their schedules and the infrequency of their visits to campus, part-time students report, "Many of the school-life activities are not available to MBA students, especially those of us who are working professionals." Those who do have the time to enjoy campus life usually take in university sporting events, enroll in interest-based and background-based clubs and organizations, and participate in the frequent spiritual retreats offered by the campus ministry. Hometown Scranton is located in the Pocono Mountains, approximately 125 miles from New York City, Philadelphia, Syracuse, and Trenton. This city of 75,000 is large enough to provide students with valuable internship and practicum opportunities.

Brennan Hall serves as the home to Scranton's business graduates and undergraduates. The facility, completed in 2000, boasts up-to-date computer labs and high-tech classrooms, as well as ample executive meeting rooms. A campus-wide voice, video, and data network allows students Internet access from just about anywhere on campus.

The University of Scranton's MBA program attracts a large international population; approximately one in three students here originates from outside the United States.

Admissions

According to The University of Scranton website, admissions decisions here are based on a combination of four factors: previous academic performance, as indicated by transcripts; GMAT score, used to "measure certain mental abilities which have been found to be indicators of success" in graduate business programs of business; three letters of recommendation; and, when applicable, prior work experience (work experience is not a prerequisite to admission to the program). Of the four factors, previous academic performance and GMAT scores are considered most important. International students whose first language is not English must provide TOEFL scores in addition to academic records, test scores, and letters of recommendation. A minimum score of 550 paper-and-pencil or 213 computer-based is required for unconditional admission to the program. A score of at least 500 paper-and-pencil/173 computer-based allows conditional admission contingent on the completion of an English language proficiency course. The IELTS English proficiency exam is also accepted. The minimum score is 6.0.

FINANCIAL FACTS

Annual tuition	$17,472
Fees	$2,500
Cost of books	$1,733
Room & board (on/off-campus)	$10,950/$14,495
% of students receiving aid	10
Average award package	$26,278

ADMISSIONS

Admissions Selectivity Rating	61
# of applications received	101
% applicants accepted	83
% acceptees attending	24
Average GMAT	510
Average GPA	3.3
TOEFL required of international students	Yes
Minimum TOEFL (paper/computer)	550/213
Application fee	$50
Regular application deadline	Rolling
Regular notification	Rolling
Deferment available	Yes
Maximum length of deferment	2 years
Transfer students accepted	Yes
Transfer application policy	A transfer from an AACSB-accredited school Jesuit school; otherwise 6 credits max.
Non-fall admissions	Yes

EMPLOYMENT PROFILE	
Career Rating	79

UNIVERSITY OF SOUTH CAROLINA
MOORE SCHOOL OF BUSINESS

GENERAL INFORMATION
Type of school   Public
Environment   City
Academic calendar   Semester

SURVEY SAYS . . .
Good social scene
Good peer network
Solid preparation in:
OperationsTeamwork
Doing business in a global economy

STUDENTS
Enrollment of parent institution	27,390
Enrollment of business school	750
% male/female	66/34
% out-of-state	35
% part-time	39
% minorities	12
% international	13
Average age at entry	27
Average years work experience at entry	4

ACADEMICS
Academic Experience Rating	**83**
Student/faculty ratio	30:1
Profs interesting rating	80
Profs accessible rating	92
% female faculty	22
% minority faculty	3.3

Joint Degrees
JD/IMBA 4 years, JD/MHR 3 years, JD/MA (economics) 3 years, JD/MACC 3 years.

Prominent Alumni
Larry Wilson, CEO, IT Company; Shigeru Sekine, president, Nikko Chemicals; Whitney MacEachern, vice president, Latin American affairs, Citigroup; Larry Kellner, president, Continental Airlines. Kellie Cooper Johnson, senior product manager, GlaxoSmithKline; William Timmerman, chairman, president, & CEO, SCANA.

Academics

"If international exposure is what you are looking for, the Moore School of Business is top-notch," MBAs at University of South Carolina agree, citing "the international focus of all course matter from the very beginning of the curriculum." Moore's flagship program is its international MBA (IMBA), in which "The MBA is integrated with foreign language studies and international focus. It's more than just an MBA plus international electives or an MBA plus language study." IMBA students choose from among two program tracks. The language track emphasizes multilingualism, international internships, and geopolitical issues. The global track focuses more intensely on political, business, and economic issues that impact international investment; it, too, includes an international internship.

All students complete a core curriculum that "is well integrated with respect to individual disciplines (accounting, management, etc.) and international realities." Moore also offers several specialized master's degrees and a professional MBA. Students cite finance, accounting, and operations as Moore's strongest areas ("We learn more in operations here than most managers would within 2 years on the job," one student opines), while marketing and information systems are sometimes deemed "less than satisfactory."

Students place their international internships in the asset column, telling us that "the school gives 5 months for an international internship to every student." The experience is "second to none." Professors also score high marks with students: "[They] have fabulous forward-thinking planning about curriculum possibilities for the electives that are offered after the internship, during the second year. The professors want to maintain cutting-edge competitive advantages in what they impart to students as 'deep skills sets.'" Moore's administration "is excellent," placing it in stark contrast to the administration of the university at large, which students deem "two stone-throws away from Neanderthal. Even for a state university it is average at best." Students also complain that "the school really needs to improve its facilities and separate the IMBA program from the rest of the university." "A new building is supposedly on its way in the next several years. Let's just hope this occurs."

Career and Placement

Students tell us that Moore's Career Management "has actually turned things around in the last 2 or 3 years" and is now "Outstanding. Resources for finding jobs and job search help are both readily available." Students report that "the Graduate Career Management Office does a fantastic job of focusing their company contact efforts on employers requested by current students, and they present many on-campus opportunities for students in addition to offering $300 per student in the second year to attend an approved job fair or recruiting event." Students are especially pleased that "there have been more multinational companies coming to school this year," although they note that these companies "generally hire for local jobs and are not open to putting students in international locations."

Students observe that "the international students who come to the Moore School find it very difficult to find employment in the U.S. because most of the companies will not

REENA LICHTENFELD, DIRECTOR, GRADUATE ADMISSIONS AND ENROLLMENT MANAGEMENT
1705 COLLEGE STREET, COLUMBIA, SC 29208 UNITED STATES
PHONE: 803-777-4346 • FAX: 803-777-0414
E-MAIL: GRADADMIT@MOORE.SC.EDU • WEBSITE: MOORESCHOOL.SC.EDU

sponsor a work visa." One such international student notes, "Approximately 99 percent of the companies coming to recruit on campus are looking either for U.S. citizens or permanent residents. I am a Romanian citizen and would like very much to work somewhere in Europe, but none of the companies present on campus seem to have any opportunities for me in this direction." Top employers of Moore MBAs include: Ingersoll Rand, CHEP, Citibank, Bank of America, Hilti, BBandT, PPG, Michelin, ExxonMobil and Liberty Mutual.

Student Life and Environment

Moore places its core classes into cohorts, and "This, along with class size, makes students an extremely close group." Students endure a first semester with "an extremely heavy and accelerated course load," but afterwards "Things ease up," and by second year "Things can be very relaxed, and students may find that they can easily balance part-time work and school." Students also find time for extracurriculars "or finance clubs that organize different social events, tours, wine tastings, and other activities. Moreover, students are enjoy getting to know each other at events like tailgates, birthday parties, or other get-togethers. The balance between studies and relaxation is very good, especially during the second year."

Admissions

Applications to the IMBA program at Moore must include: an official application to the USC Graduate School, including letters of recommendation and personal essays; official transcripts documenting all postsecondary academic work; and satisfactory GMAT scores. At least 2 years of meaningful professional experience is strongly preferred. International applicants whose first language is not English must submit official score reports for the TOEFL, unless they have a degree from an American college or university. In addition to the IMBA, the Moore School also offers a Master of Accountancy, a Master of Human Resources, a Master of Arts in Economics, and a Professional MBA. Admissions requirements are most stringent for the IMBA program and personal interview may be required.

FINANCIAL FACTS

Annual tuition (in-state/ out-of-state)	$35,000/$52,000
Fees (in-state/ out-of-state)	$525/$525
Cost of books	$2,000
Room & board	$10,000
% of students receiving aid	82
% of first-year students receiving aid	89
% of students receiving loans	72
% of students receiving grants	47
Average award package	$38,000
Average grant	$14,000
Average student loan debt	$36,000

ADMISSIONS

Admissions Selectivity Rating	85
# of applications received	268
% applicants accepted	64
% acceptees attending	62
Average GMAT	623
Range of GMAT	560–685
Average GPA	3.29
TOEFL required of international students	Yes
Minimum TOEFL (paper/computer)	600/250
Application fee	$40
International application fee	$40
Regular application deadline	11/15
Regular notification	12/7
Application Deadline/Notification	
Round 1:	11/15 / 12/7
Round 2:	2/15 / 3/8
Round 3:	5/15 / 6/8
Early decision program	Yes
ED Deadline/Notification	11/15 / 12/07
Transfer students accepted	Yes
Transfer application policy Can transfer up to a maximum of 12 credit hours (4 courses)	
Non-fall admissions	Yes
Need-blind admissions	Yes

Applicants Also Look At

Georgetown University, Thunderbird, University of Georgia, University of Virginia, Vanderbilt University.

EMPLOYMENT PROFILE

Career Rating	89	Grads Employed by Function	%	Avg. Salary
Primary Source of Full-time Job Acceptances		Finance/Accounting	38	$77,443
School-facilitated activities	54%	Human Resources	1	NR
Graduate-facilitated activities	46%	Marketing/Sales	17	$71,000
Average base starting salary	$76,000	MIS	5	NR
Percent employed	88	Operations/Production	17	$74,400
		Consulting	11	$70,500
		General Management	9	$83,583
		Other	2	NR

Top 5 Employers Hiring Grads
Bank of America; Clariant; Ingersoll Rand; ExxonMobil; Liberty Mutual.

UNIVERSITY OF SOUTH DAKOTA
BEACON SCHOOL OF BUSINESS

GENERAL INFORMATION
Type of school	Public
Environment	Village
Academic calendar	Semester

SURVEY SAYS . . .
Happy students
Smart classrooms
Solid preparation in:
Finance
Accounting
Teamwork
Quantitative skills

STUDENTS
Enrollment of parent institution	8,400
Enrollment of business school	400
% male/female	50/50
% out-of-state	15
% part-time	55
% minorities	3
% international	10
Average age at entry	26

ACADEMICS
Academic Experience Rating	**68**
Student/faculty ratio	15:1
Profs interesting rating	85
Profs accessible rating	71
% female faculty	15
% minority faculty	2

Joint Degrees
JD/MBA 3 years.

Prominent Alumni
John Thune, U.S. senator, South
Dakota

Academics

If you're looking for an accredited MBA program in South Dakota, there's only one game in town. It's the MBA program at USD, the only one in the state to receive AACSB international accreditation. That distinction places the USD MBA among the top 10 percent of all business programs in the United States. Students frequently cite the school's "strong reputation," both locally and nationally, when asked why they choose this program over others.

USD's curriculum stresses "decision-making, problem-solving, understanding the role of business in society, and developing the leadership ability and social responsibility" to help its students "progress to positions of executive responsibility," according to university materials. The goal is not only to "develop future executive leadership for business, industry, and government," but also to "encourage those who have an interest in college teaching and an aptitude for an academic career to continue their work at the doctoral level." For the convenience of its students—many of whom work full-time in addition to attending school—USD offers both a part-time and full-time program, with full-time participation in Vermillion and part-time participation in Vermillion, Sioux Falls or online.

In Spring 2005, USD introduced the Cohort Express, available in Sioux Falls, is a program designed to combine the convenience of part-time instruction with the benefits of cohort learning. Participants will complete the entire 22-month program with the same peer group, allowing them to develop the same strong long-term relationships and networking contacts that full-time students enjoy. They'll accomplish this without having to increase the amount of time they spend on campus. Cohort Express requires students to attend classes only one evening a week. Plus, they'll be able to do so for the same low tuition and fees that other MBAs here pay.

USD MBAs brag that "the professors are terrific [and] the administration has been flawless. They are very friendly and helpful and have made registration easy." They especially appreciate the school's "no-nonsense approach to learning. It is understood that we are all working adults and there is very little fluff." They report that a new b-school facility is in the planning stages.

Career and Placement

USD MBAs receive career and placement services from the Business School Employment Services Office, which coordinates its efforts with the university's Career Development Center. The office provides assistance with job-search strategy, job listings, a weekly e-mail of useful info, on-campus interviews, resume reviews, mock interviews, resume referrals, career counseling, and an electronic resume book. In 2003, the last year for which such figures were available, a job fair cosponsored by the Employment Services Office and the South Dakota Career Planning and Placement Association brought 130 employers to recruit business undergraduates and graduate students. In that same year, the median starting salary for MBAs was approximately $40,500. Employers of USD business students include AFLAC, Aramark, Citibank, New York Life, Northwestern Mutual, Wells Fargo, Pitney Bowes, and Fidelity.

DR. ANGELINE LAVIN, MBA PROGRAM DIRECTOR
414 E. CLARK, SCHOOL OF BUSINESS, VERMILLION, SD 57069 UNITED STATES
PHONE: 866-890-1622 • FAX: 605-677-5058
E-MAIL: MBA@USD.EDU • WEBSITE: WWW.USD.EDU/BUSINESS/MBA

Student Life and Environment

Students at USD evince "strong Midwest values and are very caring individuals" who are "personable and understanding of work and home commitments." The student body is split among adults with considerable professional experience and younger students "fresh out of undergraduate school with few years of experience and the idea of having fun prominently on their minds."

USD is small by state-school standards, with a typical full-time enrollment of just under 8,000. The school competes in NCAA Division II athletics and supports a strong arts community active in music and theater, as well as "a wide range of other recreational, cultural, social, and professional activities and organizations." Hometown Vermillion is small and quiet, a typical city of 10,000. The surrounding area is gorgeous and offers plenty of outdoor fun, but more urbane entertainments are in relatively short supply. For those, students head southeast to Sioux City, Iowa, or north to Sioux Falls.

Admissions

Applicants to the MBA program at the University of South Dakota must submit two official transcripts for all prior academic work, GMAT scores, two letters of recommendation, a resume, a statement of purpose, and a completed application. A minimum undergraduate GPA of 2.7 is required. All international applicants must also submit a Statement of Finance form, a certified bank statement or sponsor's letter, and TOEFL scores if their native language is other than English (minimum acceptable score is 550 on the written exam). Applicants must have completed all of the following before beginning the MBA program: principles of micro and macroeconomics, six hours; principles of accounting I & II, six hours; business finance, three hours; management (principles or organizational theory), three hours; business statistics, three hours; calculus, three to four hours; introduction to management information systems, three hours; production and operations management, three hours; legal environment or American government, three hours; and marketing, three hours. Equivalent foundation courses are available at USD, but cannot be counted toward the MBA degree. According to printed material from the school, the School of Business reviews applications, then "recommends the admission status of the applicant to the dean of the Graduate School based on the applicant's undergraduate record, GMAT score, and recommendations. Students may be accepted to a University of South Dakota Graduate School degree program with full admission or provisional admission."

FINANCIAL FACTS

Annual tuition (in-state/ out-of-state)	$3,960/$11,715
Fees	$3,135
Cost of books	$1,300

ADMISSIONS

Admissions Selectivity Rating	**70**
# of applications received	53
% applicants accepted	83
% acceptees attending	91
Average GMAT	500
Average GPA	3.3
TOEFL required of international students	Yes
Minimum TOEFL (paper/computer)	550/213
Application fee	$35
Regular application deadline	6/1
Regular notification	Rolling
Deferment available	Yes
Maximum length of deferment	3 years
Transfer students accepted	Yes
Transfer application policy Maximum of 9 credit hours from an-accredited institution may be transferred.	
Non-fall admissions	Yes
Need-blind admissions	Yes

EMPLOYMENT PROFILE	
Career Rating	71
Primary Source of Full-time Job Acceptances	
Percent employed	95

UNIVERSITY OF SOUTHERN CALIFORNIA
MARSHALL SCHOOL OF BUSINESS

GENERAL INFORMATION

Type of school	Private
Environment	Metropolis
Academic calendar	Semester

SURVEY SAYS . . .
Good social scene
Good peer network
Helpful alumni
Solid preparation in:
Doing business in a global economy

STUDENTS

Enrollment of parent institution	33,400
Enrollment of business school	1,255
% male/female	68/32
% part-time	65
% minorities	33
% international	22
Average age at entry	28
Average years work experience at entry	5

ACADEMICS

Academic Experience Rating	**93**
Student/faculty ratio	3:1
Profs interesting rating	81
Profs accessible rating	87
% female faculty	20
% minority faculty	19

Joint Degrees
Dual degree programs: MBA/DDS, MBA/MA, MBA/MSG, MBA/MSISE, MBA/MA, MBA/JD/, MBA/MD, MBA/MPL, MBA/PharmD, MBA/MRED, MBA/MSW, MBA/EdD, MBT/JD.

Prominent Alumni
Cho Yang Ho, chairman and CEO, Korean Air Lines Co., Ltd.; Stephen C. Goodall, CEO, J.D. Power and Associates; J. Terrence Lanni, chairman and CEO, MGM MIRAGE; Paul Orfalea, founder and chairman emeritus, Kinko's; Robert B. McKnight, chairman and CEO, Quicksilver, Inc.

Academics

Offering "international business learning opportunities not available elsewhere" as well as solid programs in entrepreneurship, real estate, marketing, and entertainment, the University of Southern California's Marshall School of Business excels in a broad range of areas. Best of all, perhaps, USC boasts "the most amazing alumni network in the nation," a huge asset when the time for job searches arrives. As one student explains, "I have never met another Trojan anywhere in the world who wasn't excited to meet another fellow Trojan!" "The Trojan Network is enormous and expansive, providing a lifetime equity of resources."

Marshall offers a 2-year full-time program as well as a part-time evening MBA, an executive MBA, and a 1-year international MBA (called the IBEAR MBA). The school "combines a rigorous curriculum" with "the personal attention of a private college." The MBA program here "has a strong emphasis on providing students an international perspective on business issues. It is more than just saying 'We think it is important that you consider other cultures.' At Marshall, it's mandatory that all students work on a consulting project for a company overseas and travel to that region through the PRIME program. As a result of PRIME and other programs, I've had meaningful work, educational, and fun experiences in Singapore, Thailand, Vietnam, and in Western Europe."

Marshall professors "are outstanding. They bring new research into the classroom and encourage students to actively participate in class." The faculty represents "a mixture of academics and recent career switchers from their fields in business . . . they do a very good job giving us a base to learn from." Course work is demanding; one student warns, "Marshall is much more difficult than I expected. I have 9 years of work experience and consider myself a fairly bright individual. If I put in a decent amount of work and keep up with the reading, I can get a B-plus in our classes with relative ease, but it really is difficult to break the A barrier." Administrators "are committed to growth and innovation as an institution." As a result, "Chaos is inherent when new programs and classes are initiated. . . . This is a leading school's greatest challenge, and USC Marshall does everything in its power to attend to students' individual needs as well as meet their own goals and expectations."

Career and Placement

Marshall's Career Resources Center "has already made incredible changes" since bringing on a new director in 2004. "The resources and energy the Career Coaches bring to the students are head and shoulders above what students at [another prominent area business school] have. While I'm sure the CRC will continue to improve and bring in more high-profile companies, it is already a premier organization." Students praise the center's 1-week winter inter-term program for first-years, through which "students learn how to fine tune their resume and interview skills. Additionally, they learn about networking, discover their inner interests, and come up with a value proposition. I believe this gives Marshall students a leg up in recruiting."

Companies most likely to employ Marshall MBAs include: Deloitte Touche Tohmastu, Wells Fargo, Mattel, The Walt Disney Company, Warner Brothers, Bank of America, Countrywide, Neutrogena, JPMorgan Chase, Intel, Booz Allen Hamilton, McKinsey & Company, Ernst & Young, Nissan North America, and Goldman Sachs.

Student Life and Environment

Full-time students tell us that "there are numerous professional and social club opportunities in which to be involved at Marshall." Several point out that "being involved with

KEITH VAUGHN, DIRECTOR OF MBA ADMISSIONS
POPOVICH HALL, ROOM 308, LOS ANGELES, CA 90089-2633 UNITED STATES
PHONE: 213-740-7846 • FAX: 213-749-8520
E-MAIL: MARSHALLMBA@MARSHALL.USC.EDU • WEBSITE: WWW.MARSHALL.USC.EDU

the community is easy and fun due to the Challenge 4 Charity Club, which schedules regular volunteer days for junior achievement and hosts parties at popular LA night clubs where the entry fees are donated to the Special Olympics." One student adds, "With the numerous clubs and organizations, USC students are really only limited by the amount of time and energy they possess. Personally, I wanted to take a leadership role in the community, and have had the opportunity to do just that. That makes my schedule a little bit more hectic than normal, but that was a personal decision. Really, life at Marshall is as challenging as one has the ambition to make it." Throughout the program and the campus, students enjoy "a very communal atmosphere. Football season is amazing."

Los Angeles is a great hometown, "a fun and vibrant city" with "fabulous weather all year round." Students note that "living in LA requires a car" and tell us that there are "nice apartments by the ocean for a decent price" within a 20-minute commute of the campus. The city provides many opportunities "to spend time together outside of class." "There are parties or small get-togethers almost every weekend."

Admissions

The Marshall Admissions Office warns that its MBA programs are "highly selective," and that the Admissions Committee "carefully assesses each candidate on a number of dimensions, including prior academic, professional, and personal accomplishments." All applicants must provide the school with official transcripts for all postsecondary academic work, an official GMAT score report, an official TOEFL score report (for international students who have not previously attended an English-language undergraduate or graduate program), an online application, a current resume, three required essays (a fourth optional essay is available), and two letters of recommendation (at least one from a direct supervisor is preferred).

FINANCIAL FACTS

Annual tuition	$38,245
Fees	$1,634
Cost of books	$2,400
Room & board	$14,000

ADMISSIONS

Admissions Selectivity Rating	94
# of applications received	1,483
% applicants accepted	36
% acceptees attending	41
Average GMAT	680
Range of GMAT	650–710
Average GPA	3.3
TOEFL required of international students	Yes
Minimum TOEFL (paper/computer)	600/250
Application fee	$150
Regular application deadline	4/1
Regular notification	5/25
Application Deadline/Notification	
Round 1:	12/1 / 2/1
Round 2:	1/15 / 3/30
Round 3:	2/15 / 4/27
Round 4:	4/1 / 5/25
Need-blind admissions	Yes

Applicants Also Look At

New York University, Stanford University, University of California, Berkeley, University of California, Los Angeles (UCLA).

EMPLOYMENT PROFILE

Career Rating	93	Grads Employed by Function	%	Avg. Salary
Primary Source of Full-time Job Acceptances		Finance/Accounting	39	$88,436
Average base starting salary	$87,944	Human Resources	5	NR
Percent employed	91	Marketing/Sales	21	$84,310
		MIS	1	NR
		Operations/Production	3	$79,143
		Consulting	16	$98,551
		General Management	6	$81,250
		Other	9	$87,269

Top 5 Employers Hiring Grads

General Electric; Intel; Nestle; Toyota NA; Bank of America.

UNIVERSITY OF SOUTHERN MAINE
SCHOOL OF BUSINESS

Academics

The MBA program at the University of Southern Maine focuses its attention primarily on students "who wish to advance their careers and contribute to their companies." It serves a largely part-time student body whose members hold full-time jobs in the area and seek a degree that will help them "develop cross-functional business solutions to real-world problems [and] cultivate a broad critical perspective, interpersonal skills, and the analytical tools of management." USM's full-time student body is primarily enrolled in the 3-2 MBA program, which allows undergraduates to earn a bachelor's degree and an MBA in five years.

Part-time students can complete USM's 33-credit sequence in two years, although some take longer. The curriculum consists of nine three-hour core courses and two three-hour electives. "All classes are held in the evening" so that working students can attend the MBA program, which students appreciate. One such student writes, "This school is well-located for part-time students and it caters well to them. The administration strongly supports the students." Because of the limited number of electives available, students cannot fashion an area of concentration here, a situation some would like to see addressed. One says, "I work in the financial services industry and would love to be able to come out of USM with a finance concentration MBA."

USM professors "are well integrated into the local business community, opening up several great opportunities for enriching projects." Their quality as classroom instructors varies; "Some seem to teach to the lowest common denominator, but generally they are good to very strong," students tell us. They single out instructors in operations, accounting, and finance for their expertise and "ability to inspire learning in their students." Many agree the b-school facility "needs to be vastly improved," adding that "the school desperately needs a new building of their own with more modern, comfortable facilities."

Career and Placement

USM's website states: "Because many of our students are already employed in management positions, we do not have a formal placement service for MBA or MSA students." The site adds that "opportunities for employment often come to our attention," and these opportunities "are passed on to students for consideration." Students may use the services of the USM Career Services Office, which serves the entire university population. Students may also work with the Office of Graduate Studies, which employs a career advisor to administer career assessments, counsel students in resume building and interviewing skills, and arrange networking opportunities.

Student Life and Environment

Because "the University of Southern Maine is mainly a commuter college," "there is really very little in the way of organized outside activities. We all have a local life outside of school which demands our time." One student observes, "There isn't a whole lot of school spirit and clubs like at other universities. The only club I've heard of for the MBA program is the MBA Association. Unfortunately, any clubs that students are asked to participate in have meetings when many students are in class. That also goes for most networking opportunities that are available." Extracurricular life isn't totally dead, though; according to one MBA, "The school does try to bring students together for occasional special events, and many professors hold off-campus gatherings on the last night of class that provide a good networking opportunity with other students."

ALICE B. CASH, GRADUATE PROGRAMS DIRECTOR
96 FALMOUTH STREET, PO BOX 9300, PORTLAND, ME 04104 UNITED STATES
PHONE: 207-780-4184 • FAX: 207-780-4662
E-MAIL: MBA@USM.MAINE.EDU • WEBSITE: WWW.USM.MAINE.EDU/SB

USM's MBA program is a small one, the majority of whose students attend part time. They are "good-natured, intelligent individuals" who are "motivated but not extremely driven in a business sense. They are hard-working and striving for knowledge," creating "a positive learning environment." The mix of "older students with families and substantial professional backgrounds and younger students with less work experience but more recent educational experience" is a "positive mix," students say. They also love that "the academic community is quiet and the scenery is wonderful, very relaxing."

Portland is home to the School of Business' main campus. With a population just under a quarter of a million, Portland is the largest city in Maine. It serves as the state's financial, business, and retail center; its major industries include tourism, telecommunications, technology, light manufacturing, and insurance.

Admissions

All applicants to the MBA program at USM must submit a completed application, two copies of official transcripts for all postsecondary work (including work at USM), GMAT scores, three letters of recommendation, a resume, and a personal essay. In addition, international students must also submit a certificate of finances and, if English is not their first language, TOEFL scores. Fully admitted students must have a formula score of 1,100 under the formula [(undergraduate GPA × 200) + GMAT score] and a minimum GMAT score of 500. The GMAT requirement is waived for students who have completed a terminal degree (e.g. PhD, JD, MD). The admissions office considers rigor of undergraduate field of study, reputation of undergraduate institution, potential, likelihood of enhancing the educational environment at USM, demonstrated leadership, evidence of creativity, and record of accomplishment in business in making its admissions decisions. Prior to commencing the MBA program, all students must complete, or demonstrate competency in, the following 'foundation' areas: managing organizational behavior, IT/MIS, economics, accounting, probability and statistics, finance, marketing, and management science. Students with deficiencies in these areas will be notified at the time of their admission.

FINANCIAL FACTS

Annual tuition (in-state/ out-of-state)	$4,860/$13,572
Fees	$561
Cost of books	$1,000
Room & board (on-campus)	$7,800
% of students receiving aid	68
% of first-year students receiving aid	47
% of students receiving loans	35
% of students receiving grants	47
Average award package	$8,779
Average grant	$5,479

ADMISSIONS

Admissions Selectivity Rating	73
# of applications received	59
% applicants accepted	83
% acceptees attending	84
Average GMAT	544
Range of GMAT	490–580
Average GPA	3.3
TOEFL required of international students	Yes
Minimum TOEFL (paper/computer)	550/213
Application fee	$50
Regular application deadline	8/1
Regular notification	Rolling
Deferment available	Yes
Maximum length of deferment	1 year
Transfer students accepted	Yes
Transfer application policy A maximum of 6 semester hours of transfer credit may be accepted. Please see catalog at www.usm.maine.edu/catalogs/grad uate/.	
Non-fall admissions	Yes
Need-blind admissions	Yes

Applicants Also Look At
EMBA, University of Maine, University of New Hampshire.

THE UNIVERSITY OF TAMPA
JOHN H. SYKES COLLEGE OF BUSINESS

GENERAL INFORMATION

Type of school	Private
Environment	Metropolis
Academic calendar	Semester

SURVEY SAYS . . .
Students love Tampa, FL
Smart classrooms
Solid preparation in:
Marketing
Teamwork
Communication/interpersonal skills

STUDENTS

Enrollment of parent institution	5,300
Enrollment of business school	412
% male/female	64/36
% out-of-state	15
% part-time	66
% minorities	6
% international	47
Average age at entry	30
Average years work experience at entry	5

ACADEMICS

Academic Experience Rating	**77**
Student/faculty ratio	12:1
Profs interesting rating	81
Profs accessible rating	67
% female faculty	33

Joint Degrees
MS-ACC/MBA, MS-FIN/MBA, MS-IM/MBA, MS-MKT/MBA, MSN/MBA, MBA/BS (chemistry).

Prominent Alumni
Dennis Zank, COO, Raymond James; John M. Barrett, president and CEO, First Citrus Bank; William N. Cantrell, president, Peoples Gas System; Jorgen Adolfsson, Swedish technology entrepreneur; Lyndon Martin, member, Legislative Assembly, Cayman Islands.

Academics

MBAs considering the John H. Sykes College of Business at the University of Tampa have three options: a full-time program that can be completed in 16 months, a part-time program that is typically completed in about three years, and a six-term Saturday professional MBA program. Roughly one-third of the student body attends full time.

All MBA programs at Sykes consist of foundation courses, which can be waived for students completing equivalent undergraduate courses in the prior five years with a minimum grade of B, or by passing a departmental examination. The integrated core curriculum here "stresses case studies and group work, allowing students to obtain knowledge and corporate values." All students also complete course work leading to a concentration, a leadership development program centered on mentoring and one-on-one coaching, and a capstone team project in which students create a strategic business assessment and present it to the top leadership of an area company. Concentrations are available in accounting, economics, entrepreneurship, finance, information systems management, international business, management, marketing, and nonprofit management and innovation.

"Teamwork and leadership skills" are "the focus of this MBA program," students tell us. Professors here "have a genuine interest in students' success and academic endeavors" and "find ways to stimulate our thinking. They're not just giving us required material. If one doesn't understand the class material, he or she can always talk to professor during consultation hours. If even that is not enough, there is free tutoring available." Students praise Sykes' "strong relationship with the business community" and its "ability to include local area businesses in projects." Many, however, complain that "the school doesn't offer enough electives each semester," making it difficult to complete some concentrations.

Career and Placement

UT's Office of Career Services provides Sykes MBAs with a battery of services, including assessment tests, workshops in business etiquette and business dress, one-on-one counseling, and job fairs. Attendees of a recent on-campus career fair included Tampa Electric, Franklin Templeton, Ernst & Young, Deloitte Services, Inc., HSBC, Citigroup, Geico, Smith Barney, Depository Trust and Clearing Corp., Am South Bank, and Sun Trust Bank.

FERNANDO NOLASCO, DIRECTOR, GRADUATE STUDIES
401 W. KENNEDY BOULEVARD, BOX O, TAMPA, FL 33606-1490 UNITED STATES
PHONE: 813-258-7409 • FAX: 813-259-5403
E-MAIL: UTGRAD@UT.EDU • WEBSITE: GRAD.UT.EDU

Student Life and Environment

A "beautiful campus" with "state-of-the-art facilities" makes the University of Tampa a pleasant and supportive place for students pursuing their MBAs. Many here do not get to enjoy the extra amenities very often, however. Part-time students have too many other responsibilities (e.g. work, family) to linger on campus a second longer than necessary, although they do appreciate that "there are plenty of places to relax or grab a bite to eat for a student coming from a full-time job to school."

Full-time students "are typically on campus all day. Many live on campus." And since there are "a lot of activities to do," why shouldn't they? For example, "There is the Student Organization of MBAs (SOMBA), which meets about once every two weeks. Any MBA student can come, and pizza and sodas are served. The Dean of Graduate Studies always comes. Meetings have a very relaxed yet very productive atmosphere: We talk about how to promote our school, what events we would like to happen and how to organize them, and what we would like to see different in our school." An MBA lounge is another "great feature because it is a place where MBA students can study and meet for group projects. You can usually always find a seat there because it isn't flooded with undergrads."

Sykes MBAs are predominantly from the Southeast U.S., although "a lot of international students" are in the mix as well. This "enthusiastic, diverse group of professionals from all around the globe, brought together to share in growth and learning" is "competitive, but in a cooperative atmosphere: lots of e-mails, phone calls, and meetings." Full-time students tend to have "little to no work experience," while "evening classes have many working professionals in them." Nearly everyone feels that Tampa Bay is the place to be, a metropolis that "is showing very strong signs of healthy growth to use MBAs in the coming years."

Admissions

Admission to the full-time and part-time MBA programs at Sykes is based on undergraduate work (a minimum GPA of 3.0 is required of degree-seeking students; non-degree seeking students need a minimum GPA of 3.0 for their final 60 hours of undergraduate credit); GMAT score (a minimum score of 450 is required) or GRE score (a minimum combined verbal-quantitative score of 1,000 is required); demonstration of proficiency in mathematics, computers, and written and oral communications skills; and professional experience. International students must demonstrate proficiency in English by scoring at least 577 on the written TOEFL or 230 on the computer-based TOEFL. Admission to the Saturday MBA program requires relevant work experience. Applicants to the Saturday program who have a minimum undergraduate GPA of 3.0 may receive a waiver on the GMAT requirement. Applicants to all programs must submit two letters of recommendation, a resume, and a personal statement.

FINANCIAL FACTS

Annual tuition	$6,816
Fees	$70
Cost of books	$602
Room & board (on/off-campus)	$7,254/$4,700
% of students receiving aid	53
% of first-year students receiving aid	16
% of students receiving loans	40
% of students receiving grants	30
Average award package	$11,016
Average grant	$9,818
Average student loan debt	$21,712

ADMISSIONS

Admissions Selectivity Rating	75
# of applications received	254
% applicants accepted	67
% acceptees attending	73
Average GMAT	529
Range of GMAT	470–563
Average GPA	3.36
TOEFL required of international students	Yes
Minimum TOEFL (paper/computer)	577/230
Application fee	$40
Regular application deadline	6/15
Early decision program?	Yes
ED Deadline/Notification	11/1 / 11/15
Deferment available	Yes
Maximum length of deferment	1 year
Transfer students accepted	Yes
Transfer application policy Up to 9 hours from an AACSB-accredited school.	
Non-fall admissions	Yes
Need-blind admissions	Yes

Applicants Also Look At

University of Florida, University of South Florida.

EMPLOYMENT PROFILE				
Career Rating	75	Grads Employed by Function	%	Avg. Salary
Primary Source of Full-time Job Acceptances		Finance/Accounting	63	$48,700
Percent employed	77	Operations/Production	12	$55,000
Average base starting salary	$64,258	General Management	25	$39,000

THE UNIVERSITY OF TENNESSEE AT CHATTANOOGA
COLLEGE OF BUSINESS ADMINISTRATION

Academics

Change is coming to the MBA program at The University of Tennessee at Chattanooga. The school recently revamped its MBA curriculum, with changes to be implemented in the fall of 2006. The new curriculum increases the length of the program from a minimum of 30 class hours to a minimum of 36 class hours. The school has reduced the number of foundation/background courses (classes that cover pre-MBA material and which can be waived by students with undergraduate business degrees), increased the number of core and elective options, and added a second capstone class (in entrepreneurship). Students admitted after August 2006 must complete the new curriculum to graduate.

UTC's predominantly part-time student body will most likely be satisfied with the changes so long as the school maintains "a reputation for academic rigor" and, perhaps more importantly, the "great convenience of evening class scheduling, which makes it possible to work full-time while attending." As one student observes, "The program is tailored to individuals who work full-time. The faculty and staff go above and beyond to help make the program feasible without compromising the quality of the academics." Even without the coming upgrades, students here are "very impressed" by the perception that "for a small school, this program has some professors who are high profile and important in their field, yet also accessible to the students. The professors really seem to love teaching."

Other assets here include "modern classroom facilities and computer labs" and "an administration that is professional and meticulous." While some here feel that the school should get a little pickier about "whom they select for the program, because some students are not quite ready" and others wish that "there were more options for students who aren't engineers, computer scientists, or in the manufacturing and production industries," most here recognize UTC as "an excellent value for the money. The professors have real-world experience and want to help you be as prepared as possible. The work for each course is designed to give real-world experience and help you understand better the macro business perspective. Overall this is an excellent school that will only get better as more money is funded toward it."

Career and Placement

UTC maintains a Career Resource Center for all students. The center houses a library of job-search related materials, including literature, annual reports, and job postings. The school's Placement and Student Employment Center also hosts on-campus recruitment interview sessions, one major annual career fair, and a number of special career fairs each year. Students and alumni may post their resumes online with the Placement Center.

Student Life and Environment

Students at UTC tell us that they experience an "excellent atmosphere for learning." Facilities "have integrated multimedia capability and are thoroughly up-to-date" and "small class sizes are conducive to student participation and enhance learning." Students here "for the most part take classes at night and are not a part of the life of the university." And while "the Grad School is attempting to create more of a community for all of the graduate students on campus by distributing interest surveys and planning activities," "not that many people participate."

MELISSA BLAZEK, GRADUATE PROGRAM LIAISON
GRADUATE SCHOOL, DEPARTMENT 5305, 615 MCCALLIE AVENUE, CHATTANOOGA, TN 37403 U.S.
PHONE: 423-425-4667 • FAX: 423-425-5223
E-MAIL: MELISSA-BLAZEK@UTC.EDU • WEBSITE: WWW.UTC.EDU/ACADEMIC/BUSINESS

Many simply don't have the time for extracurricular commitments. Most students here "are working professionals who are committed to achieving the highest grade possible." These "hard workers are here to learn everything they can," and they "take the MBA program very seriously." Work and family obligations leave them with just enough time to study, but not to do much else. Students report that "there seem to be a lot of engineers in the program, but there are also many people from local insurance companies and other businesses in the area. It is not unusual to have classes with engineers, nurses, teachers, computer science professionals, etc."

Chattanooga is located on Tennessee's southern border, about halfway between Nashville and Atlanta. The city is home to a number of colleges and universities. UTC, the second-largest school in The University of Tennessee system, is the biggest. Others include Tennessee Temple University and Covenant College (located just outside the city, on Lookout Mountain).

Admissions

Applicants to the MBA program at UTC must provide the Admissions Committee with two official copies of transcripts for all academic work completed after high school and an official GMAT score report. The academic record must show either a minimum GPA of 2.5 for the applicant's entire undergraduate career or a GPA of at least 3.0 during the senior year in order for the applicant to gain unconditional admission. Successful applicants must have a minimum "admissions index" score of 950, calculated under the formula [(undergraduate GPA x 200) + GMAT Score]. Students who do not meet the above-mentioned qualifications may still earn conditional admission. International students whose first language is not English must submit an official score report for the TOEFL (minimum grade required: 550, paper-based; 213, computer-based).

FINANCIAL FACTS

Annual tuition (in-state/ out-of-state)	
% of students receiving aid	72
% of first-year students receiving aid	70
% of students receiving loans	61
% of students receiving grants	4
Average grant	$9,500

ADMISSIONS

Admissions Selectivity Rating	**68**
# of applications received	199
% applicants accepted	92
% acceptees attending	74
Average GMAT	537
Range of GMAT	450–700
Average GPA	3.22
TOEFL required of international students	Yes
Minimum TOEFL (paper/computer)	550/213
Application fee	$25
Regular application deadline	Rolling
Regular notification	Rolling
Deferment available	Yes
Maximum length of deferment	1 year
Transfer students accepted	Yes
Transfer application policy Students can transfer up to 6 hours from an AACSB-accredited school. All transfer courses are subject to departmant approval.	
Non-fall admissions	Yes
Need-blind admissions	Yes

Applicants Also Look At

East Tennessee State University, Georgia State University, Middle Tennessee State University, Tennessee Tech University, University of Georgia, The University of Tennessee, Vanderbilt University.

THE UNIVERSITY OF TENNESSEE AT KNOXVILLE
COLLEGE OF BUSINESS ADMINISTRATION

GENERAL INFORMATION

Type of school	Public
Environment	City
Academic calendar	Semester

SURVEY SAYS . . .
Friendly students
Good social scene
Good peer network
Happy students
Solid preparation in:
Teamwork

STUDENTS

Enrollment of parent institution	25,474
Enrollment of business school	140
% male/female	66/34
% out-of-state	32
% minorities	8
% international	18
Average age at entry	26
Average years work experience at entry	4

ACADEMICS

Academic Experience Rating	**89**
Student/faculty ratio	4:1
Profs interesting rating	73
Profs accessible rating	87
% female faculty	18
% minority faculty	9

Joint Degrees
JD/MBA 4 years, MBA/Masters in Engineering 2 years. MBA/MS Sports Management 2 years.

Prominent Alumni
Ralph Heath, vice president and COO, Lockheed Martin Aeronautics; Kiran Patel, CFO, Solectron; Joseph O'Donnell, CEO, Artesyn Technology; Bob Hall, CEO, Jewelry Television by ACN; Scott Parish, CFO, Alcon Entertainment.

Academics

The University of Tennessee's College of Business Administration has an easy time attracting the MBA-seeking masses with its 17 month program. Though "compressed in time," the school assures that "this program maintains all of the quality instruction that has made our graduates attractive to corporate recruiters." And students agree wholeheartedly that this is one of the school's "greatest strengths." "It is so stressful and fun at the same time that I think these 17 months would be one of the best times in my life," says one student.

UTK was the first MBA program in the nation to implement an integrated core curriculum, taught by a "cross-functional faculty team," that some students praise for always "moving and changing," making it "much more like business." They also appreciate that since "Classes for first-year students are lockstep," they have the opportunity to "become very familiar with peers." Meanwhile, others find it "frustrating" as "It hinders learning because it is all over the place." The list of possible concentrations for students includes finance, logistics, marketing, operations management, entrepreneurship, JD/MBA, an MS/MBA in engineering and in sports management. "So far," one student says, "I have learned volumes and have been exposed to a plethora of different real-world case scenarios. I feel that this has been a fabulous investment."

The extras are what makes the program stand out. The school offers a cultural exchange program for "academic purposes" and "credit hours" that has been hosted in locations as far-flung as Prague and Chile. After-class activities "provide the opportunity to hear speakers or participate in activities that enhance the learning experience," and "Professors always make themselves available to the students, sometimes even missing a lunch if time is pressing." In addition, "There are plenty of finance courses now included in the core curriculum" and "a large focus on entrepreneurship." All in all, students appreciate the emphasis placed on "great teamwork" and how the school is "very up-to-date with the current happenings in the business world." "I love how much attention is put in communication and presentation skills," one student explains. "The true-to-life work atmosphere allows us to prepare very well for real jobs."

Career and Placement

Although it had something of a rocky past, students praise Career Services now, noting that "under new direction" it really began "picking up." However, they do feel that more could be done to promote "the value of our program to more Fortune 100 companies." For the 2005–2006 year, the average salary for MBA graduates was $69,392.

Companies who have recruited on campus recently include Accenture, Amazon.com, AmSouth Bank, Burke, Deloitte Touche Tohmatsu, Eli Lilly and Company, FedEx, Hewlett-Packard, Milliken & Company, New York Life, and Wells Fargo, among many others.

DONNA POTTS, DIRECTOR OF ADMISSIONS, MBA PROGRAM
527 STOKELY, MANAGEMENT CENTER, KNOXVILLE, TN 37996-0552 UNITED STATES
PHONE: 865-974-5033 • FAX: 865-974-3826
E-MAIL: MBA@UTK.EDU • WEBSITE: MBA.UTK.EDU

Student Life and Environment

Knoxville, Tennessee is consistently recognized as one of the "best places to live in the United States" and UT is noted for being "a very large university in a growing, mid-major city." This may have something to do with the fact that it's nestled between the Great Smokey Mountains and the Cumberland Mountains, or that it's about a 2-hour drive from five national parks, seven state parks, and seven lakes. It is the largest city in east Tennessee and the third largest in the state. The shelter of the mountain ranges ensures that the climate is relatively temperate, with an annual average temperature of about 60 degrees (F). Students call the "downtown scene" "excellent with lots of bars, clubs, and entertainment venues." Even students coming from big cities have come to enjoy life in a smaller city. "I am enjoying the pace of life and getting to relive college to a certain degree, but this time I have a plan and more responsibility," one former New Yorker says.

Football consumes much of a UTK MBA's free time, but rest assured that "besides football games, there's plenty to do." Students say that "there are events taking place every-day, whether cultural or athletic," and that the social scene is "what you make of it." That is, if you plan on taking a break from the books. Despite staying busy with the 17-month program, many are able to find "a good balance between school and social life." "I have made great contacts," says one student. Another agrees, "They are the greatest bunch of people I have ever met! They are very smart but fun at the same time. I know for sure that I will miss my MBA life a lot after graduation."

Admissions

For the 80-odd students of the class of 2007, 66 percent were male, 34 percent were female, with 18 percent of the student body consisting of international students. The average age of an incoming student was 26, and the average undergraduate GPA was a 3.35. In addition, the average GMAT score was 600 and the average amount of work experience was 3 years. The international students came from places as diverse as Brazil, China, India, Japan, South Korea, Taiwan, and Thailand.

FINANCIAL FACTS

Annual tuition (in-state/ out-of-state)	$5,376/$15,156
Fees	$1,000
Cost of books	$3,000
Room & board (on/off-campus)	$7,400/$12,500
% of students receiving aid	43
% of first-year students receiving aid	27
% of students receiving grants	14
Average award package	$17,784
Average grant	$8,514

ADMISSIONS

Admissions Selectivity Rating	88
# of applications received	230
% applicants accepted	45
% acceptees attending	62
Average GMAT	600
Range of GMAT	560–640
Average GPA	3.3
TOEFL required of international students	Yes
Minimum TOEFL (paper/computer)	600/250
Application fee	$35
Regular application deadline	2/1
Regular notification	Rolling
Need-blind admissions	Yes

Applicants Also Look At

Arizona State University, Pennsylvania State University, University of Georgia, Vanderbilt University, Wake Forest University.

EMPLOYMENT PROFILE

Career Rating	76	Grads Employed by Function	%	Avg. Salary
		Finance/Accounting	17	$54,300
		Marketing/Sales	22	$52,000
		Operations/Production	31	$59,800
		Consulting	6	$60,300
		General Management	20	$53,600
		Other	4	$45,200

THE UNIVERSITY OF TEXAS AT ARLINGTON
COLLEGE OF BUSINESS ADMINISTRATION

GENERAL INFORMATION
Type of school	Public
Environment	Metropolis
Academic calendar	Semester

SURVEY SAYS . . .
Friendly students
Helpful alumni
Smart classrooms
Solid preparation in:
Accounting

STUDENTS
Enrollment of parent institution	25,297
Enrollment of business school	457
% male/female	54/46
% part-time	66
% minorities	28
% international	35
Average age at entry	31
Average years work experience at entry	5

ACADEMICS
Academic Experience Rating	**78**
Student/faculty ratio	20:1
Profs interesting rating	80
Profs accessible rating	70
% female faculty	16
% minority faculty	5

Joint Degrees
May combine any two degrees (usually MBA and specialized program) or a business degree with others, such as engineering, architecture, science, nursing. Can obtain second degree with as few as 18 additional hours. May pursue MBA at UTA with MIM at Thunderbird, the American Graduate School, or international management, with reduced requirements.

Prominent Alumni
John McMichael, executive vice president and CFO, Finley Resources, Inc.; Lee Thurburn, president, NetOffer.com.

Academics

In its efforts to meet the needs of its diverse student population, the College of Business Administration at The University of Texas at Arlington offers several MBA options. There's the Flexible MBA–often referred to simply as "the MBA" because it is regarded as the default option. The Flexible MBA can be completed part-time or full-time, and it jettisons the conventional lockstep MBA curriculum and cohort learning to maximize convenience. This option is offered only on the Arlington campus. Then there's the Accelerated MBA (also known as the Cohort MBA, because students travel through the program with the same group of peers), with its mini-terms scheduled for the convenience of its part-time-student/full-time-worker student body. The Accelerated MBA is offered only at UTA/Fort Worth. UTA also offers an online MBA, which can be completed "without ever setting foot on campus," and the school participates in an Executive MBA (EMBA) program in Taipei, Beijing, and Shanghai.

Students in the Flexible MBA program may choose a specialization from among the following: finance, accounting, information systems, international business, marketing research, real estate, human resource management, electronic commerce, and enterprise resource planning. Current students praise the economics department ("the professors are producing advanced research and presenting it in class along with other new research done in the field"), the accounting and operations management department, and the marketing research program, which "is offered only in limited schools across the country."

The Accelerated MBA program receives even more enthusiastic endorsements from students, one tells us, "There is tremendous value in being in with the same classmates for 2.5 years and who all have industry experience. Through presentations from classmates with experience in the field, I have learned more about the defense industry, the pharmaceutical industry, the health care industry, the banking industry, and manufacturing in general." This "extremely focused" program "is excellent for working adults." Students in the online MBA programs can earn only general MBAs without concentrations.

In all programs, students love "the overall value, [the] up-to-date technology, [and the] user-friendly registration, enrollment, and work processes." Professors here "are really good and very engaging with the class. They come from all walks of life: Some write their own textbooks, some have owned their own businesses, some are teaching for fun, some have taught forever! Given the strong professional presence of the students, they are always kept on their toes and questioned regarding anything that might not make sense."

Career and Placement

Career Services at UTA include "comprehensive assessment, industry analysis, career exploration and informational interviews, managing in a diverse environment, career-focused academic advising, and internships," the school tells us. In addition, students take a careers class that "presents both practical and theoretical perspectives on careers and managing in a changing work environment." Students gripe that "the school still needs to work hard on getting more known companies to visit the campus for recruitment." They also identify alumni connections as an area needing improvement. Employers most likely to hire UTA MBAs include Alcon Laboratories, Sabre Group Holdings, Inc, Nokia, American Airlines, and Bank of America.

Student Life and Environment

UTA's MBA programs are "made for working professionals looking to earn a degree, but not necessarily a second "college experience." Students yearning to meet new friends and embellish another undergraduate experience should look for more personalized service at other institutions. To be sure, UTA is a very large, growing institution that offers all the facilities and resources of most major academic institutions at a much lower cost. However, "most students are part-times with full-time jobs, so mingling is not a top priority." The full-timers in the Flexible MBA program are the exception—they do spend considerable time together. They tell us that "life at school is moderately paced, which allows most students to get into other activities apart from academics." One full-time student explains, "There are many opportunities for students to get involved, if they want them. UTA is a school where you have to seek out the opportunities—you will find them if you look. I am very involved on campus on the part of the graduate school. Yet such opportunities are not always advertised and made known to all the students eligible."

All programs at UTA boast impressive diversity stats. One student reports, "The school is extremely diverse; almost any class has a spread of Asians, Africans, Europeans, Middle Easterners, and Hispanics." Students in the Flexible MBA program are "a mixed bag. Like any academic program, you have foreign students, students with a lot of work experience, and students who are fresh out of undergrad. It's a very stimulating and rewarding combination." Cohort MBAs are all "industry professionals from the Dallas/Fort Worth area," notes a part-timer. They are all very vocal, intelligent, and engaging in the classroom. I've never had this much fun in a real classroom before. Vacations, gatherings, and celebrations among students is common." Everyone here is "very career-oriented and outgoing. Many students have families and are married."

Students observe that "one of the greatest strengths of UTA is that we are located in a very active business market. This large metroplex allows for many opportunities to go outside the classroom as well as bring in local experts."

Admissions

Admissions officers at UTA consider all of the following: GMAT score, undergraduate GPA and curriculum, work experience, essays (including a 200-word statement of academic intent), and letters of recommendation. Applicants are ranked using the formula [(undergraduate GPA × 200) + GMAT score], and the average admitted student scores approximately 1,100 (which, of course, means that many admitted students score lower than 1,100). Students whose first language is not English must also submit TOEFL scores (this requirement is waived for students who have earned a postsecondary degree from a U.S. college or university). International students must also provide a bank affidavit and financial statement. To promote diversity within the student body, UTA College of Business Education supports activities sponsored by the McNair Scholar Program and the National Black MBA Association.

FINANCIAL FACTS

Annual tuition (in-state/ out-of-state)	$4,944/$13,998
Fees (in-state/ out-of-state)	$2,058/$2,253
Cost of books	$1,000
Room & board (on/off-campus)	$4,800/$6,000
% of students receiving aid	20
Average award package	$8,500
Average grant	$1,000
Average student loan debt	$23,475

ADMISSIONS

Admissions Selectivity Rating	**80**
# of applications received	413
% applicants accepted	49
% acceptees attending	65
Average GMAT	530
Range of GMAT	470–620
Average GPA	3.28
TOEFL required of international students	Yes
Minimum TOEFL (paper/computer)	550/213
Application fee	$30
International application fee	$60
Regular application deadline	6/10
Regular notification	Rolling
Early decision program?	Yes
ED Deadline/Notification	Rolling / 6/15
Deferment available	Yes
Maximum length of deferment	1 year
Transfer students accepted	Yes
Transfer application policy Maximum number of transferable credits is 9; grades 'B' or better from an AACSB-accredited university.	
Non-fall admissions	Yes
Need-blind admissions	Yes

THE UNIVERSITY OF TEXAS AT AUSTIN
McCOMBS SCHOOL OF BUSINESS

Academics

For a combination of an excellent graduate business program and an equally fine quality of life, it's hard to beat the McCombs School of Business at The University of Texas at Austin. Students here agree that "Austin is a very cool town, Texas is a great state, and UT has a top 20 MBA program." They also praise "an atmosphere that is very collaborative and laid-back, but still professional." Students also love the fact that the larger university is big enough to be strong in many disciplines. Our survey respondents see strengths in such b-school staples as accounting, IT, entrepreneurship, real estate and marketing; they're also enthusiastic about the school's unique offerings in investment management, private equity, and energy finance.

The McCombs curriculum consists of 27 credits of core requirements and a minimum of 33 elective credits. If 15 of those credits are devoted to one of five specific functional areas (accounting, finance, management, information technology, or marketing), then one graduates with a concentration. In addition to concentrations, McCombs offers students the option of a specialization, which is basically a "specifically designed set of courses" within a particular discipline. Teamwork and group projects figure heavily in the McCombs curriculum; observes one student, "The cooperative and team environment is the greatest attribute of McCombs. Most classes require some form of group interaction, which is important to life in the professional world." Students report that "most professors use the methods most appropriate for their specific fields of study; from the case method to class discussion, lectures to problem sets, they use them all as required by the material."

Among McCombs' standout features is the Plus Program, a relatively recent addition to the curriculum spurred on by "the school's commitment to hands-on learning and market-driven education." The Plus Program consists of short programs "ranging from international business tours to professional development seminars." Future MBAs report that the Plus Program "helps us gain real-world experience very quickly." Writes one student, the "program gives students excellent opportunities to improve communications skills and work on real-life projects with local companies outside of the academic schedule."

Career and Placement

According to the school, each year "recruiters from hundreds of the world's leading companies" visit the Ford Career Center to recruit Texas MBAs. Corporate relationships, including "affiliations with high-tech companies," mean employers are a major presence on campus all year round, not just at recruiting time. This allows students to forge strong relationships with potential employers, which, unsurprisingly, pleases McCombs students quite a bit. Almost all the students in our survey reported satisfaction with McCombs' ability to attract recruiters and to place students in internships and jobs.

Top employers of Texas MBAs include American Airlines; Capital One; Citibank; Dell; Deloitte Consulting; Exelon; Frito Lay; General Mills; HEB; IBM; Johnson & Johnson; Procter & Gamble; SBC Communications; Samsung; Standard & Poor's; and Union Bank of Switzerland. About half of all graduates remain in the Southwest; the remaining students scatter pretty evenly around the country and the world for their first post-degree jobs.

Tina Mabley, Directors of Admission, MBA Programs
Admissions, MBA Program Office, 1 University Station, B6004, Austin, TX 78712 U.S.
Phone: 512-471-7612 • Fax: 512-471-4243
E-mail: McCombsMBA@mccombs.utexas.edu • Website: mba.mccombs.utexas.edu

Student Life and Environment

Like seemingly everyone else who lives in Austin, students love their school's hometown. Explains one student, "It's unlike any other environment. It is not New York City, so it doesn't stress you out, and it's not rural America, so it doesn't bore you to death. If you are outgoing, then this is the place to be. *Forbes* rated Austin as the best city for singles, and that kind of explains it." Students here laud the "many outdoor activities, like biking, running, hiking, and camping that are available in the city. There's also a big lake that provides a great place to relax during the spring and summer." They also praise the "incredible Tex-Mex food" (the barbecue's not half bad, either) and "the night life on Sixth Street, which is better than just about anywhere." If you like live music, you'll love Austin.

On campus, "social life is excellent" at McCombs, with "a great deal of camaraderie among the students." Student organizations "are very involved and very well run," and extracurricular fun is always close at hand, as "Every Thursday night we have Think and Drinks which allow students to mingle at a bar over a beer or two. It's a work hard, play hard culture." Tailgate parties before football games "are always fantastic, with free food, free drinks, and free fun." Married students happily note that "The Student and Significant Others Group is great for those students who bring a partner. The school has great programs for my spouse as well as for my kids."

"Teamwork and cooperation overshadows intense competition" at McCombs; students' awareness that they are in a top-flight program that can yield good jobs for all of them, and also helps keep competitiveness low. A large portion of the student body originates from outside the United States; writes one American student, "I was amazed at the broad spectrum of countries and nationalities represented. This alone has been a tremendous learning experience."

Admissions

Application to McCombs must be submitted online. Admission is extremely competitive. A completed application must include: a resume detailing work history; personal essays; official copies of transcripts for all postsecondary academic work; letters of recommendation; an official score report for the GMAT; and, for international students whose first language is not English, an official score report for the TOEFL. Programs designed to increase minority and disadvantaged populations at McCombs include Jump Start, "which targets undergraduate seniors who are academically qualified for a top-ranked MBA but lack the required work experience;" Explore McCombs, "a three-day preview of the School for qualified African American, Hispanic American, and Native American applicants;" and participation in a number of alliances, associations, and consortia dedicated to the goal.

FINANCIAL FACTS

Annual tuition (in-state/ out-of-state)	$13,320/$30,242
Fees (in-state/ out-of-state)	$6,036/$7,436
Cost of books	$1,477
Room & board (off-campus)	$13,500
% of students receiving aid	64
% of first-year students receiving aid	64
% of students receiving loans	58
% of students receiving grants	20
Average award package	$33,952
Average grant	$13,252
Average student loan debt	$60,590

ADMISSIONS

Admissions Selectivity Rating	**94**
# of applications received	1,440
% applicants accepted	37
% acceptees attending	47
Average GMAT	669
Range of GMAT	600–740
Average GPA	3.38
TOEFL required of international students	Yes
Minimum TOEFL (paper/computer)	620/260
Application fee	$125
Regular application deadline	4/1
Regular notification	5/1
Deferment available	Yes
Maximum length of deferment	1 year
Need-blind admissions	Yes

Applicants Also Look At

Duke University, Harvard University, Northwestern University, University of California, Berkeley, University of Michigan, The University of North Carolina at Chapel Hill, University of Pennsylvania.

EMPLOYMENT PROFILE

Career Rating	91	Grads Employed by Function	%	Avg. Salary
Primary Source of Full-time Job Acceptances		Finance/Accounting	40	$89,207
School-facilitated activities	163 (63%)	Marketing/Sales	26	$80,866
Graduate-facilitated activities	96 (37%)	MIS	1	$95,000
Average base starting salary	$87,692	Operations/Production	3	$76,750
Percent employed	90	Consulting	16	$103,915
		General Management	9	$80,126
		Other	5	$77,083

Top 5 Employers Hiring Grads

Dell; Deloitte Consulting; McKinsey & Co.; PricewaterhouseCoopers; Intel Corporation.

THE UNIVERSITY OF TEXAS AT DALLAS
SCHOOL OF MANAGEMENT

Academics

Most students attend The University of Texas at Dallas' MBA program on a part-time basis, enrolling in either the professional part-time MBA program (available either on-site or online) or one of a number of executive MBA options. Sixty students each year enter the more competitive cohort full-time MBA program, a relatively new offering at the school (the program was established in 1996).

Full-time students call the cohort MBA "one of the best bang-for-the-buck programs out there," one that benefits from "truly outstanding professors, many of whom have real-world work experience as business leaders. Also, all of them are excited about what they teach, and that enthusiasm rubs off on the students." Part-time students agree that professors are "very good and very knowledgeable," and also appreciate that "the school runs a tight ship." Reports one global leadership executive MBA (GLEMBA) student, "The supportive administrators really help out making the 'chore' of all the paperwork much easier so students can concentrate on learning."

All students follow the same basic curriculum, commencing with a "heavy" 29-credit core: "Some of us would rather be able to pick and choose some courses to have a more customized educational experience." Electives allow students to develop specializations in accounting, innovation and entrepreneurship, finance, international management, managerial economics, marketing management, MIS, operations management, or organization and strategy. Students single out the school's "analytic and quantitative approach to business management, with a full scope of leadership/soft skills" as its greatest curricular strength. Writes one student, "Materials are highly relevant and contemporary, the delivery is high quality and interactive, the assignments build upon the material, and the core courses build on one another." Graduate study is further enhanced by the fact that "UTD is a highly research-oriented school, and we have many professors who are well noted for their excellence in research."

Career and Placement

Students at UTD's School of Management have access to two Career Services Offices: the SOM Career Management Center (CMC), and the UTD Career Center. The offices coordinate efforts to serve both undergraduates and graduate students in business; the CMC focuses primarily on the needs of graduate students. The CMC coordinates career fairs, company information sessions, and on-campus interviews. The office also maintains online bulletin boards and job databases. Students looking for more are encouraged to use school resources to achieve their goals; writes one MBA, "The administration is wonderful. They helped a group I was in develop, implement, and finance a career fair for MBAs specifically."

Employers most likely to hire UTD MBAs include Alliance Data Systems, Bank of New York, Dell, Deloitte Touche Tohmatsu, Ernst & Young, KPMG, Lennox, Nortel, and Sabre Holdings.

Student Life and Environment

UTD's School of Management "recently transitioned into a single on-campus facility" that "has everything we need for the business school." Amenities include "wireless Internet, technologically advanced classrooms, plenty of computer labs," "a nice lounge area," breakout rooms, and a 350-seat auditorium. Despite the upgrade, some here are not entirely satisfied; they complain that "the campus is boring. The atmosphere within the buildings is not welcoming, there are few trees around, and there are few places to sit outside and enjoy the day while studying."

Ms. Jyoti Mallick, Director of the Cohort MBA Program
School of Management Building, PO Box 830688, SM21, Richardson, TX 75080 U.S.
Phone: 972-883-6191 • Fax: 972-883-6823
E-mail: CMBA@UTDALLAS.EDU • Website: SOM.UTDALLAS.EDU/GRADUATE/COHORTMBA/INDEX.HTM

Because "the majority of graduate students commute" at UTD, "there is not a strong community" among most MBA students. Reports one part-time student, "The professional MBA program is more geared toward working professionals. Classes are in the evening or on weekends, and the professors are well aware that most of the students are working 40 to 60 hours per week (as well as traveling)." Full-time students are more likely to spend free time on campus. They tell us that "there are a lot of activities going on all the time. There are several student academic and nonacademic clubs. Every Friday, the International Student Services Office arranges for the celebration of the culture of a country, with food, song, [and] dance. The school frequently organizes CEO lecture series. The Institute for Excellence in Corporate Governance in the school organizes seminars from time to time where top management people from big corporations come for brainstorming on contemporary business issues. Field trips to companies are organized."

UTD's part-time student body "mostly consists of working, married people, many with children. They are interested in performing well in school, but are not highly competitive for grades. In fact, some just want the degree and don't care about the grades. Most students already have a career path and are attending school to further careers that have been started, so you don't feel that you are competing for jobs with them." In the full-time program, "the atmosphere is very family-like. The batches work together in community outreach programs, form study groups, and have parties at each other's homes." Both programs have substantial international populations who "lend interesting insights and viewpoints."

Admissions

All applicants to UTD business graduate programs must submit the following: an online application; official copies of all postsecondary transcripts; an official score report for the GMAT; three letters of recommendation; and a personal statement/essay. International students whose native language is not English must provide an official score report for the TOEFL in addition to the materials listed above. The UTD admissions office looks most closely at the undergraduate transcript and GMAT scores; letters of recommendation and the essay are also considered important factors. Other aspects of the application are considered but are given less weight in the final decision. Admission to the full-time cohort program is more competitive than is admission to part-time programs. All programs require calculus as a prerequisite.

FINANCIAL FACTS

Annual tuition (in-state/ out-of-state)	$7,100/$13,700
Fees (in-state/ out-of-state)	$1,000/$1,000
Cost of books	$1,200
Room & board (on/off-campus)	$10,000/$10,000
% of students receiving aid	63
% of first-year students receiving aid	75
% of students receiving grants	61
Average award package	$11,796
Average grant	$11,796

ADMISSIONS

Admissions Selectivity Rating	95
# of applications received	189
% applicants accepted	33
% acceptees attending	63
Average GMAT	650
Range of GMAT	600–680
Average GPA	3.4
TOEFL required of international students	Yes
Minimum TOEFL (paper/computer)	550/213
Application fee	$50
International application fee	$100
Regular application deadline	5/1
Regular notification	6/15
Application Deadline/Notification	
Round 1:	1/15 / 3/1
Round 2:	3/1 / 4/15
Round 3:	6/1 / 6/15
Deferment available	Yes
Maximum length of deferment	1 year
Need-blind admissions	Yes

Applicants Also Look At

Southern Methodist University, University of Dallas, University of North Texas, The University of Texas at Arlington, The University of Texas at Austin.

EMPLOYMENT PROFILE

Career Rating	82	**Grads Employed by Function% Avg. Salary**	
Primary Source of Full-time Job Acceptances		Finance/Accounting 48	$72,960
School-facilitated activities	20 (80%)	Marketing/Sales 12	$71,061
Graduate-facilitated activities	5 (20%)	MIS 8	NR
Average base starting salary	$65,408	Operations/Production 12	$65,567
Percent employed	96	Consulting 12	$71,667
		General Management 8	R
		Top 5 Employers Hiring Grads	
		Deloitte; Countrywide; KPMG; PriceWaterhouse; Bank of America.	

THE UNIVERSITY OF TEXAS—PAN AMERICAN

COLLEGE OF BUSINESS ADMINISTRATION

GENERAL INFORMATION

Type of school	Public
Environment	Town
Academic calendar	Semester

SURVEY SAYS . . .
Friendly students
Happy students
Solid preparation in:
Teamwork
Communication/interpersonal skills
Presentation skills
Computer skills

STUDENTS

Enrollment of parent institution	17,500
Enrollment of business school	186
% male/female	68/32
% part-time	69
% minorities	75
% international	15
Average age at entry	31
Average years work experience at entry	2

ACADEMICS

Academic Experience Rating	**67**
Student/faculty ratio	27:1
Profs interesting rating	66
Profs accessible rating	65
% female faculty	30

Academics

The College of Business Administration at The University of Texas—Pan American offers both an evening MBA program and an online MBA program. The college and the MBA program are accredited by the American Assembly of Collegiate Schools of Business (AACSB).

UTPA's evening MBA program may be completed on either a full-time or a part-time basis. Full-time students with undergraduate degrees in business may complete the program in as little as 18 months. Part-time students may take up to six years to earn their degrees. Those lacking an academic background in business are required to commence the program with a sequence of foundation courses that cover principles of accounting, economics, management, marketing, statistics, and finance. All students must complete nine core courses and three electives for a total of 36 course hours of work. Students may choose to write a thesis instead of taking six of the nine hours of required electives; thesis topics are approved by the committee. Students in the program praise its emphasis on teamwork and the "good availability of classes at night."

The online MBA is administered jointly with seven other UT campuses (Arlington, Brownsville, Dallas, El Paso, Permian Basin, San Antonio, and Tyler). The online curriculum consists of 48 course hours. Students with sufficient backgrounds in business may have up to four core courses waived, reducing the number of required hours to 36. Online students must take at least two courses in person at their home campuses; all other courses can be completed at home via computer.

Career and Placement

Because UTPA's MBA program is relatively small, graduate students here share a university-wide Career Services Office with business undergraduates. Another support office, called the Center for Advisement, Recruitment, Internships and Retention (CARIR), provides career counseling services, job-related reference materials, and assistance in internship placements. The office participates in numerous regional and national online job databases, which students may access through their UTPA accounts. CARIR also organizes on-campus recruitment events each semester, although most of the recruitment is geared toward alumni.

Dr. Kai Koong, Director of MBA Program
1201 West University Drive, Edinburg, TX 78541-2999 United States
Phone: 956-381-3313 • Fax: 956-381-2970
E-mail: mbaprog@utpa.edu • Website: www.coba.panam.edu/mba/index.htm

Student Life and Environment

UTPA is "a commuter campus" that "is not very eventful for graduate students." Aside from "occasional group meetings," MBAs here spend little time on campus. They attend classes, take care of other school-related obligations, and then head home. For all of the students who commute, the school has plenty of new parking lots on campus.

UTPA is located in Edinburg, Texas, a city of nearly 58,000 in the southernmost section of the state. Edinburg is the county seat of Hidalgo County. The majority population is Hispanic, with most residents of Mexican descent. Education and health care are the area's major employment sectors; retail trade capitalizes on the city's location near the Mexico border.

The "career-minded" students in the program are "varied in nationalities and goals," according to their peers. These "resourceful, energetic, focused, and interesting" future MBAs "are typically employed full time, many with families and major commitments. We are nearly all night students. Students are disciplined and group-oriented."

Admissions

Applicants to University of Texas—Pan American must submit all the following materials to the Admissions Committee: an application to the UTPA Graduate School; sealed copies of official transcripts for all previously attended postsecondary institutions; a sealed copy of an official GMAT score report. In addition, international students whose first language is not English must submit a sealed copy of an official TOEFL score report. Applicants who receive a score of at least 1,000 under the formula [(undergraduate GPA for final 60 semester hours of academic work × 200) + GMAT score] have the best chance of gaining admission to the program. Those who fail to meet this benchmark may still be admitted on the basis of "strong supporting documentation," such as letters of recommendation, resume, and "other evidence of potential success based on relevant work and leadership experience."

FINANCIAL FACTS

Annual tuition (in-state/ out-of-state)	$2,797/$8,900
Fees (in-state/ out-of-state)	$314/$402
Cost of books	$1,500
Average grant	$9,999

ADMISSIONS

Admissions Selectivity Rating	**73**
# of applications received	78
% applicants accepted	47
% acceptees attending	73
Average GMAT	450
Average GPA	3.00
TOEFL required of international students	Yes
Minimum TOEFL (paper/computer)	500/173
Application fee	$35
Regular application deadline	7/1
Regular notification	Rolling
Transfer students accepted	Yes
Transfer application policy Accept maximum 3 courses.	
Non-fall admissions	Yes
Need-blind admissions	Yes

THE UNIVERSITY OF TEXAS AT SAN ANTONIO
COLLEGE OF BUSINESS

GENERAL INFORMATION
Type of school	Public
Environment	Metropolis
Academic calendar	Semester

SURVEY SAYS . . .
Students love San Antonio, TX
Smart classrooms
Solid preparation in:
General management
Quantitative skills

STUDENTS
Enrollment of parent institution	28,379
Enrollment of business school	396
% male/female	61/39
% part-time	71
% minorities	30
% international	29
Average age at entry	27

ACADEMICS
Academic Experience Rating	**75**
Student/faculty ratio	26:1
Profs interesting rating	78
Profs accessible rating	68
% female faculty	31
% minority faculty	51

Prominent Alumni
Gilbert Gonzalez, undersecretary for rural development, U.S. Department of Agriculture; Ernest Bromley, president and CEO, Bromley and Associates; Susan Evers, general counsel, USAA; William Morrow, president and vice chairman, Grande Communications; Jeanie Wyatt, CEO, South Texas Money Management.

Academics

You can earn your MBA at exactly the speed you choose at The University of Texas at San Antonio, a "self-paced" program geared toward the needs of busy area professionals. "Most students work full-time and take one or two classes a semester (three or six semester credit hours) and finish in approximately two years," according to the school's website. Students may take up to six years to complete the degree. Classes are usually offered on weekday evenings and on weekends.

The UTSA MBA program enjoys a boost from the school's PhD programs in accounting, marketing, applied statistics, finance, management and organizational studies, and information technology. Faculty in these areas are active in current research in their fields. In addition, faculty members in economics and real estate also publish frequently. The school also positions itself at the vanguard of business education by seeking new and promising disciplines; it has developed an expertise and an academic program in infrastructure assurance and security. Students here praise their professors, noting that "the majority of professors are PhDs with published work and prior experience in their field. Their real-world experience allows them to relate teachings to real-world situations, which help students assimilate new material." They appreciate how "most of the professors are very interested in making sure that their students learn the material and are very accessible and very willing to help." One MBA reports, "Several professors took time on weekends for additional exam preparation for students." Students also love the relatively low cost of the program. One writes, "The greatest strength of this program is the value when comparing tuition costs to the quality of the education and the resources available."

UTSA offers three basic MBA options: a general MBA, nonthesis; a general MBA with a thesis; and a nonthesis MBA with a concentration. All options require 33 hours of course work (beyond preparatory core courses), 21 hours of which are devoted to Foundations of Knowledge requirements (advanced courses in accounting, managerial economics, financial management, management and behavior, strategy, marketing, and decision analysis). The thesis option requires an additional six hours of electives and six hours of master's thesis credit. The nonthesis option requires 12 hours of electives. Students may use their electives to concentrate in business economics, finance, health care management, information systems, management accounting, management of technology, management science, marketing management, project management, and taxation.

Career and Placement

UTSA employs a career officer dedicated to providing counseling and placement services to graduate business students. Services include career assessment; one-on-one counseling; library services; online resume books and job postings; resume reviews; mock interviews; internships; career fairs and on-campus recruiting; career skills workshops; and networking events. UTSA MBAs appreciate the efforts but wish for something more; "We need more activities for graduate business students, more networking with alumni, and better companies to come recruit on campus," writes one student. Employers most likely to hire UTSA business graduates include HEB Grocery Company, USAA, and Dell Computers.

REBECAA MEDINA, MANAGER OF GRADUATE ADMISSIONS
ONE UTSA CIRCLE, SAN ANTONIO, TX 78249-0603 UNITED STATES
PHONE: 210-458-4330 • FAX: 210-458-4332
E-MAIL: GRADUATESTUDIES@UTSA.EDU • WEBSITE: BUSINESS.UTSA.EDU/GRADUATE

FINANCIAL FACTS

Annual tuition (in-state/ out-of-state)	$6,036/$15,936

ADMISSIONS

Admissions Selectivity Rating	**78**
# of applications received	218
% applicants accepted	63
% acceptees attending	63
Average GMAT	557
Range of GMAT	510–600
Average GPA	3.26
TOEFL required of international students	Yes
Minimum TOEFL (paper/computer)	500/173
Application fee	$45
International application fee	$80
Regular application deadline	7/1
Regular notification	Rolling
Deferment available	Yes
Maximum length of deferment	2 terms
Transfer students accepted	Yes
Transfer application policy Please refer to current graduate catalog.	
Non-fall admissions	Yes
Need-blind admissions	Yes

Student Life and Environment

UTSA is a school in transition; it "was established as a commuter school," but students note that "the last few years have seen a trend towards more traditional students and programs. It is exciting to be on a campus that is becoming a real college campus for the first time. The gym is busy even at 10:00 or 11:00 at night, and it's amazing to see the amount of activity that persists on campus even in the afternoon and evening." Students also report that "the addition of the downtown campus in the urban center has allowed for full-time professionals to more efficiently intermix the professional with the academic lives." Even so, this is hardly a lively extracurricular scene for MBA. One student explains, "Most of the courses are offered after 5:00 P.M., which lends itself to many working, commuting students. In this type of environment, it is sometimes difficult to establish a sense of community." However, approximately one-third of the students in the graduate program attend school on a full-time basis. These students tend to work on campus as research and teaching assistants and are on campus most of the day. The MBA Association does its best; it is "active and aggressive in providing MBA students with access to lectures, etiquette dinners, networking opportunities, resume seminars, [and] job fairs."

UTSA's facilities earn students' praise; MBAs tell us the campus "is beautiful and safe," and that "the business building has excellent learning technology in the classrooms. Also, access to computers and research materials is widely available throughout the campus." Things are so good here that many students identify the lack of a football team as the university's most glaring weakness.

The population of the MBA program at UTSA "is very diverse," although "the predominant type is the full-time employed individual, [typically] married, in [their] late 20s or early 30s, and whose time is at a premium." Students represent "an incredibly diverse mix of professions as well as backgrounds. For example, I had a physicist from MIT and an Air Force Colonel in the same class." says one MBA. The school attracts many internationals; one student writes, "There are people from Asia, the U.S., India, and Mexico."

Admissions

Applicants to the UTSA MBA program are required to provide the school with a completed application form, official copies of transcripts from all colleges and universities attended, official GMAT scores, and a personal statement stating the applicant's career and academic goals. A current resume and two letters of reference are officially optional but are "strongly recommended" by the Admissions Office. Applicants need not have majored in business as undergraduates to gain admission. Students with non-business undergraduate degrees are typically required to complete core courses in accounting, business law, economic theory, business finance, information systems, marketing, and quantitative methods prior to beginning work on the MBA. Students who completed undergraduate work in a business field more than seven years prior to admission may also be required to complete some or all core courses.

THE UNIVERSITY OF TOLEDO
COLLEGE OF BUSINESS ADMINISTRATION

GENERAL INFORMATION
Type of school   Public
Environment   City
Academic calendar   Semester

SURVEY SAYS . . .
Friendly Students
Solid preparation in:
Computer skills

STUDENTS
Enrollment of parent
  institution   19,374
Enrollment of
  business school   302
% male/female   59/41
% out-of-state   39
% part-time   55
% minorities   62
% international   34
Average age at entry   28
Average years work
  experience at entry   5

ACADEMICS
Academic Experience Rating   64
Student/faculty ratio   10:1
Profs interesting rating   72
Profs accessible rating   83
% female faculty   30

Joint Degrees
JD/MBA 3 years.

Prominent Alumni
Edward Kinsey, co-founder, Ariba,
Inc.; Ora Alleman, vice president,
National City Bank; Michael Durik,
executive vice president, The
Limited Stores, Inc.; Marvin Herb,
CEO, Coca-Cola Bottling Company;
Julie Higgins, Exective vice presi-
dent, The Trust Company of Toledo.

Academics

Offering a "good education at a very competitive price with convenient scheduling," the College of Business Administration at The University of Toledo fits the needs of area businesspeople in search of a quality MBA. One student explains, "The program is very accommodating toward people who work full-time. The majority of classes are taught at night, so I have been able to continue to work full-time while taking one or two classes at night." And, with a "low cost of living and low tuition fees when compared to other business schools," a UT MBA isn't a wallet buster.

UT distinguishes its MBA program with a number of cutting-edge concentrations. Students here may specialize in CRM and marketing intelligence, human resource management, information systems, operations and supply chain management, and professional sales as well as in the more traditional areas of administration, finance, international business, and marketing. Still, students warn that despite this apparent variety of choices, "The grad-level courses are fairly limited, [with] not enough variety/electives available to really customize our education. Classes are usually only offered once per semester at one specific time, so time conflicts between class and work schedules are quite common."

Students agree that "the greatest strengths of the UT MBA program come from its people. Overall, students are helpful, and it is easy to make connections through classmates. Professors follow a 40-40-20 rule with their time: 40 percent on research, 40 percent on preparing for classes, and 20 percent on advising students. This allows teachers to be student-centric." One student adds, "Receiving individual attention is a norm, be it in the Advising Office or from a professor."

Career and Placement

MBA students at Toledo may choose from an assortment of career support options. The school coordinates both academic graduate assistantships and corporate assistantships with employers like ProMedica Health System, Therma-Tru Doors, SSOE, Mercy Medical, Paramount Medical, and Goodwill. The school also sponsors regular networking events at which current students can meet and greet alumni. Finally, the Business Career Programs Office organizes on-campus recruiting, conducts mock interviews, performs resume reviews, provides counseling services, and manages a biannual Business Career Fair that brings more than 90 recruiters to campus.

Recent employers of UT MBAs include Calphalon, Chrysler, Dana Corp., DTE Energy, Ernst & Young, GM Powertrain, KeyBank, Heartland Information Systems, Hickory Farms, National City Corporation, Owens Corning, Owens Illinois, and Pilkington.

Student Life and Environment

"Life at UT is comfortable," students assure us. One praises, "Classrooms are clustered centrally so travel time between classes is quick. Most buildings have a computer lab, and the library has many quiet places to study. The fitness center is one of the largest I've seen for a college, and workouts are great. There aren't too many students crowding resources, so long lines are never a problem." If there's one area that needs help, students tell us it's the traffic and parking. One student warns, "There's an extreme lack of parking available. . . On days/nights when a major event such as a basketball or football game is going on, the school allows outsiders (nonstudents) to park on campus for a fee. This usually keeps students from being able to go to class as there's so much spillover of vehicles sometimes that parking in grass or restricted areas is common. I've had to turn

DAVID CHATFIELD, DIRECTOR MBA AND EMBA PROGRAMS
COLLEGE OF BUSINESS ADMINISTRATION, THE UNIVERSITY OF TOLEDO, TOLEDO, OH 43606-3390 U.S.
PHONE: 419-530-2775 • FAX: 419-530-7260
E-MAIL: MBA@UTOLEDO.EDU • WEBSITE: WWW.UTOLEDO.EDU/BUSINESS

around and go home, missing class, due to not being able to park or to get through traffic in a timely manner to park." To top it off, "The traffic situation on campus is horrendous."

Most students attend UT's MBA program on a part-time basis, arriving after a full day of work. Consequently, they have little time or inclination to participate in activities other than classes and group projects. Full-time students tell us that "there are many organizations to be involved in if you choose to. There are also department social functions quite frequently that are highly advertised." As for evenings and weekends, they are "what you make of them. Most people settle for simply just going to house parties or campus bars, which grows old fast. The downtown area offers good times, but most of that area is dead."

Toledo MBAs "come from diverse backgrounds, including majors, universities, religions, and ethnicity." While they "are competitive in their pursuit of high-quality jobs," they also enjoy "an atmosphere of mutual respect and teamwork between students in the program. Students are very comfortable approaching other students for help in their studies. In exchange, it is expected that every student pulls his or her own weight on the many team-based assignments." About one in three students originates from outside the United States, "providing a unique and interesting perspective on major business topics of the day."

Admissions

Applicants to the MBA program at UT must submit the following materials: a completed application; official copies of transcripts from each undergraduate and graduate institution attended; three letters of recommendation (letters should speak to academic potential); and an official score report for the GMAT. In addition to the above, all international applicants must submit a financial statement and supporting documents. International applicants from countries in which English is not the primary language must submit an official score report for the TOEFL. Students are encouraged to complete their applications online.

FINANCIAL FACTS

Annual tuition (in-state/ out-of-state)	$10,147/$18,958
Fees	$1,180
Cost of books	$1,200
Room & board (off-campus)	$5,830
Average grant	$17,646

ADMISSIONS

Admissions Selectivity Rating	**71**
# of applications received	190
% applicants accepted	71
% acceptees attending	65
Average GMAT	510
Range of GMAT	450–780
Average GPA	3.2
TOEFL required of international students	Yes
Minimum TOEFL (paper/computer)	550/213
Application fee	$45
Regular application deadline	Rolling
Regular notification	Rolling
Deferment available	Yes
Maximum length of deferment	1 semester
Transfer students accepted	Yes
Transfer application policy	
Maximum 9 credit hours with at least a B from an AACSB-accredited school.	
Non-fall admissions	Yes
Need-blind admissions	Yes

Applicants Also Look At
Bowling Green State University, The University of Findlay.

THE UNIVERSITY OF TULSA
COLLEGE OF BUSINESS ADMINISTRATION

GENERAL INFORMATION
Type of school	Private
Environment	Metropolis
Academic calendar	Semester

SURVEY SAYS . . .
Students love Tulsa, OK
Happy students
Smart classrooms
Solid preparation in:
Accounting
Quantitative skills
Computer skills

STUDENTS
Enrollment of parent institution	4,125
Enrollment of business school	167
% male/female	56/44
% out-of-state	17
% part-time	46
% minorities	12
% international	22
Average age at entry	27
Average years work experience at entry	2

ACADEMICS
Academic Experience Rating	**72**
Student/faculty ratio	17:1
Profs interesting rating	80
Profs accessible rating	93
% female faculty	24
% minority faculty	24

Joint Degrees
MBA/JD, MTAX/JD, MBA/MSF.

Academics

A small private school with a great local reputation, the College of Business Administration at The University of Tulsa offers a well-rounded MBA curriculum, an enviably low student/faculty ratio, and an intimate and supportive academic atmosphere. A true teaching college, TU professors are dedicated to their students and "very willing to help, often giving a home or cell phone number for after-hours questions." A current student insists, "Every professor that I have ever taken a course with knows me by name and makes themselves available for help, even if I do not currently have a course with them." Another agrees, "Young professors and senior professors alike all truly are dedicated to our learning experience. They strive for us to succeed."

The TU curriculum is fairly structured, consisting of 18 credit hours of foundation courses in subjects such as accounting concepts, economic concepts, statistics, and marketing (though students with an educational background in business may be able to waive some of the core requirements). After the foundation is complete, students take 25 credit hours of advanced curriculum courses in more specific subject areas, including classes like behavioral sciences in administration and management information systems. Finally, students complete the degree requirements with elective course work—some in more unusual subject areas such as nursing, athletic training, accounting, taxation, statistics, management, and quantitative methods. Throughout the curriculum, practical applications to business are emphasized, and TU professors "all have valuable work experience to share with their students and are extremely intelligent."

In order to meet the needs of a diverse student population, the school offers flexible scheduling and the opportunity to pursue a degree part-time, full-time, and online. In addition to the traditional MBA, the school also offers a couple of opportunities to pursue a joint degree, including the JD/MBA which, through overlapping course content, can reduce the degree requirements for both programs by up to 16 credit hours. Professors "assign quite a bit of reading each week" and students warn that "6 hours of course work plus a demanding full-time job is difficult." Even so, they reassure us that the "Faculty [are] aware that many of the students work and are very helpful."

Although it is a private school, many students can comfortably afford their University of Tulsa MBA because "TU offers great graduate assistantships to pay for tuition and provides a great stipend." In addition to coordinating assistantships, students appreciate the fact that the "administration is concerned with improving the university and attracting high-caliber students." In fact, students are sure that their top-notch program will soon be recognized, and "as the school grows, it will be able to offer even more opportunities."

Career and Placement

The University of Tulsa enjoys a "very good reputation in the community," and current students say its "easy to get jobs through your professors and get involved with high-powered executives in the business community." On campus, the Office of Career Services offers workshops on resume writing, interviewing, and negotiating, as well as career assessment and counseling. The Office of Career Services also sponsors on-campus interviews and annual career fairs, through which more than 200 companies visit the TU campus. In addition, TU students may access the Office of Career Services online database of more than 2,500 employers and companies.

In recent years, companies that have interviewed students at the College of Business Administration include: American Airlines, Chevron, PricewaterhouseCoopers, Ernst & Young, IBM, Koch Industries, MCI, Phillips Petroleum, and State Farm. When it comes

Dr. Mark Collins, Associate Dean of Academic Programs
BAH 217, 600 S. College Avenue, Tulsa, OK 74104-3189 United States
Phone: 918-631-2242 • Fax: 918-631-2142
E-mail: graduate-business@utulsa.edu • Website: www.cba.utulsa.edu

to recruiting, students feel that TU could expand their reputation nationally, explaining "TU has great relationships with companies in the Midwest/central region of the United States, but there are few recruiters that come to TU from the coasts."

Student Life and Environment

As with the academic experience, social life at TU is defined by the school's intimate atmosphere. A current student explains, "TU has a great student life because of the small size. It is easy to make friends even in different colleges across the campus because there are so many activities and ways to get involved." Through the business school and beyond, extracurricular activities are "plentiful and well advertised," and students appreciate the school's "beautiful campus with many new facilities." "All of the sports facilities are brand new on campus and foster a fun game atmosphere for attending sporting events." However, married students and students with families (who comprise a large percentage of the student population) feel the school could improve by providing "more activities for students and their families or partners."

TU students enjoy life in hometown Tulsa, describing it as "a fantastic city with a huge amount of growth potential." Thanks to the school's small size and cosmopolitan atmosphere, students benefit from "the perfect mixture of big-city social life and small-city relationships" at TU. When it comes to their classmates, "Tulsa and TU both have a vibrant population" and students hail from diverse backgrounds personally and professionally. On the business school campus, you'll find students who "are married with children and have worked in corporations for 5 years," and others who are "single socialites straight from undergrad."

Admissions

To apply to the MBA program at the University of Tulsa, students must submit official GMAT scores, undergraduate transcripts, a current resume, three letters of recommendation from professional or academic sources, and a completed graduate school application form. Younger applicants may be pleased to learn that professional work experience isn't required for entry into the program, nor is an undergraduate degree in business. Students may apply to enter during the fall, spring or summer term.

FINANCIAL FACTS

Annual tuition	$14,004
Fees	$54
Cost of books	$1,000
Room & board	
(on/off-campus)	$7,404/$8,314
% of students receiving aid	59
% of first-year students	
receiving aid	67
% of students receiving loans	22
% of students receiving grants	43
Average award package	$10,402
Average grant	$7,151
Average student loan debt	$25,681

ADMISSIONS

Admissions Selectivity Rating	**75**
# of applications received	84
% applicants accepted	86
% acceptees attending	85
Average GMAT	573
Range of GMAT	530–610
Average GPA	3.4
TOEFL required of	
international students	Yes
Minimum TOEFL	
(paper/computer)	575/232
Application fee	$40
Regular application deadline	Rolling
Regular notification	Rolling
Deferment available	Yes
Maximum length of	
deferment	1 year
Transfer students accepted	Yes
Transfer application policy	
Up to 6 credit hours may be transferred.	
Non-fall admissions	Yes
Need-blind admissions	Yes

Applicants Also Look At
Oklahoma State University, University of Oklahoma.

EMPLOYMENT PROFILE

Career Rating	**66**	**Top 3 Employers Hiring Grads**
Primary Source of Full-time Job Acceptances		Bank of Oklahoma; KPMG International;
Percent employed	30	Williams.

UNIVERSITY OF UTAH
DAVID ECCLES SCHOOL OF BUSINESS

GENERAL INFORMATION

Type of school	Public
Environment	City
Academic calendar	Semester

SURVEY SAYS . . .

Students love Salt Lake City, UT
Friendly students
Good peer network
Happy students
Solid preparation in:
OperationsTeamwork

STUDENTS

Enrollment of parent institution	30,000
Enrollment of business school	416
% male/female	70/30
% out-of-state	49
% part-time	75
% minorities	5
% international	21
Average age at entry	28
Average years work experience at entry	6

ACADEMICS

Academic Experience Rating	**88**
Student/faculty ratio	5:1
Profs interesting rating	80
Profs accessible rating	94
% female faculty	28
% minority faculty	16

Joint Degrees

MBA/JD 3 to 4 years, MBA/master of architecture 3 to 4 years, MBA/master of health administration.

Prominent Alumni

Pierre Lassonde, president, Franco-Nevada Mining; Spencer Kirk, CEO (retired), Megahertz Corporation; Robert McDonald, vice chair global operations, Proctor & Gamble; Jerry Atkin, president, CEO, Skywest Airlines; Geoffrey Wooley, founding partner, Dominion Ventures.

Academics

The David Eccles School of Business (DESB) at the University of Utah is a "smaller, and still very personable" program that "is striving hard to compete with larger, more well-known business schools." By many students' accounts, it is succeeding in its efforts. The school is particularly strong in the field of entrepreneurship, in which it offers "a lot of resources and opportunities for entrepreneurs." It sponsors the Utah Entrepreneur Challenge and run a Venture Development Fund. DEBS is also home to the Lassonde New Venture Center, a "great experience that allows business students to partner with researchers on campus to commercialize technology."

Entrepreneurship isn't the only game in town here, however. DESB has become strong in operations management over the past few years, as "Professors of top schools have been hired" in the field. Students also note that the university at large accommodates MBAs who are interested in health care and international business. (Students tell us that Utah has a "good Middle East Center.") A "focus on technology management and corporate strategy" throughout the curriculum leaves students feeling prepared for the challenges of the twenty-first-century business environment.

DEBS offers "a small daytime program (120 students)" that lets students "get to know the faculty and other students really well and get personalized instruction and attention." In addition to professors who know their students "by name," "The courses and structure allow for a flexible program that can be customized to individual needs." A part-time professional MBA program, with classes held in the evening, offers additional convenience and flexibility. In either program, "The faculty are extremely accessible, and I have been impressed by how they want to help the students succeed," says one student. The majority take an interest in students' schooling "outside of the classroom. For example, one of my professors has gone above and beyond in using his professional network to place students with top firms in the field. This same attitude is pervasive throughout the administration and faculty."

Career and Placement

The Office of Career Services for Graduate Business Students works in conjunction with the university's Career Services Office to provide counseling and career placement services including career fairs and on-campus recruiting events. Many students, however, report dissatisfaction with the services, telling us that "students typically do not find jobs until the last minute, and most jobs are within Utah. Those who want to get out of the state have a very difficult time doing so." As one MBA studying health services management observes, the majority of placement opportunities "are in the fields of accounting and finance. For those of us who don't do the number-crunching thing, opportunities are further apart." Students also feel that "the alumni network needs to improve so that students who are graduating have people to turn to when they are looking for jobs."

Employers who most frequently hire Utah MBAs include Ford Motor Company, KPMG International, PacifiCorp, Select Portfolio Services, Zions Bank, UBS, Utah Jazz, Albertsons, St. Mark's Hospital, McLean Quality, Mercer Health, MyFamily.com, Daifuku, and George S. Mays Consulting.

Student Life and Environment

Utah's different MBA programs have different cultures; full-time day students "have the time to engage in activities outside of the classroom" while "Professional MBAs work full-time so they rarely, if ever, engage in extracurriculars." Full-timers report that "there are so many activities and clubs and so few students that you quickly find yourself involved to a degree that would be difficult to imagine at other schools." These "activities include basketball and football games, golf clinics, visits to local businesses, and conferences. . . . Networking opportunities are endless, and, of course, we have the 'Attitude Adjustment Networking' event," a four-time-a-year at which "students and spouses meet and mingle." Otherwise, though, "Family activities are lacking" here.

The DESB MBA program holds classes in several buildings. One "is fully modern and fabulous; the other two are not. The school is in the midst of a capital campaign to help construct new buildings." The Utah campus is "beautiful" and "close to the mountains." Students agree that the "Wasatch Mountains can't be beat for convenient, year-round outdoor recreation." Some here even credit the ski-friendly mountains with attracting some of the program's prominent faculty.

Utah's full-time students "are friendly and always willing to help each other—there is very little overt competitiveness. Many students are married with families, but still find time to socialize, at least on campus." According to one student there are "two specific types of people who attend here." One is "Mormon, married, and has kids." The other is "outdoorsy, outgoing, adventurous, and is living here to get a great education and ski the best mountains in the U.S." Because of the nature of the program, there is a pronounced entrepreneurial trend among students. The evening program draws area professionals.

Admissions

The Eccles Admissions Department requires applicants to provide the following: an undergraduate transcript demonstrating a GPA of at least 3.0 (students failing to meet this requirement may gain entry based on evaluation of their performance during the final two years of undergraduate work); proof of successful completion of a college-level statistics course; GMAT scores (minimum 50th percentile score in math required); two recommendations, submitted online; responses to essay questions; and a resume. International students whose first language is not English must take the TOEFL (minimum score: 600, paper-based test; 250, computer-based test). Two years of post-undergraduate professional experience are strongly encouraged but not required. The school reports that it administers "several privately donated scholarships reserved for underrepresented groups and to help us build the gender, ethnic, and geographic diversity of our student body."

FINANCIAL FACTS

Annual tuition (in-state/ out-of-state)	$9,291/$20,936
Fees	$341
Cost of books	$1,500
Room & board (on/off-campus)	$8,000/$11,000
% of students receiving aid	44
% of first-year students receiving aid	44
% of students receiving grants	44
Average award package	$14,350
Average grant	$14,350

ADMISSIONS

Admissions Selectivity Rating	87
# of applications received	159
% applicants accepted	53
% acceptees attending	61
Average GMAT	601
Range of GMAT	540–640
Average GPA	3.4
TOEFL required of international students	Yes
Minimum TOEFL (paper/computer)	600/250
Application fee	$45
International application fee	$65
Regular application deadline	2/15
Regular notification	4/10
Transfer students accepted	Yes
Transfer application policy In special circumstances, up to 6 credit hours may be transferred into the program from another program.	
Need-blind admissions	Yes

Applicants Also Look At
Brigham Young University.

EMPLOYMENT PROFILE

Career Rating	78	Grads Employed by Function	%	Avg. Salary
Primary Source of Full-time Job Acceptances		Finance/Accounting	30	$52,833
School-facilitated activities	28 (88%)	Human Resources	10	$53,667
Graduate-facilitated activities	2 (6%)	Marketing/Sales	16	$56,400
Unknown	2 (6%)	Consulting	3	$80,000
Average base starting salary	$58,823	Other	9	$56,167
Percent employed	94	Nonprofit	3	$35,000

Top 5 Employers Hiring Grads
Ford Motor Company; KPMG; PacifiCorp; Select Portfolio Services; Zions Bank.

THE UNIVERSITY OF VERMONT
SCHOOL OF BUSINESS ADMINISTRATION

GENERAL INFORMATION

Type of school	Public
Environment	City
Academic calendar	Semester

SURVEY SAYS . . .
Students love Burlington, VT
Friendly students

STUDENTS

Enrollment of parent institution	10,391
Enrollment of business school	55
% male/female	53/47
% part-time	69
% international	24
Average age at entry	30
Average years work experience at entry	8

ACADEMICS

Academic Experience Rating	**81**
Student/faculty ratio	2:1
Profs interesting rating	78
Profs accessible rating	65
% female faculty	37

Prominent Alumni
Doug Goldsmith, CFO and vice president, finance and admin, corp. finance, Rock of Ages; Elisabeth Robert, president, CFO and treasurer, Vermont Teddy Bear, Inc.; Katherine B. Crosett, principal, Kalex Enterprises, Inc.; Alexander D. Crosett, III, principal, Kalex Enterprises, Inc.

Academics

"The best—make that 'only'—MBA program in Burlington" is how one student at the UVM School of Business Administration wryly encapsulates his school, but this program has a lot more going for it than just its geographic monopoly. With approximately 70 students in the program, UVM can offer its MBA students all the personal attention they desire. Plus, with a large university (and large university resources) looming in the background, UVM MBAs can benefit from "interaction with other programs." An environmental engineer earning his MBA here, for example, praises his easy access to the Rubenstein School of Environment and Natural Resources and the Gund Institute of Ecological Economics.

UVM offers both full-time and part-time options in the MBA but schedules classes for the convenience of part-timers, most of whom have full-time jobs. Nearly all classes meet twice weekly in 75-minute evening sessions. "The night classes offer more flexibility to those who work," one student explains. The program is divided into two parts: the core level, comprised of six required courses covering business fundamentals (marketing, accounting, organization, finance, business law, and production and operations management); and the advanced level, comprised of six distribution requirements covering six functions, three electives, and an integrative capstone course.

Students praise the UVM faculty for "bringing in current events into the classroom." They also appreciate that "professors are very accessible, willing to help with course work or networking, and are generally good at encouraging stimulating discussion in the classroom." Administrators are also "readily accessible. In fact, the director of the program offers to talk with every student at course-registration time." There are, of course, drawbacks to all small programs, and UVM is no exception. One student warns, "The frustrating part is the limited number of courses offered each semester. Moreover, many of the courses are offered at the same time, making it impossible to take all the courses you want."

Career and Placement

The Career Services Office at UVM, students tell us, "puts very little effort into graduate placement for careers. The people currently in career services are trying hard, but they are starting from scratch in the graduate area as there is no history of on-campus recruiting. There needs to be!" The office could start, one student suggests, by "offering more networking events. I think that they are trying to improve on this area by putting career counselors in place in the business building. We'll see."

Student Life and Environment

Students tell us that "there is a big difference between part-time students," who make up about two-thirds of the UVM MBA student body, "and full-time students. Part-timers and older, have full-time jobs and have done little or no prior business course work. Full-timers are younger, typically have a business-related undergraduate degree, and are unemployed. Full-timers and part-timers mingle well despite being in different life stages. They frequently hang out together outside of school." Part-timers "often work, attend classes at night, and have families to attend to. They burn the candle at both ends—and look like it!" The student body boasts a solid contingent of engineers as well as a sizeable international population.

RALPH SWENSON, DIRECTOR OF GRADUATE ADMISSIONS AND ADMINISTRATION
333 WATERMAN BUILDING, BURLINGTON, VT 05405 UNITED STATES
PHONE: 802-656-4119 • FAX: 802-656-4078
E-MAIL: STUDENTSERVICES@BSAD.UVM.EDU • WEBSITE: WWW.BSAD.UVM.EDU/_COMM/MBA

Full-timers here report "a healthy balance of work and leisure. We work hard but have plenty of valuable diversions, such as snowboarding at nearby mountains." While some feel that "it would be better to have more events for the MBA students so that [they] could network amongst [them]selves as well as potentially other members in the community," most here accept the current situation as the unavoidable result of a tiny MBA program. Students tell us, "Burlington is a great small city with lots to offer, especially the quality and variety of live music and restaurants." Montreal is only a two-hour drive from Burlington; Ottawa, Ontario, and Albany, NY, can be reached in three hours.

Admissions

The Admissions Committee for the UVM MBA program considers academic record, previous work experience, GMAT scores, writing ability, and letters of recommendation in making its decisions. Applicants must submit official transcripts for all college and graduate work, an official GMAT score report, a resume, a personal essay, and a completed application. The average GMAT score of admitted students is 600; their average undergraduate GPA is 3.2. No student may begin the MBA program without first completing prerequisite courses in macroeconomics, microeconomics, calculus, statistics, and computer usage. Students who have completed undergraduate degrees in business within the last five years may waive the prerequisite courses; others may place out of the classes by passing qualifying examinations.

FINANCIAL FACTS

Annual tuition (in-state/ out-of-state)	$9,832/$24,816
Fees	$1,492
Cost of books	$670
Room & board	$7,642
% of students receiving aid	20
% of first-year students receiving aid	26
% of students receiving loans	5
% of students receiving grants	11
Average award package	$9,803
Average grant	$5,197

ADMISSIONS

Admissions Selectivity Rating	83
# of applications received	43
% applicants accepted	67
% acceptees attending	79
Average GMAT	571
Range of GMAT	510–610
Average GPA	3.14
TOEFL required of international students	Yes
Minimum TOEFL (paper/computer)	550/213
Application fee	$45
Regular application deadline	Rolling
Regular notification	Rolling
Deferment available	Yes
Maximum length of deferment	1 year
Transfer students accepted	Yes
Transfer application policy	
Transfer credit is reviewed based upon each individual set of circumstances.	
Non-fall admissions	Yes
Need-blind admissions	Yes

Applicants Also Look At

Bentley College, Boston College, Boston University, Georgetown University, University of Connecticut, University of Massachusetts Amherst, University of New Hampshire.

UNIVERSITY OF VIRGINIA
DARDEN GRADUATE SCHOOL OF BUSINESS ADMINISTRATION

GENERAL INFORMATION

Type of school	Public
Environment	City
Academic calendar	Semester

SURVEY SAYS . . .
Good peer network
Helpful alumni
Smart classrooms
Solid preparation in:
Finance
General management
Teamwork

STUDENTS

Enrollment of parent institution	20,397
Enrollment of business school	648
% male/female	74/26
% minorities	13
% international	30
Average age at entry	28
Average years work experience at entry	4

ACADEMICS

Academic Experience Rating	**99**
Student/faculty ratio	7:1
Profs interesting rating	99
Profs accessible rating	99
% female faculty	21
% minority faculty	6

Joint Degrees
MBA/JD, 4 years, MBA/MA (Asian studies) 3 years, MBA/MA (government or foreign affairs) 3 years, MBA/ME 3 years MBA/MSN 3 years, MBA/PhD 4 years, MBA/MD, MBA/MPH.

Prominent Alumni
Douglas R. Lebda, founder and former CEO, Lending Tree, Inc.; Steven S. Reinemund, chairman of the board, PepsiCo, Inc.; Warren M. Thompson, president and chairman, Thompson Hospitality; Thomas J. Baltimore Jr., co-founder and president, RLJ Development.

Academics

Offering a unique, challenging, and spirited MBA program, the Darden School of Business at the University of Virginia distinguishes itself through "the outstanding reputation of the faculty and students, the rigorous and exciting case method, and the broad focus on general management that the school offers." Hailed as "one of the toughest programs in the world," the hallmark of a Darden education is the case-based curriculum—an intensive, discussion-based teaching method with an emphasis "on experiential learning in a collaborative environment and through teamwork." Sounds fun, but students warn that "the first-year curriculum is rigorous, and the case method demands students be prepared and take leadership positions." Not to mention that curricular requirements are incredibly time consuming. First-year students typically spend the day at school: Classes run from 8:00 A.M. to 2:00 P.M. and related activities can run until 10:00 P.M.

It's a challenge, but a Darden education is well worth the effort as "you really gain mastery of the material." Encouraging a lively and interactive classroom environment, the school's savvy professors "are outstanding at leading a case conversation and covering all of the key learning points." A second-year student raves, "The faculty at Darden has revolutionized my life. They have challenged me to think differently, to go deeper to find solutions to complex problems and stimulate my mind each day." Darden really distinguishes itself in its commitment to the student experience: "Professors at Darden are there because they want to teach. Students are the priority, not research." A current student enthuses, "Professors have enormous levels of experience and are ridiculously available outside class. I've gone in unscheduled and been able to spend over an hour working on an issue—the professor just made the time."

Teamwork is integral to the Darden experience, and each new student is assigned to a learning team of 5 or 6 students with whom they prepare for class each day. Working together, students say that Darden's "intense and competitive" academic atmosphere is counterbalanced by the fact that "Darden has an extremely helpful and collegial environment." In this stimulating campus setting, "The common thread running through the student body is a general sense of appreciation for the atmosphere, enthusiasm toward the learning experience, and a desire to collaborate with the learning experience through student-led review sessions, informal help sessions, etc."

Career and Placement

Students say "the Career Development Center has improved to a great extent," bringing a "record number of recruiters and companies on grounds this [past] fall." The center offers a variety of services to MBA students, including Career Discovery Forums, individual career consultations, a professional development series, and workshops and special events. Through the Career Development Center, students also have access to the Darden Networking Partnership, a database of nearly 2,000 alumni who have volunteered to help fellow grads in career searches.

In 2006, 87 percent of graduates seeking employment had received a job offer by graduation, and 95 percent had received a job offer within 3 months of graduation. Finance was the most popular career choice, drawing 41 percent of students; consulting drew 20 percent. Among the top recruiters were: A.T. Kearney, Booz Allen Hamilton, Deloitte Touche Tohmatsu, The Boston Consulting Group, Everest, General Mills, Johnson & Johnson, Kraft Foods, Bank of America, Citigroup, Merrill Lynch, McKinsey & Company, Bain and Company, Standard and Poor's, UTC, Progressive, Danaher Corp., Mass Mutual Financial Group, Goldman Sachs, Lehman Brothers, DuPont, General Electric, JPMorgan Chase, The McGraw-Hill Companies, Centex, Target, Dell, EDS, Intel, and Sprint Nextel.

SARA E. NEHER, DIRECTOR OF ADMISSIONS
PO BOX 6550, CHARLOTTESVILLE, VA 22906 UNITED STATES
PHONE: 434-924-7281 • FAX: 434-243-5033
E-MAIL: DARDEN@VIRGINIA.EDU • WEBSITE: WWW.DARDEN.VIRGINIA.EDU

Student Life and Environment

For those who thrive under pressure, Darden is an ideal environment as "The rhythm is extremely hectic, but the atmosphere is jovial, and there is a real palpable energy and excitement about learning in the place." In fact, Darden students seem to take a masochistic pleasure in the hectic pace of life where "Sleep is a rare commodity." In the hearty words of one first-year student: "Although the workload seems unbearable at times, and I have to schedule phone calls with my spouse, I really wouldn't trade this experience for any other." While acknowledging the rigors of the workload, students continually emphasize the kindness of the Darden community, where "Everything from the computer services to the dining hall is done for the students and with their best interests at heart."

When it comes to extracurricular activities, students reassure us that "even with the demanding workload students are very active in clubs, social events, MBA case competitions, and the community." They also manage to sneak in a moment of socializing during the daily First Coffee, "a break between classes in which you can catch up with classmates in other sections, friends, or professors. Everyone in the Darden community comes by for a cup of joe (partners and children included at times)." When it's time to relax, "Saturdays during the fall are a time for attending football games, the Chili Cook-Off, or the International Food Festival." Another favorite is "the Thursday Night Drinking Club where the majority of students meet up at a different bar every Thursday." An ideal college town, "Charlottesville is a great place to live; it has a really low cost of living without sacrificing culture."

Admissions

Darden evaluates a student's readiness for business school in three broad areas: academics, professional experience, and personal qualities and characteristics. These competencies are measured through the applicant's undergraduate record, GMAT scores, resume and work experience, letters of recommendation, and admissions essays. In addition, interviews are required and are considered an important part of the application. While there are no minimum requirements for admission, last year's entering class had a mean GMAT of 677, with a range between 600 and 750. The mean GPA was 3.27, and every person had full-time work experience before entering the program.

FINANCIAL FACTS

Annual tuition (in-state/ out-of-state)	$34,398/$39,398
Fees	$102
Cost of books	$2,577
Room & board	$13,923
% of students receiving aid	79
% of first-year students receiving aid	83
% of students receiving loans	76
% of students receiving grants	45
Average award package	$34,684
Average grant	$15,189
Average student loan debt	$66,665

ADMISSIONS

Admissions Selectivity Rating	96
# of applications received	2,465
% applicants accepted	25.5
% acceptees attending	45.2
Average GMAT	689
Average GPA	3.3
TOEFL required of international students	No (recommended)
Minimum TOEFL (paper/computer)	650/270
Application fee	$190
Application Deadline/Notification	
Round 1:	See website
Round 2:	See website
Round 3:	See website
Round 4:	See website
Deferment available	No
Maximum length of deferment	N/A
Transfer students accepted	Yes
Transfer application policy	
Transfer students are accepted but credits cannot be transferred.	
Need-blind admissions	Yes

EMPLOYMENT PROFILE

Career Rating	97	Grads Employed by Function	%	Avg. Salary
Primary Source of Full-time Job Acceptances		Finance/Accounting	44	$94,141
School-facilitated activities	136 (78%)	Marketing/Sales	9	$84,710
Graduate-facilitated activities	39 (22%)	Consulting	22	$107,020
Average base starting salary	$95,706	General Management	22	$92,052
Percent employed	94	Other	3	$96,363

Top 5 Employers Hiring Grads
McKinsey & Co.; Bank of America; JPMorgan, Merrill Lynch; IBM Strategy and Change Org.

UNIVERSITY OF WASHINGTON
BUSINESS SCHOOL

GENERAL INFORMATION
Type of school	Public
Environment	Metropolis
Academic calendar	Quarter

SURVEY SAYS . . .
Students love Seattle, WA
Friendly students
Good peer network
Solid preparation in:
Finance
Accounting
Teamwork

STUDENTS
Enrollment of parent institution	39,864
Enrollment of business school	374
% male/female	62/38
% out-of-state	62
% part-time	43
% minorities	7
% international	34
Average age at entry	29
Average years work experience at entry	5

ACADEMICS
Academic Experience Rating	**95**
Student/faculty ratio	8:1
Profs interesting rating	87
Profs accessible rating	90
% female faculty	28
% minority faculty	7

Joint Degrees
MP accounting 3 years, MBA/JD 4 years, MBA/MAIS 3 years, MBA/MHA (health administration) 3 years.

Prominent Alumni
William Ayer, CEO, Alaska Airlines; Dan Nordstrom, CEO, Nordstrom.com; Charles Lillis, former CEO, Media One Group; Gary Neale, chairman, Nisource.

Academics

The Business School at the University of Washington draws on its Seattle locale to inform the focus of its program. The curriculum emphasizes a global perspective (especially as it pertains to countries in the Pacific Rim), and there is an overall focus on technology reflecting UW's proximity to such tech heavyweights as Microsoft and Amazon ("Think tons of Microsoft alums"). There are also numerous opportunities to learn about entrepreneurship, in keeping with the city's relaxed and independent vibe. In fact, many students choose UW for its "entrepreneurship and technology focus." This plays out in case studies, projects, and real-world examples drawn from these areas during core courses, as well as in areas of concentration.

Those core courses comprise about half of UW's MBA program. Foundation subjects such as accounting, finance, human resources, ethics, and marketing are included in the required core. Toward the end of the first year, each student selects three Bridge Electives, which allow closer exploration of areas available for concentration in the second year of the program. Students say, "All classes require a good bit of teamwork." "The level of involvement is left up to individuals, but most take part in a lot of the activities." Most students take an internship between their first and second years and return for the second year to specialize in fields such as entrepreneurship and innovation, international business, e-commerce, or marketing.

Washington's MBA students are happy with the quality of teaching, as well as the support from the university's administration. "UW has excellent professors who value teaching and helping students learn. That means everything!" The "mix of case and lecture method and small class size" also are helpful, as are professors who "go beyond to make sure that students get all the education they want." That same student adds, "I haven't met more dedicated professors than the professors at UW." Another MBA candidate says, "The core professors are superstars—far and away the best instructors I've ever had in my life." The evening MBA program is also well staffed: The "Evening program generally is taught by full-time established professors who are very good at their fields, and have made themselves available via e-mail if 'in person' is not convenient for working students."

Career and Placement

The Business Connections Center in the University of Washington program offers network events, career-evaluation tools, a mentorship program with local business leaders, an online jobs data base, and personal career counseling. They "excel at connecting students with alums and other business leaders in the community and elsewhere. They stress the importance of networking and help students to establish a network." The center boasts "great connections to the Seattle business community," and "relationships with world-class companies like Microsoft, Starbucks, [and] Amazon.com." "In most cases, students are extremely successful in landing desirable internships and jobs."

Students also say there's room for improvement: "UW could improve getting access to companies and jobs outside the Pacific Northwest," one student says, and others' comments echo his opinion. He adds, "UW concentrates on networking with local companies, and doesn't seem to put much effort [into] encouraging students to recruit with national companies outside the Northwest."

Cingular, Alaska Airlines, Hewlett-Packard, Washington Mutual, Intel, Microsoft, Hitachi Consulting, Samsung, Starbucks, Tektronix, and Wells Fargo are among the companies that recruit on campus.

SUNNI BANNON, DIRECTOR OF ADMISSIONS
110 MACKENZIE HALL, BOX 353200, SEATTLE, WA 98195-3200 UNITED STATES
PHONE: 206-543-4661 • FAX: 206-616-7351
E-MAIL: MBA@U.WASHINGTON.EDU • WEBSITE: WWW.MBA.WASHINGTON.EDU

Student Life and Environment

Students find much to like about their classmates, the lifestyle, and the opportunities offered at the University of Washington. "UW has a collaborative, rigorous, and challenging academic environment, plus a sense of work/life balance that many schools do not have," says one student. "When I visited [before enrolling], I met several students, faculty, and staff, who all impressed me with their intelligence, enthusiasm, kindness, and humor. I knew that this was the type of community I wanted to be a part of."

"Smart people without the attitude," is how another MBA candidate described his classmates. Another says, "One of the greatest things about the MBA program is that there were activities and clubs for my wife. Some of these activities were social, while others were community-related." But improving the "quality of child care or providing child care for all students" is area that needs to be addressed, student agree.

Another issue is facilities. "The buildings are the ugliest ones on campus," one student complains. Another says, "UW is behind the curve for business school facilities. A new building is in the works but will not be completed for several more years." Another student adds, "The business school buildings are getting up there in terms of age and facilities. There is a plan to upgrade these, but it probably won't happen while I am a student there. Future students will certainly benefit from the improvements, though."

Admissions

Those making admissions decisions for the UW MBA program look for leadership potential, academic strength, communicative ability, and intellectual ability. They evaluate quantitative and language skills through transcripts, GMAT scores, GPAs, and, if needed, TOEFL scores. UW does not have minimum GMAT score or GPA requirement. "If a student is lacking in one area but strong in others, he or she may still be admitted," the school says on its website. For the class admitted in 2006, the average GMAT score was 679, and the average GPA was 3.5. These students averaged 5 and a half years of work experience.

FINANCIAL FACTS

Annual tuition (in-state/ out-of-state)	$17,300/$27,000
Fees	$528
Cost of books	$1,800
Room & board	$10,600
% of students receiving aid	68
% of first-year students receiving aid	82
% of students receiving loans	62
% of students receiving grants	42
Average award package	$12,898
Average grant	$8,683
Average student loan debt	$20,480

ADMISSIONS

Admissions Selectivity Rating	95
# of applications received	748
% applicants accepted	30
% acceptees attending	39
Average GMAT	679
Range of GMAT	630–720
Average GPA	3.54
TOEFL required of international students	Yes
Minimum TOEFL (paper/computer)	600/250
Application fee	$75

Application Deadline/Notification

Round 1:	10/15 / 12/15
Round 2:	11/15 / 1/15
Round 3:	1/15 / 3/15
Round 4:	3/15 / 5/15
Transfer students accepted	Yes

Transfer application policy
Transfer applicants should apply as any other new student. The status of a transfer student is determined on a case by case basis, depending on the work completed at another school.

Need-blind admissions	Yes

Applicants Also Look At

Arizona State University, University of California, Berkeley, University of California, Los Angeles (UCLA), University of Illinois, The University of North Carolina at Chapel Hill, University of Southern California, The University of Texas at Austin.

EMPLOYMENT PROFILE

Career Rating	90	Grads Employed by Function	%	Avg. Salary
Primary Source of Full-time Job Acceptances		Finance/Accounting	33	$77,292
School-facilitated activities	49 (71%)	Marketing/Sales	26	$80,474
Graduate-facilitated activities	20 (29%)	Consulting	8	$82,000
Average base starting salary	$84,089	General Management	11	$115,625
Percent employed	96	**Top 5 Employers Hiring Grads**		

Microsoft; Hitachi Consulting; Accenture; Amazon.com; Autodesk.

University of West Georgia
Richards College of Business

GENERAL INFORMATION

Type of school	Public
Environment	City
Academic calendar	Semester

SURVEY SAYS . . .

Friendly students
Smart classrooms
Solid preparation in:
General management

STUDENTS

Enrollment of parent institution	10,163
Enrollment of business school	29
% male/female	67/33
% out-of-state	56
% part-time	69
% minorities	67
% international	60
Average age at entry	25

ACADEMICS

Academic Experience Rating	**61**
Student/faculty ratio	18:1
Profs interesting rating	85
Profs accessible rating	70
% female faculty	21
% minority faculty	17

Academics

The MBA program at University of West Georgia is designed primarily to address the needs of part-time students who work full-time in the area (the school's Carrollton campus is located about 40 miles west of Atlanta). A number of full-time students also attend. Their ranks include American students making the jump directly from undergraduate programs and international students who "usually return to their own country after graduation," according to the school catalogue.

West Georgia offers both an MBA and a masters of professional accounting. Either program can be completed in 12 months by a full-time student who is entering with an undergraduate degree in business. Students whose undergraduate work is in a non-business related discipline typically must complete 24 semester hours of preparation-level course work (covering the basics of marketing, statistics, information systems, corporate finance, business law, accounting theory, microeconomics, and macroeconomics). Excluding prep-level courses, the MBA requires 30 semester hours of course work, 24 of which are dedicated to required classes. Students may choose elective courses from the fields of economics, information technology, finance, international business, cost accounting, theory and philosophy of management, and business and society.

Students attending classes at the Carrollton campus tell us that "the school has a lot of good professors who are from all over the country and the world. The teachers are very knowledgeable in what they do." Professors are also "surprisingly easy to reach, and most are willing to provide time and energy to help students succeed." Small classes create a "great learning environment," as do "the many guest speakers who lecture about their field or a topic in [their] field."

University of West Georgia also offers a web MBA, in which "all classes are taught online via the Web." Admission to the web MBA program requires a minimum of two years of post-baccalaureate professional work experience (though admission to the traditional MBA program carries no such requirement). The web MBA curriculum roughly mirrors the conventional MBA curriculum; however, no electives are available to web MBA students. One student in the program tells us that "I chose the web MBA program because it was affordable and allowed me flexibility in my study schedule. I travel during the week and would not be able to attend classes in a traditional setting."

Career and Placement

MBA students at West Georgia use the Department of Career Services, which provides "a comprehensive career development and employment plan for all students and alumni" of the school. The office provides assistance with job searches and career strategy, resume referrals, and help with finding internships. It also coordinates on-campus recruitment events, maintains job listings and a career resource library, offers seminars and workshops in resume writing and interviewing, and organizes career and job fairs.

Jonathan R. Anderson, Director, MBA Program, Associate Dean
1601 Maple Street, Carrollton, GA 30118-3000 United States
Phone: 678-839-6467 • Fax: 678-839-5040
E-mail: janderson@westga.edu • Website: www.westga.edu

Student Life and Environment

The University of West Georgia campus in Carrollton "is attractive and well located. It's outside of Atlanta but within an easy commute [from] work." Students enjoy "a relaxed, easygoing mood on the campus and in the MBA program," although they complain that "parking on campus is horrible." Because the program here is small and predominantly part-time, there is little extracurricular life for MBAs. Beginning in Fall 2007 the university will also be offering an MBA in Newnan, Georgia.

The conventional MBA program includes "a great diversity of international students." One MBA writes, "I have classes with students from Bulgaria, Turkey, India, and Colombia. I didn't have this much diversity as an undergraduate in a school of 25,000 students." Most of the American students in the program "have little work experience, and many have lived in Georgia all their lives." Students in the web MBA bring more experience to their studies, partly due to the nature of the requirements. Writes one student in the program, "We have a diverse group in our virtual team. The fact that our ages, life experiences, and backgrounds are so different seems to add to our focus and enables us to leverage individual strengths when tackling group projects. I'd say we are a friendly bunch, [and] willing to lean on each other when necessary, but also [to] hold each individual accountable for [his or her] share of work."

Admissions

All applicants to the MBA program at the University of West Georgia must submit official copies of transcripts for all postsecondary academic work, an official GMAT score report, and letters of recommendation. Applicants must meet the following minimum requirements to be considered for admission with "regular status": an analytical writing score of at least 3.0 on the GMAT, a total GMAT score of at least 450, and an admissions score of at least 950 under the formula [(undergraduate GPA × 200) + GMAT score] or a score of at least 1,000 under the formula [(undergraduate GPA for final 60 semester hours of undergraduate work × 200) + GMAT score]. International students whose first language is not English must earn at least a 550 on the paper-based TOEFL or at least a 213 on the computer-based TOEFL. Students not meeting these minimum requirements may be granted admission with "provisional status." Such students are "reviewed for retention on regular status after completing nine hours toward the MBA," according to the school.

FINANCIAL FACTS

Annual tuition (in-state/ out-of-state)	$3,044/$12,172
Fees	$900
Cost of books	$1,545
Room & board (on-campus)	$5,162
% of students receiving aid	7
% of first-year students receiving aid	6
% of students receiving loans	4
% of students receiving grants	2
Average award package	$5,340
Average grant	$1,179
Average student loan debt	$19,444

ADMISSIONS

Admissions Selectivity Rating	**60***
Average GMAT	520
Range of GMAT	450–650
Average GPA	3.08
TOEFL required of international students	Yes
Minimum TOEFL (paper/computer)	550/213
Application fee	$20
Regular application deadline	7/1
Deferment available	Yes
Maximum length of deferment1 year without re-applying	
Transfer students accepted	Yes
Transfer application policy A maxium of 6 semester hours of graduate credit may be transferred from another-accredited institution. See catalog for more information.	
Non-fall admissions	Yes

UNIVERSITY OF WISCONSIN—MADISON
SCHOOL OF BUSINESS

GENERAL INFORMATION
Type of school	Public
Environment	City
Academic calendar	Semester

SURVEY SAYS . . .
Friendly students
Good social scene
Smart classrooms
Solid preparation in:
Finance
Teamwork

STUDENTS
Enrollment of parent institution	41,466
Enrollment of business school	356
% male/female	68/32
% out-of-state	59
% part-time	30
% minorities	9
% international	26
Average age at entry	28
Average years work experience at entry	4

ACADEMICS
Academic Experience Rating	**93**
Student/faculty ratio	3:1
Profs interesting rating	79
Profs accessible rating	88
% female faculty	21
% minority faculty	12

Joint Degrees
JD/MBA 4 years.

Prominent Alumni
Steve Bennett, president and CEO, Intuit; Curt Culver, chairman and CEO, MGIC; Tadashi Okamura, chairman, Toshiba Corporation; Thomas J. Falk, chairman of the board and CEO, Kimberly Clark Corporation; John P. Morgridge, chairman of the board, Cisco Systems.

Academics

The University of Wisconsin—Madison offers a unique and challenging MBA program, well suited to highly focused students with clear career goals. Whereas most MBA programs require a wide array of course work in general management topics, the Wisconsin curriculum is designed around career specializations, through which students focus their studies on a single business area such as real estate, entrepreneurship, brand management, or marketing research. Through their career specialization, students work within the business school's Centers for Expertise, which "ensure that students have lots of exposure to alumni, specific industry news, and professionals at various levels." A current student explains, "I chose the University of Wisconsin because they have a specialized program in marketing research that would give me the specialized skill set to continue in this field."

While career specializations are the hallmark of the Wisconsin curriculum, "The program emphasizes strong learning within a specific discipline while allowing flexibility to learn cross-functional skills." Before beginning their studies within a specific center, students must complete the general management core curriculum, which provides a solid foundation in management essentials. Even so, those looking for a more varied education will probably find a better match elsewhere. Students warn that "The specified 'center' does make it difficult at times to expand into other departments." Throughout the curriculum, applied learning is an important component of the Wisconsin MBA, and students participate in live business projects for a wide range of companies. For example, students may conduct market research for leading companies, manage stock portfolios, or manage a portfolio of real estate securities.

The business school draws a team of top-notch faculty "committed to up-to-date teaching styles and topics." Student input here is valued. "Feedback is taken from the students at the end of every semester and the recommended changes are implemented for the next incoming class," says one MBA. "It's a constantly evolving and improving program that is viewed as a collaborative effort between the administration and students." On the whole, "Wisconsin represents a culture of collaboration and teamwork," and students reassure us that "when students compete, there is a general collegiate respect for one another." Another major perk of a UW education is its public school price tag, made better by the fact that through assistantships "The tuition is covered, benefits are covered, and you get a stipend." A student exclaims, "You might find it hard to catch your breath, but it's a great way to avoid loans."

Career and Placement

During the first semester at Wisconsin, students take a 6-week course to help them plan and initiate their internship search, including instruction on resume writing, interviewing, researching companies and more. After that, students have access to the Career Center's Internet database as well as one-on-one career advising with professional counselors. However, the program's unique in-depth focus is what really makes the difference in career placement. A current student explains, "Access to corporate recruiters is unprecedented since we have a program which consists of specializations, rather than a generic MBA. You get put on a niche career track right away, so recruiters know exactly what they're getting during interviews."

With strong ties in the region, 60 percent of students take jobs in the Midwest. However, for those looking to expand their horizons, students reassure us that "last year and the current year, we have been utilizing our alumni and board member connections to send a significant number of finance students out to New York for positions with bulge bracket

BETSY KACIZAK, DIRECTOR OF ADMISSIONS AND FINANCIAL AID
3150 GRAINGER HALL, 975 UNIVERSITY AVENUE, MADISON, WI 53706 UNITED STATES
PHONE: 608-262-4000 • FAX: 608-265-4192
E-MAIL: MBA@BUS.WISC.EDU • WEBSITE: WWW.BUS.WISC.EDU/MBA

firms." Currently, the top 15 recruiters at UW are: Proctor & Gamble, General Electric Company, Kraft Foods, Johnson & Johnson, Guidant, Abbott Laboratories, Nestlé, Best Buy, General Mills, SC Johnson, R.W. Baird, IBM, Cisco, UBS, and Starbucks.

Student Life and Environment

When they aren't hitting the books, Wisconsin students say there are "plenty of activities to become involved in, such as fundraising events, guest lecturers and social get-togethers." Even if you aren't into extracurricular activities, it's easy to get to know your classmates, because "In addition to clubs, classes, and social events, most students are well connected with the other students in their centers." Most Wisconsin students maintain a balanced perspective on life, work, and studies. A current student elaborates, "The students in the business school are very serious about their studies and put in long, dedicated hours to get things done. Then they go party. It takes a mature kind of mindset to be able to effectively balance the two." Another chimes in, "It's not uncommon to work on group projects until two or three in the morning."

At this famous university, the business school is located "in the middle of campus with the 35,000 other students, so there is a constant buzz of activity." The consummate college town, students love Madison, "a city with a thriving arts and cultural scene, and plenty of opportunities for recreation and entertainment." And the school's downtown location means "you get the undergraduate as well as the professional demographic all within seven blocks." With so many entertainment options and a 4-day school week, it's no surprise that "most of the MBA students go out every Thursday night for a beverage—a great way to get to know everyone."

Admissions

The University of Wisconsin—Madison seeks students from diverse personal, professional, and cultural backgrounds, who have demonstrated success in business and management. Last year's class had an average GMAT score of 661 and average work experience of 3.6 years. In addition to their academic and professional achievements, Wisconsin looks for students who demonstrate intellectual curiosity, motivation, leadership, communication skills, and analytical ability. Academic record, standardized test scores, and work experience are among the most important factors in an admissions decision.

FINANCIAL FACTS

Annual tuition (in-state/ out-of-state)	$9,180/$25,348
Fees	$730
Cost of books	$890
Room & board (on-campus)	$9,893
% of students receiving aid	77
% of first-year students receiving aid	77
% of students receiving grants	35
Average award package	$17,241
Average grant	$17,281

ADMISSIONS

Admissions Selectivity Rating	94
# of applications received	405
% applicants accepted	43
% acceptees attending	70
Average GMAT	661
Range of GMAT	630–700
Average GPA	3.37
TOEFL required of international students	Yes
Minimum TOEFL (paper/computer)	600/250
Application fee	$45
Regular application deadline	
Regular notification	
Application Deadline/Notification	
Round 1:	11/15 / 12/18
Round 2:	1/10 / 2/12
Round 3:	2/28 / 4/2
Round 4:	4/18 / 5/21
Need-blind admissions	Yes

Applicants Also Look At

Indiana University—Bloomington, New York University, Northwestern University, University of Minnesota.

EMPLOYMENT PROFILE

Career Rating	90	Grads Employed by Function	%	Avg. Salary
Primary Source of Full-time Job Acceptances		Finance/Accounting	38	$83,880
School-facilitated activities	75 (80%)	Human Resources	2	NR
Graduate-facilitated activities	19 (20%)	Marketing/Sales	28	$82,785
Average base starting salary	$82,917	MIS	2	NR
Percent employed	95	Operations/Production	11	$80,712
		Consulting	9	$90,505
		General Management	3	NR
		Other	4	$83,000
		Internet/New Media	1	NR
		Nonprofit	2	NR

Top 5 Employers Hiring Grads

Procter and Gamble; General Mills; Guidant; Kraft Foods; Abbott Laboratories.

University of Wisconsin—Milwaukee
Sheldon B. Lubar School of Business

GENERAL INFORMATION

Type of school	Public
Environment	City
Academic calendar	Semester

SURVEY SAYS . . .

Students love Milwaukee, WI
Helpful alumni
Happy students
Smart classrooms

STUDENTS

Enrollment of parent institution	28,356
Enrollment of business school	299
% male/female	100/0
% part-time	100
Average age at entry	28
Average years work experience at entry	5

ACADEMICS

Academic Experience Rating	**81**
Student/faculty ratio	9:1
Profs interesting rating	76
Profs accessible rating	66
% female faculty	30
% minority faculty	6

Joint Degrees

Master of human resources and labor relations 2 to 7 years, master of public administration, nonprofit management 2 to 7 years, MBA/MS (nursing) 3 to 7 years, MS-MIS/MBA 3 to 7 years.

Prominent Alumni

Robert Probst, executive vice president, Tamarack Petroleum Co.; Mary Ellen Stanek, managing director, Robert Baird and Co; Roger Fitzsimonds, chairman and CEO (retired), Firstar Corporation; Keith Nosbusch, CEO, Rockwell Automation; Dennis Glaso, president and CEO, Jefferson Pilot Corporation.

Academics

Students choose the MBA program at the University of Wisconsin—Milwaukee's Sheldon B. Lubar School of Business because it is convenient and affordable, and because it can be completed on a flexible schedule. Students here agree that "the greatest strength of the program is the school's ability to accommodate the full-time working student via flexible class times, and the next greatest strength is the low cost." MBAs here also appreciate that the university "has a strong connection to the surrounding community, and the school and community often work together on initiatives to make both better places."

Offering classes in the evening, UW—Milwaukee's MBA program is designed for the part-time student who can complete the program in two years by taking three courses per semester (provided the student has an undergraduate degree in business—students with non-business degrees must complete introductory courses before beginning work on the MBA). The program offers the option of graduating with a career-focused concentration in health care management, international business, supply chain management, or managing change. Students may also opt for a general MBA. Either way, students are required to complete 39 to 42 semester credits.

UW—Milwaukee offers "a great atmosphere" with "classes that are filled with discussion and group work." Instruction is "very case study-focused so you get a lot of real world applications for the concepts you are learning." Students also appreciate "the many different academic resources available here, including the computer labs, library, and faculty." Some complain, however, that "many of the courses seem limited in scope" and that "some core courses could be combined to form one comprehensive course. "Students tell us that the program could benefit from "improv[ing] the quality of the courses," "more mandatory academic counseling," and "better instructors" for "a handful of classes."

UW—Milwaukee students may also opt to pursue the MBA at Waukesha. This program, taught by the same faculty who teach at the Milwaukee campus, is a cohort-based program that takes 16 months to complete. The program consists of 24 to 27 semester credits worth of core courses and 12 credits of electives, which are chosen as a group by each cohort.

Career and Placement

The Sheldon B. Lubar School of Business Career Services Center serves undergraduates, graduate students, and alumni of the UW Milwaukee business school. The staff includes two career advisors and a director of career services. The office schedules on-campus interviews online via the eRecruiting system; coordinates internships; organizes career fairs; maintains a list of job postings; conducts workshops on resume writing, interviewing, and job-search skills; and hosts company information sessions.

SARAH M. SANDIN, MBA/MS PROGRAM MANAGER
PO BOX 742, MILWAUKEE, WI 53201-0742 UNITED STATES
PHONE: 414-229-5403 • FAX: 414-229-2372
E-MAIL: MBA-MS@UWM.EDU • WEBSITE: WWW.UWM.EDU/BUSINESS

Student Life and Environment

UW—Milwaukee is "mainly a commuter school," with "the majority of all students (graduate and undergraduate) living off campus. Some drive one hour each way to class." As one MBA candidate puts it, "Students tend to identify as members of society first, and students at this school second. Even though people come to class and leave, there are no slackers here. They are dedicated, sincere academics." Students "range in age from 22 to 40. Many are married or engaged, and all are friendly. Most are employed by major firms around Milwaukee (Briggs, GE Medical, Harley, Kohler, SC Johnson, US Bank, etc.) and want to differentiate themselves."

The UW—Milwaukee campus is not without its amenities. Students report that "the library is great for research, the student union is great for relaxing and eating, and parking isn't all that difficult. The school offers a comfortable atmosphere." There are "lots of student activities going on in the union for the campus at large," though "business school activities seem more career-focused, more concerned with additional learning and career opportunities than with socialization. There are not as many social opportunities for graduate students as there are for undergrads." Students also point out that some "campus services do not revolve around the evening class time period, nor are there standard accommodations for those who attend classes from 5:30 P.M. to 8:10 P.M. or 6:00 P.M. to 8:40 P.M."

UW—Milwaukee is located "on the east side of the city" and "it would be difficult to find a better location. There is always plenty to do, with bars and clubs everywhere. There is plenty of live music as well."

Admissions

Applicants to UW—Milwaukee's MBA program must apply to the university's Graduate School, which refers b-school applications to the School of Business Administration for review and recommendation. The Graduate School Admissions Office makes all final admissions decisions. All applicants must submit a completed application form, an official GMAT score, two official copies of transcripts for all undergraduate work, and two copies of a personal statement. Students must achieve a minimum undergraduate GPA of 2.75 and have a "satisfactory" score on the GMAT to be considered for "admission in good standing." Applicants who fail to meet these minimum requirements may be granted "admission on probation" status. International students must meet all of the above requirements and must also submit an official TOEFL score report (the minimum required score is 550 on the paper test, 213 on the computer test).

FINANCIAL FACTS

Annual tuition (in-state/ out-of-state)	$10,320/$24,756
Cost of books	$800
Room & board (on/off-campus)	$9,000/$10,000
% of students receiving aid	60
% of first-year students receiving aid	42
% of students receiving loans	55
% of students receiving grants	5
Average award package	$15,420
Average grant	$12,325

ADMISSIONS

Admissions Selectivity Rating	84
# of applications received	187
% applicants accepted	51
% acceptees attending	74
Average GMAT	555
Range of GMAT	510–610
Average GPA	3.3
TOEFL required of international students	Yes
Minimum TOEFL (paper/computer)	550/213
Application fee	$45
International application fee	$85
Regular application deadline	Rolling
Regular notification	Rolling
Deferment available	Yes
Maximum length of deferment	1 year
Transfer students accepted	Yes
Transfer application policy The application process is the same for all applicants.	
Non-fall admissions	Yes
Need-blind admissions	Yes

Applicants Also Look At
Marquette University, University of Wisconsin, University of Wisconsin—Whitewater.

EMPLOYMENT PROFILE

Career Rating	61	Grads Employed by Function	%	Avg. Salary
		Finance/Accounting	20	$50,288
		Marketing/Sales	10	$53,720
		General Management	30	$60,409
		Global Management	5	$80,000
		Other	10	$45,986
		Nonprofit	5	$37,000

Top 5 Employers Hiring Grads
Ernst & Young; Johnson Controls, Inc.; Deloitte Touche Tohmatsu; GE Health care; Northwestern Mutual.

UNIVERSITY OF WISCONSIN—WHITEWATER
COLLEGE OF BUSINESS AND ECONOMICS

GENERAL INFORMATION

Type of school	Public
Environment	Village
Academic calendar	Semester

SURVEY SAYS . . .

Cutting-edge classes
Happy students
Solid preparation in:
General management
Teamwork
Communication/interpersonal skills
Doing business in a global economy

STUDENTS

Enrollment of parent institution	10,520
Enrollment of business school	460
% male/female	45/55
% out-of-state	10
% part-time	85
% minorities	1
% international	30
Average age at entry	34
Average years work experience at entry	7

ACADEMICS

Academic Experience Rating	**66**
Student/faculty ratio	28:1
Profs interesting rating	75
Profs accessible rating	68
% female faculty	29
% minority faculty	22

Academics

Since the early 1900s, University of Wisconsin—Whitewater has been known as "the state business school of Wisconsin," a place where students can receive solid, affordable undergraduate and graduate business degrees at a reasonable cost. Whitewater serves its admirable role with distinction; its accounting department, for example, is widely regarded as one of the most effective in the nation due to its graduates' excellent success rate on the CPA exam. Whitewater also excels in several technology-driven areas. Its Management Computer Systems Program is consistently ranked among the best of its kind by the Association of Information Technology Professionals, while the joint-degree offered by the Department of Business Education and the Computer and Network Administration has been repeatedly recognized as a Program of Excellence by the National Association for Career and Technical Education (ACTE).

The Whitewater MBA program offers concentrations in finance, human resource management, international business, IT management, management, marketing, technology and training, and operations and supply chain management, as well as a master of professional accountancy. Students appreciate the breadth of choices as well as the variety of full-time and part-time options the school provides for their convenience. Most students opt for either part-time evening courses (offered at both the Whitewater and Waukesha Center campuses) or distance learning, which is growing increasingly popular despite the fact that distance courses are more expensive. One MBA writes, "I chose UW—Whitewater for the flexible class times and the multiple locations. The school truly understands the demanding schedules of students who work full-time and/or have children." Another adds, "The online program is great because it allows you to complete the entire degree off campus."

Satisfaction rates are high among MBAs, who regard Whitewater as "an excellent school with an excellent administration [that] helps you achieve your academic goals by suggesting classes and providing other valuable assistance." They praise professors who "are extremely knowledgeable, yet easy to interact with on a daily basis, [are] very accessible at all times, [and who] strive to have students participate and work together in groups." Most important, they appreciate how "IT is used very well, the subject matter is always current and relevant, and the skills/techniques are easily transferred into the business environment."

Career and Placement

The Career Services Office at Whitewater provides career counseling and placement services to all undergraduate and graduate students at the university. The office coordinates on-campus interviews, career fairs, online job-search tools, the administration of self-assessment instruments, and advisement in resume creation, interviewing, and job-search strategies. Many students tell us that the quality of the office is not a major concern to them, as their primary goal in attending Whitewater is to improve their status at their current jobs.

Donald K. Zahn, Associate Dean
800 West Main Street, Whitewater, WI 53190 United States
Phone: 262-472-1945 • Fax: 262-472-4863
E-mail: zahnd@uww.edu • Website: www.uww.edu

Student Life and Environment

The Whitewater MBA program is home to "a diverse student body that includes single, married, and international students" who "really bring the global work environment into perspective." There is also "a good mix of full-time and part-time students" as well as "a wide variety of ages and experience from students in their 50s to new undergrads." Teamwork is important here, so it's fortunate that "most students are friendly and work well in teams [and] "most everyone has a great sense of humor and is willing to compromise for the better of group projects."

Because so many students attend part-time, "there really is no 'presence' of graduate student organizations on campus. Most students seem to be interested only in school; there really aren't any graduate student activities offered to students." Full-timers—there are about 80 of them here—note that "you can be involved in a variety of business organizations or the Graduate Student Organization" if you choose to be. One student writes, "I particularly love the assistantship I have on campus because I get to continue to interact with undergraduates and watch them grow as well." The school is in the early stages of planning a new dedicated business facility. The completion of the facility should lead to an uptick in MBA-related extracurricular activity.

Whitewater is a popular vacation destination, especially for boating and fishing enthusiasts. The town is also known as "the hang gliding capital of the Midwest" due to the popularity of the sport here. One student notes, "There is not a great deal of crime in Whitewater. It is isolated and peaceful." Although Whitewater is a small town, its proximity to large cities provides access to valuable internships. Both Milwaukee and Madison are 45 minutes off by car; Chicago is 100 miles to the southeast.

Admissions

To gain admission to the MBA program at Whitewater, students must have either 1) at least a 2.75 GPA for all undergraduate work; 2) at least a 2.90 GPA for the final half of their undergraduate work; 3) 12 credits of graduate work completed successfully at Whitewater; 4) at least a 2.50 GPA for all undergraduate work, a minimum GMAT score of 570, and a minimum of five years of professional experience; 5) a formula score of at least 1,000 under the formula [(undergraduate GPA × 200) + GMAT score]; or 6) a formula score of at least 1,050 under the formula [(GPA for last half of undergraduate work × 200) + GMAT score]. Students who have previously completed graduate work at Whitewater must have a minimum GPA of 3.00 in those classes with no grades of 'I' (Incomplete) or 'P' (Pending). Non-native English speakers must demonstrate proficiency by achieving a minimum TOEFL score of 550.

FINANCIAL FACTS

Annual tuition (in-state/ out-of-state)	$7,176/$17,812
Cost of books	$2,600
Room & board (on-campus)	$4,800
Average grant	$500

ADMISSIONS

Admissions Selectivity Rating	**64**
# of applications received	134
% applicants accepted	88
% acceptees attending	92
Average GMAT	482
Range of GMAT	210-730
Average GPA	3.13
TOEFL required of international students	Yes
Minimum TOEFL (paper/computer)	550/213
Application fee	$45
Regular application deadline	Rolling
Regular notification	Rolling
Deferment available	Yes
Maximum length of deferment	1 year
Transfer students accepted	Yes
Transfer application policy	
They must meet the same requirements as a non-transfer student. 9 credits may be transferred into the program.	
Non-fall admissions	Yes
Need-blind admissions	Yes

Applicants Also Look At

Marquette University, University of Wisconsin, University of Wisconsin—Oshkosh, University of Wisconsin—Parkside, University of Wisconsin—Milwaukee.

EMPLOYMENT PROFILE	
Career Rating	63

VALPARAISO UNIVERSITY
COLLEGE OF BUSINESS ADMINISTRATION

GENERAL INFORMATION

Type of school	Private
Affiliation	Lutheran

SURVEY SAYS . . .

Cutting-edge classes
Solid preparation in:
Accounting
General management
Presentation skills
Doing business in a global economy

STUDENTS

Enrollment of parent institution	4,300
Enrollment of business school	87
% male/female	60/40
% out-of-state	58
% part-time	66
% minorities	7
% international	1
Average age at entry	27
Average years work experience at entry	4

ACADEMICS

Academic Experience Rating	**79**
Student/faculty ratio	2:1
Profs interesting rating	79
Profs accessible rating	89
% female faculty	33
% minority faculty	19

Joint Degrees

JD/MBA 4 years.

Academics

A fresh and fairly new MBA program (the first class entered in 2002), the College of Business Administration at Valparaiso University provides a strong "values-centered education" to a small class of about 85 graduate students. The Valparaiso MBA provides a thorough introduction to business topics; however, the focus on ethics and environmental stewardship is what makes a Valpo education unique. Throughout the core curriculum and elective offerings, "Professors take every opportunity to stress these concerns and develop thoughtful and caring future business leaders."

Classes at Valparaiso are small and dynamic, taught by "innovative faculty who understand the business world and incorporate those aspects into their classrooms." Students laud their teachers' ability to "engage students, involve their own personal experiences, and develop thoughts through class discussion." Indeed, group work and discussion are integral to the learning experience at Valparaiso, so students appreciate that their classmates "come from a variety of backgrounds and are able to share numerous experiences in course discussions that provide value and growth not only in the academic areas, but in the 'real world' areas." A current student attests, "I have found all of my courses to be well-run and relevant to today's business environment."

The Valparaiso MBA is specially designed to accommodate both full- and part-time students, offering 2-unit courses in short 7-week blocks. Students can complete the program in as few as 1 or as many as 5 years, and throughout their studies, students can enroll in core courses alongside elective or "enhancement" courses. Enhancement courses run the gamut from Brand Management to Global Supply Chain Management; however, some students would like to see the program include more specialized business topics. A current student explains, "Our program is small and fairly young, and thus it is not yet able to offer a large range of diverse courses. All the necessities are there of course, but as we expand hopefully there will be more focused and deeper courses in particular areas."

When it comes to the higher-ups, students agree that the "administrative system is set up well," even allowing "students the freedom to take care of their own registration and accounts." A current MBA candidate enthuses, "The overall program runs very smoothly, almost by itself. From application, to advising, to registration—it all flows."

Career and Placement

With just a few years in operation, students admit that "the word has not spread about Valpo," and the business community is just beginning to catch on to this new source of talented recruits. However, with the power of the Valparaiso name behind it and the strength of the MBA curriculum, students know it's just a matter of time before their program begins to draw its rightful share of attention from recruiters.

Many Valpo students are already employed when they begin their MBA and plan to continue at their current company after graduation. However, those who are looking for a new position have access to the Valparaiso University Career Center. The Career Center serves the school's graduate and undergraduate community and offers a variety of professional development workshops and career counseling, an annual campus career fair, and a job search database. The Career Center also helps students contact employers and schedule on-campus interviews. According to statistics published by the Career Center, the MBA program had an overall placement rate of 97.4 percent (including students who were previously employed, those who entered new positions, and those who continued with more graduate work).

ERIN L. C. NICKELSBURG, ASSISTANT DIRECTOR GRADUATE PROGRAMS IN MANAGEMENT
104 URSCHEL HALL, 1909 CHAPEL DRIVE, VALPARAISO, IN 46383 UNITED STATES
PHONE: 800-599-0840 • FAX: 219-464-5789
E-MAIL: MBA@VALPO.EDU • WEBSITE: WWW.VALPO.EDU/MBA

Student Life and Environment

While they come from different academic, professional, and personal backgrounds, "Students interact well with each other" at Valparaiso and find the academic atmosphere to be both stimulating and pleasant. "Since the program is fairly new, there are not many clubs and activities targeted to graduate MBA students." On top of that, many students are busy balancing the demands of work, school, and family; as a result, "Valpo MBA students tend to keep to themselves" and don't make time to hang out with their classmates. Not surprisingly, many students feel that Valpo should do more to promote extracurricular interaction "through more networking events and otherwise encouraging students to get together outside of class." Since the MBA program is so small, students also suggest that the business school could "promote more interaction between the different graduate schools."

For those seeking fun and friendship there is "a small group of people will gather after class at the end of the week to socialize." In addition, the school has made a modest effort to encourage non-academic interaction and "There have been some fun activities for MBA students outside of class," such as trips to see the Chicago Bulls. However, with such an engaged and effective administration at its helm, the program will surely grow its extracurricular offerings as the program expands.

Admissions

Admissions decisions are made on a rolling basis and—thanks to the program's 7-week course schedule—there are six different entry dates during the year. When making an admissions decision, Valparaiso assesses the whole person, weighing the strength of an applicant's undergraduate and postgraduate academic performance, applicable professional experience, letters of recommendation, and GMAT scores. In addition, Valparaiso requests a one-page personal statement explaining why the applicant wants to pursue an MBA at Valpo. The entering class of 2006 had an average GMAT score of 580 and an average GPA of 3.32. The average age was 27, and the average amount of professional work experience among admits was 3.6 years.

FINANCIAL FACTS

Annual tuition	$20,900
Fees	$60
Cost of books	$1,000
% of students receiving aid	87
% of first-year students receiving aid	60
% of students receiving loans	87
% of students receiving grants	87
Average student loan debt	$11,887

ADMISSIONS

Admissions Selectivity Rating	**84**
# of applications received	92
% applicants accepted	59
% acceptees attending	69
Average GMAT	580
Average GPA	3.32
TOEFL required of international students	Yes
Minimum TOEFL (paper/computer)	575/236
Application fee	$30
International application fee	$50
Deferment available	Yes
Maximum length of deferment	1 year
Transfer students accepted	Yes
Transfer application policy Students must meet admissions requirements and be in good standing at their current institution. Up to 6 credit hours may be transferred.	
Non-fall admissions	Yes
Need-blind admissions	Yes

VANDERBILT UNIVERSITY
OWEN GRADUATE SCHOOL OF MANAGEMENT

GENERAL INFORMATION

Type of school	Private
Environment	Metropolis
Academic calendar	Module

SURVEY SAYS . . .

Students love Nashville, TN
Good peer network
Cutting-edge classes
Happy students
Solid preparation in:
Teamwork
Communication/interpersonal skills

STUDENTS

Enrollment of parent institution	11,481
Enrollment of business school	374
% male/female	75/25
% minorities	9
% international	33
Average age at entry	28
Average years work experience at entry	5

ACADEMICS

Academic Experience Rating	**88**
Student/faculty ratio	10:1
Profs interesting rating	79
Profs accessible rating	96
% female faculty	14
% minority faculty	20

Joint Degrees

MBA/JD 4 years, MBA/MD 5 years, MBA/MSN 2.5 years, MBA/ME 2.5 years, MBA/MLAS 3 years, MBA/BA or MBA/BS 5 years, MBA/DIV 3.5 years.

Prominent Alumni

David Farr, CEO, Emerson Electric; David Ingram, chairman and president, Ingram Entertainment; Brad Martin, chairman and CEO, Saks, Inc.; Doug Parker, chairman, president and CEO, America West Airlines.

Academics

MBA students at Vanderbilt praise the "small class size, warm culture, and strong finance faculty" at the first-rate Owen Graduate School of Management. "There is competition here, and fellow students and faculty do not let you off easily, but they also help you through the challenges," one student explains. "Whether it is helping you prepare for an interview that they are preparing for themselves or tutoring you in finance because you tutored them in marketing, students are there for each other." It's not just the student body immersed in community spirit; the administration and faculty also join in. One MBA writes, "The beauty of going to a smaller school like Owen is that our professors know the students well, and we know our professors well. I believe this gives us a competitive advantage because we can graduate not only with fellow student contacts, but also faculty contacts." Students also appreciate that "the school is run very much like a business." "The professors are evaluated based on student feedback . . . [and] part of a professor's compensation and tenure decision is based on these reviews," notes one student. "Most of the professors at Vanderbilt have years of experience and are very easy to meet with or talk to outside of class."

Such personal touches are rarely accompanied by top-rate research, but Owen is also a leader in a variety of fields thanks to its professors' cutting-edge work. The faculty excels in finance and marketing, along with e-commerce, operations management, and organizational management. One MBA writes, "The greatest strengths of Owen are the various strong concentrations, along with a well-organized academic calendar. Moreover, if we want, we can take more electives depending on personal special interest." The strength of other Vanderbilt divisions adds further value to the program, since "Owen offers jointly taught courses with other highly ranked programs in the Vanderbilt system like the law, medical, and engineering schools." Some do wish, though, that Owen would improve "the speed at which [it] adds new classes."

Vanderbilt's MBAs rate the professors as "stellar" and the academic curriculum as "very rewarding and challenging." Many here note the "real-world practices and situations" that are incorporated "into the courses," which not only make them "fun" but encourage "active participation among students." Across the board, students love that the school is "designed for the students and all activities have that in mind. From administration through Career Management Office, everything is set up to help students succeed." One student sums it up concisely, "I couldn't have chosen a better MBA program."

Career and Placement

Owen's Career Management Center "has been completely transformed and is more confident with their opportunities and placements of students." Many find that "the CMC office does a great job" and trusts its "creativity" in how it deals with "the changing needs of the students." That said, there's always more work to be done, and "Although the school does a spectacular job in career management, it should work"—and is working—"on attracting more companies to actively recruit at the school."

Employers most likely to hire Owen MBAs include American Express, Banc America Securities, Citigroup, Dell, Deloitte Touche Tohmatsu, Deutsche Bank, Eli Lilly and Company, Emerson Electric, Ford Motor Company, Gaylord Entertainment, GE Capital, Harrah's Entertainment, Hewlett-Packard, The Home Depot, Honeywell, IBM, Johnson & Johnson, Mattel, Merrill Lynch, Procter & Gamble, Smith Barney, Sara Lee, Southern Company, SunTrust Bank, Unilever, and Wachovia.

JOHN ROEDER, DIRECTOR OF ADMISSIONS
401 21ST AVENUE SOUTH, NASHVILLE, TN 37203 UNITED STATES
PHONE: 615-322-6469 • FAX: 615-343-1175
E-MAIL: ADMISSIONS@OWEN.VANDERBILT.EDU • WEBSITE: OWEN.VANDERBILT.EDU

Student Life and Environment

The place changes but the cliché remains the same: students at Vanderbilt "work hard and play hard." But with an MBA curriculum this time-consuming, that's very welcome news to students here. "At Vanderbilt, you don't only live with books," explains one student. "The community helps you to keep a balanced life, so you also have time to play sports or meet outside the school." As one student put it, "One minute you're doing bond arbitrage, another minute you're playing flag football with the same great people." "My classmates are very intelligent and work really hard yet save enough energy to have fun," One student states, "Aside from business clubs, we have a variety social and interest clubs. This year students have started Owen Culinary Society that once a month prepares a dinner for about 40 students—cooked by the students. Also we have weekly kegs in the lobby sponsored by faculty or recruiting companies."

Students also make time to enjoy hometown Nashville, "a terrific place to go to school." The city "has the best music scene in the country," one MBA who's "not even a huge country music fan" writes, noting that "there's all types of music here because Nashville attracts incredible musicians." Another appreciates that "it is not too expensive to live in and it is very easy to navigate." Nashville also offers "good food, great parks, and a surprising number of very good employment opportunities." The city is home to big league hockey and football teams, as well as an AAA minor league baseball team.

Admissions

Vanderbilt bases admissions decisions on several factors, namely the applicant's "caliber of undergraduate institution, difficulty of major, quality and duration of prior work experience, professional responsibilities and accomplishments, career advancement, career goals, extracurricular/professional/community involvement, leadership potential, interpersonal skills, communication skills, team orientation, diversity, and cross-cultural awareness/understanding/experience/appreciation." The school encourages minorities and disadvantaged students to apply and attend its "Diversity Weekend," which the school states is "open to all prospective students, but specially targeted to prospective U.S. minority students."

FINANCIAL FACTS

Annual tuition	$33,830
Fees	$686
Cost of books	$1,484
Room & board (off-campus)	$11,268
% of students receiving aid	71
% of first-year students receiving aid	71
% of students receiving loans	51
% of students receiving grants	50
Average award package	$38,688
Average grant	$14,017
Average student loan debt	$65,652

ADMISSIONS

Admissions Selectivity Rating	**89**
# of applications received	779
% applicants accepted	45
% acceptees attending	46
Average GMAT	642
Range of GMAT	600–690
Average GPA	3.23
TOEFL required of international students	Yes
Minimum TOEFL (paper/computer)	600/250
Application fee	$100
Regular application deadline	3/1
Regular notification	4/1
Application Deadline/Notification	
Round 1:	11/14 / 1/15
Round 2:	1/15 / 3/15
Round 3:	3/1 / 4/1
Deferment available	Yes
Maximum length of deferment	1 year
Need-blind admissions	Yes

Applicants Also Look At

Duke University, Emory University, Georgetown University, Indiana University—Bloomington, The University of North Carolina at Chapel Hill, The University of Texas at Austin, University of Virginia.

EMPLOYMENT PROFILE

Career Rating	89	Grads Employed by Function	%	Avg. Salary
Primary Source of Full-time Job Acceptances		Finance/Accounting	44	$85,423
School-facilitated activities	83 (64%)	Human Resources	4	$74,700
Graduate-facilitated activities	42 (33%)	Marketing/Sales	23	$83,578
Unknown	4 (3%)	Operations/Production	5	$93,983
Average base starting salary	$85,378	Consulting	15	$89,528
Percent employed	87	General Management	9	$82,855
		Top 5 Employers Hiring Grads		
		Bank of America; Citigroup; Deloitte Consulting; Wachovia; Goldman Sachs.		

VILLANOVA UNIVERSITY
SCHOOL OF BUSINESS

GENERAL INFORMATION
Type of school	Private
Affiliation	Roman Catholic
Environment	Village
Academic calendar	Semester

SURVEY SAYS . . .
Good peer network
Smart classrooms
Solid preparation in:
Communication/interpersonal skills

STUDENTS
Enrollment of parent institution	10,274
Enrollment of business school	526
% part-time	94
Average age at entry	28
Average years work experience at entry	5

ACADEMICS
Academic Experience Rating	**81**
Student/faculty ratio	12:1
Profs interesting rating	78
Profs accessible rating	80
% female faculty	22

Joint Degrees
JD/MBA 3 to 4 years.

Academics

MBA students at Villanova University consider their School of Business to be "the most reputable business school in Philadelphia not named 'Wharton,'" with "a good overall philosophy and a good approach to education" that emanates from the university's Augustinian tradition. Students are also impressed by VU's strong "alumni connections in major cities on the Eastern Seaboard, especially in New York City." Students here feel confident that "the Villanova name will serve [them] well after graduation."

Most MBAs at Villanova attend part-time, primarily in the school's professional MBA (PMBA) program, which they describe as "a very robust program conducted at a pace that is conducive to people who cannot devote the time needed for a 2-year intensive program." PMBA students also like that their program offers a specialization option; "The e-business and international business specialization options" are especially appealing. Villanova's PMBA maintains a sense of class unity by kicking off with a Leadership Weekend; one participant notes, "In the part-time program, it is easy to not meet fellow students, but this course offers students the opportunity to meet multiple students, making group work and class discussion easier throughout the program."

VU's FTE MBA is a cohort-based program with a prescribed curriculum of 12 classes. Students "truly love the cohort aspect," telling us that "our class is extremely close and the caliber of student is high." Program requirements "are largely the same as a professional MBA, although we do not take electives during the program. However, we may return for electives/specialty courses that would be listed as a postgraduate certificate." Full-timers "are segregated from the PMBA students" because of the cohort nature of their program.

Participants in both programs agree that "the greatest strength of Villanova is the professors," whose ranks include "many who have their own businesses on the side or are active consultants with regional or national business clients. Their ability to show real-world examples of theories and principles is key to the value of a Villanova MBA." The school's "ambitious administration is actively seeking to enhance the school's reputation," a fact that pleases students here.

Career and Placement

Villanova's MBA candidates say the Career Services Office "leaves something to be desired." Students report that "recruiting efforts are 98 percent targeted toward undergraduate students." Reinforcing that perception is that fact that the office's website lists placement data for undergraduates only. The school participates in joint recruiting ventures such as the Graduate Business Talent Finder Fair, which allows employers to recruit for jobs and internships from 11 Philadelphia-area MBA programs.

Student Life and Environment

Villanova's business school facility "is very conveniently located for working professionals to access via car or public transportation from downtown Philadelphia or the suburbs." Students also like how "the building [where classes are held] has a place to purchase cooked meals or sandwiches and snacks as well as a Pete's Coffee Shop open late, all very convenient for working professionals who go to class directly from the office." The actual classroom facilities, however, "are subpar. Electrical outlets do not work, and many Ethernet ports are broken. The wireless routers are offline more than they are online."

The majority part-time population here "all work full-time, meaning our interactions

Ms. Elizabeth Eshleman, Associate Director
800 Lancaster Avenue, Bartley Hall, Villanova, PA 19085 United States
Phone: 610-519-4336 • Fax: 610-519-6273
E-mail: gradbusiness@villanova.edu • Website: www.gradbusiness.villanova.edu

with school are primarily during class and group study hours." PMBA students tell us that "professors are very understanding of the things we are all trying to balance, and are very flexible and work with each student to make the most of the class." Classmates are "friendly and make themselves available to work on group learning projects and presentations."

FTE MBA students enjoy a more robust extracurricular life. They tell us that "students are encouraged to get active in the community, as the school provides opportunities for MBA students to provide pro-bono services to nonprofits." As one student explains, "There is a huge amount of community-based activities [available] in addition to a myriad of school-related clubs and groups. I like being surrounded by these constant giving-back activities and reinforcement of good human behavior."

Villanova draws "a broad range of students, from age to background to personal life." There are "some just out of college, and many with 2 to 6 years [of] work experience. Many students have work experience in finance and pharmaceuticals (both big in the Philadelphia area)." Across the board, "Students tend to be very helpful, willing to answer questions and share thoughts. They also make sure to have someone copy notes if a student misses class, even if they aren't asked to do so. It is a very equal environment, and everyone wants each other to get ahead." In terms of students who are married versus students who are single, "It varies. Some have kids and are married, some aren't married and don't have kids." Spouses "are encouraged to come to social functions," which students appreciate. Students say the student body has "a good mix of women and men."

Admissions

Applicants to Villanova's MBA programs must submit official transcripts for all postsecondary academic work, an official GMAT score report, an official TOEFL score report (international students whose first language is not English only), two personal essays (at a maximum of 600 words each), two letters of recommendation, a resume, and a completed application.

FINANCIAL FACTS

Annual tuition	$20,250
Fees	$60
Cost of books	$800

ADMISSIONS

Admissions Selectivity Rating	**81**
# of applications received	346
% applicants accepted	66
% acceptees attending	76
Average GMAT	580
Average GPA	3.2
TOEFL required of international students	Yes
Minimum TOEFL (paper/computer)	600/250
Application fee	$50
Regular application deadline	7/15
Regular notification	Rolling
Deferment available	Yes
Maximum length of deferment	Up to one year
Transfer students accepted	Yes
Transfer application policy Up to 9 credits from AACSB-accredited MBA programs.	
Non-fall admissions	Yes
Need-blind admissions	Yes

Applicants Also Look At

Drexel University, Temple University.

VIRGINIA COMMONWEALTH UNIVERSITY
SCHOOL OF BUSINESS

GENERAL INFORMATION
Type of school	Public
Environment	Metropolis
Academic calendar	Semester

SURVEY SAYS . . .
Good peer network
Cutting-edge classes

STUDENTS
Enrollment of parent institution	30,452
Enrollment of business school	187
% male/female	63/37
% part-time	74
% international	33
Average age at entry	27
Average years work experience at entry	4

ACADEMICS
Academic Experience Rating	**79**
Student/faculty ratio	20:1
Profs interesting rating	73
Profs accessible rating	87
% female faculty	15
% minority faculty	5

Joint Degrees
BS/master of accountancy 5 years,
BS engineering/MBA, PharmD/MBA,
MBA/MSIS.

Academics

"The greatest strength [of the MBA program] is the school's connection with the local business community" at Virginia Commonwealth University, a school that capitalizes on "the many major corporations headquartered in Richmond." Students here report that "networking with prospective employers is widely available" and that "networking with other students working in various industries" is also one of the program's great benefits. A "strong regional reputation" increases the likelihood that networking opportunities here will yield positive results.

Although "VCU might be the biggest university in the state of Virginia," its MBA program is designed to create "an individualized experience. You're not just a cog or a number. You get the great facilities and resources of a big school with the close, personal touches of a small school." Those touches include "professors who are here to teach. They truly want the students to excel. Every teacher makes a strong effort to make sure each student masters the material. There is no such thing as remote teaching here; it's really hands-on, make-a-connection"-style learning. VCU professors "incorporate real-world insight into their course material and the information is there for the taking."

VCU's MBA program design also earns high marks from students for its "integrated approach rather than a silo subject-based approach" with "multiple topics per module." This type of approach allows students "to better understand how to tie multiple disciplines together to become an effective business executive." VCU's cross-functional approach includes a heavy emphasis on information technology across the curriculum.

VCU offers both a full-time and part-time MBA. With four out of five students attending part-time, students say that "the blend of part-time and full-time students provides opportunities to share different perspectives on various topics among students"). The school also offers an executive MBA that participants describe as "an exceptionally well-run program. From administration down to support staff, they do a tremendous job to help ensure each student gets the best possible education." Students here also agree that the price is right.

Career and Placement

The VCU Career Center serves all undergraduate and graduate students at the university. The office provides a wide range of counseling and placement services. Area businesses also contact the School of Business directly to post internship and career opportunities available to MBA students here. Students can keep up to date on such notifications by subscribing to the School of Business Listserv. About 80 percent of VCU's MBA students attend part-time; nearly all work part-time or full-time, many with companies with whom they intend to remain after graduation.

Student Life and Environment

A typical day in the life of a full-time MBA student at VCU, according to one such student, includes a morning internship (typically running from 9:00 A.M. to 1:00 P.M.), an extended study and preparation period through mid- to late-afternoon, "attending an employer speaker series sponsored by the graduate school networking group or employer information meet-and-greet sponsored by the Career Center," or grabbing "a snack at the Student Commons" or a local restaurant during the dinner hour, classes from 7:00 to 9:40 P.M., and then more studying until bedtime. Part-timers follow a slightly different schedule: Most work full-time jobs, arrive at campus just in time for class, and then either study or try to squeeze in some quality family time before hitting the sack. No matter what type of student you're talking about, it's a very full schedule.

Jana P. McQuaid, Director, Graduate Studies in Business
1015 Floyd Avenue, PO Box 844000, Richmond, VA 23284-4000 United States
Phone: 804-828-4622 • Fax: 804-828-7174
E-mail: gsib@vcu.edu • Website: www.gsib.vcu.edu

VCU students tell us that campus life involves "many things happening all the time. You can watch free movies at night, go to the gym, pool, tennis, etc." or hit the "eateries and cafés on every corner," which include the "fine dining at Shafer Court for the price of a canteen." The school is enjoying a period of major renovation. Says one b-student, "The building in which I have attended all of my classes is being torn down next year after a new, state-of-the-art business school opens." Students brag that "the area around the business school is one of the most attractive places in the area for young students to live," offering access to anything you could need. They also appreciate that "the campus is safe." One student observes, "If you like small cities that offer everything that big cities do without the traffic and headaches, you will like the location."

Admissions

Applicants to all MBA programs at VCU must submit a completed application, official transcripts for all postsecondary academic work, an official GMAT score report, a resume, a personal statement, and three letters of recommendation. International applicants must also provide proof of English proficiency (the school accepts both the TOEFL and the IELTS and evidence of sufficient financial support to cover the cost of attending and expenses while at VCU. The school reports that "students who were admitted to and completed course work at other AACSB-accredited institutions may apply to VCU and seek transfer of up to 6 semester hours of work toward the VCU graduate degree. Students must have earned no less than a B in each class to be transferred. The decision to transfer courses is left to the discretion of the Director of Graduate Studies in Business."

FINANCIAL FACTS

Annual tuition (in-state/ out-of-state)	$6,782/$15,904
Fees (in-state/ out-of-state)	$1,558/$1,678
Cost of books	$800
Room & board (on/off-campus)	$5,000/$8,000

ADMISSIONS

Admissions Selectivity Rating	**82**
# of applications received	172
% applicants accepted	53
% acceptees attending	55
Average GMAT	567
Range of GMAT	490–640
Average GPA	3.2
TOEFL required of international students	Yes
Minimum TOEFL (paper/computer)	600/250
Application fee	$50
Regular application deadline	7/15
Regular notification	8/1
Early decision program?	Yes
ED Deadline/Notification	4/1 / 05/1
Deferment available	Yes
Maximum length of deferment	1 year
Transfer students accepted	Yes
Transfer application policy Students who were admitted to and completed course work at other AACSB-accredited institutions may apply to VCU and seek transfer of up to 6 semester hours of work toward the VCU graduate degree. Students must have earned no less than a "B" in each class to be transferred. The decision to transfer courses is left to the discretion of the director of graduate studies in business.	
Non-fall admissions	Yes
Need-blind admissions	Yes

Applicants Also Look At

College of William and Mary, James Madison University, University of Richmond, Virginia Tech.

VIRGINIA POLYTECHNIC INSTITUTE AND STATE UNIVERSITY
PAMPLIN COLLEGE OF BUSINESS

GENERAL INFORMATION

Type of school	Public
Environment	Town

SURVEY SAYS...

Students love Blacksburg, VA
Friendly students
Happy students
Smart classrooms
Solid preparation in:
Teamwork

STUDENTS

Enrollment of parent institution	26,370
% male/female	75/25
% out-of-state	57
% minorities	2
% international	50
Average age at entry	24
Average years work experience at entry	2

ACADEMICS

Academic Experience Rating	**85**
Profs interesting rating	90
Profs accessible rating	76
% female faculty	12
% minority faculty	2

Joint Degrees

MBA/master of international management.

Academics

"It's a combination of everything"—including "an outstanding MBA program with very nice faculty, staff, and students; a beautiful campus where you can do a lot of activities (sports, cultural); and a program small enough to give you personal attention in a school that's big enough to put everything at your fingertips"—that makes the Pamplin MBA at Virginia Tech so appealing to students. MBAs here also love that their program is a "great value" and that the curriculum places an emphasis "particularly on liking what you do and doing what's important to you, and on building not only a career but a life."

Pamplin offers both a full-time and part-time MBA. The curricula for the two are identical; each requires 50 credit hours divided almost evenly among required core courses and electives. The full-time program is cohort-based; the part-time program is not. Full-time students praise the cohort system, which gets them "focused on learning from the other students in the program, in addition to the normal course material." Part-timers enjoy the convenience of their program, which offers classes in Falls Church, VA. Students in both programs tell us that "the curriculum is much more technical and hands-on as opposed to theoretical" and that "the integration of technology to courses is remarkable." Finance and IT departments both receive high marks. Across departments, professors are described as "very knowledgeable and willing to answer any questions we have, willing to give extra help when required, and available for questions and conversations outside of class." The administration "is active as well, keeping in frequent contact by sending out announcements and asking for feedback from students."

Asked how they would improve their program, most students here suggest tweaks rather than an overhaul. A typical student proposes that "the MBA program would benefit from a larger number of students. There are currently less than 50 first-year MBAs in the full-time program. This can cause problems with some concentrations not being offered due to lack of interest. The program would benefit from having closer to 100 students in each class." The school lists the following available concentrations: corporate financial management, investment and financial services management, marketing, organizational leadership, systems engineering management, and general management.

Career and Placement

Pamplin MBAs receive placement help both from the university's Career Services Office and from the MBA-dedicated Career Advising Office, which students call "perhaps the program's greatest strength. Barry O'Donnell is in charge of the program and teaches one-credit courses on career search. It's an incredible program." His office also plans MBA recruitment campaigns, "including posting MBA internships and career opportunities," as well as a speaker series.

Employers most likely to hire Pamplin MBAs include Capgemini, Deloitte Touche Tohmatsu, Ernst & Young, U.S. General Accounting Office, Wachovia, IBM, and Booze Allen Hamilton.

ADMISSIONS CONTACT: MELANIE JOHNSTON, ASSOCIATE DIRECTOR
ADDRESS: 1044 PAMPLIN HALL, VIRGINIA TECH, BLACKSBURG, VA 24061 UNITED STATES
PHONE: 540-231-6152 • FAX: 540-231-4487
E-MAIL: MBA_INFO@VT.EDU • WEBSITE: WWW.MBA.PAMPLIN.VT.EDU

Student Life and Environment

"Because of the large size of VT, there is an abundance of things to get involved with" around the Blacksburg campus, including "lots of outdoor activities" such as hiking, camping, skiing, and whitewater rafting in the nearby mountains. One parent/student notes that the campus itself offers "lots of green spaces where our kids can run and play" and plenty of opportunities to participate in intramural sports and pickup games. Social life among full-time MBAs is "active, partly because there are a lot of bars around here." One writes, "We have a dependable social circle and do many things together like going out on Thursday nights, eating dinner together at our favorite Mexican restaurant, and tailgating before football games." Many students here note that "Virginia Tech is a big football school. Especially in the fall, life around here seems to revolve around the Hokies." The MBA Association is "very active," and many MBAs devote some of their spare time to community service. Overall, as one student sums up, "life at school is really enjoyable; not too stressful, but learning a lot."

VT MBAs include "many students with engineering backgrounds," including a number of international students. One MBA observes, "Our class is very ethnically diverse, with many [students] from India and Asia, but all the different cultures seem to mesh extremely well" and the mix creates "a great learning atmosphere." Students also represent a variety of experience levels; "Many students came straight from undergrad while several others have worked for years and have children," students report. Most importantly, "students generally cooperate with one another and help each other. They don't try to run each other down in competition. There is a good camaraderie among first-year students and second-year students are very helpful to first-years."

Admissions

All applications to the Pamplin MBA program must include a completed application form, official GMAT scores, a resume, and interview, and two copies of official transcripts from all postsecondary institutions attended. Students must also submit two letters of recommendation; International students whose first language is not English must also submit TOEFL scores. The Admissions Office considers all pieces of the application, with emphasis placed on academic record and preparedness for graduate business work, GMAT scores, professional experience, communication skills, goals, and compatibility with the program. One semester of calculus and two semesters of undergraduate accounting are prerequisite to commencing the MBA program.

FINANCIAL FACTS

Annual tuition (in-state/ out-of-state)	$8,540/$14,057
Fees (in-state/ out-of-state)	$1,350/$1,419
Room & board (off-campus)	$7,200
% of students receiving grants	71
Average award package	$7,300
Average grant	$3,671

ADMISSIONS

Admissions Selectivity Rating	86
# of applications received	152
% applicants accepted	59
% acceptees attending	45
Average GMAT	631
Range of GMAT	580–676
Average GPA	3.2
TOEFL required of international students	Yes
Minimum TOEFL (paper/computer)	550/213
Application fee	$45
Regular application deadline	Rolling
Regular notification	Rolling
Deferment available	Yes
Maximum length of deferment	1 year
Need-blind admissions	Yes

Applicants Also Look At

College of William and Mary, George Mason University, The George Washington University, University of Maryland, University of Virginia, Virginia Commonwealth University.

EMPLOYMENT PROFILE

Career Rating	82	Grads Employed by Function	%	Avg. Salary
Primary Source of Full-time Job Acceptances		Finance/Accounting	36	$50,942
School-facilitated activities	9 (41%)	Marketing/Sales	9	$58,350
Graduate-facilitated activities	13 (59%)	MIS	23	$58,000
Percent employed	91	Operations/Production	5	$57,000
		Consulting	27	$60,800

Top 5 Employers Hiring Grads

US Governement Accountability Office; IBM; Cap Gemini; Booz Allen Hamilton; Wachovia.

WAKE FOREST UNIVERSITY
BABCOCK GRADUATE SCHOOL OF MANAGEMENT

Academics

A small program in a private university setting, the Babcock Graduate School of Management at Wake Forest University provides a business education that is focused on teamwork, entrepreneurship, experiential learning, and hands-on management. No matter what their academic preparation or business interest, all students are required to take the first-year core courses, which include such essentials as International Business Management, Financial Management, Macroeconomics, Operations Management, and Quantitative Methods. In the second year, students choose a career concentration within the broader areas of consulting/general management, finance, entrepreneurship, marketing, operations management, information technology management (available only as a second-ary concentration), or an individually designed concentration in an area such as health care management.

With only 90 students per class, Wake Forest maintains "an intimate feel and incredible exposure to top-notch faculty and alums in incredible positions." Students love the "entrepreneurial, collegial atmosphere that provides everyone with the opportunity to excel and invoke innovation and change." In fact, students say the school's small size works to their advantage in many ways, including "the development of stronger rela-tionships with peers, better rapport with the faculty, and higher levels of access to the resources on campus." While a Wake Forest education comes with a private school price tag, students appreciate the little perks, like the fact that "everyone gets a Dell computer and [is] linked into the same network. This makes school assignments very easy to com-plete, and our IT support staff is fantastic."

Focusing on quantitative skills and boasting strong programs in IT and strategy, students say the workload at Wake Forest can be "very intense." However, the academic stress is counterbalanced by the fact that "professors are extremely dedicated to providing a pos-itive learning environment and experience." A current student explains: "The school fos-ters a competitive environment which is key in the business world today; however, it also encourages a helpful and empowering attitude in individuals. If anyone is ever falling behind in a particular course or not understanding material, study groups are immedi-ately formed."

Despite their years of experience in the classroom, Wake Forest professors are "surpris-ingly up to date on their integration of current business trends into classroom study." However, some say they "would like to see Wake Forest faculty spend much more time applying the case study method" rather than "relying too heavily on lectures." The curriculum is further augmented by a series of school-sponsored events and lectures, providing "excellent opportunities to hear reputable outside speakers talk on relevant business topics."

Career and Placement

The Career Management Center at Wake Forest works closely with students to define their goals and help make corporate contacts. The university also maintains a list of more than 4,700 MBA alumni, among the school's approximately 6,000 total MBA graduates, who are considered active and accessible in helping current students find positions. Babcock students acknowledge that there is a trade-off in attending a smaller school, as "Increased class size would help attract more companies, but would decrease intimacy." Even so, students assure us that "the school is small; however it pulls in many large com-panies to recruit on campus."

Having built strong ties in the finance industry, Wake Forest is currently "placing a strong emphasis on marketing and consulting." But on the whole, students report, "The Career Services team has done a fantastic job of assembling a wide variety of professional

STACY POINDEXTER OWEN, DIRECTOR OF ADMISSIONS
WORRELL PROF. CENTER, RM. 2119, 1834 WAKE FOREST RD., WINSTON-SALEM, NC 27106 U.S.
PHONE: 336-758-5422 • FAX: 336-758-5830
E-MAIL: ADMISSIONS@MBA.WFU.EDU • WEBSITE: WWW.MBA.WFU.EDU

opportunities." In 2006, the mean salary for graduating students was $80,311. Fifty-two percent of grads took jobs in finance and accounting, and 20 percent took jobs in marketing and sales.

Student Life and Environment

Life at Wake Forest is a mix of work, play, and professional development, and students enjoy plenty of "well-balanced days with strong academics and a warm, friendly class." Drawing "a diverse mix of individuals across all kinds of work experience, backgrounds, race, nationality, and even age," Wake Forest students describe their classmates as "smart, fun, socially vibrant, extremely supportive, and helpful in both academic and personal issues." Encouraging an intimate and tight-knit culture, the sense of community at Wake Forest "permeates every level of [students'] academic and social lives."

Outside the classroom, "There are many student-run activities for personal and career development. These include minority interest clubs, business function clubs, and social clubs." As a result, students enjoy "multiple outlets to be a leader in a club, work with admissions, and help the surrounding community." Notable student-run activities include social enterprise projects and trips, the Wake Forest MBA Marketing Summit and an accompanying MBA Marketing Case Competition, and the Elevator Competition, a business plan/venture capital event. When looking for a little down time, "Winston is a good town with plenty to do—good restaurants, good bars, good climate, and it's close to the beach and mountains." A current student enthuses, "One of the best things is that I am always busy, whether it's from being immersed in challenging studies or hanging out with new friends."

Admissions

Wake Forest admits students who have proven academic ability, professional experience, and community involvement. Sought-after qualities include focus, motivation, leadership ability, strong values, and teamwork skills. Postgraduate work experience is highly important to an admissions decision. Last year, the entering class had an average GMAT score of 647, with a range of 610 to 680, and average work experience of 3 years.

For students who want to jump-start the admissions process, Wake Forest offers "Done in a Day" admissions, wherein prospective candidates participate in a day-long interview session in November or December. For these applicants, the admissions essays are waived, but candidates must be prepared to discuss essay topics in person.

FINANCIAL FACTS

Annual tuition	$31,500
Fees	$150
Cost of books	$1,500
Room & board (off-campus)	$7,000
% of students receiving aid	79
% of first-year students receiving aid	86
% of students receiving loans	56
% of students receiving grants	65
Average award package	$33,364
Average grant	$14,527
Average student loan debt	$47,362

ADMISSIONS

Admissions Selectivity Rating	88
# of applications received	432
% applicants accepted	53
% acceptees attending	39
Average GMAT	647
Range of GMAT	610–680
Average GPA	3.2
TOEFL required of international students	Yes
Minimum TOEFL (paper/computer)	600/250
Application fee	$75
Regular application deadline	4/1
Regular notification	Rolling
Early decision program?	Yes
ED Deadline/Notification	11/1 / 11/22
Need-blind admissions	Yes

Applicants Also Look At

Duke University, Indiana University—Bloomington, The University of North Carolina at Chapel Hill, University of Virginia, Vanderbilt University.

EMPLOYMENT PROFILE

Career Rating	89	Grads Employed by Function	%	Avg. Salary
Primary Source of Full-time Job Acceptances		Finance/Accounting	52	$80,038
School-facilitated activities	71%	Marketing/Sales	20	$73,770
Graduate-facilitated activities	29%	Operations/Production	8	NR
Average base starting salary	$80,311	Consulting	12	$78,333
Percent employed	81	General Management	4	NR
		Other	4	NR

Top 5 Employers Hiring Grads

Bank of America and Bank of America Securities; Wachovia and Wachovia Securities; IBM Consulting; Philip Morris; Lowe's.

WASHBURN UNIVERSITY
SCHOOL OF BUSINESS

GENERAL INFORMATION
Type of school	Public
Academic calendar	Semester

SURVEY SAYS . . .
Cutting-edge classes
Solid preparation in:
Finance
Accounting

STUDENTS
Enrollment of parent institution	7,400
Enrollment of business school	96
% male/female	96/4
% out-of-state	5
% part-time	85
% minorities	10
% international	12
Average age at entry	28
Average years work experience at entry	9

ACADEMICS
Academic Experience Rating	**83**
Student/faculty ratio	20:1
Profs interesting rating	84
Profs accessible rating	90
% female faculty	29
% minority faculty	18

Joint Degrees
MBA/JD 4 years.

Prominent Alumni
Greg Brenneman, CEO, president, Burger King; Mayo Schmidt, CEO, president, Saskatchewan Wheat Pool; Dale Pond, vice president marketing, Lowe's; Ken, vice president marketing, Domino's Pizza.

Academics

Located in Topeka, Kansas, Washburn University's broad-based MBA program seeks to improve a student's skills in quantitative analysis, teamwork, and technology while providing a strong academic foundation in accounting, economics, finance, information systems, management, marketing, legal and ethic issues, and global business. Attracting many working professionals as well as a considerable population of full-time, international students, Washburn teaches students how to think like business leaders and gives them the skills and confidence they need to succeed in the business world. "Upon completion of the program, I will feel confident in my abilities to provide outstanding analysis, negotiation, coordination, troubleshooting and communications skills," attests a student. "I have learned to demonstrate ethical and professional conduct coupled with excellent leadership skills."

The MBA program begins with the core-level curriculum, which covers quantitative methods and accounting. After completing the core, students begin the upper-level curriculum, comprising 30 semester hours in more specialized business topics. While eight courses in the upper-level curriculum are required, students may also take two or more electives in an area of special interest. However, be forewarned that elective offerings comprise a very small portion of the MBA program. In fact, students looking for more specialized business knowledge say the school should offer "more classes targeted to specific areas of study instead of a general overview." A current student admits, "The diversity of electives is nonexistent. Our electives would be more appropriately named requirements."

Quality teaching is fundamental to the Washburn experience, and the school's top-notch faculty is "a diverse group that have many years of experience in teaching." A dynamic classroom environment, professors "provide insight, facilitate discussion and group work resembling the workplace, and use situation analysis to make points." On top of that, students appreciate the fact that the small program facilitates personal relationships with the faculty. A current student elaborates, "Your professors will know your name. They will answer your call or e-mail. They have a genuine desire to see you succeed and do well."

Drawing students from a variety of academic and professional backgrounds, Washburn MBAs are "high-energy, results-oriented, self-motivated team players." The majority of students also work full-time while completing their MBA, which means that class discussions are loaded with real-world insights. Despite the rigors of balancing life, school, and a personal life, Washburn professors go out of their way to accommodate working students. A student explains, "It is geared toward the nontraditional working student and has a lot of flexibility for students who have to travel for their jobs." Another agrees, "Professors demand a lot, but most have been very aware and accommodating to school/life balances."

Career and Placement

Many MBA students at Washburn are currently employed and plan to stay with their current company after graduation from the program. However, those looking for a new position can receive assistance through the Washburn University Career Services Office, which serves the undergraduate and graduate community at the school, as well as alumni. Though Career Services, students have access to numerous career fairs and interview days, interview and resume preparation assistance, and job search information. A number of prominent companies have offices in Topeka, including Blue Cross and Blue

SHIRLEY GORMAN, DIRECTOR OF STUDENT AFFAIRS/MBA ADVISOR
1700 SW COLLEGE, HENDERSON ROOM 114, TOPEKA, KS 66621 UNITED STATES
PHONE: 785-670-1308 • FAX: 785-670-1063
E-MAIL: MBA@WASHBURN.EDU • WEBSITE: WWW.WASHBURN.EDU/BUSINESS

Shield Association, Burlington Northern & Santa Fe Railway, Hills Pet Foods, Southwestern Bell, Western Resources, Frito-Lay, Goodyear, and as well as a variety of smaller companies and medical resources.

Student Life and Environment

Students appreciate the amiable and non-competitive culture on the Washburn campus, describing their classmates as "friendly, personable, and enthusiastic." Group work is an important part of the Washburn MBA, giving students ample opportunity to meet and work with their classmates throughout the course of the program. Students enjoy interacting with their talented cohorts, telling us, "Almost everyone pulled their weight with regard to team projects, and the interaction of differing opinions and backgrounds was very interesting."

Of the 120 graduate students in Washburn's MBA program, about 80 percent are full-time professionals who take classes at night. As a result, there isn't much of a social buzz on campus, and most students don't participate in extracurricular activities. In fact, one student who came directly to the program out of undergrad laments, "I wish there were more of a social atmosphere outside of the classroom, but other students are too busy."

However, as a part of a larger college and university, there are plenty of ways to enjoy campus life at Washburn and, for those who are interested, "There is strong encouragement for involvement in activities and in the community." In addition to campus clubs and activities, MBA students can take advantage of the school's excellent facilities, including a new Student Recreation and Wellness Center, an art museum, and an observatory. The surrounding capital city of Topeka is a low-cost, medium-sized city of about 150,000 inhabitants, and an excellent place to balance the rigors of work and school.

Admissions

To be considered for admission to the Washburn MBA, students must submit official undergraduate transcripts, a completed application form, official GMAT scores, and two letters of recommendation from academicians, employers, or other sources who can attest to your ability to succeed in graduate school. Students with outstanding promise but incomplete applications may be considered for provisional admission to the program. International students make up 15 percent of the student population and, in addition to the preceding materials, must submit the International Student Application and TOEFL scores. Students from all major fields are welcome at Washburn.

FINANCIAL FACTS

Annual tuition (in-state/out-of-state)	$241/$490
	(per credit hour)
% of students receiving aid	25
% of first-year students receiving aid	10
% of students receiving grants	20

ADMISSIONS

Admissions Selectivity Rating	**83**
# of applications received	42
% applicants accepted	60
% acceptees attending	100
Average GMAT	535
Range of GMAT	470–630
Average GPA	3.56
TOEFL required of international students	Yes
Minimum TOEFL (paper/computer)	550/213
Application fee	$40
International application fee	$100
Regular application deadline	7/1
Regular notification	7/1
Transfer students accepted	Yes
Transfer application policy	
Up to 6 hours of MBA hours from an AACSB-accredited school may be accepted upon approval.	
Non-fall admissions	Yes
Need-blind admissions	Yes

Applicants Also Look At

Kansas State University, University of Kansas.

EMPLOYMENT PROFILE

Career Rating	84	Top 3 Employers Hiring Grads
Primary Source of Full-time Job Acceptances		Payless ShoeSource; Security Benefit
Percent employed	100	Companies; Westar Energy.

WASHINGTON STATE UNIVERSITY
COLLEGE OF BUSINESS

GENERAL INFORMATION
Type of school	Public
Environment	Town
Academic calendar	Semester

SURVEY SAYS . . .
Friendly students
Good peer network
Smart classrooms
Solid preparation in:
General management
Teamwork

STUDENTS
Enrollment of parent institution	18,000
Enrollment of business school	48
% male/female	0/100
% out-of-state	12
% international	50
Average age at entry	24

ACADEMICS
Academic Experience Rating	**69**
Student/faculty ratio	40:1
Profs interesting rating	68
Profs accessible rating	80

Joint Degrees
JD/MBA (with University of Idaho) 4 years.

Academics

Washington State's College of Business has gained a strong national reputation for its "fantastic" study environment and "relatively low tuition," but its many attributes are no secret to WSU undergrads. Many students like the school so much that they decide to remain Cougars. "I completed my undergrad at WSU and enjoyed the experience so much that I wanted to complete my graduate degree here as well," one student says.

The school offers classes at WSU's main campus in Pullman, and at its satellite campuses in Spokane, Vancouver, Washington, and the Tri-Cities area in the southeastern part of the state. Course work is offered in accounting, finance; insurance and real estate; information systems; management and operations; marketing; and hospitality business management. Master of Accounting, Master of Business Administration (MBA), Master of Technology Management, and Doctor of Philosophy (in business administration) degrees are available.

The recently revamped MBA program is "directed toward non-business undergraduate majors" and "accepts students with less than 1 year [of work] experience." Opinions of the intro-level courses are mixed: One student said his first semester was "a bit weak." Though difficult, it was "really just busywork." By all accounts, things pick up from there, with course work "designed around the issues and direction of the changing business world." There's an "emphasis on teamwork," and assignments are connected to "real-life experience." Professors are "highly experienced." One student says, "The quality of [the] faculty is by far the biggest asset." Professors maintain close contact with students through a "cohort system that allows for smaller classes and greater [student] teacher interaction." This can be a mixed blessing, however. While the faculty includes "some of the best research minds" in the field, some professors "don't know the first thing about teaching," one student says. Fortunately, "The program coordinators listen to and respect student feedback." The school's administrative staff is "on a first-name basis with all the students." They "will go out of their way to help you solve/remedy a problem," though their "speed of handling affairs" could improve.

Career and Placement

The Carson Center for Professional Development encourages student involvement in meaningful extracurricular activities. The center also polishes students' resume and interviewing skills and utilizes "alumni and faculty connections" to help students gain real-world experience through jobs and internships. These efforts are, for the most part, successful. The "proud alumni base" is particularly helpful; many here believe that WSU's greatest strength is the "dedication to each other" shown by fellow Cougars. Some students, however, would like to see more direct "interaction with outside companies." Another student says the program is "so new [that] they do not have the reputation with employers that some other MBA programs have."

Student Life and Environment

Students at WSU hail from "extremely diverse backgrounds." However, as most students "lack real working experience," this diversity is generally of the cultural variety: "About half" the students in some years are foreign-born, and "All of the students are friendly and intelligent." Students describe their classmates as "mature individuals"—the average age at entry into the program is 25—"who are attending business school to better themselves for their future careers." They're "open-minded," perhaps to a fault: "They do not have very strong opinions about much in the world," one student reports. Many have part-time jobs on campus, and almost all are "willing to help others" with course

CHERYL OLIVER, MBA@WSU.EDU
PO BOX 644744, PULLMAN, WA 99164-4744 UNITED STATES
PHONE: 509-335-7617 • FAX: 509-335-4735
E-MAIL: MBA@WSU.EDU • WEBSITE: WWW.WSU.EDU/MBA

work. While a few students believe that "the course load is usually too heavy to take part in extracurricular activities," "Most manage their time very well." Students say that because of the smaller groups in the cohort system, peers in the program "turn into life-long friends."

There are two camps here. The first could be described as the nothing-to-do camp, which claims that life here "is just going to school for classes and returning home [to] study—there's not much entertainment in this city." The other camp says Pullman is a "wonderful college town," and that the campus is "very lively." The campus reportedly has a "perfect gym" that houses "great sports programs." Some students are "involved in organized sports and activities with [the] professors and administration." One student writes, "I am involved in two organizations on campus (MBA Association and Delta Sigma Pi business fraternity). I currently hold two jobs totaling 25 hours a week. I live with other MBA students so that we can do much [of] our homework together."

Admissions

WSU's MBA program accepts applications from those with a bachelor's degree from a regionally accredited undergraduate institution. All undergraduate fields of study are considered. To be qualified for regular admission, an applicant must have a GPA of 3.0 on a 4.0 scale for the final 60 hours of undergraduate course work, or for 12 or more credits of recognized graduate-level course work. International applicants also must have a score of 580 or better on the TOEFL. GMAT scores and three letters of recommendation are required of all applicants. In addition to the above requirements, to be qualified for regular admission to the Master of Accounting program, an applicant must have a bachelor's degree in business administration with a concentration in accounting.

FINANCIAL FACTS

Annual tuition (in-state/ out-of-state)	$10,000/$19,000
Fees	$683
Cost of books	$1,080
Room & board	$8,720
Average grant	$4,000

ADMISSIONS

Admissions Selectivity Rating	**81**
# of applications received	128
% applicants accepted	58
% acceptees attending	38
Average GMAT	570
Range of GMAT	480–650
Average GPA	3.72
TOEFL required of international students	Yes
Minimum TOEFL (paper/computer)	580/237
Application fee	$35
Regular application deadline	3/1
Regular notification	4/1
Transfer students accepted	Yes
Transfer application policy Transfer students will only be able to apply 6 credits of elective course work to the WSU MBA on a case by case basis.	
Non-fall admissions	Yes
Need-blind admissions	Yes

WASHINGTON UNIVERSITY IN ST. LOUIS
JOHN M. OLIN SCHOOL OF BUSINESS

GENERAL INFORMATION

Type of school	Private
Environment	City
Academic calendar	Semester

SURVEY SAYS . . .
Friendly students
Happy students
Smart classrooms
Solid preparation in:
General management
Teamwork
Quantitative skills

STUDENTS

Enrollment of parent institution	13,527
Enrollment of business school	593
% male/female	70/30
% part-time	56
% minorities	14
% international	37
Average age at entry	28
Average years work experience at entry	4

ACADEMICS

Academic Experience Rating	**91**
Student/faculty ratio	14:1
Profs interesting rating	96
Profs accessible rating	92
% female faculty	12
% minority faculty	6

Joint Degrees
MBA/MS (architecture) 3 years, MBA/MA (East Asian studies) 3 years, MBA/MS (social work) 3 years, MBA/JD 4 years, MBA/MS (biomedical engineering) 3 years.

Prominent Alumni
Paulino Do Rego Barros Jr., president, AT&T Global Operations; Edward A. Mueller, CEO, Williams-Sonoma, Inc.; Steven F. Leer, president and CEO, Arch Coal, Inc.; W. Patrick McGinnis, president and CEO, Nestlé Purina Pet Care; William J. Shaw, president and COO, Marriott International.

Academics

Offering the unbeatable combination of a strong reputation, small class sizes, and a dedicated and talented teaching staff, students at Washington University's Olin School of Business say theirs is the "best and most recognized business school in St. Louis." Get ready to hit the ground running: "Since the MBA program is front loaded with many classes," the first semester can be "very challenging." In fact, during the first semester, students complete all but two required core courses, which comprise a third of the required units for the MBA. After that, students can take advantage of the flexible curriculum to tailor their studies through ample elective course work, including a "strong program in international business and brand management."

Despite the "grueling schedule which doesn't seem to let up," Olin's decidedly "collaborative atmosphere" and consistently small class sizes make the experience both manageable and intimate. At Olin, students have "the ability to truly learn and get involved in the learning process, both from fellow classmates and the professors." As one current student explains, "After completing each class I can truly say that I have learned something new and useful, which makes the grueling schedule bearable." A diverse and talented faculty, Olin professors "each bring a unique perspective and personality to the classroom," teaching material that is "contemporary and relevant to the business world."

Boasting a student body that is "hardworking, competitive, driven, and opinionated," fellow students play a very large role in the Washington University experience, especially in the beginning of the program. Employing a cohort study system, "The first semester is based largely on loads of group work with a pre-selected group of four to five students." These groups are selected by the administration to ensure a diversity of background and experience amongst team members, which most students find extremely edifying.

At this small, private school "The entire program is very student-centered," and the "administration is extremely open to student suggestions." Program administrators even handle all the red tape, "taking pressure off students for items like financial aid, course selection, or other issues that may take away from time that can be used for course work." Even in the classroom student concerns are taken seriously, and "Teachers issue evaluation forms every 6 weeks so that they can adapt teaching styles midway through their courses if students feel it is needed."

Career and Placement

At Olin, the focus on career planning and placement begins in the first semester, during which all first-year students must take a course entitled Career Developer, which helps refine their career goals through expert panels, self-assessments, and instruction in "soft skills" like emotional intelligence. Thereafter, the Weston Career Center offers a host of resources, including an alumni and corporate database, advising by professional career counselors, skill-building activities, and workshops on topics such as interviews, evaluating offers, and cover letter and resume editing. Some feel "The school could bring more recruiters to campus" but appreciate the fact that "alumni are always happy to help and the Career Center does an excellent job making sure that [students] are positioned to talk to recruiters even if [they] have to go to their city."

In 2006, graduates from Washington University received a median base salary of $82,000, with an average signing bonus of $14,065. Over half of students (53 percent) took positions in the Midwest. Jobs in financial services, consumer products, and manufacturing drew the most students, at 21 percent, 15 percent, and 14 percent respectively. Top employers included IBM, Johnson & Johnson, AT&T, General Mills, Merrill Lynch, and Samsung.

EVAN BOUFFIDES, DIRECTOR OF MBA ADMISSIONS AND FINANCIAL AID
1 BROOKINGS DRIVE, CAMPUS BOX 1133, ST. LOUIS, MO 63130 UNITED STATES
PHONE: 314-935-7301 • FAX: 314-935-6309
E-MAIL: MBA@OLIN.WUSTL.EDU • WEBSITE: WWW.OLIN.WUSTL.EDU

Student Life and Environment

With a student body that is "friendly, eager to learn and approachable," it's easy to fit in at the Olin School of Business. A current student raves: "They're a great bunch, whether in class, in our cohort groups, or relaxing at the bar!" Despite the challenging course material, the average Olin student "works hard but realizes that every sane and normal person should put the books aside for a while to have some fun." A first-year student explains, "You could study here 24/7 if you wanted to but most students are able to find a nice balance." On weekends, business students enjoy a weekly get-together with free food and a keg, thanks to the school-sponsored "Friday Afternoon Clubs."

On campus, the environment is both pleasant and stimulating, as "The facilities are top-notch, and the school is always buzzing with activity, from conferences to club meetings." As one current student explains, "Our day actually starts when we get out of class as we meet with our groups, go to speaker events, company info sessions, club events, work on practicum projects, and much more." Located next to Forest Park in the center of St. Louis, Missouri, "There are tons of restaurants and bars very close by, and housing is VERY affordable in the area."

Admissions

Olin looks for self-directed, disciplined professionals who will be highly involved in the MBA community as demonstrated by their academic proficiency, leadership potential, communication skills, and history of participation in extracurricular activities. To apply to Olin, students must submit a completed application form (which includes several essays and a resume), official transcripts from college, two letters of recommendation, GMAT scores, and, for international students, TOEFL scores. Though there are no official minimums for entry into the program, last year's incoming class had an average GMAT score of 654 and an average GPA of 3.37. There is also no minimum work requirement, though the average work experience for students in last year's entering class was 4.3 years.

FINANCIAL FACTS

Annual tuition	$35,950
Fees	$1,410
Cost of books	$2,500
Room & board (off-campus)	$16,500
% of students receiving aid	88
% of first-year students receiving aid	86
% of students receiving loans	62
% of students receiving grants	76

ADMISSIONS

Admissions Selectivity Rating	89
# of applications received	568
% applicants accepted	54
% acceptees attending	46
Average GMAT	654
Range of GMAT	590–720
Average GPA	3.37
TOEFL required of international students	Yes
Minimum TOEFL (paper/computer)	590/243
Application fee	$100
Application Deadline/Notification	
Round 1:	11/6 / 1/2
Round 2:	1/08 / 3/2
Round 3:	3/12 / 4/27
Round 4:	5/1 / 6/15
Deferment available	Yes
Maximum length of deferment	1 year (if approved)
Transfer students accepted	Yes
Transfer application policy	Up to 9 credits from an AACSB-accredited graduate program (with approval).
Need-blind admissions	Yes

Applicants Also Look At

Emory University, Georgetown University, Indiana University—Bloomington, University of Michigan, The University of North Carolina at Chapel Hill, The University of Texas at Austin, Vanderbilt University.

EMPLOYMENT PROFILE

Career Rating	86	Grads Employed by Function	%	Avg. Salary
Primary Source of Full-time Job Acceptances		Finance/Accounting	34	$81,435
School-facilitated activities	59 (63%)	Human Resources	3	$74,667
Graduate-facilitated activities	32 (34%)	Marketing/Sales	27	$79,750
Unknown	3 (3%)	Operations/Production	4	$84,333
Average base starting salary	$82,183	Consulting	18	$88,554
Percent employed	86	General Management	10	$84,733
		Other	4	NR

Top 5 Employers Hiring Grads
Anheuser-Busch; Johnson & Johnson; Citigroup; Harrah's Entertainment, Inc. A.G. Edwards and Sons, Inc.

WAYNE STATE UNIVERSITY
SCHOOL OF BUSINESS ADMINISTRATION

GENERAL INFORMATION
Type of school   Public
Environment   Metropolis
Academic calendar   Semester

SURVEY SAYS . . .
Cutting-edge classes
Solid preparation in:
Accounting
General management
Teamwork

STUDENTS
Enrollment of parent
  institution   32,982
Enrollment of
  business school   1,239
% male/female   60/40
% part-time   89
Average age at entry   28
Average years work
  experience at entry   5

ACADEMICS
Academic Experience Rating   66
Student/faculty ratio   35:1
Profs interesting rating   68
Profs accessible rating   80
% female faculty   10
% minority faculty   18

Joint Degrees
JD/MBA 3 years.

Prominent Alumni
Paul Glantz, president and CEO,
Proctor Financial, Inc.; Jack Martin,
chief financial officer, U.S.
Department of Education; Sandra E.
Pierce, president and CEO, Charter
One Bank; Stephen Strome, chair-
man and CEO, Handleman
Company; Susan J. Unger, senior
vice president and chief information
officer, DaimlerChrysler; James H.
Vandenberghe, vice chairman, Lear
Corporation.

Academics

Located in the heart of Detroit and associated with a "large, research-based university," the School of Business Administration at Wayne State University provides a progressive MBA program to a serious population of working professionals. The MBA curriculum consists of a minimum of 12 courses (or 36 credits) split between core courses and elective course work. However, students who do not have an educational background in business may be required to take up to eight foundation courses before beginning the core. After completing the foundation and core courses, students complete their credit requirements with electives in accounting, finance, marketing, human resources management, international business, leadership and organizational behavior, management information systems, quality management, and taxation. While the school doesn't offer specific concentrations, students say the elective offerings are impressive: "The excellent quality of the international business electives are the greatest strengths that WSU's MBA program has to offer its students."

Ninety percent of students in the graduate program at Wayne State University are working professionals, pursuing a graduate degree in the evenings while working part-time or full-time during the day. In order to "effectively accommodate working students," graduate courses are offered in the afternoon and evening, on Saturdays, and online. The extremely flexible schedule includes classes at the 203-acre, landscaped main campus, as well as at the satellite campus in Farmington Hills. Students can even pursue the MBA online, or through a combination of on-site and online courses.

Drawing students with strong career goals and diverse career experience, the varied composition of the student body brings an additional dynamic to the classroom, and many report, "The interaction with a diverse student body has been a very positive experience." Located in America's auto city, "A large percentage of Wayne State University MBA students come from the automotive industry and many are engineers by trade." Nevertheless, "other fields such as finance, telecommunications, pharmaceuticals, IT, advertising, and others are well represented." Students immediately apply class lessons to their jobs, saying the MBA course work "is pertinent to my profession, and I take what I learn and use it every day in the workplace."

Thinking like the business mavens they are training to be, Wayne State's students say, "The cost/benefit of attending this school versus another public university is excellent; it's half the cost, and the professors are just as qualified." There are nearly 60 full-time professors teaching courses in the MBA program, whom students describe as "open-minded teachers who are knowledgeable and enthusiastic about the subject matter." What's more, the professors are "very approachable and encouraging," fostering a non-competitive atmosphere in the classroom. In addition to course work, the school keeps the business program relevant to the modern business world, hosting field trips and inviting distinguished business executives to speak to the student community. Lastly, Wayne State University is the 29th largest public, doctoral-granting institution in the United States.

Career and Placement

Dedicated solely to students in the School of Business Administration, the SBA Planning and Placement Office offers career counseling and professional development assistance to undergraduate and graduate students, as well as alumni of Wayne State. The center hosts a variety of on-campus interviews, career days, and meet-and-greet events, and

LINDA S. ZADDACH, ASSISTANT DEAN OF STUDENT SERVICES
OFFICE OF STUDENT SERVICES, 5201 CASS, ROOM 200, DETROIT, MI 48202 UNITED STATES
PHONE: 313-577-4505 • FAX: 313-577-5299
E-MAIL: L.S.ZADDACH@WAYNE.EDU • WEBSITE: WWW.BUSADM.WAYNE.EDU

benefits from the fact that the school's "ties to the business community are strong." The center also offers career counseling services and comprehensive online resources.

A vast majority of Wayne State students are already working in a full-time, professional capacity when they begin their MBA. In fact, 70 percent of Wayne State graduate students are receiving tuition reimbursement from their current company. Therefore, many students are more focused on progressing in their current job, rather than making a career change or finding new positions. Whether seeking a new career or continuing in their current job, 90 percent of Wayne State graduates stay in Michigan, most in the Detroit area.

Student Life and Environment

Balancing schoolwork, a full-time career, and family life can be incredibly challenging; even so, most Wayne State students maintain a positive, go-getter attitude throughout their studies. A current student explains, "Since most people have jobs, and are thus part-time students, everyone is busy—but at the same time very determined to get through the degree." Thanks to their demanding schedules, few Wayne State students have time for extracurricular or social activities at school. However, for those who can make the time, there are a number of student clubs and honor societies at the School of Business Administration, including the MBA Association. Plus, the larger university lends a sense of excitement and action to the business school atmosphere, as there are a plethora of "young adults all over campus studying and moving from one class to another."

Students take advantage of the recreation center and the undergraduate and graduate libraries campus, and at mealtimes there are "pretty good places to eat nearby and a lounge with machines and a microwave in the library." Wayne State's business-minded grad students are pleased with the school's strategic "location, location, location, in the heart of Detroit, near downtown." However, students also warn that the current classrooms are a bit run-down and that the school "needs more security in the buildings." The School of Business Administration has responded to student and faculty needs by beginning renovations of its current building and adding undercover security, since the facility is open daytimes through late evening for classes. A new state-of-the-art, technologically advanced building is scheduled for groundbreaking in 2009.

Admissions

One of the largest part-time MBA programs in the world, there are over 1,250 students enrolled in Wayne State's graduate program. For entry, students must score at least 450 on the GMAT and have an undergraduate GPA of at least 2.5. The Admissions Committee also evaluates a student's leadership potential and professional experience when making an admissions decision. Students may apply for admission in the fall, spring, or summer semesters.

FINANCIAL FACTS

Annual tuition (in-state/ out-of-state)	$8,162/$15,930
Fees	$701
Cost of books	$1,000
Average grant	$5,373

ADMISSIONS

Admissions Selectivity Rating	**73**
# of applications received	358
% applicants accepted	68
% acceptees attending	76
Average GMAT	510
Average GPA	3.15
TOEFL required of international students	Yes
Minimum TOEFL (paper/computer)	550/213
Application fee	$50
Regular application deadline	8/1
Regular notification	Rolling
Transfer students accepted	Yes
Transfer application policy Meet admission standards.	
Non-fall admissions	Yes

EMPLOYMENT PROFILE			
Career Rating	**80**		
Primary Source of Full-time Job Acceptances		**Grads Employed by Function% Avg. Salary**	
School-facilitated activities	75%	Accounting	17% $82,800
% employed (by 3 months		Business Logistics	3% $54,300
after graduation)	989	Finance	29% $75,900
		Information Systems	
		Management	10% $63,200

WEBER STATE UNIVERSITY
JOHN B. GODDARD SCHOOL OF BUSINESS AND ECONOMICS

GENERAL INFORMATION

Type of school	Public
Environment	Village

SURVEY SAYS . . .
Friendly students
Good peer network
Cutting-edge classes
Happy students
Smart classrooms

STUDENTS

Enrollment of parent institution	16,837
Enrollment of business school	22
% male/female	81/19
% minorities	N/A
% international	2
Average age at entry	30
Average years work experience at entry	5

ACADEMICS

Academic Experience Rating	**82**
Student/faculty ratio	13
Profs interesting rating	76
Profs accessible rating	79
% female faculty	18

Academics

The MBA program at Weber State University's John B. Goddard School of Business and Economics is specially designed to meet the needs of working professionals looking to advance their careers in business. The curriculum consists of hybrid courses which combine classroom instruction with online tools, helping to enhance delivery of class material and reduce class time. All MBA classes are taught in the evenings, and the extremely flexible curriculum allows students to switch between full-time and part-time study and even arrange leaves of absence, as necessary. Therefore, Weber State is an excellent choice for returning students, as "Nontraditional students are able to complete the courses while continuing on with their busy personal lives."

Students who completed an undergraduate degree in business in the past 10 years are eligible for the fast-track MBA, a streamlined 36-credit-hour curriculum. Full-time students can complete this program in as little as 1 year. Those who do not have an undergraduate degree in business—comprising roughly half of the current business students at Goddard—are eligible for The Goddard School MBA, a 54 credit-hour program. However, if you are hoping to power through your MBA while working full-time, "The classes are structured so that I as a part time student can take two classes per semester consecutively so that I work really hard and fast and study one class at a time."

Given their professional background, students at Goddard are looking for solid, practical business expertise, and appreciate the fact that "all of the professors have great, real-life, industry knowledge to apply to their teaching skills." Fulfilling the role of academic instructor as well as professional mentor, "The professors at Weber State are much more involved in the lives and education of their students. These professors take time to get to know their students and provide guidance when students are in need." While students say there can be some headaches associated with the larger university administration, the business school is well run and student friendly. Like Weber State's affable teaching staff, "The administration seems attentive to our needs and open to our thoughts and concerns."

Not surprisingly, the academic atmosphere at Goddard is influenced by the fact that the vast majority of students are professionals. Students insist that their classmates add depth to the learning experience, describing their peers as "smart, sophisticated, and enlightening. They spur thoughts and dialogues that are unique and beneficial." "Almost every student in the program works full-time, so there is an immediate application of the subjects taught." In fact, "All students are already networking because they are almost all currently employed." Plus, there is a wide range of diversity, which further enhances the classroom discussions. A current student attests, "The undergraduate degrees in my program range from nursing to family studies. Our discussions are interesting and help me see things from different perspectives."

Career and Placement

Within the Wattis Business Building, Goddard operates a Career Services Office exclusively for business students. Staff at the Career Services Office work with Human Resources Directors to place graduates in new positions, coordinate on-campus recruiting events and interviews, and host seminars, workshops, and provide personal counseling services to business students. Their annual career fair is the largest in the region. Though most students enroll at Weber State University while continuing to work in a professional capacity, those looking for a new position reported an average starting salary of $55,025 following graduation.

Dr. Mark A. Stevenson, MBA Enrollment Director
3806 University Circle, Ogden, UT 84408-3806 United States
Phone: 801-626-7545 • Fax: 801-626-7423
E-mail: MBA@WEBER.EDU • Website: GODDARD.WEBER.EDU/DP/MBA

Student Life and Environment

Attracting a student body that is "educated, diverse, older, mature, married, busy," life at Weber State is anything but the typical college experience. In fact, students estimate that, "Most (98 percent) of my classmates are working adults with jobs. I guess that 75 percent of them have mortgages and families." As a result, most don't have time to get involved in extracurricular activities on campus, and there is "not much social interaction between students, just classwork." However, if you enjoy a lively academic atmosphere and meeting diverse and talented people, you'll have your share of fun.

For those who can find the time, "There are many opportunities to get involved in different activities" through the larger university and the business school. As the school is sensitive to the curricular needs of older students, it also understands their unique social and personal needs; in fact, "The university does a good job of providing activities, such as family-friendly movies and comedy, that the family can attend. There is also collegiate football, basketball, etc. that the family can attend for a reasonable cost."

Admissions

To apply to the Goddard School of Business and Economics, students must possess a bachelor's degree from an accredited university. The primary criteria for selection are the student's undergraduate record and GMAT performance. Current students have an average GMAT score between 560–570 and an average GPA of 3.4 on a 4.0 scale. Other factors, such as work experience and professional progression will also be considered by the Admissions Committee. Each application is evaluated individually for the applicant's ability to succeed, potential for success, and possible strengths to contribute to the program. Currently, Goddard has a 60–70 percent admissions rate.

FINANCIAL FACTS

Annual tuition (in-state/ out-of-state)	$1,793/$6,276
Cost of books	$2,000
Average grant	$3,145

ADMISSIONS

Admissions Selectivity Rating	**79**
# of applications received	63
% applicants accepted	75
% acceptees attending	94
Average GMAT	571
Range of GMAT	530–620
Average GPA	3.4
TOEFL required of international students	Yes
Minimum TOEFL (paper/computer)	550/213
Application fee	$30
Regular application deadline	7/15
Regular notification	Rolling
Deferment available	Yes
Maximum length of deferment	1 year
Transfer students accepted	Yes
Transfer application policy Transfer credits from AACSB-accredited programs accepted.	
Non-fall admissions	Yes
Need-blind admissions	Yes

Applicants Also Look At

University of Utah, Utah State University.

WEST VIRGINIA UNIVERSITY
COLLEGE OF BUSINESS AND ECONOMICS

GENERAL INFORMATION
Type of school	Public
Environment	Town
Academic calendar	Semester

SURVEY SAYS . . .
Happy students
Smart classrooms
Solid preparation in:
Teamwork

STUDENTS
Enrollment of parent institution	26,600
Enrollment of business school	216
% male/female	78/22
% out-of-state	18
% part-time	77
% minorities	20
% international	18
Average age at entry	28
Average years work experience at entry	5

ACADEMICS
Academic Experience Rating	**89**
Student/faculty ratio	17:1
Profs interesting rating	93
Profs accessible rating	77
% female faculty	18
% minority faculty	2

Joint Degrees
MBA/JD 3 years.

Prominent Alumni
John Chambers, CEO, Cisco Systems; Glen Hiner, CEO, Owens Corning; Homer Hickam, author; Ray Lane, former president and COO, Oracle; Jerry West, general manager, LA Lakers.

Academics

West Virginia University offers two distinct MBA options, each designed for a specific demographic. For young students with little professional experience and a desire to move forward quickly, WVU has designed a full-time MBA program that can be completed in just over a year. For more experienced students with a stronger business background and ongoing professional obligations, WVU offers a part-time executive MBA in eight West Virginia cities.

Both MBA options stress the integral nature of technology in modern business. One student observes, "The greatest strength of this program is the broad use of technology in the classes. I would have rated myself as an advanced user of information technology in my role of managing a number of databases before this class, and yet I have learned so much more and become even more comfortable with technology and common software packages." Although the curricula for the two programs vary, both stress the importance of teamwork and cover all major functions of business study.

The full-time program, located in Morgantown, begins with a pre-professional session designed to polish necessary business skills. It then moves through the curriculum thematically, covering such subjects as business planning, organizational skills, implementation, control, and change. Students "take one class for a period of weeks, and then a different class begins. It's a really great structure that allows you to fully concentrate on the material." The program's emphasis on "practical thinking and experience," MBAs tell us, is helpful. One explains, "I am young and do not have much business and working experience, and the MBA program has done an excellent job of easing me into the business atmosphere while challenging me to go further." Professors "make themselves available to help each student, even into the late hours of the evening, and go above and beyond the call of duty for the WVU MBA students"—another plus.

The part-time EMBA brings students to a satellite classroom, where interactive technology allows them to participate in classes with each other and the professor. Classes are videotaped to accommodate working professionals who miss class due to travel. An MBA tells us that "given the complexity of coordinating things, it is amazing how well everything has worked. Any time you are heavily dependent on technology, you expect a certain amount of inconvenience, but I have been pleasantly surprised at how well-maintained the systems are and how committed the school has been to making sure that we are all comfortable with the learning experience." Students also appreciate that "professors visit the various sites during the classes so that we actually meet them and each site gets to experience being remote and being on-site." They also tell us, "The online support given is outstanding. Anything and everything you need to know can be found by a simple Internet connection." A student complains that "too many group projects are required, meaning that additional travel to a central meeting place (one hour for me) was a common occurrence. Usually 20 to 40 percent of your grade is based upon group efforts. This undercuts a lot of the convenience of the program."

Career and Placement

The College of Business and Economics at WVU has its own dedicated Career Development Center to serve business undergraduates and graduate students. The office provides counseling services, workshops, seminars, and on-campus recruiting events.

BONNIE ANDERSON, ASSOCIATE DIRECTOR
PO BOX 6027, MORGANTOWN, WV 26506-6027 UNITED STATES
PHONE: 304-293-5408 • FAX: 304-293-2385
E-MAIL: MBA@WVU.EDU • WEBSITE: WWW.BE.WVU.EDU

Students tell us that the office seems geared mostly toward the needs of undergraduates. One writes, "The largest improvement to the program could be made with career services tailored specifically to the MBA students. The MBA program would benefit greatly by bringing reputable companies to directly meet with business students. The accounting program at WVU has an excellent relationship with the big four accounting firms. The MBA program should seek to achieve a similar relationship with a selected group of organizations."

Student Life and Environment

WVU is a pretty typical large state university, with plenty of extracurricular options for those who seek them. One student notes, "There are many things that WVU offers as special activities. They offer movies, up-all-night activities, that sort of thing. They also have a lot of shows and performers that come to campus." Football games "are always great," and "keg parties, bar crawls, and burning couches are fairly regular affairs. This is a renowned party school." Most MBAs, though, "do not have as much time to enjoy these activities as [they] did as undergrads." Hometown Morgantown "is the kind of wonderful town that you never tire of. It offers absolutely anything and everything you could want, while still holding true to a small-town atmosphere. You would have to search long and hard to match all that it offers."

It's a different story for EMBAs, whose students are "not very focused on campus life. Most people have non-university centered lives."

WVU MBAs are "a diverse group," with "work experience from a number of industries, government, and health care. Some are managers, directors, or vice presidents, while others are in staff positions. They are all willing to share their experiences and opinions." One student writes, "Even though we are so different in the class, we all pull together and work as a team and learn from each other just as much as we learn in the classes. It has been amazing."

Admissions

Applicants to the MBA program must submit official transcripts for all postsecondary academic work, an official GMAT score report, and a resume. Letters of recommendation and a statement of purpose are optional. All students must have full use of a laptop PC that meets prescribed minimum software, memory, and processor-speed requirements; contact the school or visit the website for details. Applicants to the EMBA program must have at least two years of "significant work experience." For applicants with less than five years experience, GPA and GMAT figure most heavily in the admissions decision. Professional experience, especially managerial experience, is the greater factor for applicants with at least five years of experience.

FINANCIAL FACTS

Annual tuition (in-state/ out-of-state)	$11,090/$30,114
Cost of books	$1,500
Room & board	$7,200

ADMISSIONS

Admissions Selectivity Rating	87
# of applications received	253
% applicants accepted	40
% acceptees attending	88
Average GMAT	540
Range of GMAT	488–573
Average GPA	3.4
TOEFL required of international students	Yes
Minimum TOEFL (paper/computer)	580/237
Application fee	$50
Regular application deadline	3/1
Regular notification	3/15
Early decision program?	Yes
ED Deadline/Notification	10/15 / 10/30
Deferment available	Yes
Maximum length of deferment	1 year
Transfer students accepted	Yes
Transfer application policy	
Applicants request transfer credits and the admission committee reviews the request.	
Non-fall admissions	Yes
Need-blind admissions	Yes

Applicants Also Look At

Marshall University, Rutgers, The State University of New Jersey, Syracuse University, Temple University, University of Kentucky, University of Pittsburgh, Virginia Tech.

EMPLOYMENT PROFILE

Career Rating	72	Grads Employed by Function	%	Avg. Salary
Primary Source of Full-time Job Acceptances		Finance/Accounting	2	$65,000
Average base starting salary	$53,000	Marketing/Sales	14	$41,000
		MIS	2	$55,000
		Operations/Production	6	$54,600
		General Management	2	$52,000
		Other	28	$21,000

WESTERN CAROLINA UNIVERSITY
COLLEGE OF BUSINESS

GENERAL INFORMATION
Type of school	Public
Environment	Rural
Academic calendar	Semester

SURVEY SAYS . . .
Students love Cullowhee, NC
Smart classrooms
Solid preparation in:
Accounting
General management

STUDENTS
Enrollment of parent institution	8,861
Enrollment of business school	128
% male/female	48/52
% part-time	61
% international	22
Average age at entry	28
Average years work experience at entry	7

ACADEMICS
Academic Experience Rating	**71**
Student/faculty ratio	15:1
Profs interesting rating	74
Profs accessible rating	63
% female faculty	28
% minority faculty	2

Academics

Students may pursue the Western Carolina University MBA at the school's main campus in Cullowhee or at its resident credit center in Asheville. WCU also offers a master of accountancy at the Asheville campus and a master of entrepreneurship and a master of project management as web-based programs.

WCU keeps MBA class sizes below 35 students, with many classes having as few as 15 students. Small classes free professors to employ a range of teaching techniques including team projects, case studies, in-class discussion, and lecture. Students tell us that the small size of their program means that "administration and professors are always available and easy to talk to. Most students have very good relationships with their professors. Since the MBA program here at Western is not too large, students can get to know their professors other than just in the classroom."

The WCU MBA curriculum consists of 24 credits in core courses covering managerial accounting, decision support systems, managerial economics, financial management, organizational behavior and analysis, quantitative analysis for business, strategic management, and marketing management. Students must also successfully complete 12 hours of course work in electives. Elective classes are available in the following areas: accounting; business law; information systems; economics; entrepreneurship; finance; international business; management; and marketing. Instruction is provided by "professors who are at the PhD level and are experienced teachers," though some here "wish the instructors had more experience with big business." The administration earns student praise for being "helpful in every way it can be, from signing students up for classes to sending out job vacancies from businesses."

Career and Placement

The Office of Career Services and Cooperative Education handles counseling and placement services for all undergraduate and graduate students at WCU. Services include a career library, co-op placement, one-on-one counseling, interviewing workshops, resume critiquing, online job listings, career-related personality assessment, career days, and on-campus recruitment events. Companies recruiting on campus in 2004 included Allegis Group, BB&T, Builders First Source, Cintas Corporation, Consolidated Electrical Distributors, Edward Jones, Ferguson Enterprises, Home Trust Bank, and Liberty Mutual.

Student Life and Environment

Western Carolina's main campus is located in Cullowhee, which has a "small-town atmosphere that makes it easy to focus on your studies." Cullowhee is surrounded by a rural valley between the Great Smoky Mountains and the Blue Ridge Mountains. Nearby amenities include the Blue Ridge Parkway, the Cherokee Indian Reservation, Great Smoky Mountain National Park, and a number of resorts offering golf, fishing, skiing, and other outdoor activities. Not everyone sees the town's merits, however. Complains one MBA, "To me, the town WCU is a little small. Some people enjoy that there aren't a lot of buildings and cars and people, but I enjoy larger cities with a little more going on. However, Asheville, NC is only 45 minutes away, and [it has] a lot to offer." For a real taste of city life, Atlanta, Georgia, lies two and a half hours to the southwest.

MICHAEL SMITH, DIRECTOR OF MBA PROGRAM
112 FORSYTH BUILDING, CULLOWHEE, NC 28723 UNITED STATES
PHONE: 828-227-3588 • FAX: 828-227-7414
E-MAIL: FDEITZ@EMAIL.WCU.EDU • WEBSITE: WWW.WCU.EDU/COB/MBA

WCU's MBA program includes "many students from all over the world, including Germany, Ireland, Egypt, and India" who "are very friendly and are as curious about our culture as we are of theirs." Writes one American MBA, "Here at WCU, I have learned a lot about different cultures by just simply getting to know my fellow students. It has been a fun and educational experience for me." The program also attracts many "younger part-time students with families." Most have been "pleasantly surprised by the qualities of [their] fellow students" who are, as one student puts it, "bright, friendly, motivated, and interesting people. They come from a variety of backgrounds and work experiences and are well-rounded."

WCU hosts "many clubs and organizations" and has "a movie theater on campus," all of which help to foster a "close-knit community" among full-time students. The many part-timers here, however, have little time for such diversions; explains one, "My life at school is insignificant compared to my life at work and [as] a mother of three children. However, if I had the time, there would be many opportunities to do really cool stuff at school. I read the announcements of events longingly."

Admissions

Applicants to the MBA program at Western Carolina University must submit official copies of transcripts for all academic work completed after high school and an official score report for the GMAT, and two letters of recommendation. International applicants must also submit official score reports for the TOEFL and achieve a minimum score of 79–80 on the Internet-based test, 550 on the paper test, or 213 on the computer test. International applications are due by April 1 for the fall semester and by September 1 for the spring semester.

FINANCIAL FACTS

Annual tuition (in-state/ out-of-state)	$2,173/$11,758
Fees	$2,423
Cost of books	$3,000
Room & board	$7,000
% of students receiving aid	57
% of first-year students receiving aid	75
% of students receiving loans	8
% of students receiving grants	31
Average award package	$6,730
Average grant	$2,904
Average student loan debt	$19,923

ADMISSIONS

Admissions Selectivity Rating	71
# of applications received	71
% applicants accepted	77
% acceptees attending	80
Average GMAT	505
Range of GMAT	470–550
Average GPA	3.28
TOEFL required of international students	Yes
Minimum TOEFL (paper/computer)	550/213
Application fee	$40
Regular application deadline	Rolling
Regular notification	Rolling
Deferment available	Yes
Maximum length of deferment	1 year
Transfer students accepted	Yes
Transfer application policy	Up to 6 hours of graduate credit may be transferred from an AACSB institution.
Non-fall admissions	Yes
Need-blind admissions	Yes

Applicants Also Look At

Appalachian State University, University of North Carolina at Charlotte.

WICHITA STATE UNIVERSITY
BARTON SCHOOL OF BUSINESS

Academics

At the W. Frank Barton School of Business at Wichita State University, students benefit from a traditional, management-based MBA program that offers a broad range of course work in accounting, economics, finance, management, and marketing. Depending on a student's academic background (those who studied business as an undergraduate may be able to waive some requirements), the MBA is comprised of 36 to 48 credit hours, beginning with a core curriculum that covers business fundamentals. Throughout the core curriculum, particular attention is given to understanding the organization as an integrated system. Later, students may choose an area of concentration, taking up to 19 credit hours of electives in finance, marketing, entrepreneurship, technology and operations management, or health care administration.

The school offers a fast-paced executive MBA program for high-level professionals, as well as a traditional, 2-year MBA program. Whether enrolled in the accelerated or traditional program, a majority of students work full-time while attending school in the evenings. In fact, "Most of them are professionals with aircraft industries in the Wichita area," which means a double dose of work and responsibility. However, the school is aware of its students' special needs and "is very adept at offering programs that fit the schedules of its students." On top of that, students reassure us that the workload is manageable—"substantial at times, but for the most part, the average workload is within the expected output of a graduate program."

Reporting on the great classroom experience, WSU students generally describe their professors as "candid, well spoken, knowledgeable, prepared, and fun." Unfortunately, students admit that a few staff members don't deserve such rave reviews. "There are some professors' classes I wish I could get a refund on, simply because the professors seem to be there only to earn a paycheck or a boosted ego," grumbles one student. In addition to their professors, classmates form an essential part of the learning experience at WSU. Drawing "a mix of mid-career business people and young business students," Witchita State students enjoy the fact that "everyone is very opinionated, which makes for great class discussions."

The "only AACSB-accredited school in the Wichita area," WSU is an excellent match for those who work or wish to start a career in the region, and WSU promotes a great deal of "community involvement with local businesses and entrepreneurs." Students appreciate the fact that "the school brings in wonderful special speakers and has a good reputation in the community." For example, "Recently, the CEOs of Wal-Mart and PepsiCo visited the business school." Beyond Kansas, the school also runs an "international project with Berlin School of Economics, where students taking the advanced strategic management course go to Berlin, Germany for one week and do the project there in conjunction with Berlin students."

Career and Placement

The Career Services office at Wichita State University serves the school's undergraduate and graduate community, including the business school. Through Career Services, students have access to career counseling, an online job database, and an alumni database. The office also hosts several campus career fairs and on-campus interviews.

DOROTHY HARPOOL, DIRECTOR OF GRADUATE STUDIES IN BUSINESS
1845 N. FAIRMOUNT, WICHITA, KS 67260-0048 UNITED STATES
PHONE: 316-978-3230 • FAX: 316-978-3767
E-MAIL: MBA@WICHITA.EDU • WEBSITE: WICHITA.EDU/MBA

At Wichita State, "Many students seem to be earning their MBAs in order to receive a raise or progress upward with their current employers," with a number of them also receiving tuition assistance. For those looking for a position with a new company after graduation, major employers in Wichita include Bank of America, Boeing, Bombardier Aerospace Learjet, Cargill Meat Solutions, Cessna Aircraft Company, The Coleman Company, Hawker Beechcraft, INTRUST Bank, Koch Industries, Spirit AeroSystems, Via Christi Health Systems, and York International.

Student Life and Environment

Those looking for a close-knit and community-oriented business school may be disappointed by "commuter-school" Wichita State. While they get a great business education, students admit that "the opportunities for networking are not particularly strong, as most students are too busy with work and families to attend mixers or be involved on campus." On the other hand, the atmosphere is pleasantly casual and friendly, and the community is "very diverse with local, national, and international students." A current student shares: "Even though we come from very different backgrounds and experiences, everyone seems to be incredibly open-minded and accepting to all students in the program."

The university provides plenty of extracurricular and recreational opportunities. In fact, students assure us that "if you want to do an activity and you look for one, you can find one." A case in point: One student who went from part-time to full-time status in his second year tells us, "I was surprised when I concentrated life to studies. . . . I learned a lot that I missed when I was working in my first year." Off campus, Wichita is a pleasant, low-cost, medium-sized city with plenty of cultural, financial, shopping, performing arts, festivals, and entertainment options for graduate students.

Admissions

To be considered for admissions at Wichita State University, students must possess a 4-year degree from an accredited college or university and be proficient in word processing, spreadsheet, and presentation software. Admissions decisions are made by evaluating the following: official GMAT scores, undergraduate transcript, an applicant's personal goals statement, two letters of recommendation, and a current resume. For the traditional MBA, career experience is a plus in an application package but is not required. Applicants to the executive MBA must have at least 5 years of relevant work experience. Students may apply for entry in the spring and fall semesters.

FINANCIAL FACTS

Annual tuition (in-state/ out-of-state)	$198.30/$548.20
	per credit hour
Cost of books	$1,200
Average grant	$6,000

ADMISSIONS

Admissions Selectivity Rating	**83**
# of applications received	93
% applicants accepted	60
% acceptees attending	89
Average GMAT	559
Average GPA	3.35
TOEFL required of international students	Yes
Minimum TOEFL (paper/computer)	570/230
Application fee	$35
International application fee	$50
Regular application deadline	7/1
Deferment available	Yes
Maximum length of deferment	1 year
Transfer students accepted	Yes
Transfer application policy Only AACSB-accredited classes may be transferred in.	
Non-fall admissions	Yes
Need-blind admissions	Yes

EMPLOYMENT PROFILE	
Career Rating	66

WILFRID LAURIER UNIVERSITY
SCHOOL OF BUSINESS AND ECONOMICS

GENERAL INFORMATION
Type of school   Public
Academic calendar

SURVEY SAYS . . .
Good peer network
Happy Students

STUDENTS
Enrollment of
  business school   488
% male/female   70/30
% part-time   84
% international   5
Average age at entry   30
Average years work
  experience at entry   7

ACADEMICS
Academic Experience Rating   **74**
Profs interesting rating   68
Profs accessible rating   82

Joint Degrees
MBA/CMA (certified management accountant) 3.3 years, MBA/CFA (certified financial analyst) 3.3 years, MBA/FCIP (fellow chartered insurance professional) 3.3 years.

Academics

As Canada's largest full classroom-contact MBA program, there is something for everyone at the School of Business and Economics at Wilfrid Laurier University. Whether you want to take courses during the week, during the weekend, during the day, at night, on a part-time basis, on a full-time basis, at the Waterloo campus, or at the satellite campus in Toronto, chances are there is going to be an MBA format option at Laurier that suits your needs. In addition, the school's many MBA options cater to students from all professional and academic backgrounds. At Laurier, business executives have the opportunity to get a high-speed degree though the school's accelerated MBA program, while students with no previous work experience may apply to the "co-op" program, designed to help business newcomers develop their managerial and organizational skills. In addition, many students come to Laurier because it offers "the ability to get a professional designation (i.e., CMA, CFA) along with the MBA" through several joint-degree programs.

No matter how, when, or where they pursue an MBA, Laurier students appreciate the school's commitment to the case-based learning method, which "requires that you understand both the theory and then apply them in real-world situations." Emphasizing practical competence over strict academic theory, "The Laurier experience builds your thinking skills and allows you to attack complex problems from many angles." Discussion and debate are fundamental to the program, and "Almost all courses include a group work component which promotes the teamwork abilities within each student." This interaction is an undeniable asset to the MBA education, since many "Students are already at the manager/director level in their careers." A current student praises the professors, saying, "Not only do they contribute to the learning experience due to their vast work experiences, but they are very willing to help out both within the classroom and outside of it (networking)."

The core curriculum takes an "integrated" approach to business topics, which "allows you to cement concepts since you are dealing with them in multiple courses at the same time." After completing the core, students can tailor their education through a concentration in a number of fields (such as finance, accounting, brand communication management, supply chain management, or international business to name a few) by completing at least four courses in that subject area. They may also add breadth to their education through one of the school's international programs in Europe and Asia, or through the school's ample list of special seminars.

At the top of their field, Laurier professors are an excellent "mix of tenured professors and recognized, practicing professionals." Most "are PhDs and have recent/relevant consulting or real business experience." Friendly, down to earth, and well run, administrators at Laurier "communicate frequently with students and have always responded to questions very quickly."

Career and Placement

Career Services for the School of Business and Economics Graduate Programs provides assistance to MBA and MABE students and alumni. Their services include one-on-one career counseling and specialized workshops on topics such as resume writing, networking, interviewing, and cocktail and dining etiquette. Career Services also hosts special events, such as executive recruiter panels.

Students agree that their school enjoys a great reputation in Canada, telling us that "employers love Laurier MBA students because they are much better educated and

Maureen Ferraro or Susan Manning-Faber, MBA Marketing Coordinator's
75 University Avenue West, Waterloo, ON N2L3C5 Canada
Phone: 519-884-0710 • Fax: 519-886-6978
E-mail: mbawlu@wlu.ca • Website: www.wlu.ca/mba

friendlier to work with." The following companies are among the extensive list of organizations recruiting Laurier MBAs from 2004 to 2005: Accenture, American Express Canada, Bank of Canada, Canada Revenue Agency, CIBC World Markets, CPP Investment Board, Dell Canada, Deloitte Touche Tohmatsu, FedEx Canada, GE Canada, General Mills Canada, General Motors Canada, IBM Canada, The Loyalty Group, Managerial Design, Manulife Financial, National Bank Financial, Proctor & Gamble, Raytheon Canada, RLG International, Scotiabank Group, and TD Securities.

Student Life and Environment

With such a large and diverse student population, it's hard to summarize life at Laurier. Not surprisingly, there is something of a split between students who attend the program part-time and those who chose to pursue their studies full-time. There are two campuses in the Wilfrid Laurier University MBA program. One is on the Waterloo-based university campus and the other is a satellite campus right in downtown Toronto. Part-timers attending school at the Toronto MBA campus sometimes feel a little cut off from the main campus. However, Toronto students are required to participate in MBA events and competitions at the Waterloo campus.

In both locations, the majority of students are "mature with an established career and family life." For most, "Life happens off campus," and students admit that there isn't much enthusiasm for campus activities or after-hours socializing. "Social activities with the satellite or main campus are limited due to work/family commitments in addition to academic demands," explains a current MBA candidate.

With many personal and professional commitments, most students at Laurier are talented multitaskers, who "are very good at balancing personal, work, and school life." However, they warn that the many group assignments, homework, and classes can make it difficult to juggle your educational, professional, and personal life. A student laments, "You have to be tough skinned to do an MBA on a part-time basis at WLU."

Admissions

To be considered for admission to Wilfrid Laurier University's MBA program, students must possess a 4-year, undergraduate degree (in any field of study) with at least a B average in the last 10 half-credit courses taken. Except for the MBA with co-op option (for which no work experience is required), applicants must have at least 2 years of full-time work experience to apply for an MBA at Laurier. Students must also submit a GMAT score of at least 550. In addition to test scores and transcripts, students must send three letters of recommendation from professional and academic references.

FINANCIAL FACTS
Annual tuition (in-state/ out-of-state)	$17,100/$20,470
Cost of books	$5,120

ADMISSIONS
Admissions Selectivity Rating	**81**
# of applications received	474
% applicants accepted	69
% acceptees attending	65
Average GMAT	600
Range of GMAT	550–710
Average GPA	3.3
TOEFL required of international students	Yes
Minimum TOEFL (paper/computer)	573/230
Application fee	$100
Regular application deadline	5/1
Regular notification	Rolling
Deferment available	Yes
Maximum length of deferment	1 year (case-by-case)
Non-fall admissions	Yes
Need-blind admissions	Yes

Applicants Also Look At
Brock University, McMaster University, Queen's University, University of Toronto, York University.

EMPLOYMENT PROFILE	
Career Rating	77

WILLAMETTE UNIVERSITY
ATKINSON GRADUATE SCHOOL OF MANAGEMENT

Academics

Willamette University is an excellent place for early-career professionals to get their feet wet in the world of business. This small MBA program is "tailored more to those students with less work experience"; therefore, business theory and academic course work is heavily augmented by hands-on projects. Of the numerous experiential learning programs at Willamette, many mention the excellence of the school's Private, Public, and Community Enterprise program (or PACE program), through which students develop business plans for venture capitalist approval and provide management consulting for a client organization. Through such projects, students develop their skills in "teamwork, time-management, managing expectations, presentation, HR, organizational development, market research, delegation, consulting, and a view of the world of an entrepreneur." A current student attests, "My overall experience has allowed me to grow a lot, and given me the skills that I will need to leverage into the workplace."

In the classroom, professors "make it a point to stay on top of the latest trends and make learning about business fun." Group work is fundamental to the core curriculum, during which students "are paired with 12 other students for the first year to work on various team assignments." Boasting a student body that is "motivated, driven, ethical, friendly, and non-competitive," team-building opportunities are among the most attractive aspects of the Willamette MBA. One student describes it this way: "One of the biggest benefits of Atkinson is the ability to gain cross-cultural understanding. Herding cats? Try reaching consensus in a group made up of people from India, Japan, Romania, and Texas." Another adds, "For being a small school in Oregon's pristine nature, the program is intellectually diverse with a global outlook."

While the program is excellent for newbies, those with a more extensive professional background are less satisfied with Willamette, complaining that "students with previous work experience shouldn't have to be forced to take a career class." Though the class does provide tools needed for successful transitions to internships and future professional positions. For more experienced students, Atkinson recently opened a professional MBA program in Portland, Oregon. However, full-timers also warn us that the school is still ironing out the kinks: "The same professors are used at both locations, and it is obvious to full-time students that the professors feel very overwhelmed and compromised for out-of-class availability." To address these growing pains, the school has hired additional faculty.

Career and Placement

When it's time to look for a job, Willamette students benefit from their school's "great regional reputation" and loyal alumni network. "If you want to work in the Pacific Northwest after graduation, our alumni network is going to be so valuable to you," insists a current student.

From day one, career development is taken seriously, and a course entitled Integration and Professional Development is a required part of the core curriculum. In addition, Career Services at Willamette helps MBAs define and achieve their career goals through career counseling, career fairs, professional organizations, peer advisors, workplace site visits, networking events, Internet resources, and more. Career Services also operates a mentorship program, which "allows for additional contacts and networking opportunities." While they are loaded down with tools and resources, students suggest you be somewhat of a self-starter when it comes to the career search, as "on-campus recruiting seems almost nonexistent." Many Northwest companies prefer to interview at their own site and through the Northwest MBA Career Day consortium while working with the school's career services office.

JUDY O'NEILL, DIRECTOR OF ADMISSION
900 STATE STREET, SALEM, OR 97301 UNITED STATES
PHONE: 503-370-6167 • FAX: 503-370-3011
E-MAIL: MBA-ADMISSION@WILLAMETTE.EDU • WEBSITE: WWW.WILLAMETTE.EDU/MBA

In 2006, 66 percent of full-time MBA students had accepted a job offer by graduation, and 88 percent had accepted a job offer within three months of graduation. Companies that recently hired Willamette grads include Digimarc, Ernst & Young, The Gallup Organization, Harrah's Lake Tahoe, Intel, Kaiser Permanente, Microsoft, Nordstrom, Russell Investments, Saber, The Boeing Company, US Bank, and Vision Plastics.

Student Life and Environment

Life as a Willamette MBA is "intense, rewarding, and worthwhile." Be prepared for some late nights and coffee drinking. "The first year is a pressure cooker," and students say you can expect 80 or more hours of academic activities per week. Fortunately, studying and socializing go hand-in-hand at Willamette, where students "spend a lot of time working together, and, hence, we also relax together."

In this tiny program, "Students build strong relationships in the first-year core classes," and during the course of their 22 months of study, students "become a big family." In addition, "There is a good camaraderie among business students and law students, whose college is directly across the street from the Atkinson building. We participate in joint courses, which diversify the perspectives and group learning in class. The two graduate schools even participate in extracurricular functions together, such as a bowling league."

Outside the classroom, "There are more than enough ways to get involved and be social with our classmates," whether it's tipping back a beer at the bar or playing on an intramural sports team. An oft-mentioned pleasure is the weekly Thursday Night Out, "where staff, faculty, students, and spouses/others network and socialize," at a local venue. While Salem is a small town, students say it enjoys an idyllic location close to the charming city of Portland and lies "only an hour from the beach and an hour and a half from the mountains."

Admissions

Applicants to the full-time MBA must submit the application, GMAT or GRE score, references, and undergraduate transcripts. Qualified applicants are invited to interview. Last year's entering class had a mean GMAT score of 597 and a mean undergraduate GPA of 3.3. Thirty-eight percent of Willamette MBAs studied liberal arts or social sciences in college. The full-time MBA program is designed for students with little or no professional experience. Applicants to the Professional MBA Program must submit the application, GMAT score, references and undergraduate transcripts. A minimum of three years of professional experience is required for the Professional MBA.

FINANCIAL FACTS

Annual tuition	$23,330
Fees	$50
Cost of books	$1,200
Room & board (on/off-campus)	$12,000/$11,000
% of students receiving aid	79
% of first-year students receiving aid	79
% of students receiving loans	70
% of students receiving grants	70
Average award package	$19,392
Average grant	$13,000
Average student loan debt	$31,941

ADMISSIONS

Admissions Selectivity Rating	81
# of applications received	143
% applicants accepted	67
% acceptees attending	52
Average GMAT	597
Range of GMAT	543–638
Average GPA	3.3
TOEFL required of international students	Yes
Minimum TOEFL (paper/computer)	570/230
Application fee	$50
Regular application deadline	5/1
Regular notification	Rolling
Application Deadline/Notification	
Round 1:	1/12 / Rolling
Round 2:	3/1 / Rolling
Round 3:	5/1 / Rolling
Deferment available	Yes
Maximum length of deferment	1 year
Transfer students accepted	Yes
Transfer application policy	
May transfer up to six credits of MBA course work to the full-time MBA program with the approval of the dean.	
Need-blind admissions	Yes

Applicants Also Look At

Oregon State University, Pepperdine University, Portland State University, Stanford University, University of Oregon, University of Portland, University of Washington.

EMPLOYMENT PROFILE

Career Rating	65	Grads Employed by Function	%	Avg. Salary
Primary Source of Full-time Job Acceptances		Finance/Accounting	33	$56,828
School-facilitated activities	10 (27%)	Human Resources	8	$43,333
Graduate-facilitated activities	26 (73%)	Marketing/Sales	11	$50,750
Percent employed	21	Operations/Production	14	$66,250
		Consulting	8	$68,533
		Entrepreneurship	4	NR
		General Management	3	$92,000
		Other	12	NR
		Nonprofit	7:	$64,260

Top 5 Employers Hiring Grads
Saber Consulting; Ernst & Young; Intel Corporation; Providence Health Systems; Nike, Inc.

WORCESTER POLYTECHNIC INSTITUTE
DEPARTMENT OF MANAGEMENT

GENERAL INFORMATION
Type of school   Private
Academic calendar   Semester

SURVEY SAYS . . .
Cutting-edge classes
Solid preparation in:
Finance
Accounting
General management
Presentation skills
Quantitative skills

STUDENTS
Enrollment of parent institution	3,903
Enrollment of business school	225
% male/female	70/30
% out-of-state	50
% part-time	95
% minorities	14
% international	25
Average age at entry	32
Average years work experience at entry	8

ACADEMICS
Academic Experience Rating	**80**
Student/faculty ratio	11:1
Profs interesting rating	82
Profs accessible rating	83
% female faculty	46
% minority faculty	4

Joint Degrees
BS/MBA 5 years

Prominent Alumni
Paul Allaire, chairman and CEO, Xerox Corporation; Judith Nitsch, president, Judith Nitsch Engineering, Inc.; Windle Priem, president and CEO, Korn/Ferry International; Stephen Rubin, president and CEO, Intellution, Inc.; Ronald Zarella, president, GM North America.

Academics

The MBA program at Worcester Polytechnic Institute unites a broad-based degree in business essentials with highly specialized instruction on technology and technology management. One of the oldest technical universities in the United States, "WPI is an engineering school first and foremost" that built its reputation on its strong programs in science and technology. Given the school's legacy, students agree that "the addition of a technology-oriented business program is a natural progression that WPI is uniquely suited to provide." The 49-credit hour MBA program begins with foundation courses, such as economics and accounting, followed by a set of core courses, designed to integrate foundational concepts. Naturally, all course work is taught from a technological perspective and practical applications to business theory are emphasized. After completing the core requirements, students tailor their education through a concentration in challenging fields such as information security management, operations management, or technological innovation. In addition to electives offered through the business school, WPI students can enroll in graduate-level electives in other departments, including computer science, biomedical engineering, and electrical engineering. While students choose WPI for its highly pointed focus on technical subject areas, they also suggest that the school make an effort to "team with other universities nationwide to provide an even more diverse curriculum."

Offering the opportunity to pursue an MBA entirely online or through a mix of classroom and online courses, many students gravitate to Worcester Polytechnic Institute for its flexible scheduling options. At Worcester, busy professionals appreciate "the ability to take classes remotely even if my career required me to travel around the world from time to time." Offering a web-based program since 1998, students reassure us that the school maintains high academic standards, even for virtual students. In the words of one, "I am currently an online student and find the online classes very thorough, organized, and convenient." As if we would expect any less, students also report that "the technical support is phenomenal. They make the whole thing work so seamlessly that you feel spoiled. If all IT/IS departments were this effective, the world would be a much more efficient place."

In the classroom, students appreciate the quality of the teaching staff, saying their professors are "extremely up to date and have a genuine affection toward their students. They work very hard to make the experience positive and exciting." The program's extensive project-based work "gives a good amount of experience in applying the theories taught and prepares students well for applying lessons in the real world." Teamwork is also a crucial part of the learning experience, and even online courses include "virtual teams," who meet via the Internet. Across the board, students agree that "WPI is a well-run institution that exhibits a high degree of consistency." A current student adds, "The administration is also top-notch. They have an unusually quick response time to problem resolution and provide excellent advice."

Career and Placement

A high percentage of WPI students work full-time, many receiving tuition reimbursement from their current company while pursuing the MBA. Therefore, most will continue at the same company after completing the WPI program. However, those considering a career change can receive support and guidance through the university's Career Development Center, which serves the undergraduate, graduate, and alumni population. The CDC offers career counseling, workshops, and assessments, and maintains contact with regional employers and WPI alumni. The CDC also hosts several annual campus career fairs.

Norm Wilkinson, Director, Graduate Management Programs
100 Institute Road, Worcester, MA 01609 United States
Phone: 508-831-5218 • Fax: 508-831-5720
E-mail: gmp@wpi.edu • Website: www.mgt.wpi.edu

According to statistics published by the Career Development Center, MBA graduates in 2005 were offered an average salary of $91,500.

Student Life and Environment

At WPI, students are "mostly male in their 30s," pursuing a degree part-time or online while continuing to work in a professional capacity. Those who attend classes on campus enjoy the company of their classmates, saying they "come from various backgrounds and work experiences, but all seem bright and eager to be part of the MBA program." There are plenty of clubs and activities offered through the larger university—though be forewarned that the technology focus extends well beyond the classroom. A student elaborates, "Like most schools there are the sports and social clubs, but there are also many opportunities for students with a passion for science to feed their 'inner geek.'"

Set on 80 acres in the small New England town of Worcester, Massachusetts, the WPI campus boasts a pleasant collegiate atmosphere, excellent student facilities, and, of course, first-rate technological resources. A part-time student shares, "Being part-time, I spend time on campus once or twice a week and find the classrooms and student center to be quite usable and very inviting." Since there isn't a virtual campus (yet), most distance students aren't involved in the community and "do not go to campus except to meet with professors." While they certainly keep busy with school and work, some say they'd like the school to "find ways to connect the off-campus part-time students with on-campus activities."

Admissions

The MBA program at Worcester Polytechnic Institute accepts students whose academic and professional record demonstrates the ability to excel in a challenging, technology-focused graduate program. Students are analyzed on the basis of their academic and professional performance, as well as their career goals and personal statement. In addition, all applicants must have demonstrated capacity to succeed in a technology-driven management program; therefore, a minimum of three semesters of college-level math or two semesters of college-level calculus are a prerequisite of the program. To apply, students must submit undergraduate transcripts, official GMAT scores, three letters of recommendation, and a completed application form.

FINANCIAL FACTS

Annual tuition	$24,427
Fees	$85
Cost of books	$1,100
Room & board (off-campus)	$8,100
% of students receiving aid	65
% of first-year students receiving aid	75
% of students receiving loans	33
% of students receiving grants	65
Average award package	$4,800
Average grant	$35,000

ADMISSIONS

Admissions Selectivity Rating	78
# of applications received	84
% applicants accepted	77
% acceptees attending	52
Average GMAT	610
Range of GMAT	580–690
Average GPA	3.35
TOEFL required of international students	Yes
Minimum TOEFL (paper/computer)	550/213
Application fee	$70
Regular application deadline	8/1
Regular notification	Rolling
Deferment available	Yes
Maximum length of deferment	1 year
Transfer students accepted	Yes
Transfer application policy	
Accepted transfer applicants may transfer in up to 9 prior graduate-level credits toward the WPI MBA.	
Non-fall admissions	Yes
Need-blind admissions	Yes

Applicants Also Look At

Babson College, Bentley College, Boston College, Boston University, Massachusetts Institute of Technology, Northeastern University, University of Massachusetts Amherst.

EMPLOYMENT PROFILE

Career Rating	96	Grads Employed by Function	%	Avg. Salary
Primary Source of Full-time Job Acceptances		Operations/Production	50	$105,000
School-facilitated activities	1 (50%)	Communications	50	$78,000
Graduate-facilitated activities	1 (50%)			
Average base starting salary	$91,500			

XAVIER UNIVERSITY
WILLIAMS COLLEGE OF BUSINESS

Academics

The Williams College of Business at Xavier University combines three things that students respect: "academic excellence," a "strong reputation," and "scheduling convenience" to fit in the lives of working professionals. All students at Xavier are required to have a foundation in basic business skills courses, which comprise 20 of the 36 to 60 credit hours required for graduation. Students may then concentrate in e-business, finance, business administration, international business, management information systems, or marketing. They may take courses offered in the evening, generally meeting one day a week, or they may choose a weekend MBA option. With substantial work experience (and usually financial support from an employer), students may also choose an executive MBA option, which meets one full day a week for 19 months.

Whatever option they choose, students like the fact that Xavier has "the best reputation in the Midwest for an MBA," and they find the quality of teaching upholds that reputation. "Professors are very passionate about their respective subjects, and most seem to have tremendous past work experience to help shed light on them," a student says. "Talented faculty who are experts in their areas," and "instructors who understand what is happening in the real world and have experience to share" make students feel their investment in working toward an MBA is worthwhile. Xavier is a private school based on centuries of Jesuit educational tradition, and students find "no hard-bitten civil servants here. Professors get who their students are," and "they have high expectations" as well being as "accessible outside the classroom and going the extra mile when you need help." Some, however, "wish classes were more in-depth and more technical," and they would like to see Xavier "offering more graduate-level electives and concentrations that apply to the business community."

Across the board, students praise a concerned administrative staff. "They are very good about facilitating learning rather than just throwing you out there and hoping you can swim," one student points out, and another offers that "Xavier's administration of the MBA program is exceptional. From communication with students to outside seminars and career development and skills workshops, Xavier goes above and beyond to provide students with the tools they need to succeed." When problems do arise, "Any road bumps encountered along the way" are "quickly resolved," and "This school makes all administrative matters a snap," students agree.

Career and Placement

Three out of four MBA students at Williams College of Business attend part-time because they are already working; still, many feel the Professional Development Center, as well as Xavier's alumni network, is helpful to them as they consider new opportunities. In addition to the career fairs, workshops, and networking events offered by the center, students may also tap into the networking resources of other members of a consortium of Jesuit business schools. "Strong alumni ties to corporate community," is an aspect many students point to as an asset, although "helping students with job placements and internships outside of Cincinnati" is an area that some students feel needs improving. In general, though, students are satisfied with the assistance they receive in career planning and placement. "The administration is constantly keeping students in the loop regarding career opportunities," one student says, summing up the feelings of colleagues.

GE, Proctor & Gamble, Hewlett-Packard, Fifth Third Bank, Convergys, and International Paper are among the companies which have employed Xavier's MBA graduates.

JENNIFER BUSH, EXECUTIVE DIRECTOR, MBA PROGRAMS
3800 VICTORY PARKWAY, CINCINNATI, OH 45207 UNITED STATES
PHONE: 513-745-3525 • FAX: 513-745-2929
E-MAIL: XUMBA@XAVIER.EDU • WEBSITE: WWW.XAVIER.EDU/MBA

Student Life and Environment

In common with most graduate programs where the majority of students attend part-time, there's a mixed bag of feelings about student life among those in Xavier's MBA program. Besides course work "The only other interaction is maybe going out for a beer after class"; one student says, "We spend time in classes together but have other lives, and so we do not interact or network as much I would like in order to make connections that would help my career advancement," though the school does provide options. "Everyone is going through the same experience, and everyone is understanding of this. Everyone is helpful in classes and out. Easy to network with and helpful in that respect as well." Most Xavier MBA students agree that "students are hardworking but friendly. Most are open to, and expect to, learn from other students and their experiences. Everyone strives to do well and is [more] interested in helping others succeed [than hoping they fail]." It's no surprise that the program is made up of "very driven, type-A personalities." Students find that "Xavier has the feeling of a small town where everyone knows everyone. It has a relaxed atmosphere where academics are a priority."

Admissions

Williams College of Business at Xavier offers paper and online application methods. Either way, students must submit a resume, transcripts, and scores on the GMAT, with an optional personal statement. While prior work experience is not required for the weekend and weeknight MBA programs, the executive MBA requires that students have substantial management experience, or hold a PhD, JD, or other higher-level degree. Those admitted to that program recently have 8 years of work experience. Across all programs, the average undergraduate GPA of those admitted in 2006 is 3.2, and the average GMAT score is 550.

FINANCIAL FACTS

Annual tuition	$11,340
Cost of books	$900
% of students receiving aid	25
% of students receiving loans	25
% of students receiving grants	38
Average grant	$975

ADMISSIONS

Admissions Selectivity Rating	**78**
# of applications received	666
% applicants accepted	67
% acceptees attending	83
Average GMAT	550
Range of GMAT	470–640
Average GPA	3.2
TOEFL required of international students	Yes
Minimum TOEFL (paper/computer)	550/213
Application fee	$35
Deferment available	Yes
Maximum length of deferment	1 year
Transfer students accepted	Yes
Transfer application policy 6 hours of core curriculum from AACSB-accredited programs only; up to 18 hours of core curriculum from AACSB-accredited Jesuit MBA Network Schools.	
Non-fall admissions	Yes
Need-blind admissions	Yes

Applicants Also Look At

Miami University Ohio, Northern Kentucky University, University of Cincinnati.

EMPLOYMENT PROFILE

Career Rating	84	Grads Employed by Function	%	Avg. Salary
Primary Source of Full-time Job Acceptances		Finance/Accounting	30	$63,300
School-facilitated activities	68 (83%)	Human Resources	21	$60,000
Graduate-facilitated activities	11 (13%)	Marketing/Sales	9	$63,200
Average base starting salary	$90	MIS	20	$61,100
Percent employed	15	Operations/Production	16	$61,200
		Consulting	3	$63,100
		Other	1	$62,100

Top 4 Employers Hiring Grads
Procter & Gamble; GE Aircraft Engines; Cintas; Fidelity Investments.

YALE UNIVERSITY
SCHOOL OF MANAGEMENT

GENERAL INFORMATION

Type of school	Private
Environment	City
Academic calendar	Semester

SURVEY SAYS . . .
Good social scene
Good peer network
Cutting-edge classes
Helpful alumni
Happy students
Solid preparation in:
Finance
General management
Teamwork

STUDENTS

Enrollment of parent institution	11,483
Enrollment of business school	425
% male/female	64/36
% minorities	10
% international	21
Average age at entry	28

ACADEMICS

Academic Experience Rating	**98**
Student/faculty ratio	5:1
Profs interesting rating	83
Profs accessible rating	95
% female faculty	17
% minority faculty	1

Joint Degrees
JD/MBA (with Yale Law School) 4 years, MBA/MD (with Yale School of Medicine) 5 years, MBA/MARCH (with Yale School of Architecture) 4 years, MBA/MFA (with Yale School of Drama) 4 years, MBA/MDIV or MAR (with Yale Divinity School) 3 years, MBA/MEM or MF (with Yale School of Forestry and Environmental Studies) 3 years, MBA/MPH (with Yale School of Public Health) 3 years, MBA/PhD (with Yale Graduate School of Arts and Sciences). MBA/MA international relations, Eastern European studies (with Yale Graduate School of Arts and Sciences).

Academics

An MBA program "outside the box," Yale University's School of Management distinguishes itself though an unparalleled "emphasis on social issues and integrity" coupled with the prestige and quality of the Yale name. "Top ranked for social enterprise and nonprofit management" as well as for its finance programs, the school aims to educate global leaders for business and society, promoting purpose, creativity, passion, and accountability among its students and faculty. Attracting a diverse and accomplished student body, Yale's talented business students are "not number-crunching machines or ultra-competitive politicians"; rather they are intelligent leaders and innovators, who "strive for excellence, but still care about the ethical implications of how things are done."

The core MBA curriculum at Yale recently underwent a serious overhaul, the result of which is a first-year program that presents a "highly interdisciplinary, integrated approach to learning the fundamentals of business management." Built around eight multidisciplinary courses called Organizational Perspectives, the new core curriculum is cutting edge—the product of the "commitment to curriculum innovation among faculty and administration." In fact, the new program is so enticing that a second-year student laments, "I totally have 'core envy' and wish I could go back and take the core as it currently is!"

Beyond core courses, "a wide range of electives provide ample opportunity to expand my horizons." Plus, lucky Yale students "don't have to worry about getting into classes; this semester 99.9 percent of second-year students got into all of their first-choice classes." Part of a renowned university, there are "many different ideas and paths here outside the traditional-stereotype MBA track," including the "opportunity to integrate classes from other schools at Yale." In particular, many students mention the school's "strong joint-degree program with the Yale School of Forestry and Environmental Studies."

When it comes to faculty, Yale draws big names in every subject area, and some "classes are taught by 'executives in residence'—the former CEO of JPMorgan Capital or the co-founder of Marakon Associates." The rigorous course work is counterbalanced by the fact that "the professors are excellent instructors and are very accessible outside of class." On top of that, the "warm, interpersonal dynamic" on campus creates the perfect salve for business school slavery. In addition, students dole out praises for the school's "open and innovative" administration—especially the dynamic Dean Podolny, who "makes it a priority to be available for the students, be it through monthly breakfasts or over e-mail in which he responds within 24 hours."

Career and Placement

The Career Development Office at the Yale School of Management helps place students in a variety of positions and industries. Through the CDO, students have access to one-on-one career counseling, mock interviews, and special workshops on resume writing, career searches, networking, and negotiation. The CDO also hosts career fairs, company presentations, and on-campus interviews. Needless to say, Yale students enjoy a "huge brand name," which adds some serious sparkle to your postgraduate career search.

In 2006, 46 percent of Yale grads took jobs in financial services, and another 15 percent in consulting. The top hiring companies were: Lehman Brothers, Citigroup, Washington Mutual, General Electric Company, Hartford Financial Services, Merrill Lynch, American Express Company, Standard & Poor's, Technoserve, Banc of America Securities, Barclay's Capital, JPMorgan Chase, Johnson & Johnson, MBIA, PepsiCo, and Proctor & Gamble. Grads in 2006 earned a median base salary of $95,000 with a median signing bonus of $20,000.

BRUCE DELMONICO, DIRECTOR OF ADMISSIONS
135 PROSPECT STREET, PO BOX 208200, NEW HAVEN, CT 06520-8200 UNITED STATES
PHONE: 203-432-5635 • FAX: 203-432-7004
E-MAIL: MBA.ADMISSIONS@YALE.EDU • WEBSITE: WWW.MBA.YALE.EDU

Student Life and Environment

The friendliness, talent, and diversity of the student body is one of the most unique and enviable aspects of a Yale education. Hardly cookie-cutter future executives, "Students come from a wide range of backgrounds, have a variety of job and life experiences, and have a broad range of professional and personal interests, passions, and hobbies." On the whole, Yale students are "more liberal in their thinking and progressive in their politics" than you would traditionally find at a business school program. This year's class tried to level the playing field with the addition of a Conservative Club—though, to date, they have only two members.

An active academic and social environment, "students are usually involved in half a dozen different clubs, consulting and research projects. Often, students spend as much on organizing and participating nonclass activities as in actual class time." From dinners to ski trips, there are tons of regular social events for business students, including an "excellent happy hour every Thursday, with faculty and administrators joining in the fun."

Yale is "a great place to make lifelong friendships," boasting a highly friendly and inclusive atmosphere. A current student exclaims, "It is hard to have a party without inviting the whole class—both because you want to include everyone, and because it is such a tight-knit group!" Off campus, there is plenty of nightlife in this bustling college town, and students admit that "the small city of New Haven facilitates stronger networking and relationship-building with classmates." However, when they are ready for the bright lights, Yale is situated "close enough to New York and Boston to take advantage of the big city during the weekends."

Admissions

The Admissions Committee at Yale University School of Management seeks accomplished students with highly diverse professional and academic experience. Recent admits come from a range of backgrounds (69% private, 22% public, and 9% government), including such unlikely fields as jewelry design, athletics, medicine, nonprofit organizations, and the performing arts. The school does not publish any specific admissions standards; however, the class of 2008 had an average GMAT score of 701 and an average college GPA of 3.4. Women comprise 38 percent of the entering class at Yale School of Management.

Prominent Alumni

John Thornton, former co-COO and president, Goldman Sachs; Nancy Peretsman, managing director, Allen and Company; Indra Nooyi, CEO, PepsiCo Inc.; Fred Terrell, managing partner and CEO, Provender Capital Group; Timothy Collins, CEO and senior managing director, Ripplewood Holding.

FINANCIAL FACTS

Annual tuition	$39,500
Fees	$1,700
Cost of books	$7,200
Room & board	$13,000
% of students receiving aid	77
% of first-year students receiving aid	75
% of students receiving loans	71
% of students receiving grants	48
Average award package	$34,860
Average grant	$16,360
Average student loan debt	$76,456

ADMISSIONS

Admissions Selectivity Rating	**98**
# of applications received	2,220
% applicants accepted	22
% acceptees attending	43
Average GMAT	701
Average GPA	3.46
TOEFL required of international students	Yes
Minimum TOEFL (paper/computer)	600/250
Application fee	$180
Application Deadline/Notification	
Round 1:	10/25 / 1/19
Round 2:	1/10 / 4/5
Round 3:	3/14 / 5/18
Need-blind admissions	Yes

Applicants Also Look At

Harvard University, University of Pennsylvania.

EMPLOYMENT PROFILE

Career Rating	94	Grads Employed by Function	%	Avg. Salary
Primary Source of Full-time Job Acceptances		Finance/Accounting	49	$94,217
Average base starting salary	$92,213	Marketing/Sales	12	$90,675
Percent employed	92	Operations/Production	12	$101,333
		Consulting	25	$95,826
		General Management	7	$84,135
		Other	5	$70,924

Top 5 Employers Hiring Grads

Credit Suisse; IBM Strategy; Microsoft; Standard and Poor's; Lehman Brothers.

Part III-B
Business School Data
Listings

ARIZONA STATE UNIVERSITY— WEST

SCHOOL OF GLOBAL MANAGEMENT & LEADERSHIP

ADMISSIONS CONTACT: *Graduate Programs Admissions*
ADDRESS: *PO Box 37100, Phoenix, AZ 85069-7100*
PHONE: *602-543-6201 • Fax: 602-543-6249*
E-MAIL: *GRADPROGRAMS@ASU.EDU*
WEBSITE: *WWW.WEST.ASU.EDU/SGML/GRAD*

GENERAL INFORMATION
Type of School: public **Environment:** city **Academic Calendar:** semester

STUDENTS
Enrollment of Parent Institution: 55,000 **Male/female:** 100/0 % **Part-time:** 100 **Average Age at Entry:** 35 **Average Years Work Experience at Entry:** 9

ACADEMICS
Student/faculty Ratio: 20:1 **% Female Faculty:** 29 **% Minority Faculty:** 12

FINANCIAL FACTS
Tuition (in-state/out-of-state): $194/$510 (per credit hour)

ADMISSIONS
Admissions Selectivity Rating: 76

Applicants Accepted: 93 **% Acceptees Attending:** 100 **GMAT Range (25th to 75th percentile):** 450–700 **Average GMAT:** 590 **Average GPA:** 3.5 **TOEFL Required of Int'l Applicants:** yes **Minimum TOEFL (paper/computer):** 600/250 **Application Fee:** $50 **Non-fall Admissions:** yes **Applicants Also Look At:** Arizona State University, Northern Arizona University, University of Arizona.

EMPLOYMENT PROFILE
Grads Employed by Industry:.......%

Finance/Accounting	15
Human Resources	1
Marketing/Sales	20
MIS	6
Operations/Production	24
Strategic Planning	1
Consulting	6
Communications	1
General Management	7
Other	10

ARKANSAS STATE UNIVERSITY

COLLEGE OF BUSINESS

ADMISSIONS CONTACT: *Dr. Thomas Wheeler, Dean, Graduate School*
ADDRESS: *PO Box 60, State University, AR 72467*
PHONE: *870-972-3029 • Fax: 870-972-3857*
E-MAIL: *GRADSCH@CHOCTAW.ASTATE.EDU*
WEBSITE: *BUSINESS.ASTATE.EDU*

GENERAL INFORMATION
Type of School: public **Environment:** town **Academic Calendar:** semester

STUDENTS
Enrollment of Business School: 104

ACADEMICS
Student/faculty Ratio: 25:1 **% Female Faculty:** 24 **% Minority Faculty:** 1

FINANCIAL FACTS
Tuition (in-state/out-of-state): $1,488/$3,744 **Books and Supplies:** $2,100 **Room & Board (on):** $3,500 **Average Grant:** $6,427

ADMISSIONS
Admissions Selectivity Rating: 60*

# of Applications Received: 53 **% Applicants Accepted:** 85 % **Acceptees Attending:** 80 **TOEFL Required of Int'l Applicants:** yes **Minimum TOEFL (paper):** 550 **Regular Application Deadline:** rolling **Regular Notification:** rolling

ASHRIDGE (UNITED KINGDOM)

ASHRIDGE BUSINESS SCHOOL

ADMISSIONS CONTACT: *MBA Admissions*
ADDRESS: *Berkhamsted, Hertfordshire, HP4 1NS England*
PHONE: *001 44 1442 841143 • Fax: 001 44 1442 841144*
E-MAIL: *MBA@ASHRIDGE.ORG.UK*
WEBSITE: *WWW.ASHRIDGE.ORG.UK*

GENERAL INFORMATION
Type of School: private **Academic Calendar:** January to December

STUDENTS
Enrollment of Business School: 69 % **Male/female:** 64/36 **% Part-time:** 61 **% International:** 80 **Average Age at Entry:** 35 **Average Years Work Experience at Entry:** 12

ACADEMICS
Student/faculty Ratio: 1:1 **% Female Faculty:** 31 **Prominent Alumni:** Mark Harris, chief executive, National Lottery Commission; Rob Williams, finance director, *The Economist*; Nigel Pears, operations & safety director, First Group PLC; Sue Latham, director of nursing, Clemintine Hospital.

FINANCIAL FACTS

Tuition: $57,945 **Books and Supplies:** $880 **Room & Board (on/off campus):** $6,719/$8,959 **Average Award Package:** $50,000

ADMISSIONS

Admissions Selectivity Rating: 77

% Acceptees Attending: 100 **GMAT Range (25th to 75th percentile):** 520–640 **Average GMAT:** 560 **TOEFL Required of Int'l Applicants:** yes **Minimum TOEFL (paper/computer):** 600/250

Deferment Available: yes **Maximum Length of Deferment:** 1 year **Non-fall Admissions:** yes

BALL STATE UNIVERSITY
MILLER COLLEGE OF BUSINESS

ADMISSIONS CONTACT: DR. GAYLE HARTLEROAD, DIRECTOR OF STUDENT SERVICES
ADDRESS: WB 147, MUNCIE, IN 47306
PHONE: 765-285-5329 • FAX: 765-285-8818
E-MAIL: MBA@BSU.EDU
WEBSITE: WWW.BSU.EDU/MBA

GENERAL INFORMATION

Type of School: public **Environment:** city **Academic Calendar:** semester

STUDENTS

Enrollment of Parent Institution: 18,161 **Enrollment of Business School:** 173 % **Male/female:** 73/27 **% Out-of-state:** 11 **% Part-time:** 68 **% Minorities:** 4 **% International:** 15 **Average Age at Entry:** 27 **Average Years Work Experience at Entry:** 4

ACADEMICS

Student/faculty Ratio: 30:1

FINANCIAL FACTS

Tuition (in-state/out-of-state): $8,272/$21,040 **Fees:** $675 **Books and Supplies:** $1,700 **Room & Board (on/off campus):** $9,000/$9,500

ADMISSIONS

Admissions Selectivity Rating: 70

# of Applications Received: 41 **% Applicants Accepted:** 78 **GMAT Range (25th to 75th percentile):** 420–720 **Average GMAT:** 532 **Average GPA:** 3.32 **TOEFL Required of Int'l Applicants:** yes **Minimum TOEFL (paper/computer):** 550/213 **Application Fee:** $35 **International Application Fee:** $40 **Regular Application Deadline:** rolling **Regular Notification:** rolling **Deferment Available:** yes **Maximum Length of Deferment:** 2 years **Transfer Students Accepted:** yes **Non-fall Admissions:** yes **Need-Blind Admissions:** yes **Applicants Also Look At:** Butler University, Indiana University Kokomo, Indiana University–Purdue University at Fort Wayne, Indiana University–Purdue University Indianapolis.

BOISE STATE UNIVERSITY
COLLEGE OF BUSINESS AND ECONOMICS

ADMISSIONS CONTACT: J. RENEE ANCHUSTEGUI, PROGRAMS ADMINISTRATOR
ADDRESS: BUSINESS GRADUATE STUDIES, 1910 UNIVERSITY DRIVE, B318, BOISE, ID 83725-1600
PHONE: 208-426-3116 • FAX: 208-426-1135
E-MAIL: GRADUATEBUSINESS@BOISESTATE.EDU
WEBSITE: COBE.BOISESTATE.EDU/GRADUATE

GENERAL INFORMATION

Type of School: public **Environment:** city **Academic Calendar:** semester

STUDENTS

Enrollment of Parent Institution: 18,876 **Enrollment of Business School:** 119 % **Male/female:** 57/43 **% Out-of-state:** 40 **% Part-time:** 82 **% Minorities:** 1 **% International:** 17 **Average Age at Entry:** 32 **Average Years Work Experience at Entry:** 6

ACADEMICS

Student/faculty Ratio: 28:1 **% Female Faculty:** 20 % **Minority Faculty** 7

Prominent Alumni: Jan Packwood, president & COO, Idaho Power Company; William Glynn, president, Intermountain Gas; Steve Heyl, vice president strategic planning, Arby's; Norm Schlachter, vice president finance, Micron Technology; Mary Schofield, controller, Boise Division, Hewlett Packard

FINANCIAL FACTS

Tuition (out-of-state): $7,778 **Fees (in-state/out-of-state):** $5,936/$7,778 **Books and Supplies:** $2,000 **Room & Board (on/off campus):** $6,800/$7,200 **% of Students Receiving Aid:** 30 **% of First-year Students Receiving Aid:** 12 **% of Students Receiving Loans:** 18 **% of Students Receiving Grants:** 12 **Average Award Package:** $20,020 **Average Grant:** $22,130 **Average Student Loan Debt:** $12,000

ADMISSIONS

Admissions Selectivity Rating: 90

# of Applications Received: 81 **% Applicants Accepted:** 38 **% Acceptees Attending:** 87 **GMAT Range (25th to 75th percentile):** 530–640 **Average GMAT:** 585 **Average GPA:** 3.3 **TOEFL Required of Int'l Applicants:** yes **Minimum TOEFL (paper/computer):** 587/240 **Application Fee:** $55 **Regular Application Deadline:** 6/1 **Regular Notification:** 7/15 **Early Decision Program:** yes **Deferment Available:** yes **Maximum Length of Deferment:** 1 year **Transfer Students Accepted:** yes **Non-fall Admissions:** yes **Need-Blind Admissions:** yes **Applicants Also Look At:** Brigham Young University, Idaho State University.

EMPLOYMENT PROFILE

Average Base Starting Salary: $76,000

Percent Employed: 100

Grads Employed by Industry:.......% avg. salary:

Finance/Accounting.........................25 $96,000

Human Resources...........................8 $85,000

Marketing/Sales 17 $75,000

MIS 8 $63,000

Operations/Production 17 $63,500

Global Management 8 $70,000

Other...17 $64,500

Top 2 Employers Hiring Grads: Blue Cross of Idaho; Micron Technology

BRADLEY UNIVERSITY
FOSTER COLLEGE OF BUSINESS ADMINISTRATION

ADMISSIONS CONTACT: DR. EDWARD SATTLER, DIRECTOR OF GRADUATE PROGRAMS
ADDRESS: BAKER HALL, PEORIA, IL 61625
PHONE: 309-677-2253 • FAX: 309-677-3374
E-MAIL: ADE@BRADLEY.EDU
WEBSITE: WWW.BRADLEY.EDU/FCBA/INDEX.HTML

GENERAL INFORMATION

Type of School: private **Environment:** city **Academic Calendar:** semester

FINANCIAL FACTS

Tuition: $8,832 **Fees:** $15 **Books and Supplies:** $700

ADMISSIONS

Admissions Selectivity Rating: 60*

# of Applications Received: 47 **% Applicants Accepted:** 100 **% Acceptees Attending:** 57 **TOEFL Required of Int'l Applicants:** yes **Minimum TOEFL (paper):** 500 **Application Fee:** $50 **Regular Application Deadline:** rolling **Regular Notification:** rolling **Deferment Available:** yes **Maximum Length of Deferment:** 1 year **Non-fall Admissions:** yes **Need-Blind Admissions:** yes **Applicants Also Look At:** Illinois State University, University of Phoenix On-Line.

CALIFORNIA STATE UNIVERSITY— BAKERSFIELD
SCHOOL OF BUSINESS AND PUBLIC ADMINISTRATION

ADMISSIONS CONTACT: DEBBIE BLOWERS, EVALUATIONS
ADDRESS: 9001 STOCKDALE HIGHWAY, BAKERSFIELD, CA 93311-1099
PHONE: 661-664-3036 • FAX: 661-664-3389
E-MAIL: ADMISSIONS@CSUB.EDU
WEBSITE: WWW.CSUBAK.EDU/BPA/

GENERAL INFORMATION

Type of School: public **Environment:** village **Academic Calendar:** quarter

STUDENTS

Enrollment of Parent Institution: 6,700 **Enrollment of Business School:** 84 **% Male/female:** 33/67 **% Part-time:** 86 **% Minorities:** 25 **% International:** 25 **Average Age at Entry:** 32

ACADEMICS

Student/faculty Ratio: 17:1 **% Female Faculty:** 10 **% Minority Faculty:** 10

FINANCIAL FACTS

Tuition (in-state/out-of-state): $2,126/$6,646 **Books and Supplies:** $2,200 **Room & Board (on/off campus):** $4,950/$7,679

ADMISSIONS

Admissions Selectivity Rating: 87

# of Applications Received: 80 **% Applicants Accepted:** 28 **% Acceptees Attending:** 73 **GMAT Range (25th to 75th percentile):** 490–570 **Average GMAT:** 530 **Average GPA:** 3.3 **TOEFL Required of Int'l Applicants:** Yes **Minimum TOEFL (paper):** 550 **Application Fee:** $55 **Regular Application Deadline:** rolling **Regular Notification:** rolling **Non-fall Admissions:** yes

California State University— Los Angeles

College of Business and Economics

Admissions Contact: Joan Woosley, Admissions Officer
Address: 5151 State University Drive, Los Angeles, CA 90032
Phone: 323-343-3904 • Fax: 323-343-6306
E-mail: admissions@calstatela.edu
Website: cbe.calstatela.edu/

GENERAL INFORMATION

Type of School: Public **Environment:** metropolis **Academic Calendar:** quarter

STUDENTS

Enrollment of Parent Institution: 18,849 **Enrollment of Business School:** 330 **% Male/female:** 47/53 **% Part-time:** 100 **% Minorities:** 50 **Average Age at Entry:** 31

ACADEMICS

Student/faculty Ratio: 20:1

FINANCIAL FACTS

Tuition (in-state/out-of-state): $3,949/$12,096 **Books and Supplies:** $500 **Average Grant:** $12,000

ADMISSIONS

Admissions Selectivity Rating: 83
# of Applications Received: 388 **% Applicants Accepted:** 43 **% Acceptees Attending:** 52 **Average GMAT:** 560 **Average GPA:** 3.00 **TOEFL Required of Int'l Applicants:** yes **Minimum TOEFL (paper/computer):** 550/213 **Application Fee:** $55 **Regular Application Deadline:** 6/15 **Regular Notification:** 1/1 **Non-fall Admissions:** yes

California State University— Northridge

College of Business and Economics

Admissions Contact: Oscar W. DeShields, Jr., PhD, Director of Graduate Programs
Address: 18111 Nordhoff Street, Northridge, CA 91330-8380
Phone: 818-677-2467 • Fax: 818-677-3188
E-mail: mba@csun.edu
Website: csun.edu/mba

GENERAL INFORMATION

Type of School: public **Environment:** city **Academic Calendar:** semester

STUDENTS

Enrollment of Parent Institution: 33,000 **Enrollment of Business School:** 269 **% Male/female:** 56/44 **% Out-of-state:** 19 **% Part-**time: 84 **% International:** 17 **Average Age at Entry:** 29 **Average Years Work Experience at Entry:** 7

ACADEMICS

Student/faculty Ratio: 22:1 **% Female Faculty:** 18 **% Minority Faculty:** 6

FINANCIAL FACTS

Fees: $3,618 **Books and Supplies:** $1,300 **Room & Board (off campus):** $9,328

ADMISSIONS

Admissions Selectivity Rating: 90
# of Applications Received: 249 **% Applicants Accepted:** 27 **% Acceptees Attending:** 70 **GMAT Range (25th to 75th percentile):** 460–690 **Average GMAT:** 560 **Average GPA:** 3.3 **TOEFL Required of Int'l Applicants:** yes **Minimum TOEFL (paper/computer):** 550/213 **Application Fee:** $55 **Regular Application Deadline:** 5/1 **Regular Notification:** rolling **Deferment Available:** yes **Maximum Length of Deferment:** 1 semester **Transfer Students Accepted:** yes **Non-fall Admissions:** yes **Need-Blind Admissions:** yes **Applicants Also Look At:** California State University, Long Beach, California State University, Los Angeles, Pepperdine University, University of California, Los Angeles (UCLA).

California State University— Sacramento

College of Business Administration

Admissions Contact: Jeanie Allam, Graduate Program Academic Counselor
Address: 6000 J Street, Sacramento, CA 95819-6088
Phone: 916-278-6772 • Fax: 916-278-4233
E-mail: cbagrad@csus.edu
Website: www.csus.edu/cbagrad/index.html

GENERAL INFORMATION

Type of School: public **Environment:** metropolis **Academic Calendar:** semester

STUDENTS

Enrollment of Parent Institution: 28,375 **Enrollment of Business School:** 311 **% Male/female:** 56/44 **% Part-time:** 63 **% Minorities:** 49 **% International:** 10 **Average Age at Entry:** 30 **Average Years Work Experience at Entry:** 3

ACADEMICS

Student/faculty Ratio: 13:1 **% Female Faculty:** 28 **Joint Degrees:** MBA/JD (with McGeorge School of Law) 4.5 years. **Prominent Alumni:** Dennis Gardemeyer, executive vice president, Zuckerman-Hertog; Tom Weborg, chief executive officer, Cucina Holdings; William Keever, president, Vodafone Airtouch; Margo Murray, president, CEO/MMHA The Mangers' Mentors Inc.; Scott Syphax, president, CEO/Nehemiah Corporation.

FINANCIAL FACTS

Tuition (in-state/out-of-state): $3,310/$9,160 **Books and Supplies:** $1,700 **Room & Board (on/off campus):** $9,400/$8,400

ADMISSIONS

Admissions Selectivity Rating: 81

# of Applications Received: 247 **% Applicants Accepted:** 61 **% Acceptees Attending:** 66 **GMAT Range (25th to 75th percentile):** 420–750 **Average GMAT:** 575 **Average GPA:** 3.1 **TOEFL Required of Int'l Applicants:** yes **Minimum TOEFL (paper/computer):** 550/213 **Application Fee:** $55 **Regular Application Deadline:** 4/1 **Regular Notification:** 5/30 **Transfer Students Accepted:** yes **Non-fall Admissions:** yes **Need-Blind Admissions:** yes

CANISIUS COLLEGE
RICHARD J. WEHLE SCHOOL OF BUSINESS

ADMISSIONS CONTACT: LAURA MCEWEN, DIRECTOR, GRADUATE BUSINESS PROGRAMS
ADDRESS: CANISIUS COLLEGE, 2001 MAIN STREET, BAGEN HALL 201, BUFFALO, NY 14208-1098
PHONE: 716-888-2140 • FAX: 716-888-2145
E-MAIL: GRADUBUS@CANISIUS.EDU
WEBSITE: WWW.CANISIUS.EDU/MBA

GENERAL INFORMATION

Type of School: private **Affiliation:** Roman Catholic-Jesuit **Environment:** metropolis **Academic Calendar:** semester

STUDENTS

Enrollment of Parent Institution: 4,979 **Enrollment of Business School:** 261 **% Male/female:** 51/49 **% Part-time:** 74 **% Minorities:** 9 **% International:** 9 **Average Age at Entry:** 28

ACADEMICS

% Female Faculty: 13 **% Minority Faculty:** 8 **Joint Degrees:** BA/MBA 5 years.

FINANCIAL FACTS

Tuition: $32,251 **Books and Supplies:** $500 **Room & Board:** $8,300

ADMISSIONS

Admissions Selectivity Rating: 60*

GMAT Range (25th to 75th percentile): 410–550 **Average GMAT:** 474 **TOEFL Required of Int'l Applicants:** yes **Minimum TOEFL (paper/computer):** 500/200 **Application Fee:** $25 **Regular Application Deadline:** rolling **Regular Notification:** rolling

Deferment Available: yes **Maximum Length of Deferment:** 1 year **Transfer Students Accepted:** yes **Non-fall Admissions:** yes **Applicants Also Look At:** State University of New York-University at Buffalo.

CENTRAL MICHIGAN UNIVERSITY
COLLEGE OF BUSINESS ADMINISTRATION

ADMISSIONS CONTACT: PAMELA STAMBERSKY, DIRECTOR OF GRADUATE PROGRAMS
ADDRESS: 105 WARRINER HALL, MOUNT PLEASANT, MI 48859
PHONE: 517-774-3150 • FAX: 517-774-2372
E-MAIL: CBAWORK@CMICH.EDU
WEBSITE: WWW.CBA.CMICH.EDU

GENERAL INFORMATION

Type of School: public **Environment:** town **Academic Calendar:** semester

STUDENTS

Enrollment of Parent Institution: 16,613 **Enrollment of Business School:** 471 **% Male/female:** 59/41 **% Part-time:** 50 **% Minorities:** 1 **% International:** 34 **Average Age at Entry:** 28

FINANCIAL FACTS

Tuition (in-state/out-of-state): $418.15/$621.05 (per credit hour) **Books and Supplies:** $9,999

ADMISSIONS

Admissions Selectivity Rating: 60*

# of Applications Received: 151 **% Applicants Accepted:** 80 **TOEFL Required of Int'l Applicants:** yes **Minimum TOEFL (paper):** 550 **Application Fee:** $30 **Regular Application Deadline:** rolling **Regular Notification:** rolling **Deferment Available:** yes

CLARION UNIVERSITY
COLLEGE OF BUSINESS ADMINISTRATION

ADMISSIONS CONTACT: DR. ROBERT S. BALOUGH, DIRECTOR OF MBA PROGRAM
ADDRESS: 302 STILL HALL, CLARION UNIVERSITY, CLARION, PA 16214
PHONE: 814-393-2605 • FAX: 814-393-1910
E-MAIL: MBA@CLARION.EDU
WEBSITE: WWW.CLARION.EDU/MBA

GENERAL INFORMATION

Type of School: public **Environment:** village **Academic Calendar:** semester

STUDENTS

Enrollment of Parent Institution: 6,338 **Enrollment of Business School:** 36 **% Male/female:** 64/36 **% Out-of-state:** 8 **% Part-time:** 14 **% Minorities:** 6 **% International:** 31 **Average Age at Entry:** 23 **Average Years Work Experience at Entry:** 6

ACADEMICS

Female Faculty: 18 **% Minority Faculty:** 23

FINANCIAL FACTS

Tuition (in-state/out-of-state): $5,888/$9,422 **Fees (in-state/out-of-state):** $1,778/$1,843 **Books and Supplies:** $3,650 **Room & Board (on/off campus):** $5,246/$4,000

Admissions Selectivity Rating: 65

# of Applications Received: 36 **% Applicants Accepted:** 86 %
Acceptees Attending: 65 **Average GMAT:** 489 **Average GPA:** 3.44
TOEFL Required of Int'l Applicants: yes **Minimum TOEFL
(paper/computer):** 550/213 **Application Fee:** $30 **Regular
Application Deadline:** rolling **Regular Notification:** rolling
Deferment Available: yes **Maximum Length of Deferment:** 1 year
Transfer Students Accepted: yes **Non-fall Admissions:** yes **Need-
Blind Admissions:** yes

CLARK ATLANTA UNIVERSITY
SCHOOL OF BUSINESS ADMINISTRATION

*ADMISSIONS CONTACT: SARBETH J. FLEMING,
 DIRECTOR OF ADMISSIONS AND STUDENT AFFAIRS
ADDRESS: 223 JAMES P. BRAWLEY DRIVE, ATLANTA, GA 30314
PHONE: 404-880-844/ • FAX. 404-880-6159
E-MAIL: SFLEMING@CAU.EDU
WEBSITE: WWW.SBUS.CAU.EDU*

GENERAL INFORMATION

Type of School: private **Affiliation:** Methodist **Environment:** city
Academic Calendar: semester

STUDENTS

Enrollment of Parent Institution: 5,000 **Enrollment of Business
School:** 120 **% Male/female:** 38/62 **% Part-time:** 10 **% Minorities:**
90 **% International:** 10 **Average Age at Entry:** 28 **Average Years
Work Experience at Entry:** 5

ACADEMICS

Student/faculty Ratio: 11:1 **% Female Faculty:** 39 **% Minority
Faculty:** 92

FINANCIAL FACTS

Tuition: $19,127 **Fees:** $550 **Books and Supplies:** $800 **Room &
Board (off campus):** $4,875 **% of Students Receiving Aid:** 95 **% of
First-year Students Receiving Aid:** 95 **% of Students Receiving
Loans:** 95 **% of Students Receiving Grants:** 95 **Average Award
Package:** $32,000 **Average Grant:** $32,000 **Average Student Loan
Debt:** $65,000

ADMISSIONS

Admissions Selectivity Rating: 72

# of Applications Received: 134 **% Applicants Accepted:** 67 %
Acceptees Attending: 69 **GMAT Range (25th to 75th percentile):**
340–520 **Average GMAT:** 430 **Average GPA:** 3.00 **TOEFL Required
of Int'l Applicants:** yes **Minimum TOEFL (paper):** 175 **Application
Fee:** $40 **International Application Fee:** $55 **Regular Application
Deadline:** 4/1 **Regular Notification:** rolling **Deferment Available:**
yes **Maximum Length of Deferment:** 1 year **Transfer Students
Accepted:** yes **Applicants Also Look At:** Emory University, Georgia
State University, Kennesaw State University.

EMPLOYMENT PROFILE

Primary Source of Full-time Job Acceptances

School-facilitated Activities 7 (25%)
Graduate-facilitated Activities 15 (50%)
Unknown.......................................7 (25%)

Grads Employed by Industry:......% avg. salary:

Finance/Accounting........................30 $82,000
Human Resources..........................7 $75,000
Marketing/Sales 52 $80,000
Operations/Production 7 $75,000
Other...4 $50,000

Top 5 Employers Hiring Grads

Chevron/Texaco; Coca-Cola; American Express Company; Union
Pacific; Delta Airlines.

CLEVELAND STATE UNIVERSITY
JAMES J. NANCE COLLEGE OF BUSINESS
ADMINISTRATION

*ADMISSIONS CONTACT: BRUCE M. GOTTSCHALK, MBA PROGRAMS
 ADMINISTRATOR
ADDRESS: 2121 EUCLID AVENUE, BU 219, CLEVELAND, OH 44115
PHONE: 216-687-3730 • FAX: 216-687-5311
E-MAIL: CBAGSII@CSUOHIO.EDU
WEBSITE: WWW.CSUOHIO.EDU/CBA/MBA*

GENERAL INFORMATION

Type of School: public **Environment:** city **Academic Calendar:**
semester

STUDENTS

Enrollment of Parent Institution: 15,450 **Enrollment of Business
School:** 645 **% Male/female:** 61/39 **% Out-of-state:** 40 **% Part-
time:** 78 **% Minorities:** 19 **% International:** 35 **Average Age at
Entry:** 27 **Average Years Work Experience at Entry:** 5

ACADEMICS

Student/faculty Ratio: 27:1 **% Female Faculty:** 22 **% Minority
Faculty:** 15

Joint Degrees: JD/MBA 4 years, MBA/MSN 3 years. **Prominent
Alumni:** Monte Ahuja, chair, president& CEO, Transtar Industries;
Michael Berthelot, chair and CEO Transtechnolgy Corporation; Ted
Hlavaty, chair and CEO, Neway Stamping and Manufacturing;
Thomas Moore, president, Wolf Group; Kenneth Semelsberger, pres-
ident, COO and director, Scott Fetzer, Inc.

FINANCIAL FACTS

Tuition (in-state/out-of-state): $9,936/$18,840 **Books and Supplies:**
$1,300 **Room & Board (on/off campus):** $10,000/$12,000 **% of
Students Receiving Aid:** 4 **% of First-year Students Receiving Aid:**
8 **% of Students Receiving Loans:** 39 **% of Students Receiving
Grants:** 1 **Average Award Package:** $20,000

ADMISSIONS

Admissions Selectivity Rating: 68

# of Applications Received: 402 **% Applicants Accepted:** 74 **% Acceptees Attending:** 54 **GMAT Range (25th to 75th percentile):** 460–590 **Average GMAT:** 500 **Average GPA:** 3.14 **TOEFL Required of Int'l Applicants:** yes **Minimum TOEFL (paper/computer):** 550/213 **Application Fee:** $30 **Regular Application Deadline:** 7/1 **Regular Notification:** rolling **Deferment Available:** yes **Maximum Length of Deferment:** 1 year **Transfer Students Accepted:** yes **Non-fall Admissions:** yes **Need-Blind Admissions:** yes **Applicants Also Look At:** Case Western Reserve University, DeVry University, John Carroll University, Kent State University, The University of Akron, University of Phoenix.

EMPLOYMENT PROFILE

Primary Source of Full-time Job Acceptances

School-facilitated Activities 20 (34%)

Graduate-facilitated Activities 48 (66%)

Grads Employed by Industry: ......% avg. salary:

Finance/Accounting 10 $56,000

Human Resources 3 $56,000

Marketing/Sales 7 $58,000

MIS 7 $63,800

Operations/Production 4 $57,600

General Management 5 $86,000

Other 12 $51,000

Top 5 Employers Hiring Grads

Progressive Insurance; National City Bank; Federal Reserve Bank of Cleveland; Rockwell Automation; Sherwin Williams.

CRANFIELD UNIVERSITY
CRANFIELD SCHOOL OF MANAGEMENT

ADMISSIONS CONTACT: EILEEN FISHER, ADMISSIONS EXECUTIVE
ADDRESS: CRANFIELD SCHOOL OF MANAGEMENT, CRANFIELD, BEDFORD, MK43 0AL ENGLAND
PHONE: 0044-1234-754431 • FAX: 0044-1234-752439
E-MAIL: MBAADMISSIONS@CRANFIELD.AC.UK
WEBSITE: WWW.CRANFIELDMBA.INFO

GENERAL INFORMATION

Type of School: public **Academic Calendar:** year long

STUDENTS

Enrollment of Business School: 209 **% Male/female:** 77/23 **% Part-time:** 50 **% International:** 70 **Average Age at Entry:** 31 **Average Years Work Experience at Entry:** 8

ACADEMICS

Student/faculty Ratio: 2:1 **% Female Faculty:** 26

Prominent Alumni: Ted Tuppen, CEO, Enterprise Inns; Nigel Doughty, CEO, Doughty Hanson; John McFarlane, CEO, ANZ Banking Group; Andy Bond, chief executive, Asda; Michael Wemms, chair, House of Fraser.

FINANCIAL FACTS

Tuition (in-state/out-of-state): $51,120/$51,122 **Books and Supplies:** $1,000 **Room & Board (on-campus):** $10,000 **% of Students Receiving Aid:** 78 **% of First-year Students Receiving Aid:** 82 **% of Students Receiving Grants:** 78 **Average Grant:** $12,290

ADMISSIONS

Admissions Selectivity Rating: 87

# of Applications Received: 299 **% Applicants Accepted:** 56 **% Acceptees Attending:** 62 **GMAT Range (25th to 75th percentile):** 620–690 **Average GMAT:** 659 **TOEFL Required of Int'l Applicants:** yes **Minimum TOEFL (paper/computer):** 600/250 **Regular Application Deadline:** rolling **Regular Notification:** rolling **Deferment Available:** yes **Maximum Length of Deferment:** 2 years **Need-Blind Admissions:** yes **Applicants Also Look At:** INSEAD, University of Cambridge, University of London, University of Manchester, University of Oxford, University of Warwick.

EMPLOYMENT PROFILE

Primary Source of Full-time Job Acceptances

School-facilitated Activities 23 (27%)

Graduate-facilitated Activities 54 (64%)

Unknown 8 (9%)

Average Base Starting Salary: $98,826

Percent Employed: 72

Grads Employed by Industry: ......% avg. salary:

Finance/Accounting 8 $113,444

Human Resources 2 $129,146

Marketing/Sales 8 $89,006

MIS 1 $99,583

Operations/Production 8 $95,987

Strategic Planning 9 $99,477

Consulting 24 $92,500

Entrepreneurship...........................2 NR

General Management 16 $109,953

Other 22 $71,553

Top 5 Employers Hiring Grads

CHEP UK; Credit Suisse; American Express Company; UBS; P A Consulting.

CREIGHTON UNIVERSITY
COLLEGE OF BUSINESS ADMINISTRATION

ADMISSIONS CONTACT: GAIL HAFER, COORDINATOR OF GRADUATE BUSINESS PROGRAMS
ADDRESS: COLLEGE OF BUSINESS ADMINISTRATION, ROOM 212C, 2500 CALIFORNIA PLAZA, OMAHA, NE 68178
PHONE: 402-280-2853 • FAX: 402-280-2172
E-MAIL: COBAGRAD@CREIGHTON.EDU
WEBSITE: COBWEB.CREIGHTON.EDU

GENERAL INFORMATION

Type of School: private **Affiliation:** Roman Catholic **Environment:** metropolis

STUDENTS

Enrollment of Parent Institution: 6,723 **Enrollment of Business School:** 118 **% Male/female:** 58/42 **% Part-time:** 84 **% Minorities:** 1 **% International:** 31 **Average Age at Entry:** 25 **Average Years Work Experience at Entry:** 3

ACADEMICS

Student/faculty Ratio: 2:1 **% Female Faculty:** 10

Joint Degrees: MBA/JD 3 years, MBA/Doctor of Pharmacy 4 years, MBA/Master of International Relations 3 years, MBA/MS.

FINANCIAL FACTS

Tuition: $10,206 **Fees:** $764 **Books and Supplies:** $1,600 **Room & Board (on/off campus):** $7,000/$6,000 **% of Students Receiving Aid:** 15 **% of First-year Students Receiving Aid:** 8 **Average Award Package:** $19,653

ADMISSIONS

Admissions Selectivity Rating: 72

# of Applications Received: 24 **% Applicants Accepted:** 96 **% Acceptees Attending:** 78 **Average GMAT:** 570 **Average GPA:** 3.4 **TOEFL Required of Int'l Applicants:** yes **Minimum TOEFL (paper/computer):** 550/213 **Application Fee:** $40 **Regular Application Deadline:** rolling **Regular Notification:** rolling **Deferment Available:** yes **Maximum Length of Deferment:** 1 year **Transfer Students Accepted:** yes **Non-fall Admissions:** yes **Applicants Also Look At:** University of Nebraska at Omaha.

DEPAUL UNIVERSITY
KELLSTADT GRADUATE SCHOOL OF BUSINESS

ADMISSIONS CONTACT: ROBERT RYAN, ASSISTANT DEAN
ADDRESS: 1 EAST JACKSON BOULEVARD, SUITE 7900, CHICAGO, IL 60604
PHONE: 312-362-8810 • FAX: 312-362-6677
E-MAIL: KGSB@DEPAUL.EDU
WEBSITE: WWW.KELLSTADT.DEPAUL.EDU

GENERAL INFORMATION

Type of School: private **Affiliation:** Roman Catholic **Environment:** metropolis **Academic Calendar:** quarter

STUDENTS

Enrollment of Parent Institution: 23,148 **Enrollment of Business School:** 1,682 **% Male/female:** 74/26 **% Part-time:** 97 **% Minorities:** 8 **% International:** 18 **Average Age at Entry:** 28 **Average Years Work Experience at Entry:** 5

ACADEMICS

Student/faculty Ratio: 11:1 **% Female Faculty:** 24 **% Minority Faculty:** 23

Joint Degrees: MBA/JD 2.8 to 3.8 years. **Prominent Alumni:** Jim Jenness, CEO, Kellogg's; Richard Driehaus, president, Driehaus

Capital Management; Edward Bosowski, president, USG Corporation; Daniel Ustian, chair, president and CEO, Navistar International.

FINANCIAL FACTS

Tuition: $36,920 **Fees:** $200 **Books and Supplies:** $1,300 **Room & Board (on/off campus):** $12,316/$10,800 **Average Award Package:** $21,120 **Average Grant:** $16,080 **Average Student Loan Debt:** $46,005

ADMISSIONS

Admissions Selectivity Rating: 71

# of Applications Received: 750 **% Applicants Accepted:** 84 **% Acceptees Attending:** 58 **GMAT Range (25th to 75th percentile):** 452–640 **Average GMAT:** 547 **Average GPA:** 3.14 **TOEFL Required of Int'l Applicants:** yes **Minimum TOEFL (paper/computer):** 550/213 **Application Fee:** $60 **Regular Application Deadline:** 7/1 **Regular Notification:** rolling **Deferment Available:** yes **Maximum Length of Deferment:** 1 year **Transfer Students Accepted:** yes **Non-fall Admissions:** yes **Need-Blind Admissions:** yes **Applicants Also Look At:** Loyola University Chicago, Northwestern University, The University of Chicago.

EMPLOYMENT PROFILE

Average Starting Salary $63,000

Primary Source of Full-time Job Acceptances

School-facilitated Activities.............9 (50%)

Graduate-facilitated Activities 9 (50%)

Average Base Starting Salary: $63,000

Grads Employed by Industry:.......% avg. salary

Finance/Accounting........................12 $74,833

Marketing/Sales 2 $72,500

Consulting...1 $93,000

General Management 1 $83,000

Top 5 Employers Hiring Grads

Lehman Brothers; Grant Thornton; Motorola; Northern Trust; Morningstar.

DRAKE UNIVERSITY
COLLEGE OF BUSINESS AND PUBLIC ADMINISTRATION

ADMISSIONS CONTACT: DANETTE KENNE, DIRECTOR OF GRADUATE PROGRAMS
ADDRESS: 2507 UNIVERSITY AVENUE, ALIBER HALL, SUITE 211, DES MOINES, IA 50311
PHONE: 515-271-2188 • FAX: 515-271-2187
E-MAIL: CBPA.GRADPROGRAMS@DRAKE.EDU
WEBSITE: WWW.CBPA.DRAKE.EDU/ASPX/PROGRAMS/PROGRAMDETAIL.ASPX?ID=6

GENERAL INFORMATION

Type of School: private **Environment:** metropolis **Academic Calendar:** semester

STUDENTS

Enrollment of Parent Institution: 5,366 **Enrollment of Business School:** 231 % **Male/female:** 40/60 % **Part-time:** 66 % **Minorities:** 8 % **International:** 19 **Average Age at Entry:** 26

ACADEMICS

Student/faculty Ratio: 19:1 % **Female Faculty:** 1 **Joint Degrees:** MBA/PharmD 6 years, MBA/JD 3 years, MPA/JD 3 years, MPA/PharmD 6 years. **Prominent Alumni:** Robert D, Ray, former governor, Iowa; Sherrill Milnes, Opera; Daniel Jorndt, former chairman/CEO, Walgreen Co.; Dwight Opperman, former CEO, West Publishing; Marie Wilson, president, MS Foundation for Women.

FINANCIAL FACTS

Tuition: $8,600 **Fees:** $306 **Books and Supplies:** $800 **Room & Board (on/off campus):** $5,870/$6,170 % **of Students Receiving Loans:** 10 % **of Students Receiving Grants:** 1

ADMISSIONS

Admissions Selectivity Rating: 67

# of Applications Received: 57 % **Applicants Accepted:** 96 % **Acceptees Attending:** 78 **GMAT Range (25th to 75th percentile):** 430–590 **Average GMAT:** 500 **Average GPA:** 3.27 **TOEFL Required of Int'l Applicants:** yes **Minimum TOEFL (paper/computer):** 550/213 **Application Fee:** $25 **Regular Application Deadline:** 7/6 **Regular Notification:** rolling **Deferment Available:** yes **Maximum Length of Deferment:** 1 term **Transfer Students Accepted:** yes **Non-fall Admissions:** yes **Need-Blind Admissions:** yes **Applicants Also Look At:** Iowa State University, University of Iowa.

FINANCIAL FACTS

Tuition (in-state/out-of-state): $5,138/$15,000 **Fees:** $1,100 **Books and Supplies:** $1,000 **Room & Board (on/off campus):** $5,000/$6,000 % **of Students Receiving Aid:** 25 % **of First-year Students Receiving Aid:** 25 % **of Students Receiving Grants:** 25 **Average Award Package:** $6,000 **Average Grant:** $6,000 **Average Student Loan Debt:** $10,000

ADMISSIONS

Admissions Selectivity Rating: 66

# of Applications Received: 70 % **Applicants Accepted:** 77 % **Acceptees Attending:** 85 **GMAT Range (25th to 75th percentile):** 450–700 **Average GMAT:** 535 **Average GPA:** 3.3 **TOEFL Required of Int'l Applicants:** yes **Minimum TOEFL (paper/computer):** 550/213 **Application Fee:** $25 **International Application Fee:** $35 **Regular Application Deadline:** 6/1 **Regular Notification:** rolling **Deferment Available:** yes **Maximum Length of Deferment:** 1 year **Transfer Students Accepted:** yes **Non-fall Admissions:** yes **Need-Blind Admissions:** yes **Applicants Also Look At:** University of Tennessee, Virginia Tech.

EMPLOYMENT PROFILE

Primary Source of Full-time Job Acceptances

Grads Employed by Industry:	.......%	avg. salary:
Human Resources	10	$30,000
Marketing/Sales	10	$38,000
Entrepreneurship	10	$35,000
General Management	50	$30,000

EAST TENNESSEE STATE UNIVERSITY
COLLEGE OF BUSINESS AND TECHNOLOGY

ADMISSIONS CONTACT: DR. MARTHA POINTER, DIRECTOR OF GRADUATE STUDIES
ADDRESS: PO BOX 70699, JOHNSON CITY, TN 37614
PHONE: 423-439-5314 • FAX: 423-439-5274
E-MAIL: BUSINESS@BUSINESS.ETSU.EDU
WEBSITE: WWW.ETSU.EDU/CBAT/

GENERAL INFORMATION

Type of School: public **Environment:** town **Academic Calendar:** semester

STUDENTS

Enrollment of Parent Institution: 12,156 **Enrollment of Business School:** 71 % **Male/female:** 55/45 % **Out-of-state:** 10 % **Part-time:** 70 % **Minorities:** 10 % **International:** 10 **Average Age at Entry:** 28 **Average Years Work Experience at Entry:** 3

ACADEMICS

Student/faculty Ratio: 7:1 % **Female Faculty:** 10 % **Minority Faculty:** 2 **Prominent Alumni:** Pal Barger, Food Services.

EASTERN ILLINOIS UNIVERSITY
LUMPKIN COLLEGE OF BUSINESS AND APPLIED SCIENCES

ADMISSIONS CONTACT: DR. CHERYL NOLL, COORDINATOR, GRADUATE BUSINESS STUDIES
ADDRESS: 600 LINCOLN AVENUE, 4025 LUMPKIN HALL, CHARLESTON, IL 61920-3099
PHONE: 217-581-3028 • FAX: 217-581-6642
E-MAIL: MBA@EIU.EDU
WEBSITE: WWW.EIU.EDU/~MBA

GENERAL INFORMATION

Type of School: public **Environment:** village

STUDENTS

Enrollment of Parent Institution: 12,000 **Enrollment of Business School:** 134 % **Male/female:** 57/43 % **Part-time:** 36 % **Minorities:** 2 % **International:** 17 **Average Age at Entry:** 26 **Average Years Work Experience at Entry:** 4

ACADEMICS

Student/faculty Ratio: 22:1 % **Female Faculty:** 36 % **Minority Faculty:** 14

FINANCIAL FACTS

Tuition (in-state/out-of-state): $5,590/$16,770 **Fees:** $2,226 **Books and Supplies:** $325 **Room & Board (on/off campus):** $7,000/$8,000 **% of Students Receiving Aid:** 31 **% of First-year Students Receiving Aid:** 41 **% of Students Receiving Grants:** 31 **Average Grant:** $7,000

ADMISSIONS

Admissions Selectivity Rating: 73

# of Applications Received: 81 **% Applicants Accepted:** 77 % **Acceptees Attending:** 84 **GMAT Range (25th to 75th percentile):** 430–680 **Average GMAT:** 516 **Average GPA:** 3.26 **TOEFL Required of Int'l Applicants:** yes **Minimum TOEFL (paper/computer):** 550/213 **Application Fee:** $30 **Regular Application Deadline:** rolling **Regular Notification:** rolling **Deferment Available:** yes **Maximum Length of Deferment:** 1 year **Transfer Students Accepted:** yes **Non-fall Admissions:** yes **Need-Blind Admissions:** yes

EASTERN KENTUCKY UNIVERSITY

ADDRESS: COATES CPO 5-A, 521 LANCASTER AVENUE, RICHMOND, KY 40475
PHONE: (859) 622-1742
E-MAIL: GRADUATESCHOOL@EKU.EDU
WEBSITE: WWW.GRADSCHOOL.EKU.EDU/

GENERAL INFORMATION

Type of School: public **Academic Calendar:** semester

STUDENTS

Enrollment of Parent Institution: 15,763 **Enrollment of Business School:** 67 % **Male/female:** 50/50 **% Part-time:** 91

ACADEMICS

Student/faculty Ratio: 7:1 **% Female Faculty:** 32 **% Minority Faculty:** 5 **Prominent Alumni:** Howard Thompson, Dean, College of Business, Eastern Kentucky University; Steve Pence, Lieutenant Govenor, Kentucky.

FINANCIAL FACTS

Tuition (in-state/out-of-state): $5,610/$15,910 **Books and Supplies:** $750 **Room & Board (on-campus):** $5,000

ADMISSIONS

Admissions Selectivity Rating: 68

# of Applications Received: 31 **% Applicants Accepted:** 87 % **Acceptees Attending:** 93 **GMAT Range (25th to 75th percentile):** 450–540 **Average GMAT:** 504 **Average GPA:** 3.31 **TOEFL Required of Int'l Applicants:** yes **Minimum TOEFL (paper/computer):** 550/213 **Application Fee:** $35 **Regular Application Deadline:** 7/9 **Deferment Available:** yes **Maximum Length of Deferment:** 5 years **Transfer Students Accepted:** yes **Non-fall Admissions:** yes

EDHEC BUSINESS SCHOOL
THESEUS-EDHEC MBA

ADMISSIONS CONTACT: MAUREEN BYRNE, ADMISSIONS MANAGER
ADDRESS: CAMPUS LILLE, 58 RUE DU PORT, LILLE, 59046 FRANCE
PHONE: 011-33 3 2015 4465 • FAX: 011-33 3 2015 4841
E-MAIL: MAUREEN.BYRNE@EDHEC.EDU
WEBSITE: WWW.THESEUS-MBA.COM

GENERAL INFORMATION

Type of School: private

STUDENTS

Enrollment of Business School: 17 % **Male/female:** 83/17 % **International:** 72 **Average Age at Entry:** 34

FINANCIAL FACTS

Tuition: $27,000 **Room & Board (off campus):** $700

ADMISSIONS

Admissions Selectivity Rating: 67

Acceptees Attending: 100 **Average GMAT:** 600 **TOEFL Application Fee:** $27,000 **International Application Fee:** $27,000 **Regular Application Deadline:** 5/31 Application Deadline/Notification Round 1: December/January, Round 2: February/March, Round 3: April/May, Round 4: May/June.

EM LYON (FRANCE)

ADMISSIONS CONTACT: CHRISTÈLE FERNAND, HEAD OF DEVELOPMENT & RECRUITMENT
ADDRESS: 23, AV. GUY DE COLLONGUE, ECULLY, 69134 FRANCE
PHONE: 0033 4 78 33 77 83 • FAX: 0033 4 78 33 61 69
E-MAIL: IMBA@EM-LYON.COM
WEBSITE: WWW.EM-LYON.COM

GENERAL INFORMATION

Type of School: private

STUDENTS

Enrollment of Parent Institution: 2,800 **Enrollment of Business School:** 112 % **Male/female:** 70/30 **% Part-time:** 71 % **International:** 65 **Average Age at Entry:** 33 **Average Years Work Experience at Entry:** 8

ACADEMICS

Student/faculty Ratio: 3:1 **% Female Faculty:** 28 **Prominent Alumni:** Jean Pascal Tricoire, president, Schneider Electric; Didier Barret, president, MERCK Generique; Christian Seux, CEO, Becton Dickinson.

FINANCIAL FACTS

Tuition: $32,837 **Room & Board (off campus):** $10,500

Admissions Selectivity Rating: 85

# of Applications Received: 95 **% Applicants Accepted:** 51 %
Acceptees Attending: 67 **Average GMAT:** 610 **TOEFL Required of Int'l Applicants:** yes Minimum TOEFL (computer): 240 **Application Fee:** $131 **Application Deadline:** Round 1 1/15, Round 2 2/19, Round 3 4/2, Round 4 5/7.

Deferment Available: yes **Maximum Length of Deferment:** 1 year
Transfer Students Accepted: yes **Need-Blind Admissions:** yes
Applicants Also Look At: HEC School of Management–Paris, IMD (International Institute for Management Development), RSM Erasmus University.

EMPORIA STATE UNIVERSITY
SCHOOL OF BUSINESS

ADMISSIONS CONTACT: MARY SEWELL, GRADUATE ADMISSIONS COORDINATOR
ADDRESS: EMPORIA STATE UNIVERSITY, CAMPUS BOX 4003, 1200 COMMERCIAL STREET, EMPORIA, KS 66801
PHONE: 620-341-5403 • FAX: 620-341-5909
E-MAIL: GRADINFO@EMPORIA.EDU
WEBSITE: WWW.EMPORIA.EDU

GENERAL INFORMATION
Type of School: public

STUDENTS
Enrollment of Parent Institution: 6,473 **Enrollment of Business School:** 94 % **Male/female:** 59/41 **% Out-of-state:** 1 **% Part-time:** 16 **% Minorities:** 2 **% International:** 32 **Average Age at Entry:** 26

ACADEMICS
Student/faculty Ratio: 5:1 **% Female Faculty:** 5 **% Minority Faculty:** 19 **Prominent Alumni:** Donna Jacobs, vice president, nuclear services, Diablo Corporation; Shawn Keough, PhD, professor, University of Texas–Tyler.

FINANCIAL FACTS
Tuition (in-state/out-of-state): $4,162/$11,222 **Fees:** $724 **Books and Supplies:** $720 **Room & Board:** $6,260 **Average Grant:** $6,752

ADMISSIONS
Admissions Selectivity Rating: 62

# of Applications Received: 65 **% Applicants Accepted:** 92 %
Acceptees Attending: 47 **GMAT Range (25th to 75th percentile):** 420–600 **Average GMAT:** 498 **Average GPA:** 3.12 **TOEFL Required of Int'l Applicants:** yes **Minimum TOEFL (paper/computer):** 550/213 **Application Fee:** $30 **International Application Fee:** $75

Deferment Available: yes **Transfer Students Accepted:** yes **Non-fall Admissions:** yes **Need-Blind Admissions:** yes **Applicants Also Look At:** Institute of Undergraduate Business Studies.

ESCP-EAP EUROPEAN SCHOOL OF MANAGEMENT
ESCP-EAP PARIS LONDON MADRID BERLIN TORINO

ADMISSIONS CONTACT: FRANCYNE MARCAR, UK MARKETING COMMUNICATIONS MANAGER
ADDRESS: 527, FINCHLEY ROAD, HAMPSTEAD, LONDON, NW3 7BG ENGLAND
PHONE: 011-44-207-443-88-73 • FAX: 011-44-207-443-88-74
E-MAIL: UKADMISSION@ESCP-EAP.NET
WEBSITE: WWW.ESCP-EAP.NET

GENERAL INFORMATION
Type of School: private

STUDENTS
Enrollment of Parent Institution: 3,300 **Enrollment of Business School:** 229 % **Male/female:** 45/55 **% International:** 86 **Average Age at Entry:** 25 **Average Years Work Experience at Entry:** 1

ACADEMICS
Student/faculty Ratio: 20:1 **% Female Faculty:** 25 **Prominent Alumni:** Jean Pierre Raffarin, former prime minister, France; Henri Sturtz, president, Capgemini Ernst & Young; Ignacio Garcia Alves, president, Arhur D.Little; Werner Josef Lübberink, director, Deutsche Bahn; Antoine Riboud, Danone.

FINANCIAL FACTS
Tuition: $15,000 **Books and Supplies:** $1,000 **Room & Board (off campus):** $10,000

ADMISSIONS
Admissions Selectivity Rating: 60*

# of Applications Received: 523 **% Applicants Accepted:** 62 %
Acceptees Attending: 70 **Application Fee:** $200 **International Application Deadline/Notification:** round 1: 3/1 / 5/1, round 2 5/1 / 6/1, round 3 6/5 / 7/1.

Deferment Available: yes **Maximum Length of Deferment:** 1 year
Need-Blind Admissions: yes

EMPLOYMENT PROFILE
Primary Source of Full-time Job Acceptances

School-facilitated Activities 45 (20%)
Graduate-facilitated Activities 75 (34%)
Unknown 103 (46%)

Percent Employed: 13

Top 5 Employers Hiring Grads

L'Oréal; Société Générale; PSA Peugeot Citroën; BNP Paribas; Capgemini.

FAIRLEIGH DICKINSON UNIVERSITY—COLLEGE AT FLORHAM
SILBERMAN COLLEGE OF BUSINESS

ADMISSIONS CONTACT: SUSAN NEIHART, DIRECTOR OF GRADUATE RECRUITMENT & MARKETING
ADDRESS: 285 MADISON AVENUE (M-MS1-03), MADISON, NJ 07960
PHONE: 973-443-8905 • FAX: 973-443-8088
E-MAIL: GRAD@FDU.EDU
WEBSITE: WWW.FDU.EDU

GENERAL INFORMATION
Type of School: private

STUDENTS
Enrollment of Parent Institution: 3,587 **Male/female:** 58/42 **% Out-of-state:** 7 **% Part-time:** 71 **% Minorities:** 17 **% International:** 9 **Average Age at Entry:** 28

ACADEMICS
Student/faculty Ratio: 25:1 **% Female Faculty:** 17 **Joint Degrees:** MBA (management)/MA (corporate and organizational communications), MBA (human resource management)/MA (industrial/organizational psychology). **Prominent Alumni:** Michael King, KingWorld, television syndicator; Patrick Zenner, former president and CEO, Hoffman-LaRoche, Inc.; Anthony Cuti, chairman, president, CEO, Duane Reade Corp.; George Martin, captain, NFL Giants; Gary Balkema, president, Worldwide Bayer, Cust. Care Div., Bayer Corp.

FINANCIAL FACTS
Tuition: $15,102 **Fees:** $572 **Books and Supplies:** $2,000 **Room & Board (on campus):** $9,806 **% of Students Receiving Aid:** 60 **% of Students Receiving Loans:** 33 **% of Students Receiving Grants:** 35 **Average Award Package:** $3,500 **Average Grant:** $3,250

ADMISSIONS
Admissions Selectivity Rating: 60*
# of Applications Received: 181 **% Applicants Accepted:** 67 **% Acceptees Attending:** 363 **TOEFL Required of Int'l Applicants:** yes **Minimum TOEFL (paper/computer):** 550/213 **Application Fee:** $40 **Regular Application Deadline:** rolling **Regular Notification:** rolling **Deferment Available:** yes **Transfer Students Accepted:** yes **Non-fall Admissions:** yes **Need-Blind Admissions:** yes

FU JEN CATHOLIC UNIVERSITY
COLLEGE OF MANAGEMENT

ADMISSIONS CONTACT: PEI-GI SHU, ASSOCIATE DEAN
ADDRESS: NO. 510, CHUNG-CHENG ROAD, HSINGCHUANG, TAIPEI HSIEN, 24205 TAIWAN
PHONE: 011-886-2-2905-2613 • FAX: 011-886-2-2905-2186
E-MAIL: CLARE@MAILS.FJU.EDU.TW
WEBSITE: WWW.MANAGEMENT.FJU.EDU.TW

GENERAL INFORMATION
Type of School: private Affiliation: Roman Catholic-Jesuit

STUDENTS
Enrollment of Business School: 116 **% Male/female:** 60/40 **% Out-of-state:** 1 **% Part-time:** 40 **% International:** 1 **Average Age at Entry:** 30 **Average Years Work Experience at Entry:** 2

ACADEMICS
% Female Faculty: 45 **Prominent Alumni:** Yi-Jeng Peng, vice president, Bank of Overseas Chinese; Wan-Li Wang, vice president, CFSB; Wen-Zong Shu, general manager, Home Box; Ying-Chung Lyu, senior vice president; Yen-Mu Chen, president, furniture company.

FINANCIAL FACTS
Tuition: $4,063 **Books and Supplies:** $625 **% of Students Receiving Aid:** 25 **% of First-year Students Receiving Aid:** 10 **% of Students Receiving Grants:** 12

ADMISSIONS
Admissions Selectivity Rating: 97
# of Applications Received: 2,497 **% Applicants Accepted:** 5 **% Acceptees Attending:** 98 **Average GPA:** 3.00 **Application Fee:** $65 **International Application Fee:** $65 Regular

EMPLOYMENT PROFILE
Primary Source of Full-time Job Acceptances
Graduate-facilitated Activities 2 (9%)
Unknown.......................................21 (91%)
Percent Employed: 85

GEORGE MASON UNIVERSITY
SCHOOL OF MANAGEMENT

ADMISSIONS CONTACT: ANGEL BURGOS, MBA DIRECTOR
ADDRESS: 4400 UNIVERSITY DRIVE, MSN 5A2, ENTERPRISE HALL, ROOM 28,
FAIRFAX, VA 22030
PHONE: (703) 993-2136 • FAX: 703-993-1778
E-MAIL: MBA@GMU.EDU
WEBSITE: WWW.SOM.GMU.EDU

GENERAL INFORMATION

Type of School: public **Environment:** city **Academic Calendar:** semester

STUDENTS

Enrollment of Parent Institution: 29,889 **Enrollment of Business School:** 264 % **Male/female:** 54/46 **% Part-time:** 86 % **International:** 56 **Average Age at Entry:** 29 **Average Years Work Experience at Entry:** 6

ACADEMICS

Prominent Alumni: Michael G. Anzilotti, president/CEO, First Virginia Bank; William Page Johnson, II, Commissioner for Revenue, City of Fairfax, VA; Terri Malone, Washington National Opera, Northrop Grumman executive; Bill Henry, national president, The American Society of Civil Engineers; Walter Howell, senior vice president, Computer Associates International, Inc.

FINANCIAL FACTS

Tuition (in-state/out-of-state): $12,240/$21,600 **Fees:** $260 **Books and Supplies:** $1,000

ADMISSIONS

Admissions Selectivity Rating: 86

# of Applications Received: 292 **% Applicants Accepted:** 45 % **Acceptees Attending:** 68 **Average GMAT:** 583 **Average GPA:** 3.00 **TOEFL Required of Int'l Applicants:** yes **Minimum TOEFL (paper/computer):** 600/230 **Application Fee:** $60 **Regular Application Deadline:** 4/1 **Regular Notification:** 5/15 Application Deadline/Notification: round 1 4/1 / 5/15, round 2 6/1 / 6/30. **Deferment Available:** yes **Maximum Length of Deferment:** 1 semester **Non-fall Admissions:** yes **Need-Blind Admissions:** yes

GEORGIA COLLEGE & STATE UNIVERSITY
THE J. WHITNEY BUNTING SCHOOL OF BUSINESS

ADMISSIONS CONTACT: MIKE AUGUSTINE, DIRECTOR OF ADMISSIONS
ADDRESS: GC&SU CAMPUS BOX 23, MILLEDGEVILLE, GA 31061
PHONE: 478-445-6289 • FAX: 478-445-1914
E-MAIL: CHRISTY.SMITH@GCSU.EDU
WEBSITE: WWW.GCSU.EDU

GENERAL INFORMATION

Type of School: public **Environment:** town **Academic Calendar:** semester

STUDENTS

% Part-time: 100 **Average Age at Entry:** 26

ACADEMICS

Student/faculty Ratio: 17:1 **% Female Faculty:** 35 **Prominent Alumni:** Tony Nicely, president and CEO, GEICO; Alex Gregory, president and CEO, YKK Corporation of America; Mike Garrett, president and CEO, Georgia Power Company.

FINANCIAL FACTS

Tuition (in-state/out-of-state): $4,185/$13,365 **Fees:** $700 **Books and Supplies:** $700 **Room & Board (on/off campus):** $6,282/$6,850 **Average Award Package:** $7,005 **Average Grant:** $2,336

ADMISSIONS

Admissions Selectivity Rating: 66

# of Applications Received: 71 **% Applicants Accepted:** 83 % **Acceptees Attending:** 75 **GMAT Range (25th to 75th percentile):** 430–510 **Average GMAT:** 485 **Average GPA:** 3.2 **TOEFL Required of Int'l Applicants:** yes **Minimum TOEFL (paper/computer):** 500/173 **Application Fee:** $25 **Deferment Available:** yes **Maximum Length of Deferment:** 1 year **Transfer Students Accepted:** yes **Non-fall Admissions:** yes

Grenoble École de Management (France)
Grenoble Graduate School of Business

ADMISSIONS CONTACT: MS. CHLOË THOMAS, MARKETING AND ADMISSIONS
ADDRESS: 12 RUE PIERRE SÉMARD, BP 127, GRENOBLE, 38003 FRANCE
PHONE: 011 33 (0) 4 76 70 60 23 • FAX: 011 33 (0) 4 76 70 61 77
E-MAIL: CHLOE.THOMAS@GGSB.COM
WEBSITE: WWW.GRENOBLE-EM.COM

GENERAL INFORMATION
Type of School: private

STUDENTS
Enrollment of Business School: 214 **% Male/female:** 66/34 **%**
International: 83 **Average Age at Entry:** 32 **Average Years Work**
Experience at Entry: 9

FINANCIAL FACTS
Tuition: $24,762 **Room & Board (on campus):** $800

ADMISSIONS
Admissions Selectivity Rating: 97
# of Applications Received: 805 **% Applicants Accepted:** 6 **%**
Acceptees Attending: 92 **GMAT Range (25th to 75th percentile):**
660–700 **Average GMAT:** 610 **Average GPA:** 3.4 **TOEFL Required of**
Int'l Applicants: yes **Minimum TOEFL (paper/computer):** 507/210
Application Fee: $85 **International Application Fee:** $85 **Regular**
Application Deadline: 5/10 **Regular Notification:** 5/10 Application
Deadline: round 1 2/19, round 2 3/22, round 3 4/12, round 4 5/10.
Deferment Available: yes **Maximum Length of Deferment:** 1 year
Transfer Students Accepted: yes **Non-fall Admissions:** yes

EMPLOYMENT PROFILE
Primary Source of Full-time Job Acceptances
School-facilitated Activities 22%
Graduate-facilitated Activities 12%
Unknown..66%

Groupe ESC Toulouse
ESC Toulouse Graduate School
of Management

ADMISSIONS CONTACT: DIRECTOR ESC TOULOUSE
ADDRESS: 20, BD LASCROSSES, BP 7010, TOULOUSE, 31068, FRANCE
WEBSITE: WWW.ESC-TOULOUSE.FR

GENERAL INFORMATION
Type of School: private **Academic Calendar:** trimester

STUDENTS
Enrollment of Parent Institution: 1,424 **Enrollment of Business**
School: 850 **% Male/female:** 52/48 **% International:** 16 **Average**
Age at Entry: 23

FINANCIAL FACTS
Tuition: $9,999

ADMISSIONS
# of Applications Received: 2,500 **% Applicants Accepted:** 20 **%**
Acceptees Attending: 90 **Regular Application Deadline:** 7/30
Deferment Available: yes

Henderson State University
School of Business Administration

ADMISSIONS CONTACT: MISSIE BELL, GRADUATE SCHOOL, ADMINISTRATIVE
ASSISTANT
ADDRESS: 1100 HENDERSON STREET, BOX 7802, ARKADELPHIA,
AR 71999-0001
PHONE: (870) 230-5126 • FAX: (870) 230-5479
E-MAIL: GRAD@HSU.EDU
WEBSITE: WWW.HSU.EDU/SCHOOLOFBUSINESS/

GENERAL INFORMATION
Type of School: public **Environment:** rural

STUDENTS
Enrollment of Parent Institution: 3,754 **Enrollment of Business**
School: 45 **% Male/female:** 50/50 **% Out-of-state:** 5 **% Part-time:**
25 **% Minorities:** 10 **% International:** 20

ACADEMICS
Student/faculty Ratio: 6:1 **% Female Faculty:** 38 **Prominent**
Alumni: Junious Babbs, Assistant Superintendent, Little Rock
School District; Richard Hoover, NASA; Billy Hudson, professor,
Vanderbilt University; Bob Fisher, president, Belmont University.

FINANCIAL FACTS
Tuition (in-state/out-of-state): $2,916/$5,832 **Fees:** $411 **Room &**
Board: $3,874

ADMISSIONS
Admissions Selectivity Rating: 61
# of Applications Received: 19 **% Acceptees Attending:** 32 **Average**
GMAT: 450 **Average GPA:** 3.00 **TOEFL Required of Int'l Applicants:**
yes **Minimum TOEFL (paper/computer):** 550/213 **International**
Application Fee: $40 **Transfer Students Accepted:** yes **Non-fall**
Admissions: yes **Need-Blind Admissions:** yes

IDAHO STATE UNIVERSITY
COLLEGE OF BUSINESS

ADMISSIONS CONTACT: GORDON B. BROOKS, SR.,
ASSISTANT DEAN FOR GRADUATE PROGRAMS
ADDRESS: BOX 8020, POCATELLO, ID 83209
PHONE: 208-282-2504 • FAX: 208-236-4367
E-MAIL: BROOGORD@ISU.EDU
WEBSITE: COB.ISU.EDU

GENERAL INFORMATION

Type of School: public **Environment:** town **Academic Calendar:** semester

STUDENTS

Enrollment of Parent Institution: 13,977 **Enrollment of Business School:** 109 **% Male/female:** 75/25 **% Part-time:** 56 **% Minorities:** 4 **% International:** 10 **Average Age at Entry:** 32

ACADEMICS

Student/faculty Ratio: 23:1 **% Female Faculty:** 20 **% Minority Faculty:** 2

FINANCIAL FACTS

Tuition (in-state/out-of-state): $5,520/$13,220 **Books and Supplies:** $1,000 **Room & Board:** $7,500

ADMISSIONS

Admissions Selectivity Rating: 82

# of Applications Received: 73 **% Applicants Accepted:** 59 **% Acceptees Attending:** 74 **Average GPA:** 3.4 **TOEFL Required of Int'l Applicants:** yes **Minimum TOEFL (paper/computer):** 550/213 **Regular Application Deadline:** 6/1 **Regular Notification:** 6/7 **Deferment Available:** yes **Maximum Length of Deferment:** 2 years **Transfer Students Accepted:** yes **Non-fall Admissions:** yes

INCAE
GRADUATE PROGRAM

WEBSITE: WWW.INCAE.AC.CR

GENERAL INFORMATION

Type of School: private **Academic Calendar:** trimester

STUDENTS

Enrollment of Parent Institution: 441 **Enrollment of Business School:** 441 **% Male/female:** 70/30 **% Part-time:** 20 **Average Age at Entry:** 28

ACADEMICS

Student/faculty Ratio: 15:1

FINANCIAL FACTS

Tuition: $11,500 **% of Students Receiving Aid:** 3

ADMISSIONS

Admissions Selectivity Rating: 60*

# of Applications Received: 530 **% Applicants Accepted:** 60 **% Acceptees Attending:** 37 **Application Fee:** $50 **Regular Application Deadline:** 7/15 **Regular Notification:** rolling **Deferment Available:** yes

INDIANA UNIVERSITY—
NORTHWEST
SCHOOL OF BUSINESS AND ECONOMICS

ADMISSIONS CONTACT: JOHN GIBSON, DIRECTOR, UNDERGRADUATE
AND GRADUATE PROGRAMS IN BUSINESS
ADDRESS: 3400 BROADWAY, GARY, IN 46408-1197
PHONE: 219-980-6635 • FAX: 219-980-6916
E-MAIL: JAGIBSON@IUN.EDU
WEBSITE: WWW.IUN.EDU/~BUSNW

GENERAL INFORMATION

Type of School: Academic Calendar: semester

STUDENTS

Enrollment of Parent Institution: 4,300 **Enrollment of Business School:** 115 **% % Part-time:** 99 **Average Age at Entry:** 35

ACADEMICS

Student/faculty Ratio: 10:1 **% Female Faculty:** 26 **% Minority Faculty:** 37

FINANCIAL FACTS

Tuition (in-state/out-of-state): $3,750/$8,750 **Fees:** $375 **Books and Supplies:** $999 **% of Students Receiving Loans:** 30 **Average Grant:** $999

ADMISSIONS

Admissions Selectivity Rating: 63

# of Applications Received: 50 **% Applicants Accepted:** 70 **% Average GMAT:** 470 **TOEFL Required of Int'l Applicants:** yes **Minimum TOEFL (paper):** 550 **Application Fee:** $25 **International Application Fee:** $55 **Deferment Available:** yes **Maximum Length of Deferment:** 1 semester **Transfer Students Accepted:** yes **Non-fall Admissions:** yes **Need-Blind Admissions:** yes **Applicants Also Look At:** Purdue University Calumet, Valparaiso University.

Indiana University–Purdue University Fort Wayne

SCHOOL OF BUSINESS AND MANAGEMENT

ADMISSIONS CONTACT: SANDY FRANKE, SECRETARY, MBA PROGRAM
ADDRESS: NEFF 366, 2101 COLISEUM BOULEVARD EAST, FORT WAYNE, IN 46805-1499
PHONE: 260-481-6498
E-MAIL: EMAIL@SCHOOL.EDU
WEBSITE: WWW.IPFW.EDU/BMS/MBA1.HTM

GENERAL INFORMATION

Type of School: public **Environment:** village **Academic Calendar:** semester

STUDENTS

Enrollment of Parent Institution: 10,749 **Enrollment of Business School:** 191 % **Male/female:** 65/35 **% Part-time:** 91 **Average Age at Entry:** 32

ACADEMICS

Student/faculty Ratio: 1:1

FINANCIAL FACTS

Tuition (in-state/out-of-state): $218.75/$474.90 (per credit hour)

ADMISSIONS

Admissions Selectivity Rating: 60*

# of Applications Received: 45 **% Applicants Accepted:** 91 % **Acceptees Attending:** 95 **Application Fee:** $30 **Regular Application Deadline:** 7/15 **Regular Notification:** 1/1 **Deferment Available:** yes **Non-fall Admissions:** yes Need-Blind

Instituto de Empresa

ADMISSIONS CONTACT: JULIAN TRIGO, DIRECTOR OF ADMISSIONS
ADDRESS: MARÍA DE MOLINA 11-13-15, MADRID, MA 28006 SPAIN
PHONE: 011 34 91 568 9610 • FAX: 011 34 91 568 9710
E-MAIL: ADMISSIONS@IE.EDU
WEBSITE: WWW.IE.EDU

GENERAL INFORMATION

Type of School: private

STUDENTS

Enrollment of Business School: 219 % **Male/female:** 64/36 % **International:** 87 **Average Years Work Experience at Entry:** 4

ACADEMICS

Student/faculty Ratio: 11:1 **Prominent Alumni:** Fernando Barnuevo, head of global investment management, JPMorgan Chase; Pilar de Zulueta, southern europe director, Warner Bros.; José María Cámara, president, Sony Music, Spain; Juan PableSan Agustín, vice president, CEMEX; Isabel Aguilera, COO, NH Hoteles.

FINANCIAL FACTS

Tuition : $33,950 **Books and Supplies:** $400 **Average Grant:** $17,000

ADMISSIONS

Admissions Selectivity Rating: 98

# of Applications Received: 1,044 **% Applicants Accepted:** 26 % **Acceptees Attending:** 81 **Average GMAT:** 685 **Average GPA:** 3.7 TOEFL **Application Fee:** $120 **Regular Application Deadline:** rolling **Regular Notification:** rolling **Deferment Available:** yes **Maximum Length of Deferment:** 2 years **Non-fall Admissions:** yes **Need-Blind Admissions:** yes **Applicants Also Look At:** IMD (International Institute for Management Development), INSEAD, London Business School.

EMPLOYMENT PROFILE

Top 5 Employers Hiring Grads

BBVA; Telefónica; Accenture; Bayer; Pfizer.

Instituto Tecnologico y de Estudios Superiores de Monterrey (ITESM)

EGADE, MONTERREY CAMPUS

ADMISSIONS CONTACT: LIC. OLGA RENÉE DE LA TORRE, ACADEMIC SERVICES DIRECTOR
ADDRESS: AV. FUNDADORES Y RUFINO TAMAYO, COL. VALLE ORIENTE, SAN PEDRO GARZA GARCÍA, NL 66269 MEXICO
PHONE: 011-52-818-625-6204 • FAX: 011-52-818-625-6208
E-MAIL: ADMISIONES.EGADE@ITESM.MX
WEBSITE: WWW.EGADE.ITESM.MX

GENERAL INFORMATION

Type of School: private **Academic Calendar:** quarter

STUDENTS

Enrollment of Parent Institution: 19,358 **Enrollment of Business School:** 597 % **Male/female:** 79/21 **% Part-time:** 90 % **International:** 66 **Average Age at Entry:** 28 **Average Years Work Experience at Entry:** 5

ACADEMICS

Student/faculty Ratio: 14:1 **% Female Faculty:** 25 **Joint Degrees:** Double degree MBA (1 year more than the regular length).
Prominent Alumni: Eugenio Clariond Reyes-Retana, general director, IMSA Group; Fernando Canales Clariond, Ministery of Economic Affairs; Jose Antonio Rivero Larrea, president of administration board, Autlan Group; Jose Antonio Fernandez Carbajal, general director, FEMSA Group; Luis Sada Gonzalez, general director, John Deere Mexico.

FINANCIAL FACTS

Tuition: $17,500 **Books and Supplies:** $780 **Room & Board (on/off campus):** $7,800/$6,400 **% of Students Receiving Aid:** 26 % of

First-year Students Receiving Aid: 24 % of Students Receiving Loans: 3 % of Students Receiving Grants: 23 Average Grant: $11,375

ADMISSIONS

Admissions Selectivity Rating: 84

# of Applications Received: 199 **% Applicants Accepted:** 73 % **Acceptees Attending:** 74 **Average GMAT:** 615 **Average GPA:** 3.5 **Application Fee:** $115 **Regular Application Deadline:** 5/1 **Regular Notification:** 6/1 **Deferment Available:** yes **Maximum Length of Deferment:** 1 year **Transfer Students Accepted:** yes **Non-fall Admissions:** yes

IOWA STATE UNIVERSITY
COLLEGE OF BUSINESS

ADMISSIONS CONTACT: AMY HUTTER, DIRECTOR, MBA RECRUITMENT & MARKETING
ADDRESS: 1360 GERDIN BUSINESS BUILDING, AMES, IA 50011
PHONE: 515-294-8118 • FAX: 515-294-2446
E-MAIL: BUSGRAD@IASTATE.EDU
WEBSITE: WWW.BUS.IASTATE.EDU/MBA

GENERAL INFORMATION

Type of School: public **Environment:** town **Academic Calendar:** semester

STUDENTS

Enrollment of Parent Institution: 26,380 **Enrollment of Business School:** 94 % **Male/female:** 62/38 **% Out-of-state:** 8 **% Part-time:** 62 **% International:** 31 **Average Age at Entry:** 26 **Average Years Work Experience at Entry:** 3

ACADEMICS

Student/faculty Ratio: 4:1 **% Female Faculty:** 9 **% Minority Faculty:** 12 **Joint Degrees:** MBA/MS (Statistics) 3 years, MBA/MS (Community and Regional Planning) 3 years, MBA/BS (Engineering) 5 years.

FINANCIAL FACTS

Tuition (in-state/out-of-state): $7,718/$18,132 **Fees:** $930 **Books and Supplies:** $1,000 **Room & Board:** $10,200 **% of Students Receiving Aid:** 50 **% of First-year Students Receiving Aid:** 50 **Average Award Package:** $8,120

ADMISSIONS

Admissions Selectivity Rating: 82

# of Applications Received: 210 **% Applicants Accepted:** 69 % **Acceptees Attending:** 65 **Average GMAT:** 595 **Average GPA:** 3.41 **TOEFL Required of Int'l Applicants:** yes **Minimum TOEFL (paper/computer):** 600/250 **Application Fee:** $30 **International Application Fee:** $70 **Regular Application Deadline:** rolling **Regular Notification:** rolling **Deferment Available:** yes **Maximum Length of Deferment:** 1 year **Non-fall Admissions:** yes **Need-Blind Admissions:** yes **Applicants Also Look At:** Drake University, University of Iowa.

EMPLOYMENT PROFILE

Primary Source of Full-time Job Acceptances

School-facilitated Activities 23 (69%)
Graduate-facilitated Activities 12 (31%)
Unknown.......................................35 (100%)

Average Base Starting Salary: $57,848

Percent Employed: 94

Grads Employed by Industry:.......% avg. salary:

Finance/Accounting........................21 $51,800
Human Resources.........................3 NR
Marketing/Sales 11 $61,667
MIS..12 $74,500
Operations/Production 33 $53,000
Consulting.....................................6 $68,000
General Management 14 $43,500

JACKSON STATE UNIVERSITY
SCHOOL OF BUSINESS

ADMISSIONS CONTACT: JESSE PENNINGTON, DIRECTOR OF GRADUATE PROGRAMS
ADDRESS: PO BOX 18660, JACKSON, MI 39217
PHONE: 601-432-6315 • FAX: 601-987-4380
E-MAIL: GADMAPPL@CCAIX.JSUMS.EDU
WEBSITE: CCAIX.JSUMS.EDU/BUSINESS/

GENERAL INFORMATION

Type of School: public **Environment:** metropolis **Academic Calendar:** semester

STUDENTS

Enrollment of Parent Institution: 6,292 **Enrollment of Business School:** 1,104

FINANCIAL FACTS

Tuition: $1,920

ADMISSIONS

Admissions Selectivity Rating: 60*

# of Applications Received: 160 **% Applicants Accepted:** 77 % **Acceptees Attending:** 89 **TOEFL Required of Int'l Applicants:** yes **Minimum TOEFL (paper):** 525 **Regular Application Deadline:** rolling **Regular Notification:** rolling **Deferment Available:** yes

James Madison University
College of Business

ADMISSIONS CONTACT: KRISTA D. DOFFLEMYER, ADMINISTRATIVE ASSISTANT
ADDRESS: ZANE SHOWKER HALL, MSC 0206, ROOM 616, HARRISONBURG, VA 22807
PHONE: 540-568-3253 • FAX: 540-568-3587
E-MAIL: MBA@JMU.EDU
WEBSITE: WWW.JMU.EDU/MBA

GENERAL INFORMATION

Type of School: public **Environment:** town

STUDENTS

Enrollment of Parent Institution: 17,393 **Enrollment of Business School:** 103 % **Male/female:** 69/31 **% Out-of-state:** 44 **% Part-time:** 84 **% Minorities:** 6 **% International:** 19 **Average Age at Entry:** 31

ACADEMICS

% Female Faculty: :30 **% Minority Faculty:** 4

FINANCIAL FACTS

Tuition (in-state/out-of-state): $6,336/$17,832 **Books and Supplies:** $2,000 **% of Students Receiving Aid:** 60 **% of First-year Students Receiving Aid:** 46 **% of Students Receiving Loans:** 39 **% of Students Receiving Grants:** 33 **Average Award Package:** $11,252 **Average Grant:** $5,981 **Average Student Loan Debt:** $17,563

ADMISSIONS

Admissions Selectivity Rating: 76

# of Applications Received: 37 **% Applicants Accepted:** 84 **% Acceptees Attending:** 77 **GMAT Range (25th to 75th percentile):** 520–670 **Average GMAT:** 575 **Average GPA:** 3.2 **TOEFL Required of Int'l Applicants:** yes **Minimum TOEFL (paper/computer):** 550/280 **Application Fee:** $55 **Regular Application Deadline:** 7/1 **Regular Notification:** rolling **Deferment Available:** yes **Maximum Length of Deferment:** 1 year **Transfer Students Accepted:** yes

Kansas State University
College of Business Administration

ADMISSIONS CONTACT: LYNN WAUGH, GRADUATE STUDIES ASSISTANT
ADDRESS: 107 CALVIN HALL, MANHATTAN, KS 66506-0501
PHONE: 785-532-7190 • FAX: 785-532-7216
E-MAIL: LWAUGH@KSU.EDU
WEBSITE: WWW.CBA.KSU.EDU

GENERAL INFORMATION

Type of School: public **Environment:** village **Academic Calendar:** semester

STUDENTS

Enrollment of Business School: 91 % **Male/female:** 70/30 **% Out-of-state:** 4 **% Part-time:** 18 **% Minorities:** 9 **% International:** 22 **Average Age at Entry:** 24 **Average Years Work Experience at Entry:** 2

ACADEMICS

Student/faculty Ratio: 5:1 **% Female Faculty:** 22 **% Minority Faculty:** 4

FINANCIAL FACTS

Tuition (in-state/out-of-state): $6,855/$19,340 **Fees:** $666 **Books and Supplies:** $1,000 **Room & Board (on/off campus):** $5,000/$6,000 **% of Students Receiving Aid:** 18 **% of First-year Students Receiving Aid:** 12 **Average Grant:** $2,500

ADMISSIONS

Admissions Selectivity Rating: 89

# of Applications Received: 86 **% Applicants Accepted:** 40 **% Average GMAT:** 548 **Average GPA:** 3.4 **TOEFL Required of Int'l Applicants:** yes **Minimum TOEFL (paper/computer):** 550/213 **Application Fee:** $50 **International Application Fee:** $60 **Regular Application Deadline:** 9/1 **Regular Notification:** 7/15 **Deferment Available:** yes **Maximum Length of Deferment:** 1 year **Transfer Students Accepted:** yes **Need-Blind Admissions:** yes **Applicants Also Look At:** Oklahoma State University, University of Kansas, University of Nebraska–Lincoln, University of Oklahoma, Wichita State University.

EMPLOYMENT PROFILE

Grads Employed by Industry:	.......%	avg. salary:
Finance/Accounting	30	$46,000
Human Resources	8	$52,000
Marketing/Sales	8	$42,000
MIS	8	$55,000
Consulting	22	$42,000
Communications	8	$57,000
Entrepreneurship	8	$38,000

King Fahd University of Petroleum and Minerals (Saudi Arabia)
College of Industrial Management

ADMISSIONS CONTACT: ASSISTANT DEAN FOR GRADUATE PROGRAMS, CIM, ASSISTANT DEAN FOR GRADUATE PROGRAMS
ADDRESS: P. O. BOX: 1570, DHAHRAN, 31261 SAUDI ARABIA
PHONE: 011-966-3-860-1143 • FAX: 011-966-3-860-3850
E-MAIL: SGHAMDI@KFUPM.EDU.SA
WEBSITE: WWW.KFUPM.EDU.SA/

GENERAL INFORMATION

Type of School: public **Academic Calendar:** Sept. to June

STUDENTS

Enrollment of Business School: 193 **% Out-of-state:** 10 **% Part-time:** 87 **% Minorities:** 23 **% International:** 23 **Average Age at Entry:** 29

ACADEMICS

Student/faculty Ratio: 20:1 **% Minority Faculty:** 60 **Prominent Alumni:** K. Alfaleh, vice president, Aramco; A. Al Khuraimi, vice president, SABIC; A. Alothman, vice president, Fin-Aramco; T. Batteeri, CEO, Saudi Electric; S. Sheikh, chief economist, NCB.

FINANCIAL FACTS

Tuition: $40 (per credit hour) **Room & Board (on/off campus):** $6,500/$11,000

ADMISSIONS

Admissions Selectivity Rating: 71

# of Applications Received: 108 **% Applicants Accepted:** 62 **% Average GMAT:** 450 **Average GPA:** 3.1 **TOEFL Required of Int'l Applicants:** yes **Minimum TOEFL (paper/computer):** 520/190 **Regular Application Deadline:** 10/31 **Regular Notification:** 11/21 **Deferment Available:** yes **Transfer Students Accepted:** yes **Non-fall Admissions:** yes

EMPLOYMENT PROFILE

Primary Source of Full-time Job Acceptances

School-facilitated Activities 20%

Graduate-facilitated Activities 80%

KUWAIT UNIVERSITY
COLLEGE OF BUSINESS ADMINISTRATION

ADMISSIONS CONTACT: ADMISSIONS OFFICER
ADDRESS: KUWAIT UNIVERSITY, COLLEGE OF GRADUATE STUDY, KHALDIA-BULDING 2, KUWAIT PO BOX 5969, SAFAT 13060 KUWAIT
PHONE: 965-498-7102 • FAX: 965-481-0499
E-MAIL: GRADADM@KUC01.KUNIV.EDU.KW
WEBSITE: WWW.GRADUATE.EDU.KW

GENERAL INFORMATION

Type of School: public

STUDENTS

Enrollment of Parent Institution: 45 **Enrollment of Business School:** 145 **% Male/female:** 30/70 **% Part-time:** 95 **% International:** 30 **Average Age at Entry:** 25 **Average Years Work Experience at Entry:** 3

ACADEMICS

Student/faculty Ratio: 7:1

FINANCIAL FACTS

Tuition (in-state): $1,060 **Fees (in-state):** $320

ADMISSIONS

Admissions Selectivity Rating: 65

# of Applications Received: 12 **% Applicants Accepted:** 100 **% Acceptees Attending:** 100 **GMAT Range (25th to 75th percentile):** 450–559 **Average GMAT:** 520 **Average GPA:** 3.2 **TOEFL Required of Int'l Applicants:** yes **Minimum TOEFL (paper/computer):** 550/213 **Regular Application Deadline:** 1/31 **Regular Notification:** 5/15

Application Deadline/Notification: 1/31 / 5/15 **Deferment Available:** yes **Maximum Length of Deferment:** 1 year **Transfer Students Accepted:** yes

LA SALLE UNIVERSITY
SCHOOL OF BUSINESS ADMINISTRATION

ADMISSIONS CONTACT: KATHY BAGNELL, DIRECTOR, MARKETING AND GRADUATE ENROLLMENT
ADDRESS: 1900 WEST OLNEY AVENUE, PHILADELPHIA, PA 19141
PHONE: 215-951-1057 • FAX: 215-951-1886
E-MAIL: EMAIL@SCHOOL.EDU
WEBSITE: WWW.LASALLE.EDU/ACADEM/SBA/GRAD/INDEX.SHTML

GENERAL INFORMATION

Type of School: private **Environment:** metropolis **Academic Calendar:** trimester

STUDENTS

Enrollment of Parent Institution: 5,408 **Enrollment of Business School:** 687 **% Male/female:** 59/41 **% Part-time:** 90 **% Minorities:** 12 **% International:** 11 **Average Age at Entry:** 32

FINANCIAL FACTS

Tuition: $12,800 **Fees:** $85

ADMISSIONS

Admissions Selectivity Rating: 60*

# of Applications Received: 142 **% Applicants Accepted:** 85 **% Acceptees Attending:** 89 **TOEFL Required of Int'l Applicants:** yes **Minimum TOEFL (paper):** 550 **Application Fee:** $35 **Regular Application Deadline:** 8/14 **Regular Notification:** rolling **Deferment Available:** yes **Non-fall Admissions:** yes

LEHIGH UNIVERSITY
COLLEGE OF BUSINESS AND ECONOMICS

ADMISSIONS CONTACT: CORINN MCBRIDE, DIRECTOR OF RECRUITMENT AND ADMISSIONS
ADDRESS: 621 TAYLOR STREET, BETHLEHEM, PA 18015
PHONE: 610-758-3418 • FAX: 610-758-5283
E-MAIL: MBA.ADMISSIONS@LEHIGH.EDU
WEBSITE: WWW.LEHIGH.EDU/MBA

GENERAL INFORMATION

Type of School: private **Environment:** city **Academic Calendar:** semester

STUDENTS

Enrollment of Parent Institution: 6,858 **Enrollment of Business School:** 259 **% Male/female:** 71/29 **% Part-time:** 86 **% Minorities:** 6 **% International:** 63 **Average Age at Entry:** 32 **Average Years Work Experience at Entry:** 8

ACADEMICS

Student/faculty Ratio: 6:1 **% Female Faculty:** 20 **% Minority Faculty:** 27

Joint Degrees: MBA/Engineering, MBA/MEd. **Prominent Alumni:** Dexter Baker, chairman & CEO (retired), Air Products & Chemicals; Stephen A. Riordan, editor, *The Boston Globe*; William H. Glenn, vice president finance, CFO, Dresser Rand Co.; E. Joseph Hochreiter, chairman and CEO, M. Cubed Technolgies, Inc; John E. McGlade, president and COO, Air Products and Chemicals.

FINANCIAL FACTS

Tuition: $11,340 **Fees:** $300 **Books and Supplies:** $1,300 **Room & Board (off campus):** $10,800 **% of Students Receiving Aid:** 8 **% of First-year Students Receiving Aid:** 15 **Average Award Package:** $24,260 **Average Grant:** $11,000

ADMISSIONS

Admissions Selectivity Rating: 86

# of Applications Received: 226 **% Applicants Accepted:** 68 **% Acceptees Attending:** 76 **GMAT Range (25th to 75th percentile):** 580–670 **Average GMAT:** 626 **Average GPA:** 3.28 **TOEFL Required of Int'l Applicants:** yes **Minimum TOEFL (paper/computer):** 600/250 **Application Fee:** $65 **Regular Application Notification:** rolling **Deferment Available:** yes **Maximum Length of Deferment:** 1 year **Transfer Students Accepted:** yes **Non-fall Admissions:** yes **Need-Blind Admissions:** yes

EMPLOYMENT PROFILE

Primary Source of Full-time Job Acceptances

School-facilitated Activities	3 (27%)
Graduate-facilitated Activities	2 (18%)
Unknown	6 (55%)

Grads Employed by Industry:	% avg. salary:
Finance/Accounting	37 $109,000
Marketing/Sales	9 NR
MIS	9 NR
Operations/Production	9 $76,000
Consulting	9 $145,000
Entrepreneurship	9 $60,000
Other	9 $80,000

LOUISIANA STATE UNIVERSITY— SHREVEPORT
COLLEGE OF BUSINESS ADMINISTRATION

ADMISSIONS CONTACT: SUSAN WOOD, MBA DIRECTOR
ADDRESS: ONE UNIVERSITY PLACE, SHREVEPORT, LA 71115
PHONE: 318-797-5213 • FAX: 318-797-5017
E-MAIL: SWOOD@PILOT.LSUS.EDU
WEBSITE: WWW.LSUS.EDU/BA/MBA/

GENERAL INFORMATION

Type of School: public **Environment:** city **Academic Calendar:** semester

STUDENTS

Enrollment of Parent Institution: 4,237 **Enrollment of Business School:** 150 **% Male/female:** 47/53 **% Part-time:** 93 **% Minorities:** 10 **% International:** 5

ACADEMICS

Student/faculty Ratio: 20:1

FINANCIAL FACTS

Tuition (in-state/out-of-state): $3,245/$9,420 **% of Students Receiving Aid:** 60

ADMISSIONS

Admissions Selectivity Rating: 60*

# of Applications Received: 70 **% Applicants Accepted:** 71 **% Acceptees Attending:** 80 **TOEFL Required of Int'l Applicants:** yes **Minimum TOEFL (paper):** 550 **Application Fee:** $10 **Regular Application Deadline:** 6/30 **Regular Notification:** rolling **Non-fall Admissions:** yes

LOUISIANA TECH UNIVERSITY
COLLEGE OF ADMINISTRATION AND BUSINESS

ADMISSIONS CONTACT: DR. REBECCA BENNETT, INTERIM ASSOCIATE DEAN OF GRADUATE STUDIES
ADDRESS: PO BOX 10318, RUSTON, LA 71272
PHONE: 318-257-4528 • FAX: 318-257-4253
E-MAIL: GSCHOOL@CAB.LATECH.EDU
WEBSITE: WWW.CAB.LATECH.EDU

GENERAL INFORMATION

Type of School: public **Environment:** rural **Academic Calendar:** quarter

STUDENTS

Enrollment of Parent Institution: 11,232 **Enrollment of Business School:** 83 **% Male/female:** 70/30 **% Part-time:** 13 **% International:** 8

ACADEMICS

Student/faculty Ratio: 25:1 **% Female Faculty:** 10 **% Minority Faculty:** 8

FINANCIAL FACTS

Tuition (in-state/out-of-state): $3,376/$6,956 **Fees :** $40 **Books and Supplies:** $900 **Room & Board (on campus):** $6,580

ADMISSIONS

Admissions Selectivity Rating: 83

# of Applications Received: 38 **% Applicants Accepted:** 39 **% Acceptees Attending:** 113 **Average GMAT:** 530 **Average GPA:** 3.2 **TOEFL Required of Int'l Applicants:** yes **Minimum TOEFL (paper/computer):** 550/213 **Application Fee:** $20 **International Application Fee:** $30 **Regular Application Deadline:** 8/1 **Deferment Available:** yes **Maximum Length of Deferment:** 1 year **Transfer Students Accepted:** yes **Non-fall Admissions:** yes

Marshall University
Lewis College of Business

ADMISSIONS CONTACT: DR. MICHAEL A. NEWSOME, MBA DIRECTOR
ADDRESS: CORBY HALL 217, 400 HAL GREER BOULEVARD, HUNTINGTON, WV
25755-2305
PHONE: 304-696-2613 • FAX: 304-696-3661
E-MAIL: EMAIL@SCHOOL.EDU
WEBSITE: LCOB.MARSHALL.EDU/

GENERAL INFORMATION
Type of School: public **Environment:** town **Academic Calendar:** semester

STUDENTS
Enrollment of Business School: 80 % **Male/female:** 40/60 % **Minorities:** 15 % **International:** 30

ACADEMICS
Student/faculty Ratio: 5:1 **% Female Faculty:** 10 **% Minority Faculty:** 10

FINANCIAL FACTS
Tuition (in-state/out-of-state): $2,020/$5,653 **Fees (in-state/out-of-state):** $1,100/$1,250 **Books and Supplies:** $1,000 **Room & Board (off campus):** $4,000 **% of Students Receiving Aid:** 50 **% of First-year Students Receiving Aid:** 50

ADMISSIONS
Admissions Selectivity Rating: 73

# of Applications Received: 100 **% Applicants Accepted:** 84 % **Acceptees Attending:** 95 **Average GMAT:** 530 **Average GPA:** 3.5 **TOEFL Required of Int'l Applicants:** yes **Minimum TOEFL (paper/computer):** 525/195 **Application Fee:** $30 **International Application Fee:** $25 **Regular Application Deadline:** rolling **Regular Notification:** rolling **Transfer Students Accepted:** yes **Non-fall Admissions:** yes

McNeese State University
MBA Program

ADMISSIONS CONTACT: TAMMY PETTIS, UNIVERSITY ADMISSIONS
ADDRESS: BOX 92495, LAKE CHARLES, LA 70609-2495
PHONE: 337-475-5145 • FAX: 337-475-5189
E-MAIL: INFO@MCNEESE.EDU
WEBSITE: WWW.MCNEESE.EDU/COLLEGES/BUSINESS/MBA

GENERAL INFORMATION
Type of School: public **Environment:** city **Academic Calendar:** semester

STUDENTS
Enrollment of Parent Institution: 8,423 **Enrollment of Business School:** 78 % **Male/female:** 68/32 % **Out-of-state:** 3 % **Part-time:** 64 % **Minorities:** 1 % **International:** 36 **Average Age at Entry:** 30

ACADEMICS
Student/faculty Ratio: 16:1 **% Female Faculty:** 1 **% Minority Faculty:** 45

FINANCIAL FACTS
Tuition (in-state/out-of-state): $3,054/$9,120 **Books and Supplies:** $1,000 **Room & Board (on/off campus):** $3,200/$3,600

ADMISSIONS
Admissions Selectivity Rating: 62

# of Applications Received: 36 **% Applicants Accepted:** 97 % **Acceptees Attending:** 51 **Average GMAT:** 480 **Average GPA:** 3.6 **TOEFL Required of Int'l Applicants:** yes **Minimum TOEFL (paper/computer):** 500/173 **Application Fee:** $20 **International Application Fee:** $30 **Regular Application Deadline:** rolling **Regular Notification:** rolling **Deferment Available:** yes **Maximum Length of Deferment:** 1 year **Transfer Students Accepted:** yes **Non-fall Admissions:** yes **Need-Blind Admissions:** yes

Memorial University of Newfoundland
Faculty of Business Administration

ADMISSIONS CONTACT: LISA SAVAGE, MBA PROGRAM ASSISTANT
ADDRESS: FACULTY OF BUSINESS ADMINISTRATION, MEMORIAL UNIVERSITY OF
NEWFOUNDLAND, ST. JOHN'S, NL A1B 3X5 CANADA
PHONE: 709-737-8522 • FAX: 709-737-2467
E-MAIL: MBA@MUN.CA
WEBSITE: WWW.BUSINESS.MUN.CA/

GENERAL INFORMATION
Type of School: public

STUDENTS
Enrollment of Parent Institution: 17,800 **Enrollment of Business School:** 124 **% Male/female:** 40/60 **% Part-time:** 62 % **International:** 28 **Average Age at Entry:** 25 **Average Years Work Experience at Entry:** 7

ACADEMICS
Student/faculty Ratio: 15:1 **% Female Faculty:** 35

FINANCIAL FACTS
Tuition (in-state): $2,000 **Fees (in-state):** $610 **Books and Supplies:** $1,300 **Room & Board (on/off campus):** $3,500/$5,200 **Average Grant:** $1,200

ADMISSIONS
Admissions Selectivity Rating: 87

# of Applications Received: 82 **% Applicants Accepted:** 40 % **Acceptees Attending:** 70 **Average GMAT:** 600 **TOEFL Required of Int'l Applicants:** yes **Minimum TOEFL (paper/computer):** 580/237 **Application Fee:** $40 **Regular Application Deadline:** 3/15 **Deferment Available:** yes **Maximum Length of Deferment:** 1 year **Transfer**

Students Accepted: yes Non-fall Admissions: yes Need-Blind Admissions: yes

MICHIGAN STATE UNIVERSITY
THE ELI BROAD GRADUATE SCHOOL
OF MANAGEMENT

ADMISSIONS CONTACT: JEFF MCNISH, DIRECTOR, MBA ADMISSIONS
ADDRESS: FULL-TIME MBA PROGRAM, 215 EPPLEY CENTER, EAST LANSING, MI 48824-1121
PHONE: 517-355-7604 • FAX: 517-353-1649
E-MAIL: MBA@MSU.EDU
WEBSITE: MBA.MSU.EDU

GENERAL INFORMATION

Type of School: public Environment: town Academic Calendar: semester

STUDENTS

Enrollment of Parent Institution: 43,401 Enrollment of Business School: 181 % Male/female: 69/31 % Out-of-state: 67 % Minorities: 14 % International: 40 Average Age at Entry: 28 Average Years Work Experience at Entry: 5

ACADEMICS

Student/faculty Ratio: 05:1 % Female Faculty: 20 % Minority Faculty: 5

Joint Degrees: JD/MBA (in conjunction with Michigan State University College of Law) 4 years, MBA/Masters in Global Management (in conjuction with Thunderbird, School of Global Management). Prominent Alumni: Matthew Barnhill, senior vice president, market research, BET; Susan Oaks, vice president, A. T. Kearney; Robert A. Olstein, chairman, The Olstein Financial Alert Fund; Toichi Takenaka, president and CEO, Takenaka Corp.; Robert A. Chapek, president, Buena Vista Home Entertainment.

FINANCIAL FACTS

Tuition (In-state/out-of-state): $17,750/$24,850 Fees: $31 Books and Supplies: $1,700 Room & Board: $7,752 % of Students Receiving Aid: 87 % of First-year Students Receiving Aid: 90 % of Students Receiving Loans: 49 % of Students Receiving Grants: 63 Average Award Package: $17,750 Average Grant: $6,358 Average Student Loan Debt: $36,997

ADMISSIONS

Admissions Selectivity Rating: 93

# of Applications Received: 594 % Applicants Accepted: 33 % Acceptees Attending: 52 GMAT Range (25th to 75th percentile): 580–700 Average GMAT: 636 Average GPA: 3.3 TOEFL Required of Int'l Applicants: yes Minimum TOEFL (paper/computer): 600/250 Application Fee: $85 Application Deadline/Notification: round 1 11/1 / 12/18, round 2 1/9 / 2/23, round 3 2/20 / 3/30, round 4 4/10 / 5/11. Need-Blind Admissions: yes Applicants Also Look At: Arizona State U., The Ohio State U., Penn State U., Purdue U., U. of Michigan, U. of Wisconsin, Vanderbilt U.

EMPLOYMENT PROFILE

Primary Source of Full-time Job Acceptances
School-facilitated Activities............74 (83%)
Graduate-facilitated Activities 15 (17%)
Average Base Starting Salary: $83,588
Percent Employed: 13
Grads Employed by Industry:.......% avg. salary:
Finance/Accounting.........................27 $84,019
Human Resources...........................3 $76,167
Marketing/Sales 18 $82,467
MIS 3 $85,333
Operations/Production 29 $82,606
Consulting.......................................15 $89,815
General Management ....5 NR

Top 5 Employers Hiring Grads

Cummins Inc.; Ford Mortor Company; Intel; Johnson & Johnson; Procter & Gamble.

MICHIGAN TECHNOLOGICAL UNIVERSITY
SCHOOL OF BUSINESS AND ECONOMICS

ADMISSIONS CONTACT: NANCY REHLING, DIRECTOR OF ADMISSIONS
ADDRESS: ADMISSIONS OFFICE, 1400 TOWNSEND DRIVE, HOUGHTON, MI 49931
PHONE: 906-487-2335 • FAX: 906-487-2125
E-MAIL: MTU4U@MTU.EDU
WEBSITE: WWW.SBE.MTU.EDU

GENERAL INFORMATION

Type of School: public

ACADEMICS

Student/faculty Ratio: 14:1
Joint Degrees: BA/MBA.

FINANCIAL FACTS

Tuition (in-state): $7,776 Room & Board (on campus): $8,830

ADMISSIONS

Admissions Selectivity Rating: 80
# of Applications Received: 150 % Applicants Accepted: 63 % Acceptees Attending: 68 Average GMAT: 570 Average GPA: 3.3 Application Fee: $40 International Regular Application Deadline: rolling Regular Notification: rolling

MIDDLE TENNESSEE STATE UNIVERSITY
JENNINGS A. JONES COLLEGE OF BUSINESS

ADMISSIONS CONTACT: TROY A. FESTERVAND, DIRECTOR, GRADUATE BUSINESS STUDIES
ADDRESS: PO BOX 290, BAS N222, MURFREESBORO, TN 37132
PHONE: 615-898-2368 • FAX: 615-904-8491
E-MAIL: GBS@MTSU.EDU
WEBSITE: WWW.MTSU.EDU/~GRADUATE/PROGRAMS/BUAD.HTM

GENERAL INFORMATION
Type of School: public **Environment:** village

STUDENTS
Enrollment of Business School: 396 % **Male/female:** 77/23 % **Minorities:** 12 **Average Age at Entry:** 24

ACADEMICS
Student/faculty Ratio: 20:1

FINANCIAL FACTS
Tuition (in-state/out-of-state): $2,250/$6,100 **Fees:** $300 **Books and Supplies:** $1,000 **Room & Board:** $2,500

ADMISSIONS
Admissions Selectivity Rating: 63
# of Applications Received: 231 % **Applicants Accepted:** 83 % **Acceptees Attending:** 105 **Average GMAT:** 490 **Average GPA:** 3.2 **TOEFL Required of Int'l Applicants:** yes **Minimum TOEFL (paper/computer):** 525/197 **Application Fee:** $25 **International Application Fee:** $30 **Regular Application Deadline:** 7/1 **Regular Notification:** 8/1 **Deferment Available:** yes **Transfer Students Accepted:** yes **Non-fall Admissions:** yes

ACADEMICS
Student/faculty Ratio: 3:1 % **Female Faculty:** 32 % **Minority Faculty:** 11
Joint Degrees: MBA (project management) 1 to 2 years. **Prominent Alumni:** John Grisham, best-selling author; Bailey Howell, Hall of Fame basketball player; Hartley Peavey, founder, Peavey Electronics; Turner Catledge, former executive editor, *The New York Times*; Pat Spainhour, chairman & CEO (retired), Ann Taylor Stores.

FINANCIAL FACTS
Tuition (in-state/out-of-state): $6,894/$15,828 **Books and Supplies:** $950 **Room & Board:** $7,760 **% of Students Receiving Aid:** 68 **% of First-year Students Receiving Aid:** 73 **% of Students Receiving Loans:** 31 **% of Students Receiving Grants:** 35 **Average Award Package:** $13,333 **Average Grant:** $2,886

ADMISSIONS
Admissions Selectivity Rating: 72
# of Applications Received: 71 % **Applicants Accepted:** 70 % **Acceptees Attending:** 72 **GMAT Range (25th to 75th percentile):** 475–540 **Average GMAT:** 498 **Average GPA:** 3.42 **TOEFL Required of Int'l Applicants:** yes **Minimum TOEFL (paper/computer):** 575/232 **Application Fee:** $30 **International Application Fee:** $30 **Regular Application Deadline:** 7/1 **Regular Notification:** rolling **Deferment Available:** yes **Maximum Length of Deferment:** 1 year **Transfer Students Accepted:** yes **Non-fall Admissions:** yes **Need-Blind Admissions:** yes

EMPLOYMENT PROFILE
Primary Source of Full-time Job Acceptances
School-facilitated Activities 9 (47%)
Graduate-facilitated Activities 10 (53%)
Unknown.......................................4
Percent Employed: 67

MISSISSIPPI STATE UNIVERSITY
COLLEGE OF BUSINESS AND INDUSTRY

ADMISSIONS CONTACT: DR. BARBARA SPENCER, DIRECTOR OF GRADUATE STUDIES IN BUSINESS
ADDRESS: PO DRAWER 5288, MISSISSIPPI STATE, MS 39762
PHONE: 662-325-1891 • FAX: 662-325-8161
E-MAIL: GSB@COBILAN.MSSTATE.EDU
WEBSITE: WWW.CBI.MSSTATE.EDU/GSB

GENERAL INFORMATION
Type of School: public **Environment:** town **Academic Calendar:** semester

STUDENTS
Enrollment of Parent Institution: 16,206 **Enrollment of Business School:** 91 % **Male/female:** 53/47 % **Out-of-state:** 12 % **Part-time:** 21 % **Minorities:** 8 % **International:** 7 **Average Age at Entry:** 27

MOREHEAD STATE UNIVERSITY
COLLEGE OF BUSINESS

ADMISSIONS CONTACT: JESSICA THOMPSON, ADMISSIONS SPECIALIST
ADDRESS: 701 GINGER HALL, MOREHEAD, KY 40351
PHONE: 606-783-2039 • FAX: 606-783-5061
E-MAIL: GRADUATE@MOREHEADSTATE.EDU
WEBSITE: WWW.MOREHEADSTATE.EDU

GENERAL INFORMATION
Type of School: public

STUDENTS
Enrollment of Parent Institution: 9,100 **Enrollment of Business School:** 161 % **% Out-of-state:** 19 **% Part-time:** 91 **% International:** 3

FINANCIAL FACTS
Tuition: $5,940

ADMISSIONS

Admissions Selectivity Rating: 81

# of Applications Received: 250 **% Applicants Accepted:** 13 **% Acceptees Attending:** 28 **Average GMAT:** 498 **Average GPA: TOEFL Required of Int'l Applicants:** Yes **Minimum TOEFL (paper/computer):** 525/61 **Regular Application Deadline:** 8/1 **Regular Notification:** 8/1 **Deferment Available:** yes **Maximum Length of Deferment:** 1 year **Transfer Students Accepted:** yes **Non-fall Admissions:** yes

MURRAY STATE UNIVERSITY
COLLEGE OF BUSINESS AND PUBLIC AFFAIRS

ADMISSIONS CONTACT: DR. GERRY NKOMBO MUUKA, ASSISTANT DEAN AND MBA DIRECTOR
ADDRESS: 109 BUSINESS BUILDING, GRADUATE ADMISSIONS OFFICE, SPARKS HALL, MURRAY, KY 42071
PHONE: 270-762-6970 • FAX: 270-762-3482
E-MAIL: CBPA@MURRAYSTATE.EDU
WEBSITE: WWW.MURSUKY.EDU/QACD/CBPA/MBA/INDEX.HTM

GENERAL INFORMATION

Type of School: public **Environment:** village **Academic Calendar:** semester

STUDENTS

Enrollment of Parent Institution: 9,000 **Enrollment of Business School:** 160 **% Part-time:** 53 **Average Age at Entry:** 31

ACADEMICS

Student/faculty Ratio: 20:1

FINANCIAL FACTS

Tuition (in-state/out-of-state): $4,185/$11,700 **Room & Board (on campus):** $3,800

ADMISSIONS

Admissions Selectivity Rating: 60*

# of Applications Received: 121 **% Applicants Accepted:** 75 **% Acceptees Attending:** 52 **TOEFL Required of Int'l Applicants:** yes **Minimum TOEFL (paper):** 525 **Application Fee:** $25 **Regular Application Deadline:** rolling **Regular Notification:** rolling **Deferment Available:** yes **Transfer Students Accepted:** yes **Non-fall Admissions:** yes

NANYANG TECHNOLOGICAL UNIVERSITY
NANYANG BUSINESS SCHOOL

ADMISSIONS CONTACT: ASSOCIATE PROFESSOR OOI LEE LEE, DIRECTOR (MBA)
ADDRESS: THE NANYANG MBA, NANYANG BUSINESS SCHOOL, NANYANG AVENUE, SINGAPORE, 639798 SINGAPORE
PHONE: 011-65-67906183 • FAX: 011-65-67913561
E-MAIL: NBSMBA@NTU.EDU.SG
WEBSITE: WWW.NANYANGMBA.NTU.EDU.SG

GENERAL INFORMATION

Type of School: public

STUDENTS

Enrollment of Parent Institution: 27,652 **Enrollment of Business School:** 298 **% Male/female:** 67/33 **% Part-time:** 42 **% International:** 84 **Average Age at Entry:** 29 **Average Years Work Experience at Entry:** 6

ACADEMICS

Student/faculty Ratio: 30:1 **% Female Faculty:** 31

Joint Degrees: NTU-Waseda double MBA 1 year, NTU-St Gallen double MBA 1.5 years, NTU-ESSEC double MBA 1.5 years. **Prominent Alumni:** Ms. Jill Lee, senior executive vice president & CFO, Siemens; Mr. Yeo Tiong Eng, senior regional financial director, Molex Far East South Mgt. P/L; Ms. Francine Lim, director (group CFO), Neptune Orient Lines Ltd.; Mr. Terence Chan, CEO, CAD-IT Consultants (Asia) Pte. Ltd.; Mr. Chew Hong Gian, senior vice president, Singapore Exchange.

FINANCIAL FACTS

Tuition: $17,000 **Books and Supplies:** $9,000 **Room & Board (on/off campus):** $3,500/$5,500 **% of Students Receiving Grants:** 7

ADMISSIONS

Admissions Selectivity Rating: 93

# of Applications Received: 719 **% Applicants Accepted:** 32 **% Acceptees Attending:** 53 **GMAT Range (25th to 75th percentile):** 600–680 **Average GMAT:** 650 **TOEFL Required of Int'l Applicants:** yes **Minimum TOEFL (paper/computer):** 600/250 **Application Fee:** $35 **Regular Application Deadline:** 2/28 **Regular Notification:** 3/31 **Deferment Available:** yes **Maximum Length of Deferment:** 1 year **Transfer Students Accepted:** yes **Non-fall Admissions:** yes

EMPLOYMENT PROFILE

Primary Source of Full-time Job Acceptances

School-facilitated Activities 17 (22%)

Graduate-facilitated Activities 54 (69%)

Unknown.......................................7 (9%)

Percent Employed: 40

Top 5 Employers Hiring Grads

Accenture; Bayer; DBS Bank; Citibank; Frost & Sullivan.

NATIONAL SUN YAT-SEN UNIVERSITY
COLLEGE OF MANAGEMENT

ADMISSIONS CONTACT: PROFESSOR PING-YI CHAO, COLLEGE OF MANAGEMENT
ADDRESS: 70 LIEN-HAI ROAD, KAOHSIUNG, 804-24, TAIWAN
E-MAIL: CHAOPY@MAIL.NSYSU.EDU.TW
WEBSITE: WWW.CM.NSYSU.EDU.TW

GENERAL INFORMATION
Type of School: public

STUDENTS
Enrollment of Parent Institution: 9,830 **Enrollment of Business School:** 617 % **Male/female:** 52/48 **% Part-time:** 51 **Average Age at Entry:** 25 **Average Years Work Experience at Entry:** 2

ACADEMICS
Student/faculty Ratio: 17:1 **% Female Faculty:** 20 **Prominent Alumni:** Chu Chen, mayor, Kaohsiung; Bo-Chang Chen, president, Tong Lung Metal Industry Co., Ltd.; Chin-Nan Hsieh, president, Lung Ching Steel Enterprist Co., Ltd.; Chao-Dong Ong, manager, China Steel Structure Co., Ltd.; Yu -Chang Hu, cognoscente, CMMI.

FINANCIAL FACTS
Tuition: $3,400 **Fees:** $1,046 **Books and Supplies:** $175 **Room & Board (on/off campus):** $3,000/$4,300 **% of Students Receiving Grants:** 38 **Average Grant:** $1,050

ADMISSIONS
Admissions Selectivity Rating: 60*
# of Applications Received: 5,663 **% Applicants Accepted:** 11 % **Regular Application Deadline:** 4/30 **Regular Notification:** 5/30

NEW YORK UNIVERSITY
STERN EXECUTIVE MBA PROGRAM

ADMISSIONS CONTACT: PETER TODD, ADMISSIONS COORDINATOR
ADDRESS: 44 WEST FOURTH STREET, SUITE 10–66, NEW YORK, NY 10012
PHONE: 212-998-0789 • FAX: 212-995-4222
E-MAIL: EXECUTIVE@STERN.NYU.EDU
WEBSITE: WWW.STERN.NYU.EDU/EXECUTIVE/EMBA

GENERAL INFORMATION
Type of School: private

STUDENTS
Enrollment of Business School: 100 % **Male/female:** 71/29 % **Minorities:** 12 % **International:** 20 **Average Age at Entry:** 33 **Average Years Work Experience at Entry:** 10

FINANCIAL FACTS
Tuition: $128,000 (for 2 years)

ADMISSIONS
Admissions Selectivity Rating: 96
# of Applications Received: 600 **% Applicants Accepted:** 25 % **Acceptees Attending:** 67 **Average GMAT:** 660 **Average GPA:** 3.4 **Application Fee:** $150 **International Application Fee:** $150 **Regular Application Deadline:** 2/27 **Regular Notification:** rolling **Deferment Available:** yes **Maximum Length of Deferment:** 1 year **Non-fall Admissions:** yes

NIAGARA UNIVERSITY
COLLEGE OF BUSINESS ADMINISTRATION

ADDRESS: COLLEGE OF BUSINESS ADMINISTRATION, MASTER OF BUSINESS ADMINISTRATION, NIAGARA UNIVERSITY, NY 14109
PHONE: (716) 286-8300
E-MAIL: SQC@NIAGARA.EDU
WEBSITE: WWW.NIAGARA.EDU/MBA/

GENERAL INFORMATION
Type of School: private

FINANCIAL FACTS
Tuition (in-state/out-of-state): $7,440

ADMISSIONS
Admissions Selectivity Rating: 60*
Application Fee: $35 **Regular Application Deadline:** rolling **Regular Notification:** rolling

NICHOLLS STATE UNIVERSITY
COLLEGE OF BUSINESS ADMINISTRATION

ADMISSIONS CONTACT: BECKY LEBLANC-DUROCHER, DIRECTOR OF ADMISSIONS
ADDRESS: PO BOX 2004, THIBODAUX, LA 70310
PHONE: 877-642-4655 • FAX: 985-448-4929
E-MAIL: ESAI-BL@NICHOLLS.EDU
WEBSITE: WWW.NICHOLLS.EDU

GENERAL INFORMATION
Type of School: public **Environment:** village **Academic Calendar:** semester

STUDENTS
Enrollment of Parent Institution: 7,482 **Enrollment of Business School:** 116 % **Male/female:** 49/51 **% Out-of-state:** 1 **% Part-time:** 59 **% Minorities:** 6 **% International:** 12

ACADEMICS
Student/faculty Ratio: 15:1 **% Female Faculty:** 19
Prominent Alumni: Barry Melancon, president, AICPA; John Weimer, justice, Louisiana Supreme Court; Billy Tauzin, U.S. Representative.

FINANCIAL FACTS

Tuition (in-state/out-of-state): $3,075/$8,523 **Books and Supplies:** $2,000 **Room & Board (on campus):** $4,584 **% of Students Receiving Aid:** 20 **Average Grant:** $4,000

ADMISSIONS

Admissions Selectivity Rating: 61

# of Applications Received: 70 **% Acceptees Attending:** 57 **Average GMAT:** 486 **Average GPA:** 3.1 **TOEFL Required of Int'l Applicants:** yes **Minimum TOEFL (paper/computer):** 550/213 **Application Fee:** $20 **International Application Fee:** $30 **Regular Application Deadline:** 7/1 **Regular Notification:** rolling **Deferment Available:** yes **Maximum Length of Deferment:** 1 semester **Transfer Students Accepted:** yes **Non-fall Admissions:** yes **Need-Blind Admissions:** yes

NORTH DAKOTA STATE UNIVERSITY
COLLEGE OF BUSINESS ADMINISTRATION

ADMISSIONS CONTACT: PAUL BROWN, MBA DIRECTOR
ADDRESS: PO BOX 5137, FARGO, ND 58018
E-MAIL: PAUL.BROWN@NDSU.EDUX
WEBSITE: WWW.NDSU.EDU/CBA/

GENERAL INFORMATION

Type of School: public **Environment:** city

STUDENTS

Enrollment of Business School: 537 % **Male/female:** 60/40 **% Part-time:** 89 **% International:** 8 **Average Age at Entry:** 29

ACADEMICS

Student/faculty Ratio: 19:1 **Joint Degrees:** MBA/JD 3.5 to 5 years.

FINANCIAL FACTS

Tuition (in-state/out-of-state): $4,600/$10,800 **Fees:** $340

ADMISSIONS

Admissions Selectivity Rating: 60*

# of Applications Received: 162 **% Applicants Accepted:** 90 % **Acceptees Attending:** 80 **TOEFL Required of Int'l Applicants:** yes **Minimum TOEFL (paper):** 550 **Application Fee:** $35 **Regular Application Deadline:** 7/15 **Regular Notification:** rolling **Deferment Available:** yes **Non-fall Admissions:** yes

NORTHERN ILLINOIS UNIVERSITY
COLLEGE OF BUSINESS

ADMISSIONS CONTACT: MONA SALMON, ASSISTANT DIRECTOR
ADDRESS: BARSEMA 203, DEKALB, IL 60115
PHONE: 866-648-6221 • FAX: 815-753-1668
E-MAIL: MBA@NIU.EDU
WEBSITE: WWW.COB.NIU.EDU/MBAPROGRAMS

GENERAL INFORMATION

Type of School: public **Environment:** rural

STUDENTS

Enrollment of Parent Institution: 25,000 **Enrollment of Business School:** 528 **% Part-time:** 99 **Average Age at Entry:** 32 **Average Years Work Experience at Entry:** 9

ACADEMICS

Student/faculty Ratio: 24:1 **% Female Faculty:** 19 **% Minority Faculty:** 4

FINANCIAL FACTS

Tuition (in-state/out-of-state): $8,154/$11,538 **Books and Supplies:** $750

ADMISSIONS

Admissions Selectivity Rating: 67

# of Applications Received: 262 **% Applicants Accepted:** 97 **% Acceptees Attending:** 70 **Average GMAT:** 550 **Average GPA:** 3.2 **TOEFL Required of Int'l Applicants:** yes **Minimum TOEFL (paper/computer):** 550/213 **Application Fee:** $30 **Regular Application Deadline:** 6/1 **Regular Notification:** rolling **Deferment Available:** yes **Maximum Length of Deferment:** 2 years **Transfer Students Accepted:** yes **Non-fall Admissions:** yes **Need-Blind Admissions:** yes

NORTHERN KENTUCKY UNIVERSITY
COLLEGE OF BUSINESS

ADMISSIONS CONTACT: SHANE JAYEMANNE, GRADUATE ASSISTANT
ADDRESS: COLLEGE OF BUSINESS, NUNN DRIVE, HIGHLAND HEIGHTS, KY 41099
PHONE: 859-572-6336 • FAX: 859-572-6177
E-MAIL: MBUSINESS@NKU.EDU
WEBSITE: COB.NKU.EDU/MBA/

GENERAL INFORMATION

Type of School: public **Environment:** metropolis

STUDENTS

Enrollment of Parent Institution: 14,000 **Enrollment of Business School:** 235 % **Male/female:** 58/42 **% Out-of-state:** 16 **% Part-time:** 85 **Average Age at Entry:** 27

ACADEMICS

Student/faculty Ratio: 20:1 **Joint Degrees:** MBA/JD 2.8 years.

FINANCIAL FACTS

Tuition (in-state/out-of-state): $312/$643 (per credit hour) **% of Students Receiving Aid:** 33 **% of Students Receiving Loans:** 23 **% of Students Receiving Grants:** 10 **Average Award Package:** $8,356 **Average Grant:** $3,359 **Average Student Loan Debt:** $27,880

ADMISSIONS

Admissions Selectivity Rating: 60*

# of Applications Received: 109 **% Applicants Accepted:** 66 **% Acceptees Attending:** 72 **GMAT Range (25th to 75th percentile):** 440–630 **Average GMAT:** 529 **Average GPA:** 3.28 **TOEFL Required of Int'l Applicants:** yes **Minimum TOEFL (paper/computer):** 550/213 **Regular Application Deadline:** 8/1 **Regular Notification:** rolling **Deferment Available:** yes **Transfer Students Accepted:** yes **Non-fall Admissions:** yes **Need-Blind Admissions:** yes **Applicants Also Look At:** University of Cincinnati, Xavier University.

NYENRODE BUSINESS UNIVERSITEIT

ADMISSIONS CONTACT: VICTORIA BRESSERS, HEAD OF ADMISSIONS
ADDRESS: PO BOX 130, BREUKELEN, 3620 AC NETHERLANDS
PHONE: 00 31 346 291 291 • FAX: 00 31 346 291 450
E-MAIL: INFO@NYENRODE.NL
WEBSITE: WWW.NYENRODE.NL

GENERAL INFORMATION

Type of School: private

STUDENTS

% Male/female: 65/35 **% International:** 71 **Average Age at Entry:** 28 **Average Years Work Experience at Entry:** 5

ACADEMICS

Student/faculty Ratio: 4:1 **Prominent Alumni:** Kai Jin, general manager, Nokia, China; Pierro Overmars, member of the board, ABN AMRO.

FINANCIAL FACTS

Tuition: $38,500 **Fees:** $1,308 **Books and Supplies:** $1,950 **Room & Board (on campus):** $15,000 **Average Grant:** $13,000

ADMISSIONS

Admissions Selectivity Rating: 60*

Average GMAT: 580 **TOEFL Required of Int'l Applicants:** yes **Minimum TOEFL (paper/computer):** 600/250 **Application Fee:** $80 **Regular Application Deadline:** 8/31 **Regular Notification:** rolling **Deferment Available:** yes **Maximum Length of Deferment:** 2 years

EMPLOYMENT PROFILE

Primary Source of Full-time Job Acceptances

School-facilitated Activities 4
Unknown 18

OAKLAND UNIVERSITY
SCHOOL OF BUSINESS ADMINSTRATION

ADMISSIONS CONTACT: PAUL M. TRUMBULL, COORDINATOR OF GRADUATE
  BUSINESS PROGRAMS
ADDRESS: 432 ELLIOTT HALL, ROCHESTER, MI 48309-4493
PHONE: 248-370-3287 • FAX: 248-370-4964
E-MAIL: GBP@LISTS.OAKLAND.EDU
WEBSITE: WWW.SBA.OAKLAND.EDU

GENERAL INFORMATION

Type of School: public **Environment:** town **Academic Calendar:** semester

STUDENTS

Enrollment of Parent Institution: 17,736 **Enrollment of Business School:** 470 **% Male/female:** 66/34 **% Out-of-state:** 5 **% Part-time:** 95 **% International:** 5 **Average Age at Entry:** 28 **Average Years Work Experience at Entry:** 5

ACADEMICS

Student/faculty Ratio: 19:1 **% Female Faculty:** 19 **% Minority Faculty:** 5

FINANCIAL FACTS

Tuition (in-state/out-of-state): $7,452/$12,902 **Books and Supplies:** $826 **Room & Board (on campus):** $7,170 **Average Grant:** $4,500

ADMISSIONS

Admissions Selectivity Rating: 73

# of Applications Received: 116 **% Applicants Accepted:** 84 **% Acceptees Attending:** 90 **Average GMAT:** 535 **Average GPA:** 3.23 **TOEFL Required of Int'l Applicants:** yes **Minimum TOEFL (paper/computer):** 550/213 **Application Fee:** $50 **Regular Application Deadline:** 8/1 **Regular Notification:** rolling **Deferment Available:** yes **Maximum Length of Deferment:** 1 year **Transfer Students Accepted:** yes **Non-fall Admissions:** yes **Need-Blind Admissions:** yes **Applicants Also Look At:** Wayne State University.

OHIO UNIVERSITY
COLLEGE OF BUSINESS

ADMISSIONS CONTACT: JAN ROSS, ASSISTANT DEAN, GRADUATE PROGRAM
ADDRESS: 514 COPELAND HALL, ATHENS, OH 45701
PHONE: 740-593-4320 • FAX: 740-593-1388
E-MAIL: ROSSJ@OHIO.EDU
WEBSITE: WWW.COB.OHIOU.EDU/GRAD/

GENERAL INFORMATION

Type of School: public **Environment:** rural **Academic Calendar:** quarters

STUDENTS

Enrollment of Parent Institution: 19,000 **Enrollment of Business School:** 105 **% Male/female:** 55/45 **% Out-of-state:** 50

Minorities: 7 % International: 20 Average Age at Entry: 25 Average Years Work Experience at Entry: 2

ACADEMICS

Student/faculty Ratio: 10:1 % Female Faculty: 10 % Minority Faculty: 10

Joint Degrees: MBA/MSpAd 2 years, MBA/MA (International Affairs) 2 years.

FINANCIAL FACTS

Tuition (in-state/out-of-state): $8,800/$18,400 Fees: $4,000 Books and Supplies: $4,700 Room & Board: $10,000 % of Students Receiving Aid: 70 % of First-year Students Receiving Aid: 70 Average Award Package: $15,000 Average Grant: $8,000

ADMISSIONS

Admissions Selectivity Rating: 77

# of Applications Received: 264 % Applicants Accepted: 64 % Acceptees Attending: 62 GMAT Range (25th to 75th percentile): 470–670 Average GMAT: 555 Average GPA: 3.00 TOEFL Required of Int'l Applicants: yes Minimum TOEFL (paper/computer): 600/250 Application Fee: $30 Regular Application Deadline: 1/15 Regular Notification: 4/1 Deferment Available: yes Maximum Length of Deferment: 1 year Need-Blind Admissions: yes

OKLAHOMA STATE UNIVERSITY
SPEARS SCHOOL OF BUSINESS

ADMISSIONS CONTACT: JANICE ANALLA, ASSISTANT DIRECTOR, MBA PROGRAM
ADDRESS: OKLAHOMA STATE UNIVERSITY, 102 GUNDERSEN HALL, STILLWATER, OK 74078-4022
PHONE: 405-744-2951 • FAX: 405-744-7474
E-MAIL: MBA-OSU@OKSTATE.EDU
WEBSITE: SPEARS.OKSTATE.EDU/MBA/

GENERAL INFORMATION

Type of School: public Environment: town Academic Calendar: semester

STUDENTS

Enrollment of Business School: 319 % Male/female: 65/35 % Part-time: 72 % Minorities: 1 % International: 22 Average Age at Entry: 24 Average Years Work Experience at Entry: 5

ACADEMICS

Student/faculty Ratio: 25:1

Joint Degrees: MBA/MSTM 2.5 years, MBA/DO 1.5 years.

Prominent Alumni: Tiffany Sewell Howard, chief operating officer, The Charles Machine Works; Dennis Reilley, CEO, Praxaire; Charlie Eitel, chairman & CEO, Simmons Companies; Don Humphries, vice president and treasurer, ExxonMobil.

FINANCIAL FACTS

Tuition (in-state/out-of-state): $3,601/$12,610 Fees: $1,754 Books and Supplies: $4,460 Room & Board (on campus): $6,780 Average

Award Package: $4,000 Average Grant: $1,000 Average Student Loan Debt: $8,000

ADMISSIONS

Admissions Selectivity Rating: 79

# of Applications Received: 95 % Applicants Accepted: 66 % Acceptees Attending: 68 GMAT Range (25th to 75th percentile): 510–610 Average GMAT: 560 Average GPA: 3.47 TOEFL Required of Int'l Applicants: yes Minimum TOEFL (paper/computer): 575/233 Application Fee: $40 International Application Fee: $75 Regular Application Deadline: 7/1 Regular Notification: rolling Deferment Available: yes Maximum Length of Deferment: 1 year Transfer Students Accepted: yes Non-fall Admissions: yes Need-Blind Admissions: yes Applicants Also Look At: University of Arkansas-Fayetteville, University of Kansas, University of Oklahoma, The University of Tulsa.

EMPLOYMENT PROFILE

Primary Source of Full-time Job Acceptances

School-facilitated Activities............18 (45%)
Graduate-facilitated Activities 23 (55%)

Percent Employed: 15

OREGON STATE UNIVERSITY
COLLEGE OF BUSINESS

ADMISSIONS CONTACT: JIM COAKLEY, MBA PROGRAM COORDINATOR
ADDRESS: 200 BEXELL HALL, CORVALLIS, OR 97330
PHONE: 541-737-3716 • FAX: 541-737-4890
E-MAIL: OSUMBA@BUS.OREGONSTATE.EDU
WEBSITE: WWW.BUS.OREGONSTATE.EDU/

GENERAL INFORMATION

Type of School: public Environment: town Academic Calendar: quarter

STUDENTS

Enrollment of Parent Institution: 19,362 Enrollment of Business School: 78 % Male/female: 56/44 % Minorities: 10 % International: 32 Average Age at Entry: 29

ACADEMICS

Student/faculty Ratio: 3:1 % Female Faculty: 15 % Minority Faculty: 18

FINANCIAL FACTS

Tuition (in-state/out-of-state): $9,366/$15,603 Fees (in-state/out-of-state): $1,266/$1,323 Books and Supplies: $1,350 Room & Board (on campus): $6,336

ADMISSIONS

Admissions Selectivity Rating: 83

# of Applications Received: 142 % Applicants Accepted: 50 % GMAT Range (25th to 75th percentile): 520–625 Average GMAT: 563 Average GPA: 3.34 TOEFL Required of Int'l Applicants: yes Minimum TOEFL (paper/computer): 575/233 Application Fee: $50

Regular Application Deadline: 3/5 Regular Notification: rolling
Deferment Available: yes Transfer Students Accepted: yes Non-fall
Admissions: yes Need-Blind Admissions: yes Applicants Also Look
At: Portland State University, University of Oregon.

PACE UNIVERSITY
LUBIN SCHOOL OF BUSINESS

ADMISSIONS CONTACT: SUSAN FORD-GOLDSCHEIN,
ASSOCIATE DIRECTOR OF GRADUATE ADMISSION
ADDRESS: ONE PACE PLAZA, EXECUTIVE MBA, NEW YORK, NY 10038
PHONE: 212-346-1531 • FAX: 212-346-1585
E-MAIL: GRADNYC@PACE.EDU
WEBSITE: WWW.PACE.EDU/LUBIN/

GENERAL INFORMATION
Type of School: private Environment: metropolis Academic
Calendar: semester

STUDENTS
Enrollment of Parent Institution: 13,463 Enrollment of Business
School: 836 % Male/female: 48/52 % Out-of-state: 15 % Part-
time: 82 % Minorities: 5 % International: 50 Average Age at Entry:
24 Average Years Work Experience at Entry: 2

ACADEMICS
Student/faculty Ratio: 23:1 % Female Faculty: 17 % Minority
Faculty: 21
Joint Degrees: MBA/JD. Prominent Alumni: Ivan G. Seidenberg,
president and CEO, Verizon Communications; John R. Danieli, presi-
dent, CEO, owner, Computer Merchant LTD.; Richard Zannino, CEO,
Dow Jones & Co.; Mel Karmazin, CEO, Sirius Satellite Radio Inc.;
Marie J. Toulantis, CEO, Barnes & Noble.

FINANCIAL FACTS
Tuition: $857 (per credit hour) Books and Supplies: $3,450 Room &
Board (on/off campus): $10,490/$19,427 % of Students Receiving
Aid: 54 % of First-year Students Receiving Aid: 63 % of Students
Receiving Loans: 30 % of Students Receiving Grants: 33 Average
Award Package: $14,710 Average Grant: $5,443 Average Student
Loan Debt: $20,963

ADMISSIONS
Admissions Selectivity Rating: 76
# of Applications Received: 878 % Applicants Accepted: 54 %
Acceptees Attending: 46 GMAT Range (25th to 75th percentile):
470–550 Average GMAT: 516 Average GPA: 3.21 TOEFL Required
of Int'l Applicants: yes Minimum TOEFL (paper/computer): 570/230
Application Fee: $65 International Application Fee: $65 Regular
Application Deadline: 8/1 Regular Notification: rolling Transfer
Students Accepted: yes Non-fall Admissions: yes Need-Blind
Admissions: yes

EMPLOYMENT PROFILE
Primary Source of Full-time Job Acceptances
Grads Employed by Industry:......% avg. salary:
Finance/Accounting........................65 $55,990
Human Resources.........................2 $68,500
Marketing/Sales 17 $83,193
MIS 1 $60,000
Operations/Production 2 $72,333
Consulting.....................................6 $92,000
General Management 7 $75,600
Top 5 Employers Hiring Grads
Deloitte Touche Tohmatsu; Ernst & Young; JPMorgan Chase; Grant
Thornton; KPMG International.

PENNSYLVANIA STATE
UNIVERSITY—HARRISBURG
SCHOOL OF BUSINESS ADMINISTRATION

ADMISSIONS CONTACT: DR. THOMAS STREVELER, DIRECTOR OF ENROLLMENT
SERVICES
ADDRESS: 777 WEST HARRISBURG PIKE, MIDDLETOWN, PA 17057
PHONE: 717-948-6250 • FAX: 717-948-6325
E-MAIL: HBGADMIT@PSU.EDU
WEBSITE: WWW.HBG.PSU.EDU/SBUS

GENERAL INFORMATION
Type of School: public Environment: village Academic Calendar:
semester

STUDENTS
Enrollment of Parent Institution: 3,239 Enrollment of Business
School: 207 % Male/female: 64/36 % Out-of-state: 5 % Part-time:
88 % Minorities: 7 % International: 5 Average Age at Entry: 27

ACADEMICS
Student/faculty Ratio: 12:1

FINANCIAL FACTS
Tuition (in-state/out-of-state): $12,000/$17,592 Books and
Supplies: $4,170 Average Grant: $4,200

ADMISSIONS
Admissions Selectivity Rating: 67
# of Applications Received: 76 % Applicants Accepted: 91 %
Acceptees Attending: 90 Average GMAT: 520 Average GPA: 3.00
TOEFL Required of Int'l Applicants: yes Minimum TOEFL
(paper/computer): 550/213 Application Fee: $50 Regular Application
Deadline: 7/18 Regular Notification: rolling Deferment Available:
yes Maximum Length of Deferment: 3 years Transfer Students
Accepted: yes Non-fall Admissions: yes Need-Blind Admissions: yes

PURDUE UNIVERSITY CALUMET
SCHOOL OF MANAGEMENT

ADMISSIONS CONTACT: PAUL MCGRATH, COORDINATOR,
GRADUATE MANAGEMENT PROGRAMS
ADDRESS: SCHOOL OF MANAGEMENT, PURDUE UNIVERSITY CALUMET,
HAMMOND, IN 46323-2094
PHONE: 219-989-2425 • FAX: 219-989-3158
E-MAIL: PMCGRAT@CALUMET.PURDUE.EDU
WEBSITE: WWW.CALUMET.PURDUE.EDU

GENERAL INFORMATION

Type of School: public **Environment:** city **Academic Calendar:** semester

STUDENTS

Enrollment of Parent Institution: 9,500 **Enrollment of Business School:** 213 **% Part-time:** 96 **Average Age at Entry:** 28 **Average Years Work Experience at Entry:** 5

ACADEMICS

Student/faculty Ratio: 10:1 **% Female Faculty:** 43 **% Minority Faculty:** 24

FINANCIAL FACTS

Tuition (In-state/out-of-state): $4,325/$9,322 **Books and Supplies:** $6,000

ADMISSIONS

Admissions Selectivity Rating: 70

# of Applications Received: 102 **% Applicants Accepted:** 93 **% Acceptees Attending:** 98 **Average GMAT:** 538 **Average GPA:** 3.2 **TOEFL Required of Int'l Applicants:** yes **Minimum TOEFL (paper/computer):** 550/213 **Application Fee:** $55 **Regular Application Deadline:** 8/1 **Regular Notification:** 8/1 **Deferment Available:** yes **Maximum Length of Deferment:** 1 year **Transfer Students Accepted:** yes **Non-fall Admissions:** yes **Need-Blind Admissions:** yes **Applicants Also Look At:** Indiana University Northwest, Valparaiso University.

RIDER UNIVERSITY
COLLEGE OF BUSINESS ADMINSTRATION

ADMISSIONS CONTACT: JAMIE MITCHELL, DIRECTOR, GRADUATE ADMISSIONS
ADDRESS: PJ CIAMBELLI HALL, 2083 LAWRENCEVILLE ROAD, LAWRENCEVILLE,
NJ 08648-3099
PHONE: 609-896-5036 • FAX: 609-895-5680
E-MAIL: GRADADM@RIDER.EDU
WEBSITE: WWW.RIDER.EDU/CBA

GENERAL INFORMATION

Type of School: private **Environment:** village **Academic Calendar:** semester

STUDENTS

Enrollment of Parent Institution: 5,790 **Enrollment of Business School:** 289 **% Male/female:** 69/31 **% Out-of-state:** 29 **% Part-time:** 82 **% Minorities:** 35 **% International:** 18 **Average Age at Entry:** 28

ACADEMICS

Student/faculty Ratio: 9:1 **% Female Faculty:** 53 **% Minority Faculty:** 23

Joint Degrees: BS/BA/MBA 5 years, BS/BA/MAcc 5 years.
Prominent Alumni: Michael Cardillo, former president, Aetna U.S. Healthcare; Clare Hart, chair, executive vice president, president, Dow Jones and Co. Inc.; Terry McEwen, director, NJ State Department of Banking and Insurance; Donald Noe, managing director, global head, JPMorgan Chase; Michael S. Spector, vice president, GlaxoSmithKline.

FINANCIAL FACTS

Tuition: $680 (per credit hour) **Books and Supplies:** $5,320 **% of Students Receiving Aid:** 67 **% of First-year Students Receiving Aid:** 31 **% of Students Receiving Loans:** 57 **% of Students Receiving Grants:** 18 **Average Award Package:** $19,837 **Average Grant:** $4,944 **Average Student Loan Debt:** $8,654

ADMISSIONS

Admissions Selectivity Rating: 73

# of Applications Received: 127 **% Applicants Accepted:** 65 **% Acceptees Attending:** 75 **GMAT Range (25th to 75th percentile):** 420–550 **Average GMAT:** 488 **Average GPA:** 3.34 **TOEFL Required of Int'l Applicants:** yes **Minimum TOEFL (paper/computer):** 585/240 **Application Fee:** $45 **International Application Fee:** $45

Application Deadline: round 1 8/1, round 2 12/1, round 3 5/1. **Deferment Available:** yes **Maximum Length of Deferment:** 1 year **Transfer Students Accepted:** yes **Non-fall Admissions:** yes **Need-Blind Admissions:** yes **Applicants Also Look At:** Rowan University, Rutgers, The State University of New Jersey.

SAINT MARY'S UNIVERSITY (CANADA)
SOBEY SCHOOL OF BUSINESS

ADMISSIONS CONTACT: LEAH RAY, MANAGING DIRECTOR, MBA PROGRAM
ADDRESS: 923 ROBIE STREET, HALIFAX, NS B3H 3C3 CANADA
PHONE: 902-420-5002 • FAX: 902-420-5119
E-MAIL: MBA@SMU.CA
WEBSITE: WWW.SOBEY.SMU.CA

GENERAL INFORMATION

Type of School: private **Academic Calendar:** semester

STUDENTS

Enrollment of Parent Institution: 8,000 **Enrollment of Business School:** 82 **% Male/female:** 40/60 **% Out-of-state:** 60 **% Part-time:** 68 **% International:** 40 **Average Age at Entry:** 28 **Average Years**

Work Experience at Entry: 6

ACADEMICS

Student/faculty Ratio: 5:1 **Joint Degrees:** MBA/CMA 2.3 years.

FINANCIAL FACTS

Tuition: $9,235 **Fees:** $480 **Books and Supplies:** $1,000 **% of Students Receiving Aid:** 20 **% of First-year Students Receiving Aid:** 10 **% of Students Receiving Grants:** 20 **Average Grant:** $2,500

ADMISSIONS

Admissions Selectivity Rating: 85

# of Applications Received: 114 **% Applicants Accepted:** 64 **% Acceptees Attending:** 78 **GMAT Range (25th to 75th percentile):** 550–720 **Average GMAT:** 610 **Average GPA:** 3.3 **TOEFL Required of Int'l Applicants:** yes **Minimum TOEFL (paper/computer):** 580/237 **Application Fee:** $70 **International Application Fee:** $70 **Regular Application Deadline:** 5/31 **Regular Notification:** rolling **Early Decision Program:** yes **ED Deadline/notification:** 1/31, 3/7 (for Chinese applications) **Deferment Available:** yes **Maximum Length of Deferment:** 1 year **Transfer Students Accepted:** yes **Need-Blind Admissions:** yes

SAINT MARY'S UNIVERSITY OF MINNESOTA
SCHOOL OF GRADUATE AND PROFESSIONAL PROGRAMS

ADMISSIONS CONTACT: SARAH LANG, DIRECTOR OF ADMISSIONS
ADDRESS: 2500 PARK AVENUE, MINNEAPOLIS, MN 55404-4403
PHONE: 612-728-5100 • FAX: 612-728-5121
E-MAIL: TC-ADMISSION@SMUMN.EDU
WEBSITE: WWW.SMUMN.EDU/GRADPRO

GENERAL INFORMATION

Type of School: private Affiliation: Roman Catholic **Environment:** rural

STUDENTS

Enrollment of Business School: 134

ACADEMICS

Student/faculty Ratio: 12:1

FINANCIAL FACTS

Tuition: $8,520 **Books and Supplies:** $500 **Average Award Package:** $18,090

ADMISSIONS

Admissions Selectivity Rating: 60*

# of Applications Received: 50 **% Applicants Accepted:** 80 **TOEFL Required of Int'l Applicants:** yes **Minimum TOEFL (paper/computer):** 550/213 **Application Fee:** $25 **Regular Application Deadline:** rolling **Regular Notification:** rolling **Transfer Students Accepted:** yes **Non-fall Admissions:** yes

SALISBURY UNIVERSITY
FRANKLIN P. PERDUE SCHOOL OF BUSINESS

ADMISSIONS CONTACT: JANINE VIENNA, MBA DIRECTOR
ADDRESS: 1101 CAMDEN AVENUE, SALISBURY, MD 21801-6837
PHONE: 410-548-3983 • FAX: 410-548-2908
E-MAIL: JMVIENNA@SALISBURY.EDU
WEBSITE: MBA.SALISBURY.EDU

GENERAL INFORMATION

Type of School: public **Environment:** town **Academic Calendar:** semester

STUDENTS

Enrollment of Parent Institution: 7,000 **Enrollment of Business School:** 75 **% Male/female:** 61/39 **% Part-time:** 56 **% Minorities:** 1 **% International:** 21 **Average Age at Entry:** 24 **Average Years Work Experience at Entry:** 2

ACADEMICS

Student/faculty Ratio: 22:1 **% Female Faculty:** 5

FINANCIAL FACTS

Tuition (in-state/out-of-state): $7,800/$16,380 **Fees:** $1,470 **Books and Supplies:** $1,000 **Room & Board (off campus):** $8,000 **Average Grant:** $9,680

ADMISSIONS

Admissions Selectivity Rating: 70

# of Applications Received: 61 **% Applicants Accepted:** 77 **% Acceptees Attending:** 89 **Average GMAT:** 490 **Average GPA:** 3.22 **TOEFL Required of Int'l Applicants:** yes **Minimum TOEFL (paper/computer):** 550/213 **Application Fee:** $45 **Regular Application Deadline:** 3/1 **Regular Notification:** 4/1 **Transfer Students Accepted:** yes **Non-fall Admissions:** yes **Need-Blind Admissions:** yes

SAM HOUSTON STATE UNIVERSITY
COLLEGE OF BUSINESS ADMINISTRATION

ADMISSIONS CONTACT: DR. LEROY ASHORN, ASSOCIATE DEAN/COORDINATOR OF GRADUATE STUDIES
ADDRESS: PO BOX 2056, HUNTSVILLE, TX 77341-2056
PHONE: 936-294-1239 • FAX: 936-294-3612
E-MAIL: BUSGRAD@SHSU.EDU
WEBSITE: COBA.SHSU.EDU/

GENERAL INFORMATION

Type of School: public **Environment:** town

STUDENTS

Enrollment of Business School: 164 **% Male/female:** 49/51 **% Part-time:** 71 **% Minorities:** 7 **% International:** 5

FINANCIAL FACTS

Tuition (in-state/out-of-state): $6,822/$11,466

ADMISSIONS

Admissions Selectivity Rating: 62

# of Applications Received: 108 **% Applicants Accepted:** 71 **%
Acceptees Attending:** 53 **GMAT Range (25th to 75th percentile):**
460–550 **Average GMAT:** 504 **TOEFL Required of Int'l Applicants:** yes
Minimum TOEFL (paper/computer): 550/213 **Application Fee:** $20
International Application Fee: $20 **Regular Application Deadline:**
8/1 **Regular Notification:** rolling **Transfer Students Accepted:** yes
Non-fall Admissions: yes **Need-Blind Admissions:** yes

SAMFORD UNIVERSITY
SAMFORD UNIVERSITY SCHOOL OF BUSINESS

*ADMISSIONS CONTACT: MR. LARRON C. HARPER, DIRECTOR OF GRADUATE
STUDIES*
*ADDRESS: DBH 203E, SCHOOL OF BUSINESS, 800 LAKESHORE DRIVE,
BIRMINGHAM, AL 35229*
PHONE: 205-726-2040 • FAX: 205-726-2464
E-MAIL: LEPHILLI@SAMFORD.EDU
WEBSITE: WWW.SAMFORD.EDU/BUSINESS

GENERAL INFORMATION

Type of School: private **Affiliation:** Baptist **Environment:** town

STUDENTS

Enrollment of Parent Institution: 4,440 **Enrollment of Business
School:** 136 **% Part-time:** 100 **Average Age at Entry:** 31 **Average
Years Work Experience at Entry:** 7

ACADEMICS

Student/faculty Ratio: 12:1 **% Female Faculty:** 23 **% Minority
Faculty:** 10
Joint Degrees: MBA/MAcc (concentrations in management,
accounting) 1.5 to 7 years, MBA/JD.

FINANCIAL FACTS

Tuition: $500 (per credit hour) **Books and Supplies:** $600

ADMISSIONS

Admissions Selectivity Rating: 76

% Applicants Accepted: 59 **Average GMAT:** 520 **Average GPA:** 3.45
Application Fee: $25 **International Application Fee:** $25 **Regular
Application Deadline:** rolling **Regular Notification:** rolling
Deferment Available: yes **Maximum Length of Deferment:** 1 year
Transfer Students Accepted: yes **Non-fall Admissions:** yes **Need-
Blind Admissions:** yes **Applicants Also Look At:** University of
Alabama at Birmingham.

SOUTHEAST MISSOURI STATE UNIVERSITY
DONALD L. HARRISON COLLEGE OF BUSINESS

ADMISSIONS CONTACT: DR. KENNETH HEISCHMIDT, DIRECTOR, MBA PROGRAM
*ADDRESS: MBA PROGRAM; SOUTHEAST MISSOURI STATE UNIVERSITY, 1
UNIVERSITY PLAZA, MS 5890, CAPE GIRARDEAU, MO 63701*
PHONE: 573-651-5116 • FAX: 573-651-5032
E-MAIL: MBA@SEMO.EDU
WEBSITE: WWW6.SEMO.EDU/MBA

GENERAL INFORMATION

Type of School: public **Environment:** town **Academic Calendar:**
semester

STUDENTS

Enrollment of Parent Institution: 10,000 **Enrollment of Business
School:** 79 **% Male/female:** 55/45 **% Out-of-state:** 11 **% Part-time:**
35 **% Minorities:** 5 **% International:** 13 **Average Age at Entry:** 27

ACADEMICS

Student/faculty Ratio: 19:1 **% Female Faculty:** 40 **% Minority
Faculty:** 10
Joint Degrees: MBA/Masters in International Business and
Economics (offered with University of Applied Sciences,
Schmalkalden, Germany).

FINANCIAL FACTS

Tuition (in-state/out-of-state): $5,064/$8,952 **Books and Supplies:**
$500 **Room & Board:** $4,800 **Average Award Package:** $11,200
Average Grant: $11,200

ADMISSIONS

Admissions Selectivity Rating: 92

# of Applications Received: 62 **% Applicants Accepted:** 85 **%
Acceptees Attending:** 79 **GMAT Range (25th to 75th percentile):**
410–620 **Average GMAT:** 515 **Average GPA:** 3.56 **TOEFL Required
of Int'l Applicants:** yes **Minimum TOEFL (paper/computer):** 550/213
Application Fee: $20 **International Application Fee:** $100 **Regular
Application Deadline:** rolling **Regular Notification:** rolling
Deferment Available: yes **Maximum Length of Deferment:** 1 year
Transfer Students Accepted: yes **Non-fall Admissions:** yes **Need-
Blind Admissions:** yes **Applicants Also Look At:** Missouri State
University (formerly SW MSU), Saint Louis University, Southern
Illinois University, University of Missouri-Columbia, University of
Missouri–St. Louis.

EMPLOYMENT PROFILE

Percent Employed: 95

SOUTHEASTERN LOUISIANA UNIVERSITY
COLLEGE OF BUSINESS

ADMISSIONS CONTACT: SANDRA MEYERS, GRADUATE ADMISSIONS ANALYST
ADDRESS: SLU 10752, HAMMOND, LA 70402
PHONE: 800-222-7358 • FAX: 985-549-5632
E-MAIL: SMEYERS@SELU.EDU
WEBSITE: WWW.SELU.EDU/ACAD_RESEARCH/COLLEGES/BUS

GENERAL INFORMATION
Type of School: public **Environment:** village **Academic Calendar:** semester

STUDENTS
Enrollment of Parent Institution: 15,118 **Enrollment of Business School:** 172 % **Male/female:** 54/46 % **Part-time:** 35 % **Minorities:** 26 % **International:** 21 **Average Age at Entry:** 25

ACADEMICS
Student/faculty Ratio: 6:1 % **Female Faculty:** 22 % **Minority Faculty:** 19

Prominent Alumni: Robin Roberts, ESPN sportscaster; Russell Carollo, Pulitzer Prize winner; Harold Jackson, president (retired), Sunsweet Products; James J. Brady, former president, National Democratic Party; Carl Barbier, federal judge.

FINANCIAL FACTS
Tuition (in-state/out-of-state): $2,216/$6,212 **Fees:** $986 **Books and Supplies:** $1,000 **Room & Board (on/off campus):** $5,750/$7,632 % **of Students Receiving Aid:** 51 % **of First-year Students Receiving Aid:** 66 % **of Students Receiving Loans:** 17 **Average Award Package:** $6,152

ADMISSIONS
Admissions Selectivity Rating: 67
# of Applications Received: 65 % **Applicants Accepted:** 78 % **Acceptees Attending:** 63 **GMAT Range (25th to 75th percentile):** 440–538 **Average GMAT:** 497 **Average GPA:** 3.17 **TOEFL Required of Int'l Applicants:** yes **Minimum TOEFL (paper/computer):** 525/195 **Application Fee:** $20 **International Application Fee:** $30 **Regular Application Deadline:** 7/15 **Regular Notification:** rolling **Deferment Available:** yes **Maximum Length of Deferment:** 1 year **Transfer Students Accepted:** yes **Non-fall Admissions:** yes **Need-Blind Admissions:** yes

SOUTHERN UTAH UNIVERSITY
SCHOOL OF BUSINESS

ADMISSIONS CONTACT: STEVE ALLEN, DIRECTOR OF ADMISSION
ADDRESS: 351 WEST UNIVERSITY BOULEVARD, CEDAR CITY, UT 84720
PHONE: 435-586-7740 • FAX: 435-865-8223
E-MAIL: ADMINFO@SUU.EDU
WEBSITE: WWW.SUU.EDU/BUSINESS

GENERAL INFORMATION
Type of School: public

STUDENTS
Enrollment of Parent Institution: 7,000 **Enrollment of Business School:** 24 % **Male/female:** 85/15 % **Part-time:** 50 **Average Age at Entry:** 25 **Average Years Work Experience at Entry:** 2

FINANCIAL FACTS
Tuition (in-state/out-of-state): $4,872/$16,078 **Fees:** $550 **Books and Supplies:** $800 **Room & Board (on/off campus):** $4,166/$2,916

ADMISSIONS
Admissions Selectivity Rating: 64
# of Applications Received: 69 % **Applicants Accepted:** 87 % **Acceptees Attending:** 40 **Average GMAT:** 508 **Average GPA:** 3.38 **TOEFL Required of Int'l Applicants:** yes **Minimum TOEFL (paper/computer):** 500/173 **Application Fee:** $50 **Regular Application Deadline:** 3/31 **Regular Notification:** 4/1 **Deferment Available:** yes **Maximum Length of Deferment:** 1 year **Transfer Students Accepted:** yes **Non-fall Admissions:** yes **Need-Blind Admissions:** yes **Applicants Also Look At:** Utah State University, Weber State University.

ST. BONAVENTURE UNIVERSITY
SCHOOL OF BUSINESS

ADMISSIONS CONTACT: CONNIE C. HORAN, SR. ASSOCIATE DIRECTOR OF ADMISSIONS
ADDRESS: OFFICE OF GRADUATE ADMISSIONS, PO BOX D, ST. BONAVENTURE, NY 14778
PHONE: 716-375-2021 • FAX: 716-375-4015
E-MAIL: GRADSCH@SBU.EDU
WEBSITE: WWW.GRAD.SBU.EDU

GENERAL INFORMATION
Type of School: private **Affiliation:** Roman Catholic

STUDENTS
Enrollment of Business School: 129 % **International:** 3

FINANCIAL FACTS
Tuition: $650 (per credit hour) **Books and Supplies:** $600 **Room & Board (on campus):** $8,000 **Average Student Loan Debt:** $25,738

ADMISSIONS

Admissions Selectivity Rating: 60*

TOEFL Required of Int'l Applicants: yes **Minimum TOEFL (paper/computer):** 550/213 **Application Fee:** $30 **International Application Fee:** $30 **Deferment Available:** yes **Maximum Length of Deferment:** 1 year **Transfer Students Accepted:** yes **Non-fall Admissions:** yes **Need-Blind Admissions:** yes

ST. CLOUD STATE UNIVERSITY
HERBERGER COLLEGE OF BUSINESS

ADMISSIONS CONTACT: GRADUATE STUDIES OFFICE—ANNETTE DAY, GRADUATE ADMISSIONS MANAGER
ADDRESS: 720 FOURTH AVE. SOUTH, AS-121, ST. CLOUD, MN 56301-4498
PHONE: 320-308-2112 • FAX: 320-308-3986
E-MAIL: GRADUATESTUDIES@STCLOUDSTATE.EDU
WEBSITE: WWW.STCLOUDSTATE.EDU/MBA/

GENERAL INFORMATION

Type of School: public **Academic Calendar:** semester

STUDENTS

Enrollment of Parent Institution: 16,334 **Enrollment of Business School:** 166 % **Male/female:** 71/29 **% Out-of-state:** 18 **% Part-time:** 75 **% Minorities:** 10 **% International:** 48 **Average Age at Entry:** 28 **Average Years Work Experience at Entry:** 5

ACADEMICS

Student/faculty Ratio: 25:1 **% Female Faculty:** 27 **% Minority Faculty:** 20

FINANCIAL FACTS

Tuition: $14,292 **Fees:** $165 **Books and Supplies:** $1,800

ADMISSIONS

Admissions Selectivity Rating: 80

% Acceptees Attending: 48 **Average GMAT:** 525 **Average GPA:** 3.3 **TOEFL Required of Int'l Applicants:** yes **Minimum TOEFL (paper/computer):** 550/213 **Application Fee:** $35 **Regular Application Deadline:** rolling **Regular Notification:** rolling **Early Decision Program:** yes **ED Deadline/notification:** 4/15 / 6/15 **Deferment Available:** yes **Maximum Length of Deferment:** 2 years **Non-fall Admissions:** yes

ST. JOHN FISHER COLLEGE
RONALD L. BITTNER SCHOOL OF BUSINESS

ADMISSIONS CONTACT: OFFICE OF GRADUATE ADMISSIONS, MBA ADMISSIONS COORDINATOR
ADDRESS: 3690 EAST AVENUE, OFFICE OF GRADUATE ADMISSIONS, ROCHESTER, NY 14618
PHONE: 585-385-8161 • FAX: 585-385-8344
E-MAIL: GRAD@SJFC.EDU
WEBSITE: WWW.SJFC.EDU/BITTNER/

GENERAL INFORMATION

Type of School: private

STUDENTS

Enrollment of Parent Institution: 3,704 **Enrollment of Business School:** 88 % **Male/female:** 38/62 **% Part-time:** 61 **% Minorities:** 18 **Average Age at Entry:** 33

FINANCIAL FACTS

Tuition: $46,000 **Average Award Package:** $29,967

ADMISSIONS

Admissions Selectivity Rating: 76

# of Applications Received: 74 **% Applicants Accepted:** 61 **% Acceptees Attending:** 80 **GMAT Range (25th to 75th percentile):** 460–550 **Average GMAT:** 501 **Average GPA:** 3.33 **TOEFL Required of Int'l Applicants:** yes **Application Fee:** $30 **International Application Fee:** $30 **Regular Application Deadline:** 7/1 **Deferment Available:** yes **Maximum Length of Deferment:** 1 year **Transfer Students Accepted:** yes **Non-fall Admissions:** yes **Need-Blind Admissions:** yes **Applicants Also Look At:** University of Rochester–Simon School of Business.

STATE UNIVERSITY OF NEW YORK—OSWEGO
SCHOOL OF BUSINESS

ADMISSIONS CONTACT: GRADUATE OFFICE, DAVID W.KING, DEAN GRADUATE STUDIES
ADDRESS: 602 CULKIN HALL, SUNY OSWEGO, OSWEGO, NY 13126
PHONE: 315-312-3692 • FAX: 315-312-3577
E-MAIL: MBA@OSWEGO.EDU
WEBSITE: WWW.OSWEGO.EDU/BUSINESS/MBA

GENERAL INFORMATION

Type of School: public **Academic Calendar:** semester

STUDENTS

Enrollment of Parent Institution: 8,183 **Enrollment of Business School:** 76 % **Male/female:** 70/30 **% Part-time:** 40 **% Minorities:** 7 **% International:** 24 **Average Age at Entry:** 26 **Average Years Work Experience at Entry:** 5

ACADEMICS

Student/faculty Ratio: 19:1 **% Female Faculty:** 17 **% Minority Faculty:** 33 **Joint Degrees:** . **Prominent Alumni:** Al Roker, NBC Meteorologist; Alice McDermott, Award Winning Author; Ken Auleta, New Yorker Columnist & critically acclaimed author; Kendis Gibson, CNN Anchor; Heraldo Munoz, Ambassador of Chile to the United Nations.

FINANCIAL FACTS

Tuition (in-state/out-of-state): $7,100/$11,340 **Fees:** $721 **Books and Supplies:** $800 **Room & Board (on campus):** $8,840 **% of**

Students Receiving Aid: 45 % of First-year Students Receiving Aid: 14 % of Students Receiving Loans: 29 % of Students Receiving Grants: 18 **Average Award Package:** $13,650 **Average Grant:** $533 **Average Student Loan Debt:** $30,120

ADMISSIONS

Admissions Selectivity Rating: 68

# of Applications Received: 86 **% Applicants Accepted:** 90 % **Acceptees Attending:** 29 **Average GMAT:** 520 **Average GPA:** 3.00 **TOEFL Required of Int'l Applicants:** yes **Minimum TOEFL (paper/computer):** 560/220 **Application Fee:** $50 **Regular Application Deadline:** 4/15 **Regular Notification:** 6/1 **Deferment Available:** yes **Maximum Length of Deferment:** 1 year **Transfer Students Accepted:** yes **Non-fall Admissions:** yes **Need-Blind Admissions:** yes **Applicants Also Look At:** State University of New York at Albany, State University of New York—University at Buffalo.

STEPHEN F. AUSTIN STATE UNIVERSITY
NELSON RUSCHE COLLEGE OF BUSINESS

ADMISSIONS CONTACT: MICHAEL D. STROUP, MBA DIRECTOR
ADDRESS: PO BOX 13004, SFA STATION, STEPHEN F. AUSTIN STATE UNIVERSITY, NACOGDOCHES, TX 75962-3004
PHONE: 936-468-3101 • FAX: 936-468-1560
E-MAIL: MBA@SFASU.EDU
WEBSITE: WWW.COB.SFASU.EDU

GENERAL INFORMATION

Type of School: public **Environment:** town

STUDENTS

Enrollment of Parent Institution: 10,000 **Enrollment of Business School:** 45 % **Male/female:** 60/40 **% Out-of-state:** 5 **% Part-time:** 50 **% Minorities:** 25 **% International:** 15 **Average Age at Entry:** 25 **Average Years Work Experience at Entry:** 3

ACADEMICS

Student/faculty Ratio: 10:1 **% Female Faculty:** 30 **% Minority Faculty:** 10

FINANCIAL FACTS

Tuition (in-state/out-of-state): $1,134/$7,236 **Fees (in-state/out-of-state):** $126/$804 **Books and Supplies:** $1,000 **Room & Board (on/off campus):** $5,000/$6,500 **% of Students Receiving Aid:** 15 **% of First-year Students Receiving Aid:** 5 **% of Students Receiving Loans:** 5 **Average Award Package:** $3,500 **Average Grant:** $3,500

ADMISSIONS

Admissions Selectivity Rating: 60*

# of Applications Received: 60 **% Applicants Accepted:** % **Acceptees Attending:** **Average GMAT:** 510 **Average GPA:** 3.00 **TOEFL Required of Int'l Applicants:** yes **Minimum TOEFL (paper/computer):** 550/213 **Application Fee:** $25 **International**

Application Fee: $50 **Regular Application Deadline:** 8/1 **Regular Notification:** 8/15 **Deferment Available:** yes **Maximum Length of Deferment:** 1 year **Transfer Students Accepted:** yes **Non-fall Admissions:** yes **Need-Blind Admissions:** yes **Applicants Also Look At:** Northwestern University, Sam Houston State University, Texas State Univeristy–San Marcos, University of North Texas.

EMPLOYMENT PROFILE

Primary Source of Full-time Job Acceptances

Grads Employed by Industry:......% avg. salary:

Finance/Accounting	15	$65,000
Marketing/Sales	25	$45,000
General Management	20	$45,000

TENNESSEE STATE UNIVERSITY

ADMISSIONS CONTACT: LISA SMITH, DIRECTOR OF PUBLIC SERVICE
ADDRESS: 330 TENTH AVENUE NORTH, SUITE K, NASHVILLE, TN 37203
PHONE: 615-963-7137 • FAX: 615-963-7139
E-MAIL: LSMITH11@TNSTATE.EDU
WEBSITE: WWW.COB.TNSTATE.EDU

GENERAL INFORMATION

Type of School: public **Environment:** city

STUDENTS

Enrollment of Business School: 100

ACADEMICS

Student/faculty Ratio: 12:1 **Prominent Alumni:** Nicole Dunigan, vice president, First Tennessee Bank; Thelma Harper, Senator, Tennessee; Kevin Williams, vice president, General Motors; Karen Isabel, CEO, Dalmatian Creative Agency, Inc; Darren Johnson, author, entrepreneur.

FINANCIAL FACTS

Tuition (in-state/out-of-state): $2,569/$4,847 **Fees (in-state/out-of-state):** $428/$2,937 **Books and Supplies:** $2,000 **Room & Board (on/off campus):** $3,160/$4,000

ADMISSIONS

Admissions Selectivity Rating: 60*

Average GMAT: 510 **Average GPA:** 3.2 **TOEFL Required of Int'l Applicants:** yes **Minimum TOEFL (paper/computer):** 500 **Application Fee:** $25 **Regular Application Deadline:** 1/1 **Regular Notification:** 1/1 **Deferment Available:** yes **Transfer Students Accepted:** yes **Non-fall Admissions:** yes **Need-Blind Admissions:** yes

Texas A&M University— Commerce
College of Business and Technology

Admissions Contact: Vicky Turner, Graduate Admissions
Address: PO Box 3011, Commerce, TX 75429
Phone: 903-886-5167 • Fax: 903-886-5165
E-mail: graduate_school@tamu-commerce.edu
Website: www.tamu-commerce.edu/graduateprograms

GENERAL INFORMATION
Type of School: public **Academic Calendar:** semester

STUDENTS
Enrollment of Parent Institution: 7,678 **Enrollment of Business School:** 489 % **Male/female:** 56/44 **% Part-time:** 61 **% Minorities:** 53 **% International:** 23 **Average Age at Entry:** 22

ACADEMICS
Student/faculty Ratio: 27:1 **% Female Faculty:** 10 **% Minority Faculty:** 10
Joint Degrees: MBA/BPA (emphasis in accounting) 5 years.
Prominent Alumni: Sam Rayburn, former Speaker of the House of Represntation; Sheryl Leach, creator of Barney; Durwood Merril, baseball umpire, Texas Baseball Hall of Fame; Duane Allen, lead singer, Oak Ridge Boys; Wade Wilson, quaterback coach, Chicago Bears.

FINANCIAL FACTS
Tuition (in-state/out-of-state): $6,800/$15,050 **Books and Supplies:** $700 **Room & Board (on/off campus):** $2,850/$2,170

ADMISSIONS
Admissions Selectivity Rating: 69
# of Applications Received: 1,215 **% Applicants Accepted:** 60 **% Acceptees Attending:** 65 **Average GMAT:** 460 **Average GPA:** 3
TOEFL Required of Int'l Applicants: Yes **Minimum TOEFL (paper/computer):** 500/173 **Application Fee:** $35 **International Application Fee:** $50 **Regular Application Deadline:** 6/1 **Regular Notification:** rolling
Deferment Available: yoc **Maximum Length of Deferment:** 1 year
Transfer Students Accepted: yes **Non-fall Admissions:** yes
Applicants Also Look At: Baylor University, Southern Methodist University, Texas Christian University (TCU), University of Dallas, University of North Texas, University of Phoenix Online, The University of Texas at Arlington.

Texas State Univeristy—San Marcos
Emmett and Miriam McCoy College of Business

Address: The Graduate College, 601 University Drive, San Marcos, TX 78666
E-mail: gradcollege@txstate.edu
Website: www.business.txstate.edu/

GENERAL INFORMATION
Type of School: public

STUDENTS

FINANCIAL FACTS
Tuition (in-state/out-of-state): $4,390/$8,980 **Books and Supplies:** $770 **Room & Board:** $6,800

ADMISSIONS
Admissions Selectivity Rating: 60*
Application Fee: $40 **Regular Application Deadline:** 6/1

Tilburg University
Faculty of Economics and Business Administration

Admissions Contact: Mrs. Nettie Cools,
Address: B234, Warandelaan 2, PO Box 90153, Tilburg, 5000 LE Netherlands
Phone: 011 31 13 466 2512 • Fax: 011 31 13 466 3072
E-mail: InfoFEB@uvt.nl
Website: www.tilburguniversity.nl

GENERAL INFORMATION
Type of School: public

FINANCIAL FACTS
Tuition: $38,900

ADMISSIONS
Admissions Selectivity Rating: 60*
TOEFL Required of Int'l Applicants: yes **Minimum TOEFL (paper/computer):** 575/233 **International Application Fee:** $100 **Regular Application Deadline:** 6/1

UNION GRADUATE COLLEGE
SCHOOL OF MANAGEMENT

ADMISSIONS CONTACT: RHONDA SHEEHAN, DIRECTOR, GRADUATE ADMISSIONS AND REGISTRAR
ADDRESS: LAMONT HOUSE, 807 UNION STREET, SCHENECTADY, NY 12308
PHONE: 518-388-6148 • FAX: 518-388-6686
E-MAIL: INFO@UNIONGRADUATECOLLEGE.EDU
WEBSITE: WWW.UNIONGRADUATECOLLEGE.EDU

GENERAL INFORMATION

Type of School: private **Environment:** town **Academic Calendar:** trimester

STUDENTS

Enrollment of Parent Institution: 484 **Enrollment of Business School:** 245 **% Male/female:** 50/50 **% Out-of-state:** 2 **% Part-time:** 62 **% Minorities:** 12 **% International:** 5 **Average Age at Entry:** 26 **Average Years Work Experience at Entry:** 3

ACADEMICS

Student/faculty Ratio: 15:1 **% Female Faculty:** 38 **% Minority Faculty:** 9 **Joint Degrees:** JD/MBA 4 years, BA/BS/MBA 5 years, PharmD/MS or MBA 6 years. **Prominent Alumni:** Michael Keegan, president, M&T Bank; Wayne McDougall, DFO, MapInfo; James Mandell, president, Boston Children's Hospital; James Figge, medical director, CDPHP-HMO.

FINANCIAL FACTS

Tuition: $22,000 **Fees:** $125 **Books and Supplies:** $15,000 **Room & Board (off campus):**/$10,000 **% of Students Receiving Aid:** 35 **% of First-year Students Receiving Aid:** 61 **% of Students Receiving Loans:** 22 **% of Students Receiving Grants:** 20 **Average Award Package:** $18,000 **Average Grant:** $4,000 **Average Student Loan Debt:** $21,000

ADMISSIONS

Admissions Selectivity Rating: 68

# of Applications Received: 116 **% Applicants Accepted:** 72 **% Acceptees Attending:** 81 **GMAT Range (25th to 75th percentile):** 460–560 **Average GMAT:** 545 **Average GPA:** 3.44 **TOEFL Required of Int'l Applicants:** yes **Minimum TOEFL (paper/computer):** 550/213 **Application Fee:** $60 **International Application Fee:** $60 **Deferment Available:** yes **Maximum Length of Deferment:** 1 year **Transfer Students Accepted:** yes **Non-fall Admissions:** yes **Need-Blind Admissions:** yes **Applicants Also Look At:** Rensselaer Polytechnic Institute, State University of New York at Albany.

EMPLOYMENT PROFILE

Average base starting salary: $50,000

Top 5 Employers Hiring Grads: The Ayco Company, LP; GE Lockheed Martin; Morgan Stanley; Bank of America.

UNIVERSITÉ LAVAL
FACULTÉ DES SCIENCES DE L'ADMINISTRATION

ADMISSIONS CONTACT: BERNARD GARNIER, DIRECTOR, MBA PROGRAMS
ADDRESS: PAVILLON PALASIS-PRINCE, QUÉBEC, QC G1K 7P4 CANADA
PHONE: 418-656-3080 • FAX: 418-656-5216
E-MAIL: REG@REG.ULAVAL.CA
WEBSITE: WWW.FSA.ULAVAL.CA/HTML/FORMATION.HTML

GENERAL INFORMATION

Type of School: public **Academic Calendar:** semester

STUDENTS

Enrollment of Parent Institution: 38,226 **Enrollment of Business School:** 1,111 **% Male/female:** 56/44 **% Out-of-state:** 21 **% Part-time:** 67 **% International:** 31 **Average Age at Entry:** 35 **Average Years Work Experience at Entry:** 4

ACADEMICS

Student/faculty Ratio: 25:1 **% Female Faculty:** 32

FINANCIAL FACTS

Tuition (in-state/out-of-state): $2,118/$12,272 **Books and Supplies:** $3,000 **Room & Board (on campus):** $2,301

ADMISSIONS

Admissions Selectivity Rating: 79

# of Applications Received: 1,351 **% Applicants Accepted:** 53 **% Acceptees Attending:** 49 **Average GPA:** 3.00 **TOEFL Required of Int'l Applicants:** yes **Minimum TOEFL (paper/computer):** 550/213 **Application Fee:** $30 **International Application Fee:** $30 **Regular Application Deadline:** 2/1 **Regular Notification:** rolling **Deferment Available:** yes **Maximum Length of Deferment:** 1 year **Non-fall Admissions:** yes

THE UNIVERSITY OF ALABAMA IN HUNTSVILLE
COLLEGE OF ADMINISTRATIVE SCIENCE

ADMISSIONS CONTACT: DR. J. DANIEL SHERMAN, ASSOCIATE DEAN
ADDRESS: ASB 102, HUNTSVILLE, AL 35899
PHONE: 256-824-6681 • FAX: 256-890-7571
E-MAIL: GRADBIZ@UAH.EDU
WEBSITE: WWW.UAH.EDU

GENERAL INFORMATION

Type of School: public **Environment:** city **Academic Calendar:** semester

STUDENTS

Enrollment of Business School: 110 **% Male/female:** 58/42 **% Minorities:** 12 **% International:** 7 **Average Age at Entry:** 29 **Average Years Work Experience at Entry:** 6

ACADEMICS

Student/faculty Ratio: 5:1 **% Female Faculty:** 23 **% Minority Faculty:** 10

FINANCIAL FACTS

Tuition (in-state/out-of-state): $5,866/$9,432 **Books and Supplies:** $900

ADMISSIONS

Admissions Selectivity Rating: 71

# of Applications Received: 66 **% Applicants Accepted:** 77 **% Acceptees Attending:** 82 **Average GMAT:** 514 **Average GPA:** 3.29 **TOEFL Required of Int'l Applicants:** yes **Minimum TOEFL (paper):** 550 **Application Fee:** $40 **Regular Application Deadline:** 8/1 **Regular Notification:** 1/1 **Transfer Students Accepted:** yes **Non-fall Admissions:** yes **Need-Blind Admissions:** yes

UNIVERSITY OF ALASKA— ANCHORAGE
COLLEGE OF BUSINESS AND PUBLIC POLICY

ADMISSIONS CONTACT: AL KASTAR, DIRECTOR OF ADMISSIONS
ADDRESS: PO BOX 141629, ANCHORAGE, AK 99514-1029
PHONE: 907-786-1480 • FAX: 907-786-4000
E-MAIL: ANMBS1@UAA.ALASKA.EDU
WEBSITE: WWW.CBPP.UAA.ALASKA.EDU

GENERAL INFORMATION

Type of School: public **Environment:** city

STUDENTS

Enrollment of Business School: 66 **% Male/female:** 35/65 **% Part-time:** 74 **% Minorities:** 12 **% International:** 24 **Average Years Work Experience at Entry:** 5

ACADEMICS

Student/faculty Ratio: 20:1 **% Female Faculty:** 20 **% Minority Faculty:** 22

FINANCIAL FACTS

Tuition (in-state/out-of-state): $4,824/$9,846 **Fees:** $464 **Books and Supplies:** $500 **Room & Board (on campus):** $7,930 **Average Grant:** $6,057

ADMISSIONS

Admissions Selectivity Rating: 77

# of Applications Received: 53 **% Applicants Accepted:** 60 **% Acceptees Attending:** 88 **GMAT Range (25th to 75th percentile):** 450–640 **Average GMAT:** 524 **Average GPA:** 3.3 **TOEFL Required of Int'l Applicants:** yes **Minimum TOEFL (paper):** 550 **Application Fee:** $45 **Regular Application Deadline:** rolling **Regular Notification:** rolling **Deferment Available:** yes **Maximum Length of Deferment:** 1 semester **Transfer Students Accepted:** yes **Non-fall Admissions:** yes **Need-Blind Admissions:** yes

UNIVERSITY OF ALASKA— FAIRBANKS
SCHOOL OF MANAGEMENT

ADMISSIONS CONTACT: NANCY DIX, DIRECTOR
ADDRESS: PO BOX 757480, FAIRBANKS, AK 99775
PHONE: 907-474-7500 • FAX: 907-474-5379
E-MAIL: ADMISSIONS@UAF.EDU
WEBSITE: WWW.UAFSOM.COM/GPMBA.HTML

GENERAL INFORMATION

Type of School: public **Environment:** city

STUDENTS

Enrollment of Parent Institution: 5,025 **Enrollment of Business School:** 30 **Average Age at Entry:** 32 **Average Years Work Experience at Entry:** 10

ACADEMICS

Student/faculty Ratio: 3:1 **% Female Faculty:** 30 **% Minority Faculty:** 20

FINANCIAL FACTS

Tuition (in-state/out-of-state): $4,824/$9,846 **Fees:** $670 **Books and Supplies:** $1,076 **Room & Board (on/off campus):** $6,030/$10,413 **Average Grant:** $16,928 **Average Student Loan Debt:** $12,166

ADMISSIONS

Admissions Selectivity Rating: 90

% Acceptees Attending: 92 **Average GMAT:** 547 **Average GPA:** 3.51 **TOEFL Required of Int'l Applicants:** yes **Minimum TOEFL (paper/computer):** 550/213 **Application Fee:** $50 **Regular Application Deadline:** 8/1 **Deferment Available:** yes **Maximum Length of Deferment:** 1 year **Transfer Students Accepted:** yes **Non-fall Admissions:** yes **Need-Blind Admissions:** yes **Applicants Also Look At:** University of Alaska–Anchorage.

UNIVERSITY OF ANTWERP
MANAGEMENT SCHOOL

ADMISSIONS CONTACT: WIM VAN DRIESSEN, ADMISSIONS OFFICER
ADDRESS: SINT JACOBSMARKT 9-13, ANTWERPEN, 2000 BELGIUM
PHONE: 32-0-3-220-4942 • FAX: 32-0-3-220-4953
E-MAIL: UAMS-MASTER@UA.AC.BE
*WEBSITE: WWW.UAMS.BE/MAIN.ASP?C=*UAMSENG*

GENERAL INFORMATION

Type of School: private

FINANCIAL FACTS

Tuition: $14,500

Admissions Selectivity Rating: 60*

Application Fee: $60 **Regular Application Deadline: Deferment Available:** yes **Maximum Length of Deferment:** 1 year

UNIVERSITY OF ARKANSAS
AT LITTLE ROCK
COLLEGE OF BUSINESS

ADMISSIONS CONTACT: DR. KEN GLACHUS, MBA ADVISOR
ADDRESS: 2801 SOUTH UNIVERSITY AVENUE, LITTLE ROCK, AR 72204
PHONE: 501-569-3356 • FAX: 501-569-8898
WEBSITE: WWW.CBA.UALR.EDU

GENERAL INFORMATION

Type of School: public **Environment:** city **Academic Calendar:** semester

STUDENTS

Enrollment of Parent Institution: 9,925 **Enrollment of Business School:** 225 **% Male/female:** 58/42 **% Out-of-state:** 1 **% Part-time:** 87 **% Minorities:** 8 **% International:** 15 **Average Age at Entry:** 29

FINANCIAL FACTS

Tuition: $30,500

ADMISSIONS

Admissions Selectivity Rating: 60*

# of Applications Received: 87 **% Applicants Accepted:** 66 **% Acceptees Attending:** 74 **TOEFL Required of Int'l Applicants:** yes **Minimum TOEFL (paper):** 550 **Regular Application Deadline:** rolling **Regular Notification:** rolling **Deferment Available:** yes **Applicants Also Look At:** Babson College, Indiana University South Bend, Rensselaer Polytechnic Institute.

UNIVERSITY OF BALTIMORE
MERRICK SCHOOL OF BUSINESS

ADMISSIONS CONTACT: JEFFREY ZAVRONTY, ASSISTANT DIRECTOR OF ADMISSIONS
ADDRESS: 1420 NORTH CHARLES STREET, BALTIMORE, MD 21201
PHONE: 877-277-5982 • FAX: 410-837-4793
E-MAIL: ADMISSIONS@UBMAIL.UBALT.EDU
WEBSITE: BUSINESS.UBALT.EDU/GRADUATEPROGRAMS/MBA.HTML

GENERAL INFORMATION

Type of School: public **Environment:** metropolis **Academic Calendar:** semester

STUDENTS

Enrollment of Parent Institution: 4,639 **Enrollment of Business School:** 506 **% Male/female:** 57/43 **% Out-of-state:** 16 **% Part-time:** 54 **% Minorities:** 18 **% International:** 33 **Average Age at Entry:** 29

ACADEMICS

Student/faculty Ratio: 15:1 **% Female Faculty:** 25 **% Minority Faculty:** 34 **Joint Degrees:** MBA/MS (Nursing) 2 to 7 years, MBA/PhD (Nursing) 2 to 7 years, MBA/PharmD 2 to 7 years, MBA/JD 3 to 7 years. **Prominent Alumni:** William Donald Schaefer, former govenor, Maryland; Peter Angelos, owner, Baltimore Orioles; J. Joseph Curran, Jr., former attorney general, Maryland; Vernon Wright, vice chairman, MBNA America Bank.

FINANCIAL FACTS

Tuition (in-state/out-of-state): $374/$569 (per credit hour) **Books and Supplies:** $900

ADMISSIONS

Admissions Selectivity Rating: 73

# of Applications Received: 376 **% Applicants Accepted:** 62 **% Acceptees Attending:** 63 **GMAT Range (25th to 75th percentile):** 470–520 **Average GMAT:** 500 **Average GPA:** 3.00 **TOEFL Required of Int'l Applicants:** yes **Minimum TOEFL (paper/computer):** 550/213 **Application Fee:** $30 **International Application Fee:** $30 **Regular Application Deadline:** rolling **Regular Notification:** rolling **Deferment Available:** yes **Maximum Length of Deferment:** 1 year **Transfer Students Accepted:** yes **Non-fall Admissions:** yes **Need-Blind Admissions:** yes **Applicants Also Look At:** Loyola College in Maryland, University of Maryland.

UNIVERSITY OF CENTRAL
MISSOURI
HARMON COLLEGE OF BUSINESS ADMINISTRATION

ADMISSIONS CONTACT: LAURIE DELAP, ADMISSIONS EVALUATOR, GRADUATE SCHOOL
ADDRESS: WARD EDWARDS 1800, WARRENSBURG, MO 64093
PHONE: 660-543-4328 • FAX: 660-543-4778
E-MAIL: DELAP@UCMO.EDU
WEBSITE: WWW.UCMO.EDU/GRADUATE

GENERAL INFORMATION

Type of School: public **Environment:** rural **Academic Calendar:** semester

STUDENTS

Enrollment of Parent Institution: 10,711 **Enrollment of Business School:** 53 **% Male/female:** 57/43 **% Out-of-state:** 40 **% Part-time:** 38 **% Minorities:** 8 **Average Age at Entry:** 26 **Average Years Work Experience at Entry:** 3

ACADEMICS

Student/faculty Ratio: 2:1 **% Female Faculty:** 29 **% Minority Faculty:** 2

FINANCIAL FACTS

Tuition (in-state/out-of-state): $5,784/$11,232 **Books and Supplies:** $1,200 **Room & Board:** $5,412 **% of Students Receiving Grants:** 50

Admissions Selectivity Rating: 76

# of Applications Received: 74 **% Applicants Accepted:** 66 **%**
Acceptees Attending: 51 **GMAT Range (25th to 75th percentile):**
440–540 **Average GMAT:** 482 **Average GPA:** 3.32 **TOEFL Required**
of Int'l Applicants: yes **Minimum TOEFL (paper/computer):** 550/213
Application Fee: $30 **International Application Fee:** $50 **Regular**
Application Deadline: rolling **Regular Notification:** rolling
Deferment Available: yes **Maximum Length of Deferment:** 1 year
Transfer Students Accepted: yes **Non-fall Admissions:** yes **Need-**
Blind Admissions: yes **Applicants Also Look At:** Missouri State
University (Formerly SW MSU), Southeast Missouri State University,
University of Missouri–Kansas City.

UNIVERSITY COLLEGE DUBLIN
UCD MICHAEL SMURFIT SCHOOL OF BUSINESS

ADMISSIONS CONTACT: ELAINE MCAREE, MBA ADMISSIONS MANAGER
ADDRESS: UCD SMURFIT SCHOOL OF BUSINESS, CARYSFORT AVENUE,,
* BLACKROCK, CO. DUBLIN, IRELAND*
PHONE: 00 353 1 7168862 • FAX: 00 353 1 7168981
E-MAIL: MBA@UCD.IE
WEBSITE: WWW.UCD.IE/SMURFITSCHOOL

GENERAL INFORMATION

Type of School: Public Affiliation: **Environment: Academic**
Calendar: 2006/2007 Schedule:

STUDENTS

Enrollment of Parent Institution: 22,000 **Enrollment of Business**
School: % **Male/female:** 73/27 **% International:** 30 **Average Age**
at Entry: 32 **Average Years Work Experience at Entry:** 8

ACADEMICS

Student/faculty Ratio: 3:1 **% Female Faculty:** 23 **Joint Degrees:**
CEMS (Masters Community of European Management Schools) 1
year. **Prominent Alumni:** Patrick Haren, MBA, group chief executive,
Viridian; Cathal McGloin, CEO and founder, Perform; JP Donnelly,
managing director, Ogilvy & Mather.

FINANCIAL FACTS

Tuition (in-state): $35,548 **Fees (in-state):** $35,548 **Books and**
Supplies: $1,317 **Room & Board (on/off campus):** $11,203/$12,000
% of Students Receiving Grants: 20

ADMISSIONS

Admissions Selectivity Rating: 60*

# of Applications Received: 162 **% Applicants Accepted:** 23 **GMAT**
Range (25th to 75th percentile): 560–730 **Average GMAT:** 620
TOEFL Required of Int'l Applicants: yes **Minimum TOEFL**
(paper/computer): 600/250 **Application Fee:** $35 **Application**
Deadline/Notification: round 1 1/31 / 2/14, round 2 3/16 / 3/30,
round 3: 5/11 / 5/25, round 4: 7/9 / 7/23. **Deferment Available:** yes
Maximum Length of Deferment: 1 year **Transfer Students**
Accepted: yes **Non-fall Admissions: Need-Blind Admissions:** yes
Applicants Also Look At: IESE Business School, INSEAD, RSM

Erasmus University, Trinity College, University of Dublin, University
of London, University of Oxford, University of Warwick.

EMPLOYMENT PROFILE

Primary Source of Full-time Job Acceptances
Percent Employed: 96
Top 5 Employers Hiring Grads
IBM Consulting; Dell; Procter & Gamble; Davy Stockbrokers;
Airtricity.

UNIVERSITY OF COLORADO
AT BOULDER
LEEDS SCHOOL OF BUSINESS

ADMISSIONS CONTACT: TOBY HEMMERLING, ASSOCIATE DIRECTOR, MBA
* ADMISSIONS & MARKETING*
ADDRESS: UCB 419, BOULDER, CO 80309
PHONE: 303-492-8397 • FAX: 303-492-1727
E-MAIL: LEEDSMBA@COLORADO.EDU
WEBSITE: LFFDS.COLORADO.EDU/MBA

GENERAL INFORMATION

Type of School: public **Environment:** city **Academic Calendar:**
semester

STUDENTS

Enrollment of Parent Institution: 29,151 **Enrollment of Business**
School: 175 **% Male/female:** 66/34 **% Out-of-state:** 46 **% Part-**
time: 35 **% Minorities:** 16 **% International:** 10 **Average Age at**
Entry: 28 **Average Years Work Experience at Entry:** 5

ACADEMICS

Student/faculty Ratio: 4:1 **% Female Faculty:** 12 **% Minority**
Faculty: :20

Joint Degrees: MBA/JD 4 years, MBA/MS (Telecommunications
and/or Computer Science) 3 to 3.5 years, MBA/MA (Fine Arts) 3
years, MBA/MA (Theater and Dance) 3 years, MBA/MA (Germanic
Languages) 3 years, MBA/MS (Environmental Studies) 3 years,
MBA/MA (Anthropology) 3 years. **Prominent Alumni:** Kevin Burns,
managing principle, Lazard Technology Partners; John Puerner,
president & CEO, *Los Angeles Times*; Patrick Tierney, CEO, Reed
Elsevier; Dick Fuld, CEO, Lehman Brothers; Michael Leeds, president
and CEO, Flightstar.

FINANCIAL FACTS

Tuition (in-state/out-of-state): $8,982/$24,156 **Fees:** $869 **Books**
and Supplies: $3,000 **Room & Board:** $13,000 **% of Students**
Receiving Aid: 60 **% of First-year Students Receiving Aid:** 74 **% of**
Students Receiving Loans: 69 **% of Students Receiving Grants:** 72
Average Award Package: $23,103 **Average Grant:** $4,132 **Average**
Student Loan Debt: $29,956

ADMISSIONS

Admissions Selectivity Rating: 83

# of Applications Received: 224 **% Applicants Accepted:** 63 **% Acceptees Attending:** 35 **GMAT Range (25th to 75th percentile):** 610–690 **Average GMAT:** 630 **Average GPA:** 3.2 **TOEFL Required of Int'l Applicants:** yes **Minimum TOEFL (paper/computer):** 600/250 **Application Fee:** $70 **Regular Application Deadline:** 4/1 **Regular Notification:** 6/15 **Application Deadline/Notification:** round 1: 12/1 / 2/15, round 2: 2/1 / 4/15, round 3: 4/1 / 6/15. **Early Decision Program:** yes **ED Deadline/notification:** 12/1 / 2/15 **Transfer Students Accepted:** yes **Need-Blind Admissions:** yes **Applicants Also Look At:** Arizona State University, Colorado State University, University of California, Berkeley, University of Colorado at Denver and HSC, University of Denver, The University of Texas at Austin, University of Washington.

EMPLOYMENT PROFILE

Primary Source of Full-time Job Acceptances

School-facilitated Activities 27 (84%)

Graduate-facilitated Activities 5 (16%)

Average Base Starting Salary: $78,863

Percent Employed: 82

Grads Employed by Industry: ......% avg. salary:

Finance/Accounting 32 $72,200

Marketing/Sales 32 $91,575

Operations/Production 6 $73,500

Consulting.......................................6 $68,500

General Management 9 $73,667

Other..12 $75,500

UNIVERSITY OF COLORADO AT COLORADO SPRINGS
GRADUATE SCHOOL OF BUSINESS ADMINISTRATION

ADMISSIONS CONTACT: MAUREEN CATHEY, MBA PROGRAM DIRECTOR
ADDRESS: 1420 AUSTIN BLUFFS PARKWAY, COLORADO SPRINGS, CO 80918
PHONE: 719-262-3408 • FAX: 719-262-3100
E-MAIL: BUSADVSR@UCCS.EDU
WEBSITE: WEB.UCCS.EDU/BUSINESS

GENERAL INFORMATION

Type of School: public **Environment:** metropolis **Academic Calendar:** semester

STUDENTS

Enrollment of Parent Institution: 7,407 **Enrollment of Business School:** 273 **% Part-time:** 100 **Average Age at Entry:** 29 **Average Years Work Experience at Entry:** 7

ACADEMICS

Student/faculty Ratio: 8:1 **% Female Faculty:** 15 **% Minority Faculty:** 3

FINANCIAL FACTS

Tuition (in-state/out-of-state): $227/$824 (per credit hour) **Room & Board (off campus):** $8,000

ADMISSIONS

Admissions Selectivity Rating: 69

# of Applications Received: 79 **% Applicants Accepted:** 90 **% Acceptees Attending:** 76 **GMAT Range (25th to 75th percentile):** 490–560 **Average GMAT:** 540 **Average GPA:** 3.2 **TOEFL Required of Int'l Applicants:** yes **Minimum TOEFL (paper/computer):** 550/213 **Application Fee:** $60 **International Application Fee:** $75 **Regular Application Deadline:** 6/1 **Regular Notification:** rolling **Deferment Available:** yes **Maximum Length of Deferment:** 1 year **Transfer Students Accepted:** yes **Non-fall Admissions:** yes **Need-Blind Admissions:** yes

UNIVERSITY OF COLORADO AT DENVER AND HEALTH SCIENCES CENTER
BUSINESS SCHOOL

ADMISSIONS CONTACT: SHELLY TOWNLEY, GRADUATE ADMISSIONS COORDINATOR
ADDRESS: CAMPUS BOX 165, PO BOX 173364, DENVER, CO 80217-3364
PHONE: 303-556-5900 • FAX: 303-556-5904
E-MAIL: GRAD.BUSINESS@CUDENVER.EDU
WEBSITE: WWW.BUSINESS.CUDENVER.EDU

GENERAL INFORMATION

Type of School: public **Environment:** metropolis **Academic Calendar:** semester

STUDENTS

Enrollment of Parent Institution: 11,050 **Enrollment of Business School:** 1,249 **% Male/female:** 89/11 **% Out-of-state:** 1 **% Part-time:** 71 **% Minorities:** 10 **% International:** 14 **Average Age at Entry:** 25

ACADEMICS

Student/faculty Ratio: 35:1

FINANCIAL FACTS

Tuition (in-state/out-of-state): $463/$1,096 (per credit hour) **% of Students Receiving Aid:** 29 **Average Grant:** $1,000

ADMISSIONS

Admissions Selectivity Rating: 60*

# of Applications Received: 547 **% Applicants Accepted:** 74 **% Acceptees Attending:** 64 **TOEFL Required of Int'l Applicants:** yes **Minimum TOEFL (paper/computer):** 525/197 **Application Fee:** $50 **International Application Fee:** $75 **Regular Application Deadline:** 6/1 **Regular Notification:** rolling **Deferment Available:** yes **Maximum Length of Deferment:** 1 year **Transfer Students Accepted:** yes **Non-fall Admissions:** yes **Need-Blind Admissions:** yes

University of Delaware
Alfred Lerner College of Business and Economics

Admissions Contact: Denise Waters, Director Recruitment & Admissions
Address: 103 Alfred Lerner Hall, Newark, DE 19716
Phone: 302-831-2221 • Fax: 302-831-3329
E-mail: mbaprogram@udel.edu
Website: www.mba.udel.edu

GENERAL INFORMATION

Type of School: public **Environment:** town **Academic Calendar:** semester

STUDENTS

Enrollment of Parent Institution: 20,000 **Enrollment of Business School:** 359 % **Male/female:** 55/45 **% Out-of-state:** 61 **% Part-time:** 80 **% Minorities:** 14 **% International:** 37 **Average Age at Entry:** 27 **Average Years Work Experience at Entry:** 4

ACADEMICS

Student/faculty Ratio: 30:1 **% Female Faculty:** 14 **% Minority Faculty:** 3

Joint Degrees: MBA/MA (economics), MBA/MS OEDC, MBA/MS ISTM. **Prominent Alumni:** Thomas R. Carper, governor, Delaware; Leonard Quill, CEO & chairman of the board, Wilmington Trust Corp.; Howard Cosgrove, chairman and CEO, Conectlv; Dennis Sheehy, partner, Deloitte Touche Tohmatsu.

FINANCIAL FACTS

Tuition (in-state/out-of-state): $8,552/$17,690 **Fees:** $760 **Books and Supplies:** $1,600 **Room & Board (on/off campus):** $9,000/$10,200 **% of Students Receiving Aid:** 37 **% of First-year Students Receiving Aid:** 15

ADMISSIONS

Admissions Selectivity Rating: 77

# of Applications Received: 242 **% Applicants Accepted:** 59 **% Acceptees Attending:** 46 **Average GMAT:** 553 **Average GPA:** 3.1 **TOEFL Required of Int'l Applicants:** yes **Minimum TOEFL (paper/computer):** 600/260 **Application Fee:** $60 **Regular Application Deadline:** 5/1 **Regular Notification:** rolling **Deferment Available:** yes **Maximum Length of Deferment:** 1 year **Transfer Students Accepted:** yes **Non-fall Admissions:** yes **Need-Blind Admissions:** yes **Applicants Also Look At:** Drexel University, Temple University, Villanova University.

University of Detroit Mercy
College of Business Administration

Admissions Contact: Tyra Rounds, Director of Recruiting
Address: PO Box 19900, Detroit, MI 48219-0900
Phone: 313-993-1245 • Fax: 313-993-3326
E-mail: admissions@udmercy.edu
Website: www.business.udmercy.edu

GENERAL INFORMATION

Type of School: private **Affiliation:** Roman Catholic **Environment:** city **Academic Calendar:** semester

STUDENTS

Enrollment of Parent Institution: 5,415 **Enrollment of Business School:** 144 % **Male/female:** 91/9 **% Part-time:** 69 **% Minorities:** 5 **% International:** 10 **Average Age at Entry:** 32

ACADEMICS

Student/faculty Ratio: 30:1 **% Female Faculty:** 17 **% Minority Faculty:** 13

Joint Degrees: JD/MBA 3 years. **Prominent Alumni:** Thomas Angott, chairman of the board, C.F. Burger Co.; Thomas Capo, Dollar Thrifty Automotive Group; Armando Cavazos, president and CEO, Credit Union One; James Padilla, president, Ford Motor Co.; Emil Simon, owner, The Rollick Beverage Co.

FINANCIAL FACTS

Tuition: $15,750 **Fees:** $570 **Books and Supplies:** $1,200 **Room & Board (on campus):** $7,622 **Average Grant:** $40,000

ADMISSIONS

Admissions Selectivity Rating: 66

# of Applications Received: 91 **% Applicants Accepted:** 87 **% Acceptees Attending:** 68 **GMAT Range (25th to 75th percentile):** 450–650 **Average GMAT:** 500 **Average GPA:** 3.35 **Application Fee:** $30 **International Application Fee:** $50 **Application Deadline:** round 1: 8/15, round 2: 12/15, round 3: 4/15, round 4: 5/15.

Deferment Available: yes **Maximum Length of Deferment:** 2 years **Transfer Students Accepted:** yes **Non-fall Admissions:** yes **Applicants Also Look At:** Oakland University, University of Michigan–Dearborn, Wayne State University.

UNIVERSITY OF HAWAII—MANOA
SHIDLER COLLEGE OF BUSINESS

ADMISSIONS CONTACT: CHERI HONDA, GRADUATE COORDINATOR
ADDRESS: 2404 MAILE WAY, HONOLULU, HI 96822
PHONE: 808-956-8266 • FAX: 808-956-9890
E-MAIL: MBA@HAWAII.EDU
WEBSITE: WWW.SHIDLER.HAWAII.EDU

GENERAL INFORMATION
Type of School: public **Environment:** metropolis **Academic Calendar:** semester

STUDENTS
Enrollment of Parent Institution: 17,532 **Enrollment of Business School:** 319 **% Male/female:** 61/39 **% Out-of-state:** 8 **% Part-time:** 49 **% Minorities:** 18 **% International:** 21 **Average Age at Entry:** 29 **Average Years Work Experience at Entry:** 4

ACADEMICS
Student/faculty Ratio: 25:1 **% Female Faculty:** 5 **% Minority Faculty:** 10

Joint Degrees: MBA/JD 4 years, MBA/Nursing 3 years. **Prominent Alumni:** Brenda Lei Foster, president and CEO, ULU Group, Inc; Sharon Weiner, vice president, DFS Hawaii; C. Dudley Pratt, Jr., former trustee, Campbell Estate; David McCoy, former CEO, Campbell Estate.

FINANCIAL FACTS
Tuition (in-state/out-of-state): $10,896/$16,272 **Fees:** $172 **Books and Supplies:** $900 **Room & Board (on/off campus):** $12,000/$14,000 **Average Award Package:** $12,281 **Average Grant:** $25,000 **Average Student Loan Debt:** $7,644

ADMISSIONS
Admissions Selectivity Rating: 88

# of Applications Received: 313 **% Applicants Accepted:** 39 **% Acceptees Attending:** 55 **GMAT Range (25th to 75th percentile):** 500–710 **Average GMAT:** 575 **Average GPA:** 3.3 **TOEFL Required of Int'l Applicants:** yes **Minimum TOEFL (paper/computer):** 600/250 **Application Fee:** $50 **Regular Application Deadline:** 5/7 **Regular Notification:** rolling Early Decision Program: yes ED Deadline/notification: 3/7 / 5/7 **Deferment Available: Maximum Length of Deferment: Transfer Students Accepted:** yes **Non-fall Admissions:** yes **Need-Blind Admissions:** yes

UNIVERSITY OF HOUSTON— CLEAR LAKE
SCHOOL OF BUSINESS

ADMISSIONS CONTACT: KEVIN McKISSON, REGISTRAR
ADDRESS: 2700 BAY AREA BOULEVARD, HOUSTON, TX 77058-1098
PHONE: 281-283-2500 • FAX: 281-283-2522
E-MAIL: ADMISSIONS@UHCL.EDU
WEBSITE: WWW.UHCL.EDU

GENERAL INFORMATION
Type of School: public **Environment:** metropolis **Academic Calendar:** semester

STUDENTS
Enrollment of Parent Institution: 7,706 **Enrollment of Business School:** 401 **% Out-of-state:** 12 **% Part-time:** 65 **% Minorities:** 18 **% International:** 19 **Average Age at Entry:** 31 **Average Years Work Experience at Entry:** 5

ACADEMICS
Student/faculty Ratio: 18:1 **% Female Faculty:** 31 **% Minority Faculty:** 19

Joint Degrees: MBA/Master of Healthcare Administration 3 years.

FINANCIAL FACTS
Tuition (in-state/out-of-state): $3,312/$10,980 **Fees:** $5,004 **Books and Supplies:** $1,800 **Room & Board:** $12,836 **% of Students Receiving Aid:** 20 **Average Award Package:** $8,300 **Average Grant:** $1,000 **Average Student Loan Debt:** $26,916

ADMISSIONS
Admissions Selectivity Rating: 75

# of Applications Received: 236 **% Applicants Accepted:** 53 **% Acceptees Attending:** 67 **GMAT Range (25th to 75th percentile):** 440–0530 **Average GMAT:** 492 **Average GPA:** 3.12 **TOEFL Required of Int'l Applicants:** yes **Minimum TOEFL (paper/computer):** 550/213 **Application Fee:** $35 **International Application Fee:** $75 **Regular Application Deadline:** 8/1 **Regular Notification:** rolling **Deferment Available:** yes **Maximum Length of Deferment:** 1 year **Transfer Students Accepted:** yes **Non-fall Admissions:** yes **Need-Blind Admissions:** yes **Applicants Also Look At:** Houston Baptist University, University of Houston, University of St. Thomas.

UNIVERSITY OF LONDON
LONDON BUSINESS SCHOOL

ADMISSIONS CONTACT: DAVID SIMPSON, SENIOR MANAGER, MBA MARKETING AND ADMISSIONS
ADDRESS: REGENT'S PARK, LONDON, NW1 4SA ENGLAND
PHONE: 011-44-20-7000-7500 • FAX: 011-44-20-7000-7501
E-MAIL: MBAINFO@LONDON.EDU
WEBSITE: WWW.LONDON.EDU

GENERAL INFORMATION
Type of School: private

STUDENTS
% International: 90 **Average Age at Entry:** 28 **Average Years Work Experience at Entry:** 5

ACADEMICS
Student/faculty Ratio: 8:1
Joint Degrees: EMBA-Global (with Columbia University) 1.5 years.

FINANCIAL FACTS
Tuition: $35,675 **Books and Supplies:** $500 **Room & Board (off campus):** $25,500 **% of Students Receiving Loans:** 56 **Average Grant:** $17,980

ADMISSIONS
Admissions Selectivity Rating: 60*
# of Applications Received: 1,849 **% GMAT Range (25th to 75th percentile):** 650–710 **Average GMAT:** 680 **Average GPA:** 3.3 **TOEFL Required of Int'l Applicants:** yes **Application Fee:** $280 **International Application Fee:** $280 **Regular Application Deadline:** 4/27 **Regular Notification:** 5/18 Application Deadline/Notification: round 1 10/20 / 11/17, round 2 1/5 / 2/9, round 3 2/23 / 4/3, round 4 4/27 / 5/18. **Deferment Available:** yes **Maximum Length of Deferment:** 1 year **Need-Blind Admissions:** yes **Applicants Also Look At:** Columbia University, Harvard University, INSEAD, New York University, Northwestern University, Stanford University, University of Pennsylvania.

UNIVERSITY OF LOUISIANA AT MONROE
COLLEGE OF BUSINESS ADMINSTRATION

ADMISSIONS CONTACT: MIGUEL PEREZ, COORDINATOR OF ASSESSMENT AND INTERNAL AFFAIRS
ADDRESS: 700 UNIVERSITY AVENUE, MONROE, LA 71209-0100
PHONE: 318-342-1100 • FAX: 318-342-1101
E-MAIL: PEREZ@ULM.EDU
WEBSITE: ELE.ULM.EDU/MBA/

GENERAL INFORMATION
Type of School: public **Academic Calendar:** semester

STUDENTS
Enrollment of Parent Institution: 10,942 **Enrollment of Business School:** 77 % **Male/female:** 60/40 **% Out-of-state:** 11 **% Part-time:** 19 **% Minorities:** 5 **% International:** 40 **Average Age at Entry:** 27

ACADEMICS
% Female Faculty: 30 **% Minority Faculty:** 4

FINANCIAL FACTS
Tuition (in-state/out-of-state): $1,900/$7,858 **Fees:** $382 **Books and Supplies:** $600 **Room & Board (on campus):** $2,560 **Average Grant:** $5,000

ADMISSIONS
Admissions Selectivity Rating: 73
# of Applications Received: 77 **% Applicants Accepted:** 58 **% Acceptees Attending:** 78 **Average GMAT:** 480 **Average GPA:** 3.00 **TOEFL Required of Int'l Applicants:** yes **Minimum TOEFL (paper/computer):** 480/157 **Application Fee:** $20 **International Application Fee:** $30 **Regular Application Deadline:** 7/1 **Regular Notification:** 7/15 **Deferment Available:** yes **Maximum Length of Deferment:** 1 year **Transfer Students Accepted:** yes **Non-fall Admissions:** yes

UNIVERSITY OF MAINE
MAINE BUSINESS SCHOOL

ADMISSIONS CONTACT: MAXINE EWANKUW, PROGRAM ASSISTANT, BUSINESS GRADUATE PROGRAMS
ADDRESS: 5723 DP CORBETT BUSINESS BUILDING, ORONO, ME 04469-5723
PHONE: 207-581-1973 • FAX: 207-581-1930
E-MAIL: MBA@MAINE.EDU
WEBSITE: WWW.UMAINE.EDU/BUSINESS

GENERAL INFORMATION
Type of School: public **Environment:** village **Academic Calendar:** semester

STUDENTS
Enrollment of Parent Institution: 11,300 **Enrollment of Business School:** 79 % **Male/female:** 61/39 **% Out-of-state:** 1 **% Part-time:** 37 **% Minorities:** 1 **% International:** 23 **Average Age at Entry:** 27 **Average Years Work Experience at Entry:** 6

ACADEMICS
Student/faculty Ratio: 4:1 **% Female Faculty:** 40 **Prominent Alumni:** Bernard Lown, Nobel Peace Prize winner; Steven King, writer; Olympia Snowe, U.S. Senator.

FINANCIAL FACTS
Tuition (in-state/out-of-state): $5,328/$15,210 **Fees:** $644 **Books and Supplies:** $800 **Room & Board:** $7,150 **Average Grant:** $5,000

ADMISSIONS
Admissions Selectivity Rating: 81
# of Applications Received: 42 **% Applicants Accepted:** 64 **% Acceptees Attending:** 56 **GMAT Range (25th to 75th percentile):**

530–610 **Average GMAT:** 576 **Average GPA:** 3.47 **TOEFL Required of Int'l Applicants:** yes **Minimum TOEFL (paper/computer):** 550/213 **Application Fee:** $50 **Regular Application Deadline:** 6/1 **Regular Notification:** 7/1 **Deferment Available:** yes **Maximum Length of Deferment:** 1 year **Transfer Students Accepted:** yes **Non-fall Admissions:** yes **Need-Blind Admissions:** yes **Applicants Also Look At:** University of New Hampshire, University of Southern Maine.

UNIVERSITY OF MANCHESTER
MANCHESTER BUSINESS SCHOOL

ADMISSIONS CONTACT: GAER BUCHANAN, ADMISSIONS ADMINISTRATOR
ADDRESS: MBA ADMISSIONS OFFICE, BOOTH STREET WEST, MANCHESTER, M15 6PB ENGLAND
PHONE: 00-44-161-275-6364 • FAX: 00-44-161-275-6556
E-MAIL: GAER.BUCHANAN@MBS.AC.UK
WEBSITE: WWW.MBS.AC.UK/MBA

GENERAL INFORMATION
Type of School: public

ACADEMICS
Prominent Alumni: Rijkman Groenink, chairman of the managing board, ABN AMRO; Robert H. Herz, chairman, U.S. Financial Accounting Standards Board; Sir Terry Leahy, chief executive, Tesco; Paul Skinner, chairman, Rio Tinto; David Varney, executive chairman, Her Majesty's Revenue and Cust.

FINANCIAL FACTS
Tuition: $53,100

ADMISSIONS
Admissions Selectivity Rating: 60*

TOEFL Required of Int'l Applicants: yes **Minimum TOEFL (paper/computer):** 600/250 **Regular Application Deadline:** 7/9 **Regular Notification:** 7/30 Application Deadline/Notification: round 1 2/26 / 4/30, round 2 03/26 / 5/14, round 3 5/28 / 7/30 round 4 7/9 / 7/30. **Deferment Available:** yes **Maximum Length of Deferment:** 1 year

EMPLOYMENT PROFILE
Primary Source of Full-time Job Acceptances

School-facilitated Activities 43%
Graduate-facilitated Activities 57%
Grads Employed by Industry:.......% avg. salary:
Finance/Accounting.........................22 $110,240
Marketing/Sales 21 $92,100
Operations/Production 12 $93,900
Strategic Planning.........................5 $106,950
Consulting......................................26 $91,800
General Management 14 $73,550

UNIVERSITY OF MANITOBA
I.H. ASPER SCHOOL OF BUSINESS

ADMISSIONS CONTACT: EWA MORPHY, GRADUATE PROGRAM MANAGER
ADDRESS: 324 DRAKE CENTER, WINNIPEG, MB R3T 5V4 CANADA
PHONE: 204-474-8448 • FAX: 204-474-7544
E-MAIL: ASPERMBA@UMANITOBA.CA
WEBSITE: WWW.UMANITOBA.CA/ASPER

GENERAL INFORMATION
Type of School: public **Environment:** city

STUDENTS
Enrollment of Parent Institution: 26,000 **Enrollment of Business School:** 120 **% Male/female:** 60/40 **% Part-time:** 72 **% International:** 9 **Average Age at Entry:** 32 **Average Years Work Experience at Entry:** 10

ACADEMICS
Student/faculty Ratio: 30:1 **% Female Faculty:** 18 **% Minority Faculty:** 32

Prominent Alumni: F. Ross Johnson, chair/CEO RJM Group; Robert W. Pollock, chair, Drake International; Gerald W. Schwartz, chair, president and CEO, Onyx Corp.; Martin S. Weinberg, president, CEO Assante Corporation; Bill McCallum, president and CEO, Great-West Life Annuity Insurance.

FINANCIAL FACTS
Tuition: $16,201 **Books and Supplies:** $2,543 **Room & Board (on/off campus):** $5,800/$10,174 **% of First-year Students Receiving Aid:** 10 **Average Grant:** $4,000

ADMISSIONS
Admissions Selectivity Rating: 76

# of Applications Received: 67 **% Applicants Accepted:** 72 **% Acceptees Attending:** 62 **GMAT Range (25th to 75th percentile):** 444–633 **Average GMAT:** 566 **Average GPA:** 3.00 **TOEFL Required of Int'l Applicants:** yes **Minimum TOEFL (paper/computer):** 550/213 **Application Fee:** $75 **International Application Fee:** $90 **Regular Application Deadline:** 6/1 **Regular Notification:** rolling **Transfer Students Accepted:** yes **Non-fall Admissions:** yes

EMPLOYMENT PROFILE
Primary Source of Full-time Job Acceptances

School-facilitated Activities 4 (15%)
Graduate-facilitated Activities 14 (50%)
Unknown..10 (35%)
Percent Employed: 12
Grads Employed by Industry:.......% avg. salary:
Finance/Accounting.........................5 $62,500
Marketing/Sales 5 $97,500
Communications 5 $77,500
General Management 36 $82,143
Quantitative 24 $91,250
Other..11 $75,000
Internet/New Media.......................5 $102,500

University of Michigan— Dearborn
School of Management

ADMISSIONS CONTACT: CHRISTINE BRZEZINSKI, GRADUATE ADMISSIONS COORDINATOR
ADDRESS: SCHOOL OF MANAGEMENT, 19000 HUBBARD DRIVE, DEARBORN, MI 48126-2638
PHONE: 313-593-5460 • FAX: 313-271-9838
E-MAIL: GRADBUSINESS@UMD.UMICH.EDU
WEBSITE: WWW.SOM.UMD.UMICH.EDU

GENERAL INFORMATION

Type of School: public **Environment:** city **Academic Calendar:** semester

STUDENTS

Enrollment of Parent Institution: 8,566 **Enrollment of Business School:** 435 % **Male/female:** 60/40 % **Part-time:** 91 % **Minorities:** 22 **Average Age at Entry:** 30 **Average Years Work Experience at Entry:** 7

ACADEMICS

Student/faculty Ratio: 30:1 % **Female Faculty:** 38 % **Minority Faculty:** 25

Joint Degrees: MBA/Master of Science (Finance) 2 to 5 years, MBA/MS (Industrual Engineering) 4-5 years, MBA/Master of Health Services Administration.

FINANCIAL FACTS

Tuition (in-state/out-of-state): $443.90/$843.50 (per credit hour)
Books and Supplies: $1,200 **Average Grant:** $1,500

ADMISSIONS

Admissions Selectivity Rating: 77

# of Applications Received: 116 % **Applicants Accepted:** 76 % **Acceptees Attending:** 78 **Average GMAT:** 571 **Average GPA:** 3.21 **TOEFL Required of Int'l Applicants:** yes **Minimum TOEFL (paper/computer):** 560/220 **Application Fee:** $60 **International Application Fee:** $75 **Regular Application Deadline:** 8/1 **Regular Notification:** rolling **Deferment Available:** yes **Maximum Length of Deferment:** 1 year **Transfer Students Accepted:** yes **Non-fall Admissions:** yes **Need-Blind Admissions:** yes **Applicants Also Look At:** Eastern Michigan University, Michigan State University—College of Law, Oakland University, University of Detroit Mercy, University of Michigan, Wayne State University.

University of Minnesota
Carlson School of Management

ADMISSIONS CONTACT: JEFF BIEGANEK, DIRECTOR OF ADMISSIONS & BUSINESS DEVELOPMENT
ADDRESS: 321 NINETEENTH AVENUE SOUTH, SUITE 4—106, MINNEAPOLIS, MN 55455
PHONE: 612-625-5555 • FAX: 612-626-7785
E-MAIL: FULL-TIMEMBAINFO@CARLSONSCHOOL.UMN.EDU
WEBSITE: WWW.CARLSONSCHOOL.UMN.EDU

GENERAL INFORMATION

Type of School: public **Environment:** metropolis **Academic Calendar:** semester

STUDENTS

Enrollment of Parent Institution: 50,402 **Enrollment of Business School:** 1,922 % **Male/female:** 65/35 % **Part-time:** 89 % **Minorities:** 10 % **International:** 40 **Average Age at Entry:** 29 **Average Years Work Experience at Entry:** 5

ACADEMICS

Student/faculty Ratio: 15:1 % **Female Faculty:** 22 % **Minority Faculty:** 20

Joint Degrees: MBA/JD 4 years, MBA/MHA 3 years, MD/MBA 5 years. **Prominent Alumni:** Charles W. Mooty, CEO, International Dairy Queen; William G. Van Dyke, chairman, president and CEO, Donaldson Company, Inc.; Curtis C. Nelson, president and COO, Carlson Companies; Robert A. Kierlin, chairman, Fastenal Company; Barbara J. Mowry, president & CEO, TMC Consulting.

FINANCIAL FACTS

Tuition (in-state/out-of-state): $21,300/$30,320 **Fees:** $2,500 **Books and Supplies:** $4,000 **Room & Board (on/off campus):** $13,000/$15,000 % **of Students Receiving Aid:** 77 % **of Students Receiving Loans:** 41 % **of Students Receiving Grants:** 63 **Average Award Package:** $29,260 **Average Grant:** $19,200 **Average Student Loan Debt:** $41,877

ADMISSIONS

Admissions Selectivity Rating: 88

# of Applications Received: 418 % **Applicants Accepted:** 53 % **Acceptees Attending:** 56 **Average GMAT:** 641 **Average GPA:** 3.3 **TOEFL Required of Int'l Applicants:** yes **Minimum TOEFL (paper/computer):** 580/240 **Application Fee:** $60 **International Application Fee:** $90 **Regular Application Deadline:** 4/15 **Regular Notification:** 5/15 **Application Deadline/Notification:** round 1: 12/15 / 2/15, round 2: 2/15 / 4/15, round 3: 4/15 / 5/15.

Early Decision Program: yes ED Deadline/notification: 12/15 / 2/15 **Deferment Available:** yes **Maximum Length of Deferment:** 1 year **Need-Blind Admissions:** yes

Primary Source of Full-time Job Acceptances

School-facilitated Activities 68 (77%)

Graduate-facilitated Activities 20 (23%)

Average Base Starting Salary: $82,436

Percent Employed: 97

Top 5 Employers Hiring Grads: Northwest Airlines; Best Buy Co., Inc.; Ecolab; Cargill.

UNIVERSITY OF MINNESOTA— DULUTH
LABOVITZ SCHOOL OF BUSINESS AND ECONOMICS

ADMISSIONS CONTACT: CANDY FURO, ASSOCIATE ADMINISTRATOR
ADDRESS: 21 LSBE, 412 LIBRARY DRIVE, DULUTH, MN 55812
PHONE: 218-726-8986 • FAX: 218-726-6789
E-MAIL: GRAD@D.UMN.EDU
WEBSITE: WWW.D.UMN.EDU/SBE/DEGREEPROGS/MBA/

GENERAL INFORMATION

Type of School: public **Environment:** village **Academic Calendar:** semester

STUDENTS

Enrollment of Parent Institution: 11,190 **Enrollment of Business School:** 61 **% Part-time:** 100 **Average Age at Entry:** 30 **Average Years Work Experience at Entry:** 5

ACADEMICS

Student/faculty Ratio: 20:1 **% Female Faculty:** 24

Prominent Alumni: Jon Gerlach, CFO; Chris Mahai, president/CEO; Elaine Hansen, director; Jim Vizanko, CFO.

FINANCIAL FACTS

Tuition: $739 (per credit hour) **Books and Supplies:** $1,000 **Room & Board (off campus):** $6,000

ADMISSIONS

Admissions Selectivity Rating: 76

# of Applications Received: 19 **% Applicants Accepted:** 89 **% Acceptees Attending:** 94 **GMAT Range (25th to 75th percentile):** 530–640 **Average GMAT:** 585 **Average GPA:** 3.24 **TOEFL Required of Int'l Applicants:** yes **Minimum TOEFL (paper/computer):** 550/213 **Application Fee:** $55 **International Application Fee:** $75 **Regular Application Deadline:** 7/15 **Regular Notification:** 9/1 Application Deadline/Notification: round 1 7/15 / 8/31, round 2 11/1 / 12/31, round 3 5/1 / 5/30.

Deferment Available: yes **Maximum Length of Deferment:** 1 year **Transfer Students Accepted:** yes **Non-fall Admissions:** yes **Need-Blind Admissions:** yes **Applicants Also Look At:** St. Cloud State University, University of Minnesota, University of St. Thomas.

THE UNIVERSITY OF MONTANA— MISSOULA
SCHOOL OF BUSINESS ADMINISTRATION

ADMISSIONS CONTACT: KATHLEEN SPRITZER, ADMINISTRATIVE OFFICER
ADDRESS: SCHOOL OF BUSINESS ADMINISTRATION, UNIVERSITY OF MONTANA, MISSOULA, MT 59812
PHONE: 406-243-4983 • FAX: 406-243-2086
E-MAIL: KATHLEEN.SPRITZER@BUSINESS.UMT.EDU
WEBSITE: WWW.MBA-MACCT.UMT.EDU

GENERAL INFORMATION

Type of School: public **Environment:** city **Academic Calendar:** semester

STUDENTS

Enrollment of Parent Institution: 13,564 **Enrollment of Business School:** 184 **% Male/female:** 46/54 **% Part-time:** 47 **% Minorities:** 5 **% International:** 10 **Average Age at Entry:** 29 **Average Years Work Experience at Entry:** 3

ACADEMICS

Student/faculty Ratio: 26:1 **% Female Faculty:** 31 **% Minority Faculty:** 1

Joint Degrees: JD/MBA 3 years, MBA/PharmD 5 years.

FINANCIAL FACTS

Tuition (in-state/out-of-state): $6,150/$14,230 **Books and Supplies:** $1,800 **Room & Board (on campus):** $8,750 **% of Students Receiving Aid:** 10 **% of Students Receiving Grants:** 10 **Average Grant:** $9,000

ADMISSIONS

Admissions Selectivity Rating: 60*

# of Applications Received: 146 **% Applicants Accepted:** 75 **% Acceptees Attending:** 88 **Average GMAT:** 566 **Average GPA:** 3.2 **TOEFL Required of Int'l Applicants:** yes **Minimum TOEFL (paper/computer):** 580/237 **Application Fee:** $45 **International Application Fee:** $45 **Regular Application Deadline:** 4/15 **Regular Notification:** 5/1 **Deferment Available:** yes **Maximum Length of Deferment:** 1 year **Transfer Students Accepted:** yes **Non-fall Admissions:** yes **Need-Blind Admissions:** yes **Applicants Also Look At:** Idaho State University, Montana State University, University of Oregon, University of Washington, Washington State University.

University of Nebraska at Kearney
College of Business and Technology

Admissions Contact: Linda Johnson, Director, Graduate Admissions & Programs
Address: 905 W 25th St, Founders Hall Room 2131, Kearney, NE 68849
Phone: 800-717-7881 • Fax: 308-865-8837
E-mail: johnsonli@unk.edu
Website: www.unk.edu/acad/MBA

GENERAL INFORMATION
Type of School: public **Academic Calendar:** semester

STUDENTS
Enrollment of Parent Institution: 6,468 **Enrollment of Business School:** 44 **% Male/female:** 60/40 **% Out-of-state:** 13 **% Part-time:** 66 **% International:** 27 **Average Age at Entry:** 25 **Average Years Work Experience at Entry:** 2

ACADEMICS
Student/faculty Ratio: 2:1 **% Female Faculty:** 38

FINANCIAL FACTS
Tuition (in-state/out-of-state): $2,889/$5,976 **Fees:** $670 **Books and Supplies:** $700 **Room & Board (on/off campus):** $6,700/$7,500

ADMISSIONS
Admissions Selectivity Rating: 73

# of Applications Received: 23 **% Applicants Accepted:** 83 **% Acceptees Attending:** 100 **GMAT Range (25th to 75th percentile):** 460–580 **Average GMAT:** 520 **Average GPA:** 3.42 **TOEFL Required of Int'l Applicants:** yes **Minimum TOEFL (paper/computer):** 550/213 **Application Fee:** $45 **Regular Application Deadline:** 5/1 **Regular Notification:** rolling **Deferment Available:** yes **Maximum Length of Deferment:** 1 year **Transfer Students Accepted:** yes **Non-fall Admissions:** yes **Applicants Also Look At:** Creighton University, University of Nebraska–Lincoln, University of Nebraska at Omaha.

University of Nebraska— Lincoln
College of Business Administration

Admissions Contact: Judy Shutts, Graduate Adviser
Address: CBA 125, Lincoln, NE 68588-0405
Phone: 402-472-2338 • Fax: 402-472-5180
E-mail: cgraduate@unlnotes.unl.edu
Website: www.cba.unl.edu

GENERAL INFORMATION
Type of School: public **Environment:** city **Academic Calendar:** semester

STUDENTS
Enrollment of Parent Institution: 22,106 **Enrollment of Business School:** 124 **% Male/female:** 66/34 **% Out-of-state:** 12 **% Part-time:** 45 **% Minorities:** 3 **% International:** 32 **Average Age at Entry:** 25 **Average Years Work Experience at Entry:** 5

ACADEMICS
Student/faculty Ratio: 6:1 **% Female Faculty:** 17 **% Minority Faculty:** 13
Joint Degrees: MBA/JD 4 years, MBA/Arch 3 years.

FINANCIAL FACTS
Tuition (in-state/out-of-state): $5,076/$13,674 **Fees:** $757 **Books and Supplies:** $944 **Room & Board (on/off campus):** $7,106/$7,500 **% of Students Receiving Aid:** 80 **% of First-year Students Receiving Aid:** 76 **% of Students Receiving Loans:** 28 **% of Students Receiving Grants:** 56 **Average Award Package:** $15,000 **Average Grant:** $12,312

ADMISSIONS
Admissions Selectivity Rating: 84

# of Applications Received: 101 **% Applicants Accepted:** 70 **% Acceptees Attending:** 62 **GMAT Range (25th to 75th percentile):** 580–640 **Average GMAT:** 620 **Average GPA:** 3.48 **TOEFL Required of Int'l Applicants:** yes **Minimum TOEFL (paper/computer):** 550/213 **Application Fee:** $45 **Regular Application Deadline:** 6/15 **Regular Notification:** rolling **Deferment Available:** yes **Maximum Length of Deferment:** 1 semester **Transfer Students Accepted:** yes **Non-fall Admissions:** yes **Need-Blind Admissions:** yes **Applicants Also Look At:** Arizona State University, Creighton University, University of Iowa, University of Kansas, University of Nebraska at Omaha.

EMPLOYMENT PROFILE
Primary Source of Full-time Job Acceptances
Average Base Starting Salary: $65,122
Percent Employed: 100

Grads Employed by Industry:	%	avg. salary:
Finance/Accounting	20	$67,364
Human Resources	4	$53,939
Marketing/Sales	7	$50,500
MIS	10	$68,250
Operations/Production	14	$50,833
Consulting	10	$96,250
Entrepreneurship	7	$50,000
General Management	8	$68,100
Other	2	$35,000
Nonprofit	17	$60,929

UNIVERSITY OF NEBRASKA AT OMAHA
COLLEGE OF BUSINESS ADMINISTRATION

ADMISSIONS CONTACT: LEX KACZMAREK, DIRECTOR, MBA PROGRAM
ADDRESS: 6001 DODGE STREET, OMAHA, NE 68182-0048
PHONE: 402-554-2303 • FAX: 402-554-3747
E-MAIL: MBA@UNOMAHA.EDU
WEBSITE: CBA.UNOMAHA.EDU/MBA

GENERAL INFORMATION

Type of School: public **Environment:** metropolis **Academic Calendar:** semester

STUDENTS

Enrollment of Parent Institution: 14,667 **Enrollment of Business School:** 293 **% Part-time:** 100 **Average Age at Entry:** 28 **Average Years Work Experience at Entry:** 5

ACADEMICS

Student/faculty Ratio: 15:1 **% Female Faculty:** 40 **% Minority Faculty:** 5

Prominent Alumni: James R. Young, president and COO, Union Pacific Railroad; R. Craig Hoenshell, former CEO, Avis and American Express International; Ronald J. Burns, former president and CEO, Union Pacific; Bernard R. Reznicek, former chairman, president and CEO, Boston Edison Comp.; Samuel G. Leftwich, former president, K-Mart Corporation.

FINANCIAL FACTS

Tuition (in-state/out-of-state): $163.50/$430 (per credit hour) **Room & Board (on/off campus):** $6,500/$9,500 **Average Award Package:** $8,414 **Average Grant:** $2,981 **Average Student Loan Debt:** $7,625

ADMISSIONS

Admissions Selectivity Rating: 77

# of Applications Received: 86 **% Applicants Accepted:** 79 **% Acceptees Attending:** 78 **GMAT Range (25th to 75th percentile):** 500–610 **Average GMAT:** 568 **Average GPA:** 3.45 **TOEFL Required of Int'l Applicants:** yes **Minimum TOEFL (paper/computer):** 550/213 **Application Fee:** $45 **International Application Fee:** $45 **Regular Application Deadline:** 7/1 **Regular Notification:** rolling **Deferment Available:** yes **Maximum Length of Deferment:** 1 year **Transfer Students Accepted:** yes **Non-fall Admissions:** yes **Need-Blind Admissions:** yes **Applicants Also Look At:** Creighton University, University of Nebraska–Lincoln.

UNIVERSITY OF NEW MEXICO
ROBERT O. ANDERSON GRADUATE SCHOOL OF MANAGEMENT

ADMISSIONS CONTACT: MARY BERGER, GRADUATE PROGRAMS MANAGER
ADDRESS: THE UNIVERSITY OF NEW MEXICO, 1924 LAS LOMAS BOULEVARD, ALBUQUERQUE, NM 87131
PHONE: 505-277-3888 • FAX: 505-277-9356
E-MAIL: MBA@MGT.UNM.EDU
WEBSITE: WWW.MGT.UNM.EDU/

GENERAL INFORMATION

Type of School: public **Environment:** metropolis **Academic Calendar:** semester

STUDENTS

Enrollment of Parent Institution: 26,339 **Enrollment of Business School:** 507 **% Male/female:** 55/45 **% Out-of-state:** 24 **% Part-time:** 48 **% Minorities:** 43 **% International:** 16 **Average Age at Entry:** 29 **Average Years Work Experience at Entry:** 5

ACADEMICS

Student/faculty Ratio: 26:1 **% Female Faculty:** 31

Joint Degrees: MBA/MA (Latin American Studies) 3 to 4 years, MBA/JD 4 years. **Prominent Alumni:** Daniel L. Jorndt, CEO, Walgreen Co.; Ann Rhoades, president, PeopleInk; Judith Rogala, president & CEO, La Petite Academy; Waneta Tuttle, CEO, Exagen Diagnostics; Milton H. Ward, president & CEO (retired), Cyprus Amax Minerals Co.

FINANCIAL FACTS

Tuition (in-state/out-of-state): $4,110/$12,811 **Fees:** $280 **Books and Supplies:** $2,000 **Room & Board (on/off campus):** $10,270/$8,520 **% of Students Receiving Aid:** 55 **% of First-year Students Receiving Aid:** 52 **% of Students Receiving Loans:** 36 **% of Students Receiving Grants:** 30 **Average Award Package:** $5,424 **Average Grant:** $2,849 **Average Student Loan Debt:** $25,134

ADMISSIONS

Admissions Selectivity Rating: 87

# of Applications Received: 168 **% Applicants Accepted:** 51 **% Acceptees Attending:** 100 **Average GMAT:** 561 **Average GPA:** 3.54 **TOEFL Required of Int'l Applicants:** yes **Minimum TOEFL (paper/computer):** 550/213 **Application Fee:** $50 **Regular Application Deadline:** 6/1 **Regular Notification:** rolling **Deferment Available:** yes **Maximum Length of Deferment:** 1 year **Transfer Students Accepted:** yes **Non-fall Admissions:** yes

UNIVERSITY OF NEW ORLEANS
COLLEGE OF BUSINESS ADMINSTRATION

ADMISSIONS CONTACT: ROSLYN SHELEY, DIRECTOR OF ADMISSIONS
ADDRESS: ADMIN BUILDING ROOM 103, NEW ORLEANS, LA 70148
PHONE: 504-280-6595 • FAX: 504-280-5522
E-MAIL: ADMISSIONS@UNO.EDU
WEBSITE: WWW.UNO.EDU

GENERAL INFORMATION

Type of School: public **Environment:** metropolis **Academic Calendar:** semester

STUDENTS

Enrollment of Parent Institution: 17,360 **Enrollment of Business School:** 810 % **Male/female:** 51/49 **% Out-of-state:** 30 **% Part-time:** 46 **% Minorities:** 25 **% International:** 26 **Average Age at Entry:** 30

ACADEMICS

Student/faculty Ratio: 24:1 **Prominent Alumni:** Dr. James Clark, chairman of the board, Netscape Communications; Michael Fitzpatrick, CEO, Rohm & Haas; Erving Johnson, starting center, Milwaukee Bucks; Mike Kettenring, president and general manager, Gillett Broadcasting; Dr. Reuben Arminana, president, Sonoma State University.

FINANCIAL FACTS

Tuition (in-state/out-of-state): $3,300/$10,800 **Books and Supplies:** $1,150 **Room & Board:** $4,122 **Average Grant:** $2,697

ADMISSIONS

Admissions Selectivity Rating: 66

# of Applications Received: 575 **% Applicants Accepted:** 67 **% Acceptees Attending:** 62 **GMAT Range (25th to 75th percentile):** 400–510 **Average GMAT:** 459 **Average GPA:** 3.00 **TOEFL Required of Int'l Applicants:** yes **Minimum TOEFL (paper/computer):** 550/213 **Application Fee:** $40 **Regular Application Deadline:** 7/1 **Regular Notification:** 9/1 **Deferment Available:** yes **Maximum Length of Deferment:** 1 semester **Transfer Students Accepted:** yes **Non-fall Admissions:** yes **Need-Blind Admissions:** yes

UNIVERSITY NEW SOUTH WALES
AUSTRALIAN GRADUATE SCHOOL OF MANAGEMENT

ADMISSIONS CONTACT: BRONWYN ALLAN, TEAM LEADER, ADMISSIONS
ADDRESS: AGSM, UNSW, SYDNEY NSW, 2052 AUSTRALIA
PHONE: 011-61-2-9931-9490 • FAX: 011-61-2-9931-9205
E-MAIL: ADMISSIONS@AGSM.EDU.AU
WEBSITE: WWW.AGSM.EDU.AU

GENERAL INFORMATION

Type of School: public

STUDENTS

Enrollment of Business School: 50 % **Male/female:** 80/20 **% International:** 59 **Average Age at Entry:** 30 **Average Years Work Experience at Entry:** 7

ACADEMICS

Student/faculty Ratio: 4:1 **% Female Faculty:** 29 **Joint Degrees:** MBA/LLM 2 years.

FINANCIAL FACTS

Tuition: $41,378 **Books and Supplies:** $4,310 **% of First-year Students Receiving Aid:** 68

ADMISSIONS

Admissions Selectivity Rating: 60*

# of Applications Received: 153 **% Applicants Accepted:** 46 **% Acceptees Attending:** 70 **GMAT Range (25th to 75th percentile):** 590–700 **Average GMAT:** 640 **Average GPA:** 3.00 **Minimum TOEFL (paper/computer):** 600/250 **Application Fee:** $75 **Regular Application Deadline:** 8/30 **Regular Notification:** rolling **Application Deadline:** round 1: 8/30, round 2: 10/15. **Deferment Available:** yes **Maximum Length of Deferment:** 1 year **Transfer Students Accepted:** yes

EMPLOYMENT PROFILE

Primary Source of Full-time Job Acceptances

School-facilitated Activities 15 (23%)
Graduate-facilitated Activities 51 (77%)

UNIVERSITY OF NORTH TEXAS
COLLEGE OF BUSINESS ADMINISTRATION

ADMISSIONS CONTACT: DENISE GALUBENSKI OR KONNI STUBBLEFIELD, GRADUATE ACADEMIC ADVISORS
ADDRESS: P.O. BOX 311160, DENTON, TX 76203
PHONE: 940-369-8977 • FAX: 940-369-8978
E-MAIL: MBA@COBAF.UNT.EDU
WEBSITE: WWW.COBA.UNT.EDU

GENERAL INFORMATION

Type of School: public **Environment:** city **Academic Calendar:** semester

STUDENTS

Enrollment of Parent Institution: 31,155 **Enrollment of Business School:** 515 **% Part-time:** 63 **Average Age at Entry:** 32 **Average Years Work Experience at Entry:** 5

ACADEMICS

Student/faculty Ratio: 45:1 **% Female Faculty:** 22 **% Minority Faculty:** 17

Joint Degrees: MBA (Operations Management Science)/MS (Engineering Technology), MBA/MS (Merchandising), MBA/MS (Hospitality Management).

FINANCIAL FACTS

Tuition (in-state/out-of-state): $2,126/$4,448

ADMISSIONS

Admissions Selectivity Rating: 60*

# of Applications Received: 533 **% Applicants Accepted:** 55 **Average GMAT:** 527 **TOEFL Required of Int'l Applicants:** yes **Minimum TOEFL (paper/computer):** 550/213 **Application Fee:** $50 **International Application Fee:** $75 **Regular Application Deadline:** 7/15 **Deferment Available:** yes **Maximum Length of Deferment:** 1.5 years **Transfer Students Accepted:** yes **Non-fall Admissions:** yes **Need-Blind Admissions:** yes

UNIVERSITY OF QUEENSLAND
UQ BUSINESS SCHOOL

ADMISSIONS CONTACT: THE MANAGER, STUDENT ADMINISTRATOR
ADDRESS: UQ BUSINESS SCHOOL, THE UNIVERSITY OF QUEENSLAND, ST LUCIA, Q 4072 AUSTRALIA
PHONE: 011-617-3365 6475 • FAX: 011-617-3365 6988
E-MAIL: POSTGRAD_ENQUIRIES@BUSINESS.UQ.EDU.AU
WEBSITE: WWW.BUSINESS.UQ.EDU.AU

GENERAL INFORMATION

Type of School: private

FINANCIAL FACTS

Tuition: $17,050

ADMISSIONS

Admissions Selectivity Rating: 60*

Regular Application Deadline: 1/30 **Regular Notification:** 1/30

UNIVERSITY OF SAN DIEGO
SCHOOL OF BUSINESS ADMINISTRATION

ADMISSIONS CONTACT: MS. KACY KILNER, ADMISSIONS DIRECTOR, MBA PROGRAMS
ADDRESS: 5998 ALCALA PARK, SAN DIEGO, CA 92110-2492
PHONE: 619-260-4860 E-MAIL: MBA@SANDIEGO.EDU
WEBSITE: WWW.SANDIEGO.EDU/BUSINESS

GENERAL INFORMATION

Type of School: private **Affiliation:** Roman Catholic **Environment:** metropolis

STUDENTS

Enrollment of Parent Institution: 7,483 **Enrollment of Business School:** 219 **% Male/female:** 62/38 **% Part-time:** 92 **% Minorities:** 8 **% International:** 18 **Average Age at Entry:** 26 **Average Years Work Experience at Entry:** 4

ACADEMICS

% Female Faculty: 25 **% Minority Faculty:** 15

Joint Degrees: MBA/JD 4 years, MBA/MSN 3 years, MBA/MSRE 2.5 years, MBA/MSGL 2.5 years, IMBA/JD 4 years.

FINANCIAL FACTS

Tuition (in-state/out-of-state): $35,700 **Fees:** $136 **Books and Supplies:** $1,300 **Room & Board (on/off campus):** $10,960/$8,910 **% of Students Receiving Aid:** 100 **% of First-year Students Receiving Aid:** 100 **% of Students Receiving Loans:** 44 **% of Students Receiving Grants:** 100 **Average Award Package:** $26,845 **Average Grant:** $15,981

ADMISSIONS

Admissions Selectivity Rating: 91

# of Applications Received: 156 **% Applicants Accepted:** 37 **% Acceptees Attending:** 31 **GMAT Range (25th to 75th percentile):** 608–675 **Average GMAT:** 646 **Average GPA:** 3.23 **TOEFL Required of Int'l Applicants:** Yes **Minimum TOEFL (paper/computer):** 580/237 **Application Fee:** $45 **Regular Application Deadline:** 6/15 **Regular Notification:** rolling **Deferment Available:** yes **Maximum Length of Deferment:** 1 year **Need-Blind Admissions:** yes

UNIVERSITY OF SAN FRANCISCO
MASAGUNG GRADUATE SCHOOL OF MANAGEMENT

ADDRESS: 2130 FULTON STREET, LONE MOUNTAIN, SAN FRANCISCO, CA 94117-1045
PHONE: 415-422-2089 • FAX: 415-422-2066
E-MAIL: GRADUATE@USFCA.EDU
WEBSITE: WWW.USFCA.EDU/SOBAM

GENERAL INFORMATION

Type of School: private **Affiliation:** Jesuit **Environment:** metropolis

STUDENTS

Enrollment of Parent Institution: 8,110 **Enrollment of Business School:** 275 **% Part-time:** 27 **% Minorities:** 28 **% International:** 40 **Average Age at Entry:** 28 **Average Years Work Experience at Entry:** 4

ACADEMICS

Student/faculty Ratio: 3:1 **% Female Faculty:** 20 **% Minority Faculty:** 25

Joint Degrees: JD/MBA, MBA/MAPS (Asian Pacific Studies), MBA/MSEM (Master of Science in Environmental Management), MBA/MSFA. **Prominent Alumni:** Gordon Smith, CEO, PG&E; Lip Bu-Tan, founder, Walden International Investment Group; Mary Callanan, retired treasurer for the County/City of San Francisco; Angela Alioto, attorney, political leader; Pierre Salinger, former press secretary to the U.S. President.

FINANCIAL FACTS

Tuition: $24,875 **Fees:** $444 **Books and Supplies:** $1,250 **Room & Board (on campus):** $8,830

ADMISSIONS

Admissions Selectivity Rating: 76

# of Applications Received: 373 **% Applicants Accepted:** 67 **% Acceptees Attending:** 42 **GMAT Range (25th to 75th percentile):** 500–680 **Average GMAT:** 573 **Average GPA:** 3.2 **TOEFL Required of Int'l Applicants:** yes **Minimum TOEFL (paper/computer):** 600/250 **Application Fee:** $55 **International Application Fee:** $65 **Application Deadline/Notification:** round 1: 11/15 / 12/31, round 2: 1/15 / 2/28, round 3: 3/15 / 5/31, round 4: 5/15 / 6/30. **Deferment Available:** yes **Maximum Length of Deferment:** 1 year **Transfer Students Accepted:** yes **Applicants Also Look At:** Pepperdine University, Santa Clara University, University of California—Irvine, University of San Diego.

EMPLOYMENT PROFILE

Primary Source of Full-time Job Acceptances

Grads Employed by Industry:.......% avg. salary:

Finance/Accounting	14 $72,000
Marketing/Sales	39 $70,000
MIS	7 $63,000
Consulting	4 $65,000
General Management	4 $50,000
Other	31 $55,000
Nonprofit	1 $52,000

UNIVERSITY OF SOUTH ALABAMA
MITCHELL COLLEGE OF BUSINESS

ADMISSIONS CONTACT: OFFICE OF ADMISSIONS,
ADDRESS: MEISLER HALL, SUITE 2500, MOBILE, AL 36688-0002
PHONE: 251-460-6141 • FAX: 251-460-7876
E-MAIL: ADMISS@USOUTHAL.EDU
WEBSITE: MCOB.SOUTHALABAMA.EDU/

GENERAL INFORMATION

Type of School: public

STUDENTS

Enrollment of Parent Institution: 13,500 **Enrollment of Business School:** 135 **% Male/female:** 55/45 **% Minorities:** 55 **% International:** 10 **Average Age at Entry:** 28

ACADEMICS

Student/faculty Ratio: 31:1 **% Female Faculty:** 21 **% Minority Faculty:** 10

FINANCIAL FACTS

Tuition (in-state/out-of-state): $4,008/$8,016 **Fees:** $2,460 **Books and Supplies:** $1,200 **Room & Board (on/off campus):** $4,750/$7,200

ADMISSIONS

Admissions Selectivity Rating: 75

# of Applications Received: 80 **% Applicants Accepted:** 78 **% Acceptees Attending:** 73 **Average GMAT:** 550 **Average GPA:** 3.4 **TOEFL Required of Int'l Applicants:** yes **Minimum TOEFL (paper):** 525 **Application Fee:** $25 **Regular Application Deadline:** 7/15 **Regular Notification:** 7/25 **Transfer Students Accepted:** yes **Need-Blind Admissions:** yes

UNIVERSITY OF SOUTH FLORIDA
COLLEGE OF BUSINESS ADMINISTRATION

ADMISSIONS CONTACT: WENDY BAKER, ASSISTANT DIRECTOR OF GRADUATE STUDIES
ADDRESS: 4202 E. FOWLER AVENUE, BSN 3403, TAMPA, FL 33620
PHONE: 813-974-3335 • FAX: 813-974-4518
E-MAIL: MBA@COBA.USF.EDU
WEBSITE: WWW.COBA.USF.EDU

GENERAL INFORMATION

Type of School: public **Environment:** metropolis **Academic Calendar:** semester

STUDENTS

Enrollment of Parent Institution: 44,038 **Enrollment of Business School:** 396 **% Male/female:** 57/43 **% Part-time:** 67 **% Minorities:** 8 **% International:** 30 **Average Age at Entry:** 28 **Average Years Work Experience at Entry:** 3

ACADEMICS

Student/faculty Ratio: 4:1 **% Female Faculty:** 25 **% Minority Faculty:** 7 **Joint Degrees:** MBA/MSM (Management Information Systems) 2 to 5 years.

FINANCIAL FACTS

Tuition (in-state/out-of-state): $6,048/$21,552 **Fees:** $37 **Books and Supplies:** $800 **Room & Board:** $13,200 **Average Grant:** $6,500

ADMISSIONS

Admissions Selectivity Rating: 74

# of Applications Received: 238 **% Applicants Accepted:** 77 **% Acceptees Attending:** 68 **GMAT Range (25th to 75th percentile):** 490–610 **Average GMAT:** 549 **Average GPA:** 3.27 **TOEFL Required of Int'l Applicants:** yes **Minimum TOEFL (paper/computer):** 550/213 **Application Fee:** $30 **Regular Application Deadline:** 6/1 **Regular Notification:** 6/1 **Deferment Available:** yes **Maximum Length of Deferment:** 1 year **Transfer Students Accepted:** yes **Non-fall Admissions:** yes **Need-Blind Admissions:** yes **Applicants Also Look At:** The University of Tampa.

UNIVERSITY OF SOUTH FLORIDA—ST. PETERSBURG
COLLEGE OF BUSINESS

ADMISSIONS CONTACT: KEVIN COUGHLIN, DIRECTOR OF ADMISSIONS AND RECORDS
ADDRESS: 140 7TH AVENUE SOUTH, BAY 104, ST. PETERSBURG, FL 33701
PHONE: 727-873-4143 • FAX: 727-873-4525
E-MAIL: KEVINC@STPT.USF.EDU
WEBSITE: WWW.STPT.USF.EDU

GENERAL INFORMATION

Type of School: public

STUDENTS

Enrollment of Business School: 104 **% Part-time:** 100 **Average Age at Entry:** 31

ACADEMICS

% Female Faculty: 30 **% Minority Faculty:** 13 **Joint Degrees:** MBA/CPA 2 years.

FINANCIAL FACTS

Tuition (in-state/out-of-state): $230.64/882.05 (per credit hour)

ADMISSIONS

Admissions Selectivity Rating: 82

# of Applications Received: 51 **% Applicants Accepted:** 69 **% Acceptees Attending:** 71 **GMAT Range (25th to 75th percentile):** 500–640 **Average GMAT:** 586 **Average GPA:** 3.46 **Minimum TOEFL (paper/computer):** 550/213 **Application Fee:** $30 **Regular Application Deadline:** 7/1 **Deferment Available:** yes **Maximum Length of Deferment:** indefinite **Transfer Students Accepted:** yes

Non-fall Admissions: yes **Applicants Also Look At:** University of Florida, University of South Florida.

UNIVERSITY OF SOUTHERN INDIANA
COLLEGE OF BUSINESS

ADMISSIONS CONTACT: DR. PEGGY HARREL, DIRECTOR OF GRADUATE STUDIES
ADDRESS: 8600 UNIVERSITY BOULVARD, EVANSVILLE, IN 47712
PHONE: 812-465-7015 • FAX: 812-464-1956
E-MAIL: GSSR@USI.EDU
WEBSITE: BUSINESS.USI.EDU

GENERAL INFORMATION

Type of School: public **Environment:** city **Academic Calendar:** semester

STUDENTS

Enrollment of Parent Institution: 10,021 **Enrollment of Business School:** 91 **% Part-time:** 96 **Average Age at Entry:** 31 **Average Years Work Experience at Entry:** 7

ACADEMICS

Student/faculty Ratio: 26:1 **% Female Faculty:** 27 **% Minority Faculty:** 9

FINANCIAL FACTS

Tuition (in-state/out-of-state): $3,888/$7,668 **Fees:** $220 **Books and Supplies:** $900 **Room & Board (on/off campus):** $6,368/$7,872 **% of Students Receiving Aid:** 24 **% of First-year Students Receiving Aid:** 4 **% of Students Receiving Loans:** 18 **% of Students Receiving Grants:** 9 **Average Award Package:** $5,522 **Average Grant:** $2,422

ADMISSIONS

Admissions Selectivity Rating: 73

# of Applications Received: 26 **% Applicants Accepted:** 85 **% Acceptees Attending:** 73 **GMAT Range (25th to 75th percentile):** 520–590 **Average GMAT:** 547 **Average GPA:** 3.29 **TOEFL Required of Int'l Applicants:** yes **Minimum TOEFL (paper/computer):** 550/213 **Application Fee:** $25 **International Application Fee:** $25 **Regular Application Deadline:** rolling **Regular Notification:** rolling **Transfer Students Accepted:** yes **Non-fall Admissions:** yes **Need-Blind Admissions:** yes

The University of Southern Mississippi
College of Business

ADMISSIONS CONTACT: GABRIEL McPHEARSON, ASSISTANT TO THE DIRECTOR
ADDRESS: 118 COLLEGE DRIVE #5096, HATTIESBURG, MS 39406-5096
PHONE: 601-266-4653 • FAX: 601-266-5814
E-MAIL: MBA@USM.EDU
WEBSITE: WWW.USM.EDU/MBA

GENERAL INFORMATION
Type of School: public **Environment:** city **Academic Calendar:** semester

STUDENTS
Enrollment of Parent Institution: 15,030 **Enrollment of Business School:** 93 % **Male/female:** 58/42 % **Out-of-state:** 24 % **Part-time:** 59 % **Minorities:** 8 % **International:** 8 **Average Age at Entry:** 27

ACADEMICS
Student/faculty Ratio: 30:1 % **Female Faculty:** 25 % **Minority Faculty:** 15
Joint Degrees: MBA/MPH 2 to 6 years.

FINANCIAL FACTS
Tuition: $4,312 **Fees (in-state/out-of-state):** $0/$5,430 **Books and Supplies:** $1,600 **Room & Board (on/off campus):** $5,800/$7,600 % **of Students Receiving Aid:** 75 % **of Students Receiving Grants:** 25 **Average Grant:** $8,690

ADMISSIONS
Admissions Selectivity Rating: 77

# of Applications Received: 73 % **Applicants Accepted:** 56 % **Acceptees Attending:** 76 **GMAT Range (25th to 75th percentile):** 450–560 **Average GMAT:** 508 **Average GPA:** 3.36 **TOEFL Required of Int'l Applicants:** yes **Minimum TOEFL (paper/computer):** 550/213 **Application Fee:** $25 **Regular Application Deadline:** 7/15 **Regular Notification:** rolling **Deferment Available:** yes **Maximum Length of Deferment:** 1 year **Transfer Students Accepted:** yes **Non-fall Admissions:** yes **Need-Blind Admissions:** yes

EMPLOYMENT PROFILE
Top 5 Employers Hiring Grads

Cintas; Frito Lay; Walgreen Co.; Sherman Williams; AmSouth Bank.

University of Strathclyde—Glasgow
Graduate School of Business

ADMISSIONS CONTACT: 141-553- 6118, LUCY REYNOLDS
ADDRESS: 199 CATHEDRAL STREET, GLASGOW, G4 0QU SCOTLAND
PHONE: 141-553-6118 • FAX: 141-553-6162
E-MAIL: ADMISSIONS@GSB.STRATH.AC.UK
WEBSITE: WWW.GSB.STRATH.AC.UK

GENERAL INFORMATION
Type of School: private

STUDENTS
Enrollment of Business School: 107 % **Male/female:** 86/14 % **Part-time:** 37 % **Minorities:** 88 % **International:** 84 **Average Age at Entry:** 32 **Average Years Work Experience at Entry:** 9

ACADEMICS
Student/faculty Ratio: 4:1 % **Female Faculty:** 11 **Joint Degrees:** MBA (with a specialism in Leadership Studies) 2.5 to 3 years.

FINANCIAL FACTS
Fees: $31,600 **Books and Supplies:** $150 **Room & Board (on/off campus):** $13,500/$15,300

ADMISSIONS
Admissions Selectivity Rating: 69

# of Applications Received: 280 % **Applicants Accepted:** 90 % **Acceptees Attending:** 42 **Average GMAT:** 560 **Average GPA:** 3.4 **TOEFL Required of Int'l Applicants:** yes **Minimum TOEFL (paper/computer):** 600/250 **Regular Application Deadline:** rolling **Regular Notification:** rolling **Deferment Available:** yes **Maximum Length of Deferment:** 2 years **Non-fall Admissions:** yes

EMPLOYMENT PROFILE
Top 5 Employers Hiring Grads

Mott McDonald; BT; RBoS; Standard Life; Prince and Princess of Wales Hospice.

The University of Tennessee at Martin
College of Business and Public Affairs

Admissions Contact: Kevin Hammond, College of Business & Public Affairs Graduate Program
Address: 103 Business Administration Building, Martin, TN 38238-5015
Phone: 888-293-5822 • Fax: 731-587-7241
E-mail: bagrad@utm.edu
Website: www.utm.edu/departments/soba/

GENERAL INFORMATION
Type of School: public **Environment:** rural **Academic Calendar:** semester

STUDENTS
Enrollment of Parent Institution: 6,900 **Enrollment of Business School:** 123 % **Male/female:** 62/38 **% Part-time:** 78 % **International:** 73 **Average Age at Entry:** 26

FINANCIAL FACTS
Tuition (in-state/out-of-state): $4,668/$9,470 **Fees (in-state):** $732 **Books and Supplies:** $1,000

ADMISSIONS
Admissions Selectivity Rating: 60*

% Acceptees Attending: 78 **Average GMAT:** 516 **Average GPA:** 3.04 **TOEFL Required of Int'l Applicants:** yes **Minimum TOEFL (paper):** 525 **Application Fee:** $30 Rolling **Regular Notification:** rolling **Deferment Available:** yes **Transfer Students Accepted:** yes **Non-fall Admissions:** yes

The University of Texas at El Paso
College of Business Administration

Admissions Contact: Laura Uribarri, Director of MBA Programs
Address: Room 103, College of Business Administration, El Paso, TX 79968
Phone: 915-747-5379 • Fax: 915-747-5147
E-mail: lmuribarri@utep.edu.
Website: mba.utep.edu

GENERAL INFORMATION
Type of School: public **Environment:** metropolis **Academic Calendar:** semester

STUDENTS
Enrollment of Parent Institution: 19,900 **Enrollment of Business School:** 209 **Average Age at Entry:** 32 **Average Years Work Experience at Entry:** 4

ACADEMICS
Student/faculty Ratio: 4:1 **% Female Faculty:** 10 **% Minority Faculty:** 29
Joint Degrees: MBA/MPA 2 to 6 years.

FINANCIAL FACTS
Tuition (in-state/out-of-state): $173.50/$448.50 (per credit hour) **% of Students Receiving Aid:** 30 **% of First-year Students Receiving Aid:** 30 **% of Students Receiving Loans:** 24

ADMISSIONS
Admissions Selectivity Rating: 62

# of Applications Received: 140 **% Applicants Accepted:** 90 % **Acceptees Attending:** 71 **Average GMAT:** 538 **TOEFL Required of Int'l Applicants:** yes **Minimum TOEFL (paper/computer):** 600/250 **Application Fee:** $15 **Regular Application Deadline:** 7/1 **Regular Notification:** rolling **Deferment Available:** yes **Maximum Length of Deferment:** 2 years **Transfer Students Accepted:** yes **Non-fall Admissions:** yes **Need-Blind Admissions:** yes

The University of Texas at Tyler
School of Business Administration

Admissions Contact: Dr. Mary Fischer, Coordinator of Graduate Programs in Business
Address: 3900 University Boulevard, Tyler, TX 75799
Phone: 903-566-7433 • Fax: 903-566-7372
E-mail: mfischer@uttyler.edu
Website: www.uttyler.edu/cbt/mba.htm

GENERAL INFORMATION
Type of School: public **Environment:** city **Academic Calendar:** semester

STUDENTS
Enrollment of Parent Institution: 5,926 **Enrollment of Business School:** 187 **% Part-time:** 99 **Average Age at Entry:** 30

ACADEMICS
Student/faculty Ratio: 20:1 **% Female Faculty:** 47 **% Minority Faculty:** 53
Joint Degrees: MSN/MBA 2 to 6 years, MBA/MEng 2 to 6 years.

FINANCIAL FACTS
Tuition (in-state/out-of-state): $50/$325 (per credit hour) **Books and Supplies:** $975

ADMISSIONS
Admissions Selectivity Rating: 77

# of Applications Received: 98 **% Applicants Accepted:** 69 % **Acceptees Attending:** 100 **Average GMAT:** 535 **Average GPA:** 3.29 **TOEFL Required of Int'l Applicants:** yes **Minimum TOEFL (paper/computer):** 550/213 **Application Fee:** $25 **International Application Fee:** $50 **Regular Application Deadline:** rolling **Regular

Notification: rolling **Deferment Available:** yes **Maximum Length of Deferment:** 1 semester **Non-fall Admissions:** yes

UNIVERSITY OF TORONTO
JOSEPH L. ROTMAN SCHOOL OF MANAGEMENT

ADMISSIONS CONTACT: CHERYL MILLINGTON, DIRECTOR OF MBA RECRUITING AND ADMISSIONS
ADDRESS: 105 ST. GEORGE STREET, TORONTO, ON M5S 3E6 CANADA
PHONE: 416-978-3499 • FAX: 416-978-5812
E-MAIL: MBA@ROTMAN.UTORONTO.CA
WEBSITE: WWW.ROTMAN.UTORONTO.CA

GENERAL INFORMATION
Type of School: public **Environment:** metropolis

STUDENTS
Enrollment of Parent Institution: 67,000 **Enrollment of Business School:** 330 % **Male/female:** 73/27 **% Part-time:** 19 **% Minorities:** 50 **% International:** 40 **Average Age at Entry:** 28 **Average Years Work Experience at Entry:** 5

ACADEMICS
Student/faculty Ratio: 7:1 **% Female Faculty:** 22
Joint Degrees: JD/MBA 4 years, BASC/MBA 5 years, 8 months, MBA/MA (Russian and Eastern European Studies) 4 years.
Prominent Alumni: Joseph L. Rotman, founder & chairman, Clairvest Group Inc.; Ian Locke, general partner, Jefferson Partners; Don Morrison, COO, Research In Motion; John Cassaday, president & CEO, Corus Entertainment; Richard Nesbitt, CEO, TSX Group.

FINANCIAL FACTS
Tuition (in-state/out-of-state): $21,800/$29,800 **Books and Supplies:** $5,000 **Room & Board:** $10,000 **% of Students Receiving Aid:** 70 **% of First-year Students Receiving Aid:** 70 **% of Students Receiving Loans:** 70 **% of Students Receiving Grants:** 20 **Average Grant:** $8,000

ADMISSIONS
Admissions Selectivity Rating: 60*
# of Applications Received: 1,010 **GMAT Range (25th to 75th percentile):** 550–770 **Average GMAT:** 642 **Average GPA:** 3.4 **TOEFL Required of Int'l Applicants:** yes **Minimum TOEFL (paper/computer):** 600/250 **Application Fee:** $150 **Regular Application Deadline:** 4/30 **Regular Notification:** 7/1 **Application Deadline/Notification:** round 1: 1/15 / 3/15, round 2: 4/30 / 7/1. **Early Decision Program:** yes **ED Deadline/notification:** 1/15 (domestic students only) / 3/15 **Deferment Available:** yes **Maximum Length of Deferment:** 1 year **Need-Blind Admissions:** yes **Applicants Also Look At:** McGill University, Queensland University of Technology, University of Western Ontario, York University.

EMPLOYMENT PROFILE
Primary Source of Full-time Job Acceptances
School-facilitated Activities 53%
Graduate-facilitated Activities 47%

Percent Employed: 93
Top 5 Employers Hiring Grads
CIBC; RBC Financial Group; TD Bank Financial Group; BMO Financial Group; Johnson & Johnson.

UNIVERSITY OF WARWICK
WARWICK BUSINESS SCHOOL

ADMISSIONS CONTACT: JO MOUND, MBA MARKETING AND RECRUITMENT TEAM
ADDRESS: WARWICK BUSINESS SCHOOL, COVENTRY, CV4 7AL ENGLAND
PHONE: 011-44-0-24-7652-4100 • FAX: 011-44-0-24-7657-4400
E-MAIL: WARWICKMBA@WBS.AC.UK
WEBSITE: WWW.WBS.AC.UK

GENERAL INFORMATION
Type of School: public **Academic Calendar:** trimester

STUDENTS
Enrollment of Parent Institution: 18,000 **Enrollment of Business School:** 460 % **Male/female:** 65/35 **% Part-time:** 90 **% International:** 82 **Average Age at Entry:** 31 **Average Years Work Experience at Entry:** 8

ACADEMICS
Student/faculty Ratio: 12:1 **Prominent Alumni:** Svein Stokke, director, Citigroup; Keith Bedell-Pearce, chair, Norwich & Peterborough Building Society; Mike O'Driscoll, president, Aston Martin, Jaguar, Land Rover; Steven Falk, director of financial services, Manchester United FC; Roger Lovering, head of card services, HSBC Bank plc.

FINANCIAL FACTS
Tuition: $38,305 **Books and Supplies:** $2,500 **Room & Board:** $11,000 **% of Students Receiving Aid:** 20 **% of Students Receiving Grants:** 20 **Average Award Package:** $21,000 **Average Grant:** $230,000

ADMISSIONS
Admissions Selectivity Rating: 86
# of Applications Received: 220 **% Applicants Accepted:** 45 **% Acceptees Attending:** 50 **GMAT Range (25th to 75th percentile):** 550–680 **Average GMAT:** 620 **TOEFL Required of Int'l Applicants:** yes **Minimum TOEFL (paper/computer):** 620/200 **Application Fee:** $132 **International Application Fee:** $132 **Regular Application Deadline:** rolling **Regular Notification:** rolling **Deferment Available:** yes **Maximum Length of Deferment:** 1 year **Applicants Also Look At:** Cranfield University, London Business School, University of Cambridge, University of Manchester, University of Oxford.

EMPLOYMENT PROFILE
Primary Source of Full-time Job Acceptances
Percent Employed: 93

UNIVERSITY OF WEST FLORIDA
COLLEGE OF BUSINESS

ADMISSIONS CONTACT: GRADUATE ADMISSIONS OFFICE, REGISTRAR OFFICER
ADDRESS: 11000 UNIVERSITY PARKWAY, PENSACOLA, FL 32514
PHONE: 850-474-2230 • FAX: 850-474-3360
E-MAIL: ADMISSIONS@UWF.EDU
WEBSITE: UWF.EDU/MBA

GENERAL INFORMATION
Type of School: public **Environment:** city

STUDENTS
Enrollment of Business School: 178 % **Male/female:** 43/57 % **Out-of-state:** 52 % **Part-time:** 89 % **International:** 52 **Average Age at Entry:** 18

ACADEMICS
Student/faculty Ratio: 25:1 % **Female Faculty:** 27 % **Minority Faculty:** 14
Joint Degrees: MBA/Master of Science (with Nyenrode University in the Netherlands) 2.3 to 4 years.

FINANCIAL FACTS
Tuition (in-state/out-of-state): $8,072/$29,206 **Books and Supplies:** $650 **Average Grant:** $1,400

ADMISSIONS
Admissions Selectivity Rating: 75
# of Applications Received: 75 % **Applicants Accepted:** 57 % **Acceptees Attending:** 77 **GMAT Range (25th to 75th percentile):** 440–544 **Average GMAT:** 478 **Average GPA:** 3.37 **TOEFL Required of Int'l Applicants:** yes **Minimum TOEFL (paper/computer):** 550/213 **Application Fee:** $30 **Regular Application Deadline:** 6/1 **Regular Notification:** rolling **Deferment Available:** yes **Maximum Length of Deferment:** 1 year **Transfer Students Accepted:** yes **Non-fall Admissions:** yes **Applicants Also Look At:** Florida State University, Troy University, University of Florida.

UNIVERSITY OF WISCONSIN— EAU CLAIRE
SCHOOL OF BUSINESS

ADMISSIONS CONTACT: MS. JAN STEWART, MBA PROGRAM ASSISTANT
ADDRESS: 105 GARFIELD AVENUE, EAU CLAIRE, WI 54702-4004
PHONE: 715-836-4733 • FAX: 715-836-2409
E-MAIL: ADMISSIONS@UWEC.EDU
WEBSITE: WWW.UWEC.EDU/COB/ACADEMICS/MBA/INDEX.HTM

GENERAL INFORMATION
Type of School: public **Environment:** town **Academic Calendar:** semester

STUDENTS
Enrollment of Parent Institution: 10,500 **Enrollment of Business School:** 130 % **Male/female:** 55/45 % **Out-of-state:** 80 % **Part-time:** 90 % **Minorities:** 5 % **International:** 80 **Average Age at Entry:** 28 **Average Years Work Experience at Entry:** 7

ACADEMICS
Student/faculty Ratio: 5:1 % **Female Faculty:** 30 **Joint Degrees:** Partner in the University of Wisconsin Internet Consortium MBA Program. Students may combine online courses with on campus courses.

FINANCIAL FACTS
Tuition (in-state/out-of-state): $6,223/$16,833 **Books and Supplies:** $1,000 **Room & Board (on campus):** $4,266

ADMISSIONS
Admissions Selectivity Rating: 60*
Average GMAT: 530 **Average GPA:** 3.2 **TOEFL Required of Int'l Applicants:** yes **Minimum TOEFL (paper/computer):** 550/213 **Application Fee:** $45 International **Regular Application Deadline:** rolling **Regular Notification:** rolling **Deferment Available:** yes **Maximum Length of Deferment:** 1 year **Transfer Students Accepted:** yes **Non-fall Admissions:** yes **Need-Blind Admissions:** yes

UNIVERSITY OF WISCONSIN— LA CROSSE
COLLEGE OF BUSINESS ADMINISTRATION

ADMISSIONS CONTACT: KATHY KIEFER, DIRECTOR
ADDRESS: 1725 STATE STREET, LA CROSSE, WI 54601
PHONE: 608-785-8939 • FAX: 608-785-6695
E-MAIL: ADMISSIONS@UWLAX.EDU
WEBSITE: WWW.UWLAX.EDU

GENERAL INFORMATION
Type of School: public **Academic Calendar:** semester

STUDENTS

Enrollment of Parent Institution: 8,509 **Enrollment of Business School:** 44 **% Part-time:** 3 **Average Age at Entry:** 29

ACADEMICS

Student/faculty Ratio: 25:1 **% Female Faculty:** 28 **% Minority Faculty:** 22

FINANCIAL FACTS

Tuition (in-state/out-of-state): $7,196/$17,806 **Books and Supplies:** $500 **Room & Board:** $4,800

ADMISSIONS

Admissions Selectivity Rating: 75

# of Applications Received: 34 **% Applicants Accepted:** 76 **% Acceptees Attending:** 65 **Average GMAT:** 552 **Average GPA:** 3.3 **TOEFL Required of Int'l Applicants:** yes **Minimum TOEFL (paper/computer):** 550/213 **Application Fee:** $48 **Regular Application Deadline:** rolling **Regular Notification:** rolling **Deferment Available:** yes **Maximum Length of Deferment:** rolling **Transfer Students Accepted:** yes **Non-fall Admissions:** yes **Need-Blind Admissions:** yes

UNIVERSITY OF WISCONSIN— OSHKOSH

COLLEGE OF BUSINESS ADMINSTRATION

ADMISSIONS CONTACT: LYNN GRANCORBITZ, MBA PROGRAM ASSISTANT DIRECTOR AND ADVISOR
ADDRESS: 800 ALGOMA BOULEVARD, OSHKOSH, WI 54901
PHONE: 800-633-1430 • FAX: 920-424-7413
E-MAIL: MBA@UWOSH.EDU
WEBSITE: WWW.UWOSH.EDU/COLLEGES/COBA/ASSETS/GRAD/INDEX.PHP

GENERAL INFORMATION

Type of School: public **Environment:** village **Academic Calendar:** semester

STUDENTS

Enrollment of Parent Institution: 10,528 **Enrollment of Business School:** 525 **% Male/female:** 55/45 **% Out-of-state:** 2 **% Part-time:** 95 **% Minorities:** 2 **% International:** 3 **Average Age at Entry:** 32

ACADEMICS

Student/faculty Ratio: 11:1 **% Female Faculty:** 15 **% Minority Faculty:** 5

FINANCIAL FACTS

Tuition (in-state/out-of-state): $4,664/$13,622 **% of Students Receiving Aid:** 5 **% of First-year Students Receiving Aid:** 5 **% of Students Receiving Loans:** 5

ADMISSIONS

Admissions Selectivity Rating: 70

# of Applications Received: 115 **% Applicants Accepted:** 90 **% Acceptees Attending:** 93 **GMAT Range (25th to 75th percentile):** 470–610 **Average GMAT:** 540 **Average GPA:** 3.1 **TOEFL Required of Int'l Applicants:** yes **Minimum TOEFL (paper):** 550 **Application Fee:** $45 **Regular Application Deadline:** 7/1 **Regular Notification:** rolling **Deferment Available:** yes **Maximum Length of Deferment:** 3 years **Transfer Students Accepted:** yes **Non-fall Admissions:** yes **Applicants Also Look At:** Marquette University.

EMPLOYMENT PROFILE

Primary Source of Full-time Job Acceptances
Graduate-facilitated Activities 100 (100%)
Percent Employed: 50

UNIVERSITY OF WISCONSIN— PARKSIDE

SCHOOL OF BUSINESS AND TECHNOLOGY

ADMISSIONS CONTACT: BRAD PIAZZA, ASSISTANT DEAN
ADDRESS: 900 WOOD ROAD, BOX 2000, KENOSHA, WI 53141-2000
PHONE: 262-595-2046 • FAX: 262-595-2680
E-MAIL: PIAZZA@UWP.EDU
WEBSITE: WWW.UWP.EDU/DEPARTMENTS/BUSINESS

GENERAL INFORMATION

Type of School: public **Environment:** city **Academic Calendar:** semester

STUDENTS

Enrollment of Parent Institution: 5,000 **Enrollment of Business School:** 81 **% Male/female:** 60/40 **% Part-time:** 87 **% Minorities:** 16 **% International:** 2 **Average Age at Entry:** 33

ACADEMICS

Student/faculty Ratio: 6:1 **% Female Faculty:** 35 **% Minority Faculty:** 30

FINANCIAL FACTS

Tuition (in-state/out-of-state): $6,730/$17,500 **Fees:** $277 **Books and Supplies:** $300

ADMISSIONS

Admissions Selectivity Rating: 62

# of Applications Received: 28 **% Applicants Accepted:** 96 **% Acceptees Attending:** 93 **GMAT Range (25th to 75th percentile):** 330–680 **Average GMAT:** 460 **Average GPA:** 3.00 **TOEFL Required of Int'l Applicants:** yes **Minimum TOEFL (paper/computer):** 550/213 **Application Fee:** $45 **Regular Application Deadline:** 8/1 **Regular Notification:** rolling **Deferment Available:** yes **Maximum Length of Deferment:** 1 year **Transfer Students Accepted:** yes **Non-fall Admissions:** yes **Need-Blind Admissions:** yes

UNIVERSITY OF WYOMING
COLLEGE OF BUSINESS

ADMISSIONS CONTACT: TERRI L. RITTENBURG, DIRECTOR OF MBA PROGRAM
ADDRESS: PO BOX 3275, LARAMIE, WY 82071
PHONE: 307-766-2449 • FAX: 307-766-4028
E-MAIL: MBA@UWYO.EDU
WEBSITE: BUSINESS.UWYO.EDU/MBA

GENERAL INFORMATION

Type of School: public **Environment:** town **Academic Calendar:** semester schedule: full-time/part-time/evening

STUDENTS

Enrollment of Parent Institution: 11,904 **Enrollment of Business School:** 63 % **Male/female:** 64/36 % **Part-time:** 48 % **International:** 18 **Average Age at Entry:** 28

ACADEMICS

Student/faculty Ratio: 3:1

FINANCIAL FACTS

Tuition (in-state/out-of-state): $2,988/$8,676 **Fees (in-state/out-of-state):** $246/$298 **Books and Supplies:** $300 **Room & Board (on campus):** $6,212 **% of Students Receiving Loans:** 34

ADMISSIONS

Admissions Selectivity Rating: 60*

Average GMAT: 558 **Average GPA:** 3.2 **TOEFL Required of Int'l Applicants:** yes **Minimum TOEFL (paper/computer):** 525/197 **Application Fee:** $40 **Regular Application Deadline:** 2/1 **Regular Notification:** rolling **Deferment Available:** yes **Maximum Length of Deferment:** 1 year **Transfer Students Accepted:** yes **Need-Blind Admissions:** yes

UTAH STATE UNIVERSITY
COLLEGE OF BUSINESS

ADMISSIONS CONTACT: SCHOOL OF GRADUATE STUDIES, ADMISSIONS OFFICER
ADDRESS: 900 OLD MAIN HILL, LOGAN, UT 84322-0900
PHONE: 435-797-1189 • FAX: 435-797-1192
E-MAIL: GRADSCH@CC.USU.EDU
WEBSITE: WWW.USU.EDU/COB

GENERAL INFORMATION

Type of School: public **Environment:** town **Academic Calendar:** semester

STUDENTS

Enrollment of Parent Institution: 23,623 **Enrollment of Business School:** 137 % **Male/female:** 78/22 % **Out-of-state:** 3 % **Part-time:** 77 % **International:** 16 **Average Age at Entry:** 28 **Average Years Work Experience at Entry:** 5

ACADEMICS

Student/faculty Ratio: 4:1 % **Female Faculty:** 16 % **Minority Faculty:** 10

Joint Degrees: International MBA (in food and agribusiness in cooperation with Royal Agricultural College in Cirencester, England). **Prominent Alumni:** Ron Labrum, president and CEO, Cardinal Health; Annette Herman, CEO, United Healthcare Utah; Kay Toolson, CEO, Monaco Coach; Mark James, vice president human resources, Honeywell; Michael Kraupp, vice president finance, SkyWest Airlines.

FINANCIAL FACTS

Tuition (in-state/out-of-state): $4,557/$14,523 **Fees (in-state/out-of-state):** $792/$798 **Books and Supplies:** $1,650 **Room & Board:** $4,400 **% of Students Receiving Aid:** 20 **% of First-year Students Receiving Aid:** 20 **% of Students Receiving Grants:** 20 **Average Award Package:** $5,300 **Average Grant:** $1,500 **Average Student Loan Debt:** $7,500

ADMISSIONS

Admissions Selectivity Rating: 82

# of Applications Received: 145 % **Applicants Accepted:** 62 % **Acceptees Attending:** 64 **GMAT Range (25th to 75th percentile):** 450–690 **Average GMAT:** 570 **Average GPA:** 3.56 **TOEFL Required of Int'l Applicants:** yes **Minimum TOEFL (paper/computer):** 550/213 **Application Fee:** $55 **International Application Fee:** $55 **Regular Application Deadline:** 2/15 **Regular Notification:** 3/15 **Deferment Available:** yes **Maximum Length of Deferment:** 1 year **Transfer Students Accepted:** yes **Need-Blind Admissions:** yes **Applicants Also Look At:** Brigham Young University, University of Utah, Weber State University.

EMPLOYMENT PROFILE

Primary Source of Full-time Job Acceptances

Grads Employed by Industry:	%	avg. salary:
Finance/Accounting	17	$42,333
Marketing/Sales	13	$33,000
Operations/Production	8	$60,000
Entrepreneurship	5	NR
General Management	13	$55,000
Other	17	$54,250

VALDOSTA STATE UNIVERSITY
LANGDALE COLLEGE OF BUSINESS ADMINISTRATION

ADMISSIONS CONTACT: JUDY TOMBERLIN, GRADUATE SCHOOL
ADDRESS: 903 N. PATTERSON STREET, VALDOSTA, GA 31698-0005
PHONE: (229) 333-5696 • FAX: (229) 245-3853
E-MAIL: MBA@VALDOSTA.EDU
WEBSITE: WWW.VALDOSTA.EDU/LCOBA/GRAD/

GENERAL INFORMATION

Type of School: public **Environment:** city **Academic Calendar:** semester

STUDENTS

Enrollment of Parent Institution: 10,500 **Enrollment of Business School:** 31 % **Male/female:** 50/50 % **Part-time:** 100 % **International:** 8 **Average Age at Entry:** 30 **Average Years Work Experience at Entry:** 8

ACADEMICS

Student/faculty Ratio: 3:1 % **Female Faculty:** 20

FINANCIAL FACTS

Tuition (in-state/out-of-state): $3,766/$12,544 **Fees:** $708 **Books and Supplies:** $800 **Room & Board:** $2,684 **Average Grant:** $1,000

ADMISSIONS

Admissions Selectivity Rating: 82

# of Applications Received: 21 % **Applicants Accepted:** 48 % **Acceptees Attending:** 80 **GMAT Range (25th to 75th percentile):** 500–640 **Average GMAT:** 534 **Average GPA:** 3.3 **TOEFL Required of Int'l Applicants:** yes **Minimum TOEFL (paper/computer):** 550/213 **Application Fee:** $25 **Regular Application Deadline:** rolling **Regular Notification:** rolling **Deferment Available:** yes **Maximum Length of Deferment:** 1 semester **Transfer Students Accepted:** yes **Non-fall Admissions:** yes **Need-Blind Admissions:** yes

WESTERN ILLINOIS UNIVERSITY
COLLEGE OF BUSINESS AND TECHNOLOGY

ADMISSIONS CONTACT: DIRECTOR OF MBA PROGRAM
ADDRESS: 1 UNIVERSITY CIRCLE, 115 SHERMAN HALL, MACOMB, IL 61455
PHONE: 309-298-3157 • FAX: 309-298-3111
E-MAIL: ADMISSIONS@WIU.EDU
WEBSITE: WWW.WIU.EDU/USERS/MICOBTD/

GENERAL INFORMATION

Type of School: public **Environment:** village **Academic Calendar:** semester

STUDENTS

Enrollment of Parent Institution: 132 **Enrollment of Business School:** 132 % **Male/female:** 58/42 % **Out-of-state:** 1 % **Part-time:** 37 % **Minorities:** 1 % **International:** 15 **Average Age at Entry:** 24

FINANCIAL FACTS

Tuition (in-state/out-of-state): $3,287/$6,574 % **of Students Receiving Aid:** 34

ADMISSIONS

Admissions Selectivity Rating: 60*

# of Applications Received: 250 % **Applicants Accepted:** 50 % **Acceptees Attending:** 60 **TOEFL Required of Int'l Applicants:** yes **Minimum TOEFL (paper):** 550 **Application Fee:** $30 **Regular Application Deadline:** rolling **Regular Notification:** rolling **Deferment Available:** yes **Non-fall Admissions:** yes

WESTERN MICHIGAN UNIVERSITY
HAWORTH COLLEGE OF BUSINESS

ADMISSIONS CONTACT: HAL BATES, HCOB ACADEMIC ADVISING AND ADMISSIONS
ADDRESS: 2130 SCHNEIDER HALL, MS #5411, KALAMAZOO, MI 49008-5411
PHONE: 269-387-5075 • FAX: 269-387-5710
E-MAIL: BUS-ADV-OFFICE@WMICH.EDU
WEBSITE: WWW.HCOB.WMICH.EDU

GENERAL INFORMATION

Type of School: public **Environment:** city **Academic Calendar:** semester

STUDENTS

Enrollment of Parent Institution: 24,841 **Enrollment of Business School:** 321 % **Male/female:** 60/40 % **Out-of-state:** 1 % **Part-time:** 65 % **Minorities:** 6 % **International:** 20 **Average Age at Entry:** 29 **Average Years Work Experience at Entry:** 6

ACADEMICS

Student/faculty Ratio: 30:1 % **Female Faculty:** 16

FINANCIAL FACTS

Tuition (in-state/out-of-state): $7,776/$17,524 **Fees:** $690 **Books and Supplies:** $5,006 **Room & Board:** $6,850 **Average Award Package:** $4,340 **Average Grant:** $10,420

ADMISSIONS

Admissions Selectivity Rating: 76

# of Applications Received: 205 % **Applicants Accepted:** 59 % **Acceptees Attending:** 74 **GMAT Range (25th to 75th percentile):** 480–590 **Average GMAT:** 520 **Average GPA:** 3.1 **TOEFL Required of Int'l Applicants:** yes **Minimum TOEFL (paper/computer):** 550/213 **Application Fee:** $40 **International Application Fee:** $55 **Regular Application Deadline:** 7/1 **Regular Notification:** 8/1 **Deferment Available:** yes **Maximum Length of Deferment:** 1 year **Transfer Students Accepted:** yes **Non-fall Admissions:** yes **Applicants Also Look At:** Michigan State University–College of Law, University of Michigan, Wayne State University.

WESTERN NEW ENGLAND COLLEGE
COLLEGE OF BUSINESS

ADDRESS: 1215 WILBRAHAM ROAD, SPRINGFIELD, MA 01119
PHONE: 413-782-3111 • FAX: 413-782-1746
WEBSITE: WWW1.WNEC.EDU/BUSINESS

GENERAL INFORMATION

Type of School: private

FINANCIAL FACTS

Tuition: $5,988

WESTERN WASHINGTON UNIVERSITY
COLLEGE OF BUSINESS AND ECONOMICS

ADMISSIONS CONTACT: PROGRAM MANAGER
ADDRESS: 516 HIGH STREET, PARKS HALL 419, BELLINGHAM,
WA 98225-9072
PHONE: 360-650-3898 • FAX: 360-650-4844
E-MAIL: MBA@WWU.EDU
WEBSITE: WWW.CBE.WWU.EDU/MBA

GENERAL INFORMATION

Type of School: public **Environment:** city

STUDENTS

Enrollment of Business School: 76 **% Male/female:** 57/43 **% Part-time:** 47 **% Minorities:** 2 **% International:** 12 **Average Age at Entry:** 29

FINANCIAL FACTS

Tuition (in-state/out-of-state): $6,608/$16,844

ADMISSIONS

Admissions Selectivity Rating: 60*

# of Applications Received: 78 **Average GMAT:** 545 **TOEFL Required of Int'l Applicants:** yes **Minimum TOEFL (paper/computer):** 567/227 **Application Fee:** $50 **Regular Application Deadline:** 5/1 **Regular Notification:** 6/1 **Deferment Available:** yes **Maximum Length of Deferment:** 1 year **Non-fall Admissions:** yes

WIDENER UNIVERSITY
SCHOOL OF BUSINESS ADMINISTRATION

ADMISSIONS CONTACT: LISA BUSSOM, ASSISTANT DEAN
ADDRESS: 1 UNIVERSITY PLACE, CHESTER, PA 19013
PHONE: 610-499-4305 • FAX: 610-499-4615
E-MAIL: SBAGRADV@MAIL.WIDENER.EDU
WEBSITE: WWW.WIDENER.EDU/SBA

GENERAL INFORMATION

Type of School: private **Environment:** town **Academic Calendar:** semester

STUDENTS

Enrollment of Parent Institution: 6,460 **Enrollment of Business School:** 122 **% Male/female:** 74/26 **% Part-time:** 78 **% International:** 13 **Average Age at Entry:** 29 **Average Years Work Experience at Entry:** 7

ACADEMICS

Student/faculty Ratio: 6:1 **% Female Faculty:** 39 **% Minority Faculty:** 5

Joint Degrees: MBA/JD 3 to 4 years, MBA/Master of Engineering 2 to 5 years, MBA/Doctor of Clinical Psychology 5 years, MBA (Health Care Management)/Doctor of Clinical Psychology 5 years. **Prominent Alumni:** Leslie C. Quick, founder, Quick & Reilly; H. Edward Hanway, CEO, Cigna Corporation; Paul Biederman, chair, Mellon Mid-Atlantic; Tiffany Tomasso, vice president, Sunrise Assisted Living.

FINANCIAL FACTS

Tuition: $20,400 **Fees:** $200 **Books and Supplies:** $850 **Room & Board (off campus):** $7,650 **% of Students Receiving Aid:** 9 **% of First-year Students Receiving Aid:** 3 **% of Students Receiving Loans:** 8 **% of Students Receiving Grants:** 5 **Average Award Package:** $19,174 **Average Grant:** $9,660

ADMISSIONS

Admissions Selectivity Rating: 76

# of Applications Received: 139 **% Applicants Accepted:** 62 **% Acceptees Attending:** 62 **GMAT Range (25th to 75th percentile):** 450–540 **Average GMAT:** 533 **Average GPA:** 3.2 **TOEFL Required of Int'l Applicants:** yes **Minimum TOEFL (paper/computer):** 550/213 **Application Fee:** $25 **Regular Application Deadline:** 5/1 **Regular Notification:** rolling **Deferment Available:** yes **Maximum Length of Deferment:** 1 year **Transfer Students Accepted:** yes **Non-fall Admissions:** yes **Need-Blind Admissions:** yes **Applicants Also Look At:** DUPE–Drexel University–Professional MBA, La Salle University, Penn State University–Great Valley Campus, Saint Joseph's University, Temple University, University of Delaware, Villanova University.

WINSTON-SALEM STATE UNIVERSITY
SCHOOL OF BUSINESS AND ECONOMICS

ADMISSIONS CONTACT: TOMIKIA LEGRANDE, DIRECTOR OF GRADUAGE
ENROLLMENT MANAGEMENT
ADDRESS: GRADUATE SCHOOL, ANDERSON CENTER, WINSTON-SALEM STATE
UNIVERSITY, WINSTON- SALEM, NC 27110
PHONE: 336-750-2021 • FAX: 336-750-2355
E-MAIL: GRADUATE@WSSU.EDU
WEBSITE: WWW.WSSU.EDU/WSSU/GRADUATESTUDIES/GRADUATE+PROGRAMS/
EVENING+MBA/

GENERAL INFORMATION

Type of School: public

STUDENTS

Enrollment of Parent Institution: 5,700 **Enrollment of Business School:** 42 **% Male/female:** 50/50 **% Part-time:** 100 **% Minorities:** 48 **% International:** 2 **Average Age at Entry:** 38 **Average Years Work Experience at Entry:** 10

ACADEMICS

Student/faculty Ratio: 15:1 **% Female Faculty:** 22

ADMISSIONS

Admissions Selectivity Rating: 77

% Acceptees Attending: 93 **Average GMAT:** 480 **Average GPA:** 3.00 **TOEFL Required of Int'l Applicants:** yes **Minimum TOEFL (paper/computer):** 550/213 **Application Fee:** $40 **Regular Application Deadline:** 7/15 **Deferment Available:** yes **Maximum Length of Deferment:** 2 years **Transfer Students Accepted:** yes **Non-fall Admissions:** yes **Need-Blind Admissions:** yes

WINTHROP UNIVERSITY
COLLEGE OF BUSINESS ADMINISTRATION

ADMISSIONS CONTACT: PEGGY HAGER, DIRECTOR OF GRADUATE PROGRAMS
ADDRESS: 213 THURMOND BUILDING, ROCK HILL, SC 29733
PHONE: 803-323-2409 • FAX: 803-323-2539
E-MAIL: MBAOFFICE@WINTHROP.EDU
WEBSITE: CBA.WINTHROP.EDU

GENERAL INFORMATION

Type of School: public **Environment:** town **Academic Calendar:** semester

STUDENTS

Enrollment of Parent Institution: 7,304 **Enrollment of Business School:** 250 **% Male/female:** 100/0 **% Part-time:** 40 **Average Age at Entry:** 29 **Average Years Work Experience at Entry:** 5

FINANCIAL FACTS

Tuition (in-state/out-of-state): $4,216/$7,753

ADMISSIONS

Admissions Selectivity Rating: 64

# of Applications Received: 53 **% Applicants Accepted:** 92 **% Acceptees Attending:** 73 **Average GMAT:** 490 **Average GPA:** 3.3 **TOEFL Required of Int'l Applicants:** yes **Minimum TOEFL (paper):** 550 **Application Fee:** $50 **Regular Application Deadline:** 7/15 **Regular Notification:** rolling **Deferment Available:** yes **Maximum Length of Deferment:** 1 year **Transfer Students Accepted:** yes **Non-fall Admissions:** yes

WRIGHT STATE UNIVERSITY
RAJ SOIN COLLEGE OF BUSINESS

ADMISSIONS CONTACT: MICHAEL EVANS, DIRECTOR, MBA PROGRAMS
ADDRESS: 110 RIKE HALL, 3640 COLONEL GLENN HIGHWAY, DAYTON, OH 45435-0001
PHONE: 937-775-2437 • FAX: 937-775-3545
E-MAIL: MBA_DIRECTOR@WRIGHT.EDU
WEBSITE: WWW.WRIGHT.EDU/BUSINESS

GENERAL INFORMATION

Type of School: public **Environment:** city **Academic Calendar:** quarter

STUDENTS

Enrollment of Business School: 470 **% Male/female:** 57/43 **% Part-time:** 32 **Average Age at Entry:** 31

ACADEMICS

Student/faculty Ratio: 8:1 **% Female Faculty:** 24

Joint Degrees: MBA/MS (Nursing) 2 to 5 years, MBA/MS (Economics) 2 to 5 years, MBA/MD 4 years.

FINANCIAL FACTS

Tuition (in-state/out-of-state): $10,500/$17,796 **Books and Supplies:** $1,300

ADMISSIONS

Admissions Selectivity Rating: 68

# of Applications Received: 416 **% Applicants Accepted:** 84 **% Acceptees Attending:** 67 **Average GMAT:** 525 **Average GPA:** 3.1 **TOEFL Required of Int'l Applicants:** yes **Minimum TOEFL (paper/computer):** 550/213 **Application Fee:** $25 **Regular Application Deadline:** 8/1 **Regular Notification:** 8/2 **Deferment Available:** yes **Maximum Length of Deferment:** 1 year **Transfer Students Accepted:** yes **Non-fall Admissions:** yes **Need-Blind Admissions:** yes

School Says

In this section you'll find schools with extended listings describing Admissions, curriculum, internships, and much more. This is your chance to get in-depth information on programs that interest you. The Princeton Review charges each school a small fee to be listed, and the editorial responsibility is solely that of the university.

AMERICAN UNIVERSITY
Kogod School of Business

AT A GLANCE

American University's Kogod School of Business is among the best business schools in the Washington, DC area and is the school of choice for interdisciplinary business education. The Kogod School of Business was established in 1955 as Washington, DC's first university-level school of business.

Kogod offers graduate business degrees with an unmatched opportunity to integrate business education with other renowned AU disciplines such as international services, law, and politics. Kogod's dual degrees and programs, strong co-curricular programs, endowed scholarships, thought-leading research, and comprehensive career services attract high-quality students and faculty.

CAMPUS AND LOCATION

American University's Kogod School of Business is situated on a beautiful, 84-acre campus in one of the most desirable residential neighborhoods of Northwest Washington, DC. There are 37 buildings on campus, and the Kogod building offers classrooms, student lounges, and a computer lab. Over the next year Kogod is expanding and adding almost 20,000 square feet of learning space, including seven classrooms, a career-management center, a student lounge, a financial services and information technology lab, two seminar rooms, and three break-out rooms.

DEGREES OFFERED

MBA (full-time); MBA (part-time); MS in Taxation; MS in Information Technology Management; MS in Accounting; LLM/MBA; JD/MBA; MBA/MA in International Studies

PROGRAMS AND CURRICULUM

The Kogod MBA program is flexible and provides a solid grounding in theory and practice. The program focuses on the managerial aspects of information technology and global business practices.

The Kogod MBA is a 51-credit-hour program, including 31.5 credit hours of required courses and 19.5 credit hours of electives. Students entering the full-time program in the fall semester should complete the curriculum in 21 months. To learn more about the MBA program, visit www.kogod.american.edu/grad.

FACILITIES

The Kogod School of Business is situated in the center of American University's beautiful 84-acre campus. The Kogod School of Business is expanding. The present Kogod building will be connected to an adjacent existing classroom structure. The existing classroom structure will be completely renovated with an additional story and a new facade. Construction is scheduled to begin in the spring of 2007, and the goal is to complete the expansion for the Fall 2008 academic term.

The expansion will include seven new classrooms, a career management center, a student lounge area, a financial services and information technology lab, two seminar rooms and three break-out rooms. For more information, please visit www.kogod.american.edu/expansion.

COSTS AND EXPENSES

Costs 2006–2007

The tuition fee for the Kogod School of Business of American University is $27,404 per semester for full-time MBA students and $1,048 per credit hour for part-time MBA students.

Tuition

Fewer than 9 credit hours: $1048 per credit hour

12 or more credit hours: $13,702 per semester

Graduate Student Fees

Graduate student fee (all students): $30 per semester

Sports center fee (full-time students): $65 per semester

Sports center fee (part-time students): $30 per semester

Technology fee (full-time) $95 per semester

Technology fee (part-time) $30 per semester

FACULTY

Kogod's Faculty members are internationally recognized scholars, outstanding lecturers and researchers, and advisors who are committed to the highest standards of teaching. They bring real business challenges into the classroom for you to solve. You will find many faculty members serving as consultants to major corporations and governments, or actively engaged in research.

STUDENT BODY

At Kogod we believe education should extend beyond the classroom. Hands-on experiences enhance leadership ability, communication skills, and self-confidence. K-LAB (Kogod Leadership and Applied Business) allows students to learn valuable professional skills in real-world settings and includes options to participate in graduate study abroad, the annual case competition, and a variety of advisory boards.

ADMISSIONS

The application process for the Kogod School of Business is an electronic process. Complete the online application at www.kogod.american.edu/apply.

Kogod application requirements include the following: a bachelor's degree from a regionally accredited college or university, official GMAT score (international students: TOEFL paper-based score of 600 or computer-based score of 250), an interview, resume, personal statement, two letters of recommendation, and a $75 application fee.

Applicants may also be considered for admission without reference to their undergraduate average if they have maintained a 3.3 cumulative grade point average in a master's program completed at an accredited institution.

SPECIAL PROGRAMS

Kogod offers an extensive set of interdisciplinary programs that include three dual-degree programs: LLM/MBA, JD/MBA, and the MA/MBA. Visit www.kogod.american.edu/dualdegree.

Kogod graduate students may also decide to design their own Career Tracks. Career Tracks may be combined with up to nine credits taken outside of Kogod. Visit www.kogod.american.edu/careertracks.

ADDITIONAL INFORMATION

American University
Kogod School of Business
Attn: Graduate Admissions
4400 Massachusetts Avenue Northwest
Washington, DC 20016
Telephone: 202-885-1913
Fax: 202-885-1078
E-mail: kogodmba@american.edu
www.kogod.american.edu

CAREER SERVICES AND PLACEMENT

Preparation for life after graduation begins on your first day at Kogod, and we offer a number of services to help make your employment search as successful as possible. These services include career counseling, development workshops, on-campus recruiting, career fairs, and networking events.

ARIZONA STATE UNIVERSITY
W.P. Carey School of Business

AT A GLANCE

The W.P. Carey MBA at Arizona State University (ASU) prepares you for success by grounding you with business essentials and teaching you to develop relevant specialized knowledge based on your career goals.

The intensive first year of the W. P. Carey MBA—Full-time Program is an integrated academic experience that builds advanced managerial knowledge and skills, essential for your career. During the second year, students structure a flexible learning experience that addresses their individual goals. Courses selected from diverse focus areas in the second year complement the deep foundation of primary business knowledge built in the first-year core curriculum. The W.P. Carey MBA emphasizes experiential, applied knowledge and best practices from a Faculty with a wealth of cumulative experience and scholarship. Alumni tell us year after year that the W.P. Carey MBA prepared them well for their next step after graduation, and that it has continued to fuel professional advancement years later.

CAMPUS AND LOCATION

The W.P. Carey School of Business is headquartered on the university's Tempe campus, adjacent to Phoenix, Arizona, the fifth-largest city in the U.S. Classes and program services are also offered at satellite locations throughout Greater Phoenix. The metro area provides students with access to companies in high-tech, aerospace, financial services, manufacturing, telecommunications, transportation and tourism-related service industries. The thriving population also supports an active cultural environment and a wide range of professional sports.

DEGREES OFFERED

The W.P. Carey School of Business offers a Master of Business Administration (W.P. Carey MBA) degree, as well as undergraduate and doctoral (PhD) studies in a number of disciplines.

ACADEMIC PROGRAMS

The W.P. Carey MBA builds and strengthens a student's knowledge, skills and managerial abilities by means of technical, analytical and case materials that inform about the functional areas of business. Students put new knowledge into practice through applied projects, business presentations, and case competitions.

In the first year of the program, skill development is grounded in fundamental disciplines such as accounting, marketing, ethics, statistics, and management. Integrated courses elevate learning as students discover the way business disciplines relate to one another and how singular decisions affect company success across functions.

During the second year, courses selected from diverse focus areas complement the deep foundation of primary business knowledge built in the first-year core curriculum. Second-year students can elect to concentrate their studies in one area or build a customized experience from a blend of electives in these disciplines. Students may also take advantage of a number of concurrent degree options.

FACILITIES

The W.P. Carey School of Business is housed in two buildings that contain an auditorium, lecture halls, seminar rooms, several computer resource centers, and a coffee house. The business complex is equipped with wireless access points (WAP) throughout its two buildings including the external patio and fountain areas.

The Ford Graduate Suite, a dedicated resource for graduate business students, includes a student center, fully mediated team rooms, computer lab, open study areas and student organization offices.

EXPENSES AND FINANCIAL AID

W.P. Carey MBA—Full-time Program tuition and fees for the 2006–2007 academic year are $16,028 for Arizona residents and $26,614 for nonresidents.

The W. P. Carey MBA is fortunate to have an array of financial resources such as grants, fellowships, scholarships, assistantships and out-of-state tuitions waivers available to students based on various criteria including need and merit.

FACULTY

W.P. Carey School Faculty elevate the quality of research, the effectiveness of teaching and the opportunities that develop for the students and business partners associated with the school of business. W.P. Carey Faculty are in the top ranks for research productivity as measured by the premier academic journals. These thought leaders develop new knowledge through research, consulting and other interactions with major corporations. They bring their intellectual energy and real-world research experiences to bear on the school's curriculum and student experience—shaping new business and community leaders.

STUDENT BODY

W.P. Carey MBA—Full-time Program students have diverse backgrounds. For the Fall 2006 entering class, the average student age was 28, with 4.4 years of professional, postbaccalaureate work experience. 24 percent are international students, 13 percent are members of ethnic minority groups, and 24 percent are women.

ADMISSIONS

Application to the W.P. Carey MBA is open to individuals with at least two years of full-time work experience who hold a bachelor's degree or its equivalent in any discipline from an accredited college or university.

The W.P. Carey MBA Admissions Committee looks for well-rounded individuals with leadership skills, strong academic credentials, managerial experience or potential, and the ability to contribute to the diversity of the class. Transcripts, GMAT scores, TOEFL scores (for international students), work history, essay questions, letters of recommendation, and a required interview all influence the admission decision.

W.P. Carey MBA is on rolling admissions and will review applications until all seats are filled. Admission is for the fall term only.

CAREER SERVICES AND PLACEMENT

Resources offered by the Graduate Career Management Center help students compete successfully in the employment marketplace include individual career consulting, professional development seminars, and networking opportunities with regional business professionals.

Over 95 percent of the class of 2006 was placed within three months of graduation.

BABSON COLLEGE
F.W. Olin Graduate School of Business

AT A GLANCE

At the F.W. Olin Graduate School of Business at Babson College, we have a rich tradition of excellence in cultivating entrepreneurial thinking. While some of our graduates pursue start-up ventures, far more of our graduates use their entrepreneurial training to succeed in the corporate environment. Here, entrepreneurship isn't about starting a business; it's a state of mind. Babson features four unique degree programs that prepare students to become superior managers and to meet the needs of progressive organizations. In 2006, *BusinessWeek* named Babson "One of the Best MBA Programs" for entrepreneurship and ranked Babson in the top 40 MBA programs overall. Babson is the MBA that delivers.

CAMPUS AND LOCATION

Babson College is located in Wellesley, Massachusetts, 12 miles from Boston. Babson's Fast Track MBA is also offered in Portland, Oregon.

ACADEMIC PROGRAMS

The Two-Year MBA program stresses innovation, creative problem-solving, and the ability to recognize opportunity. The first year takes students through the business development cycle. The second year allows students to focus on their interests with electives. The One-Year MBA is an accelerated program that allows students with undergraduate business degrees to complete their MBA in three full-time semesters (12 months). The One-Year MBA begins with an intensive summer program. Students then join second-year students in the Two-Year MBA program to complete their elective course work in the fall and spring semesters. The Fast Track MBA is a part-time program combining traditional classroom instruction with web-based, distance learning. You earn your degree in just 24 months—much faster than a traditional part-time MBA. Students attend classes on campus during intensive, two-day sessions approximately every six weeks. Its convenience and flexibility make Fast Track the perfect choice if you're balancing work, long-term career goals, and other demands. Fast Track is now offered in both Wellesley, Massachusetts and Portland, Oregon. The Babson Evening MBA program is among the top-ranked part-time MBA programs in the country. It builds on a more compact core of ten courses, four of which feature a cross-disciplinary approach. The Evening MBA provides students the greatest opportunity to adjust their program pace to fit their personal and professional lives.

FACILITIES

The library subscribes to a browsing collection of 700 periodicals and newspapers; thousands more are available from any computer on campus through Internet subscriptions with Dow Jones Interactive, InfoTrac Web, LexisNexis Universe, ProQuest Direct, FirstSearch, and Primark's Global Access. Using the WEBnet Library Catalog, students can select books in both management and liberal arts topics from Babson's stacks or for delivery from other area college libraries. Horn Library is a wireless environment. Students can meet with their peers in group study rooms, some of which have LCD projectors and VCRs, or work independently in the Horn Computer Center. The Stephen D. Cutler Investment Management Center, located in Horn Library, is a working lab for students pursuing financial analysis.

EXPENSES AND FINANCIAL AID

Two-Year MBA nine-month academic year cost estimates (2007–2008)
Tuition: $35,110
Books and supplies: $2,270
Living expenses: approximately $18,200
One-Year MBA 12-month academic year cost estimates (2007–2008)
Tuition and fees: $48,688
Books and supplies: $2,632
Living expenses: $24,000

Fast Track tuition estimate (September 2007): $49,800
Evening MBA tuition: $1,041 (per-credit)

Merit awards include Olin Fellowships and Scholarships, Babson Fellowships and Scholarships, Forte Foundation Fellowships, Women's Leadership Awards, and several awards based on entrepreneurial accomplishments.

FACULTY

Babson's Faculty is an internationally and professionally diverse group. The Faculty includes seasoned corporate executives, visionary entrepreneurs, and academic thought leaders.

STUDENT BODY

Students in the Two-Year MBA program are, on average, 29 years old and have about 5 years of work experience. The average GMAT score is 630, and women make up 22 percent of the class. Students come from diverse industries and represent 26 countries. International students compose 49 percent of the Two-Year MBA program. International students participate in an intensive Pre-MBA program before beginning the MBA. This consists of familiarization with the campus and resources, and Faculty members present a basic introduction to economics, marketing, and the case method. Recreational and social events are scheduled.

ADMISSIONS

Students are admitted to the program based on a careful evaluation of academic records, professional qualifications, GMAT scores, and personal attributes. Interviews are required for admission to full-time MBA programs. The current two-year class's GMAT scores range from 560–710, and the average undergraduate GPA is 3.05. International students must submit TOEFL results and official English translations of all academic documents. All candidates should have strong mathematics, computer, economics, and business writing skills. Application deadlines (two-year program): November 15, January 15, March 15, and April 15. For application deadlines and decision dates for all programs, visit www3.babson.edu/MBA/admission/TimeTable.cfm.

For more information, applicants should contact:

Office of Graduate Admission
F.W. Olin Graduate School of Business
Babson Park, MA 02457
Telephone: 781-239-4317 or 800-488-4512 (toll-free within the U.S.)
Fax: 781-239-4194
E-mail: mbaadmission@babson.edu
Website: www.babson.edu/mba

SPECIAL PROGRAMS

The Global Management Program gives MBA students the chance to work as project managers and consultants with more than 250 companies operating in 40 countries. This program is application-based and is available to full-time MBA students and full-time Evening MBA students who have completed 30 credit hours.

Successful business partnerships have always been a major component of Babson's programs. First-year student teams consult with Boston-area organizations through the year-long Babson Consulting Alliance Program. The Management Consulting Field Experience offers a variety of second-year consulting projects.

CAREER SERVICES AND PLACEMENT

The Center for Career Development's Relationship Management team will work with you in planning a career strategy, including developing your personal marketing communication plan and preparing for networking activities and interviews.

BAYLOR UNIVERSITY
Hankamer School of Business

AT A GLANCE
Where you choose to attain your MBA is an important decision. Baylor University can be a valuable partner on your journey in achieving your highest personal and professional potential. Baylor offers MBA students the exceptional resources of a premier institution recognized worldwide for academic quality, superior teaching, and a reputation for graduating persons of both competence and character. Baylor's distinctiveness lies in the university's continual pursuit of intellectual excellence and a faithfulness to the Christian tradition which, together, inspire action on behalf of the world. Small classes, hosted at the university's state-of-the-art Hankamer School of Business in Waco, Texas, set the stage for an integrated learning experience that balances leading-edge business theory with practical, hands-on, real-world challenges.

CAMPUS AND LOCATION
Chartered in 1845, Baylor University is the oldest institution of higher learning in continuous operation in Texas. Baylor has grown to a 735-acre campus with 14,000 students. With an area population of 208,000, Baylor is centrally located in Waco, Texas, within 150 miles of four major metropolitan cities: Dallas, Houston, Austin and San Antonio.

DEGREES OFFERED
Master of Business Administration (MBA); Executive MBA Program in Dallas (EMBA); Executive MBA Program in Austin-Waco (EMBA); MBA—International Management (MBA—IM); MBA—Information Systems Management (MBA—ISM); MBA/Master of Science in Information Systems (MBA/MSIS); Juris Doctorate/MBA (JD/MBA); MBA—Master of Engineering (MBA/ME)
Details are available at www.baylor.edu/mba/degreeoptions.

ACADEMIC PROGRAMS
The fully integrated MBA curriculum incorporates theory, application, personal development and career management into three core "lockstep" semesters. Each "lockstep" semester focuses on a different perspective of the business process: define, discover, and deliver.

FACILITIES
The Hankamer School of Business features seminar-style classrooms, a 75-seat videoconferencing room, and the Graduate Center that maximizes discussion and interaction between students and Faculty. With Baylor's wireless data network, AirBear, students can connect their notebook computers to the Internet from any location on campus, unencumbered by a physical network connection.

EXPENSES AND FINANCIAL AID
More than half of the MBA students receive some form of merit-based scholarships or graduate assistantship awards. Merit-based scholarships or assistantships are awarded ranging from 50 to 100 percent tuition remission. Additionally, students can earn a stipend in exchange for working 10 hours per week for a professor in the Business School.

Tuition and Fees for 2007–2008
$22,220 per academic year (fall and spring)
$643 per hour in the summer semester
Estimated student fees for an academic year are $2,900. An additional $1,500 for the notebook computer is required. You need to purchase a new computer.

FACULTY
Baylor MBA students can expect a personalized and integrative educational experience administered by a highly supportive academic community. The MBA Faculty is accessible, involved, and intent on your success. Your relationship with Faculty members will help you sharpen your ambitions and form a solid basis upon which to develop the business acumen to succeed.

All professors teaching in the MBA programs hold doctorate degrees, are active in their professional fields, are business consultants, and are well published.

STUDENT BODY
Baylor offers an environment that will challenge you academically and nourish you personally. A culturally diverse learning environment, which includes people from around the world, gives students the global perspective necessary to succeed in today's world market.

ADMISSIONS
Admission to Baylor Business is competitive. We're looking for individuals with professional work experience, outstanding scholarship, a commitment to community service, and a motivation to pursue an intense graduate business program. MBA candidates should have strong analytical capabilities and communication skills.

SPECIAL PROGRAMS
The adage is true: The best way to learn something is through practice. It is the concept behind both the corporate-alliance practicum known as Focus Firm and the "Practicum in Portfolio Management" finance class.

In the Focus Firm project, students research, critically assess and recommend viable solutions to an identified business dilemma for an actual business. See www.baylor.edu/mba/focusfirm.

In the portfolio management class, students manage a live fund valued at more than $6 million. See www.baylor.edu/business/financial_markets.

The advantage of both practica over simulation exercises or case study is that students practice multidisciplinary expertise, with expectations of real-time business delivery.

ADDITIONAL INFORMATION
Baylor Business—Our commitment to the personal as well as professional development of our students is distinctive. Values-based guidance of Faculty mentors and innovative program design allow you to take your career—and your life—wherever you want to go. Baylor's graduate business programs provide the comprehensive learning experience you need to achieve your career objectives, within the context of greater personal development goals designed to serve you for life. Discover the difference Baylor can make.

CAREER SERVICES AND PLACEMENT
Each semester MBA students take a career management class. Seminars address critical areas such as self-assessment, job-search strategies and resume development, as well as provide valuable instruction on appropriate interviewing behavior, negotiating successfully and accepting a job offer in a professional manner. Topics such as Strategy-Driven Career Plans, Cover Letters That Work, and Pounding The Pavement are presented by recruiters, alumni and career professionals who have volunteered to share strategies that will facilitate your professional success. A pivotal function of Career Management is matching our graduates with the perfect job opportunity. To accomplish this objective, each MBA develops a personalized plan of action based on his or her unique qualifications, talent, experience and vocational leanings. Internships present opportunities to apply the management theory learned in the first year of your MBA program to the marketplace within a large or small corporation. At the same time, internship employers have an opportunity to discover an outstanding candidate with a proven record of expertise. Experience gained through internships aids both students and employers by providing each with what they need: the skills and expertise to get the job done.

CALIFORNIA POLYTECHNIC STATE UNIVERSITY—SAN LUIS OBISPO
Orfalea College of Business

AT A GLANCE

The Orfalea College of Business at California Polytechnic State University—San Luis Obispo (Cal Poly) offers one-year MBA programs that follow the educational philosophy of "learn by doing". The programs' in-class experience includes simulations of management decision-making scenarios, case studies, team exercises, extensive interaction with Faculty and other students, and personal communication and presentation skills enhancement. The Orfalea College of Business' (OCOB) MBA programs are accredited by the AACSB and admit a limited number of students each year. Students accepted into and enrolled in Cal Poly's OCOB MBA programs may:

- Enter the program without an undergraduate business degree and without completing prerequisite business course requirements.

- Choose an accelerated option (Track One) that allows full-time students to follow a prescribed course of study and complete the program in less than a year, or a traditional, nonaccelerated option (Track Two)

- Study relevant, current, challenging, and intellectually stimulating courses.

- Enroll in short intensive summer sessions to complete the MBA program and/or follow the accelerated option requirements.

- Enroll in a 2.5-week business study tour to mainland China

- Work with renowned faculty in a friendly and professional academic atmosphere.

- Live and study on California's beautiful Central Coast

In addition to a General Management MBA, Cal Poly offers an MBA with a specialization in Agribusiness, an MBA with a specialization in Graphic Communication Document Systems Management, and an MS in Accounting—Taxation. Two-year dual-degree options are also available for students wishing to pursue two graduate degrees simultaneously. For example, a formal, joint MBA/MS program in Engineering Management (EMP) and various other informal MBA/MS or MBA/MA dual-degree options are available. Beginning in Fall 2008, a Master's of Science in Economics will be offered.

CAMPUS AND LOCATION

Cal Poly is located in San Luis Obispo, an idyllic city of 45,000 located on the beautiful Central Coast of California, midway between San Francisco and Los Angeles. San Luis Obispo's small-town casual atmosphere makes it an excellent location in which to study and socialize away from the large metropolitan areas; however, it is close enough for easy interviews and contacts.

DEGREES OFFERED

The Cal Poly Orfalea College of Business offers a general management Masters in Business Administration (MBA), as well as specializations in agribusiness and graphic communication document systems management. Also available, an MBA and MS in Engineering Management (EMP) dual degree, and Masters of Science in Accounting—Taxation, and a Masters in Industrial and Technical Studies (MS in I and TS). In addition, Cal Poly offers a variety of informal dual-degree options where a student can link the MBA degree with certain other graduate degree programs on campus. Beginning in Fall 2008, a Masters of Science in Economics will be offered.

ACADEMIC PROGRAMS

The Cal Poly MBA program is a 60–64 unit program that provides students who are willing to commit to a rigorous schedule of prescribed courses the option to complete the program in less than 11 months (Track I). A traditional MBA model (Track II) for those not pursing this accelerated option and/or simultaneously pursuing joint/dual degrees is also offered.

FACILITIES

The Orfalea College of Business, named after Paul Orfalea, the founder of Kinko's, is a modern building offering over 13,000 square feet of computer lab space and teaching facilities. Cal Poly offers on-campus housing for 2,783 students in 13 residence halls; has library holdings of 2,576,3000; computer access of 1,800 student workstations in labs, classrooms, and residence halls; and a modern 91,559-square-foot recreation center.

EXPENSES AND FINANCIAL AID

MBA Program Tuition and Fees (nine-month academic year)

California Residents	$5,244
Nonresidents	$16,092
Optional Session Course	$ 3,020

Optional International Business Tour $ 4,200

Housing, transportation, books, and personal living costs are approximately $13,000.

Cal Poly students have a variety of financial aid programs available for assistance. Programs vary in eligibility criteria, award amounts, and repayment options.

FACULTY

Outstanding faculty teach in Cal Poly's MBA programs. Each Faculty member has a terminal degree in his/her discipline (e.g., PhD or JD). Furthermore, each faculty member is active and engaged in his or her discipline, whether it's research and publication work, consulting, and/or community and professional service.

STUDENT BODY

With 300 clubs on campus, MBA students have many opportunities for activities outside the classroom. The MBA Association organizes a Professional Speaker Series, giving students the opportunity to network with industry professionals. Cal Poly MBA students participate annually in the International Collegiate Business Strategy Competition and the MBA Business Ethics Competition, which they won in 2006. In 2005, Cal Poly's team won the Bank of America Low-Income Housing Challenge competition, defeating teams from Stanford and UC—Berkeley.

ADMISSIONS

The Cal Poly MBA program seeks candidates who are bright, motivated, and demonstrate the ability to successfully complete a rigorous academic program. While admission is primarily based on GPA and GMAT achievement, we do consider additional factors such as work experience, leadership qualities, and letters of recommendation in order to develop an overall assessment of the applicant. Interviews are optional.

SPECIAL PROGRAMS

Two-year dual-degree options are available for students wishing to pursue two graduate degrees simultaneously. A joint MBA/MS program in Engineering Management (EMP) and various other MBA/MS or MBA/MA dual-degree options are available.

ADDITIONAL INFORMATION

Our MBA programs have a distinctly Cal Poly character—course work emphasizing the fundamentals and consistent with our "learn by doing" philosophy, integrative learning, and the opportunity for international study. Our methods of instruction entail extensive interaction; thus, we limit the number of students admitted to our programs to foster a real sense of community. We invite you to visit our campus, business school and the San Luis Obispo community to sample what we have to offer.

CAMPBELLSVILLE UNIVERSITY
School of Business and Economics

AT A GLANCE

The School of Business and Economics is part of Campbellsville University—a private liberal arts institution that offers over 40 undergraduate majors and 9 graduate degrees. The goal of Campbellsville University's MBA program is to prepare students to play a leadership role in the rapidly changing, technologically advanced global marketplace.

Campbellsville University celebrated its centennial year during the 2006–2007 school year. Campbellsville University is a private, liberal arts comprehensive institution in the Christian tradition. Founded in 1906, Campbellsville University is affiliated with the Kentucky Baptist Convention and has an enrollment of over 2,300 students who represent 95 Kentucky counties, 27 states, and 34 foreign nations. Campbellsville University has received numerous awards for its excellence in academics and athletics and has been recognized as one of the nation's best values in higher education.

LOCATION AND ENVIRONMENT

The physical campus of Campbellsville University is located in the idyllic rolling hills of south central Kentucky. Campbellsville University is located 82 miles southwest of Lexington, Kentucky, and 80 miles southeast of Louisville, Kentucky.

On-campus MBA classes take place on weekends to accommodate our students' work schedules.

Campbellsville University also offers MBA courses through an online format so that you can earn your degree from anywhere and at a time that is convenient to you.

DEGREES OFFERED

We offer five MBA degrees: a general MBA and four MBAs with concentrations. Specializations are available in health care management, international business, human resource management, and marketing.

ACADEMIC PROGRAMS

Each program is comprised of 12 courses, or 36 credit hours. The on-campus program is designed to be completed in as little as 18 months, and the online program can be completed in one calendar year.

Our programs have earned professional accreditation by IACBE, the International Assembly for Collegiate Business Education, and our university is accredited by the Commission on Colleges of the Southern Association of Colleges and Schools, ensuring the highest academic standards for our programs.

FACILITIES

The School of Business and Economics is located on the top floor of the university's historic administration building. We have state-of-the-art, high-tech classrooms, a student lounge, and a computer lab for our students. Campbellsville University's Montgomery Library provides a vast collection of resources to students both on campus and online.

EXPENSES AND FINANCIAL AID

The MBA program at Campbellsville University is incredibly affordable, especially compared to other online MBA options. Current graduate tuition for MBA courses is $365 per credit hour. Online MBA courses also require a $100 technology fee. Total tuition costs for the MBA is $13,140 for the on-campus program and $14,340 for the online program.

Most of our students receive some form of financial aid or tuition reimbursement.

FACULTY

Faculty in our MBA program have excellent credentials and expertise. All of our MBA faculty hold PhDs in their respective fields and combine rigorous scholarship with practical real-world experience. Our faculty have held significant positions with *Fortune* 500 firms and International Organizations. The faculty at Campbellsville University enjoy working with students on a one-to-one basis, mentoring them and helping them "find their calling" and reach their goals. Our MBA Faculty have been nationally recognized for their teaching excellence.

STUDENT BODY

Most of our students pursue their MBA while working full-time. Our student population includes a diverse mix of local professionals and international students, providing you with a rich experience to prepare you for the global marketplace.

ADMISSIONS

Applicants to the MBA program must have a bachelor's degree from a regionally accredited four-year college or university, and official transcripts for the baccalaureate work must be mailed directly to the Office of Admissions. While the GMAT is the preferred entrance exam, the school will also accept results from the GRE or the Miller Analogies Test. The Admissions test must have been taken within the last five years. Applications must submit a resume that includes education and work history and a typewritten statement of professional goals. Two letters of reference must be mailed to the Office of Admissions, and the applicant must submit an application form (available online at www.campbellsville.edu).

International applicants whose primary language is not English and who are not graduates of a college or university in the U.S. must submit a score of 550 (paper) on the Test of English as a Foreign Language. An official, independent evaluation of academic work completed at foreign institutions must be sent to the Office of Admissions from World Education Services, and international students who do not hold a U.S. permanent resident visa must submit evidence of financial support before an I-20 form can be processed.

CAREER SERVICES

Graduates from the School of Business and Economics have secured employment with major firms in a variety of roles.

ADDITIONAL INFORMATION

For Additional Information, please contact Dr. Patricia H. Cowherd, Dean, School of Business and Economics or Dr. Rick E. Corum, Director of the MBA Program.

One University Drive

Campbellsville, KY 42718-2799

E-mail: mba@campbellsville.edu

Phone: 270-789-5553

Toll-free: 800-264-6014

Fax: 270-789-5066

Website: www.campbellsville.edu

CENTRAL MICHIGAN UNIVERSITY
School of Business

AT A GLANCE

The Master of Business Administration at Central Michigan University prepares graduate students for leadership positions in today's global economy. The program is accredited by the Association to Advance Collegiate Schools of Business (AACSB International).

Many courses are taught by Six Sigma Black Belt—certified faculty, and SAP Enterprise Software for Management is integrated into the curriculum.

CAMPUS AND LOCATION

Central Michigan University's 480-acre campus is accommodating, friendly, and conveniently located in the heart of a classic college town. CMU faculty, staff, students, and community residents care about each other and feel quite safe to walk on and off campus, to shop, and to attend sporting events or other recreational opportunities.

DEGREES OFFERED

The College of Business Administration offers three graduate degree programs: the Master of Business Administration (MBA), the Master of Science in Information Systems (MSIS) and the Master of Arts in Economics (MA in Economics).

ACADEMIC PROGRAMS

The MBA program requires 30 credit hours. The accelerated 8-week courses allow full-time students to complete the program in 12 months. Part-time students can expect to complete the program in two or three years. Individuals who possess an undergraduate degree in business will be most prepared to begin the program; those with other undergraduate degrees and business credits will be asked to meet prerequisite requirements.

Students will specify a primary area of concentration in one of the following areas: accounting, business economics, consulting, finance, general business, international business, management information systems (SAP emphasis), marketing, and human resources management.

Students will also complete an applied, integrated project in which skills and competencies are applied to actual business problems.

The MSIS program is also accredited by AACSB International. The program is designed for individuals who do not have previous information systems or computing-related degrees. The program prepares students to enter various information systems positions in business, consulting, government, or nonprofit organizations; to teach computer applications and information systems at community colleges; or to enter doctoral programs in information systems-related areas after graduation. The program requires 30 credit hours and is open to full-time or part-time students.

Students will specify a primary area of concentration in one of the following areas: business processing engineering, systems applications, general business, and teaching/training. SAP Enterprise Software for Management is used in several courses in the business processing engineering concentration.

The MA in Economics is designed for students who wish to gain marketable skills in applied economics and for students who wish to strengthen their preparation in order to continue work toward a doctorate in economics. The program requires 30 credit hours and is open to full-time or part-time students.

FACILITIES

Located at the center of campus, Park Library provides state-of-the-art Facilities for students. The adjacent Bovee University Center is a hub of vibrant activity, with auditoriums, restaurant services, and a variety of student service offices and student organizations.

Expenses and Financial Aid

In-state tuition: $366 per credit hour

Out-of-state tuition: $678 per credit hour

International students must provide proof of funding of $23,500 for an academic year.

Domestic students—estimate for housing, food, utilities, tuition, books and supplies: $19,492.

Domestic students and international students may apply for graduate assistantships and fellowships. International students may be eligible for Out-of-State Tuition Merit Awards. For more information, visit: www.grad.cmich.edu

STUDENT BODY

Students in the program come from a wide variety of academic, professional, and personal backgrounds. The diversity of the international and domestic students offers a rewarding learning environment by adding numerous perspectives and insights to teamwork situations.

ADMISSIONS

The college accepts applications from students who have earned a baccalaureate degree from an accredited university or college. To be admitted to the MBA program, a student must present both an acceptable score on the Graduate Management Admission Test (GMAT) and an acceptable grade point average (GPA). Our college uses a set index formula to determine a candidate's eligibility for admission. Applicants must achieve at least 1,050 points based on this formula: 200 times the undergraduate GPA plus the GMAT score, which must be independently 450 or higher. International students must also submit a score of at least 79 (internet-based test), 213 (computer-based test) or 550 (paper-based test) or higher on the Test of English as a Foreign Language (TOEFL).

All application procedures take place through CMU's College of Graduate Studies (www.grad.cmich.edu). Domestic students should apply for admission at least six weeks prior to the start of the semester of entry. International students should apply at least six months in advance of a semester start date.

SPECIAL PROGRAMS

Housed within CMU's Applied Business Studies Complex, our LaBelle Entrepreneurial Center helps small businesses reorganize and competitively reposition themselves and provides real-world connections between graduate students, corporations, and small businesses.

CAREER SERVICES AND PLACEMENT

CMU provides a variety of career services, including scheduling of on-campus interviews with potential employers. Students can register for e-recruiting services, resumes are critiqued, and mock interviews are provided to help you better prepare for real interviews. Career advising services are provided as well (www.careers.cmich.edu).

CITY UNIVERSITY OF NEW YORK—BARUCH COLLEGE

Zicklin School of Business

AT A GLANCE

The Zicklin School offers degree programs leading to the BBA, MBA, Executive MBA, MS, Executive MS in Finance, and the Baruch/Mt. Sinai MBA in Health Care Administration, which is accredited by the CAHME (Commission on Accreditation of Health Care Management Education). Among its exciting new initiatives are the Zicklin Full-Time MBA program, which enrolls a select group of candidates whose credentials and average GMAT scores of 647 place them among the top students in the nation. Its combined, five-year undergraduate/MS degree program in accountancy meets the latest education requirements for the CPA exam. The Zicklin School houses the City University's PhD in business and offers a joint-degree program leading to the JD/MBA degrees in conjunction with both Brooklyn Law School and The New York Law School.

The Zicklin MBA features a core curriculum that spans all the major business areas and a specialization that permits students to explore a specific area in greater depth.

Zicklin's MS degree programs offer in-depth study in a range of areas. Unlike the broader MBA curriculum, students are often not required to do course work in disciplines included in the MBA core. The MS is a more focused degree and usually requires fewer courses.

CAMPUS AND LOCATION

Located in Manhattan's historic Gramercy Park neighborhood and the leading-edge Flatiron District, Baruch is at the heart of one of the world's most dynamic business and cultural centers—within easy reach of Wall Street, "Silicon Alley," and the headquarters of major business and financial firms and nonprofit organizations.

DEGREES OFFERED

The Zicklin School offers degree programs leading to the BBA, MBA, Executive MBA, MS, Executive MS in Finance, and the Baruch/Mt. Sinai MBA in Health Care Administration.

ACADEMIC PROGRAMS

Besides the BBA degree, Zicklin offers the MBA degree in three different formats: the Full-Time Honors MBA, a highly selective full-time, primarily daytime program; the Accelerated Part-Time format for those who wish to complete their degree in 28 months; and the Flex-Time format for full- or part-time students who need a wider range of options in scheduling their graduate study.

The Zicklin School also offers Master of Science programs, an Executive MBA, and Executive MS programs in finance and industrial and labor relations.

FACILITIES

Baruch's 17-floor academic complex is home to the Zicklin School. The award-winning design encloses modern, multimedia-equipped classrooms; two large production-level theaters; a fitness center with a gym and a swimming pool; a television studio; and an enhanced Center for Student Life.

Baruch's Information and Technology Building houses the award-winning William and Anita Newman Library, the Baruch Computing and Technology Center, and the Subotnick Financial Services Center/Bert W. and Sandra Wasserman Trading Floor.

EXPENSES AND FINANCIAL AID

Tuition for New York State residents for the Fall 2006 term was $4,400 per semester for full-time and $400 per credit for part-time MBA study; $3,200 per semester for full-time and $270 per credit for part-time MS study.

For out-of-state residents and international students, tuition was $600 per credit for full- or part-time MBA study; and $500 per credit for full- or part-time MS study. Tuition and fees are subject to change without notice.

Average estimated annual cost for books, supplies, transportation, and personal expenses is $15,500 per year.

Financial aid is available and is merit based. Honors MBA Tuition Scholarships and Graduate assistantships are awarded to the most qualified students in the Full-Time Honors MBA program. International students are eligible for both honors scholarships and graduate assistantships.

Additional financial aid information is available at www.baruch.cuny.edu/financialaid.

FACULTY

The faculty of the Zicklin School of Business is large, distinguished, and diverse. They include noted scholars, authors, sought-after consultants, and master teachers. See our website at http://aux.zicklin.baruch.cuny.edu/hires/ for the bios of our newest faculty members.

STUDENT BODY

Baruch's reputation for excellence extends to all parts of the world, attracting students from New York, neighboring states, and abroad. The diverse group of men and women doing graduate work at Baruch hold undergraduate degrees from more than 200 colleges and universities.

The average graduate student is 29 years old, with an average of at least 2 years of full-time work experience. Many MBA students at Baruch have undergraduate degrees in business, but the majority have majored in the liberal arts, the sciences, or engineering. Professional experience varies widely. Over 40 percent of the students are women, while members of minority groups represent almost 30 percent of the Student Body. International students make up close to 50 percent of the full-time MBA student population.

ADMISSIONS

Applicants must submit application forms, an essay, a resume, official transcripts from every college or university attended, two letters of recommendation, a nonrefundable application fee, and current GMAT scores. International students whose native language is not English must take the TOEFL/TWE.

Application deadlines for fall admission: June 30 for Health Care MBA students, May 31 for domestic Flex-Time students, and April 30 for all other applicants. For spring, the deadline is October 31 for all Flex-Time students. Only the Flex-Time programs offer spring admission.

Application materials can be obtained at http://zicklin.baruch.cuny.edu/Admissions/grad/apply.

For more information regarding Admissions, contact us at http://zicklin.baruch.cuny.edu/Admissions/grad or http://zicklin.baruch.cuny.edu/programs/exec.

SPECIAL PROGRAMS

In addition to our regular MBA and MS programs, the Zicklin School also offers a joint JD/MBA in conjunction with New York Law School or Brooklyn Law School; the Baruch/Mt. Sinai MBA in Health Care Administration; and Executive Master degrees in countries such as China, Singapore, Taiwan, and Israel.

CAREER SERVICES AND PLACEMENT

The Graduate Career Management Center offers students a range of job search services. A core curriculum of workshops is offered to all students. On-campus recruiting is held throughout the year, and career fairs are held as the market warrants. Students have unlimited access to the various full-time and internship position openings that are posted regularly on E-Recruiting and in the office resource center. Special events, such as career seminars, company information sessions, and other networking opportunities, are also held throughout the year.

CLARK UNIVERSITY
Graduate School of Management

AT A GLANCE

Clark University Graduate School of Management Offers the MBA with choice of six concentrations and the Master of Science in Finance (MSF). As a student at Clark, you will benefit from small class sizes and close interactions with talented Faculty who are dedicated researchers, practitioners and educators. As a Clark graduate you will join an international alumni network of people who have taken leadership roles in multinational corporations, revitalized family businesses, and started ventures of their own.

CAMPUS AND LOCATION

Clark University is located in Worcester, Massachusetts in the heart of New England. Within an hour's drive of Boston and three hours from New York City Clark, Clark is positioned near major technology, financial services, health care, life sciences, manufacturing, and insurance industry centers.

Clark University's main campus is thoroughly integrated into the surrounding urban neighborhood creating a thriving academic community within the city of Worcester. Facilities on campus include extensive library holdings and research resources, athletic facilities, computing and digital multimedia production space, wireless network capability, and a strong on-campus extracurricular tradition. Graduate business students will have access to all campus-wide resources in addition to dedicated interactive classrooms, wireless network, and GSOM team project space.

In addition to the main campus, the Graduate School of Management also maintains a satellite campus in Framingham, Massachusetts serving part-time students in the Metro-West region. While serving part-time student needs, this location also further connects Clark to the business community of central Massachusetts and the Metro-West region.

DEGREES OFFERED

Master of Business Administration (MBA) with six concentrations: Accounting, Global Business, Finance, Marketing, Management Information Systems, and General Management.

Master of Science in Finance (MSF)

ACADEMIC PROGRAMS

Programs Offered

MBA

MSF (Master of Science in Finance)

Management Fellows (Post-MBA Certificate)

The Clark MBA provides students with the skills and vision to make strategic business decisions in the global business environment. Courses are cross-functional and focus on developing the perspective necessary to conquer the toughest business challenges. Choose to concentrate your MBA degree in one of six different fields: accounting, finance, marketing, global business, management information systems, or general management.

The Clark MSF develops skills in applied finance theory. The program curriculum addresses corporate finance, securities markets, risk management and derivatives markets, statistics and modeling, and global finance. Upon completion of the program students will have a portfolio of advanced technical skills and quantitative tools combined with an integrative perspective on the world of finance.

EXPENSES AND FINANCIAL AID

Tuition is charged on a per-unit basis. For the 2007–2008 academic year, tuition is $3,020 per unit. The MBA program is 16 units. The MSF program is 10 units.

Clark University Graduate School of Management offers merit-based awards ranging from 25–100 percent of tuition to approximately 40 percent of full-time students. Part-time students are also eligible for partial scholarship awards.

In addition to merit scholarships and graduate assistantships, full-time domestic students are eligible for a variety of student loan programs. Clark University's Financial Aid staff assists MBA and MSF students in identifying and applying for these funds.

FACULTY

Clark Graduate School of Management's faculty are dedicated teachers, practitioners, and researchers. Our full-time faculty advance their respective fields through unique research, extensive corporate consulting, and active participation in professional associations. Each day they bring this experience into the classroom to the benefit of our MBA and MSF students. Additionally, our full-time faculty is supplemented by an accomplished group of adjunct faculty, many who are practicing professionals in the region's technology, biotech, financial services, and insurance industries.

STUDENT BODY

Clark Graduate School of Management is proud to welcome a diverse student population who represent the multinational nature of business today. Generally between 60 and 70 percent of our full-time students are from countries other than the United States. They come to Clark from a wide variety of industry and functional backgrounds, from large multinational corporations and small family-run enterprises, and at different stages in their careers. This multiplicity of experiences and backgrounds benefits our students as they learn firsthand how to manage in a diverse community.

Clark Graduate School of Management draws heavily on local industries for their part-time student population including technology, financial services, biotechnology, banking, health care, manufacturing, and the non-profit sector.

CLEMSON UNIVERSITY
School of Business

AT A GLANCE

Clemson University is ranked thirty-fourth among the nation's public doctoral-granting universities. The Clemson MBA consistently ranks in the top 50 public MBA programs nationally and the top 90 among all institutions nationwide. Clemson's Career Launch MBA provides an intensive first year in business fundamentals and advanced concepts followed by a second year in a designated focus area. Students pursuing a dual master's degree, earning an MBA and at the same time another master's degree, may choose to focus their MBA on the subject covered by the second master's. Clemson's Career Accelerator MBA is designed for the convenience of experienced working professionals, delivering advanced business concepts one night a week per class in Greenville, South Carolina. Both programs are designed to integrate theoretical knowledge with applied, hands-on experiences.

CAMPUS AND LOCATION

Clemson University is located in South Carolina's lake and mountain region on more than 1,400 wooded acres of the former plantation of John C. Calhoun, on Lake Hartwell. The adjacent town of Clemson is a small college community of around 35,000. The campus is within 45 minutes of Greenville, South Carolina and roughly 2 hours from both Atlanta, Georgia and Charlotte, North Carolina.

DEGREES OFFERED

The Clemson MBA offers a full-time, Career Launch program on the Clemson campus for individuals just starting their career, and a Career Accelerator program for experienced professionals, taught on campus and in the evenings in Greenville, South Carolina at the University Center. MBA students may pursue a dual degree in conjunction with another master's degree, including those from engineering, social science, business, or humanities.

ACADEMIC PROGRAMS

Internationally recognized faculty bring applied and creative knowledge into the learning environment; a seminar series broadens students' exposure to different industries and critical issues; internships, assistantships, and project courses enhance hands-on experience and critical-thinking abilities; a flexible curriculum allows students to follow a designated specialization or pursue a second, dual master's degree, both of which can usually be earned in 2.5 years; and a full-time Career Services Office provides personalized support for effective interviewing, resume writing and help with finding the right internship and job. The Clemson MBA Program is accredited by AACSB International. Participants in the Career Launch curriculum (full-time, on-campus for individuals just starting their career) take an intensive 62-semester-hour program over two years. The first year provides foundation knowledge in core business areas. The second year is flexible, with designated specializations in innovation and entrepreneurial leadership, supply chain and information management, real estate, and marketing management; or courses in a second master's degree. Clemson's Career Accelerator curriculum (part-time or full-time) is for professionals with at least two years of career-relevant work experience. The part-time option is offered in the evening at the University Center in Greenville, South Carolina. Some individuals elect to take this curriculum full-time on-campus, completing their MBA in about a year.

FACILITIES

On campus, the MBA program is offered in historic Sirrine Hall. In Greenville, the program is delivered through the University Center. Clemson Facilities provide modern classroom settings, multimedia capabilities and instructional technologies.

EXPENSES AND FINANCIAL AID

Graduate assistantships are awarded on a competitive basis to highly qualified full-time students, regardless of citizenship. Assistantships pay a stipend of $6,000 per year (2 semesters) for 15 hours per week of work and reduce the student's tuition to a flat fee of, currently, $950 per semester ($1,900 per year). This represents an annual savings in tuition of $7,386 (in state) and $16,610 (out of state).

Full-time students (12 credit hours or more) who do not hold assistantships pay tuition and medical fees as follows:

- SC resident, $4,642/semester
- Out-of-state resident, $9,255/semester

Tuition at the Greenville University Center: $535/credit hour; $918/credit hour.

FACULTY

The Clemson MBA faculty includes Fulbright Scholars, top researchers, research center directors, innovative entrepreneurs, and award-winning teachers and scholars. They have broad work experience and collaborate with industry and government leaders. Over 98 percent of MBA faculty hold a PhD.

STUDENT BODY

Clemson's MBA students hail from all over the world. Overall, about 60 percent of students have science or engineering undergraduate degrees, with 40 percent from social science, humanities, or business. About 30 percent of students are women and roughly 30 percent of students are international, representing more than 15 countries. Hiring companies typically include Michelin, Bank of America, Blackbaud, Ryobi, KPMG International, Wachovia, Newell Rubbermaid, and many other well-known companies.

ADMISSIONS

A number of factors are considered when reviewing applications: work experience (resume), academic credentials (transcripts), standardized tests (GMAT, TOEFL), written essays, interview, and letters of recommendation. A score of at least 550 on the TOEFL is required for all students whose native language is not English. Applicants with more than two years of work experience are a good fit for the Career Accelerator curriculum. Individuals with a non-business undergraduate degree and little or no work experience are candidates for the Career Launch curriculum. Application deadlines for the full-time program are April 15 for international students and June 15 for domestic students. For the part-time program, deadlines are April 15, July 15, and November 1. Visit our Admissions and application website at www.clemson.edu/business/mba/apply.htm for details.

Clemson MBA Office
124 Sirrine Hall
Clemson, SC 29634-1315
Phone: 864-656-3975
Fax: 864-656-0947
Admissions e-mail: mba@clemson.edu
Web address: www.clemson.edu/business/mba

SPECIAL PROGRAMS

Through their graduate assistantships or class projects, most MBA students work with these centers on a variety of real-life projects.

- Center for the Advancement of Marketing and the Social Sciences
- Center for International Trade
- Small Business Development Center
- Spiro Institute for Entrepreneurial Leadership
- Strom Thurmond Institute of Government and Public Affairs

DUQUESNE UNIVERSITY
John F. Donahue Graduate School of Business

AT A GLANCE

Duquesne University's Donahue Graduate School of Business challenges students to reach their potential as strategic, ethical leaders in a global economy. Our destination quality MBA programs emphasize cross-discipline integration for addressing contemporary business issues. Accredited by AACSB International since 1962, the Donahue School is ranked among the top three MBA programs for ethics, and Duquesne University is listed among the top 20 small universities for Faculty Scholarly Productivity. Our graduate business programs are designed to encourage growth, ignite innovation, and connect you with success.

Evening and Saturday MBA programs feature convenient class times and locations for busy professionals. The curriculum provides relevant preparation for confronting today's marketplace challenge. Eleven possible concentrations include supply chain, finance, marketing, health care management, international business, information systems, and more.

An innovative full-time MBA program combines the rigor of an MBA with the economic power of sustainability. It is designed for new generation leaders who want to increase profits while being socially and environmentally responsible. Two concentrations are offered—finance or supply chain—along with hard- and soft-skill development, practical projects, and international study of global best practices.

We also grant masters degrees in taxation, accountancy and information systems management and joint degrees with law, pharmacy, environmental science, health management and other professional schools within the university.

CAMPUS AND LOCATION

Duquesne University's campus overlooks downtown Pittsburgh, the country's "Most Livable City" according to Rand McNally's 2007 Places Rated Almanac. Located a few blocks from headquarter offices of H. J. Heinz, ALCOA, U.S. Steel, PNC Financial, Mellon Financial, Federated Investors, PPG Industries, Deloitte Touche Tohmatsu and other leading corporations, our campus is a convenient choice for part-time students who work in the city and full-time students seeking internships. Shopping, dining, theaters, and professional sports venue are within walking distance.

DEGREES OFFERED

The Donahue Graduate School of Business offers the MBA, MS—Information Systems Management, MS in Taxation, and MS in Accountancy.

Joint degrees include: MBA/JD, MBA/Doctorate in Pharmacy, MBA/MS—Information Systems Management, MBA/MS—Accountancy, MBA/MS—Taxation, MBA/MS—Environmental Science, MBA/MS—Health Management Systems, MBA/MS—Nursing, MBA/MA—Communications, MBA/MA—Social and Public Policy, MBA/MA—Leadership and Liberal Studies.

PROGRAMS AND CURRICULUM

The MBA program features a challenging, well-rounded curriculum. Students may waive some or all of the foundation courses based on academic and professional preparation.

MBA Foundation:

Knowledge and Skills (20 credits): Statistical Thinking, Communication—Written, Communication—Presentation, Applied Ethics, External Financial Reporting, Strategic Uses of Accounting Information, Law for the Executive, Marketing Management, Managing Operations

MBA Core (22 credits): Understanding the Value Chain, Economics for Decision Making, Assessing the Financial Health of the Firm, Information Systems for Managers, Managing a Diverse Workforce, Global Economy, Public Affairs Management, Leading Change in Organizations, Strategy Formulation and Implementation

Electives (15 credits): Students customize their program by choosing from over 80 electives in 11 areas of concentration.

FACILITIES

Rockwell Hall houses technology-rich classroom learning centers that provide access to Enterprise Resource Planning software applications, and networking laboratories. The Investment Center supplies real-time data feeds, news and market data on stocks, bonds, international markets, futures, options, and other securities.

The university's Gumberg Library houses over 500,000 volumes and more than 3,700 journal titles and enables remote access to e-resources and databases.

EXPENSES AND FINANCIAL AID

Tuition is $715 per credit plus a $71-per-credit university fee. Graduate assistantships are available to full-time students on a competitive basis. Student loans are secured through the Office of Financial Aid.

FACULTY

Thirty-one full-time faculty members bring outstanding academic and professional qualifications to the classroom. Our professors hold degrees from prestigious schools such as Princeton, Yale, the University of Michigan, Carnegie Mellon, the University of Pennsylvania, and others. Esteemed adjunct faculty and business executives add real-world experience. Actively engaged in research and publications, many faculty serve as consultants to regional businesses.

STUDENT BODY

350 students are currently enrolled in graduate business programs. Seventy-five percent of the students study part-time. Twenty-five percent of the school's full-time students come from abroad and promote a cosmopolitan environment. The Donahue School is also a school of choice for students sponsored by Fulbright Scholars, Peace Corp Fellows and Muskie Programs.

ADMISSIONS

Applicants are accepted to the Donahue Graduate School of Business on a competitive basis. Admissions criteria include:

- A completed application ($50 application fee waived for on-line applicants)
- Official college transcript(s)
- Two letters of recommendation from employers or former professors
- A two-part essay
- The GMAT (waived for applicants holding a graduate degree or who have demonstrated 10 years of managerial experience)

SPECIAL PROGRAMS

The full-time MBA program emphasizes sustainability. It features rigorous course work, international study, live projects and training in the practical hard and soft skills that employers value most. The school also offers several joint-degree programs in cooperation with other graduate schools at Duquesne University, including Law, and Environmental Sciences.

CAREER SERVICES

Lifetime placement opportunities interview training workshops are offered through Career Services. Career Link enables students and graduates to access online job postings for thousands of employment positions nationwide. The Donahue School's Business Development Director arranges internships and consulting partnerships. The annual MBA Career Fair and fall and spring job fairs provide regular opportunities for networking with alumni and the corporate community.

FLORIDA INTERNATIONAL UNIVERSITY
Alvin H. Chapman School of Business

AT A GLANCE

The Chapman Graduate School of Business is characterized by its rich active learning environment extending beyond the classroom. Miami is recognized worldwide as the "Gateway to the Americas"; students enrolled in the Chapman School's programs are completely immersed in this world-class trade and commerce hub. BusinessWeek has consistently ranked the Chapman Graduate School as the leading business school in South Florida.

According to *U.S. News & World Report's* "America's Best Graduate Schools" (2006) the Chapman School is ranked among the top 20 of international specializations. Courses in the International MBA (full-time) program are taught by faculty who are experts in their field and bring a global business perspective to the classroom. The study abroad and internship opportunities provide students with practical international business experience. The curriculum includes a foreign language component, where students choose between Chinese (Mandarin), Spanish, Advanced Business English or Portuguese. Students electing the China Track participate in a semester-long study abroad and take Chinese language courses both during their year at the Chapman Graduate School and for one month in China.

PARTNER INSTITUTIONS

Fomenting international partnerships is a priority for the Chapman School. The school continues to expand its list of first-class partner institutions. Talks are underway with schools in Australia, The United Kingdom, China, Croatia, Germany, Italy, Poland, and Spain. Members of a global network combine their academic strengths through Faculty exchanges and dual degrees available to outstanding students.

PROGRAMS

Evening MBA, Downtown MBA, Professional MBA, International MBA (full-time), Executive MBA, Executive Master of Science in Taxation, Master of Accounting, Master of International Business, Master of Science in Finance, Master of Science in International Real Estate, Master of Science in Management Information Systems, Master of Science in Human Resource Management, Doctor of Philosophy in Business Administration

CAMPUS AND LOCATION

Florida International University has two major campuses. University Park is the university's main campus and administrative headquarters; the Center for Engineering and Applied Science adjoins University Park. Biscayne Bay Campus in North Miami is Florida International University's other major campus.

The College of Business Administration and the Chapman Graduate School are headquartered in the Ryder Business Building and the Management and Advanced Research Building at University Park. We also offer programs at the Biscayne Bay Campus, Pembroke Pines Campus and the Downtown Center.

ACADEMIC PROGRAMS

At the Chapman School you'll find a set of innovative programs that provide you with the knowledge and skills to advance your career in today's dynamic global marketplace.

Evening MBA—Designed for working professionals with two or more years of professional work experience.

Downtown MBA—Designed for working professionals in the downtown Miami area, classes meet two evenings per week at the Downtown Center.

Professional MBA—A lock-step program offering classes on Saturdays for working professionals with four or more years of professional work experience.

International MBA—A full-time, lock-step program with classes being offered during the day.

Executive MBA—A lock-step program offering classes on Saturdays tailored to the mid-level executive with eight or more years of work experience.

MBA for Public Managers—Tailored for city, county, federal, and state employees. Classes meet Friday evenings and Saturday mornings.

Executive Master of Science in Taxation—Catering to tax professionals and accountants, the program satisfies the requirement for the CPA exam in the state of Florida.

Master of Accounting—Tailored for students who have an undergraduate degree in accounting, the program satisfies the requirement for the CPA exam in the state of Florida.

Master of International Business—Designed for professionals with a business background who wish to further their career in a global business environment. Classes are offered Monday– Thursday evenings.

Master of Science in Finance—Designed for working professionals who wish to broaden their understanding of domestic and global financial services, classes meet Friday evenings and Saturdays in a lock-step format.

Master of Science in Management Information Systems—A lock-step program offering classes on Saturdays for working IT professionals who wish to advance their knowledge of the latest technological advancements in MIS and management of information technology.

Master of Science in Human Resource Management—Tailored for those with careers in Human Resources or those who wish to pursue a career in Human Resource Management, classes are offered on Saturdays in a lock-step format.

Master of Science in International Real Estate—A lock-step program offering classes two evenings per week designed for working professionals who wish to acquire skills necessary in today's international real estate marketplace.

Doctor of Philosophy in Business Administration

FACILITIES

The Chapman Graduate School is located on the 344 acre University Park campus of Florida International University. This is the university's main campus, featuring lush tropical landscaping and impressive architecture. Currently under construction is an 80,000-square-foot facility that will incorporate the latest technology with state-of-the-art classrooms and ample meeting and social spaces for our graduate business students. Students have access to over 100 computers and a wireless network. Also available is an eight-story library that contains more than 1.5 million volumes in addition to substantial holdings of federal, state, local and international documents, periodical and journal subscriptions, institutional archives, maps, microforms, and curriculum materials.

FACULTY

A dynamic force for excellence within Miami's only public, multicampus research university. The dedicated, multicultural faculty of more than 100 in the College of Business Administration includes seven eminent scholars and a cadre of internationally distinguished experts in international business, information systems, operations research, knowledge management, e-commerce, international banking and trade, financial derivatives, consumer marketing and research, global marketing, human resource management, and corporate responsibility.

ADMISSIONS

Particular program-specific requirements are listed on our program websites, which are accessible at: http://business.fiu.edu/chapman.To be eligible for admission, prospective must hold a bachelor's degree or equivalent from an accredited institution and a minimum undergraduate GPA of 3.0 in upper division courses (last 60 credit hours). Official transcripts from all previously attended institutions are required to be submitted in a sealed university envelope. Applications and more information can be found online at http://gradschool.fiu.edu.

GEORGETOWN UNIVERSITY
The McDonough School of Business

AT A GLANCE:

Offering unparalleled access to global business, policy, and thought leaders, the McDonough School of Business is seated at one of the nation's most prestigious universities in one of the world's most influential cities. Founded in 1789, Georgetown University is the oldest Catholic and Jesuit university in America.

The Georgetown MBA Program develops leaders capable of making complex business decisions in a global environment and who are dedicated to serving their companies, society, and humanity. Students gain solid grounding in all core management disciplines, with an emphasis on the global, ethical, and political environment of business. Our commitment to understanding international business is demonstrated by the global curricula, strong presence of international students (more than one-third), and opportunities provided to study business and management in other parts of the world.

CAMPUS AND LOCATION

For more than 200 years, Georgetown University has welcomed aspiring leaders to its campus along the banks of the Potomac River, overlooking the nation's capital. Known for its distinctive energy and style, Washington, DC is home to and abundance of museums, monuments, world-class culture, and big-time sports.

DEGREES OFFERED

The McDonough School offers the following programs: MBA Full-Time, MBA Evening, and International Executive MBA. Additional offerings include the Executive Master's in Leadership and customized executive programs. Georgetown University has many outstanding graduate level programs, and MBA Full-Time students may pursue the following joint degrees: JD/MBA, MD/MBA, MBA/Master's in Public Policy, MBA/MS Foreign Service, and BA/PhD Physics.

ACADEMIC PROGRAMS

Georgetown MBA provides a general management framework with an emphasis on the global business environment. The curriculum's organization—into intensive team-based experiences, courses that integrate various functional areas and elective courses that offer choice—is designed to give students the tools and skills they need to anticipate, analyze, and solve increasingly interrelated, complex business challenges. Students may choose courses according to individual interests and career goals and also pursue summer internships or study abroad programs. All students are required to undertake a foreign residency, the Global Integrative Experience, in which teams work on real consulting projects for companies in cities around the world. Recent locations have included Dubai, Ho Chi Minh City, Johannesburg, Prague, and Sao Paulo.

FACILITIES

Currently, the Georgetown MBA program is located just two blocks from the main campus in the historic Car Barn, a modern facility named for its origin as a streetcar depot. In March 2006, the school broke ground on a new facility at the heart of Georgetown's main campus. To be completed in early 2009, this five-story, state-of-the-art structure will unite the graduate and undergraduate programs under one roof.

Georgetown MBA Full-Time Tuition and Fees for 2007–2008

Tuition (15 credits per semester)°	$37,800
Yates fee	$296
Health insurance	$1,921
Average room and board	$13,650
Average books	$2,260
Average personal expenses	$3,815
Average travel	$2,360
Total	**$62,102**

Merit-Based Financial Assistance: All admitted applicants are considered for partial- and full- tuition scholarships (based primarily on scholastic performance, work experience, and other factors demonstrating leadership potential).

Assistantships: Over $1.5 million is invested to provide opportunities for students to work with faculty and to support administrative offices.

Need-Based Assistance: The Office of Student Financial Services attempts to assists qualified applicants who have financial eligibility to meet their educational and living costs. All U.S. citizens and permanent residents of the U.S. may be considered for federally funded programs.

FACULTY

With an emphasis on global business, innovation, and ethical decision-making, Georgetown MBA faculty prepare students to be leaders of the future. Georgetown's tradition of strong student-faculty interaction is illustrated by faculty accessibility and involvement—collaborating on research projects, advising student organizations, and assisting in career decision-making.

STUDENT BODY

Teamwork, cooperation, and friendly competition are emphasized. Because classes are smaller, students develop close relationships with one another, Faculty, and administrators. This atmosphere of easy camaraderie extends to an active social life, both on Georgetown's campus and in Washington, DC. Students actively shape the future of the school. Through participation in student organizations, students demonstrate leadership skills by planning special events such as professional development activities (including functional days and career treks to domestic and international locations), networking opportunities, and social events.

We enroll smart, hardworking students with some important traits in common: demonstrated leadership ability and accomplishments, cross-cultural awareness, clear career goals, and desire to make a difference in the world. The typical student has worked five years prior to joining Georgetown MBA.

ADMISSIONS

Georgetown University seeks a diverse Student Body and encourages applications from a wide variety of backgrounds. A number of factors are considered, including: intellectual capacity and academic achievement as indicated by transcripts, letters of recommendation, and results of standardized tests (GMAT and, for international students, TOEFL, or IELTS); professional accomplishments and personal strengths as demonstrated by distinctive and useful achievements, ideas, talents, and motivation for graduate business education; and the Admissions interview.

CAREER SERVICES AND PLACEMENT

The MBA Career Management Center is an invaluable resource for Georgetown MBA students. The center has two core functions—career advising/counseling services and recruiting/employer relations—which benefit students in distinct but complimentary ways. Students have access to career counseling services, topical workshops, resume/cover letter critiques, mock interviews, and more. Students also benefit from on-campus employer presentations and interviews for internships and full-time employment as well as 24-hour access to job posting from employers seeking Georgetown MBA applicants.

GISMA BUSINESS SCHOOL

AT A GLANCE

GISMA Business School offers two highly international AACSB-accredited MBA programs in cooperation with Purdue University's Krannert School of Management, Indiana, USA.

The full-time program lasts 11 months; the on-the-job Executive Program lasts 22 months. Both programs are internationally accredited (AACSB, AMBA) and represented in rankings all over the world (e.g., *Financial Times* ranked GISMA's Executive MBA Program twelfth in the world).

GISMA's programs provide a combination of theory and business-related topics moving beyond typical lectures and exams to experiential learning exercises, computer simulations, student consulting projects with real companies and off-site trips to young professionals with work experience. Study groups are diverse with regards to first academic degrees, cultural background, and work experience. For more details please go to www.gisma.com.

CAREER SERVICES AND PLACEMENT

Besides its top-notch academic program, GISMA Business School also offers extensive career counseling and job-finding services. Right from the start, professional coaches are there to help students target careers which are a close match for their individual wishes, abilities, and strengths.

GISMA's 90 percent job-placement rate within three months of graduation says a lot about the effectiveness of Career Center support in areas such as potential evaluation, interview coaching, and assessment center training.

THE CAREER CENTER SERVICE PORTFOLIO AT A GLANCE:

- Potential evaluation, resume and interview coaching, assessment center training.

- Distribution of resumes to key HR contacts at international corporations, both via online portals and in the form of a printed resume book.

- Daily updates on job offers and online job portals, recruiting events, and European programs for young professionals.

- Contacts to GISMA alumni working in global enterprises.

- Free phone, fax, and videoconferencing services for staying in touch with potential employers and recruiters.

- Frequent in-house presentations and visits to companies for valuable insight into the personnel needs of global enterprises. In-house presentations occur four to five times per module (with the program consisting of five modules), while field visits to companies take place once during each module.

- Participation in the annual MBA Career Fair staged in collaboration with other business schools in Germany. Here students get to know potential employers face-to-face in workshops, presentations, and interviews. As a rule, 15 percent of all participating students receive one or more job offers right after the fair.

HOFSTRA UNIVERSITY
Frank G. Zarb School of Business

AT A GLANCE
A university large enough to have extensive resources yet small enough to give students individual attention—this is Hofstra University. With an outstanding faculty, advanced technological resources, and state-of-the-art facilities, Hofstra has a growing national reputation. Yet our average graduate class size is just 13. Hofstra offers a dynamic, vibrant campus life on a 240-acre campus that is a registered national arboretum.

A suburban university just 25 miles from New York City and all the cultural and business opportunities it has to offer. Find your edge at Hofstra University.

CAMPUS AND LOCATION
Hofstra's distinctive 240-acre campus, an accredited arboretum, is located in suburban Long Island, just 25 miles from New York City.

With New York City just a short ride by train or car, students take advantage of the theaters, museums, concerts, and professional sports as well as business internships the city offers. Students can also explore Long Island, which offers world-class beaches, museums, shopping, plus many internship and employment opportunities.

DEGREES OFFERED
MBA in accounting, business computer information systems, finance, health services management, international business, management, marketing, quality management, sports and entertainment management, and taxation

Executive Master of Business Administration (EMBA)

Juris Doctor/Master of Business Administration (JD/MBA) (with the Hofstra School of Law)

MS in accounting, computer information systems, finance, human resources management, marketing, marketing research, quantitative finance, and taxation

Combined BBA/MS in Accounting, Marketing, Marketing Research, and Taxation

ACADEMIC PROGRAMS
The Frank G. Zarb School of Business' accounting and general business programs are accredited by AACSB International. The school offers a challenging 41–48 credit MBA program that includes a 15-credit concentration in a major discipline. Our unique curriculum focuses on analysis, decision making, and management, through which students gain the knowledge they need to succeed in business. The Hofstra MBA program provides students with broad exposure to the functional areas of business, opportunities to gain hands-on experience in a specific field and specialized instruction in the leadership aspects of business.

FACILITIES
The Hofstra campus houses 112 buildings, including 37 residence halls and a fully computerized library containing 1.2 million volumes. C.V. Starr Hall, home to the Zarb School of Business, features a state-of-the-art academic trading room complete with Bloomberg terminals and Internet access at every student seat. Additionally, through Hofstra's online library, students have access 24/7 to about 30 business databases.

EXPENSES AND FINANCIAL AID
Tuition is assessed on a per-credit basis and is $820 for each credit for 2007–2008, with courses carrying two and three credits each. Hofstra is a private institution, so tuition is the same for residents and nonresidents of New York State. Financial aid is available in the form of fellowships, which provide partial tuition credit, and graduate assistantship positions.

FACULTY
The Zarb School employs more than 85 full-time, highly credentialed faculty—90 percent of whom hold the highest degrees in their fields. At the Zarb School every course is taught by a member of the faculty. Students benefit from their teachers' years of experience in business and research and their understanding of the day-to-day challenges of business.

STUDENT BODY
Students enrolled in the graduate programs at the Zarb School form a dynamic, achievement-oriented community. These students represent 10 states and 23 countries. About 25 percent are members of minority groups, 24 percent are international students, and 37 percent are women. Many students in these graduate programs have previous work experience.

ADMISSIONS
Admission is selective. Candidates are required to complete the graduate application and all supporting forms and to submit two letters of recommendation, a resume, a statement of professional objectives, official transcripts from every college or university attended, and scores obtained on the Graduate Management Admission Test (GMAT). International students are also required to submit scores obtained on the TOEFL.

For the most recently admitted class, the middle 80 percent range of GMAT scores was from 450 to 630; the average undergraduate grade point average was 3.2 on a 4.0 scale. All credentials submitted in support of the application for admission are carefully considered in making the admission decision.

Hofstra subscribes to a rolling admissions policy, with suggested filing deadlines of May 1 for fall admission and November 1 for spring admission. Candidates are generally advised of admission decisions no later than four weeks after the application is completed.

SPECIAL PROGRAMS
The Zarb School of Business offers a number of Special Programs designed to meet the needs of its students. We recently added MBA programs in Health Services Management, Quality Management, and Sports and Entertainment Management, and an MS in Quantitative Finance.

Other innovative programs include a JD/MBA program, offered in conjunction with the Hofstra School of Law; and an Executive MBA program, which features a schedule designed to allow working professionals to complete their degrees.

The school's internship program takes advantage of the proximity of New York City, allowing students to gain on-the-job experience in areas such as finance, business, media, advertising, and entertainment.

CAREER SERVICES AND PLACEMENT
A wide variety of career placement opportunities and resources are available to graduate students at the Zarb School. The MBA Career Services actively assists students with a range of services including internships, part-time employment, recruitment activities, and general career counseling. These services are supplemented by the MBA/MS resume book and website.

IMPAC UNIVERSITY
School of Business

AT A GLANCE

IMPAC University develops both its academic curricula and training programs using the strictest standards of quality education and state-of-the-art business practices. The academic curriculum includes master's degrees in business administration, organizational behavior and human resource development, and management information systems, as well as certificate programs in business administration and management information systems.

IMPAC University is accredited by the DETC (Distance Education and Training Council) which is recognized by the Council for Higher Education and authorized by the United States Department of Education.

CAMPUS AND LOCATION

900 West Marion Avenue
Punta Gorda, Florida 33950
USA

DEGREES OFFERED

Master of Business Administration (MBA)

Develop an in-depth understanding of fundamental business knowledge through functional approaches such as accounting, finance, marketing, strategic thinking, and quantitative methods of decision analysis.

Master of Business Administration in Public Administration

A concentration in Public Administration approaches the disciplines of administration and management in the public sector from a broad perspective; ideal for students interested in working for government agencies, city, state, and federal governing units.

Master of Science in Organizational Behavior and Human Resource Development (OBHR)

Discover the consultation process and methods designed to improve an organization's effectiveness, professional and career development, issues related to workforce diversity, transformation of organizational cultures, understanding individual and group behavior in the context of the organization. Examine and engage in the practice of change strategies such as team building, conflict resolution, role analysis, job design, organizational design, and instructional design.

Master of Science in Management Information Systems (MIS)

Focuses on the application of information system concepts to the collection, retention, and dissemination of information for management planning and decision making. A blend of theory and practice that develops skills applicable to complex real-world problems.

ACADEMIC PROGRAMS

IMPAC University offers customized certificate programs for all types of businesses demands. Let us design a Certificate Program to meet your needs. Certificates are offered in the following: Business Administration, Management Information Systems, Executive Leadership Development, Business Basics—Health Care, Business Basics—Retail, Business Basics—Financial Services, Business Basics—Manufacturing

FACILITIES

While IMPAC University is primarily online in its delivery of courses, the university's campus occupies a 60,000-square-foot modern facility in the city of Punta Gorda, Florida. The campus is an educational and training facility that reflects a holistic approach to education. Facilities include several classrooms; a large auditorium; computer support; a research library; formal presentation rooms; and athletic facilities consisting of racquetball, basketball, and volleyball courts; swimming pool; and workout rooms.

The campus is located in historic Punta Gorda on the Peace River, within walking distance of the Fishermen's Village.

EXPENSES AND FINANCIAL AID

Students are expected to pay one-half of tuition and fees at the time of registration each term. Full payment of all tuition and fees is due by the first day of the term for which the student is enrolled.

Payment options: check, money order, cashier's check or credit card.

IMPAC University will make credit-based student loan options available to students who qualify, through specified financial institutions. The university does not currently participate in Title IV federal loan programs.

FACULTY

Our professors are worldwide business professionals, authors, and lecturers who bring their expertise and experience to the classroom. They have worked with our administration to develop a twenty-first-century learning experience based on real-world application of knowledge and skills that will form the basis for your future career success.

ADMISSIONS

Apply online now or download an application at our website, www.impacu.edu. Mail the completed application and the $35 nonrefundable application fee to IMPAC University.

Individuals interested in information about IMPAC University, its programs, and the application process are invited to contact the Admissions Department at Admissions@impac.edu or 941-639-7512.

Students are expected to pay a $250 tuition deposit within two weeks of acceptance to a degree program at IMPAC University. The deposit will be credited toward tuition and fees upon initial registration.

SPECIAL PROGRAMS

Our Center for Organizational Excellence is committed to meeting the educational needs of business. Educational/training needs, consistent with corporate mission and strategic objectives, are determined. Curricula are tailored to address executive education, leadership, supervisory, sales/sales management training, and organizational assessment.

ADDITIONAL INFORMATION

Please contact:

Dr. Joseph Mazurkiewicz Jr., Vice President of Academic Affairs
941-639-7512/941-833-3475
jmazurkiewicz@impacu.edu

P.J. Getchell, Director of Admissions/Records/Registrar
941-639-7512/941-833-3473
pjgetchell@impacu.edu

Barbara Trubenbach, Director of Student Services
941-639-7512/941-833-3474
btrubenbach@impacu.edu

CAREER SERVICES AND PLACEMENT

Office of Student Services provides assistance with the search of career choice for a student, and helps develop resumes and cover letters. The university also provides a role-play room for practicing interview techniques and the interview can be video taped for critique.

INDIANA UNIVERSITY OF PENNSYLVANIA
Eberly College of Business and Information Technology

AT A GLANCE

The Eberly College of Business and Information Technology MBA program (accredited by AACSB International), with its global strategy focus and highly international student and Faculty composition, is designed to sharpen students' managerial, analytical, and decision-making skills so that they can compete in today's global environment. The Eberly MBA program has a long tradition of providing cost-effective preparation for a successful career in business. *Consumers Digest* magazine ranks IUP as number four in the magazine's June 2007 rankings of the "Best Values in Public Colleges and Universities." IUP is the highest-ranked university in Pennsylvania, and is ranked at 40 out of 100 colleges and universities selected for *Kiplinger's Personal Finance* magazine's February 2007 "Best Values in Public Colleges" listing.

CAMPUS AND LOCATION

Indiana University of Pennsylvania enrolls 14,000 students from across the nation and around the globe. With 30,000 residents in the rolling foothills of the Allegheny Mountains, the community of Indiana has been commended in terms of safety. It is a place of tree-lined streets, pleasant neighborhoods, and friendly shops and restaurants. Pittsburgh is a short drive to the southwest from IUP. A variety of recreational activities are available year-round, such as skiing in the winter and swimming or baseball in the summer.

DEGREES OFFERED

Eberly College offers a full-time, on-campus MBA program for young professionals and recent college graduates that can be completed in 12 months. In addition, an executive MBA program for experienced working professionals is available at IUP's off-campus sites in the Pittsburgh area. Other graduate programs include a Master of Science in Information Technology (MSIT) and a Master of Education in Business and Workforce Development (MEd) The college also offers undergraduate bachelor's degrees in accounting, business education, business technology support, entrepreneurship and small business management, finance, general management, human resource management, industrial management, international business, management information systems, and marketing.

ACADEMIC PROGRAMS

The Eberly MBA is a 36-credit integrated general management program with an option to complete concentrations (9 additional credits) in accounting, finance, management information systems, supply chain management, international business, human resource management, and marketing. The MBA courses focus on business applications, current analytical tools and techniques, and a strong emphasis on information technology utilization in managerial problem solving. A wide variety of elective courses are available in the concentration areas, including opportunities for MBA internships with local, national, and international organizations.

FACILITIES

A state-of-the-art $12 million facility houses the MBA classrooms. The Eberly Complex is a beautiful, four-story facility that offers spacious atriums for student interaction and studying, wireless access, a café, a 450-seat auditorium, and a 24-hour computing lab operation. Students of the Eberly College study in one of the most technologically advanced business schools in the country. The Eberly complex houses over 600 computer workstations, over 20 file servers, nine computing labs including a digital production studio, wireless technology, and access to comprehensive online business periodicals and journals databases. The college has a partnership with SAP America, the worldwide leader in ERP (Enterprise Resource Planning) software.

A new Financial Trading Room in Eberly offers students databases and related software to conduct financial analysis and learn valuation techniques, arbitrage techniques, and portfolio risk-management strategies.

EXPENSES AND FINANCIAL AID

Tuition, Pennsylvania residents, 2006–2007: $3024/semester
Tuition, non-Pennsylvania residents, 2006–2007: $4,839/semester
Miscellaneous fees are approximately $500/semester.
On-campus housing costs: from $1,575/semester (double) to $2,208/semester (single)
More than 30 percent of full-time MBA students receive graduate assistantships on a competitive basis that include a full- or partial-tuition waiver and stipend. International students are eligible to compete for partial-tuition waiver during the first semester of study.

FACULTY

Eberly MBA courses are taught by faculty members who have doctoral degrees in their fields of specialization and extensive research and publication track records. Their international backgrounds and/or exposure, experience in industry, and current research projects bring an ideal blend of theory and practice to the MBA courses. Eberly faculty serve as editors to nine national and international journals.

STUDENT BODY

Eberly provides students with an opportunity to learn with a diverse group of individuals. More than 35 percent of the students are from 22 countries other than the U.S., 35 percent have previous business work experiences, and 10 percent are currently working full-time in professional careers. Eberly College takes great pride in the activities and initiatives of its College of Business Student Advisory Council and the members of its 14 student organizations. In addition to having the opportunity to serve on university-wide committees, students serve on Eberly College committees for strategic planning, technology, curriculum, outcomes assessment, student services, and programming.

ADMISSIONS

Requirements for admission include a completed undergraduate degree in any field with a superior academic track record from an accredited institution, GMAT scores, academic/professional letters of recommendation, and the applicant's career goal statement. The average GMAT score of admitted candidates is 530; the average undergraduate grade point average is 3.1. International applicants must also submit an official TOEFL score report with a minimum score of 200 (computer-based test score) and an affidavit of financial support indicating availability of funds to study in the U.S. For information and a complete application packet, visit www.eberly.iup.edu/mba; contact Dr. Krish Krishnan, Eberly College MBA Program, 301 Eberly College of Business and Information Technology, IUP, 664 Pratt Drive, Indiana, PA 15705; or e-mail iup-mba@iup.edu or Krishnan@iup.edu.

CAREER PLACEMENT AND SERVICES

IUP assists MBA students with job placement through its recruiting programs, computerized job-search database, resume referrals, individual counseling, workshops, and job fairs. Many major corporations recruit on the IUP campus, and recent MBA graduates have accepted positions with companies such as Accenture, Arthur Anderson, BearingPoint, Citizens Bank, Coca- Cola, Deloitte Touche Tohmatsu, Deutsche Bank, Dow Chemical, GE, IBM, Merrill Lynch, MetLife, Novell, Renault, Rockwell International, Siemens, Symantec, Walt Disney, and World Bank. During 2006–2007, the Eberly College held two major career fairs that attracted over 35 businesses and governmental agencies. Separately, 34 employers came to campus for one-on-one interviews.

JACKSONVILLE STATE UNIVERSITY
College of Commerce and Business Administration

AT A GLANCE
Jacksonville State University's College of Commerce and Business Administration offers a Master of Business Administration (MBA) degree that ranks in the top 10 percent of all MBA programs in the world. The program allows for students to obtain either a general MBA or the MBA with a concentration in accounting.

Students are attracted from around the world to our program; approximately 20 percent of JSU's MBA's are international students. While at JSU, students enhance their knowledge of business fundamentals and further their professional development. The end results are successful graduates that are tomorrow's business leaders.

CAMPUS AND LOCATION
JSU is located in a diverse community of 10,000 set in the natural scenic beauty of the southern Appalachians. The local community, as well as the university's proximity to large cities (75 miles from Birmingham, Alabama and 125 miles from Atlanta, Georgia), provides a rich variety of activities and resources for students.

Business programs are housed in the 69,794-square-foot Merrill Building. Multimedia capabilities and instructional technology are integrated throughout the classrooms and Facilities.

DEGREES OFFERED
The CCBA offers the MBA degree with options for either a general degree or a concentration in accounting. The MBA is offered as an evening program and serves both part-time and full-time students. Classes are offered in 3-hour blocks, one evening per week. Traditional courses are available on campus, and an online MBA is also available.

ACADEMIC PROGRAMS
The JSU MBA is a program with a broad-based appeal. Students are provided with a quality program and an outstanding educational value. Opportunities exist for students to participate in internships and independent studies in addition to the traditional courses in the basic business disciplines. Exciting, real-world case studies are incorporated throughout many of the courses. Ten courses (30 semester hours), including electives make up the general MBA, while the accounting concentration requires an additional 3 semester hours and includes 9 semester hours of accounting courses. With careful planning, the program may be completed in 12 to 18 months.

FACILITIES
The state-of-the-art facilities of the Merrill Building provide an outstanding arena for learning. The CCBA uses the latest communications and course delivery technology to help students network effectively.

EXPENSES AND FINANCIAL AID
The CCBA provides one of the best returns on investment available. This nationally accredited program provides a top-notch, affordable education as it prepares students to enhance their careers.

2006–2007 Academic Year Tuition and Fees

In-state students: $225/semester hour

Out-of-state students: $450/semester hour

Housing, textbooks, and personal living costs: approximately $10,000/year

Merit-based financial aid is offered to outstanding candidates each year. The criteria for these awards mirror requirements for admission: academic record, work history, leadership experience, and test scores. Domestic and international applicants are eligible for graduate assistantships. Graduate assistantships provide a salary of approximately $520 per month and paid tuition for six hours of course work each semester.

FACULTY
Engaging. Experienced. World-renowned. CCBA MBA Faculty combine exemplary teaching and academic research, bringing expertise, talent, and dedication to the program. Many are involved with consulting practices that keep them "in-the-know" and on the pulse of innovative practices and emerging business trends. Course content combines the latest trends in business management with traditional theories that have withstood the tests of time. MBA Faculty hold doctoral degrees from leading academic institutions and bring a diverse mix of business experiences into the classroom, assisting students both academically and professionally.

STUDENT BODY
CCBA MBAs are not passive recipients of education but active players in determining the type of MBA experience delivered. Due to the large number of part-time students enrolled in the program and the fact that many students work full-time, little time is available for club participation. However, students use the classroom and interactions with other students to demonstrate leadership, involvement, and collaboration.

MBA students average nearly 3 years of work experience, a GPA of approximately 3.15 (4.0 scale), and an average GMAT score of approximately 450.

ADMISSIONS
The CCBA MBA seeks candidates who have demonstrated the ability to complete a rigorous academic program and who possess the potential for success in a professional environment. The admission review process includes consideration of a number of factors that are all important in the admission decision: academic background; standardized tests (GMAT and TOEFL); references; and the student's reason for desiring an MBA.

CAREER SERVICES AND PLACEMENT
JSU's Career Placement Services staff assists in helping students achieve their career goals. Each fall, they sponsor a Career Fair for all business students and each spring a panel of very successful JSU alumni are brought to campus to interact with graduates in an effort to assist with career preparation. Staff members are advocates, consultants, and marketers, assisting with on-campus interviews and resume preparation. They are coaches that believe that a person's most important asset is the ability to learn to effectively market himself or herself.

LOYOLA UNIVERSITY—NEW ORLEANS

Joseph A. Butt, S.J. College of Business

AT A GLANCE

The business environment of today, and surely that of tomorrow, is characterized as one of constant change, uncertainty, and greater connectivity through technology. Our MBA program has been designed to prepare individuals to thrive in this dynamic, global marketplace.

At Loyola University—New Orleans, we provide a distinctive mix of faculty excellence and individualized attention to create a superb learning environment in which you can excel. By studying with us, you will enhance your ability to critically analyze business issues, work in a team environment, appropriately apply technology, and effectively communicate your ideas. Equally important is the emphasis we place on providing you the foundation necessary to make ethical decisions in today's complex society.

CAMPUS AND LOCATION

Loyola University—New Orleans is located in the heart of the old residential section of New Orleans. This gracious Southern city is one of the most fascinating in the United States. Often described as more European than American in nature, it is known for its jazz, cuisine, the French Quarter, café au lait, the architecture, streetcars, riverboats, a bustling seaport, the history, the writers, and Mardi Gras. New Orleans offers world-class events and Facilities such as the New Orleans Jazz and Heritage Festival, the Crescent City Classic, the Sugar Bowl, the Audubon Zoo, and the Aquarium of the Americas. Music weaves through every aspect of life in the Crescent City, from one of the oldest opera companies in the nation to jazz bands in street parades.

Our school is located five miles, by streetcar, from the Central Business District on a historic avenue in the heart of one of the most beautiful neighborhoods. Across the street you will find Audubon Park, a perfect place to enjoy jogging and picnicking among ancient oak trees or strolling past tranquil lagoons to the Audubon Zoo and the Mississippi River.

DEGREES OFFERED

Loyola University—New Orleans offers a traditional MBA program that can be taken at a full-time or part-time basis. Additionally, we offer a JD/MBA program in coordination with the law school.

MARYMOUNT UNIVERSITY

AT A GLANCE

Marymount's School of Business Administration offers graduate programs that provide a strong foundation in business principles, as well as instruction in the latest technological advances. Faculty advising, peer networking, and a cutting-edge education afford a wide array of professional opportunities. Marymount graduates find employment in the many government, corporate, and technology organizations that are constantly recruiting qualified employees in the Washington, DC region and beyond. Graduate students can take advantage of full- or part-time study options, with an emphasis placed on evening and Saturday classes that are convenient for the working professional. Classes are small and taught by expert faculty with "real-world" experience who work closely with students to help them achieve their educational and professional goals. At the graduate level, Marymount offers career-advancing programs in Business Administration (MBA), Health Care Management, Human Resource Management, Legal Administration, Information Technology, and Management. Graduate certificates are also available in many of these disciplines. Highlights of Marymount's graduate programs are detailed in the Special Programs section of this profile.

LOCATION AND ENVIRONMENT

Marymount's Main Campus and Ballston Center are located in Arlington, Virginia, just minutes from Washington, DC. The public Metrorail system connects the university with the entire metropolitan Washington area. The university also maintains a free shuttle service that connects the Main Campus, Ballston Center, and Ballston-MU Metro station. The university's proximity to the nation's capital provides countless cultural and research resources, as well as professional opportunities. Marymount's Reston Center opened in Spring 2007 and is located in western Fairfax County where the strong northern Virginia economy has created a demand for a well-educated, capable workforce.

DEGREES OFFERED

For 2007–2008, the following graduate degree and certificate programs will be offered:

- Business Administration (MBA) with tracks in finance, health care management, human resource management, information technology, international business, legal administration, and marketing

- Health Care Management (MS)

- Human Resource Management (MA)

- Information Technology (MS), with tracks in computer security, project management and technology leadership, and software engineering

- Legal Administration (MA)

- Management (MS)

GRADUATE CERTIFICATE PROGRAMS

Computer Security and Information Assurance, Health Care Informatics, Human Resource Management, Information Technology, IT Project Management and Technology Leadership, Instructional Design, Leadership, Leading and Managing Change, Management Studies, Organization Development, Paralegal Studies, and Project Management.

ACADEMIC PROGRAMS

The Marymount MBA allows students to tailor their studies to meet specific career objectives with specializations in finance, general business, health care management, human resource management, information technology, international business, legal administration, and marketing. As of Fall 2007, Marymount offers bachelor's and master's degrees in Information Technology (IT) to support the increased demand for IT professionals in the region and across the country. The new program builds on previous programs in computer science and information systems to provide employees with graduates who have strong technical skills as well as business knowledge in such areas as project management. The MA in Human Resource Management is recognized as a premier program in the DC region. Beginning in Fall 2007, the university will offer an HRM leadership cohort program at the Reston Center for mid- and executive-level HR professionals. The MS in Health Care Management applies core business principles to the health care industry. The program is fully accredited by the Commission on Accreditation of Health Care Management Education.

FACILITIES

The Main Campus consists of the Main House, academic buildings, residence halls, the Emerson G. Reinsch Library, and the Lee Center. Academic Facilities on the Main Campus include computer labs and wireless access areas. The Reinsch Library provides print, electronic, and audiovisual material to supplement Marymount's curriculum as well as computers, video viewing stations, and study rooms. Marymount's Ballston Center, located in the Ballston professional district, is home to Marymount's School of Business Administration. The Ballston Center houses classrooms, seminar rooms, computer labs, the Truland Auditorium, the Electronic Learning Center, and the Verizon Information Security Lab. This state-of-the-art security lab provides students with hands-on experience with cybersecurity challenges. The Reston Center, an adult education center located in northern Virginia's thriving business and technology region, has eight classrooms, including two executive conference/seminar rooms, a computer lab, student lounge, and administrative offices.

TUITION AND FEES

Graduate tuition for the 2007–2008 academic year is $655 per credit hour. Each term students will be assessed $6.70 per credit up to a maximum fee of $80.40 per semester to support computer enhancement. There is a one-time new student fee of $30.

FINANCIAL AID

Financial aid is available through graduate assistantships, loans, federal work study, and several program-specific scholarships. These include the National Science Foundation Scholarship for Service in Information Assurance and Computer Security, the HR Leadership Scholarship, and The William G. McGowan Scholarship. The Virginia Tuition Assistance Grant (TAG) is available to Virginia residents.

FACULTY

88 percent of all full-time instructional faculty have terminal degrees. In the School of Business Administration, 97 percent of all full-time instructional faculty have terminal degrees.

ADMISSIONS

Students are admitted on a full- or a part-time basis for the September and January semesters and for the summer sessions. All applicants must submit an application with a $40 fee, transcripts of postsecondary work, and two letters of recommendation. (The letters of recommendation are optional for School of Business students, but a resume is requested.) Most programs also require standardized tests and interviews. Contact Graduate Admissions for specific details.

ADDITIONAL INFORMATION

For more information about Marymount's graduate business programs, contact the Office of Graduate Admissions at 703-284-5901 or 800-548-7638, e-mail grad.Admissions@marymount.edu, or visit www.marymount.edu.

MCMASTER UNIVERSITY
DeGroote School of Business

AT A GLANCE

The DeGroote School of Business has earned a strong reputation as a center for academic excellence and innovation. An integral part of our innovative culture is our focus on experiential learning that enables students to gain hands-on experience through co-op work terms; internships; and assignments that stimulate learning, lead to personal development and discovery, and enhance their ability to function effectively very quickly after moving into their career paths.

As a pioneer in the creation of the Co-op MBA model of learning, the DeGroote School of Business is the premier co-op MBA school in Canada. We also offer full-time and part-time MBA options that meet the complex needs and learning styles of the leaders of tomorrow.

Our Health Services Management MBA specialization is the only program of its kind in Canada. It combines expertise found in McMaster's renowned Faculty of Health Sciences and the School of Business with hands-on training gained through work experience in health care organizations.

The DeGroote School of Business is also home to the AIC Institute for Strategic Business Studies which includes an endowed Chair in Investment and Portfolio Management, two Professorships, an MBA program with specific focus on strategic business studies, and a certificate program on business valuation in continuing education for industry professionals. Generous scholarships have also been established in order to help recruit top talent into this competitive program.

CAMPUS AND LOCATION

McMaster campus is at the western end of Lake Ontario. Area attractions include Cootes Paradise, the Bruce Trail, the Niagara Escarpment, the Waterfront Trail, and the Royal Botanical Gardens.

DEGREES OFFERED

We offer a general MBA as well as specializations in accounting and financial management services, finance, strategic marketing, the management of innovation and new technology, supply chain management, e-business, strategic business valuation, and health services management. Additionally, we offer a joint CMA/MBA program specializing in management accounting. The goal of the MBA Program at DeGroote is to develop innovative leaders in the field of management.

ACADEMIC PROGRAMS

In our first year we emphasize the learning of business fundamentals in a variety of areas. As an introduction to our program, students will learn fundamental skills, which they will use and develop throughout our program and their future careers. Our orientation activities include communication and thinking skills workshops as well as modules on team-building, presentation skills and the case study method, as well as career planning, and MBA student survival skills.

The second year of our program offers several options (specializations) which allow a student to choose a course of study which optimally enhances his/her current skills profile.

FACILITIES

The McMaster University Library consists of Mills Memorial Library (humanities and social sciences), Innis Library in Kenneth Taylor Hall (business), the H.G. Thode Library of Science and Engineering, and the Health Sciences Library in the Health Sciences Centre. The university library is a member of the Association of Research Libraries.

Officially opened to the public in June 1994, the museum contains five exhibition galleries, a paper center and an educational access gallery. The Museum of Art offers a year-round program of exhibitions, ranging from historical displays to present-day artistic investigations either organized by the McMaster Museum or loaned by such institutions as the Art Gallery of Ontario and the National Gallery of Canada. The museum also hosts its own lunchtime talks, visiting artist talks, seminars, tours, workshops, and concerts.

TUITION AND FINANCIAL AID

Financial assistance is available to our students in the form of teaching assistantships, scholarships, bursaries, and loans. Preference is given to advanced-level students in awarding teaching assistantships, while the majority of scholarship offers are made to entering students.

FACULTY

Our faculty members are selected for their research, teaching skills and their ability to generate new business knowledge. Their connections in the business community help to provide students with the opportunities they need to pursue the practical side of their business education and to facilitate their post-graduate activities.

STUDENT BODY

MBA students come from a variety of undergraduate backgrounds in the sciences, arts, and engineering, representing both experienced professionals and new graduates, and have interests in all areas of business. MBA Co-op students are ideally suited for special project assignments for a variety of organizations and can also handle on-going operational responsibilities as needed.

ADMISSIONS

Requirements for entrance to this program depend on the option chosen. The core requirements are based on academic performance in the student's final two years of undergraduate work as well as the GMAT score. On the margin, work experience and community leadership are also considered. Our goal is to ensure that our graduates all complete the program with a base of work experience, either prior to their MBA or within the MBA through the co-op program.

Candidates for the MBA Co-op Program are selected through a personal interview with co-op staff in which communications and interpersonal skills, initiative, leadership, and general experience are assessed to ensure they can both succeed and benefit from their co-op experience.

SPECIAL PROGRAMS

The Management Accounting Specialization prepares students for a career and certification as CMAs (Certified Management Accountants), the strategic financial management professionals in business.

CAREER SERVICES AND PLACEMENT

We are very committed to developing strong relationships with our employer partners by meeting their needs on several levels. In addition to the Commerce Internship and MBA Co-op Programs, we provide, through a joint venture with our own student organizations, full Business Employment Services, which include on-campus recruiting services, excellent on-site interview facilities, company information sessions, job postings, and customized services as required. We can also connect employers with student groups for educational/promotional seminars, student projects, and short-term contract work.

All these services are available within the School of Business, which allows us to provide the employer with in-depth information about our students, their academic programs and statistics on our graduates.

MONMOUTH UNIVERSITY
School of Business Administration

AT A GLANCE

A comprehensive and scholarly environment. A blend of rich tradition and advanced technologies. A community of individuals, unique in their strengths, united in their goal to succeed—and to lead. These are some of the ingredients driving our dynamic, interactive, personalized approach to education.

We look forward to your arrival at Monmouth University. Here you can develop your strengths; energize your life; define your future. Monmouth University: Where leaders look forward.

CAMPUS AND LOCATION

The university is located in the safe residential town of West Long Branch, New Jersey—an attractive community near the Atlantic Ocean, about an hour and a half from New York City and Philadelphia. Monmouth enjoys close proximity to many high-technology firms and financial institutions, and a thriving business-industrial sector. The university's 156-acre campus, considered one of the most beautiful in New Jersey, includes a blend of historic and contemporary architectural styles.

We offer graduate information sessions in the evenings, library visits, and other opportunities to meet with admission representatives. Check the website for details: www.monmouth.edu/visit.

DEGREES OFFERED

- Master of Business Administration (MBA), with optional tracks in accounting, finance, or real estate
- Accelerated MBA
- MBA with concentration in health care management
- Post-MBA certificates in health care management or accounting

ACADEMIC PROGRAMS

The School of Business Administration is accredited by the Association to Advance Collegiate Schools of Business (AACSB). Alumni include more than 3,300 successful entrepreneurs, managers, and executives from a broad spectrum of the business world. Monmouth's MBA program includes courses in the key business disciplines of accounting, finance, economics, marketing, management, and business law. The program is constantly improved to reflect evolving business practices and theories. Strong emphases are placed on international, ethical, and technological perspectives within a broad strategic framework.

FACILITIES

While always meeting our community's evolving and expanding needs with new facilities and modern technologies, Monmouth also celebrates history. Wilson Hall, Monmouth's administrative center, is designated a National Historic Landmark. The Guggenheim Cottage, a wing of the Library, is on the National Register of Historic Places. Monmouth features a campus-wide computer network, numerous computer labs and cybercafés, and wireless technologies. Monmouth offers a technologically advanced academic environment with a growing number of web-enhanced courses and online tools.

EXPENSES AND FINANCIAL AID

Students may qualify for federal financial aid by filing the Free Application for Federal Student Aid (FAFSA), available online at www.fafsa.ed.gov.

The cost per credit for graduate classes during the 2007–2008 academic year is $710. Additional Information about expenses is available online at www.monmouth.edu/admission/financialaid/pay/tuitionfees/gtuitionfees.asp. Academic scholarships are available to graduate students in selected majors.

FACULTY

Recognized for their scholarly achievements by peers in their fields, the Faculty members of the School of Business Administration provide a challenging classroom environment. They bring insight from their research and real-world professional experience into the classroom. Faculty members also serve as advisors and mentors to students, in many cases not only during the course of their studies but also after they graduate from the university.

STUDENT BODY

Approximately 6,000 undergraduate and graduate students are members of the Monmouth University community. Our graduate students are a blend of working professionals, and recent graduates of undergraduate programs who have chosen to move directly into graduate study.

ADMISSIONS

Graduates of colleges of recognized standing, whose records show evidence of ability to do graduate work, may apply for admission.

Regular admission requirements for graduate degree programs offered through the School of Business Administration include either of the following:

1. Possession of a four-year baccalaureate degree and either
   a. GMAT minimum score of 500, or
   b. GMAT minimum score of 450, and a minimum total of 1000 when a GMAT is added to 200 times the GPA, or
   c. CPA or CFA licensure
2. Possession of a master's or doctoral degree (MS, MD, JD, PhD, EdD, etc.)

The Accelerated MBA requires appropriate academic business preparation for admission.

The deadline for application is July 15 for the fall semester; November 15 for the spring semester; and May 1 for summer sessions. Qualified applicants are given consideration after the deadline on a space-available basis.

SPECIAL PROGRAMS

The Accelerated MBA is a 30-credit, fast-track program designed for students looking for a time-saving alternative to a traditional two-year MBA program. Applicants must have earned a bachelor's degree in business within the last seven years from a recognized business program and meet other admission requirements. The Master of Business Administration with a concentration in health care management combines the generalized management preparation of an MBA with intensive training necessary to successfully manage within the health care industry. If you already have your MBA and are interested in the health care field, consider the certificate program in health care management. Monmouth's Kislak Real Estate Institute offers two options: a certificate program, designed for real estate professionals who want to round out their education, and a track in real estate as part of the university's MBA program. The REI is the only academic credit-bearing real estate program in New Jersey. All real estate courses are taught by credentialed practitioners.

ADDITIONAL INFORMATION

Kevin Roane, Director of Graduate Admission
Monmouth University
West Long Branch, NJ 07764-1898
Telephone: 800-320-7754, 732-571-3452
E-mail: kroane@monmouth.edu
www.monmouth.edu

PACIFIC LUTHERAN UNIVERSITY
School of Business

AT A GLANCE

Pacific Lutheran University has a long tradition of providing excellent undergraduate (BBA) and graduate (MBA) business education. Nearly all faculty come from industry and have doctorate degrees; in addition, 95 percent of the faculty have significant international experience. The school program has been accredited by AACSB International since 1976 and enjoys a strong reputation among businesses locally and globally. Alumni can be found all over the world leading businesses.

The PLU MBA program is distinctly different in approach and design to meet the specific needs of working professionals. Classes are conveniently held in the evenings; the program takes just 20–22 months to complete (or just 16 months for the accelerated program); and students have the option of tailoring their course work to earn a general management MBA or an MBA with an emphasis in technology and innovation management (TIM), entrepreneurship and closely held business, or health care management.

The dynamic curriculum is designed around the latest trends and theories in business and focuses on these four foundational cornerstones: 1) a global perspective and appreciation for diversity, 2) an ethical and responsible approach to business decisions, 3) a focus on effective leadership, and 4) a predisposition for innovation and change within any organization.

The BBA program combines a rigorous upper-division curriculum with a strong liberal arts foundation. Students tailor their degree with one of the four concentrations: professional accounting, finance, human resources and organizations, and marketing management. The BBA program takes a hands-on approach to education emphasizing internships and international study away programs. Classes are small (averaging 22 students), and students are encouraged to join one of the many clubs or organizations to enhance their learning and experience.

CAMPUS AND LOCATION

Pacific Lutheran University is located in Tacoma, Washington. Tacoma is just one hour south of Seattle and a 30-minute drive north of Olympia, the capital of the state. Residents of Washington enjoy the natural beauty of the Pacific Northwest and the easy access to nearly all outdoor activities: skiing, biking, hiking, kayaking, and sailing, to name just a few. Tacoma and Seattle also enjoy thriving theater and arts communities.

DEGREES OFFERED

Master of Business Administration (MBA)

Areas of emphasis: General Management; Technology and Innovation Management; Entrepreneurship and Closely Held Business; Health Care Management; Academic Programs; MBA—General Management; MBA—Technology and Innovation Management; MBA—Health Care Management; MBA—Entrepreneurship and Closely Held Business

FACILITIES

The Morken Center for Learning and Technology is home to the School of Business and Departments of Math and Computer Science, and Engineering. The $21 million facility is LEED Certified Gold by the U.S. Green Building Council for environmental friendliness and conservation. The center has wireless access, lab classrooms, research labs, project workrooms, a multimedia lab, electronics lab, a café selling organic foods, and a public events room for guest speakers and conferences.

EXPENSES AND FINANCIAL AID

Choosing a university is among the most important, most life-shaping investments you will ever make. Given that PLU offers academically rigorous classes, a supportive campus community unlike any other, and prepa-

ration for success in the world, you'll find that it is time and money well spent. The MBA program charges a per-course tuition rate of $2,350, which is guaranteed for six consecutively enrolled semesters. The overall MBA program costs $35,250. All tuition rates reflected are accurate for the 2006–2007 academic year.

FACULTY

The School of Business faculty is PhD qualified, and nearly all have significant industry and international experience. Faculty members are not only leading researchers and publishers in their fields, but are also dedicated to the learning experience of the student. All PLU classes are taught by professors—there are no teaching assistants in front of the classroom. Professors are accessible and hold office hours for students who need extra help with course work, and they are often invaluable resources for internship and job leads as they maintain their active roles in the business community.

STUDENT BODY

PLU is known as a selective university. The average incoming undergraduate GPA is 3.60, and graduate GPA is 3.30.

The MBA program recommends at least two years of work experience prior to applying. This creates a slightly older population of students with a wealth of work experience to share in the classroom. The average age in the MBA program is 29–30.

ADMISSIONS

Admission Requirements for Graduate MBA Students

The PLU MBA program is competitive and selection is based on several criteria. The Graduate Admission Committee bases decisions on a holistic assessment of the individual merits of each applicant. We look for students who:

- Have demonstrated proven success in a challenging undergraduate or master's level program
- Desire academic, personal, and career challenges
- Communicate clearly and demonstrate leadership capability in a variety of settings
- Serve in their community, workplace, church, or school
- Will bring a unique perspective to the classroom environment

For application information please visit http://www.plu.edu/mba/admission.html.

SPECIAL PROGRAMS

The MBA program, with the support of the PLU Business Network Alumni Association and the Dwight Zulauf Fund, puts on the annual MBA Executive Leadership Series bringing in business executives to share their insights and stories with MBA students. This is not only a networking opportunity but also an invaluable experience for students to hear about the current trends in industry firsthand.

CAREER SERVICES AND PLACEMENT

The School of Business partners with the Career Development and Student Employment Office to mentor students in the job search. The School of Business also has a mentorship program that matches alumni with students interested in specific industries as well as the PLU Business Network Alumni Association that puts on four networking events per year for students and alums. The PLU Business Network also supports student workshops throughout the year that relate to career planning, financial management and networking.

PURDUE UNIVERSITY
Krannert School of Business

AT A GLANCE

When you're ready to take your career to the next level with an MBA or other master's-level business degree, your choice of a school should be the same as the organizations you could one day help lead. That choice is Krannert. What makes our graduates a top pick of recruiters and other business professionals? Companies know that when they hire Krannert students, they'll get employees who work hard and work smart—team players with strong analytical skills, entrepreneurial drive, and a solid ethical foundation. Initially, the choice is yours to make. It begins with your application to one of Krannert's three full-time master's programs in management or one of its three part-time executive programs. It continues with your exploration of the school's diverse option areas and elective course work, study abroad and internship opportunities, and career services offerings.

CAMPUS AND LOCATION

Founded in 1869 and named after benefactor John Purdue, Purdue University began its journey with 6 instructors, 39 students, and a mission to provide agriculture and mechanic arts education.

STUDENT BODY

System-wide enrollment of 69,098 students; West Lafayette enrollment of 38,712 students (Fall 2005); students from 50 states and 130 countries.

LOCATION

Main campus in West Lafayette, Indiana (126 miles southeast of Chicago, 65 miles north of Indianapolis). Statewide university system includes five campuses and numerous teaching and research sites.

DEGREES OFFERED

Master of Business Administration (two years); Master of Science of Industrial Administration (11 months); Master of Science in Human Resource Management (two years); Master of Science in Finance (one year); Executive Master of Business Administration (two years); Executive International Master of Management (two years); Weekend Master of Business Administration (three years); PhD in Economics and Management; Master of Business Administration—International Management (11 months, offered in Germany only)

ACADEMIC PROGRAMS

The synergistic MBA program is stimulating, intense, and develops highly effective business management professionals. The in-class experience includes numerous simulations of management decision-making scenarios, extensive interaction between the faculty and the students, personal communication and presentation skills enhancement, and team exercises. In addition to the in-class experience, there are various programs for continued growth, including a Friday Management Development Series aimed at bringing leading-edge practices and emerging topics to the students.

FACILITIES

Rawls Hall houses 13 electronically equipped classrooms, a professional career center, a multimedia-based auditorium, 25 breakout rooms, distance-learning facilities, and sophisticated computer labs. The building is named for Krannert master's alum, Jerry S. Rawls in recognition of his generosity. Rawls, the president and CEO of Finisar Corp., donated $10 million to Krannert, the largest gift in Krannert's history.

EXPENSES AND FINANCIAL AID

The Krannert School provides two types of merit-based financial support.

Graduate Awards: Graduate awards are awarded on the basis of academic merit and other criteria that may be specified by the sponsoring organization.

Some awards are restricted to U.S. citizens or permanent residents. Applicants who are identified as award candidates during the Admissions review process will be invited to campus, upon admission, to further assess their eligibility for an award. Graduate awards are awarded to first-year students only.

Graduate Assistantships: Graduate assistantships within the Krannert Graduate School of Management are traditionally awarded to competitive applicants at the time of admission. This gives students the chance to earn a monthly stipend and tuition remittance by working for Krannert Faculty and staff. Some students secure graduate assistantships outside of the School of Management based upon their special skills and expertise. These assistantship opportunities outside of Krannert are not advertised and are obtained through an individual job search.

FACULTY

Faculty is the cornerstone of Krannert's programs. In addition to the knowledge faculty convey, they are dedicated to providing students with a positive educational experience. That means moving beyond typical lectures and exams to experiential learning exercises, computer simulations, and field trips. They also supervise off-site projects with corporate partners. Krannert faculty are more than educators, they are also recognized leaders in their fields of study. They serve as editors or on the editorial boards of more than 50 professional journals, and the research productivity of the school's management program is ranked among the world's best. Many of our faculty members provide consulting services to *Fortune* 500 companies, while others work on projects funded by government agencies, private foundations, and corporate sponsors.

STUDENT BODY

When asked to describe the atmosphere at Krannert, students often use words such as "diverse," "welcoming," "family-friendly," and "team oriented." With fewer than 400 students enrolled at any given time, we're relatively small compared to other top-ranked institutions. People say hello when you walk through the halls. Faculty and staff members know your name and freely share their time. Krannert encourages informal interaction through weekly social hours, club events, evening and weekend outings, and other recreational activities. The opportunities extend to the Purdue campus and surrounding community, which provide a safe, clean environment and a variety of cultural offerings. Those who desire the occasional bustle of a big city don't have far to travel, either. Chicago is a two-hour drive to the north, while Indianapolis is only an hour south.

ADMISSIONS

The high quality of Krannert students drives the success of the school's programs. We offer an outstanding program precisely because we accept only those applicants with the most outstanding backgrounds. Our review of your application begins with an emphasis on these factors: academic record, GMAT scores, work experience, and additional requirements for international applicants.

These factors will help us determine your ability to take on the challenges of a master's program. Just as important, we look at your ability to contribute to a dynamic learning environment and Krannert's ability to help you reach your personal and professional goals. For that reason, we ask applicants for essays, letters of recommendation, and information about community involvement. Occasionally, our Admission Committee will also request interviews to get to know a student better.

CAREER SERVICES AND PLACEMENT

For information on Krannert Graduate Career Services, please visit www.krannert.purdue.edu/departments/gcs/Home.asp.

ST. JOHN'S UNIVERSITY
The Peter J. Tobin College of Business

AT A GLANCE
For nearly 80 years, the Tobin College has offered future business leaders a strong foundation in management education. Our flexible curriculum, network of over 35,000 alumni worldwide, talented and dedicated faculty, outstanding resources, and commitment to a values-based business education all make the college unique in providing business leadership skills for life.

CAMPUS AND LOCATION
Tobin has three residential campuses in exciting New York City as well as a campus in Rome, Italy.

Queens Campus
8000 Utopia Parkway
Jamaica, NY 11439
Tel: 718-990-2600
One of the city's most recognized campuses, St. John's 105-acre Queens campus is in a quiet residential area. On-campus residents halls are an attractive addition and make New York City easily accessible.

Staten Island Campus
300 Howard Avenue
Staten Island, NY 10301
Tel: 718-390-4500
Overlooking New York harbor, the Staten Island campus is in New York's most suburban borough. Manhattan is easily accessible and apartment-style housing is available for students.

Manhattan Campus
101 Murray Street
New York, NY 10007
Tel: 212-277-5113
This 10-story building in lower Manhattan is just a few blocks from Wall Street, Battery Park City, and the city's Financial Center.
Ideally located at Murray Street and the West Side Highway, the distinctive building features athletic facilities, a caféteria, and a library with one of the world's largest collections of insurance-related texts. There are a limited number of student residences available and, due to high demand, are available on a first-come, first-served basis.

Rome Campus
Rome Graduate Center
Via Santa Maria Mediatrice, 24
Rome, Italy 00165
Tel: 011-39-06-393-842
Located at the historic Pontificio Oratorio San Pietro, the Rome Campus offers St. John's first overseas MBA program. The program, launched in Fall 1995, is designed to provide students with access to the professional expertise of international corporate leaders. A master's program in International Relations also is offered at the Graduate Center.

DEGREES OFFERED
The MBA degree is offered with specializations in accounting, taxation, decision sciences, executive management, finance, financial services, international business, international finance, marketing management, insurance, actuarial sciences, risk management, and computer information systems for managers. Successful completion requires a minimum of 36 credit hours; additional credits may be required, depending on previous business and economics course work. The degree can be completed on either a part- or full-time basis. The Master of Science (MS) degree is offered in taxation, accounting and in risk and insurance. Advanced Professional Certificates (APCs) are available to individuals who have completed the MBA degree and are interested in accruing additional skills. Eighteen credits are required for completion of the APC.

ACADEMIC PROGRAMS
St. John's recognized early on the importance of globalization for future business leaders and, as a result, is one of the first American business schools to establish a presence internationally in Rome, Italy. Today, it is a thriving center for students interested in the intersection of business and international markets. The MBA curriculum offers enhanced flexibility for students to design a program that best meets their own professional and personal objectives. Courses in social responsibility, managing in today's complex environment, and the ethics of management are required of all students and serve as its foundation. The Tobin College is fully accredited by AACSB International—The Association to Advance Collegiate Schools of Business.

FACILITIES
The Main Library of the university is on the Queens campus. Together with the collections of the Loretto Memorial Library on the Staten Island campus, the Law School Library, the Oakdale Campus Library, the Kathryn and Shelby Cullom Davis Library in Manhattan, and the Rome campus library, the total university library collection numbers 1.7 million volumes and includes more than 6,000 periodic subscriptions. Extensive computer facilities include over 90 multimedia classrooms and more than 2,000 computers available for student use.

EXPENSES AND FINANCIAL AID
Tuition in 2007–2008 is $830 per credit. An additional $75 general fee per term is due at the time of registration. A limited number of graduate assistantships are awarded, based on academic merit.

FACULTY
The faculty at the Tobin College of Business is drawn from leading institutions all over the world. They are complemented by business practitioners who regularly serve as adjunct instructors or co-teachers. Ninety percent of the faculty members hold the highest terminal degree in their fields and six members are internationally recognized Fulbright Scholars; numerous others are frequent consultants to business and the business news media.

STUDENT BODY
The Tobin College has succeeded in launching the careers of more than 35,000 business leaders worldwide. Special opportunities exist for students to network with alumni of the college for the purposes of career information, development, and internships.

ADMISSIONS
All applicants must possess a baccalaureate from an accredited institution or the international equivalent. Candidates are encouraged to begin the application process early and should submit, in addition to the $40 nonrefundable application fee, official transcripts from all undergraduate, graduate, and professional schools attended. In addition, results of the GMAT taken within the last five years, a resume, letters of recommendation, and a personal statement should also be submitted. Details of these requirements are available at the Office of Admissions or from the college's website. Applicants whose native language is not English must also submit the results of the TOEFL.

SPECIAL PROGRAMS
In addition to study abroad programs, selected students can participate in the Executive-in-Residence program, which provides special opportunities to serve as consultants in partnership with senior corporate executives in solving business challenges. An alumni-funded Student Investment Fund also enables students to obtain hands-on investing experience under the guidance of seasoned Faculty members and alumni with vast Wall Street experience.

SYRACUSE UNIVERSITY
Marvin J. Whitman School of Management

AT A GLANCE
This is a time of great momentum and excitement in the history of our school. With a revamped curriculum, construction underway for our new building, and a significant gift that has resulted in a named school, the Martin J. Whitman School of Management is strengthening its reputation and raising its prominence among business schools worldwide. The Whitman School is proud to nurture graduates who—like our namesake, trailblazing financier Martin Whitman—mix a shirtsleeves work ethic and entrepreneurial mindset with high integrity, exceptional business acumen, social conscience, and a lifelong commitment to mentoring and learning. Our focus is simple—developing entrepreneurial managers who will become leaders in an era of global competitiveness and technological advancements. We do this in an environment that promotes firsthand experiences where students can hone their communication and interpersonal skills as well as their analytic and problem-solving capabilities, giving our students a dynamic and relevant business education.

CAMPUS AND LOCATION
One of the oldest schools in the state of New York, SU is also one of only 62 research universities in the U.S. to be elected to the prestigious Association of American Universities (AAU). SU offers a remarkable combination of academic excellence and a relaxed lifestyle in upstate New York.

The 220-acre campus rests on a hill overlooking the city of Syracuse, providing an ideal blend of urban and peaceful environments. SU consists of 170 buildings surrounding a historic central quadrangle. The university has more than 15,000 students; over 70 percent live in the 13 residence halls on campus. The student/faculty ratio is 12:1.

SU is a 20-minute walk from downtown Syracuse, a midsized city with many recreational and cultural options, including parks, museums, art galleries, and a symphony orchestra. Syracuse enjoys four distinct seasons and is only a four-hour drive from New York City.

DEGREES OFFERED
Full-Time MBA: This program is traditionally completed in two academic years, with the summer between the first and second years spent in an internship.

Independent Study MBA (iMBA): This is a limited-residency program that is typically completed in three years. Students from around the world spend a week on the Syracuse campus prior to the start of each trimester (August, January, May) in intense class sessions with faculty and classmates.

Part-Time MBA: Students can complete this program in three years, taking classes in the evenings. Courses are offered Monday through Thursday and meet either once or twice a week.

Accelerated MBA: MS in Accounting

This program is completed in one to three years—the number of credits required varies and depends upon the candidate's academic preparation

MS in Media Management: Typically completed full-time in one calendar year, this program may be reduced to 36 credits for candidates who have successfully completed coursework in communications

PROGRAMS AND CURRICULUM
The Whitman School's two-year MBA curriculum integrates the teaching of traditional management fundamentals and the innovations necessary for success in today's rapidly changing business world. All degree programs are accredited by AACSB International—The Association to Advance Collegiate Schools of Business.

The second year of the program offers students a high degree of flexibility. Students have the opportunity to select one or two areas of concentration such as accounting, finance, marketing management, and general management, as well as several progressive concentrations, including entrepreneurship, innovation management, management of technology, and supply chain management. Students spend the summer between their first and second years in either an internship placement or in a study abroad program.

The school also works in cooperation with other graduate schools at Syracuse University to offer combined degrees in law, environmental science, media, public administration, and other disciplines.

FACILITIES
Classrooms facilitate creative use of educational technologies. Quality spaces for public events and informal interactions, including a state-of-the-art auditorium, a Grand Hall, a café, plentiful team breakout rooms, and comfortable conversation areas tucked throughout the building. A lounge and a computer cluster specifically for graduate students will builds identity and cohesion.

EXPENSES AND FINANCIAL AID
The Whitman School of Management offers students numerous forms of financial assistance, including scholarships, fellowships, assistantships, and loans. Scholarships, fellowships, and assistantships are all awarded on a merit basis. The application deadline for fellowship consideration is January 15. The application deadline for scholarships is March 1. Loans can be applied for at any time.

STUDENT BODY
International students comprise 50 percent of the Student Body at the Whitman School. The Office of International Students (OIS) offers services ranging from immigration advice to personal counseling. OIS is housed in its own building and is a friendly place for all students to visit, relax, read a newspaper, and talk with staff. The office organizes many social and cultural events to promote on-campus diversity.

ADMISSIONS
Admission to the Whitman School of Management MBA and MS programs is highly selective. The Whitman School seeks candidates who can contribute to the school and who aim to assume leadership roles in organizations around the world—individuals who have displayed the drive, the leadership potential, and the intellectual capacity to achieve their goals.

Individuals who have obtained the equivalent of a U.S. bachelor's degree from a fully accredited university are eligible for admission to the Whitman School.

The Admissions Committee uses several criteria in their admissions decisions, including the applicant's academic achievement, communication skills, previous work history, and standardized test scores. A completed application form must be accompanied by two letters of recommendation preferably from past supervisors, a current resume, all academic transcripts, a GMAT score, essays, and a $65 application fee. The Whitman School strongly encourages students to participate in an evaluative interview, which is usually conducted on campus. Since the admissions decision involves several criteria, there are no set minimums for the GMAT or GPA average. The 2003 entering class had an average GPA of 3.1 (on a 4.0 scale) and an average GMAT score of 576.

The Whitman School strongly encourages students to apply online through www.princetonreview.com. The deadline for applications is March 1.

TEMPLE UNIVERSITY
The Fox School of Business and Management

AT A GLANCE

With more than 5,500 students and 154 full-time faculty, The Fox School is the largest, most comprehensive business school in the region and among the largest in the world. Established in 1918, the school has a long history of innovation in education, introducing new curriculum and programs in advance of current business trends.

With over 42,000 graduates, two-thirds of whom live and work in the Philadelphia metropolitan area, The Fox School is the primary source of management talent in the region. This important network of business associates continues to connect with The Fox School by mentoring and advising students; speaking at events; introducing employers to the school, resulting in internship, recruitment and hands-on learning opportunities; and providing financial support.

CAMPUS AND LOCATION

The city of Philadelphia is the cornerstone of life at Temple. One of the largest cities on the East Coast, Philadelphia is home to a variety of forward-looking businesses, progressive work in technology and science, and thriving artistic output. While the city is the product of a rich history, it is also a center for twenty-first-century innovation and culture.

Temple delivers its full-time MBA program entirely at the smaller downtown campus in Center City, while the part-time MBA program is conducted at both Center City and the Fort Washington Campus. Classes at Center City are held during the day and in the evening, while only evening classes are offered in Fort Washington.

DEGREES OFFERED

MBA, PhD—Business Administration; MS—Actuarial Sciences; MS—Accounting and Financial Management; MA, PhD—Economics; MS—Finance; MS—Financial Engineering; MS—Healthcare Finance; MS—Human Resource Management; MS—Management Information Systems; MS—Marketing; MS, PhD—Statistics

ACADEMIC PROGRAMS

The Fox School of Business offers 11 areas of concentration to a mix of both full-time and part-time students. With programs in accounting, business administration, economics, finance, general and strategic management, health care management, human resource administration, international business administration, international business (tri-continent), management—information systems, and risk management and insurance, Fox gives graduate students an unusually wide array of choices.

The Fox MBA is a full-time, two-year cohort program, and The Fox Professional MBA provides management education to working professionals on a part-time basis. Both programs prepare individuals to assume leadership roles in corporations, as well as in governmental and nongovernmental organizations which also require business management skills.

The Fox School also offers specialized master's degrees which provide an educational experience with a more concentrated scope in a specific business discipline.

FACILITIES

Temple University's facilities are on the cutting edge of technology and expose today's students to tomorrow's innovation. Home to the TECH Center, the largest student computer lab in the country, Temple students have access to nearly 2,000 computers in over a dozen computer labs across campus. With a campus that is nearly 90 percent wireless students have limitless access to information and 24-hour access to their courses through the Temple Blackboard system. Temple also strives to bring technology into the classroom by outfitting them with "smart" technology as can be seen in Temple's Tuttleman Learning Center, which offers 20 high-tech classrooms.

EXPENSES AND FINANCIAL AID

At current tuition rates, in-state students can expect to pay about $27,500 USD for a Fox MBA degree, while out-of-state and international students can expect to pay $40,500 USD in tuition for the entire degree program. Tuition for specialized master's degree programs can range from $15,000 to $25,000 for Pennsylvania residents and $22,000 to $36,000 for non-Pennsylvania residents, depending upon the number of prerequisite courses needed to complete the program.

Temple University's Office of Student Financial Services assists eligible MBA students in obtaining State and Federal Government grants and guaranteed loans. Students may begin to file the FAFSA for 2006–2007 during the application process, and can file for loans with lenders after being offered admission to the MBA.

The Fox School of Business and Management has a limited number of scholarships for full-time students with high academic grades and test scores. Scholarships are offered at the time of acceptance into the Fox School. The Fox School also has a limited number of graduate externships for assignments in academic and administrative departments.

FACULTY

On all of our campuses, the Temple Faculty includes instructors who are distinguished and active members in their fields. Professors bring the critical perspective of scholars and the practical knowledge of their discipline to their classrooms.

ADMISSIONS

Application Deadlines for MBA, MA, or MS Applicants

Full-time, fall semester only: June 1 (March 15 if you possess international credentials requiring evaluation)

Part time MBA/MS, fall semester: June 1

Part time MBA, Full time MA/MS spring semester: September 30

JD/MBA MD/MBA applicants: April 1

At The Fox School we have rolling Admissions, meaning the open positions for candidacy fill up with each round. Even though we do not have a pre-established quota for accepted students; we do try to establish a target amount each year. Applying early allows you to be considered among the first applicants for candidacy at The Fox School of Business.

It usually takes two weeks for an Admissions decision after we determine that the application is complete. This is exclusive of the time it takes the graduate school to evaluate the applications. For international transcripts it can take up to an additional four weeks to receive an answer.

TEXAS CHRISTIAN UNIVERSITY

The M.J. Neeley School of Business

AT A GLANCE

At the Neeley School, we bring together highly motivated professionals and exceptional faculty in a personalized, interactive environment. Neeley is one of an elite group of accredited business schools to offer a 12-Month Accelerated MBA degree along with the 2-year Full-Time MBA. Learning here goes beyond the classroom to hands-on experiences that impact the bottom line. Our students stay on top of the quickly changing business environment through frequent and meaningful interaction with business leaders. Our commitment to you is an experience that is personal, connected, and real.

ACADEMIC PROGRAMS

At Neeley, we make sure that our MBA isn't a "one-size-fits-all" program. We understand that students have different backgrounds and career goals, and have crafted options to best meet your needs.

- The 12-Month Accelerated MBA is targeted to individuals with significant academic and professional background in business who are looking to move forward within their career field. This option allows you to build upon your business background and focus your course work on your specific career interest. The Accelerated MBA provides the benefits of a full-time MBA without an extended absence from the job market and with less impact on your financial, career, and personal life.

- If you are planning to make a broader career change, the comprehensive two year Full-Time MBA programs allows you to explore career options and add new experiences to your résumé. Whether your degree is in business, engineering or ballet, the Full-Time MBA gives you the academic background, practical experience, professional development, career coaching, and networking opportunities you need to position yourself for your next career move.

WHAT YOU LEARN

A Neeley MBA taps into your existing strengths and shores up your shortcomings to create an extraordinary skill set. Not a cookie-cutter skill set but a dynamic package of hard and soft skills, analytical and intangible assets that represent the best of you. You learn how to make insightful decisions in a world of perpetual change, and how to communicate, collaborate, and lead diverse groups to turn those decisions into action.

HOW YOU LEARN

Not only do you work day to day with faculty who are recognized leaders in their fields, you put that knowledge to work outside the classroom. We call it Experiential Learning, and it's based on real-world experiences that recruiters tell us they look for when filling top positions. You do real work for real clients with real life challenges. Combine all of that with high-profile internships, interaction with leading executives and international business trips. It's only natural to think outside the box when you don't spend all your time inside of one.

PERSONAL

We're small by design at Neeley, so the lessons you learn here will reach much farther than the glow of a PowerPoint presentation in a two hundred-seat lecture hall. Not only will you know your professors—you'll also come to know that these are the very people improving and transforming business in the real world. The same holds true for the hundreds of business executives who visit here. You can discuss ideas in actual conversations with C-level executives—not just sit in the same room with them. We take a personal approach to your career too. Throughout your time here, we give you one-on-one coaching with hiring experts, charting a course for your self-improvement that yields the greatest results.

CAREER AND PLACEMENT

It's impossible to be at Neeley and not make important connections. We bring top companies to you for internships and jobs, and we even take you to top companies. Our alumni know that Neeley students excel in the workplace. Plus, Neeley is right at home in the thriving Dallas/Fort Worth Metroplex. Literally hundreds of big-name businesses are located here, and more are coming every day. But we don't stop there. With international trips (Chile, Italy, Germany, China, and India are some of the places we visit), you gain insight into just how the business world is intricately connected. You learn to spot new opportunities in unexpected places, and to value new insights and old customs.

What good is knowledge if you can't put it into action? Lots of people can read books and take tests. The real test is how you perform in a business organization. Companies turn to our MBA students to work on real-world projects, to identify challenges, evaluate opportunities and generate strategies. These projects intensify your business knowledge and sharpen your skills. They look pretty good on a resume, too.

UNION GRADUATE COLLEGE
School of Management

AT A GLANCE

Union's emphasis is on highly effective education that provides the skills and knowledge that today's employers want. As a result, Union students graduate ready to make an impact in their chosen professions—immediately and over the long term. Union Graduate College is a leader in innovative professional graduate education. Our master's degree programs are selective, student-centered, and taught by committed teacher-scholars. Because our programs are rooted in strong community partnerships, they also take full advantage of the economic and cultural opportunities of New York's Capital Region.

CAMPUS AND LOCATION

Union Graduate College offers a unique blend of strong, traditional liberal-arts-based graduate education with cutting-edge programming that leverages the cultural and economic vibrancy of New York's Capital Region/Tech Valley. Union Graduate College is located in the city of Schenectady, New York, about 150 miles north of New York City. Centrally located, the Graduate College is close to many metropolitan cities; Albany is located 15 miles from the campus. New York City and Boston are only a three-hour drive away; Montreal, Canada is only a four-hour drive away. The Adirondack Region (a camping and recreational area) is about a one-hour drive from Schenectady.

DEGREES OFFERED

The Master of Business Administration programs prepare students for functional, managerial, and executive-level positions in a wide variety of manufacturing, service, and public policy enterprises. The Master of Business Administration is accredited by the AACSB International; one of only 28 graduate-only accredited MBA programs in the world. The MBA in Health Systems Administration prepares graduates for careers as administrators and analysts in health care, governmental, and private-sector organizations with strong health care interests. The program is accredited by both the Accrediting Commission on Education for Health Services Administration (ACEHSA) and AACSB International. It is one of only 21 prestigious dually accredited health administration programs worldwide. The Graduate College offers three joint-degree programs: With Albany Law School, students can obtain a JD and MBA; with Albany College of Pharmacy they offer a joint pharmacy degree. In cooperation with Union College, Union's undergraduates can earn a bachelor's degree and MBA.

PROGRAMS AND CURRICULUM

MBA (General): The MBA core courses provides a solid foundation in all aspects of business administration including Probability, Statistics, Financial Accounting, Managerial Accounting and Finance, Economics, Marketing, Operations Management, Managing People and Business Law. The MBA courses beyond the core allows the student to tailor the program to his or her individual interests with a specific focus on Finance, Economics, Marketing, Operations, General Management or Global Business. Capstone course's principle is the development of a comprehensive business plan for a real company.

MBA Program Course Requirements: 10 required core; 2 required advanced; 8 elective advanced; MBA Health Care Management

MBA Health Care Management core courses include Introduction to Health Systems, Health Systems Management, and Managing Ethically in a Global Environment.

MBA Health Care Management required courses beyond the core include Health Care Finance, Health Economics, and Health Systems Marketing and Information Systems.

MBA Health Care Management elective courses include Quality Systems Management, Management for Information Systems, Group Practice Administration, Issues in Long Term Care, and Biomedical Ethics.

Capstone course is typically the last course taken and is intended to integrate all the courses studied in the MBA Healthcare Management program.

Program Course Requirements: 10 required core; 7 required advanced; 3 elective advanced

Both Programs: 12 of the 20 courses must be completed at the Graduate College.

A maximum of 8 waivers and transfers combined are allowed.

The internship is a valuable component of both MBA Programs and is required of all full-time MBA students. Most full-time students complete a 400-hour internship while in the MBA Program.

FACILITIES

Schaffer Library holds over 570,000 volumes, 3,400 current serials, government documents, a periodicals reading room, faculty studies, and individual study spaces. The Murray and Ruth Reamer Campus Center provides space for social and community activities and services for the entire campus.

EXPENSES AND FINANCIAL AID

Tuition for the MBA program for the academic year 2006–2007 is $22,000. Resource fees are $150. There is no on-campus housing for graduate students.

Merit-based assistance is available to both U.S. and non-U.S. citizens. Competitive scholarships are awarded. Graduate student loans, co-op opportunities, part-time employment, and affordable graduate housing are available.

FACULTY

The Graduate College's distinguished faculty are readily accessible to students outside the classroom. With an average class size of 15, classes include open discussion and intensive feedback.

STUDENT BODY

There is almost an even number of full- and part-time students, ranging from accelerated undergraduates to CEOs, doctors, lawyers, and entrepreneurs. Nineteen percent are international students.

ADMISSIONS

Applicants may seek admission to the MBA programs as matriculated graduate students throughout the year on a rolling basis. Notification of an Admissions decision is made within four weeks of receipt of a completed application. Students may begin their study in any term. International students whose native language is not English must take the TOFEL exam.

Criteria for Admissions in to the MBA programs include a student's postsecondary academic record, career objectives, personal recommendations, and standardized test scores. In general, a minimum GPA of 3.0 is expected in previous academic work. Applicants must submit a $60 application fee, essays, three letters of recommendation, official GMAT test scores, and official transcripts of all previous academic work.

CAREER SERVICES AND PLACEMENT

MBA Faculty, the Associate Dean for Career Placement, and the Career Development Center offer a variety of opportunities for MBA students and alumni to explore career paths and learn the job search and career development skills needed to advance in their longer-term careers. Services and resources include one-on-one career counseling, self-assessment, workshops, videotaped mock interviews, resume development and critique, an online resume referral services, and on-campus recruiting.

UNIVERSITY OF CALIFORNIA—LOS ANGELES
Anderson School of Business

AT A GLANCE

Consistently ranked among the top-tier business schools in the world, UCLA Anderson School of Management provides management education to some 1,600 students enrolled in full-time, part-time, and executive MBA programs, as well as academic master's and doctoral programs. Award-winning Faculty renowned for their research and teaching, highly selective admissions, successful alumni, and world-class Facilities designed by the architectural firm of Pei Cobb Freed & Partners combine to provide an extraordinary learning environment.

As a leader in advancing knowledge about business models, decision making and market behavior, UCLA Anderson's faculty and research centers are influential in shaping theoretical and practical developments in critical areas ranging from global capital markets, information technology management and organizational strategy to entrepreneurship and leadership.

CAMPUS AND LOCATION

Just five miles from the ocean, UCLA lies in one of the most attractive areas of Southern California. It is bordered on the north by the protected wilderness of the Santa Monica Mountains and on the south by Westwood Village. Some 313 buildings on 419 acres house the College of Letters and Science plus 11 professional schools and serve more than 37,563 students.

DEGREES OFFERED

Master of Business Administration (MBA); Master of Science (MS); Doctor of Philosophy (PhD), Concurrent Degree Programs; Management MBA/Computer Science MS; Management MBA/Latin American Studies MA; Management MBA/Law JD; Management MBA/Library and Information Science MLIS; Management MBA/Medicine MD; Management MBA/Nursing MSN; Management MBA/Public Health MPH; Management MBA/Public Policy MPP; Management MBA/Urban Planning MA

ACADEMIC PROGRAMS

The school offers a variety of programs leading to graduate degrees at the master's and doctoral levels. These include both an academic (MS) and professional (MBA) master's, as well as a 21-month Executive MBA Program designed for working managers who are moving from specialized areas into general management, and a three-year Fully Employed MBA Program for emerging managers. A PhD in management is also offered, as are a certificate Executive Program and research conferences and seminars for experienced managers.

A rigorous, flexible curriculum allows each student to learn the fundamentals of business and management and at the same time to customize the program by selecting specialized subjects for exploration in greater depth.

FACILITIES

The Center for Health Services Management is operated jointly by the Anderson School and the School of Public Health. Organized as a partnership with the health services management community, the center's activities are designed to be supportive of management practitioners in the health care community.

The Center for International Business Education and Research (CIBER) actively increases international business research across the campus through the direct funding of Faculty research travel, graduate student research assistantships, and academic conferences.

The Center for Management in Information Economy (CMIE) focuses on current management processes and practices being used in businesses and organizations involved in the creation, management, and delivery of digital information as a key component of their products and services.

The Harold Price Center for Entrepreneurial Studies provides academic and extracurricular activities that prepare MBA candidates for the challenge of business management in entrepreneurial environments.

EXPENSES AND FINANCIAL AID

At this time, the mandatory student fees for the Anderson MBA Program are $26,039 for California residents and $35,576 for non-California residents. These fees are subject to change and do not include mandatory health insurance, course material fees or activity fees. The total cost for the FEMBA program for the academic year 2007–2008 is $27,500 (estimated). This year-one total cost covers tuition, university fees, books and supplies, use of the Anderson School's computing Facilities, selected speaker events and campus parking.

All admitted full-time students who are U.S. citizens or permanent residents may apply for need-based financial aid. A limited number of research assistant and teaching assistant positions are available. Students may apply for these positions once they arrive on campus. All admitted students are automatically considered for Dean's Fellowships, which are based on the overall strength of the application for admission. A limited amount of fellowship support is available to exceptional applicants. No separate application is needed.

FACULTY

The mainstay of UCLA Anderson's high-quality management education programs is its esteemed, international faculty. Each year, UCLA Anderson faculty members publish papers in leading scholarly journals, receive recognition for research excellence, provide leadership in and beyond UCLA, and serve as inspirational teachers and mentors.

STUDENT BODY

John E. Anderson Graduate School of Management students come from diverse professional and educational backgrounds and seek equally diverse personal and professional goals. Whether they pursue the professional MBA, the academic MS, or a PhD in management, they graduate with a broad understanding of people and organizations and with a sound technical background in the economic and mathematical concepts of management planning and decision making.

ADMISSIONS

To be considered for admission, candidates must hold a four-year bachelor's degree from an accredited college or university and must submit a fully completed application for admission (see application checklist for details). International applicants should check for degree equivalency on the Admissions website.

The Admissions Committee evaluates applicants' prospects as leaders in management and their projected ability succeed in, benefit from and contribute to the UCLA Anderson MBA Program. Committee members carefully consider personal and academic background information, GMAT scores, TOEFL scores (for most international applicants), achievements, awards and honors, employment history, letters of recommendation, and college and community involvement, especially where candidates have served in leadership capacities.

Candidates are strongly encouraged to apply early. We began accepting applications on September 1, 2006. Candidates may apply to only one Anderson MBA program in a given year. There are separate application processes for each program.

For more information, contact the UCLA Anderson Admissions Office at 310-825-6944 or via e-mail at mba.Admissions@anderson.ucla.edu.

UNIVERSITY OF CALIFORNIA—RIVERSIDE
A. Gary Anderson Graduate School of Management

AT A GLANCE

Balancing the Art and Science of Management: At the A. Gary Anderson Graduate School of Management (AGSM), our MBA curriculum provides a balance of the art and science of management. This recognition of the dual challenges that face today's manager permeates one's educational experience at AGSM. The Anderson School offers an intimate educational environment were classes are small by typical MBA standards, professors are accessible to students, and the business community is very supportive and closely involved with the school's myriad of activities.

CAMPUS AND LOCATION

The 1,200-acre Riverside campus of the University of California is conveniently located some 50 miles east of Los Angeles, within easy driving distance of most of the major cultural and recreational offerings in Southern California. Enrollment at UCR is approximately 13,000, nearly 10 percent graduate students. The campus, with modern classroom buildings, beautiful commons, and 161-foot Carillon Tower, is designed to support the academic and research programs as part of its assigned mission in the University of California system.

A city of 250,000, Riverside has several major shopping malls, a symphony orchestra, an opera association, two community theaters, an art center, and many restaurants in proximity to the campus.

ACADEMIC PROGRAMS

The MBA curriculum balances the art and science of management, with an emphasis on managing through information, and recognizes the global context of management. The program stresses the essential interdependencies that exist across functional areas, emphasizing the development of superior management skills as well as theoretical foundations. Great importance is placed on teamwork, relationships, and communication.

The program is designed to accommodate the unique requirements of both career professionals and full-time students. Courses are offered in the evenings to permit career professionals to complete the MBA on a part-time basis. In this way, full-time and part-time students take classes together, enriching the educational experience of both.

FACILITIES

The university library is the focal point of research and study at UCR. The collection includes more than 1.8 million bound volumes, 13,316 serial subscriptions, and 1.6 million microforms.

The MBA program is housed in Anderson Hall. MBA students have access to the latest computing equipment, including PC platforms and powerful UNIX workstations.

EXPENSES AND FINANCIAL AID

Several kinds of financial assistance are available. These include fellowships, teaching assistantships, and research assistantships. Applicants indicate interest in support on the application form. Loans and work study may be applied for through the UCR Financial Aid Office.

FACULTY

The A. Gary Anderson Graduate School of Management has a renowned, multicultural Faculty, representing excellence in its respective areas. Faculty members have doctorates from world-class universities and publish research in top journals in their fields. Faculty members also have industry and consulting experience and teach in executive programs and workshops.

STUDENT BODY

Diverse backgrounds and experiences are characteristic of students in the AGSM MBA program. The average age of students is 27, with an age range from 21 to 46. Approximately 50 percent are women, and 16 percent are members of minority groups. Sixty-five percent of the students have an average of three years' work experience in fields ranging from medicine to manufacturing; 35 percent come directly from undergraduate programs.

Approximately 50 percent of AGSM's MBA students are international students. The International Services Center provides special assistance to international students and their dependants.

ADMISSIONS

Admission is open to eligible students from all undergraduate majors. Admission is based on several criteria, including the quality of previous academic work as measured by GPA for the last two years of undergraduate work, scores on the Graduate Management Admission Test(GMAT), letters of recommendation, and potential for success in the program.

A course in quantitative methods is a prerequisite to the program. Students may be admitted without this course but must meet this requirement during their first two quarters in residence.

Application deadlines for domestic students are May 1 for fall, September 1 for winter, and December 1 for spring. Deadlines for international students are February 1 for fall, July 1 for winter, and October 1 for spring. Applications are processed on a rolling basis, and decisions are made when files are complete. For further information, go to www.agsm.ucr.edu.

SPECIAL PROGRAMS

Global Focus: Most AGSM required courses include a global perspective, with recognition of the international issues that affect each functional area. In addition, electives in many of the functional areas provide opportunities for in-depth studies of international topics.

The management synthesis course at the end of the first year of study and the required internship are key elements of the AGSM MBA program.

ADDITIONAL INFORMATION

Technology Environment: The AGSM Microcomputer facility consists of 50 Intel-based microcomputers. Within the School, the facility is utilized for teaching, class demonstrations, theses, statistical analysis and Faculty research projects and as a tool for effective management decision making. One of AGSM's goals is to graduate students with wide-ranging computer skills that help them become successful in the modern business world.

The Business School Network: Relationships with the corporate community are an integral part of the AGSM MBA program. The AGSM Advisory Council assists the school with developing and maintaining a relevant curriculum and interacts with MBA students at numerous events. Every year, the school also names two distinguished business leaders as AGSM Fellows. Each Fellow spends one day each quarter speaking to classes and consulting with MBA students. These and other activities ensure that each MBA student has the opportunity to develop a network of business contacts prior to graduation.

A full range of career planning and placement services is offered through the MBA Career Management Center. The center is staffed by professional counselors to address the specific career needs of graduate business students. Services available include on-campus interviews, career seminars and workshops, individual counseling, an alumni career network, a resume directory, and an extensive career library including computerized employment databases.

UNIVERSITY OF COLORADO AT BOULDER
Leeds School of Business

AT A GLANCE

The Leeds School of Business develops people who are knowledgeable in the best business practices, can think critically, communicate effectively, adapt to and lead change, act ethically, value diversity, and are competitive in the global economy. The school promotes academic excellence, fosters strong relationships with the surrounding business community, and emphasizes ongoing business research.

Strong historical ties to the business community enable the school to provide students with the most practical educational experience during their academic careers. The Business Advisory Council (BAC) is composed of high-level executives who provide advice, counsel, and an outside perspective to the dean and his administration while advocating for the school within the external community. Council members spearhead major parts of development programs, strengthen the school's nationwide network in business and political arenas, and provide significant input to curriculum design.

CAMPUS AND LOCATION

Boulder is widely rated as one of the best places to live, and it was recently ranked third among the "Smartest Small Towns" by Bizjournals.com. The campus has been ranked fourth "Most Architecturally Successful" campus in the country, and *Outside* magazine rated CU Boulder the second-best college in turning out "smart grads with top-notch academic credentials, a healthy environmental ethos and an A-plus sense of adventure."

DEGREES OFFERED

The Leeds School of Business offers programs leading to the Master of Business Administration (MBA), Master of Science (MS) emphasis in accounting, and Doctor of Philosophy in business administration (PhD) degrees. The Leeds School also offers a part-time MBA program called the Evening MBA that leads to the same degree as the full-time MBA program. Dual-degree options available in the MBA program include Juris Doctor/Master of Business Administration (JD/MBA), Master of Business Administration/Master of Arts (MBA/MA) in fine arts, Master of Business Administration/Master of Arts (MBA/MA) in anthropology, Master of Business Administration/Master of Arts (MBA/MA) in Germanic and Slavic Languages, Master of Business Administration/Master of Science (MBA/MS) in environmental studies, Master of Business Administration/Master of Science (MBA/MS) in computer science, Master of Business Administration/Master of Science (MBA/MS TLEN) in telecommunications. Dual-degree options are not available in the Evening MBA program.

ACADEMIC PROGRAMS

The MBA program is rigorous and comprehensive, and demands student commitment. The core curriculum provides a set of broad-based, integrative skills, rather than narrowly focused, highly specialized skills. Core courses provide a solid foundation in both business management and analytical disciplines, a foundation that fosters continued career growth. In addition to core courses stressing key functional areas of business, students can choose electives specific to their chosen area of concentration.

The Evening MBA program is specifically designed for the working professional in the Boulder/Denver metro region. Course work combines theoretical background with practical knowledge students can use in their jobs the next day. Taught by the same nationally renowned Faculty who teach in our full-time MBA program, the Evening MBA program gives students and their companies access to the latest cutting-edge business knowledge and practices.

FACILITIES

The Leeds School of Business houses several resources for the specific needs of business students. The Facilities include: the William M. White Business Library, the Douglas H. Buck Electronic Media Center, computerized classrooms, the MBA Business Center, a student lounge, food center, Faculty and administrative offices, the Business Research Division, the Robert H. and Beverly A. Deming Center for Entrepreneurship, the Real Estate Center, the Burridge Center for Securities Analysis and Valuation, and the Center for Business and Society.

EXPENSES AND FINANCIAL AID

Cost of Full-time Tuition for the 2007–2008 Academic Year

Resident: $9,792

Nonresident: $24,390

Tuition for the class that will enroll in the Evening program in 2007 will be $5,250 per term for eight terms, for a total of $42,000.

The University of Colorado Financial Aid Office manages the determination of need, as based on the FAFSA reports, and any federal loan applications and awards (both subsidized and unsubsidized). They also provide counseling for students and make adjustments to student budgets as needed and as allowed by federal and university guidelines. You may contact that office directly at 303-492-5091 or visit their website at www.colorado.edu/finaid.

FACULTY

The faculty of the school is made up of talented men and women who offer a diverse range of expertise and research activities. The faculty publishes frequently and is internationally recognized for the quality of its research. In addition, many maintain strong ties within the business community and bring a current business perspective to the classroom. Business faculty members strive to deliver the most effective teaching in management theory and real-world applications to ensure a quality learning experience for business graduates.

ADMISSIONS

The Leeds MBA is a competitive program. Our Admissions Committee considers each candidate's entire record of achievement. We look at undergraduate and graduate transcripts, GMAT scores, essays, letters of recommendation, personal interviews, work experience, and extracurricular and community activities. Professional work experience is strongly encouraged as it adds relevance and depth to the learning process and enables candidates to contribute to, and benefit from, the knowledge of fellow classmates.

Applications for the Leeds MBA programs at the University of Colorado at Boulder are accepted for the fall semester only. For applications submitted by March 1, decision letters will be mailed on May 15. For applications submitted by May 1, decision letters will be mailed on July 15.

UNIVERSITY OF CONNECTICUT
School of Business

AT A GLANCE

Educating leaders for more than 125 years, the University of Connecticut (UConn) is ranked among the top 5 percent of business schools worldwide according to *BusinessWeek, U.S. News & World Report, The Wall Street Journal,* and The Princeton Review. UConn's highly regarded MBA Program is known for its innovative curriculum design that incorporates distinctive learning accelerators to leverage traditional academic instruction with high-profile corporate partnering in solving practical, real-time challenges. Working alongside research faculty and corporate executives to develop solutions to real industry problems, these unique experience-based opportunities allow students to acquire a business education like no other. Ultimately, UConn MBA graduates have it all: the fundamental knowledge, skills, and practical experience necessary to compete in business today.

CAMPUS AND LOCATION

UConn has grown from a strong regional school in recent years to a prominent national academic institution with over 28,000 students, 170,000 alumni, and 120 major buildings on 3,100 acres at the main campus in Storrs. The state capital and metropolitan area of Hartford is 30 minutes away, Boston is a 90 minute drive, and New York City is a 3-hour drive.

DEGREES OFFERED

UConn offers MBA and MS (accounting) degrees, as well as a variety of dual-degree programs including: MBA/JD, MBA/MD, MBA/MA in international studies, MBA/MSW, MBA/MS in nursing, and MBA/MA of international management (MIM).

ACADEMIC PROGRAMS

UConn's MBA curriculum requires a total of 19 courses (57 credits), which takes 2 academic years. Assigned to groups from day one, students work together throughout their first year of core courses as members of cross-functional teams. The spring semester culminates in a live, real-company integration project that draws upon formal course instruction as well as pre-program work experience. Presentations are made to faculty members and business leaders, and students are given structured feedback to hone their technical, analytical, and interpersonal skills. Partnering companies have included Aetna, Hamilton Sundstrand, GE, Pitney Bowes, Pratt & Whitney, and Xerox. During the second year, students focus their studies in any two of the five MBA concentrations: operations and information management, finance, health care management and insurance studies, venture consulting, and marketing intelligence.

FACILITIES

UConn students study in state-of-the-art research and learning facilities. Classrooms are outfitted with broad multimedia capability reflecting the school's commitment to meet the demands of the information era.

EXPENSES AND FINANCIAL AID

2006–2007 tuition and fees for the full-time MBA program for the academic year (two semesters) are $9,510 for Connecticut residents and $22,290 for nonresidents. Housing and living costs vary among candidates but are approximately $4,948 for graduate resident housing and $3,916 for meals. Additional costs including required health insurance, textbooks, mobile computer, laundry and incidentals (estimated at $7,000) bring the total yearly cost of attending the MBA program to approximately $25,000 for Connecticut residents and $37,000 for nonresidents.

Financial aid is available in the form of loans, scholarships, and graduate assistantships. Most financial aid is awarded on the basis of established need, primarily determined through an analysis of an applicant's Free Application for Federal Student Aid (FAFSA). For further information, students may also contact the University of Connecticut's Financial Aid Office at 860-486-2819 or via the web at www.financialaid.uconn.edu.

FACULTY

UConn's faculty offer a wealth of academic and business experience to students. Over 96 percent of them have earned a PhD or the highest degree in their field. Most are actively involved in scholarly activities that enable them to stay current in and contribute to their fields of knowledge, as well as to bring a balanced perspective between theory and practice into the classroom.

STUDENT BODY

UConn MBA students come from a wide variety of undergraduate institutions, both domestic and international. Their undergraduate degrees represent majors in many diverse areas—from engineering and English, sciences and fine arts, to business to economics. In a typical class of students, 34 percent are women, the average age is 28, and approximately 35 percent are international students. Friendliness and informality characterize student life at the main campus. Social and professional organizations, including the Graduate Business Association (GBA), offer a variety of activities to satisfy the needs of students.

ADMISSIONS

Admission is very competitive. The minimum requirements for admission include two years of postgraduate professional work experience; a minimum 3.0 GPA on a 4.0 scale, or the equivalent, from a four-year accredited institution; and a total GMAT score of at least 560. For international students whose native language is not English, a TOEFL score of at least 233 (computer-based) is required. The application deadline for international applicants is February 1 and for domestic applicants, April 15.

SPECIAL PROGRAMS

UConn's experiential learning accelerators are what distinguish it from other top-quality MBA programs. These dynamic multipartner initiatives create a dynamic environment that significantly leverages the learning process, allowing students to acquire a business education like no other. Learning accelerators include the aforementioned MBA Integration Project; GE edgelab; SS&C Technologies Financial Accelerator; Innovation Accelerator; $2 million Student Managed Fund; and Corporate MBA Assistantship.

ADDITIONAL INFORMATION

The UConn School of Business is nationally accredited by AACSB International—The Association to Advance Collegiate Schools of Business and is a member of the Graduate Management Admissions Council (GMAC) and the European Foundation for Management Development (EFMD).

CAREER SERVICES AND PLACEMENT

UConn's career planning activities begin during orientation and continue throughout the MBA program. Primary recruiters include General Electric, CIGNA, Aetna, IBM, United Technologies Corp., Wachovia, Hartford Financial Services, PricewaterhouseCoopers, Gerber Technologies, ESPN, and UBS Warburg. For the class of 2006, the median salary was $70,000 and went as high as $95,000 plus bonus.

UNIVERSITY OF DENVER
Daniels College of Business

AT A GLANCE

The nation's eighth-oldest accredited collegiate business school, Daniels offers one of the nation's premier MBA programs in an exciting learning environment that prepares you for leadership in today's global business environment. Daniels built a curriculum based on ethics and leadership long before it became the norm. *The Wall Street Journal* has recognized the college for four consecutive years, most recently ranking us third in the world for producing students with high ethical standards.

CAMPUS AND LOCATION

The University of Denver is the largest independent private university in the Rocky Mountain region with more than 10,850 students. Founded in 1864 by John Evans, the Colorado Territorial Governor for Abraham Lincoln, the 125-acre University of Denver campus is located in a quiet neighborhood in Denver. Students enjoy an academic atmosphere with access to the cosmopolitan activities and lifestyle of Denver and the nearby Rocky Mountains.

Metro Denver is the center for finance, commerce, and business in Colorado. The Daniels College of Business is 15 minutes from two business hubs: downtown Denver and the Denver Technological Center.

In September 1999, the $25 million Daniels College of Business building opened. This beautiful facility fosters teamwork and collaboration, with breakout team study rooms, a commons for informal gatherings, wireless Internet, over 3,400 data and voice ports, and an Advanced Technology Center.

The Suitts Center for Career Placement at Daniels provides extensive resources to help students assess career choices and develop effective strategies—from workshops and counseling to career forums, alumni networking, and an alumni mentor program.

ACADEMIC PROGRAMS

At the Daniels College of Business, academic excellence and a commitment to values-based leadership come together. Recognizing that ethics and values-based leadership, along with technical business knowledge, are prerequisites for success in business today, Daniels requires students to take the Daniels Compass, courses that integrate values, global perspective and innovation.

Our faculty strikes a balance between disseminating useful theory and demonstrating compelling ways to use it in business-world situations. Mix this with a true love for teaching and a commitment to teamwork and communications, and the result is a balanced learning environment of engaged teachers and scholars. Daniels brings relevance to the classroom through case studies, integration of business disciplines, teamwork and communication, and experiential learning.

Our integrated curriculum helps develop creative critical thinking and decision making through a continued focus on applying business tools in an interrelated format. Students move from the Daniels Compass and foundational courses into elective or specialization courses. Specializations in accounting, construction management, electronic commerce, entrepreneurship, finance, information technology, marketing and real estate are available, or students may create their own specializations.

A part-time MBA program is offered, along with an International MBA, an MBA/JD joint-degree program and a dual-degree program that allows students to combine their MBA degree with programs from other University of Denver schools and departments. Daniels also offers an 18-month Executive MBA.

Our 83 full-time faculty members have a balance of industry experience and academic dedication. They have developed the curriculum in collaboration with business leaders and continue to refine our programs while maintaining excellence in teaching, research, and consulting.

EXPENSES AND FINANCIAL AID

Tuition is based on a cost per credit hour. (The exception is the Executive MBA, which is a single fee.) For academic year 2007–2008, tuition is $873 per credit hour. Expenses for books, supplies, fees, housing, and meals vary, depending on courses per quarter and extracurricular activities. Although Denver is the largest city in the Rocky Mountain region, the cost of living is well below other major U.S. cities. Financial aid and merit-based scholarships are available to qualified students.

STUDENT BODY

Daniels students come from across the country and have a wide range of academic and professional backgrounds. Of the approximately 670 MBA students in the Full-Time, Part-Time, Executive and International MBA programs, 52 percent are working professionals, 35 percent are women, and 18 percent are international students.

Prominent alumni include Peter Coors, chairman of Coors Brewing Company; Tom Marsico, founder, CEO, and CIO of Marisco Capital Management; and Carol Tome, executive vice president and CFO of Home Depot.

ADMISSIONS

The Daniels College of Business is looking for candidates who demonstrate a commitment to advanced learning and high ethical standards, display leadership potential, and show promise in their chosen career. Applications are evaluated through a comprehensive process that considers previous academic performance and undergraduate academic record, professional/extracurricular experience, and GMAT (and in some cases, GRE) scores. Requirements include an undergraduate degree from an accredited college or university, results of the GMAT (or, if applicable, GRE), responses to essay questions, two letters of recommendation and a completed application.

Admission to the Daniels College of Business is selective, and decisions are based on a qualitative evaluation of each candidate's potential professional, intellectual, and interpersonal contributions to the Daniels learning environment. No specific undergraduate major is considered preferable, however, prior business study is helpful.

There are three application deadlines for fall and spring Admissions (spring admission is not offered for all programs): Early Action/Decision; priority scholarship consideration; and the space-only consideration. Candidates are strongly encouraged to apply early in the process.

UNIVERSITY OF HAWAII—MANOA
Shidler College of Business

AT A GLANCE

A leader among U.S. business schools in its focus on the Asia-Pacific region, the Shidler College of Business at the University of Hawaii—Manoa provides students with an in-depth understanding of the best business practices, an awareness of languages and cultures, and a solid comprehension of emerging technologies within today's complex global economic environment. Founded in 1949, the college offers students a wide selection of degree, certificate and high-impact executive programs in a unique multicultural learning environment enhanced by collaborative learning, research projects, international speakers, internships, study abroad opportunities, and career services. In the past several years, *U.S. News & World Report* has ranked the college among the top 25 U.S. graduate business schools for international business.

The graduate program offers an integrated curriculum in five fields: accounting, finance, marketing, management, and information technology to accentuate the practical application of business theories. The curriculum incorporates the latest technology, offers specific concentration fields such as the recently added Entrepreneurship and Innovation courses and is designed with an Asia-Pacific perspective to respond to the changing economic conditions.

For more information, call 808-956-8266 or visit www.shidler.hawaii.edu.

CAMPUS AND LOCATION

The Shidler College of Business at the University of Hawaii—Manoa is located in Honolulu on the Island of Oahu. Nestled in beautiful Manoa Valley, the college is just minutes away from Waikiki, downtown Honolulu, and most major cultural centers.

DEGREES OFFERED

Bachelor of Business Administration; Master of Business Administration—Full-Time; Master of Business Administration—Part-Time; Master of Accounting; Master of Human Resource Management; Executive MBA; Executive Neighbor Island MBA; Executive MBA—Vietnam; Japan-focused MBA; China-International MBA; Joint JD/MBA; Joint MS in Nursing Admin/MBA; PhD in International Management

ACADEMIC PROGRAMS

The Shidler College of Business at the University of Hawaii—Manoa offers the only AACSB International—accredited graduate programs in the state.

The inaugural Full-Time MBA program commences Fall 2007 and is a full-time program. The Part-Time MBA has both spring and fall admission and may be pursued on either a full- or part-time basis, allowing students greater flexibility to work or pursue an internship during the day. Both are 48-credit-hour programs with either a thesis or nonthesis option.

The Executive MBA program is an intensive experience that allows working professionals the opportunity to complete their degree within 22 months, attending class one night a week and every other Saturday.

The China International MBA is a 21-month cohort program that provides intensive study in the language, culture, and business practices of China.

The Japan-focused MBA (now in its fifteenth class) is a 15-month cohort program that provides intensive study in the language, culture, and business practices of Japan.

The Vietnam Executive MBA program, which is held in Hanoi, Vietnam, is offered jointly by the University of Hawaii and the Hanoi School of Business and is open to U.S., Vietnamese, and international applicants.

The Master of Accounting program is a 30-credit-hour program that is designed to prepare students for careers in professional accounting.

The PhD program in international management offers specializations in Asian finance, international accounting, international marketing, global information technology management, and international organization and strategy.

EXPENSES AND FINANCIAL AID

Full-time graduate tuition for the Evening MBA 2006–2007 academic year is $10,896 for state residents and $16,272 for nonresidents. Part-time tuition is $454 per credit hour for residents and $678 for nonresidents. Fees are approximately $85 per semester; books and other materials cost around $300. Tuition for the China International MBA is $30,888. The total cost of the Japan-focused MBA is $31,000, which covers tuition, fees, books, and class materials. The MAcc tuition for 2006–2007 is $412 per credit for residents and $647 for nonresidents.

Over 1 million dollars in merit-based scholarship aid is available to all qualified applicants.

FACULTY

The Shidler College of Business faculty is a diverse group of internationally accomplished researchers and highly recognized teachers, holding doctoral degrees from Columbia, Carnegie-Mellon, MIT, Stanford, Purdue, Harvard, and other major universities. Our faculty's international experience and business research in the Asia-Pacific region provide an exceptional learning experience for students.

STUDENT BODY

Total enrollment in the Part-Time MBA and MAcc programs is 367, with 70–80 new MBA and 40–50 new MAcc students entering each semester. More than a third of these students are women, and 60 percent are part-time students. The average MBA student is 29 years old with four years of work experience beyond the bachelor's degree. The Japan-focused and China International MBA programs attract another 30–40 students each fall. The Executive MBA program generally draws 35–40 students; the typical Executive MBA student is 36 years old with 12 years' work experience.

ADMISSIONS

The ideal student entering the program has a solid academic record, high test scores, strong motivation, and well-thought-out career goals. Admission requirements include a minimum grade point average of 3.0 or higher (on a 4.0 scale) in the last 60 credits of undergraduate or graduate course work. Applicants whose native language is not English must submit official TOEFL scores. Work experience of at least two years is required for the MBA programs, and four years is required for the Executive MBA; no work experience is required for the MAcc. All applicants are required to submit official GMAT scores, statement of objectives, resume, and letters of recommendation.

For further information on admissions, please visit our website at www.shidler.hawaii.edu.

ADDITIONAL INFORMATION

The Shidler College of Business Alumni and Friends group was formed to broaden career opportunities and support the college's academic programs. An extensive network of alumni—from the 50-plus years of the college's existence—spans the globe and provides a helpful link to international opportunities.

CAREER SERVICES AND PLACEMENT

The college houses a full-service Internship and Career Development Center offering internships in Hawaii, mainland and aboard, full-time employment placement, on-campus interviews, career fairs and workshops on resume building, interview skills, negotiating salary, business etiquette and dressing for success.

UNIVERSITY OF HOUSTON—VICTORIA
School of Business Administration

AT A GLANCE

The University of Houston—Victoria School of Business Administration is accredited by AACSB International, the hallmark of excellence in management education. We have been ranked number two for the Greatest Opportunity for Minority Students, as well as named one of the "Top 25 Ranked Best Buys" in distance learning by GetEducated.com for the past three years. Our business programs are taught face-to-face in the Victoria and Houston areas, as well as completely online. We are considered to be a national leader in distance education and online course delivery. The convenient format of our business programs offers students the opportunity to continue their education while still gaining experience in the workforce.

CAMPUS AND LOCATION

Business programs are offered at our main campus in Victoria, Texas, as well as at two teaching centers located in Sugar Land and Katy, Texas. Physical addresses for each campus are listed below:

University of Houston—Victoria
3007 North Ben Wilson
Victoria, Texas 77901

University of Houston—Victoria
University of Houston System Sugar Land
14000 University Boulevard
Sugar Land, Texas 77479

University of Houston—Victoria
University of Houston System Cinco Ranch
4242 South Mason Road
Katy, Texas 77450

DEGREES OFFERED

Graduate Programs

Strategic MBA: Accounting, Finance, General Business, International Business, Management, Marketing

Global MBA: Finance, Management, Master of Science in Economic Development and Entrepreneurship

Undergraduate Programs

Bachelor of Business Administration: Accounting, General Business, Management, Marketing

ACADEMIC PROGRAMS

The University of Houston—Victoria School of Business Administration allows students to develop the business competencies and global mindset for success in today's competitive business environment, thus preparing future leaders who are capable of managing in environments market by constant change. Our business programs are taught face-to-face in the evenings in the Victoria and Houston areas, as well as completely online. Our convenient teaching methods provide students with an opportunity to engage in teamwork with others from the United States, and around the world. The mission of the UHV MBA program is to provide individuals with the knowledge and skills needed to successfully manage organizations in a dynamic environment by offering an integrated curriculum that blends theoretical concepts with practical applications. Specifically, the MBA program seeks to develop in each the graduate the capacity to:

1. Understand and adapt to the changing business, political, and social environments

2. Evaluate and respond to emerging threats and opportunities

3. Interact with and effectively lead diverse groups

4. Analyze and evaluate business operations and processes

5. Synthesize and apply cross-functional approaches to organizational issues

Integration and cross-functional approaches to organizational issues are embedded throughout the MBA core through close coordination of course content using the strategic planning process. Strategic management consists of the analysis, decisions, and actions an organization undertakes in order to create shareholder value and sustain competitive advantages. Each course in the MBA program will enhance students' understanding of the strategic management process and assist students in acquiring the tools and skills needed to be a successful manager. The syllabi for the MBA core courses explain how they connect to the mission and objectives of the MBA program and to other courses.

EXPENSES AND FINANCIAL AID

As of April 2007, Texas residents pay about $819 per course in tuition and fees for the MBA program; out-of-state and international students pay about $1,494 per course in tuition and fees. The University of Houston—Victoria School of Business Administration has been named one of the "Top 25 Ranked Best Buys" in distance learning by GetEducated.com for the past three years. UHV offers numerous scholarships, grants and loan options, as well as payment plans to assist students with funding their education. A limited number of graduate assistantships and fellowships are also available.

FACULTY

Our programs are taught by faculty with PhDs as well as current research in their fields. Most importantly, our faculty are known for their dedication, responsiveness, accessibility, and adaptability—a primary reason that many of our students and alumni chose UHV.

ADMISSIONS

The individual attention for which UHV School of Business Administration is known begins with the admission process. Admission requirements for the MBA program include the following:

- An overall GPA of 2.5 or a GPA of 2.5 based on your last 60 hours of course work.

- A GMAT score of 450. Students may enroll in up to 12 hours without their official GMAT scores on file. For those students who qualify, a GMAT waiver is available.

- International students need a TOEFL score of 550 (written), 213 (computer based), or 79 (IBT).

- There is no application fee.

SPECIAL PROGRAMS

In addition to the Strategic MBA, UHV offers a Global MBA and a Master of Science in Economic Development and Entrepreneurship. The MS-EDE is the only program of its kind, combining traditional economic development (attracting businesses) with entrepreneurship (starting businesses). The 36-hour curriculum may be completed part-time in 2 years, and is available entirely online.

THE UNIVERSITY OF IOWA
Henry B. Tippie School of Management

AT A GLANCE

The University of Iowa's Henry B. Tippie School of Management offers a Master of Business Administration (MBA) degree consistently ranked in the top 50 MBA programs in the world. Many characteristics contribute to the quality of the Tippie MBA, including a flexible curriculum and great placement results. Here are a few of the attributes that set Tippie apart from other programs.

A Personal Touch

Or students are never just a face in the crowd. They form relationships with classmates, faculty, and staff that continue long after the formal program is complete. In fact, our students are on a first-name basis with the dean. By limiting class size, we provide a program that meets individual needs.

Reputation

The Tippie School of Management is for its quality by attracting the best and brightest students from around the world. While at Tippie, students enhance their knowledge of business fundamentals, develop leadership experience, and further their professional development. We produce graduates that go on to business success across the country and the world.

Environment

Iowa City has a cosmopolitan atmosphere and rich culture, contributing to the city's selection by *Forbes* as one of the nation's best "small cities". Enjoy Big Ten athletics, world-class cultural events, ethnic restaurants, and parks all within easy driving distance of Chicago, Minneapolis, St. Louis, and Kansas City.

The Tippie MBA is one-of-a-kind. Taught by world-class faculty in a dynamic, Big Ten town, the Tippie MBA is an outstanding value.

CAMPUS AND LOCATION

Iowa City is a diverse, highly cosmopolitan community of 60,000 set in the natural scenic beauty of Iowa's rolling hills and woods. It was selected the number-one place to live in the nation by *Editor & Publisher* magazine, named one of the 10 most enlightened towns in the country by *Utne Reader*, and listed in the book *The 100 Best Small Art Towns in America*.

The University of Iowa campus is seamlessly integrated with the Iowa City community. The 1,900-acre campus is located along both sides of the Iowa River. The campus community provides a rich variety of activities and resources for students.

ACADEMIC PROGRAMS

The Tippie MBA Program emphasizes applied business learning in a collaborative, team-based environment. The curriculum is founded on a core of courses that includes key functional areas of finance, marketing, accounting, statistics, organizational behavior, operations management, economics, and strategic management. Students select a concentration from one of the following areas: accounting, entrepreneurship, finance, strategic management and consulting, management information systems, marketing or operations management. An individually designed concentration is also an option for those with more specific interests.

FACILITIES

The state-of-the-art facilities of the John Pappajohn Business Building provide a comfortable arena for learning. The Internet conferencing system allows students to work in real-time on a project.

Some building highlights:

- The Marvin A. Pomerantz Business Library provides a 30,000-volume resource area with electronic access to libraries around the world

- Laptop computers are available for checkout from the library for use throughout the building

- A wireless LAN provides Internet access to any student with a network-enabled laptop

- Our Instructional Technology Center features 100 computer workstations (the largest on campus), two 32-seat computer classrooms, and a computerized operations/behavioral laboratory

EXPENSES AND FINANCIAL AID

The Tippie MBA provides one of the best returns on investment available. This nationally accredited program provides a top-notch education that can help students take their career to the next level.

2007–2008 Academic Year Tuition and Fees

Annual Tuition

  Iowa residents: $13,162

  Nonresidents: $24,142

Computer fees: $237

Health fees: $202

Student Union, activities, and service fees: $220

Building fee: $119

Merit-based Financial Aid

Merit-based financial aid is offered to outstanding candidates each year. The criteria for these awards mirror those for admission—academic record, work history, leadership experience, test scores—although only those with the highest qualifications receive offers for aid. Both domestic and international applicants are eligible for awards. Awards may consist of a scholarship, a graduate assistantship, or both. Most scholarships vary from $1,000 to $4,000. Graduate assistantships provide a salary of approximately $8,000, a contribution toward health insurance costs, and resident tuition status for non-Iowa residents.

STUDENT BODY

Tippie MBAs are active players in determining the type of MBA experience delivered. Student organizations offer an opportunity to develop their leadership potential and team building skills. Student clubs organize professional development events, career networking opportunities, social events, and many other activities that enhance the Tippie MBA experience.

The entering class in the fulltime MBA Program averages more than three years of work experience, a GPA of approximately 3.3 (4.0 scale), and a GMAT score of 640.

ADMISSIONS

The Tippie MBA seeks candidates demonstrating the ability to complete a rigorous academic program and the potential for success.

UNIVERSITY OF MIAMI
School of Business Administration

AT A GLANCE

The University of Miami MBA Program is ranked among the best MBA programs by *The Wall Street Journal* and *The Financial Times*. Our Business School is one of 549 schools in North America that is fully accredited by AACSB International—The Association to Advance Collegiate Schools of Business, and it is also accredited by CAHME—The Commission on Accreditation of Health Care Management Education.

LOCATION AND ENVIRONMENT

Coral Gables, home of the University of Miami, infuses Old World ambiance with New World technology. Our unique location, in the midst of one of the most dynamic areas of international business growth in the Western Hemisphere, contributes to the classroom environment.

DEGREES OFFERED

The University of Miami, School of Business Administration offers a full-time, 48-credit Two-Year MBA Program, and a 32-credit One-Year MBA Program designed for students who graduated within the last 5 years with an undergraduate degree in business. Executives and professionals may earn an MBA degree by attending Saturday or Saturday/Monday evening classes in one of the following areas: health administration and policy, international business, management, or MBA/Master of Science in Industrial Engineering (MBA/MSIE). For more information please visit us at **www.bus.miami.edu/grad.**

ACADEMIC PROGRAMS

At the School of Business Administration, the curriculum provides a decidedly flexible framework for learning. A variety of teaching methods are utilized: lecture, discussion, case method, and team projects. Classes are small in order to encourage exchange of ideas between teacher and student, and among students.

OFF-CAMPUS OPPORTUNITIES

Off-campus MBA programs are currently offered in Tampa, Orlando, Delray Beach, and to residents of Nassau, Bahamas. Visit our website at **www.bus.miami.edu/grad** for program schedule, curriculum, and information sessions.

FACILITIES AND EQUIPMENT

The School of Business Administration's $24 million, award-winning complex, built for the exclusive use of graduate business students, provides the most advanced technology and sophisticated academic environment. This facility is complete with computer access at every seat, and a virtual library, a computer lab exclusive to MBA students and hi-tech classrooms with executive seating. The Ziff Graduate Career Services Center is exclusively dedicated to helping graduate business students find employment opportunities, obtain internships, and prepare to compete for top job positions.

TUITION, ROOM AND BOARD, AND FEES

Graduate tuition for the 2007–2008 academic year is $1,350 per credit hour.

FINANCIAL AID

A limited number of graduate assistantships, offered to outstanding applicants in the fall semester only, usually include both a tuition scholarship and a monthly stipend. The Graduate Assistantship can cover up to 75 percent of the tuition cost. Graduate students are eligible to apply for student loans and work-study assistance through the university's Office of Financial Assistance Services.

FACULTY

Educated at some of the world's finest academic institutions, the School of Business Administration faculty are world-renowned and prestigious. The UM Faculty serve as consultants to *Fortune* 500 companies and international corporations across the globe.

STUDENT ORGANIZATIONS AND ACTIVITIES

The University of Miami values its multicultural community and student organizations. The Graduate Business Student Association is the foremost business organization for MBA students. In addition, a variety of student organizations are available within the University of Miami community such as; the Council of International Students and Organizations, Colombian Student Association, Hispanic Heritage Month Association, Latin American Student Association, Latino Greek Council, United Dominicans Association, and Federación de Estudiantes Cubanos to name a few.

ADMISSIONS

The Graduate Business Admissions Committee welcomes applications from individuals whose undergraduate degrees are from accredited colleges or universities. Student applications are reviewed on an individual basis to determine the applicant's potential for success in the MBA Program. A competitive GMAT score and GPA are essential to be considered for admission. Other factors considered by the Admissions Committee include an essay, letters of recommendation, work experience, and community involvement. Students applying to the MBA Programs for Executives and Professionals are not required to take the GMAT; however, they are required to have a minimum of three years of professional work experience.

THE UNIVERSITY OF NORTH CAROLINA AT CHARLOTTE
Belk College of Business

AT A GLANCE

The MBA Program at UNC Charlotte offers students the opportunity to invest in themselves and their careers by earning a highly respected MBA. As an MBA student at the Belk College of Business, you will learn more than management, finance, and marketing. Our program is distinguished by its full and engaging curriculum taught by our outstanding resident faculty. It is designed to teach you to think strategically, to communicate effectively and to work productively as part of a team—giving you the tools to succeed in today's complex, fast-paced business environment.

The MBA is self-paced, allowing students the option of completing the degree in as few as 18 months and as many as 6 years. All courses meet one evening per week, allowing students seeking a balance between work, graduate school, family, and other commitments maximum flexibility.

You may concentrate your MBA in one of nine defined areas (business finance, information and technology management, international business, management, marketing, economics, real estate finance and development, financial institutions/commercial banking, supply chain management) as well as the option to define your own. These choices allow you to customize your MBA to help you achieve your individual career goals and develop additional depth in an area of particular interest.

The MBA program at UNC Charlotte is fully accredited by AACSB International, the premier accrediting agency for programs in business administration and accounting. This prestigious distinction is achieved as a result of the world-class faculty and highest caliber students that make up the Belk College of Business.

CAMPUS AND LOCATION

The University of North Carolina at Charlotte is located in one of the largest financial centers of the United States. In addition, many of the nations leading service, manufacturing, retail and nonprofit corporations are headquartered in the area. The area is rapidly growing and expanding, as is UNC Charlotte.

The main campus (9201 University City Boulevard) sits on more than 1,000 acres in northern Charlotte. The university also has an Uptown Charlotte location (220 North Tryon) where about 50 percent of the MBA courses are delivered.

DEGREES OFFERED

Master of Business Administration (MBA)

MBA in Sports Marketing/Management (beginning 2007)

Master of Accountancy

Master of Science in Economics

Master of Science in Math Finance

PhD in Business Administration

ACADEMIC PROGRAMS

The MBA is a 37-credit-hour program that begins with developing a comprehensive understanding of the functions of an organization then builds upon this foundation to develop effective strategic management. The concentration allows candidates to specialize their degree to further individual goals. Additional course work may be required of students in a preparatory component based on academic preparation and experience.

ADMISSIONS

Admission to the UNC Charlotte MBA program is highly selective. We seek candidates who are motivated and aim to assume leadership roles in organizations locally and around the world. Candidates must have obtained the equivalent of a U.S. bachelor's degree from a fully accredited university to be eligible for admission to the UNC Charlotte MBA.

Previous study of business is not required, as the program offers a 10-credit preparatory component that provides non-business majors the background they need to be successful in the rest of the program. These preparatory courses are waived for candidates with sufficient undergraduate preparation.

Admissions decisions are based on several criteria, including the applicant's academic achievement, previous work history, and standardized test scores. A completed application form must be accompanied by three letters of recommendation, a current resume, all academic transcripts, a GMAT score, statement of purpose, and a $55 application fee.

Work experience is not required for admission to the MBA program, however it is strongly recommended. The average UNC Charlotte MBA student has more than 7 years of professional work experience. Since the Admissions decision involves several criteria, there are no set minimums for the GMAT or GPA average. The Fall 2005 entering class had an average undergraduate GPA of 3.2 (on a 4.0 scale) and an average GMAT score of 575.

In addition to the above, international students must also submit an official financial statement verifying sufficient resources to cover education and living expenses. International students are also required to provide TOEFL scores (557 on paper-based test or 220 on the computer-based test).

Applications to the MBA are accepted for fall, spring, and summer entry on a rolling admissions basis.

UNIVERSITY OF NOTRE DAME
Mendoza College of Business

AT A GLANCE
The Mendoza College of Business is home to more than 2,300 students engaged in undergraduate, graduate, and executive studies. Its programs are defined by three attributes: academic excellence, implementation effectiveness, and a commitment to integrity and community. Our purpose here is not only to build careers but to build lives rooted in purpose and in faith.

The Institute for Ethical Business Worldwide seeks to promote positive illustrations of ethical and socially responsible business conduct throughout the world. We stress the importance of ethical leadership as a cornerstone to building a stronger sense of integrity and values into all business firms.

The Center for Ethics and Religious Values seeks to strengthen ethical foundations in business and public policy decisions by fostering dialogue among academic and corporate leaders, as well as by research and publications. The center's ethics curriculum, ranked in the top four in Business Week, is integrated throughout Notre Dame's business course work.

The Gigot Center for Entrepreneurial Studies fosters innovation among current and aspiring entrepreneurs. Through a unique curriculum, business plan competitions, and mentoring opportunities with Notre Dame alumni, students gain vital experience and the skills necessary to build successful businesses.

The Fanning Center for Business Communication provides course work in all facets of human communication, from writing and speaking to listening and group interaction. In addition to classroom success—*The Wall Street Journal* ranked Notre Dame MBAs number two worldwide in communications skills—Fanning Center faculty have also earned an international reputation for their research and publications.

CAMPUS AND LOCATION
The University of Notre Dame is an independent, national Catholic university located in Notre Dame, Indiana. Located adjacent to the city of South Bend and approximately 90 miles southeast of Chicago, Notre Dame offers students the best of both worlds: a small, Midwestern town and large metropolitan city within close proximity. Notre Dame's campus, considered one of the most beautiful in the country, contains 1,250 acres, 2 lakes, and nearly 140 buildings with a total property replacement value of $2 billion.

DEGREES OFFERED
The Master in Business Administration (MBA) serves more than 300 students in three programs of study: a Two-Year MBA degree, a One-Year MBA degree for students with an undergraduate business degree, and an MBA/JD degree offered jointly with the University of Notre Dame's Law School.

The Executive MBA (EMBA) is a flexible master's in business administration degree program designed for executive students who are employed full-time.

The Master of Science in Administration (MSA) program prepares students for leadership in social service organizations.

The Master of Science in Accountancy is a two semester, 30-hour program in which students earn a master's degree while fulfilling the education requirement for CPA exam eligibility.

PROGRAMS AND CURRICULUM
The University of Notre Dame MBA program offers concentration tracks in business-to-business marketing, corporate finance, consulting, consumer marketing, entrepreneurship, general management, investments, and operations management.

The classroom delivery of these concentrations is done via three primary methods: case study, lecture, and team work. Ethical studies and evaluations are a component of most if not all classes.

EXPENSES AND FINANCIAL AID
Graduate students who apply and who demonstrate financial need may qualify for a Subsidized Federal Stafford Loan up to a maximum of $8,500 per year. A graduate student may also qualify for an Unsubsidized Federal Stafford Loan at a maximum level of $18,500 per year minus the student's Subsidized Federal Stafford Loan.

FACULTY
Mendoza's faculty are recognized not only for outstanding teaching, but also for the value of their research contributions. All of Notre Dame's Mendoza professors bring a spirit of passion and exploration to their interactions with students and their collaborative research.

STUDENT BODY
If you're going to spend the time to get an MBA; wouldn't it be nice if you could enjoy yourself as well? Notre Dame boasts several advantages including the following:

- The Basilica of the Sacred Heart is a designated national monument.

- Notre Dame's Football Saturdays are unlike any school in the country.

- The MBA Tailgate Party is a great opportunity to mix with alumni, professors, and recruiters in a fairly casual setting.

- MBA club activities relating to careers in technology, investments, marketing, entrepreneurship, MBA Association governance or other timely interests.

- MBA faculty, students and their spouses, of all denominations and faiths, are invited to take part in a weekend spirituality retreat.

ADMISSIONS
The Two-Year MBA program is open to domestic and international applicants who hold a bachelor's degree or its international equivalent from an accredited college or university in any area of concentration.

Applicants to the One-Year MBA program are expected to hold an undergraduate degree in business from an accredited college or university in the United States. At a minimum, applicants must have the following academic background:

- 6.0 credit hours each in accounting, economics, and mathematics

- 3.0 credit hours each in finance, marketing, and MIS/computers

Courses are offered on a full-time basis only. The One-Year program starts in late May and is completed in May of the following year. Admission is granted for the summer semester only for the One-Year program.

SPECIAL PROGRAMS
The Notre Dame MBA community supports a number of student-led clubs and committees.

ADDITIONAL INFORMATION
With more than 240 alumni clubs worldwide, Notre Dame's network is among the strongest in the country, and the almost-fanatic pride that graduates take in their school means that most alumni are more than willing to lend a hand to a fellow Domer.

CAREER SERVICES AND PLACEMENT
At the University of Notre Dame, the number one priority of the MBA Career Development Center is our students. Students drive our process as we consistently provide individualized career counseling and advising.

UNIVERSITY OF ROCHESTER
William E. Simon Graduate School of Business

AT A GLANCE
The William E. Simon Graduate School of Business Administration at the University of Rochester in Rochester, New York offers an integrated, cross-functional approach to management, which uses economics as both the framework and common language of business, and the skills to become an effective leader. Programs offered are full-time MBA and MS programs, Executive MBA and Part-Time MBA and MS programs.

The school is accredited by the AACSB—The International Association for Management Education since 1966. Simon: where thinkers become leaders.

CAMPUS AND LOCATION
The Simon School is situated on the River Campus of the University of Rochester, near the banks of the Genesee River, and three miles from downtown Rochester, New York. The Simon School is one of seven schools and colleges within the University of Rochester.

DEGREES OFFERED
Full-Time Study: The MBA degree requires 67 hours of study and a 3.0 grade-point average. There are two entrance dates, September or January. The degree requirements for the January entrance are the same as those for fall entry.

Part-Time Study: Applicants to the Part-Time MBA Program may matriculate in any quarter. They may also take up to four classes before matriculating to the program. The part-time MBA degree requires 64 hours of study and a 3.0 grade-point average.

Executive MBA Programs: Offers candidates a fully accredited MBA degree without career interruption. Classes meet every other Friday/Saturday for two academic years in Rochester, New York; and Bern, Switzerland. (22 months).

MS Programs: Nine Master of Science in Business Administration programs are offered: Accountancy, Marketing, General Management, Medical Management, Manufacturing Management, Service Management, Information Systems Management, Technology Transfer and Commercialization and Finance.

Each M.S. degree is offered on a full-time or part-time basis. Certificate Programs are offered in five areas of study.

ACADEMIC PROGRAMS
The Simon School's MBA programs are designed to train individuals to solve management problems as team members in a study-team structure. It is a place where thinkers become leaders. The curriculum emphasizes learning the principles of economics and effective decision making through a mix of lecture, case study, and project courses. Nine core courses are required. A three-credit course over two quarters in business communications is required of all full-time students. Eleven elective courses are required.

FACILITIES
Schlegel Hall is a four-story classroom and student-services building. The building contains nine case-style classrooms, which seat 35 to 100 students, and 21 rooms for group study. Classrooms are equipped with state-of-the-art audio and visual technology.

Carol G. Simon Hall houses the school's administration, faculty and PhD students. Carol G. Simon Hall is linked to Schlegel and Gleason Halls by the Florescue-von Manstein Plaza and is also connected to it by a tunnel. The building contains more than 75 offices, several conference rooms, and a variety of lounge spaces for Faculty and staff.

James S. Gleason Hall is the 38,000-square-foot classroom building linked to Schlegel Hall. Gleason Hall houses five new classrooms, up to 16 study rooms, and a significantly expanded Career Management Center suite, including eight dedicated interview rooms.

EXPENSES AND FINANCIAL AID
In addition to the $125 application fee, tuition is $1,228 per credit hour, or $36,840 per year, for 2007–2008. The cost of books and supplies averages $1,500 a year, and living expenses (rent, food supplies, personal expenses, and health insurance) were estimated at less than $10,000 for the 2007–2008 academic year. Both U.S. and international applicants are eligible for merit awards.

STUDENT BODY
Each September approximately 120 students enter the Simon community. Another 50 students join their classmates in January. September entrants complete the first-year core courses during the fall, winter, and spring quarters; the majority of January entrants complete core courses during the winter, spring, and summer quarters. Within each cohort, students are assigned to a study team of 4 or 5 members. Each team always includes representatives from at least three countries.

In the class of 2007, 17 countries are represented. Prior full-time work experience averages 4.1 years, and the average age is 27. Women comprise 30 percent of the class. Thirty-eight percent of Simon students are members of American minority groups.

ADMISSIONS
A Simon School Admissions Committee reads each application individually and evaluates recommendations, teamwork and communication skills, the nature and scope of prior work experience, the undergraduate academic record, GMAT scores. All undergraduate majors are represented in the program.

SPECIAL PROGRAMS
During the two-week Orientation Program, students participate in self-assessment exercises, personal selling and communication skills instruction, corporate leadership training, and one-on-one career counseling. In addition, students participate in several VISION (the student-managed portion of a Simon MBA) modules designed to enhance leadership skills in the areas of team building, training in diversity issues, ethical decision making, and social responsibility.

ADDITIONAL INFORMATION
Year after year, the Simon School consistently ranks high on the lists of top b-school programs. These rankings include: *BusinessWeek*, *U.S. News & World Report*, *Financial Times of London*, *Forbes*, and *The Wall Street Journal*.

CAREER SERVICES AND PLACEMENT
The Career Management Center team works diligently to develop new and enhance existing corporate partnerships to provide a wide range of career opportunities for both summer internships and full-time career positions.

The Career Management Center's Counseling and Education staff offers targeted, personalized counseling to assist students in identifying, initiating, and implementing highly effective career plans.

UNIVERSITY OF SOUTH CAROLINA
Moore School of Business

AT A GLANCE:

Moore School of Business is known for its expertise and experience in international business. Top-ranked in national and international surveys, Moore School's undergraduate and graduate programs offer students opportunities to learn and work in a global business environment.

Moore School of Business is a comprehensive business school offering a full range of options for business education, including degree programs at the undergraduate, master's, and doctoral levels, plus executive education, distance education, research centers, and outreach support.

The 2,600 undergraduate and 800 graduate students are taught by 96 full-time faculty plus qualified full-time lecturers in specialty areas of business and technology. The school is housed in a modern nine-story building that contains offices, research labs and centers, classrooms, presentation and seminar rooms, television classrooms, computer labs, and a full business library. Offices and classrooms are connected by the campus digital and/or video network.

In March of 1998, Moore School of Business became the first major business school named for a woman, honoring University of South Carolina alumna and business executive Darla Moore. The school builds on its long history of innovation and achievement, serving as an asset to South Carolina by being part of the global network of business.

CAMPUS AND LOCATION

Moore School of Business has an urban campus with green space and gardens, historic buildings, and easy access to recreation and cultural events. With its location in the heart of Columbia, the capital of South Carolina, students can take advantage of water sports on the nearby rivers and lakes, hiking and skiing in the mountains, and fishing and sailing on the Atlantic Coast. In town, the Columbia Museum of Art provides traveling exhibitions and a substantial permanent collection. The Town Theatre, the Workshop Theatre, and the Koger Center are among the many venues offering theater beyond the very active university performances. Columbia is home to the world-class Riverbanks Zoo and Botanical Garden and the historic State Museum. Nightlife abounds around campus, with live bands performing rock, jazz, and blues, and the area is the origin of popular groups such as Hootie and the Blowfish. The gentle Southern climate makes outdoor sports and recreation a year-round pursuit.

DEGREES OFFERED

Bachelor of Science in Business Administration; International Master of Business Administration; Master of Business Administration; Master of Human Resources; Master of Accountancy; Master of Arts in Economics; Doctor of Philosophy in Business Administration; Doctor of Philosophy in Economics

ACADEMIC PROGRAMS

The school is noted for its innovative International Master of Business Administration (IMBA) which now offers more flexibility in curriculum and length of program. IMBA provides two options: language track or global track.

FACILITIES

Moore School of Business at the University of South Carolina is housed in a nine-story building with offices and classrooms in close proximity to foster interaction between students and faculty.

Facilities include the Elliott White Springs Business Library, Japan Business Library, Center for Entrepreneurship, James C. Self Computer Lab, Center for Business Communication, auditoriums, media classrooms, television studio classrooms, meeting rooms, and teleconference facilities.

EXPENSES AND FINANCIAL AID

Moore School of Business has been rated a "Best Buy" and best "ROI" at various times by *Forbes* and *BusinessWeek*. A set program fee for each program in lieu of tuition and strong merit-based financial aid packages and work grants make Moore attractive to talented students.

IMBA Language and Global Track program fees are $35,000 for SC residents, and $52,000 for nonresident students.

FACULTY

Moore School of Business has 14 endowed chairs and named professorships plus 24 fellowships. Many of the faculty have lived and worked in other countries, and all have professional or doctoral-level degrees. Many professors are members or directors of academic or professional boards, and are contributors to or editors of professional journals. Core graduate courses are taught exclusively by professors. Currently Moore has 87 tenure and track professors, and 19 teaching lecturers.

STUDENT BODY

Students in the IMBA program tend to be about 26–30 years old (27 years average), with 2 to 7 years of work experience. Thirty percent of the students are women, and about 30 percent of the students are foreign nationals. About 43 percent of the students have an undergraduate major of business, but majors also include economics, engineering, international studies, political science, languages, and liberal arts. The diverse student population draws students from South America, Western and Eastern Europe, Asia, Africa, and Australia in addition to the U.S. population.

IMBA students have an average GMAT of 638, and an average GPA of 3.40 for undergraduate studies.

ADMISSIONS

GMAT scores, undergraduate GPA, work experience, and essays are the most important elements of a graduate application portfolio. Depending on the competitiveness of the program to which the student is applying, the GMAT should be between 570 and 680, the TOEFL has a minimum requirement of 600 (250 CAT, 100 IB), and the undergraduate GPA should be about 3.3 or higher. Most graduate programs prefer students with two or more years work experience. The application deadlines for the IMBA are November 15 (round I) and February 15 (round II) for best consideration and financial aid.

Web address: Mooreschool.sc.edu

SPECIAL PROGRAMS

Moore School of Business offers specialized master's degrees in accounting (Master of Accountancy), economics (MA in Economics), and human resources (Master of Human Resources).

Also offered is an MBA for working professionals, the Professional MBA, distributed by satellite to 23-plus receiving locations throughout South Carolina. This program has been ongoing for more than 30 years and features professors teaching by live television with interactive audio.

Flexibility of start date, class time, curriculum, and location, attracts working professionals in business, engineering, and accounting who want to enhance their careers by earning an MBA from an accredited university.

CAREER SERVICES AND PLACEMENT

Moore School of Business Graduate Career Management Office partners with students to achieve their career goals. A highly structured Career Development Curriculum prepares students for their job search soon after they come to campus.

THE UNIVERSITY OF TAMPA

John H. Sykes School of Business

AT A GLANCE

The John H. Sykes College of Business is accredited by AACSB International—The Association to Advance Collegiate Schools of Business. The university is also accredited by Southern Association of Colleges and Schools to award associate's, baccalaureate, and master's degrees. The university was founded in 1931 by visionary community leaders who wanted to provide the best possible educational opportunity for their community. UT has excelled in its mission of preparing a growing and culturally diverse Student Body for rewarding careers and responsible citizenship.

CAMPUS AND LOCATION

The 100-acre University of Tampa campus offers a full-service educational setting that includes a comprehensive library, a broad range of technology and support, an active Career Services and Placement Center, and many student programs. There is much more to Tampa's location than beautiful beaches and pleasant year-round temperatures. Tampa Bay is among the top 10 fastest-growing areas in the U.S. and a great place to be for career building. Tampa is Florida's West Coast center for the arts, banking, real estate, law, transportation, international business, education, communications, health care, and scientific research.

DEGREES OFFERED

MBA: part-time, full-time, and Saturday formats; Master of Science in Accounting (MSA); Master of Science in Finance (MS-FIN); Master of Science in Innovation Management (MS-IM); Master of Science in Marketing (MS-MKT)

ACADEMIC PROGRAMS

MBA program elements include:

- Fast Start Workshop
- Leadership Development Program
- Integrated Core
- MBA Concentrations offered in accounting, economics, entrepreneurship, finance (with tracks in Investment Analysis and CFA and Corporate Financial Strategy and Management), international business, information systems management, management, marketing, and nonprofit management and innovation
- Capstone Experience

FACILITIES

The John H. Sykes College of Business is an 80,000-square-foot facility with more than 30 classrooms and faculty offices. The Macdonald-Kelce Library offers UTOPIA, an online catalog that provides Web access to library holdings and links to e-books and several databases. The Vaughn Center has a multicuisine dining facility, campus store, cybercafé, game rooms, and computer labs. Housing is available for graduate students in Straz Hall and Kennedy Place.

EXPENSES AND FINANCIAL AID

Tuition for 2007–2008 is $450 per credit hour (Saturday MBA tuition is $565 per credit hour.) In addition, a $35 student services fee is required each term. The cost of books, supplies, health insurance, parking, and personal expenses is additional. Graduate Assistantships are available each academic year to qualified full-time MBA students. Assistantships provide tuition waiver for up to six classes per year plus a $3,000 stipend. Recipients must be full-time students and work 20 hours per week. The university offers a variety of financial aid programs. Graduate students who are not currently employed may apply for a noncredit internship with a local business.

FACULTY

All graduate faculty members have PhDs. More than half of our graduate Faculty have won awards for teaching and professional excellence. Many of our faculty have owned their own businesses, have helped lead and build major companies, or are engaged in consulting at the highest leadership levels.

ADMISSIONS

Admission to UT's graduate business programs is competitive and is based on a number of factors. Application deadlines are:

- Fall semester: priority June 1; final July 15; international June 1
- Spring semester: priority November 1; final December 15; international November 1

All students admitted must have earned four-year undergraduate degrees from a regionally accredited college or university. A specific undergraduate degree is not required.

The Graduate Management Admissions Test (GMAT) is required but may be waived for the Saturday MBA, MS in Finance, MS in Innovation Management and MS in Marketing programs depending upon the applicant's academic background and work experience.

To be considered for graduate admissions, applicants must submit the following information:

- Completed application
- $40 application fee
- Official transcripts of all previous college work received directly from each institution
- Two professional reference forms completed by individuals that attest to the applicant's professional background and academic potential.
- Resume
- Personal Statement
- Test of English as a Foreign Language (TOEFL) score report (international applicants only)
- Graduate Management Admissions Test (GMAT) score report is required for full-degree admission. Students with degree higher than bachelor's are exempt from taking the test.
- Individual interviews are recommended, but not required, except for the MS-IM program.

Applicants should submit materials to:

The University of Tampa
Graduate Studies
Box O
401 West Kennedy Boulevard
Tampa, FL 33606-1490
Telephone: 813-258-7409
Fax: 813-259-5403
E-mail: utgrad@ut.edu
Website: grad.ut.edu

SPECIAL PROGRAMS

Interaction with local community leaders and organizations is part of UT's graduate business education. The university is woven into the Tampa Bay community through internships, experiential learning opportunities, community forums, advisory boards, business outreach programs, and several centers and institutes. Among the discussion and speaker groups that meet regularly on campus are the Fellows Forum and the Business Network Symposium.

THE UNIVERSITY OF TOLEDO
College of Business Administration

AT A GLANCE

One of the best in the Midwest, the MBA program at The University of Toledo features affordability and flexibility that help you expand your skills and opportunities without interrupting your career. The college's history of excellence in practical, relevant education based on cutting-edge research and business engagement will take your career to the next level. The UT MBA curriculum is designed to equip the future leaders of business with relevant, real-world knowledge about the workings and motivations of every level of the enterprise: employees, customers, the firm itself, and all levels of the economy.

CAMPUS AND LOCATION

The University of Toledo was established in 1872 and became a member of the state university system in 1967. UT is a community built around 11 academic colleges and professional programs matched only by a handful of public universities nationwide. UT's main campus, located along the banks of the Ottawa River in a residential section of the city, includes historic buildings, modern Facilities and abundant green space. The university's campus was also named one of the 100 most beautifully landscaped university campuses in the country by the American Society of Landscape Architects.

DEGREES OFFERED

The College of Business Administration offers the following degrees: Bachelor of Business Administration (12 different fields); MBA (full-time and part-time); JD/MBA Dual Degree; Executive MBA; Master of Science in Accountancy (MSA); PhD in Manufacturing Management

MBA Specializations are available in: Administration; Finance; Human Resource Management; Information Systems; International Business; Marketing (3 tracks); CRM and Marketing Intelligence; Marketing Management, Sales Leadership, Operations and Supply Chain Management; Sales Leadership

The UT MBA program is the first AACSB-accredited MBA program in the country to offer a specialization in Professional Sales Leadership. The concentration builds on the expertise of the pioneering Edward Schmidt School of Professional Sales within the UT College of Business Administration, one of about 10 similar programs nationwide.

ACADEMIC PROGRAMS

You can earn an MBA program at UT in as little as one calendar year by completing 11 courses. Since we offer all of our core courses in the fall, spring, and summer, you will find that the UT MBA program is designed specifically for your busy schedule, allowing you to take the courses you need when you want to take them. Every UT MBA student is able to customize their MBA by taking their 9 credits of electives in one specific specialization.

The Executive MBA program is designed specifically for working professionals with three to five years of experience in a managerial role. EMBA students work in a cohort and complete the program in only 15 months working in weekend residencies on Friday nights and Saturdays.

The Master of Science in Accountancy (MSA) degree program is designed to meet the needs of the professional in accounting and to qualify candidates to sit for the CPA examination in Ohio. The UT MSA degree is a 30-semester-hour program and typically includes 21 semester hours of accounting classes and nine semester hours of diversification electives. Every MSA applicant's background is evaluated and an individualized plan of study is developed with the program director.

We also offer a joint JD/MBA degree program in conjunction with the College of Law, consistently ranked in the top 100 programs in the country by U.S. News & World Report.

All of The University of Toledo's business degree programs can be completed without career interruption.

FACILITIES

The College of Business Administration is fully equipped to instruct students in a cutting-edge learning environment that integrates technology into the curriculum. Over 100 laptop computers are available for students to check out on a daily basis. All of our laptops have integrated wireless network access, which allows students to get online in Stranahan Hall, the college's main building. The John Neff Stock Trading Floor is one of only 30 such facilities in the country and gives students real- and delayed-access to feeds from stock exchanges around the world. The college is also breaking ground in the fall of 2007 on the $12 million Savage and Associates Complex for Business Learning and Engagement expansion.

EXPENSES AND FINANCIAL AID

2006–2007 Academic Year Tuition and Fees (approximate)

Ohio residents: $7,600

Nonresidents: $14,220

Please visit the Bursar's Office webpage at http://bursarsoffice.utoledo.edu for the most current information on tuition and fees. Merit-based scholarships, Federal Stafford Loans, and private educational loans and graduate assistantships are available to eligible students.

Graduate students who are regularly admitted to a degree program from Hillsdale, Lenawee, Macomb, Monroe, Oakland, Washtenaw, and Wayne Counties in Michigan are eligible for the Michigan In-State Tuition Initiative, which allows students with permanent residency in those counties to attend UT at the in-state tuition rate.

ADMISSIONS

Admission to the MBA and MSA programs takes place in all three semesters: fall (August), spring (January), and summer (May).

We encourage prospective students to apply online. The Admissions Committee requires the following documents in order to evaluate an application:

- Application for admission
- Application fee
- Three letters of recommendation
- One official transcript from each university attended
- Official GMAT results
- Official TOEFL results (if necessary)

Applicants are encouraged to apply as early as possible to ensure that their applications are processed and that they can be admitted for the term they want.

Since the Executive MBA is a cohort-based program, applicants can only enter the program in August of each calendar year. Applications are considered on a space-available basis.

CAREER SERVICES AND PLACEMENT

The MBA program features special opportunities and resources to enhance your education and career. Through the Corporate Graduate Assistantship Program, highly qualified students work 16 hours a week at a local company while pursuing an MBA full-time. MBA students can also utilize the resources of the Business Career Programs Office, which organizes on-campus recruiting, resume reviews, walk-in advising, mock interviews, and the biannual Business Career Fair, which attracts more than 90 companies.

VIRGINIA COMMONWEALTH UNIVERSITY
School of Business

AT A GLANCE

Located on two downtown campuses in Richmond, Virginia, Virginia Commonwealth University ranks among the top 100 universities in the country in sponsored research and enrolls 30,000 students in more than 195 certificate, undergraduate, graduate, professional, and doctoral programs in 15 schools and one liberal arts college.

The School of Business is located on VCU's main academic campus in Richmond's historic Fan District. It employs 100 full-time faulty and enrolls more than 2,100 undergraduate and 480 graduate students. Students receive instruction primarily from graduate faculty, over 95 percent of whom hold a doctorate or equivalent professional degree.

The School of Business is accredited by the AACSB—The International Association for Management Education. The VCU School of Business is an integral part of the Richmond business community. Students regularly participate in local internships and workshops, and are heavily recruited by local companies.

CAMPUS AND LOCATION

Richmond, the capital of Virginia, is a diverse cultural city, surrounded by historic neighborhoods, parks, and a thriving James River. The city consistently ranks among "Best Places to Live and Work in America" in several national publications.

DEGREES OFFERED

Master of Business Administration
Master of Science in Business with concentrations in Finance, Decision Sciences, Global Marketing Management, Human Resource Management and Industrial Relations, and Real Estate Valuation
Master of Accountancy
Master of Arts in Economics
Master of Science in Information Systems
Master of Taxation
Dual Degrees
MBA/PharmD
MBA/MSIS
Doctor of Philosophy in Business with the following concentrations:
Information Systems
Accounting
Management

PROGRAMS AND CURRICULUM

The Master of Business Administration (MBA) focuses on the development of functions and techniques of management, as well as an understanding of environmental and economic forces that influence administration and decision making. Students may choose to concentration in a particular area or complete a general concentration. The Master of Science in Business programs focus on a particular discipline. Most require four foundation courses and ten advanced courses. The Master of Accountancy degree was revised in the spring of 2000 to address a requirement that future candidates for the CPA exam must have completed at least 150 credit hours of college study to be eligible to sit for the examination. Most undergraduates complete 120 credit hours, so students intending to take the CPA examination are encouraged to consider earning the additional credit hours of study in the integrated Master of Accountancy program. The Master of Taxation program includes a comprehensive study of tax laws and regulations, administrative practice and procedure, and tax research fundamentals, and is designed to develop both technical knowledge and conceptual understanding within the field of taxation. Ethical considerations are stressed within the framework of individual courses.

The Master of Science program in Information Systems is designed to prepare students for specialized roles in information systems. The MS program is offered in both the traditional semester format, and in an executive (alternate weekend) format. The executive program (Fast Track Executive MS in IS) focuses on Information Technology Management and is designed for students with six or more years professional experience.

Graduates of the Master of Arts in Economics will have the knowledge and experience to qualify for a wide and rapidly expanding range of analyst positions in the private or public sectors.

FACILITIES

The School of Business is currently housed in the VCU Business Building, a facility that offers state-of-the-art technology classrooms, computer Facilities, and team meeting rooms. University Library Services administers the James Branch Cabell and Tompkins-McCaw research libraries on both campuses and provides numerous electronic resources, federal and state documents, patents, and a wide variety of microform and media resources.

EXPENSES AND FINANCIAL AID

For the 2006–2007 academic year, in-state tuition and fees for full-time students were $4,170.50 per semester. Out-of-state tuition and fees for full-time students totaled $8,791 per semester. In-state tuition rates for part-time students were set at $435.35 per credit hour. Out-of-state part-time students paid $947.50 per credit hour.

A limited number of master's assistantships are available through the Graduate Studies in Business office for full-time master's-level students with exemplary academic credentials. Endowed scholarships are also available through GSIB on an annual basis.

FACULTY

The School of Business has 102 full-time faculty members. Many faculty have been recognized nationally for their teaching effectiveness, research contributions, and service to professional organizations. Faculty members are best known for their contributions in information systems, organizational behavior, financial research, global marketing management, and international business activities.

STUDENT BODY

Approximately 500 students are currently enrolled in the master's and doctoral programs of VCU's School of Business. Seventy-two percent of our master's students are fully employed in the greater Richmond area and study on a part-time basis. Women make up 40 percent of the graduate student population, and students have an average of six years of work experience beyond their undergraduate degrees.

ADMISSIONS

Applicants to graduate programs in the VCU School of Business must submit the following:

Application for admission and fee
Two copies of official transcripts from each university or college attended
Three letters of recommendation
A current resume
A personal statement
A current GMAT score (except MA in Economics which requires the GRE)
Application procedures vary slightly by degree program.

WILLAMETTE UNIVERSITY
Atkinson Graduate School of Management

AT A GLANCE

As a Willamette MBA student, you will participate in an MBA program noted for excellent teaching and experiential learning. You will have multiple opportunities to learn "to do" and build your resume of professional experience. While the distinct design of Willamette's MBA programs develop the real-world experience and interpersonal skills sought by employers, the curriculum offers the added benefit of more choices—you can pursue your individual career goals in business, government or not-for-profit enterprises, and in one or more functional career areas of interest.

CAMPUS AND LOCATION

Willamette University is located in Salem, Oregon, and has an off-campus facility in the Pearl District of Portland, Oregon. Salem and Portland offer an excellent quality of life, friendly people, mild climate and quick access to the recreational and professional benefits of the beautiful Pacific Northwest—one of the fastest-growing areas in the United States for young, college-educated people.

DEGREE OFFERED

Willamette offers the Master of Business Administration degree. The Willamette MBA is one of only two programs in the world dually accredited for business (AACSB International) and public administration (NASPAA). Willamette is also profiled as one of the best business schools by *BusinessWeek*, *U.S. News & World Report*, The Princeton Review, Vault.com, and Beyond Grey Pinstripes.

ACADEMIC PROGRAMS

Full-time MBA: 21-month program that builds the knowledge and real-world experience needed for your first professional position or career change. Areas of interest include: accounting, finance, general management, human resources, information systems, international management, marketing, organizational analysis, public management, and quantitative analysis.

Accelerated MBA: 12-to-15 month program for students seeking career change or advancement who have strong knowledge of business and professional experience. Accelerated students focus their studies in the elective courses of the Full-Time MBA program.

MBA/JD: Four-year joint-degree that combines Willamette's Full-Time MBA and Doctor of Jurisprudence programs.

Professional MBA: 24-month program for working professionals with three or more years of experience who want to complete their MBA while employed. Students develop an enterprise wide view of management and immediately apply what they learn to their work place. Willamette's Professional MBA program is available in Portland and Salem.

FACILITIES

Classrooms are spacious and modern. Students have wireless access to the Internet, e-mail and network software and printing services. A laptop computer with wireless LAN capability and a standard suite of software is required.

The Salem campus includes two libraries, state-of-the art classrooms, recreational and fitness facilities, dining centers, a student center, a concert hall, an art museum, student apartments, and more. The Portland Center is conveniently located in the Pearl District with easy access to public transportation and public parking.

TUITION

2007–2008 tuition for the Full-Time MBA program is $12,600 per semester, or $25,200 for the two semester academic year. Tuition for Professional MBA is approximately $6,480 per semester, or $19,440 for the three semester academic year.

FINANCIAL AID

Merit-based scholarships, Federal Stafford Loans, Federal Graduate Plus Loans, private educational loans and graduate assistantships are available to eligible students enrolled in the Full-Time MBA program.

Federal Stafford Loans, Federal Graduate Plus Loans, and private educational loans are available to eligible students enrolled in the Professional MBA program.

FACULTY

Faculty are excellent teachers who are committed to their students and to the educational model of "learning by doing." They are easily accessible to students and alumni. They are also leaders of community and professional organizations; award-winning teachers and researchers; authors of books, articles, and software; editors and reviewers of professional journals; entrepreneurs; and consultants. They make Willamette an exciting place to learn.

STUDENT BODY

"Dedicated, creative, ethical, exceptional, friendly, hardworking, leader, professional, respected, team player": these are words used to describe Willamette MBA students. Our students come from around the world and throughout the U.S. to prepare for the next step in their career. Some have academic backgrounds in liberal arts and sciences, while others have a background in business or engineering. Some are pursuing careers as managers of large corporations. Others are seeking opportunities in small business, entrepreneurial ventures, government, or not-for-profit agencies.

ADMISSIONS

Applicants are evaluated on an individual basis. All applicants must submit the application for admission, official GMAT score, official copies of all college/university transcripts, two references, and essays. International applicants must also submit financial documents required for an I-20, a photocopy of the name page of their passport, and a TOEFL score of 230 or higher. Applicants should check our web site at www.willamette.edu/mba for specific information.

For more information, contact:

MBA Admission Office

Willamette University

Telephone Toll Free: 866-MBA-AGSM

E-mail: mba-admission@willamette.edu or pmba@willamette.edu

Web: www.willamette.edu/mba

CAREER SERVICES AND PLACEMENT

Career services include an organized program of the best practices of career management, workshops, internship programs, on-campus interviews, employment postings, databases, individual counseling, mentoring programs, career/networking fairs, and student professional organizations.

Eighty-eight percent of 2006 graduates received a job offer within three months of graduation. A sample of employers includes Ernst & Young, The Gallop Organization, Mentor Graphics, Microsoft, KPMG international, Hewlett-Packard, Key Bank, Intel Corporation, Tektronix, and Providence Health Systems.

Nearly 100 percent of students participate in an internship. A sample of recent internship employers includes Sony BMG Music, Columbia Sportswear, ESCO, Flir Systems, Merrill Lynch, Microsoft, Morgan Stanley, Nike, Oregon Zoo, Saber Consulting, Spacekraft, T-Mobile, Tektronix, U.S. Department of State, and the State of Oregon.

DECODING DEGREES

Many business programs offer a number of degrees, including joint- or combined-degree programs with other departments (or with other schools) that you can earn along with your MBA. You'll find the abbreviations for these degrees in the individual school profiles, but we thought we'd give you a little help in figuring out exactly what they are.

AGSIM	American Graduate School of International Management	IMBA	International MBA
AM	Social Service Administration	IPD	Interdisciplinary Product Development
APC	Advanced Professional Certificate	JD	Juris Doctorate
BA	Bachelor of Arts	LLB	Bachelor of Law
BASC	Bachelor in Engineering	MA	Master of Arts
BBA	Bachelor of Business Administration	MAB	Master of Agribusiness
BPA	Bachelor of Public Affairs	MAcc	Master of Accountancy (or Accounting)
BS	Bachelor of Science	MAAE	Master of Arts in Applied Economics
BSB	Bachelor of Science in Business	MAEcon	Master of Arts in Economics
BSBA	Bachelor of Science in Business Administration	MAg	Master of Agriculture
CIS	Computer Information Systems (or Sciences)	MAIB	Master of Arts in International Business
DBA	Doctor of Business Administration	MAIS	Master of Accounting and Information Systems
DDS	Doctor of Dental Surgery	MALL	Master of Arts in Language Learning
DMD	Doctor of Dental Medicine	MAPS	Master of Asian Pacific Studies
DO	Doctor of Osteopathic Medicine	MAR	Master of Arts in Religion
DPS	Doctor of Professional Studies	MArch	Master of Architecture
EdD	Doctor of Education	MAS	Master of Actuarial Science
EDM	Executive Doctor of Management	MBA	Master of Business Administration
EMBA	Executive MBA	MBE	Master of Business Education
EMIB	Executive Master of International Business	MBI	Master of Business Informatics
EMPA	Executive Master of Public Administration	MBS	Master of Business Studies
EMS	Executive Master of Science	MD	Doctor of Medicine
EMSM	Executive Master of Science in Management	MDIV	Master of Divinity
EMSMOT	Executive Master of Science in Management of Technology	ME	Master of Engineering
EMST	Executive Master of Science in Taxation	MECOM	Master of Electronic Commerce
GDPA	Graduate Diploma in Accounting	MEd	Master of Educational Leadership/ Master of Education
GEMBA	Global Executive Master of Business Administration	MEM	Master of Engineering and Management
HRIM	Hotel, Restaurants and Institutional Management	MEng	Master of Engineering
IAMBA	Information Age Master of Business Administration	MF	Master of Forestry
		MFA	Master of Fine Arts
		MHA	Master of Health Administration
		MHR	Master of Human Resources
		MHRM	Master of Human Resources Management

MIA	Master of International Affairs	MSG	Master of Science in Gerontology
MIAS	Master of International and Area Studies	MSGFA	Master of Science in Global Financial Analysis
MIB	Master of International Business	MSHA	Master of Science in Health Administration
MIE	Master of Industrial Engineering	MSHFID	Master of Science in Human Factors in Information Design
MILR	Master of Industrial and Labor Relations		
MIM	Master of International Management	MSIAM	Master of Science in Information Age Marketing
MIS	Management Information Systems		
MISM	Master of Information Systems Management	MSIB	Master of Science in International Business
MLAS	Master of Liberal Arts and Science	MSIE	Master of Science in Industrial Engineering
MMIS	Master of Management Information Systems	MSIM	Master of Science in Industrial Management
MMR	Master of Marketing Research	MSIMC	Master of Science in Integrated Marketing Communications
MMS	Master of Management Science	MSIR	Master of Science in Industrial Relations
MNO	Master of Nonprofit Organizations	MSIS	Master of Science in Information Systems
MOD	Master of Science in Organizational Development	MSISE	Master of Science in Industrial and Systems Engineering
MPA	Master of Public Administration	MSISM	Master of Science in Information Systems Management
MPAcc	Master of Professional Accounting		
MPH	Master of Public Health	MSIT	Master of Science in Information Technology
MPIA	Master of Public and International Affairs	MSITM	Master of Science in Information Technology Management
MPL	Master of Planning		
MPP	Master of Public Policy	MSM	Master of Science in Management
MRED	Master of Real Estate Development	MSMIS	Master of Science in Management Information Systems
MS	Master of Science	MSMOT	Master of Science in Management of Technology
MSA	Master of Science in Accountancy (or Accounting)		
MSAIS	Master of Science in Accounting Information Systems	MSN	Master of Science in Nursing
		MSOD	Master of Science in Organization Development
MSAT	Master of Science in Accountancy, Taxation	MSpAd	Master of Sports Administration
MSB	Master of Science in Business	MSRE	Master of Science in Real Estate
MSBA	Master of Science in Business Administration	MSS	Master of Social Science
		MSSA	Master of Science in Social Administration
MSE	Master of Science in Engineering	MST	Master of Science in Taxation
MSEC	Master of Science in Electronic Commerce	MSTM	Master of Science in Telecommunications Management
MSF	Master of Science in Finance		
MSFA	Master of Science in Financial Analysis	MSW	Master of Social Work
MSFS	Master of Science in Foreign Services	MTAX	Master of Taxation

MTLM	Master of Transportation and Logistics Management
NEMBA	National Executive Master of Business Administration
PharmD	Doctor of Pharmacy
PhD	Doctor of Philosophy
SM	Master of Science
TSM	Telecommunications Systems Management
VMD	Doctor of Veterinary Medicine

INDEX

ALPHABETICAL INDEX

R

S

T

V

W

X

Y

INDEX BY LOCATION

INDEX BY COST

$15,000–$30,000

MORE THAN $30,000

ABOUT THE AUTHOR

Nedda Gilbert is a graduate of the University of Pennsylvania and holds a master's degree from Columbia University. She has worked for The Princeton Review since 1985. In 1987, she created The Princeton Review corporate test preparation service, which provides Wall Street firms and premier companies tailored educational programs for their employees. She currently resides in New Jersey.

NOTES

FINDING THE FUNDS
What you should know about paying for your graduate school education

Furthering your education is an investment in your future. Laying down $120,000 — probably more — in exchange for a top-notch graduate school education requires just as much research and planning as deciding which school you'll hand that money over to.

The good news is that you still have a little time before you have to really worry about signing on the dotted line for any type of financial assistance. That gives you some time to research options, to properly calculate the actual costs of going to graduate school beyond just the sticker price, and to create a plan so that your potential future earnings cover your costs of living when you're out of school and using that degree you will have worked so hard for.

You're going to be responsible for the choices you make. Cutting your ancillary expenses for the next few years and building up an out-of-pocket school fund before you ever register for that first class might save you thousands of dollars in interest payments down the road. But how will you know if you don't come up with a plan?

No doubt you've accumulated some sort of credit history, most likely through undergrad student loans and/or some high-interest credit card debt, so you might think you have it all figured out when it comes to paying for graduate school. While you might understand the basics about how federal loans work and how scholarships, grants, and fellowships can help to cut down the final bill, there are lesser-known and fairly new options out there that can make your postgraduate life a little easier to enjoy.

OTHER PEOPLE'S MONEY

Scholarships and Grants

These are the best form of financial aid because they don't have to be paid back. Remember, though, that most scholarships require a minimum GPA and that some grants are good for only one year. When evaluating your payment options, make sure there is a reasonable expectation that the financial aid package being offered will be available for the full term of the degree requirement or that you have a way of managing funds if they are not enough.

Fellowships and Stipends

Fellowships come in many different forms. Sometimes partial tuition scholarships are called fellowships. These university-sponsored fellowships consist of a cash award that is promptly subtracted from your tuition bill. You can earn the amount of the award by teaching for a department or by completing research for a faculty member. The percentage of students who receive this type of fellowship and the amount paid to each will vary depending on the intended degree and field, enrollment status (full- or part-time), and years of enrollment.

It is important to note that survival on a fellowship alone is unlikely. Fellowships are taxable income — federal, state, county, and city — and you may be expected to pay for school fees, supplies, and books out of your fellowship, as well as tuition. If the fellowship doesn't cover the full cost of your attendance, you'll have to explore other financing options.

Employer-financed Opportunities:

Some employers will offer a tuition reimbursement or a limited financial sum for employees to attend graduate school part time. Employers expect the advanced degree to enhance your performance on the job or to make you eligible for a different job within the company. Be sure you understand all aspects of your employer's tuition reimbursement program before you sign on and be prepared to meet any commitments expected of you.

LOANS

When scholarships, grants, and fellowships don't cover the full cost of attendance, many students take out loans to help out with the rest.

Avoid loans if you can. A loan can best be described as renting money. There's a cost and it may not be an easy cost to bear.

Here's an interesting anecdote. Many students graduate without knowing what types of loans they received, who the lender was and how much they owe. The first time many students become aware of the scope of their obligation is when they receive their first bill—six months after graduation.

This is often because students are passive participants in the financial aid process and do not educate themselves or ask questions. Most students receive a list of "preferred lenders" from their financial aid office and simply go with the lender recommended to them. Over the course of the previous year, relationships between financial aid offices and lenders have been called into question by State Attorneys General, the Department of Education, and regulators. Financial aid offices in certain cases received revenue from lenders in exchange for being placed on the "preferred lender list." Some schools have even rented out their name and logo for use on loan applications. These practices occur without disclosure to parents and students.

It is important to know that the "preferred lenders" may not offer the best deals on your loan options. While your financial aid office may be very helpful with scholarships and grants, and is legally required to perform certain duties with regard to federal loans, many do not have staff researching the lowest cost options at the time you are borrowing.

Remember that your tuition payment equals revenue for the school. When borrowing to pay tuition, you can choose to borrow from any lender. That means you can shop for the lowest rate. Keep reading. This will tell you how.

TYPES OF LOANS

The federal government and private commercial lenders offer educational loans to students. Federal loans are usually the "first resort" for borrowers because many are subsidized by the federal government and offer lower interest rates. Private loans have the advantage of fewer restrictions

on borrowing limits, but may have higher interest rates and more stringent qualification criteria.

Federal Loans:

There are three federal loan programs. The Federal Perkins Loan Program where your school lends you money made available by government funds, the Federal Direct Loan Program (FDLP) where the government lends its money directly to students, and the Federal Family Education Loan Program (FFELP) where financial institutions such as MyRichUncle lend their own money but the government guarantees them. While most schools participate in the Federal Perkins Program, institutions choose whether they will participate in either the FFELP or FDLP. You will borrow from FFELP or FDLP depending on which program your school has elected to participate in.

The Federal Perkins Loan is a low-interest (5%) loan for students with exceptional need. Many students who do not qualify or who may need more funds can borrow FFELP or FDLP student loans. Under both programs, the Stafford loan is the typical place to start. The Stafford loan program features a fixed interest rate and yearly caps on the maximum amount a student can borrow. Stafford loans can either be subsidized (the government pays the interest while the student is in school) or unsubsidized (the student is responsible for the interest that accrues while in school). Starting July 1, 2007, the maximum amount a student can borrow for graduate school is $20,500.

It is often assumed that the government sets the rate on student loans. The government does not set the rate of interest. It merely indicates the maximum rate lenders can charge. These lenders are free to charge less than the specified maximum rate of 6.8% for Stafford loans. There is also a maximum origination fee of up to 2% dropping to 1.5% on July 1, 2007. In some cases you may also be charged up to a 1% guarantee fee. Any fees will be taken out of your disbursement.

Historically lenders have hovered at the maximum rate because most loans were distributed via the financial aid office

> The government only lends money directly to you under the Federal Direct Loan Program. Lenders provide loans guaranteed by the federal government in the Federal Family Education Loan Program.

whereby a few lenders received most of the loans. The end result was limited competition. At 1,239 institutions, one lender received more than 90% of the number of Stafford loans in 2006.

The GradPLUS loan is a federal loan that is another option for graduate and professional students. GradPLUS loans can be used to cover the full cost of attendance and have a fixed interest rate. The maximum rate a lender can charge for a GradPLUS loan is 8.5%. GradPLUS loans also have an origination fee of up to 3%, and a guarantee fee of up to 1%. Any fees will be taken out of your disbursement. Getting approved for one might be easier than getting approved for a private loan, so long as you don't have an adverse credit history.

For either program, the borrower submits a federal application known as the Free Application for Federal Student Aid (FAFSA). The application is available online at www.fafsa.ed.gov.

Certain lenders offer rate reductions, also known as borrower benefits, conditioned on the borrower making a certain number of on-time payments. Unfortunately, it is estimated that 90% of borrowers never qualify for these reductions.

Last year, MyRichUncle challenged this process by launching a price war. The company cut interest rates on Stafford loans and Graduate PLUS loans and introduced widespread price competition. These interest rate cuts are effective when students enter repayment and do not have any further qualification requirements. In addition, students only lose the rate reduction if they default.

Your financial aid office is legally required to certify for lenders that you are enrolled and based on your financial aid package, the amount in Federal loans you are eligible to borrow. You are free to choose any lender even if the lender is not on your financial aid office's preferred lender list.

To shop for low cost Federal loans, call a number of lenders before applying to determine their rates and fees. This is an effective approach because your application will not impact the price. Once you are comfortable that you have the lowest

cost option, apply and submit the Master Promissory Note to your lender of choice.

Private Loans:

Private student loans can make it possible to cover the costs of higher education when other sources of funding have been exhausted. Additionally, when you apply for federal loans, you can borrow up to what your institution has pre-defined as the annual cost of attendance. If your anticipated expenses are above and beyond this predefined cost because of your unique needs, it will take a series of appeals before your institution will allow you to borrow more federal loans. Private loans help you meet your true expectation of what you will need financially. Private loans can pay expenses that federal loans can't, such as application and testing fees and the cost of transportation.

When you apply for a private loan, the lending institution will check your credit history including your credit score and determine your capacity to pay back the money you borrow. For individuals whose credit history is less than positive, lenders may require a co-borrower: a credit-worthy individual who also agrees to be accountable to the terms of the loan. While private loans do not have annual borrowing limits, they often have higher interest rates, and interest rate caps are higher than those set by Federal loans. Generally, the loans are variable rate loans, so the interest rate may go up or down, changing the cost.

To shop for a private loan, after you've researched several options, apply to as many of them as you feel comfortable. Once you are approved, compare rates. Pick the lowest cost option.

EXTRA LESSONS

Borrow the minimum:

Just because someone is offering to lend you thousands upon thousands of dollars doesn't mean you should necessarily take them up on that offer. At some point, you'll have to repay the debt and you'll have to do it responsibly. Wouldn't it be better to use your money for something more worthwhile to you?

Know your rights:

Currently, student lending is an industry that is under heavy scrutiny. It is important, now more than ever, for parents and students to have an active voice and to make educational and financial choices that are right for them.

Some schools work with "preferred lenders" when offering federal and private loans. You are not required to choose a loan from one of these lenders if you can find a better offer. With respect to Federal loans, the financial aid office has a legislated role which is to certify for the lending institution that you the borrower are indeed enrolled and the amount you are eligible for. They are not legally empowered to dictate your choice of lender and must certify your loan from the lender of your choice. You have the right to shop for and to secure the best rates possible for your loans. Don't get bullied into choosing a different lender simply because it is preferred by an institution. Instead, do your homework and make sure you understand all of your options.

Know what you want:

When it's all said and done, you will have to take a variety of factors into account in order to choose the best school for you and for your future. You shouldn't have to mortgage your future to follow a dream, but you also shouldn't downgrade this opportunity just to save a few bucks.

MYRICHUNCLE
STUDENT LOANS

Call us:
1-800-926-5320

or learn more online:
MYRICHUNCLE.COM/BUSINESS

MYRICHUNCLE

Who we are:

MyRichUncle is a national student loan company offering federal (Stafford, PLUS and GradPLUS) and private loans to undergraduate, graduate, and professional students. MyRichUncle knows that getting a student loan can be a complicated and intimidating process, so we changed it. We believe students are credit-worthy borrowers, and that student loan debt should be taken seriously by borrowers and lenders alike. We propose changes in the student loan industry that will better serve parents, schools, and most importantly, students.

Why it matters:

Your student loan will be your responsibility. When you enter into a loan agreement, you're entering into a long-term relationship with your lender — 15 years, on average. The right student loan with the right lender can help you avoid years of unnecessary fees and payments.

What we do:

MyRichUncle pays close attention to the obstacles students face. Removing these obstacles drives everything we do. MyRichUncle discounts federal loan rates at repayment rather than requiring years of continuous payments to earn the discount, which saves you money right from the start. We help you plan ahead, so you can choose the best loans and save.

Our credentials:

MyRichUncle is a NASDAQ listed company. Our symbol is UNCL. In 2006, MyRichUncle was featured in FastCompany Magazine's Fast 50 and in Businessweek's Top Tech Entrepreneurs. MyRichUncle and its parent company, MRU Holdings, are financed by a number of leading investment banks and venture capitalists, including subsidiaries of Merrill Lynch, Lehman Brothers, Battery Ventures and Nomura Holdings.

More expert advice from  The Princeton Review

G ive yourself the best chances for getting into the business school of your choice with The Princeton Review. We can help you get higher test scores, make the most informed choices, and make the most of your experience once you get there. We can also help you make the career move that will let you use your skills and education to their best advantage.

CRACKING THE GMAT
2008 EDITION
978-0-375-76610-7 $21.00/C$27.00

CRACKING THE GMAT WITH DVD
2008 EDITION
978-0-375-76611-4 $37.95/C$47.00

MATH WORKOUT FOR THE GMAT
2ND EDITION
978-0-375-76463-9 $19.00/C$27.00

VERBAL WORKOUT FOR THE GMAT
2ND EDITION
978-0-375-76462-2 $19.00/C$27.00

BEST 290 BUSINESS SCHOOLS
2008 EDITION
978-0-375-76627-8 $22.95/C$29.95

MATH SMART FOR BUSINESS
978-0-679-78391-6 $12.00/C$16.95

Available at Bookstores Everywhere.